# Horror
# Film

**CineBooks Home Library Series**
**No. 4**

# The Horror Film

## A guide to more than 700 films on videocassette

CineBooks

CineBooks, Inc.
Evanston, Illinois, 1989

**Editor in Chief:** James J. Mulay

**President:** Anita L. Werling; **Editorial Director:** William Leahy; **Editors:** Daniel Curran, Jeffrey H. Wallenfeldt, Jenny Mueller; **Research Director:** William C. Clogston; **Associate Editors:** Jeannette Hori, Jennifer Howe, Michaela Tuohy.

**Business Manager:** Jack Medor; **Assistants:** Bernie Gregoryk, Lena Hicks. **Advertising Manager:** Craig Carter.

Editorial & Sales Offices
CINEBOOKS
990 Grove Street
Evanston, Illinois 60201

ISBN: 0-933997-23-X

CINEBOOKS, INC. is a McPherson's Publishing Company

Printed in the United States
First Edition

1      2      3      4      5      6      7      8      9      10

# Table of Contents

# Foreword

Horror movies have changed since I did the original FLY or the first re-make of THE MYSTERY OF THE WAX MUSEUM, which was titled THE HOUSE OF WAX. They have become more gory, if less logical, but they still appeal to audiences of all ages. I think this appeal is based, perhaps subconsciously, on an inherent need to be frightened. Fright heightens the humdrum experiences of everyday life. It sharpens our awareness of the extra-ordinary and, at the same time, it warns us to be wary of complacency.

Some of the earliest films were horror or science fiction subjects. They were chosen, I believe, because of their universal appeal as well as the challenge they afforded the technical experts of motion pictures. Fright is a very delicate subject from every aspect. To go overboard in the areas of acting or directing is as dangerous as to underplay. To frighten an audience successfully is to suggest that the unreal is real (logical) and, at the same time, that there is always the hope, the chance of escaping from it back to reality. A good horror film demands that we be kept in suspense from beginning to end just as subtly as we are in day-to-day life.

My memories of horror films always have appeared contradictory, evoking hard work and discipline, and, at the same time moments of great joy. I worked on them with some of the finest, most versatile and jolly people I have ever known—yes, Jolly!. . .For, to survive the making of them requires above all a highly honed sense of humor verging on the ridiculous. My compatriots in their making—Boris Karloff, Peter Lorre, Basil Rathbone, etc.—were gentlemen above all and endowed with the above senses to the highest degree. Many of their best moments will be found in this excellent guide.

— Vincent Price

# Introduction

*"To conceive the horror of my sensations is, I presume, utterly impossible; yet a curiosity to penetrate the mysteries of these awful regions, predominates even over my despair, and will reconcile me to the most hideous aspect of death."*

—Edgar Allen Poe
*Ms. Found In a Bottle*

Despite its significant place in the development of the cinema, the horror film and its devotees have been much maligned by many serious film scholars and even the general public. Occasionally, there may come a film that manages to break through to a mainstream audience, such as THE EXORCIST (1973), but mostly the horror movie is seen as the domain of a select and loyal audience. This has been especially true in the last 20 years as mindless, misogynistic, and extremely graphic gore films have flooded the market, providing the antihorror faction with plenty of ammunition. While the genre certainly boasts more than its share of outright trash, the reactionary stance is a shame, for such horror films as THE CABINET OF DR. CALIGARI (1919) and NOSFERATU (1921), which were crucial in the development of film as an art form, do not always get the respect or attention they deserve. What is often ignored is that the horror genre has always been a refuge for commercial filmmakers with an experimental bent. While the industry and the public do not accept radical cinematic experimentation in a big-budget, all-star production, the horror director usually has free reign to indulge in wild camera moves, erratic editing, and nonlinear narrative structure. In a fantasy format, anything goes. This is especially true in the 1980s, when most Hollywood films have fallen into prepackaged formulas that stifle genuine creativity or artistic expression. By contrast, the entire "Nightmare on Elm Street" series is proof that cinematic experimentation and ingenuity live, through horror, in the commercial cinema, veering as it does between dreams and reality and back again at will, unafraid of losing its audience.

In this reference work, we have attempted to assemble a useful guide to the horror films available on videocassette. Because of the VCR, horror films that were once screened only in drive-ins or remote theaters are now readily available at your local rental house. The same is true of such important, but rarely seen, films as WITCHCRAFT THROUGH THE AGES (1922) and VAMPYR (1931), as well as such remarkable obscurities as MANIAC (1934); CARNIVAL OF SOULS (1962); and SPIDER BABY (1964). While the vast majority of horror films available to Americans are from either the US or Great Britain, we have also included films from Italy, Spain, and Mexico by such directors as Mario Bava, Dario Argento, Lucio Fulci, Amando De Ossorio, and Rene Cardona. With literally hundreds of independent video dealers hawking every obscure or commercially unavailable title imaginable, the dedicated horror fan can ferret out titles that the average renter or buyer would never have the chance to see. Since the product of these dealers is probably illegal and a definite risk in terms of quality, however, we have chosen to include only those video titles most readily available through accepted commercial video distributors and some respected independents.

This, of course, begs the question: Just what is a horror film? The films in this book have one thing in common: they explore human fears. Be it fear of death, dismemberment, sexuality, or simply things that go bump in the night, the horror film has always been a cathartic outlet for us to face the darker reaches of the human soul and exorcise them...at least for a short while. The horror film deals in the macabre, grotesque, and supernatural in the same way science fiction explores the potential and limitations of science. Fantastic films all share certain qualities, and many genres, such as horror and science fiction, tend to overlap. While we have included most "mad scientist" and "giant monster" movies here, films with futuristic, outer-space, alien-visitation, or atomic themes have been left to an upcoming volume on science-fiction and fantasy films, as has most of the Ray Harryhausen canon (usually set in a mythical time and place). Some titles—such as Mario Bava's incredible PLANET OF THE VAMPIRES (1965) or the "Alien" films—were a very tough call, but it was decided that since they are set either in the future or in outer space (or both), they are more sci-fi than horror. In any case, the reader may find some titles included here that are borderline cases, but since there are really no concrete guidelines, the selection process here has been somewhat subjective.

In addition to listing titles, years, running times, casts, credits, and synopses of the films, we have also made use of a star-rating system as a guide to which films are actually worth seeing. While the star-rating format is limiting—often a one-star or zero-rated film is more fun to watch than a five-star entry—readers have come to expect it over the years and it makes the task of selecting which reviews to read much easier for the casual consumer. While we do take the genre seriously, we have not forgotten the pure pleasure of being frightened, grossed out, or merely amused by spectacular ineptitude, and the reviews often reflect that aspect of the horror movie experience. Readers will note that the acknowledged "classics" of the genre—the Universal and Hammer horror series, the Val Lewton RKO films, the Roger Corman Poe series—continue to be rated highly, while certain subgenres, such as slasher movies like FRIDAY THE 13TH and its ilk, are taken to task for their basic worthlessness. This critical approach may alienate the "gorehounds," but the gross-out factor is only part of what makes a film work and far too many recent horror movies have adopted a gore-for-gore's-sake standard that severely limits the genre's appeal. This is not a prudish reaction; the reader will find the work of George Romero, David Cronenberg, and Wes Craven—directors known for their stomach-churning viscera—rated quite highly. Yet there has to be an intelligent sensibility behind the gore for it to rise above the merely inane and exploitative.

As of this writing, a shocking number of seminal horror films remain unavailable on videotape. Most notably absent are such titles as ISLAND OF LOST SOULS (1932); DR. JEKYLL AND MR. HYDE (1932); MURDERS IN THE RUE MORGUE (1932); THE OLD DARK HOUSE (1932); THE WEREWOLF OF LONDON (1935); MAD LOVE (1935); DRACULA'S DAUGHTER (1936); the majority of Hammer's excellent "Dracula" and "Frankenstein" series; THE REPTILE (1966); PLAGUE OF THE ZOMBIES (1966); THE DEVIL RIDES OUT (1967); and SUSPIRIA (1976). Luckily, the video market place is burgeoning with new titles every week, and one can only hope that soon some of the greatest films the genre has produced will make their way into your living rooms, uninterrupted and uncensored.

—James J. Mulay

# FILMS BY STAR RATING

Movies included in this volume are listed below by their star ratings. Ratings indicate:
*****—masterpiece; ****—excellent; ***—good; **—fair; *—poor; zero—without merit

## *****

BLACK CAT, THE
BODY SNATCHER, THE
BRIDE OF FRANKENSTEIN, THE
CABINET OF DR. CALIGARI, THE
CURSE OF THE DEMON
DAWN OF THE DEAD
DEAD RINGERS
ERASERHEAD
EVIL DEAD, THE
EVIL DEAD 2: DEAD BY DAWN
FREAKS
HILLS HAVE EYES, THE
HORROR CHAMBER OF DR.
  FAUSTUS, THE
HORROR OF DRACULA, THE
HUNCHBACK OF NOTRE DAME,
  THE
I WALKED WITH A ZOMBIE
KING KONG
MARTIN
NIGHT OF THE LIVING DEAD
NIGHTMARE ON ELM STREET, A
NOSFERATU, THE VAMPIRE
PEEPING TOM
PSYCHO
REPULSION
ROSEMARY'S BABY
SEVENTH VICTIM, THE
TEXAS CHAIN SAW MASSACRE,
  THE
VAMPYR

## ****

ABBOTT AND COSTELLO MEET
  FRANKENSTEIN
ALICE, SWEET ALICE
ASSAULT ON PRECINCT 13
BASKET CASE
BIRD WITH THE CRYSTAL
  PLUMAGE, THE
BIRDS, THE
BLOOD AND BLACK LACE
BROOD, THE
CARNIVAL OF SOULS
CAT PEOPLE
CONQUEROR WORM, THE
CRAZIES, THE
CURSE OF FRANKENSTEIN, THE
CURSE OF THE CAT PEOPLE, THE
DAY OF THE DEAD
DEAD OF NIGHT
DEATHDREAM
EATING RAOUL

EXORCIST, THE
FLY, THE
FRANKENSTEIN
GOLEM, THE
HALLOWEEN
HANDS OF THE RIPPER
HOUSE OF USHER
ISLE OF THE DEAD
JAWS
KWAIDAN
LADY IN WHITE
MASQUE OF THE RED DEATH, THE
MONKEY SHINES: AN EXPERIMENT
  IN FEAR
MS. 45
MUMMY, THE
MYSTERY OF THE WAX MUSEUM,
  THE
NEAR DARK
PHANTASM
PHANTOM OF THE OPERA, THE
PIT AND THE PENDULUM, THE
Q
SEANCE ON A WET AFTERNOON
SHINING, THE
SISTERS
SON OF FRANKENSTEIN
SPIDER BABY
STEPFATHER, THE
THEATRE OF BLOOD
TOMB OF LIGEIA, THE
VIDEODROME
WHATEVER HAPPENED TO BABY
  JANE?
WOLF MAN, THE
YOUNG FRANKENSTEIN

## ***1/2

ABOMINABLE DR. PHIBES, THE
ANGUISH
BEETLEJUICE
BLACK ROOM, THE
BLACK SABBATH
BLACK SUNDAY
BLUE SUNSHINE
BLUEBEARD
BRAIN DAMAGE
CREATURE FROM THE BLACK
  LAGOON
CURSE OF THE WEREWOLF, THE
DAUGHTERS OF DARKNESS
DEMENTIA 13
DEVIL DOLL, THE
DOCTOR PHIBES RISES AGAIN

DR. JEKYLL AND MR. HYDE
DOCTOR X
DON'T LOOK NOW
DRACULA
FEAR NO EVIL
FLY, THE
FRIGHT NIGHT
FROM BEYOND
GANJA AND HESS
GHOSTBUSTERS
GORGON, THE
HORROR EXPRESS
HOUSE OF WAX
HOWLING, THE
HUMAN MONSTER, THE
HUSH . . . HUSH, SWEET
  CHARLOTTE
INVISIBLE MAN, THE
IT LIVES AGAIN
IT'S ALIVE
LAST HOUSE ON THE LEFT
LEOPARD MAN, THE
LITTLE SHOP OF HORRORS
LOST WORLD, THE
MASSACRE AT CENTRAL HIGH
MUMMY, THE
NINTH CONFIGURATION, THE
NOSFERATU, THE VAMPIRE
NUTTY PROFESSOR, THE
OTHER, THE
PICTURE OF DORIAN GRAY, THE
PLUMBER, THE
RAVEN, THE
RAVEN, THE
RE-ANIMATOR
SERPENT AND THE RAINBOW, THE
SON OF DRACULA
TALES OF TERROR
TARGETS
TWINS OF EVIL
WICKER MAN, THE
WOLFEN

## ***

ALLIGATOR
ANDY WARHOL'S DRACULA
ASYLUM
BEDLAM
BEYOND THE DOOR II
BLACULA
BLOOD DEMON
BLOOD ON SATAN'S CLAW, THE
CAPTAIN KRONOS: VAMPIRE
  HUNTER

CARRIE
CAT AND THE CANARY, THE
CHANGELING, THE
CHILDREN SHOULDN'T PLAY WITH
 DEAD THINGS
CHILD'S PLAY
CIRCUS OF HORRORS
CORRIDORS OF BLOOD
COUNT YORGA, VAMPIRE
CREEPERS
CREEPING FLESH, THE
CRIME OF DR. CRESPI, THE
DEAD ZONE, THE
DEMENTIA
DIE! DIE! MY DARLING
DR. JEKYLL AND MR. HYDE
DRESSED TO KILL
EATEN ALIVE
FADE TO BLACK
FRANKENSTEIN MEETS THE WOLF
 MAN
FUNHOUSE, THE
GATE, THE
GHOST STORY
GHOUL, THE
GREAT GABBO, THE
HALLOWEEN IV: THE RETURN OF
 MICHAEL MYERS
HAUNTED STRANGLER, THE
HAUNTING, THE
HELLRAISER
HOMEBODIES
HORROR HOTEL
HOUSE ON HAUNTED HILL
HOUSE THAT DRIPPED BLOOD,
 THE
HUNCHBACK OF NOTRE DAME,
 THE
INFERNO
IT'S ALIVE III: ISLAND OF THE
 ALIVE
KINGDOM OF THE SPIDERS
LEGEND OF THE SEVEN GOLDEN
 VAMPIRES, THE
LITTLE GIRL WHO LIVES DOWN
 THE LANE, THE
MAN THEY COULD NOT HANG,
 THE
MARK OF THE VAMPIRE
MURDERS IN THE RUE MORGUE
NIGHTMARE ON ELM STREET 3:
 DREAM WARRIORS, A
NIGHTMARE ON ELM STREET 4:
 THE DREAM MASTER, A
OBLONG BOX, THE
PHANTOM OF THE OPERA
PREMATURE BURIAL, THE
PREMONITION, THE
PRINCE OF DARKNESS
PSYCHO III

PULSE
PYX, THE
RABID
RETURN OF THE VAMPIRE, THE
SCANNERS
SCREAM AND SCREAM AGAIN
SENDER, THE
SHOUT, THE
SON OF KONG
SQUIRM
STRANGE BEHAVIOR
SURVIVOR
TALES FROM THE CRYPT
TELL-TALE HEART, THE
TENANT, THE
TO THE DEVIL A DAUGHTER
UNHOLY THREE, THE
VAMPIRE BAT, THE
WHEN A STRANGER CALLS
WHITE ZOMBIE

**1/2

ABBOTT AND COSTELLO MEET DR.
 JEKYLL AND MR. HYDE
ALONE IN THE DARK
AMERICAN WEREWOLF IN
 LONDON, AN
AMITYVILLE HORROR, THE
ANDY WARHOL'S FRANKENSTEIN
ANGEL HEART
ASPHYX, THE
BEAST WITHIN, THE
BEFORE I HANG
BEN
BLACK DRAGONS
BLOW OUT
BODY DOUBLE
BOOGEY MAN, THE
BOOGEYMAN II
BOWERY AT MIDNIGHT
BRAIN THAT WOULDN'T DIE, THE
BRIDE, THE
CHRISTINE
CORPSE VANISHES, THE
CREATURE FROM THE HAUNTED
 SEA
CREEPSHOW
CURSE OF THE AZTEC MUMMY,
 THE
DAUGHTER OF DR. JEKYLL
DEAD MEN WALK
DEADLY BLESSING
DEADLY EYES
DEVIL BAT, THE
DEVIL DOLL
DEVONSVILLE TERROR, THE
DIE, MONSTER, DIE
DR. BLACK AND MR. HYDE
DR. HECKYL AND MR. HYPE
DR. JEKYLL AND SISTER HYDE

DR. TARR'S TORTURE DUNGEON
DR. TERROR'S HOUSE OF
 HORRORS
DRILLER KILLER
DUNWICH HORROR, THE
ENTITY, THE
EQUINOX
EVIL, THE
EVILSPEAK
EXORCIST II: THE HERETIC
FLESH EATERS, THE
FOG, THE
FRANKENSTEIN 1970
FROGS
FROM BEYOND THE GRAVE
FURY, THE
GHOST SHIP
GHOST STORY
GRAVE OF THE VAMPIRE
GREMLINS
HALLOWEEN III: SEASON OF THE
 WITCH
HATCHET FOR A HONEYMOON
HAUNTING OF JULIA, THE
HELL NIGHT
HELLO MARY LOU, PROM NIGHT II
HORROR OF THE ZOMBIES
HOUSE OF SEVEN CORPSES, THE
HUMANOIDS FROM THE DEEP
HUNGRY WIVES
I DRINK YOUR BLOOD
INVISIBLE GHOST, THE
JAWS II
LAIR OF THE WHITE WORM
LAST HORROR FILM, THE
LET'S SCARE JESSICA TO DEATH
LOST BOYS, THE
LOVE AT FIRST BITE
MAD MONSTER PARTY
MONSTER WALKS, THE
MOTEL HELL
NESTING, THE
NIGHTMARE CASTLE
NIGHTMARE IN BLOOD
NIGHTMARE ON ELM STREET
 PART 2: FREDDY'S REVENGE
NOMADS
OF UNKNOWN ORIGIN
ONE DARK NIGHT
PACK, THE
PATRICK
PHANTOM OF THE PARADISE
PICTURE MOMMY DEAD
PIRANHA
POLTERGEIST
POLTERGEIST II
PRISON
PSYCHO II
RACE WITH THE DEVIL
RAZORBACK

RETURN OF THE FLY
RETURN TO SALEM'S LOT, A
ROAD GAMES
RUBY
SCREAM, BLACULA, SCREAM
SHOCK WAVES
SILENT SCREAM
SLAUGHTER HIGH
SLUMBER PARTY MASSACRE
SLAYER, THE
STRAIT-JACKET
STREET TRASH
STUFF, THE
TEEN WOLF
THEY CAME FROM WITHIN
THIRST
THIRTEEN GHOSTS
TORTURE GARDEN
TWO THOUSAND MANIACS
VAMPIRE LOVERS, THE
VAMPYRES, DAUGHTERS OF
   DRACULA
VAULT OF HORROR, THE
WHO SLEW AUNTIE ROO?
WILLARD

**

AMERICAN GOTHIC
AMITYVILLE 3-D
AMITYVILLE II: THE POSSESSION
AND NOW THE SCREAMING
   STARTS
APE, THE
APRIL FOOL'S DAY
AUDREY ROSE
BABY, THE
BAD DREAMS
BARON BLOOD
BELIEVERS, THE
BERSERK
BEYOND THE FOG
BILLY THE KID VS. DRACULA
BLACK CHRISTMAS
BLOOD FEAST
BLOOD SPATTERED BRIDE, THE
BOOGENS, THE
BRIDE OF THE GORILLA
BROTHERHOOD OF SATAN, THE
BRUTE MAN, THE
BUTCHER, BAKER (NIGHTMARE
   MAKER)
CAR, THE
CAT PEOPLE
CAT'S EYE
CAULDRON OF BLOOD
CHAMBER OF HORRORS
CHOPPING MALL
COUNT DRACULA
CREATURE FROM BLACK LAKE,
   THE

CRUCIBLE OF TERROR
CUJO
CURSE OF THE LIVING CORPSE,
   THE
DAMIEN—OMEN II
DEAD AND BURIED
DEADLY FRIEND
DEEP RED, HATCHET MURDERS
DEMENTED
DEVIL'S NIGHTMARE, THE
DEVIL'S RAIN, THE
DON'T LOOK IN THE BASEMENT
DRACULA
ELVIRA: MISTRESS OF THE DARK
EVIL OF FRANKENSTEIN, THE
FINAL CONFLICT, THE
FLESH AND BLOOD SHOW, THE
FLESH FEAST
FRIGHTMARE (1974)
GHOST TOWN
GHOSTS ON THE LOOSE
GHOUL, THE
GRAVEYARD SHIFT
HALLOWEEN II
HELLBOUND: HELLRAISER II
HITCHER, THE
HORROR HOSPITAL
HOUSE OF EXORCISM, THE
HOUSE OF THE LONG SHADOWS
HOUSE THAT VANISHED, THE
HOWLING IV: THE ORIGINAL
   NIGHTMARE
HUNGER, THE
IN THE SHADOW OF KILIMANJARO
INCENSE FOR THE DAMNED
JAWS 3-D
KEEP, THE
KILLING HOUR, THE
KING OF THE ZOMBIES
LEGEND OF BOGGY CREEK, THE
LEGEND OF HELL HOUSE, THE
LITTLE SHOP OF HORRORS
LOVE BUTCHER, THE
LUST FOR A VAMPIRE
MAD MONSTER, THE
MADHOUSE
MAGIC
MAN WHO HAUNTED HIMSELF,
   THE
MAN WITH TWO BRAINS, THE
MANIAC
MANIAC
MANITOU, THE
MIDNIGHT
MONSTER IN THE CLOSET
MONSTER SQUAD, THE
MURDER CLINIC, THE
NIGHT OF A THOUSAND CATS, THE
NIGHTMARES
OFFSPRING, THE

OMEN, THE
PHANTASM II
PROWLER, THE
PSYCHIC KILLER
PSYCHOMANIA
PUMPKINHEAD
RETURN OF THE LIVING DEAD
RETURN OF THE LIVING DEAD
   PART II
ROBOT VS. THE AZTEC MUMMY,
   THE
SCALPEL
SCARED TO DEATH
SCARED TO DEATH
SCARS OF DRACULA, THE
SCHLOCK
SCREAMTIME
SILENT NIGHT, BLOODY NIGHT
SISTER SISTER
SLUMBER PARTY MASSACRE II
SOMETHING WICKED THIS WAY
   COMES
STRANGER IS WATCHING, A
STRANGLER, THE
SUPERNATURALS, THE
SWAMP THING
TERROR, THE
TERROR HOUSE
TERROR TRAIN
THEATRE OF DEATH
TOO SCARED TO SCREAM
TRICK OR TREAT
TRICK OR TREATS
TWILIGHT ZONE—THE MOVIE
UNCANNY, THE
UNSEEN, THE
VAMP
VIRGIN WITCH, THE
WARNING SIGN
WITCHBOARD
WITCHES OF EASTWICK, THE
YOU BETTER WATCH OUT
ZOMBIES OF MORA TAU

*1/2
ATOM AGE VAMPIRE
AWAKENING, THE
BEAST IN THE CELLAR, THE
BEYOND THE DOOR
BLACK ROOM, THE
BLADE IN THE DARK, A
BLOOD BEACH
BLOOD OF DRACULA'S CASTLE
BLUE MONKEY
BOGGY CREEK II
BRAIN OF BLOOD
CELLAR DWELLER
CHILDREN OF THE CORN
CHOSEN, THE
COLOR ME BLOOD RED

# FILMS BY YEAR

Movies included in this volume are listed below by their year of release.

## 1988
AMERICAN GOTHIC
CELLAR DWELLER
DEADLY DREAMS
DRACULA'S WIDOW
ELVIRA: MISTRESS OF THE DARK
FRANKENSTEIN GENERAL
  HOSPITAL
GHOST TOWN
LAIR OF THE WHITE WORM, THE
PULSE
SEVENTH SIGN, THE
SLAUGHTERHOUSE
SLAUGHTERHOUSE ROCK
UNINVITED, THE
ANGUISH
BAD DREAMS
BEETLEJUICE
BERSERKER
BRAIN DAMAGE
CHILD'S PLAY
DEAD HEAT
DEAD RINGERS
FRIDAY THE 13TH PART VII—THE
  NEW BLOOD
GHOULIES II
HALLOWEEN IV: THE RETURN OF
  MICHAEL MYERS
HELLBOUND: HELLRAISER II
HOWLING IV: THE ORIGINAL
  NIGHTMARE
IT'S ALIVE III: ISLAND OF THE
  ALIVE
LADY IN WHITE
MANIAC COP
MONKEY SHINES: AN EXPERIMENT
  IN FEAR
NIGHTMARE ON ELM STREET 4:
  THE DREAM MASTER, A
PHANTASM II
POLTERGEIST III
PRISON
PUMPKINHEAD
RETRIBUTION
RETURN OF THE LIVING DEAD
  PART II
RETURN TO SALEM'S LOT, A
SERPENT AND THE RAINBOW, THE
SISTER SISTER
SLEEPAWAY CAMP 2: UNHAPPY
  CAMPERS
UNHOLY, THE

## 1987
ANGEL HEART
BELIEVERS, THE
BLOOD DINER
BLOOD SISTERS
BLUE MONKEY
BORN OF FIRE
CREEPSHOW 2
CURSE, THE
DEADTIME STORIES
DEATHROW GAMESHOW
DOLLS
DREAMANIAC
ESCAPES
EVIL DEAD 2: DEAD BY DAWN
GATE, THE
GOTHIC
GRAVEYARD SHIFT
HELLO MARY LOU, PROM NIGHT II
HELLRAISER
HOUSE II: THE SECOND STORY
HOWLING III, THE
I WAS A TEENAGE ZOMBIE
JAWS: THE REVENGE
LOST BOYS, THE
MONSTER IN THE CLOSET
MONSTER SQUAD, THE
MUNCHIES
MY DEMON LOVER
NAIL GUN MASSACRE
NEAR DARK
NIGHTMARE ON ELM STREET 3:
  DREAM WARRIORS, A
OFFSPRING, THE
OPEN HOUSE
OUTING, THE
PRINCE OF DARKNESS
PSYCHOS IN LOVE
RAWHEAD REX
RETURN TO HORROR HIGH
ROCK 'N' ROLL NIGHTMARE
SILENT NIGHT, DEADLY NIGHT
  PART II
SLAUGHTER HIGH
SLUMBER PARTY MASSACRE II
STEPFATHER, THE
STREET TRASH
SUPERNATURALS, THE
TEEN WOLF TOO
WITCHBOARD
WITCHES OF EASTWICK, THE

## 1986
APRIL FOOL'S DAY
BLADE IN THE DARK, A
BLOODY BIRTHDAY
CARNAGE
CHOPPING MALL
CLASS OF NUKE 'EM HIGH
CRAWLSPACE
DEADLY FRIEND
DEMONS 2: THE NIGHTMARE
  RETURNS
FLY, THE
FRIDAY THE 13TH PART VI: JASON
  LIVES
FROM BEYOND
GIRLS SCHOOL SCREAMERS
HAUNTED HONEYMOON
HITCHER, THE
HOUSE
IN THE SHADOW OF KILIMANJARO
KILLER PARTY
KING KONG LIVES
LITTLE SHOP OF HORRORS
MANHATTAN BABY
MAXIMUM OVERDRIVE
MONSTER DOG
MOUNTAINTOP MOTEL MASSACRE
MOVIE HOUSE MASSACRE
NIGHTMARE WEEKEND
POLTERGEIST II
PSYCHO III
REVENGE
SHADOWS RUN BLACK
SORORITY HOUSE MASSACRE
TEXAS CHAINSAW MASSACRE
  PART 2, THE
TRICK OR TREAT
TROLL
VAMP
WITCHFIRE
WRAITH, THE

## 1985
BOGGY CREEK II
BRIDE, THE
CAT'S EYE
CREEPERS
DAY OF THE DEAD
DEMONS
FRIDAY THE 13TH, PART V—A NEW
  BEGINNING
FRIGHT NIGHT
GHOULIES
HILLS HAVE EYES II, THE
HOWLING II . . . YOUR SISTER IS A
  WEREWOLF
MUTILATOR, THE
NIGHTMARE ON ELM STREET
  PART 2: FREDDY'S REVENGE, A

NOMADS
ONCE BITTEN
RE-ANIMATOR
RETURN OF THE LIVING DEAD
SCREAMTIME
STEPHEN KING'S SILVER BULLET
STUFF, THE
SUPERSTITION
TEEN WOLF
TERMINAL CHOICE
TOO SCARED TO SCREAM
TOXIC AVENGER, THE
TRANSYLVANIA 6-5000
WARNING SIGN

## 1984
BLACK ROOM, THE
BODY DOUBLE
CHILDREN OF THE CORN
DADDY'S DEADLY DARLING
DON'T OPEN TILL CHRISTMAS
FRIDAY THE 13TH—THE FINAL
   CHAPTER
GHOSTBUSTERS
GIRLS NIGHT OUT
GREMLINS
HOUSE BY THE CEMETERY, THE
INITIATION, THE
INVISIBLE STRANGLER, THE
LAST HORROR FILM, THE
MIRRORS
NIGHTMARE ON ELM STREET, A
POWER, THE
PREY, THE
RAZORBACK
SILENT NIGHT, DEADLY NIGHT
SPLATTER UNIVERSITY

## 1983
AMITYVILLE 3-D
BOOGEYMAN II
CHRISTINE
CITY OF THE WALKING DEAD
CUJO
CURTAINS
DEAD ZONE, THE
DEVONSVILLE TERROR, THE
DORM THAT DRIPPED BLOOD, THE
EVIL DEAD, THE
FINAL TERROR, THE
FOREST, THE
FRIGHTMARE
GATES OF HELL, THE
HOUSE OF THE LONG SHADOWS
HOUSE ON SORORITY ROW, THE
HUNGER, THE
HYSTERICAL
I SPIT ON YOUR GRAVE
JAWS 3-D
KEEP, THE

MAN WITH TWO BRAINS, THE
MARDI GRAS MASSACRE
MAUSOLEUM
MICROWAVE MASSACRE
MIDNIGHT
MORTUARY
NIGHTMARES
OF UNKNOWN ORIGIN
ONE DARK NIGHT
PSYCHO II
SCALPS
SLEEPAWAY CAMP
SOMETHING WICKED THIS WAY
   COMES
SWEET SIXTEEN
TWILIGHT ZONE—THE MOVIE
VIDEODROME
WACKO

## 1982
ALONE IN THE DARK
AMITYVILLE II: THE POSSESSION
BASKET CASE
BEAST WITHIN, THE
BLOOD TIDE
BUTCHER, BAKER (NIGHTMARE
   MAKER)
CAT PEOPLE
CREEPSHOW
DEADLY EYES
DR. BUTCHER, M.D.
DR. JEKYLL'S DUNGEON OF DEATH
EATING RAOUL
ENTITY, THE
EVILSPEAK
FRIDAY THE 13TH PART III
FUNERAL HOME
HALLOWEEN III: SEASON OF THE
   WITCH
HOSPITAL MASSACRE
HOUSE WHERE EVIL DWELLS, THE
HUMONGOUS
INCUBUS, THE
JEKYLL AND HYDE . . . TOGETHER
   AGAIN
KILLING HOUR, THE
LOVE BUTCHER, THE
MADMAN
NEXT OF KIN
PANDEMONIUM
POLTERGEIST
Q
SENDER, THE
SLAYER, THE
SLUMBER PARTY MASSACRE
SPASMS
STRANGER IS WATCHING, A
SWAMP THING
TRICK OR TREATS
VISITING HOURS

## 1981
AMERICAN WEREWOLF IN
   LONDON, AN
BEYOND THE FOG
BLOOD BEACH
BLOW OUT
BOOGENS, THE
BURNING, THE
DEAD AND BURIED
DEADLY BLESSING
DEMON, THE
DEMONOID
FEAR NO EVIL
FINAL CONFLICT, THE
FINAL EXAM
FRIDAY THE 13TH PART II
FUNHOUSE, THE
GHOST STORY
GRADUATION DAY
GRIM REAPER, THE
HALLOWEEN II
HAND, THE
HAPPY BIRTHDAY TO ME
HELL NIGHT
HOWLING, THE
MONSTER CLUB, THE
MY BLOODY VALENTINE
NESTING, THE
NIGHT OF THE ZOMBIES
NIGHTMARE
PIECES
PIRANHA II: THE SPAWNING
PLAY DEAD
POSSESSION
PROWLER, THE
ROAD GAMES
SATURDAY THE 14TH
SAVAGE WEEKEND
SCANNERS
SCARED TO DEATH
STRANGE BEHAVIOR
STUDENT BODIES
UNSEEN, THE
WOLFEN

## 1980
ALLIGATOR
AWAKENING, THE
BEYOND EVIL
BLOODEATERS
BOOGEY MAN, THE
CHANGELING, THE
CHILDREN, THE
DEATH SHIP
DEMENTED
DR. HECKYL AND MR. HYPE
DON'T ANSWER THE PHONE
DON'T GO IN THE HOUSE
DRESSED TO KILL
EYES OF A STRANGER

FADE TO BLACK
FIEND
FOG, THE
FRIDAY THE 13TH
GODSEND, THE
GREAT ALLIGATOR, THE
HE KNOWS YOU'RE ALONE
HEARSE, THE
HUMAN EXPERIMENTS
HUMANOIDS FROM THE DEEP
INFERNO
JUST BEFORE DAWN
KEEP MY GRAVE OPEN
LAST RITES
MANIAC
MOTEL HELL
MOTHER'S DAY
MS. 45
NEW YEAR'S EVIL
NINTH CONFIGURATION, THE
PHOBIA
PLUMBER, THE
PROM NIGHT
SCHIZOID
SHINING, THE
SILENT SCREAM
SURVIVOR
TERROR ON TOUR
TERROR TRAIN
TO ALL A GOODNIGHT
VISITOR, THE
WATCHER IN THE WOODS, THE
YOU BETTER WATCH OUT
ZOMBIE

## 1979
AMITYVILLE HORROR, THE
BEYOND THE DOOR II
BROOD, THE
DAWN OF THE DEAD
DRACULA
DRILLER KILLER
FRIDAY THE 13TH . . . THE
    ORPHAN
LEGACY, THE
LOVE AT FIRST BITE
NIGHTWING
NOCTURNA
NOSFERATU, THE VAMPIRE
PHANTASM
PROPHECY
SCREAMS OF A WINTER NIGHT
THIRST
TOURIST TRAP, THE
WHEN A STRANGER CALLS
WOLFMAN

## 1978
ALICE, SWEET ALICE
CHOSEN, THE

DAMIEN—OMEN II
DRACULA'S DOG
ERASERHEAD
EVIL, THE
FURY, THE
HALLOWEEN
HILLS HAVE EYES, THE
IT LIVES AGAIN
JAWS II
JENNIFER
MAGIC
MANITOU, THE
MARTIN
NIGHTMARE IN BLOOD
PATRICK
PIRANHA
SCREAMERS
SHOUT, THE
TERROR
TOOLBOX MURDERS, THE

## 1977
AUDREY ROSE
BLUE SUNSHINE
CAR, THE
CATHY'S CURSE
CHILD, THE
DAY OF THE ANIMALS
DEMON LOVER, THE
EXORCIST II: THE HERETIC
HAUNTS
ISLAND OF DR. MOREAU, THE
KINGDOM OF THE SPIDERS
LAST HOUSE ON DEAD END
    STREET
LITTLE GIRL WHO LIVES DOWN
    THE LANE, THE
MEAT CLEAVER MASSACRE
ORCA
PACK, THE
PSYCHIC, THE
RUBY
SATAN'S CHEERLEADERS
SENTINEL, THE
SHOCK WAVES
TENTACLES
TOWN THAT DREADED SUNDOWN,
    THE
UNCANNY, THE
WORM EATERS, THE

## 1976
ASSAULT ON PRECINCT 13
BLOODSUCKING FREAKS
BURNT OFFERINGS
CARNIVAL OF BLOOD
CARRIE
CREATURE FROM BLACK LAKE,
    THE
DR. BLACK AND MR. HYDE

DRIVE-IN MASSACRE
EATEN ALIVE
GRIZZLY
HAUNTED
HAUNTING OF JULIA, THE
HOUSE OF EXORCISM, THE
KEEPER, THE
KING KONG
LAND OF THE MINOTAUR
MANSION OF THE DOOMED
MASSACRE AT CENTRAL HIGH
OMEN, THE
RABID
RATTLERS
REDEEMER, THE
SCALPEL
SCHIZO
SQUIRM
TENANT, THE
THEY CAME FROM WITHIN
TO THE DEVIL A DAUGHTER
TRACK OF THE MOONBEAST

## 1975
BEYOND THE DOOR
CONFESSIONAL, THE
DEEP RED: HATCHET MURDERS
DEVIL'S RAIN, THE
FORCED ENTRY
GHOUL, THE
JAWS
MARY, MARY, BLOODY MARY
PEOPLE WHO OWN THE DARK
PREMONITION, THE
PSYCHIC KILLER
RACE WITH THE DEVIL
THIRSTY DEAD, THE
VAMPYRES, DAUGHTERS OF
    DRACULA

## 1974
ANDY WARHOL'S DRACULA
ANDY WARHOL'S FRANKENSTEIN
BEAST MUST DIE, THE
BLACK CHRISTMAS
BLOOD SPATTERED BRIDE, THE
CAPTAIN KRONOS: VAMPIRE
    HUNTER
CRAZE
DEMON WITCH CHILD
FRIGHTMARE
FROM BEYOND THE GRAVE
GHOST STORY
HOMEBODIES
HORROR OF THE ZOMBIES
HOUSE OF SEVEN CORPSES, THE
HOUSE OF WHIPCORD
HOUSE ON SKULL MOUNTAIN, THE
HOUSE THAT VANISHED, THE
I DISMEMBER MAMA

INN OF THE DAMNED
IT'S ALIVE
MADHOUSE
NIGHT OF A THOUSAND CATS, THE
NIGHT OF THE COBRA WOMAN
PHANTOM OF THE PARADISE
SHRIEK OF THE MUTILATED
SILENT NIGHT, BLOODY NIGHT
SPECTRE OF EDGAR ALLAN POE,
    THE
TEMPTER, THE
TEXAS CHAIN SAW MASSACRE,
    THE
WICKER MAN, THE
YOUNG FRANKENSTEIN

## 1973
AND NOW THE SCREAMING
    STARTS
ARNOLD
BABY, THE
BLACKENSTEIN
BLOOD ORGY OF THE SHE-DEVILS
CRAZIES, THE
CREEPING FLESH, THE
CRYPT OF THE LIVING DEAD
DEVIL'S WEDDING NIGHT, HE
DOCTOR DEATH: SEEKER OF
    SOULS
DON'T LOOK IN THE BASEMENT
DON'T LOOK NOW
ENCOUNTER WITH THE UNKNOWN
EXORCIST, THE
GANJA AND HESS
HORROR HOSPITAL
HOUSE OF FREAKS
HOUSE OF PSYCHOTIC WOMEN,
    THE
HOUSE OF THE LIVING DEAD
HUNGRY WIVES
LEGEND OF BOGGY CREEK, THE
LEGEND OF HELL HOUSE, THE
LEGEND OF THE SEVEN GOLDEN
    VAMPIRES, THE
PYX, THE
SCHLOCK
SCREAM, BLACULA, SCREAM
SISTERS
STANLEY
THEATRE OF BLOOD
TORSO
TWITCH OF THE DEATH NERVE
VAULT OF HORROR, THE
WEREWOLF OF WASHINGTON

## 1972
ASPHYX, THE
ASYLUM
BARON BLOOD
BEN

BLACULA
BURKE AND HARE
CHILDREN SHOULDN'T PLAY WITH
    DEAD THINGS
CORPSE GRINDERS, THE
DEAR, DEAD DELILAH
DEATHDREAM
DISCIPLE OF DEATH
DOCTOR PHIBES RISES AGAIN
DR. TARR'S TORTURE DUNGEON
FLESH AND BLOOD SHOW, THE
FROGS
GARDEN OF THE DEAD
GRAVE OF THE VAMPIRE
HORROR EXPRESS
INVASION OF THE BLOOD
    FARMERS
LAST HOUSE ON THE LEFT
MAN WITH TWO HEADS, THE
OTHER, THE
PSYCHOMANIA
RATS ARE COMING! THE
    WEREWOLVES ARE HERE!, THE
SCREAM BLOODY MURDER
SCREAMING DEAD, THE
TALES FROM THE CRYPT
TERROR HOUSE

## 1971
ABOMINABLE DR. PHIBES, THE
BEAST IN THE CELLAR, THE
BIG FOOT
BRAIN OF BLOOD
BROTHERHOOD OF SATAN, THE
CAULDRON OF BLOOD
COUNT DRACULA
CRUCIBLE OF HORROR
CRUCIBLE OF TERROR
DAUGHTERS OF DARKNESS
DEVIL'S NIGHTMARE, THE
DR. JEKYLL AND SISTER HYDE
HANDS OF THE RIPPER
HOUSE THAT DRIPPED BLOOD,
    THE
I DRINK YOUR BLOOD
LADY FRANKENSTEIN
LET'S SCARE JESSICA TO DEATH
LUST FOR A VAMPIRE
MURDERS IN THE RUE MORGUE
OCTAMAN
POINT OF TERROR
TWINS OF EVIL
VELVET VAMPIRE, THE
WEREWOLVES ON WHEELS
WHO SLEW AUNTIE ROO?
WILLARD

## 1970
BIRD WITH THE CRYSTAL
    PLUMAGE, THE

BLOOD ON SATAN'S CLAW, THE
BLOODTHIRSTY BUTCHERS
COUNT YORGA, VAMPIRE
DORIAN GRAY
DRACULA VS. FRANKENSTEIN
DUNWICH HORROR, THE
EQUINOX
FLESH FEAST
HORROR OF FRANKENSTEIN, THE
INCENSE FOR THE DAMNED
LUST FOR A VAMPIRE
MAN WHO HAUNTED HIMSELF,
    THE
MARK OF THE DEVIL
SCARS OF DRACULA, THE
TORTURE DUNGEON
VAMPIRE LOVERS, THE
VIRGIN WITCH, THE
WEREWOLF VS. THE VAMPIRE
    WOMAN, THE
WIZARD OF GORE, THE

## 1969
HATCHET FOR A HONEYMOON
MAD DOCTOR OF BLOOD ISLAND,
    THE
NIGHT OF BLOODY HORROR
NIGHTMARE IN WAX
OBLONG BOX, THE
SCREAM AND SCREAM AGAIN
WITCHMAKER, THE

## 1968
BLOOD BEAST TERROR, THE
CONQUEROR WORM, THE
FEAR CHAMBER, THE
GHASTLY ONES, THE
GRUESOME TWOSOME
HOUSE OF EVIL
NIGHT OF THE BLOODY APES
NIGHT OF THE LIVING DEAD
ROSEMARY'S BABY
SPIDER BABY
TARGETS

## 1967
BERSERK
BLOOD DEMON
BLOOD OF DRACULA'S CASTLE
CASTLE OF EVIL
DEATH CURSE OF TARTU
HILLBILLYS IN A HAUNTED HOUSE
MAD MONSTER PARTY
SOMETHING WEIRD
TORTURE GARDEN

## 1966
BILLY THE KID VS. DRACULA
CURSE OF THE SWAMP
    CREATURE

JESSE JAMES MEETS
   FRANKENSTEIN'S DAUGHTER
MURDER CLINIC, THE
PICTURE MOMMY DEAD
THEATRE OF DEATH

## 1965
BLOOD AND BLACK LACE
COLOR ME BLOOD RED
CURSE OF THE AZTEC MUMMY,
   THE
DIE! DIE! MY DARLING
DIE, MONSTER, DIE
DR. TERROR'S HOUSE OF
   HORRORS
NIGHTMARE CASTLE
ORGY OF THE DEAD
REPULSION
THRILL KILLERS, THE

## 1964
ATOMIC BRAIN, THE
CURSE OF THE LIVING CORPSE,
   THE
DEVIL DOLL
EVIL OF FRANKENSTEIN, THE
FLESH EATERS, THE
GORGON, THE
HORROR OF PARTY BEACH, THE
HUSH . . . HUSH, SWEET
   CHARLOTTE
KWAIDAN
MASQUE OF THE RED DEATH, THE
SEANCE ON A WET AFTERNOON
STRAIT-JACKET
STRANGLER, THE
TOMB OF LIGEIA, THE
TWO THOUSAND MANIACS
WRESTLING WOMEN VS. THE
   AZTEC MUMMY, THE

## 1963
BIRDS, THE
BLACK SABBATH
BLOOD FEAST
DEMENTIA 13
HAUNTING, THE
MANIAC
NUTTY PROFESSOR, THE
RAVEN, THE
TERROR, THE

## 1962
CARNIVAL OF SOULS
PREMATURE BURIAL, THE
TALES OF TERROR
TELL-TALE HEART, THE
WHATEVER HAPPENED TO BABY
   JANE?

## 1961
ATOM AGE VAMPIRE
CREATURE FROM THE HAUNTED
   SEA

CURSE OF THE WEREWOLF, THE
LITTLE SHOP OF HORRORS
LIVING HEAD, THE
PIT AND THE PENDULUM, THE

## 1960
BLACK SUNDAY
CIRCUS OF HORRORS
HORROR HOTEL
HOUSE OF USHER
LITTLE SHOP OF HORRORS
PEEPING TOM
PSYCHO
THIRTEEN GHOSTS

## 1959
BRAIN THAT WOULDN'T DIE, THE
HORROR CHAMBER OF DR.
   FAUSTUS, THE
MONSTER OF PIEDRAS BLANCAS,
   THE
MUMMY, THE
NIGHT OF THE GHOULS
RETURN OF THE FLY

## 1958
CORRIDORS OF BLOOD
CURSE OF THE DEMON
FLY, THE
FRANKENSTEIN 1970
FRANKENSTEIN'S DAUGHTER
GIANT FROM THE UNKNOWN
HAUNTED STRANGLER, THE
HORROR OF DRACULA, THE
HOUSE ON HAUNTED HILL
ROBOT VS. THE AZTEC MUMMY,
   THE

## 1957
AZTEC MUMMY, THE
CURSE OF FRANKENSTEIN, THE
DAUGHTER OF DR. JEKYLL
UNEARTHLY, THE
ZOMBIES OF MORA TAU

## 1955
DEMENTIA

## 1954
ABBOTT AND COSTELLO MEET DR.
   JEKYLL AND MR. HYDE
CREATURE FROM THE BLACK
   LAGOON

## 1953
GHOST SHIP
HOUSE OF WAX

## 1951
BRIDE OF THE GORILLA

## 1948
ABBOTT AND COSTELLO MEET
   FRANKENSTEIN

## 1947
SCARED TO DEATH

## 1946
BEDLAM
BRUTE MAN, THE
DEAD OF NIGHT

## 1945
BODY SNATCHER, THE
ISLE OF THE DEAD
PICTURE OF DORIAN GRAY, THE

## 1944
BLUEBEARD
CURSE OF THE CAT PEOPLE, THE
RETURN OF THE VAMPIRE, THE

## 1943
APE MAN, THE
DEAD MEN WALK
FRANKENSTEIN MEETS THE WOLF
   MAN
GHOSTS ON THE LOOSE
I WALKED WITH A ZOMBIE
LEOPARD MAN, THE
PHANTOM OF THE OPERA
SEVENTH VICTIM, THE
SON OF DRACULA

## 1942
BLACK DRAGONS
BOWERY AT MIDNIGHT
CAT PEOPLE
CORPSE VANISHES, THE
MAD MONSTER, THE

## 1941
CHAMBER OF HORRORS
DEVIL BAT, THE
DR. JEKYLL AND MR. HYDE
INVISIBLE GHOST, THE
KING OF THE ZOMBIES
WOLF MAN, THE

## 1940
APE, THE
BEFORE I HANG
HUMAN MONSTER, THE

## 1939
DEMON BARBER OF FLEET
   STREET, THE
HUNCHBACK OF NOTRE DAME,
   THE
MAN THEY COULD NOT HANG,
   THE
SON OF FRANKENSTEIN

## 1936
CRIME OF DR. CRESPI, THE
DEVIL DOLL, THE

REVOLT OF THE ZOMBIES

## 1935
BLACK ROOM, THE
BRIDE OF FRANKENSTEIN, THE
MARK OF THE VAMPIRE
RAVEN, THE

## 1934
BLACK CAT, THE
MANIAC

## 1933
GHOUL, THE
INVISIBLE MAN, THE
KING KONG
MYSTERY OF THE WAX MUSEUM,
   THE
SON OF KONG
VAMPIRE BAT, THE

## 1932
DOCTOR X
FREAKS
MONSTER WALKS, THE
MUMMY, THE
VAMPYR
WHITE ZOMBIE

## 1931
DRACULA
FRANKENSTEIN

## 1930
UNHOLY THREE, THE

## 1929
GREAT GABBO, THE

## 1927
CAT AND THE CANARY, THE

## 1925
LOST WORLD, THE
PHANTOM OF THE OPERA, THE

## 1923
HUNCHBACK OF NOTRE DAME,
   THE

## 1922
NOSFERATU, THE VAMPIRE
WITCHCRAFT THROUGH THE
   AGES

## 1920
CABINET OF DR. CALIGARI, THE
DR. JEKYLL AND MR. HYDE
GOLEM, THE

# The Horror Film

**Film Reviews**

# A

## ABBOTT AND COSTELLO MEET DR. JEKYLL AND MR. HYDE**½

(1954) 76m UNIV bw

Bud Abbott *(Slim)*, Lou Costello *(Tubby)*, Boris Karloff *(Dr. Henry Jekyll)*, Craig Stevens *(Bruce Adams)*, Helen Westcott *(Vicky Edwards)*, Reginald Denny *(Inspector)*, John Dierkes *(Batley)*, Patti McKay, Lucille Lamarr *(Dancers)*, Henry Corden *(Javanese Actor)*, Marjorie Bennett *(Militant Woman)*, Carmen de Lavallade *(Javanese)*, Arthur Gould-Porter *(Bartender)*, Herbert Deans *(Victim)*, Judith Brian *(Woman on Bike)*, Clyde Cook, John Rogers *(Drunks)*, Gil Perkins *(Man on Bike)*, Hilda Plowright *(Nursemaid)*, Keith Hitchcock *(Jailer)*, Harry Cording *(Rough Character)*, Donald Kerr *(Chimney Sweep)*, Clive Morgan, Tony Marshe, Michael Hadlow *(Bobbies)*.

As two American cops sent to London to study crowd control, Abbott and Costello inadvertently become involved with mad scientist Dr. Henry Jekyll (Boris Karloff), who has been busy transforming animals into weird hybrids (a cat that moos like a cow, a rabbit that barks like a dog) and murdering colleagues who have mocked his theories. Jekyll does this by injecting a special serum that turns him into the evil Mr. Hyde (stuntman Eddie Parker played the monster for the 66-year-old Karloff in the more athletic scenes). Of course, comedic chaos ensues as Jekyll/Hyde becomes more crazed and decides to kill the Americans. In the climactic chase, Costello is jabbed with a syringe containing Jekyll's formula and turns into a snarling, hairy Mr. Hyde himself. By this—the seventh—entry in the "Abbott and Costello Meet" series, the concept had long run out of gas. One point in this film's favor is the appearance of Boris Karloff, here playing a monster for the first time in 14 years. Unfortunately, the Mr. Hyde makeup by Bud Westmore, who inherited the Universal makeup department from the masterful Jack Pierce, is little more than an immobile mask and must be considered a disappointment. The next "A&C Meet" entry, ABBOTT AND COSTELLO MEET THE MUMMY (1955), would be the last.

p, Howard Christie; d, Charles Lamont; w, Lee Loeb, John Grant (based on the novel *Dr. Jekyll and Mr. Hyde* by Robert Louis Stevenson); ph, George Robinson; ed, Russell Schoengarth; m, Joseph Gershenson.

(PR:A MPAA:NR)

## ABBOTT AND COSTELLO MEET FRANKENSTEIN****

(1948) 83m UNIV bw (GB: ABBOTT AND COSTELLO MEET THE GHOSTS)

Bud Abbott *(Chick Young)*, Lou Costello *(Wilbur Grey)*, Lon Chaney, Jr. *(Lawrence Talbot/The Wolf Man)*, Bela Lugosi *(Dracula)*, Glenn Strange *(The Monster)*, Lenore Aubert *(Sandra Mornay)*, Jane Randolph *(Joan Raymond)*, Frank

Ferguson *(McDougal)*, Charles Bradstreet *(Dr. Stevens)*, Howard Negley *(Harris)*, Clarence Straight *(Man in Armor)*, Helen Spring *(Woman)*, Harry Brown *(Photographer)*, Paul Stader *(Sergeant)*, Bobby Barber *(Waiter)*, Vincent Price *(Voice of the Invisible Man)*.

In this spoof of Universal horror series, Abbott and Costello play railway porters who unwittingly deliver the "undead" bodies of Frankenstein's monster (Glenn Strange) and Dracula (Bela Lugosi) to a wax museum, where the bodies are revived. Thus awakened, Dracula becomes intent on replacing the catatonic Monster's brain with dim-witted Costello's, because it would make the beast easier to control. Lawrence Talbot (Lon Chaney, Jr.) attempts to help the boys, but he's got problems of his own: he turns into a wolfman whenever there's a full moon. Never were horror and comedy mixed more successfully than in this, the best of the Abbott and Costello movies. Although very funny, the film is a rather ignoble end for the excellent Universal horror series, which, after 17 years, had finally limped into self-parody with this effort. Horror buffs will note that in one scene Chaney, Jr., who had played the Monster in THE GHOST OF FRANKENSTEIN (1942), filled in for Strange in the shot where the Monster tosses actress Lenore Aubert out a window. Strange had broken his foot in an accident, and rather than lose three days' worth of shooting, Chaney volunteered to don the makeup once again. After this film's incredible success at the box office, Abbott and Costello made seven more pictures in which they "met" Hollywood monsters, but none were as lively and entertaining as this effort.

p, Robert Arthur; d, Charles T. Barton; w, Robert Lees, Frederic I. Rinaldo, John Grant (based on the novel *Frankenstein* by Mary Shelley); ph, Charles Van Enger; ed, Frank Gross; m, Frank Skinner.

(PR:A MPAA:NR)

## ABOMINABLE DR. PHIBES, THE***½

(1971, Brit.) 93m AIP c

Vincent Price *(Dr. Anton Phibes)*, Joseph Cotten *(Dr. Vesalius)*, Hugh Griffith *(Rabbi)*, Terry-Thomas *(Dr. Longstreet)*, Virginia North *(Vulnavia)*, Audrey Woods *(Goldsmith)*, Susan Travers *(Nurse Allan)*, Alex Scott *(Dr. Hargreaves)*, Peter Gilmore *(Dr. Kitaj)*, Edward Burnham *(Dr. Dunwoody)*, Peter Jeffrey *(Inspector Trout)*, Maurice Kaufman *(Dr. Whitcombe)*, Norman Jones *(Sgt. Schenley)*, Derek Godfrey *(Crow)*, John Cater *(Waverly)*, Barbara Keogh *(Mrs. Frawley)*, Sean Bury *(Lem Vesalius)*, Walter Horsbrugh *(Ross)*, Caroline Munro *(Mrs. Victoria Phibes)*, David Hutcheson *(Dr. Hedgepath)*, Dallas Adams, Alan Zipson *(Police Officials)*.

A delightfully goofy horror film set in England circa 1929, THE ABOMINABLE DR. PHIBES stars Vincent Price as Dr.

Anton Phibes, a horribly disfigured madman who enacts an insidious revenge on the team of physicians who failed to save the life of his dear, departed wife (Caroline Munro, seen mostly in photos). His face and voice destroyed in an auto accident, Phibes reconstructs his mutilated visage over the bones that remained, and repairs his lost vocal cords by plugging a cord extended from his neck into a Victrola! His devilishly devised gruesome ends for the doctors are patterned after the plagues brought down on Ramses in ancient Egypt (killer locusts, blood-sucking bats, rabid rats, locusts, etc.). Price has never been more wonderfully hammy than in what was billed as his 100th film. Kept at a snappy pace by "Avengers" director Robert Fuest and given a bizarre art deco look by art director Bernard Reeves and set designer Brian Eatwell, this movie is a kitschy homage to the sillier horror pictures of the 1930s and well worth a look. An equally entertaining sequel, DR. PHIBES RISES AGAIN, was released in 1972.

p, Louis M. Heyward, Ronald S. Dunas; d, Robert Fuest; w, James Whiton, William Goldstein; ph, Norman Warwick; ed, Tristam Cones; m, Basil Kirchin.

(PR:C   MPAA:PG)

## ALICE, SWEET ALICE****

(1978) 108m AA c (AKA: COMMUNION; HOLY TERROR)

Paula Sheppard (Alice), Brooke Shields (Karen), Linda Miller (Catherine), Jane Lowry (Aunt Annie), Alphonso DeNoble (Alphonso), Rudolph Willrich (Father Tom), Mildred Clinton (Mrs. Tredoni), Niles McMaster (Dom Spages), Michael Hardstark (Detective), Gary Allen (Uncle), Tom Signorelli (Brenner), Louisa Horton (Psychiatrist), Antonino Rocco (Funeral Attendant), Lillian Roth (Pathologist).

ALICE, SWEET ALICE is an excellent low-budget horror film from director Alfred Sole, whose impressive grasp of filmmaking technique and eye for the grotesque keeps the viewer on edge throughout the entire movie. Set in Paterson, New Jersey, in the early 1960s, the film focuses on a series of bizarre and horrible murders committed in and around the local Catholic church. Although all the evidence seems to point to sullen and alienated 12-year-old Alice (Paula Sheppard), the true culprit is actually much less obvious. This is a truly unsettling film. Sole presents us with a society diseased by blind devotion, jealousy, repression, and guilt. In ALICE, SWEET ALICE, the family unit is hopelessly corrupted, the Catholic church is fundamentally hypocritical, and the forces of law and order are useless. His startling imagery combines religious iconography, grotesque characters, and gruesome killings, with a visual style that effectively evokes Hitchcock and Polanski without blatantly stealing from either. Rereleased twice under two different titles in an effort to exploit the appearance of the preteen Brooke Shields (her character is murdered in church just before her first communion), ALICE, SWEET ALICE has had a spotty distribution history, but is widely available on home video. Highly recommended.

p, Richard K. Rosenberg; d, Alfred Sole; w, Rosemary Rityo, Alfred Sole; ph, John Friberg, Chuck Hall (Technicolor); ed, Edward Salier; m, Stephen Lawrence.

(PR:O   MPAA:R)

## ALLIGATOR***

(1980) 94m Group 1 c

Robert Forster (David Madison), Robin Riker (Marisa Kendall), Michael Gazzo (Police Chief Clark), Perry Lang (Kelly), Jack Carter (Mayor), Henry Silva (Col. Brock), Bart Braverman (Kemp, the Reporter), Dean Jagger (Slade, the Tycoon), Sue Lyon, Angel Tompkins (News Reporters), Sidney Lassick (Guichei), James Ingersoll (Helms), Robert Doyle (Bill), Patti Jerome (Madeline), Leslie Brown (Young Marisa), John Lisbon Wood (Mad Bomber), Buckley Norris (Bob), Royce D. Applegate (Callan), Jim Brockett (Gator Wrestler), Jim Boeke (Shamsky), James Arone (Sloan), Ed Brodow (Ross), Simmy Bow (Seedy), Stan Haze (Meyer), Peter Miller (Sparks), Pat Peterson (Joey), Micol (Joey's Mother), Tom Kindle (Announcer), Philip Luther (Purdy), Larry Margo (Stanley), John F. Goff (Ashe), Elizabeth Halsey (Policewoman), Barry Chase, Richard Partlow (Policemen), Kendall Carly Browne (Ann), Mike Mazurki (Gatekeeper), Bella Bruck (Dot), Corky Ford (Chi Chi).

The title creature, after being flushed down a toilet as a baby, grows to monstrous proportions over a 12-year period by feasting on the discarded bodies of animals chock full of illegal growth hormones, with which a chemical company has been experimenting. After a while, the big guy gets hungry and wreaks reptilian havoc on Los Angeles, even getting some sort of revenge by slurping down the chemical plant's owner (Dean Jagger). Cop David Madison (Robert Forster) and a female scientist (Robin Riker) team up to destroy the gator and start up a romance as well. Sure, this sounds stupid, and it is—but it's quite a bit of fun, too. Screenwriter John Sayles, whose own work as a director (MATEWAN; EIGHT MEN OUT) has been critically acclaimed, and director Lewis Teague have loaded ALLIGATOR with visual puns, film-buff jokes, and a few frightening moments as well. Forster is very likable as the problem-ridden cop and Riker, an attractive but tough redhead, is wonderfully charismatic as the herpetologist whose mom and dad threw that little thing down the toilet in the first place. All in all, a fine example of what a sense of humor can do with a low budget and an old idea.

p, Brandon Chase; d, Lewis Teague; w, John Sayles; ph,

Joseph Mangine (Deluxe Color); ed, Larry Block, Ronald Medico; m, Craig Hundley.

(PR:O  MPAA:R)

## ALONE IN THE DARK**½

(1982) 92m New Line c

Jack Palance (Frank Hawkes), Donald Pleasenoo (Dr. Leo Bain), Martin Landau (Bryon "Preacher" Sutcliff), Dwight Schultz (Dan Potter), Erland Van Lidth (Ronald "Fatty" Elster), Deborah Hedwall (Nell Potter), Lee Taylor-Allen (Tonie Potter), Phillip Clark (Tom Smith/Skaggs).

Four killers (Jack Palance, Martin Landau, Erland Van Lidth, and Phillip Clark) escape from an asylum during a statewide blackout and join looters who have broken into a sporting goods store. Armed with a variety of weapons from the store, the psychos proceed to the home of Dr. Dan Potter (Dwight Schultz), the hated staff psychologist of the asylum, to terrorize him and his family. This was the promising directorial debut of Jack Sholder, who would go on to helm both A NIGHTMARE ON ELM STREET PART 2: FREDDY'S REVENGE (1985) and the excellent science-fiction film THE HIDDEN (1987). Sholder, who wrote the script as well, sees his psychopaths as no better or worse than supposedly sane members of society and sets his climax at a punk rock club where the SicF*cks blare out tunes like "Chop up Your Mother." This black sense of humor, combined with the playful performances of its excellent cast (especially Donald Pleasance, as the head of the asylum), raises ALONE IN THE DARK a cut above the average maniacs-on-the-loose entry.

p, Robert Shaye; d, Jack Sholder; w, Jack Sholder; ph, Joseph Mangine; ed, Arline Garson; m, Renato Serio.

(PR:O  MPAA:R)

## AMERICAN GOTHIC**

(1988, Brit./Can.) 90m Manor Ground/Vidmark c

Rod Steiger (Pa), Yvonne De Carlo (Ma), Sarah Torgov (Cynthia), Michael J. Pollard (Woody), Fiona Hutchinson (Lynn), William Hootkins (Teddy), Janet Wright (Fanny), Terry Kelly (Psychiatrist), Mark Ericksen (Jeff), Caroline Barclay (Terri), Mark Lindsay Chapman (Rob), Stephen Shelley (Paul).

A group of friends, including the mentally unstable Cynthia (Sarah Torgov), fly off together for a camping trip, only to experience engine trouble, forcing them to make an unscheduled landing on a remote island. They discover a house at the other end of the island, all furnished straight out of the 1920s, complete with Victrola and photos of the Gish sisters. Soon the occupants—Pa (Rod Steiger) and Ma (Yvonne De Carlo)—arrive, and insist that everyone stay for supper and the night. Eventually the guests are introduced to the elderly couple's daughter, Fanny (Wright), and son, Woody (Michael J. Pollard), who soon thereafter knock off the first camper. By the finale everyone is dead but Cynthia, whose nuttiness nearly matches that of the backwoods clan. Despite the rather obvious plotting, derivative of everything from PSYCHO and more recent spam-

in-a-cabin epics to THE MOST DANGEROUS GAME, this Canadian-made effort does manage to incorporate some interesting facets. Without a doubt, however, what makes the film most noteworthy are the performances of Steiger and Torgov. Steiger's Bible-spouting, moralizing patriarch is superb, given the weakness of the material in general. Torgov's part is better written and she makes the most of it, letting us see madness in her eyes better than anyone since the glory days of Barbara Steele. And Michael J. Pollard is always weird, even in non-horror films.

p, John Quested, Christopher Harrop; d, John Hough; w, Bert Wetanson, Michael Vines; ph, Harvey Harrison; ed, John Victor Smith; m, Alan Parker.

(PR:O  MPAA:R)

## AMERICAN WEREWOLF IN LONDON, AN**½

(1981) 97m UNIV c

David Naughton (David Kessler), Jenny Agutter (Alex Price), Griffin Dunne (Jack Goodman), John Woodvine (Dr. Hirsch), Brian Glover (Chess Player), David Schofield (Dart Player), Lila Kaye (Barmaid), Paul Kember (Sgt. McManus), Don McKillop (Inspector Villiers), Frank Oz (Mr. Collins), Anne Marie Davies (Nurse Gallagher), Paula Jacobs (Mrs. Kessler), Gordon Sterne (Mr. Kessler), Mark Fisher (Max), Michele Brisigotti (Rachel).

This schizophrenic horror/comedy suffers under the cloddish direction of John Landis, but is almost redeemed by the truly ground-breaking special makeup effects of Rick Baker, which won him the first Academy Award for Best Makeup in 1981. Basically a sendup of old werewolf movies, the film begins as two American tourists, David Kessler (David Naughton) and Jack Goodman (Griffin Dunne), hike through the English moors and are attacked by a werewolf. Jack is killed and David is bitten while slaying the beast. Once in a London hospital, Jack meets and falls in love with a nurse, Alex (Jenny Agutter), who tends his wounds. She takes him into her home, where he begins to have lycanthropic seizures, turning into a werewolf and stalking the residents of London. Between transformations, David is visited by the ghost of Jack—decomposing more each time he shows up—who urges him to commit suicide and end the string of lycanthropy. A filmmaker seemingly incapable of constructing a balanced narrative, Landis once again relies on a scattershot approach by which every half-baked gag to pop into his head makes it to the screen. AMERICAN WEREWOLF is loaded with potentially good ideas, but Landis never takes the time to develop his situations, characters, or themes. Instead he presents several show-stopping sequences that are impressive in and of themselves, but rarely fit together to form a satisfying whole. Baker's effects, which were somewhat overshadowed by those of Rob Bottin in THE HOWLING (which was released first), are excellent and alone worth the price of admission.

p, George Folsey, Jr.; d, John Landis; w, John Landis; ph, Robert Paynter (Technicolor); ed, Malcolm Campbell; m, Elmer Bernstein.

(PR:O  MPAA:R)

AMITYVILLE HORROR, THE—

## AMITYVILLE HORROR, THE**½

(1979) 126m AIP c

James Brolin *(George Lutz)*, Margot Kidder *(Kathleen Lutz)*, Rod Steiger *(Fr. Delaney)*, Don Stroud *(Fr. Bolen)*, Natasha Ryan *(Amy)*, K.C. Martell *(Greg)*, Meeno Peluce *(Matt)*, Michael Sacks *(Jeff)*, Helen Shaver *(Carolyn)*, Val Avery *(Sgt. Gionfriddo)*, Amy Wright *(Jackie)*, Murray Hamilton *(Fr. Ryan)*, John Larch *(Fr. Nuncio)*, Irene Dailey *(Aunt Helena)*.

THE AMITYVILLE HORROR is the occasionally effective haunted house movie that made a fortune for its studio, American International, just before it went out of business. Based on a sensational best seller that purported to be based on fact, the film chronicles the trials and tribulations of the hapless Lutz family (Margot Kidder, James Brolin, Natasha Ryan, Meeno Peluce, and K.C. Martell) as they discover that the new house they purchased for a steal in Amityville, N.Y., is plagued by evil demons that manifest themselves in a variety of disgusting ways (flies, black gook, doors opening and closing by themselves, and so on). As it turns out, the previous family was murdered by their eldest son, and before *that* the house was owned by Satanists. Good Catholics, the Lutz family calls upon the unlikely clerical duo of Rod Steiger and Don Stroud to drive the demons out. Though undeniably spooky in spots, mainly due to the atmospheric direction of Stuart Rosenberg, THE AMITYVILLE HORROR simply can't escape the overall silliness of its plot. Luckily, the earnest efforts of its solid cast keep the potential for unintentional humor at a minimum, with the exception of Steiger's usual over-the-top histrionics. Ironically, the town of Amityville, fed up with the publicity caused by Jay Anson's book, refused to allow the filmmakers to shoot there, forcing the production to move to Tom's River, New Jersey. Two inferior sequels followed.

p, Ronald Saland, Elliot Geisinger; d, Stuart Rosenberg; w, Sandor Stern (based on the book by Jay Anson); ph, Fred J. Koenekamp; ed, Robert Brown; m, Lalo Schifrin.

(PR:O  MPAA:R)

## AMITYVILLE 3-D**

(1983) 105m Dino DeLaurentiis/Orion c

Tony Roberts *(John Baxter)*, Tess Harper *(Nancy Baxter)*, Robert Joy *(Elliot West)*, Candy Clark *(Melanie)*, John Beal *(Harold Caswell)*, Leona Dana *(Emma Caswell)*, John Harkins *(Clifford Sanders)*, Lori Loughlin *(Susan Baxter)*, Meg Ryan *(Lisa)*.

Yet another sequel to THE AMITYVILLE HORROR, this time starring Tony Roberts as a cynical reporter determined to debunk the notion that the house is possessed by moving into it with his teenaged daughter (Meg Ryan). Of course, he's wrong, and the usual catalog of terrors ensues. Veteran director Richard Fleischer demonstrates a keen understanding of the potentials of the 3-D gimmick here, but there is little else to recommend this dull retread.

p, Stephen F. Kesten; d, Richard Fleischer; w, William

Wales; ph, Fred Schuler (DeLuxe Color); ed, Frank J. Urioste; m, Howard Blake.

(PR:C  MPAA:PG)

## AMITYVILLE II: THE POSSESSION**

(1982) 104m Dino DeLaurentiis/Orion c

Burt Young *(Anthony Montelli)*, Rutanya Alda *(Deloris Montelli)*, James Olson *(Fr. Adamski)*, Jack Magner *(Sonny Montelli)*, Diane Franklin *(Patricia Montelli)*, Andrew Prine *(Fr. Tom)*, Leonardo Cimino *(Chancellor)*, Brent Katz *(Mark Montelli)*, Erica Katz *(Jan Montelli)*, Moses Gunn *(Detective Turner)*.

This prequel to the amazingly successful THE AMITYVILLE HORROR is actually a low-budget Italian effort that presents audiences with what happened in the house *before* the Lutz family moved in. Sonny Montelli (Jack Magner) is the troubled teenaged son of a middle-class clan lorded over by a brooding and oppressive patriarch (Burt Young). Anguished by the usual teen frustrations and his crummy home life, Sonny becomes possessed by some form of evil lurking in his house's basement. The kid finally goes off the deep end and hacks apart his entire family. The themes of incest and family abuse give the final grisly scenes a nasty, disturbing quality in an otherwise laughable film. Director Damiano Damiani occasionally manages to convey a few genuine chills between bouts of unintentional laughter, but overall the film is a failure.

p, Ira N. Smith, Stephen R. Greenwald; d, Damiano Damiani; w, Tommy Lee Wallace (based on a book by Hans Holzer); ph, Franco DiGiacomo (DeLuxe Color); ed, Sam O'Steen; m, Lalo Schifrin.

(PR:O  MPAA:R)

## AND NOW THE SCREAMING STARTS**

(1973, Brit.) 87m Amicus/Cinerama c (AKA: I HAVE NO MOUTH BUT I MUST SCREAM; FENGRIFFIN; BRIDE OF FENGRIFFIN; SCREAMING STARTS, THE)

Peter Cushing *(Dr. Pope)*, Herbert Lom *(Henry Fengriffen)*, Patrick Magee *(Dr. Whittle)*, Ian Ogilvy *(Charles Fengriffen)*, Stephanie Beacham *(Catherine Fengriffen)*, Guy Rolfe *(Maitland)*, Geoffrey Crutchley *(Silas)*, Rosalie Crutchley *(Mrs. Luke)*, Janet Key *(Bridget)*, Gillian Lind *(Aunt Edith)*, Sally Harrison *(Sarah)*.

Amicus, known for its string of omnibus horrors such as ASYLUM and TALES FROM THE CRYPT, broke with that tradition for this old-fashioned gothic chiller involving a curse on a young newlywed, Catherine (Stephanie Beacham), who has just moved into the ancestral mansion of her husband, Charles Fengriffen (Ian Ogilvy). It seems that a few generations ago Charles' relative Henry Fengriffen (Herbert Lom) raped a virgin servant girl, and now a disembodied hand takes its revenge on all the heirs to the estate. This standard old dark house story hasn't much to recommend it; however, the dullness of the central characters is offset somewhat by the typically solid contributions of Peter Cushing, Lom, and Patrick Magee. Stunning art direction and excellent camerawork do give the proceedings a lift.

p, Milton Subotsky, Max J. Rosenberg; d, Roy Ward Baker; w, Roger Marshall; ph, Denys Coop; ed, Peter Tanner.

(PR:C MPAA:PG)

## ANDY WARHOL'S DRACULA***

(1974, Fr./It.) 90m CC Champion & 1-Carlo Ponti-Jean Yanne-Jean-Pierre Rassam/CFDC c (DRACULA CERCA SANGUE DI VERGINE E. . .MORI DI SETE; DRACULA VUOLE VIVERE: CERCA SANGUE DI VERGINA; AKA: BLOOD FOR DRACULA; YOUNG DRACULA; ANDY WARHOL'S YOUNG DRACULA)

Joe Dallesandro (Mario), Udo Kier (Dracula), Arno Juerging (Anton, Count's Assistant), Maxime McKendry (Lady Difiore), Vittorio De Sica (Lord Difiore), Dominique Darel (Rubinia), Stefania Cassini (Saphiria), Roman Polanski (Man in Inn), Gil Cagne (Townsman), Milena Vukotic (Esmeralda), Silvia Dionisio (Perla), Eleonora Zani, Emi Califri.

Shot immediately after ANDY WARHOL'S FRANKEN-STEIN with much of the same cast and crew, DRACULA is definitely the better of the two. More like a drug addict than a monster, Dracula (Udo Kier) needs "wirgin" blood to survive and virgins in his native Romania are in short supply. With his assistant, Anton (Arno Juerging), and his sister (in a coffin), Dracula travels to Roman Catholic Italy, where virgins should be more prevalent, and winds up at the crumbling estate of a destitute marquis and his four unmarried daughters. Eager to marry one of his daughters off to the rich Romanian count, the marquis gives Dracula a warm welcome. Unbeknownst to the vampire, however, the two middle daughters have already lost their virginity to socialist handyman Mario (Joe Dallesandro), and when Dracula sinks his teeth into them the sullied blood makes him vomit. Eventually, Mario deduces that the count is a vampire and rushes to deflower the 14-year-old daughter before Dracula can get to her. Not as outright disgusting as Warhol's FRANKENSTEIN, DRACULA is stylishly directed, wonderfully atmospheric, hysterically funny, and intense enough to please gorehounds—especially at the climax. Kier makes a wonderful Dracula with his thick accent and goofy mannerisms, but Vittorio De Sica (director of such neo-realist classics as SHOESHINE and THE BICYCLE THIEF) nearly steals the show as the eccentric marquis who lets the name Dra-cu-la roll off his tongue for nearly five minutes. Once again, Paul Morrissey's distinctive stamp is on the script, but many European sources credit Antonio Margheriti as the director. Look for director Roman Polanski in a goofy cameo as a villager wanting to play "You can't do what I can do" with the bewildered Juerging. Originally rated "X" by the MPAA and later changed to an "R".

p, Carlo Ponti, Andrew Braunsberg, Jean-Pierre Rassam, Jean Yanne; d, Paul Morrissey, Antonio Margheriti; w, Paul Morrissey; ph, Luigi Kuveiller (Eastmancolor); ed, Jed Johnson, Franca Silvi; m, Claudio Gizzi.

(PR:O MPAA:R)

## ANDY WARHOL'S FRANKENSTEIN**½

(1974, Fr./It.) 95m CC Champion & 1-Carlo Ponti-Jean Yanne-Jean-Pierre Rassam/CFDC c (IL MOSTRO E IN TAVOLA. . .BARONE FRANKENSTEIN; CARNE PER FRANKENSTEIN; AKA: FLESH FOR FRANKENSTEIN; FRANKENSTEIN; FRANKENSTEIN EXPERIMENT, THE; WARHOL'S FRANKENSTEIN; UP FRANKENSTEIN; DEVIL AND DR. FRANKENSTEIN, THE)

Joe Dallesandro (Nicholas), Monique Van Vooren (Katrin), Udo Kier (Frankenstein), Srdjan Zelenovic (Farmer/Male Zombie), Dalila DiLazzaro (Girl Zombie), Arno Juerging (Otto), Liu Bozizio (Maid), Carla Mancini (Daughter), Marco Liofredi (Son), Nicoletta Elmi, Christina Gaioni, Fiorella Masselli, Rosita Torosh, Imelda Marani.

This is a totally revolting, but nonetheless fascinating, spin on the Frankenstein legend, which Andy Warhol himself had nothing to do with other than lending his name to the title. Taking pains to break every social taboo in the books, the film finds the crazed baron (played in delightfully hammy fashion by the bug-eyed Udo Kier, whose accent sounds like a cross between Peter Lorre and Arnold Schwarzenegger) tinkering with internal organs in his basement, assisted by his doltish servant, Otto (Arno Juerging). Obsessed with creating a master race, Baron Frankenstein constructs two creatures, male and female, in the hopes of breeding them. When local shepherd Nicholas (Joe Dallesandro), who has been sleeping with the baron's wife-sister, notices his best friend's head on the shoulders of the male creature, he begins to smell a rat. Shot using Arch Oboler's Spacevision 3-D process (first used in BWANA DEVIL, 1952), WARHOL'S FRANKENSTEIN contains an unprecedented amount of explicit gore and spills it in viewers' laps. In addition to the grand guignol, the film assaults the audience with enough weird sex, eccentric performances, and hilarious black humor to last a lifetime. Although the script bears the unmistakable imprint of Warhol Factory compatriot Paul Morrissey, European sources credit prolific Italian filmmaker Antonio Margheriti with the direction. A companion film, ANDY WARHOL'S DRACULA, immediately followed. Both films were originally rated "X" by the MPAA and then later changed to "R" for rerelease in 1982.

p, Carlo Ponti, Andrew Braunsberg, Jean-Pierre Rassam, Jean Yanne; d, Paul Morrissey, Antonio Margheriti; w, Paul Morrissey; ph, Luigi Kuveiller (Eastmancolor); ed, Jed Johnson, Franca Silvi; m, Claudio Gizzi.

(PR:O MPAA:R)

## ANGEL HEART**½

(1987) 113m Winkast-Union-Carolco Intl./Tri-Star c

Mickey Rourke (Harry Angel), Robert De Niro (Louis Cyphre), Lisa Bonet (Epiphany Proudfoot), Charlotte Rampling (Margaret Krusemark), Stocker Fontelieu (Ethan Krusemark), Brownie McGhee (Toots Sweet), Michael Higgins (Dr. Fowler), Elizabeth Whitcraft (Connie), Eliott Keener (Sterne), Charles Gordone (Spider Simpson),

Dann Florek (Winesap), Kathleen Wilhoite (Nurse), George Buck (Izzy), Judith Drake (Izzy's Wife), Gerald L. Orange (Pastor John), Peggy Severe (Mammy Carter), Pruitt Taylor Vince (Deimos), David Petitjean (Baptism Preacher), Rick Washburn (Cajun Heavy), Neil Newlon (2nd Cajun Heavy), Oakley Dalton (Big Jacket), Yvonne Bywaters (Margaret's Maid), Loys T. Bergeron (Mike), Joshua Frank (Toothless), Karmen Harris (Harlem Mourner), Nicole Burdette (Ellie), Kendell Lupe, Percy Martin (Oyster Cajuns), Viola Dunbar (Concierge), Murray Bandel (Bartender), Jarrett Narcisse (Epiphany's Child), Ernest Watson (Oyster Bar Saxophonist), Rickie Monie (Oyster Bar Pianist), Roselyn Lionhart (Voodoo Musician), Sugar Blue, Pinetop Perkins, Deacon Johnmoore, Richard Payne, W. Alonzo Stewart, Lillian Boutte (Toots Sweet Band), Joel Adam, Stephen Beasley, Jerome Reddick (Tap Dancers), Louis Freddie Kohlman, Kufaru Aaron Mouton (Voodoo Drums), Marilyn Banks, Lula Elzy, Francesca J. Ridge, Arlena Rolant, Karen Davis, Shirleta Jones, Mark Taylor (Voodoo Dancers).

New York City, 1955. Harry Angel (Mickey Rourke) is a cheap private eye who specializes in divorce and insurance claims. He is asked to go to Harlem to meet wealthy, mysterious Louis Cyphre (Robert De Niro) by his lawyer, Winesap (Dann Florek). The intellectual, goateed Cyphre pays Angel to find a 1940s crooner named Johnny Favorite, who reneged on a contract and disappeared 12 years ago. Angel goes to a New York sanitarium but finds that the singer, injured during the war and suffering from amnesia, has been transferred, according to hospital records. The trail leads to New Orleans, and what ensues is an ever-deepening mystery that comes to involve voodoo, Satanism, and the supernatural. Notorious for the "X" rating imposed by the MPAA because of a torrid love scene between Rourke and Lisa Bonet in which blood drips from the ceiling (the producers trimmed 10 seconds from the scene and won an "R"), ANGEL HEART is a convoluted combination of film noir and horror that, although expertly filmed by director Alan Parker, seems more an exercise in flashy visuals than mature cinematic storytelling. Both the R-rated version and the infamous "uncut" version are available on videocassette.

p, Alan Marshall, Elliott Kastner; d, Alan Parker; w, Alan Parker (based on the novel Falling Angel by William Hjortsberg); ph, Michael Seresin (Technicolor); ed, Gerry Hambling; m, Trevor Jones.

(PR:O  MPAA:R)

## ANGUISH***½

(1988, Sp.) 91m Pepon Cormina/Spectrafilm c (ANGUSTIA)

Zelda Rubinstein (Mother), Michael Lerner (John), Talia Paul (Polly), Angel Jove (Killer), Clara Pastor (Linda), Isabel Garcia Lorca (Caroline), Nat Baker (Teaching Doctor), Edward Ledden (Doctor), Janet Porter (Laboratory Nurse), Patricia Manget, Merche Gascon (Nurses at Clinic), Jose M. Chucarro (Boy Friend), Antonella Murgia (Ticket Girl), Josephine Borchaca (Concession Girl), Georgie Pinkley (Laura), Francesco Rabella (Don), Diane Pinkley (Popcorn Woman), Benito Pocino (Popcorn Husband), Joy Blackburn (Concession Girl), Marc Maloney (Elderly Man), Jasmine Parker (Elderly Woman), Jean Paul Soto (Manny), Javier Ducan (Moe), Marc Auba (Jack), Randall Stewart (First Murder), Eva Heald (Granny), Rose Sherpac (Granny's Friend), Emi Matias (Hairy Woman), Elisa Crehvet (Ann), Mingo Rafols (Chicano), Maribel Martinez (Hysterical Woman), Gustavo Guarino (Hysterical Husband), Frank Craven (Sleepy), Mario Fernandez (Black Boy), May Vives (Blond Girl), Craig Hill (Doctor at Hospital), Ricardo Azulay (Police Captain), Joe Wolberg (Swat Commander).

A masterful example of audience manipulation, ANGUISH is a terrifically suspenseful horror film containing not one, but two classic gimmicks: a William Castle-style warning that the film may cause mental distress due to the hypnotic tricks onscreen, and the film-within-a-film trick most recently seen in Lamberto Bava's DEMONS. While the first gimmick is silly, Spanish director Bigas Luna employs the second extremely well. The movie begins as a loutish optometrist orderly (Michael Lerner) louses up on the job and is dismissed. His mother (Zelda Rubinstein) is an odd little woman who totally dominates her docile son. Using a form of hypnosis, mother merges her mind with her son's and sends him out to get revenge on the patient (Isabel Garcia Lorca) who caused his dismissal. At this point, director Bigas pulls back from the image to reveal that it is merely a horror film being watched by a small matinee crowd in a movie theater. As it happens, one of the patrons is a real lunatic, who begins killing off theater employees and patrons in a manner that parallels the action on screen. Although basically an empty-headed exercise in cinematic style, ANGUISH is a superbly crafted film and lots of fun to watch. Because mainstream audiences have no interest in experimental filmmaking techniques, commercial directors of an adventurous bent have found the horror genre an incredibly flexible venue in which to dabble with the unconventional. With a built-in audience whose only requirement is that the film be scary, directors have been able to get away with virtually plotless essays in style in which they can indulge in any trick they care to as long as they deliver the occasional jolt. Shot in 1986 on locations in Spain, New York, and Los Angeles, ANGUISH, for some unimaginable reason, didn't receive much of a release in the US and turned up on the home video heap. This is a great shame, for the film's effect would have been heightened for audiences actually sitting in a theater while this movie-within-a-movie-within-a-movie—in which everyone is killed while watching a movie—flickered on a big screen. It would be impossible not to look over one's shoulder while watching ANGUISH at the local triplex. Unfortunately, home is where most people will see this unique little film, and although it is still quite effective, the cinematic experience won't be as complete.

p, Pepon Coromina; d, Bigas Luna; w, Bigas Luna; ph, Josep Maria Civit (Eastmancolor, Agfa Color); ed, Tom Sabin; m, J.M. Pagan.

(PR:O  MPAA:R)

## APE, THE**

(1940) 63m MON bw

Boris Karloff *(Dr. Bernard Adrian)*, Maris Wrixon *(Frances Clifford)*, Gertrude Hoffman *(Mrs. Clifford)*, Henry Hall *(Sheriff Jeff Holliday)*, Gene O'Donnell *(Danny Foster)*, Dorothy Vaughan *(Jane)*, Jack Kennedy *(Tomlin)*, Jessie Arnold *(Mrs. Brill)*.

Kindly doctor Bernard Adrian (Boris Karloff), who has become obsessed with finding a cure for polio after his daughter's death, is convinced that the elusive cure can be found in the spinal fluid of human beings. Killing an escaped circus ape, Adrian dons the animal's hide and murders innocent townspeople, draining them of the precious fluid for his serum. THE APE was just one of *nine* Karloff films released in 1940 and it was easily one of the worst of his entire career. This picture came at the end of his contract with Monogram, where he had languished in the ''Mr. Wong'' detective series, and his eagerness to get it over with shows. This is the kind of film Bela Lugosi was making on a regular basis and, in fact, it is often confused with Lugosi's THE APE MAN (1943).

p, Scott R. Dunlap; d, William Nigh; w, Curt Siodmak, Richard Carroll (based on a play by Adam Hull Shirk); ph, Harry Neumann; ed, Russell Schoengarth; m, Edward Kay.

(PR:A MPAA:NR)

## APE MAN, THE*

(1943) 64m MON bw (GB: LOCK YOUR DOORS)

Bela Lugosi *(Dr. Brewster)*, Wallace Ford *(Jeff Carter)*, Louise Currie *(Billie Mason)*, Minerva Urecal *(Agatha Brewster)*, Henry Hall *(Dr. Randall)*, Ralph Littlefield *(Zippe)*, J. Farrell MacDonald *(Captain)*, George Kirby *(Butler)*, Wheeler Oakman *(Brady)*, Emil Van Horn *(The Ape)*.

Mad scientist Dr. Brewster (Bela Lugosi), long thought dead, is actually working away in his basement laboratory on a serum derived from gorilla spinal fluid. Experimenting on himself, Dr. Brewster is dismayed to discover that the injections have given him a bushy beard and begun to force his spine into a distinctly simian posture. With an actual gorilla as an accomplice, Brewster seeks to counteract the effects of his serum by draining the spinal fluid from murdered humans and using it as the catalytic ingredient in changing back to his ''normal'' self. A pair of gutsy reporters (Wallace Ford and Louise Currie) investigates the killings. This unintentionally hilarious Lugosi outing was directed by the infamous hack William Beaudine and is reminiscent, at times, of Monogram's 1940 Boris Karloff vehicle THE APE. Although a failure as horror, THE APE MAN is a roaring success as a camp classic and is recommended on that basis. Monogram never used the talents of Karloff and Lugosi well, and both stars' best work can be seen in their classics for Universal.

p, Sam Katzman, Jack Dietz; d, William Beaudine; w, Barney Sarecky (based on ''They Creep in the Dark'' by Karl Brown); ph, Mack Stengler; ed, Carl Pierson; m, Edward Kay.

(PR:A MPAA:NR)

## APRIL FOOL'S DAY**

(1986) 88m Hometown/PAR c

Jay Baker *(Harvey)*, Pat Barlow *(Clara)*, Lloyd Berry *(Ferryman)*, Deborah Foreman *(Muffy/Buffy)*, Deborah Goodrich *(Nikki)*, Tom Heaton *(Potter/Uncle Frank)*, Michael Nomad *(Buck)*, Ken Olandt *(Rob)*, Griffin O'Neal *(Skip)*, Leah King Pinsent *(Nan)*, Clayton Rohner *(Chaz)*, Amy Steel *(Kit)*, Thomas F. Wilson *(Arch)*.

Not content to simply disgust audiences with his ultraviolent, ultramindless FRIDAY THE 13TH series of slasher movies, producer Frank Mancuso decided to put a spin on the tired formula by making a comedy out of it with the help of screen writer Danilo Bach (BEVERLY HILLS COP). Eight college friends (Jay Baker, Deborah Goodrich, Ken Olandt, Griffin O'Neal, Leah King Pinsent, Clayton Rohner, Amy Steel, and Thomas F. Wilson) are invited for an April Fool's weekend party at the exclusive island mansion of heiress and fellow classmate Muffy (Deborah Foreman). Muffy greets her friends with a sly smile that betrays the fact that they will soon be subjected to a seemingly endless series of April Fool's jokes, including collapsing chairs, whoopee cushions, dribble glasses, squirting faucets, and the like. Things suddenly turn serious as the guests are whittled away like Agatha Christie's ''Ten Little Indians,'' each dispatched in a bloody manner by an unseen assassin. Mostly played for laughs, APRIL FOOL'S DAY is clever enough, but, as is the case with all stalk-and-slash films, it becomes repetitive and boring very quickly. The gross-out effects are kept to a minimum, and the standard sexual scenes are handled fairly discreetly and obviously meant to parody those in other slasher films.

p, Frank Mancuso, Jr.; d, Fred Walton; w, Danilo Bach; ph, Charles Minsky (Panavision, Metrocolor); ed, Bruce Green; m, Charles Bernstein.

(PR:O MPAA:R)

## ARNOLD*

(1973) 94m Cinerama c

Stella Stevens *(Karen)*, Roddy McDowall *(Robert)*, Elsa Lanchester *(Hester)*, Shani Wallis *(Jocelyn)*, Farley Granger *(Evan Lyons)*, Victor Buono *(Minister)*, John McGiver *(Governor)*, Bernard Fox *(Constable Hooks)*, Patric Knowles *(Douglas Whitehead)*, Jamie Farr *(Dybbi)*, Norman Stuart *(Arnold)*, Ben Wright *(Jonesy)*, Wanda Bailey *(Flo)*, Steven Marlo, Leslie Thompson *(Dart Players)*.

This dull-witted comedy stars Stella Stevens as the mistress of a deceased nobleman who marries the stiff posthumously to inherit his fortune. While the dead man lies in state, a series of killings occur. The victims are: playboy brother Robert (Robert McDowall), flaky sister Hester (Elsa Lanchester), lawyers Lyons (Farley Granger) and Whitehead (Patric Knowles), handyman Dybbi (Jamie Farr), and widow Jocelyn (Shani Wallis). The whole thing comes off like a cheap made-for-TV movie of the week. The title song is performed by Wallis.

p, Andrew J. Fenady; d, Georg Fenady; w, Jameson Brewer, John Fenton Murray; ph, William Jurgenson (DeLuxe Color); ed, Melvin Shapiro; m, George Duning.

**(PR:A   MPAA:PG)**

## ASPHYX, THE**½

(1972, Brit.) 93m Paragon c (AKA: SPIRIT OF THE DEAD; HORROR OF DEATH, THE)

Robert Stephens *(Hugo Cunningham)*, Robert Powell *(Giles Cunningham)*, Jane Lapotaire *(Christina Cunningham)*, Alex Scott *(President)*, Ralph Arliss *(Clive Cunningham)*, Fiona Walker *(Anna Wheatly)*, Terry Scully *(Pauper)*, John Lawrence *(Mason)*, Davis Gray *(Vicar)*, Tony Caunter *(Warden)*, Paul Bacon *(lst Member)*.

An unusual horror movie with an intriguing premise, THE ASPHYX is, unfortunately, marred by a weak script and unimaginative direction. Set in England in the late 1870s, the film follows nobleman Hugo Cunningham (Robert Stephens) as he uses the emerging arts of photography and cinematography to uncover the existence of the legendary asphyx, which, according to Greek mythology, is a protoplasmic being that hovers near living things at moments of great peril, ready to capture their souls. Hugo is able to isolate the asphyx of a guinea pig by using a special blue light, then seals it in an airtight container, making the tiny animal immortal. Obsessed with making himself and his family likewise immortal, Hugo begins experimenting on humans. While the concept alone makes the film worth watching, THE ASPHYX is ultimately frustrating as a result of its distracting lapses of logic, talkiness, dull direction, and missed opportunities. It's more an exercise in the intellectual than the visceral, and if thought about too intently the movie begins to unravel. The film is beautifully photographed in wide-screen by Freddie Young (LAWRENCE OF ARABIA), but, regrettably, much of the effect is lost on videocassette.

p, John Brittany; d, Peter Newbrook; w, Brian Comfort; ph, Freddie Young (Todd-AO 35); ed, Colin Hobson; m, Bill McGuffie.

**(PR:C   MPAA:PG)**

## ASSAULT ON PRECINCT 13****

(1976) 91m Turtle Releasing Co. c

Austin Stoker *(Bishop)*, Darwin Joston *(Wilson)*, Laurie Zimmer *(Leigh)*, Martin West *(Lawson)*, Tony Burton *(Wells)*, Charles Cyphers *(Starker)*, Nancy Loomis *(Julie)*, Peter Bruni *(Ice Cream Man)*, John J. Fox *(Warden)*, Kim Richards *(Kathy)*, Henry Brandon.

Not really a horror film, but one that often comes up during discussions of George Romero's NIGHT OF THE LIVING DEAD (1968), this early John Carpenter movie still holds up as one of the director's best works. A low-budget and taut update of the classic Howard Hawks western RIO BRAVO, set in modern-day Los Angeles, the story concerns a lengthy siege by a multiracial street gang on a soon-to-be-closed police station. The gang has murdered a young girl, whose father has run to the station for help. This man is in a state of shock and cannot speak to the lone cop, Bishop (Austin Stoker), and two secretaries, Leigh (Laurie Zimmer) and Julie (Nancy Loomis), waiting for the moving vans to take what's left of the station's file cabinets. Unexpectedly, two death-row prisoners arrive and are put in holding cells until authorities can find a place for them, since the state prison is overcrowded. As night falls, the gang attacks in full force, peppering the station with bullets shot from silencers. The gang cuts the electricity and phone lines, leaving the station helpless in the center of the neighborhood. The inmates demand to be let loose so they can defend themselves, and prove to be honorable men. The shadowy photography, great editing, snappy dialog, and a moody synthesizer score by Carpenter himself make this one of the most successful homages to the Hawks' brand of filmmaking, and a very impressive film in its own right. The parallels with Romero's film are obvious (the street gang is reminiscent of the Romero's zombies), and Carpenter, who often borrows character names and situations from films and filmmakers he admires, may well have intended it that way.

p, J.S. Kaplan; d, John Carpenter; w, John Carpenter; ph, Douglas Knapp (Metrocolor); ed, John T. Chance; m, John Carpenter.

**(PR:C-O   MPAA:R)**

## ASYLUM***

(1972, Brit.) 88m Amicus/Cinerama c (AKA: HOUSE OF CRAZIES)

Peter Cushing *(Smith)*, Britt Ekland *(Lucy)*, Herbert Lom *(Byron)*, Patrick Magee *(Dr. Rutherford)*, Barry Morse *(Bruno)*, Barbara Parkins *(Bonnie)*, Robert Powell *(Dr. Martin)*, Charlotte Rampling *(Barbara)*, Sylvia Syms *(Ruth)*, Richard Todd *(Walter)*, James Villiers *(George)*, Geoffrey Bayldon *(Max)*, Ann Firbank *(Anna)*, John Franklyn-Robbins *(Stebbins)*, Megs Jenkins *(Miss Higgins)*.

The best of the horror anthologies from Amicus was written by Robert Bloch (from his own stories) and has a surprisingly effective framing story. Set in a madhouse, the movie begins as a new doctor (Robert Powell) arrives and is given the task of identifying one of the doctors, who has recently gone mad, from the patients. As he interviews the inmates, their terrifying stories unfold. In the first episode, a man (Richard Todd) dismembers his wife and wraps the pieces in paper, which he then places in the freezer. Soon the parts come to life and crawl around seeking revenge. The second story stars Peter Cushing as a grieving father who brings some special cloth to a tailor (Barry Morse) for a suit that will bring his dead son back to life. The third is a tale of schizophrenia featuring Britt Ekland as the evil half of Charlotte Rampling, while the final chapter features Herbert Lom as an insane inventor who makes tiny robot dolls that murder at his command. The twist ending of the framing story is truly a surprise and makes a great capper to the four eerie tales presented here. Buoyed by a distinguished cast of horror veterans, Bloch's well-written script, and Roy Ward Baker's deft direction, ASYLUM is the most satisfying of the horror anthologies of the 1970s.

p, Max J. Rosenberg, Milton Subotsky; d, Roy Ward Baker; w, Robert Bloch; ph, Denys Coop (Technicolor); ed, Peter Tanner.

**(PR:C    MPAA:PG)**

## ATOM AGE VAMPIRE*½

(1961, It.) 87m Topaz Films bw (SEDDOK, L'EREDE DI SATANA)

Alberto Lupo (Prof. Levyn), Susanne Loret (Jeannete), Sergio Fantoni (Pierre), Roberto Berta (Sacha, Prof. Levyn's Man), Franca Paridi Strahl (Monique), Ivo Garrani (Police Commissioner), Andrea Scotti (Gardener).

This typically bizarre Italian horror offering, produced by Mario Bava, stars Alberto Lupo as a berserk professor who falls in love with torch singer Jeanette (Susanne Loret). When she is horribly disfigured in a car accident, he restores her marred face by injecting her with serum from the glands of the dead, causing her to turn into a vampire. The professor also regularly transforms himself, inexplicably, into a reptilian monster, supposedly as a result of his exposure to Hiroshima victims he has been treating. Pierre (Sergio Fantoni) and friends finally seek out the awful pair and destroy them. Highly derivative of George Franju's classic THE HORROR CHAMBER OF DR. FAUSTAS (LES YEUX SANS VISAGE), ATOM AGE VAMPIRE is a lame imitation that lacks the kind of visual verve producer Bava brought to his own work. Although the film is a failure cinematically, some perverse delight can be had in the pure luridness of the premise. The original Italian cut ran 105 minutes.

p, Mario Bava; d, Anton Guilio Majano, Richard McNamara; w, Anton Guilio Majano, Piero Monviso, Gino de Sanctis, Alberto Befilacqua, John Hart; ph, Aldo Giordano; m, Armando Trovajoli.

**(PR:C    MPAA:NR)**

## ATOMIC BRAIN, THE*

(1964) 72m Emerson bw (AKA: MONSTROSITY)

Frank Gerstle (Doctor), Erika Peters (Nina), Judy Bamber (Bee), Marjorie Eaton (Hazel), Frank Fowler (Victor), Margie Fisco (Zombie).

Cinematographer Joseph V. Mascelli, the man who shot Ray Dennis Steckler's classic THE INCREDIBLY STRANGE CREATURES WHO STOPPED LIVING AND BECAME MIXED-UP ZOMBIES (1965) and wrote an essential handbook for professional cinematographers, branched off on his own to cowrite and direct this obscure mad scientist epic. Marjorie Eaton plays a wealthy but aging widow seeking eternal youth. She employs a mad doctor (Frank Gerstle), to put her brain into the body of a young woman—any young, beautiful woman will do—and he operates on three abducted females, two of whom become zombies that kill off townsfolk. The third victim is his own pet project; he inserts a cat's brain into the woman

and she turns into a carnivorous feline. While Mascelli's cinematography was surprisingly good on the Steckler films, he's not much of a director. Worthwhile if taken as camp.

p, Jack Pollexfen, Dean Dillman, Jr.; d, Joseph V. Mascelli; w, Vi Russell, Sue Dwiggens, Dean Dillman, Jr..

**(PR:C    MPAA:NR)**

## AUDREY ROSE**

(1977) 112m UA c

Marsha Mason (Janice Templeton), Anthony Hopkins (Elliot Hoover), John Beck (Bill Templeton), Susan Swift (Ivy Templeton), Norman Lloyd (Dr. Lipscomb), John Hillerman (Scott Velie), Robert Walden (Brice Mack), Philip Sterling (Judge Langley), Ivy Mones (Mary Lou Sides), Stephen Pearlman (Russ Rothman), Aly Wassil (Maharishi Gupta Pradesh), Mary Jackson (Mother Veronica), Richard Lawson, David Wilson (Policemen), Tony Brande (Detective Fallon), Elizabeth Farley (Carole Rothman), Ruth Manning (Customer in Store), Stanley Brock (Cashier in Store), David Fresco (Dominick), Pat Corley (Dr. Webster), Eunice Christopher (Mrs. Carbone), Karen Anders (Maria).

The happy lives of ritzy New York City couple Janice (Marsha Mason) and Bill (John Beck) are disrupted when stranger Elliott Hoover (Anthony Hopkins) appears, claiming that their daughter, Ivy (Susan Swift) is the reincarnated spirit of his dead little girl. They dismiss his strange tale, then begin to notice that their daughter has been acting a little odd lately. A surprisingly weak outing for veteran director Robert Wise, whose CURSE OF THE CAT PEOPLE (1944), THE BODY SNATCHER (1945), and THE HAUNTING (1963) are classics of the horror genre. Part of the problem is Frank De Felitta's script, which is based on his own feeble novel, which is almost evangelical in its promotion of belief in reincarnation. To his credit, Wise took a subtle approach to the material, but AUDREY ROSE remains a rather uninteresting tale of the supernatural and contains little of what made THE HAUNTING so successful.

p, Joe Wizan, Frank De Felitta; d, Robert Wise; w, Frank De Felitta (based on his novel); ph, Victor J. Kemper (DeLuxe Color); ed, Carl Kress; m, Michael Small.

**(PR:C    MPAA:PG)**

## AWAKENING, THE*½

(1980) 102m Orion/WB c

Charlton Heston (Matthew Corbeck), Susannah York (Jane Turner), Jill Townsend (Anne Corbeck), Stephanie Zimbalist (Margaret Corbeck), Patrick Drury (Paul Whittier), Bruce Myers (Dr. Khalid), Nadim Sawalha (Dr. El Sadek), Ian McDiarmid (Dr. Richter), Ahmed Osman (Yussef), Miriam Margolyes (Kadira), Michael Mellinger (Hamid), Leonard Maguire (John), Ishia Bennison (Nurse), Madhav Sharma (Doctor), Chris Fairbanks (Porter), Michael Halphie, Roger Kemp (Doctors).

Archeologist Matthew Corbeck (Charlton Heston), obsessed with the legend of Egyptian princess Kara—who was forced into an incestuous affair with her father and later killed him—travels to the Middle East to uncover her tomb. Disregarding the curse associated with the legend, Corbeck pillages the burial site and brings the loot back to a London museum, unaware that his daughter was born at the very moment he broke the seal on Kara's tomb. After a quick 18 years fly by, Corbeck's daughter, Margaret (Stephanie Zimbalist), becomes possessed by the long-dormant spirit of Kara and the bodies start to pile up. Adapted from Bram Stoker's novel *The Jewel of the Seven Stars* (which also inspired Hammer's BLOOD FROM THE MUMMY'S TOMB), THE AWAKENING attempts to revive the mummy film while at the same time emulating the kind of goriness made popular by THE OMEN. Although given a big-budget production with excellent set design, gorgeous cinematography by veteran Jack Cardiff (a Michael Powell fave), and a first-rate musical score, the film is predictable, unrelentingly dull, and padded with tedious Egyptian travelog footage. Heston, in his only horror film, gives a rather ridiculous impersonation of a British scientist; Zimbalist, however, imbues her character with an eerie quality that, when combined with the incestuous theme, suggests that the film could have been a disturbing horror story in different hands.

p, Robert Solo, Andrew Scheinman, Martin Shafer; d, Mike Newell; w, Allan Scott, Chris Bryant, Clive Exton (based on the novel *The Jewel of Seven Stars* by Bram Stoker); ph, Jack Cardiff (Technicolor); ed, Terence Rawlings; m, Claude Bolling.

(PR:O   MPAA:R)

## AZTEC MUMMY, THE*

(1957, Mex.) 65m Cinematografica Calderon bw (LA MOMIA; LA MOMIA AZTECA; AKA: ATTACK OF THE MAYAN MUMMY; MUMMY STRIKES, THE; MUMMY, THE)

Ramon Gay, Rosita Arenas, Luis Aceves Castaneda, Arturo Martinez, Jesus Murcielago Velazquez, Salvador Lozano, Crox Alvarado, Guillermo Hernandez, Alejandro Cruz.

This was the first entry in the Mexican mummy series (THE CURSE OF THE AZTEC MUMMY and THE ROBOT VS. THE AZTEC MUMMY followed), all of which were directed by Rafael Lopez Portillo, starred Ramon Gay, and were released in 1957. Having hypnotized his lover, Flor (Rosita Arenas), and discovered that in a past life she was an Aztec princess killed for having an illicit affair with the warrior Popoca, Dr. Almada (Gay) and his assistant (Crox Alvarado) attempt to uncover the princess' tomb. Popoca, who was buried with the princess as her guard, is revived and mistakes Flor for his ancient lover. Enter yet another villain, the masked and evil Dr. Krupp (Luis Aceves Casteneda) and you've got one of the strangest mummy movies ever made. Completely bizarre and cheaply made, the Mexican mummy series isn't exactly high quality, but they are certainly engaging and well worth a look for those with a taste for the offbeat. The Lopez Portillo mummy series

is not to be confused with the "Wrestling Women" series directed by Rene Cardona—the highlight of which was THE WRESTLING WOMEN VS. THE AZTEC MUMMY (1964).

p, Guillermo Calderon; d, Rafael Portillo; w, Guillermo Calderon, Alfredo Salazar; ph, Enrique Wallace.

(PR:A   MPAA:R)

# B

## BABY, THE**

(1973) 102m Scotia International c

Anjanette Comer, Ruth Roman, Mariana Hill, Suzan Zenor, David Manzy.

Ruth Roman plays an alcoholic psycho whose husband ran off years earlier, leaving her with an infant son. To express her hatred for men, she keeps her so-called "baby" (a mentally retarded teenager) in diapers, gurgling in his play pen. A social worker (Anjanette Comer) uncovers the situation and attempts to rescue the youth. Competently directed by the always-interesting Ted Post (HANG 'EM HIGH; GO TELL THE SPARTANS), THE BABY, despite its occasional lapses into genuine bad taste (exploiting the retarded) is fairly effective and contains a truly surprising twist ending. Star Comer was also featured in THE LOVED ONE (1965), RABBIT RUN (1970), and the unforgettable Spanish horror epic NIGHT OF A THOUSAND CATS (1974).

p, Milton Polsky, Abe Polsky; d, Ted Post; w, Abe Polsky; m, Gerald Fried.

(PR:C   MPAA:PG)

## BAD DREAMS**

(1988) 84m American Entertainment Partners II-No Frills/FOX c

Jennifer Rubin *(Cynthia)*, Bruce Abbott *(Dr. Alex Karmen)*, Richard Lynch *(Harris)*, Dean Cameron *(Ralph)*, Harris Yulin *(Dr. Berrisford)*, Susan Barnes *(Connie)*, John Scott Clough *(Victor)*, E.G. Daily *(Lana)*, Damita Jo Freeman *(Gilda)*, Louis Giambalvo *(Ed)*, Susan Ruttan *(Miriam)*, Sy Richardson *(Detective Wasserman)*, Missy Francis *(Young Cynthia)*, Sheila Scott Wilkinson *(Hettie)*, Ben Kronen *(Edgar)*, Charles Fleischer *(Ron the Pharmacist)*, Brian Katkin *(Physical Therapist)*, Stephen Anderson, Chip Johnson, Diane Zolten Wiltse *(Reporters)*, Coleen Maloney *(Unity House Nurse)*, Annie Waterman *(Female Unity)*, Rex Lee Waddell, Jr., Tim Trella, Philip Granger *(Male Unities)*.

This well-crafted and promising directorial debut from recent NYU film school graduate Andrew Fleming concentrates more on mood than on gore. BAD DREAMS begins in the early 1970s as the leader of a Jim Jonesish religious cult, Harris (Richard Lynch), ceremonially douses his followers with gasoline, then sets them and himself aflame. Twenty-seven men, women, and children die in the horrible fire, but there is one survivor, Cynthia, a 13-year-old girl who escapes the inferno but sinks into a coma. Fifteen years later, the girl (Jennifer Rubin) awakens from her coma and is placed in a group therapy session geared to the suicidal. Soon she begins having visions of the charred cult leader, who urges her to kill herself to make the sacrifice complete. When she refuses, Harris kills off the members of her therapy group one at a time. Although much of this is very familiar territory, BAD DREAMS' cowriter-director Fleming does come up with some surprisingly effective moments. Producer Gale Ann Hurd (THE TERMINATOR; ALIENS) and Fleming use their low ($4.5 million) budget to their advantage, capitalizing on the claustrophobic nature of the production, which basically employs only two sets: the old house where the fire takes place and the hospital. The cult scenes are particularly memorable, benefitting from Fleming's clever use of the Chambers Brothers' classic rock tune "Time Has Come Today" as the segue between the 1973 and 1988 sections of the film. Unfortunately, the narrative's gimmick—a therapy group bumped off by a nightmare bogeyman—bears a striking resemblance to last year's NIGHTMARE ON ELM STREET PART III: DREAM WARRIORS, which also featured Rubin as one of the Dream Warriors.

p, Gale Anne Hurd; d, Andrew Fleming; w, Andrew Fleming, Steven E. de Souza (based on a story by Andrew Fleming, Michael Dick, Yuri Zeltser, P.J. Pettiette); ph, Alexander Gruszynski (DeLuxe Color); ed, Jeff Freeman; m, Jay Ferguson.

(PR:O   MPAA:R)

## BARON BLOOD**

(1972, It.) 90m AIP c (GLI ORRORI DEL CASTELLO DI NOREMBERGA; AKA: TORTURE CHAMBER OF BARON BLOOD, THE)

Joseph Cotten *(Becker/The Baron)*, Elke Sommer *(Eva)*, Massimo Girotti *(Uncle Karl)*, Antonio Cantafora *(Peter Kleist)*, Alan Collins *(Fritz)*, Nicoletta Elmi *(Gretchen)*, Rada Rassimov *(Occult Lady)*, Dieter Tressier *(Castle Owner)*, Humi Raho *(Inspector)*.

Not one of Mario Bava's better efforts, this film follows college students Peter (Antonio Cantafora) and Eva (Elke Sommer) as they work to restore for the tourist trade an ancient castle once owned by the notorious sadist Baron Otto von Kleist. The couple hold a seance and wake up the ghost of the evil baron (Joseph Cotten), who subsequently goes on a rampage, introducing his guests to the good old-fashioned torture chamber in the basement. Although it contains a few effective moments, Bava's typically impressive visuals (marred somewhat by the excessive use of zooms) fail to bring this material to life. Sommer spends the entire film dressed in a miniskirt and screaming at the top of her lungs, while Cotten wanders around looking embarrassed. Two minutes of gore was cut by AIP for the American release (the film got a "PG" rating), and Stelvio Cipriani's original score was replaced with one by AIP vet-

eran Les Baxter. Available on videotape as THE TORTURE CHAMBER OF BARON BLOOD.

p, Alfred Leone; d, Mario Bava; w, Vincent Forte, William A. Bairn; ph, Emilio Varriano (Technicolor); ed, Carlo Reali; m, Les Baxter.

(PR:C   MPAA:PG)

## BASKET CASE****

(1982) 90m Analysis Releasing c

Kevin Van Hentenryck *(Duane Bradley)*, Terri Susan Smith *(Sharon)*, Beverly Bonner *(Casey)*, Lloyd Pace *(Dr. Harold Needleman)*, Diana Browne *(Dr. Judith Kutter)*, Robert Vogel *(Hotel Manager)*, Bill Freeman *(Dr. Julius Lifflander)*, Joe Clarke *(Brian "Mickey" O'Donovan)*, Dorothy Strongin *(Josephine)*, Ruth Neuman *(Aunt)*, Richard Pierce *(Mr. Bradley)*, Kerry Ruff *(Detective)*.

This 16mm, ultra-low-budget production, which was shot over the course of six months on location in the streets, apartments, and flophouses of New York City, became a hit on the midnight show circuit and is certainly one of the best horror films of the 1980s. Directed by Frank Henenlotter with as much style possible on a minuscule budget, the film centers on Duane (Kevin Van Hentenryck), a young man from Glens Falls, New York, who checks into a fleabag hotel on 42nd St. carrying a wicker basket. Inside the basket is Duane's small, horribly misshapen siamese twin, Belial, who was cut from Duane's side by a team of hack doctors when they were just children. Communicating with Duane telepathically, Belial is determined to wreak vengeance on the physicians that separated him from his twin. Meanwhile, however, Duane has met a nice girl (Terri Susan Smith) and begun to make a life of his own, one that doesn't include Belial . . . Disturbing, grotesque, and very funny at times, BASKET CASE is a truly unique work in which imagination triumphs over the limitations of budget. Blown up to 35mm from the 16mm original, the film's grainy, cheap look only enhances the seediness of Henenlotter's milieu, while, in Belial, Henenlotter has come up with one of the most memorable and sympathetic screen monsters since KING KONG. A rather cheap-looking puppet created by Kevin Haney and John Caglione, Belial has a certain shabby charm that has endeared him to horror fans throughout the world. A few brief sequences in which Belial is animated via stop-motion techniques were handled by Henenlotter himself. In a film that contains many unforgettable images, perhaps the most startling—and most moving—is a flashback to Belial's childhood, in which the monster's kindly aunt lets the mutant child sit on her lap while reading aloud to him. Although some gore was cut from the theatrical release to appease the MPAA, the uncut version is available on video. The film is dedicated to Herschell Gordon Lewis.

p, Edgar Ievins; d, Frank Henenlotter; w, Frank Henenlotter; ph, Bruce Torbet; ed, Frank Henenlotter; m, Gus Russo.

(PR:O   MPAA:NR)

## BEAST IN THE CELLAR, THE*½

(1971, Brit.) 87m Tigon/Cannon c (AKA: ARE YOU DYING YOUNG MAN?; YOUNG MAN, I THINK YOU'RE DYING)

Beryl Reid *(Ellie Ballantyne)*, Flora Robson *(Joyce Ballantyne)*, Tessa Wyatt *(Joanna Sutherland)*, John Hamill *(Cpl. Alan Marlow)*, T.P. McKenna *(Supt. Paddick)*, David Dodimead *(Dr. Spencer)*, Christopher Chittell *(Baker)*, Peter Craze *(Roy)*, John Kelland *(Sgt. Young)*, Vernon Dobtcheff *(Sir Bernard Newsmith)*, Dafydd Harvard *(Stephen Ballantyne)*.

In the 1930s, two English spinster sisters, Joyce (Flora Robson) and Ellie (Beryl Reid), brick up their brother, Stephen (Dafydd Harvard), in the cellar so that he won't have to go to war. Thirty years later, Stephen, now quite insane, breaks out of his prison and terrorizes the neighborhood, committing a series of gory murders. The somewhat embarrassed sisters must now clean up after their maniacal sibling. The potentially interesting premise, a gore version of ARSENIC AND OLD LACE, is undone by an extremely chatty script in which even the simplest expository passages are verbally explained to the audience in minute detail.

p, Graham Harris; d, James Kelly; w, James Kelly; ph, Harry Waxman; ed, Nicholas Napier-Bell; m, Tony Macauley.

**(PR:C MPAA:NR)**

## BEAST MUST DIE, THE*

(1974, Brit.) 93m Cinerama c

Calvin Lockhart *(Tom Newcliffe)*, Peter Cushing *(Dr. Christopher Lundgren)*, Charles Gray *(Bennington)*, Anton Diffring *(Pavel)*, Marlene Clark *(Caroline Newcliffe)*, Ciaran Madden *(Davina Gilmore)*, Tom Chadbon *(Paul Foote)*, Michael Gambon *(Jan Jamokowksi)*, Sam Mansaray *(Butler)*, Andrew Lodge *(Pilot)*, Carl Bohun, Eric Carte *(Hunters)*.

A dull, overly talky attempt to combine a werewolf movie with THE MOST DANGEROUS GAME, THE BEAST MUST DIE concerns a millionaire big-game hunter (Calvin Lockhart) who invites an odd assortment of guests to his English manor. Believing one of his guests is a werewolf, the millionaire plans to unmask the monster and then hunt him down. The only point of interest here is a William Castle-type gimmick, introduced in the prolog, which informs viewers that they have been chosen as detectives who must deduce the identity of the werewolf, using clues sprinkled through the film. Later, there is a 30-second break in the action during which the audience is to guess who the werewolf is. We wouldn't want to spoil what little fun there is here by giving the answer away. A rather sorry excuse for a horror film—even Peter Cushing's distinguished presence doesn't help.

p, Max J. Rosenberg, Milton Subotsky; d, Paul Annett; w, Michael Winder; ph, Jack Hildyard (Technicolor); ed, Peter Tanner; m, Douglas Gamley.

**(PR:A MPAA:PG)**

## BEAST WITHIN, THE**½

(1982) 90m MGM/UA c

Ronny Cox *(Eli MacCleary)*, Bibi Besch *(Caroline MacCleary)*, Paul Clemens *(Michael MacCleary)*, Dan Gordon *(Judge Curwin)*, R.G. Armstrong *(Doc)*, Kitty Moffat *(Amanda)*, L.Q. Jones *(Sheriff)*, Ramsay King *(Edwin)*, John Dennis Johnston *(Horace)*, Ron Soble *(Tom)*, Luke Askew *(Dexter)*, Meshach Taylor *(Deputy)*.

Caroline (Bibi Besch) and Eli MacCleary (Ronny Cox) are honeymooning in Mississippi (which may have been their first mistake) when the former is raped by someone or something with hairy legs. Seventeen years later, their son (Paul Clemens) is not the kind of kid you'd like to introduce to your daughter. Matter of fact, he's weird and not feeling too well, so Mom and Dad take him back to Mississippi to see if there's any connection between what's bothering him and that hairy thing we met in reel one. There is, of course, and the teen soon transforms (in some disgustingly effective cheap effects by Tom Burman) into a giant insect creature that roams the area, ripping the limbs off passersby. Written by Tom Holland, who would go on to write and direct FRIGHT NIGHT and CHILD'S PLAY, the script does a nice job of translating the awkwardness of adolescence into a horrifying event, while Australian director Philippe Mora (THE HOWLING III) concentrates on the exploiting of the creepy atmospherics of the Deep South. A strong cast of veteran character actors (Cox, R.G. Armstrong, Luke Askew, L.Q. Jones) lends credibility to the outrageous premise. Made on location in Raymond, Mississippi, and produced by THE OMEN's Harvey Bernhard.

p, Harvey Bernhard, Gabriel Katzka; d, Philippe Mora; w, Tom Holland (based on a novel by Edward Levy); ph, Jack L. Richards (DeLuxe Color); ed, Robert Brown, Bert Livitt; m, Les Baxter.

**(PR:O MPAA:R)**

## BEDLAM***

(1946) 78m RKO bw

Boris Karloff *(Master Sims)*, Anna Lee *(Neil Rowen)*, Billy House *(Lord Mortimer)*, Glen Vernon *(The Gilded Boy)*, Jason Robards, Sr. *(Oliver Todd)*, Joan Newton *(Dorothea)*, Richard Fraser *(Hannay)*, Ian Wolfe *(Sidney Long)*, Leyland Hodgson *(John Wilkes)*, Elizabeth Russell *(Mistress Simms)*.

Another strong chiller from the brilliant producer Val Lewton, BEDLAM stars Boris Karloff as the sadistic head of London's infamous St. Mary of Bethlehem Hospital for the Insane, which was nicknamed Bedlam after its horrible conditions. When an actress (Anna Lee) goes on a crusade to change conditions, she winds up an inmate. Inspired by Plate no. 8 of William Hogarth's "The Rake's Progress," BEDLAM is fairly accurate historically (if not psychologically), but not as effective as some of Lewton's earlier horrors, despite a superb performance from Karloff. After years of making a great deal of money for RKO with such low-budget supernatural masterpieces as THE CAT PEOPLE (1942) and I WALKED WITH A ZOMBIE (1943), Lewton aimed to pull himself out of B movies with BED-

LAM by focusing on realistic social horrors rather than the supernatural. Unfortunately, the movie lost money for the studio and Lewton's career at RKO was over. He produced only three more films, none of them notable, and died of a heart attack at the age of 46.

p, Val Lewton; d, Mark Robson; w, Mark Robson, Carlos Keith; ph, Nicholas Musuraca; ed, Lyle Boyer; m, Roy Webb.

**(PR:C    MPAA:NR)**

## BEETLEJUICE***½

(1988) 92m Geffen/WB c

Alec Baldwin *(Adam Maitland)*, Geena Davis *(Barbara Maitland)*, Michael Keaton *(Betelgeuse)*, Catherine O'Hara *(Delia Deetz)*, Glenn Shadix *(Otho)*, Winona Ryder *(Lydia Deetz)*, Jeffrey Jones *(Charles Deetz)*, Sylvia Sidney *(Juno)*, Patrice Martinez *(Receptionist)*, Robert Goulet *(Maxie Dean)*, Dick Cavett *(Bernard)*, Annie McEnroe *(Jane Butterfield)*, Simmy Bow *(Janitor)*, Maurice Page *(Ernie)*, Hugo Stanger *(Old Bill)*, Rachel Mittelman *(Little Jane)*, J.J. Saunders, Mark Ettlinger *(Moving Men)*, Cynthia Daly *(Three-fingered Typist)*, Douglas Turner *(Char Man)*, Carmen Filpi *(Messenger)*, Susan Kellermann *(Grace)*, Adelle Lutz *(Beryl)*.

The long-awaited second film from the promising 27-year-old director Tim Burton (PEE-WEE'S BIG ADVENTURE) is a wildly inventive, unique horror/comedy that plays like a demented, surrealistic, cartoon remake of TOPPER (1937). In it, a recently deceased yuppie couple (Geena Davis and Alec Baldwin) are horrified to learn while haunting their quaint country farmhouse that an obnoxious New York City family has bought the place and plans to move in. Attempting to rid their house of the horrid new owners, the ghostly couple are forced to hire repulsive "bio-exorcist" Betelgeuse (Michael Keaton), the self-proclaimed "ghost with the most," to drive the annoying humans away. His film brimming with hilariously ghastly special effects, director Burton gleefully charges through the expository twists of the script and serves up a strictly visual carnival of craziness, like a kid with his finger on the fast-forward button who wants to get to the good stuff. A former Disney animator, Burton brings an animator's sensibilities to his work and creates worlds in which surrealism and expressionism are the norms. Working closely with cinematographer Thomas Ackerman, the superb production designer Bo Welch, and a cadre of special effects wizards led by Robert Short and Chuck Gaspar, Burton presents a distinct and personal cinematic vision populated by eccentric characters, strange locations, and warped sets. Although the entire cast is excellent, BEETLEJUICE's insane energy is embodied by Keaton as the title foul-mouthed, rip-snorting maniac. On-screen for less than half the film, Keaton makes up for lost time with a gruff, growling performance that grabs viewers by the throat and blows the moldy breath of the angry dead in their faces. His character would be perfectly at home in the equally wild and woolly netherworlds of EVIL DEAD director Sam Raimi's demented imagination. In fact, Keaton is such a

deranged presence that he actually drives the film's initially light mood into darkly dangerous waters.

p, Richard Hashimoto, Larry Wilson, Michael Bender; d, Tim Burton; w, Michael McDowell, Warren Skaaren (based on a story by McDowell, Larry Wilson); ph, Thomas Ackerman (Technicolor); ed, Jane Kurson; m, Danny Elfman.

**(PR:C    MPAA:PG)**

## BEFORE I HANG**½

(1940) 62m COL bw

Boris Karloff *(Dr. John Garth)*, Evelyn Keyes *(Martha Garth)*, Bruce Bennett *(Dr. Paul Ames)*, Edward Van Sloan *(Dr. Ralph Howard)*, Ben Taggart *(Warden Thompson)*, Pedro de Cordoba *(Victor Sondini)*, Wright Kramer *(George Wharton)*, Barton Yarborough *(Stephen Barclay)*, Don Beddoe *(Captain McGraw)*, Robert Fiske *(District Attorney)*, Kenneth McDonald *(Anson)*, Frank Richards *(Otto Kron)*.

Yet another Boris Karloff vehicle, this film stars the actor as a kindly doctor whose noble experiments go awry, causing much death and despair. In this outing, the elderly Dr. Garth (Karloff) searches for a cure for mortality via plasma injections. Sentenced to death for a mercy killing, Garth is allowed to continue his experiments in prison under the supervision of prison doctor Howard (Edward Van Sloan). Needing blood for the experiments, Howard gets it from the corpse of a prisoner who had just been hanged. Knowing he is to be executed the next day, he injects himself with the serum, only to learn that his sentence has been commuted to life. The serum causes Garth to appear younger, but there is a rather nasty side affect: the kindly medical man becomes homicidal now that the blood of a murderer courses through his veins. This standard mad scientist tale, given an unimaginative treatment by director Nick Grinde, gets a significant boost through the subtly effective performance from Karloff as the kindly old doctor turned youthful maniac.

p, Wallace MacDonald; d, Nick Grinde; w, Robert D. Andrews; ph, Benjamin Kline; ed, Charles Nelson; m, Morris W. Stoloff.

**(PR:A    MPAA:NR)**

## BELIEVERS, THE**

(1987) 114m Orion c

Martin Sheen *(Dr. Cal Jamison)*, Helen Shaver *(Jessica Halliday)*, Harley Cross *(Chris Jamison)*, Robert Loggia *(Lt. Sean McTaggert)*, Elizabeth Wilson *(Kate Maslow)*, Harris Yulin *(Donald Calder)*, Lee Richardson *(Dennis Maslow)*, Richard Masur *(Marty Wertheimer)*, Carla Pinza *(Mrs. Ruiz)*, Jimmy Smits *(Tom Lopez)*, Raul Davila *(Sezine)*, Malick Bowens *(Palo)*, Janet-Laine Green *(Lisa)*, Larry Ramos *(Diner Counterman)*, Philip Corey, Jennifer Lee *(Calder's Assistants)*, Nonnie Griffin, Bob Clout *(Cigar Couple)*, Harvey Chao, Christine Pak *(Chinese Couple)*, Joan Kaye *(Woman in Park)*, Eddie Jones *(Police Patient)*, John Bendel *(Theater Detective)*, Joseph Pentangleo,

Joseph Wilkens *(Theater Cops)*, Robert Clohessy *(Diner Detective)*, Dick Martinsen *(Diner Cop)*, Robert Connelly, Tony Desantis *(Precinct Detectives)*, Frank Rivers *(Park Cop)*, Ana Maria Quintana *(A.C.H.E. Secretary)*, Ray Paisley *(Customs Agent)*, Dick Callahan *(Bartender)*, Christopher Brown *(Carpenter)*, Shirley Anthony *(Marty's Secretary)*, Elizabeth Hanna *(Doctor at Hospital)*, Micki Moore, Richard Spiegelman, Fernando Queija, Maria Lebb *(Believers)*, Khali Keyi *(African Shaman)*, Leroy Radcliffe *(Chief Dancer)*.

This misfired big-budget horror movie from respected director John Schlesinger is, given its sensationalistic premise, surprisingly dull. Psychologist Cal Jamison (Martin Sheen), who is widowed in the very effective opening scene, moves his young son (Harley Cross) to New York City, where he gets a job with the police department. Soon he is embroiled in an investigation of NYC's *santeria* religious community and its evil sect, *brujeria*, which has been sacrificing humans. As Cal digs deeper, he learns that the cult has designs on his son for their next sacrifice. Although THE BELIEVERS does contain a few effective moments, it is marred by some unfortunate racism and a misleading presentation of *santeria*, a complex religion created by African slaves that combines Catholic iconography with their native beliefs. Although there is an attempt to delineate between the "good" and "bad" aspects of the religion (the script also tries to negate accusations of racism by making the true evildoers a group of wealthy, decadent whites who exploit and pervert *santeria* to their own ends), nearly every person of color in the film is portrayed as some sort of fanatical cultist mumbling threatening incantations that can only mean trouble for the white-bread hero. While the film completely unravels shortly after the opening scene, there a few good performances (notably from Robert Loggia) and the gorgeous cinematography of Robby Muller to cling to as it sinks into the confused abyss.

p, John Schlesinger, Michael Childers, Beverly Camhe; d, John Schlesinger; w, Mark Frost (based on the novel *The Religion* by Nicholas Conde); ph, Robby Muller (Deluxe Color); ed, Peter Honess; m, J. Peter Robinson.

**(PR:O   MPAA:R)**

## BEN**½

(1972) 95m Cinerama c

Lee Montgomery *(Danny Garrison)*, Joseph Campanella *(Cliff Kirtland)*, Arthur O'Connell *(Bill Hatfield)*, Rosemary Murphy *(Beth Garrison)*, Meredith Baxter *(Eve Garrison)*, Kaz Garas *(Joe Greer)*, Paul Carr *(Kelly)*, Richard Van Fleet *(Reade)*, Kenneth Tobey *(Engineer)*, James Luisi *(Ed)*, Lee Paul *(Careu)*, Norman Alden *(Policeman)*, Scott Garrett *(Henry Gary)*, Arlen Stuart *(Mrs. Gray)*, Richard Drasin *(George)*.

The sequel to the popular killer-rat movie WILLARD (1971) picks up right where its predecessor left off, as an army of rats devours their hapless trainer, Willard. With the cops in hot pursuit, the rats hide out in the city sewers and lay low for awhile. The rodents' leader, Ben, surfaces periodically to hunt for food, and while out on one of his wander-

ings he meets young Danny (Lee Harcourt Montgomery), a lonely boy with a heart condition. Ben and Danny become fast friends, and a genuinely touching relationship develops between the rat and boy while Ben's minions stage commando raids on the surrounding community. As is to be expected, adults just don't understand Danny and Ben's special relationship and the authorities attempt to force Danny to reveal where the rats—4,000 of them—are hiding. Now remembered mainly for its Michael Jackson theme song, which became a huge hit, BEN is actually a fairly effective and surprisingly sentimental nature-on-the-loose movie that manages to deliver the genre goods while making the audience go all misty-eyed over the boy-rat relationship. Veteran crime film director Phil Karlson (THE PHENIX CITY STORY, 1955; THE BROTHERS RICO, 1957; WALKING TALL, 1973) handles this potentially laughable material with aplomb and presents some genuinely creepy scenes, especially the one in which Ben introduces Danny to his army of rats in the sewer. Although neither WILLARD nor BEN has held up particularly well over the years, both are a lot of fun to watch and work better than they have any right to.

p, Mort Briskin; d, Phil Karlson; w, Gilbert A. Ralston (based on characters created by Stephen Gilbert); ph, Russell Metty (DeLuxe Color); ed, Henry Gerstad; m, Walter Scharf.

**(PR:A-C   MPAA:PG)**

## BERSERK**

(1967) 98m COL c

Joan Crawford *(Monica Rivers)*, Ty Hardin *(Frank Hawkins)*, Diana Dors *(Matilda)*, Michael Gough *(Dorando)*, Judy Geeson *(Angela Rivers)*, Robert Hardy *(Supt. Brooks)*, Geoffrey Keen *(Comm. Dalby)*, Sidney Tafler *(Harrison Liston)*, George Claydon *(Bruno)*, Ambrosine Philpotts *(Miss Burrows)*, Ted Lune *(Skeleton Man)*, Philip Madoc *(Lazlo)*, Peter Burton *(Gustavo)*, Golda Casimir *(Bearded Lady)*, Milton Reid *(Strong Man)*, Marianne Stone *(Wanda)*, Miki Iveria *(Gypsy Fortune Teller)*, Howard Goorney *(Emil)*, Reginald Marsh *(Sgt. Hutchins)*, The Billy Smart Circus.

Another in the string of bizarre horror films starring Joan Crawford that pockmarked the end of her career (STRAIT-JACKET, 1964; TROG, 1970), this one features Joan as the icy and ambitious owner of a traveling circus who finds that all her star attractions are getting bumped off one by one. *See* a spike driven through Michael Gough's skull! *See* Diana Dors literally sawed in half! *See* Ty Hardin fall off his tightrope onto a bed of knives! *Guess* whose psychopathic 16-year-old daughter is responsible for the crimes! Producer Herman Cohen had a penchant for horror films in which the cast is killed off in a variety of creative ways (HORRORS OF THE BLACK MUSEUM, 1959), and does not disappoint in this garishly color-photographed effort. While not particularly gory, the film is a camp delight as Crawford chews the scenery like a mad dog. The then 63-year-old actress is truly a kitsch vision here, with her hair put up in a vise-like bun and her body outfitted in ringmaster's garb that consists of a black leotard, scarlet tail-coat, and top hat. Padded out with a lot of circus performance footage, BESERK may prove slow going for modern-day horror enthusiasts, but for fans of STRAITJACKET and TROG this one is essential.

p, Herman Cohen; d, Jim O'Connor; w, Aben Kandel, Herman Cohen; ph, Desmond Dickinson (Technicolor); ed, Raymond Poulton; m, Patrick John Scott.

**(PR:C  MPAA:NR)**

## BERSERKER zero

(1988) 85m American Video-Paradise Filmworks/ Shapiro c

Joseph Johnson, Valerie Sheldon, Greg Dawson.

BERSERKER is routine spam-in-a-cabin with a gimmick: this time it's actually the reincarnated spirit of a cannibalistic Viking warrior that's doing the mincing. Six interchangeable teenagers set out from the city for a week of camping in a remote valley originally settled by Norwegians—or "descendants of the Vikings," as the smart kid portentously reads aloud from a book. He goes on to relate the legend of the "berserkers," fierce warriors who were so feared even by their own comrades that they were kept chained in the bows of longboats until they hit the beaches and were unloosed upon the populace. The brainy teen continues to read some mumbo-jumbo about the spirits of these warriors being doomed because they practiced cannibalism, never to find rest but to pass from generation to generation until the last of their descendants is killed. The other kids laugh it off, of course—until they arrive at the campground and begin dying one by one. There's nothing here to attract even the most indiscriminate of horror fans, and the performances are all far below even the mediocre standard of the slice-and-dice genre. The kids are idiotic, becoming hopelessly lost in the woods only steps away from their cabin and running around in circles over the same terrain without realizing they've been there just moments before. BERSERKER is poorly plotted and lackadaisically directed, and it's little wonder that this one never graced a commercial screen and instead appeared straight on the video racks to lure the unwary into wasting $2, as well as valuable time that could be spent organizing sock drawers or playing Nintendo.

p, Jules Rivera; d, Jef Richard; w, Jef Richard; ph, Henning Shellerup; ed, Marcus Manton; m, Chuck Francour, Gary Griffin.

**(PR:O  MPAA:R)**

## BEYOND EVIL*

(1980) 94m IFI/Scope III c

John Saxon (Larry), Lynda Day George (Barbara), Michael Dante (Del), Mario Milano (Albanos), Janice Lynde (Alma), David Opatoshu (Dr. Solomon), Anne Marisse (Leia), Zitto Kazaan (Esteban).

This terribly tepid haunted-house movie follows married couple Barbara (Lynda Day George) and Larry (John Saxon) as they move into an island mansion that hasn't been

inhabited for 100 years, and for good reason. It seems that, a century ago, Alma (Janice Lynde) made a pact with the devil and was involved in black magic before she was murdered by her philandering husband. Alma came back from the dead to break her evil spouse's neck, and now Barbara begins to have visions of her, too. The dull direction by Herb Freed (GRADUATION DAY) fails to wring any scares out of this mundane material and only the musical score by Pino Donaggio (CARRIE; DRESSED TO KILL) will hold any interest for fans of the genre.

p, David Baughn, Herb Freed; d, Herb Freed; w, Paul Ross, Herb Freed (based on a story by David Baughn); ph, Ken Plotin (Metrocolor); ed, Rick Westover.

**(PR:C  MPAA:R)**

## BEYOND THE DOOR*½

(1975, It./US) 100m Film Ventures c (CHI SEI?; AKA: DEVIL WITHIN HER, THE; WHO?)

Juliet Mills (Jessica), Richard Johnson (Dimitri), David Colin, Jr. (Robert), Elizabeth Turner, Gabriele Lavia, Nino Segurini, Carla Mancini, Barbara Fiorini, Joan Acti, Vittoria Fanfoni.

This Italian rip-off of both THE EXORCIST (1973) and ROSEMARY'S BABY (1968) stars Juliet Mills as Jessica, the bored wife of a record producer, who enters into an affair with a mysterious stranger and becomes pregnant. Her lover, of course, has made a pact with the devil and the fetus in Jessica's womb is satanic. This causes Jessica to start looking and behaving like Linda Blair in THE EXORCIST, while the little devil inside her causes toys to move on their own and doors to slam. Complete with spinning heads and green puke, this blatant plagiarization made a surprising amount of money in the US, coming in second behind JAWS at the box office for several weeks in New York City. When not reprising events from the Friedkin and Polanski films, BEYOND THE DOOR fails to make much sense, but director Oliver Hellman (Ovidio G. Assonitis) manages to inject a bit of atmosphere into the familiar proceedings, and fans of "Nanny and the Professor" may get a kick out of seeing Mills spew green goo all over the room. Exteriors were filmed in San Francisco, interiors in Rome. A sequel directed by Mario Bava (see below) is a sequel in name only.

p, Ovidio Assonitis, Giorgio Rossi; d, Ovidio Assonitis; w, Roberto d'Ettore Piazzoli, Ovidio Assonitis, Antonio Troisio, Giorgio Marini, Aldo Crudo, Sonia Molteni; ph, Roberto d'Ettore Piazzoli (Deluxe Color); m, Riz Ortolani.

**(PR:O  MPAA:R)**

## BEYOND THE DOOR II***

(1979, It.) 92m Film Ventures c (AKA: SHOCK)

Daria Nicolodi (Dora), John Steiner (Bruno), David Colin, Jr. (Marco), Ivan Rassimov (Carlos), Nicola Salerno.

Made in Italy in 1977 and marketed in the US as a sequel to BEYOND THE DOOR, this film is wholly original and has nothing to do with Ovidio Assonitis' EXORCIST/

ROSEMARY'S BABY rip-off, save for the fact that young actor David Colin, Jr., is in both films. The last feature directed by the legendary Mario Bava, this movie finds a young boy (Colin) who has supernatural powers living with his mother, Dora (Daria Nicolodi), who is quietly insane. Although it's assumed that the boy's father, a drug addict, committed suicide, it is later revealed that Dora killed her husband so that she could marry her lover, Bruno (John Steiner). Bruno was her accomplice in the crime, and it was he who walled up the body in the basement. The boy, however, may be possessed by his dead father, and uses his powers to drive his mother slowly into dementia by coming on to her sexually and making her see rotting hands grabbing at her from unexpected places. As with any Bava film, the nonsensical plot is secondary to the dazzling visuals that accompany it. Bava was a master of cinematic manipulation and mood is everything here, from the mobile camera to the atmospheric soundtrack. Continuing to explore his perverse obsessions (mainly sex and death) to the end, Bava holds nothing back and even manages to coax a strong performance from female lead Nicolodi. Codirecting here with his son, Lamberto, who would later go on to make DEMONS (1985), Bava would only have time to make one more film, a made-for-television movie, before his death in 1980.

p, Juri Vasile; d, Mario Bava, Lamberto Bava; w, Lamberto Bava, Francesco Barbieri, Paolo Briganti, Dardano Sacchetti; ph, Alberto Spagnoli.

**(PR:O MPAA:R)**

## BEYOND THE FOG**

(1981, Brit.) 86m Independent-International c (AKA: TOWER OF EVIL; HORROR ON SNAPE ISLAND)

Bryant Haliday (Brent), Jill Haworth (Rose), Anna Palk (Nora), Jack Watson (Hamp), Mark Edwards (Adam), Derek Fowlds (Dan), John Hamill (Gary), Candace Glendenning (Penny), Dennis Price (Bakewell), George Coulouris (Gurney), Robin Askwith (Des), Serretta Wilson (Mac), Fredric Abbott (Saul), Mark McBride (Michael), William Lucas (Det. Hawk), Anthony Valentine (Dr. Simpson), Marianne Stone (Nurse).

Originally released in Britain in 1972 as HORROR ON SNAPE ISLAND, this film was rereleased in the US in 1981 as BEYOND THE FOG, an attempt to capitalize on the success of John Carpenter's THE FOG (1980). After a young American woman appears to have gone mad and killed her companions on Snape Island, which is rumored to contain a fortune in buried treasure, a private investigator (Bryant Halliday) and a team of archaeologists (there is a Phoenician temple on the island) visit the scene to investigate. Once on the island, of course, they are viciously slaughtered one by one. The main suspect is a horribly scarred lighthouse keeper who is quite insane and keeps the rotting corpse of his wife in a rocking chair. Gratuitous nudity and gory violence are exploited to the fullest by director Jim O'Connolly, who penned the script based on a story by respected horror writer George Baxt (BURN WITCH BURN). Unfortunately, the performances are subpar, even for this genre, and O'Connolly has a penchant

for shock-cuts and zooms that tends to be overbearing and that date the film badly. For gorehounds only.

p, Richard Gordon; d, Jim O'Connolly; w, Jim O'Connolly (based on a story by George Baxt); ph, Desmond Dickinson (Eastmancolor); ed, Henry Richardson; m, Ken Jones.

**(PR:O MPAA:R)**

## BIG FOOT*

(1971) 95m Gemini-American/Ellman c

Chris Mitchum (Rick), John Carradine (Jasper B. Hawks), Joi Lansing (Joi Landis), Lindsay Crosby (Wheels), Ken Maynard (Mr. Bennett), Joy Wilkerson (Peggy), John Mitchum (Elmer Briggs), Doodles Weaver (Forest Ranger), Haji Lamme (Haji), James Stellar (Big Foot).

This pretty silly monster picture made decent money at the box office, because interest in the fabled Big Foot peaked just as the film, shot in 1969, was released. Joi Landis (played by the homophonous Joi Lansing) is forced to parachute into the dense woods of Northern California after her private plane has engine trouble. There she finds herself confronted by the legendary missing link, Big Foot (in a laughably ratty costume), who is looking to breed and carts her off to his lair. Meanwhile, weekend biker Rick (Chris Mitchum) is attacked by another Big Foot, and when he comes to discovers that his girl friend has also been kidnapped by the tattered creatures. Rick goes back to town and drafts a posse to rescue the girls, while two local backwoods types (John Carradine and John Mitchum) plot to capture the beasts and exhibit them in a sideshow. Terminally dumb, the film does contain some priceless moments of high camp and is worth a look for that alone. B western fans will note that Ken Maynard plays the owner of the General Store. Although he had been inactive for several decades, the elderly Maynard came out of retirement to appear in BIG FOOT, only to beat a hasty retreat back to the home where he died four years later.

p, Anthony Cardoza; d, Robert F. Slatzer; w, Robert F. Slatzer, James Gordon White; ph, Wilson S. Hong (Deluxe Color); ed, Bud Hoffman, Hugo Grimaldi; m, Richard A. Podolor.

**(PR:C MPAA:PG)**

## BILLY THE KID VS. DRACULA**

(1966) 73m EM/Circle c

Chuck Courtney (Billy the Kid), John Carradine (Vampire Uncle), Melinda Plowman (Betty), Walter Janovitz (Franz Oster), Harry Carey Jr. (Ben), Roy Barcroft (Marshal Griffin), Olive Carey (Dr. Henrietta Hull), Hannie Landman (Lila Oster), Marjorie Bennett (Mrs. Ann Bentley), William Forrest (James Underhill), George Cisar (Joe Blake), Charlita (Nana), Virginia Christine (Eva Oster), Richard Reeves, Max Kleven, Jack Williams, William Challee.

This film and its companion piece, JESSE JAMES MEETS FRANKENSTEIN'S DAUGHTER (1966), comprise one of the weirdest genre hybrids in cinema history, and both were directed by the infamous Hollywood hack William Beaudine. John Carradine, who hadn't played Dracula since THE HOUSE OF DRACULA in 1945, stars once again as the world's most famous vampire. This time out of the casket, however, the locale has switched from central Europe to the American Old West. Dracula arrives in town on a stagecoach and sets himself up as the uncle of attractive ranch owner Betty (Melinda Plowman) by hypnotising her. Meanwhile, a reformed Billy the Kid (Chuck Courtney), who has landed a job as the foreman of Betty's ranch and fallen in love with his boss, begins to suspect that Betty's "uncle" is up to no good. This truly bad movie is, nonetheless, good fun and Carradine contributes a delightfully hammy performance. More western than horror film, the action climaxes in a silver mine as Dracula is cornered by Billy the Kid and the town doctor—who, inexplicably, just happens to know everything there is to know about vampires.

p, Carroll Case; d, William Beaudine; w, Carl Hittleman (based on his story); ph, Lothrop Worth (Pathe Color); ed, Roy Livingston; m, Raoul Kraushaar.

(PR:A  MPAA:NR)

## BIRD WITH THE CRYSTAL PLUMAGE, THE****

(1970, It./Ger.) 98m Glazier/UM c (L'UCELLO DALLE PLUME DI CRISTALLO; AKA: PHANTOM OF TERROR, THE)

Tony Musante (Sam Dalmas), Suzy Kendall (Julia), Eva Renzi (Monica), Enrico Maria Salerno (Morosini), Mario Adorf (Berto), Renato Romano (Dover), Umberto Rano (Ranieri).

Sam Dalmas (Tony Musante) is an American writer in Rome who, while walking home one night, sees a man dressed in black attempting to murder Monica (Eva Renzi) in an art gallery. He can't make out the killer's face, but the police decide to hold on to Sam's passport and force him to cooperate with their investigation, since this is but one of several murders of lone women. At first resentful of the police, Sam soon becomes obsessed with the case and sets out on his own to find the killer. The directorial debut of one of Italy's most successful directors, Dario Argento, this film was ahead of its time and immeasurably influenced what would come to be known as the "slasher" genre in the 1980s. Inspired by Alfred Hitchcock but never derivative, Argento presents the viewer with a streamlined narrative structure that, in the end, isn't as important as its cinematic presentation. Superb work by cinematographer Vittorio Storaro and a memorable score by the prolific Ennio Morricone aid Argento as he skillfully heightens every suspenseful moment and visualizes scenes in a unique and surprising way, without ever becoming self-consciously "arty." Argento demonstrates a great sense of humor as well, and stocks the film with several eccentric and amusing characters. While Brian De Palma is frequently noted for his slavish devotion to Hitchcock, he borrows just as liberally (and obviously) from Dario Argento.

p, Salvatore Argento; d, Dario Argento; w, Dario Argento;

ph, Vittorio Storaro (Eastmancolor); ed, Franco Fraticelli; m, Ennio Morricone.

(PR:C  MPAA:PG)

## BIRDS, THE****

(1963) 120m UNIV c

Rod Taylor (Mitch Brenner), Tippi Hedren (Melanie Daniels), Jessica Tandy (Lydia Brenner), Suzanne Pleshette (Annie Hayworth), Veronica Cartwright (Cathy Brenner), Ethel Griffies (Mrs. Bundy), Charles McGraw (Sebastian Sholes), Ruth McDevitt (Mrs. MacGruder), Joe Mantell (Salesman), Doodles Weaver (Fisherman), Richard Deacon (Man in Elevator), Alfred Hitchcock (Man in Front of Pet Shop with White Poodles).

Alfred Hitchcock's follow-up to PSYCHO (1960) was yet another ground-breaking addition to the horror genre and further revealed the master director's darker obsessions. Loosely based on a Daphne De Murier short story, the action is set in Bodega Bay and follows bored, spoiled socialite Melanie Daniels (Tippi Hedren) as she romantically pursues dashing lawyer Mitch Brenner (Rod Taylor). There is much tension among Melanie; Mitch's former flame, schoolteacher Annie Hayworth (Suzanne Pleshette); and Mitch's domineering mother (Jessica Tandy), but the emotional interplay is interrupted (and reflected) by the sudden and unexplained attack of thousands of birds on the area. Hailed as Hitchcock's masterpiece by some and despised by others, THE BIRDS is certainly one of the director's most complex and fascinating works. Volumes have been written about the film, with each writer picking it apart scene by scene in order to prove his or her particular critical theory—mostly of the psychoanalytic variety. Be that as it may, even those who cringe at some of the performances and are bored by the somewhat stilted scenes between the bird attacks cannot deny the extreme power of many of the film's haunting images: the bird point-of-view shot of Bodega Bay, the birds slowly gathering on the jungle gym, the attack on the children's birthday party, Melanie trapped in the attic, and the final ambiguous shot of the defeated humans leaving Bodega Bay while the thousands of triumphant birds gathered on the ground watch them go.

p, Alfred Hitchcock; d, Alfred Hitchcock; w, Evan Hunter (based on the story by Daphne du Maurier); ph, Robert Burks (Technicolor); ed, George Tomasini; m, Bernard Herrmann.

(PR:C  MPAA:NR)

## BLACK CAT, THE*****

(1934) 70m UNIV bw (AKA: THE VANISHING BODY; GB: HOUSE OF DOOM)

Boris Karloff (Hjalmar Poelzig), Bela Lugosi (Dr. Vitus Verdegast), David Manners (Peter Allison), Jacqueline Wells (Joan Allison), Lucille Lund (Karen), Egon Brecher (Majordomo), Henry Armetta (Sergeant), Albert Conti (Lieutenant), Anna Duncan (Maid), Herman Bing (Car Steward), Andre Cheron (Train Conductor), Luis Alberni

(Train Steward), Harry Cording (Thalmar), George Davis (Bus Driver), Alphonse Martell (Porter), Tony Marlow (Patrolman), Paul Weigel (Stationmaster), Albert Polet (Waiter), Rodney Hildebrand (Brakeman), John Carradine (Man Playing Organ), King Baggot, Michael Mark, Paul Panger.

The first and best teaming of Universal horror stars Boris Karloff and Bela Lugosi was this bizarre, haunting, and hypnotic film by director Edgar G. Ulmer. The story concerns a young couple, Peter (David Manners) and Joan (Jacqueline Wells), who meet mysterious scientist Dr. Vitus Verdegast (Lugosi) while on their honeymoon in Budapest. The trio wind up at the home of Verdegast's old friend Hjalmar Poelzig (Karloff), an architect living atop a mountain in a modernistic, art deco mansion. As it turns out, Poelzig is the leader of a satanic cult who, as a commander during WW I, caused the capture of Verdegast and the deaths of thousands of their countrymen in a bloody battle. Poelzig has built his house on the battlefield, which he calls "the greatest cemetery in the world." While Verdegast rotted in prison, the architect stole his wife, who later died (he keeps her corpse in a glass case), then married Verdegast's daughter. Verdegast has now come for revenge, and Peter and Joan find themselves caught in a deadly game of cat and mouse. A remarkable study of evil, THE BLACK CAT is still one of the most affecting horrors the genre has ever produced. With supreme directorial skill, Ulmer infuses the film with an overwhelming sense of unease, eroticism, and dread that remains powerful to this day. The literate script, magnificent set design, superbly fluid camerawork, and stunning performances by Karloff (whose character was inspired by occult hedonist Aleister Crowley) and Lugosi (in one of his finest roles) lend the film a timeless quality. The early use of incidental music is extremely effective, with most of the score derived from the works of Tchaikovsky, Liszt, and Schumann. Ulmer had worked with the classic German Expressionist filmmakers of the 1920s, and their influence is pervasive. Karloff and Lugosi would never work as well together again. Ulmer would go on to direct such low-budget classics as DETOUR (1945), but this is his masterpiece.

p, Carl Laemmle; d, Edgar G. Ulmer; w, Edgar G. Ulmer, Peter Ruric (based on the story by Edgar Allan Poe); ph, John Mescall; ed, Ray Curtis.

(PR:C   MPAA:NR)

## BLACK CHRISTMAS**

(1974, Can.) 93m Ambassador c (AKA: SILENT NIGHT, EVIL NIGHT; STRANGER IN THE HOUSE)

Olivia Hussey (Jess), Keir Dullea (Peter), Margot Kidder (Barb), Andrea Martin (Phyl), John Saxon (Lt. Fuller), Marian Waldman (Mrs. Mac), Art Hindle (Chris), Lynne Griffin (Clare Harrison), James Edmond (Mr. Harrison).

DEATHDREAM (1972) director Bob Clark helmed this fairly effective slasher movie, featuring Margot Kidder as a sorority sister whose annual Christmas party is ruined by a madman (Keir Dullea) hiding upstairs. As the holiday festivities commence and the various coeds practice carnal knowledge, the killer knocks them off one by one. Although strictly standard fare, the material is elevated somewhat through Clark's skillful handling of such plot devices as the killer making obscene phone calls to the girls via the upstairs phone and a nicely handled twist ending, which provides a genuine shock. "SCTV" fans will note Andrea Martin among the sorority girls.

p, Bob Clark; d, Bob Clark; w, Roy Moore; ph, Reginald H. Morris; ed, Stan Cole; m, Carl Zittrer.

(PR:O   MPAA:R)

## BLACK DRAGONS**½

(1942) 61m MON bw

Bela Lugosi (Dr. Melcher Colomb), Joan Barclay (Alice), Clayton Moore (Don Martin), George Pembroke (Saunders), Robert Frazer (Hanlin), I. Stanford Jolley (The Dragon), Max Hoffman, Jr. (Kerney), Irving Mitchell (Van Dyke), Edward Peil (Wallace), Bob Fiske (Ryder), Kenneth Harlan (Colton), Joe Eggenton (Stevens), Bernard Gorcey (Cabby).

This bizarre wartime horror/espionage film stars Bela Lugosi as Dr. Melcher Colomb, a Nazi plastic surgeon sent to Japan to give Japanese spies a Caucasian look so they can move about freely while committing their heinous acts of sabotage in the US. The surgery is a success, but the untrustworthy Japs throw the doctor in the hoosegow to make sure the whole thing stays secret. The angry surgeon eventually escapes, however, and travels to America to seek his revenge on the sly Japanese. The whole thing is pretty silly (not to mention racist, as were most films of this period) and unnecessarily complicated by a convoluted structure that depends on a lengthy flashback at the climax to explain Lugosi's motivation. Not a particularly good film, but definitely an oddity and worth a look for the historically curious.

p, Sam Katzman, Jack Dietz; d, William Nigh; w, Harvey Gates; ph, Art Reed; ed, Carl Pierson.

(PR:A   MPAA:NR)

## BLACK ROOM, THE***½

(1935) 73m COL bw

Boris Karloff (Baron Gregor de Berghmann/Anton de Berghmann), Marian Marsh (Thea Hassel), Robert Allen (Lt. Albert Lussan), Thurston Hall (Col. Hassel), Katherine De Mille (Mashka), John Buckler (Beran), Henry Kolker (Baron Frederick de Berghmann), Colin Tapley (Lt. Hassel), Torben Meyer (Peter), Egon Brecher (Karl), John Bleifer (Franz), Frederick Vogeding (Josef), Edward Van Sloan (Doctor).

Boris Karloff is superb in a dual role as twin brothers (one evil, one good) in one of the few horror films produced by Columbia Pictures in the 1930s. The action takes place in the early 1800s in Czechoslovakia, where twins Gregor and Anton are born to the ruling de Berghmann family. Anton, the good child, is born with a paralyzed arm and is taken away when very young to be educated abroad. The evil brother, Gregor, grows to inherit the castle and becomes infamous for his sadistic behavior. Many of the young women in the village have entered his domain never to return, and the populace is beginning to turn nasty. The villagers rejoice when Anton returns, and Gregor steps down and allows his sibling to assume control of the castle to avoid being lynched by the peasants. But Gregor has a plan. He takes his twin to a hidden part of the house known as the Black Room and murders him, assuming his identity so that he may continue his heinous acts in the good brother's guise. Directed with a great sense of style by Roy William Neill, this is first-rate gothic horror, with Karloff giving one of his greatest performances, especially in the scene in which the evil Gregor rehearses his portrayal of his crippled brother. Karloff's skillful portrayals plus good optical work and excellent editing succeed in creating the illusion of two Karloffs interacting. As a comparison of special effects and acting, THE BLACK ROOM and David Cronenberg's DEAD RINGERS (1988) would make a fascinating double bill.

p, Robert North; d, Roy William Neill; w, Arthur Strawn, Henry Myers (based on a story by Arthur Strawn); ph, Al Seigler; ed, Richard Cahoon.

(PR:A  MPAA:NR)

## BLACK ROOM, THE*½

(1984) 87m CI Films c

Stephen Knight *(Jason)*, Cassandra Gaviola *(Bridget)*, Jim Stathis *(Larry)*, Clara Perryman *(Robin)*, Geanne Frank *(Sandy)*, Charlie Young *(Lisa)*, Christopher McDonald *(Terry)*, Linnea Quigley *(Milly)*.

This early straight-to-video release, shot in 1981, features brother and sister team Jason (Stephen Knight) and Bridget (Cassandra Gaviola), who own a mansion in the Hollywood Hills and lure swingers into the "Black Room" so that they can voyeuristically photograph sex acts and then kill them. The blood of the victims is used in transfusions for Jason, who suffers from a rare blood disease. A sleazy low-budget item, the film attempts to combine soft-core thrills with explicit team action and fails on both accounts. The only points of interest are the casting of beautiful model Gaviola (who played the witch who turns into a fireball while making love to Arnold Schwarzenegger in 1982's CONAN THE BARBARIAN) and a bit part by current Queen of the Bs Linnea Quigley.

p, Aaron C. Butler; d, Elly Kenner, Norman Thaddeus Vane; w, Norman Thaddeus Vane; ph, Robert Harmon; ed, David Kern; m, Art Podell, James Achley.

(PR:O  MPAA:R)

## BLACK SABBATH***½

(1963, It.) 99m AIP bw (I TRE VOLTI DELLA PAURA; AKA: THREE FACES OF TERROR, THE; THREE FACES OF FEAR, THE; BLACK CHRISTMAS)

Jacqueline Pierreux *(Helen Corey)*, Milli Monti *(Maid)*, Michele Mercier *(Rosy)*, Lidia Alfonsi *(Mary)*, Boris Karloff *(Gorca)*, Susy Anderson *(Sdenka)*, Mark Damon *(Vladimir*

*d'Urfe)*, Glauco Onorato *(Giorgio)*, Rika Dialina *(Wife)*, Massimo Righi *(Pietro)*.

Mario Bava's horror anthology presents three episodes introduced by Boris Karloff, who also stars in the last (and best) segment. The first story concerns a nurse (Jacqueline Pierreux) who is summoned to the home of a dying clairvoyant. Upon her arrival, she discovers that the medium has already died, greedily steals a diamond ring from the body, and wears it home. That night she is haunted by the ghost of the deceased woman. The second episode features Michele Mercier as Rosy, a prostitute who is harassed by phone calls made by a man she helped send to prison. The escaped killer murders the hooker's friend by mistake, giving Rosy a chance to kill him. The final episode stars Karloff as Gorca, the patriarch of an Eastern European family who has gone off to kill a local bandit. Before his departure, Gorca informed his family that if he were gone longer than five days he might return as a Wurdalak—i.e., a vampire who thirsts for the blood of his loved ones—and that no matter how strong his demands he must not be let into the house. He returns on the fifth day and the family is horrified to discover that their father has, indeed, returned as a Wurdalak. Gorca proceeds to kill the whole bunch, including his young grandson, turning them into vampires. While all the episodes have terrifying moments, the finale is the standout, with the most disturbing scenes being those in which Karloff, having turned his grandson into a vampire, uses the child's cries to lure the other members of the family into his deadly trap. Bava's stylistic experiments, especially in the final story, remain effective and fascinating to this day.

p, Salvatore Billitteri; d, Mario Bava; w, Marcello Fondato, Alberto Bevilacqua, Mario Bava (based on "The Drop of Water" by Anton Chekov, "The Telephone" by F.G. Snyder, "The Wurdalak" by Leo Tolstoy); ph, Ubaldo Terzano; ed, Mario Serandrei; m, Roberto Nicolosi (Ital.), Les Baxter (US).

(PR:C  MPAA:NR)

## BLACK SUNDAY*****

(1960, It.) 84m Galatea-S.P.A./AIP bw (LA MASCHERA DEL DEMONIO; AKA: DEMON'S MASK, THE; REVENGE OF THE VAMPIRE; HOUSE OF FRIGHT)

Barbara Steele *(Witch Princess Asa/Katia)*, John Richardson *(Dr. Andre Gorobec)*, Ivo Garrani *(Prince Vaida)*, Andrea Cecchi *(Dr. Choma)*, Arturo Dominici *(Javutich)*, Enrico Olivieri *(Constantin)*, Antonio Pierfederici *(The Pope)*, Clara Bindi *(Innkeeper)*, Germana Dominici *(His Daughter)*, Mario Passante *(Nikita)*, Tino Bianchi *(Ivan)*.

Mario Bava's undisputed masterpiece of horror, BLACK SUNDAY contains some unforgettable imagery and remains extremely powerful to this day. In 1630, a beautiful witch princess, Asa (Barbara Steele), who is a vampire, and her lover, Juvato (Arturo Dominici), are put to death by her vengeful brother. He has iron devil-masks with spikes on the inside placed on both of their faces and then sledgehammered home. Two hundred years later, blood is accidentally spilled on Asa's face and she rises from the dead along with Juvato to wreak revenge on the descendants of those who executed her—including her lookalike, Katia (also played by Steele). Beautifully photographed in black and white by Bava himself, BLACK SUNDAY is a hypnotically compelling horror film, a kind of lyrical nightmare. From the brutal opening to the resurrection of the vampires and the horrors that follow, Bava's camera effortlessly glides through the fogbound sets, presenting one incredible image after another. In addition to the visuals, Bava's use of sound and music—or even the lack thereof—is impressive as well, with entire sequences played out in virtual silence. Steele is magnificent in her dual role as vengeful female sexuality and vestal virgin. As the resurrected Asa, her beautiful face is both seductive and horrifying, bearing the terrible holes savagely punched by the iron mask. The role catapulted her to horror movie stardom and even today she remains the reigning queen of the genre. Unfortunately, when released in the US by American International Pictures, BLACK SUNDAY was badly dubbed and a bombastic Les Baxter score was imposed over the original by Roberto Nicolosi. Not widely available on tape, but well worth seeking out. California-based video company Sinister Cinema has just announced release of a version that differs from the American AIP release in dubbing and music.

p, Massimo de Rita; d, Mario Bava; w, Ennio De Concini, Mario Bava, Marcello Coscia, Mario Serandrei (based on the story "The Vij" by Nikolai Gogol); ph, Mario Bava, Ubaldo Terzano; ed, Mario Serandrei; m, Roberto Nicolosi, Les Baxter (English Version).

**(PR:C  MPAA:NR)**

## BLACKENSTEIN*

(1973) 93m Exclusive International c (AKA: BLACK FRANKENSTEIN)

John Hart *(Dr. Frankenstein),* Joe DiSue *(The Monster),* Ivory Stone, Andrea King, Liz Renay, Roosevelt Jackson, James Cougar, Cardella Di Milo, Nick Bolin.

Blaxploitation producers went on a brief foray through the horror genre, and although BLACKENSTEIN is one of their worst efforts, it's at least interesting on a conceptual level. Combining the horrors of Vietnam with the more gothic variety, the film stars Joe DiSue as a black Vietnam vet who comes home a paraplegic. There is hope for a cure, however, when his fiancee's boss, Dr. Frankenstein (John Hart), offers to graft a new arm and leg on the injured veteran. All goes well until the good doctor's crazed assistant, who is in love with the patient's fiancee, feeds his rival a potion that turns him into . . . Blackenstein. Sporting a hip box haircut that makes his head look flat, the monster wanders the neighborhood tearing the blouses off his well-endowed female victims before killing them. This is as bad—and unintentionally funny—as it sounds. Given a scant release when it first opened, BLACKENSTEIN disappeared without a trace until the miracle of videotape reintroduced it to an anxious horror public. Old horror film buffs will note that special effects expert Ken Strickfaden, who created the electronic gadgets in the original Universal FRANKENSTEIN movies, came out of retirement to do more of the same here.

p, Frank R. Saletri; d, William A. Levy; w, Frank R. Saletri.

**(PR:O  MPAA:R)**

## BLACULA***

(1972) 92m AIP c

William Marshall *(Blacula),* Vonette McGee *(Tina),* Denise Nicholas *(Michelle),* Thalmus Rasulala *(Gordon Thomas),* Gordon Pinsent *(Lt. Peters),* Charles McCauley *(Dracula),* Emily Yancy *(Nancy),* Lance Taylor Sr. *(Swenson),* Ted Harris *(Bobby),* Rick Metzler *(Billy),* Ji-tu Cumbuka *(Skillet),* Ketty Lester *(Juanita),* Elisha Cook, Jr. *(Sam).*

If BLACKENSTEIN was one of the worst blaxploitation films ever made, BLACULA is easily one of the best. Respected stage actor William Marshall is outstanding in this subtle tongue-in-cheek version of the vampire legend. Action begins in the 18th century, when an African prince, Mamuwalde (Marshall), is visiting Transylvania. There he is attacked by Count Dracula, who makes him into one of the undead and renames him Blacula. Two hundred years later the story picks up in Los Angeles, where a couple of fey interior designers have bought the contents of Castle Dracula, including Blacula's coffin. Soon Blacula is romping around LA, biting necks and chasing after the beautiful Tina (Vonette McGee), who he believes is his reincarnated wife. Enter police pathologist Dr. Gordon Thomas (Thalmus Rasulala) who thinks he has a vampire on his hands and is determined to end Blacula's reign of terror. Although BLACULA is surprisingly conventional (given the concept's potential) and painfully low-budget, the hammy performance by William Marshall makes it an enjoyable outing. A sequel, SCREAM, BLACULA, SCREAM, followed in 1973.

p, Joseph T. Naar; d, William Crain; w, Joan Torres, Raymond Koenig; ph, John Stevens (Movielab Color); ed, Allan Jacobs; m, Gene Page.

**(PR:C  MPAA:PG)**

## BLADE IN THE DARK, A*½

(1986, It.) 96m National Cinematografica-Nuovo Dania/Lightning Video c (LA CASA CON LA SCALA NEL BUIO; AKA: HOUSE OF THE DARK STAIRWAY)

Andrea Occhipinti *(Bruno),* Anny Papa, Fabiola Toledo, Michele Soavi, Valeria Cavalli, Stanko Molnar, Lara Naszinski.

Produced in 1983 (at 110 minutes) but unreleased in the US until Lightning Video debuted it on cassette, A BLADE IN THE DARK is an early film by Lamberto Bava, son of Mario Bava. Bruno (Andrea Occhipinti) is a young composer who has been hired by a female movie director to score her latest horror epic. Alone in a rented villa, Bruno begins to notice some strange goings-on, all of which seem to relate to the previous tenant, a psychotic woman named Linda who may have returned to continue her crimes. The film is yet another boring Italian retread of Hitchcock's PSYCHO, with most of its running time devoted to solitary characters walking down dark, shadowy hallways and staircases, intercut with shots of the blade of a knife held by the unseen killer waiting nearby. Bava never diverges from the standard formula here, and he is not yet (and probably never will be) the accomplished visual stylist that his father was or that producer Argento is. Some may find the self-reflexive, film-within-a-film angle intriguing, but it's all been done before and Bava later beat it to death in DEMONS. The performances are serviceable, with Occhipinti making a fairly appealing hero (he's best known to American audiences as the impotent bullfighter in Bo Derek's disastrous BOLERO), and Lara Naszinski, cousin of Nastassja Kinski, making her debut as one of the many victims.

d, Lamberto Bava; w, Dardano Sacchetti, Elisa Briganti; ph, Gianlorenzo Battaglia (Luciano Vittori Color); ed, Lamberto Bava; m, Guido De Angelis, Maurizio De Angelis.

**(PR:O  MPAA:NR)**

## BLOOD AND BLACK LACE****

(1965, It.) 88m Lou Moss/AA c (SEL DONNE PER L'ASSASSINO)

Cameron Mitchell *(Max Marlan)*, Eva Bartok *(Christina)*, Thomas Reiner *(Inspector Silvester)*, Arianna Gorini *(Nicole)*, Dante De Paolo *(Frank Sacalo)*, Mary Arden *(Peggy)*, Franco Ressel *(Marquis Richard Morell)*, Claude Dantes *(Taoli)*, Lea Krugher *(Isabella)*, Massimo Righi *(Marco)*, Guiliano Raffaelli *(Zenchin)*, Harriet Medin *(Clarica)*.

For all the praise that's been heaped upon Herschell Gordon Lewis' BLOOD FEAST for being years ahead of its time, Mario Bava's BLOOD AND BLACK LACE is just as important—and certainly much better. As plotless as most of Bava's other work, the film is set in a high-fashion agency run by Christina (Eva Bartok) and her lover, Max (Cameron Mitchell), who uses their business as a front for a drug ring. Without warning, the agency's beautiful models are murdered one by one, stalked by a masked killer wearing a glove fitted with metal claws. With its systematic disposal of beautiful-but-characterless women, graphic bloodletting, and sweeping, sumptuous camera work, BLOOD AND BLACK LACE is truly a groundbreaking horror film and it set the stage for the slasher films of the 1970s and 80s. But while Bava inspired the sort of mindless mayhem that would characterize the majority of slasher films to follow, there is an intelligence and complexity to his work that makes it more deeply disturbing than any high-tech gore could possibly be. In BLOOD AND BLACK LACE he lovingly constructs a cinematic pantheon to misogyny. Bava is obsessed with the idea that sexual desire provokes violence, and expresses it through beautiful photography that draws the viewer in with its stunning artfulness. By making his killer faceless—the black fabric mask he wears has no eye or mouth holes—Bava implicates all males in the audience and accuses them of sharing his perverse obsession. We are all guilty.

p, Lou Moss; d, Mario Bava; w, Marcello Fondato, Joe Barilla, Mario Bava; ph, Herman Tarzana (Technicolor); ed, Mark Suran; m, Carlo Rustichelli.

**(PR:C-O  MPAA:NR)**

## BLOOD BEACH*½

(1981) 89m Jerry Gross c

David Huffman *(Harry Caulder)*, Mariana Hill *(Catherine)*, John Saxon *(Pearson)*, Otis Young *(Piantadosi)*, Stefan Gierasch *(Dimitros)*, Burt Young *(Royko)*, Darrell Fetty *(Hoagy)*, Lynne Marta *(Jo)*, Eleanor Zee *(Mrs. Elden)*, Lena Pousette *(Marie)*.

People keep disappearing on Santa Monica Beach and local police chief Pearson (John Saxon) wants to find out why. As it turns out, the victims are sucked beneath the sand by a shabby-looking monster, the progeny of a rather uninspired special effects team. Yet another rip-off of JAWS (1975), BLOOD BEACH even went so far as to co-opt the advertising campaign for JAWS II ("Just when you thought it was safe to go back into the water . . .") by proclaiming, "Just when you thought it was safe to go back in the water—you can't get to it." Unfortunately, the film never rises to the level of its advertising.

p, Steven Nalevansky; d, Jeffrey Bloom; w, Jeffrey Bloom (based on a story by Jeffrey Bloom, Steven Nalevansky); ph, Steve Poster (Movielab Color); ed, Gary Griffen; m, Gil Melle.

**(PR:C  MPAA:R)**

## BLOOD BEAST TERROR, THE*

(1968, Brit.) 88m Tigon/Eastman c (AKA: VAMPIRE-BEAST CRAVES BLOOD, THE)

Peter Cushing *(Inspector Quennell)*, Robert Flemyng *(Prof. Mallinger)*, Wanda Ventham *(Clare Mallinger)*, Vanessa Howard *(Meg Quennell)*, Roy Hudd *(Morgue Attendant)*, David Griffin *(William)*, Kevin Stoney *(Grainger)*, Glynn Edwards *(Sgt. Allan)*, John Paul *(Warrander)*, Russell Napier *(Landlord)*.

Set in mid-19th century England, THE BLOOD BEAST TERROR stars Robert Flemyng as Prof. Mallinger, a somewhat daffy entomologist whose daughter has the uncanny ability to change herself into a giant moth that needs human blood to survive. In a rather odd attempt to thwart his daughter's assault on the entire village, Dad tries to create another mega-moth for her to play with. Peter Cushing plays a Scotland Yard inspector sent to solve the perplexing murders. This silly mad scientist drama is undone by an incompetent production team, which utterly fails to persuade an audience to suspend their disbelief of the outlandish concept. Poor Cushing gives it the old college try, but even he can't overcome the film's fundamental flaws.

p, Tony Tenser, Arnold Louis Miller; d, Vernon Sewell; w, Peter Bryan; ph, Stanley A. Long (Eastmancolor); ed, Howard Lanning; m, Paul Ferris.

**(PR:C  MPAA:NR)**

## BLOOD DEMON***

(1967, Ger.) 81m Hemisphere bw (DIE SCHLANGENGRUBE UND DAS PENDEL; AKA: TORTURE CHAMBER OF DR. SADISM, THE; SNAKE PIT, THE; SNAKE PIT AND THE PENDULUM, THE; TORTURE ROOM, THE)

Christopher Lee *(Count Regula)*, Karin Dor *(Lilian' Von Brandt)*, Lex Barker *(Roger Montelis)*, Carl Lange *(Anatole)*, Vladimir Medar *(Fabian)*, Christiane Rucker *(Babette)*, Dieter Eppler *(Kutscher)*.

Nightmarish horror, German style, this film features Christopher Lee as the gleefully sadistic Count Regula, who has been rejuvenated by his loyal servant, Anatole (Carl Lange), 40 years after being decapitated and dismembered for murdering 12 virgins in the hope that their blood would give him eternal life. Unfortunately, Regula was one shy of the required *13* virgins, and now he's back to finish the job, having summoned a castle full of guests to torment, including Baroness von Brandt (Karin Dor, wife of director Harold Reinl) and her lawyer, Roger (ex-Tarzan Lex Barker). Very loosely based on Poe's "The Pit and the Pendulum," BLOOD DEMON has little going for it in terms of plot, but makes up for it with some fascinatingly perverse visuals, including an eerie forest of the dead. Good makeup job on Lee. On videocassette as THE TORTURE CHAMBER OF DR. SADISM.

p, Wolfgang Kuhnlenz; d, Harold Reinl; w, Manfred R. Kohler (based on the story "The Pit and the Pendulum" by Edgar Allan Poe); ph, Ernst W. Kalinke; ed, Hermann Haller; m, Peter Thomas.

(PR:O   MPAA:NR)

## BLOOD DINER*

(1987) 90m Lightning-PMS Filmworks/Vestron c

Rick Burks *(Michael Tutman)*, Carl Crew *(George Tutman)*, Roger Dauer *(Mark Shepard)*, LaNette La France *(Sheba Jackson)*, Lisa Guggenheim *(Connie Stanton)*, Max Morris *(Chief Miller)*, Roxanne Cybelle *(Little Michael)*.

This cartoonish, gory tribute to the films of Herschell Gordon Lewis details the attempts of two siblings to provide a body for an ancient goddess out of the hacked-up parts of dozens of scantily clad girls. The Tutman brothers (Rick Burks and Carl Crew) follow the practices taught them in childhood by their uncle, who later died in a hail of police bullets after going on a murderous rampage. Their first step in raising the goddess Sheetar is to dig up their uncle's moldering corpse and remove his brain, which they restore with incantations and place in a jar of liquid. The brain instructs them to prepare the Blood Banquet, which has a menu of teenager niblets, and to build the body for Sheetar out of the other human parts. The lads serve the leftovers at their health food restaurant, attracting a large and dedicated clientele. Although directed by a woman, BLOOD DINER's consciousness is no more heightened than that of I SPIT ON YOUR GRAVE or MANIAC. Jackie Kong watched most of H.G. Lewis' gore-fests before making this, and admits that BLOOD FEAST (see below) was the primary source for the plot; moreover, director Kong in-

jects the sort of contempt for the original material that ruins most horror satires. There's nothing the least bit redeeming about BLOOD DINER.

p, Jimmy Maslon, Jackie Kong; d, Jackie Kong; w, Michael Sonye; ph, Jurg Walther; ed, Thomas Meshelski; m, Don Preston.

(PR:O   MPAA:R)

## BLOOD FEAST**

(1963) 58m Box Office Spectaculars c

Thomas Fair *(Pete Thornton)*, Mal Arnold *(Ramses)*, Connie Mason *(Suzette)*, Scott H. Hall *(Police Captain)*, Lyn Bolton *(Mrs. Fremont)*, Toni Calvert *(Trudy)*, Gene Courtier *(Tony)*, Ashlyn Martin *(Girl on Beach)*, Sandra Sinclair *(Girl in Apartment)*, Jerome Eden *(High Priest)*.

Heralded as the original splatter film, BLOOD FEAST has become the temple at which gorehounds pay homage. Unfortunately, while it certainly broke new ground in terms of explicit gore, it isn't a very good film. The preposterous plot details the activities of an insane caterer, Fuad Ramses (Mal Arnold), who, in his spare time, has authored the book *Ancient Weird Religious Rites*. Seeking to resurrect the arcane spirit of the Egyptian princess Ishtar, Ramses prowls about hacking—in bloody close-up—at the limbs, tongues, and brains of his female victims for use in a "Blood Feast" in Ishtar's honor. Meanwhile, Mrs. Fremont (Lyn Bolton) hires Ramses to cater the party she's throwing for her lovely daughter, Suzette (Connie Mason, the June 1963 *Playboy* playmate). Just as Ramses is about to vivisect Suzette as his final ingredient, her policeman boy friend, Pete Thornton (Wood) arrives and chases the gore-crazed caterer into the blades of a garbage truck compactor. Much, too much really, has been written about BLOOD FEAST, and Herschell Gordon Lewis must be one of the most interviewed directors in film history. Yes, the film has realistically staged gore in the best tradition of the Grand Guignol, photographed lovingly in living color, but the rest of the movie is simply bad. The script is laughable, the acting is atrocious, and if it weren't so short it would be a total bore! Luckily, it is also extremely funny (unintentionally it would seem) and the gore is truly unsettling—even to this day. Lewis went on to make several more bloody epics, most notably TWO THOUSAND MANIACS; THE GORE GORE GIRLS; and THE WIZARD OF GORE and, although long retired from moviemaking, he remains the guru of gorehounds.

p, David F. Friedman, Stanford S. Kohlberg, Herschell Gordon Lewis; d, Herschell Gordon Lewis; w, Allison Louise Down; ph, Herschell Gordon Lewis; ed, Robert Sinise, Frank Romolo; m, Herschell Gordon Lewis.

(PR:O   MPAA:NR)

## BLOOD OF DRACULA'S CASTLE*½

(1967) 84m Paragon Pictures c (AKA: DRACULA'S CASTLE)

John Carradine *(George)*, Alex D'Arcy *(Dracula)*, Paula

**THE HORROR FILM**

Raymond *(Countess)*, Ray Young *(Mango)*, Vicki Volante, Robert Dix, John Cardos, Kent Osborne.

Dracula (Alex D'Arcy) and his wife (Paula Raymond) have relocated to modern-day America and are living under the assumed name of Townsend. Their butler, George (John Carradine), and his hunchback assistant, Mango (Ray Young), are charged with the task of keeping "the Townsends" in cocktails made from blood of young girls—who are conveniently chained in the basement and sacrificed to the god Luna before serving. Yet another cheapo from the prolific Al Adamson, whose incredibly amateurish horror movies and biker flicks have become the object of much "psychotronic" admiration. Add this one to the list of B films that famed cinematographer Laszlo Kovacs cut his teeth on.

p, Al Adamson, Rex Carlton; d, Al Adamson, Jean Hewitt; w, Rex Carlton; ph, Laszlo Kovacs.

(PR:C MPAA:M)

## BLOOD ON SATAN'S CLAW, THE***

(1970, Brit.) 100m Tigon/Cannon c (AKA: SATAN'S CLAW; GB: SATAN'S SKIN)

Patrick Wymark *(Judge)*, Linda Hayden *(Angel)*, Barry Andrews *(Ralph)*, Michele Dotrice *(Margaret)*, Wendy Padbury *(Cathy)*, Anthony Ainley *(Rev. Fallowfield)*, Charlotte Mitchell *(Ellen)*, Tamara Ustinov *(Rosalind)*, Simon Williams *(Peter)*, James Hayter *(Middleton)*, Howard Goorney *(Doctor)*.

Although inferior to Michael Reeves' classic THE WITCHFINDER GENERAL (1968), which obviously inspired this effort, BLOOD ON SATAN'S CLAW has considerable virtue in its own right. Set in 17th-century England, the story concerns a beautiful blonde girl who discovers a disembodied claw of Satan and organizes a cult of teenagers to resurrect the Prince of Darkness. Directed with flair by Piers Haggard (grandson of H. Rider Haggard, the author of *King Solomon's Mines* and *She*), this tale of witchcraft is quite effective and fans of gore will be glad to note that the various tortures and brutalities are given detailed treatment. Beware cut prints.

p, Peter Andrews, Malcolm Heyworth; d, Piers Haggard; w, Robert Wynne Simmons; ph, Dick Bush; m, Marc Wilkinson.

(PR:O MPAA:R)

## BLOOD ORGY OF THE SHE-DEVILS*

(1973) 78m Gemini bw

Lila Zaborin *(Mara)*, Tom Pace *(Mark)*, William Bagdad *(Toruke)*, Leslie McRae *(Lorraine)*, Victor Izay *(Dr. Helsford)*, Ray Myles *(Rodannus)*, Paul Wilmoth *(Barth)*, Kebrine Kincade *(Sharon)*, Curt Matson *(Dr. Paxton)*, Linn Henson *(Roberta)*, John Nicolai *(Dr. Everest)*, John Ricco *(Royce Littleton)*, Vincent Barbi *(Indian Chief)*.

One of the most bizarre and eccentric ultra-low-budget directors in Hollywood history (he used to live in a castle), Ted V. Mikels is responsible for such cult classics as THE ASTRO ZOMBIES and THE CORPSE GRINDERS. Technically, his work is on par with Al Adamson and Andy Milligan. In this, one of his best-known works, Mikels presents us with Mara (Lila Zaborin), an evil witch heading a coven of scantily clad young women who, on occasion, are wont to ritualistically sacrifice hapless men seduced into their lair. Believe it or not, Mara is approached by enemy agents who ask her to put a mystical "hit" on a rival ambassador to the United Nations. Another typically loopy Mikels production, combining flesh, gore, witchcraft, ritual, and espionage to little effect—other than laughter.

p, Ted V. Mikels; d, Ted V. Mikels; w, Ted V. Mikels.

(PR:O MPAA:NR)

## BLOOD SISTERS zero

(1987) 86m Reeltime c

Amy Brentano *(Linda)*, Shannon McMahon *(Alice)*, Dan Erickson *(Russ)*, Maria Machart *(Marnie)*, Elizabeth Rose *(Bonnie)*, Cjerste Thor *(Cara)*, Patricia Finneran *(Diana)*, Gretchen Kingsley *(Ellen)*, Brigette Cossu *(Laurie)*, Randall Walden *(Jim)*, Brian Charlton Wrye *(John)*, John Fasano *(Larry)*, Pam La Testa *(The Madame)*, Mikhail Druhan *(Edna the Prostitute)*, Lynnea Benson, Ruth Collins *(Prostitutes)*, Michael Tilton *(The John)*, Seraphine Warrington *(Little Sally)*, Jesse D'Angelo *(Little Russ)*.

This poorly paced horror tale follows a group of sorority pledges forced to spend an evening in an abandoned old house, which was formerly a house of prostitution. Sorority sister Linda (Amy Brentano) is in charge of the affair, and orders the pledges to hunt through the dark house in search of a list of hidden items. As the girls wander around the twisting halls and empty rooms, they glimpse apparitions of prostitutes, and each time one of the pledges looks into a mirror, she enters a trancelike state and has a vision of the prostitutes who years ago occupied the room. As the night grows darker, the pledges disappear one by one, dying at the hands of an unseen attacker wearing a negligee. A standard slasher entry, BLOOD SISTERS is of interest only because it was directed by Roberta Findlay, one of the more legendary names in exploitation films. Findlay, who worked throughout the 1960s and 1970s with her then-husband, Michael, is perhaps best remembered for SNUFF, a movie in which the film's crew apparently murdered an actress before the cameras. It proved to be a grand hoax that sent many bloodthirsty viewers searching for *real* "snuff" films. (For the curious, none have ever been documented.) After working for some time as a porno director, Findlay delivered a 1986 entry called TENEMENT. Judging from this most recent effort, however, Findlay might as well go back to making porn—BLOOD SISTERS is one of the most boring entries to come off the slasher conveyor belt. One would think the combination of seven perky young actresses and a sexually deranged killer would, at least, produce a scare or two. Not a chance. This film consists almost exclusively of frightened girls walking slowly (very slowly) through the house with flashlights in hand. Nothing happens in BLOOD SISTERS, until the last 10 minutes. Findlay uses restraint

## BLOOD SISTERS—

(probably motivated by a small budget) in showing gore, as there are only a couple of such shots.

p, Walter Sear; d, Roberta Findlay; w, Roberta Findlay; ph, Roberta Findlay (Studio Film Color); ed, Walter Sear, Roberta Findlay; m, Walter Sear, Michael Litovsky.

**(PR:O  MPAA:R)**

## BLOOD SPATTERED BRIDE, THE**

(1974, Sp.) 83m Europix c (LA NOVIA ESANGENTADA)

Simon Andreu, Maribel Martin, Alexandra Bastedo, Dean Selmier, Monteserrat Julio, Rosa M. Rodriguez, Angel Lombarte.

This lesbian vampire tale, loosely based on Sheridan LeFanu's classic novella *Carmilla*, features Maribel Martin as a frigid newlywed who is seduced by a mysterious stranger (Alexandra Bastedo)—who turns out to be a lady vampire. The story, which has been done a dozen times (most notably in Carl Dreyer's classic VAMPYR, Hammer's THE VAMPIRE LOVERS, and Harry Kuemel's DAUGHTERS OF DARKNESS), gets the standard Spanish treatment here, with plenty of bizarre and incongruous imagery amid all the sex and gore.

p, Antonio Perez Olea; d, Vincent Aranda; w, Vincent Aranda.

**(PR:O  MPAA:NR)**

## BLOOD TIDE*

(1982) 82m 21st Century c (AKA: RED TIDE, THE)

James Earl Jones *(Frye)*, Jose Ferrer *(Nereus)*, Lila Kedrova *(Sister Anna)*, Mary Louise Weller *(Sherry)*, Martin Kove *(Neil)*, Deborah Shelton *(Madeline)*, Lydia Cornell *(Barbara)*.

Filmed in 1980 under the title "The Red Tide," this turkey didn't receive a release until 1982, when it was promptly forgotten. Gorgeous Greek locations were the excuse for several major stars to appear in this mess, which features Deborah Shelton as Madeline, an American artist who becomes fascinated with ancient Greek rites in which young virgins were sacrificed to a sea monster. Of course, the creature—a rubber monster that has been snoozing in an undersea grotto all these centuries—is awakened after American treasure hunter Frye (James Earl Jones) sets off some explosions, and the grouchy ancient demon wreaks havoc on modern-day Greece. Lots of deaths; plenty of nubile, bikini-clad bodies; and that ham, James Earl Jones, to chew up the scenery. Jose Ferrer and Lila Kedrova, both the ablest of players, act as window dressing. Model Shelton would later be featured in Brian De Palma's BODY DOUBLE (1984) and "Dallas." A generally embarrassing picture for all.

p, Nico Mastorakis, Donald Langdon; d, Richard Jeffries; w, Richard Jeffies, Donald Langdon, Nico Mastorakis; ph, Ari Stavrou (Technicolor); ed, Robert Leighton; m, Jerry Moseley.

**(PR:O  MPAA:R)**

## BLOODEATERS*

(1980) 84m CM Prod/Parker National c (AKA: FOREST OF FEAR)

Charles Austin *(Cole)*, Beverly Shapiro *(Polly)*, Dennis Heffend *(Hermit)*, Paul Haskin *(Briggs)*, John Amplas *(Phillips)*.

Another NIGHT OF THE LIVING DEAD rip-off. Not only was this filmed in George Romero's beloved Pennsylvania, it features John Amplas, who starred in Romero's MARTIN, as an FBI agent! When the government decides to spray marijuana crops with Dromax, an experimental herbicide, they inadvertently turn the dope-smoking renegade farmers into a herd of cannibalistic zombies (cannabis = cannibals?). This amateurish low-budget effort tries for gory thrills, but comes off as merely silly. Amplas is wasted in a bad role for which he is obviously too young. Originally shot on 16mm and blown up to 35mm for theatrical release.

p, Chuck McCrann; d, Chuck McCrann; w, Chuck McCrann; ph, David Sperling (Movielab Color); ed, Chuck McCrann, David Sperling.

**(PR:O  MPAA:R)**

## BLOODSUCKING FREAKS*

(1976) 88m Troma c (AKA: INCREDIBLE TORTURE SHOW, THE)

Seamus O'Brien *(Sardu)*, Louie DeJesus *(Ralphus)*, Niles McMaster *(Tom)*, Viju Krim *(Natasha)*, Alan Dellay *(Crazy Silo)*, Dan Fauci *(Det. Sgt. Tucci)*.

A genuine cult item, this gleeful exercise in total gross-out was originally released in 1976 as THE INCREDIBLE TORTURE SHOW with an "X" rating. In 1982, sleazoid New York City film production house Troma acquired the rights and rereleased it as BLOODSUCKING FREAKS, immediately raising the ire of Woman Against Pornography, who picketed its showing. Basically a bunch of incredibly gory Grand Guignol stage scenes strung together with a flimsy plot, the film stars Seamus O'Brien as the mad master of ceremonies of the Off-Off-Broadway "Theatre of the Macabre" show in SoHo. Little does the audience know that the playhouse is also a front for O'Brien's white-slavery trade. When the goofy impresario kidnaps a noted ballerina, however, the cops finally sit up and take notice. Filmed in "Ghoulovision," the movie features a dwarf, naked cannibal women, decapitations, torture, and even a woman getting her brains sucked out through a straw. You've been warned.

p, Alan Margolin; d, Joel M. Reed; w, Joel M. Reed; ph, Gerry Toll; ed, Victor Kanefsky; m, Michael Sahl.

**(PR:O  MPAA:R)**

## BLOODTHIRSTY BUTCHERS zero

(1970) 85m Constitution Films c

John Miranda, Annabella Wood, Berwick Kaler, Jane Helay, Michael Cox, Linda Driver, Jonathan Holt, Ann Arrow.

The irrepressible Andy ("I've never made a film for more than $10,000") Milligan directed this gory and typically cheap retelling of the Sweeney Todd legend. In Victorian London, a barber and a baker conspire in a series of brutal murders. Their assistant kidnaps and kills customers, who end up in "meat pies." An unsuspecting salesgirl goes to the police when her boy friend disappears, the plot is revealed, and the film ends with the barber and his assistant hacking each other to death. Bloodier than most of Milligan's efforts. The writer-director-cinematographer squeezed this one in while he was in England filming THE BODY BENEATH and THE RATS ARE COMING! THE WEREWOLVES ARE HERE!

p, William Mishkin; d, Andy Milligan; w, Andy Milligan, John Borske; ph, Andy Milligan.

(PR:O   MPAA:R)

## BLOODY BIRTHDAY*

(1986) 85m Judica c (AKA: CREEPS)

Susan Strasberg *(Mrs. Davis)*, Jose Ferrer *(Doctor)*, Lori Lethin *(Joyce Russel)*, Melinda Cordell *(Mrs. Brody)*, Julie Brown *(Beverly Brody)*, Joe Penny *(Mr. Harding)*, Billy Jacoby *(Curtis)*, Andy Freeman *(Steven Seaton)*, Elizabeth Hoy *(Debbie Brody)*, K.C. Martell *(Timmy Russel)*, Ben Marley *(Duke)*, Erica Hope *(Annie)*, Cyril O'Reilly, Shane Butterworth, Michael Dudikoff, Daniel Currie, Norman Rice, George Paul, Bill Boyett.

An unredeemed waste of everyone's time, BLOODY BIRTHDAY gets off to a dull start as Jose Ferrer delivers three infants almost simultaneously during a total eclipse of the sun. Ten years later, the terrible trio (Billy Jacoby, Andy Freeman, and Elizabeth Hoy) go on an inexplicable murder binge, killing almost everyone in the community. A real bore, with the director seemingly incapable of creating suspense. Killings simply occur, with no buildup and no rationale, and the evil children never generate any menace (though Hoy does have a disconcerting gleam in her eye). Originally shot in 1980.

p, Gerald T. Olson; d, Ed Hunt; w, Ed Hunt, Barry Pearson; ph, Stephen Posey (Panavision); ed, Ann E. Mills; m, Arlon Ober.

(PR:O   MPAA:R)

## BLOW OUT**½

(1981) 108m Filmways c

John Travolta *(Jack)*, Nancy Allen *(Sally)*, John Lithgow *(Burke)*, Dennis Franz *(Karp)*, Peter Boyden *(Sam)*, Curt May *(Frank)*, Ernest McClure *(Jim)*, Davie Roberts *(Anchor Man)*, Maurice Copeland *(Jack)*, Claire Carter *(Anchor Woman)*, John Aquino *(Detective)*, John Hoffmeister *(McRyan)*, Patrick McNamara *(Nelson)*, Terrence Currier *(Lawrence Henry)*, Tom McCarthy *(Policeman)*, Dean Bennett *(Campus Guard)*.

More than just another of Brian De Palma's Alfred Hitchcock homages, BLOW OUT is his Hitchcock-Michelangelo Antonioni homage—and a not half-bad movie at that.

Drawing on the film-school training he and his contemporaries received, De Palma sets this thriller against a film-making background. Jack Terry (John Travolta) is a sound-effects recorder who specializes in sounds for trashy porn-slasher films. While out recording one night, he hears a tire blow out and sees a car swerve off a bridge and into the water. He jumps in and saves Sally (Nancy Allen), a prostitute who was with a now-drowned politician. The media and the dead man's associates are all convinced it was an accident, but Jack hears something on his tape recording—a gunshot that precedes the blow out. Using Sally as bait, Jack begins a cat-and-mouse game to find the killer. Like most of De Palma's films, BLOW OUT is partly successful, partly a failure. It's a treat for film insiders (the stress on recording and editing techniques, the trashy film posters that cover Jack's walls) that starts off promisingly, then falls apart when its characters begin making foolish and obvious mistakes, which stretch credibility. As in Antonioni's BLOW-UP or Francis Ford Coppola's THE CONVERSATION, the process of solving the mystery is shown to be a modern, technical one, rather than a question of shadowing a suspect down a rainy street. Adding interest is Travolta, playing against type as an especially sleazy character with whom we have no choice but to sympathize, since he is the only one of the film's characters who is even remotely likable.

p, George Litto; d, Brian De Palma; w, Brian De Palma; ph, Vilmos Zsigmond (Technicolor); ed, Paul Hirsch; m, Pino Donaggio.

(PR:O   MPAA:R)

## BLUE MONKEY*½

(1987) 98m Spectrafilm c (AKA: GREEN MONKEY)

Steve Railsback *(Jim Bishop)*, Gwynyth Walsh *(Dr. Rachel Carson)*, Susan Anspach *(Dr. Judith Glass)*, John Vernon *(Roger Levering)*, Joe Flaherty *(George Baker)*, Robin Duke *(Sandra Baker)*, Don Lake *(Elliot)*, Sandy Webster *(Fred)*, Helen Hughes *(Marwella Harbison)*, Joy Coghill *(Dede Wilkens)*, Bill Lake *(Paramedic)*, Peter Van Wart *(Oscar)*, Stuart Stone *(Joey)*, Ivan E. Roth *(The Creature)*.

When a hapless gardener cuts himself on a mysterious plant and collapses, he is rushed to the emergency room of County Memorial Hospital, where he suddenly goes into convulsions and vomits up a squiggly larva. Doctors Susan Anspach and Gwynyth Walsh send the disgusting little item down to the lab, where it is cut open to reveal a small insect. Before expert entomologists have a chance to identify the strange creature, a group of mischievous children feed the bug some liquid steroids and it immediately grows to huge proportions, killing a horny orderly and his candy-striped friend, then sucking the calcium out of their bones. By now, the hospital has been quarantined, leaving those inside trapped with the creature, which has given birth to a mate, laying numerous eggs in every nook and cranny in the place. Led by brave police detective Jim Bishop (Steve Railsback), the humans attempt to defeat the monster. The only attention paid to this film during its brief theatrical release was prompted by its perplexing title, one that left many to wonder: What in the hell is a blue monkey? For what it's worth, the blue monkey used to be a *green* monkey, before the title was changed at the last minute because of calls from the media asking if the film was about the now-infamous African primates that are believed to be the originators of the AIDS virus. Which doesn't settle the issue, since the monster is not a monkey at all, but a giant entomological hybrid with the head of a wasp, the eyes of a dragonfly, the stomach of a scorpion, the back of various beetles, and the limbs of a praying mantis.

p, Martin Walters; d, William Fruet; w, George Goldsmith; ph, Brenton Spencer; ed, Michael Fruet; m, Patrick Coleman, Paul Novotny.

**(PR:O   MPAA:R)**

## BLUE SUNSHINE***½

(1977) 97m Ellanby/Cinema Shares c

Zalman King *(Jerry Zipkin)*, Mark Goddard *(Edward Flemming)*, Robert Walden *(David Blume)*, Charles Siebert *(Det. Clay)*, Ann Cooper *(Wendy Fleming)*, Ray Young *(Wayne Mulligan)*, Bill Adler *(Ralphie)*, Barbara Quinn *(Stephanie)*, Richard Crystal *(Frannie Scott)*, Alice Ghostley.

This excellent second feature from SQUIRM director Jeff Lieberman veers into early David Cronenberg territory with its harrowing combination of detective, horror, and sci-fi. Zalman King stars as Jerry Zipkin, a man on the run for a murder he committed in self-defense who uncovers the solution to a string of killings that has been plaguing a comfortable suburb. It seems that, 10 years ago, a Stanford professor named Flemming (Mark Goddard) created a form of LSD, dubbed Blue Sunshine, and administered it to several students in the name of science. Now, when all the human guinea pigs are well-to-do middle-class members of society, a delayed chromosomal imbalance is kicking, resulting in the subjects' sudden hair loss and an uncontrollable rage that makes them kill. Flemming, in the meantime, has gone into politics and it is up to Zipkin to reveal the results of his horrible experiments. Intense, but at the same time quite offbeat and humorous, BLUE SUNSHINE presents one of the most memorable and effective condemnations of American middle-class values in the annals of genre filmmaking. As in the underrated SQUIRM, Lieberman directs with genuine flair and does a nice job of keeping the audience off balance by following genuinely funny passages with unforgettable moments of sheer horror. Highly recommended.

p, George Manasse; d, Jeff Lieberman; w, Jeff Lieberman; m, Charles Gross (Movielab Color).

**(PR:O   MPAA:R)**

## BLUEBEARD***½

(1944) 71m PRC bw

John Carradine *(Gaston)*, Jean Parker *(Lucille)*, Nils Asther *(Insp. Lefevre)*, Ludwig Stossel *(Lamarte)*, George Pembroke *(Insp. Renard)*, Teala Loring *(Francine)*, Sonia Sorel *(Renee)*, Iris Adrian *(Mimi)*, Henry Kolker *(Deschamps)*, Emmett Lynn *(Le Soldat)*, Patti McCarty *(Bebette)*.

A film that can marginally be considered horror, BLUEBEARD is one of director Edgar G. Ulmer's best works and contains one of John Carradine's greatest performances. Set in 19th-century Paris, BLUEBEARD stars Carradine as Gaston Morel, the operator of a popular puppet show that stages marionette versions of the Faust legend. Unfortunately, Gaston is himself a victim of sinister urges—which drive him to strangle women with his bare hands. In flashback, we learn that Gaston, who is also an artist, murdered his first victim after he had painted her portrait, then discovered that she was not the idealized woman he had created on canvas. Gaston is now condemned to pick up models for his paintings and then murder them. In this extremely low-budget Producers Releasing Company production, Ulmer again turned monetary liabilities into advantages through his brilliant narrative sense, savvy camera placement, and skillful direction of actors. One inspired solution to the budget problem is Ulmer's effective use of the Faust puppet show. Filmed as if the puppets were actual human actors on stage, with several minutes of running time devoted to the show, the performance becomes a haunting—and inexpensive—metaphor for Gaston's plight. A must-see.

p, Leon Fromkess; d, Edgar G. Ulmer; w, Pierre Gendron (based on a script by Arnold Phillips and Werner H. Furst); ph, J.A. Feindel; ed, Carl Pierson.

**(PR:A   MPAA:NR)**

## BODY DOUBLE**½

(1984) 109m COL-Delphi II COL c

Craig Wasson *(Jake)*, Melanie Griffith *(Holly)*, Gregg Henry *(Sam)*, Deborah Shelton *(Gloria)*, Guy Boyd *(Jim McLean)*, Dennis Franz *(Rubin)*, David Haskell *(Drama Teacher)*, Rebecca Stanley *(Kimberly)*, Al Israel *(Corso)*, Douglas Warhit *(Video Salesman)*, B.J. Jones *(Douglas)*, Russ Marin *(Frank)*, Lane Davies *(Billy)*, Barbara Crampton *(Carol)*, Larry Flash Jenkins *(Assistant Director)*, Monte Landis *(Sid Goldberg)*, Linda Shaw *(Herself)*, Mindi Miller *(Tina)*, Denise Loveday *(Actress/Vampire Movie)*, Gela Jacobson *(Corso's Secretary)*, Ray Hassett, Rick Gunderson, Jerry Brutsche *(Police Officers)*, Michael Kearns *(Male Porno Star)*, Rob Paulsen *(Cameraman)*, Jeremy Lawrence *(Theater Director)*, Rod Loomis *(TV Director)*, Gary F. Griffith *(Auditioning Actor)*, Michael White *(Security Guard)*, Emmett Brown *(Studio Guard)*, H. David Fletcher *(Security Guard at Bellini's)*, Marcia Del Mar *(Production Assistant)*, Phil Redrow *(Naked Man)*, Slavitza Jovan *(Saleslady)*, Jack Mayhall *(Jake's Replacement)*, Patty Lotz, Barbara Peckinpaugh *(Girls in Holly Does Hollywood)*, David Ursin, Casey Sanders, Wes Edwards *(Men in Holly Does Hollywood)*.

Jake (Craig Wasson) is a second-rate actor who has just been released from his latest opus, a sleazy horror movie. Sam (Gregg Henry) is a colleague who gets work in Washington and offers Jake the job of house-sitting in his huge circular home atop a Hollywood mountain. Jake accepts, and spends his evenings peering through a telescope at Gloria (Deborah Shelton), a beautiful woman across the way who undresses in front of an unshaded, uncurtained window. The bored Jake watches her every night and is soon in love with the woman. One night she is murdered in gruesome fashion while Jake watches from across the street, helpless. He tells the police what he has seen, but since there is no physical evidence, his story is not believed. Investigating on his own, Jake meets Holly (Melanie Griffith), a punky porno actress who has been hired by an unknown someone to play the role of the woman doing the strip in the window. She's a body double for Gloria, but why? Contrived, shallow, distasteful, and ultimately pointless, BODY DOUBLE is more an exercise in empty cinematic style than an engrossing thriller. While cinematographer Stephen H. Burum executes some absolutely breathtaking camera moves, his effort goes for nought when pitted against director Brian De Palma and cowriter Robert J. Avrech's insipid narrative.

p, Brian De Palma; d, Brian De Palma; w, Brian De Palma, Robert J. Avrech (based on a story by Brian De Palma); ph, Stephen H. Burum (Metrocolor); ed, Jerry Greenberg, Bill Pankow; m, Pino Donaggio.

**(PR:O    MPAA:R)**

## BODY SNATCHER, THE*****

(1945) 79m RKO bw

Boris Karloff *(John Gray),* Bela Lugosi *(Joseph),* Henry Daniell *(Dr. MacFarlane),* Edith Atwater *(Meg Camden),* Russell Wade *(Donald Fettes),* Rita Corday *(Mrs. Marsh),* Sharyn Moffet *(Georgina Marsh),* Donna Lee *(Street Singer).*

The first and best of the three Val Lewton-Boris Karloff collaborations for RKO (ISLE OF THE DEAD and BEDLAM would follow), THE BODY SNATCHER is an excellent adaptation of Robert Louis Stevenson's short story, scripted by Lewton himself (under the pseudonym Carlos Keith) and directed with considerable skill and admirable restraint by Robert Wise. This chilling and atmospheric tale of grave-robbing in 1832 Edinburgh features Henry Daniell as MacFarlane, a doctor who regularly buys cadavers that are delivered to his back door by menacing cabbie Gray (Karloff). When Gray turns to murder in his quest for bodies—and delivers the still-warm corpse of a young street singer MacFarlane had seen alive and well only that morning—the frightened doctor realizes he must do something about it. MacFarlane is finally driven to murder Gray, but—haunted by the ghoul's cryptic prophecy, ''You'll never be rid of me''—is eventually driven mad. Literate, but not at the expense of the cinematic, THE BODY SNATCHER is one of Lewton's greatest works and contains what is arguably Karloff's finest performance. Lewton's obsession with historical detail is evident throughout and, although the film was shot on the lot at RKO, the filmmakers manage to create an unforgettable vision of Edinburgh through judicious use of sets, lighting, camera placement, sound, and editing. Also featured—mainly for marquee value—was Bela Lugosi in a small role as MacFarlane's servant, Joseph. Although Lugosi and Karloff had only one scene together, it was a great one, and was the last gasp of respectability in Lugosi's sad career.

p, Val Lewton; d, Robert Wise; w, Philip MacDonald, Val Lewton (based on a short story by Robert Louis Stevenson); ph, Robert DeGrasse; ed, J.R. Whittredge; m, Roy Webb.

**(PR:A    MPAA:NR)**

## BOGGY CREEK II*½

(1985) 91m Howco International c (AKA: BARBARIC BEAST OF BOGGY CREEK PART II, THE)

Charles B. Pierce *(Prof. Lockhart),* Cindy Butler *(Leslie Ann Walker),* Serene Hedin *(Tanya),* Chuck Pierce *(Tim Thorn),* Jimmy Clem *(Crenshaw),* Rick Hildreth *(Deputy Williams),* Fabus Griffin *(Adult Creature),* Victor Williams *(Young Creature).*

More than a dozen years after THE LEGEND OF BOGGY CREEK became a major exploitation success in a string of regional releases, director Charles B. Pierce returned to the scene in this sequel—in which, besides writing, directing, and producing the film, Pierce also stars, narrates, and gives his son Chuck a job. The film opens with Pierce *pere,* as Lockhart, a professor at the University of Arkansas, receiving word that a semilegendary beast similar to Big Foot and known to the locals as the Boggy Creek Monster has been spotted again. Lockhart quickly organizes a group to investigate, taking along Tim Thorn (the younger Pierce) and two coeds (Cindy Butler and Serene Hedin). There are flashbacks as previous encounters with the monster are recalled, and a few fuzzy, fleeting glimpses of the beast. The team members set up all kinds of scientific equipment in the woods, and, with the help of an old hermit who has managed to capture a baby monster, they manage to lure an adult Big Foot out of the woods. Not a thrill is to be found in this official sequel (an unofficial sequel, RETURN TO BOGGY CREEK, was even worse), and the monster, when it's finally seen, turns out to be no more than a guy in a gorilla suit. The first ''Boggy Creek'' entry had a certain power in its pseudo-documentary style, but this film—made in 1983, but released only in major trade centers two years later—has none of that, and Pierce clearly oversteps his talents in taking on almost every job in sight. Not for the discriminating.

p, Charles B. Pierce; d, Charles B. Pierce; w, Charles B. Pierce; ph, Shirah Kojayan (Movielab Color); ed, Shirah Kojayan; m, Frank McKelvey.

**(PR:C    MPAA:PG)**

## BOOGENS, THE**

(1981) 95m Taft International/Sunn Classic c

Rebecca Balding *(Trish),* Fred McCarren *(Mark),* Anne-Marie Martin *(Jessica),* Jeff Harlan *(Roger),* John Crawford *(Brian),* Med Flory *(Dan),* Jon Lormer *(Blanchard),* Peg Stewart *(Victoria),* Scott Wilkinson *(Deputy),* Marcia Reider *(Martha).*

This film concerns some Utah residents who reopen a silver mine that was closed way back in 1912 after a mysterious cave-in. When locals probing the shaft end up dead, it is discovered that they were killed by a pack of tentacled, leechlike monsters that reside in the mine. The incoherent plot merely serves to dilute whatever power this old-fashioned 1950s-style horror movie may have had, and it's a long wait to see the monsters—created by Stan Winston—which aren't fully unveiled until the very end.

p, Charles E. Sellier, Jr.; d, James L. Conway; w, David O'Malley, Bob Hunt; ph, Paul Hipp; ed, Michael Spence; m, Bob Summers.

(PR:O  MPAA:R)

## BOOGEY MAN, THE**½

(1980) 79m Jerry Ross c

Suzanna Love (Lacey), Ron James (Jake), John Carradine (Doctor), Nicholas Love (Willy), Raymond Boyden (Kevin), Felicite Morgan (Helen), Bill Rayburn (Uncle Earnest), Llewelyn Thomas (Father Reilly), Natasha Schiano (Young Lacey), Jay Wright (Young Willy), Gillian Gordon (Mother), Howard Grant (Lover), Lucinda Ziesing (Susan), Jane Pratt (Jane), David Swim (Timmy), Catherine Tambini (Kathy), Katie Casey, Ernest Meier, Stony Richards, Claudia Porcelli (Teenagers).

A fairly clever attempt to merge the slasher-movie characteristics of HALLOWEEN with the supernatural elements of THE EXORCIST and THE OMEN, THE BOOGEY MAN was directed by Ulli Lommel, a former member of German director Rainer Werner Fassbinder's stable of actors and filmmakers (he appears in Fassbinder's THE AMERICAN SOLDIER and CHINESE ROULETTE). Loaded with repressed sexuality and dark family problems, the film opens as a young boy murders his mother's evil lover while his sister, Lacy, watches. Twenty years later, Lacy—now played by Suzanna Love, the director's wife—is haunted by the ghost of the murdered man. In an attempt to purge her demons, Lacy returns to the house where the killing took place, and, to her horror, sees her mother's lover in a mirror. Lacy smashes the mirror with a chair, but, instead of destroying the ghost, she unleashes his evil force, causing several more deaths. This interesting, if not entirely successful, outing was a surprise hit at the box office and would be followed by a sequel in 1983. Director Lommel must be obsessed with the subject matter; his film A TASTE OF SIN (also 1983) has a very similar plot.

p, Ulli Lommel; d, Ulli Lommel; w, Ulli Lommel; ph, David Sperling (Metrocolor); ed, Terrell Tannen; m, Tim Krog.

(PR:O  MPAA:R)

## BOOGEYMAN II**½

(1983) 79m New West Films c

Suzanna Love (Lacey), Ulli Lommel (Mickey), Bob Rosenfarb (Bernie), Shannah Hall (Bonnie), Shoto von Douglas (Joseph), Ahley DuBay, Rhonda Aldrich, Sarah Jean Watkins, David D'Arnel, Leslie Smith, Mina Kolb, Rafael Nazario, Ann Wilkinson, Rock McKenzie, Llewellyn Thomas, Nicholas Love, John Carradine, Ron James, Felicite Morgan.

This is the bizarre and wholly self-conscious sequel to THE BOOGEY MAN (see above) wherein director Ulli Lommel attacks the Hollywood system by casting himself as a hack director constantly at odds with his producer. Beginning six months after the first picture ended, the film follows Lacey (again played by Suzanna Love) as she moves from Maryland to Los Angeles to begin a new life. After falling in with the Hollywood crowd, she is encouraged to recall the events of the first film, thus saving money by using up nearly a half an hour of running time with footage from THE BOOGEY MAN. Film director Mickey (Lommel) and his friends want to make a movie about the terrifying experience, but when a shard of mirror from the first film turns up, Lacey's new friends are slaughtered one-by-one in a variety of deliberately absurd and amusing ways. Obviously bitter and cynical in his view of the Hollywood scene, director Lommel fulfills the minimum requirements of the inevitable sequel by delivering virtually the same chills and gore from the first film, while at the same time mocking the entire process (the extensive use of footage from the original) and bitching about it publicly in the guise of a frustrated and angry director. Although at times a bit frustrating to watch—because of the already familiar flashback footage—BOOGEYMAN II is a fascinating display of utter contempt for the industry that produced it.

p, Ulli Lommel; d, Ulli Lommel, Bruce Starr; ph, Phillipe Carr Foster, David Sperling (Pacific Color); ed, Terrell Tannen; m, Tim Krog, Wayne Love, Craig Hundley.

(PR:O  MPAA:NR)

## BORN OF FIRE zero

(1987, Brit.) 84m Film Four Int'l./IFEX-Vidmark c

Peter Firth (Paul Bergson), Suzan Crowley (Anoukin), Oh-Tee (Master Musician), Stefan Kalipha, Nabil Shaban.

Paul Bergson (Peter Firth), an English flutist, begins to hear strange music in his head during a performance. Anoukin (Suzan Crowley), an astronomer, comes to tell him she's heard it too. What's more, she's convinced it's tied in with disturbances on the sun's surface and volcanic eruptions in Turkey. Interestingly, Paul's father, also a famous flutist, ventured to Turkey years before to learn the breathing secrets of the "Master Musician" and died there. Paul and Anoukin travel to the mysterious village and become involved in a preposterous stew of mumbo-jumbo that apparently will result in the use of music to lacerate the Earth's surface so that it will be consumed by fire. The trouble with BORN OF FIRE is that it is presented with such pompous, would-be philosophical earnestness that it becomes unintentionally hilarious. If the filmmakers didn't take themselves so seriously, this film wouldn't be such an offensive waste of time. Structurally, it is an elliptical mess, jumping back and forth between reality and Firth's character's visions. If there is a weighty symbolic message concerning the essence of music or the nature of the struggle between good and evil contained in the film, as its creators appear to believe there is, it is even more elusive than the secrets Firth has come to explore. To its credit, BORN OF FIRE is slickly photographed and the Turkish locations are beautiful and intriguing. The village, carved into gumdrop hills, looks like surreal cliff dwellings designed by Gaudi.

p, Jamil Dehlavi, Therese Pickard; d, Jamil Dehlavi; w, Raficq Abdulla; ph, Bruce McGowan.

**(PR:O MPAA:R)**

## BOWERY AT MIDNIGHT**½

(1942) 60m MON bw

Bela Lugosi *(Prof. Brenner)*, John Archer *(Dennison)*, Wanda McKay *(Judy)*, Tom Neal *(Frankie Mills)*, Vincent Barnett *(Charlie)*, John Berkes *(Fingers Dolan)*, Ray Miller *(Big Man)*, J. Farrell MacDonald *(Capt. Mitchell)*, Lew Kelly *(Doc Brooks)*, Lucille Vance *(Mrs. Malvern)*, Anna Hope *(Mrs. Brenner)*.

BOWERY AT MIDNIGHT is arguably one of the best of the Monogram quickies featuring Bela Lugosi, although there are so many characters and so much plot—mostly borrowed from THE HUMAN MONSTER (1940)—that most of the time it's extremely difficult to figure out just what the hell is going on. Lugosi plays Prof. Brenner, a respected psychologist who has a secret criminal alter ego that manifests itself by night. In his criminal state, Brenner runs a Bowery mission as a front for his murderous activities and buries his victims in the basement, which is rather ludicrously set up as an actual cemetery, complete with headstones. Unfortunately for Prof. Brenner, his disgruntled, drug-addicted assistant has figured out a way to revive the deceased and has turned them into zombies, hiding them in a cave *below the basement cemetery*, where they await the chance to get at their killer. Although his career was by now beginning its steep slide downward, Lugosi turns in a nicely detailed performance that required him to shift in character from a kindly, benevolent psychologist to a cruel criminal mastermind and back again.

p, Sam Katzman, Jack Dietz; d, Wallace Fox; w, Gerald Schnitzer; ph, Mack Stengler; ed, Carl Pierson.

**(PR:A MPAA:NR)**

## BRAIN DAMAGE***½

(1988) 87m Henenlotter/levins/Palisades c

Rick Herbst *(Brian)*, Gordon MacDonald *(Mike)*, Jennifer Lowry *(Barbara)*, Theo Barnes *(Morris Ackerman)*, Lucille Saint-Peter *(Martha Ackerman)*, Vicki Darnell *(Blonde in Hell Club)*, Kevin Van Hentenryck *(Man with Basket)*, Joe Gonzales *(Guy in Shower)*, Bradlee Rhodes *(Night Watchman)*, Michael Bishop *(Toilet Victim)*, Beverly Downer *(Neighbor)*, Ari Roussimoff *(Biker)*, Michael Rubenstein *(Bum in Alley)*, Angel Figueroa *(Junkie)*, John Reichert *(Policeman)*, Don Henenlotter *(Policeman)*, Kenneth Packard, Artemis Pizzaro *(Subway Riders)*, Slam Wedgehouse *(Mohawked Punk)*.

Frank Henenlotter's first film since the cult favorite BASKET CASE (1982) is another grotesque "boy and his parasite" tale. Brian (Rick Herbst) is a nice young man with a New York City apartment whose life is changed when a 1,000-year-old, brain-eating parasite named Elmer slithers into his room and attaches itself to his neck, injecting him with a blue fluid that causes pleasant hallucinations. As Brian becomes addicted to Elmer's blue fluid, he begins to suffer radical shifts in personality, and goes on nocturnal jaunts with Elmer during which the parasite attacks and sucks the brains out of assorted security guards, punk rockers, and flophouse tenants. Trouble looms, however, when Elmer's previous owners—an elderly neighbor couple—demand his return. As in BASKET CASE, director Henenlotter combines some disturbing gore with an offbeat sense of humor that makes the entire disgusting exercise a bit more palatable. In fact, the little parasite Elmer is the most engaging character in the film. With his lines spoken by an uncredited actor, Elmer is an arrogant little slug whose soothing, measured tones prove very persuasive to anyone in his reach. Like a drug dealer snaring schoolchildren, Elmer seduces Brian into accepting him. Giving the victim a taste of the drug for free and then moving in for the kill, Elmer makes a junkie out of Brian. The most haunting scene in the film is a uneasy combination of horror and laughs in which Brian lies writhing on the floor, trying to go cold turkey, while Elmer sits in the sink and happily sings the Tommy Dorsey hit "Elmer's Tune." In addition to the queasily funny scenes, there are also some out-and-out comedy bits, such as the scene in which Brian and Elmer share a bath, and Henenlotter's hilarious homage to himself, wherein Kevin Van Hentenryck, the star of BASKET CASE, with wicker basket in tow, takes a seat on the subway opposite the crazed Herbst and engages him in a wild-eyed stare-down.

p, Edgar levins; d, Frank Henenlotter; w, Frank Henenlotter; ph, Bruce Torbet (TVC Color); ed, James Y. Kwei, Frank Henenlotter; m, Gus Russo, Clutch Reiser.

**(PR:O MPAA:R)**

## BRAIN OF BLOOD*½

(1971, Phil.) 83m Hemisphere c (AKA: CREATURE'S REVENGE, THE; BRAIN, THE)

Kent Taylor *(Dr. Trenton)*, John Bloom *(Gor)*, Regina Carroll *(Tracy)*, Angelo Rossitto *(Dorro)*, Grant Williams *(Robert Nigserian)*, Reed Hadley *(Amir)*, Vicki Volante *(Katherine)*, Zandor Vorkov *(Mohammed)*, Richard Smedley *(Angel)*, Gus Peters *(Charlie)*, Margo Hope *(Pale Girl)*, Bruce Kimball *(Jim)*, Ervin Saunders *(Victim)*.

Hack director Al Adamson once again assembled his usual cast and crew for this rotten mad scientist effort, shot around the same time as DRACULA VS. FRANKENSTEIN. The corpse of fallen Arab leader Amir (Reed Hadley) is rushed to the lab of crazed scientist Dr. Trenton (Kent Taylor), who has invented a way to transplant the human brain from one body to another, then performs plastic surgery on the host body to make it look like the deceased. In a hurry to transplant Amir's brain, lest it go bad, Trenton transfers it into the body of his deformed assistant, Gor (John Bloom, who played Frankenstein's monster in DRACULA VS. FRANKENSTEIN). When Amir's mind awakens and sees that he has become an ugly monster, he goes nuts and threatens mayhem all around. A typically inept Adamson production, BRAIN OF BLOOD features most of the supporting cast from DRACULA VS. FRANKENSTEIN, including dwarf actor Angelo Rossito, the oddly named Zandor Vorkov, and, of course, the director's voluptuous wife, Regina Carrol. The resulting film is not quite as bad as DRACULA VS. FRANKENSTEIN, but darn close, and has become something of a cult favorite with late-show television viewers. Filmed at least partially in the Philippines.

p, Al Adamson, Sam Sherman; d, Al Adamson; w, Joe Van Rogers, Kane W. Lynn.

(PR:C   MPAA:NR)

## BRAIN THAT WOULDN'T DIE, THE**½

(1959) 81m STER bw (AKA: HEAD THAT WOULDN'T DIE, THE)

Jason Evers (Dr. Bill Cortner), Virginia Leith (Jan Compton), Adele Lamont (Doris), Paula Maurice (B-Girl), Bruce Brighton (Doctor), Doris Brent (Nurse), Leslie Daniel (Kurt), Bonnie Shari (Stripper), Lola Mason (Donna Williams), Audrey Devereau (Jeannie), Eddie Carmel (Monster), Bruce Kerr (Announcer).

One of the most genuinely bizarre "brain" movies, this low budget chiller begins as brilliant surgeon Bill Cortner (Herb [Jason] Evers) inadvertently decapitates his beautiful fiancee, Jan (Virginia Leith), when he crashes his sports car after speeding. Wrapping Jan's head in his jacket, he rushes back to his mansion laboratory and hooks it up to a device that allows it to live. Although the bodiless head begs to be allowed to die, Bill will have none of it and frequents seedy strip joints looking for a suitable body. He finds a real knockout, Doris (Adele Lamont), whose face happens to be disfigured. Promising to restore her good looks— although he actually plans to replace her head with Jan's—Bill brings Doris back to his mansion. Meanwhile, Jan has developed telepathic powers, and, when she learns what Bill's up to, she uses her newfound psychic ability to call upon the giant mutant locked in the closet (one of Bill's earlier failures) to break out and put the kibosh on the transplant. This is a *really strange* movie, and it contains so many outlandish, peculiar, grotesque, and incongruous moments that it becomes downright surreal. A small-but-loyal cult has formed around this truly unique film, which also made writer-director Paul Schrader's "Guilty Pleasures" list in *Film Comment*.

p, Rex Carlton; d, Joseph Green; w, Joseph Green (based on a story by Rex Carlton, Joseph Green); ph, Stephen Hajnal; ed, Leonard Anderson, Marc Anderson; m, Abe Baker, Tony Restaino.

(PR:C-O   MPAA:NR)

## BRIDE, THE**½

(1985) 119m COL c

Sting (Frankenstein), Jennifer Beals (Eva), Anthony Higgins (Clerval), Clancy Brown (Viktor), David Rappaport (Rinaldo), Geraldine Page (Mrs. Baumann), Alexei Sayle (Magar), Phil Daniels (Bela), Veruschka (Countess), Quentin Crisp (Dr. Zalhus), Cary Elwes (Josef), Tim Spaull (Paulus), Ken Campbell (Pedlar), Guy Rolfe (Count), Andrew de la Tour (Priest), Tony Haygarth (Tavern Keeper), Matthew Guinness, Tony Brutus (Patrons), Gary Shail, Carl Chase (Circus Hands), Jack Birkett (Blind Man), Fenella Fletcher (Masked Lady), Joe Kaye (Groom), Harold Coyne (Butler), Stromboli, Sally Oultram, Joel Baland, Miss Irta (Circus Performers), Andy Barrett (Circus Ringmaster), Annie Roddam (Countess' Daughter).

An extremely loose reworking of 1935's THE BRIDE OF FRANKENSTEIN, THE BRIDE is actually two movies rolled into one—a poignant tale of friendship between the Frankenstein monster (Clancy Brown) and an adventurous dwarf (David Rappaport), a la OF MICE AND MEN, and an utterly worthless morality play about a mad scientist (Sting) obsessed with fashioning his new creation (Jennifer Beals) into his image of the perfect independent woman, a la "Pygmalion." THE BRIDE must be commended for its attempt to tell two parallel stories, but unfortunately the halves do not balance, resulting in a picture in which the lead characters (Sting and Beals) become secondary to the supporting ones (Brown and Rappaport). Whenever the scenes between Brown and Rappaport get into high gear, the audience is subjected to more of the unwanted Beals-Sting story. Had Sting and Beals been completely written out, THE BRIDE would be far more tolerable. Its saving grace is Rappaport (previously seen in TIME BANDITS, 1981), who brings to the film it's only touch of humanity and warmth in his relationship with Brown. If only for Rappaport's performance, THE BRIDE should be seen. Also recommended is the superb photography by Stephen H. Burum (who so skillfully shot RUMBLEFISH, 1983), which splendidly captures the gothic European atmosphere and brings to life the film's rich and detailed production design, much of it inspired by the original Universal "Frankenstein" series.

p, Victor Drai; d, Franc Roddam; w, Lloyd Fonvielle (based on the novel *Frankenstein* by Mary Shelley); ph, Stephen H. Burum (Rank Film Lab Color); ed, Michael Ellis; m, Maurice Jarre.

(PR:C   MPAA:PG-13)

## BRIDE OF FRANKENSTEIN, THE*****

(1935) 80m UNIV bw

Boris Karloff (The Monster), Colin Clive (Henry Frankenstein), Valerie Hobson (Elizabeth Frankenstein), Elsa Lanchester (Mary Shelley/The Bride), O.P. Heggie (The Hermit), Una O'Connor (Minnie), Ernest Thesiger (Dr. Septimus Pretorious), Gavin Gordon (Lord Byron), Douglas Walton (Percy Shelley), E.E. Clive (Burgo master), Lucien Prival (Otto), Dwight Frye (Karl), Reginald Barlow (Hans), Mary Gordon (Hans' Wife), Anne Darling (Shepherdess), Gunnis Davis (Uncle Glutz), Tempe Piggott (Auntie Glutz), Ted Billings (Ludwig), Neil Fitzgerald (Rudy), Walter Brennan (Neighbor), Lucio Villegas (Priest), Edwin Mordant (Coroner), Grace Cunard (Woman), Helen Gibson (Woman), John Carradine (Huntsman), Monty Montague

*(King),* Joan Woodbury *(Queen),* Norman Ainsley *(Archbishop),* Peter Shaw *(Devil),* Billy Barty *(Baby),* Kansas De Forest *(Ballerina),* Josephine McKim *(Mermaid),* Helen Parrish *(Girl).*

This sequel to the original FRANKENSTEIN (1931) is one of the greatest films of the horror genre, and to this day it remains a lasting tribute to the unique genius of its director, James Whale. Picking up where FRANKENSTEIN left off, the film begins as the injured Dr. Frankenstein is taken back to the castle to recuperate, while the monster (Boris Karloff) is left for dead. The monster is alive, however, and wanders the countryside in search of friendship. Enter the eccentric and devious Dr. Pretorious (Ernest Thesiger). An alchemist who has also been trying to create artificial life, Pretorious blackmails the reluctant Frankenstein to aid him in the creation of a woman—a bride for the monster. A brilliant combination of gothic horror and impish black humor, THE BRIDE OF FRANKENSTEIN is Whale's masterpiece. The film is an unforgettable visual experience with its expressionistic sets, excellent costume and make-up design, special effects, chiaroscuro lighting, and shrewd camera placement. Franz Waxman's magnificent score—which Universal later used in innumerable productions, including both the "Flash Gordon" and "Buck Rogers" serials—adds immeasurably to the overall effect. The performances are uniformly excellent as well, with Karloff injecting more humanity into the monster, making him a supremely sympathetic and moving character. But it is Thesiger who nearly steals the film with his pithy portrayal of the horrible Dr. Pretorious. From its prolog—which sees young Mary Shelley (Elsa Lanchester, who also plays the Bride) spinning her horrible tale for her husband Percy and their friend Lord Byron—to its apocalyptic ending, THE BRIDE OF FRANKENSTEIN is both a genuine oddity and one of the most memorable films that Hollywood has ever produced.

p, Carl Laemmle; d, James Whale; w, William Hurlbut, John L. Balderston (based on the novel by Mary Shelley); ph, John Mescall; ed, Ted Kent; m, Franz Waxman.

**(PR:A   MPAA:NR)**

## BRIDE OF THE GORILLA**

(1951) 65m REA bw

Barbara Payton *(Dina),* Lon Chaney, Jr. *(Taro),* Raymond Burr *(Barney Chavez),* Tom Conway *(Dr. Viet),* Paul Cavanagh *(Klass Von Gelder),* Carol Varga *(Larina),* Paul Maxey *(Van Heussen),* Woody Strode *(Policeman),* Martin Garralaga *(Native Man),* Moyna MacGill *(Mrs. Van Heussen),* Felippa Rock *(Van Heusen's Daughter).*

An amusingly bad horror film, written and directed by Curt Siodmak, who seems to be cribbing from his script for THE WOLF MAN (1941). Barney Chavez (Raymond Burr) is the foreman of a rubber plantation who falls into an affair with his boss's bored wife, Dina (Barbara Payton). This leads to Chavez's murdering his boss and marrying Dina. An old servant, however, puts something in Chavez's drink that causes him to turn into a murderous gorilla-man by night and local police chief Taro (played by Lon Chaney, Jr.,

who, of course, was the wolf man in the aforementioned Siodmak effort) must solve the killings. There is only one reason to sit through this low-budget and extremely silly film, namely the camp value of watching Perry Mason turn into a snorting gorilla-man. Not one of Siodmak's better efforts.

p, Jack Broder; d, Curt Siodmak; w, Curt Siodmak; ph, Charles Van Enger; ed, Francis D. Lyon; m, Raoul Kraushaar.

**(PR:A   MPAA:NR)**

## BROOD, THE****

(1979, Can.) 91m NW c

Oliver Reed *(Dr. Raglan),* Samantha Eggar *(Nola),* Art Hindle *(Frank),* Cindy Hinds *(Candice),* Nuala Fitzgerald *(Julianna),* Henry Beckerman *(Barton Kelly),* Susan Hogan *(Ruth),* Michael McGhee *(Inspector Mrazek),* Gary McKeehan *(Mike Trellan),* Bob Silverman *(Jan),* Nicholas Campbell *(Chris),* John Ferguson, Felix Silla *(Creatures),* Larry Solway *(Resnikoff, the Lawyer),* Rainer Schwartz *(Dr. Birkin),* Mary Swinton *(Wendy),* Jerry Kostur *(Construction Worker),* Christopher Britton *(Man in Auditorium).*

Outside of Toronto, at the Somafree Institute of Psychoplasmics, controversial psychotherapist Dr. Raglan (Oliver Reed) teaches mental patients to physically manifest their subconscious anger as boils and welts on their bodies. One of his patients, Nola (Samantha Eggar), has actually begun giving birth to a small army of mutant babies—the ultimate projection of her hostilities. Raglan houses her brood in a nearby cabin, from which, dressed in their colorful Dr. Dentons, the murderous little creatures venture out and kill the objects of Nola's rage. Nola's bitter ex-husband, Frank (Art Hindle), who is trying to discredit Raglan's treatments so that he can gain custody of their daughter (Cindy Hinds), uncovers the horrible truth. THE BROOD is acclaimed Canadian director David Cronenberg's first truly brilliant film—and his most personal. Driven by the pain he felt after a nasty divorce, Cronenberg vented his resentment and frustrations through his art and came up with a mature, controlled, highly provocative, and deeply disturbing work that finds horror not only in such sacred institutions as hospitals and schools but, more specifically, in the family unit itself. While his previous work (THEY CAME FROM WITHIN and RABID) consisted of coldly clinical exercises in fear and loathing of the human body, Cronenberg presents more complex and genuinely sympathetic characters in THE BROOD, giving the film added resonance. THE BROOD also marks Cronenberg's growing confidence as a visual stylist, and the cinematic realization of his themes is remarkably effective and quite unforgettable. A must-see.

p, Claude Heroux; d, David Cronenberg; w, David Cronenberg; ph, Mark Irwin; ed, Allan Collins; m, Howard Shore.

**(PR:O   MPAA:R)**

## BROTHERHOOD OF SATAN, THE**

(1971) 92m COL c

Strother Martin *(Don Duncan)*, L.Q. Jones *(Sheriff)*, Charles Bateman *(Ben)*, Anna Capri *(Nicky)*, Charles Robinson *(Priest)*, Alvy Moore *(Tobey)*, Geri Reischl *(Kiti)*.

Character actor L.Q. Jones directed several low-budget genre films during the 1970s, most notably the science-fiction cult item A BOY AND HIS DOG (1975). This time out, Jones starred in and produced this minor effort, while Bernard McEveety (before he worked for Disney and on TV films) directed. While on a driving trip through the Southwest with his daughter and girl friend, Ben (Charles Bateman) stumbles upon a small town plagued by the disappearance of several children and the murders of their parents. Offering his services, Ben stays on to assist the local sheriff (Jones), his deputy (Alvy Moore), the local priest (Charles Robinson), and a physician (Strother Martin) as they try to solve the mystery. As it turns out, the culprits are a coven of elderly witches and warlocks who plan to transfer their evil souls into the bodies of the missing children so that they may continue their existence. Standard stuff, unimaginatively handled, although fans of Martin (who appeared in several Sam Peckinpah westerns with Jones) may want to take a look.

p, L.Q. Jones, Alvy Moore; d, Bernard McEveety; w, William Welch (based on an idea by Sean McGregor); ph, John Arthur Morrill; ed, Marvin Walowitz; m, Jaime Mendoza-Nava.

**(PR:C-O  MPAA:GP)**

## BRUTE MAN, THE**

(1946) 58m PRC bw

Rondo Hatton *(Hal Moffat)*, Jane Adams *(Helen)*, Tom Neal *(Clifford Scott)*, Jan Wiley *(Virginia)*, Peter Whitney *(Lt. Gales)*, Donald MacBride *(Capt. Donelly)*, Fred Cobey *(Hal Moffat)*, Janelle Johnson *(Joan Bemish)*, Joseph Crehan *(Commissioner Salisbury)*, Lorin Raker *(Parkington)*, Oscar O'Shea *(Mr. Haskins)*, John Gallaudet *(Police Guard)*, John Hamilton *(Prof. Cushman)*, Charles Wagenheim *(Pawnbroker)*, Patrick McVey *(Detective)*, Tristram Coffin *(Police Captain)*, Mary Ann Bricker *(Dorothy)*, Peggy Converse *(Mrs. Obringer)*, Frank O'Connor *(Officer)*, Jack Parker *(Jimmy)*.

After his appearance as "The Creeper" in the Sherlock Holmes mystery THE PEARL OF DEATH (1944), Universal decided to make disfigured character actor Rondo Hatton the star of his own B-picture series. The first of these, HOUSE OF HORRORS (1946), was immediately followed by this film, which turned out to be Hatton's last. THE BRUTE MAN shows us the origin of the Creeper, who was once Hal Moffat, a handsome and popular football star at Hampton College (played in flashback by Fred Coby). Horribly disfigured in a chemistry accident, Moffat becomes a mad killer and sets out to get revenge on all of those he holds responsible. A cult has popped up around the figure of Hatton, about whom little is known. Rumored to have once been a respected journalist, the quiet and introverted Hatton was afflicted with acromegaly, a disease of the pituitary gland that causes the progressive enlargement of the bones in the hands, feet, and face. Grotesquely disfigured, he was forced to quit work as a reporter and wound up playing bit parts in movies, usually as a villainous henchman. Just as he began to achieve a bizarre sort of stardom, Hatton finally succumbed to the disease, dying before THE BRUTE MAN was released. Although Universal produced, the studio declined to release the film for fear of being accused of exploiting Hatton and sold it to poverty-row studio PRC, which had no such compunctions. While not a particularly good film, THE BRUTE MAN remains today—because of Rondo Hatton—a distinct Hollywood oddity.

p, Ben Pivar; d, Jean Yarbrough; w, George Bricker, M. Coates Webster (based on a story by Dwight V. Babcock); ph, Maury Gertsman; ed, Philip Cahn.

**(PR:A  MPAA:NR)**

## BURKE AND HARE*

(1972, Brit.) 91m Armitage c (AKA: HORRORS OF BURKE AND HARE, THE)

Harry Andrews *(Dr. Knox)*, Derren Nesbitt *(Burke)*, Glynn Edwards *(Hare)*, Dee Sjendery, Alan Tucker, Yootha Joyce.

This is a misfired version of the story of 19th-century medical pioneer Dr. Knox (Harry Andrews), whose illicit dealings with grave-robbers Burke (Derren Nesbitt) and Hare (Glynn Edwards) became legendary. Although Andrews contributes a solid performance, his efforts are undone by the cartoonish characterizations of Burke and Hare, who are presented as a pair of moronic Irish twits and mostly played for laughs. Director Vernon Sewell attempts to distract viewers from the innate cheapness of his production by inserting pointless brothel scenes. Stick to THE BODY SNATCHER (1945).

p, Kenneth Shipman; d, Vernon Sewell; w, Ernie Bradford; ph, Desmond Dickinson (DeLuxe Color); m, Roger Webb.

**(PR:O  MPAA:NR)**

## BURNING, THE*

(1981) 90m Filmways c

Brian Matthews *(Todd)*, Leah Ayres *(Michelle)*, Brian Backer *(Alfred)*, Larry Joshua *(Glazer)*, Jason Alexander *(Dave)*, Ned Eisenberg *(Eddie)*, Carrick Glenn *(Sally)*, Carolyn Houlihan *(Karen)*, Fisher Stevens *(Woodstock)*, Lou David *(Cropsey)*.

A blatant FRIDAY THE 13TH rip-off, THE BURNING places a bevy of nubile teens at a summer camp, only to have them brutally murdered one by one. The killer turns out to be the former caretaker of the camp who was horribly burned by mischievous kids five years before and has returned to enact his revenge. A few effectively directed sequences and special makeup effects by Tom Savini (most of which were cut to avoid an "X" rating) are the only reasons to sit through this terribly familiar material. Rick

Wakeman, former keyboardist of the rock band Yes, contributes a typically grating musical score.

p, Harvey Weinstein; d, Tony Maylam; w, Peter Lawrence, Bob Weinstein (based on a story by Harvey Weinstein, Tony Maylam, Brad Grey); ph, Harvey Harrison; ed, John Sholder; m, Rick Wakeman.

**(PR:O   MPAA:R)**

## BURNT OFFERINGS*

(1976) 116m UA c

Karen Black *(Marian)*, Oliver Reed *(Ben)*, Burgess Meredith *(Brother)*, Eileen Heckart *(Roz)*, Lee Montgomery *(David)*, Dub Taylor *(Walker)*, Bette Davis *(Aunt Elizabeth)*, Anthony James *(Chauffeur)*, Orin Cannon *(Minister)*, James T. Myers *(Dr. Ross)*, Todd Turquand *(Young Ben)*, Joseph Riley *(Ben's Father)*.

This mundane haunted-house chiller was produced and directed by television's Dan Curtis, who made his name doing "Dark Shadows" and "The Night Stalker" before turning to such bloated miniseries as "The Winds Of War." Based on a best-selling novel, the plot concerns married couple Ben (Oliver Reed) and Marian (Karen Black), who rent a huge Victorian summer home in Northern California from a bizarre brother and sister (Burgess Meredith and Eileen Heckart). Once the couple move in their family, which includes their son, David (Lee Montgomery), and Ben's elderly aunt (Bette Davis), they realize why the rent was so cheap—the joint's possessed by a ghoulish creature that feeds off the residents. Overlong, talky, predictable, and dull, dull, dull.

p, Dan Curtis; d, Dan Curtis; w, William Nolan (based on the novel by Robert Marasco); ph, Jacques Marquette, Stevne Larner (Deluxe Color); ed, Dennis Verkler; m, Robert Cobert.

**(PR:C   MPAA:PG)**

## BUTCHER, BAKER (NIGHTMARE MAKER)**

(1982) 91m International Films c (AKA: NIGHT WARNING; NIGHTMARE MAKER)

Jimmy McNichol *(Billy)*, Susan Tyrrell *(Cheryl)*, Bo Svenson *(Carlson)*, Marcia Lewis *(Margie)*, Julia Duffy *(Julie)*, Steve Easton *(Coach)*, Caskey Swaim *(Phil)*, Brett Leach *(Sgt. Cook)*, Cooper Neal *(Frank)*, William Paxton *(Eddie)*, Kay Kimler *(Ann)*, Gary Baxley *(Bill, Sr.)*, Vickie Oleson *(Police Officer)*, Clemente Anchondo *(Arrestee)*, Alex Baker *(Officer Wescott)*, Randy Norton *(Tony)*, Kelly Kapp *(Student)*, Steve DoFrance *(Lab Man)*, Bill Keene *(Announcer)*, Riley Morgan *(Chuck)*.

This weird little movie concerns Billy (Jimmy McNichol), a 17-year-old boy who has been raised by his incredibly possessive aunt Cheryl (Susan Tyrrell) since the age of three, when his parents were killed in an auto wreck. Cheryl is a bit odd, as she has built a shrine to her dead lover in the basement—the centerpiece of which is his pickled head. With Billy nearing adulthood, Cheryl frets that he will desert her, she commits a series of murders designed to

keep him from leaving. Director William Asher, whose previous credits include various episodes of "I Love Lucy" and several beach party movies—most notably, BEACH BLANKET BINGO and HOW TO STUFF A WILD BIKINI—keeps the action rolling at a brisk pace, while Tyrrell turns in one of her best performances as the psychopathic aunt.

p, Stephen Breimer, Eugene Mazzola; d, William Asher; w, Stephen Breimer, Alan Jay Glueckman, Boon Collins.

**(PП:O   MPAA:R)**

# C

## CABINET OF DR. CALIGARI, THE*****

(1920, Ger.) 69m Decla-Bioscop/Goldwyn bw (DAS CABINETT DES DR. CALIGARI)

Werner Krauss *(Dr. Caligari)*, Conrad Veidt *(Cesare)*, Friedrich Feher *(Francis)*, Lil Dagover *(Jane)*, Hans Heinz von Twardowski *(Alan)*, Rudolf Lettinger *(Dr. Olson)*, Rudolph Klein-Rogge *(A Criminal)*, Ludwig Rex, Elsa Wagner, Henri Peters-Arnolds, Hans Lanser-Ludolff.

One of the landmark films in the history of cinema and one of the first self-conscious works of film art, THE CABINET OF DR. CALIGARI has had a profound and lasting impact on the world's creative community. The film opens as two pale-faced men sit on a park bench, exchanging stories. The younger, Francis (Friedrich Feher), tells a fantastic tale of horror that transports the viewer to Holstenwall, a bizarre-looking community with jagged roads, steeply pointed rooftops, and sloping walls. Into the town walks Dr. Caligari (Werner Krauss), a man of sinister appearance, who obtains a permit for his carnival, the chief attraction of which is the somnambulist Cesare (Conrad Veidt). Their arrival in Holstenwall mysteriously corresponds to a series of unexplained murders. This film, with its disturbing and ambiguous framing story told by Francis, exploded onto the art world with shocking impact. Its unique vision provided the spark needed to expand the Expressionist movement throughout Germany, and, shortly thereafter, through the rest of the world. German music, theater, painting, posters, literature, and architecture were all inspired by CALIGARI. Even more important than Robert Wiene's direction (the script was by the brilliant Carl Mayer and Czech poet Hans Janowitz, Fritz Lang was initially slated to direct, and the framing story was decided upon by producer Erich Pommer) is the stunningly original art direction by painters Hermann Warm and Walter Reimann and designer Walter Rohrig. They created in their constructed village of Holstenwall a completely artificial universe—a stifling place without a sky, where sunlight and shadows are painted onto floors and walls, and where the angular contraptions called buildings defy all laws of architecture—a universe that could exist only in the mind of a madman. Budgeted at $18,000, the finished film was first screened in Berlin in February 1920 with a musical accompaniment that included selections from Schubert and Ros-

CABINET OF DR. CALIGARI, THE—

sini. Some early prints were tinted with green, brown, and blue.

p, Erich Pommer; d, Robert Wiene; w, Carl Mayer, Hans Janowitz; ph, Willy Hameister.

(PR:A MPAA:NR)

## CAPTAIN KRONOS: VAMPIRE HUNTER***

(1974, Brit.) 91m PAR/Hammer c

Horst Janson *(Kronos)*, John Carson *(Dr. Marcus)*, Shane Briant *(Paul Durward)*, Caroline Munro *(Carla)*, John Cater *(Prof. Grost)*, Lois Daine *(Sara Durward)*, Wanda Ventham *(Lady Durward)*, Ian Hendry *(Kerro)*.

This good vampire adventure from Hammer features Horst Janson as the title character, who wields a mean sword to dispatch all manner of villains, including the nasty blood-suckers. With the aid of his loyal sidekick, the hunchback Prof. Grost (John Cater); wagon driver Dr. Marcus (John Carson); and the lovely Carla (Caroline Munro), Capt. Kronos tackles an elderly vampire woman (Wanda Ventham) who must dine on blood to maintain her youthful appearance. The film was written and directed by Brian Clemens, who wrote many of the best episodes of the popular "Avengers" television series. Fast-paced and with a good sense of humor, CAPTAIN KRONOS was shot in 1972, but left unreleased until 1974, when it was unfortunately double-billed upon release with the disastrous FRANKENSTEIN AND THE MONSTER FROM HELL (1974). Both films failed miserably.

p, Albert Fennell, Brian Clemens; d, Brian Clemens; w, Brian Clemens; ph, Ian Wilson (Humphries Labs); ed, James Needs; m, Laurie Johnson.

(PR:O MPAA:NR)

## CAR, THE**

(1977) 98m UNIV c

James Brolin *(Wade Parent)*, Kathleen Lloyd *(Lauren)*, John Marley *(Everett)*, R.G. Armstrong *(Amos)*, John Rubenstein *(John Morris)*, Elizabeth Thompson *(Margie)*, Roy Jenson *(Ray Mott)*, Kim Richards *(Lynn Marie)*, Kyle Richards *(Debbie)*, Kate Murtagh *(Miss McDonald)*, Robert Phillips *(Metcalf)*, Doris Dowling *(Bertha)*, Henry O'Brien *(Chas)*, Ronny Cox *(Luke)*, Melody Thomas, Bob Woodstock *(Cyclists)*, Eddie Little Sky *(Denson)*, Lee McLaughlin *(Marvin Fats)*, Margaret Wiley *(Navajo Woman)*, Reed Morgan *(Mac Gruder)*, Ernie Orsatti *(Dalton)*, Joshua Davis *(Jimmy)*, Geraldine Kearns *(Donna)*, Hank Hamilton *(Al)*, John Moio *(Parker)*, Melody Thomas *(Suzie)*, Bob Woodlock *(Pete)*, James Rawley *(Thompson)*, Louis Welch *(Berry)*, Bryan O'Byrne *(Wally)*, Don Keefer *(Dr. Pullbrook)*, Steve Gravers *(Mackey)*, Tony Brande *(Joe)*.

THE CAR is a laughable rip-off of Steven Spielberg's television movie "Duel" in which a driverless black car terrorizes a small southwestern town. Wade Parent (James Brolin) is the troubled deputy determined to destroy the Detroit demon, which has killed both his boss (John Mar-

ley) and his girl friend (Kathleen Lloyd). The majority of the movie is dominated by scenes of the vehicle overrunning defenseless townsfolk while the inept police department tries to determine what to do about it. The climax shows the apparent death of the demonic auto as it plunges over a cliff, exploding in a fiery ball. Good score, okay crash sequences, and lots of unintentional laughs are the only reason to sit through this.

p, Elliot Silverstein, Marvin Birdt; d, Elliot Silverstein; w, Dennis Shryack, Michael Butler, Lane Slate (based on a story by Dennis Shryack); ph, Gerald Hirschfield (Technicolor); ed, Michael McCroskey; m, Leonard Rosenman.

(PR:C MPAA:PG)

## CARNAGE zero

(1986) 91m Jaylo International/Media Home Entertainment c

Leslie Den Dooven *(Carol)*, Michael Chiodo *(Jonathan)*, John Garitt *(Walter)*, Deeann Veeder *(Susan)*, Chris Baker *(Ann)*, Jack Poggi *(Minister)*, Albert Alfano *(Tony)*, Che Moody *(Motherin-Law)*, Rosemary Egan *(Margaret)*, Ellen Orchid *(Judy)*, Chris Georges *(Mark)*, Bill Grant *(Dad)*, Judith Mayes *(Martha)*, Lola Ross *(Rose Novak)*, Lon Freeman *(Nathan Frye)*, Joseph Vitagliano *(Plumber)*, Victor Logan *(Dr. Marcus)*, Willis Karp *(Ray Trail)*, Susan Ortiz *(Secretary)*, William Cooner, David Marks *(Burglars)*.

Written, photographed, and directed in 1983 as "Hell House" by Staten Island's favorite low-budget exploitation king, Andy Milligan, this haunted-house/gore film is so bad it never saw a theatrical release and went straight to video. Shot in Milligan's usual home-movie style, CARNAGE opens as a bride and groom bid each other a passionate goodbye before he shoots her in the head and then commits suicide himself. Three years later, another newlywed couple, Carol and Jonathan (Leslie Den Dooven and Michael Chiodo), move into the first couple's house, which of course is haunted. Tedious, talky, and incredibly inept, CARNAGE is laughably amateurish. Most scenes appear to be lit by one—very bright—light source, which illuminates the actors, but leaves the rest of the set in darkness. The only way to pad out a cheap feature with a concept this lame is to have the characters talk and talk and talk without saying anything, so there are long, pointless conversations between Carol and Jonathan, then Carol and her father (on the phone), then Carol and the minister, and even a subplot from hell involving the collapsing marriage of Carol's best friend (Chris Baker), whom we watch talk with *her* mother for what seems like an eternity. These long passages of boredom are punctuated by unintentionally hilarious "special effects" sequences in which objects are supposed to be moving by themselves, but are obviously being propelled by strings or even hands just out of frame. One could make a case that all these ineptitudes combine to form a perversely charming film, sort of like the short Super-8 films that ambitious teenagers make at home. Maybe so, but just try to imagine yourself sitting through a *90-minute* home movie made by the neighbor-

34

THE HORROR FILM

hood kids. If you can take that, then you'll almost be ready to suffer through CARNAGE.

p, Lew Mishkin; d, Andy Milligan; w, Andy Milligan; ph, Andy Milligan; ed, Gerald Bronson.

**(PR:C MPAA:NR)**

### CARNIVAL OF BLOOD zero

(1976) 87m Kirk/Monarch c

Earle Edgerton *(Tom)*, Judith Resnick *(Laura)*, John Harris [Burt Young] *(Gimpy)*, Martin Barolsky *(Dan)*, Kaly Mills *(Fortune Teller)*, Gloria Spivak *(Fat Blonde)*, Eve Packer *(Prostitute)*, Glenn Kimberley *(Sailor)*, William Grinnel *(Husband)*, Linda Kurtz *(Wife)*.

In this unwatchable BLOOD FEAST rip-off, a psycho who was driven insane by his domineering mother, his face scarred from a fire, dons a rubber mask and wanders Coney Island killing women who remind him of Mom. The bloody special effects are obviously purchases from the local meat market. Since there is no plot, the actors are forced to improvise, making for lots of dialog scenes with people sitting on couches yakking away and saying nothing worth listening to. Shot in 1971 and not released until 1976, this was reportedly actor Burt Young's first film, although he's hiding behind the pseudonym "John Harris."

p, Leonard Kirman; d, Leonard Kirman; w, Leonard Kirman; m, The Brooks Group, H. Crisman.

**(PR:C MPAA:PG)**

### CARNIVAL OF SOULS****

(1962) 80m Herts-Lion bw

Candace Hilligoss *(Mary Henry)*, Herk Harvey *(The Man)*, Frances Feist *(Landlady)*, Sidney Berger *(John Linden)*, Stan Levitt *(Doctor)*, Art Ellison *(Minister)*, Tom McGinnis, Dan Palmquist, Steve Boozer, Pamela Ballard, Lamy Sneegas, Cari Conboy, Karen Pyles, Forbes Caldwell, Bill De Jarnette, T.C. Adams, Sharon Scoville, Mary Ann Harris, Peter Schnitzler, Bill Sollner.

A genuinely chilling ghost story, CARNIVAL OF SOULS was independently produced in Lawrence, Kansas, for less than $100,000 and today has a deservedly large cult following. The story opens as Mary (Candace Hilligoss) and two of her girl friends accidentally drive off a bridge to find a watery grave in the river below. Mary somehow emerges from the depths, however, and wanders into a church, where she becomes the new organist. She rents a room from the landlady (Frances Feist) and her fellow boarder across the hall (Sidney Berger, who in real life was the speech instructor at the University of Kansas) makes unsuccessful advances toward the strange woman. Suffering from visions wherein a ghoulish-looking man is following her, Mary finds herself inexplicably drawn to a battered old amusement park, where she is escorted by a dance of the dead by the man in her hallucinations. Eventually the auto accident is discovered, and when the authorities pull the car out of the river, they find the bodies of all three women, proving Mary has been one of the dead

all along. In this very atmospheric film, with great chilling moments, director Herk Harvey (who plays the leader of the dead) demonstrates an innate visual sense and lends a dreamlike quality to the proceedings. There is an oppressive sense of unease and dread throughout, which is actually enhanced by the employment of amateur actors, whose natural awkwardness before the camera merely adds to the disquieting mood. Harvey's use of actual locations—such as the huge church, the decrepit amusement park, and the abandoned ballroom—is excellent and adds immeasurably to the overall effect. The eerie score is played entirely on an church organ. Although Harvey never directed another film, CARNIVAL OF SOULS is truly the stuff of nightmares and a lasting testament to a great undiscovered talent.

p, Herk Harvey; d, Herk Harvey; w, John Clifford; ph, Maurice Prather; ed, Dan Palmquist, Bill DeJarnette; m, Gene Moore.

**(PR:C MPAA:NR)**

### CARRIE***

(1976) 97m UA c

Sissy Spacek *(Carrie White)*, Piper Laurie *(Margaret White)*, Amy Irving *(Sue Snell)*, William Katt *(Tommy Ross)*, John Travolta *(Billy Nolan)*, Nancy Allen *(Chris Hargenson)*, Betty Buckley *(Miss Collins)*, P.J. Soles *(Norma Watson)*, Sydney Lassick *(Mr. Fromm)*, Stefan Gierasch *(Principal Morton)*, Priscilla Pointer *(Mrs. Snell)*, Michael Talbot *(Freddy)*, Cameron De Palma *(Boy On Bicycle)*.

This was the overrated Brian De Palma's first big hit, and remains his best horror effort to date. Sissy Spacek (in a stunning performance that overpowers most of the movie's faults) stars as Carrie, a troubled, sexually repressed high schooler who slowly realizes that she possesses incredible telekinetic powers. Plagued with problems in school (she feels homely and nobody likes her) and at home (her mother is a religious fanatic who hates men and makes her daughter pray in a closet), she struggles to maintain her dignity and sanity, but is finally driven over the edge when cruel classmates rig things so that she is elected prom queen in an elaborate joke designed to embarrass her. At the dance, Carrie is in her glory and finally feels accepted, until three pranksters (P.J. Soles, John Travolta, and Michael Talbot) drop a bucket of pig's blood on her head as she accepts her honors. Carrie's telekinetic powers—only hinted at thus far—go wild, and she destroys most of her school and the people in it. Cleverly designed to appeal to its target teenage audience, CARRIE was the synthesis of De Palma's talent for intense, stylish, visual filmmaking. His techniques—elaborate compositions, camera moves, and slow motion—combined with a fairly literate script (due more to Stephen King's source material than De Palma's influence) make for an interesting film that successfully deals with the inner rage every teenager feels. Unfortunately, CARRIE also hints at De Palma's penchant for pointless exercises in overblown, style-for-style's-sake sequences (combined with a lack of real insight into his characters that makes its difficult to take his rip-offs of Hitchcock and Hawks seriously) and his increasingly disturbing misogyny, which would mar much of his later work. While De Palma has his legion of fans, his seems to be the marginal talent of an empty stylist.

p, Paul Monash; d, Brian De Palma; w, Larry Cohen (based on the novel by Stephen King); ph, Mario Tosi (DeLuxe Color); ed, Paul Hirsch; m, Pino Donaggio.

(PR:O   MPAA:R)

## CASTLE OF EVIL*

(1967) 80m United Pictures/WORLD c

Scott Brady *(Matt Granger),* Virginia Mayo *(Sable),* Lisa Gaye *(Carol Harris),* David Brian *(Robert Hawley),* Hugh Marlowe *(Dr. Corozal),* William Thourlby *(The Robot),* Shelley Morrison *(Lupe Tekal d'Esperanza),* Natividad Vacio *(Machado),* Ernest Sarracino *(Tunki).*

This horrible horror film's only value is its campiness. A mad scientist, wickedly disfigured by phosphorous salts, dies and leaves a will. When a group of people who are to share in his wealth visits his remote Caribbean castle, they learn that none of them will receive any of the cash until the one who disfigured him is found. A murderous robot created in the image of its scarred master is programmed to discover and kill the guilty one. The killer, in turn, ingeniously reprograms the robot to kill everyone *else* instead. This cheapie exploitation film even offered a free funeral if the viewer dropped dead while watching. Does the offer still stand?

p, Earle Lyon; d, Francis D. Lyon; w, Charles A. Wallace; ph, Brick Marquard (Eastmancolor); ed, Robert S. Eisen; m, Paul Dunlap.

(PR:C   MPAA:NR)

## CAT AND THE CANARY, THE***

(1927) 86m UNIV bw

Laura La Plante *(Annabelle West),* Creighton Hale *(Paul Jones),* Forrest Stanley *(Charles Wilder),* Tully Marshall *(Roger Crosby),* Gertrude Astor *(Cecily Young),* Arthur Edmund Carewe *(Harry Blythe),* Flora Finch *(Susan Sillsby),* Martha Mattox *("Mammy" Pleasant),* Lucien Littlefield *(Dr. Patterson),* George Siegmann *(Hendricks),* Joe Murphy *(Milkman),* Billy Engle *(Taxi Driver).*

Framed by the Gothic-arched back of a chair, the presumed legatees of an eccentric millionaire—dead these 20 years—are shown awaiting the stroke of midnight, the time at which the deceased decreed his will should be read. The closest relatives of the late recluse, a-twitter with anticipation, are appalled to learn that they have been left nothing; the entire estate is to go to distant relative Annabelle West (Laura La Plante), the only one of the clan who didn't consider the old man's mind to be twisted. One stipulation: Annabelle herself must be demonstrably in her right mind; otherwise, a second document will be opened naming another heir. Mysterious occurrences abound in the old mansion—the attorney disappears, secret panels open and close, a sinister hand with Fu Manchu fingernails menaces the assemblage—all serving to put Annabelle's

sanity in jeopardy. Gothic horror is larded liberally with humor in this benchmark silent classic that established a genre: the haunted-mansion picture. Far more cinematic than theatrical, John Willard's 1922 stage play works beautifully on the screen, and director Paul Leni pulls out all the stops with vignettes, odd camera angles, and long tracking shots in this, his first US helming. A longtime art director in his native Germany, Leni directed the Expressionistic masterpiece WAXWORKS in 1924, serving also as ... director. In THE CAT AND THE CANARY, Leni had an added advantage in the presence of another talented artist, set designer Charles D. Hall, who had worked on THE PHANTOM OF THE OPERA (1925) and who was to go on to further Gothic fame with DRACULA (1931) and FRANKENSTEIN (1932). A visual delight, alternating thrills with giggles, well paced and with fine characterizations all around.

d, Paul Leni; w, Robert F. Hill, Alfred A. Cohn (based on the play by John Willard); ph, Gilbert Warrenton.

(PR:A   MPAA:NR)

## CAT PEOPLE****

(1942) 73m RKO/UNIV bw

Simone Simon *(Irene Dubrovna),* Kent Smith *(Oliver Reed),* Tom Conway *(The Psychiatrist),* Jane Randolph *(Alice Moore),* Jack Holt *(Commodore),* Alan Napier *(Carver),* Elizabeth Dunne *(Miss Plunkett),* Elizabeth Russell *(The Cat Woman).*

CAT PEOPLE was the first of several literate, understated, and atmospheric low-budget horror films produced by Val Lewton that, despite initial box-office indifference, became seminal works of the genre. One of the first films to explicitly link horror and sexuality, CAT PEOPLE follows beautiful New York fashion designer Irena Dubrovna (Simone Simon) as she falls in love and marries handsome architect Oliver Reed (Kent Smith). The union is not a happy one, however, for Irena—who is of Balkan heritage—refuses to consummate the marriage because of her belief in an ancient legend of her homeland that maintains that, if sexually aroused, she will transform into a murderous panther and kill her lover. Brilliantly directed by Jacques Tourneur, CAT PEOPLE is a subtly terrifying film in which the horror is conveyed entirely through suggestion. Irena bumps into an oddly feline-looking woman at a restaurant and instinctively *knows* she shares the curse; a woman walks alone down a dark street with the pools of light from a streetlamp her only refuge; a woman is trapped in a swimming pool naked and alone in the dark with *something* circling her—all these moments, played mostly without dialog, are evocative of universal fears and phobias (many of them shared by producer Lewton), and are much more frightening than any blatant scares, including the use of an actual panther in the climax at the studio's insistence. The minimal budgets Lewton was forced to work with actually enhanced his films, forcing his directors to be more creative. Lewton economized by using existing RKO sets—the spooky-looking apartment house used in CAT PEOPLE is the gigantic set built for Orson Welles' THE MAGNIFICENT AMBERSONS only a few months earlier in 1942. CAT PEO-

PLE was Lewton's biggest hit, with viewers lured in by the film's bombastic advertising, which blared: "Kiss me and I'll claw you to death!" —a line more lurid than anything that ever appeared in any of his movies. A loose sequel, CURSE OF THE CAT PEOPLE, would follow, and 40 years later Paul Schrader would remake the original, unlearning everything that Lewton had taught.

p, Val Lewton; d, Jacques Tourneur; w, Dewitt Bodeen; ph, Nicholas Musuraca; ed, Mark Robson; m, Roy Webb.

**(PR:A MPAA:NR)**

## CAT PEOPLE**

(1982) 118m UNIV/RKO c

Nastassja Kinski (Irena Gallier), Malcolm McDowell (Paul Gallier), John Heard (Oliver Yates), Annette O'Toole (Alice Perrin), Ruby Dee (Female), Ed Begley, Jr. (Joe Creigh), Scott Paulin (Bill Searle), Frankie Faison (Detective Brandt), Ron Diamond (Detective Diamond), Lynn Lowry (Ruthie), John Larroquette (Bronte Judson), Tessa Richarde (Billie), Patricia Perkins (Taxi Driver), Berry Berenson (Sandra), Fausto Barajas (Otis), John H. Fields (Massage Parlor Manager), Emery Hollier (Yeatman Brewer), Stephen Marshall (Moonie), Robert Pavlovitch (Ted), Julie Denney (Carol), Arione de Winter (Indian Village Mother), Francine Segal (Churchwoman), Don Hood (Agent), David Showacre (Man in Bar), Neva Gage (Cat-like Woman), Marisa Folse, Danelle Hand (Indian Girls), John C. Isbell (Police Officer).

Paul Schrader's remake of the 1942 classic CAT PEOPLE is the antithesis of what the original's producer, Val Lewton, had contributed to the genre. Where the first film's sexual themes were understated and evocative, Schrader has made them blatant and obvious. Where the horrors were subtle and suggestive, Schrader has made them graphic and gory. Shifting the setting from New York to New Orleans, the 1982 CAT PEOPLE stars Nastassia Kinski as Irena, a young virgin who is visited by her brother, Paul (Malcolm McDowell). He informs her that, when she has sex, she will become a panther and subsequently kill her mate, unless he is a relative. This comes as bad news for Irena, who has the hots for zookeeper Oliver Yates (John Heard). Unbelievably wrong-headed, this remake virtually trashes all the elements that made the original so compelling. There is no ambiguity, no psychological complexity, and no substance. The film is merely a vehicle for ex-Calvinist Schrader to play out his various sexual obsessions (including, it would seem, bondage, as demonstrated in a scene where Heard decides to risk evisceration by having sex with Kinski, but ties her hands and feet to the bedposts first). All one is left with—besides the soft-core pornography—are some stomach-churning effects by Tom Burman and excellent camerawork by John Bailey. Scripted by Alan Ormsby, of CHILDREN SHOULDN'T PLAY WITH DEAD THINGS fame.

p, Charles Fries; d, Paul Schrader; w, Alan Ormsby (based on the story by DeWitt Bodeen); ph, John Bailey

(Technicolor); ed, Jacqueline Cambas; m, Giorgio Moroder, David Bowie.

**(PR:O MPAA:R)**

## CATHY'S CURSE*

(1977, Can.) 88m 21st Century c (AKA: CAUCHEMARES)

Alan Scarfe (George Gimble), Beverley Murray (Vivian Gimble), Randi Allen (Cathy Gimble), Hubert Noel (Doctor), Roy Witham (Paul), Dorothy Davis (Mary), Mary Morter (Medium), Renee Girard (Mrs. Burton), Sonny Forbes (Policeman), Linda Koot (Laura), Bob Gerolami (Vet), Peter McNeil (Young George), Bryce Allen, Lisa Nickelt (Cathy's Friends).

This dull Canadian EXORCIST-inspired horror film stars Randi Allen as Cathy, a little girl possessed by the spirit of her dead aunt, who was killed in a car crash when she was the same age as Cathy. The aunt's spirit enters the home through Cathy's rag doll, leading to bloody mutilations, cheesy makeup, and inept special effects.

p, N. Mathieu, Nicole Boisvert, Eddy Matalon; d, Eddy Matalon; w, Myra Clement, Eddy Matalon, A. Sens-Cazenave.

**(PR:O MPAA:R)**

## CAT'S EYE**

(1985) 93m MGM/UA c

Drew Barrymore (Girl), James Woods (Morrison), Alan King (Dr. Donatti), Kenneth McMillan (Cressner), Robert Hays (Norris), Candy Clark (Sally Ann), James Naughton (Hugh), Tony Munafo (Junk), Court Miller (Mr. McCann), Russell Horton (Mr. Milquetoast), Patricia Benson (Mrs. Milquetoast), Mary D'Arcy (Cindy), James Rebhorn (Drunk Businessman), Jack Dillon (Janitor), Susan Hawes (Mrs. McCann), Shelly Burch (Jerrilyn), Sal Richards (Westlake), Jesse Doran (Albert), Patricia Kalember (Marcia), Mike Starr (Ducky), Charles Dutton (Dom).

A rather tepid anthology film, CAT'S EYE is a pastiche of leftover Stephen King notions, connected by a ubiquitous cat that ominously appears to set off each tale. The first and best story concerns a chain-smoker (James Woods) who enrolls in the "Quitter's Inc." stop-smoking program run by Dr. Donatti (Alan King)—unfortunately, the cure is quite sadistic and requires that the smoker's poor wife (Mary D'Arcy) be hooked up to an electric chair. Episode number two is set in Atlantic City, where a brutal gambler (Kenneth McMillan), who knows that his wife has been sleeping with a man named Norris (Robert Hays), forces Norris into a bet: he must climb out of a window 20 stories high and manipulate his body along a six-inch ledge to circumnavigate the apartment; if he does so, he wins the gambler's money and wife. The final story takes place in Wilmington, North Carolina, where a young girl (Drew Barrymore) is being terrorized by a miniature troll. The whole thing was the ill-conceived notion of mogul Dino De Laurentiis; screenwriter King allegedly thought the cat angle a poor way to connect the tales. Director Lewis Teague

CAT'S EYE—

(ALLIGATOR) does a workmanlike job here, and the only thing to recommend the movie is James Woods' performance in the first episode and some nice special-effects work—particularly in the troll story.

p, Martha Schumacher; d, Lewis Teague; w, Stephen King (based on the short stories "Quitters Inc.," "The General," "The Ledge" by Stephen King); ph, Jack Cardiff (Technicolor); ed, Scott Conrad; m, Alan Silvestri.

**(PR:C MPAA:PG-13)**

## CAULDRON OF BLOOD**

(1971, Sp.) 101m Cannon c (AKA: BLIND MAN'S BLUFF; EL COLECCIONISTA DE CADAVERES)

Boris Karloff *(Franz Badulescu)*, Viveca Lindfors *(Tania Badulescu)*, Jean-Pierre Aumont *(Claude Marchand)*, Jacqui Speed *(Pilar)*, Rosenda Monteros *(Valerie)*, Ruven Rojo *(Lover)*, Dianik Zurakowska *(Elga)*, Milo Quesada, Merecedes Rojo, Mary Lou Palermo, Manuel de Blas, Eduardo Coutelen.

Boris Karloff stars here as blind sculptor Franz Badulescu, who lives in Spain with his evil wife, Tania (Viveca Lindfors), the woman who actually blinded and crippled him during a murder attempt that looked like a car crash. Badulescu is working on a massive sculpture, using the skeletons of animals and humans as his base, but unbeknownst to him, Tania and her lover (Milo Queseda), are committing a series of grisly murders, boiling the corpses in acid, and giving the artist the *fresh* bones to work with. When a travel reporter (Jean-Pierre Aumont) who has been interviewing the artist catches on to the scheme, violence erupts. One of Karloff's last films, this was shot in Spain in 1967 and wasn't released in the US until 1971, three years after the actor's death. Claude Rains was originally selected to play the role of Badulescu, but illness prevented him from taking the part.

p, Robert D. Weinbach; d, Santos Alcocer; w, John Melson, Jose Luis Bayonas, Santos Alcocer (based on a story by Santos Alcocer); ph, Francisco Sempere (Panoramica, Eastmancolor); ed, J. Antonio Rojo; m, Jose Luis Navarro, Ray Ellis.

**(PR:C MPAA:GP)**

## CELLAR DWELLER*½

(1988) 77m Dove/Empire c

Pamela Bellwood *(Amanda)*, Deborah Mullowney *(Whitney Taylor)*, Brian Robbins *(Philip)*, Cheryl-Ann Wilson *(Lisa)*, Vince Edwards *(Mr. Shelski)*, Floyd Levine *(Taxi Driver)*, Yvonne De Carlo *(Mrs. Briggs)*, Michael Deak *(Cellar Dweller)*, Jeffrey Combs *(Colin Childress)*.

This modest horror film opens in 1951, as cartoonist Colin Childress (Jeffrey Combs) is hard at work in his basement on a horror comic book, his storyboard panels showing a monster with a satanic symbol on its chest killing and eating a young woman. The inspiration for Childress' work is "The Curses of the Ancient Dead," and when he reads one of these curses, the drawing comes to life. Twenty-five

years later, Childress' mansion has become a rooming house for art students, where newcomer Whitney Taylor (Deborah Mullowney) attempts to create a comic book based on Childress' old "Cellar Dweller" series, setting up work in the basement and discovering the book of curses in the process. An enjoyable though not particularly distinguished effort, CELLAR DWELLER has a number of small worthwhile moments. Director John Carl Buechler gets the most out of a somewhat limited script, pacing the action nicely, and the special effects are adequate—but, like everything else in this film, small and limited in scale.

p, Bob Wynn; d, John Carl Buechler; w, Kit DuBois; ph, Sergio Salvati (Technicolor); ed, Barry Zetlin; m, Carlo Dante.

**(PR:O MPAA:R)**

## CHAMBER OF HORRORS**

(1941, Brit.) 85m Rialto-Pathe/MON bw (GB: DOOR WITH SEVEN LOCKS, THE)

Leslie Banks *(Dr. Manetta)*, Lilli Palmer *(June Lansdowne)*, Romilly Lunge *(Dick Martin)*, Gina Malo *(Glenda Blake)*, David Horne *(Edward Havelock)*, Richard Bird *(Inspector Sneed)*, Cathleen Nesbitt *(Ann Cody)*, J.H. Roberts *(Luis Silva)*, Aubrey Mallalieu *(Lord Selford)*, Harry Hutchinson *(Bevan Cody)*, Ross Landon *(John Selford)*, Philip Ray *(Cawler)*, R. Montgomery *(Craig)*.

Leslie Banks, in a big come-down since his glory days with Hitchcock, plays Manetta, a mad doctor and descendant of Spanish Inquisitors who eliminates the heirs to a fortune through an imaginative series of tortures and experiments. When June Lansdowne (Lilli Palmer) turns up as an unknown claimant to the estate, Manetta menaces her until police inspector Sneed (Richard Bird) puts a stop to his fiendish machinations. Banks seems thoroughly uncomfortable as a mad Spanish scientist, but Palmer does as well as could be expected in a low-budget programmer like this.

p, John Argyle; d, Norman Lee; w, Norman Lee, John Argyle, Gilbert Gunn (based on a novel by Edgar Wallace); ph, Desmond Dickinson.

**(PR:A MPAA:NR)**

## CHANGELING, THE***

(1980, Can.) 107m Pan-Canadian/Associated Film Distributors c

George C. Scott *(John Russell)*, Trish Van Devere *(Claire Norman)*, Melvyn Douglas *(Sen. Joe Carmichael)*, John Colicos *(DeWitt)*, Jean Marsh *(Joanna Russell)*, Barry Morse *(Dr. Pemberton)*, James Douglas *(Eugene Carmichael)*, Madeleine Thornton-Sherwood *(Mrs. Norman)*, Roberta Maxwell *(Eva Lingstrom)*, Berrand Behrens *(Prof. Robert Lingstrom)*, Frances Hyland *(Elizabeth Grey)*, Ruth Springford *(Minnie Huxley)*, Helen Burns *(Leah Harmon)*, Eric Christmas *(Albert Harmon)*, Chris Gampel *(Tuttle)*.

In this truly frightening haunted-house story, the ghost of a murdered boy does the terrorizing. John Russell (George

THE HORROR FILM

C. Scott) is a widowed music professor who moves into a historic Seattle mansion, only to learn that the house is haunted. With the help of local historical society worker Claire (Trish Van Devere), Russell discovers that the spirit is a boy who was murdered by his father in an attempt to collect an inheritance. When the father realized that he could not collect the cash until his son became 21, he put a substitute—or changeling—in the murdered child's place. Years later, the changeling has grown into a wealthy old industrialist (Melvyn Douglas), who thinks that Russell is trying to reveal his past and blackmail him. Directed with considerable flair by Peter Medak (THE RULING CLASS), this is a horror film made up of small moments that have lasting impact, such as an old-fashioned wheelchair creaking down the hall on its own, and a chilling seance scene. One of the most genuinely haunting ghost stories in recent years, THE CHANGELING is much eerier and more effective than the overrated and bombastic POLTERGEIST.

p, Joel B. Michaels, Garth H. Drabinsky; d, Peter Medak; w, William Grey, Diana Maddox (based on a story by Russell Hunter); ph, John Coquillon (Panavision); ed, Lilla Ledersen; m, Rick Wilkins.

(PR:O MPAA:R)

## CHILD, THE*

(1977) 73m Valiant International c (AKA: KILL AND GO HIDE!)

Laurel Barnett *(Elise)*, Rosalie Cole *(Rosalie)*, Frank Janson *(Father)*, Richard Hanners *(Len)*, Ruth Ballen *(Mr. Whitfield)*, Slosson Bing Jong *(Gardener)*.

A dull supernatural tale set in a remote woodland area in the 1930s, THE CHILD concerns sweet little girl Rosalie (Rosalie Cole), who discovers that she possesses demonic powers after her daddy pays the homicidal gardener to bump off her mother. In retaliation, Rosalie commands the bodies of the dead to rise in a nearby cemetery. New governess Alicianne (Laurel Barnett) begins to think things are strange when most of the cast gets chewed up by things that go bump in the night. The spunky nursemaid realizes that she's next, and barricades herself in the pumphouse with an axe, waiting for the newly risen dead to find her. This low-budget effort has its champions, mainly because of some nice subjective camerawork, but it simply takes too long to kick into gear and by that time one's interest is lost.

p, Robert Dadashian; d, Robert Voskanian; w, Ralph Lucas; ph, Mori Alavi (Eastmancolor); m, Rob Wallace (performed by Michael Quatro).

(PR:O MPAA:R)

## CHILDREN, THE zero

(1980) 90m World-Nortal c

Martin Shaker *(John Freemont)*, Gil Rogers *(Sheriff Billy Hart)*, Gale Garnett *(Cathy Freemont)*, Jessie Abrams, Tracy Griswold, Joy Glaccum, Suzanne Barnes, Rita Montone, Michelle Le Mothe, Shannon Bolin, Clara Evans, Jeptha Evans, Sarah Albright, Nathanael Albright, Julie Carrier, Edward Terry.

In this terribly pretentious, totally inept, and unintentionally hilarious attempt at a horror film, a busload of little kids is accidentally turned radioactive when they pass through the site of a nuclear plant leak. The kids immediately become zombies (identified as such by their tell-tale black fingernails), and turn their parents into piles of smoldering embers with a mere hug. As it turns out, the only way to stop these kids is to cut off their hands—which plays as funny as it sounds. Obviously made by individuals committed to social change, THE CHILDREN evokes a catalog of modern social ills—from unsafe nuclear power to selfish, inattentive parents—in an attempt to be relevant. In the end, a woman gives birth to a black-fingernailed baby, a rather fanciful stab at setting up a sequel from producer-director Max Kalmanowicz.

p, Max Kalmanowicz, Carlton J. Albright; d, Max Kalmanowicz; w, Carlton J. Albright, Edward Terry; ph, Barry Abrams; ed, Nikki Wessling; m, Harry Manfredini.

(PR:O MPAA:R)

## CHILDREN OF THE CORN*½

(1984) 93m Gatlin-Angeles Group-Inverness/NW c

Peter Horton *(Dr. Burt Stanton)*, Linda Hamilton *(Vicky Baxter)*, R.G. Armstrong *(Diehl)*, John Franklin *(Isaac)*, Courtney Gains *(Malachai)*, Robby Kiger *(Job)*, Annemarie McEvoy *(Sarah)*, Julie Maddalena *(Rachel)*, Jonas Marlowe *(Joseph)*, John Philbin *(Amos)*, Dan Snook *(Boy)*, David Cowan *(Dad)*, Suzy Southam *(Mom)*, D.G. Johnson *(Mr. Hansen)*, Patrick Boylan, Elmer Soderstrom, Teresa Toigo *(Hansen Customers)*.

CHILDREN OF THE CORN is another of the lame Stephen King adaptations that popped up during the first half of the 1980s, this time based on a short story. Burt (Peter Horton) and Vicky (Linda Hamilton) are a young couple driving cross-country to Seattle, where Burt—just out of medical school—will begin his internship. Somewhere in Nebraska, they find themselves in a small farming town in which the children have murdered all the adults and set themselves up as a religious cult that sacrifices grown-ups to some sort of corn-god, which burrows its way through the fields. After the opening, wherein the kids slaughter their folks just after Sunday services, the film takes a steep nosedive into tedium, leaving director Fritz Kiersch to show off his gratuitous visual style. Female lead Hamilton would score later in the year with the surprise sci-fi hit THE TERMINATOR.

p, Donald P. Borchers, Terence Kirby; d, Fritz Kiersch; w, George Goldsmith (based on the short story "Night Shift" by Stephen King); ph, Raoul Lomas (CFI Color); ed, Harry Keramidas; m, Jonathan Elias.

(PR:C-O MPAA:R)

## CHILDREN SHOULDN'T PLAY WITH DEAD THINGS***

(1972) 85m Geneni c

Alan Ormsby *(Alan)*, Jane Daly *(Terry)*, Anya Ormsby *(Anya)*, Jeffrey Gillen *(Jeff)*, Valerie Mamches *(Val)*, Paul Cronin *(Paul)*, Bruce Soloman *(Winns)*, Seth Sklarey *(Orville)*, Roy Engleman *(Roy)*, Bob Filep *(Emerson)*, Alecs Baird *(Caretaker)*.

This surprisingly good low-budget (under $100,000) zombie film stars screenwriter Alan Ormsby as Alan, the leader of a troupe of eccentric actors who travel to a small, lonely island on which there is a large cemetery and a house. Armed with the *Book of the Dead*, Alan digs up a corpse and names it "Orville," performing an elaborate ritual to bring Orville to life. Nothing happens. Disappointed but undaunted, Alan brings Orville into the house, and the troupe proceeds to have a party with the corpse as the guest of honor. After many (too many) bad cadaver jokes, the spell finally takes hold and the dead in the cemetery begin to pull themselves out of the ground—the decaying bodies, in a truly terrifying and effective sequence, slowly lumbering off in search of flesh to eat. Highly derivative of NIGHT OF THE LIVING DEAD and filled with amateurish performances, strained comedy, and zero production values, CHILDREN SHOULDN'T PLAY WITH DEAD THINGS does contain, however, an undeniable power in the rising-dead scenes, and a genuine mood of unease throughout that most big-budget horror outings fail to capture. The film was produced and directed by Bob Clark, whose incredibly spotty career boasts small gems like DEATHDREAM and A CHRISTMAS STORY, as well as such garbage as PORKY'S; RHINESTONE; TURK 182; and FROM THE HIP. Screenwriter-actor Ormsby would go on to direct the excellent—but as of yet unavailable on videocassette—Ed Gein movie DERANGED (1974) and pen the script for Paul Schrader's CAT PEOPLE (1982).

p, Bob Clark, Gary Goch; d, Bob Clark; w, Alan Ormsby, Bob Clark.

**(PR:C-O    MPAA:PG)**

## CHILD'S PLAY***

(1988) 87m UA/MGM-UA c

Catherine Hicks *(Karen Barclay)*, Chris Sarandon *(Det. Mike Norris)*, Alex Vincent *(Andy Barclay)*, Brad Dourif *(Charles Lee Ray)*, Dinah Manoff *(Maggie Peterson)*, Tommy Swerdlow *(Jack Santos)*, Jack Colvin *(Dr. Ardmore)*, Edan Gross.

Is anyone ever going to make a really good toys-coming-to-life-to-kill-people movie? Although better than Stuart Gordon's disappointing DOLLS (1987), CHILD'S PLAY once again fails to milk the situation for all it's worth and delivers only half the chills it could have. Crazed serial killer Charles Lee Ray (Brad Dourif) is tracked down by a Chicago cop (Chris Sarandon) and fatally shot in a toy store. The dying Ray invokes voodoo powers and transfers his evil spirit into a "Good Guy" doll—a large, expensive toy that responds to human commands and talks while moving its mouth and eyes. The next day, single mother Karen Barclay (Catherine Hicks) buys the doll for her son, Andy (Alex Vincent), who names it "Chucky." Soon Andy realizes Chucky is more than just a doll, however, as the "Good Guy" comes to life, uses vulgar language, prowls around the apartment, and knocks off the baby-sitter. Buoyed by a good cast, strong direction, and excellent effects, CHILD'S PLAY almost works. Unfortunately, the screenplay is full of plot holes, lapses of logic, and missed opportunities, and begins to run out of gas at the halfway point when the killing gets repetitive and the plot bogs down. Interest is added by a strong current of social satire, however, especially in the way that the "Good Guy" dolls are marketed through a cartoon show, breakfast cereal, pajamas, and the like. The effects—a combination of midgets in suits and puppets—are excellent, making Chucky the scariest and easily most convincing "living doll" to grace the screen. The filmmakers are obviously making a bid for "Freddy" status with Chucky, and considering CHILD'S PLAY's success at the box office, we're likely to see him again.

p, David Kirschner; d, Tom Holland; w, Don Mancini, John Lafia, Tom Holland (based on a story by Don Mancini); ph, Bill Butler (Technicolor, Astro Color); ed, Edward Warschilka, Roy E. Peterson; m, Joe Renzetti.

**(PR:O    MPAA:R)**

## CHOPPING MALL**

(1986) 76m Concorde-Trinity/Concorde c (AKA: KILLBOTS; R.O.B.O.T.)

Kelli Maroney *(Allison Parks)*, Tony O'Dell *(Ferdy Meisel)*, John Terlesky *(Mike Brennan)*, Russell Todd *(Rick Stanton)*, Karrie Emerson *(Linda Stanton)*, Barbara Crampton *(Suzie Lynn)*, Nick Segal *(Greg Williams)*, Suzee Slater *(Leslee Todd)*, Mary Woronov *(Mary Bland)*, Paul Bartel *(Paul Bland)*, Dick Miller *(Walter Paisley)*, Gerrit Graham *(Technician Nessler)*, Mel Welles *(Cook)*, Angela Aames *(Miss Vanders)*, Paul Coufos *(Dr. Simon)*, Arthur Roberts *(Mr. Todd)*, Ace Mask, Will Gill, Jr. *(Janitors)*, Lenny Juliano *(Burglar)*, Lawrence Guy *(Dr. Carrington)*, Morgan Douglas *(Technician Marty)*, Toni Naples *(Bathing Beauty)*, Robert Greenberg *(Big Eater)*, Maurie Gallagher *(Girl in Restaurant)*.

The Park Plaza Mall has just installed the latest in security systems, three robots that cruise the corridors at night, armed with a variety of ways of subduing malefactors, including electric stun darts, lasers, and nasty-looking steel pincers. Needless to say, things go wrong when lightning strikes the control center on the roof, and the robots kill their supervising technicians. They then go out to patrol the mall, attacking four young couples partying in the furniture store, and kill them off in standard slasher film fashion. There is nothing original or especially interesting about this film, and the victims die in predictable order, according to their likableness and sexual habits. In-jokes abound throughout the film, ranging from appearances by Paul Bartel and Mary Woronov (repeating their EATING RAOUL parts), Dick Miller in his Walter Paisley role from BUCKET OF BLOOD (now reduced to a janitor), and Mel Welles of LITTLE SHOP OF HORRORS as a none-too-sanitary pizza cook, to a visit by the boys to Peckinpah's Sporting Goods store, from which they emerge looking like something out of THE WILD BUNCH. CHOPPING MALL had the potential to be more than it turned out to be, and at times it comes close to capturing something of the capitalism gone-amok theme of the similarly located DAWN OF THE DEAD, but it drops those overtones to become another wages-of-sin dead-teenager movie almost indistinguishable from a FRIDAY THE 13TH sequel. The robots are pretty neat, though.

p, Julie Corman; d, Jim Wynorski; w, Jim Wynorski, Steve Mitchell; ph, Tom Richmond (DeLuxe Color); ed, Leslie Rosenthal; m, Chuck Cirino.

(PR:O   MPAA:R)

## CHOSEN, THE*½

(1978, Brit./It.) 102m AIP c (AKA: HOLOCAUST 2,000)

Kirk Douglas *(Caine)*, Agostine Belli *(Sara)*, Simon Ward *(Angel)*, Anthony Quayle *(Prof. Griffith)*, Virginia McKenna *(Eva)*, Alexander Knox *(Meyer)*, Romolo Valli *(Msgr. Charrier)*, Massimo Foschi *(Assassin)*.

Kirk Douglas plays the chairman of the board of a powerful multinational corporation that builds nuclear power plants around the globe. After the tycoon is shaken by a nightmare wherein the world is destroyed by a seven-headed serpent, he discovers that his son (Simon Ward) is the Antichrist. As it happens, the little devil plans to wrest control of the corporation and destroy the Earth by making all the nuclear plants go boom. This lame rip-off of THE OMEN (1976) was directed by Alberto de Martino, who, four years previously, cribbed from THE EXORCIST (1973) for his tale of demonic possession, THE TEMPTER.

p, Edmundo Amati; d, Alberto de Martino; w, Sergio Donati, Aldo Di Martino, Michael Robson; ph, Enrico Menczer (Technicolor); ed, Vincenzo Tomassi; m, Ennio Morricone.

(PR:O   MPAA:R)

## CHRISTINE**½

(1983) 116m COL c

Keith Gordon *(Arnie Cunningham)*, John Stockwell *(Dennis Guilder)*, Alexandra Paul *(Leigh Cabot)*, Robert Prosky *(Will Darnell)*, Harry Dean Stanton *(Rudolph Junkins)*, Christine Belford *(Regina Cunningham)*, Roberts Blossom *(George LeBay)*, William Ostrander *(Buddy)*, David Spielberg *(Mr. Casey)*, Malcolm Danare *(Moochie)*, Steven Tash *(Rich)*, Stuart Charno *(Vandenberg)*, Kelly Preston *(Roseanne)*, Marc Poppel *(Chuck)*, Robert Barnell *(Michael Cunningham)*.

This slick and well-made, but strangely uninvolving horror film from John Carpenter stars a killer Plymouth Fury that has a will of its own. CHRISTINE's strong first half paints an insightful portrait of modern high school life as seen through the eyes of an unpopular nerd, Arnie (Keith Gordon). The status-seeking teen finally makes a bid for independence by getting himself a hip car, which he names "Christine," but, unfortunately, the car is demonically pos-

sessed and the evil automobile begins to take over its owner's personality. Up to this point the movie is fine, but the last half of the film degenerates into a tedious and repetitious car chase in which the driverless (?) Plymouth runs down all of Arnie's enemies (shades of THE CAR). Robert Prosky is fine as the crotchety garage owner; Harry Dean Stanton is totally wasted in a thankless part that could have been played by an extra. The special effects by which the car heals itself are impressive, but much too long. Basically, CHRISTINE just boils down to another frustratingly average adaptation of increasingly weak Stephen King novels that hit Hollywood like a bad rash in 1983.

p, Richard Kobritz; d, John Carpenter; w, Bill Phillips (based on the novel by Stephen King); ph, Donald Morgan (Panavision, Metrocolor); ed, Marion Rothman; m, John Carpenter, Alan Howarth.

(PR:C-O   MPAA:R)

## CIRCUS OF HORRORS***

(1960, Brit.) 88m AIP c

Anton Diffring *(Dr. Schuler)*, Erika Remberg *(Elissa)*, Yvonne Monlaur *(Nicole)*, Donald Pleasence *(Vanet)*, Jane Hylton *(Angela)*, Kenneth Griffith *(Martin)*, Conrad Phillips *(Inspector Ames)*, Jack Gwillim *(Supt. Andrews)*, Vanda Hudson *(Magda)*, Yvonne Romain *(Melina)*, Colette Wilde *(Evelyn Morley)*, William Mervyn *(Dr. Morley)*, John Merivale *(Edward Finsbury)*, Carla Challoner *(Nicole as a Child)*, Peter Swanwick *(Inspector Knopf)*, Walter Gotell *(Von Gruber)*, Chris Christian *(Ringmaster)*, Sasha Coco *(Luis)*, Jack Carson *(Chief Eagle Eye)*, Glyn Houston *(Barker)*, Malcolm Watson *(Elderly Man)*, Kenneth Warren, Fred Haggerty *(Roustabouts)*.

Just after WW II, a brilliant-but-demented German plastic surgeon (Anton Diffring) is forced to flee England after a socialite female patient removes her bandages too early and finds her face horribly scarred. In France, the surgeon changes his name to Schuler and continues to practice clandestinely, using a traveling circus he has acquired as a front. Sexually attracted to disfigured women, Schuler seeks out badly scarred female criminals (thieves, prostitutes, murderers) and fixes their faces, making them his beautiful concubines. In return, the grateful women agree to work in his circus as aerialists, lion tamers, and equestrienne ballerinas. If they attempt to leave, however, they are met with fatal "accidents" that occur before the horrified crowd. British film studio Anglo Amalgamated produced three remarkably similar and disturbing horror pictures during 1959-60, all of which have a perverse sexual obsession with voyeurism, disfigurement, and murder. Arthur Crabtroe's HORRORS OF THE BLACK MUSEUM (1959), was followed by CIRCUS OF HORRORS, and then Michael Powell's magnificently depraved masterpiece PEEPING TOM (1960). CIRCUS OF HORRORS, while quite good, is the weakest of the lot, marred by some bad direction, poorly integrated circus footage, and two "dangerous animals"—a dancing bear and a gorilla—that are obviously stuntmen in ratty costumes.

p, Julian Wintle, Leslie Parkyn; d, Sidney Hayers; w,

## CIRCUS OF HORRORS—

George Baxt; ph, Douglas Slocombe (Eastmancolor); ed, Reginald Mills; m, Franz Reizenstein, Muir Mathieson.

**(PR:O MPAA:NR)**

## CITY OF THE WALKING DEAD*

(1983, Sp./It.) 92m 21st Century c (AKA: NIGHTMARE CITY; NIGHTMARE)

Mel Ferrer, Hugo Stiglitz, Laura Trotter, Francisco Rabal, Maria Rosaria Omaggio, Sonia Viviani, Eduardo Fajardo, Manolo Zarzo, Alejandro de Enciso.

Filmed in 1980, but not released in the US until 1983, Umberto Lenzi's CITY OF THE WALKING DEAD is another dumb Italian zombie film that suffers from some terribly meandering direction. The movie opens as a plane lands at an airport and the doors open to unleash a horde of flesh-eating zombies that terrorize the city. It seems that a professor on board the flight was suffering from radiation sickness, which in turn infected the other passengers. Even the military cannot stop the multitude of zombies, which are multiplying faster than they can be killed. Bloody and boring. Lenzi even falls back on the "It was all a dream" ending.

p, Diego Alchimede, Luis Mendez; d, Umberto Lenzi; w, Antonio Corti, Piero Regnoli, Luis Maria Delgado; ph, Hans Burman.

**(PR:O MPAA:NR)**

## CLASS OF NUKE 'EM HIGH*

(1986) 92m TNT-Troma/Troma c

Janelle Brady *(Chrissy)*, Gilbert Brenton *(Warren)*, Robert Prichard *(Spike)*, R.L. Ryan *(Mr. Paley)*, James Nugent Vernon *(Eddie)*, Brad Dunker *(Gonzo)*, Gary Schneider *(Pete)*, Theo Cohan *(Muffey)*, Gary Rosenblatt *(Greg)*, Mary Taylor *(Judy)*, Rick Howard *(Spud)*, Heather McMahan *(Taru)*, Chris McNamee *(Joe)*, Anthony Ventola *(George)*, Arthur Lorenz *(Dewy)*, Donald O'Toole *(Mr. Westly)*, Seth Oliver Hawkins *(Lumpy)*, Larae Dean *(Cathy)*, Reuben Guss *(Mr. Hyde)*, Diana DeVries *(Miss Stein)*, Lauraine Austin *(Ms. Austin)*, Dianna-Jean Flaherty *(Denise)*, Sloane Herz, Lily Hayes Kaufman *(Tromaville Kiddies)*, Don Costello *(Nuclear Worker)*, Frank Cole *(Mr. Flint)*, Sam Scardino *(Mr. Hanson)*, Barbara Ann Missbach *(Barbi)*, Andy Newton *(Beetovan)*, Skip Hamra *(Nuclear Worker in Basement)*, Donnie Reynolds *(Tom)*, Joe Severino *(Jimmy)*, Jeffrey Grossi *(Bill)*, Maezie Murphy *(Mrs. Crabtree)*, Rick Collins *(Ron Simms)*, Bob Schenck *(Harry)*, Belle Maria Wheat *(Mrs. Murphy)*, Libby Miller *(Mugged Woman)*, Ron Giles *(Dr. Herz)*.

When last we visited Tromaville, site of 1985's THE TOXIC AVENGER, the town was rocked by strange happenings after a harassed young man fell into a vat of hazardous chemical waste and became a super-strong monster. Now Tromaville, the self-dubbed "Toxic Waste Capital of the World," experiences another series of catastrophes after a leak at the nearby nuclear power plant infects the water supply. At Tromaville High, a student drinks from a water fountain, starts spewing green gunk, and later in class begins foaming at the mouth and ears, attacking a classmate before diving out a window and dissolving into a steaming pile of noxious jello. Former honor society kids are suddenly transformed into a vicious gang of heavy metal creeps, who call themselves the Cretins, who terrorize the school. Meanwhile, a monster grows in a vat of toxic waste in the basement ... CLASS OF NUKE 'EM HIGH does have a kind of loopy charm and ingenuousness that keeps its aggressive stupidity from being too offensive. The violence is explicit to the point of silliness (one memorable moment of gore occurs as the monster punches right through a girl's head, then wags its fingers to show us they came out the back of her skull). There are a number of good lines, including the nuclear plant manager solemnly telling reporters, "This plant will be here long after most of you are gone." The technical credits and production values are up to Troma's usual low standards, and the acting is laughably wooden, but it's all harmless enough, and guaranteed to make money for Troma.

p, Lloyd Kaufman, Michael Herz; d, Richard W. Haines, Lloyd Kaufman; w, Richard W. Haines, Mark Rudnitsky, Lloyd Kaufman, Stuart Strutin (based on a story by Richard W. Haines); ph, Michael Mayers (TVC color); ed, Richard W. Haines; m, Michael Lattanzi, Biohazard.

**(PR:O MPAA:R)**

## COLOR ME BLOOD RED*½

(1965) 74m Box Office Spectaculars/Jacquelin c

Don Joseph *(Adam Sorg)*, Candi Conder *(April)*, Elyn Warner *(Gigi)*, Scott H. Hall *(Farnsworth)*, Jerome Eden *(Rolf)*, Patricia Lee *(Sydney)*, James Jackel *(Jack)*, Iris Marshall *(Mrs. Carter)*, William Harris *(Gregorovich)*, Cathy Collins *(Mitri)*.

COLOR ME BLOOD RED, part three of Herschell Gordon Lewis' filmed-in-Florida gore trilogy (BLOOD FEAST; TWO THOUSAND MANIACS), concerns an artist, Adam Sorg (Don Joseph), who gains fame when he begins to use his own blood on the canvas to get a perfect shade of red. Predictably, he becomes a bit anemic and turns to killing his models for their blood, using a number of grisly methods to dispatch them. A blatant rip-off of Roger Corman's BUCKET OF BLOOD (as Lewis openly acknowledges), this was the last film for the partnership of producer David F. Friedman and Lewis. Friedman claims that the two had a falling out while shooting this picture and Lewis walked, leaving Friedman to finish it by himself. In any case, the men went their separate ways, Friedman back to nudie films like THE LUSTFUL TURK (1968) and THAR SHE BLOWS (1969), while Lewis divided his time between both nudies (THE GIRL, THE BODY, AND THE PILL, 1967; LINDA AND ABILENE, 1969) and gore (A TASTE OF BLOOD, 1967; THE GRUESOME TWOSOME, 1967; THE WIZARD OF GORE, 1970).

p, David F. Friedman; d, Herschell Gordon Lewis; w, Herschell Gordon Lewis; ph, Herschell Gordon Lewis; ed, Robert Sinise.

**(PR:O MPAA:NR)**

## CONFESSIONAL, THE*

(1975, Brit.) 104m Atlas c (AKA: HOUSE OF MORTAL SIN)

Anthony Sharp *(Meldrum)*, Susan Penhaligan *(Jenny)*, Stephanie Beacham *(Vanessa)*, Norman Eshley *(Bernard)*, Sheila Keith *(Miss Brabazon)*, Hilda Barry *(Mrs. Meldrum)*, Stewart Beven *(Terry)*, Julia McCarthy *(Mrs. Davey)*, Jon Yule *(Robert)*, Mervyn Johns *(Father Duggan)*, Victor Winding *(Dr. Gaudio)*, Kim Butcher *(Valerie)*, Bill Kerr *(Davey)*, Ivor Salter *(Gravedigger)*, Jack Allen, Jane Hayward, Andrew Sachs, Austin King, Melinda Clancy.

This trashy anti-Catholic horror entry comes from director Peter Walker, who was also responsible for such slimy classics as FRIGHTMARE (1974) and HOUSE OF WHIPCORD (1974). Once again attacking the establishment, Walker presents us with a demented priest (Anthony Sharp) who records the confessions of young women in order to blackmail them. When a few unfortunate parishioners stumble upon the priest's activities, he kills them, using a variety of religious icons. One victim—played by Stephanie Beacham—is strangled with a rosary, another has his skull bashed in with an incense burner, and the priest even kills his own mother with a poisoned host! Since Walker fails to bring any sensibility, other than the merely exploitative, to the grotesque material, this must be considered pretty irredeemable stuff, even for a horror film.

p, Peter Walker; d, Peter Walker; w, David McGillivray; ph, Peter Jessop; m, Stanley Myers.

**(PR:O MPAA:R)**

## CONQUEROR WORM, THE****

(1968, Brit.) 87m Tigon British/AIP c (AKA: EDGAR ALLAN POE'S CONQUEROR WORM; GB: WITCHFINDER GENERAL)

Vincent Price *(Matthew Hopkins)*, Ian Ogilvy *(Richard Marshall)*, Rupert Davies *(John Lowes)*, Hilary Dwyer *(Sara)*, Robert Russell *(John Stearne)*, Patrick Wymark *(Oliver Cromwell)*, Wilfrid Brambell *(Master Loach)*, Nicky Henson *(Trooper Swallow)*, Tony Selby *(Salter)*, Bernard Kay *(Fisherman)*, Godfrey James *(Webb)*, Michael Beint *(Capt. Gordon)*, John Trenaman *(Trooper Harcourt)*, Bill Maxwell *(Trooper Gifford)*, Morris Jar *(Paul)*, Maggie Kimberley *(Elizabeth Clark)*, Peter Haigh *(Lavenham Magistrate)*, John Kidd *(Magistrate)*, Hira Talfrey *(Hanged Woman)*, Ann Tirard *(Old Woman)*, Peter Thomas *(Farrier)*, Edward Palmer *(Shepherd)*, David Webb *(Jailer)*, Paul Dawkins *(Farmer)*, Lee Peters *(Infantry Sergeant)*, Martin Terry *(Hoxne Innkeeper)*, Jack Lynn *(Brandeston Innkeeper)*, Beaufoy Milton *(Priest)*, Toby Lennon *(Old Man)*, Gillian Aldham *(Young Woman in Cell)*, Paul Ferris *(Young Husband)*.

During the English Civil War, Matthew Hopkins (Vincent Price) is appointed "Witchfinder General" by the Puritans under Cromwell and empowered to travel the countryside with his henchman, Stearne (Robert Russell), collecting a fee for each witch from whom he extracts a confession.

They ride into one town where the village priest, Lowes (Rupert Davies), is accused, and proceed to torture him by driving steel spikes into his flesh, looking for "The Devil's Mark." Sara (Hilary Dwyer), Lowes' niece, offers herself to the pair, but Stearne just rapes her and hangs her uncle anyway. Marshall (Ian Ogilvy), her fiance, is a soldier with the Royalists who has sworn to protect her, and when he learns what has happened he leaves the army to hunt down Hopkins and Stearne. This masterful study in terror was directed by Michael Reeves, who made just three films before killing himself in 1969 at age 25 (various reports cite an overdose of pills, a car crash, and a fall from a window as the means). Reeves' films, THE SHE-BEAST; THE SORCERERS; and THE CONQUEROR WORM—the best of the three—all show a thoroughly depressing world in which evil runs rampant and corrupts the heroes who fight it. The performances are all quite good, with Price giving one of his finest portrayals as an intelligent, civilized madman in a place and time that encourages him to act out his darkest impulses. There was a real Matthew Hopkins, Cromwell's Witchfinder General, who, with his assistant Stearne, killed some 200 alleged witches in 1645-46 before he retired to write his memoirs and died in bed the following year. This profoundly disturbing film was played off on the American market as just another entry in AIP's Vincent Price/Edgar Allan Poe series (like THE RAVEN or THE PIT AND THE PENDULUM), with Price reading Poe's poem "The Conqueror Worm" over the opening and closing titles.

p, Arnold Louis Miller; d, Michael Reeves; w, Michael Reeves, Tom Baker, Louis M. Heyward (based on the novel *Witchfinder General* by Ronald Bassett); ph, John Coquillon (Eastmancolor); ed, Howard Lanning; m, Paul Ferris.

**(PR:O MPAA:NR)**

## CORPSE GRINDERS, THE*½

(1972) 72m Geneni c

Sean Kenney *(Dr. Howard Glass)*, Monika Kelly *(Angie Robinson)*, Sanford Mitchell *(Landau)*, J. Byron Foster *(Maltby)*, Warren Ball *(Caleb)*, Ann Noble *(Cleo)*, Vince Barbi *(Monk)*, Harry Lovejoy *(The Neighbor)*, Earl Burnam *(De Sisto)*, Zenna Foster *(Mrs. Babcock)*, Ray Dannis *(Babcock)*, Charles Fox *(Willie)*, Stephen Lester *(Mortician)*, William Kirschner *(B.K.)*, George Bowden *(David)*, Don Ellis *(Factory Workman)*, Mike Garrison *(Assistant to De Sisto)*, Andy Collings *(De Sisto's Secretary)*, Mary Ellen Burke *(Annie)*, Curt Matson *(Paul, The Stranger)*, Drucilla Hoy *(Tessie)*.

This hilariously bad horror-comedy from Ted V. Mikels concerns the owners of the Lotus Cat Food Company (Sanford Mitchell and J. Byron Foster), who become enraged after their financial backer pulls out of the deal immediately after construction of the cat-food factory. For revenge, the duo push the man into their meat grinder (an ineptly constructed papier-mache prop) and mix his flesh in with the kitty chow. The new recipe is a big hit among the local felines and the cat-food kings must now provide fresh bodies for the grinders. Meanwhile, the cats that have eaten the flavor-enhanced food begin viciously attacking their masters. Although gory, Mikels' approach to the grotesque material is satiric and gleeful in a self-consciously gross way. The film's basic ineptitude, cheaply produced and poorly shot, makes it all the more enjoyable for students of Le Bad Cinema.

p, Ted V. Mikels; d, Ted V. Mikels; w, Arch Hall, Joseph L. Cranston; ph, Bill Anneman (Eastmancolor); ed, Ted V. Mikels.

**(PR:O   MPAA:NR)**

### CORPSE VANISHES, THE**½

(1942) 64m MON bw

Bela Lugosi (Dr. Lorenz), Luana Walters (Pat Hunter), Tristram Coffin (Dr. Foster), Elizabeth Russell (Countess), Minerva Urecal (Fagah), Kenneth Harlan (Keenan), Vince Barnett (Sandy), Joan Barclay (Alice), Frank Moran (Angel).

Bela Lugosi's career was well on the skids by 1942, as this programmer testifies, but the film has a genuinely weird quality that makes it well worth investigating. Lugosi plays a mad botanist who kidnaps virgin brides from the altar to provide glandular injections needed to keep his 80-year-old wife (Elizabeth Russell) fresh and young. Assisting him are an old woman and her half-wit son (Minerva Urecal and Frank Moran) and a dwarf named Toby (Angelo Rossitto). A girl reporter (Luana Walters) finally cracks the case. What with a gothic castle, a crazy botanist, poison orchids, virgin brides, glandular injections, an old hag, and a dwarf, this is a pretty strange film. Monogram even managed to work a hint of Lugosi's Dracula image into the proceedings by having him and Russell sleep in matching coffins. This created a problem during shooting, however, for when it came time for the couple to retire for the night, Russell was afraid to step into the coffin and refused to do the scene. A double was used instead. This is also one of several films that paired Lugosi with dwarf actor Rossitto; others include BLACK DRAGONS (1942) and Lugosi's only color film, SCARED TO DEATH (1947)—another very odd movie, which would make a nice double-bill with this one.

p, Sam Katzman, Jack Dietz; d, Wallace Fox; w, Harvey Gates, Sam Robins, Gerald Schnitzer; ph, Art Reed; ed, Robert Golden.

**(PR:A   MPAA:NR)**

### CORRIDORS OF BLOOD***

(1958, Brit.) 85m Producers Associates/MGM bw (AKA: DOCTOR FROM SEVEN DIALS, THE)

Boris Karloff (Dr. Thomas Bolton), Betta St. John (Susan), Finley Currie (Dr. Matheson), Christopher Lee (Resurrection Joe), Francis Matthews (Dr. Jonathan Bolton), Adrienne Corri (Rachel), Francis De Wolff (Black Ben), Basil Dignam (Chairman), Frank Pettingell (Dr. Blount), Marian Spencer (Mrs. Matheson), Carl Bernard (Ned The Cow), Yvonne Warren (Rosa), Charles Lloyd Pack (Hardcastle), Robert Raglan (Wilkes), John Gabriel

(Dispenser), Nigel Green (Inspector Donovan), Howard Lang (Chief Inspector), Julian D'Albie (Bald Man), Roddy Hughes (Man With Watch).

Boris Karloff stars as Dr. Thomas Bolton, a humanitarian London doctor who is attempting to develop a workable anesthetic for the pain and suffering involved in surgery in the days when hospitals were like torture chambers. Unfortunately, he performs his experiments on himself and slowly becomes addicted to drugs. Thinking he has found a proper anesthetic, he performs a demonstration of his pain-killing gas for an audience of physicians and students. Unexpectedly, the gas wears off too soon, and the patient awakens during the operation and bolts from the table, attempting to attack the audience. Bolton is fired from his position and begins to become desperate for drugs, since his access to them is now cut off. In a seedy tavern, he meets shady gravediggers Black Ben (Francis De Wolff) and Resurrection Joe (Christopher Lee), who sell cadavers to hospitals. They lure Bolton into their scheme by offering to supply him with drugs if he will sign phony death certificates for them. The doctor reluctantly agrees, but soon finds himself embroiled in a murder. Shot back to back with THE HAUNTED STRANGLER, CORRIDORS OF BLOOD was produced in England in 1958, but wasn't released in the US until 1962, after bit player Lee had become a horror film superstar in his own right in the excellent Hammer films. Although this film is surprisingly gruesome, Karloff maintains his dignity throughout and contributes yet another memorable and sympathetic performance.

p, John Croydon, Charles Vetter; d, Robert Day; w, Jean Scott Rogers; ph, Geoffrey Faithfull; ed, Peter Mayhew; m, Buxton Orr.

**(PR:C-O   MPAA:NR)**

### COUNT DRACULA**

(1971, Sp./It./Ger./Brit.) 100m Filmer Compagnia Cinematografica-Phoenix-Korona c

Christopher Lee (Dracula), Herbert Lom (Van Helsing), Klaus Kinski (Renfield), Soledad Miranda, Maria Rohm, Fred Williams, Jack Taylor, Paul Muller.

For years, Christopher Lee wanted to play Dracula according to Bram Stoker's description in the novel, and with much fanfare he announced that he was finally going to do it here under the direction of Jesus Franco. One of the most prolific filmmakers working in the genre (reportedly, there are over 130 feature films to his credit), Franco is, unfortunately, also one of the worst. Shot in Spain, COUNT DRACULA was given the typically cheap Franco production, suffers from an awful and unfaithful screenplay, and contains some laughably clumsy camerawork. Lee, however, does a fairly good job under the circumstances, sporting white hair and a bushy moustache. His Dracula is an old man who grows younger with each sup of blood. Herbert Lom plays Dr. Van Helsing, and Klaus Kinski—who would later play the vampire in Werner Herzog's NOSFERATU (1979)—steals the show as Renfield, raving incoherently and munching insects in his padded cell (some of his scenes are ruined, regretfully, by the shadow of the camera on the cell wall). Everyone involved agrees it was a major disappointment, but Lee contends that, in spite of the flaws, it was the nearest approach to Stoker's story yet made.

p, Harry Alan Towers; d, Jesus Franco; w, Jesus Franco, August Finochi, Alan Towers, Carlo Fadda, Milo G. Cuccia, Dietmar Behnke (based on the novel by Bram Stoker); ph, Manuel Marion (Panavision, Eastmancolor); m, Bruno Nicolai.

**(PR:C-O MPAA:NR)**

## COUNT YORGA, VAMPIRE***

(1970) 90m AIP c

Robert Quarry *(Count Yorga)*, Roger Perry *(Hayes)*, Michael Murphy *(Paul)*, Michael Macready *(Michael)*, Donna Anders *(Donna)*, Judith Lang *(Erica)*, Edward Walsh *(Brudah)*, Julie Conners *(Cleo)*, Paul Hansen *(Peter)*, Sybil Scotford *(Judy)*, Marsha Jordan *(Mother)*, Deborah Darnell *(Vampire)*, Erica Macready *(Nurse)*, George Macready *(Narrator)*.

This modern-day vampire movie, set in Los Angeles, was a surprise hit when it was released and spawned a quick sequel, THE RETURN OF COUNT YORGA. Former child star Robert Quarry stars as the title count, who owns a huge Victorian mansion just outside LA. Considered a hip eccentric, Yorga holds seances at his home to attract young women. He is, of course, a vampire, and quickly adds Donna (Donna Anders) and Erica (Judith Lang) to his harem of vampire brides. Erica's boy friend, Paul (Michael Murphy), goes after Yorga, never to return, while Donna's beau, Michael (played by producer Michael Macready), enlists Dr. Hayes (Roger Perry) in the fight to take the castle and rescue the girls from the clutches of the evil vampire. Although rated "PG," the film is filled with shocking moments—such as when Paul stumbles upon Erica in the process of devouring a house cat—and Quarry does a credible and energetic job as the vampire. Quarry, in fact, proved so popular that he began a minicareer in 70s horror films, appearing in the YORGA sequel, opposite Vincent Price in DR. PHIBES RISES AGAIN (1974) and MADHOUSE (1974), and in the zombie film SUGAR HILL (1974). Producer-actor Macready is the son of veteran actor George Macready, best known as Rita Hayworth's sadistic husband in GILDA (1946). The senior Macready, who owned a Los Angeles art gallery with partner Vincent Price, provided the narration for COUNT YORGA, VAMPIRE.

p, Michael Macready; d, Bob Kelljan; w, Bob Kelljan; ph, Arch Archambault (Movielab Color); ed, Tony De Zarraga; m, Bill Marx.

**(PR:C MPAA:GP)**

## CRAWLSPACE*

(1986) 77m Charles Band/Empire c

Klaus Kinski *(Dr. Karl Gunther)*, Talia Balsam *(Lori Bancroft)*, Barbara Whinnery *(Harriet)*, Sally Brown *(Martha)*, Carol Francis *(Jess)*, Tane *(Sophie)*, Jack Heller *(Alfred)*, Kenneth Robert Shippy *(Joseph Steiner)*.

Klaus Kinski has made a career of playing homicidal nutcases on the big screen, whether it be in such exploitative cheapies as SCHIZOID or in such brilliant pictures as AGUIRRE, THE WRATH OF GOD and FITZCARRALDO. This time he plays Dr. Karl Gunther, the demented son of a Nazi war criminal. A physician and expert in euthanasia, Gunther runs a safe-looking boarding house for nubile young starlets. Behind the walls, however, lies a maze of crawl spaces through which Gunther slinks on his belly. For cheap thrills, he peeks through the heating vents to watch the girls undressing. To give them a little scare, he bangs on the vents, and later blames the racket on rats. But Gunther is not simply a voyeur, he is also perversely addicted to violent, sadistic, torturous murder. The good doctor *really* begins to get wacky, however, when Nazi hunter Lori Bancroft (Talia Balsam) starts snooping around. Relying on very real fears of Naziism and memories of concentration camp atrocities to heighten its horrors, CRAWLSPACE is almost a bit too depraved. Kinski's performance is, however, somewhat compelling. Gunther has convinced himself that he is meant to kill, and, after each murder, ritualistically puts a bullet into the chamber of a revolver, spins the barrel, and puts the gun to his head. He pulls the trigger, and hearing only a click, finds his life is spared again. Reading this as a sign to continue his killing, Kinski utters the words "So be it." Not as gory as most slasher entries, CRAWLSPACE is instead simply ugly and disturbing.

p, Roberto Bessi; d, David Schmoeller; w, David Schmoeller; ph, Sergio Salvati; ed, Bert Glastein; m, Pino Donaggio.

**(PR:O MPAA:R)**

## CRAZE zero

(1974, Brit.) 96m WB c (AKA: INFERNAL IDOL, THE)

Jack Palance *(Neal Mottram)*, Diana Dors *(Dolly Newman)*, Julie Ege *(Helena)*, Edith Evans *(Aunt Louise)*, Hugh Griffith *(Solicitor)*, Trevor Howard *(Supt. Bellamy)*, Michael Jayston *(Detective Sgt. Wall)*, Suzy Kendall *(Sally)*, Martin Potter *(Ronnie)*, Percy Herbert *(Detective Russet)*, David Warbeck *(Detective Wilson)*, Kathleen Byron *(Muriel)*, Venecia Day *(Dancer)*, Marianne Stone *(Barmaid)*, Dean Harris *(Ronnie's Friend)*.

This awful mad-stalker effort wastes a good cast on mundane material, but what else should one expect from the producer and director who gave us TROG (1970)? Neal Mottram (Jack Palance) is an antique shop owner who prays to the African idol Chuku, which he keeps in his basement. Believing that the god will reward him with riches if he makes live sacrifices, Mottram begins luring prostitutes to his shop and sacrifices them. Producer Herman Cohen presided over the decline of Joan Crawford's career with such pictures as BERSERK! and the aforementioned TROG.

p, Herman Cohen; d, Freddie Francis; w, Aben Kandel, Herman Cohen (based on the novel *Infernal Idol* by Henry

Seymour); ph, John Wilcox (Technicolor); ed, Henry Richardson; m, John Scott.

(PR:C    MPAA:R)

## CRAZIES, THE****

(1973) 103m Cambist c (AKA: CODE NAME: TRIXIE)

Lane Carroll *(Judy)*, W.G. McMillan *(David)*, Harold Wayne Jones *(Clank)*, Lloyd Hollar *(Col. Pockem)*, Richard Liberty *(Artie)*, Lynn Lowry *(Kathie)*, Richard France *(Dr. Watts)*, Edith Bell *(Woman Lab Technician)*, Harry Spillman *(Maj. Ryder)*, Will Disney *(Dr. Brookmyre)*, W.L. Thunhurst, Jr. *(Brubaker)*, Leland Starnes *(Shelby)*, A.C. MacDonald *(Gen. Bowden)*, Robert J. McCully *(Hawks)*, Robert Karlowsky *(Sheriff)*.

Until the advent of home video, this excellent George Romero effort went virtually unseen by the public because of its rotten theatrical distribution and total failure at the box office. Reminiscent of NIGHT OF THE LIVING DEAD, the story centers on an Army cargo plane carrying an untested chemical warfare virus that crashes near the small town of Evans City, Pennsylvania. Since the virus—which causes its victims either to die instantly or to become homicidal maniacs—is top-secret and has no cure, the government dispatches the army to isolate the spread of the virus by quarantining the entire town. Without warning, soldiers dressed in white, bacteria-proof suits and gas masks, armed with automatic weapons, invade Evans City and scare the inhabitants by herding them into the local high school. A group of people not yet affected by the virus attempt to escape from the military and get out of town, while scientists work around the clock to find a cure. Even more relevant now that it was 17 years ago, THE CRAZIES is a nightmarish expose of government omnipotence and paranoia. Romero paints a bleak picture of a bureaucracy that has nothing but contempt for the lives of private citizens, zealously harbors secrets, and gives unbelievable power to a basically incompetent military. The chaos of the situation is brilliantly conveyed by Romero, who keeps his characters—and the audience—off kilter through the entire movie. Paranoia runs rampant—who can separate the crazies from the normals when the whole world seems to have gone mad? One of Romero's most underrated efforts, THE CRAZIES is highly recommended.

p, Alvin C. Croft; d, George A. Romero; w, George A. Romero (based on an original script by Paul McCollough); ph, S. William Hinzman; ed, George A. Romero; m, Bruce Roberts.

(PR:O    MPAA:NR)

## CREATURE FROM BLACK LAKE, THE**

(1976) 95m Howco International c

Jack Elam *(Joe Canton)*, Dub Taylor *(Grandpa Bridges)*, Dennis Fimple *(Pahoo)*, John David Carson *(Rives)*, Bill Thurman *(Sheriff Billy Carter)*, Becky Smiser *(Becky Carter)*, Roy Tatum *(Fred/The Creature)*, Michelle Willingham *(Michelle)*, Jim McCullough, Jr. *(Orville Bridges)*, Evelyn Hindricks *(Mrs. Bridges)*, Roger Pancake *(H.B.)*, Karen

Brooks *(Orville's Mother)*, Chase Tatum *(Little Orville)*, Bob Kyle *(Rufus)*, Catherine McClenny *(Waitress)*, J.N. Houck, Jr. *(Dr. Burch)*.

Despite its obvious handicaps, this ultra-low-budget Bigfoot movie—a subgenre that always seem to suffer from a lack of production funds—is fairly watchable. When a Bigfoot is reported to be stomping around a Louisiana lake, two college students load up their van and head off to confirm the sighting. Entertaining performances by Jack Elam (ONCE UPON A TIME IN THE WEST) and Dub Taylor (BONNIE AND CLYDE) contribute greatly to the entertainment value. A hint of the production's lightheartedness can be found in a cast list that includes a sheriff named after then-new First Brother Billy Carter. Cinematography fans take note: this film is an early effort from Dean Cundey, who would go on to shoot such John Carpenter movies as HALLOWEEN; THE FOG; ESCAPE FROM NEW YORK; and THE THING, and who would later work with Robert Zemeckis on BACK TO THE FUTURE and WHO FRAMED ROGER RABBIT.

p, Jim McCullough, Sr.; d, Joy Houck, Jr.; w, Jim McCullough, Jr.; ph, Dean Cundey; m, Jaime Mendoza-Nava.

(PR:C    MPAA:PG)

## CREATURE FROM THE BLACK LAGOON***½

(1954) 79m UNIV bw

Richard Carlson *(David Reed)*, Julie Adams *(Kay Lawrence)*, Richard Denning *(Mark Williams)*, Antonio Moreno *(Carl Maia)*, Nestor Paiva *(Lucas)*, Whit Bissell *(Edwin Thompson)*, Ben Chapman *(Gill-Man)*, Harry Escalante *(Chico)*, Bernie Gozier *(Zee)*, Sydney Mason *(Dr. Matos)*, Julio Lopez *(Tomas)*, Rodd Redwing *(Louis)*.

While searching for fossils in the Amazonian jungle, a scientific expedition encounters a prehistoric half-man, half-amphibian that falls in love with Kay (Julia Adams), the lone female in the party. The scientists drug and capture the creature, but it later escapes, kills half the expedition, and kidnaps Kay. Head scientist David Reed (Richard Carlson) must then track the creature to its underwater lair, the Black Lagoon. Imbued with great atmosphere by director Jack Arnold, the film is genuinely frightening, but also elicits a certain amount of pathos for the creature, reminiscent of that that goes out to the unfortunate KING KONG. The creation of Bud Westmore and Jack Kevan, the creature was played on land by Ben Chapman, with swimming champ Ricou Browning taking over in the underwater sequences. Browning had to hold his breath for four minutes at a time because the tight-fitting suit did not permit the use of an aqua lung. The film was originally shot in 3-D but has been rarely seen in that format, though in the early 1980s, a few independent television stations attempted 3-D showings with the aid of special glasses. The results, however, were disappointing. Two sequels followed: REVENGE OF THE CREATURE and THE CREATURE WALKS AMONG US.

p, William Alland; d, Jack Arnold; w, Harry Essex Arthur

Ross (based on a story by Maurice Zimm); ph, William E. Snyder (in 3-D), James C. Havens; ed, Ted Kent.

**(PR:A MPAA:NR)**

## CREATURE FROM THE HAUNTED SEA**½

(1961) 63m Filmgroup bw

Anthony Carbone *(Renzo Capeto)*, Betsey Jones-Moreland *(Mary-Belle)*, Robert Towne *(Sparks Moran)*, Edmundo Rivera Alvarez *(Col Tostada)*, Robert Bean *(Jack)*, Sonya Noemi *(Mango)*, Beach Dickerson, Roger Corman.

This entertaining quickie from Roger Corman could have been called ""The Hood Who Cried Sea Monster." American criminal Renzo Capeto (Anthony Carbone) helps some loyalists escape from a revolution-torn Caribbean island with a cargo of cash. Blinded by greed, he kills the fleeing men and blames their deaths on a legendary sea monster. Nobody buys his explanation, however, until a real sea monster starts chomping up everyone in sight. CREATURE FROM THE HAUNTED SEA was made in the Corman tradition—quick, cheap, and using the same cast and crew as two previous island films, THE BATTLE OF BLOOD ISLAND and LAST WOMAN ON EARTH. Corman trivia buffs may be interested to know that Monte Hellman (TWO LANE BLACKTOP) directed the pre-credits sequence, and that screenwriter Robert Towne (CHINATOWN; TEQUILA SUNRISE) appears as an actor under the pseudonym Edward Wain.

p, Roger Corman; d, Roger Corman; w, Charles Griffith; ph, Jacques Marquette; ed, Angela Scellars; m, Fred Katz.

**(PR:A MPAA:NR)**

## CREEPERS***

(1985, It.) 83m Dacufilm/New Line c (PHENOMENA)

Jennifer Connelly *(Jennifer Corvino)*, Donald Pleasence *(John McGregor)*, Fausta Avelli, Marta Biuso, Sophie Bourchier, Paola Grooper, Ninke Hielkema, Mitzy Orsini, Geraldine Thomas *(Schoolgirls)*, Daria Nicolodi, Dalila Di Lazzaro, Patrick Bauchau, Fiore Argento, Federica Mastroianni, Fiorenza Tessari, Mario Donatone, Francesca Ottaviani, Michele Soavi, Franco Trevisi, Tanga the Chimpanzee.

Italian slasher-movie king Dario Argento's first English-language film is another stylish, if somewhat mindless, horror-thriller. Jennifer (Jennifer Connelly) is a teenager who has the ability to communicate telepathically with insects: bees crawl on her hand harmlessly; fireflies guide her way at night. The area she lives in is being terrorized by a psychotic killer who has been murdering coeds and making off with their decapitated bodies. Desperate for clues, a police inspector visits an eminent entomologist (Donald Pleasence), and eventually he and Jennifer team to find the killer. Released in Europe in 1984 as PHENOMENA, Argento's weird thriller was a huge box-office hit, and New Line Cinema picked up the US release rights, cut 28 minutes from the film, and retitled it CREEPERS. The resultant US version is still quite bizarre and contains some

very suspenseful moments. Although Argento's plot is often confused and grotesque, he has a remarkably energetic visual style (mobile camera, slow-motion, careful lighting, creative editing) that is never boring. Pleasence manages to hold his usual scenery-chewing instincts in check for this performance, but Connelly, who was so wonderful in Sergio Leone's ONCE UPON A TIME IN AMERICA (1984), seems out of place here. Regrettably, Argento miscalculates with his musical score. While most of the incidental music, provided by Argento's group, The Goblin (who contributed an effective, offbeat score to George Romero's DAWN OF THE DEAD), works well, some of the best suspense scenes are marred by the teeth-jarring sounds of such obnoxious heavy metal bands as Iron Maiden and Motorhead.

p, Dario Argento; d, Dario Argento; w, Dario Argento, Franco Ferrini; ph, Romano Albani (Panavision, Technicolor); ed, Franco Fraticelli; m, The Goblin.

**(PR:O MPAA:R)**

## CREEPING FLESH, THE***

(1973, Brit.) 91m Tigon British World Film/COL c

Christopher Lee *(James Hildern)*, Peter Cushing *(Emmanuel Hildern)*, Lorna Heilbron *(Penelope)*, George Benson *(Waterlow)*, Kenneth Warren *(Lenny)*, Duncan Lamont *(Inspector)*, Harry Locke *(Barman)*, Hedger Wallace *(Dr. Perry)*, Michael Ripper *(Carter)*, Catherine Finn *(Emily)*, Robert Swann *(Young Aristocrat)*, David Bailie *(Young Doctor)*, Maurice Bush *(Karl)*, Tony Wright *(Sailor)*, Marianne Stone *(Female Assistant)*, Alexandra Dane *(Whore)*, Jenny Runacre *(Emmanuel's Wife)*, Larry Taylor, Martin Carroll *(Warders)*, Dan Meaden *(Lunatic)*.

At the center of this surprisingly good effort from the incredibly spotty Freddie Francis is Victorian scientist Emmanuel Hildern's (Peter Cushing) attempt to develop an antidote for the blood-poisoning evil spread by an antediluvian skeleton that sprouts flesh when it come into contact with water. Fearing that his daughter will go insane like her mother, Hildern gives her the serum he has created, but instead of becoming a saint, she turns into a sex-crazed murderer. Meanwhile, Hildern's ruthless brother, James (Christopher Lee), who is head of the asylum where Hildern's wife spent her last days, is obsessed with uncovering the source of evil and steals the skeleton. A storm erupts during the coach ride from Emmanuel's lab to the asylum, and the skeleton is drenched, resulting in the return of its flesh. Brought back to life, it escapes and terrorizes the countryside. Well mounted and scary, THE CREEPING FLESH is yet another genre film that equates unchecked female sexuality with horrific consequences, though it isn't clear whether director Francis is condemning or supporting this notion.

p, Michael Redbourn; d, Freddie Franics; w, Peter Spenceley, Jonathon Rumbold; ph, Norman Wanvick; ed, Oswald Hafenrichter; m, Paul Ferris.

**(PR:C MPAA:PG)**

## CREEPSHOW**½

(1982) 129m Alpha/Laurel WB c

Hal Holbrook *(Henry)*, Adrienne Barbeau *(Wilma)*, Fritz Weaver *(Dexter)*, Leslie Nielsen *(Richard)*, Carrie Nye *(Sylvia)*, E.G. Marshall *(Upson)*, Viveca Lindfors *(Aunt Bedelia)*, Ed Harris *(Hank)*, Ted Danson *(Harry)*, Stephen King *(Jordy)*, Warner Shook *(Richard)*, Robert Harper *(Charlie)*, Elizabeth Regan *(Cass)*, Gaylen Ross *(Becky)*, Jon Lormer *(Nathan)*, Don Keefer *(Janitor)*, Bingo O'Malley *(Jordy's Dad)*, David Early *(White)*, Nann Mogg *(Mrs. Danvers)*, Iva Jean Saraceni *(Billy's Mother)*, Joe King *(Billy)*.

A difficult entry in the George Romero filmography, this collaboration with horror novelist Stephen King is a loving tribute to the E.C. comic books of the 1950s. Unfortunately, it never quite gels. The film starts off on a stormy night with an angry father's discovery that his son has been reading an E.C. comic book, which he throws into the street, where the wind opens it to the first of five vignettes, a tale about a long-buried corpse that returns to wreak havoc on his birthday. The second vignette deals with a farmer (writer King) who is slowly covered in green fungus; The third with a jealous husband who buries his wife and her lover up to their necks on the beach just before high tide. In the fourth, a college professor hides a vicious monster in a basket under some campus stairs. The last, and most effective, tale focuses on a Howard Hughes-like tycoon who is attacked by millions of cockroaches. Each vignette features a cast full of recognizable actors who play material in an appropriately broad manner. Stylistically, Romero attempts to duplicate the look of an E.C. comic book and relies heavily on exaggerated lighting schemes and angles; however, the trick simply doesn't work, and the film looks ham-handed and juvenile. Moreover, King's stories are nothing special, and with the exception of the final entry, none of the film is particulary scary. Romero is capable of much better, but, ironically, CREEPSHOW was his biggest box-office hit and inspired the "Tales of the Darkside" television series produced by his former company, Laurel. The sequel, CREEPSHOW 2 (see below), in which Romero adapted more King stories with the directorial chores handed over to CREEPSHOW cinematographer Michael Gornick, is even worse.

p, Richard P. Rubinstein; d, George A. Romero; w, Stephen King; ph, Michael Gornick (Technicolor); ed, Michael Spolan, Pasquale Buba, George A. Romero, Paul Hirsch; m, John Harrison.

**(PR:O    MPAA:R)**

## CREEPSHOW 2*

(1987) 89m Laurel/NW c

Lois Chiles *(Annie Lansing)*, George Kennedy *(Ray Spruce)*, Dorothy Lamour *(Martha Spruce)*, Tom Savini *(The Creep)*, Domenick John *(Boy Billy)*, Frank S. Salsedo *(Ben Whitemoon)*, Holt McCallany *(Sam Whitemoon)*, David Holbrook *(Fatso Gribbens)*, Don Harvey *(Andy Cavenaugh)*, Paul Satterfield *(Deke)*, Jeremy Green *(Laverne)*, Daniel Beer *(Randy)*, Page Hannah *(Rachel)*,

David Beecroft *(Annie's Lover)*, Tom Wright *(The Hitchhiker)*, Richard Parks *(George Lansing)*, Stephen King *(Truck Driver)*, Philip Dore *(Curly)*, Deane Smith *(Mr. Cavenaugh)*, Shirley Sonderegger *(Mrs. Cavenaugh)*, Chere Bryson *(Woman At Accident)*, Joe Silver *(Voice of the Creep)*.

This sequel to George Romero's CREEPSHOW doesn't repeat the mistakes of the original, but it does commit new errors all its own. Stephen King once again contributed the lame stories, which were adapted by Romero and directed by CREEPSHOW cinematographer Michael Gornick, making his helming debut. The first tale, "Old Chief Wood'nhead," is about a cigar store Indian that comes to life to avenge the murders of the sweet old couple that ran the general store he guarded. Story No. 2, "The Raft," follows a quartet of pot-smoking college students to a raft in the middle of a lake where they are attacked by an oil slick with a mind of its own. In the last story, "The Hitchhiker," a cheating wife returning from a tryst hits a hitchhiker, who survives and keeps popping up, forcing her to kill him again and again. Whereas Romero's approach to this material is distinctly tongue-in-cheek, Gornick makes the mistake of giving the stories a straightforward treatment that merely heightens their inherent weakness. Both pictures use animation to tie things together, though the cartoon work in both is weak. Tom Savini makes a cameo appearance in heavy makeup as the "Creep" (his voice dubbed by Joe Silver), and King appears in the final sequence as a truck driver. It doesn't help.

p, David Ball; d, Michael Gornick; w, George A. Romero (based on stories by Stephen King); ph, Dick Hart, Tom Hurwitz (Technicolor); ed, Peter Weatherly; m, Les Reed, Rick Wakeman.

**(PR:C-O    MPAA:R)**

## CRIME OF DR. CRESPI, THE***

(1936) 64m REP bw

Erich von Stroheim *(Dr. Crespi)*, Dwight Frye *(Dr. Thomas)*, Paul Guilfoyle *(Dr. Arnold)*, Harriet Russell *(Mrs. Ross)*, John Bohn *(The Dead Man)*, Geraldine Kay *(Miss Rexford)*, Jeanne Kelly *(Miss Gordon)*, Patsy Berlin *(Jeanne)*, Joe Verdi *(Di Angelo)*, Dean Raymond *(Minister)*.

Although it suffers from a low budget and contains a dementedly overblown performance by Erich von Stroheim, this distinctly eerie little film is well worth seeing. Loosely based on Edgar Allen Poe's ""The Premature Burial," it stars von Stroheim as Dr. Crespi, a brilliant surgeon who takes revenge on a romantic rival by injecting him with a drug that induces suspended animation. Appearing to have died on the operating table, Crespi's victim is taken to the morgue, where the doctor threatens to bury the still-conscious man alive. Although the man is, in fact, interred, two of Crespi's colleagues later exhume him. Quite insane from the experience, he returns to the hospital in a zombie-like state and proceeds to drive Crespi mad. Shot in little more than a week at the Biograph Studio in the Bronx, the film has an almost surreal quality due to Larry William's atmospheric photography, the bizarre set design, and von Stroheim's eccentric performance. Surprisingly morbid for its day, THE CRIME OF DR. CRESPI numbers among its highlights the sequence wherein the two doctors who have exhumed the body begin performing an autopsy only to have their first incision reveal warm, circulating blood!

p, John H. Auer; d, John H. Auer; w, Lewis Graham, Edward Olmstead (based on a story by John H. Auer from "The Premature Burial" by Edgar Allan Poe); ph, Larry Williams; ed, Leonard Wheeler.

(PR:C    MPAA:NR)

## CRUCIBLE OF HORROR*½

(1971, Brit.) 91m Cannon-Abacus/GN c (AKA: VELVET HOUSE; GB: CORPSE, THE)

Michael Gough (Walter Eastwood), Yvonne Mitchell (Edith), Sharon Gurney (Jane), Simon Gough (Rupert), Olaf Pooley (Reid), David Butler (Gregson), Nicholas Jones (Benjy), Mary Hignett (Sevant), Howard Goorney (Gas Attendant).

English stockbroker Walter Eastwood (Michael Gough) terrorizes his wife and daughter with tyrannical rules and daily beatings in this dull psychological horror film. During a trip to the country, the women in Walter's life decide they've had enough and poison him, making his death appear to be a suicide. But they aren't through with Walter yet, as he returns to haunt them. Slow paced and unimaginatively directed, CRUCIBLE OF HORROR does boast a few nice performances, but they simply aren't enough to keep the seen-it-all-before material interesting. Released in England in 1970, the film made it to American shores a year later.

p, Gabrielle Beaumont; d, Viktor Ritelis; w, Olaf Pooley; m, John Hotchkis.

(PR:C    MPAA:GP)

## CRUCIBLE OF TERROR**

(1971, Brit.) 79m Scotia/Barber c

Mike Raven (Victor Clare), Mary Maude (Millie), Melissa Stribling (Joanna Brent), James Bolam (John Davis), Ronald Lacey (Michael Clare), John Arnatt (Bill Cartwright), Beth Morris (Jane), Betty Alberge (Dorothy Clare), Kenneth Keeling (George Brent), Judy Matheson (Marcia), Me Me Lay (Chi San).

Former BBC disc jockey Mike Raven stars as a sculptor who creates statues by pouring molten bronze over the bodies of his unsuspecting female models. Yet another variation on the MYSTERY OF THE WAX MUSEUM theme, CRUCIBLE OF TERROR makes extensive use of picturesque Cornish locations. Cinematographer Peter Newbrook would go on to direct the interesting THE ASPHYX and THE DISCIPLE OF DEATH (both 1972), the latter employing many cast and crew members from CRUCIBLE OF TERROR.

p, Tom Parkinson; d, Ted Hooker; w, Ted Hooker, Tom Parkinson; ph, Peter Newbrook.

(PR:O    MPAA:NR)

## CRYPT OF THE LIVING DEAD*½

(1973) 75m Coast Industries c

Andrew Prince, Mark Damon, Teresa Gimpera, Patty Sheppard, Francisco Brana.

On Vampire Island, a professor is killed while excavating the tomb of Gimpera, wife of Louis VII, who was buried alive in 1269. Arriving at the site to investigate the death of his father, the professor's son uncovers the 700-year-old corpse of Gimpera, still in perfect condition. Shortly thereafter, the undead Gimpera does her thing and dead bodies begin to pile up. CRYPT OF THE LIVING DEAD was directed by actor Ray Danton, who played gangster Legs Diamond in two films—Budd Boetticher's THE RISE AND FALL OF LEGS DIAMOND (1960) and PORTRAIT OF A MOBSTER (1961)—before becoming a hack director of horror films (THE DEATHMASTER, 1972, and PSYCHIC KILLER, 1976) and television programs.

p, Lou Shaw; d, Ray Danton; w, Lou Shaw (based on a story by Lois Gibson); ph, Juan Gelpi (Metrocolor).

(PR:C    MPAA:PG)

## CUJO**

(1983) 91m WB c

Dee Wallace (Donna), Danny Pintauro (Tad), Daniel Hugh-Kelly (Vic), Christopher Stone (Steve), Ed Lauter (Joe), Kaiulani Lee (Charity), Billy Jacoby (Brett), Mills Watson (Gary), Sandy Ward (Bannerman), Jerry Hardin (Masen), Merritt Olsen, Arthur Rosenberg, Terry Donovan-Smith, Robert Elross, Robert Behling, Claire Nono, Daniel H. Blatt.

Although it has its champions, CUJO is a disappointing effort from director Lewis Teague, whose homage to ""B"" monster movies, ALLIGATOR (1980), was a surprisingly effective (and funny) film. This time the ""monster" is a bat-bitten, rabid St. Bernard that goes on a rampage, cornering a suburban housewife (Dee Wallace) and her son in a stranded Pinto station wagon, in 100-degree heat, for what seems like weeks. CUJO suffers from universally unsympathetic characters, and the dog is just not scary enough to maintain any interest. Significantly, the film also lacks the sly humor that made ALLIGATOR so appealing (Teague really misses a great opportunity to make the ultimate in dog-bites-mailman jokes when a postman ventures to the farmhouse where the woman and boy are trapped). Most of the film's weaknesses, however, are due to Stephen King's flawed source material. CUJO could have been a good film, but it isn't.

p, Daniel H. Blatt, Robert Singer; d, Lewis Teague; w, Don Carlos Dunaway, Lauren Currier (based on the novel by Stephen King); ph, Jan DeBont (CFI Color); ed, Neil Travis; m, Charles Bernstein.

(PR:O    MPAA:NR)

## CURSE, THE*½

(1987) 90m Trans World c (AKA: FARM, THE)

Wil Wheaton (Zachary Hayes), Claude Akins (Nathan

*Hayes),* Malcolm Danare *(Cyrus),* Cooper Huckabee *(Dr. Alan Forbes),* John Schneider *(Carl Willis),* Amy Wheaton *(Alice Hayes),* Steve Carlisle *(Charley Davidson),* Kathleen Jordan Gregory *(Frances Hayes),* Hope North *(Esther Forbes),* Steve Davis *(Mike).*

The directorial debut of actor David Keith (AN OFFICER AND A GENTLEMAN; THE LORDS OF DISCIPLINE; FIRESTARTER), this nauseating little movie was shot on Keith's own property in Tennessee, with interiors filmed in Rome. Set on a lonely farm, the film stars young Wil Wheaton (STAND BY ME) as an unhappy boy whose miserable home life is further complicated by a mysterious meteorite that crashes on the property and infects his family, turning them into murderous zombies. Director Keith and screenwriter David Chaskin's (A NIGHTMARE ON ELM STREET II) attempt to comment on the seedy underbelly of the American family farm is suitably claustrophobic and effective in the early going, but then collapses once the meteor hits, becoming just another predictable, gross, silly, and ultimately forgettable little horror film. The last 15 minutes are almost totally incoherent, giving the impression that the film was slapped together hastily. The gore effects by Italian Franco Ruffini are predictably disgusting.

p, Ovidio Assonitis; d, David Keith, Frank Vanorio; w, David Chaskin; ph, Robert D. Forges (Widescreen, Technicolor); ed, Claudio Cutry; m, Franco Micalizzi.

(PR:O MPAA:R)

## CURSE OF FRANKENSTEIN, THE****

(1957, Brit.) 82m Hammer/WB c

Peter Cushing *(Baron Victor Frankenstein),* Christopher Lee *(The Creature),* Hazel Court *(Elizabeth),* Robert Urquhart *(Paul Krempe),* Valerie Gaunt *(Justine),* Noel Hood *(Aunt Sophia),* Marjorie Hume *(Mother),* Melvyn Hayes *(Young Victor),* Sally Walsh *(Young Elizabeth),* Paul Hardtmuth *(Prof. Bernstein),* Fred Johnson *(Grandfather),* Claude Kingston *(Small Boy),* Henry Caine *(Schoolmaster),* Michael Mulcaster *(Werner),* Patrick Troughton *(Kurt),* Joseph Behrman *(Fritz),* Hugh Dempster *(Burgomaster),* Anne Blake *(Burgomaster's Wife),* Raymond Rollett *(Father Felix),* Alex Gallier *(Priest),* Ernest Jay *(Undertaker),* J. Trevor Davis *(Uncle),* Bartlett Mullins *(Tramp),* Eugene Leahy *(Second Priest).*

The most significant British horror film ever, THE CURSE OF FRANKENSTEIN burst upon the scene in gory color and heralded Hammer's domination of the genre for the next 10 years. Opening as Baron Victor Frankenstein (Peter Cushing) awaits execution for the murder of his wife, the story is told in flashback, presenting the megalomaniacal scientist as a man so obsessed with his goal of creating artificial life from the parts of dead bodies, that he unthinkingly destroys the lives of all those around him. Director Terence Fisher—who helmed 24 features before making his mark with this one—brought a new seriousness and verve to a genre which had collapsed into self-parody with ABBOTT AND COSTELLO MEET FRANKENSTEIN (1948). To avoid infringing on Universal's copyright of Jack Pierce's makeup for the monster, British makeup man Phil

Leakey created a much more realistic-looking creature that better resembled the description in Mary Shelley's novel. Christopher Lee is excellent as the mute monster, but this is Cushing's film all the way, and his groundbreaking portrayal of Baron Frankenstein dominated the series in five more films: THE REVENGE OF FRANKENSTEIN (1958); THE EVIL OF FRANKENSTEIN (1964); FRANKENSTEIN CREATED WOMAN (1966); FRANKENSTEIN MUST BE DESTROYED (1969); FRANKENSTEIN AND THE MONSTER FROM HELL (1973); most of which, regrettably, are not yet available on video cassette. Shot for $250,000, the film grossed millions and singlehandedly returned the horror film to prominence in an era that had been dominated by science fiction. Having successfully revived Frankenstein, Hammer and director Terence Fisher would surpass themselves with their next effort, THE HORROR OF DRACULA (1958).

p, Anthony Hinds; d, Terence Fisher; w, Jimmy Sangster (based on the novel *Frankenstein* by Mary Shelley); ph, Jack Asher; ed, James Needs; m, Leonard Salzedo.

(PR:C MPAA:NR)

## CURSE OF THE AZTEC MUMMY, THE**½

(1965, Mex.) 65m Cinematografica Calderon-AIP-TV/K. Gordon Murray bw (LA MALDICION DE LA MOMIA AZTECA)

Ramon Gay, Rosita Arenas, Crox Alvarado, Luis Aceves Castaneda, Angel d'Esteffani, Jesus Velazquez, Alejandro Cruz, Jaime Gonzalez Quinones.

The evil Dr. Krupp (Luis Aceves Castaneda) escapes from the police and unleashes a fiendish plot to steal the treasure hidden in an Aztec pyramid. Just when he has gotten the best of the good guys and his plan is on the verge of success, the Aztec mummy—named Popoca—comes out of its tomb and subdues the villain by locking him in a room with hundreds of poisonous snakes. This wholly enjoyable sequel to the wild THE AZTEC MUMMY (1963) would soon be followed by THE ROBOT VS. THE AZTEC MUMMY (1965). All three were filmed and released in Mexico between 1957 and 1958, but didn't receive north-of-the-border releases until the 1960s. Although not really part of the series, one of the most outrageous Mexican mummy movies, WRESTLING WOMEN VS. THE AZTEC MUMMY, was released in 1964. All four are great fun.

p, Guillermo Calderon; d, Rafael Portillo; w, Alfredo Salazar (based on a story by Calderon, Salazar); ph, Enrique Wallace; ed, Jorge Bustos; m, Antonio Diaz Conde.

(PR:A MPAA:NR)

## CURSE OF THE CAT PEOPLE, THE****

(1944) 70m RKO bw

Simone Simon *(Irena),* Kent Smith *(Oliver Reed),* Jane Randolph *(Alice Reed),* Ann Carter *(Amy),* Elizabeth Russell *(Barbara),* Eve March *(Miss Callahan),* Julia Dean *(Julia Farren),* Erford Gage *(State Trooper Captain),* Sir Lancelot *(Edward),* Joel Davis *(Donal),* Juanita Alvarez

(Lois), Charley Bates (Jack), Gloria Donovan, Ginny Wren, Linda Ann Bieber (Little Girls), Sarah Selby (Miss Plummett), Mel Sternlight (State Trooper).

Director Joe Dante, a Val Lewton fan, said of THE CURSE OF THE CAT PEOPLE that ""Its disturbingly Disneyesque fairy tale qualities have perplexed horror fans for decades." Ostensibly a sequel to Lewton's successful CAT PEOPLE, it is, however, less the horror film that its typically lurid title implies than a look at a child's lonely fantasies. Carrying over the character of Oliver Reed (Kent Smith) from the previous film, the sequel finds him remarried and the father of Amy (Ann Carter), a lonely, introverted six-year-old who creates an imaginary world of her own. Oliver worries that his dreamy daughter may somehow be influenced by the spirit of his first wife, Irena (Simone Simon), who believed she was descended from a race of cat people. When Amy finds an old picture of Irena, her imaginary friend suddenly has a face, and Irena becomes her confidante and playmate. At the same time, Amy makes friends with Julia (Julia Dean), an elderly actress who lives in the spooky Victorian mansion next door. Julia enjoys having the child around and tells her fantastic tales, much to the dismay of her own adult daughter, Barbara (Elizabeth Russell), who feels Amy is stealing her mother's love. In time both Oliver and the spiteful Barbara move to put an end to Amy's fantasy life. A beautiful and haunting film, THE CURSE OF THE CAT PEOPLE captures what critic James Agee called "the poetry and danger of childhood." Many of the incidents are derived from producer Lewton's own childhood, adding a personal resonance to the film. RKO editor Robert Wise made his directorial debut here, taking over from Gunther V. Fritsch early on in the production. Although not as skillfully directed as the Jacques Tourneur-Lewton collaborations, this picture remains one of the most ethereal looks at childhood the cinema has produced.

p, Val Lewton; d, Robert Wise, Gunther V. Fritsch; w, Dewitt Bodeen; ph, Nicholas Musuraca; ed, J.R. Whittredge; m, Roy Webb.

**(PR:A   MPAA:NR)**

## CURSE OF THE DEMON*****

(1958) 82m COL bw (AKA: NIGHT OF THE DEMON)

Dana Andrews (John Holden), Peggy Cummins (Joanna Harrington), Niall MacGinnis (Dr. Karswell), Maurice Denham (Prof. Harrington), Athene Seyler (Mrs. Karswell), Liam Redmond (Mark O'Brien), Reginald Beckwith (Mr. Meek), Ewan Roberts (Lloyd Williamson), Peter Elliott (Kumar), Rosamond Greenwood (Mrs. Meek), Brian Wilde (Rand Hobart), Richard Leech (Inspector Mottram), Lloyd Lamble (Detective Simmons), Peter Hobbes (Superintendent), Charles Lloyd-Pack (Chemist), John Salew (Librarian), Janet Barrow (Mrs. Hobart), Percy Herbert (Farmer), Lynn Tracy (Air Hostess).

Masterful director Jacques Tourneur made this outstanding supernatural horror film without the guidance of producer Val Lewton, with whom he had collaborated so successfully on I WALKED WITH A ZOMBIE and CAT PEO-

PLE. Skeptical American psychologist John Holden (Dana Andrews) journeys to England to assist Prof. Harrington (Maurice Denham) in his attempt to expose a satanic cult led by Dr. Julian Karswell (Niall MacGinnis). While Holden is in transit, Harrington confronts Karswell, but during his drive home, the professor is killed by a demon dispatched by Karswell. Holden is shocked to learn of Harrington's death and, although he does not believe in witchcraft or the devil, decides to continue the investigation. Exceedingly eerie and suspenseful, CURSE OF THE DEMON succeeds brilliantly despite of the ham-handedness of producer Hal E. Chester. Used to working with Lewton, both screenwriter Charles Bennett and director Tourneur were shocked by Chester's insensitivity to the material. The producer brazenly rewrote much of Bennett's script and forced Tourneur to insert shots of a smoke-breathing demon, who makes his first appearance only five minutes into the movie! So much for Lewton's horror of suggestion. Luckily, Bennett's literate script and Tourneur's atmospheric visuals overpower Chester's tinkering. As in any Tourneur horror film there are some unforgettably nightmarish sequences, including an outdoor children's birthday party which is interrupted by a terrific storm summoned by Karswell, who is dressed like a clown; Holden's solo walk through the woods at night just after confronting the satanist; and the climax, wherein Karswell chases a sacred parchment as it blows down some gloomy railroad tracks. Although CURSE OF THE DEMON's original English release had a running time of 95 minutes, its American distributors removed 13 minutes from the film; however, the uncut version has been restored on videocassette.

p, Hal E. Chester; d, Jacques Tourneur; w, Charles Bennett, Hal E. Chester (based on a story, "Casting the Ruins," by Montague R. James); ph, Ted Sciafe; ed, Michael Gordon; m, Clifton Parker.

**(PR:A   MPAA:NR)**

## CURSE OF THE LIVING CORPSE, THE**

(1964) 84m FOX bw

Helen Warren (Abigail Sinclair), Roy Scheider (Philip Sinclair), Margot Hartman (Vivian Sinclair), Robert Milli (Bruce Sinclair), Hugh Franklin (James Benson), Candace Hilligoss (Deborah Benson), Dino Narizzano (Robert Harrington), Linda Donovan (Letty Crews), J. Frank Lucas (Seth Lucas), Jane Bruce (Cook), Paul Haney (Constable Barnes), George Cotton (Constable Winters), William Blood (Minister).

Rufus Sinclair, a millionaire who suffers seizures that make him appear to be dead, lives in fear of premature burial. Contained in his will is the promise that should he be buried alive, he will return from the grave to murder his heirs in the manner they most fear. Take a guess at what happens next. An almost-forgotten early gore film (the severed head of the maid winds up on a breakfast tray), THE CURSE OF THE LIVING CORPSE is notable only because it is Roy Scheider's film debut and marks the only other known credit of actress Candace Hilligoss, the star of CARNIVAL OF SOULS (1962).

p, Del Tenney; d, Del Tenney; w, Del Tenney; ph, Richard L. Hilliard; ed, Gary Youngman; m, Bill Holmes.

**(PR:C   MPAA:NR)**

## CURSE OF THE SWAMP CREATURE*

(1966) 80m AIP-TV c

John Agar *(Barry Rogers),* Francine York, Shirley McLine, Bill Thurman, Jeff Alexander, Cal Duggan, Charles McLine, Bill McGee, Rodger Ready, Ted Mitchell, Tony Houston, Annabelle Weenick, J.V. Lee, Gayle Johnson, Michael Tolden, Pat Cranshaw, Naomi Lee.

Everyone's favorite backwoods filmmaker, Larry Buchanan, produced and directed this typically silly effort about an Everglades geological expedition that runs across a mad scientist involved in the creation of half-alligator, half-human monsters. John Agar, who is featured here, would also star in Buchanan's classic sci-fi effort ZONTAR, THE THING FROM VENUS, filmed the very same year.

p, Larry Buchanan; d, Larry Buchanan; w, Tony Houston.

**(PR:C   MPAA:NR)**

## CURSE OF THE WEREWOLF, THE***½

(1961) 91m Hammer/UNIV c

Clifford Evans *(Alfredo),* Oliver Reed *(Leon),* Yvonne Romain *(Servant Girl),* Catherine Feller *(Christina),* Anthony Dawson *(Marques Siniestro),* Josephine Llewellyn *(Marquesa),* Richard Wordsworth *(Beggar),* Hira Talfrey *(Teresa),* John Gabriel *(Priest),* Warren Mitchell *(Pepe Valiente),* Anne Blake *(Rosa Valiente),* George Woodbridge *(Dominique),* Michael Ripper *(Old Soaker),* Ewen Solon *(Don Fernando),* Peter Sallis *(Don Enrique),* Martin Matthews *(Jose),* David Conville *(Rico Gomez),* Denis Shaw *(Gaoler),* Charles Lamb *(Chef),* Serafina Di Leo *(Senora Zumara),* Sheila Brennan *(Vera),* Joy Webster *(Isabel),* Renny Lister *(Yvonne),* Justin Walters *(Leon, as a Young Child).*

Despite many efforts in the 1980s to revitalize the werewolf movie, this Hammer effort is second only to the 1941 classic, THE WOLF MAN. The product of the brutal rape of a deaf-mute servant girl by a snarling mad beggar, young Leon is adopted by a kindly professor and his wife. As the boy grows older, however, his lycanthropic tendencies emerge and his parents are forced to put bars on the windows in his room and lock him there when the moon is full. As an adult, Leon (now played by Oliver Reed) falls in love with Christina (Catherine Feller), who somehow mollifies his animal instincts. Fearing that he will harm her, Leon has himself sent to a monastery, but the chains he is kept in there are not enough to prevent him from escaping and eloping with his beloved. Christina's aristocratic father catches them, however, and sees to it that Leon is imprisoned, but the moon is full and the werewolf escapes again. Although some may find the film rather slow-paced—almost half its running time is devoted to Leon's conception—THE CURSE OF THE WEREWOLF is a fascinating horror film that grounds its terror in a firm social and historical context. Director Terence Fisher once again

takes the genre in a new direction, creating a richly detailed film that finds more horror in the tyranny of aristocratic rule than in the tragedy of its victim/monster. Oliver Reed is excellent as the sympathetic Leon, and makeup artist Roy Ashton gives the werewolf a very distinctive look.

p, Anthony Hinds; d, Terence Fisher; w, Anthony Hinds (based on the novel *The Werewolf of Paris* by Guy Endore); ph, Arthur Grant (Eastmancolor); ed, Alfred Cox; m, Benjamin Frankel.

**(PR:C   MPAA:NR)**

## CURTAINS zero

(1983, Can.) 90m Simcon/Jensen Farley c

John Vernon *(Jonathon),* Samantha Eggar *(Samantha),* Linda Thorson *(Brooke),* Anne Ditchburn *(Laurian),* Lynne Griffin *(Patti O'Connor),* Sandra Warren *(Tara),* Lesleh Donaldson *(Christie),* Deborah Burgess *(Amanda),* Michael Wincott *(Matthew),* Maury Chaykin *(Monty),* Joann McIntyre *(Secretary),* Calvin Butler *(Dr. Pendleton),* Kate Lynch *(Receptionist),* Booth Savage, William Marshall, James Kidnie, Jeremy Jenson, Donald Adams, Diane Godwin, Janelle Hutchison, Virginia Laight, Kay Griffin, Bunty Webb, Daisy White, Vivian Reis, Sheila Currie, Frances Gunn, Suzanne Russell.

This worthless slasher movie casts Samantha Eggar as an actress who can't get out of a mental institution after voluntarily committing herself to research her next film role. Her director (John Vernon) immediately invites six promising starlets to his house, subjecting them to various forms of sexual harassment as he tries to find a replacement for his strait-jacketed star. Of course a masked mad killer begins knocking off the nubile ingenues, but his identity should be obvious before a third of the film is over.

p, Peter Simpson; d, Johnathan Stryker; w, Robert Guza, Jr.; ph, Robert Paynter, Fred Guthe; ed, Michael MacLaverty; m, Paul Zaza.

**(PR:O   MPAA:R)**

## DADDY'S DEADLY DARLING zero

(1984) 83m Safia S.A./Aquarius c (AKA: DADDY'S GIRL; PIGS, THE)

Toni Lawrence *(Lynn Webster),* Marc Lawrence *(Zambrini),* Jesse Vint *(Sheriff Dan Cole),* Walter Barnes *(Doctor),* Katharine Ross *(Miss Macy),* Jim Antonio, Erik Holland, Paul Hickey, Iris Korn, William Michael.

Garbage comes in many forms, but they had to scrape the bottom of the dumpster to find this one. Zambrini (Marc Lawrence), the owner of both a roadside cafe and an adjoining pigpen, doesn't feed his animals the usual slop; instead when patrons stop in for a bite they run the risk of becoming a meal themselves. Lynn (Toni Lawrence), a traumatized escapee from a mental hospital, takes a job at the cafe and lends a helping hand . . . after all, slaughtering humans is a tough job. Shot in 1972 as THE PIGS, this one-man show—produced, written, and directed by its star, Marc Lawrence—is not only reprehensible, but boring and poorly executed.

p, Marc Lawrence; d, Marc Lawrence; w, Marc Lawrence; ph, Glenn Roland, Jr. (CFI Color); ed, Irvin Goodnoff; m, Charles Bernstein.

(PR:O  MPAA:R)

## DAMIEN—OMEN II**

(1978) 109m FOX c

William Holden *(Richard Thorn),* Lee Grant *(Ann Thorn),* Jonathan Scott-Taylor *(Damien Thorn),* Robert Foxworth *(Paul Buher),* Nicholas Pryor *(Charles Warren),* Lew Ayres *(Bill Atherton),* Sylvia Sidney *(Aunt Marion),* Lance Henriksen *(Sgt. Neff),* Lucas Donat *(Mark Thorn),* Alan Arbus *(Pasarian),* Meshach Taylor *(Dr. Kane),* John J. Newcombe *(Teddy),* John Charles Burns *(Butler),* Paul Cook *(Colonel),* Robert Ingham *(Teacher),* William B. Fosser *(Minister),* Corney Morgan *(Greenhouse Technician),* Russell P. Delia *(Truck Driver),* Judith Dowd *(Maid),* Thomas O. Erhart, Jr. *(Sergeant),* Robert J. Jones, Jr. *(Guide),* Rusdi Lane *(Jim),* Charles Mountain *(Priest),* Cornelia Sanders *(Girl),* Felix Shuman *(Dr. Fiedler),* William J. Whelehan *(Guard),* Elizabeth Shepherd *(Joan Hart),* Fritz Ford *(Murray).*

The first sequel to THE OMEN returns to the story with the young antichrist Damien (Jonathan Scott-Taylor) now thirteen years old and living with his aunt and uncle (Lee Grant and William Holden). In short order, a series of mysterious accidents results in the deaths of a number of people who are suspicious of Damien, including his elderly Aunt Marion (Sylvia Sidney) and a nosy female reporter (Elizabeth Shepherd). When his uncle sends him to an exclusive military academy, Damien reads the Book of Revelations and at last discovers his true identity. After eliminating his second set of relatives, he then becomes the heir to an industrial empire, leaving the door open for an even worse sequel, THE FINAL CONFLICT, which, like this film, more or less remakes the original, rather than forging new ground. As in the FRIDAY THE 13TH movies, the only real interest here is observing the outrageous lengths the filmmakers go to in their can-you-top-this murders.

p, Harvey Bernhard; d, Don Taylor; w, Stanley Mann, Michael Hodges; ph, Bill Butler (Panavision, Deluxe Color); ed, Robert Brown; m, Jerry Goldsmith.

(PR:O  MPAA:R)

## DAUGHTER OF DR. JEKYLL**½

(1957) 67m AA bw

John Agar *(George Hastings),* Gloria Talbot *(Janet Smith),* Arthur Shields *(Dr. Lomas),* John Dierkes *(Jacob),* Martha Wentworth *(Mrs. Merchant),* Mollie McCart *(Maggie),* Marjorie Stapp, Rita Greene, Marel Page.

A somewhat disappointing Edgar G. Ulmer effort, DAUGHTER OF DR. JEKYLL is nonetheless fascinating for the manner in which Ulmer skirts his obviously paltry budget to make a memorable—if minor—horror film. It begins with a precredit sequence in which a smokey silhouette appears on the screen while a narrator provides a short history of Dr. Jekyll and his death. We watch as Jekyll sips the serum, transforms into Mr. Hyde, and then faces the camera and cackles, "Are you sure?" Enter the title character, Janet (Gloria Talbott), and her fiance, George (John Agar), who arrive at her ancestral mansion, inhabited by her aged guardian, Dr. Lomas (Arthur Shields, brother of actor Barry Fitzgerald). Since it is Janet's 21st birthday, Lomas is dutybound to reveal to her that her father was the infamous Dr. Jekyll, whose serum turned him into a murderous werewolf. Although George thinks the whole thing is ridiculous, Janet worries that her father's lycanthropy is hereditary and calls off their wedding. And, as it turns out, Janet may be right, for that very night she has a nightmare wherein she becomes a monster and murders the maid. When Janet awakens, her nightgown is covered in blood and the maid is dead. Rather silly at times, THE DAUGHTER OF DR. JEKYLL is a bizarre hybrid horror film that mixes parts of DR. JEKYLL AND MR. HYDE; THE WOLF MAN; THE OLD DARK HOUSE; and even DRACULA (the werewolf can only be killed by a wooden stake through the heart!). Ever the visual stylist, Ulmer charges through the lengthy passages of dialog to get to the meat of the film—Janet's nightmares (rendered through effective multiple dissolves) and the mist-shrouded climax. This remarkably strange and ambiguous little movie ends just as it had begun, with Mr. Hyde turning to the camera and once again cackling, "Are you sure?"

p, Jack Pollexfen; d, Edgar G. Ulmer; w, Jack Pollexfen; ph, John F. Warren; ed, Holbrook N. Todd.

(PR:A  MPAA:NR)

## DAUGHTERS OF DARKNESS***½

(1971, Bel./Fr./Ger./It.) 87m Roxy-Mediterranea/Gemini c (LE ROUGE AUX LEVRES)

Delphine Seyrig *(Countess Elisabeth Bathory),* Daniele Ouimet *(Valerie Tardieu),* John Karlen *(Stefan Chiltern),* Andrea Rau *(Ilona Harczy),* Paul Esser *(Porter),* Georges Jamin *(The Man),* Joris Collet *(Butler),* Fons Rademakers *(Mother).*

Stylishly directed by Harry Kumel, this fascinating erotic vampire film revolves around the meeting between a honeymoon couple, Stefan and Valerie (John Karlen and Daniele Ouimet), and a pair of mysterious lesbians, Countess Elisabeth Bathory (Delphine Seyrig) and Ilona (Andrea Rau)—who may or may not be vampires. When Valerie's attraction to the beautiful countess arouses jealousy in their respective mates, sparks begin flying. Stefan, a brutal male chauvinist, who may also be homosexual, beats his wife before having sex with her, and the countess, sensing Valerie's dissatisfaction, sends Ilona to seduce Stefan. Ilona corners him in the shower, but panics, slips and falls, impales herself on his straight razor. That night the countess seduces Valerie, and the two form a bond that excludes Stefan. One of the best of many early 1970s vampire movies inspired by Sheridan Le Fanu's "Carmilla," DAUGHTER OF DARKNESS is remarkable not only for its eroticism, but for Kumel's stunning visual style, reminiscent of that of Josef von Sternberg, especially in its treatment of the countess, recalling von Sternberg's early presentation of Marlene Dietrich. Also notable are the sequences of stomach-turning violence, which are all the more effective because of their mundanity.

p, Paul Coilet, Alain C. Guilleaume; d, Harry Kumel; w, Pierre Drouot, Harry Kumel, J.J. Amiel; ph, Edward Van Der Enden; ed, Gust Verschueren, Denis Bonan; m, Francois De Roubiax.

(PR:O   MPAA:R)

## DAWN OF THE DEAD*****

(1979) 125m United Film c

David Emge *(Stephen)*, Ken Foree *(Peter)*, Scott Reiniger *(Roger)*, Gaylen Ross *(Francine)*, David Crawford *(Dr. Foster)*, David Early *(Mr. Berman)*, George A. Romero *(TV Director)*, Richard France *(Scientist)*, Howard Smith *(TV Commentator)*, Daniel Dietrich *(Givens)*, Fred Baker *(Commander)*, Jim Baffico *(Wooley)*, Rod Stouffer *(Young Officer on Roof)*, Jese Del Gre *(Old Priest)*, Clayton McKinnon, John Rice *(Officers in Project Apartment)*, Ted Bank, Patrick McCloskey, Randy Kovitz, Joseph Pilato *(Officers at Police Dock)*, Pasquale Buba, Tony Buba, "Butchie", Dave Hawkins, Tom Kapusta, Rudy Ricci, Tom Savini, Marty Schiff, Joe Shelby, Taso Stavrakos, Nick Tallo, Larry Vaira *(Motorcycle Raiders)*, Sharon Ceccatti, Pan Chatfield, Jim Christopher, Clayton Hill, Jay Stover *(Lead Zombies)*.

George Romero's brilliant sequel to NIGHT OF THE LIVING DEAD (1968) begins where the first film left off, with the US overrun by the recently dead, who have returned to life and are eating the flesh of the living. Fran (Gaylen Ross), an employee of a local television station, and her boy friend, Stephen (David Emge), the station's traffic copter pilot, try to escape the madness, accompanied by his friend, Roger (Scott Reiniger), a SWAT team member, and Peter (Ken Foree), another cop. Not knowing where to go or how far the living-dead epidemic has spread, the quartet flies over Pennsylvania in Stephen's helicopter, eventually landing atop a large, empty suburban shopping mall infested with zombies. Seeing that the mall would be easy to secure and supply all their needs, the four decide to remain, but are forced to defend their palace against both flesh-eating zombies and nomadic humans. Quite possibly the most violent film ever made, DAWN OF THE DEAD is Romero's satirical slam at rampant American consumerism. Although his film is unbelievably bloody, Romero uses violence not to shock, but to numb. To evoke the horror of an existence that requires the shooting down of risen corpses, including those of loved ones and friends, Romero barrages the viewer with image upon image of quick, violent, almost cartoonlike death. While we sympathize with the protagonists of the film, we *feel* for the zombies; the embodiment of greed, they represent humanity in general, and American consumers in particular. In a tell-

ing moment, Fran wonders why the zombies are hanging around the mall. The answer is simple: it's instinct—the mall is the place where they've always wanted to be. In DAWN OF THE DEAD, Romero has created the ultimate American nightmare. We are feeding on ourselves. A sequel, DAY OF THE DEAD, followed in 1985.

p, Richard P. Rubinstein; d, George A. Romero; w, George A. Romero; ph, Michael Gornick (Technicolor); ed, George A. Romero, Kenneth Davidow; m, Dario Argento.

(PR:O   MPAA:NR)

## DAY OF THE ANIMALS zero

(1977) 95m Film Ventures c (AKA: SOMETHING IS OUT THERE)

Christopher George *(Steve Buckner)*, Leslie Nielsen *(Mr. Jenson)*, Lynda Day George *(Terry Marsh)*, Richard Jaeckel *(Prof. MacGregor)*, Michael Ansara *(Santee)*, Ruth Roman *(Mrs. Shirley Goodwin)*, Jon Cedar *(Frank Young)*, Paul Mantee *(Roy Moore)*, Walter Barnes *(Ranger Tucker)*, Susan Backlinie *(Mrs. Young)*, Andrew Stevens *(Bob Denning)*, Kathleen Bracken *(Beth Hughes)*, Bobby Porter *(Jon Goodwyn)*, Michelle Stacy *(Little Girl)*, Garrison True *(Newscaster)*, Michael Rougas *(Military Officer)*, Gil Lamb *(Old Man in Restaurant)*, Michael Andreas *(Sheriff)*, Jan Andrew Scott *(Helicopter Pilot)*, Gertrude Lee *(Ranger's Wife)*.

William Girdler, who aped THE EXORCIST (1973) with ABBY (1974), and JAWS (1975) with GRIZZLY (1976), substituting a bear for the famous shark, turns his attention to Hitchcock's classic THE BIRDS (1963) in this laughable film. Here the animals of the world are attacking people in response to humankind's aerosol-can destruction of the ozone layer. Bad casting (Ruth Roman and Richard Jaeckel as scientists?) and inept special effects combine to produce more than a few unintentional laughs for those masochists willing to sit through this Girdler outing. See the similar FROGS (1972).

p, Edward E. Montoro; d, William Girdler; w, William Norton, Eleanor E. Norton (based on a story by Montoro); ph, Bob Sorrentino (Todd-AO 35, DeLuxe Color); ed, Bub Asman, James Mitchell; m, Lalo Schifrin.

(PR:C   MPAA:PG)

## DAY OF THE DEAD****

(1985) 102m Laurel/UFDC c

Lori Cardille *(Sarah)*, Terry Alexander *(John)*, Joseph Pilato *(Capt. Rhodes)*, Jarlath Conroy *(McDermott)*, Antone DiLeo, Jr. *(Miguel)*, Richard Liberty *(Dr. Logan)*, Howard Sherman *(Bub)*, Gary Howard Klar *(Steel)*, Ralph Marrero *(Rickles)*, John Amplas *(Fisher)*, Phillip G. Kellams *(Miller)*, Taso Stavrakos *(Torrez)*, Gregory Nicotero *(Johnson)*, Don Brockett, William Cameron, Deborah Carter, Winnie Flynn, Debra Gordon, Jeff Hogan, Barbara Holmes, David Kindlon, Bruce Kirkpatrick, William Andrew Laczko, John Vulich, R.H. Martin.

The third, and perhaps last, chapter in George Romero's

"Living Dead" series is a claustrophobic character study set almost entirely in a huge underground storage facility that has been converted into a laboratory and barracks. The military has been assigned to protect and assist the group of scientists (Lori Cardille, John Amplas, and Richard Liberty) who are working to develop a solution to the zombie epidemic, experimenting on zombies that have been herded into a holding pen. One scientist, Dr. Logan (Liberty)—nicknamed ""Frankenstein" by the soldiers—tries to modify the zombies' behavior so that humans can train them like dogs; and one zombie, whom Logan calls "Bub," seems to be the missing link between animal instinct and civilized human behavior. The operation has taken its toll on the soldiers, however, and their commander, the near-psychotic Rhodes (Joseph Pilato), tries to take over the project and put an end to it. Fans of the first two films in the series may be a bit dismayed by DAY OF THE DEAD's de-emphasis of the gory action in favor of more characterization, but the need to exploit the horror of the situation has passed and the film works by concentrating instead on its implications and possible solution. The standard 1950s science fiction-horror film conflict between science and the military is also resurrected here to good effect. One thing becomes clear in DAY OF THE DEAD—the zombies are here to stay and humanity must adapt to them if it wishes to survive. Romero's original conception of the final chapter called for the scientists to train a small army of intelligent zombies to be turned over to the military for the power struggle with the living dead and the living who now maraud the country. The epic scale of Romero's vision would have required a budget far greater than the other films of the series, and when the director could not promise distributors an ""R" rating (due to the Grand Guignol violence associated with the series the film went without an MPAA rating), financing vanished, forcing him to scale down the script. Extremely underrated—even by horror film fans—DAY OF THE DEAD ranks with Romero's best work.

p, Richard P. Rubinstein; d, George A. Romero; w, George A. Romero; ph, Michael Gornick; ed, Pasquale Buba; m, John Harrison.

**(PR:O MPAA:NR)**

## DEAD AND BURIED**

(1981) 92m Avco Embassy c

James Farentino (Dan), Melody Anderson (Janet), Jack Albertson (Dobbs), Dennis Redfield (Ron), Nancy Locke Hauser (Linda), Lisa Blout (Girl on Beach), Robert Englund (Harry), Bill Quinn (Ernie), Michael Currie (Herman), Christopher Allport (George/Freddie), Joe Medalis (Doctor), Macon McCalman (Ben), Lisa Marie (Hitchhiker), Estelle Omens (Betty), Barry Corbin (Phil), Michael Pataki

(Sam), Jill Fosse (Nurse), Mark Courtney, Michael Courtney (Jamie).

A series of vicious murders of tourists plagues a New England town and everyone seems to know what's going on except the sheriff (James Farentino). All the clues lead to Dobbs (Jack Albertson), the eccentric coroner-mortician who cuts up cadavers while listening to 1940s swing music and has somehow managed to revive the dead. Scripted by Ronald Shusett and Dan O'Bannon, the team that penned ALIEN, this Gary A. Sherman effort may have a loyal following, but it is a stupid movie nonetheless. Most of the plot twists are confusing and haphazardly developed, leaving the movie as little more than an excuse to show off Stan Winston's admittedly effective gore effects. Given Sherman's wretched subsequent track record (WANTED: DEAD OR ALIVE; POLTERGEIST III), one wonders what people see in his work. This was veteran comedian and character actor Albertson's last film before his death in the same year.

p, Ronald Shusett, Robert Fentress; d, Gary Sherman; w, Ronald Shusett, Dan O'Bannon (based on a story by Jeff Millar, Alex Stern); ph, Steve Poster (Technicolor); ed, Alan Balsam; m, Joe Renzetti.

**(PR:O MPAA:R)**

## DEAD HEAT*

(1988) 86m NW c

Treat Williams (Roger Mortis), Joe Piscopo (Doug Bigelow), Lindsay Frost (Randi James), Darren McGavin (Dr. Ernest McNab), Vincent Price (Arthur P. Loudermilk), Clare Kirkconnell (Rebecca Smythers), Keye Luke (Mr. Thule), Ben Mittleman (Bob), Peter Kent (Smitty), Robert Picardo (Lt. Herzog), Mel Stewart (Capt. Mayberry), Professor Toru Tanaka (Butcher), Martha Quinn (Newscaster), Cate Caplin (Saleswoman), Monica Lewis (Mrs. Von Heiserberg), Peggy O'Brien (Jewelry Store Manager), Chip Heller (Wilcox), Steven R. Bannister (The Thing), Lew Hopson (Whitfield), Tom Nolan (Jonas), Steve Itkin (Freman), Shane Black (Patrolman), Monty Ash (Waiter), H. Ray Huff (Cop).

A disastrous attempt at blending comedy and horror, DEAD HEAT could have been a decent time-waster had it not been for the inept direction of former editor Mark Goldblatt (THE TERMINATOR) and the crippling presence of the least funny comedian in the world, Joe "Muscles" Piscopo. Set in Los Angeles, the film follows two moronic police detectives—one uptight (Treat Williams), the other a wiseacre (Piscopo)—as they try to crack a crime ring which brings the dead back to life through the use of a mysterious machine. During the course of their investigation, however, both detectives wind up dead and are themselves brought back to life. With a horrible grimace plastered on his face and his pumped-up biceps gratuitously on display throughout the film, Piscopo sabotages the film's attempts at humor. Reportedly the former "Saturday Night Live" comedian was permitted to improvise at will, and as a result DEAD HEAT's laugh quotient is reduced to next to nothing. For a former editor, director Goldblatt's sense of pacing is atrocious and the action scenes seem to drag on forever. What keeps DEAD HEAT watchable (barely) are the inventive special effects of Steve Johnson and crew. Regrettably, some of his more graphic work was cut when the MPAA balked six different times and threatened the producers with an X rating if several gruesome items weren't removed. The trimming is obvious in the final version, and certainly doesn't help the action scenes any. Unless you're a special effects nut, avoid DEAD HEAT at all costs.

p, Michael Meltzer, David Helpern; d, Mark Goldblatt; w, Terry Black; ph, Robert D. Yeoman (Technicolor); ed, Harvey Rosenstock; m, Ernest Troost.

(PR:O    MPAA:R)

## DEAD MEN WALK**½

(1943) 63m PRC bw

George Zucco (Dr. Lloyd Clayton/Dr. Elwyn Clayton), Mary Carlisle (Gayle), Nedrick Young (Dr. Bentley), Dwight Frye (Zolarr), Fern Emmett (Kate), Robert Strange (Harper), Hal Price (Sheriff), Sam Flint (Minister).

George Zucco plays a dual role as twin doctors—one good, the other evil—in this cheap but enjoyable Poverty Row effort. The evil doctor dabbles in the occult, and after he dies, is exhumed by his hunchback assistant, Zolarr (Dwight Frye), coming back to life as a vampire. Seeking vengeance on his good brother, the vampire murders several locals and soon the inevitable angry mob is after him. Zucco, one of the hammiest actors Hollywood ever produced, is a delight to watch playing both good and evil, as is Frye in what would prove to be his final role (he died of a heart attack the very next year). Director Sam Newfield occasionally triumphs over his limitations and creates some remarkably surreal effects, especially in the climax which pits brother against brother in a burning building.

p, Sigmund Neufeld; d, Sam Newfield; w, Fred Myton; ph, Jack Greenhalgh; ed, Holbrook N. Todd.

(PR:A    MPAA:NR)

## DEAD OF NIGHT****

(1946, Brit.) 104m Rank/Ealing/UNIV bw

Mervyn Johns (Walter Craig), Roland Culver (Eliot Foley), Mary Merrall (Mrs. Foley), Frederick Valk (Dr. Van Straaten), Renee Gadd (Mrs. Craig), Antony Baird (Hugh Grainger), Judy Kelly (Joyce Grainger), Miles Malleson (Hearse Driver), Sally Ann Howes (Sally O'Hara), Michael Allan (Jimmy Watson), Robert Wyndham (Dr. Albury), Googie Withers (Joan Courtland), Ralph Michael (Peter Court-land), Esme Percy (Dealer), Michael Redgrave (Maxwell Frere), Hartley Power (Sylvester Kee), Elizabeth Welch (Beulah), Magda Kun (Mitzi), Garry Marsh (Harry Parker), Basil Radford (George Parratt), Naunton Wayne (Larry Potter), Peggy Bryan (Mary Lee), Johnny Maguire (Dummy), Allan Jeayes (Maurice Olcott).

One of the best horror anthologies ever made, this much-praised film still holds up, but suffers from the variances of pace and mood that inevitably affect all compilation efforts. Architect Walter Craig (Mervyn Johns) is called to Pilgrim's Farm, a country house he has been hired to remodel. Approaching the austere Victorian building in his car, he finds that there is something hauntingly familiar about the house. Once inside, Craig recognizes everyone present, telling them they have all been part of a recurring nightmare he has had, whereupon the guests relate their own nightmares, one by one. The first tale, "The Hearse Driver," is told by Grainger (Antony Baird). In it he is a race-track driver who purposely misses a bus, on a hunch, after which the bus crashes. Sally O'Hara (Sally Ann Howes) then reports "The Christmas Story," in which she attends a holiday party and, during a game of hide-and-seek, finds a crying child in a strange room. The teenage Sally comforts him, and later discovers that the child has been long dead, killed by his own sister. Joan Courtland (Googie Withers), in "The Haunted Mirror," chillingly relates a tale in which she is given an antique mirror by her fiance, which begins to reflect a Victorian room where a killing once took place. In "The Golfing Story"—the only piece designed for comic relief—two golfers (Basil Radford and Naunton Wayne) vie for the attentions of one woman. One golfer tricks the other into suicide, only to have the deceased return and haunt him as he is about to enjoy his wedding night. The last story, titled "The Ventriloquist's Dummy," shows a ventriloquist (Michael Redgrave) going mad, believing that his dummy is assuming his personality, while he is becoming the manipulated prop. With typical disregard for consistency, US distributors thought this excellent British import was too long and cut the golfing sequence (not a bad move, actually) and the Christmas ghost tale, confusing audiences who could not understand what Howes, Radford, and Wayne were doing in the linking story. The two tales were later reinstated. Of the four directors helming the various stories, Robert Hamer is a standout with "The Haunted Mirror" and Alberto Cavalcanti excels with his two chillers, "The Christmas Story" and "The Ventriloquist's Dummy."

p, Michael Balcon; d, Alberto Cavalcanti ("The Ventriloquist's Dummy", "The Christmas Story"), Basil Dearden ("The Linking Story", "The Hearse Driver"), Robert Hamer ("The Haunted Mirror"), Charles Crichton ("The Golfing Story"); w, John Baines, Angus MacPhail, T.E.B. Clarke (based on stories by H.G. Wells, E.F. Benson, John Baines, Angus MacPhail); ph, Jack Parker, H. Julius; ed, Charles Hasse; m, Georges Auric.

(PR:C    MPAA:NR)

## DEAD RINGERS*****

(1988, Can.) 115m Mantle Clinic II/FOX c

Jeremy Irons *(Beverly Mantle/Elliot Mantle)*, Genevieve Bujold *(Claire Niveau)*, Heidi Von Palleske *(Cary)*, Barbara Gordon *(Danuta)*, Shirley Douglas *(Laura)*, Stephen Lack *(Anders Wolleck)*, Nick Nichols *(Leo)*, Lynn Cormack *(Arlene)*, Damir Androi *(Birchall)*, Miriam Newhouse *(Mrs. Bookman)*, David Hughes *(Superintendent)*, Richard Farrell *(Dean of Medicine)*, Warren Davis *(Anatomy Class Supervisor)*, Jonathan Haley *(Beverly, Age 9)*, Nicholas Haley *(Elliot, Age 9)*, Marsha Moreau *(Raffaella)*, Denis Akiyama *(Pharmacist)*, Dee McCafferty *(Surgeon)*, Susan Markle *(Operating Room Nurse)*, Murray Chuchley *(Assisting Surgeon)*, Jane Luk *(Lecture Hall Nurse)*, Tita Trevisan *(Furniture Salesman)*, Jacqueline Hennessy, Jillian Hennessy *(Escort Twins)*, David Walden *(Director)*, Liliane Stillwell *(Wardrobe Person)*.

Quietly devastating, DEAD RINGERS is final evidence that David Cronenberg has matured into a truly great filmmaker. Continuing the detailed character study that blossomed in THE FLY and combining it with his fixation on the metaphysical, Cronenberg has created yet another vividly realized film that is powerful, moving, and rich in ideas. Surprisingly, the movie does not contain the director's trademark visceralia. Instead, it is a chilling character study, boasting a brilliant performance from Jeremy Irons and some of the most impressive (and unintrusive) special effects work yet to hit the screen. Inspired by the real-life story of respected twin New York City gynecologists Steven and Cyril Marcus (who, in 1975, were both found dead in their garbage-strewn Upper East Side apartment, a double suicide brought on by barbiturate addiction), Cronenberg introduces us to his twins, Elliot and Beverly Mantle, a pair of brilliant gynecologists who open a state-of-the-art fertility clinic and share an opulent apartment. Although physically identical, the twins possess very different personalities. Elliot is something of a cad—suave, debonair, and self-confident to the point of arrogance—while Beverly is shy, studious, and more sensitive. Elliot has always procured women for Beverly by seducing them first, then turning them over to his shy sibling when he was through—unbeknownst to the woman. The brothers discuss the details of their liaisons, more or less sharing notes, and neither really feels he has experienced anything fully unless the other has done it as well. Ultimately, the relationship is suffocating, and individual identities become confused. When a famous actress, Claire Niveau (Genevieve Bujold), arrives at the clinic looking for answers to her infertility, trouble brews between the brothers, for, while they both share her sexually, Beverly falls in love for the first time, driving a wedge between the twins. Extremely unsettling, at times amusing, cold yet personal, DEAD RINGERS slowly creeps over the viewer, revealing its horrors at a deliberate pace, rather than shocking outright with such spectacular displays of gore as the exploding heads of SCANNERS, gaping stomach cavities of VIDEODROME, or vomiting Brundleflies of THE FLY. Not your average horror roller-coaster ride, DEAD RINGERS asks some disturbing questions about the nature of individual identity, and within that net explores such outgrowths as eroticism, narcissism, and misogyny. During the last decade, Cronenberg has matured into a filmmaker of remarkable scope, able to convey his obsessions with impeccable skill without sacrificing one iota of his own remarkable individuality.

p, David Cronenberg, Marc Boyman; d, David Cronenberg; w, David Cronenberg, Norman Snider (based on the book *Twins* by Bari Wood, Jack Geasland); ph, Peter Suschitzky; ed, Ronald Sandors; m, Howard Shore.

**(PR:O   MPAA:R)**

## DEAD ZONE, THE***

(1983) 103m PAR c

Christopher Walken *(Johnny Smith)*, Brooke Adams *(Sarah Bracknell)*, Tom Skerritt *(Sheriff Bannerman)*, Herbert Lom *(Dr. Sam Welzak)*, Anthony Zerbe *(Roger Stuart)*, Colleen Dewhurst *(Henrietta Dodd)*, Martin Sheen *(Greg Stillson)*, Nicholas Campbell *(Frank Dodd)*, Sean Sullivan *(Herb Smith)*, Jackie Burroughs *(Vera Smith)*, Geza Kovacs *(Sonny Elliman)*, Simon Craig *(Christopher Stuart)*, Barry Flatman *(Walter Bracknell)*, Raffi Tchalikian, Ken Pogue, Gordon Jocelyn, Bill Copeland, Jack Messinger.

Until THE FLY (1986), this was David Cronenberg's most financially successful film, and while slick and professional, it is also one of his least interesting. Easily the best adaptation of a Stephen King novel—and that includes Stanley Kubrick's THE SHINING—THE DEAD ZONE stars Christopher Walken as Johnny Smith, a young, shy schoolteacher who leaves his fiancee one night during a rainstorm and suffers a near-fatal auto accident. Five years later Johnny comes out of a deep coma, his life forever changed. His fiancee has married another man, his mother has become a religious fanatic, and he has developed a strange power to see people's futures by touching their hands. After helping to solve a murder and saving the life of a child he saw drowning in a vision, Johnny attends a political rally, and when he shakes the hand of the candidate (Martin Sheen), he sees not only that someday this man will be president but that he will also push the nuclear button, destroying the Earth. Fed up with his life and feeling increasingly ill (plagued with painful headaches), Johnny decides to assassinate the politician and change the future. Though the film is well acted and directed, once again King's source material bites off more than it can chew. It tries to elevate a simple story of tragic, unfulfilled love into a psychic horror drama that leads to world-shaking revelations, but fails to develop any of the angles particularly well. Episodic in structure, THE DEAD ZONE bogs down in spots, and while a few sequences are quite powerful, the film never really comes together. Had any other director helmed this, it would have been an impressive achievement, but for Cronenberg it is a disappointment, bereft as it is of his own unique visionary sensibility.

p, Debra Hill; d, David Cronenberg; w, Jeffrey Boam (based on the novel by Stephen King); ph, Mark Irwin (Technicolor); ed, Ronald Sanders; m, Michael Kamen.

**(PR:O   MPAA:R)**

## DEADLY BLESSING**½

(1981) 102m Polygram/UA c

Maren Jensen *(Martha)*, Susan Buckner *(Vicky)*, Sharon Stone *(Lana)*, Jeff East *(John Schmidt)*, Lisa Hartman *(Faith)*, Lois Nettleton *(Louisa)*, Ernest Borgnine *(Isaiah)*, Colleen Riley *(Melissa)*, Doug Barr *(Jim)*, Michael Berryman *(Gluntz)*, Kevin Cooney *(Sheriff)*, Bobby Dark *(Theater Manager)*, Kevin Farr *(Fat Boy)*, Neil Fletcher *(Gravedigger)*, Jonathon Gulla *(Tom)*, Chester Kulas, Jr. *(Leopold)*, Lawrence Montaigne *(Matthew)*, Lucky Mosley *(Sammy)*, Dan Shackelford *(Medic)*, Annabelle Weenick *(Ruth)*, Jenna Worthen *(Mrs. Gluntz)*, Percy Rodriguez *(Narrator)*.

This was a disappointing outing from Wes Craven, whose previous film, THE HILLS HAVE EYES (1977), stands as a masterpiece among the modern wave of horror films. The plot concerns Martha (Maren Jensen), who lives alone near the property of a conservative, repressive religious sect—the Hittites—to which her husband once belonged. He was murdered under mysterious circumstances soon after he quit the sect, and two of Martha's friends from California (Susan Buckner and Sharon Stone) have arrived to comfort her. Soon the Hittites, led by Isaiah (Ernest Borgnine), begin harassing Martha and her friends, trying to force them to leave. The pressure begins to take its toll, and the women suffer from nightmares (one of which includes a spider dropping into the dreamer's mouth) and other, actual dangers (a snake appears in the bath water), leading to more murders. Craven builds an interesting premise, but the ending is lame and unsatisfying. Outstanding cinematography and a good musical score enhance the film's mood greatly. Craven's next outing, SWAMP THING (1982), was another disappointment, but he returned in full force in 1984 with the truly terrifying A NIGHTMARE ON ELM STREET.

p, Micheline Keller, Max Keller, Pat Herskovic; d, Wes Craven; w, Glenn M. Benest, Matthew Barr, Wes Craven; ph, Robert Jessup (Metrocolor); ed, Richard Bracken; m, James Horner.

**(PR:O MPAA:R)**

## DEADLY DREAMS*

(1988) 79m New Classics/Concorde c

Mitchell Anderson *(Alex)*, Juliette Cummins *(Maggie)*, Xander Berkeley *(Jack)*, Thom Babbes *(Danny)*, Timothy Austin *(Young Alex)*, Beach Dickerson.

This surprising and refreshingly taut low-budget horror film offers what most run-of-the-mill slasher films don't: a good story with a surprise ending. Alex's (Mitchell Anderson) parents were shot and killed 10 years earlier on Christmas Eve. Now he is plagued with nightmares of a masked hunter and begins seeing him at every turn. Though comforted by girl friend Maggie (Juliette Cummins) and best friend Danny (Thom Babbes), Alex begins a slow descent into madness, while, as the story unfolds, a conspiracy to steal Alex's inheritance is revealed. Director Kristine Peterson (a former Roger Corman protege) handles the material with a sure hand and a keen eye. The numerous horror sequences are quite frightening—the viewer is never sure of what is real and what is fantasy. Moreover, Peterson delivers the scares without overloading the blood. All of the performances are convincing, especially that of Babbes (author of the screenplay), who brings a freshness to the traditional role of the wise-guy buddy.

p, Matt Leipzig; d, Kristine Peterson; w, Thom Babbes; ph, Zoran Hochstatter (Foto-Kem color); ed, Bernard Caputo; m, Todd Boekelheide.

**(PR:O MPAA:R)**

## DEADLY EYES**½

(1982) 93m Northshore Investments/Golden Communications c (AKA: RATS, THE)

Sam Groom *(Paul Harris)*, Sara Batsford *(Kelly Leonard)*, Scatman Crothers *(George Fask)*, Lisa Langlois *(Trudy White)*, Cec Linder *(Dr. Luis Spenser)*, James B. Douglas *(Mel Dederick)*, Lesleh Donaldson *(Martha)*.

A throwback to the giant-monster movies of the 1950s, this film features a special breed of rats that grow to unusually large proportions as they terrorize the city. In between rat attacks, an affair develops between a high-school science teacher (Sam Groom) and a city health inspector (Sara Batsford). Providing a lot of polish, considering his low budget, action director Robert Clouse (ENTER THE DRAGON; THE BIG BRAWL) develops the tension at a good pace and manages to maintain interest throughout. One of the more memorable scenes occurs when the rats take over a moviehouse, which may send chills up your spine if you're the type who wonders what could be lurking beneath your seat.

p, Paul Kahnert, Charles Eglee; d, Robert Clouse; w, Charles Eglee (from the novel by James Herbert); ph, Rene Verzier; ed, Ron Wisman.

**(PR:O MPAA:R)**

## DEADLY FRIEND**

(1986) 92m Pan Arts-Layton/WB c

Matthew Laborteaux *(Paul)*, Kristy Swanson *(Samantha)*, Anne Twomey *(Jeannie Conway)*, Michael Sharrett *(Tom)*, Richard Marcus *(Harry)*, Anne Ramsey *(Elvira Williams)*, Lee Paul *(Police Sgt. Volchek)*, Russ Martin *(Dr. Johanson)*, Andrew Roperto *(Carl Denton)*, Robin Nuyen *(Thief)*, William H. Faeth *(Doctor in Sam's Room)*, Joel Hile *(Deputy)*, Tom Spratley *(Neighbor)*, Jim Ishida *(Coroner)*, Charles Fleischer *(Voice of Bee Bee)*.

Is Wes Craven incapable of directing a decent horror movie with the word "deadly" in the title? This was his first film after his 1984 triumph A NIGHTMARE ON ELM STREET, and it is a big disappointment. Something of an uneasy cross between the classic FRANKENSTEIN and the 1986 cute-robot hit SHORT CIRCUIT, the film is about a brilliant young teenager, Paul (Matthew Laborteaux), an expert on artificial intelligence who has built a robot named Bee Bee that can learn and think for itself. Unfortunately, Bee Bee also can feel hatred, and the robot rolls around the neighborhood killing off all those who have slighted its creator and his friends. When Bee Bee is eventually destroyed and Paul's girl friend killed, he puts Bee Bee's computer chip in his gal's brain—creating a monster. Just what Craven was trying to do with this material is anybody's guess. The first half of the film seems a standard teen comedy with the robot thrown in as a twist, then it turns into a rather dull mad-scientist romp. Craven's direction is nothing more than workmanlike, and it appears that he threw two nightmare sequences into the mix out of sheer boredom. Both sequences work well in themselves (they are the most frightening parts of the film), but they are poorly integrated into the narrative, ultimately annoying, and apparently inserted by Craven in a desperate attempt to generate some excitement by falling back on A NIGHTMARE ON ELM STREET's former glory. The film is almost worth watching, however, for the scene in which the robot-girl throws a basketball at Anne (THROW MOMMA FROM THE TRAIN) Ramsey, decimating her head.

p, Robert M. Sherman; d, Wes Craven; w, Bruce Joel Rubin (based on the novel *Friend* by Diana Henstell); ph, Philip Lathrop (Panavision); ed, Michael Eliot; m, Charles Bernstein.

**(PR:O    MPAA:R)**

## DEADTIME STORIES*

(1987) 81m Scary Stuff/Bedford c

Michael Mesmer *(Uncle Mike)*, Brian DePersia *(Little Brian)*, Scott Valentine *(Peter)*, Phyllis Craig *(Hanagohl)*, Anne Redfern *(Florinda)*, Kathy Fleg *(Miranda)*, Casper Roos *(Vicar)*, Barbara Seldon, Leigh Kirlton *(Seductresses)*, Lesley Sank *(Reviving Magoga)*, Lisa Cain *(Living Magoga)*, Jeff Delman *(Strangling Man)*, Nicole Picard *(Rachel)*, Matt Mitler *(Willie)*, Michael Berlinger *(Greg)*, Fran Lopate *(Grandma)*, John Bachelder *(Drugstore Clerk)*, Caroline Carrigan *(Nurse)*, Oded Carmi *(Groundskeeper)*, Heather L. Bailey *(Girl in Store)*, Thea *(Dog)*, Cathryn DePrume *(Goldi Lox)*, Melissa Leo *(Melissa "Mama" Baer)*, Kevin Hannon *(Beresford "Papa" Baer)*, Timothy Rule *(Wilmont "Baby" Baer)*, Robert Trimboli *(Lt. Jack B. Nimble)*, Harvey Pierce *(Capt. Jack B. Quick)*, Rondell Sheridan *(Looney Bin Guard)*, Beth Felty *(Reporter)*, Pat McCord *(Anchorman)*, Michele Mars *(Waitress)*, Ron Bush *(Bank Guard)*, Oded Carmi *(Postman)*, Bryant Tausek *(Man at Car)*, Suzanna Vaucher *(Weather Girl)*, Leif Wennerstrom, Jim Nocell *(Dead Bodies)*.

This lame anthology bridges three skewed fairy tales with a framing story in which a little boy (Brian DePersia) who can't sleep because he keeps seeing monsters in his dark bedroom is told scary tales by his slightly vengeful uncle (Michael Mesmer), who is upset over having to miss the Nude Miss World contest on cable TV. In the first story, "Peter and the Witches," a sturdy young lad sold into slavery as a child is the lackey of a pair of hideous witches. The next story, "Little Red Runninghood," concerns a nubile high-school girl who stops by the pharmacy to pick up a prescription for Granny. Unfortunately, the package is mixed up with that of a young man who needs powerful

sleeping pills to keep him from becoming a werewolf during the full moon. In "Goldi Lox and the Three Baers," Beresford "Papa" Baer and his idiot son, Wilmont "Baby" Baer, break out of the loony bin and head to their old house, now occupied by Goldi Lox, a fellow escaped lunatic with telekinetic powers. Miserable production values plague this film, shot over the course of four years in upstate New York and Connecticut. Director Jeffrey Delman makes his debut, and although the press kit notes that his grandfather's cousin was legendary movie music composer Bernard Herrmann, it appears that talent is not hereditary. The film does have some wacky humor going for it, but comedy is not what horror film fans are after. They look for jolts, special effects, and edge-of-the-seat tension, none of which are in evidence here.

p, Bill Paul; d, Jeffrey Delman; w, Jeffrey Delman, Charles F. Shelton (based on a story by Jeffrey Delman); ph, Daniel B. Canton; ed, William Szarka; m, Taj.

**(PR:O    MPAA:R)**

## DEAR, DEAD DELILAH zero

(1972) 95m Southern Star/AE TV c

Agnes Moorehead *(Delilah)*, Will Geer *(Roy)*, Michael Ansara *(Morgan)*, Patricia Carmichael *(Luddy)*, Dennis Patrick *(Alonzo)*, Anne Meacham *(Grace)*, Robert Gentry *(Richard)*, Elizabeth Eis *(Ellen)*, Ruth Baker *(Buffy)*, Ann Giggs *(Young Luddy)*, John Marriot *(Marshall)*.

Although a rabid cult of fans extols the virtues of this cheap, bloody attempt at Southern gothic horror, DEAR, DEAD DELILAH has no redeeming qualities. In fact, if there were a lower star rating than zero it would be bestowed on this production, which embarrasses great actors Agnes Moorehead (it was her last film before she died of lung cancer in 1974) and Will Geer in their twilight years. The plot concerns a dying, obnoxious, wheelchair-confined matriarch (Moorehead) in whose mansion a fortune is buried. Evil relatives race to see who can find the dough first; Geer's character gets his hand chopped off. Really, really lame.

p, Jack Clement; d, John Farris; w, John Farris; ph, William R. Johnson (Eastmancolor); ed, Ron Dorfman; m, Bill Justis.

**(PR:O    MPAA:R)**

## DEATH CURSE OF TARTU*

(1967) 87m Falcon International/Thunderbird International c

Fred Pinero *(Ed Tison)*, Babette Sherrill *(Julie Tison)*, Mayra Cristine *(Cindy)*, Sherman Hayes *(Johnny)*, Gary Holtz *(Tommy)*, Maurice Stewart *(Joann)*, Frank Weed *(Sam Gunter)*, Doug Hobart *(Tartu)*, William Marcos *(Billy/The Indian)*.

This cheapo late-night TV favorite concerns a group of thoughtless archaeology students who accidentally disturb the grave of a Seminole Indian witch doctor named Tartu (Doug Hobart). Tartu comes back to life and goes after the kids, alternately taking the form of a snake, a shark, an alligator, and a zombie—killing off all his victims until he is swallowed up by quicksand, thus fulfilling some obscure native prophecy. The Florida Everglades, the film's location site, provide the quicksand for the "chilling" finale. Only for the desperate.

p, Joseph Fink, Juan Hildalgo-Gato; d, William Grefe; w, William Grefe; ph, Julio C. Chavez; ed, Julio C. Chavez (Eastmancolor).

**(PR:C  MPAA:NR)**

## DEATH SHIP*

(1980, Can.) 91m AE c

George Kennedy *(Ashland),* Richard Crenna *(Trevor Marshall),* Nick Mancuso *(Nick),* Sally Ann Howes *(Margaret Marshall),* Kate Reid *(Sylvia),* Victoria Burgoyne *(Lori),* Jennifer McKinney *(Robin),* Danny Highham *(Ben),* Saul Rubinek *(Jackie).*

A luxury liner collides with a mysterious ship and sinks, leaving nine survivors, including the captain (George Kennedy). Drifting, they spot a strange black ship floating by and climb aboard. Strange things begin to happen as the vessel, which appears to be a Nazi torture ship, tries to kill its passengers, while the captain becomes possessed by the Nazi evil on board. So ludicrous it's quite funny.

p, Derek Gibson, Harold Greenberg; d, Alvin Rakoff; w, John Robins; ph, Rene Verzier; ed, Mike Campbell.

**(PR:O  MPAA:R)**

## DEATHDREAM****

(1972, Can.) 88m Europix c (AKA: DEATH OF NIGHT; NIGHT WALK; VETERAN, THE)

John Marley *(Charles Brooks),* Lynn Carlin *(Christine Brooks),* Richard Backus *(Andy Brooks),* Henderson Forsythe *(Doc Allman),* Anya Ormsby *(Cathy Brooks),* Jane Daly *(Joanne),* Michael Mazes *(Bob),* Arthur Anderson *(Postman),* Bud Hoey *(Ed),* Virginia Cortez *(Rosalie),* Arthur Bradley *(Army Captain),* David Grawlikowski *(Truck Driver),* Raymond Michel *(Policeman),* Robert Cannon *(Drunk),* Jeff Becker, Scott Becker, Kevin Schweizer, Greg Wells *(Boys),* Jeffrey Gillen *(Bartender),* Mal Jones *(Sheriff),* Edward Anderson *(Deputy),* Alan Ormsby *(Bystander),* George DeVries, Robert Noble *(TV Announcers).*

Scary low-budget horror from the makers of the equally effective CHILDREN SHOULDN'T PLAY WITH DEAD THINGS and DERANGED, DEATHDREAM opens as Andy Brooks (Richard Backus) and a buddy are killed in battle in Vietnam. Back home, his parents (John Marley and Lynn Carlin) and his sister (Anya Ormsby) are rocked by the news. Dad grimly accepts their loss, but Mom refuses to believe it and acts as though her boy were still alive. That night the family dog begins to growl and Mom suspects burglars are nearby. Instead, the family is shocked to find Andy standing at the door, in his dress uniform, alive and well. Dad brings some of the neighborhood

boys over to entice Andy into playing football (before the war he always loved having the children around). Andy ignores his visitors, who persistently ask questions about the war, but when the family dog begins snarling at him, he shocks the kids by picking the dog up by the throat and strangling it to death. Dad decides that this is enough and tells his wife that he's taking their son to a doctor. The doctor tries to take Andy's pulse, but can't find it. You see, Andy's dead, and he needs a steady supply of blood to stay reanimated, so he kills the doctor, and some friends, and . . . DEATHDREAM is a powerful, creepy film that reworks the classic tale "The Monkey's Paw," relying on mood and tension to convey the terror. It uses the horror genre quite successfully to explore the difficulty of post-Vietnam adjustment (stretched to a horrible, exaggerated limit) and the disintegration of the American family in the 1960s. While the boy's father faces reality, his mother refuses to reject her baby, and even helps him during the remarkable, unforgettable climax. Both Alan Ormsby and Tom Savini worked on the special makeup. Highly recommended.

p, Bob Clark, Tom Karr; d, Bob Clark, Tom Karr; w, Alan Ormsby; ph, Jack McGowan.

**(PR:O  MPAA:R)**

## DEATHROW GAMESHOW zero

(1987) 83m Pirromount/Crown c

John McCafferty *(Chuck Toedan),* Robin Blythe *(Gloria Sternvirgin),* Beano *(Luigi Pappalardo),* Mark Lasky *(Momma),* Darwyn Carson *(Trudy),* Debra Lamb *(Shanna Shallow),* Paul Farbman *(Dinko).*

This idiotic ripoff of THE RUNNING MAN features John McCafferty as Chuck Toedan, the host of the wildly controversial gameshow "Live or Die," in which death-row inmate contestants perform silly and dangerous tasks for reprieves or prizes for their families. The audiences applaud furiously when contestants are guillotined on the air, then examined to determine if a face-up roll of the head qualifies the victim's family for a set of major kitchen appliances. Aggressively, annoyingly stupid, the film looks like something out of another time, the days of THE GROOVE TUBE, KENTUCKY FRIED MOVIE, and the like. The film is packed with gags that aren't funny and monotonous dialog. The style is cartoonish, the acting broad (but not entirely bad), and the production values below criticism. Still, there are some undeniably funny moments of sick humor.

p, Brian J. Smith; d, Mark Pirro; w, Mark Pirro, Alan Gries; ph, Craig Bassuk; ed, Tim Shoemaker; m, Gregg Gross.

**(PR:O  MPAA:R)**

## DEEP RED: HATCHET MURDERS***½

(1975, It.) 98m Seda Spettacoli Mahler c (PROFONDO ROSSO; AKA: HATCHET MURDERS, THE; DRIPPING DEEP RED; DEEP RED; SABRE TOOTH TIGER, THE)

David Hemmings *(Marcus Daly),* Daria Nicolodi *(Gianna Brazzi),* Gabriele Lavia *(Carlo),* Clara Calamai *(Marta, Carlo's Mother),* Macha Meril *(Dr. Helga Ullmann),* Glauco

Mauri *(Prof. Giordani)*, Eros Pagni *(Dr. Calcabrini)*, Giuliana Calandra *(Amanda Righetti)*, Nicoletta Elmi *(Olga)*.

Another exercise in cinematic style from Dario Argento, whose BIRD WITH THE CRYSTAL PLUMAGE had an immense impact on the genre. Marcus Daly (David Hemmings), an English music teacher in Rome, hears screams and comes to the aid of a telepathist (Macha Meril) who has been brutally attacked. Arriving on the scene too late to save the victim, Daly joins the woman's lover (Glauco Mauri), another telepathist, and a local newswoman (Daria Nicolodi, wife of director Argento) in the search for the killer, which leads to several more murders and several attempts on Daly's own life. Once again using a murder mystery format to experiment cinematically, Argento here presents a stylish and compelling film that boasts remarkable visuals and an inventive use of sound effects and music. The edge-of-your-seat climax, in which Argento gleefully manipulates his audience, is quite impressive. Hemmings, whose strong identification with his role in Michelangelo Antonioni's BLOW-UP (1966) is used by Argento to great advantage, turns in an excellent performance as the musician drawn into a confusing, gruesomely violent world after witnessing a murder.

p, Salvatore Argento, Claudio Argento; d, Dario Argento; w, Dario Argento, Giuseppe Bassan (based on a story by Argento, Bernardo Zapponi); ph, Luigi Kuveiller (Eastmancolor); ed, Franco Fraticelli; m, Giorgio Gaslini, The Goblins.

**(PR:O   MPAA:R)**

## DEMENTED**

(1980) 93m IRC-IWDC-Four Features Partners c

Sallee Elyse *(Linda Rodgers)*, Bruce Gilchrist, Bryan Charles, Chip Matthews, Deborah Alter, Kathryn Clayton, Robert Mendel.

Barely out of the sanitarium after a traumatic gang rape, Linda (Sallee Elyse) takes some boys in monster masks to be her rapists and swings into vengeful action, using guns and knives (and a cleaver). The film gets off to a slow start, but once Linda's mind snaps and she begins seducing the kids, then dispatching them in assorted grisly fashions, the film actually becomes a fairly funny black comedy.

p, Alex Rebar, Arthur Jeffreys; d, Arthur Jeffreys; w, Alex Rebar; ph, Jim Tynes; m, Richard Tufo.

**(PR:O   MPAA:R)**

## DEMENTIA***

(1955) 55m Rizzoli/van Wolfe-API bw (AKA: DAUGHTER OF HORROR)

Adrienne Barrett *(The Gamin)*, Bruno Ve Sota *(Rich Man)*, Ben Roseman *(Father—Law Enforcer)*, Richard Barron *(Evil One)*, Ed Hinkle *(Butler)*, Lucille Howland *(Mother)*, Jebbie Ve Sota *(Flower Girl)*, Faith Parker *(Nightclub Girl)*, Gayne Sullivan *(Wino)*, Ed McMahon *(Narrator)*.

This extremely obscure expressionistic horror film stars Adrienne Barrett as a young woman who finds herself propelled through a nightmare evening. She murders her father, then encounters a mysterious rich man (Bruno Ve Sota) who takes her home to his apartment. She struggles against his advances; the man falls from his balcony to the street below. The woman realizes that the dead man has pulled her necklace off in his fall, however, and runs downstairs to wrest it from his grasp. Unable to pull his fingers open, she uses a knife to saw his hand off. Seized with a maniacal giddiness, she runs into a nearby jazz club (with music provided by trumpeter Shorty Rogers and his band, the Giants), but suddenly awakens in a cheap hotel room. Thinking it was all a dream, she opens the dresser drawer to find a severed hand clutching a necklace. Wildly experimental, DEMENTIA features not a word uttered by the actors. *Variety* called it "the strangest film ever offered for theatrical release," and the film was banned by the New York State Board of Censors in 1955. Believe it or not, it's narrated by Johnny Carson sidekick Ed McMahon.

p, John Parker; d, John Parker; w, John Parker; ph, William Thompson; ed, Joseph Gluck; m, George Antheil.

**(PR:C   MPAA:NR)**

## DEMENTIA 13***½

(1963) 81m Filmgroup/AIP bw (GB: HAUNTED AND THE HUNTED, THE)

William Campbell *(Richard Haloran)*, Luana Anders *(Louise Haloran)*, Bart Patton *(Billy Haloran)*, Mary Mitchell *(Kane)*, Patrick Magee *(Justin Caleb)*, Eithne Dunne *(Lady Haloran)*, Peter Read *(John Haloran)*, Karl Schanzer *(Simon)*, Ron Perry *(Arthur)*, Derry O'Donovan *(Lillian)*, Barbara Dowling *(Kathleen)*.

This is the first *mainstream* film Francis Ford Coppola directed (he had done several "nudies" before this), and it happens to be a little gem of gothic horror, stylishly helmed on a shoestring budget. (Producer Roger Corman gave Coppola $22,000 and three of the stars of his own THE YOUNG RACERS, which had just wrapped up shooting in Ireland. Coppola served as sound man on that picture and had written DEMENTIA 13's screenplay in his spare time). The plot concerns a crazed Irish family whose members are being mysteriously killed off by someone who wants to gain a vast inheritance. The film opens with a violent argument between John (Peter Read) and his wife, Louise (Luana Anders), over his eccentric mother's (Eithne Dunne) will. The argument becomes so heated that John is stricken with a heart attack and dies. Not wanting to lose her share of the inheritance, Louise sinks her husband's body in a nearby lake and conceals his death from other family members. Meanwhile, more relatives have arrived at the estate (Bart Patton, William Campbell, and Mary Mitchell, as Campbell's fiancee) to attend a memorial ceremony for their sister, who drowned in the lake eight years before. Louise sees her opportunity and decides to drive her mother-in-law completely insane by making her believe that she can communicate with her dead daughter from the great beyond. Before Louise has a chance to enact her scheme, however, she is axed to death and the hunt for the killer is on. Though the plot is rather silly and labored, the film rises above the somewhat confused material by virtue of Coppola's budding talent for composition and clever editing. As is typical of the Corman low-budget film factory, the film was saddled (some say at Coppola's insistence) with a ridiculous five-minute opening sequence in which a "psychiatrist" sits in his office and gives the audience a test to determine if they are mentally stable enough to see the movie.

p, Roger Corman, Charles Hannawalt, R. Wright Campbell; d, Francis Ford Coppola; w, Francis Ford Coppola; ph, Charles Hannawalt; ed, Stuart O'Brien; m, Ronald Stein.

(PR:C   MPAA:NR)

## DEMON, THE*

(1981, South Africa) 95m Gold Key-Holland c

Jennifer Holmes *(Mary)*, Cameron Mitchell *(Col. Bill Carson)*, Zoli Markey *(Jo)*, Craig Gardner, Mark Tannous, Peter Elliott, Moria Winslow, Diane Burmeister, George Korelin, Vera Blacker, John Parsonson, Ashleigh Sendin, Graham Kennard, April Galetti.

This lame entry from South Africa features a mysterious monster, wearing a lifelike rubber mask, that stalks and kills women, using his steel claw and some baggies as his weapons. Obviously inspired by HALLOWEEN, this stalk-and-slash effort will be of interest only to Cameron Mitchell devotees.

p, Percival Rubens; d, Percival Rubens; w, Percival Rubens; ph, Vincent Cox; m, Nick Labuschagne.

(PR:O   MPAA:NR)

## DEMON BARBER OF FLEET STREET, THE*½

(1939, Brit.) 66m SEL/MGM bw (GB: SWEENEY TODD, THE DEMON BARBER OF FLEET STREET)

Tod Slaughter *(Sweeney Todd)*, Eva Lister *(Johanna)*, Bruce Seton *(Mack)*, Davina Craig *(Nan)*, D.J. Williams *(Stephen Oakley)*, Jerry Verno *(Pearley)*, Stello Rho *(Mrs. Lovat)*, Johnny Singer *(The Beadle)*, Billy Holland, Norman Pierce, Ben Sonten.

This early film version of the "Sweeney Todd" story stars Tod Slaughter, Britain's preeminent horror star. Unfortunately, Slaughter's performances were very theatrical, summoning laughs rather than gasps in their histrionics. For some strange reason, a plethora of his work is readily available on home video. The story concerns the famed crazed barber, who slits the throats of his wealthier customers, then dumps them in the basement via a trap door under his barber chair. There, he robs the corpses of their valuables and turns them into meat pies to be sold in the next-door bakery. Loosely based on the real-life mass murders committed by Fritz Haarmann and Carl Denke. Produced in England in 1935, but not released in the US until 1939.

p, George King; d, George King; w, Frederick Hayward, H.F. Maltby (based on the play by George Dibdin-Pitt); ph, Ronald Neame.

(PR:A   MPAA:NR)

## DEMON LOVER, THE zero

(1977) 83m 21st Century c

Christmas Robbins *(Laval Blessing)*, Val Mayerick *(Damian Kaluta)*, Gunnar Hansen *(Professor Peckinpah)*, Tom Hutton *(Tom Frazetta)*, Dave Howard *(Charles Wrightson)*, Susan Bullen *(Susan Ackerman)*, Phil Foreman *(Alex Redondo)*, Linda Conrad *(Elaine Ormsby)*, Ron Hiveley *(Paul Foster)*, Kathy Stewart *(Janis Romero)*, Sonny Bell *(Lester Gould)*, Carol Lasowski *(Sally Jones)*, Michael McGivern *(Garrett Adams)*, Janet Porter *(Jane Corben)*.

An ultra-low-budget entry, shot in Jackson, Michigan, THE DEMON LOVER features an occultist who wreaks vengeance on his flock after they abandon him. Between cheap gore effects, the film is filled with in-jokes for movie-genre and comic-book enthusiasts. All the character names are homages to the filmmakers' favorite horror movie directors and comic-book artists: Kaluta, Frazetta, Gould, Jones, Foster, Wrightson, Corben, Adams, and Kirby are all big names in the comic-book field, and Romero, Peckinpah, and Ormsby are all directors and writers of violent films. (Ackerman refers to Forest J. Ackerman, publisher of "Famous Monsters" magazine.) Actor Gunnar Hansen is better known as "Leatherface" from THE TEXAS CHAINSAW MASSACRE; Val Mayerick is a comic-book artist known for "Howard the Duck."

p, Donald Jackson, Jerry Younkins; d, Donald Jackson, Jerry Younkins; w, Donald Jackson, Jerry Younkins.

(PR:O   MPAA:R)

## DEMON WITCH CHILD*

(1974, Sp.) 84m Coliseum c

Julian Mateos, Fernando Sancho, Marian Salgado, Lone Fleming, Angel Del Pozo.

In this Spanish EXORCIST rip-off, an old witch possesses the nine-year-old daughter of the politician who had her thrown in jail. The little girl goes through the usual paces, until she is confronted in the witch's tomb by a priest who performs an exorcism. Wholly derivative, lacking in style, and utterly dull.

d, Armando De Ossorio; w, Armando De Ossorio; ph, Urgent Meaj (Technicolor); m, Victor and Diego.

(PR:O   MPAA:R)

## DEMONOID zero

(1981) 78m Zach Motion Pictures-Panorama Films S.A./ American Panorama c (AKA: MACABRA)

Samantha Eggar *(Jennifer Baines)*, Stuart Whitman *(Father Cunningham)*, Roy Jenson *(Mark Baines)*, Narciso Busquets *(Dr. Julian Rivkin)*, Erika Carl.

A really awful "hand" movie, DEMONOID features Roy Cameron Jenson and Samantha Eggar (who's been in far too much trash like this) as a husband and wife who go to Mexico looking for silver, but instead find the Devil's left hand buried in a silver box. The hand is mobile, of course, and wanders around possessing people, who subsequently get a sudden urge to remove their own left hands. The going gets pretty ridiculous as various members of the possessed inflict all manner of pain upon themselves to remove their demonic digits. One man slams his hand in a car door, one puts his wrist on train tracks, and another bursts into a doctor's office brandishing a gun, demanding that the surgeon cut off his hand or he'll blow the doctor's head off. Eggar finally calls on a priest, Stuart Whitman (who's *really* been in too much trash like this), to exorcise the hand. Whitman outdoes a number of bad performances by demonstrating *both* his Spanish and Irish accents while playing the same character. Though DEMONOID was filmed in 1979, the producers sat on it for two years until Oliver Stone's THE HAND was released.

p, Alfred Zacharias; d, Alfred Zacharias; w, David Lee Fein, Alfred Zacharias, Amos Powell (based on a story by Zacharias); ph, Alex Phillips, Jr. (CFI Color); ed, Sandy Nervig; m, Richard Gillis.

**(PR:O MPAA:R)**

## DEMONS*½

(1985, It.) 85m DAC/Titanus c (DEMONI)

Natasha Hovey *(Cheryl),* Urbano Barberini *(George),* Karl Zinny, Fiore Argento, Paola Cozzo, Fabiola Toledo, Nicoletta Elmi, Stelio Condelli, Nicole Tessier, Geretta Giancarlo, Bobby Rhodes, Guido Baldi, Bettina Ciampolini, Giuseppe Cruciano, Sally Day.

One of the most overrated horror films of the decade, DEMONS, produced by Dario Argento and directed by Lamberto Bava, is a boring and hollow exercise in style that milks one device—the movie-within-a-movie trick—ad nauseam. A group of strangers receive free passes to a movie playing at a new theater nobody has ever heard of. The patrons run the gamut from innocent teenagers to a black pimp and two prostitutes. A strange display in the lobby features a dummy on a motorcycle with a strange Satanic mask hanging from the end of a sword. One of the prostitutes tries the mask on for a laugh, and winds up pricking her face. When the movie they are attending starts, it's a story of four teenagers who find a mask that looks exactly like the one in the lobby. One of the youths tries the mask on, pricks his face, and quickly becomes a yellow-eyed, pus-oozing, green-slime-drooling zombie out to kill anyone around him. Of course, the prostitute suddenly doesn't feel too well, and heads for the ladies' room to becomes a yellow-eyed, pus-oozing, green-slime-drooling zombie out to kill anyone around her. Soon nearly everyone in the theater is a zombie, and an excruciatingly gross and boring 50 minutes follow, with patrons dashing from room to room trying to escape the monsters and being picked off one by one. All this nonsense is accompanied by an inappropriate, grating, and persistent rock score screeched by the likes of Billy Idol and Motley Crue. Director Bava apparently learned nothing from his father, Mario, and producer Argento indulges his most annoying proclivities (the lengthy, pointless opening suspense scene, the rock score) while failing to impart his strengths as a director (his crisp, unique visualizations). Followed by

a sequel, DEMONS II. See ANGUISH, which uses the same movie-within-a-movie device to much better effect, instead.

p, Dario Argento; d, Lamberto Bava; w, Dario Argento, Lamberto Bava, Dardano Sacchetti, Franco Ferrini (based on a story by Sacchetti); ph, Gianlorenzo Battaglia (Eastmancolor); ed, Pietro Bozza; m, Claudio Simonetti.

**(PR:O MPAA:NR)**

## DEMONS 2: THE NIGHTMARE RETURNS*

(1986, It.) 94m DAC/Titanus c (DEMONI 2—L'INCUBO RITORNA; Trans: Demons 2—The Nightmare is Back)

David Kinight, Nancy Brilli, Coralina Cataldi Tassoni, Bobby Rhodes, Asia Argento, Virginia Bryant, Marco Vivo.

A virtual remake of the inexplicably successful (both financially and critically) Argento-Bava disgust-o-rama DEMONS, this film lets the slime-drooling zombies loose in a high-rise apartment building. Where DEMONS linked the zombie attack with an evening at the cinema (the film took place in a movie theater), DEMONS 2 has its first zombie emerging from a television set showing a late-night horror movie. The grisly zombie promptly attacks a teenager's birthday party, and soon the victims rise to become zombies themselves, wreaking havoc on the rest of the building's tenants—including a dog, which comes back as a canine zombie. Curiously, black actor Bobby Rhodes appeared in DEMONS as a pimp (who was killed), and now shows up in DEMONS 2 as a body builder. His very presence seems to be a homage to the take-charge black characters in the films of American horror king George Romero. While Lamberto Bava does possess a remarkable grasp of technique, his films still fail to have lasting impact and lack the psychological resonance of his father's best work. The American video release of DEMONS 2 is missing three minutes of footage from the European print.

p, Dario Argento; d, Lamberto Bava; w, Dario Argento, Lamberto Bava, Franco Ferrini, Dardano Sacchetti; ph, Gianlorenzo Battaglia (Luciano Vittorio Color); ed, Pietro Bozza; m, Simon Boswell.

**(PR:O MPAA:NR)**

## DEVIL BAT, THE**½

(1941) 68m PRC bw (AKA: KILLER BATS)

Bela Lugosi *(Dr. Paul Carruthers),* Suzanne Kaaren *(Mary Heath),* Dave O'Brien *(Johnny Layton),* Guy Usher *(Henry Morton),* Yolande Mallott *(Maxine),* Donald Kerr *("One-Shot" Maguire),* Edward Mortimer *(Martin Heath),* Gene O'Donnell *(Don Morton),* Alan Baldwin *(Tommy Heath),* John Ellis *(Roy Heath),* Arthur Q. Bryan *(Joe McGinty),* Hal Price *(Chief Wilkins),* John Davidson *(Prof. Raines),* Wally Rairdon *(Walter King).*

Okay, so it's an ultra-cheap programmer from PRC with a silly plot, a ratty-looking bat on a string, and Bela Lugosi well into his steep career slide. THE DEVIL BAT is still simply too much fun to dismiss, and you can pick it up on video at any drugstore for under $6. Bela plays Dr. Carruthers, a small-town chemist who feels he has been cheated by his business partners and decides to get revenge. Too clever merely to shoot his victims, Carruthers concocts an elaborate plan, by which he takes normal-sized bats and subjects them to an electrical gizmo that makes them grow to monstrous proportions. Having devised a special shaving lotion that the killer bats are attracted to, the mad scientist then presents the lotion to his victims as a gift, urging them to try some on in his presence. Uttering a menacing "Good . . . bye!" to his guests, Carruthers sits back and waits for his giant bats to sniff out their targets and kill them. See Bela carrying prop bats hanging upside on a little trapeze to his lab! See Bela don swimming goggles so that he can watch his electrical gizmo make the bats grow! See Bela intimidate grown men into slapping shaving lotion on their necks! Also includes a pair of nosy reporters: one to crack jokes, one to romance the girl! This film proved so popular for PRC that they cranked out a sequel, DEVIL BAT'S DAUGHTER (1946), and an unofficial remake, THE WINGED SERPENT (1946).

p, Jack Gallagher; d, Jean Yarbrough; w, John Thomas Neville (based on a story by George Bricker); ph, Arthur Martinelli; ed, Holbrook N. Todd.

**(PR:A   MPAA:NR)**

## DEVIL DOLL, THE***½

(1936) 79m MGM bw

Lionel Barrymore *(Paul Lavond)*, Maureen O'Sullivan *(Lorraine Lavond)*, Frank Lawton *(Toto)*, Robert Greig *(Coulvet)*, Lucy Beaumont *(Mme. Lavond)*, Henry B. Walthall *(Marcel)*, Grace Ford *(Lachna)*, Pedro de Cordoba *(Matin)*, Arthur Hohl *(Radin)*, Rafaela Ottiano *(Malita)*, Juanita Quigley *(Marguerite)*, Claire du Brey *(Mme. Coulvet)*, Rollo Lloyd *(Detective)*, E. Allyn Warren *(Commissioner)*.

Another excellent Tod Browning foray into the macabre, THE DEVIL DOLL stars Lionel Barrymore as Paul Lavond, a wrongly convicted prisoner who escapes Devil's Island with mad scientist Marcel (Henry B. Walthall). They take refuge in Marcel's old laboratory, where he demonstrates his miraculous invention, a serum that reduces all living things to miniature size. Before dying, the ailing Marcel passes his secret formula on to Lavond, who decides to seek vengeance on the three men who framed him. Disguised as an old woman who runs a doll shop, Lavond manages to reduce two of his enemies, but begins to lose control of the scheme because of his crazed assistant, Malita (Rafaela Ottiano), who is so spellbound by the miniaturizing process that she refuses to stop, at one point hissing, "We'll make the *whole world* small!" While THE DEVIL DOLL is no FREAKS, director Tod Browning, in his second-to-last film, adds a sinister edge to what is basically a morality play. The special effects still impress today; the oversized sets and props are expertly done, with much attention given to detail; and the film is excellently photographed by Leonard Smith. Erich Von Stroheim is credited with cowriting the screenplay, but the exact nature of his contributions have never been made clear.

p, Edward J. Mannix; d, Tod Browning; w, Garrett Fort, Guy Endore, Erich von Stroheim, Tod Browning (based on the novel *Burn Witch Burn* by Abraham Merritt); ph, Leonard Smith; ed, Frederick Y. Smith; m, Franz Waxman.

**(PR:A   MPAA:NR)**

## DEVIL DOLL**½

(1964, Brit.) 80m Galaworldfilm-Gordon/Associated Film c

Bryant Halliday *(The Great Vorelli)*, William Sylvester *(Mark English)*, Yvonne Romain *(Marianne)*, Sandra Dorne *(Vorelli's Assistant)*, Karel Stepanek *(Dr. Heller)*, Francis de Wolf *(Dr. Keisling)*, Nora Nicholson *(Aunt Eva)*, Philip Ray *(Uncle Walter)*, Alan Gifford *(Bob Garrett)*, Pamela Law *(Garrett's Girl Friend)*, Heidi Erich *(Grace)*, Antony Baird *(Soldier)*, Trixie Dallas *(Miss Penton)*, Margaret Durnell *(The Countess)*, Ray Landor *(Twist Dancer)*, Ella Tracey *(Louisa)*, Guy Deghy *(Hans)*, David Charlesworth *(Hugo Novik)*, Lorenza Coalville *(Mercedes)*, Jackie Ramsden *(The Nurse)*.

Mark English (William Sylvester), an American reporter visiting London, attends a performance by the Great Vorelli (Bryant Halliday), a ventriloquist and hypnotist who works with a dummy named Hugo (a name shared with the dummy in the final episode of DEAD OF NIGHT, 1946). There is something strange about the ventriloquist act, as the dummy seems unnaturally hostile—as if Vorelli cannot control him. As it turns out, years earlier Vorelli killed his partner and transferred his soul to the dummy. However, when Vorelli hypnotizes Mark's girl friend (Yvonne Romain) and tries to transfer her soul into a female dummy, Mark puts a stop to it. Genuinely scary in parts, this is a notable entry in the tiny subgenre of ventriloquist's dummy films, but it is marred somewhat by Lindsay Shonteff's stiff and unimaginative direction.

p, Kenneth Rive, Richard Gordon, Lindsay Shonteff; d, Lindsay Shonteff; w, George Barclay, Lance Z. Hargreaves (from a story by Frederick E. Smith); ph, Gerald Gibbs; ed, Ernest Bullingham.

**(PR:C   MPAA:NR)**

## DEVIL'S NIGHTMARE, THE**

(1971, Bel./It.) 88m Hemisphere c (AKA: VAMPIRE PLAYGIRLS)

Erica Blanc, Jean Servais, Daniel Emilfork, Luciene Raimbourg, Jacques Monseau, Ivana Novak, Shirley Corrigan.

The feature directorial debut of Jean Brismee, a film school instructor in Brussels, this film went unreleased in the US until 1974, when its distributors tried to capitalize on the success of THE EXORCIST. Erica Blanc stars as the victim of an ancient family curse, which has transformed her into a succubus. She is given the task of seducing and killing seven obnoxious tourists (representing the seven deadly sins) who wind up in her remote European villa after having been directed there by a mysterious man in black (Daniel Emilfork).

p, Charles Lecocq; d, Jean Brismee; w, Patrice Rhomm, Charles Lecocq, Andre Hunebelle.

**(PR:O    MPAA:R)**

## DEVIL'S RAIN, THE**

(1975, US/Mex.) 85m Bryanston c

Ernest Borgnine *(Corbis)*, Eddie Albert *(Dr. Richards)*, Ida Lupino *(Mrs. Preston)*, William Shatner *(Mark Preston)*, Keenan Wynn *(Sheriff Owens)*, Tom Skerritt *(Tom Preston)*, Joan Prather *(Julie Preston)*, Woodrow Chambliss *(John)*, John Travolta *(Danny)*, Claudio Brooks *(Preacher)*, Lisa Todd *(Lilith)*, George Sawaya *(Steve Preston)*, Erika Carlson *(Aaronessa Fyffe)*, Tony Cortez *(1st Captor)*, Anton La Vey *(High Priest)*, Diane La Vey *(Priscilla Corbis)*, Robert Wallace *(Matthew Corbis)*.

This cheap horror film, set in the Southwest but shot in Mexico, boasts a big cast of recognizable faces. The story concerns Tom Preston's (Tom Skerritt) efforts to locate his family, which has disappeared. The trail leads to a cult of Satanists, led by Corbis (Ernest Borgnine), who is the reincarnation of a 17th-century witch. Corbis captures a bunch of souls in a bottle, but his plan backfires when the bottle is broken, the souls are released, and the "Devil's Rain" descends upon the cult, melting them. Mostly pretty boring, except for the sight of Ernest Borgnine turning into a goat-headed demon, and John Travolta (in a small role) melting along with the rest of the cast. All you Satanists out there will no doubt recognize your guru, Anton La Vey, in a small supporting role. He was also billed as technical advisor. The film was re-released after Travolta became a star with his name given top billing, even though he is barely on-screen.

p, James V. Cullen, Michael S. Glick; d, Robert Fuest; w, Gabe Essoe, James Ashton, Gerald Hopman; ph, Alex Phillips, Jr. (ToddAO 35); ed, Michael Kahn; m, Al De Lory.

**(PR:C    MPAA:PG)**

## DEVIL'S WEDDING NIGHT, THE*

(1973, It.) 85m Dimension c

Mark Damon *(Brothers No. 1 and No. 2)*, Sarah Bay *(Countess)*, Esmeralda Barros, Francesca Romana Davila, Xiro Pappas, Alexander Getty, Sergio Pislar.

An inquisitive archaeologist and his twin brother (both played by Mark Damon) learn that the infamous Nibelungen Ring, said to have supernatural powers, is being worn by a demon countess (Sarah Bay, from LADY FRANKENSTEIN) who bathes in the blood of virgins. When one of the brothers stupidly goes off to Transylvania by himself to obtain the ring, the other follows and finds that the countess has already turned his twin into a vampire. Ineptly made, fairly gory, and with lots of nudity—mostly from Bay—this is yet another horror film based on the notorious Countess Elizabeth Bathory, who actually had virgins murdered and their throats slit, then bathed in their blood to improve her complexion. Bathory is credited with murdering 611 persons before Hungarian authorities tried her in 1611, ordering her walled up in her rooms, where three

years later she died. Unfortunately, the story you just read is more interesting than this film.

p, Massimo Pupillo; d, Luigi Batzella; w, Massimo Pupillo, Walter Bigari; ph, Aristide Massaccesi.

**(PR:O    MPAA:R)**

## DEVONSVILLE TERROR, THE**½

(1983) 84m PM/New West c

Suzanna Love *(Jenny)*, Donald Pleasence *(Dr. Warley)*, Deanna Haas *(Monica)*, Mary Walden *(Chris)*, Morrigan Hurt, Leslie Smith, Barbara Cihlar *(Witches)*, Robert Walker, Jr., Paul Willson, Angelica Rebane, Paul Bentzen.

Three hundred years to the day after three witches were burned at the stake in a New England town, a mysterious woman (Suzanna Love) appears to wreak havoc on the town's patriarchy. When they tie her to the stake and try to send her back where she came from, lightning shoots from her eyes and destroys her persecutors. This quite interesting, feminist-minded horror film was directed by former Fassbinder star Ulli Lommel, who also helmed THE BOOGEYMAN and BOOGEY MAN II.

p, Ulli Lommel; d, Ulli Lommel; w, Ulli Lommel, George T. Lindsey, Suzanna Love; ph, Ulli Lommel; m, Ed Hill, Ray Colcord.

**(PR:C    MPAA:PG)**

## DIE! DIE! MY DARLING***

(1965, Brit.) 97m Hammer/COL c (GB: FANATIC)

Tallulah Bankhead *(Mrs. Trefoile)*, Stefanie Powers *(Pat Carroll)*, Peter Vaughan *(Harry)*, Maurice Kaufmann *(Alan Glentower)*, Yootha Joyce *(Anna)*, Donald Sutherland *(Joseph)*, Gwendolyn Watts *(Gloria)*, Robert Dorning *(Ormsby)*, Philip Gilbert *(Oscar)*, Winifred Dennis *(Shopkeeper)*, Diana King *(Woman Shopper)*.

Tallulah Bankhead returned from a 12-year hiatus to make what became her final film in DIE, DIE, MY DARLING, which casts Bankhead as the eerie Mrs. Trefoile, an elderly religious fanatic whose son was killed in an auto wreck several years ago. When her son's former fiancee (Stefanie Powers) stops by the mansion for a visit, Mrs. Trefoile kidnaps her and keeps her locked up in the basement in order to cleanse the girl's soul, fitting it to be reunited with her son in heaven. Bankhead is superbly cast and performs far above par in a role that bears striking similarity to Bette Davis' in WHAT EVER HAPPENED TO BABY JANE? Donald Sutherland, in the dawn of his career, appears as a imbecilic gardener who reads his Bible upside down.

p, Anthony Hinds; d, Silvio Narizzano; w, Richard Matheson (based on the novel *Nightmare* by Anne Blaisdell); ph, Arthur Ibbetson (Eastmancolor); ed, James Needs; m, Wilfred Josephs.

**(PR:C    MPAA:NR)**

## DIE, MONSTER, DIE**½

(1965, Brit.) 78m AIP c (AKA: MONSTER OF TERROR)

Boris Karloff *(Nahum Witley)*, Nick Adams *(Stephen Reinhart)*, Freda Jackson *(Letitia Witley)*, Suzan Farmer *(Susan Witley)*, Terence De Marney *(Merwyn)*, Patrick McGee *(Dr. Henderson)*, Paul Farrell *(Jason)*, George Moon *(Cab Driver)*, Gretchen Franklin *(Miss Bailey)*.

A slow-moving but effective adaptation of H.P. Lovecraft's story "The Color out of Space," this was the first directing effort by Roger Corman's veteran art director, Daniel Haller. Boris Karloff (in another standout performance) plays Nahum Witley, a wheelchair-bound scientist who has been trying to control experiments with a radioactive meteorite that can make plants grow to enormous proportions. When Stephen Reinhart (Nick Adams), an American, arrives at Witley's English mansion to visit his fiancee—the scientist's daughter—he notices strange things happening at the house. Witley does not welcome this intrusion and tries to get the American to leave. Stephen is then begged by his fiancee's bed-ridden mother, Letitia (Freda Jackson), to take her daughter away and leave the house as soon as possible. Stephen investigates, but is attacked by the now horribly mutated Letitia, who suddenly turns into a fiery spray of ashes. Witley finally realizes he can no longer control the meteor and tries to destroy it, but in the process is mutated himself and attempts to kill his daughter and her fiance. Before Stuart Gordon burst upon the scene with RE-ANIMATOR (1985) and FROM BEYOND (1986), this film and its companion, THE DUNWICH HORROR (1970), were among the few even marginally successful adaptations of Lovecraft.

p, Pat Green; d, Daniel Haller; w, Jerry Sohl (based on the story "The Color Out Of Space" by H.P. Lovecraft); ph, Paul Beeson (Colorscope, Pathecolor); ed, Alfred Cox; m, Don Banks.

(PR:C  MPAA:NR)

## DISCIPLE OF DEATH*

(1972, Brit.) 90m AE c

Mike Raven *(The Stranger)*, Stephan Bradley *(Ralph)*, Virginia Wetherall *(Ruth)*, Ronald Lacey *(Parson)*, Marguerite Hardiman, George Belbin, Nicholas Amer.

Made by the same team that brought you THE CRUCIBLE OF TERROR, this outing features former BBC disc jockey Mike Raven as a demon from hell who is revived when virgin blood is inadvertently dropped on his grave (you see, there was this guy and a girl making love on a tombstone and . . .). Needing a virgin sacrifice, the ghoul wanders the neighborhood ritualistically killing young women. With silly gore effects that look like a *hommage* to BLOOD FEAST and some distinctly bizarre humor involving a minister and a Jewish cabbalist (Amer), this is a pretty strange mix.

p, Tom Parkinson, Charles Fairman; d, Tom Parkinson; w, Tom Parkinson, Churton Fairman.

(PR:O  MPAA:NR)

## DR. BLACK AND MR. HYDE**½

(1976) 87m Dimension c

Bernie Casey *(Dr. Pride/Hyde)*, Rosalind Cash *(Dr. Billie Worth)*, Marie O'Henry *(Linda)*, Ji-Tu Cumbuka *(Lt. Jackson)*, Milt Kogan *(Lt. O'Connor)*, Stu Gilliam *(Silky)*.

An entertaining variation on Robert Louis Stevenson's classic, DR. BLACK AND MR. HYDE stars ex-Los Angeles Rams wide receiver back Bernie Casey as Dr. Pride, a wealthy California physician whose experiments turn him into a murderous white man by night. Nothing profound, but a lot of mindless fun from the director of BLACULA. Jonathan Demme's favorite cinematographer, Tak Fujimoto (SOMETHING WILD; MARRIED TO THE MOB) did the photography. Originally tagged DR. BLACK AND MR. WHITE.

p, Charles Walker; d, William Crain; w, Larry LeBron; ph, Tak Fujimoto (Metrocolor); ed, Jack Horger; m, Johnny Pate.

(PR:O  MPAA:R)

## DR. BUTCHER, M.D.*

(1982, It.) 80m Flora/Aquarius c (AKA: QUEEN OF THE CANNIBALS)

Ian McCulloch *(Peter)*, Alexandra Cole [Alexandra delli Colli] *(Lori Ridgway)*, Sherry Buchanan *(Kelly)*, Peter O'Neal *(George)*, Donald O'Brian *(Dr. Abrera)*, Walter Patriarca, Linda Fumis, Dakan, Roberto Resra.

The "M.D." stands for "Medical Deviate" in this ultra-gross 1979 Italian gore picture with effects by the team that did ZOMBIE. When it is discovered that an Asiatic tribe is robbing Manhattan of its dead, a scientist (Ian McCulloch) ventures with a female anthropologist (Alexandra Cole) to an obscure island, where they meet mad scientist Dr. Abrera (Donald O'Brian), who is conducting the kind of experiments that got Dr. Moreau ripped limb from limb in ISLAND OF LOST SOULS (1933). Extremely gory dismemberments, brain transplants, eye-gougings, and various cannibalistic acts made this splatter fave a hit at the box office and a perennial video rental.

p, Terry Levine; d, Franco Martinelli; w, Franco Martinelli, Fabrizio de Angelis, Walter Patriarca, Romano Scandariato; ph, F. Zuccoli; m, Nico Fidenco.

(PR:O  MPAA:R)

## DOCTOR DEATH: SEEKER OF SOULS*½

(1973) 87m Cinerama c

John Considine *(Dr. Death)*, Barry Coe *(Fred Saunders)*, Cheryl Miller *(Sandy)*, Stewart Moss *(Greg Vaughn)*, Leon Askin *(Thor)*, Jo Morrow *(Laura Saunders)*, Florence Marly *(Tana)*, Sivi Aberg *(Venus)*, Jim Boles *(Caretaker Franz)*, Athena Lorde *(Spiritualist)*, Moe Howard *(Volunteer)*, Robert E. Ball *(Old Wizard)*, Patrick Dennis Leigh *(Old Man)*, Barbara Boles *(Alice)*, Pierre Gonneau *(Harry)*, Larry Rogers *(Young Man in Park)*, Denise Denise *(Girl with Flat Tire)*, Larry Vincent *(Strangler)*.

John Considine plays the title doctor who, 1,000 years ago, discovered the secret to immortality but who has to periodically transfer his soul into a new body. Overall this is a pretty bad effort, but camp fans may get some satisfaction from the cameo appearances by former Stooge Moe Howard (in his final role) and TV horror host Larry "Seymour" Vincent.

p, Eddie Saeta; d, Eddie Saeta; w, Sal Ponti; ph, Kent Wakeford, Emil Oster (Movielab Color); ed, Tony DiMarco; m, Richard LaSalle.

**(PR:O MPAA:R)**

## DR. HECKYL AND MR. HYPE**½

(1980) 99m Cannon c

Oliver Reed *(Dr. Heckyl/Mr. Hype)*, Sunny Johnson *(Coral Careen)*, Maia Danziger *(Miss Finebum)*, Mel Welles *(Dr. Hinkle)*, Virgil Frye *(Lt. MacDruck "Il Topo")*, Kedrick Wolfe *(Dr. Lew Hoo)*, Jackie Coogan *(Sgt. Fleacollar)*, Corinne Calvet *(Pizelle Puree)*, Sharon Compton *(Mrs. Quivel)*, Denise Hayes *(Liza)*, Charles Howerton *(Clutch Cooger)*, Dick Miller *(Irsil/Orson)*, Jack Warford *(Herringbone Flynn)*, Lucretia Love *(Debra Kate)*, Ben Frommer *(Sgt. Gurnisht Hilfn)*, Mickey Fox *(Mrs. Fritz L. Pitzle)*, Jacque Lynn Colton *(Mrs. Fran van Crisco)*, Lisa Zebro *(Mrs. van Crisco)*, Stan Ross *(Flash Flud)*, Joe Anthony Cox *(Bad Williams)*, Duane Thomas *(Bad Williams' Ideal)*, Michael Ciccone *(Hollowpoint)*, Steve Ciccone *(Dum-Dum)*, Candi Brough *(Teri Tailspin)*, Randi Brough *(Toni Tailspin)*.

This mildly funny satire of *Dr. Jekyll and Mr. Hyde* casts Oliver Reed as Dr. Heckyl, a genuinely nice but repulsive-looking podiatrist who works at a clinic run by Dr. Hinkle (Mel Welles, "Mr. Mushnik" from the original LITTLE SHOP OF HORRORS). Depressed by his ugliness, Heckyl attempts suicide by drinking a weight-reduction potion, but instead of killing him, the serum transforms Heckyl into the handsome and dashing Mr. Hype. Unfortunately, as Mr. Hype, he also has homicidal tendencies. DR. HECKYL AND MR. HYPE was scripted and directed "with apologies to Robert Louis Stevenson" by Roger Corman collaborator Charles B. Griffith, who also penned camp classics such as BUCKET OF BLOOD and THE LITTLE SHOP OF HORRORS. Despite its often sophomoric humor (take a gander at the character names), the movie is ultimately amusing in a vulgar sort of way, though Griffith's direction adds little and his film has a downright ugly look.

p, Menahem Golan, Yoram Globus; d, Charles Griffith; w, Charles Griffith; ph, Robert Carras (Metrocolor); ed, Skip Schoolnik; m, Richard Band.

**(PR:O MPAA:R)**

## DR. JEKYLL AND MR. HYDE***½

(1920) 63m Famous Players-Lasky bw

John Barrymore *(Dr. Jekyll/Mr. Hyde)*, Martha Mansfield *(Millicent Carew)*, Brandon Hurst *(Sir George Carew)*, Charles Lane *(Dr. Richard Lanyon)*, J. Malcolm Dunn *(John Utterson)*, Cecil Clovelly *(Edward Enfield)*, Nita Naldi *(Therese)*.

The silent cinema was rife with official and unofficial adaptations of Robert Louis Stevenson's famed novel (three in 1920 alone), but this version, starring John Barrymore, remains the most famous. The upright Dr. Henry Jekyll conducts experiments that may lead to the elimination of evil from human nature by isolating the bestial tendencies of humankind. He develops a concoction that concentrates all of the latent evil in him and drinks it, becoming the malevolent Hyde, who lopes through London satisfying his lusts and indulging his cruel caprices. Gradually, the antidote that returns him to normal becomes less effective and the evil in him burgeons beyond his control, until his virtuous side sees no solution other than suicide. Although gushingly praised at the time of its release and subsequently recalled as one of the classics of silent cinema, this film has not aged well and contains little in the way of truly innovative technique. John S. Robertson was a workmanlike director and only in brief moments does he stumble upon memorable imagery; luckily, the detailed sets and the masterful camerawork pick up the slack. The focus of all the acclaim, however, was John Barrymore's performance, which was hailed as setting a new standard for screen acting. In reality, Barrymore's performance is hammy and stage-bound. Much has been made of the actor's transformation into Hyde, achieved with a minimum of special makeup or camera technique; but while this metamorphosis is accomplished by Barrymore simply breathing heavily and contorting his face, there is still an undeniable power to it. Indeed, Barrymore does carry the picture, and his Jekyll-Hyde portrayal became the standard against which subsequent performances were judged.

d, John S. Robertson; w, Clara S. Beranger (based on the novel *The Strange Case of Dr. Jekyll and Mr. Hyde* by Robert Lewis Stevenson); ph, Roy Overbaugh.

**(PR:A MPAA:NR)**

## DR. JEKYLL AND MR. HYDE***

(1941) 127m MGM bw

Spencer Tracy *(Dr. Harry Jekyll/Mr. Hyde)*, Ingrid Bergman *(Ivy Peterson)*, Lana Turner *(Beatrix Emery)*, Donald Crisp *(Sir Charles Emery)*, Ian Hunter *(Dr. John Lanyon)*, Barton MacLane *(Sam Higgins)*, C. Aubrey Smith *(The Bishop)*, Peter Godfrey *(Poole)*, Sara Allgood *(Mrs. Higgins)*, Frederic Worlock *(Dr. Heath)*, William Tannen *(Intern Fenwick)*, Frances Robinson *(Marcia)*, Denis Green *(Freddie)*, Billy Bevan *(Dr. Weller)*, Forrester Harvey *(Old Prouty)*, Lumsden Hare *(Col. Weymouth)*, Lawrence Grant *(Dr. Courtland)*, John Barclay *(Constable)*, Doris Lloyd *(Mrs. Marley)*, Gwen Gaze *(Mrs. French)*, Hillary Brooke *(Mrs. Arnold)*, Mary Field *(Wife)*, Aubrey Mather *(Inspector)*.

The best version of Stevenson's classic, the 1932 Rouben Mamoulian-Frederic March Oscar-winner, is not yet available on videotape, and this 1941 DR. JEKYLL AND MR. HYDE is not much of a substitute. MGM gave the familiar story the big-budget, big-star treatment, but in the process drained it of all of its biting social and psychological implications. Spencer Tracy, who was assigned the Jekyll/Hyde role against his wishes, is woefully miscast and sinks into hokum characterization, rolling his eyes like loose marbles and working his jaw like a maniac. Ingrid Bergman was scheduled to play the sweet fiancee and Lana Turner the barmaid, but director Victor Fleming supposedly reversed the roles at Bergman's request, effectively casting them against type. Visually, the film is stodgy, save for a few standout moments: notably the shot wherein Turner's reflection appears inside a huge enlargement of Hyde's lustful eye, and the somewhat laughable sequence that depicts two horses, one black and one white, being wildly whipped by Hyde, their heads transformed into Bergman and Turner, two gorgeous females in the altogether (head and shoulder shots). Though he tried hard, Tracy's portrayal, which was lauded at the time, doesn't begin to approach Fredric March's superb 1932 enactment or John Barrymore's silent interpretation (see above). One visitor to the set, author Somerset Maugham, watched Tracy closely, noting his rigorous transformations, then crushingly whispered to director Fleming: ""Which one is he now, Jekyll or Hyde?"

p, Victor Fleming; d, Victor Fleming; w, John Lee Mahin (based on the novel *The Strange Case of Dr. Jekyll and Mr. Hyde* by Robert Louis Stevenson); ph, Joseph Ruttenberg; ed, Harold F. Kress; m, Franz Waxman.

(PR:A MPAA:NR)

## DR. JEKYLL AND SISTER HYDE**½

(1971, Brit.) 97m Hammer/AIP c

Ralph Bates *(Dr. Jekyll)*, Martine Beswick *(Sister Hyde)*, Gerald Sim *(Prof. Robertson)*, Lewis Fiander *(Howard)*, Dorothy Alison *(Mrs. Spencer)*, Neil Wilson *(Older Policeman)*, Ivor Dean *(Burke)*, Paul Whitsun-Jones *(Sgt. Danvers)*, Philip Madoc *(Byker)*, Tony Calvin *(Hare)*, Susan Brodrick *(Susan)*, Dan Meaden *(Town Crier)*, Virginia Wetherall *(Betsy)*, Geoffrey Kenion *(1st Policeman)*, Irene Bradshaw *(Yvonne)*, Anna Brett *(Julie)*, Jackie Poole *(Margie)*, Rosemary Lord *(Marie)*, Petula Portell *(Petra)*, Pat Brackenbury *(Helen)*, Liz Romanoff *(Emma)*.

This potentially interesting variation on Stevenson's classic 19th-century horror tale is undone by a script that fails to capitalize on the very question the film is predicated on—What if Jekyll, after drinking his potion, turned into a female Hyde? While trying to discover a method with which to prolong life, Jekyll (Ralph Bates) becomes convinced that the secret lies in female hormones. After sampling a formula he has concocted, Jekyll turns into a beautiful woman (Martine Beswick) and, claiming to be his own sister, seduces men, then kills them, so they can be used in his experiments. In time, however, Jekyll falls in love with his pretty neighbor (Susan Brodrick), while "sister" Hyde is smitten with the girl's brother (Lewis Fiander), leading to much confusion and a struggle between sexual identities. Writer Brian Clemens and director Roy Ward Baker milk the material of its inherent sensationalism and humor, but they fail to dig deeper and explore the social, political, or sexual implications of the material. Instead, what we are left with is a delightfully sexy performance from Beswick.

p, Albert Fennell, Brian Clemens; d, Roy Ward Baker; w,

Brian Clemens (based on the novel *The Strange Case of Dr. Jekyll and Mr. Hyde* by Robert Louis Stevenson); ph, Norman Warwick (Technicolor); ed, James Needs; m, David Whitaker.

(PR:A MPAA:PG)

## DR. JEKYLL'S DUNGEON OF DEATH zero

(1982) 88m Rochelle/New American c

James Mathers *(Dr. Jekyll)*, John Kearney, Tom Nicholson, Dawn Carver Kelly, Nadine Kalmes.

Set in 1959 San Francisco, this weird adaptation of *Dr. Jekyll and Mr. Hyde* transpires wholly in the basement/dungeon of the title character, played by James Mathers, who also wrote this stinker. This Dr. Jekyll is experimenting with mind control serum that was originally worked on by his great-grandfather (the original Dr. J.) and later by the Nazis. Jekyll injects criminals of both sexes with the serum, then lets them loose so he can observe their kung-fu battles. This absurd film, shot in Nevada in 1978, comes to an end in a bloody basement slaughter.

p, James Wood; d, James Wood; w, James Mathers; ph, James Wood; ed, James Wood; m, Marty Allen.

(PR:O MPAA:R)

## DOCTOR PHIBES RISES AGAIN***½

(1972, Brit.) 88m AIP c

Vincent Price *(Dr. Anton Phibes)*, Robert Quarry *(Biederbeck)*, Valli Kemp *(Vulnavia)*, Hugh Griffith *(Ambrose)*, John Thaw *(Shavers)*, Keith Buckley *(Stuart)*, Lewis Fiander *(Baker)*, Gerald Sim *(Hackett)*, Milton Reid *(Cheng, Manservant)*, Peter Jeffrey *(Inspector Trout)*, John Cater *(Supt. Waverley)*, Peter Cushing *(Captain)*, Beryl Reid *(Mrs. Ambrose)*, Terry-Thomas *(Lombardo)*, Fiona Lewis *(Diana)*, Caroline Munro *(Victoria)*.

This sequel to THE ABOMINABLE DR. PHIBES carries over the tongue-in-cheek approach of its predecessor and devises an even more outlandish series of murders. After spending three years in suspended animation lying next to his beloved late wife (Caroline Munro), Phibes (Vincent Price) awakes to find his mansion destroyed and a sacred Egyptian scroll, which reveals the way to an underground river containing the elixir of life, stolen. Phibes suspects that his arch-enemy Biederbeck (Robert Quarry) is behind the theft, and with the help of his beautiful assistant, Vulnavia (Valli Kemp)—who, inexplicably, is alive, after being killed in the original—Phibes recovers the scroll and sets out for Egypt. Biederbeck, who is several hundred years old and needs the elixir to continue living, gives chase. This is where the fun comes in, as Phibes is forced to dispatch Biederbeck's men in a variety of ingenious ways. The ending was left wide open for another sequel, but the film failed at the box office and a third Phibes film wasn't made. Instead, Price spent much of the rest of his career duplicating the Phibes format in films like THEATRE OF BLOOD (1972) and MADHOUSE (1974).

p, Louis M. Heyward; d, Robert Fuest; w, Robert Fuest,

Robert Blees (based on characters created by James Whiton, William Goldstein); ph, Alex Thomson (Movielab Color); ed, Tristam Cones; m, John Gale.

**(PR:C MPAA:PG)**

## DR. TARR'S TORTURE DUNGEON**½

(1972. Mex.) 88m Group I c (LA MANSION DE LA LOCURA)

Claude [Claudio] Brook, Ellen Sberman, Martin LaSalle, Robert Dumont, Arthur Hansel, David Silva.

Based on Poe's ""The System of Doctor Tarr and Professor Feather," this surreal Mexican horror movie was the feature film directorial debut for Juan Lopez Moctezuma, who had previously worked in theater and television. In 19th-century France, a reporter (Claude Brook) discovers that an asylum has been taken over by a lunatic who allows the inmates to indulge their insane fantasies. Several of the production's participants already had significant experience with surrealism, including Moctezuma; Brook, who was featured in Luis Bunuel's THE EXTERMINATING ANGEL and THE MILKY WAY; and producer Roberto Viskin, who had performed the same duty on Alexandero Jodorowsky's bizarre western EL TOPO.

p, Roberto Viskin, J.G. Elster; d, Juan Lopez Moctezuma; w, Juan Lopez Moctezuma, Charles Illescas (based on the story "The System of Doctor Tarr and Professor Feather" by Edgar Allan Poe); ph, Rafael Corkidi.

**(PR:O MPAA:R)**

## DR. TERROR'S HOUSE OF HORRORS**½

(1965, Brit.) 98m Amicus/RF c

Peter Cushing (Dr. Schreck), Christopher Lee (Franklyn Marsh), Roy Castle (Biff Bailey), Donald Sutherland (Bob Carroll), Neil McCallum (Jim Dawson), Alan Freeman (Bill Rogers), Max Adrian (Dr. Blake), Edward Underdown (Tod), Ursula Howells (Deirdre), Peter Madden (Caleb), Katy Wild (Valda), Ann Bell (Ann Rogers), Sarah Nicholls (Carol Rogers), Jeremy Kemp (Drake), Kenny Lynch (Sammy Coin), Harold Lang (Shine), Thomas Baptiste (Dambala), Tubby Hayes Quintet (Bailey's Band), Michael Gough (Eric Landor), Isla Blair (Pretty Girl), Jennifer Jayne (Nicolle), Al Mulock (Detective), Bernard Lee (Hopkins), Russ Henderson Steel Band, Christopher Carlos, George Mossman.

The first of the many Amicus horror anthology films, DR. TERROR'S HOUSE OF HORRORS presents five vignettes loosely connected by a train ride, on which five travelers meet bearded Dr. Schreck (Cushing), who uses tarot cards to predict how each of them will die. The first to have his destiny depicted is an architect (Neil McCallum) who Schreck predicts will be killed by a female werewolf (Ursula Howells). The next to be shown his fate is a trumpet player (Roy Castle) who is to be done in by the Haitian god Dambala for publicly performing music he heard at a voodoo ceremony. An American doctor (Donald Sutherland) is then told that he will marry a vampire, and an art critic (Christopher Lee) learns he will run over an art-

ist and be haunted by the victim's dismembered hand. The last vignette reveals a death that will be dealt by a creeping killer vine in a suburban backyard. As with any omnibus film, the episodes here are a mixed bag running from bad (the somewhat racist "voodoo" sequence) to quite good (the "hand" story, whose star, Lee, jokingly referred to the film as "Dr. Terror's House of Pancakes" while hosting "Saturday Night Live"). Onetime cinematographer Freddie Francis has always been limited as a director and his film suffers for it, though that didn't stop him from going on to direct other horror anthologies, including the disappointing TALES FROM THE CRYPT (1972).

p, Milton Subotsky, Max J. Rosenberg; d, Freddie Francis; w, Milton Subotsky; ph, Alan Hume (Techniscope, Technicolor); ed, Thelma Connell; m, Elisabeth Lutyens.

**(PR:C MPAA:NR)**

## DOCTOR X***½

(1932) 77m FN/WB bw/c

Lionel Atwill (Doctor Xavier), Lee Tracy (Lee), Fay Wray (Joan), Preston Foster (Dr. Wells), Arthur Edmund Carewe (Dr. Rowitz), John Wray (Dr. Haines), Harry Beresford (Dr. Duke), George Rosener (Otto), Leila Bennett (Mamie), Robert Warwick (Police Commissioner Stevens), Willard Robertson (O'Halloran), Thomas Jackson (Editor), Harry Holman (Policeman), Tom Dugan (Sheriff), Mae Busch (The Madame).

A rare excursion into horror for First National (later Warner Bros.), DR. X became one of the great "lost" films after its initial release and developed a glowing reputation as a masterpiece of early talkie horror during the 30 years it went unseen. When a black-and-white print was finally discovered, however, some found the film a disappointment. The story is set in a spooky old mansion atop the cliffs at Blackstone Shoals, on Long Island. Lionel Atwill plays the sinister Dr. Xavier, who runs the research laboratory where most of the action takes place. Dr. Wells (Preston Foster), his one-armed lab assistant, discovers the secret to eternal life, coats his body from head to toe with synthetic flesh that gives him abnormal powers, and slips out during full moons to strangle people. Much of the current criticism of the film is directed at its emphasis on Lee Tracy's wise-cracking newspaper reporter, who is hot on the trail of the "Moon Murderer" and ultimately comes face-to-face with him. Fay Wray, who would be paired with Atwill in two more horror films, MYSTERY OF THE WAX MUSEUM and VAMPIRE BAT, plays his daughter here and is asked to scream frequently. DR. X was released in two versions—one black and white, the other two-color Technicolor—with the color prints going only to major markets. Although it was believed the color negative had vanished, a color print finally surfaced in 1973 and has since been painstakingly restored by film historians at UCLA. Moreover, the color restoration brought back some of the prestige DR. X had lost since its rediscovery, proving that director Michael Curtiz's use of color wasn't just a gimmick, but was employed intelligently and to great effect. Further study revealed that the film's black-and-white print wasn't merely struck from the color negative, but was shot separately, usually side-by-side with the Technicolor camera. The 1939 film, THE RETURN OF DOCTOR X, is not really a sequel, but it does contain Humphrey Bogart's only horror movie appearance.

d, Michael Curtiz; w, Robert Tasker, Earl Baldwin (based on a play by Howard W. Comstock and Allen C. Miller); ph, Ray Rennahan (Technicolor), Richard Tower; ed, George Amy.

(PR:A MPAA:NR)

## DOLLS*½

(1987) 77m Taryn/Empire c

Ian Patrick Williams *(David Bower),* Carolyn Purdy-Gordon *(Rosemary Bower),* Carrie Lorraine *(Judy Bower),* Guy Rolfe *(Gabriel Hartwicke),* Hilary Mason *(Hilary Hartwicke),* Bunty Bailey *(Isabel Prange),* Cassie Stuart *(Enid Tilley),* Stephen Lee *(Ralph Morris).*

Stuart Gordon's disappointing followup to RE-ANIMATOR (1985) and FROM BEYOND (1986) was written by TROLLS screenwriter Ed Naha, author of such genre-film reference works as *Horrors from Screen to Scream* and *The Science Fictionary.* Beginning on a prototypical dark and stormy night, DOLLS centers on Judy (Carrie Lorraine), an unhappy little girl traveling through England with her father and hated stepmother. Stranded by the storm, Judy, her parents, and several other strangers seek refuge in a spooky mansion owned by an eccentric old couple (Guy Rolfe and Hilary Mason), who take an immediate liking to Judy and show her their massive collection of dolls. Of course, that night the dolls come to life and kill off the most obnoxious guests. Filmed by Gordon *before* FROM BEYOND, but released *after* it, DOLLS is merely a dull interlude between the two Lovecraft adaptations. Directed and scripted in a surprisingly perfunctory manner, this movie is incredibly tedious—even at its brief 77-minute running time—as Gordon drags out every "Old Dark House" cliche while adding nothing new. Although the concept of small dolls coming to bloodthirsty life *sounds* scary, its fear factor decreases rapidly after the initial shock. Gordon and his effects team do manage to evoke some chills, however, especially when the dolls whisper among themselves, deciding the fate of their hostages right in front of the helpless victims. Unfortunately, these nightmarish moments are few and far between, and the viewer must suffer through innumerable speeches by Rolfe and Mason extolling the virtues of childlike innocence and parental responsibility—as if this pontification justifies the ensuing carnage! For a director who has so quickly pushed his way to the forefront of the horror genre with an intelligent, no-holds-barred approach, Gordon's DOLLS is surprisingly tame and wholly disappointing.

p, Brian Yuzna; d, Stuart Gordon; w, Ed Naha; ph, Mac Ahlberg; ed, Lee Percy; m, Fuzzbee Morse.

(PR:O MPAA:R)

## DON'T ANSWER THE PHONE*

(1980) 94m Scorpion/Crown c (AKA: HOLLYWOOD STRANGLER, THE)

James Westmoreland *(Chris),* Flo Gerrish *(Dr. Gale),* Ben Frank *(Hatcher),* Nicholas Worth *(Kirk),* Stan Haze *(Adkins),* Gary Allen *(Feldon),* Pamela Bryant *(Sue),* Ted Chapman *(Bald Man),* Denise Galik *(Lisa),* Dale Kalberg, Deborah Leah Land, Tom Lasswell, Ellen Karston, Mike Levine, Chuck Mitchell, Victor Mohica, Suzanne Severeid, Paula Warner, Chris Wallace.

This wretched psycho-killer film features Nicholas Worth as a disturbed Vietnam vet who works through his aggressions by strangling nubile Los Angeles area women. Loosely based on the Hillside Strangler murders of the 1970s, the plot goes nowhere except to the vet's predictable death in the closing frames. The only reason for watching this is Worth's portrayal of this most disturbed strangler—overweight and obsessed, into weightlifting, pornography, and raving on radio call-in shows.

p, Robert Hammer; d, Robert Hammer; w, Robert Hammer, Michael Castle; ph, James Carter (Metrocolor); ed, Joseph Fineman; m, Byron Allerd.

(PR:O MPAA:R)

## DON'T GO IN THE HOUSE zero

(1980) 82m Film Ventures/Turbine c

Dan Grimaldi *(Donny),* Robert Osth *(Bobby),* Ruth Dardick *(Mrs. Kohler),* Charlie Bonet *(Ben),* Bill Ricci *(Vito),* Dennis M. Hunter, John Hedberg, Johanna Brushay, Darcy Shean, Mary Ann Chin, Jim Donnegan, Claudia Folts, Denise Woods, Pat Williams, Colin McInness, Ralph D. Bowman, Joey Peschl, Connie Oaks, David McComb, Jean Manning, Ken Kelsch, Tom Brumberger, Nikki Kollins.

When his abusive mother dies, Donny (Dan Grimaldi), a deranged incinerator operator, roasts her in his private crematorium, then dresses up her crispy corpse and moves it around the house. To keep mom company, he cruises discos picking up nubile victims who all end up similarly well-done. In the baffling finale of this worthless, repugnant film, Donny's victims all come to life and kill him. As is the case with the vast majority of "Don't" movies, don't bother.

p, Ellen Hammill; d, Joseph Ellison; w, Ellen Hammill, Joseph Ellison, Joseph Masefield; ph, Oliver Wood (DeLuxe Color); ed, Jane Kurson; m, Richard Einhorn.

(PR:O MPAA:R)

## DON'T LOOK IN THE BASEMENT**

(1973) 89m Hallmark c

Rosie Holotik *(Charlotte),* Ann McAdams *(Dr. Masters),* William Bill McGhee *(Sam),* Gene Ross *(Judge Oliver W. Cameron),* Jessie Lee Fulton *(Jane St. Claire),* Camilla Carr *(Harriet),* Harriet Warren *(Jennifer),* Hugh Feagin *(Sgt. Jaffee),* Rhea MacAdams *(Mrs. Callingham),* Betty Chandler *(Allyson)*, Jessie Kirby *(Danny)*, Robert Dracup *(Ray Daniels)*, Michael Harvey *(Dr. Stephens)*.

A perennial drive-in favorite, this is one of the original "don't" movies and features some truly gruesome killings, the highlight of which occurs as one victim is pushed eye-first into the sharp metal spike of a paper-holder. The film is set in an experimental insane asylum where the inmates are encouraged to act out their fantasies. This, of course, leads to some gross scenes, especially when an inmate who wants to make love to his long-dead wife is allowed to do so (she's disinterred and handed over to the horny husband). Shortly after the arrival of a new nurse, the director of the institution is axe-murdered by one of the inmates. The nurse takes over where her boss left off, but the inmates continue to die one by one. Despite the overall cheapness of the production, director S.F. Brownrigg does manage to convey a sense of seedy claustrophobia during the depraved proceedings. In an attempt to capitalize on the success of his previous release, Wes Craven's LAST HOUSE ON THE LEFT, distributor Hallmark used the same ad slogan, "Keep telling yourself it's only a movie," for this film. An early videotape release of this film has as much as 12 minutes of gruesomeness removed, so beware.

p, S.F. Brownrigg; d, S.F. Brownrigg; w, Tim Pope.

**(PR:O   MPAA:R)**

### DON'T LOOK NOW***½

(1973, Brit./It.) 110m Casey Productions-Eldorado Films-BL/PAR c

Julie Christie *(Laura Baxter)*, Donald Sutherland *(John Baxter)*, Hilary Mason *(Heather)*, Clelia Matania *(Wendy)*, Massimo Serato *(Bishop)*, Renato Scarpa *(Inspector Longhi)*, Giorgio Trestini *(Workman)*, Leopoldo Trieste *(Hotel Manager)*, David Tree *(Anthony Babbage)*, Ann Rye *(Mandy Babbage)*, Nicholas Salter *(Johnny Boxter)*, Sharon Williams *(Christine Baxter)*, Bruno Cattaneo *(Detective Sabbione)*, Adelina Poerio *(Dwarf)*.

John Baxter (Donald Sutherland) travels to Venice with his wife, Laura (Julie Christie), after the accidental drowning death in England of their young daughter. While completing restoration work on a church, Baxter discovers he has certain psychic abilities—abilities nourished by two very strange sisters, Wendy (Clelia Matania) and Heather (Hilary Mason), who have had visions of the couple's dead daughter. Sutherland refuses to believe in his powers, but begins to relent when he sees a small figure darting around Venice dressed in the same red raincoat that his daughter wore. These sightings, coupled with his haunting visions of a funeral boat drifting down a Venetian canal, make for a puzzling and mysterious atmosphere in which "nothing is what it seems." Based on a story by Daphne du Maurier, this enigmatic film does not really warrant classification in any specific mode, but its haunting, surreal, and gloomy elements lend it to the horror and mystery genres. Beautifully photographed and boasting two great performances (Sutherland and Christie), this is one of director Nicolas Roeg's most accessible films and one of his

best. While the vagueness of the plot may frustrate some viewers, this film should be seen for its unforgettable imagery alone. Pino Donaggio's score is a beautiful addition to Roeg's mesmerizing visions.

p, Peter Katz; d, Nicolas Roeg; w, Allan Scott, Chris Bryant (based on a short story by Daphne du Maurier); ph, Anthony Richmond (Panavision Technicolor); ed, Graeme Clifford; m, Pino Donaggio.

**(PR:O   MPAA:R)**

### DON'T OPEN TILL CHRISTMAS zero

(1984, Brit.) 86m Spectacular/21st Century c

Edmund Purdom *(Inspector Harris)*, Alan Lake *(Giles)*, Belinda Mayne *(Kate)*, Gerry Sundquist *(Cliff)*, Mark Jones *(Sgt. Powell)*, Caroline Munro *(Herself)*, Kevin Lloyd *(Gerry)*, Kelly Baker *(Experience Girl)*, Pat Astley *(Sharon)*, Des Dolan *(Detective Constable)*.

This is yet another in the series of horror movies seeking to exploit Christmas and Santa Claus for scares (none of which have been as effective as Bob Clark's sweet, nostalgic A CHRISTMAS STORY, in which children are treated to a truly nightmarish visit to an impatient department store Santa). The plot, such as it is, concerns a madman who is murdering all of the men who play Santa Claus during the holiday season; Harris (Edmund Purdom) is the Scotland Yard man assigned to track down this crazy killer and bring him to justice. The Santas are depicted as drunks and tramps who have accepted the temporary jobs and are now paying for them with their lives and/or horrible dismemberment, including a brutal scene in which one of the Santas is castrated in a public restroom. There are several suspects, including a newsman (Alan Lake) who always seems to be present at the scene of the crime just after it happens. This was the directorial debut of actor Purdom, and he demonstrates little talent for his new position. Lake, who was married to Diana Dors for many years, committed suicide shortly after she died of cancer. Genre fave Caroline Munro makes a brief appearance to sing and dance in a rock'n'roll production number that seems to have been inserted only to relieve the tedium.

p, Dick Randall, Steve Minasian; d, Edmund Purdom; w, Derek Ford, Al McGoohan; ph, Alan Pudney; ed, Ray Selfe; m, Des Dolan.

**(PR:O   MPAA:NR)**

### DORIAN GRAY zero

(1970, It./Brit./Ger./Liechtenstein) 93m Commonwealth United-Towers of London/AIP c (IL DIO CHIAMATO A DORIAN; DAS BILDNESS DES DORIAN GRAY; AKA: SECRET OF DORIAN GRAY, THE)

Helmut Berger *(Dorian Gray)*, Richard Todd *(Basil Hallward)*, Herbert Lom *(Lord Henry Wotten)*, Marie Liljedahl *(Sybil Vane)*, Margaret Lee *(Gwendolyn Wotten)*, Maria Rohm *(Alice)*, Beryl Cunningham *(Adrienne)*, Isa Miranda *(Mrs. Ruxton)*, Eleonora Rossi Drago *(Esther)*, Renato Romano *(Alan)*, Stewart Black *(James Vane)*, Francesco Tensi.

An inadvertently hilarious update of Oscar Wilde's classic novel, DORIAN GRAY stars Helmut Berger, fresh from Lucino Visconti's THE DAMNED, as a swinging student in London who sells his soul to the Devil for eternal youth. A portrait of Dorian ages in his place, getting uglier with each hedonistic act. Sleazy, poorly dubbed, and atrociously acted, this is only good for a few giggles.

p, Harry Alan Towers; d, Massimo Dallamano; w, Massimo Dallamano, Marcello Coscia, Gunter Ebert (based on the novel *The Picture of Dorian Gray* by Oscar Wilde); ph, Otello Spila (Movielab Color); ed, Nicholas Wentworth; m, Peppino DeLuca, Carlo Pes.

(PR:O  MPAA:R)

## DORM THAT DRIPPED BLOOD, THE*

(1983) 84m New Image-Wescom/Obrow c

Laurine Lapinski *(Joanne),* Stephen Sachs *(Craig),* David Snow *(Brian),* Pamela Holland *(Patti),* Dennis Ely *(Bobby Lee Tremble),* Woody Roll *(John Hemmit),* Daphne Zuniga *(Debbie),* Jake Jones *(Bill Edgar),* Robert Frederick *(Tim),* Chris Morrill *(Jack),* Chandre *(Alice),* Billy Criswell *(Rick),* Richard Cowgill *(Debbie's Father),* Kay Beth *(Debbie's Mother),* Jimmy Betz *(Officer Lewis),* Thomas Christian *(Officer Dean),* Robert Richardson *(Policeman),* Chris Schroeder *(Policeman).*

A mad killer stalks the halls of a dormitory in this dumb, boring slasher movie, knocking off his victims in a variety of clever ways, including an electric drill and a pressure cooker, and all so he can be with the woman he loves from afar. Utterly predictable and full of infuriating red herrings, the film's only point of interest is the appearance of Daphne Zuniga, who would go on to THE SURE THING and THE FLY II.

p, Jeffrey Obrow; d, Jeffrey Obrow, Stephen Carpenter; w, Jeffrey Obrow, Stephen Carpenter, Stacey Giachino; ph, Stephen Carpenter; ed, Jeffrey Obrow; m, Christopher Young.

(PR:O  MPAA:R)

## DRACULA***½

(1931) 84m UNIV bw

Bela Lugosi *(Count Dracula),* Helen Chandler *(Mina Seward),* David Manners *(John Harker),* Dwight Frye *(Renfield),* Edward Van Sloan *(Dr. Van Helsing),* Herbert Bunston *(Dr. Seward),* Frances Dade *(Lucy Weston),* Charles Gerrard *(Martin),* Joan Standing *(Maid),* Moon Carroll *(Briggs),* Josephine Velez *(English Nurse),* Michael Visaroff *(Innkeeper),* Daisy Belmore *(Coach Passenger).*

Although badly dated and somewhat dull during its talky, stagy London scenes, this is the film that started the 1930s horror cycle, secured Universal's position as *the* horror studio, and made Hungarian actor Bela Lugosi a worldwide star. Following the successful stage play more than Bram Stoker's classic novel, the film opens in Transylvania, where Renfield (Dwight Frye), a British real estate salesman, arrives to arrange the sale of a deserted English manor house to a strange nobleman, Count Dracula (Lugosi). The mysterious count turns out to be a 500-year-old vampire, and Renfield is bitten and made his slave. Arriving in London, Dracula becomes smitten with Mina Seward (Helen Chandler) and attempts to make her his bride, but her fiance, Jonathan Harker (David Manners), and vampire expert Prof. Van Helsing (Edward Van Sloan) try and put a stop to the undead count. Enormously popular when first released, DRACULA remains a classic of horror to this day, largely due to Lugosi's close association with the role—which would become something of a curse for the actor in later years. While the first part of the film is almost entirely without dialog and quite cinematic, mainly due to the brilliant cinematography of Karl Freund, the movie bogs down once it gets to England, after which it appears that director Tod Browning was intent on making a documentary of the stage play. Luckily, Freund's photography creates enough visually gripping moments to keep the film moving, and his cause is greatly aided by the skillful use of sound. While the incidental music (mostly snippets from Tchaikovsky's "Swan Lake") is kept to a minimum, the sound effects are particularly effective, with the creaking of coffin lids, opening and slamming of doors, thudding footsteps, actors' voices, and howling of wolves adding greatly to the creepy atmosphere. Studio heads felt that the film would do well abroad, so a Spanish-language version starring Carlos Villarias in the Dracula role and featuring a completely new all-Spanish cast, directed by George Melford, was produced with the same sets only days after the English version was completed. Reports have it that this version is even better than the Browning-Lugosi film. A remarkable sequel, DRACULA'S DAUGHTER, followed, but is as yet unavailable on home video.

p, Carl Laemmle; d, Tod Browning; w, Garrett Fort (based on the play by Hamilton Deane and John Balderston and the novel by Bram Stoker); ph, Karl Freund; ed, Milton Carruth, Maurice Pivar; m, Peter Illich Tchaikovsky, Richard Wagner.

(PR:A  MPAA:NR)

## DRACULA**

(1979) 109m UNIV c

Frank Langella *(Dracula),* Laurence Olivier *(Van Helsing),* Donald Pleasence *(Seward),* Kate Nelligan *(Lucy),* Trevor Eve *(Harker),* Jan Francis *(Mina),* Janine Duvitski *(Annie),* Tony Haygarth *(Renfield),* Teddy Turner *(Swales),* Kristine Howarth *(Mrs. Galloway),* Joe Belcher *(Tom Hindley),* Ted Carroll *(Scarborough Sailor),* Frank Birch *(Harbormaster),* Gabor Vernon *(Captain of Demeter),* Frank Henson *(Demeter Sailor),* Peter Wallis *(Priest).*

Frank Langella starred as Dracula in a hit Broadway revival of the stage play—distinguished by the black-and-white sets by Edward Gorey that made the sight of blood very dramatic indeed—and the idea here, as when Universal made the Lugosi version in 1931, was to capitalize on the play's popularity and transfer that success to the screen. It worked in 1931, but not this time. Gorey's striking sets—none too cinematic for the unimaginative likes of John Badham—were replaced by the next best thing, namely state-of-the-art special effects. The sight of Dracula climbing down a wall headfirst is the highlight of the entire movie; the rest of the film is just another plodding remake. The familiar story is given no new twists, save for an updated Edwardian setting and a few automobiles. Langella repeats his suave and seductive portrayal, with a hammy Laurence Olivier as Van Helsing, Kate Nelligan as Lucy, and Donald Pleasence as her father. Watch a Hammer film instead.

p, Walter Mirisch; d, John Badham; w, W.D. Richter (based on the play by Hamilton Deane and John Balderston, from the novel by Bram Stoker); ph, Gilbert Taylor (Panavision, Technicolor); ed, John Bloom; m, John Williams.

(PR:C  MPAA:R)


## DRACULA VS. FRANKENSTEIN*

(1970) 91m Independent-International bw (AKA: BLOOD OF FRANKENSTEIN; THEY'RE COMING TO GET YOU)

J. Carrol Naish, Lon Chaney, Jr., Regina Carrol, John Bloom, Anthony Eisley, Zandor Vorkov, Forrest J. Ackerman, Angelo Rossitto.

Al Adamson strikes again, this time presiding over the sad, sad end of the long and distinguished careers of both J. Carrol Naish and Lon Chaney, Jr. Naish, who came out of retirement to embarrass himself here, plays a wheelchair-bound Dr. Frankenstein, who is posing as the curator of a horror museum while working on a rejuvenating blood serum. Chaney, who spent his entire career trying to break free of typecasting after his magnificent portrayal of the imbecilic Lenny in OF MICE AND MEN (1939), ends his acting days with a pathetic parody of Lenny as Groton, Frankenstein's "mad zombie" assistant, who is sent out to kill young girls for further experiments. It just so happens that a very disco-looking Count Dracula (an actor using the unlikely pseudonym of Zandor Vorkov) is in the area, and has dug up the remains of the original Frankenstein monster (John Bloom). Teaming up with the elderly doctor, Dracula intends to use the blood serum to allow him to prowl during the day and help bring the monster back to life. Adamson's busty wife, Regina Carrol—who appeared in virtually all her husband's films—is also on hand to jiggle about, while *Famous Monsters of Filmland* editor Forrest J. Ackerman shows up long enough to get killed. To avoid infringing on Universal Studios' copyright of makeup designs for DRACULA and FRANKENSTEIN, Adamson and his crew came up with two silly-looking monsters: Dracula sports an afro and goatee, while the monster looks like a guy with a terminal case of hives who was hit upside the head with a brick.

p, Al Adamson, John Vandom; d, Al Adamson; w, William Pugsley, Samuel M. Sherman; ph, Gary Graver, Paul Glickman.

(PR:O  MPAA:GP)


## DRACULA'S DOG*

(1978) 90m Crown International c (GB: ZOLTAN, HOUND OF DRACULA)

Michael Pataki *(Michael Drake)*, Reggie Nalder *(Veidt-Smit)*, Jose Ferrer *(Inspector Branco)*, Jan Shutan *(Marla Drake)*, Libbie Chase *(Linda Drake)*, John Levin *(Steve Drake)*, Simmy Bow *(Fisherman)*, JoJo D'Amore *(Fisherman)*, Arleen Martell *(Maj. Hessle)*, Roger Schumacher *(Hiker)*, Cleo Harrington *(Mrs. Parks)*, Katherine Fitzpatrick.

Stretching the Dracula legend to its ludicrous extreme, this cheap effort from Albert Band (father of Charles Band, former head of the now-defunct Empire Pictures) begins in modern-day Transylvania, where vampire-hunter Branco (Jose Ferrer) is busy burning the coffins of the Dracula family. Unfortunately, the stakes are inadvertently removed from the remains of Zoltan, the count's dog, and Veidt-Smit (Reggie Nalder), Dracula's slave. This brings the duo back to life and they venture to Los Angeles together to find Michael Drake (Michael Pataki), the last surviving member of the Dracula bloodline. Branco, of course, give chase; Zoltan's eyes glow in the dark and he roars like a jungle beast; and the whole thing is rather silly. Viewers may recognize actor Nalder, who would go on to play the vampire in the "Salem's Lot" TV miniseries, and Pataki, who had played a vampire in the bloody GRAVE OF THE VAMPIRE (1972).

p, Albert Band, Frank Ray Perilli; d, Albert Band; w, Ray Perilli (based on characters created by Bram Stoker); ph, Bruce Logan (DeLuxe Color); ed, Harry Keramidas; m, Andrew Belling.

(PR:O  MPAA:R)


## DRACULA'S WIDOW*

(1988) 86m DEG c

Sylvia Kristel *(Vanessa)*, Josef Sommer *(Lt. Lannon)*, Lenny Von Dohlen *(Raymond Everett)*, Marc Coppola *(Brad)*, Rachel Jones *(Jenny)*, Stefan Schnabel *(Von Helsing)*, Traver Burns, Rick Warner, Candice Sims.

DRACULA'S WIDOW, the feature film debut of director Christopher Coppola (nephew of Francis Ford Coppola), is an ambitious but disappointing rehash of the Dracula myth. Vanessa (Sylvia Kristel), the widow of the notorious count, is accidentally shipped from Castle Bran in Romania to a Hollywood wax museum. Using museum owner Raymond Everett (Lenny Von Dohlen) as her pawn, she plans to return to Romania to search for her long-lost husband; however, Raymond informs her that Count Dracula is dead, killed by Dr. Von Helsing many years before. This news enrages the vamp, who embarks on a killing spree, mutilating many helpless victims. Enter the police, who are confused and angered by the mysterious murders. Lt. Lannon (Josef Sommer), who has seen it all, is assigned to the case and warned by his boss "to deliver or else," but his investigation gets nowhere until Von Helsing's grandson conveniently pops up to explain everything to the disbelieving detective. Coppola attempts a modern-day *film noir*, with Sommer's monotone voice introducing the mystery over a montage of flashing neon lights and rain-soaked streets. Giuseppe Macari's cinematography is appropriately moody, and the vivid lighting, inspired by the E.C. horror comics of the 1950s, is occasionally effective, though mostly it's distracting. From time to time, Coppola rises above his material by combining stylish camera movements with expressive editing techniques, but despite his technical bravado, the film fails on the crucial level of story content.

p, Stephen Traxler; d, Christopher Coppola; w, Kathryn Ann Thomas, Christopher Coppola; ph, Giuseppe Macari (Technicolor); ed, Tom Siiter; m, James Campbell.

**(PR:O   MPAA:R)**

## DREAMANIAC zero

(1987) 82m Taryn/Wizard Video-Infinity c

Thomas Bern *(Adam)*, Kim McKamy *(Pat)*, Sylvia Summers *(Lily)*, Lauren Peterson *(Jodi)*, Bob Pelham *(Jamie)*, Cynthia Crass *(Frances)*, Brad Laughlin *(Brad)*, Linda Watts *(Jan)*, Matthew Phelps *(Foster)*, Lisa Emery *(Rosie)*, Michael Warren *(Ace)*, Brent Black *(Doctor)*.

A young composer of heavy metal tunes conjures up a succubus who sets out on a spree of seduction, murder, and mutilation at a sorority party. Eventually the songwriter, too, comes under her spell and does some carving himself. Things look bad for the two surviving sorority sisters, but a guy in a white coat shows up and drags the demon back to the funny farm. But wait! There's a dumb twist ending! This is a relentlessly stupid gore film with nothing to recommend it. All the victims are catatonic or idiotic and it's hard to care if any of them live. Plus, the ridiculous twist ending is the kind of thing that makes one want to hurl a billiard ball through the TV screen. This was the dubious debut of young director David DeCoteau, who shot the film for Empire in 10 days on a $60,000 budget. It subsequently went straight to video—released through Empire's Wizard Video label—and was laughably marketed as "Too Terrifying for the Silver Screen." While there is no shortage of blood and breasts, there is little to terrify here.

p, David DeCoteau; d, David DeCoteau; w, Helen Robinson; ph, Howard Wexler (Fotokem Color); ed, Peter Teschner.

**(PR:O   MPAA:NR)**

## DRESSED TO KILL***

(1980) 105m Samuel Z. Arkoff/Filmways c

Michael Caine *(Dr. Robert Elliott)*, Angie Dickinson *(Kate Miller)*, Nancy Allen *(Liz Blake)*, Keith Gordon *(Peter Miller)*, Dennis Franz *(Detective Marino)*, David Margulies *(Dr. Levy)*, Ken Baker *(Warren Lockman)*, Brandon Maggart *(Cleveland Sam)*, Susanna Clemm *(Bobbi)*, Fred Weber *(Mike Miller)*.

Kate (Angie Dickinson) is a sexually dissatisfied middle-aged housewife who fantasizes about erotic encounters while in the shower. Kate's sympathetic psychiatrist (Michael Caine) advises her to indulge in an extra-marital af-

fair. Immediately after her first tryst, however, Kate is cornered in an elevator and murdered by a leather-clad blonde wielding a straight razor. Now it is up to Kate's son (Keith Gordon) to solve the murder with the help of the prostitute (Nancy Allen) who discovered his mom's corpse. Although DRESSED TO KILL is highly derivative of Alfred Hitchcock, Mario Bava, and Dario Argento, director Brian De Palma infused this film with enough sex, blood, and visual panache to make it a big hit at the box office. Gushingly praised by some critics at the time of its release, it now seems a definite case of cinematic style over any real substance. A slightly longer and more explicit version was released in Europe.

p, George Litto; d, Brian De Palma; w, Brian De Palma; ph, Ralf Bode (Panavision, Technicolor); ed, Jerry Greenberg; m, Pino Donaggio.

**(PR:O   MPAA:R)**

## DRILLER KILLER**½

(1979) 90m Rochelle Films c

Jimmy Laine *(Reno)*, Carolyn Marz, Baybi Day, Bob De-Frank, Peter Yellen, Harry Schultz, Tony Coca Cola and the Roosters, Alan Wynroth, Rodney Montreal, James O'Hara, Richard Howarth, Maria Helhoski.

The feature debut of the remarkable Abel Ferrara is, although extremely low budget, quite disturbing and powerful, definitely showing the promise that would be fulfilled in Ferrara's similar MS. 45. Hiding behind the pseudonym "Jimmy Laine," Ferrara stars as Reno, an extremely alienated New York City artist who lives in terror of winding up like his derelict father. Suffering from visions and hallucinations in which his paintings whisper to him, Reno vents his frustrations by taking to the streets and murdering bums with a power drill. As his rage spirals out of control, however, Reno moves from killing derelicts to killing those in his own life who have angered him—namely an art dealer and his girl friend. A bleak rumination on the harsh realities of urban life, DRILLER KILLER would be extremely distasteful and repugnant had not Ferrara demonstrated that he was a distinct and conscientious talent behind the camera, concerned with more than just bloody exploitation. Using his budget restrictions to best advantage, Ferrara shot much of the film with a hand-held camera, giving the picture an immediate, documentary-like urgency. Ferrara continues to be an interesting director—particularly with MS. 45—but his forays into bigger-budget territory, FEAR CITY (1984) and CHINA GIRL (1987), have been somewhat disappointing.

p, Rochelle Weisberg; d, Abel Ferrara; w, Nicholas St. John; ph, Ken Kelsch; m, Joseph Delia.

**(PR:O   MPAA:R)**

## DRIVE-IN MASSACRE*

(1976) 78m New American c

Jake Barnes, Adam Lawrence, Douglas Gudbye, Newton Naushaus, Norman Sherlock, Valdesta.

This pretty average slasher film concerns a killer who preys on the patrons of a California drive-in theater. Interwoven in the plentiful gore are police interrogations of a voyeuristic truck driver and a theater manager who despises his customers, while the final murder takes place in front of the outdoor screen during the showing of a western. Obviously inspired by Peter Bogdanovich's masterful TARGETS (1968), DRIVE-IN MASSACRE has none of its predecessor's insight, intelligence, or craft. Instead, it's an ultracheap slice-and-dice effort that even boasts the tired "They're coming to get you!" ending designed to make drive-in audiences uncomfortable. Needless to say, the effect is greatly diminished on home video.

p, Stuart Segall; d, Stuart Segall; w, John Goff, Buck Flower; ph, Kenneth Lloyd Gibb.

(PR:O    MPAA:R)

## DUNWICH HORROR, THE**½

(1970) 90m AIP c

Sandra Dee *(Nancy Walker)*, Dean Stockwell *(Wilbur Whateley)*, Ed Begley *(Dr. Henry Armitage)*, Sam Jaffe *(Old Whateley)*, Donna Baccala *(Elizabeth Hamilton)*, Joanna Moore Jordan *(Lavinia)*, Talia Shire *(Cora)*, Barboura Morris *(Mrs. Cole)*, Mike Fox *(Dr. Raskin)*, Jason Wingreen *(Police Chief)*, Michael Haynes *(Guard)*, Lloyd Bochner *(Dr. Cory)*, Beach Dickerson *(Mr. Cole)*, Toby Russ *(Librarian)*, Jack Pierce *(Reege)*.

Daniel Haller's follow-up to DIE, MONSTER, DIE (1965) is another fairly successful attempt at adapting H.P. Lovecraft for the screen. Set in modern-day New England, the film stars Sandra Dee as Nancy Walker, a young college coed who is lured into the mysterious house of Whateley by the mysterious young hipster Wilbur Whateley (Dean Stockwell). The local community has long suspected that the whole Whateley family—Wilbur, his grandfather (Sam Jaffe), and his mother, who is in an insane asylum—is unholy and soon their suspicions are confirmed. Wilbur intends to use Nancy as a human sexual sacrifice that will unleash dark powers—represented by his monstrous twin brother, who exists in another dimension—throughout the Earth. Occult professor Dr. Armitage (Ed Begley, in his last screen appearance) discovers what Wilbur's up to, and with the aid of Nancy's roommate (Donna Baccala), tries to put a stop to it. An extremely underplayed and somewhat eccentric performance by the mustachioed and curly-haired Stockwell keeps the film interesting and almost makes one forget director Haller's now-dated penchant for psychedelia.

p, James H. Nicholson, Samuel Z. Arkoff; d, Daniel Haller; w, Curtis Lee Hanson, Henry Rosenbaum, Ronald Silkosky (based on a story by H.P Lovecraft); ph, Richard C. Glouner (Movielab Color); ed, Fred Feitshans, Jr., Christopher Holmes; m, Les Baxter.

(PR:C    MPAA:M)

# E

## EATEN ALIVE***

(1976) 90m Virgo International c (AKA: DEATH TRAP; STARTLIGHT SLAUGHTER; HORROR HOTEL MASSACRE; LEGEND OF THE BAYOU)

Neville Brand *(Judd)*, Mel Ferrer *(Harvey Wood)*, Carolyn Jones *(Miss Hattie)*, William Finley *(Roy)*, Stuart Whitman *(Sheriff Martin)*, Crystin Sinclaire, Roberta Collins, Janis Lynn, Kyle Richards, Robert Englund, Marilyn Burns.

This was Tobe Hopper's first film following his masterpiece, THE TEXAS CHAINSAW MASSACRE (1974), and because of haphazard distribution and several title changes, it never really found an audience. Setting his story in Louisiana, Hooper introduces us to a new maniac, Judd (Neville Brand), the sexually repressed proprietor of the Starlight Hotel, who sports a wooden leg and likes to vent his frustrations by killing his guests with a huge scythe, then feeding them to his alligator. The film's definite sick highlight occurs when an unbearably cute puppy owned by a little girl is swallowed by Judd's alligator. Although EATEN ALIVE is not as unique or terrifying as TEXAS CHAINSAW, Hooper does a fine job of building up the Southern gothic atmosphere and continues his brilliant use of sound to enhance the sense of unease and suspense. Brand is wonderful as the muttering, psychotic hotel owner, Marilyn Burns from TEXAS CHAINSAW returns for more, William Finley plays a henpecked family man who may be as crazy as Judd, and A NIGHTMARE ON ELM STREET fans will note that Robert Englund—aka "Freddy"—also makes an appearance.

p, Mardi Rustam; d, Tobe Hooper; w, Alvin L. Fast, Mardi Rustam; ph, Robert Caramico.

(PR:O    MPAA:R)

## EATING RAOUL****

(1982) 90m Bartel/FOX c

Mary Woronov *(Mary Bland)*, Paul Bartel *(Paul Bland)*, Robert Beltran *(Raoul)*, Buck Henry *(Mr. Leech)*, Richard Paul *(Mr.Kray)*, Susan Saiger *(Doris the Dominatrix)*, Ed Begley, Jr. *(Hippy)*, Dan Barrows *(Bobbie R.)*, Dick Blackburn *(James)*, Ralph Brannen *(Paco)*, Hamilton Camp *(Mr. Peck)*, John Paragon *(Sexshop Salesman)*, Edie McClurg *(Susan)*, Allan Rich, Don Steele, Billy Curtis, Anna Mathias, John Shearin, Darcy Pulliam.

This hilarious black comedy has gained quite a cult following over the years, and it remains writer-director-star Paul Bartel's best effort yet. Set in Los Angeles, the story follows straight-laced couple Paul and Mary Bland (Bartel and the inestimable Mary Woronov) who dream of some day opening their own gourmet restaurant, *Chez Bland*, in the nearby suburb of Valencia. Repulsed by the "swinging" lifestyle of their neighbors, the Blands look forward to the day when they can leave the dirty city, but they need to raise $20,000 to do so. Since Mary is a nurse and Paul has just been fired from his job at a liquor store, realizing their dream soon seems unlikely. Fate knocks, however, when a drunken reveler stumbles into their apartment by accident and begins mauling Mary. Paul angrily conks the intruder on the head with a frying pan and kills him. While looking in the victim's wallet for some ID, Paul and Mary discover a huge wad of cash. Hitting upon a scheme to raise the money they need to leave Los Angeles, Paul and Mary place an ad in a swingers' newspaper to lure "horrible, sex-crazed perverts that nobody will miss anyway" into their home, where they will be killed for their money. The plan works better than expected, until a Hispanic locksmith, Raoul (Robert Beltran), discovers the bodies and becomes their partner, selling the corpses to the Doggie King Dogfood Company. Played totally straight, with Bartel and Woronov giving wonderfully funny deadpan performances, EATING RAOUL is a terrifically droll satire on both horror movies and American middle-class values. Amazingly, given the cannibalistic subject matter, the film is downright gentle and endearing, with Paul and Mary Bland emerging as genuinely sympathetic characters. Working independently, Bartel scraped together financing from family and friends, and shot the film in piecemeal fashion when he could afford it. After several disappointing projects, such as LUST IN THE DUST (1985) and THE LONGSHOT (1986), Bartel has recently announced that he is about to launch production of EATING RAOUL's long-awaited sequel—BLAND AMBITION.

p, Anne Kimmel; d, Paul Bartel; w, Paul Bartel, Richard Blackburn; ph, Gary Thieltges (Metrocolor); ed, Alan Toomayan; m, Arlon Ober.

(PR:O   MPAA:R)

## ELVIRA: MISTRESS OF THE DARK**

(1988) 96m NBC/NW c

Cassandra Peterson (Elvira), Edie McClurg (Chastity Pariah), Pat Crawford Brown (Mrs. Meeker), William Duell (Mr. Meeker), Susan Kellermann (Patty), Daniel Greene (Bob Redding), W.W. Morgan Sheppard (Uncle).

Cassandra Peterson, the actress-comedienne-dancer who has found fame in the 1980s hosting the syndicated television show "Movie Macabre" as Elvira, a well-endowed witch who lounges seductively on a couch and cracks bad jokes during the showing of horror and science-fiction movies, brings her TV character to the big screen in this campy comedy. The film opens as Elvira concludes one of her shows (a screening of Roger Corman's 1956 classic IT CONQUERED THE WORLD). When she rejects the sexual overtures of the TV station's new owner, she is fired. Dejected, but hopeful that her upcoming stage act in Las Vegas will rejuvenate her career, Elvira is shocked to discover that the producers in Vegas want her to come up with $50,000 for the show. Luckily, at that very moment she receives a telegram informing her that her aunt has died and left Elvira part of her estate. Her arrival at the Fallwell, Massachusetts, estate causes a major scandal and the sourpuss elderly population gives her the cold shoulder; the town's bored teenagers, however,

flock to her. Elvira and her new friends set about renovating her aunt's mansion in the hopes of selling it and using the money to finance her Las Vegas debut. Things get complicated for Elvira, however, when she discovers her aunt's involvement with witchcraft. Making full use of the freedom a PG-13 rating allows, this movie must set some kind of record for the number of sophomoric double entendres and amount of sexual innuendo spewed in a feature film. But despite its mildly raunchy tone and obsession with Elvira's considerable cleavage, the film is basically a decent, good-hearted comedy that never takes itself seriously. In fact, the screenplay is an old-fashioned 60s-style slam against the establishment that takes a playful poke at Reagan-era morality. With the town named "Fallwell" (as in Jerry Falwell), there can be little doubt as to where the film's sentiments lie. Elvira is even shown to have a definite moral code and believes in truth, justice, and romantic love—while the self-righteous, hypocritical upholders of social order are seen to be the truly sick and sex-obsessed ones.

p, Eric Gardner, Mark Pierson; d, James Signorelli; w, Sam Egan, John Paragon, Cassandra Peterson; ph, Hanania Baer (CFI color); ed, Battle David; m, James Campbell.

(PR:C   MPAA:PG-13)

## ENCOUNTER WITH THE UNKNOWN zero

(1973) 87m Centronics International/Libert c

Rosie Holotik, Gary Brockette, Gene Ross, Annabelle Weenick, Bob Ginnaven, August Sehven, Kevin Kieberly, Rod Serling (Narrator).

Rod Serling, of TV's "The Twilight Zone," steps in to do some of the narration in this cheaply made (as evidenced by the presence of actors Gene Ross and Rosie Holotik, of DON'T LOOK IN THE BASEMENT) anthology of supernatural tales—all supposedly true. The first story begins in a graveyard and follows three teenagers who are cursed, the second is about a mysterious hole in a farmer's field that contains a monster, and the third is about a man who meets a girl who turns out to be a ghost on a bridge. The film was shot silent, with the dialog entirely post-dubbed. Director Harry Thomason pads out each segment with interminable flashbacks of footage he's already used in this pretty pathetic end to the soon-to-be-deceased Serling's career.

p, Joe Glass; d, Harry Thomason.

(PR:C   MPAA:PG)

## ENTITY, THE**½

(1982) 125m Belleport Investors/FOX c

Barbara Hershey (Carla Moran), Ron Silver (Phil Schneidermann), David Labisoa (Billy), George Coe (Dr. Weber), Margaret Blye (Cindy Nash), Jacqueline Brooks (Dr. Cooley), Richard Brestoff (Gene Kraft), Michael Alldredge (George Nash), Raymond Singer (Joe Mehan), Allan Rich (Dr. Walcott), Natasha Ryan (Julie), Melanie Gaffin (Kim), Alex Rocco (Jerry Anderson), Sully Boyar (Mr. Reisz), Tom Stern (Woody Browne), Curt Lowens (Dr. Wilkes), Paula

Victor *(Dr. Chevalier)*, Lee Wilkof *(Dr. L. Hase)*, Deborah Stevenson, Mark Weiner *(Interns)*, Lisa Gurley *(Receptionist)*, Chris Howell *(Guard)*, Renee Neimark *(Nurse)*, John Branagan, Daniel Furie, Amy Kirkpatric, Todd Kutches, Pauline Lomas *(Students)*.

A great performance by Barbara Hershey fails to save this poorly directed (by the ever-inept Sidney J. Furie) tale of the supernatural, which was sold as a fictionalized account of an actual paranormal case history. Carla Moran (Hershey) is a single mother living in Los Angeles who is repeatedly assaulted and raped by an invisible presence. She tries to convince herself that it's just a hysterical reaction to childhood trauma, but eventually psychiatry fails and parapsychology wins as a big, scary thing makes an appearance. Lustful Hershey fans may enjoy the rather ingenious special effects by which invisible hands molest the actress, but Furie's direction is ham-handed as usual, with the camera swooping all over the place between dull bouts of psychological and parapsychological mumbo-jumbo.

p, Harold Schneider; d, Sidney J. Furie; w, Frank De Felitta (from his novel); ph, Stephen H. Burum (Technicolor); ed, Frank J. Urioste; m, Charles Bernstein.

**(PR:O   MPAA:R)**

## EQUINOX**½

(1970) 82m Tonylyn/VIP c (AKA: BEAST, THE)

Edward Connell *(Dave)*, Barbara Hewitt *(Susan)*, Frank Boers, Jr. *(Jim)*, Robin Christopher *(Vicki)*, Jack Woods *(Asmodeus)*, Jim Phillips *(Reporter)*, Fritz Leiber *(Dr. Waterman)*, Patrick Burke *(Branson)*, Jim Duran *(Orderly)*, Norville Brooks, Irving L. Lichenstein.

Four teenagers go to a state forest to look for a missing scientist (played by Fritz Leiber, a noted sci-fi author), where they find a strange book of ancient Persian incantations. Forest ranger Asmodeus (Jack Woods), actually King of the Demons, threatens them with a series of giant monsters (a horned, winged demon, a blue-faced giant) in an attempt to recover the book. People disappear, castles appear, and a dimensional barrier sucks them in. Told in a disjointed form, and frequently confusing, EQUINOX does contain some fine moments. Genuinely weird—more because of circumstance than design—this was an amateur film shot on 16mm in 1967, after which Jack H. Harris saw it and bought the distribution rights in 1968. Keeping the impressive special effects by Jim Danforth and David Allen intact, Harris then added new scenes, which comprised more than half of the final footage. This bizarre little film has gathered quite a cult following over the years, mainly because of extensive coverage in *Famous Monsters of Filmland* magazine and the fact that the magazine's editor, Forrest J. Ackerman, supplies the voice heard on a tape recording. On videotape as THE BEAST.

p, Dennis Muren, Jack H. Harris; d, Jack Woods; w, Jack Woods (from a story by Mark Thomas McGee); ph, Mike Hoover (DeLuxe Color); ed, John Joyce; m, John Caper.

**(PR:C   MPAA:NR)**

## ERASERHEAD*****

(1978) 90m AFI/Libra bw

John Nance *(Henry Spencer)*, Charlotte Stewart *(Mary X)*, Allen Joseph *(Mr. X)*, Jeanne Bates *(Mrs. X)*, Judith Anna Roberts *(Girl Across the Hall)*, Laurel Near *(Lady in the Radiator)*, V. Phipps Wilson *(Landlady)*, Jack Fisk *(Man in the Planet)*, Jean.

David Lynch's film ERASERHEAD has been described by its creator as a "dream of dark and troubling things," and it is, possibly, cinema's only true nightmare: disturbing, repulsive, hilarious, frightening, sensitive, challenging. ERASERHEAD is filled with thousands of haunting, nightmarish images, its characters existing in an utterly strange world. Its "plot" is almost impossible to follow. A young man, Henry (John Nance), living in a dilapidated apartment building in an industrialized city learns that his girl friend, Mary (Charlotte Stewart), is pregnant. Leaving his room (which seems to be inhabited by spermlike creatures), he visits Mary and her parents—a hyperactive father with a passion for synthetic meat and a mother obsessed with her daughter's sexuality. Grandmother sits in the kitchen, stonelike. Maybe dead. Mary moves in with Henry and they begin to take care of their "baby," a deformed, constantly crying mass of tissue and bandages that looks like a skinned lamb. The infant is repulsive, yet fascinating, and also sad. Its constant whining drives Mary out of the apartment, leaving Henry alone with the baby. He accidentally kills it, and is thrown into the nightmare world that has existed on the fringes of his "real" world since the beginning of the film. After a series of weird trials and tribulations (which cause him at one point to lose his head), Henry is united with the bleached-blonde Lady in the Radiator, a frighteningly "cute" woman with monstrous apple dumpling cheeks, who calms him by singing, "In heaven, everything is fine." ERASERHEAD is not simply a film about a man who has nasty dreams. It shows that the "dark and troubling things" that we like to repress inhabit dresser drawers, or live behind the radiator, or under the bed. They are part of the environment. There is no separation between what is dreamed and what is real, no foggy dissolves, no waking-up scenes, no escape. A former painter and true cinematic visionary, Lynch is interested in allowing richly textured things, objects, and people to inhabit the film frame, creating compositions that strike the viewer with weird power. ERASERHEAD is very popular on the cult midnight-movie circuit, its gross elements enticing bored college students initially and its mysterious qualities bringing them back again and again to a very dark dream.

p, David Lynch; d, David Lynch; w, David Lynch; ph, Frederick Elms, Herbert Cardwell; ed, David Lynch; m, Fats Waller.

**(PR:O   MPAA:NR)**

## ESCAPES zero

(1987, Brit.) 72m Visual Perceptions/Prism Ent. c

Vincent Price *(Mailman)*, Todd Fulton *(Matt Wilson)*, Jerry Grishaw *(Fisherman)*, Michael Patton-Hall *(Delivery Driver)*, John Mitchum *(Mr. Olson)*, Lee Cranfield, Roelle

Mitchell *(Young Couple)*, Nick Martin, P.K. Kearns, Vera Briggs, Arleta Johnson, Delbert Johnson, Jim Sundown, Julie Ann Daly, Bob Pittinger, Wesley Widerholt, Audrey Heyser, Albert H. Harris *(People in Cafe)*, Ken Thorley *(Jogger)*, Jeff Boudov *(Scientist)*, Mark Steensland, Shawn Hannon *(Large Creatures)*, Matthew Mattingly, Caleb Mattingly *(Small Creatures)*, Shirley O'Key *(Mary Tucker)*, Robert Elson *(Young Jonah)*, Bill Sibley *(Storekeeper)*, Gil Reade *(Bum)*, Rocky Capella *(Mugger)*, Bob Peeler *(Man in Car)*, David Newham *(Policeman)*, Neal Hahn *(Wino)*, Mike Martinez *(Driver)*.

Vincent Price narrates this limp horror anthology, telling audiences at the beginning that they will see 10 tales. Actually, there are only half that many, but audiences are unlikely to quibble on this point in their relief at finally seeing the thing come to an end. In the first story, a man out fishing picks up an apple on the shore. Taking a bite, he finds a hook in his mouth. A line leading under the water starts to pull and reels him in. In the next tale, a young messenger finds himself lost in the mountains. He disregards an old man's instructions to slow down and have a cup of coffee, and instead finds himself going around in circles until he is trapped in the local diner, somehow forced to spend eternity slowly sipping a cup of java. Next we are presented with a fat jogger who is chased through the woods by horrible beasts until he falls down and one of them runs up to him, touches him, and says, "Tag; you're it." The fourth story concerns an old woman who has tried to make a living from the meager gleanings of gold on her mountain. One night a flying saucer crashes into her barn. She goes out and clears the debris from it, and the machine takes off, leaving the ground where it crashed glittering with gold, apparently having exposed the mother lode in its crash. The last story concerns a thief who steals a magic crystal from a bum who uses it to make food appear. The robber is promptly run over by a car, but the bum recovers the stone, heals the robber, and brings a police car to arrest him, having put a purse and knife in his hands magically. Not a single one of the stories is at all worthwhile, with only the second showing a little style. Most of them are relentlessly padded to make the thin plots fill the time; all were shot in northern California with an amateurish cast.

p, David Steensland, Angela Sanders; d, David Steensland; w, David Steensland; ph, Gary Tomsic; ed, Dane Westvic, Kiplan Hall; m, Todd Popple.

**(PR:A  MPAA:NR)**

## EVIL, THE**½

(1978) 89m NW c

Richard Crenna *(C.J.)*, Joanna Pettet *(Caroline)*, Andrew Prine *(Raymond)*, Cassie Yates *(Mary)*, Lynn Moody *(Felicia)*, Victor Buono *(The Devil)*, George O'Hanlon, Jr. *(Pete)*, Mary Louise Weller *(Laurie)*, Robert Viharo *(Dwight)*, Milton Selzer *(Realtor)*, Galen Thompson *(Vargas)*, Emory Souza *(Demon)*.

A psychologist (Richard Crenna) and his wife (Joanna Pettet) rent a haunted house for use as a drug rehab center, and, when strange things start to happen, they invite a group of students to help investigate. A trap-door discovered in the cellar releases a nasty force that engulfs all and disposes of them one by one. It's all pretty expertly done, and director Gus Trikonis knows how to make a haunted-house movie. Victor Buono is sublime as the Devil himself, although his final scene has been cut out of some prints.

p, Ed Carlin; d, Gus Trikonis; w, Donald G. Thompson; ph, Mario Di Leo (Movielab Color); ed, Jack Kirshner; m, Johnny Harris.

**(PR:O  MPAA:R)**

## EVIL DEAD, THE*****

(1983) 85m Renaissance/New Line c

Bruce Campbell *(Ash)*, Ellen Sandweiss *(Cheryl)*, Betsy Baker *(Linda)*, Hal Delrich *(Scott)*, Sarah York *(Shelly)*.

Sam Raimi and company took the horror genre by storm with this amazingly exhilarating feast of horror, in which narrative was thrown to the winds in favor of pure cinematic panache. Five college students take shelter in an abandoned cabin deep in the woods. Inside, they find a strange book and a tape explaining that the book is an ancient Sumerian Book of the Dead. The tape translates some of the incantations in the book, and giant demons are unleashed in the woods. One by one, the teenagers are taken over by the demons, until only Ash (Bruce Campbell) is left to fight the evil. Shot on 16mm on a tiny budget, this film definitely has some limitations technically, but because of good, creative filmmaking it is nonetheless a masterpiece of recent American horror. THE EVIL DEAD contains more truly nightmarish imagery than *all seven* of the "Friday the 13th" movies and their offshoots combined. There are sequences and shots in this film that one will never forget and, while it's thoroughly shocking and spooky, there's also enough black humor to keep it all from getting too oppressive. To discuss the film any further would spoil things, so by all means, if you haven't already seen it—do so! Followed by an equally impressive sequel, EVIL DEAD 2: DEAD BY DAWN.

p, Robert G. Tapert; d, Sam Raimi; w, Sam Raimi; ph, Tim Philo, Joshua M. Becker (Du Art Color); ed, Edna Ruth Paul; m, Joseph Lo Duca.

**(PR:O  MPAA:NR)**

## EVIL DEAD 2: DEAD BY DAWN*****

(1987) 85m Renaissance/Rosebud c

Bruce Campbell *(Ash)*, Sarah Berry *(Annie)*, Dan Hicks *(Jake)*, Kassie Wesley *(Bobby Joe)*, Theodore Raimi *(Possessed Henrietta)*, Denise Bixler *(Linda)*, Richard Domeier *(Ed)*, John Peaks *(Prof. Raymond Knowby)*, Lou Hancock *(Henrietta)*.

Director Sam Raimi strikes again with this manic, and very funny, sequel to his stunningly inventive 1983 low-budget fever dream, THE EVIL DEAD. As in the first film, Raimi lets out all the stops and plays every cinematic trick in the book. Instead of "Dead by Dawn," the subtitle of this film should be "Help! There's a Camera Chasing Me!" More a remake than a sequel, the film opens as the lone survivor from the first film, Ash (Bruce Campbell), ventures out to a lonely cabin for a romantic weekend with his girl friend (Denise Bixler). There, Ash discovers that damn tape recorder again. When the voice reads a translation of the "Book of the Dead," a vicious evil force awakens in the woods and rushes into the house, and all hell breaks loose once more. A purely cinematic experience for those with a taste for *Grand Guignol*, the impact of EVIL DEAD 2 cannot be described. Grotesque, gory, silly, and, at times, quite funny, Raimi's creation is a relentlessly energetic nightmare world where anything can (and does) happen. By taking everything to an absurd extreme, the film frequently leaves the realm of horror and becomes a cartoon gone mad. Campbell's ultraserious performance is almost Keatonesque as he gamely tries to handle everything Raimi throws at him, and Raimi has a lot of ammo. The 26-year-old director employs a myriad of cinematic tricks and visual styles, including: stop-motion animation, undercranking the camera, point-of-view shots, crane shots, hand-held shots, Dutch angles, special makeup, turning sets on their sides, rear-screen projection, anamorphic lenses, radio-controlled mechanics, mattes, miniatures, sound effects, and good-old-fashioned dramatic lighting. The film is a breathless celebration of the possibilities of the medium and should be viewed as such. Obviously, dramatic narrative holds little interest for Raimi. The setting and story are merely functional, and most of the dialog is perfunctory—sometimes hilariously so. This is by no means a psychological horror film, nor one that seeks to examine the repressed underbelly of American society. Pure visceral impact is what this film is all about and it succeeds brilliantly.

p, Robert G. Tapert; d, Sam Raimi; w, Sam Raimi, Scott Spiegel; ph, Peter Deming, Eugene Shlugleit (Technicolor); ed, Kaye Davis; m, Joseph Lo Duca.

**(PR:O MPAA:NR)**

### EVIL OF FRANKENSTEIN, THE**

(1964, Brit.) 84m Hammer/UNIV c

Peter Cushing *(Baron Frankenstein)*, Peter Woodthorpe *(Zoltan)*, Sandor Eles *(Hans)*, Kiwi Kingston *(The Creature)*, Katy Wild-Rena *(Beggar Girl)*, David Hutcheson *(Burgomaster)*, Duncan Lamont *(Chief of Police)*, James Maxwell *(Priest)*, Caron Gardner *(Burgomaster's Wife)*, Howard Goorney *(Drunk)*, Timothy Bateson *(Hypnotized Man)*, Alister Williamson *(Landlord)*, Tony Arpino *(Bodysnatcher)*, Frank Forsyth *(Manservant)*, Kenneth Cove *(Cure)*, Michelle Scott *(Little Girl)*, Anthony Blackshaw *(Burly Constable)*, David Conville *(Young Constable)*, Steven Geray *(Dr. Sorgado)*, William Phipps *(Rena's Father)*, Maria Palmer *(Rena's Mother)*, Tracy Stratford *(Rena as a Child)*, Patrick Horgan *(David Carrell)*, Derek Martin, Robert Flynn, Anthony Poole, James Garfield *(Roustabouts)*.

The only one of the Hammer Frankenstein films not to be directed by Terence Fisher, this is, consequently, one of the weakest entries in the series. With this outing—cloddishly directed by Freddie Francis—Hammer came to an agreement with Universal over use of the monster makeup, and not only does the monster bear more resemblance to the Karloff-Pierce one this time, but the plot seems borrowed from FRANKENSTEIN MEETS THE WOLFMAN (1943). Ignoring events in the first two Hammer films (THE CURSE OF FRANKENSTEIN and THE REVENGE OF FRANKENSTEIN), the film begins as the Baron (Peter Cushing) returns to his ancestral castle, having been chased out of it years earlier by angry villagers (seen in flashback). Finding his creature frozen in an ice cave, Frankenstein thaws him out and enlists the help of hypnotist Zoltan (Peter Woodthorpe) to control him. Zoltan, however, uses the monster to wreak havoc on his own enemies. The plot is overly familiar, the makeup on the monster is laughable, and the whole thing is deadly dull—save for Cushing's performance. Fisher would return with FRANKENSTEIN CREATED WOMAN (1966), one of the best of the series. Unfortunately, most of the Fisher films are not yet available on home video, but THE EVIL OF FRANKENSTEIN is. Go figure.

p, Anthony Hinds; d, Freddie Francis; w, John Elder; ph, John Wilcox (Eastmancolor); ed, James Needs; m, Don Banks.

**(PR:A MPAA:NR)**

### EVILSPEAK**½

(1982) 89m Leisure Investment-Coronet/Moreno c

Clint Howard *(Coopersmith)*, R.G. Armstrong *(Sarge)*, Charles Tyner *(Col. Kinkaid)*, Joseph Cortese *(Rev. Jameson)*, Claude Earl Jones *(Coach)*, Lynn Hancock *(Miss Freidermyer)*, Lenny Montana *(Jake)*, Don Stark, Hamilton Camp.

The ultimate revenge-of-the-nerd movie, EVILSPEAK concerns a computer-geek military school cadet (Clint Howard), constantly tormented by his neanderthalic schoolmates, who discovers a secret book of black magic hidden in the old chapel. Fascinated by the occult, he inputs the information into his computer and somehow electronically invokes a bevy of spells and a horde of razor-tusked wild boars to get even with the cadets and drill instructors who are baiting him. The directorial debut of Eric Weston, EVILSPEAK is remarkably engaging, imaginative, and well-crafted, and contains a strong performance from Howard, plus a deliciously over-the-top nasty turn by veteran character actor R.G. Armstrong.

p, Sylvio Tabet, Eric Weston; d, Eric Weston; w, Joseph Garofalo, Eric Weston; ph, Irv Goodnoff; m, Roger Kellaway.

**(PR:O MPAA:R)**

### EXORCIST, THE****

(1973) 121m WB c

Ellen Burstyn *(Mrs. MacNeil)*, Max von Sydow *(Father Merrin)*, Jason Miller *(Father Karras)*, Lee J. Cobb *(Lt. Kinderman)*, Jack MacGowran *(Burke)*, Kitty Winn *(Sharon)*, Linda Blair *(Regan)*, Vasiliki Maliaros *(Mother Karras)*, Wallace Rooney *(Bishop)*, Titos Vandis *(Karras' Uncle)*,

Rev. William O'Malley (Father Dyer), Mercedes McCambridge (Voice of the Demon).

Extremely controversial at the time of its release, THE EXORCIST kicked off intense debate among critics, community leaders, and even religious leaders—spurring the public, of course, to make it one of the most financially successful horror films ever made. Regan (Linda Blair), the 12-year-old daughter of a famous stage actress (Ellen Burstyn), begins to suffer unexplainable fits and bouts of bizarre behavior. The girl is brought to doctors, but examinations fail to pinpoint a physical or psychiatric ailment. Regan's condition grows worse and she begins to transform physically, taking on an ugly, demonic appearance. In desperation, Regan's mother asks the help of a young priest, Fr. Karras (Jason Miller). Realizing that Regan is possessed by the Devil, and knowing that his own faith is too weak for him to deal successfully with the problem himself, Karras turns to Fr. Merrin (Max von Sydow), an elderly priest who specializes in exorcisms. Based on William Peter Blatty's runaway best-seller—which itself was based upon a reported exorcism in 1949—the film is a savvy play upon the fears and frustrations of parents, with portentous religious implications thrown into the mix. Social analysis aside, the film is a masterfully directed bit of audience manipulation, with helmsman William Friedkin pushing all the right buttons. Well controlled, the movie balances its then-state-of-the-art special effects with good old-fashioned atmospheric horror to produce an excruciating 121 minutes of dread and unease. Given the big-budget treatment by Warner Bros. and then drawing a mainstream audience, making millions, THE EXORCIST gave the horror film temporary acceptability. A slew of inferior imitations followed, and an interesting, but fatally flawed, sequel was directed by John Boorman.

p, William Peter Blatty; d, William Friedkin (based on Blatty's novel); w, William Peter Blatty; ph, Owen Roizman, Billy Williams (Metrocolor); ed, Norman Gay, Jordan Leondopoulos, Evan Lottman, Bud Smith; m, Jack Nitzsche.

**(PR:O   MPAA:R)**

## EXORCIST II: THE HERETIC**½

(1977) 117m WB c

Linda Blair (Regan), Richard Burton (Father Lamont), Louise Fletcher (Dr. Gene Tuskin), Max von Sydow (Father Merrin), Kitty Winn (Sharon), Paul Henreid (The Cardinal), James Earl Jones (Older Kokumo), Ned Beatty (Edwards), Belinda Beatty (Liz), Rose Portillo (Spanish Girl), Barbara Cason (Mr. Phalor), Tiffany Kinney (Deaf Girl), Joey Green (Young Kokumo), Fiseha Dimetros (Young Monk), Ken Renard (Abbot), Hank Garrett (Conductor), Larry Goldman (Accident Victim), Bill Grant (Taxi Driver), Shane Butterworth, Joely Adams (Tuskin Children).

Not as awful as its notorious reputation would indicate, but certainly not the neglected masterpiece its small cult of supporters have claimed, John Boorman's gorgeously shot sequel to THE EXORCIST has isolated moments of breathtaking imagery, but the parts do not add up to a satisfying whole. Regan (Linda Blair), now 18, is again possessed by the demon Pazuzu but this time is treated by a child psychologist (Louise Fletcher), who brings in a heretical priest, Fr. Lamont (Richard Burton), and hooks them both up to a mind-processing machine that melds their psyches, taking them on a bizarre exploration of the nature of good and evil. While most of the scenes involving Burton, Blair, and Fletcher are torturously inept—mainly due to the misguided performances—the hallucinatory scenes of psychic exploration have a truly visionary quality, especially in the Africa sequence, in which William A. Fraker's camera swoops through the air on the back of a locust. Unfortunately, as with any cinematic work that attempts to break with convention and try something new, the film was jeered and laughed at in its first cut, prompting the studio to panic and yank it from distribution. The film was recut and reintroduced to critical wrath and public indifference. Yet another cut was released in Europe.

p, John Boorman, Richard Lederer; d, John Boorman; w, William Goodhart (based on characters created by William Peter Blatty); ph, William A. Fraker (Technicolor); ed, Tom Priestley; m, Ennio Morricone.

**(PR:O   MPAA:R)**

## EYES OF A STRANGER zero

(1980) 85m Georgetown/WB c

Lauren Tewes (Jane), Jennifer Jason Leigh (Tracy), John DiSanti (Stanley Herbert), Peter DuPre (David), Gwen Lewis (Debbie), Kitty Lunn (Annette), Timothy Hawkins (Jeff), Ted Richert (Roger), Toni Crabtree (Mona), Bob Small (Dr. Bob), Stella Rivera (Dancer), Dan Fitzgerald (Bartender), Jose Bahamande (Jimmy), Luke Halpin (Tape Editor), Rhonda Flynn (Woman in Car), Tony Federico (Man in Car), Alan Lee (Photographer), Amy Krug (Young Jane), Tabbetha Tracey (Young Tracy), Sarah Hutcheson (Friend), Jilian Lindig (Mother), George DeVries (Father), Melvin Pape (Doctor), Robert Goodman (Crewman), Pat Warren (Susan), Kathy Suergiu (Karen).

Jane (Lauren Tewes) is a TV newswoman trying to protect her deaf, dumb, and blind sister (Jason Leigh) from the homicidal crazy next door (John DiSanti). Tewes the perky cruise director on "The Love Boat," made her big-screen bid and failed miserably in this utterly derivative, offensive, and tedious thriller, which was turned into a slasher movie at the 11th hour after producers saw how well FRIDAY THE 13TH did at the box office. Near the end of shooting, gore-effects whiz Tom Savini was hired to insert some graphic murders into the film. Unfortunately, this is merely another slobbering, mindless, and reprehensible effort that exploits the rape and murder of women for pure sensation.

p, Ronald Zerra; d, Ken Wiederhorn; w, Mark Jackson, Eric L. Bloom; ph, Mini Rojas (Technicolor); ed, Rick Shaine; m, Richard Einhorn.

**(PR:O   MPAA:R)**

F

### FADE TO BLACK***

(1980) 100m American Cinema c

Dennis Christopher *(Eric Binford)*, Linda Kerridge *(Marilyn)*, Tim Thomerson *(Dr. Moriarty)*, Morgan Paull *(Gary)*, Hennen Chambers *(Bart)*, Marya Small *(Doreen)*, Eve Brent Ashe *(Aunt Stella)*, Bob Drew *(Rev. Shick)*, Gwynn Gilford *(Anne)*, John Steadman *(Sam)*, Mickey Rourke *(Richie)*, Melinda Fee *(Talk Show Hostess)*, Jane K. Wiley *(Gofer)*, Peter Horton *(Joey)*, Norman Burton *(Marty)*, James Luisi *(Gallagher)*, Anita Converse *(Dee Dee)*, Marcie Barkin *(Stacy)*, Gilbert Lawrence Kahn *(Counterman)*, Al Tafoya *(Newscaster)*, Bruce Reed *(Franco)*.

A lonely nerd who lives with his domineering aunt, Eric Binford (Dennis Christopher), retreats from his miserable existence into the wonderful world of movies—spending all his time in his bedroom, obsessively studying everything from B oaters to classic horror films. While on one of his rare jaunts outdoors, Eric meets and falls in love with a Marilyn Monroe lookalike (Linda Kerridge) and attempts to romance her. A combination of events—including being stood up by his love—cause Eric to finally crack, however, and he begins dressing up like his favorite movie heroes and killing people. Emulating such characters as Richard Widmark's Tommy Udo in KISS OF DEATH, William Boyd as Hopalong Cassidy, Boris Karloff in THE MUMMY, and Bela Lugosi as DRACULA, Eric finally gets it in a WHITE HEAT-style conclusion atop Grauman's Chinese Theater in Hollywood. Boasting a clever, inventive, and relevant concept, with a nicely nuanced performance from BREAKING AWAY's Christopher, FADE TO BLACK is a creepy little film that, perhaps, doesn't go quite far enough. While director Vernon Zimmerman does convey Eric's pathetic obsessions, the film seems a bit too tame and appears to hold back just when it should play like an even more demented version of TAXI DRIVER. It's certainly not a bad film—in fact, it can be quite fun—but it fails to grip the gut as it should and, therefore, can be considered somewhat disappointing.

p, George Braunstein, Ron Hamady; d, Vernon Zimmerman; w, Vernon Zimmerman; ph, Alex Phillips Jr.; ed, Howard Kunin.

**(PR:O    MPAA:R)**

### FEAR CHAMBER, THE zcro

(1968, US/Mex.) 87m Azteca c (LA CAMARA DEL TERROR)

Boris Karloff, Yerye Beruite, Julissa Santanon, Carlos East, Isela Vega, Eva Muller, Sandra Chavez, Rafael Munoz, Pamela Rosas, Fuensanta.

This is one of four Mexican genre films featuring Boris Karloff, whose scenes were all shot in Los Angeles—just be-

fore his death—with the footage later incorporated into films made in Mexico. Here he plays a scientist who is stricken with a rare disease after experimenting with a "living rock" taken from a volcano. While he rests in bed, his assistants—evil Isela Vega (more famous as Warren Oates' girlfriend in Sam Peckinpah's mesmerizing BRING ME THE HEAD OF ALFREDO GARCIA), a dwarf, a hunchback, and an Arab—continue his work, waylaying strippers and feeding their blood to the rock. Karloff is only in the film for the first 15 minutes, and then again, briefly, near the end. The film itself is pathetic, poorly shot and ineptly directed, with absolutely no sense of narrative story-telling or visual awareness. Even Karloff fans should stay away.

p, Luis Enrique Vergara; d, Juan Ibanez, Jack Hill; w, Jack Hill, Luis Enrique Vergara; ph, Raul Dominguez, Austin McKinney; m, Alice Uretta.

**(PR:C    MPAA:NR)**

### FEAR NO EVIL***½

(1981) 99m Avco Embassy c

Stefan Arngrim *(Andrew)*, Elizabeth Hoffman *(Mikhail/Margaret Buchanan)*, Kathleen Rowe McAllen *(Gabrielle/Hulie)*, Frank Birney *(Father Daly)*, Daniel Eden *(Tony)*, Jack Holland *(Rafael/Father Damon)*, Barry Cooper *(Mr. Williams)*, Alice Sachs *(Mrs. Williams)*, Paul Haber *(Mark)*, Roslyn Gugino *(Marie)*, Richard Jay Silverthorn *(Lucifer)*.

FEAR NO EVIL is the excellent directorial debut of 23-year-old East Coast filmmaker Frank LaLoggia, who scraped together the $150,000 it cost to make the film on his own—only to have it interfered with by Avco Embassy just before its release. Tampering aside, FEAR NO EVIL is a remarkably assured, personal, and powerful horror film, which follows a lonely and alienated high-school student, Andrew (Stefan Arngrim), as he slowly begins to realize that he is the Antichrist. An old neighbor woman (Elizabeth Hoffman) and one of Andrew's classmates (Kathleen Rowe McAllen) are the angels sent to destroy him. The whole thing climaxes at an outdoor performance of a Passion Play, wherein Andrew, looking like Lucifer (and now played by Richard Jay Silverthorn), appears and summons up a horde of zombies from the nearby cemetery. While the scant plot description may sound absurd, LaLoggia presents the material with such conviction, skill, and panache that the film is never less than gripping. Even with its outrageous concept, FEAR NO EVIL seems an intensely personal and deeply religious film that is truly concerned with the struggle between good and evil, between (quite specifically) God and Satan. In addition to his spiritual concerns, LaLoggia is a gifted filmmaker who has a splendid visual sense, creating some unforgettable images of horror. LaLoggia also makes clever use of a punk-rock soundtrack, bringing in the music of the Sex Pistols and the Ramones at appropriate moments. It would be seven years until LaLoggia directed again, with the exceptional ghost story THE LADY IN WHITE.

p, Frank La Loggia, Charles M. La Loggia; d, Frank La

Loggia; w, Frank La Loggia; ph, Fred Goodich (CFI Color); ed, Edna Ruth Paul; m, Frank La Loggia, David Spear.

(PR:O MPAA:R)

## FIEND*

(1980) 93m Cinema Enterprises c

Don Leifert *(Eric)*, Richard Nelson *(Gary)*, Elaine White *(Marsha)*, George Stover *(Dennis)*, Greg Dohler *(Scotty)*, Del Winans *(Jimmy)*, Kim Dohler *(Kristy)*, Pam Merenda *(Jane)*, Anne Fritch *(Katie)*, Steve Vertlieb *(Announcer)*, Steve Frith *(Man in Cemetery)*, Denise Grzybowski *(Kristy's Friend)*, Debbie Vogel *(Helen Weiss)*, Richard Geiwitz *(Fred)*, Lydia Vuynovich *(Girl in Cemetery)*, Tom Griffith *(Man with Beard)*, Barbara Shuman *(Woman with Dog)*, Anna Dorbert *(Woman with Groceries)*, Phil De Flavis *(Father at Academy)*, Dannielle De Flavis *(Daughter at Academy)*.

In this dumb monster movie, the title beast is a buglike creature that lives off the dead, turning corpses into killing machines capable of extracting energy from the living. When Eric (Don Leifert) becomes the unlucky recipient of a fiend, he begins carrying on gothic rituals in his cellar. Writer-director Don Dohler (THE ALIEN FACTOR) suffers from a dual affliction: pretention and amateurishness, a deadly combination. While purporting to present a monster that is the culmination of evil throughout the ages, Dohler merely succeeds in highlighting cheap special effects that aren't particularly well done.

d, Don Dohler; w, Don Dohler; ph, Don Dohler, Richard Geiwitz; ed, Don Dohler; m, Paul Woznicki.

(PR:O MPAA:NR)

## FINAL CONFLICT, THE**

(1981) 108m FOX c

Sam Neill *(Damien Thorn)*, Rossano Brazzi *(Father DeCarlo)*, Don Gordon *(Harvey Dean)*, Lisa Harrow *(Kate Reynolds)*, Barnaby Holm *(Peter Reynolds)*, Mason Adams *(President)*, Robert Arden *(American Ambassador)*, Tommy Duggan *(Brother Matteus)*, Leueen Willoughby *(Barbara)*, Louis Mahoney *(Brother Paulo)*, Marc Boyle *(Brother Benito)*, Richard Oldfield *(Brother Simeon)*, Milos Kirek *(Brother Martin)*, Tony Vogel *(Brother Antonio)*, Arwen Holm *(Carol)*, Hugh Moxey *(Manservant)*, William Fox, John Baskcomb *(Diplomats)*, Norman Bird *(Dr. Philmore)*, Marc Smith *(Press Officer)*, Arnold Diamond *(Astronomer)*, Eric Richard *(Astronomer's Technician)*, Richard Williams *(Vicar)*, Stephen Turner *(Stigwell)*, Al Matthews *(Workman)*, Larry Martyn, Frank Coda, Harry Littlewood *(Orators)*, Hazel Court.

The third installment in the saga of Damien the Antichrist sees the Devil's kid grown up and doing well as the head of Thorn Industries. Now played by Sam Neill (who takes the role too seriously), Damien is just about ready to take over the world for his papa, but is disturbed to learn that on a recent occasion three stars joined in the night sky, and sends his minions out to kill every baby born on that night. Meanwhile, a rugged monk (Rossano Brazzi) has found those handy daggers (the same ones unsuccessfully used on Damien in OMEN I & II) and drafts six of his bravest brothers to take one dagger each and try to assassinate Damien. The monks are no match for the Antichrist, and die in a variety of ways. (One slips, falls, hooks his foot in a rope, and swings upside down on a television stage wrapped in burning plastic in full view of the folks at home, another is eaten by a bunch of beagles, etc.) At the same time, all over the world, babies are being killed in an equally sick and disgusting manner (steam irons seem to be the favored method). In the end, the Almighty finally puts an end to Damien and that's that. A dumb end to a dumb series of movies that, in retrospect, play like the paranoid ramblings of a religious fundamentalist who sees unholy anti-Christian conspiracies behind every world event.

p, Harvey Bernhard; d, Graham Baker; w, Andrew Birkin (based on characters created by Dave Seltzer); ph, Robert Paynter, Phil Meheux (Panavision, DeLuxe Color); ed, Alan Strachan; m, Jerry Goldsmith.

(PR:O MPAA:NR)

## FINAL EXAM zero

(1981) 90m Bedford/AE c

Cecile Bagdadi *(Courtney)*, Joel S. Rice *(Radish)*, Ralph Brown *(Wildman)*, Deanna Robbins *(Lisa)*, Sherry Willis-Burch *(Janet)*, John Fallon *(Mark)*, Terry W. Farren *(Pledge)*, Sam Kilman *(Sheriff)*, Don Hepner *(Dr. Reynolds)*, Jerry Rushing *(Coach)*, Timothy L. Raynor *(Killer)*.

This dull and virtually bloodless slasher film, set on a college campus, is mostly talk, talk, talk until the killer—whose point of view we share, of course—starts offing folks one by one. The standard set of characters are murdered, including nubile young coeds, some frat guys, and a token gay. Director Jimmy Huston seems either to disdain the genre entirely, or was determined to forge new territory by deemphasizing graphic bloodletting in favor of meaningful characterizations. What he got was an audience screaming for his insipid characters to be murdered so that they would finally shut up.

p, John L. Chambliss, Myron Meisel; d, Jimmy Huston; w, Jimmy Huston; ph, Darrell Cathcart (DeLuxe Color); ed, John O'Connor; m, Gary Scott.

(PR:O MPAA:R)

## FINAL TERROR, THE*

(1983) 84m Comworld-Watershed-Roth c (AKA: THE FOREST PRIMEVAL; CAMPSITE MASSACRE; BUMP IN THE NIGHT)

John Friedrich *(Zorich)*, Rachel Ward *(Margaret)*, Adrian Zmed *(Cerone)*, Darryl Hannah *(Windy)*, Joe Pantoliano *(Eggar)*, Ernest Harden, Jr. *(Hines)*, Mark Metcalf *(Mike)*, Lewis Smith *(Boone)*, Cindy Harrell *(Melanie)*, Akosua Busia *(Vanessa)*, Irene Sanders *(Sammie)*, Richard Jacobs *(Morgan)*, Donna Pinder *(Mrs. Morgan)*.

Shot in 1981 but left unreleased until 1983, this was the feature debut of director Andrew Davis, who would later go on to make several quality action films, most notably the Chuck Norris vehicle CODE OF SILENCE (1985) and the recent ABOVE THE LAW (1988). Unfortunately, Davis demonstrates little of the talent he would evidence later with this predictable slasher film, which follows a bevy of teenage campers into the redwood forest as they die one by one at the hands of a deranged woman. Davis, who may have done cinematography duty as well under the pseudonym Andreas Davidescu, quotes liberally from every other city-folks-in-the-backwoods movie, especially DELIVERANCE. The only reason to watch this is to see soon-to-be-stars Adrian Zmed, Darryl Hannah, and Rachel Ward die bloody deaths.

p, Joe Roth; d, Andrew Davis; w, Jon George, Neill Hicks, Ronald Shusett; ph, A. Davidescu; ed, Paul Rubell, Erica Flaum, Hannah Washonig; m, Susan Justin.

(PR:O   MPAA:R)

## FLESH AND BLOOD SHOW, THE**

(1972, Brit.) 91m Entertainment Ventures c (AKA: ASYLUM OF THE INSANE)

Ray Brooks, Jenny Hanley, Robin Askwith, David Howey, Penny Meredith, Luan Peters, Patrick Barr, Judy Matheson, Candace Glendenning, Tristan Rogers, Peter Walker.

Hired by a man they've never met to perform a classic Grand Guignol play, a troupe of actors arrive at a decrepit seaside resort and are killed off one at a time. It turns out that their employer (Patrick Barr) is a former actor who now hates the entire profession, having once caught his actress wife fooling around with another actor and killed them both. Fairly bloody, the film has an offbeat sense of humor and boasted a climax that was originally shown in 3-D. From the director and writer of FRIGHTMARE.

p, Peter Walker; d, Peter Walker; w, Alfred Shaunghnessy; ph, Peter Jessop.

(PR:O   MPAA:R)

## FLESH EATERS, THE**½

(1964) 92m Vulcan/Cinema bw

Martin Kosleck (Peter Bartell), Rita Morley (Laura Winters), Byron Sanders (Grant Murdock), Ray Tudor (Omar), Barbara Wilkin (Jan Letterman).

An alcoholic film queen (Rita Morley) and her secretary (Barbara Wilkin) charter a private plane piloted by Grant Murdock (Byron Sanders). Forced to crash-land on an island—actually suburban New York—the trio discover that the place is inhabited by a mad scientist (Martin Kosleck) working with tiny sea creatures that can devour human flesh in a matter of moments. Filmed in 1961, this is a pretty entertaining low-budget affair that makes up for its lack of budget through sheer dedication and imagination. The filmmakers were no novices, having come from the "nudie" film industry. Since most of the special-effects money went to making up the victims, the sea creatures were created by scratching the film stock with pins. A real oddity.

p, Jack Curtis, Terry Curtis, Arnold Drake; d, J. Curtis; w,

Arnold Drake; ph, Carson Davidson; ed, Radley Metzger, Frank Forest; m, Julian Stein.

(PR:O   MPAA:NR)

## FLESH FEAST**

(1970) 72m Viking/Cine World c

Veronica Lake (Dr. Elaine Frederick), Phil Philbin (Ed Casey), Heather Hughes (Kristine), Martha Mischon, Yanka Mann, Dian Wilhite, Chris Martell.

A truly bizarre entry in the Vernoica Lake filmography, this occasionally extremely gross horror film was coproduced by the actress, who came out of a 22-year-old retirement to appear here. Lake stars as Dr. Elaine Frederick, a Miami Beach plastic surgeon who just happens to be a former mental patient. This could explain why she chooses a somewhat radical form for restoring youthful good looks— the use of specially bred flesh-eating maggots, which chew away old skin tissue before Dr. Frederick works her medical wonders. Things proceed nicely until she discovers that her newest patient is Adolf Hitler! Dr. Frederick's mother, a victim of Nazi concentration camps, is gleefully avenged as Hitler is munched on by a myriad of maggots. Despite it's being a rather grotesque end to a distinguished career, Lake discussed FLESH FEAST rather fondly in her autobiography, Veronica. She died in 1973.

p, Vernoica Lake, Brad F. Ginter; d, Brad F. Ginter; w, Brad F. Ginter, Thomas Casey; ph, Thomas Casey, Andy Romanoff.

(PR:O   MPAA:R)

## FLY, THE***

(1958) 94m FOX c

Al Hedison [David Hedison] (Andre), Patricia Owens (Helene), Vincent Price (Francois), Herbert Marshall (Insp. Charas), Kathleen Freeman (Emma), Betty Lou Gerson (Nurse Andersone), Charles Herbert (Philippe), Eugene Borden (Dr. Ejoute), Torben Meyer (Gaston), Harry Carter (Orderly), Charles Tannen (Doctor), Franz Roehn (Police Doctor), Arthur Dulac (French Waiter).

A 1950s cult favorite, THE FLY blends sci-fi and horror in its story of an obsessed scientist (David Hedison) who likes to fiddle around with his matter-transmitting device. After zapping guinea pigs from dimension to dimension, he decides to put the transmitter to the ultimate test and enters the machine himself. He fatefully pulls the switch, failing to notice that a pesty housefly is also in the machine. That little nuisance proves to be a gross inconvenience as the scientist, now fly-headed, emerges from his experiment, while buzzing somewhere around the house is the interfering fly, now sporting a human mug. The success of THE FLY is hard to fathom. Not even the numerous plot loopholes—for example, how, if the scientist has the head of the housefly, can he still think like a human?—can lessen the film's popularity. Most memorable is the film's chilling ending, in which the housefly with the human head is glimpsed in a spiderweb trap, struggling and begging, "Help me," in its wavering, high-pitched voice. The film is both fun and frightening, and can also be viewed (however modest its intentions) as a commercialized technoversion of Franz Kafka's allegory *Metamorphosis*. Its success led to two less inspired sequels, THE RETURN OF THE FLY and CURSE OF THE FLY, and the superior 1986 David Cronenberg remake.

p, Kurt Neumann; d, Kurt Neumann; w, James Clavell (based on a story by George Langelaan); ph, Karl Struss (CinemaScope, DeLuxe Color); ed, Merrill G. White; m, Paul Sawtell.

(PR:C   MPAA:NR)

**FLY, THE****

(1986) 100m Brooksfilm/FOX c

Jeff Goldblum *(Seth Brundle)*, Geena Davis *(Veronica Quaife)*, John Getz *(Stathis Borans)*, Joy Boushel *(Tawny)*, Les Carlson *(Dr. Cheevers)*, George Chuvalo *(Marky)*, Michael Copeman *(2nd Man in Bar)*, David Cronenberg *(Gynecologist)*, Carol Lazare *(Nurse)*, Shawn Hewitt *(Clerk)*.

David Cronenberg's American mainstream breakthrough film (as DEAD ZONE was intended to be) was also his most controlled, mature, and insightful work up to that point. Obsessed with the horrifying implications of a combination of science and technology with the powerful potentials of the human mind, body, and sexuality, Cronenberg had created several highly personal films over the previous 15 years. While the concepts of these films are interesting and unique, the films themselves were sloppy, undisciplined, and sometimes incoherent, with little or no attention paid to the development of characters as complex, emotional human beings. With his decision to remake the 1958 classic THE FLY, Cronenberg found the perfect outlet for his obsessions, while at the same time finally demonstrating great compassion for both the strengths and weaknesses of the human race. Updated and improved by a more complex personal relationship between the protagonists and a more realistic examination of the science and technology involved, the new version of THE FLY pairs a young female science-magazine reporter, Veronica Quaife (Geena Davis) and a somewhat shy, awkward scientist, Seth Brundle (Jeff Goldblum), who is involved in a secret experiment to transport matter that will "change life as we know it." Although brilliant intellectually, Brundle lacks adult social skills and tries to seduce Veronica clumsily, like a nerdy high schooler trying to impress the prom queen with his science project. The pair do gradually fall in love, as Brundle continues his experiments, trying to advance from transporting things to transporting living beings. Eventually, he is driven to transport himself, but fails to notice the little fly that has traveled through space with him. THE FLY succeeds on every level. As a remake, it does what remakes rarely do and improves upon the original, taking it in new directions and exploring the unused potential of the source material. Whereas the original deteriorated into a fly-hunt, the remake opts for a slow metamorphosis from man to fly that develops as a disease would. This gives Cronenberg time to examine the implications of such an event, as the film lays bare our fear of dis-

ease, death, and change. An unrelentingly gory film that explores the "poetry of the flesh," THE FLY causes most audiences to scream with revulsion as Brundle's fly-body sheds its increasingly useless human appendages (which are kept in a medicine cabinet, humorously referred to as "The Brundle Museum of Natural History"). The orgy of gross effects may be excessive, but Cronenberg isn't interested in sparing the viewer from the disturbing realities of the situation—just as the loved one of a terminal patient must endure the day-to-day horrors of that reality. This is not an easy film to watch, and it shouldn't be. Cronenberg followed this one with an even more painful film to watch—DEAD RINGERS.

p, Stuart Cornfeld; d, David Cronenberg; w, Charles Edward Pogue, David Cronenberg (based on a story by George Langelaan); ph, Mark Irwin (DeLuxe Color); ed, Ronald Sanders; m, Howard Shore.

(PR:O   MPAA:R)

**FOG, THE**½**

(1980) 91m AE c

Adrienne Barbeau *(Stevie Wayne)*, Hal Holbrook *(Fr. Malone)*, Janet Leigh *(Kathy Williams)*, Jamie Lee Curtis *(Elizabeth Solley)*, John Houseman *(Machen)*, Tommy Atkins *(Nick Castle)*, Nancy Loomis *(Sandy Fadel)*, Charles Cyphers *(Dan O'Bannon)*, Ty Mitchell *(Andy Wayne)*, George Buck Flower *(Tommy Wallace)*, John Vick *(Sheriff Simms)*, Jim Jacobus *(Mayor)*, Jim Canning *(Dick Baxter)*, Regina Waldon *(Mrs. Kobritz)*, Darrow Igus *(Mel Sloane)*, Bill Taylor *(Bartender)*, Jim Haynie *(Hank Jones)*, Fred Franklyn *(Ashcroft)*, John Goff *(Al Williams)*, Darwin Joston *(Dr. Phibes)*, Rob Bottin *(Blake)*, Charley Nicklin *(Blake's Voice)*, John Strobel *(Grocery Clerk)*, Lee Sacks, Ric Moreno, Tommy Wallace *(Ghosts)*, Laurie Arent, Lindsey Arent, Shari Jacoby, Christopher Cunday *(Children)*.

A ghost ship occupied by 100-year-old corpses terrorizes a coastal community, which is covered in a heavy fog. Although it opens promisingly enough—with a precredits sequence in which John Houseman, playing a grizzled old sailor, tells the ghost story to a group of children gathered around a campfire—THE FOG must be considered a disappointment. While some have simply argued that a rolling fog bank just isn't scary (tell that to Val Lewton), the film's real problem is Carpenter's diffuse narrative, which introduces far too many characters—forcing the director consistently to cut away to each story strand, thus destroying much of the suspense. What does work, however, is Carpenter's unmatchable visual style and the marvelous photography of Dean Cundey. As he does in most of his films, Carpenter has inserted several in-jokes, including casting himself as a church janitor and naming one of the characters after his one-time collaborator Dan O'Bannon (DARK STAR).

p, Debra Hill; d, John Carpenter; w, John Carpenter, Debra Hill; ph, Dean Cundey (Panavision, Metrocolor); ed,

Tommy Lee Wallace, Charles Bornstein; m, John Carpenter.

(PR:C-O MPAA:NR)

## FORCED ENTRY*

(1975) 82m Century International-Productions Two-Kodiak c (AKA: LAST VICTIM, THE)

Ron Max *(Carl)*, Tanya Roberts, Nancy Allen, Brian Freilino.

The slasher film concerns Carl (Ron Max), a garage mechanic who is unable to form healthy relationships with women because his mother beat him when he was a child. Instead of going to the self-help section at the paperback stand, he kills ladies in a typically imaginative variety of methods. However, when Carl breaks into the home of a young housewife (Tanya Roberts), he ties her up but is unable to kill her—instead he tries asking for a date. She takes advantage of his hesitation and fights back. A wholly distasteful production, made only more so by the muddy photography. Filmed in 1975 as THE LAST VICTIM, the film was reissued with a new title in 1984, with Roberts and Nancy Allen top-billed in hopes of cashing in on their sudden fame. Originally rated "PG," the film was rerated "R" by a rather touchy MPAA upon its re-release.

p, Jim Sotos, Henry Scarpelli; d, Jim Sotos; w, Henry Scarpelli; ph, A. Kleinman; m, Tommy Vig.

(PR:O MPAA:R)

## FOREST, THE*

(1983) 85m Fury/Wide World of Entertainment c (AKA: TERROR IN THE FOREST)

Dean Russell *(Steve)*, Michael Brody *(John)*, Elaine Warner *(Sharon)*, John Batis *(Charley)*, Ann Wilkinson *(Teddi)*, Jeanette Kelly *(Mother)*, Corky Pigeon *(John, Jr.)*, Becki Burke *(Jennifer)*, Don Jones *(Forest Ranger)*, Tony Gee, Stafford Morgan, Marilyn Anderson.

This obscure low-budgeter gives the FRIDAY THE 13TH formula a bit of a twist, introducing both a cannibal angle and ghosts. A human-flesh-eating madman terrorizes people in a patch of woods, haunted by the ghosts of his murdered wife and children. A poorly made effort that barely saw a theatrical release and is now available everywhere on videotape for less than 10 bucks.

p, Don Jones; d, Don Jones; w, Evan Jones; ph, Stuart Asbjorsen; m, Richard Hieronymous, Alan Oldfield.

(PR:O MPAA:R)

## FRANKENSTEIN****

(1931) 71m UNIV bw

Colin Clive *(Frankenstein)*, Mae Clarke *(Elizabeth)*, John Boles *(Victor)*, Boris Karloff *(The Monster)*, Edward Van Sloan *(Dr. Waldman)*, Dwight Frye *(Fritz, the Dwarf)*, Frederick Kerr *(The Baron)*, Lionel Belmore *(The Burgomaster)*, Michael Mark *(Ludwig, Peasant Father)*, Marilyn

Harris *(Maria the Child)*, Arletta Duncan, Pauline Moore *(Bridesmaids)*, Francis Ford *(Villager)*.

Universal's second horror picture of 1931—released a mere 10 months after DRACULA—was this adaptation of Mary Shelley's classic novel *Frankenstein*. The film had, and continues to have, an immeasurable impact on the genre, and it made a little-known actor by the name of Boris Karloff a worldwide star. Dr. Henry Frankenstein (Colin Clive), along with his hunchbacked assistant, Fritz (Dwight Frye), is obsessed with the idea of scientifically creating life from parts of various corpses that have been salvaged from the gallows or robbed from graves. Unknowingly, Frankenstein installs a criminal brain into his subject, and when it is brought to life, its creator is horrified and repulsed by what he has wrought—a mute creature that moves on leaden limbs, a flat-topped, lizard-eyed, heavily scarred hulk with grotesque electrodes protruding from its neck and steel clamps affixing the top of its head. Tortured by the sadistic Fritz, the childlike monster (Karloff) quickly learns to hate, and soon escapes his prison, wreaking havoc against Frankenstein and his village. A smash hit at the box office, FRANKENSTEIN caused a major sensation that continued to last through the years, drawing huge crowds on subsequent re-releases and even sparking yet another horror boom in the late 1950s, when it was shown on television. (This was not, however, the first time *Frankenstein* had been brought to the silver screen. There was the 1910 Edison Company effort featuring Charles Ogle (long thought lost, but prints have recently resurfaced); it was filmed again in 1915 as LIFE WITHOUT SOUL; and there was an Italian version in 1920 known as IL MONSTRO DI FRANKENSTEIN.) Although James Whale's direction created a vivid nightmare world—and he would even surpass himself with the film's sequel, THE BRIDE OF FRANKENSTEIN—this movie belongs to Karloff, whose superb pantomime performance created a wholly sympathetic creature, more a victim of circumstance than an inherently evil being. The film was subjected to various cuts by the studio over the years, most notably Frankenstein's line when, ecstatic at bringing life to his misshapen creation, he cries out, "In the name of God, now I know what it feels like to *be* God!" and the scene in which the monster tosses little Maria into the lake to see if she will float. These clips have finally been restored and can be seen on the videocassette release. Sequels: THE BRIDE OF FRANKENSTEIN, 1935; SON OF FRANKENSTEIN, 1939; GHOST OF FRANKENSTEIN, 1941; FRANKENSTEIN MEETS THE WOLF MAN, 1943; HOUSE OF FRANKENSTEIN, 1945; HOUSE OF DRACULA, 1945; ABBOTT AND COSTELLO MEET FRANKENSTEIN, 1948.

p, Carl Laemmle; d, James Whale; w, Garrett Fort, Francis Edwards Faragoh, John L. Balderston, Robert Florey (based on the novel by Mary Shelley and the play by Peggy Webling); ph, Arthur Edeson; ed, Maurice Pivar, Clarence Kolster; m, David Brockman.

(PR:A MPAA:NR)

## FRANKENSTEIN GENERAL HOSPITAL zero

(1988) 92m New Star c/b&w

Mark Blankfield *(Dr. Bob Frankenstein)*, Leslie Jordan *(Iggy)*, Jonathan Farwell *(Dr. Frank Reutgar)*, Kathy Shower *(Dr. Alice Singleton)*, Irwin Keyes *(Monster)*, Hamilton Mitchell *(Dr. Andrew Dixon)*, Lou Cutell *(Dr. Saperstein)*, Katie Caple *(Nurse Verna)*, Dorothy Patterson *(Mildred Pennys)*, Bobby Pickett *(Man in Elevator)*, Mark DeCarlo *(Dr. Skip)*, Harry Murphy *(Dr. Biff)*, Rebunkah Jones *(Elizabeth Rice)*, Joleen Lutz *(Candy Stripper Patty)*, Jessica Puscas *(Cindy Swanson)*, Ben Stein *(Dr. Who)*, John Young *(Dr. Alex Hoover)*, Tom Fahn *(Zach)*, Michael Franco *(Brad)*, James Serrano, Ed Khmara *(Cops)*, Chuck Kovacic *(Anesthesiologist)*, Laura Bassett *(Cigarette Girl)*, Kay E. Kuter *(Larry)*, Ken Kallmayer *(Patient)*.

Deep in the bowels of Los Angeles General Hospital lies the laboratory of the legendary Baron von Frankenstein's great-great grandson, Bob (Mark Blankfield), a physician who has conveniently changed his name to Frankenheimer. Assisted by Iggy (Leslie Jordan), a former short order cook, Bob is secretly working on the creation of a perfect human being. Wretched in nearly every respect, FRANKENSTEIN GENERAL HOSPITAL aspires to be a spoof of horror films somewhat along the lines of YOUNG FRANKENSTEIN; however, it fails to establish even the lowest level of credibility. Blankfield, who appeared in another genre send-up flop, JEKYLL AND HYDE ... TOGETHER AGAIN, tries hard, but is given such weak material that his efforts are wasted. The rest of the grossly overplayed performances are even worse. Director Deborah Roberts seems to have no idea how to pace the jokes or finish off a scene, and her idea of enlivening the proceeding appears to be having former Playmate Kathy Shower and Katie Caple take off their blouses. FRANKENSTEIN GENERAL HOSPITAL is so bad that it induces a certain strange fascination after a while. About the only thing authentic in the picture is a brief appearance by Bobby Boris Pickett, who recorded "Monster Mash" with the Crypt Kickers in the late 1950s.

p, Dimitri Villard; d, Deborah Roberts; w, Michael Kelly, Robert Deel (based on the novel by Mary Shelley); ph, Tom Fraser; ed, Ed Cotter; m, John Ross.

(PR:O    MPAA:R)

## FRANKENSTEIN MEETS THE WOLF MAN***

(1943) 72m UNIV bw

Lon Chaney, Jr. *(The Wolf Man/Lawrence Talbot)*, Ilona Massey *(Baroness Elsa Frankenstein)*, Patric Knowles *(Dr. Mannering)*, Lionel Atwill *(Mayor)*, Bela Lugosi *(Monster)*, Maria Ouspenskaya *(Maleva)*, Dennis Hoey *(Inspector Owen)*, Don Barclay *(Franzec)*, Rex Evans *(Vazec)*, Dwight Frye *(Rudi)*, Harry Stubbs *(Gune)*, Martha Vickers *(Little Girl)*, Doris Lloyd *(Hospital Nurse)*, Adia Kuznetzoff, Beatrice Roberts *(Villager)*, Jeff Corey, Torben Meyer.

Desperate to entice audiences to its waning horror series, Universal decided to combine two of its most popular monsters—Frankenstein's monster and the Wolf Man—thus creating one sequel for two films: THE GHOST OF FRAN-

KENSTEIN (1942) and THE WOLF MAN (1941). Inexplicably alive after having been bludgeoned to death in THE WOLF MAN, Lawrence Talbot (Lon Chaney, Jr.) searches out Dr. Frankenstein to cure his lycanthropy. Although Talbot finds that the doctor—his only hope—is dead, he does stumble upon Frankenstein's monster (Bela Lugosi), frozen in the ice beneath the destroyed castle. Aided by an idealistic young scientist (Patric Knowles) who wants to re-create Frankenstein's experiments, Talbot revives the monster and prepares it for an experiment that will cure Talbot of his affliction. Unfortunately, the experiment goes awry, with Talbot becoming the Wolf Man, and a fight to the death with the revitalized monster ensues. Having played both the Wolf Man and the monster (in GHOST OF FRANKENSTEIN), Chaney was originally intended by Universal to play both parts in this film, but it was decided that this would be too difficult and expensive. Ironically, Bela Lugosi, who had originally been slated to play the monster in FRANKENSTEIN (1931), but refused the part because of the lack of dialog, was cast to replace Chaney as the monster. Not only did Curt Siodmak's script call for the monster to remain mute, but he was blind as well (as he was at the conclusion of THE GHOST OF FRANKENSTEIN)—although studio cuts later eliminated any reference to the monster's blindness. Lugosi is woefully miscast here, and his cause was not helped by either the cuts (he still played the monster as if he were blind) or the fact that the actor was sick for most of the shoot. Stuntman Eddie Parker doubled for him through much of the filming, and the first close-up of the monster is actually of Parker. Universal's marketing scheme—multiple monsters—worked, spurring the studio to toss in even more creatures for their next film, THE HOUSE OF FRANKENSTEIN (1944), which featured the monster, the Wolf Man, Dracula, and a hunchback.

p, George Waggner; d, Roy William Neill; w, Curt Siodmak; ph, George Robinson; ed, Edward Curtiss.

(PR:A    MPAA:NR)

## FRANKENSTEIN 1970**½

(1958) 83m AA bw

Boris Karloff *(Baron Victor von Frankenstein)*, Tom Duggan *(Mike Shaw)*, Jana Lund *(Carolyn Hayes)*, Donald Barry *(Douglas Row)*, Charlotte Austin *(Judy Stevens)*, Irwin Berke *(Inspector Raab)*, Rudolph Anders *(Wilhelm Gottfried)*, John Dennis *(Morgan Haley)*, Norbert Schiller *(Shuter)*, Mike Lane *(Hans)*.

Boris Karloff finally gets to play the creator instead of the created in this rather strange Frankenstein outing. As Victor von Frankenstein, grandson of the late Baron, Karloff sports horrible facial scars, his character having been disfigured by the Nazis during the war. Although he plans to re-create his grandpa's experiments, Victor needs cash to purchase an atomic reactor he needs to bring his creature to life. He therefore allows a television crew to rent his historic castle to shoot a TV show. Now, with the money and spare parts to work with (the TV cast and crew), Victor succeeds in bringing his monster (it stands about seven feet tall and is wrapped up like a mummy) to life, but the creature attacks him, and during the struggle atomic steam is released, killing them both. Karloff appears to have a good time hamming it up and the whole thing is pretty silly (including the title, which means nothing), an odd combination of classic and nuclear horror.

p, Aubrey Shenck; d, Howard W. Koch; w, Richard Landau, George Worthing Yates (based on a story by Shenck, Charles A. Moses), ph, Carl E. Guthrie; ed, John Bushelman.

(PR:A  MPAA:NR)

## FRANKENSTEIN'S DAUGHTER*

(1958) 85m Astor bw (AKA: SHE MONSTER OF THE NIGHT)

John Ashley *(Johnny Bruder),* Sandra Knight *(Trudy Morton),* Donald Murphy *(Oliver Frank),* Sally Todd *(Suzie),* Harold Lloyd, Jr. *(Don),* Felix Locher *(Carter Morton),* Wolfe Barzell *(Elsu),* John Zaremba, Robert Dix, Harry Wilson, Voltaire Perkins, Charlotte Portney, Bill Coontz, George Barrows, Page Cavanaugh Trio.

Why this film is available on videocassette while most of the Hammer Frankenstein series remains unavailable is anybody's guess. An incredibly cheap attempt to cash in on the I WAS A TEENAGE . . . craze, this wretched effort has become a late-night TV fave over the years. Set in the modern-day suburbs, the story follows Oliver Frank (Donald Murphy)—short for Frankenstein—who is a descendant of the legendary mad doctor. An assistant to elderly scientist Dr. Morton (Felix Locher), Oliver absconds with a new drug his boss has developed and tests it out on the man's teenage niece, Trudy (Sandra Knight). The drug causes the girl to wander the area at night with a case of amnesia. Unhappy with those results, Oliver stalks and kills another teenage girl, bringing her back to life as a monster (now played by a big, ugly man). Once again disappointed, Oliver goes after Trudy again, but this time her boy friend (John Ashley) and the cops try to stop him. The overall cheapness of this production (the lab is in Dr. Morton's basement!) lends a somewhat surrealistic air to the proceedings, making this an inadvertently hypnotic experience—especially at 3 a.m.

p, Marc Frederic; d, Richard Cunha; w, M.E. Barrie; ph, Meredith Nicholson; ed, Everett Dodd; m, Nicholas Carras.

(PR:A  MPAA:NR)

## FREAKS*****

(1932) 64m MGM bw (AKA: NATURE'S MISTAKES; FORBIDDEN LOVE; MONSTER SHOW, THE)

Wallace Ford *(Phroso),* Leila Hyams *(Venus),* Olga Baclanova *(Cleopatra),* Rosco Ates *(Roscoe),* Henry Victor *(Hercules),* Harry Earles *(Hans),* Daisy Earles *(Frieda),* Rose Dione *(Mme. Tetrallini),* Daisy, Violet Hilton *(Siamese Twins),* Edward Brophy, Matt McHugh *(Rollo Brothers),* Olga Roderick *(Bearded Lady),* Johnny Eck *(Boy with Half a Torso),* Randian *(Hindu Living Torso),* Schlitzie, Elvira, Jennie Lee Snow *(White Pin Heads),* Pete Robinson *(Living Skeleton),* Koo Coo *(Bird Girl),* Josephine-Joseph *(Half Woman-Half Man),* Martha Morris *(Armless Wonder),* Frances O'Connor *(Turtle Girl),* Angelo Rossitto *(Midget),* Zip, Pip, Elizabeth Green *(Specialties),* Albert Conti *(Landowner),* Michael Visaroff *(Jean the Caretaker),* Ernie Adams *(Sideshow Patron),* Louise Beavers *(Maid).*

Little seen for nearly 50 years, this was MGM's answer to the success of the Universal horror series, but public and critical revulsion to the use of actual circus freaks forced the movie from distribution, after which it was picked up by Dwain Esper (MANIAC, 1934) and given town-by-town roadshow distribution, shown in tents and seedy burlesque houses, further enhancing its notorious reputation. Masterfully directed by Tod Browning, the story follows Cleopatra (Olga Baclanova), a beautiful trapeze artist with a dark and avaricious heart who seduces and marries Hans (Harry Earles), one of the midgets in their traveling circus, to get at his inheritance. Although she is normal, the close-knit society of "freaks" warmly welcomes Cleopatra into their family at the wedding reception, chanting, "We accept you as one of us." This repels the trapeze artist, who shrinks back in disgust and insults them all, stating that she will never be one of them, a grotesque freak—while her secret lover, Hercules the strongman (Henry Victor), howls with laughter. She turns and kisses Hercules repeatedly while he fondles her, all in front of her new husband, who is now thoroughly humiliated and disgraced. Cleopatra and Hercules begin to poison Hans systematically, but the freaks rally round the midget once they begin to suspect he is being murdered, and wreak a horrible vengeance upon both Cleopatra and Hercules. Although its reputation seemed to promise a repulsive exploitation of actual handicapped people, nothing could be further from the truth, for FREAKS is a truly warm and humanistic movie in which the "freaks" are seen as normal and the "normal" people are diseased and perverse. Browning drew upon his childhood experiences when making the film; he had actually run away and joined a circus in the 1890s, befriending sideshow freaks and observing how the public reacted to them with a mixture of morbid curiosity, revulsion, and genuine empathy. The real-life freaks Browning collected for his film included Olga Roderick, the bearded lady; Johnny Eck, a boy with only half a torso; bird girl Koo Coo; Josephine-Joseph, the half-man, half-woman; Randian, the armless, legless living torso; human skeleton Pete Robinson; midgets; pinheads; dwarfs; and the incredible Daisy and Violet Hilton, Siamese twins (who would later be exploited in the cheapie CHAINED FOR LIFE, 1950). FREAKS is not a study in deformity, however, but an old-fashioned morality play in which the defenseless and hopeless triumph over evil. Although it may prove slow going for those weaned on modern-day gore, FREAKS is one of the landmarks of the horror genre and still demands to be seen.

p, Tod Browning; d, Tod Browning; w, Willis Goldbeck, Leon Gordon, Edgar Allan Woolf, Al Boasberg (based on the short story "Spurs" by Ted Robbins); ph, Merritt B. Gerstad; ed, Basil Wrangell.

(PR:C  MPAA:NR)

## FRIDAY THE 13TH zero

(1980) 95m PAR c

Betsy Palmer *(Mrs. Voorhees)*, Adrienne King *(Alice)*, Harry Crosby *(Bill)*, Laurie Bartram *(Brenda)*, Mark Nelson *(Ned)*, Jeannine Taylor *(Marcie)*, Robbi Morgan *(Annie)*, Kevin Bacon *(Jack)*, Ari Lehman *(Jason)*, Peter Brouwer *(Steve)*, Rex Everhart *(Truck Driver)*, Ronn Carroll *(Sgt. Tiemey)*, Ron Millkie *(Dorf)*, Walt Gorney *(Crazy Ralph)*, Willie Adams *(Barry)*, Debra S. Hayes *(Claudette)*, Dorothy Kobs *(Trudy)*.

Although certainly groundbreaking and influential, this is a rancid excuse for a horror film, a huge surprise hit at the box office that spawned countless imitations that were even worse and threatened to destroy the genre. In the rudimentary plot, seven young camp counselors finally open up for business Camp Crystal Lake, which has been boarded up for years following a nasty murder that was never solved. Of course, the killer is still on the loose, and proceeds to eliminate the counselors one by one in a series of tedious, repetitive, ghastly murders that leaves only one teenager left. With no intelligence, no characterization, no socially redeeming value whatsoever, FRIDAY THE 13TH embodies everything wrong with the latest cycle of horror films—it's totally mindless bloodletting. The film is cloddishly directed with no real sense of style, its only interesting aspect being the inventive and well-done special makeup effects by Tom Savini, whose talents have been used better elsewhere (especially in the horror films of George Romero). A wretched film.

p, Sean S. Cunningham; d, Sean S. Cunningham; w, Victor Miller; ph, Barry Abrams (Panavision); ed, Bill Freda; m, Harry Manfredini.

**(PR:O   MPAA:R)**

## FRIDAY THE 13TH PART II zero

(1981) 87m PAR c

Amy Steel *(Ginny)*, John Furey *(Paul)*, Adrienne King *(Alice)*, Kirsten Baker *(Terry)*, Stuart Charno *(Ted)*, Warrington Gillette *(Jason)*, Walt Gorney *(Crazy Ralph)*, Marta Kober *(Sandra)*, Tom McBride *(Mark)*, Bill Randolph *(Jeff)*, Lauren-Marie Taylor *(Vickie)*, Russell Todd *(Scott)*, Betsy Palmer *(Mrs. Voorhees)*, Cliff Cudney *(Max)*, Jack Marks *(Cop)*, David Brand, China Chen, Carolyn Loudon, Jaime Perry, Tom Shea, Jill Voight *(Counselors)*.

Somehow, this one's even worse than the first. Called a sequel, it's basically the same movie, except that this time a different cast of teenagers gets killed in the usual, very graphic manner (the excess gore was trimmed to avoid an "X" rating by the MPAA). Five years after the first film, at another camp near Camp Crystal Lake, Jason—the mutant son of the killer from the first film—goes about slicing up the cast. Once again, it made a ton of money.

p, Steve Miner, Dennis Murphy; d, Steve Miner; w, Ron Kurz (based on characters created by Victor Miller); ph, Peter Stein (DeLuxe Color); ed, Susan E. Cunningham; m, Harry Manfredini.

**(PR:O   MPAA:R)**

## FRIDAY THE 13TH PART III*

(1982) 95m PAR c

Dana Kimmel *(Chris Higgins)*, Richard Brooker *(Jason)*, Catherine Parks *(Vera)*, Paul Kratka *(Rick)*, Jeffrey Rogers *(Andy)*, Larry Zerner *(Shelly)*, Tracie Savage *(Debbie)*, Rachel Howard *(Chili)*, David Katims *(Chuck)*, Nick Savage *(Ali)*, Gloria Charles *(Fox)*, Kevin O'Brien *(Loco)*, Annie Gaybis *(Cashier)*, Cheri Maugans *(Edna)*, Steve Miner *(Newscaster)*, Gianni Standaart *(Newswoman)*.

Again, the same movie filled with different corpses, but at least this sequel boasts some decent 3-D work (probably the best 3-D effects in the new wave of 3-D movies). It also contains the same stupid, gross "plot" as its predecessors, although the gore is a bit deemphasized, with the special-effects crew concentrating on the nicely done 3-D depth work for a change. It's still trash, however, and also made an immoral amount of money. Four more sequels followed, although hopes were raised by FRIDAY THE 13TH—THE FINAL CHAPTER. (They lied.)

p, Frank Mancuso, Jr., Tony Bishop; d, Steve Miner; w, Martin Kitrosser, Carol Watson (based on characters created by Victor Miller, Ron Kurz); ph, Gerald Feil (Panavision, Movielab Color, in 3-D); ed, George Hively; m, Harry Manfredini.

**(PR:O   MPAA:R)**

## FRIDAY THE 13TH—THE FINAL CHAPTER zero

(1984) 91m PAR c

E. Erich Anderson *(Rob)*, Judie Aronson *(Samantha)*, Peter Barton *(Doug)*, Kimberly Beck *(Trish)*, Tom Everett *(Flashlight Man)*, Corey Feldman *(Tommy)*, Joan Freeman *(Mrs. Jarvis)*, Lisa Freeman *(Nurse Morgan)*, Thad Geer *(Running Man)*, Crispin Glover *(Jimmy)*, Wayne Grace *(Officer Jamison)*, Alan Hayes *(Paul)*, Bonnie Hellman *(Hitchhiker)*, Frankie Hill *(Lainie)*, Barbara Howard *(Sara)*, William Irby *(Helicopter Pilot)*, Paul Lukather *(Doctor)*, Bruce Mahler *(Axel)*, Lawrence Monoson *(Ted)*, Arnie Moore *(Medic)*, Camilla More *(Tina)*, Carey More *(Terri)*, Robert Perault *(Medic)*, Antony Ponzini *(Vincent)*, Gene Ross *(Cop)*, Abigail Shelton *(Woman)*, John Walsh *(TV Newscaster)*, Robyn Woods *(Girl in Shower)*, Kristen Baker, Richard Brooker, Peter Brouwer, Ronn Carroll, Steve Daskawisz, Marta Kober, Jack Marks, Tom McBride, Betsy Palmer.

The fact that the title calls this the "Final Chapter" didn't mean that Paramount Studios was ready to dismantle their bloody money-making machine just yet. The first three mindless exercises in graphic bloodletting grossed a total of over $42 million, with very little money spent on production. Considering all that is really needed for these films is an endless supply of teenagers willing to disrobe for some on-screen hanky panky and then submit themselves to the special-effects crew, whose job it is to devise dozens of gory ways to slice them up, the overhead is low. The studio certainly doesn't have to hire any brilliant writers, since the plot of the first film has been repeated in every sequel. This time out, as if it mattered, the crazed Jason once again stomps through the woods of a lonely summer camp carving up all the nubile young camp counselors. As usual, the open ending prepared blood-lustful viewers for another sequel, FRIDAY THE 13TH, PART V—A NEW BEGINNING, a rather laughable title considering the previous four films came out of a Xerox machine.

p, Frank Mancuso, Jr., Tony Bishop; d, Joseph Zito; w, Barney Cohen (story by Bruce Hidemi Sakow, based on characters created by Victor Miller, Ron Kurz, Martin Kitrosser, Carol Watson); ph, Joao Fernandes (Movielab Color); ed, Joel Goodman, Daniel Loewenthal; m, Harry Manfredini.

(PR:O  MPAA:R)

## FRIDAY THE 13TH, PART V—A NEW BEGINNING
zero

(1985) 91m PAR c

John Shepard (Tommy Jarvis), Melanie Kinnaman (Pam), Shavar Ross (Reggie), Richard Young (Matt), Marco St. John (Sheriff Tucker), Juliette Cummins (Robin), Carol Lacatell (Ethel), Vernon Washington (George), John Robert Dixon (Eddie), Jerry Pavlon (Jake), Caskey Swaim (Duke), Mark Venturini (Victor), Anthony Barrile (Vinnie), Dominick Brascia (Joey), Tiffany Helm (Violet), Richard Lineback (Deputy Dodd), Corey Feldman (Tommy at 12), Suzanne Bateman (Nurse Yates/Receptionist), Bob De Simone (Billy/Male Nurse), Jere Fields (Anita), Ric Mancini (Mayor Cobb), Miguel A. Nunez, Jr. (Demon), Corey Parker (Pete), Rebecca Wood-Sharkey (Lana), Ron Sloan (Junior).

When we last left Jason—the psychotic killer in the hockey mask who enjoys cutting up nubile young teenagers for his greedy bosses at Paramount Studios, who continue to fill their coffers with blood-soaked box-office dollars—he was finally done in by a 12-year-old boy trying to save his family. With Jason finally dead, how does the studio continue the lucrative series? They make somebody else the crazed hockey-masked killer. After a dream-sequence in which Jason rises from the grave while the 12-year-old watches in horror, we are introduced to the guy plagued by the nightmares—Tommy Jarvis (John Shepard). Tommy is Jason's killer, and has grown up deeply disturbed by the event. Because of his problems, he is sent to a halfway house for disturbed teenagers run by progressive minded counselors. There the standard cliched assortment of mental cases (a dangerous homicidal type, a nerd, a nymphomaniac and her equally lecherous male partner, and a few others who don't seem to demonstrate any kind of abnormality) are fodder for the special-effects crew when Jason—is it or isn't it Tommy reenacting Jason's crimes?—kills them all off. Believe it or not, the bloodletting here was toned down considerably compared to the previous films, which delighted in showing the murders in medical-school detail. This was not the choice of director Danny Steinmann, however, who shot the film in the typically gory manner, then was forced by an unusually conservative MPAA to tone it down to achieve the all-important "R" rating. To make up for the lack of blood, the film provided more gratuitous nudity than had been seen in the previous installments of the series.

p, Timothy Silver; d, Danny Steinmann; w, Martin Kitrosser, David Cohen, Danny Steinmann (based on a story by Kitrosser, Cohen); ph, Stephen Posey (Metrocolor); ed, Bruce Green; m, Harry Manfredini.

(PR:O  MPAA:R)

## FRIDAY THE 13TH PART VI: JASON LIVES*

(1986) 87m Terror/PAR c

Thom Mathews (Tommy Jarvis), Jennifer Cooke (Megan), David Kagen (Sheriff Garris), Kerry Noonan (Paula), Renee Jones (Sissy), Tom Fridley (Cort), C.J. Graham (Jason Voorhees), Darcy DeMoss (Nikki), Vincent Guastaferro (Deputy Rick Cologne), Tony Goldwyn (Darren), Nancy McLoughlin (Lizbeth), Ron Palillo (Allen Hawes), Alan Blumenfeld (Larry), Matthew Faison (Stan), Ann Ryerson (Katie), Whitney Rydbeck (Roy), Courtney Vickery (Nancy), Bob Larkin (Martin), Michael Nomad (Officer Pappas), Wallace Merck (Burt), Roger Rose (Steven), Cynthia Kania (Annette), Tommy Nowell (Tyen), Justin Nowell (Billy), Sheri Levinsky (Bus Monitor), Temi Epstein (Little Girl), Turas O'Har (Little Boy).

Just before being dismembered in this, the sixth entry in one of the most revolting film series ever made, an alcoholic grave-digger quips, "Some folks have a strange idea of entertainment." Indeed. FRIDAY THE 13TH PART VI: JASON LIVES maintains the same depressing body-count formula to which the previous films adhered, but this time writer-director Tom McLoughlin, who is new to the series, adds a refreshing (relatively speaking, of course) element—self-parody. This one begins as Tommy Jarvis (Thom Mathews), the troubled teen who dispatched the last two Jasons, inadvertently resurrects Jason—although there seems to be a bit of confusion over which Jason is resurrected in this film, is it the one killed in Part IV, or the "new" Jason killed in Part V?—by skewering his corpse with a metal rod, thus allowing lightning to strike not once, but twice, bringing Jason back to life. This leaves the hockey-masked killer (C.J. Graham) to wander back to Camp Crystal Lake, where he terrorizes cabinfuls of innocent little grade-schoolers and their teenage counselors. From the parody of the classic James Bond looking-down-the-gun-barrel credits sequence (in an iris effect, Jason strolls in, turns to the camera, and pulls his machete) to the dozens of little self-conscious jokes sprinkled throughout, PART VI: JASON LIVES proves to be a little different from its precursors. In sharp contrast to PART V, which had the most gratuitous nudity in the series, there are no female teenagers showing off their bosoms in PART VI. The violence is also toned down considerably, and with only a few bloody moments, most of the killing is suggested or done off-screen. The visual style of this film is superior as well, with cinematographer Jon R. Kranhouse doing a beautifully slick, professional job, adding some very accomplished camera moves and some good underwater footage. In addition to the humor and the technical savvy, the biggest difference between this film and the five before it is that the characters are actually allowed to live long enough for the audience to develop some sort of empathy with them. Some of these teenagers are downright likable, and we don't want to see them get killed. That element, more than any other, was the only genuine breakthrough in the entire series.

p, Don Behrns; d, Tom McLoughlin; w, Tom McLoughlin; ph, Jon R. Kranhouse (Metrocolor); ed, Bruce Green; m, Harry Manfredini.

(PR:O  MPAA:R)

## FRIDAY THE 13TH PART VII—THE NEW BLOOD
zero

(1988) 90m PAR c (GB: JASON LIVES: FRIDAY THE 13TH PART VI)

Jennifer Banko (Young Tina), John Otrin (Mr. Shepard), Susan Blu (Mrs. Shepard), Lar Park Lincoln (Tina Shepard), Terry Kiser (Dr. Crews), Kevin Blair (Nick), Jennifer Sullivan (Melissa), Heidi Kozak (Sandra), Kane Hodder (Jason Voorhees), William Clarke Butler (Michael), Staci Greason (Jane), Larry Cox (Russell), Jeff Bennett (Eddie), Diana Barrows (Maddy), Elizabeth Kaitan (Robin), Jon Renfield (David), Craig Thomas (Ben), Diane Almeida (Kate), Michael Schroeder, Debora Kessler.

The series went from self-parody back to normal with this dull entry, in which Jason kills a bunch of teenagers and a couple of adults using a variety of sharp instruments, after which a girl with CARRIE-like psychokinetic powers appears to defeat him once and for all. Sure she did.

p, Iain Paterson; d, John Carl Buechler; w, Daryl Haney, Manuel Fidello; ph, Paul Elliott (Technicolor); ed, Barry Zetlin, Maureen O'Connell, Martin Jay Sadoff; m, Harry Manfredini, Fred Mollin.

(PR:O  MPAA:R)

## FRIDAY THE 13TH ... THE ORPHAN*

(1979) 80m Gilman-Westergaard/World Northal c (AKA: KILLER ORPHAN)

Peggy Feury (Aunt Martha), Joanna Miles (David's Mother), Donn Whyte (David's Father), Stanley Church (Dr. Thompson), Eleanor Stewart (Mary), Afolabi Ajayi (Akin), Jane House (Jean Ford), David Foreman (Percy Ford), Mark Owens (David).

This stupid horror movie concerns a 10-year-old boy who is told by his aunt that he is going to be put in a boarding school. For some reason, the boy imagines he is to be put in an orphanage, and fantasizes what his confinement would be like in such a place. Of course, he gets his revenge in a bloody manner. This film was actually released before Sean S. Cunningham's rancid FRIDAY THE 13TH.

d, John Ballard; w, John Ballard; ph, Beda F. Patka; m, Ted Macero.

(PR:O  MPAA:R)

## FRIGHT NIGHT***½

(1985) 106m COL c

Chris Sarandon (Jerry Dandridge), William Ragsdale

(Charley Brewster), Amanda Bearse (Amy Peterson), Roddy McDowall (Peter Vincent), Stephen Geoffreys (Evil Ed), Jonathan Stark (Billy Cole), Dorothy Fielding (Judy Brewster), Art J. Evans (Detective Lennox), Stewart Stern (Cook), Nick Savage, Ernie Holmes, Prince A. Hughes (Bouncers), Heidi Sorenson (Hooker), Irina Irvine (Teenage Girl), Robert Corff (Jonathan), Pamela Brown (Miss Nina), Chris Hendrie (Newscaster).

An outstanding little film, FRIGHT NIGHT abandoned the mad slashers of modern horror in favor of the tried-and-true vampires of old. Told with the proper amount of chills, wit, and special effects, FRIGHT NIGHT follows the teenaged Charley (William Ragsdale) as he becomes convinced that his charming new next-door neighbor, Jerry Dandridge (Chris Sarandon), is a vampire. Dandridge is a vampire, of course, and when he discovers that Charley knows his secret he threatens the boy's life, his handsome facial features contorting horribly to reveal his true vampiric visage. Of course the police and Charley's mother won't listen to him, and even his devoted girl friend, Amy (Amanda Bearse), thinks he needs professional help. Desperate, Charley turns to the only vampire expert he can think of, Peter Vincent (Roddy McDowall, in his best role in years), a washed up horror-movie actor who now hosts a "Creature Feature"-type TV show that runs old monster movies. Although at first he only humors the boy, Vincent soon realizes that Charley is telling the truth, and the two of them must team up to defeat the vampire. FRIGHT NIGHT is wonderful fun, combining the popular teenager-in-trouble subgenre with a traditional vampire movie. Sarandon's vampire brings back to the vampire a seductive sexuality not seen in years. McDowall is terrific as the meek actor-turned-vampire hunter, and it is a joy to watch him really have fun with the role. Ragsdale, Bearse, and Stephen Geoffreys—the youths in the film—are fresh-faced and still naive enough to believe in vampires, a welcome change from the jaded, sex-and-drugs addled teenagers of the slasher films. The special effects by Richard Edlund are outstanding, satisfying the current craze for high-tech effects without stopping the show completely. First-time director Tom Holland (who wrote the script here and for CLASS OF 1984; CLOAK AND DAGGER; and PSYCHO II as well) handles it all deftly and shows a true love for horror films of years gone by. The man understands the genre and knows what makes it work. FRIGHT NIGHT was a surprise hit at the box office and a sequel was shot and slated for release in 1988, but shelved until 1989.

p, Herb Jaffe; d, Tom Holland; w, Tom Holland; ph, Jan Keisser (Metrocolor); ed, Kent Beyda; m, Brad Fiedel.

(PR:O  MPAA:R)

## FRIGHTMARE**

(1974, Brit.) 86m Ellman c (AKA: FRIGHTMARE II)

Rupert Davies (Edmund), Sheila Keith (Dorothy), Deborah Fairfax (Jackie), Paul Greenwood (Graham), Kim Butcher (Debbie), Fiona Curzon (Merle), Jon Yule (Robin), Tricia Mortimer (Lilian), Pamela Farbrother (Delia), Edward Kalinski (Alec), Victor Winding (Detective Inspector),

Anthony Hennessy *(Sergeant)*, Noel Johnson *(Judge)*, Michael Sharvell-Martin *(Barman)*, Tom Wright *(Nightclub Manager)*, Andrew Sachs *(Barry)*, Nicholas John *(Pete)*, Jack Dagmar *(Old Man)*, Leo Genn *(Dr. Lytell)*, Gerald Flood *(Matthew)*.

Just released from an insane asylum, an elderly British couple, Edmund and Dorothy (Rupert Davies and Sheila Keith), retire to a remote farmhouse—where Dorothy immediately resumes her cannibalistic activities, while Edmund covers up for her. In addition to knocking off the psychiatrist sent to check up on them, Dorothy even enlists her adult daughter (Kim Butcher) in the service of her perversion. Easily the best of notorious British gore director Peter Walker's efforts (and that's including the sadistic HOUSE OF WHIPCORD, 1974), this film is stylishly directed and contains several good performances, most notably that of Keith. Released on videocassette as FRIGHTMARE II, in an effort to confuse consumers into thinking it is a sequel to the lame 1983 horror film FRIGHTMARE.

p, Peter Walker; d, Peter Walker; w, David McGillivray (based on a story by Walker); ph, Peter Jessop (Eastmancolor); ed, Robert Dearberg; m, Stanley Myers.

**(PR:O MPAA:R)**

## FRIGHTMARE*

(1983) 86m Atlantic TV/Saturn International c (AKA: HORROR STAR, THE)

Ferdinand [Ferdy] Mayne *(Conrad)*, Luca Bercovici *(Saint)*, Nita Talbot *(Mrs. Rohmer)*, Leon Askin *(Wolfgang)*, Jennifer Starrett *(Meg)*, Barbara Pilavin *(Etta)*, Carlene Olson *(Eve)*, Scott Thomson *(Bobo)*, Donna McDaniel *(Donna)*, Jeffrey Combs *(Stu)*, Peter Kastner *(Director)*, Chuck Mitchell *(Detective)*, Jesse Ehrlich *(Professor)*.

Conrad Radzoff (Ferdinand Mayne), a hammy horror film star, murders his director and then dies himself—killed by his own overacting. When a group of Radzoff's fans, members of The Horror Film Society, exhume his body, his widow—angered that they have defiled his tomb—hires a medium to bring her beloved husband back to life, this time as a real-life zombie. Radzoff's reanimated body then goes on a mass killing spree, wreaking a terrible vengeance on the misguided teens who disturbed his eternal rest. This self-consciously silly horror movie makes the fatal mistake of referring to other, much better, horror films, thus continually reminding the viewer how lame this effort is in comparison.

p, Patrick Wright, Tallie Wright; d, Norman Thaddeus Vane; w, Norman Thaddeus Vane; ph, J. King; ed, Robert Jackson; m, Jerry Moseley.

**(PR:O MPAA:R)**

## FROGS**½

(1972) 90m AIP c

Ray Milland *(Jason Crockett)*, Sam Elliott *(Pickett Smith)*, Joan Van Ark *(Karen Crockett)*, Adam Roarke *(Clint Crockett)*, Judy Pace *(Bella Berenson)*, Lynn Borden *(Jenny*

Crockett)*, Mae Mercer *(Maybelle)*, David Gilliam *(Michael)*, Nicholas Cortland *(Kenneth)*, George Skaff *(Stuart)*, Lance Taylor Sr. *(Charles)*, Holly Irving *(Iris)*, Dale Willingham *(Tina)*, Hal Hodges *(Jay)*, Carolyn Fitzsimmons *(Lady In Car)*, Robert Sanders *(Young Boy In Car)*.

In an old mansion located on a private island in the Florida Everglades, the Crockett family has assembled on the Fourth of July to celebrate the birthday of Jason Crockett (Ray Milland), their wheelchair-bound patriarch. Uninvited, however, are the thousands of frogs, snakes, turtles, and lizards who take over the island, causing havoc. An attempt to capitalize on the success of WILLARD (1971), this silly-sounding revenge-of-nature film is surprisingly effective, with director George McCowan opting simply to let normal-sized animals attack human beings—albeit in staggering numbers—instead making the creatures atomically mutated giants (although the film's advertising was a bit misleading, showing a bullfrog with a human hand sticking out of its mouth). In fact, the film offers no explanation at all for the attacks, making it reminiscent of Hitchcock's THE BIRDS (1963).

p, George Edwards, Peter Thomas; d, George McCowan; w, Robert Hutchison, Robert Blees (based on a story by Hutchison); ph, Mario Tosi (Movielab Color); ed, Fred Feitshans, Jr.; m, Les Baxter.

**(PR:C MPAA:PG)**

## FROM BEYOND***½

(1986) 85m Empire c

Jeffrey Combs *(Crawford Tillinghast)*, Barbara Crampton *(Dr. Katherine McMichaels)*, Ted Sorel *(Dr. Edward Pretorious)*, Ken Foree *(Bubba Brownlee)*, Carolyn Purdy-Gordon *(Dr. Roberta Bloch)*, Bunny Summers *(Hester Gilman)*, Bruce McGuire *(Jordan Fields)*, Del Russel *(Ambulance Driver)*, Dale Wyatt *(Paramedic)*, Karen Christenfeld *(Nurse)*, Andy Miller *(Patient in Straitjacket)*, John Leamer *(Shock Technician)*, Regina Bleesz *(Bondage Girl)*.

Stuart Gordon, whose debut, RE-ANIMATOR, was the sleeper horror hit of 1985, returned again to the fever-dreamlike stories of H.P. Lovecraft for his source in FROM BEYOND. Dr. Edward Pretorious (Ted Sorel) and his assistant, Crawford Tillinghast (Jeffrey Combs), construct a machine designed to resonate the vestigial "third-eye," the pineal gland, and open the senses to that which lies "beyond," causing sexual excitation as every sense becomes heightened. Pretorious is obsessed with the notion that five senses simply aren't "enough" and he gives himself to the creatures revealed by the machine, becoming a hideous monster, his shape changing at will. Tillinghast is arrested for the murder of Pretorious, but he manages to persuade a female psychiatrist, Dr. Katherine McMichaels (Barbara Crampton) to return with him to the lab so that he can prove his innocence. Joined by an undercover cop (Ken Foree, from DAWN OF THE DEAD) for protection, McMichaels and Tillinghast return to discover that the evil Pretorious waits to induct others into his new state. Building on the desire to "see more," FROM BEYOND is a provocative exploration of new psychosexual dimensions. The creatures that populate the film are totally new, and the notion that they swim around us all the time—as oblivious to us as we are to them—is effectively creepy. One problem inherent in all monster movies is the fact that, once shown, a monster is never so scary as when it existed only in the imagination. Here the problem is overcome by having the chief creature, the aptly named Pretorious, change his appearance every time he turns up, and even shift his shape while we watch. The effects are good in the heads-splitting-open-with-lots-of-goo style, and were created by four separate special-effects teams, each trying to outdo the others. While perhaps not as mind-blowingly unique as RE-ANIMATOR, this is definitely one of the best horror films of the 1980s.

p, Brian Yuzna; d, Stuart Gordon; w, Dennis Paoli, Brian Yuzna, Stuart Gordon (based on the story "From Beyond" by H.P. Lovecraft); ph, Mac Ahlberg (Technicolor); ed, Lee Percy; m, Richard Band.

**(PR:O   MPAA:R)**

## FROM BEYOND THE GRAVE**½

(1974, Brit.) 98m Amicus/WB c (AKA: CREATURES FROM BEYOND THE GRAVE, THE; CREATURES)

Peter Cushing *(Proprietor)*, David Warner *(Edward Charlton)*, Wendy Allnutt *(Pamela)*, Rosalind Ayres *(Prostitute)*, Marcel Steiner *("Face")*, Donald Pleasence *(Underwood)*, Ian Bannen *(Christopher Lowe)*, Diana Dors *(Mabel Lowe)*, Angela Pleasence *(Emily Underwood)*, Margaret Leighton *(Mme. Orloff)*, Ian Carmichael *(Reggie Warren)*, Nyree Dawn Porter *(Susan Warren)*, Ian Ogilvy *(William Seaton)*, Lesley-Anne Down *(Rosemary Seaton)*, Jack Watson *(Sir Michael Sinclair)*, Tommy Godfrey, Ben Howard, John O'Farrell.

Yet another horror anthology from Amicus—their seventh—this one's once again a haphazard affair that fails to satisfy. Based on four stories by R. Chetwynd-Hayes, the episodes are linked by Peter Cushing as the proprietor of a creepy antique shop who gets revenge on cheating customers by condemning them to supernatural fates after they leave the store. In the first tale, a man is possessed by the spirit of Jack the Ripper after purchasing an antique mirror. The second shows a henpecked retired army officer falling into an affair with the daughter of a mysterious peddler (played, respectively, by Angela Pleasence and her father, Donald) who uses voodoo to dispose of his wife. In the third story, a man and his wife are tormented by an "elemental," an invisible demon that sits on his shoulder. And the fourth story concerns a man who purchases an antique door and installs it in his home, only to find that it is now a portal into the home of its original owner—a man who lived for the pursuit of evil and was given to performing human sacrifices. The directorial debut of Kevin Connor, who would go on to make the notable MOTEL HELL (1980), this film is predictably uneven, with episodes two and three a bit more successful than the ones that bookend them.

p, Max J. Rosenberg, Milton Subotsky; d, Kevin Connor;

w, Raymond Christodoulou, Robin Clarke (based on stories from *The Unbidden* by Ronald Chetwynd-Hayes); ph, Alan Hume (Technicolor); ed, John Ireland; m, Douglas Gamley.

**(PR:C   MPAA:PG)**

## FUNERAL HOME*

(1982, Can.) 93m MPM-Wescom/CFDC c (AKA: CRIES IN THE NIGHT)

Lesleh Donaldson *(Heather)*, Kay Hawtrey *(Maude)*, Barry Morse *(Davis)*, Dean Garbett *(Rick)*, Stephen Miller *(Billy)*, Harvey Atkin *(Harry)*, Alf Humphreys *(Joe)*, Peggy Mahon *(Florie)*, Doris Petrik *(Ruby)*, Les Rubie *(Sam)*, Bob Warners *(Fred)*.

Maude (Kay Hawtrey), a peculiar old woman who lives in a small motel that formerly housed a funeral home, is visited one summer by her teenage granddaughter, Heather (Lesleh Donaldson). The young girl is soon haunted by the voice of a madman coming from the cellar. As it turns out, the madman is really Grandma, who is pretending to be Grandpa, whom she killed and left to rot down there. This slow-moving and predictable PSYCHO rip-off is a total waste of time.

p, William Fruet; d, William Fruet; w, Ida Nelson; ph, Mark Irwin; ed, Ralph Brunjes; m, Jerry Fielding.

**(PR:C   MPAA:R)**

## FUNHOUSE, THE***

(1981) 96m UNIV c

Elizabeth Berridge *(Amy)*, Cooper Huckabee *(Buzz)*, Miles Chapin *(Richie)*, Largo Woodruff *(Liz)*, Sylvia Miles *(Mme. Zena)*, Kevin Conway *(The Barker)*, William Finley *(Marco The Magnificent)*, Wayne Doba *(The Monster)*, Shawn Carson *(Joey Harper)*, Jeanne Austin *(Mrs. Harper)*, Jack McDermott *(Harper)*, David Carson *(Geek)*, Sonia Zomina *(Bag Lady)*, Ralph Marino *(Truck Driver)*, Herb Robins *(Carnival Manager)*, Mona Agar *(Stripper)*, William Finley *(Marco)*, Susie Malnik *(Carmella)*, Sid Raymond *(M.C.)*, Larry Ross *(Heckler)*, Frank Grimes *(Voyeur)*, Frank Schuller *(Poker Player)*, Peter Conrad *(Midget)*, Mildred Hughes *(Tall Lady)*, Glen Lawrence, Mike Montalvo *(Spectators)*, Shawn McAllister, Sandy Mielke *(Garbage Collectors)*.

An underrated Tobe Hooper film—in fact, this has been the only *decent* movie Hooper's made in the 1980s—THE FUNHOUSE concerns a group of teenagers who stay all night in a carnival funhouse, witnessing the murder of a carnival fortune teller by the mutant son of the funhouse operator. When the monster's father realizes that the teenagers saw the crime, he sends his son after them. Although the plot conventions are disturbingly familiar, Hooper does manage to sneak in enough distinctive touches to keep the film interesting. The "monster" is a relatively sympathetic cleft-faced albino (makeup by Rick Baker and Craig Reardon) who works in the funhouse, hiding beneath a Frankenstein's monster mask. This device serves a dual purpose: first it frightens the audience by presenting a monster whose face is scarier than the mask that covers it; second, it drums up considerable sympathy for the creature by echoing Boris Karloff's sensitive portrayal of the Frankenstein monster. Stylishly directed and wonderfully shot—the climax is fairly stunning—the film is also imbued with Hooper's trademark black humor, and once again explores such themes as the horror of the American family and freak-show voyeurism. While certainly not as interesting or accomplished as THE TEXAS CHAINSAW MASSACRE, FUNHOUSE is a cut above the average slasher film.

p, Derek Powers, Steven Bernhardt; d, Tobe Hooper; w, Larry Block; ph, Andrew Laszlo (Panavision, Technicolor); ed, Jack Hofstra; m, John Beal.

(PR:O  MPAA:R)

## FURY, THE**½

(1978) 117m FOX c

Kirk Douglas *(Peter Sandza)*, John Cassavetes *(Childress)*, Carrie Snodgress *(Hester)*, Amy Irving *(Gillian Bellaver)*, Andrew Stevens *(Robin Sandza)*, Fiona Lewis *(Dr. Susan Charles)*, Charles Durning *(Dr. Jim McKeever)*, Carol Rossen *(Dr. Ellen Lindstrom)*, Joyce Easton *(Katharine Bellaver)*, William Finley *(Raymond Dunwoodie)*, Jane Lambert *(Vivian Knuckells)*, Sam Laws *(Blackfish)*, Melody Thomas *(LaRue)*, Hilary Thomas *(Cheryl)*, Patrick Billingsley *(Lander)*, Jack Callahan *(DeMasi)*, Dennis Franz *(Bob)*, Michael O'Dwyer *(Marty)*, Felix Silla *(Dr. Ives)*, J. Patrick McNamara *(Robertson)*, Bernie Kuby *(Nuckles)*, Rutanya Alda *(Kristen)*, Frank Yablans *(Goon on Radio)*.

Peter Sandza (Kirk Douglas) is a high-ranking American secret government agent visiting the Middle East with his teenage son, Robin (Andrew Stevens), who possesses amazing telekinetic powers, and his cohort, Childress (John Cassavetes), the chief of a shadowy US agency investigating psychic phenomena. Terrorists attack their resort and it looks as though Peter has been killed, so Childress becomes Robin's surrogate father. It seems, however, that Childress doesn't work for the US, but is ambitious and evil and wants to tap into Robin's powers for a scheme of his own. To that end, Childress hired the "terrorists" to erase Peter so the villain could get the lad all to himself. But Peter is not dead, and he returns to the States, hiring a psychic (William Finley) to help find his son. Meanwhile, another teenager, Gillian (Amy Irving), who is also telekinetic, is currently being studied at the Paragon Institute—which is a cover for Childress' operation. When Peter does finally manage to locate his son—who is now completely under Childress' control—he must enlist the aid of Gillian to rescue him. THE FURY is basically CARRIE expanded to include CIA-type shenanigans with geopolitical implications. While director Brian De Palma does manage to handle the convoluted plot with aplomb and the performances from Douglas and Cassavetes are good, the film is bogged down by De Palma's penchant for technically slick but overblown action scenes that call attention to themselves as virtuoso set-pieces instead of serving to advance the narrative. Although there are those who find De Palma's use of slow-motion ingenious, entire scenes shot that way

seem merely self-indulgent and tedious. Nevertheless, the film is worth watching for its explosive climax, where the impressive effects work by A.D. Flowers and Rick Baker set the stage for David Cronenberg's somewhat similar SCANNERS (1981).

p, Frank Yablans; d, Brian De Palma; w, John Farris (based on his novel); ph, Richard H. Kline (DeLuxe Color); ed, Paul Hirsch; m, John Williams.

(PR:O  MPAA:R)

# G

## GANJA AND HESS***½

(1973) 110m Kelly-Jordan c (AKA: DOUBLE POSSESSION; BLOOD COUPLE)

Duane Jones *(Dr. Hess Green)*, Marlene Clark *(Ganja)*, Bill Gunn *(George)*, Sam Waymon *(Rev. Williams)*, Leonard Jackson *(Archie)*, Candece Tarpley *(Girl in Bar)*, Richard Harrow *(Dinner Guest)*, John Hoffmeister *(Jack)*, Betty Barney *(Singer)*, Mabel King *(Queen of Myrthia)*, Betsy Thurman *(Poetess)*, Enrico Fales *(Green's Son)*, Tommy Lane *(Pimp)*, Tara Fields *(Woman With Baby)*.

One of the best black-oriented movies to come out of Hollywood in the 1970s, GANJA AND HESS stars the late Duane Jones (NIGHT OF THE LIVING DEAD) as a New York anthropologist, Dr. Hess Green, embroiled in a study of the lost ancient African culture of Myrthia, a nation that died out due to a communicable parasite that fed on human blood. During his research, Dr. Green is stabbed with a jewel-encrusted Myrthian dagger by his crazed assistant (played by director Bill Gunn) and finds that he has become infected with the virus, turning him into a vampire-like creature who is addicted to blood and fancies himself an invincible African god, and who turns his wife, Ganja (Marlene Clark), into a vampire as well. This is a fascinating picture, managing both to exploit its horror angle and explore the contrasts between Western and African cultures—the former represented as repressive and puritanical, the latter as more virile and liberating. Writer-director Gunn, who is also a painter, imbues the film with a cultural richness little seen in black-oriented films. Impressionistic, vibrant, and rhythmic (the original soundtrack used both American spirituals and African traditional music), GANJA AND HESS was a memorable and haunting film until it was recut by its distributors. Most of the thematic richness wound up on the floor, but the most heinous change was the removal of the African soundtrack in favor of bland American soul music. The uncut version plays occasionally at revival houses and film societies. The 83-minute print available on videocassette, titled BLOOD COUPLE, is, unfortunately, a butchered version.

p, Chris Schultz; d, Bill Gunn; w, Bill Gunn; ph, James E. Hinton; ed, Victor Kanefsky; m, Sam Waymon.

(PR:O  MPAA:R)

## GARDEN OF THE DEAD zero

(1972)86mClover/Entertainment Pyramid c

John Dennis, Duncan McCloud, Marland Proctor, Erik Stern.

Some prison inmates get high on formaldehyde and go into a violent frenzy that results in the guards being forced to kill them. You can't keep a con down, however, and the deceased prisoners rise from the dead, raid the prison tool shed (where the gardening implements are kept), and arm themselves to wreak vengeance on the cruel guards who killed them. A low-budget effort with zero production values or originality, this film was obviously an attempt to coopt NIGHT OF THE LIVING DEAD's reputation and popularity. Rent PRISON (1988) instead.

p, Daniel Cady; d, John Hayes; w, John Jones.

**(PR:C  MPAA:PG)**

## GATE, THE***

(1987, Can.) 92m Alliance/New Century-Vista c

Stephen Dorff *(Glen)*, Christa Denton *(Alexandra "Al", Glen's Sister)*, Louis Tripp *(Terry)*, Kelly Rowan *(Lori Lee)*, Jennifer Irwin *(Linda Lee, Lori's Sister)*, Deborah Grover *(Mom)*, Scot Denton *(Dad)*, Ingrid Veninger *(Paula)*, Sean Fagan *(Eric)*, Linda Goranson *(Terry's Mom)*, Carl Kraines *(Workman)*, Andrew Gunn *(Brad)*.

This surprisingly effective low-budget effort from Canada plays on universal childhood fears, and manages to be scary without resorting to scenes of sadism or graphic bloodletting. Instead, the film relies on its likable cast of young actors and some truly imaginative special effects. Set in a Spielbergian suburb, the film centers on young Glen (Stephen Dorff) and his older sister, Al (Christa Denton), who, for the first time, have been left in charge of the house while their parents go away for the weekend. After Al goes off to the mall with a friend, the bored Glen and his bespectacled buddy, Terry (Louis Tripp), investigate a hole in the backyard that was left behind when workmen uprooted an old tree. As it turns out, the hole is really a gate to hell—through which, if a sacrifice is made, demons will burst and attempt to take over the upper world. When the body of Glen's dog—which has died mysteriously—is inadvertently dumped into the hole, the "sacrifice" unleashes dozens of one-foot-tall mischievous minions from below who wreak havoc on the house in preparation for the coming of the Demon Lord. Despite all its dealings with the denizens of hell and the occult, THE GATE is a remarkably amiable horror movie. The message here is that love is stronger than hate, and in the end no one really dies. While hard-core horror addicts may find THE GATE rather wimpy, the film makes for a refreshing change from the rash of ultrableak, cynical, humorless, and irredeemably sadistic films that have been polluting the screens of late. Director Tibor Takacs spends plenty of time developing his characters, showing them as likable human beings who elicit viewer sympathy and support (whereas, in most recent horror films, the characters are merely fodder for the gore effects). Even more impressive is the grab-bag of superior special effects that were created quickly on a rela-

tively small budget ($6 million). Although the matte work and stop-motion animation are superior, the most impressive effect is the flawless use of forced perspective in the scenes involving the minions.

p, John Kemeny, Andras Hamori; d, Tibor Takacs; w, Michael Nankin; ph, Thomas Vamos (Medallion Film Labs Color); ed, Kit Wallis; m, Michael Hoenig, J. Peter Robinson.

**(PR:C  MPAA:PG-13)**

## GATES OF HELL, THE*½

(1983, US/It.) 93m Motion Picture Marketing/Robert Warner c (PAURA NELLA CITTA DEI MORTI VIVENTI; AKA: CITY OF THE LIVING DEAD; FEAR, THE; TWILIGHT OF THE DEAD; FEAR IN THE CITY OF THE LIVING DEAD)

Venantino Venantini, Carlo de Mejo, Daniela Doria, Robert Sampson, Christopher George, Janet Agren, Katriona MacColl, Antonella Interlenghi, Giovanni Lombardo Radice, Luca Paismer, Fabrizio Jovine.

A big hit with the hardcore gore fans, this was director Lucio Fulci's follow-up to the incredibly gory ZOMBIE and he really outdoes himself this time. Filmed in 1980, Fulci's ostensible ode to H.P. Lovecraft is laughably set in Dunwich, although it's obvious the film was shot in Italy. When a parish priest hangs himself in the church cemetery, the gates of hell open up, allowing all manner of zombies to rise up and mutilate the living. Since there is little in the way of plot, the film concentrates on the gore, presenting scalpings, maggots, a really graphic electric drill through the skull, and, most revolting of all, a woman who literally spews her guts out. If the above appeals to you, you've no doubt already seen it.

p, Giovanni Masini; d, Lucio Fulci; w, Lucio Fulci, Dardano Sacchetti; ph, Sergio Salvati; m, Fabio Frizzi.

**(PR:O  MPAA:NR)**

## GHASTLY ONES, THE zero

(1968) 81m JER c

Veronica Radbrook, Hal Belsoe, Eileen Hayes, Don Williams, Maggie Rogers, Carol Vogel, Richard Ramos, Anne Linden, Fib LaBlanque, Haal Borske, Neil Flanders, Hal Sherwood.

Three couples must stay in a haunted mansion in order to inherit a dead patriarch's estate. The three men are killed off—one is hanged, another disemboweled, and a third is jabbed in the throat with a pitchfork. Of the three girls, only two make it to the final credits, with the third having her head served on a dinner plate. The killer turns out to be an old woman who claims to be the dead man's illegitimate half-sister. She is prepared to kill the remaining gals, but is stopped by her hunchback friend. She sets the hunchback on fire; he smacks her with a cleaver. Yes, it's an Andy Milligan film shot for no money on 16mm and looks like it. The trailer for this film is available on several horror movie coming-attractions reels, such as MAD RON'S

PREVUES FROM HELL. Watch that instead; it's shorter. Believe it or not, Milligan actually remade this in 1978 as LEGACY OF BLOOD.

p, Jerome Frederick; d, Andy Milligan; w, Andy Milligan, Hal Sherwood; ph, Andy Milligan, D. Mills; ed, Gerald Jackson.

(PП:O MPAA:NR)

## GHOST SHIP**½

(1953, Brit.) 69m ABTCON/Lippert bw

Dermot Walsh (Guy), Hazel Court (Margaret), Hugh Burden (Dr. Fawcett), John Robinson (Mansel), Joss Ambler (Yard Manager), Joan Carol (Mrs. Martineau), Hugh Latimer (Peter), Mignon O'Doherty (Mrs. Manley), Laidman Browne (Coroner), Meadows White (Yard Surveyor), Pat McGrath (Bert), Joss Ackland (Ron), John King-Kelly (Sid), Colin Douglas, Patricia Owens, Melissa Stribling, Jack Stewart, Anthony Marlowe, Geoffrey Dunn, Ian Carmichael, Anthony Hayes, Barry Phelps, Robert Moore, Ewen Solon.

Director Vernon Sewell's fifth version of this material, which was cribbed from an old French Grand Guignol play, concerns a young couple, Guy and Margaret (Dermot Walsh and Hazel Court), who purchase a yacht named "The Cyclops," which, they are later told, is haunted. The unbelievers ignore this warning, and strange things begin to happen. Calling in an expert on the supernatural, Guy and Margaret discover—in flashback—that the former owner killed his wife and her lover and stored the two bodies on board. A talky but fairly atmospheric effort, GHOST SHIP is hampered by its low budget. The yacht on which the film is set is director Sewell's own. Sewell would tackle this plot one more time in 1961, with HOUSE OF MYSTERY.

p, Vernon Sewell; d, Vernon Sewell; w, Vernon Sewell, Philip Thornton; ph, Stanley Grant; ed, Francis Bieber; m, Eric Spear.

(PR:A MPAA:NR)

## GHOST STORY***

(1974, Brit.) 89m Stephen Weeks c

Murray Melvin (McFayden), Larry Dann (Talbot), Vivian Mackerall (Duller), Marianne Faithfull, Anthony Bate, Leigh Lawson, Barbara Shelley.

In 1930s England, three friends, McFayden (Murray Melvin), Duller (Vivian Mackerall), and Talbot (Larry Dann), are invited to an old country house to discern whether the ancestral mansion is haunted or not. Although Duller's special paranormal equipment fails to detect anything amiss, Talbot comes under the spell of a haunted doll, which comes to life, giving him visions of a young woman (Marianne Faithfull) forced into an insane asylum against her will by her brother (Leigh Lawson). Director Weeks does a beautiful job evoking the time period in this effectively spooky and atmospheric film, and there are several fine performances, but some viewers may find the movie

rather slow going. On videocassette as MADHOUSE MANSION.

p, Stephen Weeks; d, Stephen Weeks; w, Stephen Weeks, Rosemary Sutcliff; ph, Peter Hurst (Fujicolor); m, Ron Geesin.

(PR:C MPAA:NR)

## GHOST STORY**½

(1981) 110m UNIV c

Fred Astaire (Ricky Hawthorne), Melvyn Douglas (John Jaffrey), Douglas Fairbanks Jr. (Edward Wanderley), John Houseman (Sears James), Craig Wasson (Don/David), Alice Krige (Alma/Eva), Jacqueline Brookes (Milly), Patricia Neal (Stella), Miguel Fernandes (Gregory Bate), Lance Helcomb (Fenny Bate), Mark Chamberlin (Young Jaffrey), Tom Choate (Young Hawthorne), Kurt Johnson (Young Wanderley), Ken Olin (Young James), Brad Sullivan (Sheriff), Guy Boyd, Robert Burr, Helena Carroll, Robin Curtis, Breon Gorman, Cagle D. Green, Kyra Carleton, Deborah Offner, Russell R. Bletzer, Alfred Curven, Michael O'Neil.

Four elderly men—Fred Astaire, Melvyn Douglas, Douglas Fairbanks, Jr., and John Houseman—meet regularly in New England to tell each other ghost stories. One year, strange occurrences upset the usual routine. It's then revealed that, 50 years earlier, these men accidentally killed a lovely young tease. To cover their tracks, they put her in a car and drove it into a lake, only to see her frantically but unsuccessfully try to escape. Alice Krige (CHARIOTS OF FIRE; BARFLY) turns in an eerie performance as the vengeful ghost. The film suffers from a haphazard script by CARRIE screenwriter Lawrence Cohen, who removed all of the nuance and subtlety from Peter Straub's bestselling novel in favor of special effects. Director John Irvin does manage to evoke some mood and atmosphere from the snowy New England setting, and the performances from the four veteran lead players are enjoyable.

p, Burt Weissbourd; d, John Irvin; w, Larry Cohen (based on the novel by Peter Straub); ph, Jack Cardiff (Technicolor); ed, Tom Rolf; m, Philippe Sarde.

(PR:O MPAA:R)

## GHOST TOWN**

(1988) 85m Empire/Trans World c

Franc Luz (Langley), Catherine Hickland (Kate), Jimmie F. Skaggs (Devilin), Penelope Windust (Grace), Bruce Glover (Dealer), Zitto Kazann (Blacksmith), Blake Conway (Harper), Laura Schaeffer (Etta), Michael Aldredge (Bubba), Ken Kolb (Ned), Will Hannah (Billy).

GHOST TOWN combines elements of the horror and western genres, resulting in a mixed bag of pretty pictures and stale story-telling. Present-day deputy sheriff Langley (Franc Luz) stumbles upon a ghost town while searching for missing socialite Kate (Catherine Hickland), who, at the film's opening, was snatched up by a man in black appearing out of a dust cloud on horseback. Langley, quite to his amazement, discovers that the town is full of the undead, the townsfolk bound to an old curse that keeps them ageless. GHOST TOWN has a lot going for it. Director Richard Governor brings a sense of poignancy to the material (a quality that is, to say the least, absent from most recent horror films), the movie is beautifully photographed by Mac Ahlberg, and the performances are convincing. What starts out as an interesting premise, however, soon turns into a run-of-the-mill, Saturday afternoon bad-guy western, the only difference being that here the villains are zombies. It should have been fun, but, instead of exploiting the concept's potential, the film falls prey to western cliches and lacks the strong narrative drive that could have kept it one hoof ahead of the rest.

p, Timothy D. Tennant; d, Richard Governor; w, Duke Sandefur (based on a story by David Schmoeller); ph, Mac Ahlberg (Foto-Kem Color); ed, Peter Teschner, King Wilder; m, Harvey R. Cohen.

(PR:C-O   MPAA:R)

## GHOSTBUSTERS***½

(1984) 107m COL c

Bill Murray (Dr. Peter Venkman), Dan Aykroyd (Dr. Raymond Stantz), Sigourney Weaver (Dana Barrett), Harold Ramis (Dr. Egon Spenler), Rick Moranis (Louis Tully), Annie Potts (Janine Melnitz), William Atherton (Walter Peck), Ernie Hudson (Winston Zeddmore), David Margulies (Mayor), Steven Tash, Jennifer Runyon (Students), Slavitza Jovan (Gozer), Michael Ensign (Hotel Manager), Alice Drummond (Librarian), Jordan Charney (Dean Yeager), Timothy Carhart (Violinist), John Rothman (Library Administrator), Roger Grimsby, Larry King, Joe Franklin, Casey Kasem (Themselves), Norman Matlock (Fire Commissioner), Joe Cirillo (Police Captain), Joe Schmieg (Police Sergeant), Reggie Vel Johnson (Jail Guard), Rhoda Gemignani (Real Estate Woman), Murray Rubin (Man at Elevator), Larry Dilg (Con Edison Man), Danny Stone (Coachman), Patty Dworkin, Jean Kasem (Women at Party).

An enormously successful movie that owes much to many less successful movies that preceded it, GHOST-BUSTERS is an all-star big-budget hybrid of pictures as diverse as SPOOK CHASERS (1957); THE SENTINEL (1977); SPOOK BUSTERS (1946); SCARED STIFF (1953); THE GHOST BREAKERS (1940); GHOST CATCHERS (1944), and countless others. The difference between those films and GHOSTBUSTERS is that the latter had a huge special-effects budget and the presence of Bill Murray, whose personality makes the whole thing work. Murray, Dan Aykroyd, and Harold Ramis play a trio of New York City parapsychologists who set up their own "ghost-busting" shop—not unlike exterminators—in a downtown building, complete with a bored secretary (Annie Potts). For a fee, the trio will rid humans of any supernatural spirits haunting their residence or place of business. They are hired by Dana Barrett (Sigourney Weaver), a symphony cellist who lives in a spectacular apartment above Central Park where strange things have been happening. After capturing a large, gooey, green ghost and ex-

periencing several other weird occurrences, the busters determine that the apartment building was built by a Sumerian devil cult and that the site is actually the doorway to the spirit world. Originally planned as an Aykroyd-John Belushi vehicle, the picture was rewritten upon Belushi's death, giving Murray's character the emphasis—and it is Murray's movie all the way. With his deadpan delivery and snide quips, Murray more than holds his own amid the myriad of state-of-the-art special effects. The huge box-office success of this film spawned a popular Saturday morning children's cartoon show and a line of toys. A greatly anticipated sequel, tentatively titled GHOSTBUSTERS II, is slated for release in 1989.

p, Ivan Reitman; d, Ivan Reitman; w, Dan Aykroyd, Harold Ramis; ph, Laszlo Kovacs, Herb Wagreitch (Panavision, Metrocolor); ed, Sheldon Kahn, David Blewitt; m, Elmer Bernstein.

(PR:A-C   MPAA:PG)

## GHOSTS ON THE LOOSE**

(1943) 64m MON bw (AKA: EAST SIDE KIDS MEET BELA LUGOSI, THE; GB: GHOSTS IN THE NIGHT)

Leo Gorcey (Muggs McGinnis), Huntz Hall (Glimpy Williams), Bobby Jordan (Danny), "Sunshine Sammy" Morrison (Scruno), Billy Benedict (Skinny, Benny), Stanley Clements (Stash), Bobby Stone (Rocky, Dave), Bill Bates ("Sleepy" Dave), Bela Lugosi (Emil), Rick Vallin (John "Jack" Gibson), Ava Gardner (Betty Williams Gibson), Minerva Urecal (Hilda), Wheeler Oakman (Tony), Frank Moran (Monk), Peter Seal (Bruno), Jack Mulhall (Lt. Brady), Kay Marvis Gorcey (Bridesmaid), Robert F. Hill (Minister), Tom Herbert.

Bela Lugosi plays a Nazi spy hiding out in an abandoned New York mansion. When the Bowery Boys stumble on his abode, he tries to scare them away by making the place appear haunted. Unfortunately, there is not enough focus on Lugosi, the film centering instead on the usual high jinks and buffoonery of Leo Gorcey, Huntz Hall, and company. The subplot employs Ava Gardner as Hall's soon-to-be-wed sister, coinciding with her real-life walk down the aisle with Mickey Rooney, and some exhibitors were sharp and aggressive enough to bill her as "Mrs. Mickey Rooney" on their marquees.

p, Sam Katzman, Jack Dietz; d, William Beaudine; w, Kenneth Higgins; ph, Mack Stengler; ed, Carl Pierson.

(PR:A   MPAA:NR)

## GHOUL, THE***

(1933, Brit.) 73m GAU bw

Boris Karloff (Prof. Morlant), Sir Cedric Hardwicke (Broughton), Ernest Thesiger (Laing), Dorothy Hyson (Betty Harlow), Anthony Bushell (Ralph Morlant), Kathleen Harrison (Kaney), Harold Huth (Aga Ben Dragore), D.A. Clarke-Smith (Mahmoud), Ralph Richardson (Nigel Hartley), Jack Raine (Chauffeur).

This extremely rare Boris Karloff vehicle has been virtually unavailable in the US until Sinister Cinema video came up with a tape taken from British television. While the film has developed something of a "lost classic" reputation over time (after years of searching, a print was finally found in New York City in 1969), it is certainly no masterpiece—but quite interesting nonetheless. Karloff's first British film (he left England in 1909) casts him as Prof. Morlant, an eccentric English Egyptologist obsessed with the powers of the ancient Egyptian gods. On his deathbed he commands his servant, Laing (Ernest Thesiger), to bind the sacred jewel known as "The Eternal Light" to his hand, warning that if the jewel is stolen, he will return from the grave seeking revenge. After Morlant's death, a greedy lawyer, a bogus priest, and an Egyptian student arrive at the estate and search for the jewel. When it is wrenched out of his hand, the dead Morlant indeed comes back to life, strangles the guilty party, and returns to his tomb with the jewel. Made and released on the heels of Karloff's hit THE MUMMY, this was one of the first English attempts at horror, and the filmmakers obviously looked to the popular Universal film for inspiration. Fairly moody and atmospheric, the film relies heavily on Karloff's presence for effect, but by killing him off at the beginning, then bringing him back for the climax, it burdens itself with a long, dull stretch in the middle that has no dynamic power of its own. Luckily, the excellent cast Gaumont assembled helps move things along. Remade in 1962 as the comedy NO PLACE LIKE HOMICIDE!

p, Michael Balcon; d, T. Hayes Hunter; w, Roland Pertwee, John Hastings Turner, Rupert Downing, L. DuGarde Peach (based on the novel and play by Dr. Frank King, Leonard J. Hines); ph, Gunther Krampf; ed, Ian Dalrymple.

(PR:A  MPAA:NR)

## GHOUL, THE**

(1975, Brit.) 88m Rank c

Peter Cushing (Dr. Lawrence), John Hurt (Tom), Alexandra Bastedo (Angela), Gwen Watford (Ayah), Veronica Carlson (Daphne), Stewart Bevan (Billy), Ian McCulloch (Geoffrey), Don Henderson (The Ghoul).

Another attempt at interlocking British colonialism with horror, this effort, unimaginatively directed by Freddie Francis, is set in the 1920s and features Peter Cushing as Dr. Lawrence, a defrocked clergyman who once spent time in India. Back in England, Lawrence harbors a deep, dark family secret: his son (Don Henderson) suffers from uncontrollable cannibalism. Lawrence keeps his progeny locked in the attic, but the lad manages to escape and terrorize the countryside during a major auto race. Meanwhile, John Hurt, as the gardener, is an complete lunatic in his own right and is responsible for one death himself. Cushing and other familiar Hammer faces give this the old college try, but Francis' dull direction—endless shots of Henderson's legs creeping down the stairs—makes the cause hopeless. The film was never released in the US, later turning up on television and videotape.

p, Kevin Francis; d, Freddie Francis; w, John Elder; ph,

John Wilcox (Eastmancolor); ed, Henry Richardson; m, Harry Robinson.

(PR:C  MPAA:NR)

## GHOULIES*

(1985) 84m Empire c

Peter Liapis (Jonathan Graves), Lisa Pelikan (Rebecca), Michael Des Barres (Malcolm Graves), Jack Nance (Wolfgang), Peter Risch (Grizzel), Tamara De Treaux (Greedigut), Scott Thomson (Mike), Ralph Seymour (Mark, Toad Boy), Mariska Hargitay (Donna), Keith Joe Dick (Dick), David Dayan (Eddie), Victoria Catlin (Anastasia), Charene Cathleen (Robin), Bobbi Bresee (Temptress).

To capitalize on the success of GREMLINS—which featured dozens of crazed puppet-creatures wreaking havoc on a small town—cheapo production house Empire Pictures hustled out this silly horror movie with its own set of evil little creatures. Upon the death of his father, Jonathan Graves (Peter Liapis) inherits the family mansion and decides to live there with his girl friend (Lisa Pelikan). Unbeknownst to Jonathan, his father was a warlock, and, curious about his heritage, the new homeowner begins rummaging around through Dad's possessions. He finds books and notes pertaining to witchcraft and becomes so obsessed with the material that he quits school so that he can have more time to delve into the occult. During one of his incantations, Jonathan conjures up the "ghoulies," devilish little creatures who do his bidding. To increase his power, Jonathan calls together all his friends (one of them is played by Mariska Hargitay, the beautiful daughter of Jayne Mansfield and Mickey Hargitay), and, on the pretense of performing a party trick, has them participate in a satanic ritual. The ritual goes too far and all hell breaks loose, with ghoulies attacking the guests and Jonathan's long-dead father bursting out of his grave. GHOULIES is a fairly unimaginative horror film thrown together just to show off the ghoulie puppets—which aren't very impressive. There are only five different types of ghoulies, and since there seem to be several dozen popping up all over the place it is hard to tell them apart. The ghoulies are supposed to be articulated puppets, but their construction is so crude that they are relegated to peering around corners and from behind chairs, with the puppeteers obviously hiding just behind them. Because of their restricted movements and expressions, we never believe for a moment that the creatures exist, thus making the film an utter failure. One of the now-defunct Empire Pictures' few hits, GHOULIES spawned an even dumber sequel.

p, Jefery Levy; d, Luca Bercovici; w, Luca Bercovici, Jefery Levy; ph, Mac Ahlberg (DeLuxe Color); ed, Ted Nicolaou; m, Richard Band, Shirley Walker.

(PR:O  MPAA:PG-13)

## GHOULIES II*

(1988) 90m Charles Band/Empire c

Damon Martin (Larry), Royal Dano (Uncle Ned), Phil Fondacaro (Sir Nigel), J. Downing (P. Hardin), Kerry Remsen

*(Nicole)*, Dale Wyatt *(Dixie)*, Jon Maynard Pennell *(Bobby)*, Sasha Jensen *(Teddy)*, Starr Andreeff *(Alice)*, William Butler *(Merle)*, Donnie Jeffcoat *(Eddie)*, Christopher Burton *(Leo)*, Mickey Knox *(Ray)*, Romano Puppo *(Zampano)*, Ames Morton *(Patty)*, Michael Deak *(Bozo)*, Anthony Dawson *(Priest)*, Don Hodson *(Barker)*, Carrie Janisse *(Carol)*, Steve Pelot *(Security Guard)*, Larry Dolgin, Mark Peter D'Auria *(Policemen)*, Fidel Bauna *(Hot Dog Vendor)*, Lucilla Potasso *(Bearded Lady)*, Ettore Martini *(Shooting Gallery Owner)*, Maurizio Gaudio *(Operator)*, Fiorella Ceneetti *(Fat Lady)*, Luea Mazzaeurati *(Half & Half)*, Livia Bonelli *(Gene)*.

In this straight-to-home-video sequel to GHOULIES, the badly articulated title puppets—supposed denizens of hell—are kidnaped from a group of satanists by a priest. Although the priest tries to destroy the little demons, he fails and they wind up hiding out in a haunted house called Satan's Den. Part of a traveling carnival, Satan's Den is run by a raving alcoholic (Dano) and his nephew (Martin). Down on their luck and running their exhibit at a loss because kids today are used to graphic gore and not the more genteel scares offered by a simple haunted house, uncle and nephew find their livelihood threatened by a yuppie accountant (Downing) who represents the conglomerate that owns the carnival. If the show doesn't make a profit soon, Satan's Den will be replaced by female mud wrestlers. Things look grim until the ghoulies begin showing themselves to patrons, who mistake the vile little creatures for spectacular special effects. Patrons soon come flocking to Satan's Den for a chance to see them, until the ghoulies begin killing off their public. Certainly no improvement over the original, GHOULIES II instead offers the same dull chills, bad special effects, and juvenile humor that made its predecessor so boring. The low-budget special effects by John Buechler and his team have not improved and, just like last time, the little critters simply aren't up to carrying an entire movie by themselves. The ghoulies are still quite obviously hand-puppets intermingled with some very brief scenes of stop-motion animation done by David Allen Productions. Despite their limited technical ability, the ghoulies do have a sort of shabby charm that might endear them to small children. Unfortunately, the vicious bloodletting and crude sexual innuendo here should preclude viewing of this movie by kids. If scenes of teenagers taunting a dwarf, heavy-metal kids making out in a haunted house, and a ghoulie chewing off the private parts of a yuppie accountant while he sits on a toilet is your idea of a good time, by all means rent GHOULIES II.

p, Albert Band; d, Albert Band; w, Dennis Paoli (based on a story by Charlie Dolan); ph, Sergio Salvati (Technicolor); ed, Barry Zetlin; m, Fuzzbee Morse.

(PR:C-O    MPAA:PG-13)

## GIANT FROM THE UNKNOWN*

(1958) 76m Screencraft/Astor bw

Edward Kemmer *(Wayne Brooks)*, Sally Fraser *(Janet Cleveland)*, Buddy Baer *(Vargcs, the Giant)*, Morris Ankrum *(Prof. Cleveland)*, Bob Steele *(Sheriff Parker)*, Joline Brand *(Ann Brown)*.

An archaeologist (Morris Ankrum) ventures to a remote California village in search of the remains of a legendary Spanish conquistador—said to have been a giant. The professor uncovers the monster (Buddy Baer), who is brought back to life after being struck by lightning. This, of course, sets off another round of murder and pillaging. Produced by Arthur P. Jacobs, who went on to do the "Planet of the Apes" series, this film is a poorly written and badly directed hokey mess. The only points of interest here are makeup man Jack Pierce's work on Baer's grotesque visage and Albert Glasser's interesting score.

p, Arthur P. Jacobs; d, Richard Cunha; w, Frank Hart Taussig, Ralph Brooke; ph, Richard Cunha; m, Albert Glasser.

(PR:A    MPAA:NR)

## GIRLS NIGHT OUT zero

(1984) 96m GK/Aries c (AKA: SCAREMAKER, THE)

Julie Montgomery, James Carroll, Suzanne Barnes, Rutanya Alda, Hal Holbrook, David Holbrook, Lauren-Marie Taylor, Al McGuire, Matthew Dunn, Paul Christie, Richard Bright.

A night of fun for some sorority girls and an escaped mental patient—the killer of a sister who jilted him years before—can only add up to one thing: an hour-and-a-half of tedious mad-slasher movie cliches. It seems the killer did his ex-girl friend in on the evening of a scavenger hunt. This time out, he varies things a bit by stealing the school's bear mascot costume and attaching several knives to one of the paws. The girls start dropping and the cops investigate. Like most local police forces caught in the grip of mad-slasher slayings, they are a bunch of incompetents, so Hal Holbrook, as the original victim's father and head of campus security, goes after the killer. The ending tries for a surprise twist but scarcely succeeds. Most of the college kids are played by actors old enough to be teaching higher education. Holbrook's son began his own acting career with this picture, though it certainly wasn't an auspicious start.

p, Anthony N. Gurvis; d, Robert Deubel; w, Gil Spencer, Jr., Joe Bolster, Kevin Kurgis, Anthony N. Gurvis; ph, Joe Rivers (TVC Color); ed, Arthur Ginsberg.

(PR:O    MPAA:R)

## GIRLS SCHOOL SCREAMERS*

(1986) 85m Bandit/Troma c

Mollie O'Mara *(Jackie/Jennifer)*, Sharon Christopher *(Elizabeth)*, Mari Butler *(Kate)*, Beth O'Malley *(Karen)*, Karen Krevitz *(Susan)*, Marcia Hinton *(Adelle)*, Monica Antonucci *(Rosemary)*, Peter C. Cosimano *(Paul)*, Vera Gallagher *(Sister Urban)*, Charles Braun *(Tyler Wells)*, Tony Manzo *(Dr. Robert Fisher)*, John Turner *(Bruce)*, James Finegan, Sr. *(Paul's Father)*, Jeff Menapace *(Billy the Coma Boy)*, Colleen Harrity *(Sister Mary)*, Eva Keating

McKendrick *(Young Mother Urban)*, John McKeever, Vicki McKeever *(Coma Boy's Parents)*, Daniel J. Keating, Jr. *(Reader of Will)*, Miriam Spiller *(Sister Agnes)*, Kim Robinson *(Candy Striper)*.

This dull—even by Troma standards—haunted-house epic employs the done-to-death TEN LITTLE INDIANS formula, by which a houseful of characters disappear one by one. When it is learned that a recently deceased millionaire has left his estate to a local Philadelphia girls' college, an instructor and seven of her most trusted students are dispatched to the mansion to catalog the estate. The place is filled with valuable old statues and other priceless works of art, and they spend much of the day taking inventory. That evening, their instructor falls ill, and the girls take the opportunity to roam the dark hallways of the mansion. Of course, as the evening progresses, they disappear one by one and are murdered. As it turns out, one of the survivors (Mollie O'Mara) is the reincarnation of the dead millionaire's niece. The niece was killed in the mansion in 1939 when she spurned the advances of her amorous uncle, and her spirit has come back seeking revenge. Terribly tedious, GIRLS SCHOOL SCREAMERS offers nothing in the way of chills, and, in fact, offers little in the area of basic technical competence. Slapdash direction, production values, and performances are the order of the day here, but even these could be overcome if the script had an inkling of creative energy. Unfortunately, the script is the film's most major flaw and its lameness permeates the rest of the movie.

p, John P. Finegan, Pierce J. Keating, James W. Finegan; d, John P. Finegan; w, John P. Finegan (based on a story by John P. Finegan, Katie Keating, Pierce Keating); ph, Albert R. Jordan (DuArt color); ed, Thomas R. Rondinella; m, John Hodian.

(PR:O  MPAA:R)

## GODSEND, THE*

(1980, Can.) 90m Cannon c

Cyd Hayman *(Kate Marlowe)*, Malcolm Stoddard *(Alan Marlowe)*, Angela Pleasence *(Stranger)*, Patrick Barr *(Dr. Collins)*, Wilhelimina Green, Lee Gregory, Joanne Boorman.

Kate and Alan Marlowe (Cyd Hayman and Malcolm Stoddard) have a new arrival in the house, and the kid is a little demon. Seems its real mom (Angela Pleasence) dropped by the house, had a baby, and left before dawn. So, being the nice movie couple they are, Kate and Alan decide to adopt it. The baby is an albino but is by no means pure as snow; somehow, she's responsible for the death of the couple's four natural children, Kate's miscarriage, and Alan's mumps, which render him sterile. Although the film is directed by a woman, there is little difference between this and any other lame rip-off of THE OMEN. Well, maybe one difference. This one's duller than most.

p, Gabrielle Beaumont; d, Gabrielle Beaumont; w, Olaf Pooley (based on the novel by Bernard Taylor); ph, Norman Warwick; ed, Michael Ellis; m, Roger Webb.

(PR:O  MPAA:R)

## GOLEM, THE****

(1920, Ger.) 118m UFA bw (DER GOLEM: WIE ER IN DE WELT; AKA: THE GOLEM: HOW HE CAME INTO THE WORLD)

Paul Wegener *(The Golem)*, Albert Steinruck *(Rabbi Loew)*, Ernest Deutsch *(Famulus)*, Lyda Salmonova *(Rabbi's Daughter)*, Hans Strum *(Emperor Rudolf II)*, Fritz Feld *(Jester)*, Lathar Menthel *(Knight Florian)*.

A pivotal work of German cinema and of the horror genre, THE GOLEM is a film of history, myth, and legend that also played an important part in film's future. Upon receiving news that the tyrannical Emperor of Hapsburg (Hans Strum) plans to drive the Jews from their Prague ghetto, Rabbi Loew (Albert Steinruck) conjures up a protector for his oppressed people—the Golem (Paul Wegener), a huge creature molded from clay and given life through a mystic ritual. The Rabbi, with the creature under his control, takes a trip to the Emperor's castle and, after letting the destructive Golem show his physical strength, persuades the Emperor to reverse his decree. When the Golem, who now desires more out of life than simply to be the Rabbi's servant, falls in love with the Rabbi's daughter (Lyda Salmonova), he must fight against his creator for the right to exist. This was the third time (after versions in 1914 and 1917) that Paul Wegener had brought the Golem to the screen, each time casting himself in the lead. His superb performance (a model for Karloff's Frankenstein), the photography of the legendary Karl Freund, and the masterful set design of Hans Poelzig, who reconstructed a portion of old Prague in the UFA studios, helped make this a seminal monster film. The videotape version is listed under a variety of running times, ranging anywhere from 70 to 118 minutes.

d, Paul Wegener, Carl Boese; w, Paul Wegener, Henrik Galeen (based on a story by Gustav Meyrink); ph, Karl Freund.

(PR:A  MPAA:NR)

## GORGON, THE***½

(1964, Brit.) 83m Hammer/COL c

Peter Cushing *(Namaroff)*, Christopher Lee *(Meister)*, Richard Pasco *(Paul)*, Barbara Shelly *(Carla)*, Michael Goodliffe *(Heitz)*, Patrick Troughton *(Kanof)*, Jack Watson *(Eatoff)*, Jeremy Longhurst *(Bruno)*, Toni Gilpin *(Sascha)*, Redmond Phillips *(Hans)*, Joseph O'Conor *(Coroner)*, Alister Williamson *(Cass)*, Michael Peake *(Policeman)*, Sally Nesbitt *(Nurse)*, Prudence Hyman *(Chatelaine)*.

One of director Terence Fisher's most atmospheric films and one of his personal favorites, THE GORGON, set in Austria circa 1910, opens as a professor ventures to the mysterious town of Vandorf to investigate the suicide of his youngest son. Given the cold shoulder by the police, citizens, and local surgeon Namaroff (Peter Cushing), the professor enters the ruins of a local castle, where he encounters Megaera—the legendary Gorgon whose gaze turns men to stone. Afflicted, but still alive, the professor manages to warn his eldest son, Paul (Richard Pasco), about the Gorgon before dying. Paul continues his investigation, accompanied by his mentor, the skeptical Prof. Meister (Christopher Lee). The duo attempt to interview Namaroff, but are rebuffed. This makes Meister suspicious, while Paul is quite taken with Namaroff's beautiful assistant, Carla (Barbara Shelley). Although Paul falls in love with Carla, Meister remains distrustful of the girl, and when he manages to sneak a look at Namaroff's papers he learns that Carla—an amnesiac—is actually the Gorgon. Knowing that Paul and Carla have arranged to meet at the ruins, Meister rushes to the site to prevent his pupil from being turned to stone. Although the Gorgon itself is kept off-screen through most of the movie and once revealed, is somewhat disappointing (the snakes in the hair aren't very convincing), Fisher imbues his film with a sense of deep guilt, unease, and dread that is palpable. Both Lee and (especially) Cushing turn in fine performances, as does the beautiful Shelley as the young woman unknowingly possessed by the spirit of the mythological Gorgon.

p, Anthony Nelson Keys; d, Terence Fisher; w, John Gilling (based on a story by J. Liewellyn Devine); ph, Michael Reed (Technicolor); ed, James Needs; m, James Bernard.

(PR:A   MPAA:NR)

## GOTHIC*½

(1987, Brit.) 90m Virgin Vision/Virgin Films c

Gabriel Byrne (Lord Byron), Julian Sands (Percy Bysshe Shelley), Natasha Richardson (Mary Godwin), Myriam Cyr (Claire Clairmont), Timothy Spall (Dr. John Polidori), Andreas Wisniewski (Fletcher), Alec Mango (Murray), Dexter Fletcher (Rushton), Pascal King (Justice), Tom Hickey (Tour Guide), Linda Coggin (Turkish Mechanical Doll), Kristine Landon-Smith (Mechanical Woman), Chris Chappell (Man in Armour), Mark Pickard (Young William), Kiran Shah (Fuseli Monster), Christine Newby, Kim Tillesley (Shelley Fans).

At a Swiss villa on the night of June 16, 1816, Lord Byron (Gabriel Byrne); Percy Bysshe Shelley (Julian Sands); his 19-year-old mistress, Mary Wollstonecraft Godwin (soon to be Shelley) (Natasha Richardson); her half-sister, Claire Clairmont; and Byron's personal physician, Dr. John Polidori, gathered to invent ghost stories. That evening, two classics of gothic horror literature were born: Mary Shelley's Frankenstein and Polidori's The Vampyre, the latter an influential precursor to Bram Stoker's Dracula. In GOTHIC, this historic occasion is transformed into a deranged sex-and-blood orgy of cinematic excess by the Bacchus of filmmaking himself, Ken Russell, who takes an interesting premise and creates a film that plays more like a 1960s drug-trip romp (complete with bisexuality, homosexuality, incest, miscarriages, and suicide) than a gothic horror story. GOTHIC is a frustrating film, its premise is so full of compelling potential that Russell's subsequent mindless pretensions and wanton decadence serve only to annoy and anger. To be sure, the bizarre, tortured lives of those involved make for some perversely fascinating dramatics, but Russell presents his Romantics as if they were escapees from the local asylum. To his credit, he does manage to present some memorable horrific images, including a hallucinogenic vision in which a woman's nipples are transformed into eyeballs. Although Russell keeps the parade of vulgar images coming at a furious pace, GOTHIC becomes boring, excessive, and repetitive, leaving the viewer hoping that Mary Shelley will wake up and write a lot sooner than she finally does.

p, Penny Corke; d, Ken Russell; w, Stephen Volk; ph, Mike Southon (Eastmancolor); ed, Michael Bradsell; m, Thomas Dolby.

(PR:O   MPAA:R)

## GRADUATION DAY zero

(1981) 85m IFI/Scope III c

Christopher George (Coach George Michaels), Patch MacKenzie (Anne Ramshead), E. Danny Murphy (Kevin), E.J. Peaker (Blondie), Michael Pataki (Guglione), Virgil Frye (MacGregor), Carmen Argenziano (Halliday), Denise Cheshire (Sally), Linnea Quigley (Dolores), Hal Bokar (Ronald Corliss), Beverly Dixon (Elaine Ramshead), Richard Blaine (Roberts), Karen Abbott (Joanne), Billy Hufsey (Tony), Carl Rey (Ralph), Vanna White (Doris), Erica Hope (Diane), Ruth Ann Llorens (Laura Ramshead), Tom Hintnaus (Pete), Aaron Butler (Photographer), Viola Kates Stimpson (Mrs. Badger), Patrick White (Truck Driver), Grant Loud (Singer).

Scanning the list of available special days upon which to base an entire slasher movie (as in HALLOWEEN; MY BLOODY VALENTINE; MOTHER'S DAY; PROM NIGHT; NEW YEAR'S EVIL; BLOODY BIRTHDAY, etc., etc.), the best the producers of this film could come up with was GRADUATION DAY. Wholly derivative and uninspired, this is just another slice-and-dice film, with the members of a high-school track team killed off one by one in a variety of fiendish and gross ways, including a scene in which a clod pole vaults into a bed of spikes. The main suspects include the track coach (Christopher George) and the school principal (Michael Pataki). The only reasons to watch GRADUATION DAY are to see current horror movie queen Linnea Quigley (RETURN OF THE LIVING DEAD; HOLLYWOOD CHAINSAW HOOKERS) very, very early in her career and, more important, to get a glimpse of "Wheel of Fortune" megastar Vanna White—in the days before she landed that nifty job turning letters and had to make a living doing things like posing in see-through lingerie and wandering through splatter movies. That Hollywood sure is a rough town.

p, David Baughn, Herb Freed; d, Herb Freed; w, Anne Marisse, Herb Freed; ph, Daniel Yarussi; ed, Martin Jay Sadoff.

(PR:O   MPAA:R)

## GRAVE OF THE VAMPIRE**½

(1972) 95m Entertainment Pyramid c (AKA: SEED OF TERROR)

William Smith (James Eastman), Michael Pataki (Caleb Croft/Prof. Lockwwod), Lynn Peters (Anne Arthur), Diane Holden (Anita Jacoby), Jay Adler (Zack), Kitty Vallacher

(Leslie), Jay Scott (Paul), Lieux Dressler (Olga), Carmen Argenziano (Sam), William Guhl (Duffy), Abbi Henderson (Carol), Eric Mason (Panzer), Inga Neilsen (Tex), Margaret Fairchild (Fenwick), Frank Whiteman (Brian), Lindus Guiness (Cook).

Perverse and bizarre without being terribly bloody, this picture features Michael Pataki as a vampire who rises from the grave, accosts a couple making out in the cemetery, breaks the man's back on a tombstone, and drags the girl (Kitty Vallacher) into an open grave, where he rapes her. The now-insane woman is impregnated and has a male vampire baby, which drinks her blood out of a bottle until she finally dies of anemia. Later, the grown-up offspring, James (William Smith), is reluctant to do what his heritage commands and decides to kill his old man, who is teaching occultism at a university. Only half-vampire, James can survive on small amounts of blood and can even venture out into the sunlight for short periods of time. Father and son play a cat-and-mouse game with each other, until the incredibly brutal climax, when they go at each other with no holds barred. Although crudely put together, this is an interesting departure from standard vampire tales, with plenty of unexpected curves in the narrative to keep the viewer off guard. While some sources and advertising ad mats for the film list it as being "R"-rated, the MPAA rating directory lists it as "PG"—something of a surprise considering the opening rape and the intensity of the climactic battle.

p, Daniel Cady; d, John Hayes; w, Patrick Hayes, David Chase (based on the novel The Still Life by Chase); ph, Paul Hipp; ed, Ron Johnson.

(PR:O   MPAA:PG)

## GRAVEYARD SHIFT**

(1987) 88m Cinema Ventures-Lightshow/Shapiro c

Silvio Oliviero (Stephen Tsepes), Helen Papas (Michelle), Cliff Stoker (Eric Hayden), Dorin Ferber (Gilda), Dan Rose, Don Jones.

Made in Toronto, this film features Silvio Oliviero as Stephen Tsepes, a 350-year-old vampire who drives a cab in what is supposed to be New York. Michelle (Helen Papas) is a video director who is estranged from her husband (Cliff Stoker) and who learns that she doesn't have long to live. Looking for a last passionate sexual fling, she meets Tsepes and makes love with him in what she thinks will be a one-night stand. Instead, he turns her into a vampire, and since she was about to die anyway, she rather welcomes her initiation into the society of the undead, jumping into her new role with gusto. Her husband, however, doesn't care for the proceedings, and employs a vampire killer to knock off the blood-sucking cabbie and get his wife back. A fairly stylish combination of erotica and gore, this film seems to be designed as a calling card to the industry by director Gerard Ciccoritti. Although the film has all the right elements for current commercial appeal, Ciccoritti seems to have a bit more on his mind, using the horror genre to explore modern dating rituals and life in New York City. While his thematics aren't fully developed, he does show

interest in doing more than just grossing out his audience. Although shot with plenty of graphic gore, the film had to trimmed to avoid an "X"-rating.

p, Michael Bockner; d, Gerard Ciccoritti; w, Gerard Ciccoritti; ph, Robert Bergman; ed, Robert Bergman, Norman Smith; m, Nicholas Pike.

(PR:O   MPAA:R)

## GREAT ALLIGATOR, THE zero

(1980, It.) 90m c (IL FIUME DEL GRANDE CAIMANO)

Mel Ferrer, Barbara Bach, Richard Johnson, Claudio Cassinelli, Romano Puppo, Fabrizio Castagnoli, Enzo Fizichella.

Made by the same cast and crew that created that reprehensible rip-off SCREAMERS ("See a Man Turned Inside-Out!" Yeah, sure . . .), this JAWS-inspired effort bypassed American distribution entirely and went straight to network television, pay cable, and home video. Set in an African resort recently built by insensitive developer Mel Ferrer, the story concerns a giant alligator worshipped as a god by the local natives. Of course, the monster begins stomping around the new resort, and it is up to two tourists (Barbara Bach and Claudio Cassinelli) to defeat the monster. Not only is this movie laughably cheap, it's unforgivably racist as well, playing on white people's fears of black rituals, magic, and sexuality for its real scares.

p, Lawrence Martin; d, Sergio Martino; w, Sergio Martino, Ernesto Gastaldi, Cesare Frugoni; ph, Giancarlo Ferrando.

(PR:O   MPAA:NR)

## GREAT GABBO, THE***

(1929) 71m Sono-Ait World Wide bw

Erich von Stroheim (Great Gabbo), Betty Compson (Mary), Don Douglas (Frank), Marjorie King (Babe), Otto Gabbo (A dummy), Helen Kane.

This bizarre, often unintentionally funny, and very campy film casts Erich von Stroheim, in his first talkie performance, as The Great Gabbo, a half-crazy ventriloquist who is losing his personality to his own dummy, Otto, while punishing his pretty assistant, Mary (Betty Compson), for imagined wrongs. Gabbo becomes so jealous of his helper that he drives her from his side, the dummy actually insulting her and heaping so much abuse on her head that she quits the act, even though she loves Gabbo. The ventriloquist loses his identity to the dummy altogether and goes berserk at the end, smashing the dearest thing to his heart, Otto, the wooden extension of his personality. Poorly produced, with a grainy texture and erratic sound—talkies were then in the experimental stage—THE GREAT GABBO is fascinating merely for von Stroheim's presence. He does the best he can with the improbable story, which is awkwardly directed by James Cruze, a one-time famous silent screen helmsman who failed to make the transition to talkies. It's crude and disjointed, but there are such priceless scenes as the one in which von Stroheim sings with his dummy onstage. Some absurd attempts at dance numbers are made, including one maniacal routine titled "The Web of Love," showing scantily clad chorines trapped and writhing in a massive cobweb controlled by an actor dressed in a loose-fitting wild spider costume. To those still responding to the magic name of von Stroheim, a name of great importance during the silent era, the film was a let-down, offering only another "crazy artist" story. Von Stroheim did the film because he was desperate for money and later hated the role, coming to believe it symbolized his own crackup and failure. He tried to buy the rights to the film years later, presumably to destroy all the prints, but found that someone else had purchased the property—a real-life ventriloquist named Edgar Bergen.

p, James Cruze; d, James Cruze; w, Hugh Herbert (based on the story "The Rival Dummy" by Ben Hecht); ph, Ira Morgan.

(PR:A  MPAA:NR)

## GREMLINS**½

(1984) 111m WB c

Zach Galligan (Billy), Phoebe Cates (Kate), Hoyt Axton (Rand Peltzer), Frances Lee McCain (Lynn Peltzer), Polly Holiday (Mrs. Deagle), Keye Luke (Grandfather), John Louie (Chinese Boy), Dick Miller (Mr. Futterman), Jackie Joseph (Mrs. Futterman), Scott Brady (Sheriff Frank), Harry Carey, Jr. (Mr. Anderson), Don Steele (Rockin' Ricky Rialto), Corey Feldman (Pete), Arnie Moore (Pete's Father), Glynn Turman (Roy Hanson), Belinda Balaski (Mrs. Harris), Judge Reinhold (Gerald), Jonathan Banks (Deputy Brent), Joe Brooks (Santa), Edward Andrews (Mr. Corben), Chuck Jones (Mr. Jones), Kenny Davis (Dorry), Jim McKrell (Lew Landers), Susan Burgess (Little Girl), John C. Becher (Dr. Molinaro), Gwen Willson (Mrs. Molinaro).

Teenager Billy Peltzer (Zach Galligan) receives an unusual Christmas gift from his father (Hoyt Axton): a cute little furry creature called a "mogwai." There are three warnings concerning the care of the creature: Never get it wet, never let it into the sunlight, and never feed it after midnight, no matter how much it whines. Everyone marvels at the unusual little mogwai but, of course, the rules are soon broken and the cute creature gives birth to dozens of little mogwais, which then evolve into gremlins—totally repugnant, evil, lizard-like creatures that set about destroying the entire town. Yes, Joe Dante gleefully trashes cliches and sentimental Capraesque notions, totally subverting executive producer Steven Spielberg's more cuddly instincts—something Tobe Hooper failed to do in POLTERGEIST—but one should not forget that this movie was given a "PG" rating and cynically aimed to draw an audience of small children who would no doubt be terrorized by this myth-shattering film. While Dante's manipulation of Spielbergian conventions may thrill those bored by Sir Steven's suburban fantasies, that doesn't excuse the fact that both men failed to demonstrate any sensitivity toward the minds of those to whom this film was sold. The MPAA, which rated the film "PG" because Spielberg's name was on it, also should share the blame. The justifiable furor over this film and Spielberg's INDIANA JONES AND THE TEMPLE OF DOOM forced the MPAA to create the "PG-13" rating. The

tone of outrage above may appear hypocritical, or at least incongruous, in a book devoted to films depicting the macabre, grotesque, and gory, but most of the films detailed here were not aimed at small children. GREMLINS was, and should be judged accordingly.

p, Michael Finnell; d, Joe Dante; w, Chris Columbus; ph, John Hora (Technicolor); ed, Tina Hirsch; m, Jerry Goldsmith.

(PR:O  MPAA:PG)

## GRIM REAPER, THE zero

(1981, It.) 81m c (AKA: ANTHROPOPHAGOUS)

Tisa Farrow (Julie), Saverio Vallane, Vanessa Steiger, Luigi Montefiori, Zora Kerova, Mark Bodin, Bob Larsen, Mark Logan, Rubina Rey, Margaret Donnelly.

This low-budget Italian shocker which stars Tisa Farrow (sister of Mia and star of Lucio Fulci's ZOMBIE) as an American student vacationing in the Greek isles. The young woman watches in horror as all the nice student tourists she's traveling with are killed and eaten by a nut case (Luigi Montefiori) with bad skin who somehow thinks he's getting revenge for the deaths of his wife and child during a shipwreck, even though he's the guy who killed and ate them. The effects are gory, the creep's makeup laughable, and the photography incredibly muddy. Director Joe D'Amato [Aristide Massaccesi] is better known for his sexploitation movies featuring Laura Gemser.

p, Oscar Santaniello; d, Aristide Massaccesi; w, Luigi Montefiori, Aristide Massaccesi; ph, Enrico Birbichi; ed, Ornella Michell.

(PR:O  MPAA:R)

## GRIZZLY*½

(1976) 90m Film Ventures c (AKA: KILLER GRIZZLY)

Christopher George (The Ranger), Richard Jaeckel (The Naturalist), Andrew Prine (The Helicopter Pilot), Joan McCall (The Photographer), Joseph Dorsey (The Park Supervisor), Maryann Hearn (A Victim), Charles Kissinger (Doctor), Kermit Echols (Corwin).

Film Ventures International (FVI) specialized in turning out cheap imitations based on big blockbusters. When THE EXORCIST came out, FVI followed it with BEYOND THE DOOR, and while JAWS was a number one money-grosser they came out with this film, replacing the shark with a 15-foot bear. The meager plot follows the bear as he lumbers about slicing up tourists—and not to get their picnic baskets—pursued by a heroic forest ranger (Christopher George) and a naturalist (Richard Jaeckel). The bear manages to stay one paw ahead of the search team for most of the film, poking his muzzle out only long enough to chew up Jaeckel and Andrew Prine before he is blown to pieces by George. George, Jaeckel and Prine would star in another nature-gone-mad movie, DAY OF THE ANIMALS, the next year.

p, David Sheldon, Harvey Flaxman; d, William Girdler; w,

David Sheldon, Harvey Flaxman; ph, William Anderson (Todd-AO, Movielab Color); m, Robert O. Ragland.

(PR:C  MPAA:PG)

## GRUESOME TWOSOME*½

(1968) 72m Mayflower c

Elizabeth Davis *(Mrs. Pringle)*, Chris Martell *(Her Son)*, Gretchen Welles, Rodney Bedell.

Following his break with producer David Friedman on COLOR ME BLOOD RED (1965), H.G. Lewis took a brief hiatus from gore, making the children's films (!) JIMMY, THE BOY WONDER and SANTA VISITS THE MAGIC LAND OF MOTHER GOOSE, and a few sexploitation epics, ALLEY TRAMP; SUBURBAN ROULETTE; THE GIRL, THE BODY, AND THE PILL; BLAST-OFF GIRLS. In 1967, Lewis returned to gore with a vengeance, making SOMETHING WEIRD; A TASTE OF BLOOD; and GRUESOME TWOSOME in quick succession. While SOMETHING WEIRD combines ESP, the supernatural, and international spy rings, and A TASTE OF BLOOD is a vampire epic, GRUESOME TWOSOME is more akin to BLOOD FEAST, this time with a more obvious sense of black humor. Set in a major city, the film follows a demented old woman, Mrs. Pringle, who owns a building that houses both her residence and a wig shop. The old woman rents out spare rooms to boarders—usually beautiful young women—and her son, a murderous imbecile, kills the girls, scalps them, and gives the hair to his mother for use in wigs. From the opening, which shows two styrofoam wig-heads with cartoonish cut-paper facial features having a conversation, GRUESOME TWOSOME heralds itself as a comedy, but the gore Lewis presents here—scalpings, throats cut with electric knives, disembowelments—is some of the most disturbingly realistic of his career, a trend that would reach its apex with THE WIZARD OF GORE (1970).

p, Herschell Gordon Lewis; d, Herschell Gordon Lewis; w, Allison Louise Downe; m, Larry Wellington.

(PR:O  MPAA:NR)

# H

## HALLOWEEN****

(1978) 93m Falcon/Compass c

Donald Pleasence *(Loomis)*, Jamie Lee Curtis *(Laurie)*, Nancy Loomis *(Annie)*, P.J. Soles *(Lynda)*, Charles Cyphers *(Brackett)*, Kyle Richards *(Lindsey)*, Brian Andrews *(Tommy)*, John Michael Graham *(Bob)*, Nancy Stephens *(Marion)*, Arthur Malet *(Graveyard Keeper)*, Mickey Yablans *(Richie)*, Brent LePage *(Lonnie)*, Adam Hollander *(Keith)*, Robert Phalen *(Dr. Wynn)*, Tony Moran *(Michael at 23)*, Will Sandin *(Michael at 6)*, Sandy Johnson *(Judith)*, David Kyle *(Boyfriend)*, Peter Griffith *(Laurie's Father)*, Jim Windburn *(Stunt)*, Nick Castle *(The Shape)*.

The most influential horror film of the last 15 years, HALLOWEEN spawned dozens of imitations—none of which matched director John Carpenter's skillful control of the film frame. The story: on Halloween night, 1963, a six-year-old boy stabs his sister and her boy friend to death while they are making love. He's put away in a mental institution—until, exactly 15 years later, he escapes and returns to his small Illinois hometown to once more wreak Halloween havoc, with his doctor, Loomis (Donald Pleasence), in hot pursuit. HALLOWEEN was the surprise hit of the 1978 Chicago Film Festival and critics were full of praise for the film, comparing it with Hitchcock's classic PSYCHO (which starred Jamie Lee Curtis' mother, Janet Leigh). Unfortunately, this film simply doesn't have the intelligence, wit, or resonance of Hitchcock's classic. It does, however, share a mastery of the visual aspects of the medium (few share the brilliant use of the wide-screen frame), making Carpenter one of the most interesting directors to *watch* in the last decade—if not to *think* about. From the opening, which is a lengthy steadicam point-of-view shot seen from beneath a Halloween mask, to the climactic battle in which Curtis fends off the maniac time after time, only to have him rise again, Carpenter proves himself to be a wizard of cinematic manipulation. A low-budget film, HALLOWEEN grossed well over $50 million on its initial release, thus making it the single most successful independent feature of all time. Two sequels, both produced by Carpenter, were woefully inferior to the original, but a third—released in 1988—was actually much better than those which preceded it.

p, Debra Hill; d, John Carpenter; w, Debra Hill, John Carpenter; ph, Dean Cundey (Panavision, Metrocolor); ed, Tommy Lee Wallace, Charles Burnstein; m, John Carpenter.

(PR:O  MPAA:R)

## HALLOWEEN II**

(1981) 92m DD/UNIV c

Jamie Lee Curtis *(Laurie)*, Donald Pleasence *(Sam Loomis)*, Charles Cyphers *(Leigh)*, Jeffrey Kramer *(Graham)*, Lance Guest *(Jimmy)*, Pamela Susan Shoop *(Karen)*, Hunter Von Leer *(Gary)*, Dick Warlock *(The Shape)*, Leo Rossi *(Budd)*, Gloria Gifford *(Mrs. Alves)*, Tawny Moyer *(Jill)*, Ana Alicia *(Janet)*, Ford Rainey *(Dr. Mixter)*, Cliff Emmich *(Garrett)*, Nancy Stephens *(Marion)*, John Zenda *(Marshall)*, Catherine Bergstrom *(Producer)*, Alan Haufrect *(Announcer)*, Lucille Bensen *(Mrs. Elrod)*, Bill Warlock *(Craig)*, Jonathan Prince *(Randy)*.

Debra Hill and John Carpenter produced and wrote the screenplay, but this is still a totally unnecessary and extremely poor sequel to the original HALLOWEEN. Although Dean Cundey's photography goes a long way toward recapturing the look of the first film, director Rick Rosenthal is no Carpenter, and the emphasis here is on graphic blood and gore rather than the skillful manipulation of the audience. Picking up minutes after the last film left off, HALLOWEEN II finds the lone survivor, Laurie (Jamie Lee Curtis) being taken to a local hospital to recover from shock. The killer, Michael Myers, eludes police and hunts her down, slaughtering a bevy of nurses and doctors before Dr. Loomis (Donald Pleasence) catches up to him for an apocalyptic showdown. Rosenthal later claimed that Carpenter came in at the end of the shooting and personally directed some gore sequences, though crew members say this was done to salvage the mess Rosenthal had created. Carpenter himself kept entirely mum on the subject until recently, claiming that he had always resisted the efforts of partners Hill, Moustapha Akkad, and Irwin Yablans to involve him in the sequels, but was always "suckered in at the last minute" (*Fangoria*, No. 78). Ironically, by the time he did manage to fend them off successfully for HALLOWEEN IV, that film turned out to be the best sequel of the entire series.

p, Debra Hill, John Carpenter; d, Rick Rosenthal; w, John Carpenter, Debra Hill; ph, Dean Cundey (Panavision, Metrocolor), John Carpenter, Alan Howarth; ed, Mark Goldblatt, Skip Schoolnik.

**(PR:O  MPAA:R)**

## HALLOWEEN III: SEASON OF THE WITCH**½

(1982) 96m UNIV c

Tom Atkins *(Dr. Challis)*, Stacey Nelkia *(Ellie)*, Dan O'Herlihy *(Conal)*, Ralph Strait *(Buddy)*, Michael Currie *(Rafferty)*, Jadeen Barbor *(Betty)*, Bradley Schachter *(Little Buddy)*, Garn Stephens *(Marge)*, Nancy Kyes *(Linda)*, Jonathan Terry *(Starker)*, Patrick Pankurst *(Technician)*, Al Berry *(Harry)*, Wendy Wessberg *(Teddy)*, Dick Warlock *(Assassin)*, Norman Merrill *(Red)*, Michelle Walker *(Bella)*, Joshua Miller *(Willie)*, Essex Smith *(Jones)*, Martin Cassidy *(Watcher)*, Maidie Norman *(Nurse)*, John MacBride *(Sheriff)*, Loyd Catlett *(Charlie)*, Paddie Edwards *(Secretary)*, Jeffrey D. Henry, Michael W. Green *(Technicians)*.

Though the name's the same (as are some of the production credits) this film has nothing to do with its predecessors, for John Carpenter pushed to try something completely different. The mad slasher has been replaced by Conal (Dan O'Herlihy), an Irish mad scientist-mask maker who abhors the commercialization of Halloween and wants to return the holiday to its satanic origins. To do this, he cleverly markets a series of rubber Halloween masks that all the kiddies throughout America will be clamoring for, and implants each one with a microchip that will be activated by a television commercial for the masks broadcast on Halloween night—thus killing the children. The script was originally penned by respected British science-fiction writer Nigel Kneale (author of the excellent "Quatermass" series and a personal favorite of Carpenter's), but, dismayed by director Tommy Lee Wallace's haphazard realization of his work, he sued to have his name removed from the credits. While it certainly isn't awful, the film can't really make up its mind: does it want to be a "fun" little piece full of black humor, or does it want to go the usual blood-and-gore route? The end result was the alienation of the loyal public, who went in expecting to see another Michael Myers movie and got Dan O'Herlihy instead. Although the film made money, the producers waited a few

years and then returned to the familiar formula.

p, John Carpenter, Debra Hill; d, Tommy Lee Wallace; w, Tommy Lee Wallace; ph, Dean Cundey (Panavision, Technicolor); ed, Millie Moore; m, John Carpenter, Alan Howarth.

**(PR:O  MPAA:R)**

## HALLOWEEN IV: THE RETURN OF MICHAEL MYERS***

(1988) 88m Galaxy c

Donald Pleasence *(Dr. Loomis)*, Ellie Cornell *(Rachel Carruthers)*, Danielle Harris *(Jamie Lloyd)*, George P. Wilbur *(Michael Myers)*, Michael Pataki *(Dr. Hoffman)*, Beau Starr *(Sheriff Meeker)*, Kathleen Kinmont *(Kelly)*, Sasha Jenson *(Brady)*, Gene Ross *(Earl)*, Carmen Filpi *(Jack Sayer)*.

The best of the sequels to John Carpenter's seminal slasher movie HALLOWEEN, this one hit the screen just in time to celebrate the 10th anniversary of the original. Picking up 10 years after HALLOWEEN II left off, we learn that the infamous "Shape," Michael Myers, has survived the fiery blast that appeared to have killed both him and his perennial pursuer, the slightly mad Dr. Loomis (Donald Pleasence). Having been in a coma all these years, Myers finally comes to, slaughters his handlers, and escapes while being transferred from one federal mental hospital to another. When Loomis—who also survived the blast, with only some facial scars and a limp to show for it—hears the news, he immediately heads for Haddonfield, Illinois, the site of Myers' rampage a decade ago. Knowing that Myers has a grade-school-aged niece (Danielle Harris) in Haddonfield, Loomis assumes that the psychotic killer will go home to finish her off. Although Carpenter has disowned the "Halloween" series and had nothing whatsoever to do with this sequel, HALLOWEEN 4: THE RETURN OF MICHAEL MYERS is easily the best entry since Carpenter's original. Directed with flair by Dwight H. Little (KGB—THE SECRET WAR), who does not blatantly ape Carpenter's style, the movie delivers a number of effective chills without relying too heavily on the kinds of tired tricks and bloody gore that have made this genre a boring cliche. The solid script by Alan B. McElroy takes time to develop its characters, exploits each situation to the fullest, has a fairly complicated structure with several simultaneously running subplots, and taps into childhood fears in the way that made the first film so memorable. Pleasence turns in a delightfully hammy performance as the crazed Dr. Loomis; with his scarred face and painful limp, he has begun to take on the mantle of a modern-day Captain Ahab madly pursuing his white whale. Carpenter, who didn't want to participate in any more HALLOWEEN films and who was forced to divest his financial interest in the series after being threatened with a lawsuit by his partners, Moustapha Akkad, Irwin Yablans, and Debra Hill, didn't want his name on the film, forgoing the credit, "Based on characters created by John Carpenter and Debra Hill." The producers were determined to place Carpenter's name prominently in the credits anyhow, and his name appears by itself on-screen when the HALLOWEEN theme music is credited to him. Despite Carpenter's misgivings,

HALLOWEEN 4 is a worthy successor to his original and nothing to be ashamed of.

p, Paul Freeman; d, Dwight H. Little; w, Alan B. McElroy (based on a story by Dhani Lipsius, Larry Rattner, Benjamin Ruffner and Alan B. McElroy); ph, Peter Collister; ed, Curtiss Clayton; m, Alan Howarth.

**(PR:O   MPAA:R)**

## HAND, THE*½

(1981) 104m Orion/WB c

Michael Caine (Jon Lansdale), Andrea Marcovicci (Anne Lansdale), Annie McEnroe (Stella Roche), Bruce McGill (Brian Ferguson), Viveca Lindfors (Doctress), Rosemary Murphy (Karen Wagner), Mara Hobel (Lizzie Lansdale), Pat Corley (Sheriff), Nicholas Hormann (Bill Richman), Ed Marshall (Doctor), Charles Fleischer (David Maddow), John Stinson (Therapist), Richard Altman (Hammond), Sparky Watt (Sergeant), Tracey Walter (Cop), Brian Kenneth Hume (Boy in Classroom), Lora Pearson (Girl in Classroom), Oliver Stone (Bum), Jack Evans, Scott Evans, Randy Evans, Patrick Evans (Country Bumpkins).

Before adopting the mantle of Hollywood's last angry liberal man, writer-director Oliver Stone (SALVADOR; PLATOON; WALL STREET; TALK RADIO) made this fairly awful horror film—it's a good thing he found his true calling. Poorly adapted from Marc Brandel's The Lizard's Tail, the film follows newspaper cartoonist Jon Lansdale (Michael Caine), whose career and marriage go out the window after an auto accident claims his right hand. Abandoned, alienated, and angry, Lansdale soon discovers that his disembodied hand has returned and is crawling around killing everyone who has done him wrong. Is this merely a psychotic manifestation of Lansdale's rage? Is he, in his madness, pinning his own murders on a disembodied hand only he sees? Or is there really a loose right hand skittering about strangling Lansdale's friends and associates? Don't expect many answers from the movie, for Stone hedges his bets toward the end and vacillates—leaving the whole thing infuriatingly ambiguous. The special effects aren't very good either—in fact they're laughably worse than those in THE BEAST WITH FIVE FINGERS (1946).

p, Edward R. Pressman; d, Oliver Stone; w, Oliver Stone (based on the book The Lizard's Tail by Marc Brandel); ph, King Baggott (Technicolor); ed, Richard Marks; m, James Horner.

**(PR:O   MPAA:R)**

## HANDS OF THE RIPPER****

(1971, Brit.) 85m Hammer/UNIV c

Eric Porter (Dr. John Pritchard), Angharad Rees (Anna), Jane Merrow (Laura), Keith Bell (Michael Pritchard), Derek Godfrey (Dysart), Dora Bryan (Mrs. Golding), Lynda Baron (Long Liz), Marjorie Lawrence (Dolly), Marjorie Rhodes (Mrs. Bryant), Norman Bird (Police Inspector), Margaret Rawlings (Mme. Bullard), Elizabeth MacLennan (Mrs. Wilson), Barry Lowe (Mr. Wilson), A.J. Brown (Rev. Anderson), April Wilding (Catherine), Anne Clune, Vicki Woolf (Cell Whores), Katya Wyeth, Beulah Hughes, Tallulah Miller (Pub Whores), Peter Munt (Pleasants), Philip Ryan (Police Officer), Molly Weir (Maid), Charles Lamb (Guard).

Following TASTE THE BLOOD OF DRACULA (1969), director Peter Sasdy made his last film for Hammer, HANDS OF THE RIPPER, one of that studio's most moody, atmospheric, and haunting releases. Jack the Ripper murders his wife while their three-year-old daughter, Anna, watches. Before leaving, the notorious serial killer embraces his child and kisses her. Fourteen years later, the girl has grown into a beautiful woman (Angharad Rees), but she is forever psychologically scarred by the experience. Whenever Anna's passions are stirred by a demonstration of physical affection—a kiss, an embrace—she falls into a trance and stabs her companion. Anna encounters a Freudian psychiatrist, Dr. John Pritchard (Eric Porter), who is willing to help her overcome her homicidal compulsion, but his repressed attraction to the beautiful girl only spells trouble for them both. Bearing more than a passing resemblance to Michael Powell's masterpiece PEEPING TOM (1960), HANDS OF THE RIPPER is brimming with the same sort of psychosexual-homicidal compulsions—in both cases brought on by a parent's perversion of love. Director Sasdy skillfully manipulates the complicated material, ferreting out the psychological nuances while delivering a suspenseful and exciting film that ends in a breathtaking climax. One of Hammer's best.

p, Aida Young; d, Peter Sasdy; w, L.W. Davidson (based on a story by Edward Spencer Shewl); ph, Kenneth Talbot (Technicolor); m, Christopher Gunning.

**(PR:O   MPAA:R)**

## HAPPY BIRTHDAY TO ME*½

(1981) 108m COL c

Melissa Sue Anderson (Virginia), Glenn Ford (Dr. Faraday), Tracy Bregman (Ann), Jack Blum (Alfred), Matt Craven (Steve), Lenore Zann (Maggie), David Eisner (Rudi), Lisa Langlois (Amelia), Lawrence Dane (Hal), Frances Hyland (Mrs. Patterson), Sharon Acker (Estelle), Michel Rene LaBelle (Etienne), Richard Rabiere (Greg), Lesleh Donaldson (Bernadette), Earl Pennington (Lt. Tracy), Murray Westgate (Gatekeeper), Jerome Tiberghien (Prof. Heregard), Maurice Pedbrey (Dr. Feinblum), Vlasta Vrana (Bartender), Griffith Brewer (Verger), Alan Katz (Ann's Date), Ron Lea (Amelia's Date), Terry Haig (Feinblum's Assistant), Karen Stephen (Miss Calhoun), Louis Del Grande (Surgeon), Nick Kilvertus (Anesthetist), Damir Andrei (Junior Surgeon).

Another dull slasher movie—this one less gory than most—HAPPY BIRTHDAY TO ME is set in an exclusive boarding school, where Virginia ("Little House on the Prairie" star Melissa Sue Anderson) is plagued by the thought that she may be responsible for the horrible murders of her classmates. She turns to a psychiatrist (Glenn Ford) for help, but he's not of much use since his appearance in the film is merely a brief cameo. Director J. Lee Thompson, best known for his seemingly endless series of vigilante films starring Charles Bronson, gives a slick but unimaginative sheen to the familiar proceedings, and does manage to evoke some chills in the climactic scene, when a grotesque birthday party is attended by the corpses of all of Virginia's victims.

p, John Dunning, Andre Link; d, J. Lee Thompson; w, John Saxton, Peter Jobin, Timothy Bond (based on a story by Saxton); ph, Miklos Lente (Metrocolor); ed, Debra Karen; m, Bo Harwood, Lance Rubin.

(PR:O   MPAA:R)

## HATCHET FOR A HONEYMOON**½

(1969, Sp./It.) 83m G.G.P. c (UNA HACKA PARA LA LUNA DE MIEL; IL ROSO SEGMO DELLA POLLIAS; AKA: BLOOD BRIDES)

Stephen Forsyth, Dagmar Lassander, Laura Betti, Gerard Tichy, Luciano Pigozzi, Jesus Puente, Antonia Mas, Femi Benussi, Fortunato Pasquale, Veronica Llimera.

This lesser Mario Bava effort features Stephen Forsyth as a handsome and wealthy, but impotent, fashion designer who can't make love to his wife (Laura Betti). To work through this problem, the designer has taken to murdering young brides with an ax on their wedding night. With each murder, the killer begins piecing together a long-forgotten memory of when, as a child, he witnessed the murder of his own mother. Take a guess as to who killed Mom. Although the plot is predictable and Bava once again overuses the zoom lens, this movie has its moments, including Forsyth's secret room full of mannequins dressed in bridal gowns, and a clip of Bava's own BLACK SABBATH (1963) being shown on television.

p, Manuel Cano Sanciriaco; d, Mario Bava; w, Mario Bava, Santiago Moncada, Mario Musy; ph, Mario Bava, Antonio Rinaldi; ed, Soledad Lopez; m, Sante Romitelli.

(PR:O   MPAA:R)

## HAUNTED*

(1976) 81m Northgate Communications c (AKA: THE HAUNTED)

Aldo Ray (McCloan), Anne Michelle (Jennifer Barnes), Virginia Mayo, Jim Negele.

In 1865, an Indian woman is accused of witchcraft and sent to die in the heat of the Arizona desert. Years later, the area is plagued by a series of mysterious deaths and Jennifer Barnes (Ann Michelle), an English woman, is believed to be the reincarnated ghost of the Indian woman, just now wreaking her revenge on the descendants of those who sentenced her to death 110 years before. A town elder, McCloan (Aldo Ray), decides to stop the terror by killing Jennifer. Pretentious and terribly obtuse, this has all the earmarks of a "serious" film that just happens to have supernatural overtones—please don't call it a "horror movie." Well, that might be a pretty fair request considering there isn't much that's scary here, and aside from some fairly nifty surrealistic images, the film is mostly a confused bore.

p, Michael De Gaetano; d, Michael De Gaetano; w, Michael De Gaetano; ph, W.E. Hines; m, Lor Crane.

(PR:O   MPAA:NR)

## HAUNTED HONEYMOON*½

(1986) 82m Orion c

Gene Wilder (Larry Abbot), Gilda Radner (Vickie Pearle), Dom DeLuise (Aunt Kate), Jonathan Pryce (Charles), Paul Smith (Dr. Paul Abbot), Peter Vaughan (Francis, Sr.), Bryan Pringle (Pfister), Roger Ashton-Griffiths (Francis, Jr.), Jim Carter (Montego), Eve Ferret (Sylvia), Julann Griffin (Nora Abbot), Jo Ross (Susan), Ann Way (Rachel), Will Keaton (Werewolf), Don Fellows (Producer), Lou Hirsch (Sponsor), Christopher Muncke (Announcer), Bill Bailey (The Host), David Healy (Public Relations Man), Howard Swinson (Eddy, SFX Man), Edward Wiley (Engineer), Andrea Browne (Production Assistant), Matt Zimmerman (1st Radio Actor), Sally Osborn (Larry's Mother), Alastair Haley (Little Larry), Scampi (Toby the Dog), Andy Ross (Conductor).

Larry Abbot (Gene Wilder) and Vickie Pearle (Gilda Radner) are the stars of a popular radio show called "Manhattan Mystery Theater," and have just gotten married. Before departing on their honeymoon, Larry and Vickie learn that Larry's elderly aunt (Dom DeLuise in drag) has made him the sole beneficiary of her new will. If he should die, however, the money will be split among the surviving family members. On their honeymoon, Larry and Vickie wind up at Larry's spooky old family mansion and find that many of his greedy relatives have assembled there. During their stay, it becomes apparent that *someone* is trying to kill Larry. An innocuous comedy chiller, HAUNTED HONEYMOON isn't very chilling and, worse yet, isn't very funny. Wilder, in his fourth directorial effort, has an engaging idea here in trying to re-create a style of filmmaking long forgotten. Unfortunately, although filled with the spirit of nostalgia, this sort of film no longer works. Old Abbott and Costello or Hope and Goddard chillers are only fun to watch today because of those stars. They were vehicles, but, all in all, not very good films. HAUNTED HONEYMOON may be paying homage, but the nostalgia is hollow. Why watch Wilder and Radner doing old routines when you can see the real thing? Audiences today have, for better or worse, become far too sophisticated to accept this film's whimsy.

p, Susan Ruskin; d, Gene Wilder; w, Gene Wilder, Terence Marsh; ph, Fred Schuler (DeLuxe Color); ed, Christopher Greenbury; m, John Morris.

(PR:A   MPAA:PG)

## HAUNTED STRANGLER, THE***

(1958, Brit.) 81m Anglo-Amalgamated/MGM bw (GB: GRIP OF THE STRANGLER)

Boris Karloff (James Rankin), Jean Kent (Cora Seth), Elizabeth Allan (Barbara Rankin), Anthony Dawson (Supt. Burk), Vera Day (Pearl), Tim Turner (Kenneth McColl), Diane Aubrey (Lily), Dorothy Gordon (Hannah), Peggy Ann Clifford (Kate), Leslie Perrins (Prison Governor), Michael

Atkinson *(Styles)*, Desmond Roberts *(Dr. Johnson)*, Jessie Cairns *(Maid)*, Roy Russell *(Medical Supt.)*, Derek Birch *(Supt.)*, George Hirste *(Lost Property Man)*, John G. Heller *(Male Nurse)*, George Spence *(Hangman)*, Joan Elvin *(Can-Can Girl)*.

James Rankin (Boris Karloff) is a novelist fascinated by the 20-year-old case of the "Haymarket Strangler." He discovers that Styles, the man executed for the crimes, was really innocent, and that the blame actually belongs with Dr. Tenant, the man who performed the autopsies on the murder victims. Rankin has Styles' grave unearthed and finds the doctor's missing scalpel, the murder weapon. When he picks it up, however, he becomes possessed with the murderous thoughts of the doctor. To his horror, Rankin discovers that *he* is Tenant and that a wave of amnesia had blotted out the last 20 years from his memory. He goes on an uncontrollable spree of bloodshed, picking up where he left off. Although somewhat ineptly directed by Robert Day, the film is still worth seeing for Karloff's wonderfully energetic performance, in which he—when possessed by the spirit of the strangler—closes one eye and bites down hard on his lower lip, totally transforming his face without the use of special makeup. The effect may sound silly, but it actually works!

p, John Croydon; d, Robert Day; w, Jan Read, John C. Cooper (based on a story by Read); ph, Lionel Banes; ed, Peter Mayhew; m, Buxton Orr.

(PR:A-C  MPAA:NR)

## HAUNTING, THE***

(1963) 112m Argyle/MGM bw

Julie Harris *(Eleanor Vance)*, Claire Bloom *(Theodora)*, Richard Johnson *(Dr. John Markway)*, Russ Tamblyn *(Luke Sanderson)*, Lois Maxwell *(Grace Markway)*, Fay Compton *(Mrs. Sanderson)*, Valentine Dyall *(Mr. Dudley)*, Rosalie Crutchley *(Mrs. Dudley)*, Diane Clare *(Carrie Fredericks)*, Ronald Adam *(Eldridge Harper)*, Freda Knorr *(2nd Mrs. Crain)*, Janet Mansell *(Abigail at 6)*, Pamela Buckley *(1st Mrs. Crain)*, Howard Lang *(Hugh Crain)*, Mavis Villiers *(Landlady)*, Verina Greenlaw *(Dora)*, Paul Maxwell *(Bud)*, Claud Jones *(Fat Man)*, Susan Richards *(Nurse)*, Amy Dalby *(Abigail at 80)*, Rosemary Dorken *(Companion)*.

A bit overrated upon its initial release, THE HAUNTING is, nonetheless, undeniably effective and remains one of the best haunted-house movies. Dr. Markway (Richard Johnson) is a professor of anthropology experimenting with ESP and other forms of psychic phenomena. He arrives at Hill House, a New England mansion that is reputed to be crammed with demons and ghosts and the home of everything evil. Along with Markway is Eleanor (Julie Harris), a slim spinster who, until recently, has spent her life caring for her aged mother, and Theodora (Claire Bloom), a lesbian. Both women have experienced extra-sensory occurrences, and Markway has enlisted their aid in his quest for knowledge on the subject. Luke (Russ Tamblyn), who is the heir to the house and who hopes to sell it at a great profit, goes along for a ride he will regret. Once inside, the quartet is besieged by terror—noises, yowls, and eerie

events pour off the screen until Eleanor is convinced that Hill House is alive and wants her to stay there. Director Robert Wise, who began his directorial career under the tutelage of Val Lewton, takes the lessons learned there to a bit of an extreme, overplaying his hand through the use of extremely exaggerated angles and distorting lenses. Modern-day audiences may find all this a little silly, but if one lets the film work—it will. What does not work, however, is the oversimplified and somewhat distasteful notion that Eleanor's repressed lesbianism is the cause of her downfall.

p, Robert Wise; d, Robert Wise; w, Nelson Gidding (based on the novel *The Haunting of Hill House* by Shirley Jackson); ph, Davis Boulton (Panavision); ed, Ernest Walter; m, Humphrey Searle.

(PR:A-C  MPAA:NR)

## HAUNTING OF JULIA, THE**½

(1976, Brit./Can.) 96m Fester/Discovery c (AKA: FULL CIRCLE)

Mia Farrow *(Julia)*, Keir Dullea *(Magnus)*, Tom Conti *(Mark)*, Jill Bennett *(Lily)*, Robin Gammell *(Swift)*, Cathleen Nesbitt *(Mrs. Rudge)*, Anna Wing *(Mrs. Flood)*, Pauline Jameson *(Mrs. Branscombe)*, Peter Sallis *(Branscombe)*, Sophie Ward *(Kate)*, Samantha Gates *(Olivia)*.

Set in London, this lame haunted house effort begins promisingly enough with a truly gruesome scene in which young mother Julia (Mia Farrow) desperately tries to save her choking daughter by performing a tracheotomy with a kitchen knife. It's to no avail, however, and her daughter dies. After getting over a nervous breakdown, Julia leaves her husband (Keir Dullea) and moves into an old, creaky Victorian house where spooky things happen. Her husband is found in the basement with his throat slit. Her boy friend (Tom Conti) is electrocuted in the bathtub. Is Julia committing the murders, or is it the ghostly child who was murdered near the house 30 years ago? Filmed and released in England in 1976 as FULL CIRCLE, this movie flopped badly and went unreleased Stateside until 1981, when it was unveiled under a new title and flopped again. Given the slick-but-mundane directorial treatment by Richard Loncraine, the film sort of sputters along, becoming more and more confusing until one really doesn't care how it all turns out. Once again a work by Peter Straub is poorly adapted to the big screen.

p, Peter Fetterman, Alfred Pariser; d, Richard Loncraine; w, Dave Humphries, Harry Bromley Davenport (based on the novel *Julia* by Peter Straub); ph, Peter Hannon (Panavision, Eastmancolor); ed, Ron Wisman; m, Colin Towns.

(PR:O  MPAA:R)

## HAUNTS zero

(1977) 98m Intercontinental c (AKA: THE VEIL)

May Britt *(Ingred)*, Aldo Ray *(Sheriff)*, Cameron Mitchell *(Carl)*, William Gray Espy *(Frankie)*, Susan Nohr *(Nel)*, Ben

Hammer *(Vicar)*, E.J. Andre *(Doc)*, Kendall Jackson *(Loretta)*.

A laughable low-budget effort, HAUNTS posits a small town plagued by an unknown serial killer who is hacking up the local girls with a pair of scissors. Meanwhile, at a remote farmhouse, Ingrid (May Britt) believes that her uncle (Cameron Mitchell) is the one committing the killings. But Ingrid believes a lot of things—including that she was once raped by the family goat. You see, Ingrid is sexually repressed and her frustrations are making her a bit loony. This is almost worth sitting through to see Aldo Ray, as the town's good-for-nothing drunken sheriff, retch over a toilet bowl, and to see Mitchell's hair change color from scene to scene.

p, Herb Freed, Burt Weissbourd; d, Herb Freed; w, Herb Freed, Anne Marisse; ph, Larry Secrist (Eastmancolor).

**(PR:O   MPAA:PG)**

## HE KNOWS YOU'RE ALONE*

(1980) 92m Lansbury-Beruh/MGM-UA c

Don Scardino *(Marvin)*, Caitlin O'Heaney *(Amy)*, Elizabeth Kemp *(Nancy)*, Tom Rolfing *(Killer)*, Lewis Arlt *(Gamble)*, Patsy Pease *(Joyce)*, James Rebhorn *(Professor)*, Tom Hanks *(Elliot)*, Dana Barron *(Diana)*, Joseph Leon *(Ralph the Tailor)*, Paul Gleason *(Daley)*, James Carroll *(Phil)*, Brian Byers *(Bernie)*, Curtis Hostetter *(Tommy)*, Robin Lamont *(Ruthie)*, Robin Tilghman *(Marie)*, Peter Gumeny *(Thompson)*, John Bottoms *(Father McKenna)*, Debbie Novak, Russell Todd, Dorian Lopinto, Jamie Haskins, Barbara Quinn, Laurie Faso, Anthony Shaw, Ron Englehardt, Michael Fiorillo, Steve W. James.

More detective thriller than horror movie, this is a bad attempt at making the splatter formula fit a more mainstream approach. A mad slasher is stalking Staten Island, killing young brides-to-be. Police detective Gamble (Lewis Arlt) sees a pattern to the killings, especially since a while back his own fiancee was murdered in a similar manner. As it turns out, the killer (Tom Rolfing) is hiding out in a shop that makes wedding dresses. Director Armand Mastroianni, Marcello's American-born cousin, puts this oh-so-familiar material through its paces without injecting anything remotely resembling personal style, obsession, or wit.

p, George Manasse, Robert Di Milia, Nan Pearlman; d, Armand Mastroianni; w, Scott Parker; ph, Gerald Feil (Metrocolor); ed, George T. Norris; m, Alexander Peskanov, Mark Peskanov.

**(PR:O   MPAA:R)**

## HEARSE, THE*½

(1980) 95m Marimark/Crown c

Trish Van Devere *(Jane Hardy)*, Joseph Cotten *(Walter Pritchard)*, David Gautreaux *(Tom Sullivan)*, Donald Hotton *(Rev. Winston)*, Med Flory *(Sheriff)*, Donald Petrie *(Luke)*, Christopher McDonald *(Peter)*, Perry Lang *(Paul)*, Frederic Franklyn *(Gordon)*, Olive Dunbar *(Mrs. Gordon)*,

Al Hansen *(Bo)*, Dominic Barto *(Driver)*, Nicholas Shields *(Dr. Greenwalt)*, Chuck Mitchell *(Counterman)*, Allison Balson *(Alice)*, Jimmy Gatherum *(Boy)*, Victoria Eubank *(Lois)*, Tanya Bowers *(Schoolgirl)*.

Jane Hardy (Trish Van Devere) inherits a mansion from her late aunt and decides to leave San Francisco and move into it. She doesn't understand why the townsfolk are treating her so coldly until she notices that she looks just like the aunt, who was believed to be possessed by Satan. Jane is continually hounded by an old hearse, which keeps showing up in front of her house, and by a crotchety real estate lawyer played by Joseph Cotten. This drags out every cliche in the book, including the woman-on-the-verge-of-a-nervous-breakdown-maybe-it's-all-in-her-head device. Pretty dull; then again, if you thought THE CAR was scary, you should love this.

p, Mark Tenser, Charles Russell; d, George Bowers; w, Bill Bleich (based on an idea by Tenser); ph, Mori Kawa (Metrocolor); ed, George Berndt; m, Webster Lewis.

**(PR:A   MPAA:PG)**

## HELL NIGHT**½

(1981) 101m Compass International c

Linda Blair *(Marti)*, Vincent Van Patten *(Seth)*, Peter Barton *(Jeff)*, Kevin Brophy *(Peter)*, Jenny Neumann *(May)*, Suki Goodwin *(Denise)*, Jimmy Sturtevant *(Scott)*, Hal Ralston, Cary Fox, Ronald Gans, Gloria Hellman.

It was a long, rough road from THE EXORCIST to HELL NIGHT for starlet Linda Blair (remember ROLLER BOOGIE?), but she could take comfort in the fact that this is one of the better HALLOWEEN rip-offs, which may have something to do with the fact that it was produced by HALLOWEEN executive producer Irwin Yablans and DREAMSCAPE producer Bruce Cohn Curtis (who also, however, produced ROLLER BOOGIE). Four freshman pledges of fraternity/sorority Alpha Sigma Rho (Blair, Vincent Van Patten, Peter Barton, and Suki Goodwin) are, by way of initiation, forced to spend the night at Garth mansion, where a mass murder was once committed by a man who killed his wife and three of his four handicapped children (one deformed, one deaf and dumb, one retarded, and one a literal monster), then killed himself. Moronic frat members set out to scare the foursome—who spend much of their time frolicking in their underwear—but someone or *something* kills them one by one. While the basics are pretty familiar, director Tom DeSimone (REFORM SCHOOL GIRLS; ANGEL 3: THE FINAL CHAPTER) does manage to create a few effective moments. Although the actual gore content is low, the titillation content is high, an avenue DeSimone would continue to explore in his future exploitation movies. A relative hit at the box office; there have been recent rumblings about a sequel that would once again feature Blair.

p, Irwin Yablans, Bruce Cohn Curtis; d, Tom DeSimone; w, Randolph Feldman; ph, Mac Ahlberg (Metrocolor); ed, Tony DiMarco; m, Dan Wyman.

**(PR:O   MPAA:R)**

## HELLBOUND: HELLRAISER II**

(1988) 96m Film Futures/NW c

Ashley Laurence *(Kirsty Cotton)*, Clare Higgins *(Julia)*, Kenneth Cranham *(Dr. Channard)*, Imogen Boorman *(Tiffany)*, William Hope *(Kyle Macrae)*, Oliver Smith *(Browning)*, Sean Chapman *(Uncle Frank)*, Doug Bradley *(Skinhead Cenobite)*.

Picking up a mere two hours after HELLRAISER left off, the sequel finds young Kirsty (Ashley Laurence) in a mental hospital in the aftermath of the horrific events she witnessed at the first film's climax. Her case comes to the attention of urbane Dr. Channard (Ken Cranham), who reactivates her evil stepmother, Julia, and helps her regenerate. Together they go to hell, where Channard is put through the pain-pleasure wringer and becomes the most impressive Cenobite of all. Meanwhile, Kirsty enters hell with Tiffany (Imogen Boorman), an autistic girl who opens one of the dangerous puzzle-boxes, in an attempt to rescue Kirsty's father—avoiding the bizarre Cenobites at every turn. Although publishing commitments kept Clive Barker's participation to a minimum here (he's listed as executive producer), he did write the treatment and assigned the screenplay to fellow Liverpudlian Peter Atkins, whom Barker had known since their days together at the Dog Company theater ensemble. First-timer Tony Randel, a New World veteran who has worked at everything from the mail room to special effects to marketing to editing, was chosen to direct. While there are certainly some unforgettable images in both HELLRAISER and HELLBOUND, the glue that binds these moments together is missing, and both films tend to fall apart. The obsessive lust that drives Julia to horrific extremes in HELLRAISER was almost enough to carry that film, but there is no such straw to cling to in HELLBOUND, and the film collapses into a bloody mess of bravura set-pieces that never add up to a satisfying whole. Barker, Atkins, and director Randel may succeed when it comes to the gut-churning elements, but they fail to present Barker's peculiar psychosexual obsessions in an even remotely coherent or affecting manner, nightmare logic notwithstanding. The $4 million film is also haphazard on the purely technical level. Although Robin Vidgeon's cinematography is slick and effective, the set design and optical work in the hellbound sequences leave much to be desired. The endless series of hallways and tunnels that make up hell have a cut-rate haunted house look to them, and in several spots supposedly stone walls bend inward when actors lean against them. The glass painting and matte work look rather cheap as well, and one must assume that most of the effects budget went to the duly impressive Cenobite makeup and costumes. Gorehounds desperate for a movie they can feel good about will no doubt heap all kinds of undue praise on HELLBOUND, extolling it as an example of intelligently presented graphic bloodletting. In fact, Barker has yet to make a movie on par with the work of George Romero or David Cronenberg, though some have praised him as their equal. One shouldn't close the book on Barker yet; still, he had better fulfill his promise soon, or he may wear out his welcome.

p, Christopher Figg; d, Tony Randel; w, Peter Atkins (based on a story by Clive Barker); ph, Robin Vidgeon; m, Christopher Young.

**(PR:O MPAA:R)**

## HELLO MARY LOU, PROM NIGHT II**½

(1987, Can.) 96m Simcom/Norstar c (AKA: THE HAUNTING OF HAMILTON HIGH)

Lisa Schrage *(Mary Lou Maloney)*, Wendy Lyon *(Vicki Carpenter)*, Michael Ironside *(Principal Bill, Sr.)*, Justin Louis *(Bill, Jr.)*, Richard Monette *(Father)*.

A sequel to PROM NIGHT (1980) in name only (although Peter Simpson repeats his chores as producer), this film begins with a prolog set in 1957, as prom queen Mary Lou Maloney (Lisa Schrage) is accidentally burned to death by her jilted boy friend just as she is about to receive her tiara. Thirty years later the culprit, now played by Michael Ironside, is the principal of the school, his mild indiscretion of 30 years before evidently not having phased the educational system of Edmonton, Alberta, where the film was shot. It's just a few days prior to this year's prom and wholesome teen Vicki (Wendy Lyon) is a nominee for queen. Unfortunately, the vengeful spirit of Mary Lou possesses Vicki and we're off to a gore-a-thon. A girl friend is strangled by a cape with a life of its own, the local cleric (and former boy friend of Mary Lou) is busily praying at the shrine of his former flame (pardon the pun) when he is impaled by a crucifix, a youth is zapped by his computer, and a few other bodies are strewn about for bad measure. Shown at Cannes as THE HAUNTING OF HAMILTON HIGH, this was later retitled HELLO MARY LOU, PROM NIGHT II before its general release, and, to enhance the new title, plenty of old songs with lyrics containing the name Mary Lou are prominently featured on the soundtrack. Director Bruce Pittman, who was Oscar-nominated for his 1984 short, "The Painted Door," shows promise, and does manage to squeeze some suspense and surprise out of a few scenes, especially a confrontation between the possessed Vicki and one of her girl friends in the school locker room. There are also good special effects from Jim Doyle, who worked on A NIGHTMARE ON ELM STREET and used his budget well to achieve some fine, eerie moments, including a hobby horse that comes to life and a blackboard that suddenly turns into a swirling black pool.

p, Peter Simpson; d, Bruce Pittman; w, Ron Oliver; ph, John Herzog; ed, Nick Rotundo; m, Paul Zaza.

**(PR:O MPAA:R)**

## HELLRAISER***

(1987, Brit.) 90m Cinemarque-Film Futures/NW c

Andrew Robinson *(Larry Cotton)*, Clare Higgins *(Julia Cotton)*, Ashley Laurence *(Kirsty Swanson)*, Sean Chapman *(Frank Cotton)*, Oliver Smith *(Frank the Monster)*, Robert Hines *(Steve)*, Antony Allen *(1st Victim)*, Leon Davis *(2nd Victim)*, Michael Cassidy *(3rd Victim)*, Frank Baker *(Derelict)*, Kenneth Nelson *(Bill)*, Gay Barnes *(Evelyn)*, Niall Buggy *(Dinner Guest)*, Dave Atkins, Oliver Parker

HELLRAISER—

(Moving Men), Pamela Sholto (Complaining Customer), Doug Bradley (Lead Cenobite), Nicholas Vince (Chattering Cenobite), Simon Bamford ("Butterball" Cenobite), Grace Kirby (Female Cenobite), Sharon Bower (Nurse), Raul Newney (Doctor).

HELLRAISER was the somewhat disappointing directorial debut of the "future of horror fiction" (according to Stephen King), Clive Barker, based on his own novella The Hell-Bound Heart. Frank (Sean Chapman), a sexual adventurer in search of new carnal pleasures, purchases a mysterious Chinese puzzle box while visiting an unnamed Third World country. Back home in England, he opens the box only to discover that he has unlocked the door to hell. Frank is pulled into another dimension, whose inhabitants, known as Cenobites, push him over the fine line between pleasure and pain by ripping him apart with tiny fish hooks. Years later, Frank's brother, Larry (Andrew Robinson), moves his family into the house—to which, through some blood spilled on the attic floor, Frank returns in near-skeletal form. With the help of Julia—with whom he once had an affair—Frank begins sucking the life out of bodies in order to regenerate to his old form. Meanwhile, Larry's daughter from a previous marriage, Kirsty (Ashley Laurence), begins to suspect her hated stepmother of having an affair, and to her horror becomes involved with Frank, Julia, the puzzle box, and the Cenobites. Undoubtedly head and shoulders above average horror fare thematically, HELLRAISER is, however, extremely graphic, badly paced, and, with few exceptions, poorly acted. As a director, Barker does possess a striking visual sensibility (he performs miracles on a $2.5 million budget). The film literally drips with horrific ambience. The old house is suitably creepy and Barker does well playing on the audiences' fear of what may lie upstairs in the dark. Also intriguing is the hellish dimension inhabited by the bizarre-looking Cenobites. However, while the author's cinematic sense is a pleasant surprise, his narrative is shockingly haphazard, and the film lurches from one set piece to the next with little dramatic rhythm. Some scenes are so poorly integrated that they seem more like rehearsals than actual scenes. Seemingly significant characters appear and then suddenly disappear without further explanation, and while Barker does a respectable job of developing the characters of Julia and Frank and the lustful ties that bind them, the writer-director is clearly less interested in victims Larry and Kirsty. The film never gets a handle on these characters and never provides enough characterization so that the viewer cares about their fate—in marked contrast to Barker's fiction.

p, Christopher Figg; d, Clive Barker; w, Clive Barker (based on his novella "The Hellbound Heart"); ph, Robin Vidgeon (Technicolor); ed, Richard Marden; m, Christopher Young.

(PR:O MPAA:R)

## HILLBILLYS IN A HAUNTED HOUSE*½

(1967) 88m Woolner c

Ferlin Husky (Woody Weatherby), Joi Lansing (Boots Malone), Don Bowman (Jeepers), John Carradine (Dr. Himmil), Lon Chaney, Jr. (Maximillian), Basil Rathbone

(Gregor), Linda Ho (Madame Wong), George Barrows (Gorilla), Molly Bee, Merle Haggard, Jim Kent, Pat Patterson, Jay Jasin.

The title really says it all. Country music stars Woody Weatherby and Boots Malone (Ferlin Husky and Joi Lansing) spend the night in a haunted mansion when they are caught in a storm en route to the Nashville Jamboree. There they run into the likes of Lon Chaney, Jr., John Carradine, Basil Rathbone, and a gorilla, all controlled by the insidious Madame Wong (Linda Ho), who is out to get an atomic formula. The film wastes the talents of both the once-major horror film stars and major country-and-western singers who appeared in it in an obvious urge to make a quick buck, and is an unfortunate memorial for Rathbone, this being the actor's last film (he was in his 70s, skyrocketing the production's insurance costs), and for director Jean Yarbrough, who began his directorial career with Bela Lugosi in THE DEVIL BAT (1941) and for whom this was a final filmic effort as well.

p, Bernard A. Woolner; d, Jean Yarbrough; w, Duke Yelton; ph, Vaughn Wilkins (Technicolor); ed, Roy Livingston; m, Hal Borne.

(PR:A MPAA:NR)

## HILLS HAVE EYES, THE*****

(1978) 89m Blood Relations/Vanguard c

Susan Lanier (Brenda Carter), Robert Houston (Bobby Carter), Virginia Vincent (Ethel Carter), Russ Grieve (Bob Carter), Dee Wallace (Lynne Wood), Martin Speer (Doug Wood), Brenda Marinoff (Katie Wood), Flora (Beauty), Stricker (The Beast), James Whitworth (Jupiter), Cordy Clark (Mama), Janus Blythe (Ruby), Michael Berryman (Pluto), Lance Gordon (Mars), Arthur King (Mercury), John Steadman (Fred).

With this film and A NIGHTMARE ON ELM STREET (1984), Wes Craven assured himself a place in the pantheon of great modern American horror directors whose work has had an immense influence on the genre—a mantle, ironically, that Craven has recently been trying to shed. THE HILLS HAVE EYES opens as a typical suburban family, the Carters, drive through the desert in their wagon and mobile home headed for California. The family consists of Dad (Russ Grieve), a recently retired cop; Mom (Virginia Vincent); big sister Lynne (Dee Wallace); her husband (Martin Speer); their baby; brother and sister Brenda and Bobby; and dogs Beauty and The Beast. Trouble starts when the car's axle breaks and the travelers are left stranded in the desert, miles from help. Slowly, they begin to realize that they have invaded another family's domain. A savage, almost primitive clan lives in the desert mesas, led by Jupiter (James Whitworth), who as a baby was left to die in the wasteland after he was born mutated. His wife (Cordy Clark) is a prostitute "no one would miss" whom he kidnaped from a distant town and brought into the desert for companionship. Together the couple had three "children," now fully grown. The boys, Pluto (Michael Berryman), Mars (Lance Gordon), and Mercury (Arthur King), all assist their father in protecting their territory (aided by

110                                                                THE HORROR FILM

walkie-talkies and guns that somehow found their way into the family's possession) and gathering whatever food they can come across (including, if need be, humans). The daughter, Ruby (Janus Blythe), has seen civilization and longs to escape her savage family. Soon the rival families collide, with the desert clan attacking the suburban clan to loot, kill, and eat them (horribly, their efforts focus on the baby). THE HILLS HAVE EYES is an extremely intense and disturbing film that tears at taboos viciously and examines them with a keen, unblinking glance. The result is an exciting and thematically rich and insightful essay on the dark side of the American family that could only be done in the exploitation horror genre. A must-see.

p, Peter Locke; d, Wes Craven; w, Wes Craven; ph, Eric Saarinen; ed, Wes Craven; m, Don Peake.

**(PR:O MPAA:R)**

## HILLS HAVE EYES II, THE*½

(1985) 86m New Realm/VTC c

Michael Berryman (Pluto), Kevin Blair (Roy), John Bloom (The Reaper), Janus Blythe (Rachel/Ruby), Peter Frechette (Harry), Robert Houston (Bobby), Tamara Stafford (Cass), David Nichols (The Psychiatrist), John Laughlin (Hulk), Willard Pugh (Foster), Colleen Riley (Jane), Penny Johnson (Sue), Brenda Marinoff (Katy), Edith Fellows (Mrs. Wilson), Arden Roger Meyer (Man with Towel), Virginia Vincent (Ethel), James Whitworth (Jupiter), Susan Lanier (Brenda), Lance Gordon (Mars), Martin Speer (Doug).

It's hard to believe that the same man who wrote and directed one of the best horror films of the 1970s, THE HILLS HAVE EYES (1978), could have pulled the same duty on the sequel and come up with a film as dull, confused, unnecessary, and shockingly bad as this. Eight years after the first film's events, Ruby (Janus Blythe), who has now been integrated into normal society and is running a motorcycle shop with Bobby (Robert Houston), the survivor from Part I's "normal" family, takes a group of teenagers back into the desert that spawned her to run an important motorcycle race. When a rock ruptures the fuel line of their bus, the group is stranded and they soon find themselves under attack by her brother Pluto (Michael Berryman) and their uncle, The Reaper (John Bloom), another desert savage. The teens try to defend themselves against the onslaught, but are picked off one at a time by the vicious desert rats. There was scant reason to make a sequel to THE HILLS HAVE EYES, and the only interesting aspect of this film is to see how Bobby, Ruby, and Pluto have dealt with the events of the original. Unfortunately, Ruby's role is little more than a cameo and Pluto is dispatched after uttering just a few lines of dialog. Ruby's transformation from savage desert girl to productive and trusted member of the community is rife with dramatic possibilities, and the awakening of her animal-like instincts when she reenters the desert is fascinating, but she disappears from the film before any insightful development of her character occurs. Director Craven was unhappy with the film, because the producers ran out of money and promised that he could shoot additional scenes when

more funds were raised (this was also how THE HILLS HAVE EYES was made), then changed their minds and released the film as it was. This may explain some of the scant character development, lengthy flashbacks to footage from the first film (even the dog has a flashback!), and disjointed scenes. Nevertheless, Craven did bastardize his own work and, considering the lack of any true inspiration for a sequel, the film boils down to just another teenagers-in-trouble horror dud. The man who gave us THE HILLS HAVE EYES and A NIGHTMARE ON ELM STREET should have done better.

p, Barry Cahn, Peter Locke; d, Wes Craven; w, Wes Craven; ph, David Lewis (Movielab Color); ed, Richard Bracken; m, Harry Manfredini.

**(PR:O MPAA:R)**

## HITCHER, THE**

(1986) 97m Silver Screen-HBO/Tri-Star c

Rutger Hauer (John Ryder), C. Thomas Howell (Jim Halsey), Jennifer Jason Leigh (Nash), Jeffrey DeMunn (Capt. Esteridge), John Jackson (Sgt. Starr).

Were it not for the eerie elegance of Rutger Hauer, this film would be a complete washout. One of the more sadistic films in recent memory, THE HITCHER follows the terror-filled trip of young Jim (C. Thomas Howell) as he drives a Cadillac Seville from Chicago to San Diego to earn some extra money. Somewhere in Texas, he picks up an obviously psychotic hitchhiker, pretentiously named John Ryder and played by Hauer. Ryder calmly tells the teenager that he has just massacred the carload of folks who picked him up last time, and holds a knife to Jim's eye to prove his point. Ryder isn't going to kill Jim, though; rather, he wants Jim to kill *him* (why all this is so is never explained). Jim manages to eject his unwanted passenger, but instead of getting rid of Ryder only makes the maniac mad. Soon Ryder is playing a cat-and-mouse game with the frightened Jim, pursuing him in a variety of stolen vehicles whose owners he has slaughtered. The film is about as mindlessly vicious as they get. Despite the impressive cast, slick direction, and beautiful cinematography (by John Seale, who shot WITNESS), the picture is nothing more than a fancy-pants slasher film. First-time director Robert Harmon imbues the movie with a self-important air—as if there is much more going on here than meets the eye (Titanic social allegory? Homoerotic struggle? Supernatural huggabugga?). Unfortunately, there is *nothing* else going on here. No subtext. No characterization. No relevancy. Zip. Only hyperviolence and death on a lonely Texas highway. Hauer, however, almost makes this torturous (literally) ordeal worth sitting through. Although he could probably play this role in his sleep, Hauer injects a restrained, very pure evil into his homicidal maniac that is truly chilling (young actor Howell declared later in interviews that he was actually frightened of Hauer throughout the filming and not just acting). Screenwriter Eric Red later co-wrote NEAR DARK (1987) with Kathryn Bigelow.

p, David Bombyk, Kip Ohman; d, Robert Harmon; w, Eric

Red; ph, John Seale (Metrocolor); ed, Frank J. Urioste; m, Mark Isham.

(PR:O    MPAA:R)

## HOMEBODIES***

(1974) 96m Cinema Entertainment/AE c

Peter Brocco *(Blakely),* Frances Fuller *(Emily),* William Hansen *(Sandy),* Ruth McDevitt *(Mrs. Loomis),* Paula Trueman *(Mattie),* Ian Wolfe *(Loomis),* Linda Marsh *(Miss Pollack),* Douglas Fowley *(Crawford),* Kenneth Tobey *(Construction Boss),* Wesley Lau *(Foreman),* Norman Gottschalk *(Superintendent),* Irene Webster *(Woman in Floppy Hat),* Nicholas Lewis, John Craig, Joe De Meo *(Construction Workers),* Michael Johnson *(Policeman),* Alma Du Bus *(Super's Wife),* Eldon Quick *(Insurance Inspector),* William Benedict *(Watchman).*

HOMEBODIES is a strange little shocker about a murderous group of geriatrics. Miss Pollack (Linda Marsh) is a social worker with no soul, who evicts a number of elderly people from their Cincinnati apartment building. The building is in the way of a new construction project and simply has to go. Rather than fight City Hall, the senior citizens take a more direct approach, by which Miss Pollack is stabbed to death and construction workers are gruesomely done away with. The senior citizens as portrayed as everyday people fed up with an uncaring system—which makes the fairly graphic violence all the more shocking. Well shot and directed, the film is an impressive combination of social comment, character study, black humor, and the macabre.

p, Marshal Backlar; d, Larry Yust; w, Larry Yust, Howard Kaminsky, Bennett Sims; ph, Isidore Mankofsky; ed, Peter Parasheles; m, Bernardo Segall.

(PR:C    MPAA:PG)

## HORROR CHAMBER OF DR. FAUSTUS, THE*****

(1959, Fr./It.) 84m Champs-Elysees-Lux/Lopert bw (LES YEUX SANS VISAGE; OCCHI SENZA VOLTO; AKA: EYES WITHOUT A FACE)

Pierre Brasseur *(Prof. Genessier),* Alida Valli *(Louise),* Edith Scob *(Christiane),* Francois Guerin *(Jacques),* Juliette Mayniel *(Edna Gruber),* Beatrice Altariba *(Paulette),* Alexandre Rignault *(Inspector Parot),* Rene Genin *(Bereaved Father),* Claude Brasseur, Michel Etcheverry, Yvette Etievant, Lucien Hubert, Marcel Peres.

This eerie, haunting, poetic thriller concerns a famed plastic surgeon, Dr. Genessier (Pierre Brasseur), who is obsessed with reconstructing the face of his daughter, Christiane (Edith Scob), who was disfigured in an automobile accident. He sends his loyal female assistant, Louise (Alida Valli), to Paris's Sorbonne, where she lures young women to the doctor's laboratory. Dr. Genessier then proceeds to remove their faces, in an attempt to graft the flesh onto Christiane's scarred visage—a face hidden behind a waxen mask that reveals only her melancholy eyes. Directed by Georges Franju from a screenplay written by novelists Pierre Boileau and Thomas Narcejac (DIABOLIQUE and

VERTIGO), THE HORROR CHAMBER OF DR. FAUSTUS is a frightening, blood-curdling picture, directed at an even, distant pace that builds the tension to an almost unbearable level. Having found fame as a documentary filmmaker, Franju presented this thriller in the same manner as his gruesome, but brilliant, LES SANG DES BETES (Blood of the Beasts), a documentary about a slaughterhouse, and arrives at an unflinching, unrelenting, calm, and poetic work. The scene in which Dr. Genessier takes a scalpel to his victim's face and proceeds, in the most sickening fashion, to remove her face in one flap of grotesque flesh is not photographed with even the slightest amount of sensationalism; instead, it is as if Franju, and by extension Dr. Genessier, has seen this happen a thousand times before. Essential viewing. Available in both dubbed and subtitled versions.

p, Jules Borkon; d, Georges Franju; w, Georges Franju, Jean Redon, Claude Sautet, Pierre Boileau, Thomas Narcejac (based on the novel *Les yeux sans visage* by Jean Redon); ph, Eugene Shuftan; ed, Gilbert Natot; m, Maurice Jarre.

(PR:O    MPAA:NR)

## HORROR EXPRESS***½

(1972, Sp./Brit.) 90m Granada/Benmar-Scotia c (PANICO EN EL TRANSIBERIANO; AKA: PANIC IN THE TRANS-SIBERIAN TRAIN)

Christopher Lee *(Prof. Alex Caxton),* Peter Cushing *(Dr. Wells),* Telly Savalas *(Capt. Kazan),* Alberto de Mendoza *(Inspector),* Silvia Tortosa, Jorge Rigaud, Helga Line, Angel de Pozo, Julio Pena, Jose Jaspe.

Although at least as much science fiction as horror, HORROR EXPRESS has become a favorite in both genres, and deservedly so. It's fast-paced, inventive, and wholly entertaining. Prof. Alex Caxton (Christopher Lee), an explorer and anthropologist, has discovered the frozen body of the evolutionary "missing link" in China and is transporting it on the Trans-Siberian Express, circa 1906. On the train, the ape-man defrosts and reveals itself to be an alien that came to Earth in prehistoric times to claim the planet. The alien is able to absorb the intellect of humans merely by gazing at them. Unfortunately, the process boils the brain of the victim, causing their eyes to turn white and bleed, and turns them into zombies. The alien is also able to switch bodies, taking the identity of anyone who suits him. Soon the alien is creeping around the train possessing most of the passengers (including a small army of Cossacks led by Telly Savalas) in a desperate attempt to gather enough knowledge to build a spacecraft so it can get home. Eventually Caxton and his rival, Dr. Wells (Peter Cushing), team up to defeat the marauding alien. Directed with considerable flair by Eugenio Martin, HORROR EXPRESS is a truly unique little film, which combines both horror and sci-fi with an Agatha Christie-type situation in a DOCTOR ZHIVAGO/NICHOLAS AND ALEXANDRA setting (there's even a Rasputin character). In fact, it was because of NICHOLAS AND ALEXANDRA (1971) that the film was made at all. Producer Bernard Gordon owned the model train used in the 1971 film and wanted to get the maximum use out of the expensive prop. Lee and Cushing contribute typically enthusiastic performances here, and their roles are spiced with plenty of wit and humor—usually at their expense—while Savalas is delightfully hammy as the arrogant Cossack. Also worth noting is the haunting musical score by John Cacavas, which, in the finest Ennio Morricone tradition, contains a memorable whistled theme.

p, Bernard Gordon; d, Eugenio Martin; w, Arnaud D'Usseau, Julian Halvey; ph, Alejandro Ulloa (Eastmancolor); m, John Cacavas.

**(PR:C MPAA:R)**

## HORROR HOSPITAL**

(1973, Brit.) 91m Noteworthy/Hallmark c (AKA: COMPUTER KILLERS)

Michael Gough *(Dr. Storm)*, Robin Askwith, Vanessa Shaw, Ellen Pollock, Skip Martin, Dennis Price, Kurt Christian, Barbara Wendy, Colin Skeaping, Kenneth Benda, Martin Grace, George Herbert.

This barely funny horror spoof centers on a young pop singer (Robin Askwith) who visits a hospital to relax from his grueling schedule, only to find it is run by the mad Dr. Storm (Michael Gough, who really hams it up here) and staffed by his hideous creations. Eventually, he befriends one of the monsters (Skip Martin), a dwarf, and persuades it to help him in his bid for freedom. The potentially interesting and biting satire is sunk by a hopelessly cheap production, Gough's overacting, and mundane direction by Anthony Balch.

p, Richard Gordon; d, Anthony Balch; w, Anthony Balch, Alan Watson; ph, David McDonald (Movielab Color).

**(PR:C MPAA:PG)**

## HORROR HOTEL***

(1960, Brit.) 76m Vulcan/Trans-Lux bw (GB: CITY OF THE DEAD, THE)

Patricia Jessel *(Elizabeth Selwyn/Mrs. Newless)*, Betta St. John *(Patricia Russell)*, Christopher Lee *(Prof. Driscoll)*, Dennis Lotis *(Richard Barlow)*, Venetia Stevenson *(Nan Barlow)*, Valentine Dyall *(Jethrow Keane)*, Norman MacOwan *(Rev. Russell)*, Ann Beach *(Lottie)*, Tom Naylor *(Bill Maitland)*, Fred Johnson *(Elder)*.

Written by CIRCUS OF HORROR screenwriter George Baxt, this was the first British production from American Milton Subotsky, who would soon go on to head Amicus. Part CURSE OF THE DEMON, part PSYCHO, HORROR HOTEL is an effective, quite atmospheric witchcraft film set in the US. A young student of the occult, Nan Barlow (Venetia Stevenson), visits a rundown village in Massachusetts on the recommendation of her history professor, Driscoll (Christopher Lee). She discovers that the village inn is run by a witch who was burned at the stake in 1692, but brought back to life by the Devil. Nan now finds herself the main ingredient in a human sacrifice—presided over by none other than Prof. Driscoll. The girl is killed, and shortly

thereafter her boy friend (Tom Naylor) and brother come looking for her, eventually taking on the evil coven. Director John Moxey makes much of the fog-shrouded claustrophobic atmosphere, effectively evoking the spirit of H.P. Lovecraft. Lee turns in another finely tuned performance, this time sporting a remarkably good American accent.

p, Milton Subotsky, Donald Taylor; d, John Moxey; w, George Baxt, Desmond Dickinson (based on a story by Subotsky); ed, John Pomeroy; m, Douglas Gamley, Ken Jones.

**(PR:C MPAA:NR)**

## HORROR OF DRACULA, THE*****

(1958, Brit.) 82m Hammer/UNIV c

Peter Cushing *(Van Helsing)*, Michael Gough *(Arthur Holmwood)*, Melissa Stribling *(Mina Holmwood)*, Christopher Lee *(Count Dracula)*, Carol Marsh *(Lucy)*, John Van Eyssen *(Jonathan Harker)*, Miles Malleson *(Marx, the Undertaker)*, Valerie Gaunt *(Vampire Woman)*, Charles Lloyd Pack *(Dr. Seward)*, Janina Faye *(Tania)*, Olga Dickie *(Gerda)*, George Woodbridge *(Landlord)*, Barbara Archer *(Inga)*, George Benson *(Frontier Official)*, Guy Mills, George Merritt, William Sherwood, John Mossman, Stedwell Fulcher, Judith Nelmes, Humphrey Kent, Paul Cole, Dick Morgan, Geoffrey Bayldon.

Hammer finally gave the Dracula legend the treatment it deserved here, entrusting it to the brilliant director of THE CURSE OF FRANKENSTEIN, Terence Fisher, who injected new, glorious life into the familiar material. English librarian Jonathan Harker (John Van Eyssen) travels to Transylvania, where he is employed by the mysterious Count Dracula (Christopher Lee). Eventually, Harker learns that his employer is a vampire, one of the undead who must suck the blood of the living to survive, and he becomes one of Dracula's victims. Dracula then travels to London and tracks down Harker's fiancee, Lucy (Carol Marsh), and transforms her into one of the undead. Enter Dr. Van Helsing (played with zest by Peter Cushing) and the battle lines are drawn. Van Helsing eventually tracks Dracula down at his castle, and, in a stunningly choreographed climax, kills the vampire, using sunlight and two gold candlesticks put together in the shape of the cross. In a fantastic special-effects sequence (which still holds up even against the technological wonders of modern movies), Dracula rots away into a pile of dust. Fisher's version of the Dracula legend brought with it many innovative (and, yes, subsequently overdone) approaches to the genre. The film moves quickly and forcefully from one scene to the next, keeping the audience on the very edges of their seats. The sets are lush and magnificent looking, the musical score is terrific, the actors perfectly cast, and, of course, there's the element of blood and sex. Blood and sex in vampire films (the essential elements in the legends) had been studiously avoided by previous horror filmmakers, probably due to studio censorship. Hammer had no such restrictions and freely played up actor Lee's obvious sensuality (why else would all these beautiful women allow him to get so close and remain his slaves?) to the advantage of the character and plot motivation. The result is a terrific combination of the intellectual and visceral that continues to work today. Followed by DRACULA-PRINCE OF DARKNESS and five more sequels, few of which are available on videocassette.

p, Anthony Hinds; d, Terence Fisher; w, Jimmy Sangster (based on the novel *Dracula* by Bram Stoker); ph, Jack Asher (Eastmancolor); ed, Bill Lenny, James Needs; m, James Bernard.

**(PR:C  MPAA:NR)**

### HORROR OF FRANKENSTEIN, THE*

(1970, Brit.) 95m Hammer-MI/American Continental c

Ralph Bates *(Victor Frankenstein)*, Kate O'Mara *(Alys)*, Graham James *(Wilhelm)*, Veronica Carlson *(Elizabeth)*, Bernard Archard *(Elizabeth's Father)*, Dennis Price *(Grave Robber)*, Joan Rice *(Grave Robber's Wife)*, David Prowse *(The Monster)*.

This film represents a feeble attempt by Hammer to bring some freshness to their series of Frankenstein films by introducing black humor. The jokes are told in such a straightforward and dry manner, however, that one is never sure whether or not they're supposed to be taken seriously. Ralph Bates stars as the son of Count Frankenstein, who kills his father in order to take over the castle and the charms of the comely and buxom housekeeper (Kate O'Mara). Soon he decides to build a monster (David Prowse, who would go on to play Darth Vader in the "Star Wars" movies), requiring the gory murders of various townsfolk. Frankenstein uses a numbers system to assemble the various pieces of the monster—after first practicing by putting together a dead turtle and bringing it back to life. Terence Fisher would return to direct the last film in the series, the fascinating FRANKENSTEIN AND THE MONSTER FROM HELL (1973). Sadly, Fisher died not long after shooting was completed.

p, Jimmy Sangster; d, Jimmy Sangster; w, Jimmy Sangster, Jeremy Burnham (based on the characters created by Mary Shelley); ph, Moray Grant (Technicolor); ed, Chris Barnes; m, James Bernard.

**(PR:O  MPAA:R)**

### HORROR OF PARTY BEACH, THE*

(1964) 72m Inzom/FOX bw

John Scott *(Hank Green)*, Alice Lyon *(Elaine Gavin)*, Allen Laurel *(Dr. Gavin)*, Eulabelle Moore *(Eulabelle)*, Marilyn Clark *(Tina)*, Augustin Mayer *(Mike)*, Damon Klebroyd *(Lt. Wells)*, Monroe Wade *(Television Announcer)*, Carol Grubman, Dina Harris, Emily Laurel *(Girls in Car)*, Sharon Murphy, Diane Prizio *(Two Girls)*, The Del-Aires *(Vocal Group)*.

An all-time bad movie classic! Radioactive waste at the bottom of the ocean turns the human skeletons lying there into mutated sea monsters that surface and ruin a teenage beach party, killing the rock-'n'-rollers for their blood. Lots of silly monster costumes! Lots of bad rock'n'roll songs! Lots of bad screams from lousy teenage actresses! Lots of phony newspaper headlines explaining what is happen-

ing! Eventually, an inept scientist stumbles across the solution to the problem by pouring sodium on the beasts and dissolving them (actually, his black maid, Eulabelle, discovers the secret, but she doesn't get the credit). THE HORROR OF PARTY BEACH was heralded as "the first horror monster musical"; luckily, few followed. Really bad and really fun. The songs include "Drag," "You Are Not a Summer Love," "Elaine," "Wigglin'n' Wobblin'," and "The Zombie Stomp."

p, Del Tenney; d, Del Tenney; w, Richard L. Hilliard, Ronald Gianettino, Lou Binder; ph, Richard L. Hilliard; ed, Gary Youngman.

**(PR:A  MPAA:NR)**

### HORROR OF THE ZOMBIES**½

(1974, Sp.) 85m Independent International c (EL BUQUE MALDITO)

Maria Perschy, Jack Taylor, Carlos Lemos, Manuel de Blas, Barbara Rey, Blanca Estrada, Margarita Merino.

With TOMBS OF THE BLIND DEAD, director Armando De Ossorio introduced a new breed of horror villain, the Knights Templar, a 13th-century band of soldiers who fought bravely in the Crusades. When the group began dabbling with black magic and Satan worship, they were caught, excommunicated by the Church, and hanged, their bodies left to rot with their eyes plucked out by crows. Part vampire, part zombie, the skeletal Templars are condemned to wander the earth for eternity—sucking the blood from their victims. Although blind, the slow-moving Templars can locate victims by the sounds they make—from a scream to a heartbeat. This, then, is the second sequel to TOMBS OF THE BLIND DEAD (1971), and finds the Knights Templar on board a mysterious, fog-shrouded Spanish galleon that waylays stranded ships. When a sporting goods magnate sets two bikini-clad models adrift on the ocean as a publicity stunt, the women soon find themselves the victims of the Templars. Fearing trouble, the sporting goods owner—accompanied by his assistant, the modeling agency boss, the roommate of one of the models, and a scientist aware of the Templar legend—sails his yacht into the vicinity in an effort to rescue the girls. Although the first hour is somewhat slow, with the running time padded with the bikinied models posing for pictures and a rather incongruous scene in which the meglomaniacal magnate holds the model's roommate hostage in a dungeon-like chamber, HORROR OF THE ZOMBIES pays off when the Knights Templar rise from their shipboard tombs to attack the living. The atmospheric scenes aboard the decrepit galleon (which, unfortunately, is obviously a model in long shots) are genuinely creepy and may have been borrowed by John Carpenter for THE FOG (1980). Best of all, however, is the ending, in which the two survivors wash up on the beach, besieged by the ever-vigilant Templars, who rise up out of the ocean to attack them while their haunting theme music (a pseudo-Gregorian chant) is heard. Followed by NIGHT OF THE SEAGULLS (1975).

p, J.L. Bermudez De Castro; d, Armando De Ossorio; w,

Armando De Ossorio; ph, Raul Artigot; ed, Petra De Nieva; m, A. Garcia Abril.

(PR:C    MPAA:R)

### HOSPITAL MASSACRE zero

(1982) 90m Cannon c (AKA: WARD 13; BE MY VALENTINE, OR ELSE. . .; MASSACRE HOSPITAL; GB: X-RAY)

Barbi Benton *(Susan)*, Chip Lucia *(Harry)*, Jon Van Ness *(Jack)*, John Warner Williams *(Saxon)*, Gay Austin *(Jacobs)*, Den Surles *(Beam)*, Michael Frost *(Ned)*, Karen Smith *(Kitty)*, Billy Jacoby *(Young Harry)*, Marian Beeler, Elly Wold, Jonathan Moore, Tammy Simpson, Bill Errigo, Lanny Duncan, Thomas McClure, Beverly Hart, Jon Greene, Gloria Morrison.

This film was made under the title "Be My Valentine, or Else," which was abandoned when the film MY BLOODY VALENTINE surfaced and altered to "X-RAY." But when VISITING HOURS came out first, the title was changed again to HOSPITAL MASSACRE. Harold (Chip Lucia) is a psychotic killer who, back in 1961 when they were just kids, sent a valentine to Susan (Barbi Benton) and was embarrassed when she and her brother laughed at his attempt to get closer to her. Harold knows how to hold a grudge, so he kills the brother and waits almost two decades to exact his revenge on the comely Susan. Now, Susan has just received a job promotion, for which she had to take a physical (a good excuse for Barbi to remove her clothes). It's the week before February 14 and she arrives at a local hospital to pick up the results of the routine examination. Dr. Jacobs (Gay Austin), Susan's doctor, is killed by Harold, who is wearing medical garb. He takes Susan's X-rays, which show nothing amiss, and switches them. Another doctor (John Warner Williams) sees the switched X-rays, thinks they belong to Susan, concludes that she is quite sick, and orders her to stay in the hospital. Susan dutifully submits and Harold begins to terrorize the sparsely occupied hospital, leaving a bloody trail of bodies strewn about. Since so many people think doctors are butchers anyhow, there didn't have to be that much of a suspension of disbelief here. Unless you are a diehard Benton fan, this is a must to avoid.

p, Menahem Golan, Yoram Globus; d, Boaz Davidson; w, Marc Behm; ph, Nicholas von Sternberg; m, Arlon Ober.

(PR:O    MPAA:R)

### HOUSE*

(1986) 93m NW c

William Katt *(Roger Cobb)*, George Wendt *(Harold Gorton)*, Richard Moll *(Big Ben)*, Kay Lenz *(Sandy)*, Mary Stavin *(Tanya)*, Michael Ensign *(Chet Parker)*, Erik Silver, Marc Silver *(Jimmy)*, Susan French *(Aunt Elizabeth)*, Alan Autry, Steven Williams, Ronn Carroll *(Cops)*, Jim Calvert *(Grocery Boy)*, Mindy Sterling *(Woman in Bookstore)*, Jayson Kane *(Cheesy Stud)*, Billy Beck *(Priest)*, Bill McLean *(Older Man)*, Steve Susskind *(Frank McGraw)*, John Young *(Would-Be Writer)*, Dwier Brown *(Lieutenant)*, Joey Green *(Fitzsimmons)*, Stephen Nichols *(Scott)*, Donald Willis *(Soldier)*, Robert Joseph *(Robert)*, Curt Wilmot *(Skeleton Big Ben)*.

A surprise hit early in 1986, HOUSE is an ineptly structured effort that tries to combine both scares and laughs, succeeding at neither. Roger Cobb (William Katt) is a successful Stephen King-like horror novelist suffering from writer's block due to a recent divorce from TV actress Sandy (Kay Lenz) and the disappearance of their son, Jimmy (played by twins Erik and Mark Silver). Although urged by his agent to crank out another novel, Roger instead concentrates on writing about his experiences as a soldier in the Vietnam War. After the mysterious suicide of his rather eccentric aunt, Roger decides to move into her huge Victorian home in search of solitude, but finds that the joint is a gateway to another dimension, with all manner of special-effects spooks and monsters popping out. There are about six films going on at once in HOUSE, and none of them works. Monster, haunted-house, comedy, traumatic-divorce, search-for-a-missing-child, and Vietnam plotlines are mixed together so haphazardly that little here makes any sense. It seems as if screenwriter Ethan Wiley and director Steve Miner made this film up as they went along and never went back to check if the preceding footage shot would match the brainstorm they just had. There is no logic to the strange things that happen in the house, not even the warped logic found in horror films. Of course, horror films aren't logical when compared with normal life, but they do (and must) maintain a concrete logic within the context of the fantastic storyline. HOUSE doesn't do this and the film suffers because of it. Suspense is lost, because at any moment all the rules in this film change, and it's pointless to try to anticipate what will happen next, because anything can happen. Despite the special effects (which are mediocre—all the monsters look like silly, overstuffed rubber toys) and bizarre images, the film becomes dull and dragged out. Followed by a sequel.

p, Sean S. Cunningham; d, Steve Miner; w, Ethan Wiley (based on a story by Fred Dekker); ph, Mac Ahlberg (Metrocolor); ed, Michael N. Knue; m, Harry Manfredini.

(PR:C-O    MPAA:R)

### HOUSE II: THE SECOND STORY*

(1987) 85m NW c

Arye Gross *(Jesse McLaughlin)*, Jonathan Stark *(Charlie)*, Royal Dano *(Gramps)*, Bill Maher *(John)*, John Ratzenberger *(Bill Towner)*, Lar Park Lincoln *(Kate)*, Amy Yasbeck *(Lana)*, Gregory Walcott *(Sheriff)*, Dwier Brown *(Clarence)*, Lenora May *(Judith)*, Devin Devasquez *(Virgin)*, Jayne Modean *(Rochelle)*, Ronn Carroll *(Deputy)*, Dean Cleverdon *("Slim" Reezer)*, Doug MacHugh *(High Priest)*, Mitzi Kapture *(Cowgirl)*, David Arnott *(Banana)*, Kane Hodder *(Gorilla)*, Susan Isaac *(Cat)*, Gus Rethwisch *(Arnold the Barbarian)*, Gil Birmingham *(Featured Warrior)*.

Great title, bad movie. Director-writer Ethan Wiley makes an inauspicious debut behind the camera after coauthoring the first HOUSE. He'd been a puppeteer on GREMLINS, and someone must have thought his next career move should be directing. They were wrong. It's the old haunted-house theme again, with blood and guts substituting for intelligence and suspense: Jesse (Arye Gross) and his girl friend (Lar Park Lincoln) move into a large old house once owned by Jesse's great-great-grandpa (Royal Dano), a well-known outlaw of the Old West. Jesse's parents were murdered in the house more than 20 years ago, and if you're wondering why he would want to go into the place, the answer is: greed. It's rumored there's a treasure of precious stones buried somewhere in the house, in the skull of one of Jesse's forebears. Jesse and his best pal, Charlie (Jonathan Stark), find a coffin and open it to reveal a crystal skull, plus the mummy of Gramps, who promptly sits up and plants a kiss on his great-great-grandson, explaining that he has been kept alive by the skull and its magical properties, which can make the ancient youthful and bring the dead to life. When the kids toss a large costume party, someone steals the skull, prompting a search of the house and opening the door to a dozen different dimensions. Having worked on GREMLINS, Wiley may have thought he would do well to invent some cute critters of his own, so we are treated to several, including a baby pterodactyl named "Bippy" and a weird caterpillar/dog that attaches itself to Charlie's leg and won't let go. The special effects are from Chris Walas (THE FLY), who also supervised the makeup. The first film featured George Wendt from TV's "Cheers"; this time around, they tapped the same TV show for John Ratzenberger.

p, Sean S. Cunningham; d, Ethan Wiley; w, Ethan Wiley; ph, Mac Ahlberg (Metrocolor); ed, Marty Nicholson; m, Harry Manfredini.

(PR:C-O  MPAA:PG-13)

## HOUSE BY THE CEMETERY, THE zero

(1984, It.) 78m Fulvia/Almi c (QUELLA VILLA ACCANTO AL CIMITERO)

Catriona MacColl (Lucy Boyle), Paolo Malco (Norman Boyle), Ania Peironi (Ann), Giovanni Frezza (Bob Boyle), Dagmar Lassander (Mrs. Gittelson), Giovanni de Nari (Dr. Freudstein).

Here's another gore-fest from the prolific and wholly untalented Lucio Fulci, this time set outside Boston, where researcher Norman Boyle (Paolo Malco), his wife (Catriona MacColl), and their child (Giovanni Frezza) move into a new house. As the title indicates, the house is next to a cemetery. What the title doesn't say, however, is that a deranged killer lives in the basement and has a penchant for bloodletting. The killer, Dr. Freudenstein (Giovanni de Nari), is a crazed scientist who has lived for more than 100 years, thanks to his advances in cellular regeneration. The only catch is that he gets his cells from his victims. Fans of this sort of thing will probably enjoy THE HOUSE BY THE CEMETERY. Those who want more than spilled guts from a horror film are advised to look elsewhere.

p, Fabrizio De Angelis; d, Lucio Fulci; w, Lucio Fulci, Dardano Sacchetti, Giorgio Mariuzzo (based on a story by

Elisa Livia Briganti); ph, Sergio Salvati (Luciano Vittori Color); ed, Vincenzo Tomassi; m, Walter Rizzati.

(PR:O  MPAA:R)

## HOUSE OF EVIL*

(1968, US/Mex.) 83m Azteca/COL c

Boris Karloff (Mathias Morteval), Julissa (Lucy Durant), Angel Espinoza (Dr. Emery Horvath), Andres Garcia (Charles Beasley), Manuel Alvarado (Morgenstern Morteval), Beatrice Baz (Cordelia Rash), Quintin Bulnes (Ivar Morteval), Arturo Fernandez (Fodor).

One of the four Mexican films made by Boris Karloff shortly before his death—his scenes were shot in Los Angeles and spliced in later—HOUSE OF EVIL features the actor as the patriarch of a greedy family who calls his heirs to his mansion to collect their inheritance. After the introduction of this situation and the characters, Karloff's character dies, leaving the others to spend the rest of the film wandering around in the dark corridors of the mansion, where they are murdered by the patriarch's collection of life-sized automatons (actors pretending to be robots). With muddy photography and endless chatter, this is a difficult film to watch. There are some fairly startling moments of gore, however, including one in which a hopeful heir is shot in the face by toy cannons and another in which a woman is run through with a sword by an automaton. The climax, in which the not-really-dead Karloff insanely plays the organ as his mansion bursts into flames and falls down around him, is fairly memorable. There is plenty of unintentional laughter as well: an establishing shot of the mansion is quite obviously an illustration, and the sound-effects for the squeaky automatons sound like whimpering puppies. On videocassette as THE DANCE OF DEATH.

p, Luis Enrique Vergara, Juan Ibanez; d, Juan Ibanez, Jack Hill; w, Jack Hill, Luis Enrique Vergara; ph, Raul Dominguez, Austin McKinney; m, Henry Cabiati.

(PR:A-C  MPAA:NR)

## HOUSE OF EXORCISM, THE**

(1976, It.) 90m Peppercorn-Wormser c (LA CASA DELL' ESORCISMO; AKA: LISA AND THE DEVIL)

Telly Savalas, Elke Sommer, Robert Alda, Sylva Koscina, Alida Valli, Alessio Orano, Gabriele Tinti, Kathy Leone, Eduardo Fajardo, Carmen Silva, Franz Von Treuberg, Espartaco Santoni.

Written and perhaps partially directed by producer Alfred Leone, THE HOUSE OF EXORCISM is a real mess, part Mario Bava film and part EXORCIST rip-off, with both parts spliced together in a seemingly haphazard fashion to form a frustratingly disjointed whole. Lisa (Elke Sommer) is an innocent who spies a wax dummy and recognizes her own image. She then spots the Devil—Telly Savalas—and flees. She winds up in a strange mansion inhabited by a depraved family into sadism, nymphomania, incest, and necrophilia. To make matter worse, the butler (again Savalas, this time sucking on a lollipop, a la "Kojack") looks just like the previously seen Devil! Lisa is possessed by the

Devil and is taken to a hospital, where she is tied to the bed and where she does things like vomit up frogs and levitate until a priest (Robert Alda) comes in to perform an exorcism. Apparently, the first two-thirds of the film are Bava's (filmed in 1972) and the last part—the exorcism, starring Alda—was inserted later by producer Leone for the American release. The Bava scenes, naturally, have some real haunting power, while the exorcism is merely silly.

p, Alfred Leone; d, Mario Bava; w, Alberto Tintini, Alfred Leone, Mario Bava; ph, Cecilio Paniagua; m, Carlo Savina.

(PR:O  MPAA:R)

## HOUSE OF FREAKS zero

(1973, It.) 80m Cinerama/Aquarius c (EL CASTELLO DELL' ORRORE; AKA: FRANKENSTEIN'S CASTLE OF FREAKS)

Rossano Brazzi (Count Frankenstein), Michael Dunn (Genz), Boris Lugosi (Ook, the Neanderthal), Christiane Royce (Krista), Edmund Purdom, Luciano Pignozzi, Gordon Michael, Loren Ewing, Xiro Pappas, Lewis Garfield.

This truly awful Italian outing features Rossano Brazzi (SOUTH PACIFIC) as mad scientist Frankenstein, who is attempting to create a giant monster named, appropriately enough, Goliath. With the help of the usual bevy of misfit cretins found in these movies—including Genz the dwarf and a hunchback named Kreegin—Frankenstein succeeds in planting a brain in the giant's skull. When the dwarf (Michael Dunn, who played the memorable villain Dr. Loveless in the television series "The Wild, Wild West"), is expelled from the castle, he decides to get revenge by enlisting the aid of a Neanderthal man named Ook (played by an actor named Boris Lugosi!). Even weirder, the prehistoric gent wears tennis shorts! Mind-numbingly bad, this film is available on videocassette as DR. FRANKENSTEIN'S CASTLE OF FREAKS. Oh, yeah, there are lots of big-chested naked women, too.

p, Robert Randall; d, Robert Oliver; w, Mario Francini.

(PR:C-O  MPAA:PG)

## HOUSE OF PSYCHOTIC WOMEN, THE*

(1973, Sp.) 87m Independent International c (LOS OJOS AZULES DE LA MUNECA ROTA; AKA: BLUE EYES OF THE BROKEN DOLL, THE; HOUSE OF DOOM)

Paul Naschy, Maria Perschy, Diana Lorys, Eva Leon, Eduardo Calvo, Ines Morales, Antonio Pica, Luis Ciges.

Another cheap, bloody effort from the team of Carlos Aured and Paul Naschy, THE HOUSE OF PSYCHOTIC WOMEN features former weightlifter Naschy as an ex-con who takes a job as a handyman in a house owned by three sisters: a redheaded nymphomaniac, a brunette who is missing a hand, and a blonde confined to a wheelchair. Of course, all three women are nuts and Naschy has his hands full as the bodies of beautiful women—with their eyes gouged out—begin piling up, leaving the viewer to figure out which sister is the killer. Independent International sold the film in the US with the tag line "They're HELL ON EARTH with LOVE-LUSTS and BLOOD-LUSTS that will SHOCK YOU OUT OF YOUR SEAT and MIND!" Well, not quite, but there are lots of scenes of a bare-chested, hirsute Naschy leaving the nymphomaniac's bedroom followed by gory murders. Naschy fans—and there are quite a few   will love it

p, Modesto Perez Redondo; d, Carlos Aured; w, Jacinto Molina; ph, Francisco Sanchez.

(PR:O  MPAA:R)

## HOUSE OF SEVEN CORPSES, THE**½

(1974) 90m International Amusements c

John Ireland (Eric Hartmann), Faith Domergue (Gayle), John Carradine (Mr. Price), Carole Wells (Anne), Charles Macaulay (Christopher), Jerry Strickler (Dave), Larry Record (Tommy), Ron Foreman (Ron), Marty Hornstein (Danny), Charles Bail (Jonathan Anthony Beal/Theodore Beal), Jeff Alexander (Russell Beal), Jo Anne Mower (Allison Beal), Lucy Doheny (Suzanne Beal), Ron Garcia (Charles Beal), Wells Bond (The Ghoul).

This cheapie horror movie stars John Ireland as the director of a cheapie horror movie who takes his crew on location to the haunted mansion where the murder the script is based on actually took place. During the shoot, a secret room full of black magic paraphernalia is found, and the star of the film-within-the-film, Faith Domergue (THIS ISLAND EARTH; IT CAME FROM BENEATH THE SEA), reads a passage from the Tibetan Book of the Dead, inadvertently summoning up a ghoul that begins killing off cast and crew. John Carradine is on hand as the proprietor of the mansion, which, in real life, was once the official residence of the governor of Utah. A decent script, a better-than-usual cast for this sort of thing, and some impressive direction from low-budget auteur Paul Harrison (writer of the long-defunct "H.R. Puf 'n' Stuff" children's show) help make this a fairly watchable—albeit low-budget—effort. Too bad the color on most prints in atrocious.

p, Paul Harrison, Paul Lewis; d, Paul Harrison; w, Paul Harrison, Thomas J. Kelly; ph, Don Jones.

(PR:C  MPAA:PG)

## HOUSE OF THE LIVING DEAD*

(1973, South Africa) 87m Associated Film Producers c (AKA: DOCTOR MANIAC)

Mark Burns, Shirley Ann Field, David Oxley, Margaret Inglis, Dia Sydow, Lynne Maree.

Set in the mid-19th century, this South African entry offers Mark Burns as a maniacal scientist who corrals the souls of dead animals for his own bizarre studies. Things get out of hand when he begins experimenting with the souls of his own family—including that of his brother, whose identity he assumes. Despite its intriguing premise, this obscure film is ineptly staged and tedious.

p, Matt Druker; d, Ray Austin; w, Marc Marais; ph, Lionel Friedberg.

(PR:C    MPAA:PG)

## HOUSE OF THE LONG SHADOWS**

(1983, Brit.) 96m Cannon c

Vincent Price *(Lionel),* Christopher Lee *(Corrigan),* Peter Cushing *(Sebastian),* Desi Arnaz, Jr. *(Kenneth Magee),* John Carradine *(Lord Grisbane),* Sheila Keith *(Victoria),* Julie Peasgood *(Mary Norton).*

Centering on a bizarre family reunion at a decaying Welsh manor, this amusing, old-fashioned haunted house film is little more than an excuse to reunite the grand old stars of low-budget gothic horror films—Vincent Price, Christopher Lee, Peter Cushing, and John Carradine. A young American writer (Desi Arnaz, Jr.) is using the mansion as a quiet, atmospheric place to crank out a suspense novel. However, he is unable to write when the oddball Grisbane family arrives for its reunion. HOUSE OF THE LONG SHADOWS is a real surprise from British gorehound Peter Walker, whose HOUSE OF WHIPCORD; FLESH AND BLOOD SHOW; and FRIGHTMARE set the standard for cinematic sadism in England. This effort is amazingly gentle, with just about every haunted house cliche in the book delivered tongue-in-cheek. *Seven Keys to Baldpate,* the novel on which this film was based, came to the screen five times between 1917 and 1947.

p, Menahem Golan; d, Peter Walker; ph, Norman Langley; ed, Robert Dearberg; w, Michael Armstrong (based on the novel *Seven Keys to Baldpate* by Earl Derr Biggers), m, Richard Harvey.

(PR:O    MPAA:NR)

## HOUSE OF USHER****

(1960) 79m AIP c (AKA: THE FALL OF THE HOUSE OF USHER)

Vincent Price *(Roderick Usher),* Mark Damon *(Philip Winthrop),* Myrna Fahey *(Madeline Usher),* Harry Ellerbe *(Bristol),* Bill Borzage, Mike Jordon, Nadajan, Ruth Oklander, George Paul, David Andar, Eleanor LeFaber, Geraldine Paulette, Phil Sylvestre, John Zimeas *(Ghosts).*

A real coup for Roger Corman and AIP, HOUSE OF USHER was the first of their horror films that had a decent budget ($350,000), boasted a shooting schedule of more than 10 days (they were allowed 15), was shot in color and CinemaScope, and was "inspired" by Edgar Allan Poe. The gamble paid off and the film was a critical and commercial hit that unleashed scads of other films based on the works of Poe. The wonderful Vincent Price stars as Roderick Usher, the creepy, white-haired owner of the mysterious house of Usher, who lives in seclusion in the creaking old house with his sister, Madeline (Myrna Fahey). When Madeline announces her engagement to Philip (Mark Damon), Roderick will have none of it and informs her betrothed that he and his sister are the last of the Ushers who suffer from a bizarre madness that must not be transmitted to another generation. When Philip re-

fuses to leave the spooky house despite this warning, strange accidents befall him, and he is nearly killed. Meanwhile, Madeline falls ill, and soon after, Roderick informs Philip that she has died of a heart attack and entombs her in the family chapel. The butler, however, informs Philip that his fiancee has suffered from periodic blackouts and that she may have been buried alive. Enraged, Philip confronts Roderick with this information, but the last Usher merely shrugs off the suggestion, confident that he has done the proper thing. That night Philip learns that Madeline is indeed alive and has clawed her way out of her coffin, seeking revenge. Moody, atmospheric and effective, HOUSE OF USHER succeeds in making the house a "monster," which a desperate Corman had to make clear to skeptical executive producer Sam Arkoff when he questioned the film's lack of a menacing creature. Corman's savvy use of color, musty cobwebs, and creaking and groaning sound effects combine to make the *house* appear to be the cause of all the madness. Price is wonderful as the spooky owner, but the other three players are only competent at best. All in all, this is a superlative Corman/AIP effort and a great beginning to a fitfully artistically successful but always interesting series of horror films. On video as THE FALL OF THE HOUSE OF USHER.

p, Roger Corman; d, Roger Corman; w, Richard Matheson (based on the novel "The Fall of the House of Usher" by Edgar Allan Poe); ph, Floyd Crosby; ed, Anthony Carras; m, Les Baxter.

(PR:A    MPAA:NR)

## HOUSE OF WAX***½

(1953) 90m WB c

Vincent Price *(Prof. Henry Jarrod),* Frank Lovejoy *(Lt. Tom Brennan),* Phyllis Kirk *(Sue Allen),* Carolyn Jones *(Cathy Gray),* Paul Picerni *(Scott Andrews),* Roy Roberts *(Matthew Burke),* Angela Clarke *(Mrs. Andrews),* Paul Cavanagh *(Sidney Wallace),* Dabbs Greer *(Sgt. Jim Shane),* Charles Buchinsky [Bronson] *(Igor),* Reggie Rymal *(Barker),* Philip Tonge *(Bruce Allison),* Darwin Greenfield, Jack Kenney *(Lodgers),* Ruth Warren *(Scrubwoman),* Riza Royce *(Ma Flanagan),* Richard Benjamin, Jack Mower *(Detectives),* Grandon Rhodes *(Surgeon),* Frank Ferguson *(Medical Examiner),* Eddie Parks *(Morgue Attendant),* Oliver Blake *(Pompous Man),* Leo Curley *(Portly Man),* Mary Lou Holloway *(Millie),* Joanne Brown *(Girl Friend),* Lyle Latell *(Waiter),* Terry Mitchell, Ruth Whitney, Trude Wyler *(Women),* Merry Townsend *(Ticket Taker).*

This fine remake of the classic THE MYSTERY OF THE WAX MUSEUM (1933) was filmed in 3-D and employed "Warner Phonic Sound," a forerunner to stereo that utilized a number of speakers to direct the sound at the audience from various directions. Vincent Price plays Prof. Henry Jarrod, a wax sculptor in New York at the turn of the century, who presides over a wax museum that is floundering because of his pursuit of beauty and not sensationalism. When Jarrod again refuses partner Burke's (Roy Roberts) request to create more horrifying pieces, Burke sets fire to the museum, intent on collecting the insurance money. It is presumed that Jarrod died with his creations, but he returns, horribly scarred, and strangles Burke. Years later, Jarrod, feigning a wheelchair-confining back injury, opens a new wax museum with even more life-like displays. Because his hands have been horribly burned, he employs two assistants to do the sculpting under his supervision (one of whom is played by Charles Bronson, then billed as Buchinsky). In reality, however, Jarrod's mad sculpting Is accomplished by pouring wax over people he has murdered. HOUSE OF WAX was stunningly directed by Andre de Toth, who used the new 3-D process to its fullest potential without bogging down the narrative with too many "gee-look-what-I-can-do" tricks (although the film's paddle-ball salesman is a bit annoying). Ironically, this man who saw the potential of 3-D and who directed one of the most effective movies ever shot in that process had only one eye, which hampered his depth perception. Price is magnificent as usual and manages to steal the role of Prof. Jarrod from its creator, Lionel Atwill. Although it is now extremely difficult to see in its original format, HOUSE OF WAX is still well worth viewing in flat prints or on video.

p, Bryan Foy; d, Andre de Toth; w, Crane Wilbur (based on a play by Charles Welden); ph, Bert Glennon, Peverell Marley (Natural Vision 3-D Warner Color); ed, Rudi Fehr; m, David Buttolph.

(PR:A   MPAA:NR)


### HOUSE OF WHIPCORD zero

(1974, Brit.) 94m AIP c

Barbara Markham *(Mrs. Wakehurst)*, Patrick Barr *(Justice Bailey)*, Penny Irving *(Ann-Marie Di Verney)*, Ray Brooks *(Tony)*, Anne Michelle *(Julia)*, Sheila Keith *(Walker)*, Dorothy Gordon *(Bates)*, Ivor Salter *(Jack)*, Robert Tayman *(Mark E. Desade)*, Judy Robinson *(Claire)*, Karen David *(Karen)*, Jane Hayward *(Estelle)*, Celia Quicke *(Denise)*, Celia Imrie *(Barbara)*, David McGillivray *(Caven)*, Ron Smerczak *(Ted)*, Barry Martin *(Al)*, Tony Sympson *(Henry)*, Rose Hill *(Henry's Wife)*, Dave Butler *(Ticket Collector)*, Denis Tinsley *(Police Sergeant)*, Peter Walker *(Cyclist)*.

More of an exploitation film than out-and-out horror entry, this infamous picture is perhaps the best known of the Peter Walker-David McGillivray collaborations (FRIGHTMARE; THE CONFESSIONAL) and the most sadistic. The scant plot involves an elderly couple—a retired magistrate and a former women's prison warden—who set up their own court in the countryside, arresting, trying, convicting, imprisoning, and torturing beautiful young women whose behavior they deem immoral. If seeing girls strung up by the wrists and whipped is your idea of a good time, then this is for you.

p, Peter Walker; d, Peter Walker; w, David McGillivray; ph, Peter Jessop (Movielab Color); ed, Matt McCarthy; m, Stanley Myers.

(PR:O   MPAA:R)


### HOUSE ON HAUNTED HILL***

(1958) 75m AA bw

Vincent Price *(Frederick Loren)*, Carol Ohmart *(Annabelle Loren)*, Richard Long *(Lance Schroeder)*, Alan Marshal *(Dr. David Trent)*, Carolyn Craig *(Nora Manning)*, Elisha Cook, Jr. *(Watson Pritchard)*, Julie Mitchum *(Ruth Bridgers)*, Leona Anderson *(Mrs. Slykes)*, Howard Hoffman *(Jonas)*.

Horror producer-director William Castle churned out a series of well-made little creepies that used outrageous gimmicks to pull folks into the theaters and THE HOUSE ON HAUNTED HILL was no exception. At a specified terrifying moment theater owners were supposed to release a full-sized skeleton that would "leap" from the screen and zip over the heads of audience suspended on an invisible wire. It may have worked the first time, but clever moviegoers soon got wise, waited for the skeleton to appear, and pelted it with candy counter items, prompting theater owners to bring a quick halt to the in-house "special effects" nonsense. Luckily, Castle's films are okay even without the gimmicks. In this one, Vincent Price stars as Frederick Loren, the owner of a haunted mansion who offers $10,000 to anyone dumb enough to attempt spending an entire night there. Price is delightfully hammy as he hands the brave guests little coffins that contain handguns for their protection. While Loren happily tries to scare the wits out of his guests, his wife (Carol Ohmart) and her lover (Alan Marshal) attempt to arrange things so that Frederick will be shot "accidentally" by one of the guests. Silly, but good fun.

p, William Castle; d, William Castle; w, Robb White; ph, Carl E. Guthrie; ed, Roy Livingston; m, Von Dexter.

(PR:A   MPAA:NR)


### HOUSE ON SKULL MOUNTAIN, THE*

(1974) 89m FOX c

Victor French *(Andrew Cunningham)*, Jane Michelle *(Lorena Christophe)*, Jean Durand *(Thomas)*, Mike Evans *(Phillippe)*, Xernona Clayton *(Harriet Johnson)*, Lloyd Nelson *(Sheriff)*, Ella Woods *(Louette)*, Mary J. Todd McKenzie *(Pauline)*, Don Devendorf *(Priest)*, Jo Marie *(Doctor)*, Sen. Leroy Johnson *(Lawyer LeDoux)*.

Ex-"Gunsmoke" producer Ron Honthaner was hired by a group of black Atlanta businessmen to direct this dreadfully boring black exploitation film in which four relatives converge on the spooky mansion of a dying old hag (Mary J. Todd McKenzie) to hear the reading of her will. The voodoo-practicing butler (Jean Durand) begins bumping off the relatives one by one until the token white (Victor French)—who learns that he's got more than a few drops of black blood in him—manages to rescue lovely Lorena (Janee Michelle), with whom he's fallen in love. About what you'd expect from a horror film made by a "Gunsmoke" vet.

p, Ray Storey; d, Ron Honthaner; w, Mildred Pares; ph,

Monroe Askins (Movielab Color); ed, Gerard Wilson; m, Jerrold Immel.

(PR:C  MPAA:PG)

## HOUSE ON SORORITY ROW, THE*½

(1983) 91m VAE/Film Ventures/ARC c (AKA: SEVEN SISTERS; GB: HOUSE OF EVIL)

Kathryn McNeil *(Katherine)*, Eileen Davidson *(Vicki)*, Janis Zido *(Liz)*, Robin Meloy *(Jeanie)*, Harley Kozak *(Diane)*, Jodi Draigie *(Morgan)*, Ellen Dorsher *(Stevie)*, Lois Kelsa Hunt *(Mrs. Slater)*, Christopher Lawrence *(Dr. Beck)*, Michael Kuhn, Michael Sergio, Ruth Walsh, Larry Singer, Jean Schertler, Ed Heath, Charles Serio, Peter McClung, Brian T. Small, Alan Treadwell, Ken Myers.

The feature debut of Brian DePalma protege Mark Rosman, this sporadically interesting slasher film is better directed than most. Opening with a precredit sequence wherein a horribly deformed, mentally defective baby is born to a woman who has used a fertility drug, the film then shoots forward 20 years. The mother (Kelsa Hunt) has turned her home into a college sorority house, and her mutant son is, of course, locked in the attic and just waiting for a chance to get loose so that he can kill the nubile sorority girls one at a time. His opportunity comes when the mischievous girls accidentally bring about their mother's death as part of a prank. Although director Rosman spices up the predictable murders with some stabs at surrealism, a slasher movie is a slasher movie is a slasher movie, and this one soon wears out its welcome.

p, Mark Rosman, John G. Clark; d, Mark Rosman; w, Mark Rosman, Bobby Fine; ph, Timothy Suhrstedt (TVC Color); ed, Jean-Marc Vasseur, Paul Trejo; m, Richard Band.

(PR:O  MPAA:R)

## HOUSE THAT DRIPPED BLOOD, THE***

(1971, Brit.) 101m Amicus c

Denholm Elliott *(Charles)*, Joanna Dunham *(Alice)*, Tom Adams *(Dominick)*, Robert Lang *(Psychiatrist)*, Peter Cushing *(Philip)*, Joss Ackland *(Rogers)*, Wolfe Morris *(Waxworks Owner)*, Christopher Lee *(Reid)*, Nyree Dawn Porter *(Ann)*, Chloe Franks *(Jane)*, Jon Pertwee *(Paul)*, Ingrid Pitt *(Carla)*, Geoffrey Bayldon *(Von Hartmann)*, John Bennett *(Holloway)*, John Bryans *(Stoker)*.

Adapted by *Psycho* author Robert Bloch from his own short stories, this Amicus horror anthology is set in an English country home whose tenants all meet bloody deaths. Inspector Holloway (John Bennett) is called out to investigate, and the four stories that comprise the film are presented as part of a police file. In the first installment, "Method For Murder," a mystery writer (Denholm Elliott) falls victim to a strangler not unlike a character in one of his books. Peter Cushing and Joss Ackland star in the second segment, "Waxworks," as a pair who are lured by a living statue of Salome to a wax museum where they are axed by the museum's owner (Wolfe Morris). Christopher Lee is the victim of the third tale, "Sweets to the Sweets," his death brought about by his young daughter's voodoo vengeance. The last segment "The Cloak," is a humorous tale starring Jon Pertwee as a big-headed actor who, in his quest for authenticity, is given a cloak owned by a real vampire. Although he *thinks* that he has actually joined the undead, his leading lady (Ingrid Pitt) really is a vampire. Skillfully written by Bloch and boasting an excellent cast, this omnibus is a bit better than most and was the feature debut of television director Peter Duffell, who wound up returning to small-screen work.

p, Max J. Rosenberg, Milton Subotsky; d, Peter Duffell; w, Robert Bloch; ph, Ray Parslow (Eastmancolor); ed, Peter Tanner; m, Michael Dress.

(PR:A-C  MPAA:GP)

## HOUSE THAT VANISHED. THE**

(1974, Brit.) 95m AIP c (AKA: SCREAM AND DIE)

Andrea Allan, Karl Lanchbury, Maggie Walker.

Titled SCREAM AND DIE in Britain, this soft-core slasher effort was picked up for American release and given a "House" title in an effort to capitalize on the "House" craze then sweeping the drive-ins (LAST HOUSE ON THE LEFT; THE NEW HOUSE ON THE LEFT, etc.). Another PSYCHO rip-off tells the story of a model who witnesses a murder but can't find the house in which she saw it committed when she tries to lead her boy friend to it later. The killer, whose identity becomes pretty obvious, is totally dominated by his possessive aunt (Maggie Walker). Directed by Spanish sexploitation king Joseph Larraz, this film has more than its share of gratuitous sex and nudity, and includes a predictable and absurd twist ending. On videocassette under both this title and SCREAM AND DIE.

p, Diana Daubeney; d, Joseph Larraz; w, Derek Ford.

(PR:O  MPAA:R)

## HOUSE WHERE EVIL DWELLS, THE*½

(1982) 88m MGM/UA c

Edward Albert *(Ted)*, Susan George *(Laura)*, Doug McClure *(Alex)*, Amy Barrett *(Amy)*, Mako Hattori *(Otami)*, Toshiyuki Sasaki *(Shugoro)*, Toshiya Maruyama *(Masanori)*, Tsuyako Okajima *(Witch)*, Henry Mitowa *(Zen Monk)*.

After directing the humorous and successful MOTEL HELL, Kevin Connor missed the mark with this straightforward haunted-house horror film. In a big house in 1840 Japan, a love triangle ends in two murders and a suicide, leaving an adulterous wife (Mako Hattori), her lover (Toshiyuki Sasaki), and her husband (Toshiya Maruyama) to haunt the house forever. When the young American couple (Edward Albert and Susan George) who move into the house is visited by a diplomat friend (Doug McClure), the ghosts take possession of the modern-day inhabitants and the triangle is reenacted. A Buddhist monk is called in to exorcise the house, but the ghosts return, and take over the bodies again, leading to a violent end. Although there aren't many scary parts in this one, it has plenty of nudity and some loopy humor, especially in the exorcism scene.

p, Martin B. Cohen; d, Kevin Connor; w, Robert Suhosky (based on the novel by James Hardiman); ph, Jacques Haitkin (Technicolor); ed, Barry Peters; m, Ken Thorne.

**(PR:O MPAA:R)**

## HOWLING, THE***½

(1981) 91m AE c

Dee Wallace *(Karen White)*, Patrick Macnee *(Dr. George Waggner)*, Dennis Dugan *(Chris)*, Christopher Stone *(R. William "Bill" Neill)*, Belinda Balaski *(Terry Fisher)*, Kevin McCarthy *(Fred Francis)*, John Carradine *(Erle Kenton)*, Slim Pickens *(Sam Newfield)*, Elisabeth Brooks *(Marsha)*, Robert Picardo *(Eddie)*, Dick Miller *(Walter Paisley)*, Margie Impert *(Donna)*, Noble Willingham, James Murtaugh, Jim McKrell, Kenneth Tobey, Don McLeod, Steve Nevil, Herb Braha, Joe Bratcher, Roger Corman.

Director and Roger Corman alumnus Joe Dante (PIRANHA; GREMLINS; EXPLORERS), screenwriter (now screenwriter-director) John Sayles (BROTHER FROM ANOTHER PLANET; MATEWAN; EIGHT MEN OUT) and makeup artist Rob Bottin combined talents on this wonderful combination of horror, laughs, and state-of-the-art special effects. After being severely traumatized while investigating a story, TV anchorwoman Karen White (Dee Wallace) ventures to Dr. Waggner's (Patrick Macnee) ultra-exclusive California transcendental meditation spa accompanied by her husband (Christopher Stone). In time, however, it's revealed that Waggner's select clientele are all werewolves. The transformation scenes are incredible, especially the one in which siren Elisabeth Brooks and Stone, whom she has seduced, make love under the moonlight. Dante fills the film with hysterical cameos from Corman, Dick Miller, Kevin McCarthy, John Carradine, and Slim Pickens, and demonstrates a subtle wit and a flair for horror much more sophisticated than anything John Landis came up with in his subsequent AMERICAN WEREWOLF IN LONDON. Unfortunately, a slew of really awful sequels followed.

p, Michael Finnell, Jack Conrad; d, Joe Dante; w, John Sayles, Terence H. Winkless (based on the novel by Gary Brandner); ph, John Hora (CFI color); ed, Mark Goldblatt, Joe Dante; m, Pino Donaggio.

**(PR:O MPAA:R)**

## HOWLING II . . . YOUR SISTER IS A WEREWOLF*½

(1985) 90m Granite-Hemdale/Thorn-EMI c

Christopher Lee *(Stefan Crosscoe)*, Annie McEnroe *(Jenny Templeton)*, Reb Brown *(Ben White)*, Sybil Danning *(Stirba)*, Marsha Hunt *(Mariana)*, Judd Omen *(Vlad)*, Ferdinand [Ferdy] Mayne *(Erle)*, Babel *(Punk Group)*.

A female newscaster turns into a wolf on the air one night and attacks a cameraman before being killed. At her funeral, werewolf expert Stefan Crosscoe (Christopher Lee) convinces the dead woman's brother, Ben (Reb Brown), to accompany him to Transylvania to put an end to a cult of werewolves headed by none other than Sybil Danning. Lacking suspense, scares, and decent special effects, this

film has absolutely nothing to do with the original HOWLING. Lee is as good as usual, though that's not saying much, and Danning, the reigning queen of the B's, shows less skin and less talent than usual.

p, Steven Lane; d, Philippe Mora; w, Robert Sarno, Gary Brandner (based on the novel by Brandner); ph, G. Stephenson; m, Steve Parsons.

**(PR:O MPAA:R)**

## HOWLING III, THE*½

(1987, Aus.) 94m Bacannia Ent./Square Pictures c
(AKA: THE MARSUPIALS: THE HOWLING III)

Barry Otto *(Prof. Harry Beckmeyer)*, Imogen Annesley *(Jerboa)*, Dasha Blahova *(Olga Gorki, Ballerina)*, Max Fairchild *(Thylo, Werewolf Leader)*, Ralph Cotterill *(Prof. Sharp)*, Leigh Biolos *(Donny Martin, Assistant Director)*, Frank Thring *(Jack Citron, Film Director)*, Michael Pate *(U.S. President)*, Barry Humphries *(Dame Edna Everage)*, Carole Skinner *(Yara)*, Brian Adams *(Gen. Miller)*, Bill Collins *(Doctor)*, Christopher Pate *(Security Agent)*, Jenny Vuletic *(Goolah)*, Burnham Burnham *(Kendi)*, Alan Penney *(Spud)*.

The plight of the Australian marsupial lycanthrope (a cross between a werewolf and a koala) is given a comic treatment in this the second Philippe Mora sequel to Joe Dante's THE HOWLING (1981). Mora's last sequel, 1985's THE HOWLING II . . . YOUR SISTER IS A WEREWOLF, boasted the presence of Christopher Lee and Sybil Danning. No such luck with THE HOWLING III. But although it has a relatively unknown cast and is inept technically, THE HOWLING III makes up for its deficiencies with its intentional silliness. The ridiculous plot involves a scientist (Barry Otto, the lead from BLISS) whose raison d'etre is the study of a tribe of Australian marsupial werewolves—differentiated from their European cousins by their pouches. Eventually, the scientist and his sidekick (Ralph Cotterill) make contact with the tribe's leader (Max Fairchild), whose ballerina wife (Dasha Blahova) unexpectedly transforms into a werewolf (the Russian pouchless variety) while in mid-pirouette on the Sydney Opera House stage. Some dissent within the tribe causes the pouched Jerboa (Imogen Annesley) to pack her things and head for the big city, where she finds work as an extra on a horror film called "Shape Shifters, Part 8." It's all good, not-so-clean fun with a tongue-in-cheek (or "tongue-in-pouch," as Mora put it) sense of humor.

p, Charles Waterstreet, Philippe Mora; d, Philippe Mora; w, Philippe Mora (based on the book *Howling III* by Gary Brandner); ph, Louis Irving; ed, Lee Smith; m, Allan Zavod.

**(PR:C-O MPAA:PG-13)**

## HOWLING IV: THE ORIGINAL NIGHTMARE**

(1988, Brit.) 92m John Hough/Allied c

Romy Windsor *(Marie)*, Michael T. Weiss *(Richard)*, Antony Hamilton *(Tom)*, Suzanne Severeid *(Janice)*, Lamya Derval *(Eleanor)*, Norman Anstey *(Sheriff)*, Kate Edwards *(Mrs. Orstead)*, Clive Turner *(Tow Truck Driver)*.

It seems that any successful horror film spawns at least a few sequels. Unfortunately, as the roman numerals climb, the commitment to good filmmaking seems to deteriorate. This installment of the "Howling" series does little to reverse that trend, and even less to whet viewer appetites for a possible fifth installment. Marie (Romy Windsor) is an attractive, best-selling author plagued by unsettling visions of a young nun and a demonic wolflike creature. Convinced that the visions are the result of stress and exhaustion, Marie and her husband (Michael T. Weiss) retreat to a quaint cottage near the small town of Drago. There she begins to suspect that her visions are not stress-related hallucinations at all but warnings of danger and evil from beyond the grave. By the time she puts the pieces together, Marie falls into the clutches (and bed) of a seductive local shopkeeper who is also a werewolf. Soon afterwards, the wolves come out to devour Marie and indoctrinate her husband into wolfdom. In the film's most ambitious effects sequence, her husband is reduced to a gurgling protoplasmic puddle, from which he is resurrected as a werewolf. As Marie races here and there, vainly searching for help, she discovers that *everyone* in Drago is a werewolf. The film's special effects are cheesy at best, with the husband's big meltdown scene dragging on too long for it to have any lasting impact. The film's only truly striking aspects occur during Marie's visions, director John Hough adroitly conveying the sense that the world has stopped whenever the mysterious nun appears.

p, Harry Alan Towers; d, John Hough; w, Clive Turner, Freddie Rowe (based on a story by Turner from novels by Gary Brandner); ph, Godfrey Godar; ed, Claudia Finkle, Malcolm Burns-Errington; m, David George, Barrie Guard.

(PR:O MPAA:R)

## HUMAN EXPERIMENTS*½

(1980) 82m Crown International c (AKA: BEYOND THE GATE)

Linda Haynes *(Rachel Foster)*, Geoffrey Lewis *(Dr. Kline)*, Ellen Travolta *(Mover)*, Aldo Ray *(Mat Tibbs)*, Jackie Coogan *(Sheriff Tibbs)*, Darlene Carviotto *(Rita)*, Mercedes Shirley *(Warden Weber)*, Lurene Tuttle *(Granny)*, Marie O'Henry *(Tanya)*, Wesley Marie Tackitt *(Jimmy)*, Caroline Davies *(Pam)*, Cherie Franklin *(Cell Guard)*, Bobby Porter *(Derril Willis)*, James O'Connell *(Father)*, Rebecca Bohanon *(Mother)*, Theodora Tate *(Daughter)*, Timothy Cole *(Son)*.

Linda Haynes stars as a backroads country & western singer who stumbles onto a mass murder and is arrested and quickly imprisoned for the crime. There she is tormented by a crazed prison psychologist (Geoffrey Lewis) who tries to cure his patients by driving them insane, erasing their memories, and then creating new, happier pasts for them. Although its opening is somewhat promising, this film soon degenerates into a terribly predictable, sadistic, and decidedly sleazy combination of A CLOCKWORK ORANGE and JACKSON COUNTY JAIL, once again exploiting the torture of women in the hope of a box-office payoff.

p, Summer Brown, Gregory Goodell; d, Gregory Goodell; w, Richard Rothstein; ph, Joao Fernandes; m, Marc Bucci.

(PR:O MPAA:R)

## HUMAN MONSTER, THE***½

(1940, Brit.) 76m MON bw (AKA: DARK EYES OF LONDON)

Bela Lugosi *(Dr. Orloff)*, Hugh Williams *(Inspector Holt)*, Greta Gynt *(Diana Stuart)*, Edmond Ryan *(Lt. O'Reilly)*, Wilfrid Walter *(Jake, Monster)*, Alexander Field *(Grogan)*, Arthur E. Owen *(Dumb Lew)*, Julie Suedo *(Secretary)*, Gerald Pring *(Henry Stuart)*, Bryan Herbert *(Walsh)*, May Hallatt *(Policewoman)*, Charles Penrose *(The Drunk)*.

This surprisingly gruesome British effort was slapped with the UK's first "H" certificate (horrific, persons over 16 only). Bela Lugosi, in one of his last substantive films, plays Dr. Orloff, the evil head of an insurance company who poses as Mr. Dearborn, the sightless director of a home for the blind. When several of the home's residents sign over their insurance policies to Dearborn and are then found floating in the Thames, the police get suspicious. The ruthless Orloff, who employs a network of blind vagrants to carry out his nefarious schemes, even goes so far as to deafen one of his men, Dumb Lew (Arthur E. Owen), whom he suspects of overhearing too much. Aided by Diana (Greta Gynt), the daughter of one of the victims, the police trace the murders to Dearborn/Orloff, but the inquisitive young woman is kidnaped by the doctor's monstrous assistant, Jake (Wilfrid Walter, a respected Shakespearean actor and playwright who helped create his character's effective makeup). When it appears as if Orloff is going to kill Diana, she manages to provoke a violent struggle between Jake and Orloff. Director Walter Summers maintains an effectively eerie mood throughout his film, making optimal use of the fog-shrouded Thames setting and the grotesque society of blind vagrants. Lugosi turns in one of his best performances here, actually underplaying his role, making palatable the more contrived moments in the script.

p, John Argyle; d, Walter Summers; w, Patrick Kirwan, Walter Summers, John Argyle (based on the novel *Dark Eyes of London* by Edgar Wallace); ph, Bryan Langley; ed, E.G. Richards; m, Guy Jones.

(PR:A-C MPAA:NR)

## HUMANOIDS FROM THE DEEP**½

(1980) 80m NW c (GB: MONSTER)

Doug McClure *(Jim)*, Ann Turkel *(Dr. Susan Drake)*, Vic Morrow *(Hank Slattery)*, Cindy Weintraub *(Carol Hill)*, Anthony Penya *(Johnny)*, Denise Galik *(Linda)*, Lynn Theel *(Peggy)*, Meegan King *(Jerry)*, Breck Costin *(Tommy)*, Hoke Howell *(Deke)*, Don Maxwell *(Dickie)*, David Strassman *(Billy)*, Greg Travis, Linda Shayne, Lisa Glaser, Bruce Monette, Shawn Erler, Frank Arnold, Amy Barrett, Jo Williams, Henry T. Williams, Lyle Isom, Jonathan Lehan.

Monsters from the ocean floor surface in a seaside community, kill the men, rape the women, and generally wreak havoc. Enter scientist Susan Drake (Ann Turkel), who, aided by Jim (Doug McClure), a fisherman, sets out to learn where these creatures come from and why they are acting so abominably. The randy devils (the monsters, not Jim and Susan) attack a carnival and destroy it; however, Jim and Susan find a way to kill the beasties and the world is saved. But wait! One of the raped women gives birth and her baby looks just like . . . Obviously relishing the chance to show everything they couldn't back in the early days of exploitation horror, the New World gang breaks all the monster-movie taboos while injecting heavy doses of black humor.

p, Martin B. Cohen, A. Hunt Lowry; d, Barbara Peeters; w, Frederick James (based on a story by Frank Arnold, Cohen); ph, Daniel Lacambre (Metrocolor); ed, Mark Goldblatt; m, James Horner.

(PR:O  MPAA:R)

## HUMONGOUS zero

(1982, Can.) 91m EM c

Janet Julian *(Sandy Rawlston)*, David Wallace *(Eric Simmonds)*, Janet Baldwin *(Donna Blake)*, John Wildman *(Nick Simmonds)*, Joy Boushel *(Carla Simmonds)*, Layne Coleman *(Burt Defoe)*, Shay Garner *(Ida Parsons)*, Ed McFadyen *(Mr. Parsons)*, Garry Robbins *(Ida's Son)*.

Made by Paul Lynch, the writer-director of PROM NIGHT, this gory trash from Canada follows the familiar group of teenagers out for an illicit weekend on the folks' boat. They wind up marooned on Parsons Island, where it is rumored that 36 years before a woman was raped by a man who was subsequently ripped apart by his victim's dogs. The progeny of that unholy union is, of course, wandering around on the island and in no time teens are being hacked to bits by the giant, dog-eating, mutant madman. Not only is this stupid, it's dull.

p, Anthony Kramreither; d, Paul Lynch; w, William Gray; ph, Brian Hebb; ed, Nick Rotundo; m, John Mills Cockwell.

(PR:O  MPAA:R)

## HUNCHBACK OF NOTRE DAME, THE***

(1923) 93m UNIV-Super Jewel bw

Lon Chaney *(Quasimodo)*, Ernest Torrence *(Clopin)*, Patsy Ruth Miller *(Esmeralda)*, Norman Kerry *(Phoebus)*, Kate Lester *(Mme. De Gondelaurier)*, Brandon Hurst *(Jehan)*, Raymond Hatton *(Gringoire)*, Tully Marshall *(Louis XI)*, Nigel De Brulier *(Dom Claude)*, Harry Van Meter *(Mons. Neufchatel)*, Gladys Brockwell *(Godule)*, Eulalie Jensen *(Marie)*, Winifred Bryson *(Fleur de Lys)*, Nick De Ruiz *(Mons. le Torteru)*, Edwin Wallock *(King's Chamberlain)*, W. Ray Meyers *(Charmolou's Assistant)*, William Parke, Sr. *(Josephus)*, John Cossar *(Judge of Court)*, Roy Laidlaw *(Charmolou)*, George MacQuarrie.

Quasimodo (Lon Chaney), the horribly deformed bellringer of Notre Dame, falls in love with Esmeralda (Patsy Ruth Miller), a beautiful gypsy girl, after she treats him compassionately. Determined to act as Esmeralda's protector,

Quasimodo reciprocates her kindness when she is charged with stabbing Phoebus (Norman Kerry), the officer she loves. Seeing his beloved about to be publicly executed, Quasimodo rescues Esmeralda and spirits her to the high towers of the cathedral, which he then defends against the assault of the angry mob. Justly praised for Chaney's superb makeup job and performance, this adaptation of Hugo's classic novel is, however, so ineptly directed as to be almost unwatchable. Director Wallace Worsley, who guided Chaney through A BLIND BARGAIN the year before, squanders Universal's lavish production—which included massive sets and thousands of extras—with his rudimentary visual sense and total lack of pacing. Even worse is the script, which gives a distressingly superficial treatment to the social and political subtext of Hugo's novel. Chaney's performance is another matter, however. Deriving his characterization directly from Hugo's description of Quasimodo, the actor constructed a hideous hump from 40 pounds of rubber and coupled it to a breastplate and leather harness that added another 30 pounds and constrained his movements to a crouch. Further, his teeth were jagged and misshapen, and one sightless eye bulged grotesquely from its socket. Yet the mastery of Chaney's portrayal is not in the makeup, but in his beautifully expressive body language—the only truly cinematic aspect of the entire staid production. Despite its considerable flaws, the film was a major hit and catapulted Chaney to superstardom, leading to his most famous role in the vastly superior PHANTOM OF THE OPERA. Running times for THE HUNCHBACK OF NOTRE DAME vary, but most videocassette versions are in the 90- to 98-minute range.

p, Carl Laemmle; d, Wallace Worsley; w, Edward T. Lowe, Perley Poore Sheehan (based on the novel by Victor Hugo); ph, Robert Newhard, Tony Kornman.

(PR:A  MPAA:NR)

## HUNCHBACK OF NOTRE DAME, THE*****

(1939) 115m RKO bw

Charles Laughton *(The Hunchback)*, Sir Cedric Hardwicke *(Frollo)*, Thomas Mitchell *(Clopin)*, Maureen O'Hara *(Esmeralda)*, Edmond O'Brien *(Gringoire)*, Alan Marshal *(Proebus)*, Walter Hampden *(Claude)*, Harry Davenport *(Louis XI)*, Katharine Alexander *(Mme. De Lys)*, George Zucco *(Procurator)*, Fritz Leiber *(A Nobleman)*, Etienne Girardot *(The King's Physician)*, Helene Whitney *(Fleur)*, Minna Gombell *(Queen of Beggars)*, Arthur Hohl *(Olivier)*, Rod La Rocque *(Phillipo)*, Spencer Charters *(Court Clerk)*, Rondo Hatton.

With its lavish production and superb cast, a brilliant performance by Charles Laughton, and moody, atmospheric direction from German expatriate William Dieterle, this is the best film version of Victor Hugo's classic novel to date. Laughton is the pathetic, lonely, misshapen bellringer of Notre Dame who falls in love with the beautiful gypsy Esmeralda (Maureen O'Hara). In addition to gorgeous sets by Van Nest Polglase and breathtaking photography by Joseph H. August, the film benefits from a script that is a vast improvement over the 1923 version. Bringing Hugo's social and political concerns to the forefront, screenwriters Sonya Levien and Bruno Frank make the corrupt machinations of the church almost as important as Quasimodo's tragic love. Laughton, whom some have accused of overplaying the role's pathos, is magnificent here in one of his greatest roles. His makeup, created by George and R. Gordon Bau, is at least the equal of Lon Chaney's, with modern foam latex technology allowing for a subtler and, therefore, more jarring visage. Because few production stills of Laughton's made-up face were taken, his appearance is genuinely shocking to the unprepared viewer, even to this day. RKO spent more than $2 million on this production—one of the most expensive films ever made by the studio—and was rewarded with both critical and financial success.

p, Pandro S. Berman; d, William Dieterle; w, Sonya Levien, Bruno Frank (based on the novel by Victor Hugo); ph, Joseph August; ed, William Hamilton, Robert Wise; m, Alfred Newman.

**(PR:A  MPAA:NR)**

## HUNGER, THE**

(1983) 99m MGM/UA c

David Bowie (John), Catherine Deneuve (Miriam), Susan Sarandon (Sarah Roberts), Cliff DeYoung (Tom Haver), Beth Ehlers (Alice Cavender), Dan Hedaya (Lt. Allegrezza), Rufus Collins (Charlie Humphries), Suzanne Bertish (Phyllis), James Aubrey (Ron), Ann Magnuson, John Stephen Hill (Disco Couple), Shane Rimmer (Jelinek), Bauhaus (Disco Group), Douglas Lambert (TV Host), Bessie Love (Lillybelle), John Pankow, Willem Dafoe (Phone Booth Youths), Sophie Ward, Philip Sayer (London House Couple), Lise Hilboldt (Waiting Room Nurse), Michael Howe, Edward Wiley (Interns), Richard Robles (Skater), George Camiller (Eumenes), Oke Wambu (Egyptian Slave).

After a fascinating opening sequence—juxtaposing David Bowie and Catherine Deneuve, clad in tight leather outfits and dark glasses, with shots of a rabid test monkey and the post-punk band Bauhaus playing "Bela Lugosi Is Dead"—THE HUNGER takes a nose dive. Bowie and Deneuve do what they can with the moronic script about two vampires, John and Miriam, who must kill to retain their youth. John senses that he is growing older by the minute and pays a visit to scientist Sarah Roberts (Susan Sarandon), aging nearly 200 years as he waits to see her, a marvel of editing and makeup. Then when Sarah visits John's eerie house, she is seduced by Miriam into a lesbian encounter. Rarely can one identify the spot in a film where it falls apart, but in THE HUNGER it's easy: after Miriam sinks her teeth into Sarah's flesh, there is an abrupt and unintentionally funny cut to a knife slicing a red chunk of steak. From this point on, the picture forgets about its tale of eternal love and decides to become a vampire story, concluding with an awful resurrection of the dead in John's attic. As a result TV commercial director Tony Scott's (brother of Ridley) film is so pointlessly slick and superficial that by the time the climax rolls around it's difficult to recall the merits of the first half of the movie.

p, Richard A. Shepard; d, Tony Scott; w, Ivan Davis, Michael Thomas (based on the novel by Whitley Strieber); ph, Stephen Goldblatt (Panavision, Metrocolor); ed, Pamela Power; m, Michel Rubini, Denny Jaeger.

**(PR:O  MPAA:R)**

## HUNGRY WIVES**½

(1973) 130m Latent Image/Jack H. Harris c (AKA: JACK'S WIFE; SEASON OF THE WITCH)

Jan White (Joan), Ray Laine (Gregg), Anne Muffly (Shirley), Joedda McClain (Nikki), Bill Thunhurst (Jack), Virginia Greenwald (Marion), Neil Fisher (Dr. Miller), Esther Lapidus (Sylvia), Jean Wechsler (Gloria), Shirley Strasser (Grace), Bob Trow (Detective Mills), Dan Mallinger (Sgt. Frazer), Ken Peters (John Fuller), Marvin Lieber (Jerry), Bill Hinzman (Intruder), Daryl Montgomery, Charlotte Carter, Linda Creagan, Paul McCollough, Sue Michaels, Hal Priore, Luis Yuchum, Virginia Greenwald.

One of the most problematic entries in George Romero's filmography, this somewhat haphazard affair combines witchcraft, feminism, and suburban angst into a creepy whole that is fascinating but not quite successful. Joan (Jan White) is a bored middle-aged housewife whose marriage to her uncommunicative businessman husband (Bill Thunhurst) is on the verge of collapse. Watching her daughter (Joedda McClain) blossom into womanhood and leading an active sex life further frustrates Joan, who begins to retreat into a bizarre fantasy world. While visiting a local witch for a Tarot reading, Joan becomes intrigued by the occult and buys a copy of How to Become a Witch, A Primer. Finding herself attracted to her daughter's young college professor, Joan conjures up a spell to attract him, and soon the two are engaged in an affair. Believing that she has become a witch, Joan sinks deeper and deeper into her new life until the line between fantasy and reality blurs and tragedy results. Working from one of his most interesting scripts, Romero shot this ultra-low-budget effort in 16mm and later blew it up to 35mm. But although he had worked wonders with little money before, such is not the case here, and the production looks and sounds terribly cheap, detracting from the film's complicated psychological interplay. Romero has always had spotty luck with actors, and here, with nuanced performances required, he generally strikes out. The original 130-minute print of HUNGRY WIVES was later recut to 89 minutes by the distributor, but the film still failed miserably. In 1982, however, it was rereleased in an effort to capitalize on the success of Romero's DAWN OF THE DEAD. Deceptively marketed as a new Romero movie, the film was retitled SEASON OF THE WITCH (inspired by a Donovan song heard on the soundtrack), in what may have been an attempt to ride the coattails of the just-released HALLOWEEN III: SEASON OF THE WITCH. Romero loyalists will no doubt find this film worthwhile; all others, consider yourself warned.

p, Nancy M. Romero; d, George A. Romero; w, George A. Romero; ph, George A. Romero, Bill Hinzman; ed, George A. Romero; m, Steve Gorn.

**(PR:O  MPAA:R)**

## HUSH . . . HUSH, SWEET CHARLOTTE***½

(1964) 134m FOX bw

Bette Davis *(Charlotte)*, Olivia de Havilland *(Miriam)*, Joseph Cotten *(Drew)*, Agnes Moorehead *(Velma)*, Cecil Kellaway *(Harry)*, Victor Buono *(Big Sam)*, Mary Astor *(Jewel Mayhew)*, Wesley Addy *(Sheriff)*, William Campbell *(Paul Marchand)*, Bruce Dern *(John Mayhew)*, Frank Ferguson *(Editor)*, George Kennedy *(Foreman)*, Dave Willock *(Taxi Driver)*, John Megna *(New Boy)*, Percy Helton *(Funeral Director)*, Kelly Flynn *(2nd Boy)*, Michael Petit *(Gang Leader)*, Alida Aldrich *(Young Girl)*, Kelly Aldrich *(3rd Boy)*, William Aldrich *(Boy Dancer)*, Ellen Corby, Marianne Stewart, Helen Kleeb *(Town Gossips)*, Carol De Lay *(Geraldine)*, Mary Henderson, Lillian Randolph, Geraldine West *(Cleaning Women)*, William Walker *(Chauffeur)*, Idell James *(Ginny Mae)*, Teddy Buckner and His All-Stars.

Set in a decaying Louisiana mansion, HUSH . . . HUSH, SWEET CHARLOTTE stars Bette Davis as Charlotte, an aging, somewhat demented spinster haunted by the past. In 1927, when Charlotte was a young woman, her married lover (Bruce Dern) was murdered and dismembered. Charlotte always believed that her father (Victor Buono) committed the crime, but none of the missing body parts were ever recovered, and the crime remained unsolved. Thirty-seven years later, with her father dead and only her maid (Agnes Moorehead) around for company, Charlotte worries that the upcoming demolition of her house (making way for a highway) will uncover evidence that will prove her father to be the killer. Desperate, she calls upon her cousin Miriam (Olivia de Havilland) to help her in her fight to stop the highway commission from destroying her home. Covetous of Charlotte's inheritance, Miriam and the family doctor (Joseph Cotten) arrive and set out to drive Charlotte mad. Following the critical and financial success of WHAT EVER HAPPENED TO BABY JANE? (which gave a much needed boost to Bette Davis' and Joan Crawford's declining careers), producer-director Robert Aldrich decided to reunite the actresses in another psychological horror film. But despite their successful on-screen chemistry, Davis and Crawford didn't get along with each other, and it took some time for Aldrich to come up with a project that pleased both. When HUSH . . . HUSH, SWEET CHARLOTTE was ready to go into production, Crawford became ill and bowed out. Davis then suggested her friend de Havilland as a replacement, and Aldrich flew to Europe and convinced her to play the role. While perhaps not as creepy as WHAT EVER HAPPENED TO BABY JANE?, this effort offers much the same pleasures and is a fine addition to the southern gothic horror tradition.

p, Robert Aldrich; d, Robert Aldrich; w, Henry Farrell, Lukas Heller; ph, Joseph Biroc; ed, Michael Luciano; m, Frank De Vol.

**(PR:O   MPAA:NR)**

## HYSTERICAL zero

(1983) 86m H&W Filmworks-Cinema Group Venture/EMB c

William Hudson *(Frederick)*, Mark Hudson *(Paul)*, Brett Hudson *(Fritz)*, Cindy Pickett *(Kate)*, Richard Kiel *(Capt. Howdy)*, Julie Newmar *(Venetia)*, Bud Cort *(Dr. John)*, Robert Donner *(Ralph)*, Murray Hamilton *(Mayor)*, Clint Walker *(Sheriff)*, Franklin Ajaye *(Leroy)*, Charlie Callas *(Dracula)*, Keenan Wynn *(Fisherman)*, Gary Owens *(TV Announcer)*, Helena Makela, John Larroquette, Pat Colbert, Indy Shriner, Amanda H. Bearde, Pamela Bowman, Robert Alan Browne, Sue Casey, Natalie Core, Mary Ellen Flaherty, Annie Willette, Gene Castle, Kathy Cherry, Dick Chudnow, Maurice Sneed.

The Hudson Brothers, who try to pass themselves off as comedians, star in this mind-numbingly insipid parody of horror movies. A vacationing writer (Bill Hudson) does his best to get away from it all in a rented old lighthouse on the Oregon coast; however, Venetia (Julie Newmar), the ghost of a woman who died on Halloween night in 1882, makes life difficult for him. In short order, the writer is possessed by the spirit of Venetia's husband, Captain Howdy (played by Richard "Jaws" Kiel), while the pretty ghost sets about bringing her long-dead husband's body back to life. And when the zombie sailor begins killing locals, two detectives (Mark and Brett Hudson) show up at the lighthouse to investigate. Lots of stupid gags, bad jokes, and annoying cameos by the likes of Bud Cort, Charlie Callas, Keenan Wynn, Clint Walker, and Gary Owens. Avoid HYSTERICAL at all costs.

p, Gene Levy; d, Chris Bearde; w, William Hudson, Mark Hudson, Brett Hudson, Trace Johnston; ph, Donald Morgan (DeLuxe Color); ed, Stanley Frazen; m, Robert Alcivar, Robert O. Ragland.

**(PR:A-C   MPAA:PG)**

## I DISMEMBER MAMA*

(1974) 87m Europix c (AKA: POOR ALBERT AND LITTLE ANNIE)

Zooey Hall *(Albert)*, Geri Reischl *(Annie)*, Joanna Moore Jordan, Marlene Tracy, Greg Mullavey *(Detective)*, Frank Whiteman, Elaine Partnow, Rosella Olson, Robert Christopher.

In this low-budget psycho-killer movie, poor Albert (Zooey Hall) finally escapes the mental institution his mother put him in. Now worse than he was going in, Albert has developed a mother complex, naturally, and feels it is his duty to seek out and destroy all "immoral" women. Eventually he meets and falls in love with his "ideal" female—a nine-year-old girl. Obsessed with protecting his love's purity, Albert goes after the child's tainted older sisters; luckily, the cops track him down, and the diseased killer grabs a naked mannequin and leaps out a window to his death. A pretty shabby production overall, though Hall turns in an interesting performance. Originally released on a "Frenzy of Blood!" double bill with THE BLOOD-SPATTERED BRIDE.

p, Leon Roth; d, Paul Leder; w, William Norton; ph, William Swenning; m, Herschel Burke Gilbert.

**(PR:O MPAA:R)**

## I DRINK YOUR BLOOD**½

(1971) 83m Cinemation c

Bhaskar *(Horace Bones)*, Jadine Wong *(Sue-Lin)*, Ronda Fultz *(Molly)*, Elizabeth Marner-Brooks *(Mildred Nash)*, George Patterson *(Rollo)*, Riley Mills *(Pete)*, Iris Brooks *(Sylvia)*, John Damon *(Roger Davis)*, Richard Bowler *(Doc Banner)*, Tyde Kierney *(Andy)*, Lynn Lowry, Alex Mann, Bruno Damon, Mike Gentry.

I DRINK YOUR BLOOD is a bizarre, violent black comedy about a traveling band of Satan-worshipping hippies who invade a small town and slip some LSD to an old man for laughs. The elderly man's 12-year-old son gets revenge by injecting meat pies with rabid dog blood and then selling them to the dopers. The hippies, of course, turn rabid and cannibalistic and go on a rampage, killing each other. A few survive, however, and one of the females seduces a few conservative "America First"-type construction workers, who are soon also infected. Will the disease spread throughout America? You bet. Pretty gross and surprisingly well made, the film was initially rated "X" by the MPAA—one of the first films ever so rated for violence, rather than explicit sex—then cut by the producer, who also added 10 minutes of new footage to attain the more comfortable "R" rating. This film was also part of the infamous I DRINK YOUR BLOOD/I EAT YOUR SKIN double bill ("2 GREAT BLOOD-HORRORS To Rip Out Your Guts!") of the early 1970s. I EAT YOUR SKIN was actually an unreleased 1964 black-and-white zombie movie, originally titled "Voo-doo Blood Bath," and wasn't particularly gory. I DRINK YOUR BLOOD is not currently listed as being available on videocassette, but it was released in the VHS format early in the 1980s and some video stores may still have it.

p, Jerry Gross; d, David Durston; w, David Durston; ph, Jacques Demarecaux (Widescreen, DeLuxe Color); m, Clay Pitts.

**(PR:O MPAA:R)**

## I SPIT ON YOUR GRAVE*

(1983) 100m Cinemagic Pictures c (AKA: DAY OF THE WOMAN)

Camille Keaton *(Jennifer)*, Eron Tabor *(Johnny)*, Richard Pace *(Matthew)*, Gunter Kleeman *(Andy)*, Alexis Magnotti *(Attendant's Wife)*, Tammy Zarchi, Terry Zarchi *(Children)*, Traci Ferrante *(Waitress)*, Bill Tasgal *(Porter)*, Isac Agami *(Butcher)*, Ronit Haviv *(Supermarket Girl)*.

Jennifer (Camille Keaton), a New York City writer, goes to a Connecticut countryside retreat to finish her novel. While sunbathing in a boat, she is accosted by a quartet of slob-bering goons and dragged onto shore, where she is repeatedly raped. When the ordeal is over, Jennifer staggers through the woods back to her cabin, only to be brutalized again by the same gang. They leave her for dead, but Jennifer survives, and, instead of going to the police, arms herself and stalks her attackers, systematically killing each one off. Originally released in 1978 as DAY OF THE WOMAN, the film did no business until the Jerry Gross organization got hold of it, retitled it I SPIT ON YOUR GRAVE, and gave it a lurid advertising campaign with the tag-line, "This woman has just cut, chopped, broken, and burned five men beyond recognition . . . But no jury in America would ever convict her." (One wonders if Gross even saw the movie, since there are only four men in the film, not five.) This finally got the film noticed, especially by Chicago movie critics Roger Ebert and Gene Siskel, who knew a rabble-rousing issue when they saw one and went into fits over it on their television show, throwing a harsh, negative light on the entire genre. Subsequently, the film was a notorious hit at the box-office and video rental stores. In any case, the film is not as reprehensible as its reputation suggests, but it certainly isn't very good either. Director Meir Zarchi may have been trying to make a point about the horrors of rape, brutality, revenge, and reprisal, but he simply isn't a good enough director to extract any relevance, ambiguity, or nuance from his exploitative material. Watch Wes Craven's LAST HOUSE ON THE LEFT instead.

p, Joseph Zbeda; d, Meir Zarchi; w, Meir Zarchi; ph, Yuri Haviv (Eastmancolor); ed, Meir Zarchi.

**(PR:O MPAA:R)**

## I WALKED WITH A ZOMBIE*****

(1943) 69m RKO bw

James Ellison *(Wesley Rand)*, Frances Dee *(Betsy)*, Tom Conway *(Paul Holland)*, Edith Barrett *(Mrs. Rand)*, James Bell *(Dr. Maxwell)*, Christine Gordon *(Jessica Holland)*, Teresa Harris *(Alma)*, Sir Lancelot *(Calypso Singer)*, Darby Jones *(Carre Four)*, Jeni LeGon *(Dancer)*, Richard Abrams *(Clement)*, Martin Wilkins *(Houngan)*, Jieno Moxzer *(Sabreur)*, Arthur Walker *(Ti-Joseph)*, Katheleen Hartfield *(Dancer)*, Clinton Rosemond *(Coachman)*, Alan Edmiston *(Mr. Wilkens)*, Norman Mayes *(Bayard)*, Melvin Williams *(Baby)*, Vivian Dandridge *(Melisse)*.

I WALKED WITH A ZOMBIE was the second in the series of thought-provoking, literate horror films produced by Val Lewton in the 1940s (the first was THE CAT PEOPLE), and, under the masterful direction of Jacques Tourneur, it is an unqualified masterpiece of the horror cinema. The story idea and title were borrowed from a series of newspaper articles that detailed voodoo and witchcraft practices in Haiti. Betsy (Frances Dee) is a young nurse sent to Haiti by rich American planter Paul Holland (Tom Conway) to take care of his catatonic wife, Jessica (Christine Gordon). Paul thinks his wife has gone insane, and is ridden with guilt that he may have caused it. The locals suspect, however, that Jessica has become a zombie—one of the living dead. Betsy, who makes little progress with Jessica, meets Paul's mother (Edith Barrett), a contradictory woman torn between her strong belief in the Christian church and voodoo, and his brother, Wesley (James Ellison), who is slowly drinking himself to death as he watches his brother's mistreatment of Jessica, whom he has always secretly loved. To make matters worse, Betsy and her employer begin to fall in love. Their desire to marry is intense, but impossible as long as Jessica lives. Not wanting to lose Paul, nor to see him torture himself, Betsy attempts to cure Jessica by taking her to a voodoo ceremony, in hopes that the experience will shock her back to "life." In the memorable conclusion, Wesley, in desperation, stabs Jessica and walks with her into the ocean before the unholy voodoo priest can "take her soul." Lewton's horror was based on the suggested, the psychological—not the visceral, tangible "monsters" that characterized the Universal horror series in the 1930s and 40s. The terror was presented in a shadowy, low-key atmosphere that allowed the audience to imagine and feel the unease instead of showing it to them, making the chills much more effective. The most outstanding example of this here is director Tourneur's beautiful realization of the lengthy, haunting, and elegiac sequence in which Betsy walks through the sugar cane fields with the silent Jessica to the voodoo ceremony. The scene is played in silence, save for the distant sound of drums and the gentle rustling of the wind. Visually, it is filled with gentle, floating movements (of Jessica's white gown, of the sugar cane in the wind) that are abruptly halted with the appearance of the massive zombie guard (Darby Jones) whose presence signals the women's arrival at their destination. This scene is unforgettable, as is the entire film. Essential viewing.

p, Val Lewton; d, Jacques Tourneur; w, Curt Siodmak, Ardel Wray (based on an original story by Inez Wallace); ph, J. Roy Hunt; ed, Mark Robson; m, Roy Webb.

(PR:A MPAA:NR)

## I WAS A TEENAGE ZOMBIE*½

(1987) 92m Periclean/Horizon c

Michael Rubin (Dan Wake), George Seminara (Gordy), Steve McCoy (Mussolini), Peter Bush (Rosencrantz), Cassie Madden (Cindy Faithful), Cindy Keiter (Miss Lugae), Gwyn Drischell (Margo), Allen L. Rickman (Lieberman), Lynnea Benson (Hilda), Ray Stough (Lenny), Robert C. Sabin (Chuckie), Kevin Nagle (The Byrd), Ted Polites (Moon), Steve Reidy (Policeman), Caren Pane (Poetry Teacher), Sal Lumetta, Tom Caldoro (Gangsters), Ken Baggett (Kevin Kramer), Jim Martin (Park Druggie), Brian Doyle (Shish-Ka-Bobber), Denise Texeira, Joan Bostwick (Girls at Lake), Gail Lucas (Teacher at Dance/Cindy's Friend), Frank Devlin (Radio Announcer's Voice).

This ultra-low-budget 16mm horror comedy has become something of a minor cult hit on the midnight show circuit in New York City. Basically a take-off on the "I WAS A TEENAGE . . ." movies of the 1950s, this one opens as five high-school friends (Michael Rubin, George Seminara, Kevin Nagle, Peter Bush, and Allen L. Rickman) score some bad marijuana from an unscrupulous dealer named Mussolini (Steve McCoy). The contaminated weed makes the boys ill, so, seeking revenge, the five friends grab

baseball bats and go after Mussolini, killing him and tossing his body in a nearby river. Unbeknownst to them, however, the river has been contaminated with radioactive waste dumped by a nearby nuclear power plant. The toxic chemicals revive Mussolini, making him a green zombie. Seeking revenge, the zombie Mussolini goes after the boys with the intention of killing them off one by one. When the first of their number is killed, however, the remaining friends steal their buddy's body from the funeral home and dump it in the river, thus creating a "good-guy" zombie to fight the "bad-guy" zombie. Although cheap and juvenile, I WAS A TEENAGE ZOMBIE is amusing enough for those who enjoy the goofy films that turn up at midnight shows. Much of the film is intentionally funny and its amateurish production only adds to the overall effect. There is the requisite gore in I WAS A TEENAGE ZOMBIE, but it is relatively sparse and more cartoonish than forensic.

p, Richard Hirsh, John Elias Michalakias; d, John Elias Michalakias; w, James Martin, George Seminara, Steve McCoy; ph, Peter Lewnes; ed, John Elias Michalakias; m, Jonathan Roberts, Craig Seeman.

(PR:O MPAA:NR)

## IN THE SHADOW OF KILIMANJARO**

(1986) 97m Intermedia/Scotti Brothers c

John Rhys-Davies (Chris Tucker), Timothy Bottoms (Jack Ringtree), Irene Miracle (Lee Ringtree), Michele Carey (Ginny Hansen), Leonard Trolley (Col. Emerson Maitland), Patty Foley (Lucille Gagnon), Calvin Jung (Mitsuki Uto), Don Blakely (Julius X. Odom), Jim Boeke (Claud Gagnon), Patrick Gorman (Eugene Kurtz), Mark Watters (Carlysle Bandy), Ka Vundla (District Officer Tshombe).

Supposedly based on a true occurrence of 1984, IN THE SHADOW OF KILIMANJARO takes place in Kenya in the Amboseli National Park. Jack Ringtree (Timothy Bottoms) runs a wildlife preserve in a region inhabited by the Masai, which is suffering from a severe drought. Because there is a shortage of food and water, the animals have become difficult to control—especially the baboons, which are now traveling in packs looking for food. When the dismembered body of a young native boy is found, Jack makes an appeal to have the area's 200 residents evacuated. His wife (Irene Miracle), who has just arrived from California via Nairobi, is attacked when the angry primates try to break into her house. Eventually all the locals are gathered under one roof, with boards nailed to the windows, doors well secured, and the men armed and prepared for the attack of the baboons. Amounting to nothing more than THE BIRDS meets BORN FREE, this formula thriller combines Hitchcock's revolt-of-nature theme with a Kenyan game reserve locale. First-time director Raju Patel, an Indian-born native of Nairobi, manages to create some decent suspense, however; the use of a Steadicam to simulate the point of view of the baboons' attack is harrowing, especially when coupled with the shrieking of the baboon voices (created in the sound studio by Percy Edwards). There is also some unexpected ethnographic footage of the Masai tribe, the most memorable of which is the opening scene of a young boy in the bush killing a deadly snake with his slingshot.

p, Gautam Das, Jeffrey Sneller; d, Raju Patel; w, Jeffrey Sneller, T. Michael Harry; ph, Jesus Elizondo (Technicolor); ed, Pradip Roy Shah; m, Arlon Ober.

(PR:O    MPAA:R)

## INCENSE FOR THE DAMNED**

(1970, Brit.) 87m Lucinda-Titan International c (AKA: DOCTORS WEAR SCARLET; THE BLOODSUCKERS)

Patrick Macnee *(Maj. Derek Longbow)*, Peter Cushing *(Dr. Goodrich)*, Alex Davion *(Tony Seymour)*, Johnny Sekka *(Bob Kirby)*, Madeline Hinde *(Penelope)*, Patrick Mower *(Richard Fountain)*, Imogen Hassall *(Chriseis Constandindi)*, Edward Woodward *(Holmstrom)*, William Mervyn *(Honeydew)*, David Lodge *(Colonel)*.

Set on the Greek island of Hydra, this intriguing but problem-plagued production features Patrick Mower as Richard Fountain, an Oxford don seduced into a pagan cult by a beautiful Greek woman (Hassall). The pagans worship Satan, indulge in black magic, and include a form of vampirism among their sexual rites. When Patrick's fiancee, Penelope (Madeline Hinde), goes to the embassy for help, retired army major Derek Longbow (Patrick Macnee) agrees to look into the case and finds that a whole group of Oxford dons are members of the pagan sect. Reportedly a faithful adaptation of the novel *Doctors Wear Scarlet* by Simon Raven, this film, much like George Romero's MARTIN (1977), posits vampirism as a psychosexual illness, rather than a visitation of the supernatural. Unfortunately for director Robert Hartford-Davis, the studio took control of the project and inserted scenes of the "vampires" being staked—robbing the film of its psychological concerns and transforming it into just another vampire movie. The end result of studio tampering is a wholly confused and confusing film patched together with explanatory narration. Peter Cushing's role is no more than a disappointing cameo. On videocassette as THE BLOODSUCKERS.

p, Peter Newbrook; d, Robert Hartford-Davis; w, Julian More (based on the novel *Doctors Wear Scarlet* by Simon Raven); ph, Desmond Dickinson.

(PR:O    MPAA:R)

## INCUBUS, THE*

(1982, Can.) 92m Film Ventures/Artists Releasing c

John Cassavetes *(Dr. Sam Cordell)*, Kerrie Keane *(Laura Kincaid)*, Helen Hughes *(Agatha Galen)*, Erin Flannery *(Jenny Cordell)*, Duncan McIntosh *(Tim)*, John Ireland *(Hank)*, Harvey Atkins *(Joe)*, Dirk McLean *(Incubus)*.

A series of brutal rapes and murders have begun occurring with alarming regularity in the small town of Galen, Wisconsin. A local teenager, Tim (Duncan McIntosh), has had horrible dreams concerning the rapes and fears he is the culprit, especially since many of his friends have been victims. Dr. Sam Cordell (John Cassavetes) and the sheriff

(John Ireland) investigate, and discover that the town has a dark past, involving demonology and Satanism. After many bloody rape-murders—including one in a movie-theater restroom—we get a glimpse of the killer, a demonic-looking incubus that is on-screen for all of 30 seconds. Although potentially interesting, THE INCUBUS suffers from a moronic script, which tosses the audience a dozen different diversions in the name of "suspense." The actual result is frustration and boredom, and not even the performance of the late Cassavetes can save the film. Director John Hough (THE LEGEND OF HELL HOUSE) tries to spice things up with some floating camera moves, but to no avail.

p, Marc Boyman, John M. Eckert; d, John Hough; w, George Franklin (based on the novel by Ray Russell); ph, Albert J. Dunk (Medallion Color); ed, George Appleby; m, Stanley Meyers.

(PR:O    MPAA:R)

## INFERNO***

(1980, It.) 107m FOX c

Irene Miracle *(Rose Elliot)*, Leigh McCloskey *(Mark Elliot)*, Eleonora Giorgi *(Sara)*, Daria Nicolodi *(Countess Elise)*, Alida Valli, Sacha Pitoeff, Veronica Lazar, Feodor Chapliapin, Gabriele Lavia.

This is the second entry in a proposed trilogy of films from Dario Argento, whose masterful SUSPIRIA (still unavailable on home video) was the opening salvo. Boasting an almost incoherent narrative, the film begins in New York and follows a young poet, Rose (Irene Miracle), who has rented a gothic apartment in Manhattan. The strange-looking building was designed by an alchemist, and while researching its origins, Rose buys a book written by the architect, *The Three Mothers*, from an eccentric, crippled bookseller (Sacha Pitoeff). From the book, Rose learns that two similar buildings were constructed in Rome and Germany—all three built in honor of the Mothers of Whispers, Darkness, and Tears, evil supernatural beings who rule the Earth. When Rose is brutally murdered soon after beginning her research, her brother (Leigh McCloskey), who has been studying in Rome, comes to New York to investigate his sister's death. Loaded with additional characters and confusing subplots, INFERNO makes little narrative sense. Luckily, Argento's visual sense is what makes his films compelling. Although not as powerful, impressive, or exciting as SUSPIRIA, INFERNO, under Argento's control of sight and sound, is still intriguing, effective, and stylish enough to make the narrative unimportant. The great Mario Bava, who died in 1980, helped out with the special effects here.

p, Claudio Argento; d, Dario Argento; w, Dario Argento; ph, Romano Albani (Technicolor); ed, Franco Fraticelli; m, Keith Emerson.

(PR:O    MPAA:R)

## INITIATION, THE*½

(1984) 97m Initiation Associates/NW c

Vera Miles *(Frances Fairchild)*, Clu Gulager *(Dwight Fairchild)*, Daphne Zuniga *(Kelly Terry)*, James Read *(Peter)*, Marilyn Kagan *(Marcia)*, Patti Heider *(Nurse)*, Robert Dowdell *(Jason Randall)*, Frances Peterson *(Megan)*, Deborah Morehart *(Alison)*, Robert Stroud *(Ralph)*, Peter Malof *(Andy)*, Christopher Bradley *(Chad)*, Joy Jones *(Heidi)*, Mary Davis Duncan *(Gwen)*, Rusty Meyers *(Night Watchman)*, Christi Michelle Allen *(Kelly at Age 9)*, Dan Dickerson *(Detective)*, Ronald M. Hubner *(Cop)*, Jerry L. Clark *(Orderly)*, Kathy Lee Kennedy *(Nurse)*, Trey Strood *(Ralph)*, Paula Knowles *(Beth)*.

Boring slasher stuff: College freshman Kelly (Daphne Zuniga) is a pledge with the Delta Rho Chi sorority who has suffered from amnesia since age nine and is troubled by disturbing dreams involving her parents (Clu Gulager and Vera Miles). A teaching assistant (James Read) doing research on dreams adds Kelly to his studies and helps her recover, though not before some pledge pranks involving a department store after hours and a psycho killer running amok with a knife. Top-billed Miles and Gulager are barely in the film. This would make a terrifically dreadful double bill with the similarly plotted DORM THAT DRIPPED BLOOD (1983), also featuring Zuniga.

p, Scott Winant; d, Larry Stewart; w, Charles Pratt, Jr.; ph, George Tirl (Movielab Color); ed, Ronald LaVine; m, Gabriel Black.

**(PR:O  MPAA:R)**

## INN OF THE DAMNED*½

(1974, Aus.) 125m Terryrod/Roadshow c

Judith Anderson *(Caroline Straulle)*, Alex Cord *(Cal Kincaid)*, Michael Craig *(Paul Melford)*, Joseph Furst *(Lazar Straulle)*, Tony Bonner *(Trooper Moore)*, John Meillon *(George Parr)*, Robert Quilter *(Biscayne)*, John Nash, John Morris, Don Barkham, Carla Hoogeveen, Diana Dangerfield, Phil Avalon, Louis Wishart, Graham Corry, Jack Allan, Nat Levison, Lionel Long.

This dull Australian outing is set circa 1896 in the Outback, where loony old couple Caroline and Lazar Straulle (Judith Anderson and Joseph Furst) run an out-of-the-way stagecoach stop. The problem is guests check in but don't check out. A bounty hunter (Alex Cord) shows up to investigate. It is finally revealed that Caroline and Lazar's children were killed by an escaped convict years before and they have been driven mad in their bloodthirsty quest for revenge. Part PSYCHO, part STAGECOACH, this poorly directed effort plods along predictably, getting as much mileage as it can from the gorgeous scenery.

p, Terry Bourke, Rod Hay; d, Terry Bourke; w, Terry Bourke; ph, Brian Probyn (Eastmancolor); ed, Rod Hay; m, Bob Young.

**(PR:O  MPAA:NR)**

## INVASION OF THE BLOOD FARMERS*

(1972) 84m NMO c

Cynthia Fleming *(Onhorrid)*, Norman Kelly *(Roy)*, Tanna Hunter *(Jenny)*, Bruce Detrick *(Don)*, Frank Iovieno *(Chief)*, Warren D'Oyly-Rhind.

A self-consciously campy, ultra-low-budget effort ($40,000), INVASION OF THE BLOOD FARMERS focuses on an upstate New York cult of Druids who worship a queen interred in a glass coffin. To resurrect their leader, the Druid farmers slaughter passersby in search of the proper blood type for use in a ritual blood feast. As you may have guessed, the title is the best thing about this movie, which is pretty inept in all departments, but somewhat enjoyable nonetheless. Director Ed Adlum also penned the equally bad SHRIEK OF THE MUTILATED (1974), and was a writer for the Detroit-based *Creem* rock'n'roll magazine.

p, Ed Adlum; d, Ed Adlum; w, Ed Adlum, Ed Kelleher.

**(PR:C-O  MPAA:PG)**

## INVISIBLE GHOST, THE**½

(1941) 66m BAN/MONO bw

Bela Lugosi *(Dr. Charles Kessler)*, Polly Ann Young *(Virginia)*, John McGuire *(Ralph)*, Clarence Muse *(Evans)*, Terry Walker *(Cecile)*, Betty Compson *(Mrs. Kessler)*, Ernie Adams *(Jules)*, George Pembroke *(Williams)*, Fred Kelsey *(Ryan)*, Jack Mulhall *(Tim)*.

Bela Lugosi's first picture for Monogram is a fairly incoherent effort, plotwise, but under the helm of director Joseph H. Lewis the film at least has some fairly interesting camera placement. The woefully underdeveloped story casts Lugosi as kindly Dr. Charles Kessler, who lives in a big old mansion with his adult daughter, Virginia (Polly Ann Young). Miserable since his wife was killed in an auto accident, Kessler pines for his lost love and, once a year, pretends she is still alive by having the butler (Clarence Muse) serve him a romantic dinner for two. Little does Kessler know that the gardener found Mrs. Kessler (Betty Compson) alive after the accident, but suffering from a terrible case of amnesia. Not wanting his boss to see her in such a condition, the gardener keeps Mrs. Kessler locked in his basement until she recovers. Unfortunately, Mrs. Kessler tends to slip out on occasion and wander over to the mansion, where she stares at her husband through the window. For reasons never explained, this causes Dr. Kessler to go into a deep homicidal trance that compels him to wander the house, killing anyone who gets in his way by placing his smoking-jacket over their head and suffocating them. Although the story makes little sense, with the murders and subsequent investigation bordering on the ludicrous, director Lewis lends this silly film a decidedly dreamlike, somewhat hypnotic feel. Also interesting is the surprisingly dignified and authoritative presence of black actor Muse as the loyal butler, whose character is the antithesis of the "Yas' boss" stereotype common to films of the period. For Lugosi enthusiasts, the film is worth seeing merely to hear Bela say the line, "Apple pie? My, that would be a treat!" with his typical Hungarian gusto.

# INVISIBLE GHOST, THE—

p, Sam Katzman; d, Joseph H. Lewis; w, Helen Martin, Al Martin; ph, Marcel Le Picard; ed, Robert Golden.

**(PR:A MPAA:NR)**

# INVISIBLE MAN, THE***½

(1933) 71m UNIV bw

Claude Rains *(Jack Griffin, The Invisible One)*, Gloria Stuart *(Flora Cranley)*, William Harrigan *(Doctor Kemp)*, Henry Travers *(Dr. Cranley)*, Una O'Connor *(Mrs. Jenny Hall)*, Forrester Harvey *(Mr. Herbert Hall)*, Holmes Herbert *(Chief of Police)*, E.E. Clive *(Jaffers)*, Dudley Digges *(Chief of Detectives)*, Harry Stubbs *(Inspector Bird)*, Donald Stuart *(Inspector Lane)*, Merle Tottenham *(Milly)*, Walter Brennan *(Man With Bike)*, Dwight Frye *(Reporter)*, Jameson Thomas *(Doctor)*, John Carradine *(Informer)*, John Merivale *(Boy)*.

Claude Rains, or a brief glimpse of him, made his American debut in this macabre piece based on the H.G. Wells novel and directed by the masterful James Whale. Jack Griffin (Rains) is a English scientist who has been experimenting with a drug of his own concoction, something he calls monocaine, which, he finds, has made his entire body invisible. He goes to the small village of Ipping, wrapped in bandages and wearing dark glasses, and takes a room at the local inn to continue his research in seclusion. This subsequently arouses the curiosity of the locals, who become nosy. As Griffin continues his experiments, he begins to suffer from megalomania, which eventually becomes full-blown madness. He begins to terrorize the countryside—first playing pranks, and then turning to murder. Although this film is not as interesting or substantial as THE BRIDE OF FRANKENSTEIN, Whale's distinctive darkly comic personal stamp is on THE INVISIBLE MAN. The dialog by R.C. Sherriff (who wrote "Journey's End") and Philip Wylie (uncredited) is quite witty, and the special effects by John P. Fulton remain fairly impressive to this day. Universal would milk this film and its subsequent sequel, THE INVISIBLE MAN RETURNS (1940), with a low-budget series of invisible man films, culminating with a just-average clown vehicle, ABBOTT AND COSTELLO MEET THE INVISIBLE MAN, 1951.

p, Carl Laemmle; d, James Whale; w, R.C. Sherriff, Philip Wylie (uncredited) (based on the novel by H.G. Wells); ph, Arthur Edeson; m, W. Frank Harling.

**(PR:A MPAA:NR)**

# INVISIBLE STRANGLER, THE*

(1984) 85m Jordan Lyon-New Century/Seymour Borde c

Robert Foxworth *(Lt. Charles Barrett)*, Stefanie Powers *(Candy Barrett)*, Elke Sommer *(Chris)*, Sue Lyon *(Miss De-Long)*, Leslie Parrish *(Coleen Hudson)*, Mariana Hill *(Bambi)*, Mark Slade, Frank Ashmore, Alex Dreier, Percy Rodriguez, Jo Anne Meredith, Cesare Danova, John Hart.

This ridiculous film concerns a young lad who strangles his mother when she tells him that she wishes she had aborted him. Locked away in an asylum, he studies books on the occult (what kind of mental hospital would let a disturbed inmate have books like this is a question left unanswered) until he learns an ancient Buddhist technique for becoming invisible. He then escapes his rubber-padded room and goes on a murder spree, invisibly strangling his mother's old friends in their posh homes. These scenes are pretty funny, as women suddenly start choking and their eyes roll up in their heads, although no one is in the room, at least that the audience can see. The detective assigned to the case finally gets rid of the unseen assailant by hooking a metal handrail up to an electrical outlet and frying the fellow. Sue Lyon makes a tiny appearance with no dialog, and Elke Sommer has a slightly larger role as a cocktail waitress. Shot in 1976 under the title of THE ASTRAL FACTOR, the film languished on the shelf for eight years before being sprung on an unwanting world.

p, Earle Lyon; d, John Florea; w, Arthur C. Pierce (based on a story by Lyon, Pierce); ph, Alan Stensvold; ed, Bud S. Isaacs; m, Richard Hieronymous, Alan Oldfield.

**(PR:C-O MPAA:PG)**

# ISLAND OF DR. MOREAU, THE*

(1977) 98m Wetherly-Cinema 77/AIP c

Burt Lancaster *(Dr. Moreau)*, Michael York *(Andrew Braddock)*, Nigel Davenport *(Montgomery)*, Barbara Carrera *(Maria)*, Richard Basehart *(Sayer of the Law)*, Nick Cravat *(M'Ling)*, The Great John L. *(Boarman)*, Bob Ozman *(Bullman)*, Fumio Demura *(Hyenaman)*, Gary Baxley *(Lionman)*, John Gillespie *(Tigerman)*, David Cass *(Bearman)*.

THE ISLAND OF DR. MOREAU is an unforgivably bad remake of the 1932 classic THE ISLAND OF LOST SOULS, which remains one of the greatest films the horror genre has ever produced. In 1911, Andrew Braddock (Michael York), a British naval officer whose ship has sunk, washes up on a remote tropical island owned by Dr. Moreau (Burt Lancaster), a scientist who is experimenting on jungle animals, trying to turn them into human beings. Director Don Taylor utterly fails to evoke one iota of the macabre power of the original film, giving his effort a distressingly slick look more akin to a travelog than a horror movie. The only reason for the remake's existence are the special makeup effects created by John Chambers, who did similar duty on the "Planet of the Apes" movies. While his work is interesting, it is not complemented by the unimaginative direction. Lancaster, who is miscast, fails to be a compelling figure—either tragic or malevolent—and the entire film collapses around him. That the original version has yet to see a videotape release, while this is readily available, is both a mystery and a tragedy.

p, Skip Steloff, John Temple-Smith; d, Don Taylor; w, John Herman Shaner, Al Ramrus (based on the novel by H.G. Wells); ph, Gerry Fisher (Movielab Color); ed, Marion Rothman; m, Laurence Rosenthal.

**(PR:C MPAA:PG)**

THE HORROR FILM

## ISLE OF THE DEAD****

(1945) 72m RKO bw

Boris Karloff *(Gen. Nikolas Pherides)*, Ellen Drew *(Thea)*, Marc Cramer *(Oliver Davis)*, Katherine Emery *(Mrs. St. Aubyn)*, Helene Thimig *(Kyra)*, Alan Napier *(Mr. St. Aubyn)*, Jason Robards Sr. *(Albrecht)*, Skelton Knaggs *(Henry Robbins)*, Sherry Hall *(Colonel)*, Ernst Dorian *(Dr. Drossos)*, Erick Hanson *(Officer)*.

This film, set during the Balkan War of 1912, casts Boris Karloff as the Greek general Nikolas Pherides, who, after leading his troops in a victorious battle, travels to a nearby island to visit the grave of his wife. He finds that the coffin has been exhumed, and, along with American reporter Oliver Davis (Marc Cramer), begins a search for the remains. The two are taken in by Albrecht (Jason Robards, Sr.), who explains that some locals have taken to grave robbing. Pherides decides to go after the culprits, dismissing fellow houseguest Kyra's (Helene Thimig) peasant superstitions of "vrykolakas"—Greek vampires. Members of the household come down with the plague—caused by the hundreds of corpses that litter the nearby battlefield—and begin dying off. As the disease spreads, madness begins to grip the island and culminates in a premature burial, followed by the ill and deranged Pherides finally believing Kyra's stories and vowing to kill the "vampire" Thea (Ellen Drew). As in BEDLAM, producer Val Lewton based this film on a painting, this time a work by Swiss painter Arnold Boecklin. Claustrophobic and nightmarishly atmospheric, ISLE OF THE DEAD is kept moving along by director Mark Robson at a deliberate pace, which becomes more and more creepy, until the moment of the premature burial. The audience knows that the woman is alive, and as the camera pulls away from the wooden coffin—with no sound other than that of dripping water—the suspense becomes almost unbearable until a terrible scream is heard, followed by desperate scratching. For this scene alone, ISLE OF THE DEAD deserves an exalted place in the history of horror—it is one of the most frightening moments in any Lewton film. Karloff, like his character, was physically stricken during the production, and aggravated an old back injury, which required him to be rushed to the hospital for an emergency spinal operation.

p, Val Lewton; d, Mark Robson; w, Ardel Wray, Josef Mischel, Val Lewton (suggested by a painting by Arnold Boecklin); ph, Jack Mackenzie; ed, Lyle Boyer; m, Leigh Harline.

(PR:A-C MPAA:NR)

## IT LIVES AGAIN***½

(1978) 91m Larco/WB c (AKA: IT'S ALIVE II)

Frederic Forrest *(Eugene Scott)*, Kathleen Lloyd *(Jody Scott)*, John Ryan *(Frank Davis)*, John Marley *(Mallory)*, Andrew Duggan *(Dr. Perry)*, Eddie Constantine *(Dr. Forrest)*, James Dixon *(Detective Perkins)*.

The excellent first sequel to IT'S ALIVE expands the concept of the first film and finds a more confident Larry Cohen behind the camera. Picking up where the last film left off, IT LIVES AGAIN opens as young couple Eugene and Jody Scott (Frederic Forrest and Kathleen Lloyd) celebrate the upcoming birth of their first child with a baby shower attended by friends and family. In the living room, among the guests, is a mysterious stranger, Frank Davis (John Ryan), whom no one seems to know. After all the guests have left, the couple is surprised to see Davis still sitting in their house. The father of the first monster baby in IT'S ALIVE, Davis tells the couple who he is and that he has come to ensure the protection of their baby from the authorities, who have formed a task force to abort all suspected monster pregnancies. Gene resents the implication that they are about to have one of the "freak" kids and tries to kick Davis out of his house, but the man's obvious sincerity strikes Jody and she eventually convinces her husband to trust the stranger. Davis is convinced that the children have a superior intelligence that may be on the cutting edge of a new human evolution and that they respond to the affection only their parents can give them. He takes the couple to a secret institute run by a group of scientists that want to nurture and study the babies (they have developed their own task force, which tries to get to the parents of the monster children before the government does). The opposition is led by Mallory (John Marley), a parent of a monster child himself, who has sworn to stamp out all the killer babies after his child murdered his wife. Upon the birth of their monster child, Gene is disgusted and repulsed, and Jody maternal but wary. The parents go through a complex series of acceptances and rejections of what they have wrought, building eventually to an agonizing climax. Once again, Cohen uses his outrageous premise to insightfully explore American family life, power structures, and social mores, taking on such topics as corporate abuse of the public trust, abortion, and government omnipotence. Bernard Herrmann died before this film was made, so Laurie Johnson (writer of the score for TV's "The Avengers") reworked some of his leftover themes from IT'S ALIVE.

p, Larry Cohen; d, Larry Cohen; w, Larry Cohen; ph, Fenton Hamilton (Technicolor); ed, Curtis Burch, Louis Friedman, Carol O'Blath; m, Bernard Herrmann, Laurie Johnson.

(PR:O MPAA:R)

## IT'S ALIVE***½

(1974) 90m Larco/WB c

John Ryan *(Frank Davies)*, Sharon Farrell *(Lenore Davies)*, Andrew Duggan *(The Professor)*, Guy Stockwell *(Clayton)*, James Dixon *(Lt. Perkins)*, Michael Ansara *(The Captain)*, Robert Emhardt *(The Executive)*, William Wellman Jr. *(Charlie)*, Daniel Holzman *(Chris Davies)*, Shamus Locke *(Doctor)*, Mary Nancy Burnett *(Nurse)*, Diana Hale *(Secretary)*, Patrick MacAllister, Gerald York, Jerry Taft, Gwil Richards, W. Allen York *(Expectant Fathers)*.

The film that put maverick producer-writer-director Larry Cohen on the map, IT'S ALIVE is a justifiably praised low-budget effort that insightfully delves into the dark side of American family life from a horror-movie perspective. The film opens as proud and excited parents Frank and Lenore Davies (John Ryan and Sharon Farrell) go to the hospital to deliver their new child. Suddenly all hell breaks loose in the delivery room, as Lenore gives birth to a monstrous baby that kills several hospital personnel before scurrying off into the night. The mutated birth is the result of Lenore's intake of a new fertility drug that was obviously defective, produced by a major (and powerful) drug corporation. Frank and Lenore's marriage is ripped asunder as both try to deal with what they have brought into the world. Lenore feels strong maternal instincts for the child, while Frank wishes to kill it. Frank aids the police in their search for his monster child, but as the hunt gets warmer, he, too, begins to feel parental concern for the baby, and attempts to save it. In the end, it is announced that another monster child has been born in a different part of the country. Cohen has always been a fascinating genre screenwriter of intelligence, insight, and social perceptiveness. Here he examines the American family and its support of such potentially harmful, uncaring institutions as the drug industry, the police, and even doctors and hospitals. Though the film is well written, it is at times technically shoddy, hampering its overall effectiveness. Cohen turned this rich and terrifying concept into a trilogy with IT LIVES AGAIN and IT'S ALIVE III: ISLAND OF THE ALIVE.

p, Larry Cohen; d, Larry Cohen; w, Larry Cohen; ph, Fenton Hamilton (Panavision, Technicolor); ed, Peter Honess; m, Bernard Herrmann.

**(PR:O MPAA:PG)**

## IT'S ALIVE III: ISLAND OF THE ALIVE***

(1988) 91m Larco/WB c

Michael Moriarty *(Steve Jarvis)*, Karen Black *(Ellen Jarvis)*, Laurene Landon *(Sally)*, James Dixon *(Dr. Perkins)*, Neal Israel *(Dr. Brewster)*, Art Lund *(Swenson)*, Ann Dane *(Miss Morrell)*, Macdonald Carey *(Judge Watson)*, Gerrit Graham *(Ralston)*, William Watson *(Cabot)*, C.L. Sussex *(Hunter)*, Patch MacKenzie *(Robbins)*, Rick Garia *(Tony)*, Carlos Palomino, Tony Abatemarco *(Cubans)*, Gladys Portugese, Joann Lara *(Waitresses)*, Bobby Ramsen *(T.V. Host)*, Jill Gatsby *(Girl in Cab)*, Kevin O'Conner *(Cab Driver)*, John Woehrle, Richard Duggan *(Cops)*, Lauri Riley *(Medic)*, Marilyn Staley *(Miss Garson)*, Mitchell Edmonds *(Stewart)*, Elizabeth Sanders *(Autograph Seeker)*, Steven Alan Green *(Comic)*, Kathleen Kickya *(Girl on Beach)*, Lynda Clark *(2nd Woman)*, Dan Rycerz *(Court Officer)*, Edward Shils *(Medical Examiner)*, Charles Vandergrift III *(Driver)*, Jackie Swanson *(Tenant)*, Katja Crosby *(Girl in Court)*, Paul Stader, Jr. *(Ship's Officer)*.

When we last left the mutant killer babies of IT'S ALIVE (1974) and IT LIVES AGAIN (1978), a panicked American government was in the midst of forcing abortions on pregnant mothers suspected of carrying mutants, and executing those monster kids already born. At the opening of the third installment of the series, most of the babies have been destroyed. A few, however, have survived and have been taken to a remote island, where they will be allowed to live out their days. Years later, the father of one of the babies, Steve Jarvis (Michael Moriarty), is asked to participate in a scientific expedition to the island in order to study the development of the mutants. They are shocked to dis-

cover that the mutants have grown into adulthood and have begun to procreate. Unfortunately for the scientists, there is a rebellion among the mutants and all of the visitors are killed, save Jarvis, who is forced to pilot the boat containing the escaping mutants to Florida. Larry Cohen's latest installment in the IT'S ALIVE series, one of the most thematically rich horror series ever produced, once again tackles American political and social attitudes in a genre context, but this time in an even more mocking manner. Here Cohen takes a swipe at abortion, the Baby M case, the court system, fear of AIDS, media stardom, merchandizing (Jarvis becomes a celebrity after writing a book called *A Parent's Story*), and a host of other issues debated in the 1980s. Much of the success of the film once again lies in the incredibly strange performance of Cohen veteran Moriarty. At first a rather normal, straight-laced kind of guy, Moriarty slowly becomes harsh and cynical in his view of the society that wanted to destroy his child and made him a pariah. A project designed specifically for home video, IT'S ALIVE III was shot in only four weeks on locations in Hawaii and Los Angeles. Steve Neill's special makeup for the adult mutant babies is based on the original design by Rick Baker and is quite effective, given the limited amount of money he had to work with, as is the brief stop-motion animation by William Hedge.

p, Paul Stader; d, Larry Cohen; w, Larry Cohen; ph, Daniel Pearl (Technicolor); ed, David Kern; m, Laurie Johnson, Bernard Herrmann.

**(PR:O MPAA:R)**

## JAWS****

(1975) 124m UNIV c

Roy Scheider *(Police Chief Martin Brody)*, Robert Shaw *(Quint)*, Richard Dreyfuss *(Matt Hooper)*, Lorraine Gary *(Ellen Brody)*, Murray Hamilton *(Mayor Larry Vaughn)*, Carl Gottlieb *(Meadows)*, Jeffrey Kramer *(Deputy Hendricks)*, Susan Backlinie *(Chrissie Watkins)*, Jonathan Filley *(Cassidy)*, Ted Grossman *(Estuary Victim)*, Chris Rebello *(Michael Brody)*, Jay Mello *(Sean Brody)*, Lee Fierro *(Mrs. Kintner)*, Jeffrey Voorhees *(Alex Kintner)*, Craig Kingsbury *(Ben Gardner)*, Dr. Robert Nevin *(Medical Examiner)*, Peter Benchley *(Interviewer)*, Robert Chambers *(Charlie)*, Edward Chalmers, Jr. *(Denherder)*, Cyprien R. Dube *(Posner)*, Robert Carroll *(Polk)*, Donald Poole *(Harbor Master)*, Alfred Wilde *(Iteisel/Mr. Wiseman)*.

An East Coast resort town, Amity Island, is plagued by attacks from a huge 28-foot great white shark that has been eating swimmers. Although the mayor (Murray Hamilton) would like to keep the whole thing quiet—he doesn't want to ruin the summer tourist season—the brutal attacks soon cannot be ignored, so police chief Martin Brody (Roy Scheider), marine biologist Matt Hooper (Richard Dreyfuss), and grizzled old shark hunter Quint (Robert Shaw) go after the monstrous creature, winding up in a desperate fight for their lives. The film that put Steven Spielberg on the map, JAWS was phenomenally successful at the box office and seemed to tap into a universal fear of what lies beneath the sea. Although the story is really just a variation on *Moby Dick*, with Quint as Ahab, obsessively pursuing the same type of beast that killed off his comrades when his ship sank in WW II, Spielberg's direction turns the material into a nerve-jangling visual tour de force. From the shocking opening—in which a beautiful young woman skinny-dipping in the moonlight is devoured by the unseen shark—to the claustrophobic climax aboard Quint's fishing boat, Spielberg has us in his grip and rarely lets go (although the film does bog down momentarily in some soap-opera scenes of Brody's family life). Because the film tapped into such a common fear and played on it so skillfully, it was a worldwide hit and entered the international popular culture. JAWS has been endlessly parodied by comedians and filmmakers alike, and John Williams' effective score has now become a cliche. Three vastly inferior sequels followed.

p, Richard D. Zanuck, David Brown; d, Steven Spielberg; w, Peter Benchley, Carl Gottlieb, Howard Sackler (based on the novel by Peter Benchley); ph, Bill Butler (Panavision, Technicolor); ed, Verna Fields; m, John Williams.

(PR:C    MPAA:PG)

## JAWS II**½

(1978) 117m UNIV c

Roy Scheider *(Police Chief Martin Brody)*, Lorraine Gary *(Ellen Brody)*, Murray Hamilton *(Mayor Vaughan)*, Joseph Mascolo *(Len Peterson)*, Jeffrey Kramer *(Deputy Hendricks)*, Collin Wilcox *(Dr. Elkins)*, Ann Dusenberry *(Tina Wilcox)*, Mark Gruner *(Mike Brody)*, Barry Coe *(Andrews)*, Susan French *(Old Lady)*, Gary Springer *(Andy)*, Donna Wilkes *(Jackie)*, Gary Dubin *(Ed)*, John Dukakis *(Polo)*, G. Thomas Dunlop *(Timmy)*, David Elliott *(Larry Vaughan, Jr.)*, Marc Gilpin *(Sean Brody)*, Keith Gordon *(Doug)*, Cynthia Grover *(Lucy)*, Ben Marley *(Patrick)*, Martha Swatek *(Marge)*, Billy Van Zandt *(Bob Burnside)*, Gigi Vorgan *(Brooke Peters)*, Jerry M. Baxter *(Helicopter Pilot)*, Jean Coulter *(Ski Boat Driver)*, Daphne Dibble, David Tintle *(Swimmers)*, Christine Freeman *(Water Skier)*, April Gilpin *(Renee)*, William Griffith *(Lifeguard)*.

More a remake than a sequel, this is a pointless effort. Since the plot is virtually identical to the first film, the only real difference between the two—and it is significant—is that Steven Spielberg didn't direct. Once again, the resort town of Amity Island is held in the grip of vicious shark attacks, and again police chief Brody (Roy Scheider) tries to close the beaches, but, of course, the still moronic mayor (Murray Hamilton) refuses to allow this because it might put the kibosh on an important property development deal. Since the colorful Quint was killed in the first film, the story falls back on the Brody family soap opera and places the Brody children in jeapardy, forcing their dad to save them. Director Jeannot Szwarc, best known for BUG (1975), performs his duties in a disappointingly pedestrian manner.

Since this made enough money to justify yet another sequel, JAWS 3-D was in the offing.

p, Richard D. Zanuck, David Brown; d, Jeannot Szwarc; w, Carl Gottlieb, Howard Sackler, Dorothy Tristan (based on characters created by Peter Benchley); ph, Michael Butler (Panavision, Technicolor); ed, Neil Travis, Steve Potter, Arthur Schmidt, Freeman Davies, Jr., Michael T. Elias, Robert Hernandez, Sherrie Sanet Jacobson; m, John Williams.

(PR:C    MPAA:PG)

## JAWS 3-D**

(1983) 97m Landsburg-3-D/UNIV c

Dennis Quaid *(Mike Brody)*, Bess Armstrong *(Kathryn Morgan)*, Simon MacCorkindale *(Philip FitzRoyce)*, Louis Gossett, Jr. *(Calvin Bouchard)*, John Putch *(Sean Brody)*, Lea Thompson *(Kelly Ann Bukowski)*, P.H. Moriarty *(Jack Tate)*, Dan Blasko *(Dan)*, Liz Morris *(Liz)*, Lisa Maurer *(Ethel)*, Harry Grant *(Shelby)*, Andy Hansen *(Silver Bullet)*, P.T. Horn *(Guide)*, John Edson, Jr. *(Bob)*, Kaye Stevens *(Mrs. Kallender)*, Archie Valliere *(Leonard)*, Alonzo Ward *(Fred)*, Cathy Cervenka *(Sherrie)*, Steve Mellor *(Announcer)*, Ray Meunich *(Paramedic)*, Les Alford, Gary Anstaett *(Reporters)*, Muffett Baker *(Guide)*, William Bramley, Scott Christoffel, Debbie Connoyer, Mary David Duncan, Barbara Eden, Will Knickerbocker, Jackie Kuntarich, Edward Laurie, Ken Olson, Ronnie Parks, Al Pipkin.

Since the wholly unimaginative series needed a gimmick at this point to stay afloat, the new-but-short-lived 3-D craze came along just in time. With the action moved from Amity Island to Florida's Sea World, a new cast was in order, with police chief Brody's two sons, Mike and Sean, now old enough to be played by Dennis Quaid and John Putch. Calvin Bouchard (Louis Gossett, Jr.) runs the theme park; Kathryn Morgan (Bess Armstrong) is a marine biologist who works there and who lives with Mike. A baby great white shark is caught after some divers disappear, and the Sea Worlders think they have a great attraction in "the only great white in captivity." But they haven't reckoned on a mother's love for her offspring, and when Big Mama comes to call, things get out of hand and she wrecks the place. Although shot well and boasting some effective 3-D work, this is a woefully inadequate effort and the series began to slip into inadvertent self-parody. Joe Alves, who had been production designer on the first two JAWS features, was rewarded for his efforts by the assignment to handle the direction on this.

p, Rupert Hitzig; d, Joe Alves; w, Richard Matheson, Carl Gottlieb (based on a story by Guerdon Trueblood suggested by the novel *Jaws* by Peter Benchley); ph, James A. Contner (ArriVision 3-D, Stereovision, Technicolor); ed, Randy Roberts; m, Alan Parker (shark theme, John Williams).

(PR:C    MPAA:PG)

## JAWS: THE REVENGE*

(1987) 89m UNIV c

Lorraine Gary *(Ellen Brody)*, Lance Guest *(Michael Brody)*, Mario Van Peebles *(Jake)*, Karen Young *(Carla Brody)*, Michael Caine *(Hoagie)*, Judith Barsi *(Thea Brody)*, Lynn Whitfield *(Louisa)*, Mitchell Anderson *(Sean Brody)*, Jay Mello *(Young Sean)*, Cedric Scott *(Clarence)*, Charles Bowleg *(William)*, Melvin Van Peebles *(Mr. Witherspoon)*, Mary Smith *(Tiffany)*, Edna Billotto *(Polly)*, Fritzi Jane Courtney *(Mrs. Taft)*, Cyprian R. Dube *(Mayor)*, Lee Fierro *(Mrs. Kinter)*, John Griffin *(Man in Boat)*, Diane Hetfield *(Mrs. Ferguson)*, Daniel J. Manning *(Jesus)*, William E. Marks *(Lenny)*, James Martin *(Minister)*, David Wilson *(Tarkanian)*, Romeo Farrington *(Romeo)*, Anthony Delaney *(Charles Townsend)*, Heather Thompson *(Shirley)*, Levant Carey *(Houseman)*, Darlene Davis *(Irma)*.

As the toothy fish series plays out its string, the plots of the JAWS movies become more and more ludicrous, embarrassingly so with this, the fourth and most dismal of the group. Police chief Brody (Roy Scheider, who wisely opted to escape this endless fish story) has been eliminated from the New England town of Amity; however, his wife, the long-suffering Ellen (Lorraine Gary), has taken over the lead. One of her sons, Sean (Mitchell Anderson), has become the police chief. Sean is vexed by a terrorizing shark during the Christmas season, then killed by it. Ellen, to escape the horror of her family's shark-infested history, travels to the Bahamas to visit her surviving son Michael, (Lance Guest), a marine biologist who spends most of his waking moments looking for rare sea snails with partner Jake (Mario Van Peebles). Sure enough, the very shark that attacked Sean, has followed Ellen to the Bahamas and is out to kill her second son, all in the name of vengeance for the killing of its supposed relatives in prior JAWS films. Oh yes, Ellen falls in love with easy-living Hoagie (Michael Caine), who concludes that the shark will not give up attacking her second son unless she brings a halt to the vendetta by sacrificing herself. This is really pathetic. Even the special effects are lame in this one, offering a latex shark that is about as realistic as a fake goldfish. Poorly directed by Joseph Sargent, who relies heavily on blood and fast editing to create some tension, since there certainly isn't any written into the script.

p, Joseph Sargent; d, Joseph Sargent; w, Michael de Guzman (based on characters created by Peter Benchley); ph, John McPherson; m, Michael Small, John Williams.

**(PR:C-O   MPAA:PG-13)**

## JEKYLL AND HYDE ... TOGETHER AGAIN*

(1982) 87m PAR c

Mark Blankfield *(Jekyll/Hyde)*, Bess Armstrong *(Mary)*, Krista Errickson *(Ivy)*, Tim Thomerson *(Dr. Lanyon)*, Michael McGuire *(Dr. Carew)*, Neil Hunt *(Queen)*, Cassandra Peterson *(Busty Nurse)*, Jessica Nelson *(Barbara)*, Peter Brocco *(Hubert)*, Michael Klingher, Noelle North, David Murphy *(Students)*, Mary McCusker *(Patient)*, Liz Sheridan *(Mrs. Larson)*, Alison Hong *(Asian Girl)*,

Walter Janowitz *(Elderly Man)*, Belita Moreno *(Nurse Gonzales)*, Leland Sun *(Wong)*, George Wendy *(Injured Man)*, Glen Chin *(Sushi Chef)*, Dan Barrows *(Customer)*, Virginia Wing *(Mme. WooWoo)*, Jesse Goins *(Dutch)*, Jack Collins *(Baron)*, Michael Ensign *(Announcer)*, John Dennis Johnston *(Macho Kid)*, David Ruprecht *(Brigham)*, Clarke Coleman *(Box Boy)*, Sam Whipple *(Produce Man)*.

This inept and unfunny parody of Robert Louis Stevenson's classic tale modernizes the story by starring Mark Blankfield as a surgeon-researcher named Jekyll who invents a cocaine-like substance and snorts it accidentally, turning him into his hip alter ego. As Hyde, he sports disco clothes and jewelry, rejecting his square fiancee, Mary (Bess Armstrong), for the more exotic favors of punk rock singer Ivy (Krista Errickson). Resembling a "Saturday Night Live" sketch stretched out to feature length, the film was obviously made before all the "Say No to Drugs" hype started, since this distinctly tasteless effort tries to get laughs off the cocaine subculture and fails miserably.

p, Lawrence Gordon; d, Jerry Belson; w, Monica Johnson, Harvey Miller, Jerry Belson, Michael Lesson (based on the novel *The Strange Case of Dr. Jekyll and Mr. Hyde* by Robert Louis Stevenson); ph, Philip Lathrop (Metrocolor); ed, Billy Weber; m, Barry DeVorzon.

**(PR:O   MPAA:R)**

## JENNIFER zero

(1978) 90m AIP c (AKA: JENNIFER (THE SNAKE GODDESS))

Lisa Pelikan *(Jennifer Baylor)*, Bert Convy *(Jeff Reed)*, Nina Foch *(Mrs. Calley)*, Amy Johnston *(Sandra Tremayne)*, John Gavin *(Sen. Tremayne)*, Jeff Corey *(Luke Baylor)*, Louise Hoven *(Jane Delano)*, Ray Underwood *(Dayton Powell)*, Wesley Eure *(Pit Lassiter)*, Florida Friebus *(Miss Tooker)*, Georganne La Piere *(Deedee Martin)*.

In this blatant CARRIE rip-off, Jennifer (Lisa Pelikan) is an outcast student who gets sweet revenge on her classmates at the posh Green View School for Girls—especially a snooty blonde, the sort that everyone in the audience would like to see banished to hell. She also has a religious nut for a father, a la Piper Laurie's role in CARRIE. The film also borrows a bit from BEN and WILLARD: Jennifer is in tune with snakes and calls them to do her bidding.

p, Steve Krantz; d, Brice Mack; w, Kay Cousins Johnson (based on a story by Krantz); ph, Irv Goodnoff (CFI Color); ed, Duane Hartzell.

**(PR:C-O   MPAA:PG)**

## JESSE JAMES MEETS FRANKENSTEIN'S DAUGHTER*½

(1966) 82m Circle/EM c

John Lupton *(Jesse James)*, Cal Bolder *(Hank Tracy/Igor)*, Narda Onyx *(Maria Frankenstein)*, Steven Geray *(Rudolph Frankenstein)*, Felipe Turich *(Manuel)*, Rosa Turich *(Nina)*, Estelita *(Juanita)*, Jim Davis *(Marshal McFee)*, Raymond Barnes *(Lonny)*, William Fawcett *(Jensen the Pharmacist)*,

Page Slattery, Nestor Paiva, Dan White, Roger Creed, Fred Stromsoe, Mark Norton.

Jesse James (John Lupton), along with a gang member Hank (Cal Bolder), escapes a posse and seeks the help of a young Mexican woman, Juanita (Estelita). She takes them to some ruins owned by Maria Frankenstein (Narda Onyx), the granddaughter of Baron Frankenstein (the title wrongly calls her his daughter). In the family tradition, Maria transplants the brain from her grandfather's monster into the brawny Hank, turning him into a mindless killer outlaw named Igor. This gets the local marshal riled up and he reckons he should put a stop to this nonsense. The companion piece to the equally ludicrous horror-western BILLY THE KID VS DRACULA (1965), this was veteran hack director William Beaudine's swan song, after having helmed more than 150 feature films of a similar nature.

p, Carroll Case; d, William Beaudine; w, Carl Hittleman; ph, Lothrop Worth (Pathe Color); ed, Roy Livingston; m, Raoul Kraushaar.

(PR:A   MPAA:NR)

### JUST BEFORE DAWN*½

(1980) 90m Juniper-Picturemedia/Oakland c

Chris Lemmon, Gregg Henry, Deborah Benson, George Kennedy, Mike Kellin, Ralph Seymour, John Hunsaker, Jamie Rose.

JUST BEFORE DAWN is a crushing disappointment from director Jeff Lieberman, whose SQUIRM (1976) and BLUE SUNSHINE (1977) were two of the more interesting genre efforts of the 1970s. A group of teenagers ignore the wise words of an Oregon forest ranger played by George Kennedy and venture into the woods after dark—just as they weren't supposed to do. Their disobedience results in an encounter with a pair of mutant twins who stalk their victims and slice them with machetes. This direct rip-off of THE HILLS HAVE EYES (1977) has nothing going for it. Actor Chris Lemmon is the son of Jack Lemmon; redheaded actress Jamie Rose would go on to star in the unintentional laff-fest cop show of the 1980s, "Lady Blue."

p, David Sheldon, Doro Vlado Hreljanovic; d, Jeff Lieberman; w, Mark L. Arywitz, Gregg Irving (based on a story by Joseph Middleton); ph, J. King, D. King (Panavision); m, Brad Fiedel.

(PR:O   MPAA:R)

### KEEP, THE**

(1983) 96m Capital/PAR c

Scott Glenn (Glaeken Trismegestus), Alberta Watson (Eva), Jurgen Prochnow (Woermann), Robert Prosky (Father Fonescu), Gabriel Byrne (Kempffer), Ian McKellen (Dr. Cuza), Morgan Sheppard (Alexandru), Royston Tick-

ner (Tomescu), Michael Carter (Radu), Phillip Joseph (Oster), John Vine (Lutz), Jona Jones (Otto), Wolf Kahler (S.S. Adjutant), Rosalie Crutchley (Josefa), Frederick Warder, Bruce Payne (Border Guards), David Cardy (Alexandru's Son), Philip Bloomfield (Josefa's Son), Yashar Adem (Carlos).

A minor disaster. Director Michael Mann (THIEF, television's "Miami Vice" and "Crime Story") presents a fantastic-looking movie, filled with great production values and lush cinematography, which, unfortunately, are combined with a totally incoherent narrative, punctuated by incredibly inept performances from usually fine actors (Robert Prosky, who was so good in THIEF, is an embarrassment here, as is Ian McKellen). The film is set in Eastern Europe during WW II, but just what is going on there is hard to say. The plot has something to do with a castle in the Carpathian Mountains that possesses a powerful, evil force that sucks up every Nazi it comes across and spits out their bloody entrails. Called by psychic impulses (or something like that), a mysterious traveler (Scott Glenn) arrives to do battle with the evil force. THE KEEP is one of the more visually interesting horror films of the 1980s, making its complete narrative weakness all the more frustrating.

p, Gene Kirkwood, Howard W. Koch, Jr.; d, Michael Mann; w, Michael Mann (based on a novel by F. Paul Wilson); ph, Alex Thomson (Metrocolor); ed, Dov Hoenig; m, Tangerine Dream.

(PR:O   MPAA:R)

### KEEP MY GRAVE OPEN*

(1980) 78m Wells/Jefferson & Century c

Camilla Carr (Lesley Fontaine), Gene Ross, Stephen Tobolowsky, Ann Stafford, Annabelle Weenick, Chelsea Ross, Sharon Bunn, Bill Thurman.

Set in a spooky Gothic mansion in Texas, KEEP MY GRAVE OPEN finds the crazed Lesley (Camilla Carr) imagining herself to be her long-missing brother. Occasionally she kills stray men who make a pass at her, believing that she is her brother defending Lesley. The victims are killed with a sword stashed in the backseat of an old car. DON'T LOOK IN THE BASEMENT director S.F. Brownrigg provides some interesting moments, but never really seems to pull the undeveloped psychosexual angle past the point of mere sleazy exploitation, and since his visual style isn't anywhere near as interesting as Dario Argento's, what we have is an Argento movie without Argento.

p, S.F. Brownrigg; d, S.F. Brownrigg; w, Amos Powell; ph, John Valtenburgs; m, Robert Farrar.

(PR:O   MPAA:R)

### KEEPER, THE*

(1976, Can.) 88m Lions Gate c

Christopher Lee (The Keeper), Tell Schrieber (Dick Driver), Sally Gray (Mae B. Jones), Ross Vezarian (Inspector

Clarke), Ian Tracey (The Kid), Jack Leavy, Leo Leavy (Messrs. Big), Bing Jensen (Danny).

Yet another spoof of the genre, this film stars Christopher Lee as the crippled administrator of Underwood Asylum, who is a bit daft himself. The Keeper, as he is called, ferrets out the inmates who have large estates, then tries to kill all of their heirs so the money will revert to him. Although pretty silly, the film does boast a monstrous keyboard machine that, at the touch of a button, administers punishments to the inmates, and two seven-foot-tall twins who contribute to the mad cripple's downfall.

p, Donald Wilson; d, Tom Drake; w, Tom Drake (based on a story by David Curnick, Wilson); ph, Doug McKay; ed, Sally Patterson, George Johnson; m, Eric Hoyt.

(PR:A    MPAA:NR)

## KILLER PARTY*

(1986) 91m Marquis/UA-MGM c

Martin Hewitt (Blake), Ralph Seymour (Martin), Elaine Wilkes (Phoebe), Paul Bartel (Prof. Zito), Sherry Willis-Burch (Vivia), Alicia Fleer (Veronica), Woody Brown (Harrison), Joanna Johnson (Jennifer), Terri Hawkes (Melanie), Deborah Hancock (Pam), Laura Sherman (Sandy), Jeff Pustil (Virgil), Pat Hyatt (Mrs. Henshaw), Howard Buscang, Jason Warren (Bee Boys), Majda Rogerson (Mom), Danielle Kracy (April), Scott Coppala (Stosh), Denise Ferguson (Dr. Bain), Cynthia Gillespie (Diver), Elizabeth Hanna (Stephanie), Derek Keurvorst (Clerk), Camir Andre (Daniel), Dora Danton (Kosima), John Dee (Mr. Katz), Branco Racki (Policeman).

Ah, collegiate days in splatter films, where every campus has a hushed-up death in its closet (this one even has a guillotine in its warehouse) and a mad slasher preying on coeds and their careless dates. Jennifer (Joanna Johnson), Phoebe (Elaine Wilkes), and Vivia (Sherry Willis-Burch) are three friends who are pledges at the Sigma Alpha Pi sorority house. When the sorority plans its annual April Fool's Day dance in an old frat house—abandoned for 20 years after a pledge was decapitated in a hazing accident—the boy's spirit (he's buried in the backyard) comes back and possesses Jennifer. She dispatches hapless victims with the usual bewildering array of techniques, including drowning, decapitation (in the guillotine), a claw hammer to the head, electrocution, a shovel to the face, and an auger from a heating duct, some of the time while dressed in a deep-sea diving helmet and suit. While not exactly on a par with HALLOWEEN, KILLER PARTY does have a few moments, most of them with stuffy professor Paul Bartel (who gets an electric line shoved into his neck) or weirdo Ralph Seymour (who actually gets to survive the film by leaving the party early). The killings are virtually bloodless or off-screen and the film even comes close to generating a little tension.

p, Michael Lepiner; d, William Fruet; w, Barney Cohen; ph, John Lindley (Technicolor); ed, Eric Albertson; m, John Beal.

(PR:O    MPAA:R)

## KILLING HOUR, THE**

(1982) 90m Lansbury-Berun c

Perry King, Norman Parker, Kenneth McMillan, Elizabeth Kemp.

When the work of a crazed serial killer grips Manhattan, a television talk show host (Perry King) decides to use the terror to get higher ratings, exploiting a young artist who has premonitions of murders to be committed and then is compelled to draw them. Soon the poor girl finds herself torn between the ambitious talk-show host and the police, who are trying to solve the crimes. Originally released as THE CLAIRVOYANT, this rather gimmicky slasher movie is redeemed somewhat by its decent cast.

d, Armand Mastroianni.

(PR:O    MPAA:NR)

## KING KONG*****

(1933) 100m RKO bw

Fay Wray (Ann Darrow), Robert Armstrong (Carl Denham), Bruce Cabot (John Driscoll), Frank Reicher (Capt. Englehorn), Sam Hardy (Charles Weston), Noble Johnson (Native Chief), Steve Clemento (Witch King), James Flavin (2nd Mate Briggs), Victor Wong (Charley), Paul Porcasi (Socrates), Russ Powell (Dock Watchman), Ethan Laidlaw, Blackie Whiteford, Dick Curtis, Charles Sullivan, Harry Tenbrook, Gil Perkins (Sailors), Vera Lewis, Leroy Mason (Theatre Patrons), Frank Mills, Lynton Brent (Reporters), Jim Thorpe (Native Dancer), George MacQuarrie (Police Captain), Madame Sul-Te-Wan (Handmaiden), Etta McDaniel (Native Woman), Ray Turner (Native), Dorothy Gulliver (Girl), Carlotta Monti (Girl), Barney Capehart, Bob Galloway, Eric Wood, Dusty Mitchell, Russ Rogers (Pilots), Reginald Barlow (Engineer), Merian C. Cooper (Flight Commander), Ernest B. Schoedsack (Chief Observer).

The ultimate monster movie, and one of the greatest adventure films ever made, KING KONG is one of a handful of films that have become enduring icons of American popular culture, justly praised as a true motion picture classic. Hollywood filmmaker Carl Denham (Robert Armstrong) takes starlet Ann Darrow (Fay Wray) to a mysterious prehistoric island in search of the legendary King Kong, a giant ape worshipped as a god by the local natives. To their amazement, the two find the giant beast, and it falls in love with Ann. Denham manages to capture the monster and bring it back to New York City for display, but Kong breaks loose and wreaks havoc on Manhattan in his search for his beloved Ann. As a monster, Kong is really akin to Boris Karloff's Frankenstein monster—more victim than victimizer. Of course, Kong was a fearful monster who killed and could destroy entire cities if given a chance, but he had desires, a temper, needs, and fears, and could feel emotions that audiences to this day identify with. No man in an ape suit could convey such a complex variety of emotions—only a fine actor or a master in the art of stop-motion animation, such as Willis O'Brien, who was able to create one of the cinema's most unique and memorable characters from an inanimate 18-inch stop-motion model. On its initial release, at the height of the Great Depression, KING KONG grossed $1,761,000 and by itself saved the studio that produced it from bankruptcy. Unfortunately, RKO had little respect for its savior. In 1938, the studio decided to re-release its classic, but took several steps to tone it down. Cut were the scenes of Kong chewing and crushing human beings. Gone was the scene in which a curious Kong strips Fay Wray of her clothing. In fact, RKO made the new release prints several shades darker in an effort to tone down the incredible detail of O'Brien's work (dying dinosaurs bleeding, etc.) that made everything seem so realistic. This travesty practically obliterated the steps O'Brien took to ensure that his creations would *live* on-screen. Generations of moviegoers and television watchers were denied the true, uncut brilliance of the vision of Merian C. Cooper, Ernest B. Schoedsack, and O'Brien, until recently, when restored prints of KING KONG began to circulate both in revival houses and on home video. KING KONG remains an outstanding achievement in motion picture history and a moving testament to the human imagination that will endure as long as there is an audience to thrill to its unparalleled mastery of the medium. Avoid the 1976 remake and its 1986 sequel.

p, Merian C. Cooper, Ernest B. Schoedsack; d, Merian C. Cooper, Ernest B. Schoedsack; w, James Creelman, Ruth Rose (based on a story by Cooper and Edgar Wallace); ph, Edward Linden, Vernon Walker, J.O. Taylor; ed, Ted Cheesman; m, Max Steiner.

**(PR:A-C   MPAA:NR)**

## KING KONG*½

(1976) 134m PAR c

Jeff Bridges *(Jack Prescott)*, Charles Grodin *(Fred Wilson)*, Jessica Lange *(Dwan)*, John Randolph *(Capt. Ross)*, Rene Auberjonois *(Bagley)*, Julius Harris *(Boan)*, Jack O'Halloran *(Joe Perko)*, Dennis Fimple *(Sunfish)*, Ed Lauter *(Carnahan)*, John Agar *(City Official)*, Jorge Moreno *(Garcia)*, Mario Gallo *(Timmons)*, John Lone *(Chinese Cook)*, Garry Halberg *(Army General)*, Keny Long *(Ape Masked Man in Dance)*, Sid Conrad *(Petrox Chairman)*, George Whiteman *(Army Helicopter Pilot)*, Wayne Heffley *(Air Force Colonel)*, Rick Baker *(King Kong)*.

Without a doubt, Dino De Laurentiis' remake of Merian C. Cooper and Ernest B. Schoedsack's classic is the biggest con job ever pulled on the unsuspecting American public. Having spent somewhere in the vicinity of $24 million on his epic, De Laurentiis told the world that his Kong was a fabulously expensive and technically amazing, full-sized mechanical ape that stood 40 feet tall, when in reality the majority of Kong's scenes were played by makeup man Rick Baker in a monkey suit! The Italian producer fought hard to bring his version of the 1933 classic to the screen and was even forced to give Universal's rival production, "The Legend of King Kong," a percentage of his profits to persuade them to abandon their version, which was being produced simultaneously. The updated script was fairly clever and De Laurentiis managed to assemble a tolerable cast of performers. Wilson (Charles Grodin), an official of Petrox oil, discovers an unknown island in the Pacific that

is rumored to be brimming with oil. Seeking to secure the island's wealth of crude for his company, Wilson assembles a crew and sets sail. While at sea the crew discovers a stowaway, Jack Prescott (Jeff Bridges), a hip paleontologist. Jack informs Wilson that his expedition is actually headed for the legendary "Skull Island," a land where time has stopped and prehistoric monsters still roam. Wilson scoffs at the idea, but when Bridges tells of the tribe of vicious natives who worship a giant beast called Kong, he begins to pay attention. Soon after, the crew spots a beautiful blonde woman in the water, clinging to some debris (Jessica Lange, in her first screen appearance—a role she's still trying to live down). The girl, Dwan, is an aspiring actress and was shipwrecked when the yacht she was on sank. Of course, once on Skull Island Dwan gets kidnapped by a giant gorilla named Kong. The beast is eventually captured and brought back to New York, where it escapes and winds up climbing one of the towers of the World Trade Center. Believe it or not, De Laurentiis' debacle garnered amazingly favorable reviews from incredibly short-sighted critics, who seemed anxious to denigrate the 1933 version and praise the modernness and technical advances of the remake. Considering that throughout 99 percent of the film Kong was a man in an ape costume (albeit a very good costume), the special effects were relatively simple and not particularly well executed. Perhaps the biggest injustice of all is that Rick Baker didn't even receive screen credit.

p, Dino De Laurentiis; d, John Guillermin; w, Lorenzo Semple, Jr. (based on a screenplay by James Creelman, Ruth Rose, from a concept by Merian C. Cooper, Edgar Wallace); ph, Richard H. Kline (Panavision, Metrocolor); ed, Ralph E. Winters; m, John Barry.

**(PR:C-O   MPAA:PG)**

## KING KONG LIVES*

(1986) 105m DEG c

Peter Elliot *(King Kong)*, George Yiasomi *(Lady Kong)*, Brian Kerwin *(Hank Mitchell)*, Linda Hamilton *(Amy Franklin)*, John Ashton *(Col. Nevitt)*, Peter Michael Goetz *(Dr. Ingersoll)*, Frank Maraden *(Dr. Benson Hughes)*, Alan Sader, Lou Criscuolo *(Faculty Doctors)*, Marc Clement *(Crew Chief)*, Richard Rhodes, Debbie McLeod, Elizabeth Hayes *(Reporters)*, Natt Christian, Mac Pirkle *(Surgeons)*, Larry Sprinkle *(Journalist)*, Rod Davis *(TV Reporter)*, Robin Cahall *(Mazlansky)*, Don Law *(Security Chief)*, Jack Maloney *(1st Wrangler)*, Jimmie Ray Weeks *(Major Peete)*, Jeff Benninghofen *(1st Radioman)*, Jim Grimshaw *(Sergeant)*, Bernard Addison, Michael McLendon *(Captains)*, Jimmy Wiggins *(Boy Friend)*, Mary Swafford *(Girl Friend)*, Michael Forest *(Vance)*.

Only Dino De Laurentiis would dare to make the same colossal mistake twice. When we last saw Kong in 1976, he had taken a nosedive off New York City's World Trade Center and gone splat on the pavement below. Well, fans, Kong didn't die. You see, he just fell into a deep coma and has been kept in a huge warehouse for the last 10 years until doctors and technicians had time to invent an artificial heart the size of a Volkswagen "Bug." Before the operation can begin, however, a huge blood supply must be found. Luckily, a female Kong has just been discovered on the island of Borneo, and the big gal is shipped to the US so that she can be Kong's donor. The operation is a success (it is also one of the goofiest scenes ever committed to film) and Kong's diseased heart is replaced with a brand-spankin'-new steel-and-fiberglass one. Actually, the heart works *too* well—when Kong smells a female his size in the warehouse next door, he becomes amorous, breaks his bonds, and leaves his warehouse hospital room to rescue his newfound love. The apes then make a dash for the mountains, with the Army, led by crazed Col. Nevitt (John Ashton), in hot pursuit of the lovesick leviathans—who soon produce a baby Kong. This was all a joke, right? One can only imagine the production meeting that took place between studio chief De Laurentiis, producer Martha Schumacher, director John Guillermin (who actually came back for more after the first-remake disaster), and writers Ronald Shusett and Steven Pressfield. "I know! We'll give him an artificial heart!" "Yeah, and then we'll give him a wife!" "And to top it off, we geeve Konk a leetle baby Konk! Morea people gonna cry than last time!" To be fair, there is a lot of camp value here. Fans of truly bad cinema couldn't ask for a sillier big-budget production that was envisioned with the utmost seriousness.

p, Martha Schumacher; d, John Guillermin; w, Ronald Shusett, Steven Pressfield (based on a character created by Merian C. Cooper, Edgar Wallace); ph, Alec Mills (J-D-C Widescreen, Technicolor); ed, Malcolm Cooke; m, John Scott.

(PR:C   MPAA:PG-13)

## KING OF THE ZOMBIES**

(1941) 67m MON bw

Dick Purcell, Joan Woodbury, Mantan Moreland, Henry Victor, John Archer, Patricia Stacey, Guy Usher, Marguerite Whitten, Leigh Whipper, Madame Sul-Te-Wan, Jimmy Davis, Lawrence Criner.

Some of the strangest genre hybrids ever attempted were the horror-WW II propaganda films that began popping up in the 1940s. This lame effort is a fairly typical result. When an important American admiral flying a mission goes down somewhere over the Caribbean, the government dispatches special agent Bill Summers (Dick Purcell) and his valet, Jeff    (Mantan Moreland),  to try and find him.    Their plane crash-lands on a tiny island and they are taken in by a mysterious German doctor (Henry Victor) who claims to be trying to find a cure for his wife's trancelike state. Soon after their arrival, Jeff learns that the place is overrun by zombies. Their host scoffs at such a notion, but soon both Jeff and Mac become zombified. Achieved through hypnosis, the trick doesn't really work on Jeff, who believes he is a zombie but does not behave as one. When the maid informs him, "You ain't no zombie! Zombies can't talk," Jeff responds, "Can I hep it cause I'm loquacious?" As it turns out, the doctor is a Nazi agent who was sent to lure the American admiral to the island and capture him, using hypnosis and voodoo to obtain information on American plans to defend the canal zone. Luckily, Bill catches on to

the scheme and, together with Jeff, keeps the world safe for democracy. Although pretty tedious overall, this film is livened up considerably by the comedic presence of Moreland, who is on-screen more than any of his costars. Although the humor is slightly racist, it is not nearly as bad as what one comes to expect from films of the period, and Moreland is quite funny. Victor, who plays the Nazi agent, was featured in Tod Browning's FREAKS (1932) as Hercules the strongman. A virtually identical sequel, REVENGE OF THE ZOMBIES (1943), shifted the locale from the Caribbean to the Louisiana bayous and had the bonus of better direction and an excellent performance from John Carradine. Moreland was again on hand for laughs.

p, Lindsley Parsons; d, Jean Yarbrough; w, Edmund Kelso; ph, Mack Stengler; ed, Richard Currier.

(PR:A   MPAA:NR)

## KINGDOM OF THE SPIDERS***

(1977) 94m Arachnid/Dimension c

William Shatner *(Rack Hansen)*, Tiffany Bolling *(Diane Ashley)*, Woody Strode *(Walter Colby)*, Lieux Dressler *(Emma Washburn)*, Altovise Davis *(Birch Colby)*, David McLean *(Sheriff Smith)*, Natasha Ryan *(Linda Hansen)*, Marcy Rafferty *(Terry Hansen)*, Joe Ross *(Vern Johnson)*, Adele Malis *(Betty Johnson)*, Roy Engel *(Mayor Connors)*.

A new chemical insecticide kills off the food supply of some deadly desert tarantulas, sending them swarming into the town of Verde, Arizona. Although it sounds like another EMPIRE OF THE ANTS, this film is actually fairly effective. The script is witty and the horror, as in FROGS, is of the more realistic variety. There are no super-giant spiders like the one in TARANTULA here, merely more than 5,000 live, life-sized tarantulas, which are plenty creepy on their own without inflating their size to ridiculous proportions. The terror builds slowly, and director Bud Cardos does a nice job of balancing the chills with a sly sense of humor. William Shatner gives an ever-so-slightly tongue-in-cheek performance as Rack Hansen, a veterinarian investigating the phenomenon. The eerie ending is reminiscent of Hitchcock's THE BIRDS.

p, Igo Kanter, Jeffrey Sneller; d, John ""Bud" Cardos; w, Richard Robinson, Alan Caillou; ph, John Arthur Morrill (Eastmancolor); ed, Steve Zaillian, Kantor; m, Dorsey Burnette.

(PR:C   MPAA:PG)

## KWAIDAN****

(1964, Jap.) 125m Toho/CD c (KAIDAN)

Rentaro Mikuni *(Samurai)*, Michiyo Aratama *(1st Wife)*, Misako Watanabe *(2nd Wife)*, Katsuo Nakamura *(Hoichi)*, Ganjiro Nakamura *(Head Priest)*, Takashi Shimura *(Priest)*, Joichi Hayashi *(Yoshitsune)*.

KWAIDAN contains four short supernatural stories based on the tales of Lafcadio Hearn, an American who settled in Japan in 1890 and eventually became a citizen of that country. Directed with an eerie visual sense by Masaki Kobayashi and featuring some spectacular art direction by Shigemasa Toda, the stories each involve an encounter with a ghost—according to Hearn's tales, a supernatural being who appears to be composed of flesh and blood but who is actually one of the dear departed, left to wander aimlessly through the real world. Included are "Black Hair," the tale of a samurai (Rentaro Mikuni) who returns to the wife he deserted years before and, after sleeping with her, discovers her skeletal remains and long black hair in his bed; "The Woman of the Snow," a story missing from the American theatrical release about a young wood-cutter (Tatsuya Nakadai) saved from death by a mysteri-ous snow maiden who promises to kill him should he ever reveal what happened; "Hoichi, the Earless," a tale about a blind musician (Katsuo Nakamura) whose ears are cut off as he sings, at the request of a samurai ghost, for a dead infant lord; and finally "In a Cup of Tea," a story about a guard (Ganemon Nakamura) who sees a samu-rai's face reflected in his tea and absorbs the ghost's soul into his body by drinking it. Winner of the Special Jury Prize at the 1965 Cannes Film Festival, KWAIDAN is a celebra-tion of the marvelous from director Kobayashi, whose haunting poetry is expressed not only through the beautiful color images, but also through the chilling soundtrack. The videocassette is in Japanese with English subtitles, though the wide-screen Tohoscope compositions are lost on tape.

p, Shigeru Wakatsuki; d, Masaki Kobayashi; w, Yoko Mizuki (based on the stories of Lafcadio Hearn); ph, Yoshio Miyajima (Tohoscope, Eastmancolor); m, Toru Takemitsu.

**(PR:C   MPAA:NR)**

# L

## LADY FRANKENSTEIN zero

(1971, It.) 99m Condor/NW c (LA FIGLIA DI FRANKENSTEIN; AKA: DAUGHTER OF FRANKENSTEIN, THE; MADAME FRANKENSTEIN)

Joseph Cotten *(Baron)*, Sarah Bay *(Tanya)*, Mickey Har-gitay *(Captain)*, Paul Muller *(Marsh)*, Paul Whiteman, Herbert Fux.

This awful, but awfully funny, Frankenstein movie boasts a really goofy-looking monster and the voluptuous Sarah Bay, who shows off her considerable talents throughout much of the film. Joseph Cotten plays Dr. Frankenstein, who is still trying to create a man stitched together from various parts of dead bodies. His latest creation, an insane bulbous-headed freak with one eye lower than the other, flips out, kills his master, and then scampers off into the countryside to terrorize the villagers. The dead doctor's beautiful daughter, Tanya (Bay), who has just come home from medical school, decides to create her own mon-ster—a perfect man who will not only seek out and destroy the botched creature that killed her father, but also satisfy

her voracious sexual appetite. To do this, she plunks the brain of her brilliant-but-crippled assistant into the GQ-hunk body of the moronic family shepherd. Although things are hot and heavy for Tanya and the monster at first, trouble arises when monster No. 1 shows up back at the castle. The plot is silly, the production values nil, the acting atrocious, but the sex scenes are pretty steamy and the rest of it is unintentionally hilarious. This is an all-time favorite on late-night television and cable, but rent the vid-eo so that you can see it uncut.

p, Harry Cushing, Mel Welles; d, Mel Welles; w, Edward Di Lorenzo (based on a story by Dick Randall from a comic magazine story "For the Love of Frankenstein" by Bill Warren); ph, Riccardo Pallotini; ed, Cleo Converse; m, Alessandro Alessandroni.

**(PR:O   MPAA:R)**

## LADY IN WHITE****

(1988) 112m New Century-Vista c

Lukas Haas *(Frankie Scarlatti)*, Len Cariou *(Phil)*, Alex Rocco *(Angelo Scarlatti)*, Katherine Helmond *(Amanda)*, Jason Presson *(Geno Scarlatti)*, Renata Vanni *(Mama As-sunta)*, Angelo Bertolini *(Papa Charlie)*, Jared Rushton *(Donald)*, Gregory Levinson *(Louie)*, Joelle Jacob *(Melissa)*, Tom Bower, Lucy Lee Flippen, Sydney Lassick, Rita Zohar, Hal Bokar.

Independent filmmaker Frank (FEAR NO EVIL) LaLoggia's long-awaited second feature is an impressive, if overly am-bitious, semiautobiographical ghost story that rejects gore in favor of genuine gothic chills. Surprisingly rich in charac-ter, period, and place, LADY IN WHITE begins on Hallow-een, 1962, as the youngest son of a widower (Alex Rocco), young Frankie (Lukas Haas) is locked in the school cloak-room by pranksters who leave him there for the night. Re-signed to his fate, Frankie climbs up on the top shelf and tries to get some sleep. Suddenly he is awakened by the ghost of a little girl (Joelle Jacob) about his age who was murdered in the cloakroom many years before. To his hor-ror, Frankie watches as the murder of the child is reenact-ed before his eyes. Then, a real man, whose face is ob-scured, enters the cloakroom. It is the killer, and he has returned to the scene of the crime to remove the girl's bar-rette, which had fallen down the heating duct during the murder so many years before (the school plans to install a new heater the very next day). Unfortunately for Frankie, the intruder notices the boy and tries to strangle him. Fran-kie survives the attack and police arrest a drunken black janitor, charge him with the attempted murder of Frankie, and suspect him of being the child killer who has plagued the town for several years. Frankie knows the man is inno-cent and sets out to find the real killer, with the help of the little girl's ghost, who guides him on his way. An intensely personal film, LADY IN WHITE is an incredibly ambitious low-budget effort that attempts to combine a good ghost story with a childhood reminiscence about growing up dur-ing the early 1960s. Fortunately, writer-director-composer LaLoggia pulls off this unlikely combination, although his narrative is a bit too diffuse at times. Instead of using Fran-kie's encounter with ghosts to escape the mundane realities of everyday life, LaLoggia's film is firmly rooted in the real world. Child murders, racism, and cruelty share the spotlight here and are contrasted with the warm, loving, and secure family of which Frankie is proud to be a part—he does not want to escape. What does trouble young Frankie, however, is the death of his mother. The boy's subconscious longing for her is at the root of his quest, and he fulfills his desire to be with her again by helping the ghostly little girl become reunited with her mother. LaLoggia shares his unique vision with the viewer through an imaginative and innovative visual style that flows skillfully from traditional naturalism into surreal dreamlike fantasies and back again without ever seeming gratuitous or clumsy. A remarkable film.

p, Andrew G. La Marca, Frank La Loggia; d, Frank La Loggia; w, Frank La Loggia; ph, Russell Carpenter (DeLuxe Color); ed, Steve Mann; m, Frank La Loggia.

**(PR:C  MPAA:PG-13)**

## LAIR OF THE WHITE WORM, THE***

(1988, Brit.) 94m White Lair/Vestron c

Amanda Donohoe *(Lady Sylvia Marsh)*, Hugh Grant *(Lord James D'Ampton)*, Catherine Oxenberg *(Eve Trent)*, Sammi Davis *(Mary Trent)*, Peter Capaldi *(Angus Flint)*, Stratford Johns *(Peters, the Butler)*, Paul Brooke *(P.C. Erny)*, Imogen Claire *(Dorothy Trent)*, Chris Pitt *(Kevin)*, Gina McKee *(Nurse Gladwell)*, Christopher Gable *(Joe Grant)*, Lloyd Peters *(Jesus Christ)*, Miranda Coe, Linzi Drew, Caron Anne Kelly, Fiona O'Conner, Caroline Pope, Elisha Scott, Tina Shaw *(Maids/Nuns)*, Paul Easom, James Hicks, David Kiernan, Matthew King, Ross King, Andy Norman, Bob Smith *(Soldiers/Witchdoctors)*, Jackie Russell *(Snakewoman)*.

After having a bash at Mary Shelley in 1987's disastrous GOTHIC, director Ken Russell turned his feverish imagination loose on Bram Stoker in this very campy adaptation of Stoker's final novel. Updated and set in the Derbyshire region of modern-day England, the film begins as young Scottish archaeologist Angus Flint (Peter Capaldi) uncovers an unidentifiable skull while digging up the garden of the inn where he is staying. Run by sisters Mary (Sammi Davis) and Eve Trent (Catherine Oxenberg), whose parents have recently disappeared, the house just happens to sit on a site that, centuries ago, was a convent during the Roman occupation. Soon Flint learns of local legends regarding a giant white worm/snake creature that terrorized the area in ancient times. The ancestor of a local lord is credited with having slain the evil worm and each year there is a party celebrating the event. Strangely, the skull Flint just discovered bears a distinct resemblance to paintings of the fabled worm. Meanwhile, the mysterious and sultry Lady Silvia Marsh (Amanda Donohoe) returns to her giant mansion and reveals herself to be a vampire-like creature with huge fangs who worships the giant white worm, which still exists, living in deep tunnels beneath the earth. Given a distinctly playful treatment by Russell, who fills each frame with all manner of phallic snake/worm imagery, THE LAIR OF THE WHITE WORM is a relatively entertaining and offbeat film that, of course, delights in break-

ing every social taboo known to man. In addition to the visual puns, Russell (who scripted as well) has fun with the ludicrous situation and stretches it to its satiric limits. Russell also indulges in his usual stylistic fetishes, such as pagan ritual, sexual repression, and Grand Guignol gore.

p, Ken Russell; d, Ken Russell; w, Ken Russell (based on the novel by Bram Stoker); ph, Dick Bush (Technicolor); ed, Peter Davies; m, Stanislas Syrewicz.

**(PR:O  MPAA:R)**

## LAND OF THE MINOTAUR*½

(1976, Gr.) 88m Crown International c (AKA: DEVIL'S MEN, THE; DEVIL'S PEOPLE, THE; MINOTAUR)

Donald Pleasence *(Father Roche)*, Peter Cushing *(Baron Corofax)*, Luan Peters *(Laurie)*, Nikos Verlekis *(Ian)*, Costas Skouras *(Milo)*, Bob Behling *(Tom)*, Vanna Revilli *(Beth)*, Fernando Bislani *(Police Sergeant)*, Anna Mantzourani, Jane Lyle.

The mythic Cretan minotaur is revived in this distinctly silly effort, which contains endless scenes of shrouded cultists murmuring incantations around an altar. Baron Corofax (Peter Cushing) is the head of a modern day-Greek cult that worships the man-bull, using female human sacrifices to honor their god. An Irish priest, Fr. Roche (Donald Pleasence), comes in to stop the blasphemy by sprinkling holy water all over everything. There's enough gratuitous violence and naked female flesh to satisfy fans, and the music, surprisingly enough, is by rock/New Age composer Brian Eno.

p, Frixos Constantine; d, Costa Carayiannis; w, Arthur Rowe; ph, Ari Stavrou; m, Brian Eno.

**(PR:C-O  MPAA:PG)**

## LAST HORROR FILM, THE**½

(1984) 87m Shere/Twin Continental c (AKA: FANATIC, THE)

Caroline Munro *(Jana Bates)*, Joe Spinell *(Vinny Durand)*, Judd Hamilton *(Alan Cunningham)*, Devin Goldenberg *(Marty Bernstein)*, David Winters *(Stanley Kline)*, Stanley Susanne Benton *(Susan Archer)*, Mary Spinell *(Vinny's Mother)*, Glenn Jacobson *(Bret Bates)*, J'len Winters *(Girl in Jacuzzi)*, Sharon Hughes *(Stripper)*, Sean Casey *(Jonathan)*, Don Talley *(Cowboy)*, June Chadwick *(Reporter)*.

This self-consciously amusing slasher film stars cult favorite Caroline Munro as Jana Bates, an actress with a cult following who is visiting Cannes for the film festival. Also visiting the Riviera is Vinny Durand (Joe Spinell), a New York taxi driver and her most devoted fan, who feels that she can be a great actress under his direction. When he invades her hotel room while she is taking a shower and makes his offer, she tries to toss him out. He smashes the bottle of champagne he brought with him and holds the jagged edge up to her throat. She manages to escape and runs through the crowded lobby wrapped only in a towel, with Vinny in pursuit. The festival crowd thinks it's a publicity stunt and applauds; Vinny, taken off guard, stops and makes a hesitant bow. His psychotic pursuit of his idol claims more victims (including one unfortunate decapitated with a chainsaw) before he himself meets a messy end. A nonsensical conclusion reveals that the whole thing is a film Vinny is showing to his mother (played by actor Spinell's real mom). Shot at the 1981 Cannes Festival, the film includes scenes with stars like Kris Kristofferson, Karen Black, and Marcello Mastroianni making unwitting appearances. Munro, who had been previously harassed by Spinell in the despicable MANIAC (1981) and producer Judd Hamilton (her real-life husband) were unable to come to New York for dubbing sessions, so their voices were replaced by Americans. Since the release of this film, both Joe Spinell and his mother have died. (She in 1987 and he in early 1989). Sleazy fun for fans of blood and bad acting.

p, Judd Hamilton, David Winters; d, David Winters; w, Judd Hamilton, David Winters, Tom Clasen; ph, Tom DeNove (Technicolor); ed, Chris Barnes, Edward Salier; m, Jesse Frederick, Jeff Koz.

**(PR:O MPAA:R)**

## LAST HOUSE ON DEAD END STREET zero

(1977) 90m Cinematic-Production Concepts/L.B.S. c (AKA: FUN HOUSE, THE)

Steven Morrison, Janet Sorley, Dennis Crawford, Lawrence Bornman, Paul Phillips, Elaine Norcross, Alex Kregar, Franklin Statz, Barbara Amusen, Geraldine Sanders.

Low-budget gore, LAST HOUSE ON DEAD END STREET concerns a group of sadistic moviemakers who murder their stars to make snuff films. When the filmmakers have problems with their distributors, they kill them and incorporate the footage into a new snuff feature. This vain attempt to combine splatter with a commentary on the viciousness of the movie business fails miserably on all counts.

p, Norman F. Kaiser; d, Victor Janos; w, Brian Lawrence.

**(PR:O MPAA:R)**

## LAST HOUSE ON THE LEFT***½

(1972) 91m Hallmark/AIP c

David Hess (Krug), Lucy Grantham (Phyllis), Sandra Cassel (Mari Collingwood), Marc Sheffler (Junior), Jeramie Rain (Sadie), Fred Lincoln (Weasel), Gaylord St. James (Dr. Collingwood), Cynthia Carr (Mrs. Collingwood), Ada Washington (Lady Truck Driver).

An extremely controversial cult favorite—the original "Just keep repeating: 'It's only a movie, only a movie'"movie—especially with the gore fanatics, LAST HOUSE ON THE LEFT is a much more complex (albeit crudely made) film than its bloody reputation would suggest. Loosely based on Ingmar Bergman's THE VIRGIN SPRING, LAST HOUSE ON THE LEFT details the atrocities committed by a group of escaped convicts who kidnap, rape, and murder two teenage girls who are on their way to a rock concert. After hiding the bodies, the convicts make their way through the dense New Jersey woods and take refuge in the home of a suburban couple, posing as a family whose car has broken down. Little do the killers know that the house they have picked for their refuge happens to be owned by the parents of one of their victims. Eventually, the parents find out that these strangers have murdered their daughter, and the once-nice, gentle suburban couple enact a savage revenge on the killers that makes them just as vile as those they seek to punish. As noted above, the film was crudely made on a minuscule budget, but what LAST HOUSE ON THE LEFT lacks in technical competence, it makes up for in characterization and insight into violent behavior. The killers initially toy with (torture) the girls, as if playing a game, but when the game gets out of hand and the girls wind up dead, the killers look at their corpses with saddened confusion, as if they had broken something; these people are not unthinking monsters, but deeply disturbed, nearly childlike (though admittedly very deadly) individuals who represent the dark underbelly of American society. The moment is brief, but without it the film would be just another sickening exploitation piece. Director Wes Craven has said he wanted to resensitize Americans to violence after all the desensitization that occurred during the Vietnam war. By presenting the brutality in all its horrifying and squeamish detail, Craven hoped to force his audience to recognize that violence results in great human pain and suffering. Craven—who would go on to polish his themes in the high-budgeted and slicker THE HILLS HAVE EYES—never for a moment allows the viewer to sympathize with the killers, but he does provide a window of understanding into how senseless acts of violence occur. Then he poses a moral question to the viewer: Who is worse, the sick, depraved convicts who have made murder a way of life, or the girls' affluent, God-fearing parents, who allow themselves to throw away their values to enact a bloody, torturous revenge? Craven poses the question and leaves it hanging for the viewer to decide. A deeply disturbing film that should only be viewed by those prepared for it.

p, Sean S. Cunningham; d, Wes Craven; w, Wes Craven; ph, Victor Hurwitz (Movielab color); ed, Wes Craven; m, Steve Chapin, David Hess.

**(PR:O MPAA:R)**

## LAST RITES zero

(1980) 88m New Empire/Cannon c (AKA: DRACULA'S LAST RITES)

Patricia Lee Hammond, Gerald Fielding, Victor Jorge, Michael Lally, Mimi Weddell.

This ultra-low-budget effort out of upstate New York features a bald mortician named Lucard (do we have to tell you to spell that backwards?), who is really a vampire. In fact, Lucard is the head of a vampire coven, which includes the local sheriff and doctor, who feed off hapless motorists misfortunate enough to wreck their cars in the vicinity. The barely living victims are discovered by the sheriff, brought to the doctor, declared deceased, and then brought to Lucard's mortuary, where their blood is consumed by the hungry city officials. Lucard seem partic-

LAST RITES—

ularly obsessed with sinking his teeth into the necks of a family named Fonda. Why? No one knows. This film is incredibly inept technically and gives the audience a chance to play "spot the camera equipment," with plenty of camera cases, light stands, and microphones plainly visible throughout. May also be out on videocassette under the title DRACULA'S LAST RITES.

p, Kelly Van Horn; d, Dominic Paris; w, Ben Donnelly, Dominic Paris; ph, Dominic Paris (Deluxe Color); ed, Elizabeth Lombardo; m, Paul Jost, George Small.

**(PR:O   MPAA:R)**

### LEGACY, THE*½

(1979, Brit.) 100m UNIV c (AKA: LEGACY OF MAGGIE WALSH, THE)

Katharine Ross *(Maggie Walsh)*, Sam Elliott *(Pete Danner)*, John Standing *(Jason Mountolive)*, Ian Hogg *(Harry)*, Margaret Tyzack *(Nurse Adams)*, Charles Gray *(Karl)*, Lee Montague *(Jacques)*, Hildegard Neil *(Barbara)*, Marianne Broome *(Maria)*, William Abney *(Butler)*, Patsy Smart *(Cook)*, Mathias Kilroy *(Stable Lad)*, Reg Harding *(Gardener)*, Roger Daltrey *(Clive)*.

An American couple, Maggie and Pete (Katharine Ross and Sam Elliott), arrive in England and end up staying at a country mansion when their car is forced off the road. After the other guests at the house (Charles Gray, Hildegard Neil, Roger Daltrey, Lee Montague, and Marianne Broome) begin dying in strange ways, the new couple eventually discovers that the victims were members of a Satanic cult and had sold their souls to the Devil. Bedridden millionaire Jason Mountolive (John Standing) is the leader of the cult and the man who is collecting the debts. It seems, moreover, that Maggie is the reincarnation of Mountolive's mother and predestined to take over the sect upon his death. Pete, naturally, is a bit upset by the news and takes steps to end this nonsense. This was the feature film debut of director Richard Marquand, who would go on to make such notable films as EYE OF THE NEEDLE; RETURN OF THE JEDI; and JAGGED EDGE. Unfortunately, he demonstrates little of that talent in this film, which is dry, dull, and terribly predictable. The gore factor is surprisingly high, however, so fans of Grand Guignol may want to watch the various burnings, drownings, and impalements—especially former Who lead singer Daltrey having an impromptu tracheotomy performed on him. It fails.

p, David Foster; d, Richard Marquand; w, Jimmy Sangster, Patric Tilley, Paul Wheeler (based on a story by Sangster); ph, Dick Bush, Alan Hume (Technicolor); ed, Anne V. Coates; m, Michael J. Lewis.

**(PR:O   MPAA:R)**

### LEGEND OF BOGGY CREEK, THE**

(1973) 90m Howco International c

Vern Stearman *(Narrator)*, Willie E. Smith, John P. Hixon, John W. Oates, Jeff Crabtree, Buddy Crabtree, Herb Jones.

This docudrama features a Bigfoot-like creature that allegedly terrorizes the small town of Fouke, Arkansas, near the Texas border. Usually seen as a dark, shambling shape running across someone's headlight beams on stark country roads, the creature makes several attacks on people, tossing their garbage cans around, rocking trailer homes, and occasionally sticking his arm in someone's window and scaring the kids. The film is crudely made, but fairly effective, and its "G" rating attracted lots of little kids not usually able to see a horror movie in a theater and gave them a couple of good scares. A sequel, RETURN TO BOGGY CREEK, was released in 1977.

p, Charles B. Pierce; d, Charles B. Pierce; w, Earl E. Smith; ph, Charles B. Pierce (Technicolor); ed, Thomas Boutress; m, Jaime Mendoza-Nava.

**(PR:A   MPAA:G)**

### LEGEND OF HELL HOUSE, THE**

(1973, Brit.) 94m James H. Nicholson's Academy Pictures/FOX c

Pamela Franklin *(Florence Tanner)*, Roddy McDowall *(Ben Fischer)*, Clive Revill *(Dr. Chris Barrett)*, Gayle Hunnicutt *(Ann Barrett)*, Roland Culver *(Rudolph Deutsch)*, Peter Bowles *(Hanley)*, Michael Gough.

Four people are hired to stay in a haunted house for a week to determine whether or not ghosts are inhabiting the place. Florence (Pamela Franklin) is a medium who believes she is able to communicate with the spirit world, Ben (Roddy McDowall) is a physical medium who has stayed in the house before, and Dr. Barrett (Clive Revill) is a skeptical physicist who brings along his wife (Gayle Hunnicutt). The man who is paying for their stay is eccentric millionaire Rudolph Deutsch (Roland Culver). As it turns out, the joint is being haunted by the ghost of a long-dead decadent millionaire (Michael Gough, in an unbilled, silent cameo) who, during his life, indulged in all manner of sadistic perversions, and whose corpse now emanates evil. While director John Hough (TWINS OF EVIL) does a fine job with the things-that-go-bump-in-the-night aspects of the material, he fails to breathe any life into Richard Matheson's woefully underdeveloped screenplay, which he adapted from his own novel.

p, Albert Fennell, Norman T. Herman; d, John Hough; w, Richard Matheson (based on his novel *Hell House*); ph, Alan Hume (DeLuxe Color); ed, Geoffrey Foot; m, Brian Hodgson, Delia Derbyshire.

**(PR:C   MPAA:PG)**

### LEGEND OF THE SEVEN GOLDEN VAMPIRES, THE***

(1973, Brit./Chi.) 110m Shaw-Hammer c (AKA: DRACULA AND THE SEVEN GOLDEN VAMPIRES; SEVEN BROTHERS MEET DRACULA, THE)

John Forbes-Robertson *(Dracula)*, David Chang *(Hsu Tien-an/Hsu Ching)*, Peter Cushing *(Prof. Van Helsing)*, Shih Szu *(Hsu Meichiao)*, Robin Stewart *(Leyland)*, Julie

142

THE HORROR FILM

Ege (Vanessa Buren), Chan Shen, Robert Hanna, James Ma.

An intriguing, if not entirely successful, attempt at mixing Shaw Bros. martial-arts movies with Hammer horror fare, THE LEGEND OF THE SEVEN GOLDEN VAMPIRES is wholly entertaining and, at times, a quite effective genre hybrid—which, with the exception of the Hong Kong cinema, has not been repeated. The film opens in imperial China, circa 1880, as the High Priest of the Seven Golden Vampires visits a crypt that contains Dracula's coffin. The vampire (John Forbes-Robertson) rises from his tomb and melds his identity with that of the Chinese priest, taking on his physical appearance. Meanwhile, Dr. Van Helsing (Peter Cushing, in his last go-round with the role) comes to China to study vampires, accompanied by his son, Leyland (Robin Stewart), Leyland's girl friend (Julie Ege), and seven Chinese martial arts experts—all brothers—whose father was killed by the vampires. Camped at the town of Ping Kuei, Van Helsing and his friends find themselves under attack from the legendary Seven Golden Vampires—who wear gold masks and ride on horseback—and a horde of zombies reactivated by Dracula in his high-priest guise. Filmed in 1973, this movie was not released in the US until 1979 (under the ludicrous title THE SEVEN BROTHERS MEET DRACULA). The role of Dracula was originally slated for Christopher Lee, but he refused to don the black cape again and the part was given to Forbes-Robertson, who does well with it. The combination of gothic horrors and gymnastic fight scenes complete with exaggerated sound effects is quite fun to watch (and hear), and director Roy Ward Baker delivers a few genuine chills—especially when the vampires and the zombies dig their way out of their tombs to fight Van Helsing and his friends.

p, Don Houghton, Vee King Shaw; d, Roy Ward Baker; w, Don Houghton (based on the character created by Bram Stoker); ph, John Wilcox, Roy Ford; ed, Chiang Hising-lung, Chris Barnes; m, Wang Fu-ling.

(PR:C MPAA:NR)

## LEOPARD MAN, THE***½

(1943) 63m RKO bw

Dennis O'Keefe (Jerry Manning), Margo (Clo-Clo), Jean Brooks (Kiki Walker), Isabel Jewell (Maria), James Bell (Dr. Galbraith), Margaret Landry (Teresa Delgado), Abner Biberman (Charlie How-Come), Richard Martin (Raoul Belmonte), Tula Parma (Consuelo Contreras), Ben Bard (Chief Robles), Ariel Heath (Eloire), Fely Franquelli (Rosita), Robert Anderson (Dwight), Jacqueline De Wit (Helene), Bobby Spindola (Pedro), William Halligan (Brunton), Kate Lawson (Senora Delgado), Russell Wade (Man in Car), Jacques Lory (Philippe), Ottola Nesmith (Senora Contreras), Marguerite Sylva (Marta), Charles Lung (Manuel), John Dilson (Coroner), Mary Maclaren (Nun), Tom Orosco (Window Cleaner), Eliso Gamboa (Senor Delgado), Joe Dominguez (Cop), Betty Roadman (Clo-Clo's Mother), Rosa Rita Varella (Clo-Clo's Sister), John Piffle (Flower Vendor), Rene Pedrini (Frightened Waiter), Brandon Hurst (Gatekeeper), Rose Higgins

(Indian Weaver), George Sherwood (Police Lieutenant), John Tettemer (Minister).

THE LEOPARD MAN is another superbly atmospheric thriller from producer Val Lewton and director Jacques Tourneur (CAT PEOPLE; I WALKED WITH A ZOMBIE). Jerry Manning (Dennis O'Keefe), a public relations man for a New Mexico nightclub, rents a leopard as a publicity stunt. The animal escapes and kills a teenage girl, whose mother had locked her out of the house as punishment for returning late from an errand. The scene, shot from the inside of the house, is terrifying—when the leopard strikes, all the viewer sees is blood coming under the door. Two subsequent murders are blamed on the leopard, but Jerry investigates and unmasks the real—and very human—killer. Based on Black Alibi, the third mystery novel written by the incomparable Cornell Woolrich, this film, along with Lewton and Tourneur's other collaborations, proves once again that money is not the most essential element in good filmmaking. Robert de Grasse's gorgeously fluid camerawork creates the absolutely chilling mood. While not as challenging or thematically dense as the other Lewton-Tourneur masterworks, THE LEOPARD MAN has individual sequences that refuse to fade from memory.

p, Val Lewton; d, Jacques Tourneur; w, Ardel Wray, Edward Dein (based on the novel Black Alibi by Cornell Woolrich); ph, Robert de Grasse; ed, Mark Robson; m, Roy Webb.

(PR:O MPAA:NR)

## LET'S SCARE JESSICA TO DEATH**½

(1971) 89m Jessica-PAR c

Zohra Lampert (Jessica), Barton Heyman (Duncan), Kevin O'Connor (Woody), Gretchen Corbett (Girl), Alan Manson (Dorker), Mariclare Costello (Emily).

Jessica (Zohra Lampert) is released from a mental hospital and moves to a farmhouse in Connecticut with her husband, Duncan (Barton Heyman), and family friend Woody (Kevin O'Connor). A strange woman named Emily (Mariclare Costello) is found at their house and Jessica discovers that she's a vampire. There are also ghosts, visions, and some living dead parading around town, but since no one believes her stories, Jessica begins to think she's having another breakdown. This was the feature debut of director John Hancock (who would go on to BANG THE DRUM SLOWLY and WEEDS), and he does a fairly effective job of pulling good shocks out of this somewhat familiar material. The script doesn't help his cause any; it's badly underdeveloped and contains some confusing inconsistencies that will annoy viewers if dwelt upon. Lampert turns in a memorable performance as the put-upon Jessica, but the rest of the cast is rather bland.

p, Charles B. Moss, Jr.; d, John Hancock; w, Norman Jonas, Ralph Rose; ph, Bob Baldwin; ed, Murray Soloman, Joe Ryan; m, Orville Stoeber (electronic music, Walter Sear).

(PR:C MPAA:GP)

## LITTLE GIRL WHO LIVES DOWN THE LANE, THE***

(1977, Can.) 91m Rank/AIP c

Jodie Foster *(Rynn Jacobs)*, Martin Sheen *(Frank Hallet)*, Alexis Smith *(Mrs. Hallet)*, Mort Shuman *(Officer Miglioriti)*, Scott Jacoby *(Mario Podesta)*, Dorothy Davis *(Town Hall Clerk)*, Clesson Goodhue *(Bank Manager)*, Hubert Noel, Jacques Famery *(Bank Clerks)*, Mary Morter, Judie Wildman *(Tellers)*.

This Canadian-made film, a star vehicle for the then-13-year-old Jodie Foster, is a disturbing, wonderfully acted, well-scripted, and suspenseful study of a murderous 13-year-old girl, Rynn (Foster). Living alone in her father's home, Rynn makes up stories that her father is away, when in fact he is dead. She handles the bills, the upkeep, and her own survival, admirably putting into practice what her father taught her. When a snooping neighbor makes a nuisance of herself, Rynn knocks her down the stairs. Matter-of-factly, Rynn lets the cellar door close and gets back to her work. Soon the creepy Frank (Martin Sheen) is making a pest of himself, wanting both answers to his suspicions and Rynn's barely pubescent body. Meanwhile, Rynn becomes genuinely attracted to Mario (Scott Jacoby), a youngster her own age. Frank, knowing that something is odd about Rynn's situation, presses her for answers about her father, his insistence threatening to ruin the private, self-sustaining, child-as-adult world she has created with Mario. This leads to a fatal game of cat-and-mouse between Rynn and Frank. Tautly directed by Nicolas Gessner, the film is a showcase for the young Foster and she does not disappoint, turning in a slyly nuanced performance that is downright creepy, and at the same time oddly innocent.

p, Zev Braun; d, Nicolas Gessner; w, Laird Koenig (based on his novel); ph, Rene Verzier (Panavision); ed, Yves Langlois; m, Christian Gaubert.

**(PR:C    MPAA:PG)**

## LITTLE SHOP OF HORRORS***½

(1961) 70m Filmgroup bw

Jonathan Haze *(Seymour Krelboin)*, Jackie Joseph *(Audrey)*, Mel Welles *(Gravis Mushnik)*, Jack Nicholson *(Wilbur Force)*, Dick Miller *(Fouch)*, Myrtle Vail *(Winifred Krelboin)*, Leola Wendorff *(Mrs. Shiva)*.

This is the ultimate Roger Corman super-low-budget cult favorite, and also happens to be one of the funniest black comedies ever made. The plot details the sorry existence of a dim-witted schlepp named Seymour (Jonathan Haze) who works in Mr. Mushnik's (Mel Welles) Skid Row flower shop. To impress his girl, Audrey (Jackie Joseph), Seymour invents a carnivorous little flower, naming it Audrey, Jr. Soon Seymour's bloom is all the rage among chlorophyll critics and botanists alike. The only problem is, the little flower needs human blood to grow. After discovering this gruesome detail, and the fact that the plant can talk (when it's hungry it yells, "Feed Me!"), Seymour becomes slowly possessed by the flora and commits several murders in order to stop his plant's tummy from growling. Along with these feedings comes the plant's rapid growth,

and soon it overgrows the whole flower shop, bellowing "Feeeed Meee!" in a monstrously loud and obnoxious voice, and poor Seymour finds he can no longer handle his creation. While its story doesn't make for very funny reading, LITTLE SHOP OF HORRORS is a hilarious (and yes, quite silly) film filled to the brim with enough little vignettes and character quirks to sustain laughter throughout its brief 70-minute running time. Shot in two days on a dare by Roger Corman, who was challenged by a studio employee to come up with a script and shoot a movie in the brief time remaining before the storefront set was torn down (it was left standing from another production), LITTLE SHOP OF HORRORS is surprisingly well shot and performed. Corman contacted screenwriter Chuck Griffith from his other camp hit A BUCKET OF BLOOD and together they hacked out the killer plant story in less than a week. Aided by on-the-set inspiration, Corman and his cast and crew (including a very young Jack Nicholson in a side-splitting cameo as a masochistic dental patient begging for more pain) threw together a small masterpiece of taut, economical filmmaking in the space of two days and one night that has passed the test of time, having been revived in the 1980s as a very successful off-Broadway musical. A film version of the musical was released in 1986.

p, Roger Corman; d, Roger Corman; w, Charles Griffith; ph, Archie Dalzell; ed, Marshall Neilan, Jr.; m, Fred Katz.

**(PR:A    MPAA:NR)**

## LITTLE SHOP OF HORRORS**

(1986) 88m WB c

Rick Moranis *(Seymour Krelborn)*, Ellen Greene *(Audrey)*, Vincent Gardenia *(Mushnik)*, Steve Martin *(Orin Scrivello, D.D.S.)*, Tichina Arnold *(Crystal)*, Tisha Campbell *(Chiffon)*, Michelle Weeks *(Ronette)*, James Belushi *(Patrick Martin)*, John Candy *(Wink Wilkinson)*, Christopher Guest *(1st Customer)*, Bill Murray *(Arthur Denton)*, Stanley Jones *(Narrator)*, Bertice Reading *("Downtown" Old Woman)*, Edward Wiley, Alan Tilvern, John Scott Martin *("Downtown" Bums)*, Vincent Wong *(Chinese Florist)*, Mak Wilson, Danny Cunningham, Danny John Jules, Gary Palmer, Paul Swaby *(Doo Wop Street Singers)*, Mildred Shay, Melissa Wiltsie, Kevin Scott, Barbara Rosenblat *(Customers)*, Adeen Fogle *(Radio Station Assistant)*, Kelly Huntley, Paul Reynolds *(Audrey & Seymour's Kids)*, Miriam Margolyes *(Dental Nurse)*, Abbie Dabner *(Boy Patient)*, Frank Dux *(2nd Patient)*, Peter Whitman *(Patient on Ceiling)*, Heather Henson *(Girl Patient)*, Judith Morse *(Girl's Mother)*, Bob Sherman *(Agent)*, Levi Stubbs *(Voice of "Audrey II")*.

This is the multimillion–dollar movie version of the off-Broadway musical, which was based in turn on an old movie conceived and shot in a matter of days by Roger Corman. Although the plots are virtually identical, much of the edge was taken off of the material in its transition from screen to stage to screen, with the killer plant transformed into a being from outer space rather than a warped hybrid created by Seymour in his basement. Big-budget and bloated, the film has none of the shabby charm of Corman's effort and is memorable only for a couple of decent tunes, a parade of star cameos, some impressive special effects, and a wonderful performance from Ellen Greene as Audrey. As *Chicago Tribune* film critic Dave Kehr noted in his review, more money was probably spent on the leather jacket worn by Steve Martin here than Corman had for the entire budget of the original. The mammoth set—constructed at Pinewood Studios in England—was entirely indoors and very stylized. The special effects of Lyle Conway involved several generations of Audrey II, from a potted plant to a mammoth 12 1/2-foot-tall creature that took over the entire florist shop. It weighed, at the close, more than 2,000 pounds and used almost 12 miles of cable. The most remarkable aspect of the device were the lips, perfectly in sync with the singing and dialog. While an impressive technical achievement, the film itself is a rather overblown and overhyped affair, which—for all its expensive excess—fails to recapture the spirit of the original.

p, David Geffen; d, Frank Oz; w, Howard Ashman (based on his musical stage play); ph, Robert Paynter (Panavision, Technicolor); ed, John Jympson; m, Alan Menken, Miles Goodman.

(PR:A-C MPAA:PG-13)

## LIVING HEAD, THE*½

(1961, Mex.) 75m Cinematografica A.B.S.A./Trans-International bw (LA CABEZA VIVIENTE)

Mauricio Garces, Ana Luisa Peluffo, German Robles, Guillermo Cramer, Abel Salazar, Antonio Raxell, Eric del Castillo, Salvador Lozano, Alvaro Matute.

An archaeologist and two assistants unearth the tomb of a beheaded Aztec chief and discover not only his mummy, but the mummies of the Grand Priest and the chief's fiancee—who was buried alive. Although the last mummy disintegrates, the chief's severed head is intact and the archaeologist brings the relic home. He also gives a ring found on the finger of the female mummy to his daughter—who is the spitting image of the long-dead woman. Shortly thereafter, the archaeologist discovers that his daughter has become possessed by the head of the chief, which has come to life and commands her to kill the defilers of his tomb. This poorly directed Mexican effort sounds, as usual, more interesting than it actually is.

p, Abel Salazar; d, Chanto Urueta; w, Frederick Curiel, Adolfo Lopez Portillo; ph, Jorge Stahl, Jr., Jose Ortiz Ramos; ed, Alfredo Rosas Priego; m, Gustavo Cesar Carrion.

(PR:A-C MPAA:NR)

## LOST BOYS, THE**½

(1987) 97m WB c

Jason Patric *(Michael)*, Corey Haim *(Sam)*, Dianne Wiest *(Lucy)*, Barnard Hughes *(Grandpa)*, Edward Herrmann *(Max)*, Kiefer Sutherland *(David)*, Jami Gertz *(Star)*, Corey Feldman *(Edgar Frog)*, Jamison Newlander *(Alan Frog)*, Brooke McCarter *(Paul)*, Billy Wirth *(Dwayne)*, Alexander Winter *(Marko)*, Chance Michael Corbitt *(Laddie)*.

Part horror, part comedy, THE LOST BOYS is a vampire thriller that brings some interesting twists to the genre, but is nearly defeated by director Joel Schumacher's heavy-handed efforts to bring a hip, glitzy, MTV-like sensibility to the traditionally gothic material. The recently divorced Lucy (Dianne Wiest) packs up her belongings and, along with teenaged sons Michael (Jason Patric) and Sam (Corey Haim), moves in with her eccentric father (Barnard Hughes), who lives in the Northern California town of Santa Cruz. Rumored to be the "Murder Capital of the World," the town is dominated by an old amusement park that serves as a beacon for the bored teenagers who gravitate toward it like moths to a flame. Michael, the older of the boys, becomes infatuated with a beautiful girl (Jami Gertz) who introduces him to a creepy gang of teen bikers led by David (Kiefer Sutherland). As it turns out, the teens are vampires and, through great peer pressure, Michael becomes one of them. THE LOST BOYS adds an intriguing dimension to the traditional vampire legend by exploring the material through teenagers' eyes. Instead of the tragic Bela Lugosi-type vampire who is hopelessly cursed by his undead state, screenwriters Janice Fischer, James Jeremias, and Jeffrey Boam present vampires who seem to *want to be* hellish creatures. The script utilizes the age-old teenage themes of alienation, anger, and rebellion, the "I won't grow up" appeal of Peter Pan (hence the title), and the fervent desire to be cool, and takes them to a fantastic extreme, creating the ultimate teenage clique. The problem with THE LOST BOYS lies in the frustrating disposal of most of the thematics in favor of glitzy visuals and a slam-bang climax highly derivative of both FRIGHT NIGHT and the made-for-TV SALEM'S LOT. Despite its flaws, however, THE LOST BOYS is an interesting addition to vampire cinema.

p, Harvey Bernhard; d, Joel Schumacher; w, Janice Fischer, James Jeremias, Jeffrey Boam (based on a story by Janice Fischer, James Jeremias); ph, Michael Chapman (Panavision, Technicolor); ed, Robert Brown; m, Thomas Newman.

(PR:O MPAA:R)

## LOST WORLD, THE***½

(1925) 77m FN bw

Bessie Love *(Paula White)*, Lloyd Hughes *(Edward J. Malone)*, Lewis Stone *(Sir John Roxton)*, Wallace Beery *(Prof. Challenger)*, Arthur Hoyt *(Prof. Summerlee)*, Margaret McWade *(Mrs. Challenger)*, Finch Smiles *(Austin, Challenger's Butler)*, Jules Cowles *(Zambo, Roxton's Servant)*, Bull Montana *(Apeman)*, George Bunny *(Colin McArdle)*, Charles Wellesley *(Maj. Hibbard)*, Alma Bennett *(Gladys Hungerford)*, Virginia Browne Faire *(Half-Caste Girl)*, Nelson MacDowell *(Attorney)*.

A film that stunned and amazed audiences in 1925, THE LOST WORLD was the first feature-length movie to indulge in a staggering symphony of special effects while telling an engrossing adventure story. After years of making short fantasy films, stop-motion animation genius Willis O'Brien was finally given the budget and facilities to create this state-of-the-art adventure film based on a novel by Arthur Conan Doyle. The film opens in London, where a young reporter, Malone (Lloyd Hughes) joins an expedition to the Amazon led by Prof. Challenger (Wallace Beery). The explorers intend to search for Paula's (Bessie Love) father, a scientist who disappeared while trying to locate a legendary plateau where dinosaurs still exist. Eventually, the searchers reach the fabled plateau, where they find dozens of prehistoric beasts, including a pterodactyl, a huge brontosaurus, several vicious meat-eating allosaurs, and even an ape-man. Prof. Challenger brings the brontosaurus back to London alive, but as the giant dinosaur is being unloaded, its cage is damaged and it manages to escape, the confused beast roaming the London streets and destroying everything in its path. It is difficult to describe the impact THE LOST WORLD had on audiences in 1925. Nothing like it had ever been seen before—not just on the movie screen, but anywhere. The effects were accomplished by animating 18-inch model dinosaurs constructed by O'Brien's assistant, Marcel Delgado. These models were placed within detailed miniature jungles and then moved only a fraction of an inch per film exposure. When the film was developed and projected, the models appeared to be alive. In 1922, when O'Brien was embroiled in shooting test footage of the dinosaurs, he sent a finished reel to author Doyle. Doyle was amazed at the footage and used it to stun a meeting of the Society of American Magicians in New York. The film showing made the front page of the *New York Times* the next morning, the reporter unsure as to whether or not the monsters he saw were real. Sensing that speculation was starting to snowball, Doyle explained the true nature of the film to Harry Houdini, who was the president of the Society of American Magicians, and to the newspapers. In 1924, after finally getting major studio backing from First National, THE LOST WORLD went into full-time production. After a year of shooting and special-effects work at a staggering cost of $1 million, the film was released roadshow style to amazed audiences. Though the human drama suffers from slow pacing and silly romantic subplots, the adventure footage all but makes up for it. O'Brien's monsters were a big hit in Hollywood and in the next few years several new projects were announced, including Creation for RKO. Creation and all of the other projects never came to fruition, but O'Brien's work for RKO led to the deal that would allow him to make his monumental masterpiece, KING KONG, in 1933. An accurate running time for THE LOST WORLD seems almost impossible to determine, with 130m, 77m, and 60m all listed by credible sources, but the common videotape running time is listed as 77m.

d, Harry O. Hoyt, William Dowling; w, Marion Fairfax (based on the novel by Sir Arthur Conan Doyle); ph, Arthur Edeson; ed, George McGuire.

(PR:A    MPAA:NR)

## LOVE AT FIRST BITE**½

(1979) 96m Melvin Simon/AIP c

George Hamilton *(Count Dracula)*, Susan Saint James *(Cindy Sondheim)*, Richard Benjamin *(Dr. Jeff Rosenberg)*, Dick Shawn *(Lt. Ferguson)*, Arte Johnson *(Renfield)*, Sherman Hemsley *(Rev. Mike)*, Isabel Sanford *(Judge)*, Barry Gordon *(Flashlight Vendor)*, Ronnie Schell *(Gay in Elevator)*, Bob Basso *(TV Repairman)*, Bryan O'Byrne *(Priest)*, Michael Pataki *(Mobster)*, Beverly Sanders *(Lady in Elevator)*, Basil Hoffman *(Desk Clerk)*, Stanley Brock *(Cab Driver)*, Danny Dayton *(Billy)*, Robert Ellenstein *(W.V. Man)*, David Ketchum *(Customs Inspector)*.

This better-than-usual genre spoof places Count Dracula (George Hamilton) in modern times. Forced out of his Transylvanian castle by communist bureaucrats who want to turn it into a people's gymnasium, Dracula comes to New York City, where he scours the discos looking for victims. In the Big Apple, Dracula meets beautiful fashion model Cindy Sondheim (Susan Saint James) and falls in love. Drac and Cindy spend the night together, and the model wakes up the next morning with "a dynamite hickey." This, of course, disturbs Cindy's psychiatrist boyfriend, Jeff (Richard Benjamin), who winds up trying to dispatch the vampire through a variety of methods (hypnotism, silver bullets, etc.). Although much of this is pretty funny, the film is a scattershot affair that tries to milk laughs out of the most mundane and tired gags. For every bit that works there are three that don't, and the movie becomes somewhat tedious at times. Hamilton, however, is obviously having a good time with his role and has a field day with the Bela Lugosi accent. Made at the height of the disco craze, the film is almost worth the price of admission to see Dracula dancing to "I Love the Nightlife." This film was a surprise hit at the box office and a sequel was announced but never made.

p, Joel Freeman; d, Stan Dragoti; w, Robert Kaufman (based on a story by Kaufman, Mark Gindes); ph, Edward Rosson (CFI Color); ed, Mort Fallick, Allan Jacobs; m, Charles Bernstein.

(PR:C    MPAA:PG)

## LOVE BUTCHER, THE**

(1982) 83m Desert/Mirror Releasing c

Erik Stern *(Caleb/Lester)*, Kay Near *(Florence)*, Jeremiah Beecher *(Russell)*, Edward Roehm *(Capt. Stark)*, Robin Sherwood *(Sheila)*.

Made in 1975, this pre-HALLOWEEN low-budget slasher film was a bit ahead of its time, but it looked downright archaic when it was finally released seven years later in 1982. Caleb (Erik Stern) is a crippled gardener who is constantly mistreated by his female employers. He gets his revenge when his alter ego, Lester—a suave and handsome lad (also played by Stern)—seduces, rapes, and kills them with a gardening tool. While the filmmakers are obviously attempting something a bit more intelligent than your average slice-and-dice, the movie is wildly uneven, with heavy doses of self-conscious humor haphazardly thrown into the mix. Stern does a respectable job of handling the two roles, but the rest of the cast is typical low-budget fare.

p, Gary Williams, Micky Belski; d, Mikel Angel, Don Jones; w, Don Jones, James Evergreen; ph, Don Jones, Austin

McKinney (Techniscope, Technicolor) m, Richard Hieronymous; ed, Robert Freeman.

(PR:O   MPAA:R)

## LUST FOR A VAMPIRE**

(1970, Brit.) 95m Hammer-EMI/Levitt-Pickman c (AKA: TO LOVE A VAMPIRE)

Ralph Bates *(Giles Barton),* Barbara Jefford *(Countess Herritzen),* Suzanna Leigh *(Janet Playfair),* Michael Johnson *(Richard Lestrange),* Yutte Stensgaard *(Mircalla/Carmilla),* Mike Raven *(Count Karnstein),* Helen Christie *(Miss Simpson),* David Healy *(Pelley),* Michael Brennan *(Landlord),* Pippa Steel *(Susan),* Jack Melford *(Bishop),* Eric Chitty *(Prof. Hertz),* Luan Peters *(Trudie),* Christopher Cunningham *(Coachman),* Judy Matheson *(Amanda),* Caryl Little *(Isabel),* Christopher Neame *(Hans),* Harvey Hall *(Heinrich).*

This is the second film in the Hammer trilogy comprising THE VAMPIRE LOVERS; LUST FOR A VAMPIRE; and TWINS OF EVIL—all derived from Sheridan LeFanu's classic lesbian vampire story "Carmilla." While THE VAMPIRE LOVERS was a sincere, if somewhat skittish, attempt at exploring the sexuality of female vampires, LUST FOR A VAMPIRE, under the direction of Jimmy Sangster, collapses into mere silliness. Mircalla (Yutte Stensgaard) is a beautiful blonde vampire enrolled in an exclusive finishing school located on the grounds of Karnstein Castle, the former site of various black magic rituals. She roams the dorms by night, slyly seducing her fellow female students and sucking their blood. Barton (Ralph Bates), the school's headmaster, believes the girl is a vampire and confronts her with his suspicions. She succeeds in seducing the man and then drains him of his blood. A school professor, Lestrange (Michael Johnson), then falls in love with Mircalla, and this time she returns the emotion. Unfortunately, the townsfolk have had enough of her nonsense and they storm the school, setting it ablaze. Whatever rich Gothic flavor this material may have had is totally destroyed by Sangster's annoying direction, which relies heavily on leering zooms and garish color. To make matters worse, what should be highly-charged erotic scenes are ruined by deplorably bad songs droning away on the soundtrack. Originally rated "X" by the MPAA, the film was re-rated "R" after some extensive cuts.

p, Harry Fine, Michael Style; d, Jimmy Sangster; w, Tudor Gates (based on characters created by J. Sheridan Le Fanu in his novel *Carmilla*); ph, David Muir (Technicolor); ed, Spencer Reeve; m, Harry Robinson.

(PR:O   MPAA:R)

# M

## MAD DOCTOR OF BLOOD ISLAND, THE*

(1969, Phil./US) 86m Hemisphere c (AKA: BLOOD DOCTOR; TOMB OF THE LIVING DEAD)

John Ashley *(Bill Foster),* Angelique Pettyjohn *(Sheila Willard),* Ronald Remy *(Dr. Lorca),* Alicia Alonso, Ronaldo Valdez, Tita Munoz, Tony Edmunds, Alfonso Carvajal, Bruno Punzalan, Edward Murphy, Johnny Long, Paquito Salcedo, Felisa Salcedo, Quiel Mendoza, Ricardo Hipolito, Cenon Gonzalez, Nadja.

The first sequel to the epic BRIDES OF BLOOD (1968) sends Bill Foster (John Ashley) off to the mysterious Blood Island to investigate a report of a corpse with green blood. En route he meets a variety of people headed the same way, including the lovely Miss Sheila Willard (Angelique Pettyjohn), who's searching for her missing father. Upon arrival, they find the island under the control of the decidedly mad Dr. Lorca (Ronald Remy), who's experimenting with a chlorophyll-based drug that he claims leads to eternal youth but actually creates green-blooded, mayhem-causing zombies. After our heroes set Lorca's laboratory ablaze, they leave the island believing the madman has been killed in the fire. Wrong. He will be back again in another sequel, BEAST OF BLOOD (1969). The only film in this trilogy thus far available on home video, THE MAD DOCTOR OF BLOOD ISLAND is about what you'd expect from something with codirector Eddie Romero's name on it, complete with hopelessly insipid dialog and a variety of zoom shots, presumably employed for dramatic effect. Pettyjohn, who later appeared in adult films under the name Heaven St. John, is perhaps best remembered for her role as an ax-wielding alien in the "Star Trek" episode "The Gamesters of Triskelion."

p, Eddie Romero; d, Eddie Romero, Geraldo de Leon; w, Reuben Candy; ph, Justo Paulino; m, Tito Arevalo.

(PR:O   MPAA:M)

## MAD MONSTER, THE**

(1942) 77m PRC bw

Johnny Downs *(Tom Gregory),* George Zucco *(Dr. Lorenzo Cameron),* Anne Nagel *(Lenora),* Sarah Padden *(Grandmother),* Glenn Strange *(Petro),* Gordon DeMain *(Prof. Fitzgerald),* Mae Busch *(Susan),* Reginald Barlow *(Prof. Warwick),* Robert Strange *(Prof. Blaine),* Henry Hall *(Country Doctor),* Edward Cassidy *(Father),* Eddie Holden *(Harper),* John Elliott *(Prof. Hatfield),* Charles Whitaker *(Policeman),* Gil Patric *(Lieutenant Detective).*

In the tradition of horror/WW II propaganda movies like KING OF THE ZOMBIES (1941) and REVENGE OF THE ZOMBIES (1943), THE MAD MONSTER centers on mad-but-patriotic scientist Dr. Lorenzo Cameron's (George Zucco) attempt to develop a serum that will turn the average man into an invincible soldier. Dr. Cameron transforms his guinea pig, Petro (Glenn Strange), a large, dim-witted farmboy, into a monster by injecting him with the blood of a wolf. After sprouting plenty of excess hair and pair of fangs, Petro runs amok through the countryside, sinking his new canines into anything that moves until a clever reporter (Johnny Downs)—who has fallen for Cameron's daughter (Anne Nagel)—puts two and two together and traps the beast. Shot in a mere five days to capitalize on the success of THE WOLF MAN (1941), this is a typical poverty-row effort—meaning that the production values are nil and the plot and action are very silly, but that with the right cast it can still be a lot of fun to watch. Luckily, THE MAD MONSTER has a prime cast of B players led by Zucco and Strange, in his horror movie debut. Strange, a stuntman who previously appeared in dozens of B westerns, would go on to play the Frankenstein monster in THE HOUSE OF FRANKENSTEIN (1944); HOUSE OF DRACULA (1945); and ABBOTT AND COSTELLO MEET FRANKENSTEIN (1948).

p, Sigmund Neufeld; d, Sam Newfield; w, Fred Myton; ph, Jack Greenhalgh; ed, Holbrook N. Todd; m, David Chudnow.

(PR:A   MPAA:NR)

## MAD MONSTER PARTY**½

(1967) 94m Videocraft International/AE c

Boris Karloff *(Baron Boris von Frankenstein)*, Phyllis Diller *(Frankenstein's Wife)*, Ethel Ennis, Gale Garnett, Allen Swift.

A monster of a convention is the setting for this animated feature made using the "Animagic" process (a stop-motion photography technique that uses three-dimensional figures). The Worldwide Organization of Monsters has come together to select a new leader to replace the soon-to-be-retired Baron Boris von Frankenstein (voiced by Boris Karloff), and all the biggies are present: the Werewolf, Dracula, the Creature From the Black Lagoon, King Kong, Dr. Jekyll and Mr. Hyde, The Mummy, and parodies of Claude Rains as the Invisible Man, Charles Laughton as the Hunchback of Notre Dame, and Peter Lorre as the Igor-like "Yetch". Phyllis Diller, appropriately, is the voice of Baron Frankenstein's ghoulish wife. Conflict between the major monsters erupts, and there are some surprises for the baron's *normal* nephew, Felix Flanken, who makes the mistake of falling for one of his uncle's mechanical creations. The Animagic technique works fairly well, but nobody is going to mistake this for a Ray Harryhausen film. As with the majority of cheap animation efforts, this was made strictly with a kiddie audience in mind, although animation buffs might find it interesting for awhile.

p, Arthur Rankin, Jr.; d, Jules Bass; w, Len Korobkin, Harvey Kirtzman, Forrest J. Ackerman (based on a story by Rankin); ph, (Animagic, Eastmancolor).

(PR:AA   MPAA:NR)

## MADHOUSE**

(1974, Brit.) 89m Amicus/AIP c

Vincent Price *(Paul Toombes)*, Peter Cushing *(Herbert Flay)*, Robert Quarry *(Oliver Quayle)*, Adrienne Corri *(Faye Flay)*, Natasha Pyne *(Julia)*, Michael Parkinson *(TV Interviewer)*, Linda Hayden *(Elizabeth Peters)*, Barry Dennen *(Blount)*, Ellis Dayle *(Alfred Peters)*, Catherine Willmer *(Louise Peters)*, John Garrie *(Inspector Harper)*, Ian Thompson *(Bradshaw)*, Jenny Wright *(Carol)*, Julie Crosthwaite *(Ellen)*, Peter Halliday *(Psychiatrist)*.

This pairing of AIP's Vincent Price and Hammer's Peter Cushing promises much more that it delivers. While recovering from a nervous breakdown, Paul Toombes (Price), a washed-up horror film actor, agrees to do a TV series based on his most famous character, "Dr. Death." The shows are to be scripted by his old friend, former actor Herbert Flay (Cushing), and the producer of the series is Oliver Quayle (Robert Quarry). Soon after Toombes' arrival, cast and crew begin dying after the fashion of characters in the actor's old movies. With its behind-the-scenes setting and focus on an aging star whose glory days are behind him, this could have been a wonderful elegy to the twilight of Price's long career; unfortunately, the script and direction simply aren't up to the task and the film becomes an inferior spin-off of the "Dr. Phibes" series. Not even the interaction between Price and Cushing—two very different actors—manages to generate much interest, leaving the clips from Price's Corman-AIP films the best part of the movie. Filmed in 1972, MADHOUSE went unreleased until 1974.

p, Max J. Rosenberg, Milton Subotsky; d, Jim Clark; w, Greg Morrison, Ken Levison (based on the novel *Devilday* by Angus Hall); ph, Ray Parslow (Eastmancolor); ed, Clive Smith; m, Douglas Gamley.

(PR:C   MPAA:PG)

## MADMAN zero

(1982) 88m The Legend Lives/Farley c

Alexis Dubin *(Betsy)*, Tony Fish *(T.P.)*, Harriet Bass *(Stacey)*, Seth Jones *(Dave)*, Jan Claire *(Ellie)*, Alex Murphy *(Bill)*, Jimmy Steele *(Richie)*, Paul Ehlers *(Madman Marz)*, Carl Fredericks *(Max)*, Michael Sullivan *(Cook)*, Gaylen Ross.

Predictable, boring, and bloody, this film in the FRIDAY THE 13TH tradition concerns a crazed killer who terrorizes a secluded, long-closed summer camp that is reopened as a training facility for counselors—young, nubile counselors. By the campfire one night, the story of a crazed farmer, Madman Marz, is told:   It seems Marz went over the edge one day, slaughtered his family, and was strung up by a lynch mob, though he managed to escape, scurrying off into the woods, never to be seen again. It is said, however, that one need only call out "Madman Marz" and he will emerge from his hiding place seeking revenge. Of course, one smart-mouthed kid yells, "Madman Marz," and the bloody killings soon begin anew. Filmed on Long Island, this wholly derivative splatter movie does boast some fairly slick photography, but it isn't likely to hold anyone's attention for long.

p, Gary Sales; d, Joe Giannone; w, Joe Giannone; ph, James Momel (Cineffects Color); ed, Dan Lowenthal; m, Gary Sales, Stephen Horelick.

**(PR:O MPAA:R)**

**MAGIC\*\*\***

(1978) 106m FOX c

Anthony Hopkins *(Corky)*, Ann-Margret *(Peggy Ann Snow)*, Burgess Meredith *(Ben Greene)*, Ed Lauter *(Duke)*, E. J. Andre *(Merlin)*, Jerry Houser *(Cab Driver)*, David Ogden Stiers *(George Hudson Todson)*, Lillian Randolph *(Sadie)*, Joe Lowry *(Club M.C.)*, Beverly Sanders *(Laughing Lady)*, I.W. Klein *(Maitre d')*, Stephen Hart *(Captain)*, Patrick McCullough *(Doorman)*, Bob Hackman *(Father)*, Mary Munday *(Mother)*, Scott Garrett *(Corky's Brother)*, Brad Beesley *(Young Corky)*, Michael Harte *(Minister)*.

Terribly overrated at the time of its release, this box-office hit and a recipient of several Oscar nominations is really nothing more than an expansion of the Michael Redgrave episode of DEAD OF NIGHT (1945), and not a particularly well-done one at that. At the center of its predictable plot is Corky (Anthony Hopkins), a ventriloquist who believes his ill-tempered, foul-mouthed dummy, "Fats," is taking over both the act *and* his personality. The ventriloquist's schizophrenia and paranoia become so acute that he murders his manager (Burgess Meredith) but believes Fats to be the killer. After hiding the body, Corky flees to the Catskills, where he visits a former lover, Peggy Ann (Ann-Margret). Problems arise, however, between Corky, Fats, Peggy Ann, and her husband (Ed Lauter), and another murder results. Designed as a star vehicle for Hopkins, who performed his own ventriloquism, MAGIC has few scary moments and is really a rather maudlin examination of a nervous breakdown. William Goldman's adaptation of his own novel starts off well enough, but quickly gets bogged down in sappy romance and ends disappointingly. Aside from the obligatory shots of the dummy looking sinister, director Richard Attenborough fails to evoke an effectively eerie mood, concentrating instead on the "drama" between Corky and Peggy Ann. Watch DEAD OF NIGHT instead.

p, Joseph E. Levine, Richard P. Levine; d, Richard Attenborough; w, William Goldman (based on his novel); ph, Victor J. Kemper (Panavision, Technicolor); ed, John Bloom; m, Jerry Goldsmith.

**(PR:O MPAA:R)**

**MAN THEY COULD NOT HANG, THE\*\*\***

(1939) 64m COL bw

Boris Karloff *(Dr. Henryk Savaard)*, Lorna Gray *(Janet Saavard)*, Robert Wilcox *(Scoop Foley)*, Roger Pryor *(District Attorney Drake)*, Don Beddoe *(Lt. Shane)*, Ann Doran *(Betty Crawford)*, Joseph de Stephani *(Dr. Stoddard)*, Dick Curtis *(Kearney)*, Byron Foulger *(Lang)*, James Craig

*(Watkins)*, John Tyrrell *(Sutton)*, Charles Trowbridge *(Judge Bowman)*.

Dr. Henryk Savaard (Boris Karloff), a scientist who experiments with bringing the dead back to life through the use of an artificial heart, is hanged for the murder of one of his patients. Before long, his assistant, Lang (Byron Foulger), uses the doctor's own method to revive him, but the once-noble Savaard is now a changed man bent on revenge. Trapping the judge, jury, and witnesses that convicted him in his house, Savaard kills them off one by one. This picture is the first of three similar films Karloff made under the direction of Nick Grinde—the others being THE MAN WITH NINE LIVES and BEFORE I HANG. Although the story seems far-fetched, it is based on the real-life experiments of Dr. Robert Cornish, who, during the 1930s, was reviving dead dogs but was denied his request to do tests on executed prisoners.

p, Wallace MacDonald; d, Nick Grinde; w, Karl Brown (based on a story by Leslie T. White, George W. Sayre); ph, Benjamin Kline; ed, William Lyon.

**(PR:A MPAA:NR)**

**MAN WHO HAUNTED HIMSELF, THE\*\***

(1970, Brit.) 94m Associated British/Levitt-Pickman c

Roger Moore *(Harold Pelham)*, Hildegard Neil *(Eva Pelham)*, Alastair Mackenzie *(Michael)*, Hugh Mackenzie *(James)*, Kevork Malikyan *(Luigi)*, Thorley Walters *(Bellamy)*, Anton Rodgers *(Tony Alexander)*, Olga Georges-Picot *(Julie)*, Freddie Jones *(Dr. Harris)*, John Welsh *(Sir Charles Freeman)*, Edward Chapman *(Barton)*, Laurence Hardy *(Mason)*, Charles Lloyd Pack *(Jameson)*, Gerald Sim *(Morrison)*, Ruth Trouncer *(Pelham's Secretary)*, Aubrey Richards *(Research Scientist)*, Anthony Nicholls *(Sir Arthur Richardson)*, John Carson *(Ashton)*, John Dawson *(Barber)*, Terence Sewards *(Jeweler's Assistant)*.

Respected businessman Harold Pelham (Roger Moore) suffers a terrible car accident and momentarily "dies" on the operating table. Somehow, a double—his repressed alter ego—is unleashed and raises hell without the original Pelham's knowledge. Soon Pelham discovers that his double is having an affair with a woman he met only once, and that his business career seems to have a mind of its own. Driven to distraction by this unbridled intruder, Pelham moves to destroy his evil twin. Director Basil Dearden has a difficult time making this fairly absurd material work, preferring to concentrate on the embarrassment Pelham suffers at the hands of his double, rather than exploring the darker psychological implications of the situation. As a result, the film is downright boring, with Moore turning in his standard stoic performance as both the conservative businessman and his more gregarious doppelganger. The effects when both Pelhams appear in the same shot are dreadful. Ironically, this was Dearden's final film before dying in a car accident the following year.

p, Michael Relph; d, Basil Dearden; w, Michael Relph, Basil Dearden (based on *The Case of Mr. Pelham* by

Anthony Armstrong); ph, Tony Spratling (Technicolor); ed, Teddy Darvas; m, Michael J. Lewis.

(PR:A    MPAA:GP)

## MAN WITH TWO BRAINS, THE**

(1983) 93m Aspen/WB c

Steve Martin *(Dr. Michael Hfuhruhurr)*, Kathleen Turner *(Dolores Benedict)*, David Warner *(Dr. Necessiter)*, Paul Benedict *(Butler)*, Richard Brestoff *(Dr. Pasteur)*, James Cromwell *(Realtor)*, George Furth *(Timon)*, Peter Hobbs *(Dr. Brandon)*, Earl Boen *(Dr. Conrad)*, Bernie Hern *(Gun Seller)*, Frank McCarthy *(Olsen)*, William Traylor *(Inspector)*, Randi Brooks *(Fran)*, Don McLeod *(Gorilla)*, Merv Griffin *(Elevator Killer)*, Bernard Behrens *(Gladstone)*, Russell Orozco *(Juan)*, Natividad Vacio *(Ramon)*, David Byrd *(Desk Clerk)*, Adrian Ricard, Sparky Marcus, Perla Walter, Mya Akerling, Peter Elbling, Breck Costin, Tom Spratley, Estelle Reiner.

Following his parody of *film noir*, DEAD MEN DON'T WEAR PLAID (1982), comedian Steve Martin took on the mad-scientist films of the 1940s with mixed results. Dr. Michael Hfuhruhurr (Martin), a famed neurosurgeon, travels to Vienna with his beautiful-but-frigid wife, Dolores (Kathleen Turner), in an attempt to revive their romance. There he meets fellow scientist Dr. Alfred Necessiter (David Warner), who has devised a method to keep disembodied brains alive. Hfuhruhurr communicates telepathically with the brain of a very sweet woman who was brutally murdered and falls hopelessly in love with her. Desperate to consummate his love, Hfuhruhurr decides to plant his beloved's brain in Dolores' body, thus creating the perfect woman. The premise of this comedy sounds good on paper, but is lost somewhere in its transition to the screen. Martin and director Carl Reiner are never really in control of their wacky style of humor, and the film is both terribly diffuse and works at cross purposes, with no comedic strain properly pursued. While THE MAN WITH TWO BRAINS certainly has its moments, overall it's a disappointment. The brain's voice is provided by Oscar winner Sissy Spacek.

p, David V. Picker, William E. McEuen; d, Carl Reiner; w, Carl Reiner, Steve Martin, George Gipe; ph, Michael Chapman (Technicolor); ed, Bud Molin; m, Joel Goldsmith.

(PR:O    MPAA:R)

## MAN WITH TWO HEADS, THE zero

(1972) 80m Mishkin c

Denis De Marne *(Dr. William Jekyll/Mr. Blood)*, Julia Stratton *(April Conners)*, Gay Feld *(Mary Ann Marsden)*, Jacqueline Lawrence *(Carla)*, Berwick Kaler *(Smithers)*, Bryan Southcombe *(Oliver Marsden)*, Jennifer Summerfield *(Vicky)*.

Staten Island's favorite moviemaker, Andy Milligan, journeyed all the way to England to shoot this typically lame ultra-low-budget adaptation of *The Strange Case of Dr. Jekyll and Mr. Hyde*—easily one of the worst renditions of the Stevenson classic. While experimenting on the gray matter of a mass murderer, the good Dr. Jekyll (Denis De Marne) manages to locate and isolate the portion of the brain that causes evil impulses, creating a special solution with the material. Although he initially tries the serum out on little animals, it isn't long before Jekyll experiments with the stuff himself. As the nasty "Mr. Blood," he roams the streets, killing his laboratory assistant and a saloon singer before turning on his fiancee. Once again Milligan's ambition exceeds his talent as he attempts to make a period piece set in 1835 with a budget that wouldn't cover catering costs for one meal on a Hollywood studio production.

p, William Mishkin; d, Andy Milligan; w, Andy Milligan (based on the novel  The Strange Case of Dr. Jekyll and Mr. Hyde  by Robert Louis Stevenson); ph, Andy Milligan.

(PR:C    MPAA:PG)

## MANHATTAN BABY*

(1986, It.) 89m Fulvia c

Christopher Connelly *(Prof. George Hacker)*, Martha Taylor, Birgitta Boccoli, Giovanni Frezza, Cinzia De Ponti, Laurence Welles, Andrea Bosic, Carlo De Mejo, Vincenzo Bellanich, Mario Moretti, Lucio Fulci, Antonio Pulci.

Italian goremaster Lucio Fulci (ZOMBIE) disappointed his hardcore fans with this surprisingly conventional and relatively goreless supernatural tale. Christopher Connelly stars as Prof. George Hacker, a hapless archaeologist who loses his eyesight when he excavates the *wrong* amulet while on a dig in Egypt, though doctors promise him his condition is temporary. In the meantime, a strange woman gives Hacker's daughter a similar charm that invests her with incredible telekinetic abilities. Time to call in the parapsychologists, whose attempts to investigate her newfound powers are frustrated when another girl takes her place at the last minute. A few magic incantations and cheesy special effects later, the girl is history. Back in Egypt the whole thing starts over when another young lady is presented with a similar amulet. Lacking logic, clarity, or anything that remotely resembles intelligence, MANHATTAN BABY is a sad excuse for a horror movie. Fulci's fans will be particularly disappointed to discover that there isn't one disembowelment or maggot-covered face in the entire film. Originally shot in 1982, the film bounced from distributor to distributor before finding its way onto videocassette some four years later.

p, Fabrizio De Angelis; d, Lucio Fulci; w, Elisa Briganti, Dardano Sacchetti; ph, Guglielmo Mancori (Telecolor); ed, Vincenzo Tomassi; m, Fabio Frizzi.

(PR:O    MPAA:NR)

## MANIAC**

(1934) 67m Roadshow Attractions/Hollywood Producers & Distributors bw

Bill Woods *(Don Maxwell)*, Horace Carpenter *(Dr. Meirschultz)*, Ted Edwards *(Buckley)*, Phyllis Diller *(Mrs. Buckley)*, Thea Ramsey *(Alice Maxwell)*, Jennie Dark *(Maizie)*, Marvel Andre *(Marvel)*, Celia McGann *(Jo)*, J.P. Wade *(Mike the Morgue Attendant)*, Marion Blackton *(Neighbor)*.

Hailed today as the forbearer of modern exploitation horror, MANIAC presents its sordid tale of madness and murder as an educational essay on mental illness. Strewn throughout the film are title cards explaining the various dementia dramatized in the narrative. Shot in and around director Dwain Esper's house on Willoughby Avenue in Hollywood, MANIAC is the preposterous and frequently confusing saga of Don Maxwoll (Bill Woods), a washed-up vaudeville impersonator who falls in with Dr. Meirschultz (Horace Carpenter), a mad scientist experimenting with bringing the dead back to life. During an argument, Maxwell accidentally kills the doctor and, fearing a prison sentence, assumes the dead man's identity, using his skills as a makeup man and impersonator. As the plot thickens, Maxwell goes mad and commits several crimes in an attempt to cover up his murder of Meirschultz. In the end, the police uncover the evil deed and Maxwell is imprisoned. A truly wretched production on all levels, MANIAC remains today a captivating example of early exploitation. Although Esper's films weren't booked in quality theaters, his work traveled the roadshow circuit and was screened in burlesque houses and tents. During the scant 52 minutes of MANIAC, Esper treats viewers to attempted body snatching, uncontrollable lust, topless female nudity, graphic rape, the gouging of a cat's eye and its subsequent consumption by Maxwell ("It is not unlike an oyster," he cackles as he swallows the bloody eyeball), and a fight between two women who tear at each other's clothes while wielding hypodermic needles. Appearing throughout this opus are laughable "scientific" explanations of the psychoses supposedly experienced by Maxwell. In addition to its exhilarated indulgence in Breen Code taboos, the most amusing aspect of MANIAC is its beautifully inept realization. Esper's dialog is hilariously pretentious and his actors are total hams. Horace Carpenter, who plays Dr. Meirschultz, was a member of Cecil B. DeMille's respected stock company during the silent era. Having fallen on hard times, the former star appeared in cheap exploitation productions to pay the bills, starting a trend that actors like Bela Lugosi and John Carradine would later turn into an art form. Esper also makes allusions to Edgar Allan Poe throughout MANIAC and superimposes film clips from Fritz Lang's SIEGFRIED (1924) and Benjamin Christensen's WITCHCRAFT THROUGH THE AGES (1922) over Maxwell's face to symbolize madness. Despite the crude production, replete with blown takes that were printed and used, bad camera work, and dozens of jump cuts, there is an oddly compelling quality to MANIAC that makes it surprisingly watchable. Esper was a genuine *auteur* who could translate his own warped personal vision into truly imaginative and frequently inventive little movies. MANIAC has its own twisted logic and is, in its own way, a perfectly acceptable cinematic portrayal of madness. It remains the masterpiece of Esper's known work.

p, Dwain Esper; d, Dwain Esper; w, Hildegarde Stadie; ph, William Thompson; ed, William Austin.

(PR:C  MPAA:NR)

**MANIAC\*\***

(1963, Brit.) 87m Hammer/COL bw

Kerwin Mathews *(Geoff Farrell)*, Nadia Gray *(Eve Beynat)*, Donald Houston *(Georges Beynat)*, Liliane Brousse *(Annette Beynat)*, George Pastell *(Inspector Etienne)*, Arnold Diamond *(Janiello)*, Norman Bird *(Salon)*, Justine Lord *(Grace)*, Jerold Wells *(Giles)*, Leon Peers *(Blanchard)*.

Geoff Farrell (Kerwin Mathews), a traveling American artist, is seduced by Eve (Nadia Gray), who persuades him to help free her husband from the insane asylum where he has been confined since he burned to death the man who raped his daughter (Liliane Brousse). With the help of her husband's male nurse, they bring off the escape; however, Geoff discovers a dead body in the getaway car and assumes that the victim is the nurse and that the murderer is Eve's still-insane husband. In short order, Geoff is bound and gagged, but when he escapes, he's as surprised to discover things aren't as they seem. Producer-writer Jimmy Sangster's script is terribly convoluted and filled with so many obvious red-herrings that the viewer will quickly become annoyed with this none-too-thrilling thriller. Michael Carreras' direction is mundane, failing to build on what little real suspense the material offers.

p, Jimmy Sangster; d, Michael Carreras; w, Jimmy Sangster; ph, Wilkie Cooper (Megascope); ed, Tom Simpson; m, Stanley Black.

(PR:C  MPAA:NR)

**MANIAC zero**

(1980) 87m Magnum/Analysis c

Joe Spinell *(Frank Zito)*, Caroline Munro *(Ann D'Antoni)*, Gail Lawrence *(Rita)*, Kelly Piper *(Nurse)*, Rita Montone *(Hooker)*, Tom Savini *(Disco Boy)*, Hyla Marrow *(Disco Girl)*, James Brewster *(Beach Boy)*, Linda Lee Walter *(Beach Girl)*, Tracie Evans *(Street Hooker)*, Sharon Mitchell *(2nd Nurse)*, Carol Henry *(Deadbeat)*, Nella Bacmeister *(Carmen Zito)*, Louis Jawitz *(Art Director)*, Denise Spagnuolo *(Denise)*, Billy Spagnuolo *(Billy)*, Frank Pesce *(TV Reporter)*, Candice Clements, Diane Spagnuolo *(Park Mothers)*, Kim Hudson *(Lobby Hooker)*, Terry Gagnon *(Woman in Alley)*, Joan Baldwin, Jeni Paz *(Models)*, Janelle Winston *(Waitress)*, Randy Jurgensen, Jimmy Aurichio *(Cops)*.

Without a doubt the most reprehensible splatter film every made, MANIAC is the sleazy embodiment of everything that was wrong with the ultra-violent slasher movies of the early 1980s. Shot on location in New York City, the film stars Joe Spinell as Frank Zito, a deeply disturbed loner who vents his misogynist rage on beautiful young women. He stalks his victims, murders their male companions (one of whom is played by special effects man Tom Savini), and then scalps the women, nailing their hair on mannequins in his apartment. After the murders, Zito cries himself to sleep surrounded by the mannequins he considers his friends. In a rather incongruous subplot, Zito also manages to romance a beautiful young fashion photographer (Caroline Munro). In the end, the mannequins come to life and tear Zito limb from limb. MANIAC was made by a group of former pornographers and looks like it, with hard-core gore substituted for hardcore sex. Mindless, misogynist, and trashy, MANIAC lacks any redeeming value, save for the excellent effects work by Savini—who later disavowed the film—though director William Lustig lingers on the nauseating stuff so long that it becomes unforgivably perverse—even to the most enthusiastic gore fans. The combination of this Grand Guignol and Spinell's warped performance leaves the viewer feeling violated and ashamed. Avoid.

p, Andrew Garroni, William Lustig; d, William Lustig; w, C.A. Rosenberg, Joe Spinell (based on a story by Spinell); ph, Robert Lindsay (TVC Labs Color); ed, Lorenzo Marinelli; m, Jay Chattaway.

(PR:O   MPAA:R)

## MANIAC COP*½

(1988) 85m Shapiro Glickenhaus c

Tom Atkins (Lt. McCrae), Bruce Campbell (Jack Forrest), Laurene Landon (Theresa Mallory), Richard Roundtree (Commissioner Pike), William Smith (Capt. Ripley), Sheree North (Sally Noland), Robert Z'dar (Matt Cordell).

MANIAC COP is something of a disappointment from Larry Cohen, the one-man movie machine who has written, produced, and directed such modern genre classics as the "It's Alive" trilogy, GOD TOLD ME TO, and Q. Serving only as producer and writer here, Cohen turned over the directing chores to Bill Lustig, whose MANIAC (1980) is one of the most repulsive splatter movies ever made. Written with tongue firmly in cheek, the film begins as New York City is terrorized by a homicidal killer in a police uniform whom the press dubs "Maniac Cop." Although the police department officially denies the killer is from their ranks, homicide detective McRae (Tom Atkins) isn't so sure. As the murders continue, it becomes apparent that the killer is getting his information from inside the department and McRae begins digging for clues among his fellow officers. Meanwhile, a young married policeman, Jack Forrest (Bruce Campbell), who is carrying on a clandestine affair with female officer Theresa Mallory (Laurene Landon), is implicated in the killings and forced to prove his innocence. Cohen has made some surprisingly complex and interesting low-budget genre films that are rich in characterization and thematics. MANIAC COP, however, is basically a one-idea concept enlivened ever so slightly by fleeting moments of Cohen's patented sociopolitical subtext and goofy black humor, as his script takes potshots at the news media, police department, city hall politicians, and New Yorkers. Sadly, there is not enough freshness in Lustig's direction to elevate MANIAC COP from the level of the mere competence. Relative newcomer Campbell, whose only other films have been Sam Raimi's EVIL DEAD and EVIL DEAD II, fits right in here, while Atkins, Richard Roundtree (who appeared in Cohen's Q), Sheree North, and William Smith—all veteran genre film actors with familiar faces—lend credibility to the absurd proceedings. Also appearing in brief cameos are Jake "Raging Bull" LaMotta, as a detective, and director Raimi, as a reporter at the parade.

p, Larry Cohen; d, William Lustig; w, Larry Cohen; ph, Vincent J. Rabe (Foto-Kem Color); ed, David Kern; m, Jay Chattaway.

(PR:O   MPAA:R)

## MANITOU, THE**

(1978) 104m Weist-Simon/AE c

Tony Curtis (Harry Erskine), Michael Ansara (Singing Rock), Susan Strasberg (Karen Tandy), Stella Stevens (Amelia Crusoe), Jon Cedar (Dr. Jack Hughes), Ann Sothern (Mrs. Karmann), Burgess Meredith (Dr. Ernest Snow), Paul Mantee (Dr. Robert McEvoy), Jeanette Nolan (Mrs. Winconis), Lurene Tuttle (Mrs. Hertz), Ann Mantee (Floor Nurse), Hugh Corcoran (MacArthur), Tenaya (Singing Rock's Wife), Carole Hemingway (Prostitute), Beverly Kushida (2nd Floor Nurse), Jan Heininger (Wolf), Michael Laren (Michael), Joe Gieb (Misquamacas).

When Karen Tandy (Susan Strasberg) discovers a large tumor growing on her back she undergoes surgery to have it removed, but a strange force compels the doctor who performs the operation to stab himself in the hand with a scalpel. Out of desperation, Karen turns to her former lover, phony spiritualist Harry Erskine (Tony Curtis), who takes her to see Singing Rock (Michael Ansara), a modern-day medicine man. Singing Rock informs Karen that the tumor is actually the fetus of the reincarnation of an evil 400-year-old Indian medicine man who has chosen her to be his host. As the fetus grows larger, Singing Rock and Harry make preparations to combat the coming evil spirit. This is really very silly stuff, and the gooey special effects by Tom Burman make it ever sillier. Director William Girdler—who died in a helicopter crash before this was released—does a respectable job of making it all look rather slick and professional, but the big-budget and all-star cast only add to the overall absurdity.

p, William Girdler; d, William Girdler; w, William Girdler, Jon Cedar, Tom Pope (based on the novel by Graham Masterson); ph, Michel Hugo (Panavision, CFI Color); ed, Bub Asman; m, Lalo Schifrin.

(PR:C   MPAA:PG)

## MANSION OF THE DOOMED zero

(1976) 89m Group I c (AKA: TERROR OF DR. CHANEY, THE)

Richard Basehart (Dr. Leonard Chaney), Gloria Grahame (Nurse Katherine), Trish Stewart (Nancy Chaney), Lance Henriksen (Dr. Dan Bryan), Libbie Chase (Girl), Vic Tayback (Detective), Al Ferrara, Arthur Space.

Dr. Leonard Chaney (Richard Basehart) harbors deep guilt over an auto accident that left his daughter, Nancy (Trish Stewart), blind. Obsessed with restoring her sight, he kidnaps people, removes their eyes, and tries to transplant them to his daughter. None of the operations works, however, and Chaney ends up with a large collection of eyeless folks in his dungeon, who eventually escape and rip out his eyes. Producer Charles Band—future head of the now-defunct Empire Pictures—was 21 at the time he made this terrible remake of Georges Franju's LES YEUX SANS VISAGE, and his subsequent efforts have shown that he hasn't learned from his mistakes.

p, Charles Band; d, Michael Pataki; w, Ray Perilli; ph, Andrew Davis (Deluxe Color); m, Robert O. Ragland.

**(PR:O MPAA:R)**

## MARDI GRAS MASSACRE zero

(1983) 97m Weis c (AKA: CRYPT OF DARK SECRETS)

Curt Dawson, Gwen Arment, Laura Misch, Wayne Mack, Ronald Tanet, Cathryn Lacey, Nancy Dancer.

Filmed in 1978 but not released until 1983, this uncredited reworking of H.G. Lewis' BLOOD FEAST (1963) shifts the action from Florida to New Orleans, substituting Aztec blood rituals for the Egyptian variety. An Aztec priest travels to various festivals throughout the world to find prostitutes to sacrifice to Coatla, Goddess of the Four Directions and Queen of Evil in the Universe. Lacking production funding and inspiration, this incredibly tedious effort insists on repeating its only effect—the removal of a woman's heart—ad nauseam. Believe it or not, *anything* by H.G. Lewis is better than this.

p, Jack Weis; d, Jack Weis; w, Jack Weis; ph, Jack Weis, Don Piel, Jack McGowan; m, Dennis Coffey, Mike Theodore.

**(PR:O MPAA:NR)**

## MARK OF THE DEVIL zero

(1970, Ger./Brit.) 90m c (BRENN, HEXE, BRENN; HEXEN BIS AUFS BLUT GEQUALT; AKA: BURN, WITCH, BURN)

Herbert Lom *(Count Cumberland)*, Udo Kier *(Baron Christian von Meru)*, Olivera Vuco *(Vanessa)*, Reggie Nalder *(Albino)*, Herbert Fux *(Chief Executioner)*, Gaby Fuchs, Michael Maien, Ingeborg Schoener, Doris von Danwitz, Dorothea Carrera, Marlies Peterson, Gunther Clemens, Johannes Buzalski, Adrian Hoven.

An extremely sadistic rip-off of the excellent THE CONQUEROR WORM (1968), MARK OF THE DEVIL was produced by one of the Jesus Franco gang, Adrian Hoven. Set in Austria circa 1700, it stars Herbert Lom as Count Cumberland, a general who ferrets out witches and extracts confessions from them using any means at his disposal. His young protege, Baron Christian von Meru (Udo Kier, ANDY WARHOL'S FRANKENSTEIN and DRACULA), eventually rebels, morally outraged by the count's various torture methods, which include ripping out tongues, burning at the stake, and the use of a rack and thumb screws. A favorite among slobbering misogynists who enjoy seeing naked women tortured, this irredeemably perverse German import became something of a hit in the US when the irrepressible Hallmark Releasing Corporation packaged it with a poster showing a beautiful woman about to get her tongue cut out. Moreover, a "stomach distress bag" was appropriately offered to each customer. An equally repulsive sequel, MARK OF THE DEVIL, PART II, followed in 1972 and is virtually identical to its predecessor.

p, Adrian Hoven; d, Michael Armstrong; w, Sergio Cassner, Percy Parker; ph, Ernst W. Kalinke (Eastmancolor); m, Michael Holm.

**(PR:O MPAA:NR)**

## MARK OF THE VAMPIRE***

(1935) 60m MGM bw

Bela Lugosi *(Count Mora)*, Lionel Barrymore *(Prof. Zelen)*, Lionel Atwill *(Inspector Neumann)*, Elizabeth Allan *(Irena Borotyn)*, Holmes Herbert *(Sir Karell Borotyn)*, Jean Hersholt *(Baron Otto von Zinden)*, Carol Borland *(Luna Mora)*, Donald Meek *(Dr. Doskil)*, Ivan Simpson *(Jan)*, Egon Brecher *(Coroner)*, Henry Wadsworth *(Count Feodor Vincenty)*, Eily Malyon *(Sick Woman)*, Christian Rub *(Deaf Man)*, Torben Meyer *(Card Player)*, Zeffie Tilbury *(Grandmother)*, Rosemary Glosz *(Innkeeper's Wife)*, Claire Vedara *(English Woman)*, Guy Bellis *(English Man)*, Baron Hesse *(Bus Driver)*, James Bradbury, Jr., Leila Bennett, Franklin Ardell.

After having dropped out of the genre following FREAKS in 1932, Tod Browning made his comeback with this pseudo-vampire opus—a virtual scene-for-scene remake of his own silent film LONDON AFTER MIDNIGHT (little seen since 1927 and feared lost). MGM gave Browning a class production and provided him with an exceptional cast. The striking Carol Borland, a 21-year-old protege of Bela Lugosi who worked with him in the stage version "Dracula," was given her big break and managed to create one of the most recognizable characters in horror movies on the basis of one film. Set in Czechoslovakia, the action takes place in a spooky, cobweb-filled castle recently occupied by Sir Karell Borotyn (Holmes Herbert) and his daughter, Irena (Elizabeth Allan). Rumor has it that the previous owner, Count Mora (Lugosi), murdered his daughter, Luna (Borland), then shot himself, and that their undead spirits now haunt the castle, determined to kill any new residents. When the dead body of Sir Karell is found drained of all blood, with two puncture holes in the neck, Inspector Neumann (Lionel Atwill), Dr. Doskil (Donald Meek), and Baron Otto von Zinden (Jean Hersholt) vow to solve the crime. Though the film conveys an appropriately eerie mood through its fabulous set design by Cedric Gibbons and superior cinematography by James Wong Howe, MARK OF THE VAMPIRE is disappointing due to its "twist" ending. Given that all the spooky hocus-pocus of the plot is just an elaborate ruse by police to catch a killer (and that the vampires aren't really vampires), the illogic of the action becomes annoyingly manipulative. (Did the police persuade the townsfolk to act like they believe in vampires?) Browning shot the film as straight horror without informing his players how the film was to end, but when the twist ending was revealed, the cast urged him to reject it and stay within the horror framework. When he refused, Lugosi and Borland offered an alternative which left open the possibility that their characters were actually vampires pretending to be actors. Browning refused to give in and the hokey ending remained. Lugosi, Borland, and most horror fans took this as a slap in the face, as if Browning were saying they were silly for allowing themselves to believe in such nonsense. Not only does the ending turn the vampires into fakes, but the script leaves Lugosi speechless until the final scene when he reveals that he's an actor.

p, Edward J. Mannix; d, Tod Browning; w, Guy Endore, Bernard Schubert; ph, James Wong Howe; ed, Ben Lewis.

**(PR:C  MPAA:G)**

## MARTIN*****

(1978) 95m Laurel Group/Libra c

John Amplas *(Martin)*, Lincoln Maazel *(Tata Cuda)*, Christine Forrest *(Christina)*, Elayne Nadeau *(Mrs. Santini)*, Tom Savini *(Arthur)*, Sarah Venable *(Housewife Victim)*, Fran Middleton *(Train Victim)*, Al Levitsky *(Lewis)*, George A. Romero *(Father Howard)*, James Roy *(Deacon)*, J. Clifford Forrest, Jr. *(Father Zulemas)*, Robert Ogden *(Businessman)*, Donaldo Soviero *(Flashback Priest)*, Donna Siegal *(Woman)*, Richard Rubinstein *(Housewife Victim's Husband)*, Albert J. Schmaus, Lillian Schmaus, Frances Mazzoni *(Family)*, Vince Survinski *(Train Porter)*, Tony Buba, Pasquale Buba, Clayton McKinnon *(Drug Dealers)*, Regis Survinski, Tony Pantanello *(Hobos)*.

Always a contender for consideration as George Romero's greatest work, this superb film—one of his most controlled—is an insightful and relevant reworking of the vampire myth set in a dying modern American steel town. Martin (John Amplas) is a shy, alienated 17-year-old who thinks he may be a vampire, which seems to be confirmed by the opening scene. Aboard a Pittsburgh-bound train, Martin waylays a female passenger, injects her with sodium pentothal, and while she is in a stupor, rapes her. Lacking fangs, he then cuts her wrist with a razor blade and drinks her blood (the gruesomely realistic special makeup effects are by Tom Savini, working on his first film for Romero). When Martin arrives in Pittsburgh, he is confronted with his elderly Old World cousin, Tata Cuda (Lincoln Maazel), a religious zealot who is convinced that the boy is an 84-year-old vampire, the product of a family curse. Calling Martin "Nosferatu," Tata Cuda is determined to both save the boy's soul and destroy him. Writer-director Romero leaves Martin's real identity intriguingly up in the air. At times, the boy is convinced that he is the monster Tata Cuda believes him to be, seeing himself in Universal horror movie-type flashbacks as a Count Dracula-ish vampire eluding angry villagers. But mostly, Martin is shown to be a troubled teenager with lethal psychosexual problems that compel him to make contact with sexually desirable women through violent means. All of this is presented brilliantly by Romero, who delivers a gut-wrenching horror film that is both meaningful and moving. Combining vampire legend and Old World beliefs with the harsh realities of life in a depressed American steel town, Romero creates a deeply resonant, multifaceted film that works both as insightful social commentary and as a fascinating rumination on horror film conventions. Bleak, at times funny, always fascinating, and ultimately disturbing, MARTIN

deserves to be considered one of the best films in the genre.

p, Richard P. Rubinstein; d, George A. Romero; w, George A. Romero; ph, Michael Gornick; ed, George A. Romero; m, Donald Rubinstein.

**(PR:O  MPAA:R)**

## MARY, MARY, BLOODY MARY*

(1975, US/Mex.) 101m Translor-Proa c

Cristina Ferrare *(Mary)*, David Young *(Ben Ryder)*, Helena Rojo *(Greta)*, John Carradine *(Mary's Father)*, Arthur Hansel *(U.S. Agent)*, Enrique Lucero *(Mexican Police Lieutenant)*, Susan Kamini *(Hitchhiker)*.

Cover-girl Cristina Ferrare (better known as the ex-wife of millionaire John DeLorean) plays Mary, a bisexual vampiress who is an artist by day and a neck-stabbing blood drinker by night. Among her victims are an embassy official and both male and female lovers. In time her long-lost father (John Carradine), also a vampire, arrives on the scene to kill his daughter, thinking that he's doing her a favor by ending her miserable existence. Although director Juan Lopez Moctezuma has a flair for visuals and editing, this movie is overwhelmingly boring and contains a stunningly bad performance from Ferrare. Carradine had enough sense to bail out of this picture before production was finished and was replaced by a double who is as about as convincing as the chiropractor who stood in for Bela Lugosi in PLAN NINE FROM OUTER SPACE (1959).

p, Robert Yamin, Henri Bollinger; d, Juan Lopez Moctezuma; w, Malcolm Marmorstein (based on a story by Don Rico, Don Henderson); ph, Miguel Garzon; ed, Federico Landeras; m, Tom Bahler.

**(PR:O  MPAA:R)**

## MASQUE OF THE RED DEATH, THE****

(1964, US/Brit.) 86m Alta Vista-Anglo Amalgamated/AIP c

Vincent Price *(Prince Prospero)*, Hazel Court *(Juliana)*, Jane Asher *(Francesca)*, David Weston *(Gino)*, Patrick Magee *(Alfredo)*, Nigel Green *(Ludovico)*, Skip Martin *(Hop Toad)*, John Westbrook *(Man in Red)*, Gaye Brown *(Senora Escobar)*, Julian Burton *(Senor Veronese)*, Doreen Dawn *(Anna-Marie)*, Paul Whitsun-Jones *(Scarlatti)*, Jean Lodge *(His Wife)*, Verina Greenlaw *(Esmeralda)*, Brian Hewlett *(Lampredi)*, Harvey Hall *(Clistor)*, Robert Brown *(Guard)*, David Davies, Sarah Brackett.

One of the best of the Roger Corman Edgar Allan Poe series, this is a wondrous symphony of the macabre loosely based on two Poe stories, and contains a magnificent performance from Vincent Price. Price is at his evil quintessence, playing Prince Prospero, a 12th-century Italian despot who lives for his one true love, Satan. An intellectual sadist, Prospero uses peasants for his experiments in perversity. After jailing two locals, Ludovico (Nigel Green) and Gino (David Weston) for defying his harsh tax laws, Prospero meets the beautiful Francesca (Jane Asher), daughter of Ludovico and the fiancee of Gino, who comes to him to plead for mercy. Prospero tells her that only one will be spared and toys with her emotions for his private amusement, determined to indoctrinate her into his evil circle. When Prospero learns that the plague, or Red Death, is sweeping the village, he orders all houses burned and locks himself and his followers in his castle, where they continue their decadent parties. A figure dressed in red robes, however, arrives at the castle and bides his time outdoors, playing solitaire in the graveyard. Eventually the red-robed man—the Red Death—enters the ballroom during the most opulent of masquerade balls, welcomed by Prospero as an emissary of the Devil. But the Red Death answers to no one and soon the horrors of the plague are ravaging Prospero's guests. Weird and extremely downbeat, this undoubtedly is the most serious film ever to come from Corman, echoing as it does the work of Ingmar Bergman and Luis Bunuel—two directors Corman greatly admires. The script by Charles Beaumont and R. Wright Campbell is among the most intelligent and literate of the Poe series. With photography by future director Nicolas Roeg (DON'T LOOK NOW), the film is also one of Corman's best-looking, with its incredible sets and costumes and the brilliant use of color (reds, yellows, purples) inspired by Poe's descriptions. Best of all, however, is Price's inspired performance as the wicked, jaded, and decadent Prospero. While Corman may overreach his talent and veer dangerously close to pretention, his crisp staging and confident visual style keep the film from collapsing under its own weight.

p, Roger Corman; d, Roger Corman; w, Charles Beaumont, R. Wright Campbell (based on "The Masque of the Red Death" and "Hop-Frog, or the Eight Chained Orang-outangs" by Edgar Allan Poe); ph, Nicolas Roeg (Panavision/Pathecolor); ed, Ann Chegwidden; m, David Lee.

**(PR:C  MPAA:NR)**

## MASSACRE AT CENTRAL HIGH***½

(1976) 85m Evan/Brian-New Line c

Derrel Maury (David), Andrew Stevens (Mark), Robert Carradine (Spoony), Kimberly Beck (Teresa), Roy Underwood (Bruce), Steve Bond (Craig), Damon Douglas (Paul), Rainbeaux Smith (Mary), Lani O'Grady (Jane), Steve Sikes (Rodney), Dennis Court (Arthur), Jeffrey Winner (Oscar), Thomas Logan (Harvey).

Although only marginally a horror film, this is easily the most interesting and intelligent entry in the "dead teenager" sweepstakes—a film that actually dares to place its murders in a microcosmic political climate, the American high school. David (Derrel Maury) is the new kid in school who finds it to be run by three preppie brutes, Bruce (Roy Underwood), Craig (Steve Bond), and Paul (Damon Douglas), who terrorize the student body. When David foils a rape attempted by the brutish trio, they retaliate by crushing one of his legs. Upon his recovery, David decides the time has come to dethrone the rulers of Central High and he quietly sets about murdering the three, being careful to

make the deaths look like accidents. His mission succeeds, but David soon finds himself in the position he has loathed, as the weaklings he tried to defend attempt to gather power, court favors from their new hero, and take over the school. Fights break out and David, disgusted that the oppressed have turned into oppressors, once again begins to eliminate troublesome students, eventually opting to blow up the entire school. Shot in only three weeks on a minimal budget, MASSACRE AT CENTRAL HIGH is a fascinating little movie that delivers its expected exploitation thrills while presenting a political allegory, albeit a somewhat confused one. We are shown a world run entirely by adolescents, with hardly any adults present. Director Renee Daalder understood the average American teenager's view of high school: it is a highly structured caste system where differences are not tolerated. Adults, though present, are of little consequence. It is one's peers who ultimately decide what goes on, and woe to the fool who attempts to change this rigid hierarchy. Go into any high school in America and you'll find characters not unlike those in MASSACRE AT CENTRAL HIGH. Unfortunately, the average exploitation viewer didn't understand the film and it died an unfair box-office death.

p, Harold Sobel (Bill Lange, uncredited); d, Renee Daalder; w, Renee Daalder; ph, Burt Van Munster; ed, Harry Keramidas; m, Tommy Leonetti.

**(PR:O  MPAA:R)**

## MAUSOLEUM zero

(1983) 96m Western International/Motion Picture Marketing c

Marjoe Gortner (Oliver), Bobbi Bresee (Susan), Norman Burton (Dr. Andrews), Maurice Sherbanee (Ben), Laura Hippe (Aunt Cora), LaWanda Page (Elsie), Sheri Mann (Dr. Logan), Julie Christy Murray (Susan at Age 10), William Vail (Final Demon).

Pretty and sweet young housewife Susan (Bobbie Bresee) just happens to be the eldest daughter in a bloodline afflicted with an ancient curse that causes her to be possessed by a demon from hell. This gives Susan the urge to take on a series of lovers and then kill them in a variety of gory ways, including levitation, fire, and simply splitting their heads open via telekinesis. Her dumb husband, Oliver (Marjoe Gortner), eventually sits up and takes notice long enough to be slaughtered. The special effects by John Buechler are the only reason to sit through this, the highlight being the demon's breasts, which sport little, drooling demon heads with sharp teeth. Beautiful actress Bresee spends almost as much time with her clothes off as she does with them on.

p, Robert Barich, Robert Madero; d, Michael Dugan; w, Robert Barich, Robert Madero (based on the screenplay and story by Katherine Rosenwink); ph, Robert Barich; ed, Richard C. Bock; m, Jaime Mendoza-Nava.

**(PR:O  MPAA:R)**

## MAXIMUM OVERDRIVE zero

(1986) 97m DD c

Emilio Estevez *(Bill Robinson)*, Pat Hingle *(Hendershot)*, Laura Harrington *(Brett)*, Yeardley Smith *(Connie)*, John Short *(Curt)*, Ellen McElduff *(Wanda June)*, J.C. Quinn *(Duncan)*, Christopher Murney *(Camp Loman)*, Holter Graham *(Deke)*, Frankie Faison *(Handy)*, Pat Miller *(Joe)*, Jack Canon *(Max)*, Barry Bell *(Steve)*, John Brasington *(Frank)*, J. Don Ferguson *(Andy)*, Leon Rippy *(Brad)*, Bob Gooden *(Barry)*, R. Pickett Bugg *(Rolf)*, Giancarlo Esposito *(Videoplayer)*, Ned Austin *(Bridgemaster)*, Richard Chapman, Jr. *(Helper)*, Bob Gunter *(Coach)*, Bill Huggins *(Umpire)*.

Possibly no contemporary author has ever been as abused by the movies as Stephen King has, though this time he has no one to blame but himself for what may be the worst King adaptation yet. The plot hinges on a comet passing near the Earth and mysteriously turning some (but not all) machines into mad killers. At a Little League game a soda machine begins spitting out cans at high velocity, killing most of the players. One youngster escapes the mayhem and rides through the streets observing myriad corpses and lawnmowers, remote-control airplanes, and other appliances dripping with fake-looking blood. Meanwhile, at the Dixie Boy truck stop, several semis have besieged the patrons and staff, including peckerwood manager Hendershot (Pat Hingle), former college boy and prison parolee Bill Robinson (Emilio Estevez), tough-but-sweet hitchhiker Brett (Laura Harrington), ditzy redneck newlyweds Curt and Wanda June (John Short and Ellen McElduff), and about a dozen others whose only plot function is to act scared then become victims. At first the trucks are content to simply run down anyone who shows his face outside the restaurant, but later they muster up enough courage to attack the Dixie Boy. Without doubt one of the dumbest movies of 1986, MAXIMUM OVERDRIVE doesn't work on any level. As a comedy it's obvious and asinine, as a horror film it's simply not scary, and as an action film it's a bore. The inconsistencies of internal logic are too messy to detail, but one of the most annoying is Hingle's refusal to use more than two of the scores of anti-tank missiles he has in his basement. Does he think some bigger crisis is coming along and he doesn't want to waste them? Estevez, on the other hand, seems dead serious throughout, and therefore the biggest idiot of all as he tries to synthesize some rational explanation for events.

p, Martha Schumacher; d, Stephen King; w, Stephen King; ph, Armando Nannuzzi (Technicolor); ed, Evan Lottman; m, AC/DC, Richard Wagner.

**(PR:O    MPAA:R)**

## MEAT CLEAVER MASSACRE zero

(1977) 82m Group I c (AKA: HOLLYWOOD MEAT CLEAVER MASSACRE, THE)

Larry Justin, Bob Mead, Bob Clark, Jim Habif, Sandra Crane, Evelyn Ellis, Jonathan Grant, Christopher Lee *(Narrator)*.

The title tells it all in this low-budget splatter film. When a professor of the occult is attacked by hoodlums who murder his family and leave him paralyzed, he summons up a demon to mete out his revenge. Sort of a cross between DEATH WISH (1974) and THE EXORCIST (1973), this is an ultra-cheap production, the makers of which somehow persuaded Christopher Lee to sign on as the narrator.

p, Steven L. Singer; d, Evan Lee.

**(PR:O    MPAA:R)**

## MICROWAVE MASSACRE*

(1983) 76m Reel Life c

Jackie Vernon *(Donald)*, Loren Schein *(Roosevelt)*, Al Troupe *(Philip)*, Claire Ginsberg *(May)*, Lou Ann Webber *(Dee Dee Dee)*, Anna Marlowe *(Chick)*, Sarah Alt *(Evelyn)*, Cindy Grant *(Susie)*, Karen Marshall *(Neighbor)*, Marla Simon *(Knothole Girl)*, Phil de Carlo *(Sam)*.

This bottom-of-the-barrel production is an incompetent and grotesque black comedy about a construction worker, Donald (Jackie Vernon), who is so fed up with his nagging wife (Claire Ginsberg) that he murders her and cuts up the body parts, wrapping them in tin foil and storing them in the freezer. One night, Donald inadvertently cooks a piece of his wife in the microwave and eats it. Finding the taste pleasing to his palate, Donald brings home more women, kills them when he's having sex with them, then pops them into the microwave. The film attempts to capture the LITTLE SHOP OF HORRORS-type of black comedy, but is so ineptly made—it looks like it was shot in the director's home—that most of the laughs are unintentional. The humor is forced and cheap and everyone in the cast mugs it up in front of the camera. Shot back in 1979, the film never got a theatrical release and was one of the first titles to go directly to home video.

p, Thomas Singer, Craig Muckler; d, Wayne Berwick; w, Thomas Singer (based on a story by Muckler); ph, Karen Grossman; ed, Steven Nielson; m, Leif Horvath.

**(PR:O    MPAA:NR)**

## MIDNIGHT**

(1983) 91m Congregation/Independent-International c

Lawrence Tierney *(Bert Johnson)*, Melanie Verlin *(Nancy Johnson)*, John Hall *(Tom)*, Charles Jackson *(Hank)*, Doris Hackney *(Harriet Johnson)*, John Amplas *(Abraham)*, Robin Walsh *(Cynthia)*, David Marchick *(Cyrus)*, Greg Besnak *(Luke)*.

Nancy (Melanie Verlin) runs away from home after her cop father, Bert (Lawrence Tierney), tries to rape her. She is picked up by two young men as she heads for California, only to find that she's the captive of a Devil-worshipping family. They plan to sacrifice the young woman at midnight on Easter Sunday, but Bert shows up to save his daughter. Written and directed by John Russo, who wrote the script for George A. Romero's NIGHT OF THE LIVING DEAD, and boasting special effects by Tom Savini, this is, unfortunately, something of a disappointment. While the script is interesting and the brief effects by Savini are good, Russo isn't much of a director and he fails to translate his material to the screen effectively. Luckily, the film does contain a bravura performance from veteran Hollywood actor Tierney (DILLINGER, 1945), which makes up for a lot of the other weaknesses. Shot in Pittsburgh and finished by 1980, but undistributed until 1983.

p, Donald Redinger; d, John A. Russo; w, John A. Russo (based on his novel); ph, Paul McCollough (Eastmancolor); ed, Paul McCollough; m, The Sand Castle.

**(PR:O MPAA:R)**

## MIRRORS*

(1984) 88m First American c (AKA: MARIANNE)

Kitty Winn *(Marianne)*, Peter Donat *(Dr. Godard)*, William Swetland *(Charbonnet)*, Mary-Robin Redd *(Helene)*, William Burns *(Gary)*, Lou Wagner *(Chet)*, Don Keefer *(Peter)*, Vanessa Hutchinson *(Marie)*.

Filmed sometime in the mid-to-late 1970s under the title MARIANNE, this supernatural horror effort went unreleased until it turned up on videotape as MIRRORS in 1984. Shot on location in New Orleans, the story follows Marianne (Kitty Winn) and her husband (William Swetland) as they check into an old hotel on their honeymoon. Cursed by a voodoo priestess (Vanessa Hutchinson) who wants to capture her soul, Marianne is plagued by dreams in which she walks down a hall of mirrors in her nightgown. In desperation, Marianne and her husband turn to Dr. Godard (Peter Donat) for help, but he may not be what he seems.

p, John Parker, Stirling W. Smith; d, Noel Black; w, Sidney L. Stebel; ph, Michael D. Murphy (CFI Color); ed, Robert Estrin; m, Stephen Lawrence.

**(PR:C MPAA:PG)**

## MONKEY SHINES: AN EXPERIMENT IN FEAR****

(1988) 113m Orion c (AKA: ELLA)

Jason Beghe *(Allan Mann)*, John Pankow *(Geoffrey Fisher)*, Kate McNeil *(Melanie Parker)*, Joyce Van Patten *(Dorothy Mann)*, Christine Forrest *(Maryanne Hodges)*, Stephen Root *(Dean Burbage)*, Stanley Tucci *(Dr. John Wiseman)*, Janine Turner *(Linda Aikman)*, William Newman *(Doc Williams)*, Tudi Wiggins *(Esther Fry)*, Tom Quinn *(Charlie Cunningham)*, Chuck Baker *(Ambulance Driver)*, Patricia Tallman *(Party Guest)*, David Early *(Anesthetist)*, Michael Naft *(Young Allan)*, Tina Romero, Michael Baseman, Lia Savini *(Children Playing)*, Tim Dileo, Melanie Verlin *(Vandals)*, Dan Fallon *(Allan's Friend)*, Alice Shure, Leslie Dane Shapiro, Christina Galesi *(Nurses)*, Boo the Monkey *(Ella)*.

George Romero continues to bolster his reputation as America's preeminent horror film writer-director with this terrifying psychological horror film. Allan Mann (Jason Beghe), a handsome young track star and law student who is hit by a truck and paralyzed from the neck down, participates in an experimental health care program in which a

small, trained capuchin monkey named Ella becomes an extension of the quadriplegic's immobile limbs. Unknown to Allan, Ella is also the main participant in a scientific experiment conducted by Allan's best friend, Geoffrey (John Pankow), an idealistic med student who has tried to increase the primate's intelligence by injecting it with a serum made from human brain tissue. Gradually, as Allan grows more and more dependent on Ella, Ella becomes an extension of Allan's mind as well as his limbs, acting out his repressed anger in the most violent ways. In MONKEY SHINES, as in most of his best films, George Romero poses the question: What does it mean to be human? This notion has been the overriding concern of the "Living Dead" trilogy. In DAY OF THE DEAD, the catalyst for Romero's inquiry was an incredibly intelligent zombie named Bub, and the parallels between Bub and Ella are strong—both are nonhuman, and posited as the missing link between pure animal instinct and civilized human behavior. The character of Allan, on the other hand, is the opposite of Romero's zombies; they are brainless mobility, while he is immobile intellect. Claustrophobic, gripping, and incredibly intense throughout, MONKEY SHINES is an extremely complicated emotional drama that taps into the dark side of family ties, friendship, dependency, nurturing, and love—the last emotion represented by the four very different females (his mother, the nurse, his new girl friend, and especially Ella) who all compete to care for him. After trying for years to finance MONKEY SHINES independently, Romero was forced to turn to Hollywood, which led to a lack of control over the project. The studio imposed a sappy happy ending after test audiences were dissatisfied with Romero's dark sociopolitical conclusion (entailing an army of killer monkeys). The new ending didn't make a damn bit of difference, for the film was ineptly marketed and was yet another box-office flop for Romero.

p, Charles Evans; d, George A. Romero; w, George A. Romero (based on the novel by Michael Stewart); ph, James A. Contner (DeLuxe Color); ed, Pasquale Buba; m, David Shire.

**(PR:O MPAA:R)**

## MONSTER CLUB, THE*½

(1981, Brit.) 97m ITC c

Vincent Price *(Erasmus)*, John Carradine *(Ronald Chetwynd-Haynes)*, Roger Sloman *(Club Secretary)*, Fran Fullenwider *(Buxom Beauty)*, Anthony Steel *(Lintom Busotsky)*, Suzanna Willis *(The Stripper)*, The Viewers, B. A. Robertson, Night, Pretty Things *(Bands)*, "The Shadmock Story": James Laurenson *(Raven)*, Barbara Kellerman *(Angela)*, Simon Ward *(George)*, Geoffrey Bayldon *(Psychiatrist)*, "The Vampire Story": Donald Pleasence *(Pickering)*, Britt Ekland *(Lintom's Mother)*, Richard Johnson *(Lintom's Father)*, Warren Saire *(Lintom)*, Neil McCarthy *(Watson)*, Anthony Valentine *(Mooney)*, "The Humgoo Story": Stuart Whitman *(Sam)*, Lesley Dunlop *(Luna)*, Patrick Magee *(Innkeeper)*.

Vincent Price, who had not made a film in over five years, returned to the screen in this terribly disappointing horror anthology produced by old Amicus regular Milton Subotsky (THE HOUSE THAT DRIPPED BLOOD, 1970; TALES FROM THE CRYPT, 1972; ASYLUM, 1972). Price plays Erasmus, a vampire who brings horror-story writer Ronald Chetwynd-Haynes (John Carradine) to a disco popular with monsters. The disco setting is used as a framing device linking three tales of the macabre related by Erasmus. In "The Shadmock Story," a man (James Laurenson) who possesses a lethal whistle finds himself pursued by a woman (Barbara Kellerman) who wants to steal it from him. "The Vampire Story" finds a young man (Warren Saire) trying to defend his vampire father (Richard Johnson) from Scotland Yard inspector (Donald Pleasence) of the "Vamp Squad." And in the last tale, "The Humgoo Story," a movie director (Stuart Whitman) goes on location to shoot a horror story, only to find the place infested with real monsters. While the stories themselves aren't very good, the framing device featuring Price and the late John Carradine is particularly bad. While the two veteran performers exhibit themselves well, the concept of a monster disco is merely silly and the terribly cheap masks on the various creatures make the whole thing look as if a 12-year-old boy with a camera somehow convinced Price and Carradine to appear in a home movie shot in his basement. In addition, the scenes are padded out with performances by rock groups (including Pretty Things and UB40) and a female stripper who takes it all off—right down to her bones.

p, Milton Subotsky; d, Roy Ward Baker; w, Edward Abraham, Valerie Abraham (based on the novel by Ronald Chetwynd-Hayes); ed, Peter Tanner.

**(PR:C MPAA:NR)**

## MONSTER DOG zero

(1986) 84m Continental/Trans World Entertainment c

Alice Cooper *(Vincent Raven)*, Victoria Vera *(Sandra)*, Carlos Sanurio *(Frank)*, Pepita James *(Angela)*, Emilio Linder *(Jordan)*, Jose Sarsa *(Marilou)*, Luis Maluenda *(Deputy)*, Ricardo Palacios *(Sheriff Morrison)*, B. Barta Barri *(Old Man)*, Charley Bravo, Fernando Conde, Fernando Baeza, Nino Bastida *(Townsfolk)*.

There is usually a good reason why some films are released straight to videocassette—they stink. Shot mostly in Spain in 1984, this wretched horror film with laughable special effects is no exception. It is, however, notable for the appearance of has-been rocker Alice Cooper, who appropriately enough, plays a rock star named Vincent Raven (a small joke—Cooper's real name is Vincent Furnier) who decides to shoot his next rock video at his ancestral home—a spooky old mansion. En route there, Raven, his director girl friend, Sandra (Victoria Vera), and the cast and crew are stopped by the sheriff, who informs them that a pack of wild, rabid dogs has been wreaking havoc in the area. When Raven starts getting the creeps, Sandra chides him: "The year 2000 is just around the corner. I am a recognized expert in electronic videos, and you're the hottest rock 'n' roll star in the world—and you're afraid of werewolves!" Ah, but Raven then informs her that his father had a strange "heart ailment" that turned him into a werewolf, prompting the villagers to put a permanent end

to his midnight wandering. Meanwhile, a swarthy bunch of locals arrives to kill Raven, believing that he is a "monster dog" like his father. MONSTER DOG is about as inept as they come. The stupid script can't even decide whether its monster is a werewolf or a "monster dog," which accounts for one character's frenzied soliloquy: "You are the monster dog! You are the murdering animal! Damn you! Damn you! You are the werewolf! I know you are! I know it! Sob! Sob!"

p, Carlos Aured; d, Clyde Anderson; w, Clyde Anderson; ph, Jose Garcia Galisteo (Technicolor); ed, Antonio Jose Ochoa, Gabrio Astori, Peter Teschner; m, Grupo Dichotomy, Alice Cooper.

**(PR:O MPAA:NR)**

## MONSTER IN THE CLOSET**

(1987) 87m Closet/Troma c

Donald Grant *(Richard Clark)*, Denise DuBarry *(Diane Bennett)*, Henry Gibson *(Dr. Pennyworth)*, Howard Duff *(Father Finnegan)*, Donald Moffat *(Gen. Turnbull)*, Claude Akins *(Sheriff Ketchum)*, Paul Walker *(The Professor)*, Frank Ashmore *(Scoop Johnson)*, John Carradine *(Old Joe)*, Paul Dooley *(Roy Crane)*, Stella Stevens *(Margo Crane)*, Jesse White *(Ben Bernstein)*, Kevin Peter Hall *(The Monster)*, Stacy Ferguson *(Lucy)*, Ritchie Montgomery *(Deputy Spiro)*, Arthur Berggren *(Jimmy's Father)*, Daryle Ann Lindley *(Jimmy's Mother)*, Gordon Metcalfe *(Turnbull's Aide)*, Benny Baker *(Mr. McGinty)*, Doc Duhame *(Deputy Connor)*, Jonna Lee *(Sorority Girl)*, Richie Egan *(Charlie)*, Jonathan Aluzas *(Chip)*, Brad Kester *(Rex)*, Evan Arnold *(Beaver)*, Corky Pigeon *(Danny)*, Stephanie White *(Maggie)*.

Funnier than it has any right to be, MONSTER IN THE CLOSET is an affectionate parody of the low-budget science-fiction and horror films of the 1950s, with several jabs at Hitchcock, Spielberg, and even KING KONG. Set in San Francisco, the film begins with a pre-credits sequence in which a college coed, an old blind man (John Carradine), and a small child are yanked into their closets, never to return (no blood or gore here, just clothes spewing out of the closets). Hapless obit reporter Richard Clark (Donald Grant) is assigned to cover the strange disappearances. During his investigation, Clark meets sexy biology professor Diane Bennett (Denise DuBarry) and her precocious young son, "The Professor" (Paul Walker). Several celebrity guest-star murders later, the monster finally reveals itself to be a tall, ugly creature with a huge, gaping mouth. The Army, led by the blustering General Turnbull (Donald Moffat), blasts away at the creature, but the shells have no effect and the creature wanders over to the nearest closet. Enter Dr. Pennyworth (Henry Gibson, playing his role straight—just like those ultraserious 1950s sci-fi movie scientists), who attempts to coax the monster out of hiding by playing musical notes (a la CLOSE ENCOUNTERS OF THE THIRD KIND) on a child's xylophone. When this fails, the only thing left to do is to alert the public to "Destroy All Closets!" Scattershot and sophomoric in approach, MONSTER IN THE CLOSET somehow manages to generate enough chuckles to sustain interest. Kevin Peter Hall, who played the monsters in HARRY AND THE HENDERSONS and PREDATOR, takes on the same role here. Luckily for director Bob Dahlin, his distributor, Troma, allowed him to produce a surprisingly tame picture. Any gore or nudity would have taken this film out of the realm of goofy innocence and driven it right into the arena of tasteless exploitation.

p, David Levy, Peter L. Bergquist; d, Bob Dahlin; w, Bob Dahlin (based on a story by Bob Dahlin, Peter L. Bergquist); ph, Ronald W. McLeish; ed, Raja Gosnell, Stephanie Palewski; m, Barrie Guard.

**(PR:A-C   MPAA:PG)**

## MONSTER OF PIEDRAS BLANCAS, THE*½

(1959) 71m Vanwick/Film-Service bw

Les Tremayne (Dr. Jorgenson), Forrest Lewis (Sheriff Matson), John Harmon (Sturges, the Lighthouse Keeper), Don Sullivan (The Biochemist), Jeanne Carmen (The Girl), Frank Arvidson (The Storekeeper), Joseph La Cava (Mike), Peter Dunn (Eddie), Wayne Berwick (Little Jimmy), Jack Kevan (The Monster).

With thoughts of the popularity of CREATURE FROM THE BLACK LAGOON creeping about in the backs of their minds, the producers of this film came up with a similar monster, part man and part crustacean, which was played by producer Jack Kevan in a monster suit. The plot concerns the      superstitious lighthouse keeper Sturges (John Harmon), who leaves food for the beast—which is said to live in a nearby cave—as an appeasement. Although most of the other inhabitants of the area think he's crazy, Sturges worries that the monster might go after his beautiful teenage daughter (Jeanne Carmen). When a couple of fishermen turn up on the beach with their heads torn off (the creature lives off blood), the locals finally sit up and take notice. A distinctly subpar effort, THE MONSTER OF PIEDRAS BLANCAS' only item of interest is the monster suit, which has a face like a wild boar, the body of a lobster, and hands stolen from the costumes of THE MOLE PEOPLE (1956). Back in 1959, this film won the Shock Award of the Year from Monster Magazine.

p, Jack Kevan; d, Irvin Berwick; w, Haile Chace; ph, Philip Lathrop; ed, George Gittens.

**(PR:C   MPAA:NR)**

## MONSTER SQUAD, THE**

(1987) 82m Taft Entertainment-Keith Barish-Home Box Office/TriStar c

Andre Gower (Sean), Robby Kigor (Patrick), Stephen Macht (Del, Sean's Father), Duncan Regehr (Count Dracula), Tom Noonan (Frankenstein), Brent Chalem (Horace), Ryan Lambert (Rudy), Ashley Bank (Phoebe, Sean's Sister), Michael Faustino (Eugene), Mary Ellen Trainor (Emily), Leonardo Cimino (Scary German Guy), Jonathan Gries (Desperate Man), Stan Shaw (Detective Sapir), Lisa Fuller (Patrick's Sister), Jason Hervey (E.J.), Adam Carl (Derek), Carl Thibault (Wolfman), Tom Woodruff, Jr. (Gill-Man), Michael MacKay (Mummy), Jack Gwil-

lim (Van Helsing), David Proval (Pilot), Daryl Anderson (Co-Pilot), Brian Kestner (Rookie Cop), Denver Mattson (Beefy Cop), Diana Lewis (TV Anchorwoman), Gary Rebstock (TV Anchorman), David Wendel (Army General).

In an era when most American films are patched together from parts of last year's hits, THE MONSTER SQUAD sports a fairly innovative combination; namely, the 1986 hit STAND BY ME and a potpourri of the 1940s Universal horror epics (HOUSE OF FRANKENSTEIN; HOUSE OF DRACULA; ABBOTT AND COSTELLO MEET FRANKENSTEIN. THE MONSTER SQUAD begins as Dracula (Duncan Regehr) and Frankenstein's Monster (Tom Noonan) hook up with their pals the Mummy (Michael MacKay), the Wolfman (Carl Thibault), and the Gill-Man (Tom Woodruff, Jr.) in a Spielbergian suburb to search for an ancient amulet that will help them rule the world. Meanwhile, a group of grade-school friends devoted to Hollywood monster lore meet in their treehouse and quiz one another on the finer aspects of movie-monsterdom. When the kids learn of this horrific invasion, they turn to "The Scary German Guy" (Leonardo Cimino) for assistance, then gain an unexpected ally in the Frankenstein Monster, who is tired of being bossed around by Dracula. This second feature from director Fred Dekker (NIGHT OF THE CREEPS) is a poorly paced and haphazardly scripted (by LETHAL WEAPON writer Shane Black—yes, together they are Black & Dekker) horror-comedy that is neither scary nor particularly funny, its attempt at creating a STAND BY ME-type childhood ambience strained to the breaking point. Furthermore, the monsters are a tepid lot, and the special makeup (by Zoltan and Katalin Elek) is terribly plastic. Only Noonan scores as the Frankenstein Monster, primarily because he and the filmmakers understand that children have always seen this creature as a misunderstood victim—not as a monster.

p, Jonathan A. Zimbert, Neil A. Machlis; d, Fred Dekker; w, Shane Black, Fred Dekker; ph, Bradford May (Panavision, Metrocolor); ed, James Mitchell; m, Bruce Broughton.

**(PR:A-C   MPAA:PG-13)**

## MONSTER WALKS, THE**½

(1932) 63m Like/Action-Mayfair bw (GB: THE MONSTER WALKED)

Rex Lease (Ted Clayton), Vera Reynolds (Ruth Earlton), Sheldon Lewis (Robert Earlton), Mischa Auer (Hanns Krug), Martha Mattox (Mrs. Krug), Sidney Bracy (Herbert Wilkes), Willie Best (Exodus).

THE MONSTER WALKS is an old dark house mystery, made after the commercial successes of DRACULA (1931) and FRANKENSTEIN (1931), whose plot is much indebted to THE CAT AND THE CANARY (1927). Ruth (Vera Reynolds) inherits her father's estate (including the ape he kept for experiments) but her evil, paralyzed Uncle Robert (Sheldon Lewis) wants her killed so he can have the fortune for himself. He gets Hanns (Mischa Auer), the housekeeper's moronic son, to kill Ruth and make it look like the ape did it, but the confused boy kills his own mother instead. Hanns, upset that Robert's orders have caused him to kill his mom, is determined to get revenge on both Robert and Ruth. This is a really strange bit of poverty-row horror, effectively spiced up with some nice German-style expressionism and a bit of camp bizarreness in which heroine Reynolds is strapped to a column while Auer whips the "gorilla" (really a chimpanzee) into a killer frenzy. Worth a look.

p, Cliff Broughton; d, Frank B. Stayer; w, Robert Ellis; ph, Jules Cronjager; ed, Byron Robinson.

**(PR:A   MPAA:NR)**

## MORTUARY zero

(1983) 91m Artists Releasing/Film Ventures c

Mary McDonough *(Christie)*, David Wallace *(Greg Stevens)*, Lynda Day George *(Eve Parsons)*, Christopher George *(Dr. Hank Andrews)*, Bill Paxton *(Paul Andrews)*, Beth Schaffel, Curt Ayres, Alvy Moore.

Yet another in the series of bad splatter movies that infested the market in the late 1970s and early 1980s, MORTUARY follows Greg (David Wallace) and Christie (Mary McDonough), a young couple who get entangled with creepy mortician Dr. Hank Andrews (Christopher George) and his crazed son, Paul (Bill Paxton of ALIENS and NEAR DARK), leaders of a black magic sect. Christie can't even trust her mom (Lynda Day George), who has been seen sneaking off to the mortician's black masses herself. Not as gory as some of the other splatter films, MORTUARY has a gimmick in which an embalming tool extracts bodily fluids and replaces them with formaldehyde—a trick used again in PHANTASM II.

p, Howard Avedis, Marlene Schmidt; d, Howard Avedis; w, Howard Avedis, Marlene Schmidt; ph, Gary Graver; ed, Stanford C. Allen; m, John Cacavas.

**(PR:O   MPAA:R)**

## MOTEL HELL**½

(1980) 106m Camp Hill/UA c

Rory Calhoun *(Vincent Smith)*, Paul Linke *(Bruce Smith)*, Nancy Parsons *(Ida Smith)*, Nina Axelrod *(Terry)*, Wolfman Jack *(Rev. Billy)*, Elaine Joyce *(Edith Olsen)*, Dick Curtis *(Guy Robaire)*, Monique St. Pierre *(Debbie)*, Rosanne Katon *(Suzi)*, E. Hampton Beagle *(Bob Anderson)*, Michael Melvin *(Ivan)*, Everett Creach *(Bo)*, John Ratzenberger, Marc Silver, Victoria Hartman, Gwil Richards, Toni Gillman, Shaylin Hendrixson, Heather Hendrixson, Margo Hope, Barbara Goodson, Kim Fowler.

A film that should have been funnier, MOTEL HELL is a broad horror-comedy starring Rory Calhoun as "Farmer Vincent," who markets a famous brand of exclusive sausages from his lonely motel located far off the beaten path. Aided by his piggish sister, Ida (Nancy Parsons), Vincent prepares his meats by capturing unsuspecting victims on the highway and then burying them up to their necks with their vocal cords cut (so they can't scream for help) until they are fat enough for his smokehouse, where he slaugh-

ters them and turns them into sausage. Enter the young and beautiful Terry (Nina Axelrod), who has a motorcycle accident nearby and seeks shelter in the motel. Vincent's normal brother, Bruce (played by Paul Linke—that name can't be a coincidence), falls in love with Terry, but she is smitten with old coot Vincent and wants nothing to do with his kid brother. When Bruce learns the real home-style recipe for his brother's sausages, there is a lengthy chainsaw fight between the siblings—Vincent dons a giant pig head during the battle—leading to the film's best moment, when Vincent gives a long, hilarious speech while he lies dying with a chainsaw sticking out of his side. MOTEL HELL could have been a great black comedy, but the uneasy direction of Kevin Connor, combined with the gore that comes with this territory, fails to get most of the picture off the ground.

p, Steven-Charles Jaffe, Robert Jaffe; d, Kevin Connor; w, Steven-Charles Jaffe, Robert Jaffe; ph, Thomas Del Ruth (Technicolor); ed, Bernard Gribble; m, Lance Rubin.

**(PR:O   MPAA:R)**

## MOTHER'S DAY zero

(1980) 98m United Film Distribution c

Nancy Hendrickson *(Abbey)*, Deborah Luce *(Jackie)*, Tiana Pierce *(Trina)*, Holden McGuire *(Ike)*, Billy Rae McQuade *(Addley)*, Rose Ross *(Mother)*, Kevin Lowe *(Ted)*, Karl Sandys *(Brad)*, Ed Battle *(Doorman)*, Stanley Knapp *(Charlie)*, Marsella Davidson *(Terry)*, Robert Carnegie *(Tex)*, Scott Lucas *(Storekeeper)*, Bobby Collins *(Ernie)*.

This rancid horror film suffers from pretensions of social significance. Two repulsive brothers, Ike (Holden McGuire) and Addley (Billy Rae McQuade), live in the woods of New Jersey with their equally pathetic mother (Rose Ross). Their home is filled with sugary breakfast cereals, brand-name consumer products, and dozens of television sets (the media have driven them mad). When three young women have the misfortune to wander near the geeks' home on their way to a class reunion, the brothers capture the gals and spend the next 80 minutes or so subjecting them to various tortures until two of the girls escape and get revenge by performing even grosser acts of violence on their tormentors. The film's got a lame "twist" ending guaranteed to irritate any sensible filmgoer with its obvious lack of thought. MOTHER'S DAY has some defenders who claim it is not your run-of-the-mill horror film, and they're right. It's worse.

p, Michael Kravitz, Charles Kaufman; d, Charles Kaufman; w, Charles Kaufman, Warren D. Leight; ph, Joseph Mangine; m, Phil Gallo, Clem Vicari.

**(PR:O   MPAA:NR)**

## MOUNTAINTOP MOTEL MASSACRE zero

(1986) 95m Jim McCullough/NW c

Bill Thurman *(Rev. Bill McWilley)*, Anna Chappell *(Evelyn)*, Will Mitchel *(Al)*, Virginia Loridans *(Tanya)*, Major Brock *(Crenshaw)*, James Bradford *(Sheriff)*, Amy Hill *(Prissy)*, Marian Jones *(Mary)*, Greg Brazzel *(Vernon)*, Jill King

*(Lorie)*, Rhonda Atwood *(Bar Owner)*, Foster Litton *(Sheriff Dispatcher)*, Linda Blankenship *(Al's Secretary)*, Angela Christine *(Singing Voice)*.

The title says it all. Evelyn (Anna Chappell), a recently released middle-aged mental patient, returns home to run her mountaintop motel, where her daughter, Lorie (Jill King), who is a little strange herself, worships the Devil in the basement. When Evelyn catches Lorie praying at a satanic shrine, she has a relapse and severs her daughter's head with a sickle. Her mind completely snapped, Evelyn then murders some of her motel guests. In what must be the biggest night of the year for the out-of-the-way motel, no fewer than seven customers show up looking for lodging during a nasty rainstorm. Entering their rooms through a series of underground tunnels, Evelyn lets loose poisonous snakes, large rats, and nasty biting cockroaches, later becoming more direct and simply stabbing her guests. Instead of a homicidal Jason running through the woods of a summer camp, MOUNTAINTOP MOTEL MASSACRE offers an overweight, middle-aged crazy with a sickle. Still, all the characters here suffer from terminal stupidity and deserve what they get from Evelyn. Except for insanity, however, no motivation is given for her murderous spree, and a throwaway satanic zombie angle introduced at the end comes in from left field. The filmmakers do have some sense of visual style, but a slasher film is a slasher film no matter how good it looks. Moreover, the gore effects here are straight from the Herschell Gordon Lewis school of "cheapo," glimpsed only briefly to conceal how bad they are. Self-conscious references to PSYCHO are scattered throughout the film, but they only serve to remind viewers of just how pathetic MOUNTAINTOP MOTEL MASSACRE really is.

p, Jim McCullough, Sr., Jim McCullough, Jr.; d, Jim McCullough, Sr.; w, Jim McCullough, Jr.; ph, Joe Wilcots (Eastman Kodak); ed, Mindy Daucus; m, Ron Dilulio.

**(PR:O    MPAA:R)**

## MOVIE HOUSE MASSACRE*

(1986) 75m Movie House c

Mary Woronov, Jonathan Blakely, Lynne Darcy, Cynthia Hartline, Lisa Lindsley, Pam McCormack, Joni Barnes, Laurie Tidemanson, Barrie Metz, Terry Taylor, Joe Howard, Alice Raley.

Yet another straight-to-videocassette low-budget horror epic. Filmed in 1984, MOVIE HOUSE MASSACRE has a relatively unique (in the slasher genre) premise, in which an old theater is supposed to be haunted. Years before, when the house presented stage plays, the theater's manager went crazy, stabbed the ticket girl, and started a fire that created a mass panic. Now, a greedy 11-theater chain owner has bought the "haunted" house and intends to add it to his movie exhibition franchise. (This guy would make MPAA president Jack Valenti's hair curl: he makes illegal videotape copies of the films he exhibits.) Eager to collect the $25,000 reward offered by persons unknown who dare anyone to do business there, he dispatches three employees to clean up the dreaded cinema in time

for its gala opening night. Of course, the bodies soon pile up (one of the workers is a high-school cheerleader, so an endless parade of her bouncy teammates drop by long enough to get killed), and the usual stupid twist ending makes it all seem even more pointless. Produced, written, and directed by Alice Raley, who apparently knows nothing about making films, MOVIE HOUSE MASSACRE is incredibly inept. Only the presence of veteran low-budget star Mary Woronov, as the manager's assistant, makes this even remotely tolerable. Los Angeles locals may notice that the film was shot in the Beverly Theater in Beverly Hills and the Fairfax Theater in LA.

p, Alice Raley; d, Alice Raley; w, Alice Raley; ph, Bill Fishman.

**(PR:O    MPAA:NR)**

## MS. 45****

(1980) 84m Navaron/Rochelle c (AKA: ANGEL OF VENGEANCE)

Zoe Tamerlis *(Thana)*, Steve Singer *(Photographer)*, Jack Thibeau *(Man in Bar)*, Peter Yellen *(2nd Rapist)*, Darlene Stuto *(Laurie)*, Editta Sherman *(Landlady)*, Albert Sinkys *(Boss)*, Jimmy Laine *(1st Rapist)*, Bogey *(Phil)*.

Thana (Zoe Tamerlis) is a mute girl working in New York City's garment district. On her way home, she's raped, then is raped again at home by a burglar. She kills her rapist and, to dispose of the body, cuts it up, stores it in her refrigerator, and on a daily basis dumps parts in different sections of the city. One day, while dumping a bag, she is frightened by a man lounging on a street corner and drops the bag. The man picks it up, thinking she forgot it, then corners her in an alley, where she kills him with a .45 she took from the burglar. Thana goes on a killing spree, slaying a photographer, a pimp, gang members, a sheik, and any other man who behaves in a sexist manner. The film climaxes at a Halloween party, where Thana shows up dressed as a nun, a .45 strapped to her thigh. Director Abel Ferrara's first film after DRILLER KILLER, MS. 45 is not an easy movie to watch, not directly because of its violence, but because it's a calculated attack on the male-dominated audience of exploitation films. MS. 45 begins like any other exploitation film, with unmotivated violence (the two consecutive rapes), then throws ice water on every titillated viewer. One scene that exemplifies this attack on the audience occurs as Thana begins to take off her shirt in front of a mirror. Anticipation grows with every button undone. Then the dead rapist appears from behind her and a hand grabs for her breast. It's a startling sequence, wonderfully set up and disturbingly effective. The film also explores the darker side of the revenge-vigilante films. Thana has as much right as Charles Bronson to kill the bad guys, but Ferrara makes sure things aren't as black and white as in the "Death Wish" films. She's not just killing criminals, but also respectable business men who occasionally like to hit on women, and that can make it very uncomfortable for men who identify with the screen characters. The film touches on an interesting and unexplored issue of vigilante characters: how stable is that person with the gun, and can that person think clearly enough to be judge, jury, and executioner? Ferrara's gritty and powerful style makes MS. 45 the standout that it is. His use of music (a spine-tingling saxophone), instinctive camera techniques (the overhead shots, the slow-motion finale, the powerful bathroom scene in which the dead rapist suddenly materializes), and the colorful and humorous minor characters make this low-budget picture one of the greatest urban nightmares ever committed to film.

d, Abel Ferrara; w, Nicholas St. John; ph, James Momel (Cineffects Color); ed, Christopher Andrews; m, Joseph Delia.

**(PR:O    MPAA:R)**

## MUMMY, THE****

(1932) 72m UNIV bw

Boris Karloff *(Im-Ho-Tep/Ardeth Bey)*, Zita Johann *(Helen Grosvenor/Princess Anck-es-en-Amon)*, David Manners *(Frank Whemple)*, Edward Van Sloan *(Professor Muller)*, Arthur Byron *(Sir Joseph Whemple)*, Bramwell Fletcher *(Norton)*, Noble Johnson *(The Nubian)*, Leonard Mudie *(Professor Pearson)*, Katherine Byron *(Frau Muller)*, Eddie Kane *(Doctor)*, Tony Marlow *(Inspector)*, Arnold Gray *(Knight)*, James Crane *(Pharaoh)*, Henry Victor *(Warrior)*.

Following his triumph as the monster in FRANKENSTEIN (1931), Boris Karloff created yet another unforgettable horror character with the help of makeup man Jack Pierce and cinematographer-turned-director Karl Freund. THE MUMMY opens at an Egyptian archeological dig in 1921 as a group of scientists examine their most recent finding—a sarcophagus in an unmarked grave. The coffin in which the mummy rests has been stripped of all religious markings that would have ensured an afterlife for the deceased, proof that the 3700-year-old corpse was buried in disgrace. Interred with the mummy is a large box upon which is written a warning to those who would dare open it—this, however, is a horror movie and were no one to open the box we would never be treated to Karloff's magnificent wrappings. THE MUMMY was the directorial debut of the brilliant German cinematographer Freund who had photographed such classic German silents as THE LAST LAUGH; VARIETY; and METROPOLIS, as well as DRACULA in the US. Though THE MUMMY is not an overtly terrifying film (with the exception of the mummy's revival at the beginning), Freund creates an uneasy atmosphere of dread and foreboding. His camera is remarkably mobile, with impressive tracking and crane shots that float through the action, creating an eerie mood. Though the technical credits are excellent, it is Karloff who carries the film. Makeup genius Pierce once again molded his magic to the actor, and the combination of linen, fuller's earth, and clay used to create the recently discovered mummy took over eight hours a day to apply. The effect is startling, though Karloff only appears as the mummy briefly. Perhaps more impressive is the more subtle makeup Pierce created for Karloff in his reincarnated state. The mass of delicate wrinkles on Karloff's face and hands, combined with the actor's deliberately gentle, flowing movements, creates a being who looks as if he may fall apart at any moment. The re-creation of the days of the pharaohs is also

quite effective, and the scene wherein Karloff is wrapped alive, eyes going wider as his mouth is covered, is unforgettable. Four inferior sequels followed: THE MUMMY'S HAND; THE MUMMY'S TOMB; THE MUMMY'S GHOST; and THE MUMMY'S CURSE. Hammer Films of England revived the series beginning in 1959 with THE MUMMY.

p, Carl Laemmle; d, Karl Freund; w, John L. Balderston (based on a story by Nina Wilcox Putnam, Richard Schayer); ph, Charles Stumar; ed, Milton Carruth.

**(PR:C-O    MPAA:NR)**

## MUMMY, THE***½

(1959, Brit.) 86m Hammer/UNIV c

Peter Cushing *(John Banning)*, Christopher Lee *(Kharis, the Mummy)*, Yvonne Furneaux *(Isobel Banning/Princess Ananka)*, Eddie Byrne *(Inspector Mulrooney)*, Felix Aylmer *(Stephen Banning)*, Raymond Huntley *(Joseph Whemple)*, George Pastell *(Mehemet, Priest)*, John Stuart *(Coroner)*, Harold Goodwin *(Pat)*, Dennis Shaw *(Mike)*, Michael Ripper *(Poacher)*, Willoughby Gray, Stanley Meadows, Frank Singuineau, Frank Sieman, Gerald Lawson, David Browning, John Harrison, James Clarke, Frederick Rawlings.

This lively Hammer reworking of the classic mummy material stars Peter Cushing as John Banning, one of three British archaeologists who desecrate the tomb of an Egyptian princess, awakening Kharis (Christopher Lee), her mummified lover, who was buried alive with the princess when she died. Kharis follows the archaeologists back to England and is about to kill Banning when he sees his victim's beautiful wife, Isobel (Yvonne Furneaux), the spitting image of Kharis' lover, Princess Ananka. Stylishly directed by Terence Fisher (the action scenes, in particular, are breathtakingly choreographed), THE MUMMY features a surprisingly energetic performance from Lee, whose mummy moves swiftly and with strength, unlike his slow, shuffling 1940s predecessors. By playing the Mummy, Lee completed something of a trinity of terror, having already starred as Frankenstein's Monster and Dracula.

p, Michael Carreras; d, Terence Fisher; w, Jimmy Sangster (based on the screenplays THE MUMMY by    John L. Balderston,    THE MUMMY'S TOMB by Griffin Jay); ph, Jack Asher (Technicolor); ed, James Needs, Alfred Cox; m, Franz Reizenstein.

**(PR:C    MPAA:NR)**

## MUNCHIES zero

(1987) 85m Concorde/MGM-UA c

Harvey Korman *(Cecil/Simon)*, Charles Stratton *(Paul)*, Nadine Van Der Velde *(Cindy)*, Alix Elias *(Melvis)*, Charles Phillips *(Eddie)*, Hardy Rawls *(Big Ed)*, Jon Stafford *(Dude)*, Robert Picardo *(Bob Marvelle)*, Wendy Schaal *(Marge Marvelle)*, Scott Sherk *(Buddy Holly)*, Lori Birdsong *(Terry)*, Traci Huber Sheridan *(Amy)*, Paul Bartel *(Dr. Crowder)*, Ellen Albertini Dow *(Little Old Lady)*, Jerado De Cordovier *(Old Indian)*, Chip Heller *(Burgerland Manager)*, Roberto A. Jimenez *(Ramon)*, Michael Lee Gogin, Larry Nicholas, Kevin Thompson *(Burgerland Employees)*,

Justin Dreyfuss *(Dwight),* Jan Kuljis *(Biker Chick),* Steven Bernstein *(Dean),* Paul Short *(Head Biker),* Frank Welker *(Munchie Voices),* Fred Newman.

Steven Spielberg and Joe Dante's 1984 film GREMLINS was an indisputably violent picture chronicling the mayhem wreaked on a community by a group of strange little creatures. For all its problems, at least the film got a reaction from its audience. This bland horror comedy, an unashamed GREMLINS ripoff, doesn't even do that. The story opens in a South American cave where an anthropologist (Harvey Korman) is looking for an alien he hopes will bring him professional recognition. Accompanying him is his teenaged son (Charles Stratton), who takes a dim view of his father's activities. But, lo and behold, what should they stumble upon but a small creature hidden behind some old Aztec ruins. They capture it, dub it a "Munchie," and bring it home,where it eventually multiplies and causes more than a few problems. A subplot involves Korman in a dual role as the anthropolgist's evil brother, who has secretly been storing nuclear waste in an underground dwelling. The Munchies, simple creations at best, are the liveliest thespians in the cast, blowing away their wooden human counterparts. Even camp director Paul Bartel, who's given many a funny cameo performance, fails to bring any life to his role. The funniest thing about the entire proceedings is the first Munchie's pet name, Arnold Ziffel, after the pig from TV's "Green Acres." But then what can you say about a film in which the best performances are given by puppets?

p, Roger Corman, Ginny Nugent; d, Bettina Hirsch; w, Lance Smith; ph, Jonathan West.

**(PR:C  MPAA:PG)**

### MURDER CLINIC, THE**

(1966, It./Fr.) 86m Leone-Orphee-Societe Francaise/Europix-Consolidated c (LA LAMA NEL CORPO; LES NUITS DE L'EPOUVANTE; AKA: MURDER SOCIETY, THE; REVENGE OF THE LIVING DEAD; KNIFE IN THE BODY, THE; BLADE IN THE BODY, THE; NIGHT OF TERRORS, THE)

William Berger *(Dr. Robert Vance),* Francoise Prevost *(Claudine),* Mary Young *(Lizabeth Vance),* Barbara Wilson *(Mary),* Delphi Maurin *(Laura),* Massimo Righi *(Fred),* Harriet White *(Sheena),* Philippe Hersent, Anne Sherman, William Gold, Anne Field, Max Dean.

More gothic horror from the Italians, this time set in England at the turn of the century. William Berger stars as the crazed Dr. Robert Vance, suspected of murdering female deaf-mute patients at his clinic. His purpose is to reconstruct the once-beautiful face of his sister-in-law, who was disfigured when she fell into a vat of quicklime (though some say she was pushed in, by the good doctor himself). When a new nurse arrives at the clinic and is promptly murdered, suspicion again falls on Vance. Is he the hooded killer who stalks his victims and then dispatches them with a razor blade, or could it be his invalid wife (Mary Young), or the blackmailer (Francoise Prevost), or the homicidal patient (Max Dean)? Anyone who's seen enough of these

Italian slasher movies knows the answer to this one. Although it's all terribly predictable, directors Elio Scardamaglia and Lionello de Felice do a fairly good job of evoking a creepy mood and the period flavor is impressive.

p, Elio Scardamaglia; d, Elio Scardamaglia (English version, Lewis E. Ciannelli); w, Ernesto Gastaldi, Sergio Martino (based on the novel *The Knife in the Body* by Robert Williams); ph, Marcello Masciocchi (Techniscope, Technicolor); ed, Alberto Gallitti; m, Francesco De Masi

**(PR:C  MPAA:GP)**

### MURDERS IN THE RUE MORGUE***

(1971) 87m AIP c

Jason Robards, Jr. *(Cesar Charron),* Herbert Lom *(Marot),* Christine Kaufmann *(Madeleine Charron),* Adolfo Celi *(Inspector Vidocq),* Lilli Palmer *(Madeleine's Mother),* Maria Perschy *(Genevre),* Michael Dunn *(Pierre),* Jose Calvo *(Hunchback),* Peter Arne *(Aubert),* Werner Umburg *(Theatre Manager),* Luis Rivera *(Actor),* Virginia Stach *(Lucie),* Dean Selmier *(Jacques),* Marshall Jones *(Luigi Orsini),* Rosalind Elliot *(Gabrielle),* Ruth Platt, Xan Das Bolas *(Orsini's Assistants),* Maria Martin *(Mme. Adolphe),* Sally Longley, Pamela McInnes, Rafael Hernandez *(Members of Repertory Company).*

This was the fourth MURDERS IN THE RUE MORGUE brought to the screen, following the 1914 silent version, the first sound adaptation in 1932, and a 3-D version in 1954 (renamed PHANTOM OF THE RUE MORGUE). Based on Edgar Allan Poe's famous tale in name only, this film stars Jason Robards, Jr., as Parisian theater owner Cesar Charron, who is producing a Grand Guignol play titled "Murders in the Rue Morgue." His daughter, Madeleine (Christine Kaufmann), has recurring nightmares reminiscent of the play, only these dreams always end with a man in an ape costume swinging towards her, then falling to his death. After a series of murders among several of the theater company's former actors, the evidence points to Marot (Herbert Lom), once Charron's partner, who murdered Madeleine's mother years ago because she spurned his love and threw acid in his face, disfiguring him. It had been believed that Marot committed suicide following the murder, but his resurfacing proves that the suicide had just been an act. Marot talks Madeleine into meeting him at a secluded estate, where he confesses that he is in love with her because she so closely resembles her mother. Unbeknownst to either of them, however, Charron has followed his daughter to the estate, where he attacks Marot and kills him. But once again Marot has faked his death, and he returns to the theater one night, dressed in an ape costume to avoid detection, to enact his revenge. Although it has little to do with Poe (few Poe films really do), MURDERS IN THE RUE MORGUE is a surprisingly effective period piece that boasts an intriguingly complicated structure, shifting back and forth from reality, the stage, dreams, and flashbacks. Worth seeing.

p, Louis M. Heyward; d, Gordon Hessler; w, Christopher Wicking, Henry Slesar (based on the story by Edgar Allan

Poe); ph, Manuel Berenguer (Foto Film Color); ed, Max Benedict; m, Waldo de los Rios.

(PR:C  MPAA:GP)

## MUTILATOR, THE*

(1985) 86m OK/Ocean King c

Matt Mittler *(Ed, Jr.)*, Jack Chatham *( Ed, Sr.)*, Trace Cooper *(Younger Ed, Jr.)*, Ruth Martinez *(Junior's Girl Friend)*, Frances Raines, Bill Hitchcock, Morey Lampley, Connie Rogers *(Junior's Friends)*, Pamela Wendle Cooper *(Mother)*, Ben Moore *(Cop)*.

A boy named Ed, Jr., sits cleaning his gun, which accidentally goes off and kills Mom. Years later Ed, Jr. (Matt Mittler), has grown up and gone off to college, and brings a gang of friends home to house-sit at his father's beachfront condo. Guess what? Dad isn't really gone, and he's become a homicidal maniac since that unfortunate accident! The blood splashes on the walls as he dispatches his son's classmates in a variety of exotic ways. The performances are all substandard, even for this sort of trash. Filmed in North Carolina in 1983 under the working title FALL BREAK, this film contains some brief gore effects work by Mark Shostrom.

p, Buddy Cooper; d, Buddy Cooper, John S. Douglass; w, Buddy Cooper; ph, Peter Schnall (Movielab Color); ed, Stephen Mack; m, Michael Minard.

(PR:O  MPAA:R)

## MY BLOODY VALENTINE*½

(1981, Can.) 91m Secret/PAR c

Paul Kelman *(T.J.)*, Lori Hallier *(Sarah)*, Neil Affleck *(Axel)*, Keith Knight *(Hollis)*, Alf Humphreys *(Howard)*, Cynthia Dale *(Patty)*, Helene Udy *(Sylvia)*, Rob Stein *(John)*, Tom Kovacs *(Mike)*, Terry Waterland *(Harriet)*, Carl Marotte *(Dave)*, Jim Murchison *(Tommy)*, Gina Dick *(Gretchen)*, Peter Cowper *(Miner/Harry Warden)*, Don Francks *(Newby)*, Patricia Hamilton *(Mabel)*, Larry Reynolds *(Mayor)*, Jack Van Evera *(Happy)*, Jeff Danks *(Young Axel)*, Pat Hemingway *(Woman)*, Graham Whitehead *(Mac)*, Fred Watters, Jeff Fulton *(Supervisors)*, Pat Walsh *(Harvey)*, Marguerite McNeil *(Mrs. Raleigh)*, Sandy Leim *(Ben)*, John MacDonald *(Rescuer)*.

MY BLOODY VALENTINE is another FRIDAY THE 13TH clone, but at least this time the setting is a little different. The action takes place in a mining town called Valentine Bluffs, where an annual Valentine's Day dance is held. This year, however, a killer dressed in coal miner's garb takes his pickax and sinks it into the chests of local teens. The hearts of his victims get delivered to the police, wrapped up in candy boxes. Everyone assumes that the killer is a miner who was trapped in a cave-in some 20 years before. Having gone mad before his rescue, the miner killed the two men he blamed for the disaster, then disappeared. Although the producers attempted to make this typically gory (Tom Burman, Ken Diaz, and Tom Hoerber did the effects), they were forced to cut some of the most realistic mutilation footage to avoid an "X" rating. While

the body count averages one murder every 7 1/2 minutes—which will undoubtedly please the gorehounds it was intended for—this film is slightly better than most slice-and-dice efforts and contains several genuine surprises.

p, John Dunning, Andre Link, Stephen Miller; d, George Mihalka; w, John Beaird (based on a story concept by Miller); ph, Rodney Gibbons (Movielab Color); ed, Jean LaFleur, Kit Wallis, Gerald Vansier; m, Paul Zaza.

(PR:O  MPAA:R)

## MY DEMON LOVER*½

(1987) 86m New Line c

Scott Valentine *(Kaz)*, Michelle Little *(Denny)*, Arnold Johnson *(Fixer)*, Robert Trebor *(Charles)*, Alan Fudge *(Capt. Phil Janus)*, Gina Gallego *(Sonia)*, Calvert DeForest *(Man in Healthfood Store)*.

Kaz (Scott Valentine), a Greenwich Village derelict, has a nasty affliction—he turns into a beast whenever he's sexually aroused. While many men become beasts under similar circumstances, Kaz *really* becomes a beast—sprouting a tail, horns, fangs, etc.—the result of a curse put on him by an old Rumanian woman who found him dallying with her daughter. Eventually Kaz meets Denny (Michelle Little), a loser at love with a talent for picking the wrong men. Fearing that he'll rip her to shreds, Kaz makes Denny agree that they'll remain friends and not become lovers. While "The Fixer" (Arnold Johnson) tries to concoct a potion that will end the curse, Kaz finds himself becoming more and more attracted to Denny. It's possible that the makers of MY DEMON LOVER intended it as a *biting* satire of male sexuality; however its script and direction are so sophomoric it's hard to take seriously on any level. Nonetheless, the special makeup effects (by Carl Fullerton, John Caglione, Jr., Neal Martz, and Doug Drexler) are convincing and the East Village settings add a nice touch of authenticity.

p, Robert Shaye; d, Charles Loventhal; w, Leslie Ray; ph, Jacques Haitkin; ed, Ronald Roose; m, David Newman.

(PR:C  MPAA:PG-13)

## MYSTERY OF THE WAX MUSEUM, THE****

(1933) 73m WB c

Lionel Atwill *(Ivan Igor)*, Fay Wray *(Charlotte Duncan)*, Glenda Farrell *(Florence Dempsey)*, Frank McHugh *(Jim)*, Gavin Gordon *(Harold Winton)*, Edwin Maxwell *(Joe Worth)*, Holmes Herbert *(Dr. Rasmussen)*, Arthur Edmund Carewe *(Sparrow)*, Allen Vincent *(Ralph Burton)*, Monica Bannister *(Joan Gale)*, Matthew Betz *(Hugo)*, DeWitt Jennings *(Captain of Police)*, Thomas Jackson *(Detective)*, Bull Anderson *(The Janitor)*, Pat O'Malley *(Plain clothesman)*.

Lionel Atwill and Fay Wray are teamed here for the second time in a Michael Curtiz-directed, Warner Brothers-produced two-strip Technicolor horror film (their first pairing was in DR. X in 1932). The film opens in London, in

1921, as the brilliant sculptor Ivan Igor (Atwill) is hard at work on his latest creation, surrounded by beautiful wax sculptures of female historical figures. Having eschewed the more sensational—and, therefore, more lucrative—figures of killers like Jack the Ripper in favor of these beautiful creations, Ivan finds his wax museum on the brink of bankruptcy. A fight over finances between Ivan and his partner, Joe Worth (Edwin Maxwell), results in the museum's destruction by fire, the "death" of the wax figures, and Ivan's near death. The scene then shifts to New York City, 1933, where the grey-haired Ivan is confined to a wheelchair, his hands crippled from the fire. When a wealthy socialite dies and her corpse is stolen from the morgue, tough-talking female reporter Florence Dempsey (Glenda Farrell) investigates the case. The strange disappearance of the corpse coincides suspiciously with Ivan's preparation for the opening of his new museum,in which the wax beauties have a remarkably lifelike appearance. Feared to be lost for many years, THE MYSTERY OF THE WAX MUSEUM gained a mighty reputation when film historians' memories of the movie were jogged by the 1953 3-D remake, HOUSE OF WAX. When a print of the original film surfaced in the late 1960s, however, many critics were disappointed with it, shrugging it off as a silly mystery picture, though their initial reaction was entirely unfounded. An amazing film filled with stunning sets (by Anton Grot), exceptional moments, and perhaps Atwill's greatest performance, THE MYSTERY OF THE WAX MUSEUM is also a surprisingly adult picture that deals explicitly with drug addiction, necrophilia, and insanity. Notably, it was also one of the first horror films to be set in the everyday reality of modern-day New York and not in a mystical foreign land.

p, Henry Blanke; d, Michael Curtiz; w, Don Mullally, Carl Erickson (based on a play by Charles S. Belden); ph, Ray Rennahan (Technicolor); ed, George Amy.

(PR:C  MPAA:NR)

# N

## NAIL GUN MASSACRE*

(1987) 84m Futuristic/Reel Movies c

Rocky Patterson (Doc), Michelle Meyer (Linda), Ron Queen (Sheriff), Beau Leland (Bubba), Sebrina Lawless, Monica Lawless, Mike Coady, Staci Gordon, Randy Hayes, Joanne Hazelbarth, Roger Payne, Kit Mitchell.

The rape of a girl by a gang of construction workers opens this ultra-low-budget gorefest from Texas. Some time later a killer dressed in Army fatigues and a black motorcycle helmet goes around killing construction workers with a nail gun. Could it be the rape victim seeking a brutal revenge, or someone you would never expect? What do you think? Not surprisingly, this film never received a theatrical release and went straight to home video.

p, Terry Lofton; d, Terry Lofton, Bill Leslie; w, Terry Lofton;

ph, Bill Leslie (Ultracolor); ed, Lynn Leneau Calmes; m, Whitey Thomas.

(PR:O  MPAA:NR)

## NEAR DARK****

(1987) 95m F-M Entertainment/DEG c

Adrian Pasdar (Caleb), Jenny Wright (Mae), Lance Henriksen (Jesse), Bill Paxton (Severen), Jenette Goldstein (Diamondback), Tim Thomerson (Loy), Joshua Miller (Homer), Marcie Leeds (Sarah), Kenny Call (Deputy Sheriff), Ed Corbett (Ticket Seller), Troy Evans (Plainclothes Officer), Bill Cross (Sheriff Eakers), Roger Aaron Brown (Cajun Truck Driver), Thomas Wagner (Bartender), Robert Winley (Patron in Bar), James LeGros (Teenage Cowboy), Jan King (Waitress), Danny Kopel (Biker in Bar), Billy Beck (Motel Manager), S.A. Griffin (Police Officer at Motel), Don Pugsley (Second Truck Driver), Neith Hunter, Theresa Randle (Ladies in Car), Tony Pierce, Gordon Haight (Highway Youths), Leo Geter, Gary Wayne Cunningham (Caleb's Friends), Bob Terhune, William T. Lane, Gary Littlejohn, Paul Michael Lane, Eddie Mulder (State Troopers).

An auspicious solo directing debut from Kathryn Bigelow (she codirected THE LOVELESS in 1982), NEAR DARK combines such diverse genres as horror, western, crime, and romance into what may be the first vampire road movie. Set in the American Southwest, the film begins as Caleb (Adrian Pasdar), a bored farm boy, spots the beguiling Mae (Jenny Wright) at his usual Friday night hangout. By the break of dawn, Caleb has been bitten in the neck by Mae, turned into a vampire, and befriended by a bizarre "family" of vampires—led by Jesse (Lance Henriksen), undead since before the Civil War—who travel across the country in a Winnebago. To his horror, Caleb learns that he has been "nipped" (i.e., he is almost a full-fledged vampire), and to graduate must kill and drink blood. Sensing that Mae is in love with the boy, Jesse gives Caleb a week to perform his first kill. Although several movie genres are represented here, NEAR DARK is most obviously based on director Nicholas Ray's 1949 feature debut, THEY LIVE BY NIGHT (Bigelow's characters literally must "live by night"). Both films focus on a young couple desperately in love but trapped in a lifestyle they detest by their surrogate families (bank robbers and vampires, respectively). Bigelow and coscreenwriter Eric Red (THE HITCHER) demonstrate a keen understanding and appreciation of the history of American cinema and create a unique film, which explores the conventions of the vampire movie while moving it from dank European castles to modern-day Southwestern America. Bigelow sees the vampire (the word is never used in the film) as a nomadic outlaw, much like the fabled gunslingers of the Old West or the bands of bank robbers that roved the landscape during the Depression. Although monsters, the vampires are shown to be fiercely loyal to one another. This loyalty is born of loneliness, the fear of which binds them as a family. NEAR DARK proves Kathryn Bigelow to be one of the most exciting and valuable new American filmmakers of the coming decade.

p, Steven-Charles Jaffe, Eric Red; d, Kathryn Bigelow; w,

Eric Red, Kathryn Bigelow; ph, Adam Greenberg (CFI Color); ed, Howard Smith; m, Tangerine Dream.

(PR:O   MPAA:R)

## NESTING, THE**½

(1981) 104m Nesting/Feature c (AKA: PHOBIA)

Robin Groves *(Lauren Cochran)*, Christopher Loomis *(Mark Felton)*, Michael David Lally *(Daniel Griffith)*, John Carradine *(Col. LeBrun)*, Gloria Grahame *(Florinda Costello)*, Bill Rowley *(Frank Beasley)*, David Tabor *(Abner Welles)*, Patrick Farelley *(Dr. Webb)*, Bobo Lewis *(Catherine Beasley)*, June Berry *(Saphire)*, Cecile Lieman *(Helga)*, Ann Varley *(Gwen)*, Ron Levine *(Leland LeBrun)*, Bruce Kronenberg *(Young Abner)*, Jim Nixon *(Young Frank)*, James Saxon *(Earl)*, Cliff Cudney *(Sheriff)*.

A neurotic writer of gothic novels named Lauren (Robin Groves) manages to rid herself of her agoraphobia by finally leaving her Manhattan townhouse, only to move to a haunted Victorian mansion that was once a brothel. The ghosts of the prostitutes reveal themselves to Lauren and show her, in slow motion, the massacre that ended their lives. Lauren then finds herself being used by the ghosts to get even with their murderers. Directed by one-time pornographic filmmaker Armand Weston, THE NESTING is an intriguing effort that effectively combines traditional haunted house chills with a more modern emphasis on gore. Weston also managed to assemble a solid cast, with veterans John Carradine and Gloria Grahame—in her final role as the ghost of the brothel madam—lending a bit of class to the proceedings.

p, Armand Weston; d, Armand Weston; w, Armand Weston, Daria Price; ph, Joao Fernandes; ed, Jack Foster; m, Jack Malken, Kim Scholes.

(PR:O   MPAA:R)

## NEW YEAR'S EVIL zero

(1980) 90m Cannon c

Roz Kelly *(Diane Sullivan)*, Kip Niven *(Richard Sullivan)*, Louisa Moritz *(Sally)*, Chris Wallace *(Lt. Clayton)*, Jed Mills *(Ernie)*, Grant Cramer *(Derek Sullivan)*, Taafe O'Connell *(Jane)*, Jon Greene *(Sgt. Greene)*, Anita Crane *(Lisa)*, Alice Dhanifu *(Yvonne)*, John London *(Floor Manager)*, Barry Gibberman *(Hotel Guest)*, Teri Copley *(Teenage Girl)*, Jennie Anderson *(Nurse Robbie)*, Wendy-Sue Rosloff *(Makeup Girl)*, John Alderman *(Dr. Reed)*, Jerry Chambers *(Clerk)*, Mike Mihalich *(Policeman at Hotel)*, Jerry Zanitsch, Mark L. Rosen *(Drunks)*, Bob Jarvis, Richard E. Kald *(Policemen)*, Linda Terito *(Stunt Woman)*, Mark de Frani *(Teenage Boy)*, Richard Brown *(Swamper)*, Julie Kaye Towery *(Space Girl)*.

Another routine mad slasher film, NEW YEAR'S EVIL stars Kip Niven as Richard, a mental patient who hasn't had a very good year and attempts to vent his frustration by killing one person per hour on New Year's Eve. Diane (Roz Kelly, of TV's "Happy Days") is the disc jockey who is hosting a coast-to-coast punk rock video party on the murderous evening, and Richard, identifying himself only as

"Evil," calls repeatedly to tell her about his latest executions. In the climax Evil crashes the party and tries to do in poor Diane with an elevator. This strictly paint-by-numbers effort is further sabotaged by the grating so-called punk rock performances—actually heavy metal—that pad out the running time.

p, Menahem Golan, Yoram Globus; d, Emmett Alston; w, Leonard Neubauer (based on a story by Alston, Neubauer); m, Laurin Rinder, W. Michael Lewis.

(PR:O   MPAA:R)

## NEXT OF KIN*

(1982, Aus.) 86m SIS-Filmco/Miracle c

Jackie Kerin, John Jarratt, Alex Scott, Gerda Nicolson, Charles McCallum, Bernadette Gibson, Robert Ratti, Vince Deltito, Tommy Dysart, Debra Lawrence, Kristina Marshall, Simon Thorpe, David Allshoru, Alan Rowe, Matt Burns, Daphne Miller, Isobel Harley, Irene Hewitt, Myrtle Woods, Vic Gordon, Peter Lord, Ernest Wilson, John Strahan, Bill Marr, John Bishop, Mitchell Faircloth, Nora Toohey, Sid Krasey.

This Australian mad-slasher entry offers a twist: the inhabitants of an old people's home are the victims, rather than the usual teenie boppers. Nonetheless, the results are still predictable, as Jackie Kerin, playing the young woman in charge of the home, tries to figure out who the culprit is. Director Tony Williams tosses in a bunch of quotes from films and literature in an apparent attempt to elevate the proceedings, but instead proving yet again that the evocation of great artists' names and works does not guarantee a film of the same quality.

p, Robert Le Tet; d, Tony Williams; w, Tony Williams, Michael Heath; ph, Gary Hansen (Eastmancolor); ed, Max Lemon; m, Klaus Schulze.

(PR:O   MPAA:NR)

## NIGHT OF A THOUSAND CATS, THE**

(1974, Mex.) 95m Ellman c (LA NOCHE DE LOS MIL GATOS)

Anjanette Comer, Zulma Faiad, Hugo Stiglitz, Christa Linder, Gerardo Cepeda, Tereza Velasquez, Barbara Angel.

Though unashamedly sick, THE NIGHT OF THE THOUSAND CATS should provide plenty of unintentional laughs for those who can stomach it. Director Rene Cardona, Jr., who cowrote his father's even more disgusting NIGHT OF THE BLOODY APES (1968), sets the action in beautiful Acapulco and introduces an insane nobleman (Hugo Stiglitz) who lives in the ruins of a castle and bides his time playing chess with his Igor-like servant (Gerardo Cepeda). He also keeps a horde of hungry cats in a pit, feeding them human flesh he procures by using a helicopter to scout bikini-clad babes who he then seduces and decapitates, keeping their heads in a jar. Eventually, however, he picks up the wrong sunbather and meets his match. Cardona later turned his attention to cannibalism in SURVIVE!, in which the survivor of a plane that crashes in the Andes feasts on the bodies of his fellow passengers.

p, Mario Z. Zacaria; d, Rene Cardona, Jr.; w, Mario Marzac, Rene Cardona, Jr. (based on a story by Marzac); ph, Alex Phillips, Jr.

(PR:O  MPAA:R)

## NIGHT OF BLOODY HORROR*

(1969) 89m Taste of Blood-Cinema IV/Howco c

Gerald McRaney *(Wesley Stuart)*, Gaye Yellen *(Angelle Miliot)*, Herbert Nelson *(Dr. Bennett Moss)*, Evelyn Hendricks *(Agatha Stuart)*, Lisa Dameron *(Susan Collins)*, Charlotte White *(Kay Jensen)*, Nicholous R. Krieger *(Lt. James Cole)*, Michael Anthony *(Mario Spenelli)*, Bert Roberts *(Mark Lewis)*, Gordon Ogden *(Tucker Fredricks)*, Murray Solow *(Bartender)*, Nigel Strangeways, Burt Love, Louis Grapes *(Hoods)*, George Spelvin *(Priest)*, Anthony Herrero *(Man in Club)*, Farley Dennis *(Wesley as a Boy)*.

Shot in 16mm "Violent Vision," this inept, surprisingly gory PSYCHO rip-off involves a former mental patient whose blackouts prevent him from knowing whether he is responsible for the grisly murders of several of his female acquaintances. Institutionalized as a child after accidentally killing his brother, Wesley (Gerald McRaney) has now become the prime suspect in this multiple murder case in which the victims have been hacked apart by a meat cleaver. Since the movie really isn't any good, distributors lured patrons to the theater with good old fashioned showmanship. In addition to offering $1,000 to the family of anyone who died of fright while watching the movie, there were TV ads that merely showed the movie's title while a solemn narrator ever-so-seriously intoned, "Due to the current federal subcommittee investigation of sex and violence on television, no scenes, we repeat, no scenes of the motion picture NIGHT OF BLOODY HORROR are allowed to be shown on this station." Then a different narrator was heard describing the film as " . . . the terror of beautiful women who meet sudden, brutal horror at the hands of a blood psycho gone berserk." Not surprisingly, the ads were better than the movie.

p, Joy Houck, Jr.; d, Joy Houck, Jr.; w, Robert A. Weaver, Joy Houck, Jr.; ph, Robert A. Weaver; ed, Robert A. Weaver.

(PR:O  MPAA:R)

## NIGHT OF THE BLOODY APES*

(1968, Mex.) 82m Jerand/Unistar c (LA HORRIPLANTE BESTIA HUMANA, HORROR Y SEXO; AKA: GOMAR-THE HUMAN GORILLA)

Jose Elias Moreno, Carlos Lopez Moctezuma, Armando Silvestre, Norma Lazareno, Agustin Martinez Solares, Gina Moret, Noelia Noel, Gerard Zepeda.

Mexican horror director Rene Cardona cowrote this gross, unbelievably inept offering with his son, Rene Cardona, Jr., who would go on to make THE NIGHT OF THE THOUSAND CATS (1972). A kindly doctor (Jose Elias Moreno) transplants the heart of a gorilla into the chest of his dying son (Armando Silvestre). Holding true to the unwritten hor-

ror film principles of anatomy, the boy awakens and turns into a body-builder with the face of a gorilla, terrorizing the city, raping big-breasted women, and ripping apart every living being in sight. With its dizzying combination of hardcore gore (eye, ear, nose, and throat gougings in bloody closeup), gratuitous nudity, rampaging monster, actual footage of open-heart surgery, and masked Mexican wrestlers, this is a tough one to ignore. For a nice father-and-son double bill, watch this and THE NIGHT OF THE THOUSAND CATS back-to-back, if you can stand it.

p, Guillermo Calderon, Alfredo Salazar; d, Rene Cardona; w, Rene Cardona, Rene Cardona, Jr.; ph, Raul Martinez Solares; ed, Jorge Bustos; m, Antonio Diaz Conde.

(PR:O  MPAA:NR)

## NIGHT OF THE COBRA WOMAN*

(1974, US/Phil.) 85m NW c

Joy Bang *(Joanna)*, Marlene Clark *(Lena)*, Roger Garrett *(Duff)*, Slash Marks *(Sgt. Merkle)*, Vic Diaz *(Lope)*.

Shot in the Philippines by New York experimental filmmaker and Andy Warhol devotee Andrew Meyer, NIGHT OF THE COBRA WOMAN was made under the auspices of Roger Corman's New World Pictures. Lena (Marlene Clark), a jungle priestess, needs both the venom of cobras and constant sexual activity to remain young, and to keep from becoming a cobra herself. Joanna (Warhol favorite Joy Bang), a female biology student, is somewhat dismayed when her boy friend, Duff (Roger Garrett), is seduced by Lena and becomes one of her minions. Exhausted by all the lovemaking, Duff is forced to enlist other young men to satisfy the cobra woman—all of whom turn into skeletons after she's done with them. Filmed in "Slitherama," this silly movie has its share of laughs—intentional and unintentional—but isn't particularly scary.

p, Kerry Magness, Harvey Marks; d, Andrew Meyer; w, Andrew Meyer, Kerry Magness; ph, Nonong Rasca.

(PR:O  MPAA:R)

## NIGHT OF THE GHOULS*½

(1959) 60m Atomic/Crown International TV bw (AKA: REVENGE OF THE DEAD)

Criswell *(Himself)*, Tor Johnson *(Lobo)*, Maila "Vampira" Nurmi *(Black Ghost)*, Keene Duncan *(Dr. Acula)*, Valda Hansen *(Fake Ghost)*.

Another low-budget masterwork of unintentional hilarity from Ed Wood, Jr.—the man who gave us the greatest bad film of all time, PLAN 9 FROM OUTER SPACE—NIGHT OF THE GHOULS doesn't quite live up to its "classic" predecessor. Emerging from a coffin to relate another horrifying tale, noted *psychic* Criswell returns to the screen as the narrator and star of the film (he, Tor Johnson, Maila "Vampira" Nurmi, and Bela Lugosi appeared in nearly all of Wood's little masterpieces). The story concerns phony spiritualist Dr. Acula (Keene Duncan), his lovely assistant (Valda Hansen), and a big brute (Tor Johnson) who perform bogus seances to scare money out of dim-witted customers trying to contact deceased loved ones. These ignorant crooks have been fooling with the supernatural, however, and one night they find that they *really* have brought the dead to life. The disturbed corpses—including Nurmi—exact revenge by burying the shady spiritualist and his crew alive. This was one of Wood's last efforts and it was never released theatrically, though local TV stations had no compunction about airing it as a late-night feature, much to the delight of Wood, who used to call his friends and tell them to stay up and watch it. On cassette as both NIGHT OF THE GHOULS and REVENGE OF THE DEAD.

p, Edward Wood; d, Edward Wood; w, Edward Wood.

**(PR:A   MPAA:NR)**

## NIGHT OF THE LIVING DEAD*****

(1968) 96m Image Ten/Continental-Almi bw (AKA: NIGHT OF THE FLESH EATERS; NIGHT OF ANUBIS)

Judith O'Dea *(Barbara)*, Russell Streiner *(Johnny)*, Duane Jones *(Ben)*, Karl Hardman *(Harry Cooper)*, Keith Wayne *(Tom)*, Judith Ridley *(Judy)*, Marilyn Eastman *(Helen Cooper)*, Kyra Schon *(Karen Cooper)*, Bill Hinzman *(Cemetery Zombie)*, Charles Craig *(Newscaster)*, Frank Doak *(Scientist)*, George Kosana *(Sheriff McClelland)*, Bill "Chilly Billy" Cardille *(Field Reporter)*, Vince Survinski *(Posse Gunman)*, John A. Russo *(Zombie in House/ Military Aide in Washington)*, George A. Romero *(Reporter in Washington)*, A.C. MacDonald, Samuel R. Solito, Mark Ricci.

Pittsburgh-based industrial filmmaker George Romero gathered together a loyal cast and crew of local talent, scrounged up enough money to shoot on weekends, and committed to film one of the most terrifying pictures ever to hit the screen. After Barbara (Judith O'Dea) and her brother (Russell Streiner) are attacked by an odd-looking man while visiting their father's grave in a remote cemetery, she runs to a deserted farm house where she is joined by Ben (Duane Jones), a black man who is being pursued by other strange-looking men. He then sets about a fortifying the house by nailing boards over doors and windows without much help from Barbara, whose mind has snapped. While working, Ben explains that most of the nearby towns have been infested with these deadly maniacs and many people have been killed by them. After securing the main floor, Ben is shocked to learn that a group of people has been huddled in the basement all along, led by Harry (Karl Hardman), a cowardly family man who took refuge with his wife, Helen (Marilyn Eastman), and a young teenage couple, Tom and Judy (Keith Wayne and Judith Ridley), after Harry's daughter was bitten by one of the creatures. The TV news announces that the crazed people are not escaped mental patients, but actually dead people who have come back to life seeking the flesh of the living. Trapped in the house and rife with dissent, the tiny group must pull together if they want to survive. Produced for less than $150,000 and shot in black and white, Romero's film, one of the most important horror movies ever made, sent shock waves throughout the movie-going community. Stodgy bastions of film criticism such as *Variety* spat out

scathingly negative reviews, but other critics hailed the film as a masterpiece of modern horror. After being booked in a haphazard manner—rejected by Columbia because it wasn't in color and by American International Pictures because it had no romance and a downbeat ending—the film turned up at kiddie matinees, scaring the daylights out of the unprepared youngsters. NIGHT OF THE LIVING DEAD then found its niche on the midnight show circuit and went on to become one of the most successful independent films of all time. Despite its humble origins, it set a new standard for horror and inspired literally hundreds of imitations. Romero used all the budget handicaps to his advantage: the black-and-white film stock only enhances the film's nightmarish quality, while his visual style relies on skillfully framed compositions edited together for maximum impact. The film's underlying premise is horror at its most basic: a group of strangers trapped together in a small house being attacked by the living dead—once friends, relatives and neighbors—who want only to devour them. Much has been made of the gore level in NIGHT OF THE LIVING DEAD, but most of the horror is actually suggested or off-screen, with a few, sparse visualizations brought in to punctuate the proceedings. In fact, the much-touted gore has now become so tame by today's standards that the film is often shown on TV untouched by censors' scissors. With his zombies, Romero hit upon a subject that is rich in metaphor and meaning, and he continued to explore the implications of his concept in two excellent sequels DAWN OF THE DEAD (1979) and DAY OF THE DEAD (1985).

p, Russell Streiner, Karl Hardman; d, George A. Romero; w, George A. Romero, John A. Russo (based on a story by Romero); ph, George A. Romero; ed, George A. Romero; m, Karl Hardman.

**(PR:O   MPAA:NR)**

## NIGHT OF THE ZOMBIES zero

(1981) 88m NMD c (AKA: GAMMA 693; NIGHT OF THE WEHRMACHT ZOMBIES)

Jamie Gillis *(Nick Monroe)*, Ryan Hilliard *(Dr. Proud)*, Samantha Grey *(Susan)*, Ron Armstrong *(Capt. Fleck)*, Richard de Faut *(Sgt. Freedman)*, Juni Kulis *(GRO Officer Schuller)*, Alphonse de Noble *(C.I.A. Agent)*, Joel M. Reed *(Neo-Nazi)*, Shoshana Ascher *(Prostitute)*, Lorin E. Price *(Priest)*, Ron Dorfman *(C.I.A.Chief)*, Ranate Schlessinger *(Madame)*, Kuno Sponholtz *(Doorman)*, Dick Carballo *(Man in Bar)*, John Barilla, Michael Casconi, Gordon C. Dixon, Bob Laconi, Charlene Matus, Lee Moore, Glen A. Pence, Donald K. Wallace, Bill Williams, Carl Woerner, Kai Wulff.

This really cheap zombie film was made by the man who brought you BLOODSUCKING FREAKS, Joel M. Reed. Porno star Jamie Gillis plays a CIA agent hot on the trail of a bunch of cannibalistic Nazi zombie soldiers who have continued to fight WW II despite the fact that it's been over for nearly 40 years. The soldiers were preserved by an experimental nerve gas called Gamma 693, and it is up to Gillis to stop them. This one would be great on a double bill with the similarly plotted Dana Andrews classic THE

FROZEN DEAD (1966); unfortunately, the Andrews film is not yet available on home video.

p, Lorin E. Price; d, Joel M. Reed; w, Joel M. Reed; ph, Ron Dorfman (TVC Color); ed, Samuel Pollard, Victor Kanefsky; m, Onomatopoeia, Inc., Matt Kaplowitz, Maggie Nolin.

(PR:O   MPAA:R)

## NIGHT OF THE ZOMBIES zero

(1981, Sp./It.) 100m Dara/MPM-Beatrice c
(APOCALIPSIS CANIBAL; INFERNO DEI MORTI-VIVENTI; VIRUS, INFERNO DEI MORTI-VIVENTI; AKA: HELL OF THE LIVING DEAD; ZOMBIE CREEPING FLESH)

Margit Evelyn Newton *(Lea),* Franco Giraldi, Selan Karay, Robert O'Neil, Luis Fonoll, Gaby Renom, Ester Mesina, Victor Israel, Piero Fumelli, Patrizia Costa.

Once again foreign horror filmmakers jumped on the George Romero zombie bandwagon and came up with another stinker. Borrowing ideas from Romero's "Living Dead" films *and* THE CRAZIES, this offering details the results of a disastrous chemical leak in Papua, New Guinea, that has turned the natives into flesh-eating zombies. Soon an Italian TV crew led by a tough female reporter (Margit Evelyn Newton) turns up to cover the story and quickly needs to be rescued by a squad of trigger-happy soldiers. With the arrival of the military, the gore really begins to splatter. Cheap makeup effects, unintentionally funny dialog, and lots of blood are the order of the day for this film. While director Bruno Mattei (hiding behind the pseudonym "Vincent Dawn" in the American release prints) may have gotten the inspiration for this trash from Romero's movies, he certainly displays no understanding of the humor, social insight, or skillful visual style that make Romero's films work. Released with a self-imposed X rating.

p, Sergio Corotona; d, Bruno Mattei; w, Claudio Fragasso, J.M. Cunilles; ph, John Cabrera (Telecolor); ed, Claudio Borroni; m, The Goblin.

(PR:O   MPAA:NR)

## NIGHTMARE zero

(1981) 97m 21st Century c

Baird Stafford *(George Tatum),* Sharon Smith *(Susan Temper),* C.J. Cooke *(C.J. Temper),* Mik Cribben *(Bob Rosen),* Kathleen Ferguson *(Barbara),* Danny Ronan *(Kathy the Babysitter),* John L. Watkins *(Man with Cigar).*

Given its earnest claims to Freudian psychological complexity, this pretentious gorefest (recipient of a self-imposed X rating), would be laughable if it wasn't so repulsive. George (Baird Stafford) is a New York mental patient who, as a kid, witnessed his father and his mistress participating in violent sexual acts and was so shaken that he later hacked them to pieces with an axe. Although he is put on antipsychotic drugs to calm his homicidal tendencies, they wear off and George kills a woman for her car and drives to Florida to terrorize his ex-wife (Sharon Smith) and her new family. The ads for this totally reprehensible film boasted gore effects by expert Tom Savini, who claimed he was no more than a consultant and threatened to sue, prompting the advertising to be altered pronto. In reality, the gore effects were handled by the inept Ed French (BREEDERS, 1986). The participation of director Romano Scavolini, a former adult filmmaker, ensures that this is a sleazebag production from start to finish.

p, John L. Watkins; d, Romano Scavolini; w, Romano Scavolini; ph, Gianni Fiore (Technicolor); ed, Robert T. Megginson; m, Jack Eric Williams.

(PR:O   MPAA:NR)

## NIGHTMARE CASTLE**½

(1965, It.) 90m Produzione Cinematografica Emmeci/AA bw (AMANTI D'OLTRETOMBA; AKA: FACELESS MONSTERS, THE; LOVERS FROM BEYOND THE TOMB; GB: NIGHT OF THE DOOMED)

Barbara Steele *(Muriel/Jenny),* Paul Miller *(Dr. Stephen Arrowsmith),* Helga Line *(Solange),* Lawrence Clift *(Dr. Derek Joyce),* Rik Battaglia *(David),* Giuseppe Addobbati *(Jonathan).*

The lovely Barbara Steele plays Muriel, the unfortunate wife of crazed scientist Dr. Arrowsmith (Paul Miller), who uses his wife and her lover (Rik Battaglia) in his experiments involving human blood and electricity. After electrocuting them, he drains their blood and injects it into his faithful, aging servant, Solange (Helga Line), who is suddenly rejuvenated and beautiful. He then places the hearts of Muriel and her lover in an urn. Shocked when he learns that Muriel's fortune was left to her mentally unbalanced half-sister, Jenny (also played by Steele, this time with blonde hair), Arrowsmith marries her and tries to drive her mad so he can collect the inheritance. Jenny's doctor, Derek Joyce (Lawrence Clift), however, refuses to declare her insane and begins to sense danger in the house. Arrowsmith, meanwhile, is preparing another blood solution to prolong Solange's rejuvenation. When Joyce discovers the hearts in the urn and unleashes the ghosts of Muriel and her lover, they take their revenge. While certainly not up to the level of Steele's work with the masterful Mario Bava, this is a worthwhile effort for her, and NIGHTMARE CASTLE finds its greatest success in showing the beautiful horror icon in as many extreme situations and personas as possible.

p, Carlo Caiano; d, Mario Caiano; w, Carlo Caiano, Fabio de Agostini; ph, Enzo Barboni; ed, Renato Cinquini; m, Ennio Morricone.

(PR:C   MPAA:NR)

## NIGHTMARE IN BLOOD**½

(1978) 90m Xeromega/PFE c

Kerwin Matthews *(Prince Zaroff),* Jerry Walter *(Malakai),* Dan Caldwell *(Prof. Seabrook),* Barrie Youngfellow *(Cindy*

O'Flaherty), John J. Cochran *(Scotty)*, Ray K. Goman *(B.B.)*, Hy Pyke *(Harris)*, Irving Israel *(Ben-Halik)*, Drew Eshelman *(Arlington)*, Morgan Upton *(George Wilson)*, Justin Bishop *(Dr. Unworth)*, Stan Ritchie *(Marsdon)*, Charles Murphy *(Flannery)*, Yvonne Young *(Barbara)*, Mike Hitchcock *(Lt. Driscoll)*, Erika Stanley *(Girl in Graveyard)*.

A delight for the convention-going horror movie fan, this film was cowritten and directed by John Stanley, who hosted the popular "Creature Feature" television show in San Francisco for six years and knows of what he speaks. The action takes place during a movie memorabilia convention in San Francisco. The guest of honor at the event is Malakai (Jerry Walter), a popular horror movie actor best known for his vampire roles. As it turns out, Malakai really is a vampire and his adoring fans are forced to play amateur Van Helsings to rid the convention of the bloodsucker. Not particularly well done, this really low-budget affair is nonetheless loaded with effective inside jokes and was made with a fondness for fans that is difficult to find in the majority of cynically produced horror product.

p, John Stanley, Kenn Davis; d, John Stanley; w, John Stanley, Kenn Davis; ph, Charles Rudnick (Techniscope, Technicolor); ed, Alfred Katzman.

(PR:O  MPAA:R)


## NIGHTMARE IN WAX*½

(1969) 95m A&E Film-Paragon-Productions Enterprises/ Crown c (AKA: CRIMES IN THE WAX MUSEUM)

Cameron Mitchell *(Vincent)*, Anne Helm *(Marie)*, Scott Brady *(Detective Haskell)*, Berry Kroeger *(Max Black)*, Victoria Carroll *(Carissa)*, Phillip Baird *(Tony Deane)*, Hollis Morrison *(Nick)*, John Cardos *(Sgt. Carver)*, James Forrest *(Alfred)*, The T-Bones, The Gazzari Dancers, Reni Martin.

This substandard rip-off of HOUSE OF WAX (itself a remake of MYSTERY OF THE WAX MUSEUM) features the ubiquitous Cameron Mitchell as Vincent, the badly scarred, psychotic owner of a wax museum who abducts the stars of a movie studio as revenge for his disfigurement (he was injured by the studio head during an argument over a pretty actress). Vincent, of course, doesn't just kill his victims and dump their bodies in the river; he injects them with a suspended animation formula, and then uses them as exhibits. Eventually this scheme is figured out (all the cops have to do is make the obviously unstatuesque actors blink or twitch, which they can clearly be seen doing, despite editing), and Vincent gets his comeuppance at the hands of his waxy victims. Amateurish in all respects, this one will probably interest only die-hard Mitchell fans. Filmed at Movieland Wax Museum in Los Angeles.

p, Herbert Sussan, Martin B. Cohen; d, Bud Townsend; w, Rex Carlton; ph, Glen Smith (Pathe); ed, Leonard Kwit.

(PR:C  MPAA:PG)


## NIGHTMARE ON ELM STREET, A*****

(1984) 91m New Line c

John Saxon *(Lt. Thompson)*, Ronee Blakley *(Marge Thompson)*, Heather Langenkamp *(Nancy Thompson)*, Amanda Wyss *(Tina Gray)*, Nick Corri *(Rod Lane)*, Johnny Depp *(Glen Lantz)*, Charles Fleischer *(Dr. King)*, Joseph Whipp *(Sgt. Parker)*, Robert Englund *(Freddy Krueger)*, Lin Shaye *(Teacher)*, Joe Unger *(Sgt. Garcia)*, Mimi Meyer-Craven *(Nurse)*, Jack Shea *(Minister)*, Edward Call *(Mr. Lantz)*, Sandy Lipton *(Mrs. Lantz)*, David Andrews *(Foreman)*, Jeffrey Levine *(Coroner)*, Donna Woodrum *(Tina's Mom)*, Shashawnee Hall, Carol Pritikin, Brian Reise *(Cops)*, Jason Adam, Don Hannah *(Surfers)*, Leslie Hoffman *(Hallguard)*, Paul Grenier *(Tina's Mom's Boyfriend)*.

"One, two; Freddy's comin' for you / Three, four; better lock your door / Five, six; grab your crucifix / Seven, eight; gonna stay up late / Nine, ten; never sleep again." A NIGHTMARE ON ELM STREET, one of the most intelligent and terrifying horror films of the 1980s, begins and ends with this haunting children's song. This was the film that introduced the world—the real world and the dream world—to Freddy Krueger, the horribly scarred man with the ragged slouch hat, dirty red and green striped sweater, and metal gloves with knives at the tips. Freddy (Robert Englund), a genius of a monster who exists in his victims' dreams and preys on them in the vulnerability of sleep, has returned to the town where, living as a child-killer years before, he was burnt alive by locals who took the law into their own hands. Now he's back to take revenge on their kids. In an era in which the horror film has become little more than a mindless exercise in gratuitous high-tech bloodletting, A NIGHTMARE ON ELM STREET (like most of Wes Craven's films) has brought some hope to those concerned about the fate of the genre. The film intelligently probes into the audience's terror of nightmares and combines them with another horrific element, the very real fear of killers in one's own neighborhood. The teenagers in the film, who are paying for the sins of their parents, are not simply fodder for the special-effects crew, but have distinct personalities and are independent and intelligent. The initial success of the film was based on the audience's insecurity: we are never sure whether the characters are dreaming, because the line between nightmare and reality is blurred, and, as a result, the terror is almost nonstop. The success of the sequels, while still based in the dream-versus-reality premise, has become increasingly dependent on the heroic pose of Freddy Krueger, played with energy and humor by Robert Englund.

p, Robert Shaye, Sara Risher; d, Wes Craven; w, Wes Craven; ph, Jacques Haitkin (DeLuxe color); ed, Rick Shaine; m, Charles Bernstein.

(PR:O  MPAA:R)


## NIGHTMARE ON ELM STREET PART 2: FREDDY'S REVENGE, A**½

(1985) 85m Heron-Smart Egg/New Line c

Mark Patton *(Jesse Walsh)*, Kim Myers *(Lisa Poletti)*, Robert Rusler *(Grady)*, Clu Gulager *(Mr. Walsh)*, Hope

Lange *(Mrs.Walsh)*, Marshall Bell *(Coach Schneider)*, Melinda Fee *(Mrs.Poletti)*, Tom McFadden *(Mr. Poletti)*, Sydney Walsh *(Kerry)*, Hart Sprager *(Teacher)*, Steve Eastin *(Policeman)*, Christie Clark *(Angela)*, Robert Englund *(Freddy Krueger)*.

This is the surprisingly good first sequel to Wes Craven's terrifying horror film of 1984, A NIGHTMARE ON ELM STREET. Directed by Jack Sholder, the story continues five years after the evil spirit of neighborhood child-murderer Freddy Krueger (Robert Englund)—who had been invading the dreams of the community's teenagers and killing them—was defeated by a clever young woman. Now the Walsh family has moved into the cursed house on Elm Street, and their teenage son, Jesse (Mark Patton), begins having horrible nightmares featuring Freddy. A worthy successor to the original film, NIGHTMARE PART 2 is surprisingly optimistic and moral. The power of love and kindness wins out over evil and violence—something not often seen in the new cycle of horror films. The effects in the film are stunning, never halting the flow of the narrative to let the audience gawk at the high-tech work involved, and the young cast give solid performances (though it takes some time to get over Kim Myers' strong resemblance to Meryl Streep). Though not as thought-provoking and stylish as its predecessor, A NIGHTMARE ON ELM STREET PART 2 is much better than expected.

p, Robert Shaye, Sara Risher; d, Jack Sholder; w, David Chaskin; ph, Jacques Haitkin (DeLuxe Color, prints by Technicolor); ed, Arline Garson, Bob Brady; m, Christopher Young.

**(PR:O MPAA:R)**

## NIGHTMARE ON ELM STREET 3: DREAM WARRIORS, A***

(1987) 96m New Line-Heron-Smart Egg/New Line c

Heather Langenkamp *(Nancy Thompson)*, Patricia Arquette *(Kristen Parker)*, Larry Fishburne *(Max)*, Priscilla Pointer *(Dr. Elizabeth Simms)*, Craig Wasson *(Dr. Neil Goldman)*, Brooke Bundy *(Elaine Parker)*, Rodney Eastman *(Joey)*, Bradley Gregg *(Phillip)*, Ira Heiden *(Will)*, Ken Sagoes *(Kincaid)*, Penelope Sudrow *(Jennifer)*, Jennifer Rubin *(Taryn)*, Clayton Landey *(Lorenzo, Orderly)*, Nan Martin *(Nun)*, Stacey Alden *(Marcie)*, Kristin Clayton *(Little Girl)*, Sally Piper, Rozlyn Sorrell *(Nurses)*, James Carroll *(Neurosurgeon)*, Jack Shea *(Priest at Funeral)*, Michael Rougas *(Priest in Church)*, Robert Englund *(Freddy Krueger)*, John Saxon *(Lt. John Thompson)*, Dick Cavett, Zsa Zsa Gabor *(Themselves)*.

This third chapter of the phenomenally successful horror series marks the return of the original's director, Wes Craven (he had nothing to do with PART II). Craven cowrote Part III's script and served as associate producer, and, though he didn't direct, his influence is quite apparent. The film takes place in a small town, which is experiencing a rash of teenage suicides. Kristen Parker (Patricia Arquette, younger sister of Rosanna), a teenager plagued by horrible nightmares, tries to slash her wrists and is admitted to a psychiatric hospital, where she is put under the care of

Dr. Goldman (Craig Wasson), a young doctor who specializes in treating disturbed teenagers, especially teens who refuse to sleep at night for fear of their nightmares. What is odd is that the teens insist that the same nightmarish figure appears in all their dreams—Freddy Krueger, "the bastard son of a hundred maniacs," who preys on his victims' deepest fears. Produced on a mere $4.5 million budget, NIGHTMARE 3 grossed $8.8 million on its opening weekend, one of the most successful openings in independent distribution history. The film went on to take in more than $40 million, making New Line Cinema one of the most successful independent production companies in Hollywood. Part of this success is no doubt due to the cult status attained by the character of Freddy Krueger. While Jason, of the FRIDAY THE 13TH movies, proved popular, his character is merely a lunk in a hockey mask with no personality. Freddy, however, is an energetic, clever killer with a warped sense of humor who seems to really enjoy tormenting teenagers. As played by the classically trained Robert Englund, Freddy is a vital killer who brings a sense of creepy fun to his demented work—moviegoers actually *like* the guy. The nightmares themselves are another reason for the series' success. Seldom have films explored the nightmare world with such effect, style, and panache. In NIGHTMARE 3, the wizardly special-effects team created a variety of bizarre images, including a teen who is literally tongue-tied to his bed, a television that turns into Freddy, Freddy's transformation into a marionette, and a huge Freddy head that tries to swallow Kristen whole. Unfortunately, these images have become the set pieces of the series, with increasingly less attention paid to the scenes that precede and follow them.

p, Robert Shaye, Sara Risher; d, Chuck Russell; w, Wes Craven, Bruce Wagner, Chuck Russell, Frank Darabont (based on a story by Wes Craven, Bruce Wagner and characters created by Wes Craven); ph, Roy Wagner (Deluxe Color); ed, Terry Stokes, Chuck Weiss; m, Angelo Badalamenti.

**(PR:O MPAA:R)**

## NIGHTMARE ON ELM STREET 4: THE DREAM MASTER, A***

(1988) 93m New Line-Heron-Smart Egg/New Line c

Robert Englund *(Freddy Krueger)*, Rodney Eastman *(Joey)*, Danny Hassel *(Danny)*, Andras Jones *(Rick)*, Tuesday Knight *(Kristen)*, Toy Newkirk *(Sheila)*, Ken Sagoes *(Kincaid)*, Brooke Theiss *(Debbie)*, Lisa Wilcox *(Alice)*, Brooke Bundy *(Kristen's Mother)*, Jeffrey Levine *(Paramedic)*, Nicolas Mele *(Johnson)*, Hope Marie Carlton *(Waterbed Bunny)*.

Although this latest installment in the series broke the box office record set by the previous "Nightmare" entry ($12,833,403 the first three days—the most successful opening weekend of any independently released film), it seems that with Part 4, Freddy Krueger has just about run out of gas. Getting further and further away from creator Wes Craven's original concept, the series has declined into a plotless series of special-effects set pieces featuring Freddy slicing and dicing a variety of teenagers in their dreams. What the films lack in narrative, however, they make up for with pure cinematic panache, and the latest installment is no exception; Finnish director Renny Harlin (PRISON) contributes what may be the best-directed "Nightmare" film since Craven's. Picking up where NIGHTMARE 3 left off, we see the three surviving teenage Dream Warriors suddenly being plagued in their dreams by the supposedly dead and buried Freddy (Robert Englund), who is now moving into new territory and invading the dreams of mousy teen Alice (Lisa Wilcox). What the child-killer doesn't anticipate, however, is that Alice begins taking on the strongest characteristics of her friends and soon becomes a complete Dream Warrior blessed with impressive athletic prowess, physical strength, and intelligence. In the original A NIGHTMARE ON ELM STREET, Freddy Krueger was the embodiment of pure evil. Since then, his appearance and behavior have been softened to make him more of a cartoon figure—still very lethal, but less threatening, more playful. What was once the ultimate, unforgiving horror has now become the real hero of the series, the guy teens love to hate. Which brings us to the basic problem of the "Nightmare" series: it has become an extremely lucrative, money-making industry and as such is the glue that holds New Line Cinema together. Therefore, it must become more middle-of-the-road, tamer, more able to reach across genre barriers and attract people who don't necessarily like horror films. And that is why, with each entry, the films become more removed from their source. Freddy just isn't scary anymore.

p, Robert Shaye, Rachel Talalay; d, Renny Harlin; w, Scott Pierce, Brian Helgeland (based on a story by William Kotzwinkle, Brian Helgeland); ph, Steven Fierberg; ed, Michael N. Knue, Chuck Weiss; m, Craig Safan.

(PR:O    MPAA:R)

## NIGHTMARE WEEKEND zero

(1986, Brit./U.S./Fr.) 85m Vision Communications-English-G.I.G.-Les Films des Lions/Troma c

Debbie Laster *(Julie Clingstone)*, Dale Midkiff *(Ken)*, Debra Hunter *(Jessica Brake)*, Lori Lewis *(Annie)*, Preston Maybank *(Bob)*, Wellington Meffert *(Edward Brake)*, Kim Dossin *(Mary-Rose)*, Andrea Thompson *(Linda)*, Kimberly Stahl *(Pamela)*, Bruce Morton *(Tony)*, Karen Mayo *(Sue)*, Nick James *(Gary)*, Robert Burke *(Dave)*, Scott Proctor *(Ralph)*, John Sandford *(Harry)*, Joan Krosche *(Linda's Mother)*, Jason *(Doberman)*, Barbara Lee *(James Winn)*, Lori Strup *(Karl Kunz)*, Marc Pacheco *(Jack Adams)*, Tarantula *(Himself)*, George *(George)*, Dean Gates, Mark Gotlieb *(Gas Pump Attendants)*.

Genius scientist Edward Brake (Wellington Meffert) has invented a device that can—among its other capabilities—change any object into a silver attack sphere that shoots down a person's throat and transforms him into a mindless, computer-controlled zombie. The benign uses Brake envisions for the invention are perverted when his evil but beautiful assistant, Julie (Debbie Laster), tests it on a trio of beautiful college coeds who have been invited to the house for the weekend. When some boys they picked up at a bar show up, they, too, are turned into "neuropaths,"

as is a maid who's afraid of spiders. One day, while roller-skating, Jessica (Debra Hunter), Brake's nubile daughter, glides into the same bar where the coeds picked up the unlucky guys and falls in love with Ken (Dale Midkiff), who is in cahoots with Julie, and to whom Jessica loses her virginity. Not surprisingly, the vengeful Julie then turns practically everyone into a neuropath and sends them after Jessica. Watching this sleazy, unscary, pseudo-softcore stab at filmmaking is both a confusing and excruciating experience. The characters are indistinguishable, the nudity gratuitous and ample, and the shocks few and feeble. Moreover, the editing is incomprehensible, and the action limited to just three locations, though it seems like fewer. Simply put, NIGHTMARE WEEKEND is a waste of time, yours and the filmmakers'.

p, Bachoo Sen; d, Henry Sala; w, George Faget-Benard; ph, Denis Gheerbrant, Bob Baldwin (Eastmancolor); ed, David Gilbert; m, Martin Kershaw.

(PR:O    MPAA:R)

## NIGHTMARES**

(1983) 99m UNIV c

Cristina Raines *(Wife)*, Joe Lambie *(Husband)*, Anthony James *(Clerk)*, Claire Nono *(Newswoman)*, Raleigh Bond *(Neighbor)*, Robert Phelps *(Newsman)*, Dixie Lynn Royce *(Little Girl)*, Lee James Jude *(Glazier)*, Emilio Estevez *(J.J.)*, Mariclare Costello *(Mrs. Cooney)*, Louis Giambalvo *(Cooney)*, Moon Zappa *(Pamela)*, Billy Jacoby *(Zock)*, Joshua Grenrock *(Willie)*, Gary Cervantes *(Mazenza)*, C. Stewart Burns *(Root)*, Andre Diaz *(Pedro)*, Rachel Goslins *(Phyllis)*, Joel Holman *(Z-Man)*, Christopher Bubetz *(Jeffrey)*, Rudy Negretl *(Emiliano)*, James Tolkan *(Bishop's Voice)*, Lance Henriksen *(MacLeod)*, Tony Plana *(Del Amo)*, Timothy Scott *(Sheriff)*, Robin Gammell *(Bishop)*, Rose Marie Campos *(Mother)*, Richard Masur *(Steven)*, Veronica Cartwright *(Claire)*, Bridgette Andersen *(Brooke)*, Albert Hague *(Mel)*, Howard F. Flynn *(Announcer)*.

This quartet of scary tales is, like any compilation film, a mixed bag. Two stories work and two don't. One of those that does, "Bishop of Battle," features Emilio Estevez as a teenager who becomes so good at a video game that he actually becomes part of the game itself. The other successful story, "Night of the Rat," starring Richard Masur and Veronica Cartwright, is a strange bit of black humor about a suburban couple who try to fight off a pony-sized rat that has invaded their home fresh from its stint in the 17th century. The other stories, "Terror in Topanga" and "The Benediction," are a simplistic mad slasher tale and a "Duel"-inspired fantasy, respectively, showing little imagination or wit. Produced by Christopher Crowe, who would go on to direct the misfired Vietnam murder mystery OFF LIMITS (1988), and directed by veteran helmsman Joseph Sargent (THE FORBIN PROJECT, 1970), this was never given much of a release in either Britain or US and has mostly been seen on home video.

p, Christopher Crowe; d, Joseph Sargent; w, Christopher Crowe, Jeffrey Bloom; ph, Mario DiLeo, Gerald Perry

Finnerman (Panavision, Technicolor); ed, Rod Stephens, Michael Brown; m, Craig Safan.

(PR:C MPAA:PG)

## NIGHTWING*

(1979) 103m COL c

Nick Mancuso (Youngman Duran), David Warner (Phillip Payne), Kathryn Harrold (Anne Dillon), Stephen Macht (Walker Chee), Strother Martin (Selwyn), George Clutesi (Abner Tasupi), Ben Piazza (Roger Piggott), Donald Hotton (John Franklin), Charles Hallahan (Henry), Judith Novgrod (Judy), Alice Hirson (Claire Franklin), Pat Corley (Vet), Charlie Bird (Beejay), Danny Zapien (Joe), Peter Prouse (Doctor), Jose Toledo (Harold), Richard Romancito (Ben), Flavio Martinez III (Isla Lalama), Virginia P. Maney, Wade Stevens, Robert Dunbar.

What do you get when you cross THE BIRDS with JAWS, adding just a touch of WILLARD? Right. The influence of the three is obvious in this boring effort in which a group of rabid bats goes on the rampage on a New Mexico Indian reservation. Payne (David Warner) is the aptly named, surly, ever-wisecracking scientist who's tracking the flying rodents in an effort to avenge the death of his father, who was eaten by them. Duran (Nick Mancuso) is a reservation cop who doesn't believe the tribal lore that explains the bats' strange behavior as part of some sort of spiritual revenge. Actor George Clutesi, fresh from his role as an native American seer in the equally insipid PROPHECY, once more finds himself in a similar part. All of the attempts to make this nonsense scary are ultimately defeated by cheesy special effects and gaping logic holes in the script penned by Bud Shrake, Steve Shagan (SAVE THE TIGER) and Martin Cruz Smith (on whose novel the film is based). The location shooting in the American Southwest is nicely photographed, though poorly used. Arthur Hiller (LOVE STORY; MAN OF LA MANCHA; TEACHERS) is one of the worst directors around under normal circumstances and has no business trying to make a horror film.

p, Martin Ransohoff; d, Arthur Hiller; w, Steve Shagan, Bud Shrake, Martin Cruz Smith (based on the novel by Martin Cruz Smith); ph, Charles Rosher (Metrocolor); ed, John C. Howard; m, Henry Mancini.

(PR:C MPAA:PG)

## NINTH CONFIGURATION, THE***½

(1980) 105m WB c (AKA: TWINKLE, TWINKLE, KILLER KANE)

Stacy Keach (Col. Kane), Scott Wilson (Capt. Cutshaw), Jason Miller (Lt. Reno), Ed Flanders (Col. Fell), Neville Brand (Groper), George Di Cenzo (Capt. Fairbanks), Moses Gunn (Maj. Nammack), Robert Loggia (Lt. Bennish), Joe Spinell (Spinell), Alejandro Rey (Lt. Gomez), Tom Atkins (Sgt. Krebs), Steve Sandor (1st Cyclist), Richard Lynch (2nd Cyclist).

William Peter Blatty, best known as author of THE EXORCIST makes his debut as producer, director, and screenwriter with this adaptation of his own novel. Colonel Kane (Stacy Keach), an Army psychiatrist assigned to a remote castle-cum-military asylum in the Pacific Northwest, encourages his patients to enact their fantasies as part of their therapy, but he has his own reasons for telling them to do so. The dialog is really weird and often incomprehensible in this very strange, personal film, but Blatty has a good sense of the absurd, and handles the direction well, making sure that things are never quite what they seem to bo. The supporting cast is excellent, especially Scott Wilson as an astronaut who tipped out on the launching pad and aborted his mission. Offbeat, visionary, and challenging, THE NINTH CONFIGURATION was never understood by the studio, which released several different versions of varying length: 140 minutes, 105 minutes, 99 minutes, 104 minutes, or 118 minutes. The last was the cut Blatty approved and, luckily, is available on videocassette.

p, William Peter Blatty; d, William Peter Blatty; w, William Peter Blatty (based on the novel by Blatty); ph, Gerry Fisher; ed, T. Battle Davis, Peter Lee-Thompson, Robert Silvi; m, Barry De Vorzon.

(PR:O MPAA:R)

## NOCTURNA zero

(1979) 85m Compass International c (AKA: NOCTURNA, GRANDDAUGHTER OF DRACULA)

Nai Bonet (Nocturna), John Carradine (Count Dracula), Yvonne De Carlo (Jugulia), Tony Hamilton (Jimmy), Brother Theodore (Theodore), Sy Richardson (RH Factor), Ivery Bell, Michael Harrison, Norris Harris, William H. Jones, Jr. (The Moment of Truth), Adam Keefe (BSA President), Monica Tidwell (Brenda), Tony Sanchez (Victim), Thomas Ryan (Policeman), Ron Toler (Taxi Driver), Pierre Epstein (John), Albert M. Ottenheimer (Dr. Bernstein), John Blyth Barrymore, Toby Handman, Angelo Vignari, Shelly Wyant (BSA Members), Frank Irizarry (DiscJockey), Irwin Keyes, Marcus Anthony (Transylvania Characters), Al Sapienza, Jerry Sroka, A.C. Weary (Musicians).

Nai Bonet, a former belly dancer who traded in her navel diamond for some cheap plastic fangs, plays Nocturna, the granddaughter of the famous Count Dracula (John Carradine, at an all-time low), in this horror comedy which she executive produced. Tired of the old man's outdated ways, Nocturna becomes involved with a disco musician (Tony Hamilton) and runs away to Manhattan where she enlists the support of one of her grandfather's oldest lovers, Jugulia (Yvonne De Carlo), who is laid out in a crypt beneath the Brooklyn Bridge. Dracula follows and puts a curse on all those involved, but Jugulia's got a soft spot for the crazy kids and she subverts Drac's authority. This incredibly cheap-looking and inept disco horror-comedy was made and released the same year as the similar—and much better—LOVE AT FIRST BITE. Fans of TV's "Late Night" will note the presence of Letterman regular Brother Theodore.

p, Vernon Becker; d, Harry Tampa; w, Harry Tampa; ph, Mac Ahlberg (Metrocolor); ed, Ian Maitland.

(PR:O MPAA:R)

## NOMADS**½

(1985) 95m Cinema 7/PSO c

Pierce Brosnan *(Pommier)*, Lesley-Anne Down *(Dr. Flax)*, AnnaMaria Montecelli *(Niki)*, Adam Ant *("Number One")*, Hector Mercado *(Ponytail)*, Josie Cotton *(Silver Ring)*, Mary Woronov *(Dancing Mary)*, Frank Doubleday *(Razor)*, Jeannie Elias *(Cassie)*, Paul Anselmo, Michael Gregory *(Cops in Apartment)*, Alan Autry *(Olds)*, Frances Bay *(Bertrill)*, Josee Beaudry, Freddie Duke, Anita Jesse, Gayle Vance, Helen Vick *(Nurses)*, Dana Chelette *(Orderly)*, Nina Foch *(Real Estate Agent)*, Junero Jennings *(Gas Station Attendant)*, Anthan Karras *(Apartment Manager)*, Reed Morgan *(Cop)*, Elizabeth Russell *(Cathy)*, Kario Salem *(Schacter)*, J.J. Saunders *(Cort)*, John Vidor *(Kid in Park)*, Tim Wallace *(Intern)*.

This supernatural thriller tries hard to be different, but winds up collapsing under the effort. Set in modern-day Los Angeles, the film opens as Dr. Flax (Lesley-Anne Down) is called in to deal with an emergency patient who was picked up wandering the streets. The man, Pommier (Pierce Brosnan), babbles in French and struggles violently with the nurses and orderlies. When Flax tries to calm him, he bites her, whispers something in French in her ear, and suddenly dies. Police discover that Pommier was a French anthropologist who had worked all over the world, studying the habits of nomadic tribes. Flax begins having visions of Pommier, and sees the events leading up to his death—events that involve a group of punk rockers (including Adam Ant, Josie Cotton, and Mary Woronov) who are actually the evil spirits of ancient nomads. Though handled with flair by first-time helmer John McTiernan (who later directed PREDATOR and DIE HARD), NOMADS' complicated structure doesn't really work. Pommier and his story are much more interesting than Flax, whose character keeps annoyingly interrupting the narrative flow to stare bug-eyed around the room as she senses what Pommier experienced. Though the concept of urban nomads is a fascinating one, the film really never exploits our interest in these strange creatures, and aside from one night's rather mundane wanderings nothing regarding their existence in modern-day America is explored. Kathryn Bigelow's 1987 NEAR DARK addresses some of the same ideas and themes with much more success.

p, Elliott Kastner; d, John McTiernan; w, John McTiernan; ph, Stephen Ramsey (Eastmancolor); ed, Michael John Bateman; m, Bill Conti, Ted Nugent.

**(PR:O   MPAA:R)**

## NOSFERATU, THE VAMPIRE*****

(1922, Ger.) 63m Prana Co. bw (DIE ZWOELFTE STUNDE; EINE NACHT DES GRAUENS; NOSFERATU—EINE SYMPHONIE DES GRAUENS; AKA: TERROR OF DRACULA; DRACULA; TWELFTH HOUR, THE; NOSFERATU—A SYMPHONY OF TERROR; NOSFERATU—A SYMPHONY OF HORROR)

Max Schreck *(Graf Orlok, Nosferatu)*, Alexander Granach *(Knock)*, Gustav von Wangenheim *(Hutter)*, Greta Schroeder *(Ellen)*, G.H. Schnell *(Harding)*, Ruth Landshoff

*(Annie)*, John Gottowt *(Prof. Bulwer)*, Gustav Botz *(Prof. Sievers)*, Max Nemetz *(Captain of the "Demeter")*, Wolfgang Heinz, Albert Venohr *(Seamen)*, Guido Herzfeld *(Innkeeper)*, Hardy von Francois *(Doctor)*.

The first "Dracula" (the title was changed to avoid copyright problems) is a wonderfully atmospheric work, made more eerie by virtue of its authentic location shooting. Hutter (Gustav von Wangenheim), a real estate clerk in the city of Bremen, must leave his bride to conduct a little business in the distant Carpathian mountains with an "eccentric" client, Graf Orlok (Max Schreck). The journey is filled with ominous warnings, especially the fact that the mysterious coach that finally delivers the young man to the Graf's castle is shot by director F.W. Murnau in fast motion and on negative stock. At the castle, Murnau's splendid sense of composition establishes a mood of creepy neo-reality guaranteed to make the skin of the most devoted horror fan crawl. After a few evenings of blood-letting, the weakened but finally wise Hutter manages to escape Nosferatu's clutches. But the vampire follows him home, bringing terror and pestilence with him. Murnau's visualization of the Dracula saga is vastly different from the 1931 Tod Browning-Bela Lugosi adaptation, and the disconcerting, almost ratlike appearance of the appropriately named Schreck (whose surname is also the German word for "fright") greatly enhances the film's considerable present-day power.

d, F.W. Murnau; w, Henrik Galeen (based on the novel *Dracula* by Bram Stoker); ph, Fritz Arno Wagner.

**(PR:C   MPAA:NR)**

## NOSFERATU, THE VAMPIRE***½

(1979, Fr./Ger.) 107m FOX c (NOSFERATU, PHANTOM DER NACHT; AKA: NOSFERATU, THE VAMPYRE)

Klaus Kinski *(Count Dracula)*, Isabelle Adjani *(Lucy Harker)*, Bruno Ganz *(Jonathan Harker)*, Roland Topor *(Renfield)*, Walter Ladengast *(Dr. Van Helsing)*, Dan Van Husen *(Warden)*, Jan Groth *(Harbormaster)*, Carsten Bodinus *(Schrader)*, Martje Grohmann *(Mina)*, Ryk De Gooyer *(Town Official)*, Clemens Scheitz *(Town Employee)*, Lo Van Hartingsveld *(Councilman)*, Tim Beekman *(Coffinbearer)*, Jacques Dufilho *(Captain)*, Beverly Walker *(Nun)*.

After capturing the attention of the American critics and public with ambitious, unique, and powerful films, German director Werner Herzog remade what he considers to be the most visionary and important of all German films, F.W. Murnau's silent masterpiece of 1922, NOSFERATU. Held together by the sheer power of Klaus Kinski's performance as the vampire, NOSFERATU, THE VAMPIRE evokes several scenes (practically shot-for-shot) from the Murnau classic while slightly altering some of the original's thematics. In Murnau's film, the vampire is pure evil invading a small German community (Herzog feels that the 1922 film predicted the rise of Naziism in Germany). Herzog's vampire is much more sympathetic. An outcast from society (as are all of Herzog's protagonists), Kinski's Nosferatu longs for contact, acceptance, and even love from the humans who fear and revile him. Sadly, his curse and death's-head appearance forever prevent this. The vampire's undead state and need for blood seem to be presented as a horrible, irreversible *disease*, rather than an inherently evil harbinger of hell. While this isn't exactly a fresh innovation in the development of the horror film (Tod Browning's DRACULA, 1931, starring Bela Lugosi, had moments of pathos, as does George Romero's MARTIN, 1978), Herzog and Kinski succeed here because they convey a sense of pity for a creature so visually repulsive it's hard to look at him. As with most of Herzog's films, the story behind the production is almost more interesting than the film itself. Unable to shoot in Bremen, as Murnau did in 1922, Herzog had to settle for the Dutch town of Delft. Still bitter over the occupation by the Nazis during WW II, the citizens of Delft were less than enthusiastic about welcoming this small army of German filmmakers into their town. When Herzog announced his plan to release 11,000 rats into the streets of Delft for the scene in which Nosferatu arrives (the director wanted grey rats, but ended up with white ones, so he had his crew paint them grey), the Delft *burgermeister* categorically refused and told the apparently insane German that his town had just spent months clearing the canals of their own home-grown rats, and had little enthusiasm for reinfesting the area with laboratory rats from Hungary. Nonplussed, Herzog moved his rats to a more accommodating city, Schiedam, where he was allowed to shoot, albeit on a smaller scale. In German with English subtitles.

p, Werner Herzog; d, Werner Herzog; w, Werner Herzog (based on the novel *Dracula* by Bram Stoker and the film script NOSFERATU by Henrik Galeen); ph, Jorg Schmidt-Reitwein (Eastmancolor); ed, Beate Mainka-Jellinghaus; m, Popol Vuh, Florian Fricke, Richard Wagner, Charles Gounod.

**(PR:C-O  MPAA:PG)**

## NUTTY PROFESSOR, THE***½

(1963) 107m PAR c

Jerry Lewis *(Prof. Julius Ferris Kelp/Buddy Love)*, Stella Stevens *(Stella Purdy)*, Del Moore *(Dr. Hamius R. Warfield)*, Kathleen Freeman *(Millie Lemmon)*, Ned Flory, Skip Ward, Norman Alden *(Football Players)*, Howard Morris *(Father Kelp)*, Elvia Allman *(Mother Kelp)*, Milton Frome *(Dr. Leevee)*, Buddy Lester *(Bartender)*, Marvin Kaplan *(English Boy)*, David Landfield, Celeste Yarnall, Francine York, Julie Parrish, Henry Gibson *(College Students)*, Dave Willock *(Bartender)*, Doodles Weaver *(Rube)*, Mushy Callahan *(Cab Driver)*, Gavin Gordon *(Salesman Clothier)*, Joe Forte *(Faculty Member)*, Terry Higgins *(Cigarette Girl)*, Murray Alper *(Judo Instructor)*, Gary Lewis *(Boy)*, Les Brown and His Band of Renown.

Jerry Lewis' best film stars the often moronic comic as Julius F. Kelp, a bumbling professor of chemistry at a small college who falls hopelessly in love with one of his more popular students, Stella Purdy (Stella Stevens). Seeking to improve his looks, Kelp whips up a chemical potion and is transformed into an overbearing and obnoxious but dashing singer who calls himself Buddy Love. Though totally

conceited, Buddy Love (Lewis in a dual role) succeeds in winning over Stella. Unfortunately, his formula has a way of wearing off at the wrong times. Although only tangentially related to horror films, THE NUTTY PROFESSOR can be seen as a strange companion piece to the *Dr. Jekyll and Mr. Hyde* films—in which the dark, menacing side of an otherwise harmless character seeps through to the forefront. Much has been made of Buddy Love's resemblance to Lewis' former partner, Dean Martin, but the person Love really resembles is the pompous, self-important, and bitter Jerry Lewis of talk shows and telethons.

p, Jerry Lewis, Ernest D. Glucksman; d, Jerry Lewis; w, Jerry Lewis, Bill Richmond (based on a story by Lewis); ph, W. Wallace Kelley (Technicolor); ed, John Woodcock; m, Walter Scharf.

**(PR:A  MPAA:NR)**

## OBLONG BOX, THE***

(1969, Brit.) 91m AIP c (AKA: EDGAR ALLEN POE'S "THE OBLONG BOX")

Vincent Price *(Julian Markham)*, Christopher Lee *(Dr. Neuhartt)*, Alistair Williamson *(Sir Edward Markham)*, Hilary Dwyer *(Elizabeth Markham)*, Peter Arne *(Samuel Trench)*, Harry Baird *(N. Galo)*, Carl Rigg *(Mark Norton)*, Maxwell Shaw *(Tom Hackett)*, Michael Balfour *(Ruddock)*, Godfrey James *(Weller)*, Rupert Davies *(Joshua Kemp)*, Sally Geeson *(Sally Baxter)*, Ivor Dean *(Hawthorne)*, Uta Levka, James Mellor, Danny Daniels, John Barrie, Hira Talfrey, John Wentworth, Betty Woolfe, Martin Terry, Anne Clune, Jackie Noble, Tara Fernando, Tony Thawton, Anthony Bailey, Richard Cornish, Colin Jeavons, Andreas Maladrinos.

After being captured by natives and horribly mutilated in Africa, Sir Edward Markham (Alistair Williamson) goes mad, forcing his brother, Julian (Vincent Price), to keep him locked in an upstairs room upon their return to England. Desperate to escape, Edward concocts a scheme to that end. With the help of an African witch doctor and several other confederates, Edward takes a pill whose effects simulate death. Once the coffin is removed from the house, his cohorts will release him. Unfortunately, Edward's partners double-cross him and allow him to be buried alive. Luckily, a pair of grave-robbers who supply fresh corpses for anatomist Dr. Neuhartt (Christopher Lee), dig Edward up and deliver him to the doctor, and when Edward awakens, he blackmails the grave-robbing Neuhartt into giving him sanctuary. Donning a cloth crimson mask, the insane Edward prowls the area by night, cutting the throats of those who betrayed him. This was to have been directed by Michael Reeves (THE CONQUEROR WORM), who began production, but then died of a barbiturate overdose. Gordon Hessler stepped in, and while one can only wonder what Reeves would have done with the material, the film remains a fairly effective chiller. Although purportedly based on Poe's "The Premature Burial," the film's plot is much closer to Rudyard Kipling's short story "The Mark of the Beast," with the evil specter of British colonialism driving the narrative. Price and Lee are billed prominently, but the film really belongs to Williamson, who cuts a rather menacing figure with his crimson mask. Indeed, the film's biggest disappointment is the much-anticipated PHANTOM OF THE OPERA-like unmasking scene, which reveals Sir Edward's scarcely horrible visage. Lee later claimed he took the small supporting role merely for the opportunity to work with Price. Unfortunately, they have only one fleeting scene together, played out as Lee lies on the floor with his throat cut.

p, Gordon Hessler; d, Gordon Hessler; w, Lawrence Huntingdon, Christopher Wicking (based on the story by Edgar Allan Poe); ph, John Coquillon (Berkey Pathe Color); ed, Max Benedict; m, Harry Robinson.

**(PR:C   MPAA:M)**

## OCTAMAN zero

(1971) 90m Filmers Guild c (AKA: OCTOMAN)

Kerwin Matthews, Pier Angeli, Jeff Morrow, Jerry Guardino, Norman Fields, Robert Warner, David Essex.

This laughable film was directed by Harry Essex, who borrowed heavily from his own screenplay for THE CREATURE FROM THE BLACK LAGOON, written nearly 20 years before. Brave-but-stupid explorers Kerwin Matthews, Pier Angeli, and company venture into the wilds of Mexico, where they discover a rather silly looking monster-octopus that lumbers about the terra firma on two legs like a man. Not only is the Octaman malformed, he possesses only six tentacles as opposed to the usual eight (a budgetary consideration makeup man Rick Baker was forced to contend with), which makes the creature less than terrifying. The usual monster-wreaks-havoc-on-the-expedition scenes are filmed with little skill or imagination. Angeli, the former James Dean flame, came out of semiretirement to star in this one, but died tragically from a barbiturate overdose while the film was still in production.

p, Michael Kraike; d, Harry Essex; w, Lawrence Morse; ph, Robert Caramico; m, Post Production Associates.

**(PR:O   MPAA:NR)**

## OF UNKNOWN ORIGIN**½

(1983, Can.) 88m David-Nesis-CFDC/WB c

Peter Weller *(Bart),* Jennifer Dale *(Lorrie),* Lawrence Dane *(Eliot),* Kenneth Welsh *(James),* Louis Del Grande *(Clete),* Shannon Tweed *(Meg),* Keith Knight *(Salesman),* Maury Chaykin *(Dan),* Leif Anderson *(Peter),* Jimmy Tapp *(Meg's Father),* Gayle Garfinkle *(Janis),* Earl Pennington *(Thompson),* Bronwen Mantel *(Florence),* Monik Nantel *(Secretary),* Jacklin Webb *(News Vendor).*

A surprisingly effective little man vs. vermin story, OF UNKNOWN ORIGIN pits a successful advertising executive named Bart (Peter Weller) against a super-intelligent fe-

male rat—females being the more vicious rat gender—in his newly renovated Manhattan townhouse. After his wife and son go off on vacation, Weller is left home alone to do battle with the huge sewer rat that has invaded his home. The battle grows into a full-fledged obsession, with Bart coming home from work each night looking forward to another evening of search-and-destroy tactics. Directed with flair by George Pan Cosmatos (RAMBO) and filled with sly references to *Moby Dick* and *The Old Man and the Sea,* this film is a successful blend of terror and humor, played with some real fervor by Weller. It's also better than any of the Cosmatos-Sylvester Stallone team-ups.

p, Claude Heroux; d, George Pan Cosmatos; w, Brian Taggert (based on the novel *The Visitor* by Chauncey G. Parker III); ph, Rene Verzier; ed, Robert Silvi; m, Ken Wannberg.

**(PR:O   MPAA:R)**

## OFFSPRING, THE**

(1987) 96m Conquest Entertainment/TMS c (AKA: FROM A WHISPER TO A SCREAM)

Vincent Price *(Julian White),* Clu Gulager *(Stanley Burnside),* Terry Kiser *(Jesse Hardwicke),* Harry Caesar *(Felder Evans),* Rosalind Cash *(The Snake Woman, Sideshow Owner),* Cameron Mitchell *(Sgt. Gallen),* Susan Tyrrell *(Bess Chandler),* Martine Beswicke *(Katherine White),* Angelo Rossitto *(Carny Barker),* Lawrence Tierney *(Official at Execution),* Ron Brooke *(Stephen Arden),* Didi Lanier *(Amaryllis).*

This effective low-budget horror anthology, which features an ensemble cast of familiar faces, manages to capture the look and feel of the classic E.C. horror comics of the 1950s without resorting to the kind of overly dramatic "comic-book" lighting used by George Romero in CREEPSHOW. In the small town of Oldfield, Tennessee, Julian White (Vincent Price) relates four hideous tales to curious news reporter Bess Chandler (Susan Tyrrell). The first concerns Stanley Burnside (Clu Gulager), a bespectacled middle-aged nerd who finally works up enough nerve to ask a beautiful young coworker out on a date, then strangles her to death before the evening ends. The second story shows small-time hood Jesse Hardwicke (Terry Kiser) suffering from a gunshot wound and seeking refuge in the swamps, where he is rescued by an eccentric old black man, Felder Evans (Harry Caesar), who is revealed to be 200 years old. The third tale takes place in an obscure carny and features a handsome young man—the glass-eater in the freak show—who is in love with a local girl. When he runs off with her, the voodoo priestess who runs the carnival gets revenge by making everything the boy has ever eaten explode from his body. The final episode, set at the end of the Civil War, stars Cameron Mitchell as a mean and surly Union sergeant who is captured, along with three comrades, by a band of children whose parents were killed in the war. Although the war has just ended, the children will not rest until all adults are made to pay for starting the fighting. Although the subjects of these loathsome little tales run the gamut from necrophilia to cannibalism, first-time director Jeff Burr presents them in a slightly tongue-in-cheek manner that captures the ghoulish spirit of horror comic books. He imbues each sequence with a different feel, and juggles his obviously low budget with considerable skill. Despite the emphasis on gore and some pretty vile subject matter, Burr has a definite appreciation for the history of the horror genre and presents more here than just your average slasher film.

p, Darin Scott, William Burr; d, Jeff Burr; w, Courtney Joyner, Darin Scott, Jeff Burr; ph, Craig Greene (United Color); ed, W.O. Garrett; m, Jim Manzie, Pat Regan.

**(PR:O   MPAA:R)**

## OMEN, THE**

(1976) 111m FOX c (AKA: BIRTHMARK)

Gregory Peck *(Robert Thorn)*, Lee Remick *(Katherine Thorn)*, David Warner *(Jennings)*, Billie Whitelaw *(Mrs. Baylock)*, Leo McKern *(Bugenhagen)*, Harvey Stevens *(Damien)*, Patrick Troughton *(Father Brennan)*, Martin Benson *(Father Spiletto)*, Anthony Nichols *(Dr. Becker)*, Holly Palance *(Young Nanny)*, John Stride *(Psychiatrist)*, Robert MacLeod *(Mr. Horton)*, Sheila Raynor *(Mrs. Horton)*, Tommy Duggan *(Priest)*, Robert Rietty *(Monk)*, Roy Boyd *(Reporter)*, Nancy Manningham *(Nurse)*, Nicholas Campbell *(Marine)*.

This silly and bloody, but at times very effective, horror film takes THE EXORCIST one step further by concentrating, not on possession by the Devil, but on the Antichrist himself. Robert Thorn (Gregory Peck) is a highly respected American ambassador to England whose wife, Katherine (Lee Remick), gives birth to a stillborn child. Thorn is encouraged by a priest to switch his dead child with the living baby of a mother who died during childbirth. Five years later, strange things begin happening in the Thorn household—all of which can be traced to their boy, Damien (Harvey Stevens), who, unbeknownst to his surrogate parents, is the Antichrist. Regardless of its rather questionable premise, execution (unintentionally funny dialog abounds), or taste, THE OMEN is a fairly entertaining horror picture that made an obscene amount of money and spawned two sequels, DAMIEN—OMEN II and THE FINAL CONFLICT, neither of which was very good. The films were originally conceived as four parts, tracing Damien's rise to power from his childhood through adulthood and eventually to Armageddon, but patron interest slacked off considerably after the second film, forcing the wise producers to cut the saga short at three.

p, Harvey Bernhard; d, Richard Donner; w, David Seltzer; ph, Gilbert Taylor (Panavision, DeLuxe Color); ed, Stuart Baird; m, Jerry Goldsmith.

**(PR:O   MPAA:R)**

## ONCE BITTEN*

(1985) 97m Samuel Goldwyn c

Lauren Hutton *(Countess)*, Jim Carrey *(Mark Kendall)*, Karen Kopins *(Robin Pierce)*, Cleavon Little *(Sebastian)*, Thomas Ballatore *(Jamie)*, Skip Lackey *(Russ)*, Jeb Adams *(WW I Ace Vampire)*, Joseph Brutsman *(Confederate*

*Vampire)*, Stuart Charno *(Cabin Boy Vampire)*, Robin Klein *(Flowerchild Vampire)*, Glen Mauro, Gary Mauro *(Twin Vampires)*, Carey More *(Moll Flanders Vampire)*, Peter Elbling *(Bookseller)*, Richard Schaal *(Mr.Kendall)*, Peggy Pope *(Mrs. Kendall)*, Anna Mathias *(Daphne)*, Kate Zentall *(Tanya)*, Laura Urstein *(Darlene)*, Megan Mullally *(Suzette)*, Garry Goodrow *(Wino)*, Dan Barrows *(Harry)*, Alan McRae *(Man in Drag)*, Ruth Silveira *(Instructor)*, Ron Vernan *(Man at Table)*, Terry Wills *(Principal)*.

This attempt to combine elements of vampire lore with the limited format of the teen sex comedy is a monstrous movie all right, a frighteningly awful horror comedy. The Countess (Lauren Hutton) is a centuries-old vampire who requires a triple feeding of virgin blood before every Halloween to maintain a youthful appearance. She now lives in 1980s Los Angeles, where, in an oft-repeated joke, teenage virgins are a rare commodity. Mark Kendall (Jim Carrey) is a high school student who desperately wants to bed his reluctant girl friend, Robin (Karen Kopins). Fate intervenes when Mark ventures to a freaky Hollywood bar and meets the Countess—both characters finding the perfect mate to satisfy their desires. Hutton makes a sensual vampire, but this comedy wastes what she brings to the part by consistently relying on cheap laughs to provide the bulk of the film. Carrey brings some humor to his part—considering the script limitations—but his efforts, too, simply aren't enough to overcome the lame jokes, which rely heavily on sex gags.

d, Dimitri Villard, Robby Wald, Frank E. Hildebrand, Howard Storm; w, David Hines, Jeffrey Hause, Jonathan Roberts (based on a story by Villard); ph, Adam Greenberg (Metrocolor); ed, Marc Grossman; m, John Du Prez.

**(PR:O   MPAA:PG-13)**

## ONE DARK NIGHT**½

(1983) 89m ComWorld c

Meg Tilly *(Julie)*, Melissa Newman *(Olivia)*, Robin Evans *(Carol)*, Leslie Speights *(Kitty)*, Donald Hotton *(Dockstader)*, Elizabeth Daily *(Leslie)*, David Mason Daniels *(Steve)*, Adam West *(Allan)*, Leo Gorcey, Jr. *(Barlow)*, Rhio H. Blair *(Coroner)*, Larry Carroll *(TV Reporter)*, Katee McLure *(Reporter)*, Kevin Peter Hall *(Eddie)*, Ted Lehman *(Drunk)*, Nancy Mott *(Lucy)*, Martin Nosseck *(Caretaker)*, Albert Cirimele *(Reporter)*, Shandor *(Russian Minister)*, Julie Chase, Peaches Johnson.

Julie (Meg Tilly) is a sweet girl desperate to be accepted by her peers, a rather tough and nasty bunch. One of them, Carol (Robin Evans), was jilted by Julie's present boy friend, so she is anxious to make it as tough on Julie as possible. The final chore Julie must porform to gain acceptance is to spend the night in a mausoleum, where Carol plans to scare the girl out of her wits. The mausoleum mayhem really begins, however, when a dead man with telekinetic powers uses his skills to drain the energies of the pranksters.   The direction by McLoughlin manages to develop a fair amount of tension, the cast is better than average, and the special makeup effects by Tom Burman and company make ONE DARK NIGHT a cut above the usual dreck.

p, Michael Schroeder; d, Tom McLoughlin; w, Tom McLoughlin, Michael Hawes; ph, Hal Trussel (Movielab Color); ed, Charles Tetoni, Michael Spence; m, Bob Summers.

(PR:C  MPAA:PG)

## OPEN HOUSE*

(1987) 95m Intercontinental c

Joseph Bottoms *(Dr. David Kelley)*, Adrienne Barbeau *(Lisa Grant)*, Rudy Ramos *(Rudy Estevez)*, Mary Stavin *(Katie Thatcher)*, Scott Thompson Baker *(Joe Pearcy)*, Darwyn Swalve *(Harry)*, Robert Miano *(Shapiro)*, Page Moseley *(Toby)*, Johnny Haymer *(Paul Bernal)*, Leonard Lightfoot *(T.J.)*, Barry Hope *(Barney Resnick)*, Stacey Adams *(Tracy)*, Roxanne Baird *(Allison)*, Tiffany Bolling *(Judy Roberts)*, Dena Drotar *(The Fan)*, Christina Gallegos *(Pilar)*, Cathryn Hartt *(Melody)*, Lee Moore *(Donald Spectre)*, Stephen Nemeth *(Tommy)*, Joanne Norman *(Agent # 1)*, Richard Parnes *(Lenny)*, Sheila Ryan *(Ellen)*, A. Gerald Singer *(Capt. Blake)*, Bryan Utman *(Policeman)*, Susan Widem *(Policewoman)*, Eddie Wong *(Mr. Yoshida)*.

This low-budget, independent slasher film stars Joseph Bottoms as Dr. David Kelley, a pop psychologist who hosts a popular Los Angeles radio call-in show. Making headlines is a string of murders of beautiful female real estate agents, and one day the doctor gets a mysterious call from "Harry," a disturbed man who makes some brutal statements about the slain women and ends by saying that those who were killed "deserved it." Dr. David has reason to be concerned, because his girl friend, Lisa (Adrienne Barbeau), is a real estate agent. As the killings continue (in a variety of perversely imaginative—and graphic—ways) the calls from Harry become more frequent and Dr. David becomes more involved. Overlong and lacking in suspense, OPEN HOUSE is a pretty dull affair. Padded out with endless scenes of Bottoms talking to wacko callers on the radio and Playmate-calendar-type agents showing houses, the film merely grinds its gears until the next bloody killing. The gore effects are poorly done and the camera lingers on the nasty goo far too long. Bottoms turns in his usual performance—professional and unremarkable—while Barbeau surprises, not only because she is in a bargain basement slasher film (not that we expect to see her doing Shakespeare), but because she performs a brief and very gratuitous topless scene after having avoided doing so for many years.

p, Sandy Cobe; d, Jag Mundhra; w, David Mickey Evans (from a story by Jag Mundhra); ph, Robert Hayes, Gary Louzon; ed, Dan Selakovich; m, Jim Studer.

(PR:O  MPAA:R)

## ORCA*

(1977) 92m Dino De Laurentiis/PAR c (AKA: ORCA— KILLER WHALE)

Richard Harris *(Capt. Nolan)*, Charlotte Rampling *(Rachel*

Bedford,*Oceanologist)*, Will Sampson *(Umilak)*, Bo Derek *(Annie)*, Keenan Wynn *(Novak,First Mate)*, Robert Carradine *(Ken)*, Scott Walker *(Swain)*, Peter Hooten *(Paul)*, Wayne Heffley *(Priest)*, Vincent Gentile *(Gas Station Attendant)*, Don "Red" Barry *(Dock Worker)*.

Dino De Laurentiis' attempt to cash in on JAWS' popularity is a total failure. Capt. Nolan (Richard Harris) is a whaler who makes the mistake of killing the pregnant mate of a killer whale. The whale takes his revenge on everyone and everything associated with Nolan. Of course, the good captain begins behaving like a modern-day Ahab and becomes obsessed with killing the whale, which leads to a rather laughable standoff on an ice floe. The only reason to sit through this is to see the part where Bo Derek—who has a broken leg—has it bitten off, cast and all, by the whale.

p, Luciano Vincenzoni; d, Michael Anderson; w, Luciano Vincenzoni, Sergio Donati; ph, Ted Moore, Vittorio Dragonetti (Panavision, Technicolor); ed, Ralph E. Winters, John Bloom, Marion Rothman; m, Ennio Morricone.

(PR:C  MPAA:PG)

## ORGY OF THE DEAD*½

(1965) 82m Astra/F.O.G.-Crest c

Criswell *(The Emperor)*, Pat Barringer *(Shirley/Gold)*, Fawn Silver *(Black Ghoul)*, William Bates *(Bob)*, Louis Ojena *(The Mummy)*, John Andrews *(The Wolfman)*, Rod Lindeman *(Giant)*, John Bealy *(Detective)*, Arlene Spooner *(Nurse)*, Colleen O'Brien *(The Street Walker)*, Barbra Norton *(The Skeleton)*, Mickey Jines *(Hawaiian)*, Nadejda Dobrev *(The Slave)*, Dene Starnes *(The Zombie)*, Texas Starr *(The Cat)*, Bunny Glaser *(Indian)*, Rene De Beau *(Seven Veils)*, Stephanie Jones *(The Skull)*.

"This is a story of those in the twilight time, once human, now monsters, in a void between the living and the dead. Monsters to be pitied. Monsters to be despised. A night with the ghouls. The ghouls reborn from the innermost depths of the world!" So goes the introduction by the Master of the Dead (Criswell) to this "horror" film, which is basically a collection of boring striptease routines filmed on a fog-shrouded cemetery set. The plot involves a writer, Shirley (Pat Barringer), and her fiance, Bob (William Bates), who visit a cemetery one night to gather material for her next book. They run into the Master of the Dead and his partner, the Princess of Darkness (Fawn Silver, looking a lot like Elvira), who preside over a ceremony to judge recently deceased sinners. Captured by a mummy and a wolf man, Bob and Shirley are tied up and forced to watch the presentation of the accused, including an Indian maiden (Bunny Glaser) who performs erotic dances and who loved fire, a prostitute (Colleen O'Brien) who robbed and then murdered her clients, a cat lover (Texas Starr) condemned to spend eternity in a really silly cat costume, a bride (Barbra Norton) who killed her husband and now must forever remain with his skeleton, and several others, while the Master of the Dead, the Princess of Darkness, the mummy, and the wolf man look on. At one point, the

Master of the Dead cackles, "Torture! Torture! It pleasures me!" Bad dancing, bad music, bad dialog, and Criswell—it must mean only one thing: an Edward D. Wood, Jr., movie! Unfortunately, Wood only wrote this one, but his priceless dialog is more than worth the price of admission.

p, A.C. Stephen; d, A.C. Stephen; w, Edward Davis Wood, Jr. (based on the novel by Wood); ph, Robert Caramico.

(PR:O  MPAA:NR)

**OTHER, THE***½

(1972) 108m FOX c

Uta Hagen *(Ada, Grandmother)*, Chris Udvarnoky *(Niles Perry)*, Martin Udvarnoky *(Holland Perry)*, Diana Muldaur *(Alexandra Perry)*, Norma Connolly *(Aunt Vee)*, Victor French *(Angelini)*, Loretta Laversee *(Winnie)*, Lou Frizzell *(Uncle George)*, Portia Nelson *(Mrs. Rowe)*, Jenny Sullivan *(Torrie)*, John Ritter *(Rider)*, Jack Collins *(Mr. P.C. Pretty)*, Ed Bakey *(Chan-yu)*, Clarence Crow *(Russell)*.

This genuinely creepy psychological horror film is set in a small Connecticut farm town circa 1935. Ten-year-old Niles (Chris Udvarnoky) and his twin brother, Holland (Martin Udvarnoky), spend their summer playing together around their home. While Niles is a well-behaved child, Holland is mischievous and has an evilness about him that is constantly getting Niles into trouble. Eventually, Holland's pranks turn lethal and several deaths occur. It isn't until an hour into the movie that we learn that Holland has been dead for years and Niles is imagining him. Adapted by former actor Thomas Tryon from his own best-selling novel, THE OTHER is a return to the Val Lewton school of horror, where terror is mostly conveyed through subtle suggestion and an overall sense of unease and dread. Director Robert Mulligan (TO KILL A MOCKINGBIRD) does an excellent job of evoking both the historical period and the terror, aided greatly by Robert Surtees' fine photography. The performances from the Udvarnoky twins are nuanced and memorable. Well worth seeing.

p, Robert Mulligan; d, Robert Mulligan; w, Thomas Tryon (based on the novel by Tryon); ph, Robert L. Surtees (DeLuxe Color); ed, Folmar Blangsted, O. Nicholas Brown; m, Jerry Goldsmith.

(PR:C  MPAA:PG)

**OUTING, THE***½

(1987) 85m Warren Chaney-HIT/TMS c (AKA: THE LAMP)

Deborah Winters *(Eve Farrell)*, James Huston *(Dr. Al Wallace)*, Andra St. Ivanyi *(Alex Wallace)*, Scott Bankston *(Ted Pinson)*, Mark Mitchell *(Mike Daley)*, Andre Chimene *(Tony Greco)*, Damon Merrill *(Babe)*, Barry Coffing *(Ross)*, Tracye Walker *(Gwen)*, Raan Lewis *(Terry)*, Hank Amigo *(Harley)*, Brian Floores *(Max)*, Michelle Watkins *(Faylene)*, Danny D. Daniels.

Although this film may look like just another slasher-in-the-woods splatter film, it is actually about a monstrous genie in a lamp, and most of the action takes place in a natural

history museum. When an ancient lamp ends up in a museum curated by Dr. Al Wallace (James Huston), it s genie escapes and possesses the curator's teenage daughter, Alex (Andra St. Ivanyi). THE OUTING brings some badly needed variety to the splatter genre by using the antique genie to dispatch its cast of nubile young teenagers, rather than employing the usual knife-wielding psycho. The film also earns some bonus points for setting the action inside the dark museum, and director Tom Daley makes fairly good use of the creepy location. The special effects are unremarkable, with the 20-foot-tall genie (actually only eight feet tall) looking very inanimate as it is rolled around the set through an eerie cloud of liquid nitrogen gas.

p, Warren Chaney; d, Tom Daley; w, Warren Chaney; ph, Herbert Raditschnig; ed, Claudio Cutry; m, Joel Rosenbaum.

(PR:O  MPAA:R)

**PACK, THE****½

(1977) 99m WB c (AKA: LONG DARK NIGHT, THE)

Joe Don Baker *(Jerry)*, Hope Alexander-Willis *(Millie)*, Richard B. Shull *(Hardiman)*, R.G. Armstrong *(Cobb)*, Ned Wertimer *(Walker)*, Bibi Besch *(Marge)*, Delos V. Smith, Jr. *(McMinnimee)*, Richard O'Brien *(Dodge)*, Sherry Miles *(Lois)*, Paul Willson *(Tommy)*, Eric Knight *(Guy)*, Steve Lytle *(Paul)*, Rob Narke *(Husband)*, Peggy Price *(Wife)*, Steve Butts *(Bobby)*.

A group of abandoned dogs on a small vacation island revert to their natural state and become a vicious pack of killers. Joe Don Baker plays Jerry, the marine biologist who leads the humans in their fight against the wild animals. This could easily have turned into a JAWS rip-off but instead is a nicely handled little horror piece. Directed with flair by veteran action film helmsman Robert Clouse (ENTER THE DRAGON), THE PACK manages to create a creeping sense of terror that mounts to the cataclysmic climax. A cut above the usual exploitative revenge-of-nature films, it was made with the cooperation of the American Humane Society, which oversaw the treatment of the animals.

p, Fred Weintraub, Paul Heller; d, Robert Clouse; w, Robert Clouse (based on the novel by Dave Fisher); ph, Ralph Woolsey (Technicolor); ed, Peter E. Berger; m, Lee Holdridge.

(PR:O  MPAA:R)

**PANDEMONIUM zero**

(1982) 82m MGM/UA c (AKA: THURSDAY THE 12TH)

Tom Smothers *(Cooper)*, Debralee Scott *(Sandy)*, Candy Azzara *(Bambi)*, Suzanne Kent, Phil Hartmann, Michael Kless, David Lander, Ebbe Roe Smith, Miles Chapin, Marc

McClure, Pat Ast, David Becker, Paul Reubens, Gary Allen, Eve Arden, Kaye Ballard, Tab Hunter, Edie McClurg, Donald O'Connor, Richard Romanus, Carol Kane, Judge Reinhold, Randi Brough, Candi Brough.

Although directed by Alfred Sole, whose ALICE, SWEET, ALICE (1977) is one of the most remarkable horror films of the 1970s, this FRIDAY THE 13TH parody is shockingly bad. Striving for an AIRPLANE!-like sense of sheer goofiness, the film follows a mad killer as he haunts the campus of It Had To Be U., murdering the students in various silly ways (the "Cheerleader shish kebab" and "five-on-a-javelin" are the kind of gags operating here). Typically, the loaded-with-guest-stars cast ensures that this goes nowhere in a hurry. The only possible point of interest here is that Paul Reubens, better known as Pee Wee Herman, makes a guest appearance as the Pee Wee-like assistant of Tommy Smothers, who plays a Canadian Mountie.

p, Doug Chapin; d, Alfred Sole; w, Richard Whitley, Jaime Klein; ph, Michel Hugo (Panavision, Technicolor); ed, Eric Jenkins; m, Dana Kaproff.

**(PR:C   MPAA:PG)**

## PATRICK**½

(1978, Aus.) 110m Australian International/Filmways c

Susan Penhaligon (Kathy Jacquard), Robert Helpmann (Dr. Roget), Robert Thompson (Patrick), Rod Mullinar (Ed Jacquard), Bruce Barry (Dr. Wright), Julia Blake (Matron Cassidy), Helen Hemingway (Sister Williams), Maria Mercedes (Nurse Panicale), Frank Wilson (Detective Sgt. Grant), Peter Culpan (Grant's Assistant), Peggy Nichols (Night Desk Nurse), Carole-Ann Aylett (Patrick's Mother), Walter Pym (Capt. Fraser), Paul Young (The Lover).

This CARRIE-inspired telekinesis-centered film from down under stars Robert Thompson as the title character, a young man who has been in an irreversible coma for three years, ever since his mother and her lover were killed in an electrical accident. As it happens, Patrick is their killer, and although comatose, he still has a powerful sixth sense which allows him to move objects through mind-power. He falls in love with Kathy (Susan Penhaligon), the nurse who cares for him, and leaves her love notes psychically written on her typewriter. In time she concludes that Patrick is causing strange occurrences in the hospital, as doctors and nurses who would like to expedite his death beginning dying themselves. Moreover, Patrick wants his beloved to commit suicide so she can join him in death. Director Richard Franklin went on to direct the more interesting ROADGAMES and PSYCHO II. The US version of PATRICK, like MAD MAX, has poorly dubbed American voices over the Australian ones.

p, Anthony I. Ginnane, Richard Franklin; d, Richard Franklin; w, Everett De Roche; ph, Don McAlpine (Afgacolor); ed, Edward Queen-Mason; m, Brian May.

**(PR:C   MPAA:PG)**

## PEEPING TOM*****

(1960, Brit.) 109m Anglo-Amalgamated/Astor c (AKA: FACE OF FEAR)

Karl Boehm (Mark Lewis), Moira Shearer (Vivian), Anna Massey (Helen Stephens), Maxine Audley (Mrs. Stephens), Esmond Knight (Arthur Baden), Bartlett Mullins (Mr. Peters), Shirley Ann Field (Diane Ashley), Michael Goodliffe (Don Jarvis), Brenda Bruce (Dora), Martin Miller (Dr. Rosan), Pamela Green (Milly), Jack Watson (Inspector Gregg), Nigel Davenport (Sgt. Miller), Brian Wallace (Tony), Susan Travers (Lorraine), Maurice Durant (Publicity Chief), Brian Worth (Assistant Director), Veronica Hurst (Miss Simpson), Miles Malleson (Elderly Gentleman), Alan Rolfe (Store Detective), Michael Powell (Mr. Lewis), John Dunbar.

Disturbing, perverse, sadistic, voyeuristic, intensely personal, and truly brilliant, this unqualified masterpiece should be seen by everyone who has an interest in film. Mark Lewis (Karl Boehm), a focus-puller at a film studio, works part-time at a corner cigar store taking pornographic photos of women. One night, he approaches a prostitute on the street, goes to her apartment, and stabs her with the sharpened leg of the tripod of the 16mm camera he uses to record the whole affair. Then, the next morning, he films the police investigation of her murder. Mark rents out most of the house he owns, and Helen Stephens (Anna Massey), a young woman who lives there with her blind mother (Maxine Audley), takes a liking to him and the two become friendly. When he lets Helen watch home movies of him as a young boy, she is horrified to see that the films chronicle his father (played by director Michael Powell) scientifically torturing the boy—part of the psychologist's studies in fear, Mark explains. (One reel captures the young Mark being awakened by the lizard his father has thrown on his bed.) It is not long, however, before Mark kills again. This time his victim is Vivian (Moira Shearer), a dancer-actress working at his film studio. He promises her a screen test, but as the camera rolls, he places the pointy tripod at her throat, and as she watches her reflection in a mirror connected to the camera, she is killed. Increasingly attracted to Helen, Mark tries to repress his cinematic obsession by leaving his camera at home when they go out, but his perverted impulses begin to get the best of him, especially after Helen's mother confronts him. Michael Powell, one of the cornerstones of the British film industry during the 1940s, was vilified by the British press following the release of this picture. The director of STAIRWAY TO HEAVEN (1946), BLACK NARCISSUS (1947), and THE RED SHOES (1948) had made a rich and provocative psychological horror film, but critics in his homeland found it completely repugnant. The film was quickly recut (butchered is more accurate) by the studio and was shown briefly in US second-run houses. It wasn't until 1979, however, that a restored version was released due to the efforts of director Martin Scorsese, a devout fan of the picture. Powell's career never recovered from the critical attacks, and he made only a handful of features and shorts after PEEPING TOM. With its incredibly complex structure—which continually accuses the audience of sharing Mark's sickness—PEEPING TOM is a remarkable examination of the overwhelming power of cinema, and one of the most disturbing films ever made.

p, Michael Powell; d, Michael Powell; w, Leo Marks; ph, Otto Heller (Eastmancolor); ed, Noreen Ackland; m, Brian Easdale.

(PR:O MPAA:NR)

## PEOPLE WHO OWN THE DARK*

(1975, Sp.) 87m Newcal/Sean Cunningham c
(PLANETA CIEGO)

Paul Naschy, Maria Perschy, Tony Kendall, Teresa Gimpera, A. de Mendoza.

An orgy in the basement of an old house is interrupted when nuclear war breaks out and everyone above ground is blinded. Clacking their canes and bumping into each other, the sightless survivors attack the house. Paul Naschy looks dangerous as he uses a high-powered rifle to fight off the not very terrifying attackers and defends unknown starlets who are dead ringers for Sophia Loren, Britt Ekland, and other famous faces. Inspired by George Romero's NIGHT OF THE LIVING DEAD, this one is for Naschy fans only.

p, Salvadore Romero; d, Armando De Ossorio; w, Vencenzio Naranda.

(PR:O MPAA:R)

## PHANTASM****

(1979) 90m AE c

Michael Baldwin (Mike), Bill Thornbury (Jody), Reggie Bannister (Reggie), Kathy Lester (Lady in Lavender), Terrie Kalbus (Granddaughter), Ken Jones (Caretaker), Susan Harper (Girl Friend), Lynn Eastman (Sally), David Arntzen (Toby), Ralph Richmond (Bartender), Bill Cone (Tommy), Laura Mann (Double Lavender), Mary Ellen Shaw (Fortune Teller), Myrtle Scotton (Maid), Angus Scrimm (Tall Man).

This tour-de-force comes from 21-year-old filmmaker Don Coscarelli, who did just about everything on PHANTASM, a wonderfully creative, bizarre, delightfully terrifying horror film that never fails to surprise. Told as if the whole experience were a nightmare, the film centers on Mike (Michael Baldwin), a 15-year-old orphan who lives with his older brother, Jody (Bill Thornbury). After witnessing some strange happenings at the funeral of a murdered friend (shadowy, gnomelike creatures lurking around tombstones, etc.), Mike grabs his skeptical brother and returns to the creepy mausoleum to investigate. Once inside, they find it is actually the headquarters of the lanky and grotesque undertaker, known only as The Tall Man (Angus Scrimm), who is using the place as a connection into the netherworld in order to take over the Earth. The Tall Man has a number of insidious devices to ensure his success, most notably a shiny, silver sphere that flies through the air, sprouts sharp spikes, plunges into the forehead of an unsuspecting victim, and then drills his brains out. The beauty of PHANTASM is its fever-dream quality, which

paved the way for such entries as A NIGHTMARE ON ELM STREET. Perhaps because of Coscarelli's youth, PHANTASM seems the product of the warped imagination of a teenager, full of creative and original scares rooted in basic fears of abandonment, loneliness, sex, and death. Although viewers leave the theater buzzing about the flying silver sphere, it was only one element in a film filled with unique, personal, witty, and, at the same time, terrifying imagery rarely seen in low-budget horror films.

p, Don Coscarelli, Paul Pepperman; d, Don Coscarelli; w, Don Coscarelli; ph, Don Coscarelli; ed, Don Coscarelli (Technicolor); m, Fred Myrow, Malcolm Seagrave.

(PR:O MPAA:R)

## PHANTASM II**

(1988) 93m UNIV c

James Le Gros (Mike Pearson), Reggie Bannister (Reggie), Angus Scrimm (The Tall Man), Paula Irvine (Liz), Samantha Phillips (Alchemy), Kenneth Tigar (Father Meyers), Ruth C. Engel (Grandma), Mark Anthony Major (Mortician), Rubin Kushner (Grandpa), Stacey Travis (Jeri), J. Patrick McNamara (Psychologist).

Content with recycling the highlights of Don Coscarelli's 1979 cult favorite PHANTASM without ever establishing its own identity, this shockingly dull sequel only approaches the wild imagination and surreal horrors of the original when it steals from it. More a remake than a sequel, the film begins promisingly enough, with a well-crafted transition between 1979 footage and new material. The story picks up exactly where it left off, with young Mike (Michael Baldwin) being captured by The Tall Man (Angus Scrimm), a supernatural mortician with yellow embalming fluid in his veins. Years later, we see that Mike has grown into an adult (played by James Le Gros) and has been in a mental hospital since the incident. He is finally released after he declares that all the events were hallucinations. What he doesn't tell the hospital authorities, however, is that he continues to believe everything that happened was real. In addition, Mike has begun receiving psychic messages from a young woman (Paula Irvine) who shares his visions of The Tall Man, and senses that the villain is still after them. Of course, The Tall Man's deadly flying silver spheres, dubbed the "Flying Cuisinarts" by some critics, are back for the sequel, and whiz about drilling people's brains out. The original PHANTASM was an inventive fever-dream, but the sequel, unfortunately, lacks that delirious youthful imagination. There are some memorable moments along the way—fleeting images scattered throughout the film that have a cumulative effect—but when the shocks do come, they are mostly retreads of the highlights from the first film. Despite this rather mundane effort, however, Coscarelli continues to exhibit a glimmer of unique, personal cinematic vision, and that is a rare commodity these days.

p, Roberto A. Quezada; d, Don Coscarelli; w, Don Coscarelli; ph, Daryn Okada (Foto-Kem Color); ed, Peter Teschner; m, Fred Myrow, Christopher L. Stone.

(PR:O MPAA:R)

## PHANTOM OF THE OPERA, THE****

(1925) 94m UNIV bw

Lon Chaney *(The Phantom)*, Mary Philbin *(Christine Daae)*, Norman Kerry *(Raoul de Chagny)*, Snitz Edwards *(Florine Papillon)*, Gibson Gowland *(Simon)*, Edward Martindel *(Philippe de Chagny)*, Virginia Pearson *(Carlotta)*, Arthur Edmund Carewe *(Ledoux)*, Edith Yorke *(Mama Valerius)*, Anton Vaverka *(Prompter)*, Bernard Siegel *(Joseph Buguet)*, Olive Ann Alcorn *(La Sorelli)*, Cesare Gravina *(Manager)*, George B. Williams *(Mons. Ricard)*, Bruce Covington *(Mons. Moncharmin)*, Edward Cecil *(Faust)*, Alexander Bevani *(Mephistopheles)*.

One of the most famous horror movies of all time, THE PHANTOM OF THE OPERA still manages to frighten after more than 60 years. The legendary Lon Chaney is magnificent as Erik, the horribly disfigured maniac composer known only as the "Phantom," who takes an interest in Christine (Mary Philbin), an understudy at the Paris Opera. Hidden in secret passages, he coaches her, perfecting her art until she is a star. Then he forces the company's leading soprano to step down by unleashing a series of horrors, including sending an enormous chandelier crashing down on the audience during a performance. Eventually the masked Phantom lures Christine to his subterranean lair, where he professes his love for her. He also agrees to let her return to the stage on the condition that she break off her relationship with Raoul (Norman Kerry). Christine agrees, but once she is free, rushes to her lover and they make plans to flee to England following her performance. The Phantom overhears them, however, and kidnaps Christine. As he sits and plays his huge pipe organ, curiosity overwhelms Christine and she creeps up behind the Phantom and pulls off his mask, revealing the terrible skull-like visage beneath. Eventually, Raoul and a mysterious foreign agent set out to capture the Phantom, as does an enraged mob led by the brother of one of the Phantom's victims. A much stronger film than THE HUNCHBACK OF NOTRE DAME (1923), THE PHANTOM OF THE OPERA further cemented Chaney's reputation as a superstar and made Universal synonymous with horror. From the point of view of the studio's management, however, THE PHANTOM OF THE OPERA was horrific in more ways than one, taking more than two years to reach the theaters after its initial completion in 1923. When it was originally previewed in California, critics told Carl Laemmle that he would have a turkey on his hands unless he offset the scary aspects with plenty of comedy relief, so the studio head brought in Chester Conklin from the Sennett lot and additional footage was shot. These additions, however, necessitated a new set of titles, and the expensive Walter Anthony was hired to provide them. When the picture, which Universal hoped would achieve "prestige" status, was then screened in San Francisco, the consensus was that it had some wonderful moments but failed to make sense. So the whole production was turned over to a new staff of title writers and editors, who *really* tore it apart. Out came the comedy, as well as a whole subplot involving Ward Crane and a lot of sword play, until finally the studio felt they had their "big picture." With its play of light and shadow, its secret passageways, masked ball (filmed in

two-strip Technicolor), and the still-chilling unmasking scene, THE PHANTOM OF THE OPERA deserves its revered place in horror film history.

p, Carl Laemmle; d, Rupert Julian; w, Raymond Schrock, Elliott J. Clawson, Tom Reed, Frank M. McCormack (based on the novel *Le Fantome de l'Opera* by Gaston Leroux); ph, Virgil Miller, Milton Bridenbecker, Charles Van Enger; ed, Maurice Pivar.

**(PR:A   MPAA:NR)**

## PHANTOM OF THE OPERA***

(1943) 92m UNIV c

Nelson Eddy *(Anatole Garron)*, Susanna Foster *(Christine DuBois)*, Claude Rains *(Enrique Claudin)*, Edgar Barrier *(Inspector Raoul de Chagny)*, Leo Carrillo *(Signor Feretti)*, Jane Farrar *(Biancarolli)*, J. Edward Bromberg *(Amiot)*, Fritz Feld *(Lecours)*, Frank Puglia *(Villeneuve)*, Steven Geray *(Vercheres)*, Barbara Everest *(Aunt)*, Hume Cronyn *(Gerard)*, Fritz Leiber *(Franz Liszt)*, Nicki Andre *(Lorenzi)*, Gladys Blake *(Jennie)*, Elvira Curci *(Biancarolli's Maid)*, Hans Herbert *(Marcel)*, Kate Lawson *(Marie)*, Miles Mander *(Pleyel)*, Rosina Galli *(Christine's Maid)*, Walter Stahl *(Dr. Lefours)*, Paul Marion *(Desjardines)*, Tudor Williams, Anthony Marlow *(Martha Singers)*, Beatrice Roberts *(Nurse)*, Marek Windheim *(Renfrit)*, Muni Seroff *(Reporter)*, Belle Mitchell *(Feretti's Maid)*, Ernest Golm *(Office Manager)*, Renee Carson *(Georgette Pleyel's Girl Friend)*, Lane Chandler, Stan Blystone *(Officers)*.

Universal Studios' elaborate and expensive remake of their classic 1925 silent horror film THE PHANTOM OF THE OPERA boasts fabulous sets, gorgeous costumes, and stunning Technicolor photography—but fails in the horror department, because of an excess of music and low comedy. Draining much of the fear, suspense, and mystery out of the original Gaston Leroux material, this remake posits Enrique Claudin (Claude Rains)—the future "Phantom"—as a somewhat frail, middle-aged violinist with the Paris Opera who is in love from afar with Christine DuBois (Susanna Foster), a pretty and talented singer in the chorus. Although Christine doesn't even know the violinist exists, Enrique devotes his entire life to her, sacrificing his musical future and life just to make her happy. Universal spent $1.5 million on PHANTOM OF THE OPERA and every dollar is on the screen. While the opera house set is the same one used in the original, many additional sets were constructed and dressed up with elaborate and expensive wares. Rains, who had just finished playing what would later become his best-remembered role—that of Capt. Louis Renault in CASABLANCA—managed to bring a sense of pathos and menace to the Phantom. The sparse and briefly seen makeup of the disfigured violinist is merely serviceable; wisely, no attempt was made to duplicate or surpass Lon Chaney's amazing visage in the original. While this version can be quite entertaining at times, it is frustrating that the horror elements are used merely as a plot device to propel the story along to the next elaborate opera scene—a structure that pleased neither horror fans nor opera buffs. PHANTOM OF THE OPERA won Oscars for Best Color Cinematography and Best Color Interior Decoration (John B. Goodman, Alexander Golitzen, R.A. Gausman, Ira S. Webb), receiving nominations for Best Sound Recording and Best Musical Score.

p, George Waggner; d, Arthur Lubin; w, Eric Taylor, Samuel Hoffenstein (based on the novel Le Fantome de l'Opera by Gaston Leroux, adapted by John Jacoby); ph, Hal Mohr, W. Howard Greene (Technicolor); od, Russell Schoengarth; m, Edward Ward, George Waggner.

**(PR:A    MPAA:NR)**

## PHANTOM OF THE PARADISE**½

(1974) 91m Harbor/FOX c

Paul Williams (Swan), William Finley (Winslow, the Phantom), Jessica Harper (Phoenix), George Memmoli (Philbin), Gerrit Graham (Beef), Jeffrey Comanor, Archie Hahn, Harold Oblong (The Juicy Fruits, The Beach Bums, The Undeads), Gene Gross (Warden), Henry Calvert (Nightwatchman), Ken Carpenter, Sam Forney (Stagehands), Leslie Brewer, Celia Derr, Linda Larimer, Roseanne Romine (Surfgirls), Nydia Amagas, Judy Washington, Susan Weiser (Dancers), Janet Savarino, Jean Savarino (Singing Twins), Keith Allison (Country and Western Singer), Bobby Birkenfeld (Guy), Sandy Catton (Black Singer).

This rock'n'roll parody is better than THE ROCKY HORROR PICTURE SHOW, but not much better. One of director Brian De Palma's more original efforts, PHANTOM OF THE PARADISE combines elements of THE PHANTOM OF THE OPERA and the Faust legend into a fairly entertaining, but only sporadically successful, horror/musical comedy. Winslow (William Finley) is an unknown songwriter whose best composition is stolen by the evil and unscrupulous record producer Swan (Paul Williams), who wants to use it as the basis for a new "sound" with which to open his glittery rock palace, the Paradise. Winslow accuses Swan of the theft, but the record producer frames the songwriter on a phony drug charge and has him thrown into prison. When the song becomes a hit, the angry Winslow breaks out of jail and plans revenge. In the process, he suffers a horrible accident and is scarred for life. Because of his hideous visage, he is forced to wear a bizarre helmet and a black cape as he creeps about the Paradise to find Swan. While some of the attacks on the music industry, "glitter" rock, and popular success are right on target, the film suffers from a bad pace and overly complicated script that tries to comment on far too many aspects of pop culture to nail down even one of them. The film's production design and set direction was done by the husband-and-wife team of Jack Fisk and Sissy Spacek. Just two years later Spacek, who had already appeared in a couple of films (PRIME CUT; BADLANDS), would become a star as the lead in De Palma's CARRIE.

p, Edward R. Pressman; d, Brian De Palma; w, Brian De Palma; ph, Larry Pizer (Movielab Color); ed, Paul Hirsch; m, Paul Williams, George Aliceson Tipton.

**(PR:C    MPAA:PG)**

## PHOBIA*½

(1980, Can.) 94m Spiegel-Bergman/PAR c

Paul Michael Glaser (Dr. Peter Ross), John Colicos (Inspector Barnes), Susan Hogan (Jenny), Alexandra Stewart (Barbara), Robert O'Ree (Bubba), David Bolt (Henry), David Eisner (Johnny), Lisa Langlois (Laura), Kenneth Welsh (Sgt. Wheeler), Neil Vipond (Dr. Clegg), Patricia Collins (Dr. Toland), Marian Waldman (Mrs. Casey), Gwen Thomas (Dr. Clemens), Paddy Campanero, Gerry Salsberg, Peter Hicks, Joan Fowler.

Director John Huston's only foray into horror is a disappointing effort, crippled by a simpleminded script that will leave most viewers bored after the first 15 minutes. Paul Michael Glaser plays Dr. Peter Ross, a controversial psychologist who treats convicted murderers by forcing them to confess and confront their deep-rooted phobias. Unfortunately, someone is taking things a bit too far and using the patients' most basic fears to bring about their deaths. Regrettably, the whole affair is extremely contrived, with a solution even a simpleton could decipher after the credits sequence. While Huston attempts to spice things up by juggling the narrative in a fairly creative manner, the film is crippled by its unsatisfying conclusion and a distinctly weak performance from Glaser.

p, Zale Magder; d, John Huston; w, Lew Lehman, Jimmy Sangster, Peter Bellwood (based on a story by Gary Sherman, Ronald Shusett); ph, Reginald H. Morris; ed, Stan Cole; m, Andre Gagnon.

**(PR:O    MPAA:R)**

## PICTURE MOMMY DEAD**½

(1966) 88m Berkeley/EM c

Don Ameche (Edward Shelley), Martha Hyer (Francene Shelley), Zsa Zsa Gabor (Jessica), Susan Gordon (Susan Shelley), Maxwell Reed (Anthony Caretaker), Wendell Corey (Clayborn), Signe Hasso (Sister Rene), Anna Lee (Elsie Kornwald), Paule Clark (1st Woman), Marlene Tracy (2nd Woman), Steffi Henderson (3rd Woman), Robert Sherman (Father), Kelly Corcoran (Boy).

Producer-director Bert I. Gordon cast his daughter, Susan, in the lead role in this creepy thriller as a young woman who is released from a sanitarium after suffering a nervous collapse when her mother (Zsa Zsa Gabor) is killed in a fire. Her daddy (Don Ameche) has remarried in the interim, but his new bride, Francene (Martha Hyer), is really only in it for the large inheritance left to Susan (which also happens to be Ms. Gordon's character name) by her dead momma. Francene tries to drive Susan nuts again so the dough will be transferred to her father, providing the evil gold digger easy access; however, the scheme doesn't go as Francene expected. Although hardly innovative, PICTURE MOMMY DEAD is enlivened by its relatively classy cast and the usual Gordon scare tactics.

p, Bert I. Gordon; d, Bert I. Gordon; w, Robert Sherman; ph, Ellsworth Fredricks (Pathe Color); ed, John Bushelman; m, Robert Drasnin.

**(PR:C    MPAA:NR)**

## PICTURE OF DORIAN GRAY, THE***½

(1945) 110m MGM bw-c

George Sanders *(Lord Henry Wotton)*, Hurd Hatfield *(Dorian Gray)*, Donna Reed *(Gladys Hallward)*, Angela Lansbury *(Sybil Vane)*, Lowell Gilmore *(Basil Hallward)*, Peter Lawford *(David Stone)*, Richard Fraser *(James Vane)*, Reginald Owen *(Lord George Farmoor)*, Lydia Bilbrook *(Mrs. Vane)*, Morton Lowry *(Adrian Singleton)*, Douglas Walton *(Alan Campbell)*, Mary Forbes *(Lady Agatha)*, Robert Greig *(Sir Thomas)*, Lisa Carpenter *(Lady Henry Wotton)*, Moyna MacGill *(Duchess)*, Billy Bevan *(Chairman Malvolio Jones)*, Miles Mander *(Sir Robert Bentley)*, Sir Cedric Hardwicke *(Narrator)*, William Stack *(Mr. Erskine)*, Natalie Draper *(Mrs. Vandelear)*, Renee Carson *(Young French Woman)*, Lillian Bond *(Kate)*, Alan Edmiston *(Cabby)*, Charles Coleman *(Butler)*, Carol Diane Keppler *(Gladys as a Child)*, Emily Massey *(Parker the Nurse)*, Jimmy Conlin *(Piano Player)*, James Aubrey *(Cabby)*.

This subtle and frightening adaptation of the classic Oscar Wilde novel allows the audience's imagination to do most of the scaring. Hurd Hatfield stars as the title character—a young aristocrat in 19th-century London whose gentle, angelic appearance is dangerously deceptive. Coaxed by the manipulative and hedonistic Lord Henry Wotton (George Sanders), Dorian grows as evil and scandalous as his mentor, becoming a philandering louse who entertains sadistic and perverse thoughts, alluding to (unseen) orgies and unspeakable evils. At the height of his vanity, Dorian has his portrait painted, and, in a Faustian pact, trades his soul for eternal youth. As a result, the portrait ages hideously, while Dorian's appearance never changes. In much the same manner as Val Lewton's horror films, THE PICTURE OF DORIAN GRAY frightens the audience by mere suggestion, without ever resorting to distracting visual representations of the horrible. All the infamy of Hatfield's character is implied, resulting in a building up of evil so horrible that it becomes unspeakable. The only visual shock the audience is subjected to is the portrait itself (which one never expects to see when it pops onto the screen in Technicolor with a violent musical crash), painted in a brilliantly grotesque style by Ivan Albright. THE PICTURE OF DORIAN GRAY not only frightened many viewers, it also earned the respect of the Motion Picture Academy, which bestowed upon the film two Oscar nominations—one to Angela Lansbury (as Dorian's jilted fiancee) for Best Supporting Actress and another to Cedric Gibbons and Hans Peters for Best Black-and-White Art Direction—and one statuette for the deep-focus camerawork of Harry Stradling.

p, Pandro S. Berman; d, Albert Lewin; w, Albert Lewin (based on the novel by Oscar Wilde); ph, Harry Stradling; ed, Ferris Webster; m, Herbert Stothart.

**(PR:C   MPAA:NR)**

## PIECES zero

(1981, Sp./Puerto Rico) 85m FVI-Artists Releasing-Amena and Fort/Spectacular c (MIL GRITOS TIENE LA NOCHE)

Christopher George *(Lt. Bracken)*, Lynda Day George *(Mary)*, Edmund Purdom *(Dean)*, Paul Smith *(Willard)*, Frank Brana *(Sgt. Hoden)*, Ian Sera *(Kendall)*.

Bordering on parody, but too sleazy to be very funny, this mad slasher film involves a cleaver-wielding psycho who lurks in the halls of a Boston university. Christopher George plays the detective baffled by the slayings, committed because the slasher is determined to construct a jigsaw-puzzle woman out of body parts. The end comes when the segmented cadaver comes to life and takes its revenge.

p, Dick Randall, Steve Manasian; d, Juan Piquer Simon; w, Dick Randall, John Shadow; ph, Juan Marino; m, Cam.

**(PR:O   MPAA:NR)**

## PIRANHA**½

(1978) 92m New Piranha/World c

Bradford Dillman *(Paul Grogan)*, Heather Menzies *(Maggie McKeown)*, Kevin McCarthy *(Dr. Robert Joak)*, Keenan Wynn *(Jack)*, Dick Miller *(Buck Gardner)*, Barbara Steele *(Dr. Mengers)*, Belinda Balaski *(Betsy)*, Melody Thomas *(Laura)*, Bruce Gordon *(Col. Waxman)*, Barry Brown *(Trooper)*, Paul Bartel *(Dumont)*, Shannon Collins *(Suzie)*, Shawn Nelson *(Whitney)*, Richard Deacon *(Earl)*, Janie Squire *(Barbara)*, Roger Richman *(David)*, Bill Smillie *(Jailer)*, Guich Koock *(Pitchman)*, Jack Pauleson *(In Canoe)*, Eric Henshaw *(Father in Canoe)*, Robert Vinson *(Soldier)*, Virginia Dunnam *(Girl)*, Hill Farnsworth.

PIRANHA is an early effort from Joe Dante, the director of THE HOWLING; GREMLINS; and INNERSPACE; in which he successfully combines laughs and chills in a parody of JAWS. Maggie McKeown (Heather Menzies) is a female detective out to trace a missing couple who have disappeared somewhere in the woods. During her search she meets up with the reclusive Paul Grogan (Bradford Dillman) whom she enlists to help her. Together they trace the couple to a supposedly deserted army base, where they drain a pool to see what is on the bottom. Only after it's too late do they learn that they've released a school of super-bred killer piranha into the river—an indestructible strain of fish that Dr. Robert Joak (Kevin McCarthy) developed years ago for the army as a way to infest the rivers of Vietnam and slow down the Viet Cong. Now, thanks to the brilliance of Maggie and Paul, the piranha are heading for a children's summer camp, and when they're finished snacking on the kiddies, they're going to check out the grand opening of a new lakeside resort. The silliness of the whole concept is handled with a sly sense of humor by director Dante, with some tongue-in-cheek cameo appearances by Keenan Wynn, Kevin McCarthy, Paul Bartel, Barbara Steele, and Dick Miller adding to the fun. Much credit must also go to John Sayles (the director of THE RETURN OF THE SECAUCUS SEVEN; MATEWAN; and EIGHT

MEN OUT), who wrote the intelligent, witty, and purposely ludicrous script.

p, Jon Davison; d, Joe Dante; w, John Sayles (based on a story by Richard Robinson, Sayles); ph, Jamie Anderson (Metrocolor); ed, Mark Goldblatt, Joe Dante; m, Pino Donaggio.

(PR:O    MPAA:R)

## PIRANHA II: THE SPAWNING*½

(1981, Neth.) 95m Brouwersgracht-Chako/Saturn c
(AKA: PIRANHA II: FLYING KILLERS)

Tricia O'Neil (Anne), Steve Marachuk (Tyler), Lance Henriksen (Steve), Ricky G. Paull (Chris), Ted Richert (Raoul), Leslie Graves (Allison), Carole Davis, Connie Lynn Hadden, Arnie Ross, Tracy Berg, Albert Sanders, Anne Pollack, Hildy Magnasun, Phil Colby, Lee Krug, Sally Ricca, Ward White, Ancil Gloudon, Paul Drummond, Dorothy Cunningham, Aston S. Young, Capt. Kidd Brewer, Jr., Gaetano Del Grande, Jan Eisner Mannon.

Though the title suggests this is a sequel to Joe Dante's PIRANHA, it isn't. Totally unrelated to the earlier film, PIRANHA II takes place at a Caribbean resort that suddenly finds itself besieged by the ravenous fish. As in the Dante film, this strain of killer piranha is the result of a government experiment; unlike the Dante film, however, these piranha can fly. Fly??? Yes, and not only can they fly, they can also survive out of the water. Sure. Of course, the little critters gather their forces and attack the resort, leaving lots of bloody bodies behind. The special effects are awful (the piranhas are obviously hand-puppets), the script worse, and the only spawning to be seen is that of the human couples who fall into bed with each other during lulls in the action. Executive producer Ovidio Assonitis funded the picture with foreign money and hired an unknown director named James Cameron, who would go on to make a couple more films you may have heard of—THE TERMINATOR and ALIENS.

p, Chako van Leuwen, Jeff Schectman; d, James Cameron; w, H.A. Milton; ph, Roberto d'Ettore Piazzoli (Technicolor); ed, Robert Silvi; m, Steve Powder.

(PR:O    MPAA:R)

## PIT AND THE PENDULUM, THE****

(1961) 85m Alta Vista/AIP c

Vincent Price (Nicholas Medina), John Kerr (Francis Barnard), Barbara Steele (Elisabeth Barnard Medina), Luana Anders (Catherine Medina), Anthony Carbone (Dr. Charles Leon), Patrick Westwood (Maximillian Butler), Lynne Bernay (Maria), Larry Turner (Nicholas as a Child), Mary Menzies (Isabella), Charles Victor (Bartolome).

The second and one of the best films in Roger Corman's Edgar Allan Poe series stars Vincent Price as Nicholas Medina, owner of a large and spooky castle with an elaborate torture chamber built by his father during the Spanish Inquisition. Stricken with grief after the death of his wife, Elisabeth (Barbara Steele, in her American film debut),

Nicholas becomes obsessed with the notion that he accidentally buried her alive. Elisabeth's brother, Francis Barnard (John Kerr), suspects foul play and travels to the castle looking for answers. He finds Nicholas slowly going mad and claiming to hear Elisabeth's voice calling to him. Eventually it is revealed that Elisabeth is not dead at all, but has conspired with her lover, family doctor Charles Leon (Anthony Carbone), to drive her husband insane. Corman brought in THE PIT AND THE PENDULUM on a 15-day shooting schedule and the result is a very entertaining horror film with chills, humor, and a bravura performance by Price, who was just beginning to finely hone his wickedly delightful, villainous characters. Shot in lush and almost garish color by cinematographer Floyd Crosby (who also shot Corman's previous Poe film, THE HOUSE OF USHER), the picture includes some impressive techniques and camera movement. Screenwriter Richard Matheson did a fine job of adapting Poe's rather limited (for films) short story by saving the dungeon sequences for the climax and then creating a rather interesting plotline to lead up to it. One of Corman and AIP's best.

p, Roger Corman; d, Roger Corman; w, Richard Matheson (based on a story by Edgar Allan Poe); ph, Floyd Crosby (Panavision, Pathe Color); ed, Anthony Carras; m, Les Baxter.

(PR:C    MPAA:NR)

## PLAY DEAD*

(1981) 89m Rudine-Wittman and United Construction c

Yvonne De Carlo, Stephanie Dunnam, David Cullinane.

Yvonne De Carlo plays a woman who makes a pact with the Devil to get back at her family. Satan possesses her beloved doggy and trains it to attack her hated relatives—making the murders look like accidents. Although the production is fairly slick and De Carlo is fun, it's all very silly, really.

d, Peter Wittman; w, Lothrop W. Jordan; ph, Bob Bethard.

(PR:O    MPAA:R)

## PLUMBER, THE***½

(1980, Aus.) 76m South Australian Film-Australian Film Commission-TCN/Cinema Ventures c

Judy Morris (Jill Cowper), Robert Coleby (Brain Cowper), Ivar Kants (Max the Plumber), Candy Raymond (Meg), Henri Szeps (Department Head).

Australian director Peter Weir (WITNESS) shows his directorial skill here by taking the flimsiest of material and turning it into a taut, tension-packed thriller, while getting in his jabs at hypocritical college-educated liberals. The premise is a simple one—Jill Cowper (Judy Morris), a married anthropologist living in a Sydney highrise, is psychologically terrorized by Max (Ivar Kants), a plumber who invades her apartment and proceeds to drive her into a state of near-hysteria. Though neither Jill nor her university professor husband, Brian (Robert Coleby), called for a plumber, the disheveled Max appears at their door, his gear in hand. A seemingly minor repair becomes a major project and Max sticks around for a couple of days, talking about his time in prison and making an incredible, wholly impractical, design out of the bathroom pipes. In the meantime, Jill is trying to prepare a paper on the artifacts and masks of New Guinea natives, drawing on a past encounter with a witch doctor whose photograph is prominently displayed. What is most frightening in THE PLUMBER is the fear of what may happen. The viewer, like Jill, is made terribly uneasy by Max's mysterious presence; we are never quite sure what he wants, or what he is capable of doing. Photographed on 16mm for Australian television.

p, Matt Carroll; d, Peter Weir; w, Peter Weir; ph, David Sanderson (Colorfilm Color); ed, G. Tunney-Smith; m, Gerry Tolland.

(PR:C-O  MPAA:NR)

## POINT OF TERROR*

(1971) 88m Jude/Crown International c

Peter Carpenter (Tony), Dyanne Thorne (Andrea), Lory Hansen (Helayne), Paula Mitchell (Sally), Leslie Simms (Fran), Joel Marston (Martin), Roberta Robson (1st Wife), Dana Diamond (Barmaid), Tony Kent (Priest).

While lounging on a California beach, rock 'n' roller Tony Trelos (Peter Carpenter) is picked up by a pneumatic blonde named Andrea (Dyanne Thorne). As it turns out, she's the wife of a music publisher and promises the singer a recording contract if he will dump his girl friend and have an affair. This soon leads to a tangled web of deception, betrayal, and murder, with a heavy dose of the supernatural tossed in at the end. Directed by former actor Alex Nicol, the film has some stylish touches here and there, but is strictly a B effort.

p, Chris Marconi, Peter Carpenter; d, Alex Nicol; w, Tony Crechales, Ernest A. Charles (based on a story by Carpenter, Marconi); ph, Robert Maxwell (DeLuxe Color); ed, R.A. Radecki; m, John Caper.

(PR:O  MPAA:NR)

## POLTERGEIST**½

(1982) 114m MGM-UA c

Craig T. Nelson (Steve Freeling), JoBeth Williams (Diane Freeling), Beatrice Straight (Dr. Lesh), Dominique Dunne (Dana), Oliver Robins (Robbie), Heather O'Rourke (Carol Anne Freeling), Zelda Rubinstein (Tangina), Martin Casella (Marty), Richard Lawson (Ryan), Michael McManus (Tuthill), Virginia Kiser (Mrs. Tuthill), James Karen (Teague), Lou Perry, Clair Leucart, Dirk Blocker, Allan Graf, Joseph R. Walsh, Helen Baron, Noel Conlon, Sonny Landham, Jeffrey Bannister, Jaimi Gendian.

If only director Tobe Hooper had been left alone by producer-writer Steven Spielberg, this might have been a modern masterpiece of family horror, doing for suburban families what Hooper's TEXAS CHAINSAW MASSACRE did for rural clans. Instead, we're left with a vapid, silly horror movie with occasional moments of promise, which ulti-

mately fails due to an overdose of Spielbergian cuteness. Steve and Diane Freeling (Craig T. Nelson and JoBeth Williams) are a happy suburban couple who suddenly find that their perfect-house-in-the-perfect-neighborhood has begun acting funny, scaring their perfect children. They really sit up and take notice, however, when wide-eyed young daughter Carol Anne (Heather O'Rourke) becomes possessed by late-night television and gets sucked into limbo by God knows what. Enter clairvoyant Tangina (Zelda Rubenstein), who surmises that the subdivision was built on a sacred Indian burial ground and the gods aren't happy. POLTERGEIST is frustrating because one gets a hint at what Hooper really wanted to do (the face-ripping scene comes to mind), but it's obvious that he was restrained by Spielberg (who would similarly discipline Joe Dante in GREMLINS), who didn't want to spoil the big box-office potential. The problem is, some of the truly horrifying moments slip through the censorship cracks, scaring little kids (and their parents) who walked in expecting CLOSE ENCOUNTERS OF THE THIRD KIND and not THE TEXAS CHAINSAW MASSACRE, and leaving POLTERGEIST a very disjointed, uneven movie. Judging, however, from Hooper's subsequent botch jobs (LIFEFORCE; TEXAS CHAINSAW MASSACRE II; and INVADERS FROM MARS), it's hard to tell where to place the greatest blame.

p, Steven Spielberg, Frank Marshall; d, Tobe Hooper; w, Steven Spielberg, Michael Grais, Mark Victor; ph, Matthew F. Leonetti (Panavision, Metrocolor); ed, Michael Kahn; m, Jerry Goldsmith.

(PR:C-O  MPAA:PG)

## POLTERGEIST II**½

(1986) 90m UA/MGM c

JoBeth Williams (Diane Freeling), Craig T. Nelson (Steve Freeling), Heather O'Rourke (Carol Anne Freeling), Oliver Robins (Robbie Freeling), Zelda Rubinstein (Tangina Barrons), Will Sampson (Taylor), Julian Beck (Reverend Henry Kane), Geraldine Fitzgerald (Gramma Jess), John P. Whitecloud (Old Indian), Noble Craig (Vomit Creature), Susan Peretz (Daughter), Helen Boll (Mother), Kelly Jean Peters (Young Jess), Jaclyn Bernstein (Young Diane), Robert Lesser, Jamie Abbott, Ann Louise Baradach, Syd Beard, David Beaman, Hayley Taylor-Block, Pamela Gordon, Kathy Wagner (Kane's People).

Although an improvement thematically over the first film (the childlike awe of the original has been replaced by a very adult fear of impotence), POLTERGEIST II is terribly disjointed and dramatically unfulfilling. The forces of evil that demolished the Freeling house in POLTERGEIST have followed the family into this film in search of the blonde, blue-eyed little Carol Anne (Heather O'Rourke). The Freelings have fled to Arizona to live with Gramma Jess (Geraldine Fitzgerald), who shares with Carol Anne the psychic ability to "see things others cannot see." Soon after Gramma Jess dies, a soft-spoken Indian named Taylor (Will Sampson) pays a visit to the family, explaining that he has been sent by the clairvoyant Tangina (Zelda Rubenstein) to protect them from any more evil spirits. Steve (Craig T. Nelson), now an alcoholic, resists further contact with the supernatural, but Taylor tells them that they must stay and fight off the evil power that is attempting to destroy them. When the family is visited by the deathly looking Rev. Henry Kane (brilliantly played by Julian Beck), the sunny skies turn dark and it is obvious that the enemy has arrived for Carol Anne. Although the film moves along at a rapid clip, it is poorly constructed and haphazardly executed. Reportedly, several additional family scenes wound up on the cutting room floor, leaving the film to lurch from one special-effects sequence to the next with little character insight in between. The confrontation between the characters played by Nelson and Beck (the founder of the avant-garde "Living Theater") is the very core of the film, and its one redeeming moment. Despite his very brief appearance (filmed almost entirely in close-up) Beck's bone-chilling presence dominates the film. It is a tribute to Beck's considerable talents that in his all-too-limited role he manages to create an embodiment of evil so terrifying as to burn his image into the viewer's brain long after the rest of POLTERGEIST II is justifiably forgotten. Famous Swiss painter H.R. Giger, creator of the monster in ALIEN, designed the "Vomit Creature," which is seen ever so briefly as it slithers across the floor.

p, Mark Victor, Michael Grais; d, Brian Gibson; w, Mark Victor, Michael Grais; ph, Andrew Laszlo (Panavision, Metrocolor); ed, Thom Noble; m, Jerry Goldsmith.

**(PR:O    MPAA:PG-13)**

## POLTERGEIST III*½

(1988) 97m MGM/MGM-UA c

Tom Skerritt *(Bruce Gardner)*, Nancy Allen *(Patricia Gardner)*, Heather O'Rourke *(Carol Anne Freeling)*, Zelda Rubinstein *(Tangina Barrons)*, Lara Flynn Boyle *(Donna Gardner)*, Kip Wentz *(Scott)*, Richard Fire *(Dr. Seaton)*, Nathan Davis *(Kane)*, Rober May *(Burt)*, Paul Graham *(Martin)*, Meg Weldon *(Sandy)*, Stacy Gilchrist *(Melissa)*, Joey Garfield *(Jeff)*, Chris Murphy *(Dusty)*, Roy Hytower *(Nathan)*, Meg Thalken *(Deborah)*, Dean _Tokuno *(Takamitsu)*, Catherine Gatz *(Marcie)*, Paty Lombard *(Helen)*, E.J. Murray *(Mary)*, Sherry Narens *(Mrs. Seaton)*, Phil Locker *(Bill)*, Maureen Steindler *(Old Woman)*, Alan Wilder, Brent Shaphren, Mindy Bell *(Observers)*, Conrad Allan *(Young Boy)*, Maureen Mueller *(Gallery Woman)*, John Rusk *(Gallery Man)*, Sam Sanders *(Security Guard)*, Laurie V. Logan *(Elevator Woman)*, Jerry Birn *(Elevator Man)*, Jane Alderman *(Scott's Mother)*, Mary Hogan, Laura Koppel, Chris Montana, Harold Taulbee, Lynn Koppel, Mark Zweigler, Wendy Wolfman, Christy Davis.

The second sequel to the hit 1982 haunted-house extravaganza is an erratic affair, containing some promising ideas and clever effects, which, unfortunately, are haphazardly presented in a narrative so perfunctory as to be almost nonexistent. The brainchild of writer-director Gary Sherman (who had the project dumped in his lap by the studio), POLTERGEIST III shifts the focus of the series from the suburbs to the city, setting the action in Chicago, in a newly constructed, state-of-the-art high-rise complex full of shops, offices, and apartments. Little blonde-haired Carol Anne (Heather O'Rourke) lives with her Aunt Trish (Nancy

Allen), her Uncle Bruce (Tom Skerritt), and her teenage cousin (Lara Flynn Boyle). Carol Anne is enrolled in a school for highly intelligent but emotionally disturbed youngsters. Her therapist, the pithy Dr. Seaton (Richard Fire), attributes the poltergeists that have haunted Carol Anne's past to mass hypnosis caused by her suggestions and ignores her protests that the ghost of the evil Rev. Kane (Nathan Davis) has located her. Kane, however, has indeed found Carol Anne in the Windy City, appearing in mirrors and reflections and beckoning her "into the light." The little girl is frightened, but because she knows no one will listen to her, she keeps her mouth shut and tries to ignore the malicious ghost who won't go away. The movie works perfectly well as an excuse to parade a number of cleverly conceived and executed in-camera (live) special effects before the public, but when the handful of truly remarkable tricks have passed, what is left behind is an incoherent mess filled with bad dialog, weak performances, unintentional humor, and some surprisingly dull scenes of poltergeist mayhem. This was the final film for Heather O'Rourke, who died just after the film's completion. POLTERGEIST stars seem to have been cursed over the years—Dominique Dunne, Will Sampson, and Julian Beck all died after appearing in installments of the series.

p, Barry Bernardi; d, Gary Sherman; w, Gary Sherman, Brian Taggert; ph, Alex Nepomniaschy (Astro Color); ed, Ross Albert; m, Joe Renzetti.

**(PR:C-O    MPAA:PG-13)**

## POSSESSION*

(1981, Fr./Ger.) 81m Oliane-Soma-Marianne/Limelight International c

Isabelle Adjani *(Anna/Helen)*, Sam Neill *(Marc)*, Heinz Bennent *(Heinrich)*, Margit Carstensen *(Margie)*, Michael Hogben *(Bob)*, Shaun Lawton *(Zimmerman)*, Johanna Hofer *(Mother)*, Carl Duering *(Detective)*, Maximilian Ruethlein, Thomas Frey, Leslie Malton, Gerd Neubart, Kerstin Wohlfahrt, Ilse Trautschold.

An enormous number of symbols—sexual, religious, and political—collide randomly in this pretentious, incoherent horror story. Set in Berlin, it follows the alienated Anna (Isabelle Adjani) as she gives birth to a slimy tentacled monster, the tangible product of her troubled id. Her husband, Marc (Sam Neill), who has been away on a special assignment for a couple of years, comes home to find his wife acting strangely. When she admits to having a lover—ex-flower child Heinrich (Heinz Bennent)—Marc has some private detectives follow her. One detective is killed by Anna and fed to the beast, the other by the tentacled monster itself. Unaware of the monster's existence, Marc thinks that his wife has gone mad and tries to help her—despite the fact that he catches her making love to the slimy creature. Although it would like to be somber and ultraserious, POSSESSION is merely silly and disgusting. Amazingly, Adjani, one of the most beautiful women in the world, spends much of the film mutilating herself, wandering Berlin in a catatonic state, and occasionally puking torrents of blood—all for the love of the creature that was designed and built by Carlo Rambaldi. The original European cut of the film ran 127 minutes.

p, Marie-Laure Reyre; d, Andrzej Zulawski; w, Andrzej Zulawski, Frederic Tuten; ph, Bruno Nuyteen (Eastmancolor); ed, Marie-Sophie Dubus, Suzanne Lang-Willar; m, Andrzej Korzynski, Art Phillips.

(PR:O  MPAA:R)

## POWER, THE*

(1984) 84m Jeffrey Obrow/Artists Releasing-Film Ventures c

Susan Stokey (Sandy), Warren Lincoln (Jerry), Lisa Erickson (Julie), Chad Christian (Tommy), Ben Gilbert (Matt), Chris Morrill (Ron Prince), Rod Mays (Lee McKennah), J. Dinan Mytretus (Francis Lott), Jay Fisher (Raphael), Costy Basile (Jorge), Juan Del Valle (Jeep Driver), Alice Champlin (Roxanne), Gabe Cohen (Marty), Milton Robinson (Jack), Steve Nagle (Driver), Richard Cowgill (Cemetery Guard).

Three high-school students come into possession of a stolen Aztec idol and use it to try to contact the dead. When they become frightened by the evil power they have unleashed, they enlist the help of a reporter (Susan Stokey) for a sleazy tabloid. Her boy friend (Warren Lincoln) then steals the figurine and is possessed by the demon and transformed into an ugly monster, leading to the usual levitation and dismemberment. Finally it occurs to someone to smash the statuette. This low-budget, low-intelligence horror story, brought to you by the boys who made the forgettable THE DORM THAT DRIPPED BLOOD (1982), offers nothing fans of the genre haven't already seen.

p, Jeffrey Obrow; d, Jeffrey Obrow, Stephen Carpenter; w, Jeffrey Obrow, Stephen Carpenter (based on a story by Obrow, Carpenter, John Penny, John Hopkins); ph, Stephen Carpenter (Getty Color); ed, Jeffrey Obrow, Stephen Carpenter; m, Christopher Young.

(PR:O  MPAA:R)

## PREMATURE BURIAL, THE***

(1962) 81m Santa Clara/AIP c

Ray Milland (Guy Carrell), Hazel Court (Emily Gault), Richard Ney (Miles Archer), Heather Angel (Kate Carrell), Alan Napier (Dr. Gideon Gault), John Dierkes (Sweeney), Richard Miller (Mole), Brendan Dillon (Minister), Clive L. Halliday.

This was the third of Roger Corman's Poe adaptations and the only one that didn't star Vincent Price. In late 19th-century England, Dr. Guy Carrell (Ray Milland) lives in morbid fear of being buried alive, as he believes his father—a cataleptic—was. So obsessed with this notion is Guy that he even attempts to postpone his marriage to the beautiful Emily (Hazel Court), though she refuses to let him. Soon after their marriage, Guy constructs a burial vault equipped with a half-dozen escape hatches. His best friend, Miles (Richard Ney), is disturbed by Guy's obsession and,

helped by Emily, persuades him to destroy the vault. Coming to his senses, Guy even agrees to face his fear by unlocking his father's crypt to view his remains. The sight of the skeleton, however, causes him to suffer what appears to be a fatal heart attack and he is pronounced dead. However, just as he feared, Guy is alive but cannot move. He is placed in a casket and buried, but when a pair of body snatchers dig up his corpse, Guy rises from the "dead" and kills the men. He then creeps off into the misty night to mete out revenge on those who buried him. Although a solid effort, this film sorely misses Price, who would have brought a more intense sense of fear and obsession to the role. While Milland does well in the scenes in which he logically explains the various escape devices built into his crypt, a mad edge is missing. In addition to these casting problems, the film also suffers from a script by Charles Beaumont and Ray Russell that falls back on several plot twists from the previous Poe pictures, and the climax is predictable and hurried. Visually, however, the film is quite interesting, benefitting from director Roger Corman's usual sharp eye for color and composition (most of which will be lost on videotape, for the wide-screen film, like the other Corman Poe adaptations, is not letterboxed). Corman's creative use of sound—from a cat trapped in a wall to the eerily whistled "Molly Malone"— adds immeasurably to the overall creepiness, and Daniel Haller's set design is, once again, excellent.

p, Roger Corman; d, Roger Corman; w, Charles Beaumont, Ray Russell (based on the story by Edgar Allan Poe); ph, Floyd Crosby (Panavision, Eastmancolor); ed, Ronald Sinclair; m, Ronald Stein.

(PR:A  MPAA:NR)

## PREMONITION, THE***

(1975) 94m Galaxy/AE c

Sharon Farrell (Sheri Bennett), Richard Lynch (Jude), Jeff Corey (Det. Mark Denver), Ellen Barber (Andrea Fletcher), Edward Bell (Prof. Miles Bennett), Chiitra Neogy (Dr. Jeena Kingsly), Danielle Brisebois (Janie), Rosemary McNamara (Lenore), Thomas Williams (Todd Fletcher), Margaret Graham (Landlady), Roy White (Dr. Larabee), Wilmuth Cooper (Gypsy Lady), Robert Harper (Night Watchman), Mark Schneider, Stanley W. Winn, Tamara Bergdall, Bonita Chambers, Edward L. Emling, Jr..

An intriguing low-budget independent production shot in Mississippi, THE PREMONITION is a throwback to the Val Lewton school of horror, relying on mood and atmosphere rather than outright visceral shock. Sheri Bennett (Sharon Farrell from IT'S ALIVE) is the foster mother of a young girl (Danielle Brisebois) whose real mother, the insane Andrea (Ellen Barber), is intent on regaining custody. Tracking her daughter down at school, Andrea tries to make contact with her, but Sheri arrives and whisks the child away. While Sheri begins having terrible premonitions, Andrea and her friend, Jude (Richard Lynch), a scary carnival clown, plan to kidnap the girl. Blessed with a strong cast—especially Farrell and Lynch—and an excellent use of location, THE PREMONITION is an effectively creepy film which successfully preys on very real fears (the loss of a child) without exploiting the situation for cheap thrills. At times talky and a bit slow-moving, the film nonetheless builds tension steadily and contains several unforgettably eerie scenes.

p, Robert Allen Schnitzer; d, Robert Allen Schnitzer; w, Allen Schnitzer, Anthony Mahon, Louis Pastore (based on the manuscript "The Adoption"); ph, Victor C. Milt (TVC Color); ed, Sidney Katz; m, Henry Mollicone, Pril Smiley.

**(PR:C   MPAA:PG)**

## PREY, THE zero

(1984) 80m Essex International/NW c

Debbie Thureson *(Nancy)*, Steve Bond *(Joel)*, Lori Lethin *(Bobbie)*, Robert Wald *(Skip)*, Gayle Gannes *(Gail)*, Philip Wenckus *(Greg)*, Carel Struycken *(The Giant)*, Jackson Bostwick *(Mark)*, Jackie Coogan *(Lester)*, Ted Hayden *(Frank)*, Connie Hunter *(Mary)*, Garry Goodrow *(Cop)*.

The killer in this standard mad-slasher-in-the-woods effort is a crazed gypsy mutant horribly burned in a fire that occurred 30 years before. Still angry and wielding an ax, he lumbers off after a bunch of camping youths. There is not one iota of creativity here.

p, Summer Brown, Randy Rovins; d, Edwin Scott Brown; w, Summer Brown, Edwin Scott Brown; ph, Teru Hayashi; ed, Michael Barnard; m, Don Peake.

**(PR:O   MPAA:R)**

## PRINCE OF DARKNESS***

(1987) 101m Alive/UNIV c

Donald Pleasence *(Priest)*, Jameson Parker *(Brian)*, Victor Wong *(Professor Birack)*, Lisa Blount *(Catherine)*, Dennis Dun *(Walter)*, Susan Blanchard *(Kelly)*, Anne Howard *(Susan)*, Ann Yen *(Lisa, Language Expert)*, Alice Cooper *(Street-People Leader)*, Ken Wright, Dirk Blocker, Jesse Lawrence Ferguson, Peter Jason.

After a short flirtation with big-budget filmmaking, director John Carpenter returned to his low-budget horror film roots with this strange tale of religion, science, and pure evil. Veteran Carpenter performer Donald Pleasence stars as a priest who discovers the existence of a strange canister full of swirling green liquid, hidden in the basement of an old church in Los Angeles many years before. Near the container is an old book, some sort of alternate Bible, which when deciphered reveals that the canister contains the energy of Satan's son. It seems that, several thousand years ago, Satan (who was an alien) was exiled to the "dark side," a world that mirrors our own. Before leaving, Satan locked his son in a container, in preparation for his return—when the conditions are right, the son will unlatch the container from the inside and fetch his father back from his exile. Not only does Carpenter create a terrifying tale that works on the visceral level of a horror film, he also explores the fundamental conflict of religion, science, and the unknown, adding an intellectual dimension sorely lacking in most current films of this genre. Provocative plot aside, Carpenter once again proves his mastery of the visual aspects of the medium with his excellent use of the

wide-screen format and a bag of simple cinematic tricks that seem to have been forgotten in these days of high-priced, state-of-the-art effects crews. Although Carpenter names his church St. Godard's in tribute to director Jean-Luc Godard, his film bears a much greater resemblance to the masterful work of Jean Cocteau (ORPHEUS; BEAUTY AND THE BEAST) with its tilted sets (by production designer Daniel Lomino), forced perspectives, filming in reverse, and, most of all, the ability to reach into a mirror and discover an alternate reality.

p, Larry Franco; d, John Carpenter; w, John Carpenter; ph, Gary B. Kibbe (Panavision); ed, Steve Mirkovich; m, John Carpenter, Alan Howarth.

**(PR:O   MPAA:R)**

## PRISON**½

(1988) 102m Empire c

Viggo Mortensen *(Connie Burke)*, Chelsea Field *(Katherine Walker)*, Lane Smith *(Ethan Sharpe)*, Lincoln Kilpatrick *(Cresus)*, Tom Everett *(Rabbitt)*, Ivan Kane *(Lasagna)*, Andre De Shields *(Sandor)*, Tom "Tiny" Lister, Jr. *(Tiny)*, Steven E. Little *(Rhino)*, Mickey Yablans *(Brian Young)*, Larry Flash Jenkins *(Hershey)*, Arlen Dean Snyder *(Horton)*, Hal Landon, Jr. *(Wallace)*, Matt Kanen *(Johnson)*, Rod Lockman *(Kramer)*, Jeff L. Deist *(Gate Guard)*, Kane Hodder *(Charlie Forsythe/Gas-mask Guard)*, George D. Wallace *(Joe Reese)*, Luciana Capozzoli *(Claxton)*, Duke Spencer *(Scully)*, Pat Noonan *(Collins)*, Lyle D. Kelsey *(Guard)*, Rob Brox *(Pervis)*, Larry Moore *(Reptile Guard)*, John Hoke *(Old Warden)*.

Easily the best non-Stuart Gordon film to be released under the auspices of Empire Pictures, PRISON is an effective and unique chiller that successfully combines two genres: the prison film and horror. Conceived and produced by HALLOWEEN executive producer Irwin Yablans, the film begins at Creedmore Prison in 1964 as an innocent man is being executed for the murder of an inmate who was really killed by brutal prison guard Ethan Sharpe (Lane Smith). During the next 20 years Creedmore, which was built at the turn of the century, is closed down and Sharpe moves up the penal system ladder—although he is plagued by nightmares. In 1984, the state decides to re-open Creedmore and make Sharpe its warden, and before long the vengeful ghost of the executed man is unleashed. An intriguing genre hybrid boasting a stronger than usual cast and excellent, atmospheric direction from Finnish newcomer Renny Harlin, PRISON is an impressive piece of low-budget genre work. With the film played as a straight prison drama for close to half its running time, the filmmakers take the time to develop the characters and set the mood before pouring on the gore. Cold stone walls, cramped cells, low-key lighting, and flooded floors all contribute to the dank, dark, claustrophobic feel. The gore effects, while graphic, are handled with dispatch and are not lingered over any longer than need be. The entire film plays almost like a good old-fashioned horror excursion in which mood is more important than gut-churning carnage.

p, Irwin Yablans; d, Renny Harlin; w, Courtney Joyner

(based on a story by Irwin Yablans); ph, Mac Ahlberg; ed, Andy Horvitch; m, Richard Band, Christopher L. Stone.

(PR:O MPAA:R)

## PROM NIGHT*

(1980) 91m AE c

Leslie Nielsen *(Hammond),* Jamie Lee Curtis *(Kim),* Casey Stevens *(Nick),* Eddie Benton *(Wendy),* Antoinette Bower *(Mrs. Hammond),* Michael Tough *(Alex),* Robert Silverman *(Sykes),* Pita Oliver *(Vicki),* David Mucci *(Lou),* Jeff Wincott *(Drew),* Marybeth Rubins *(Kelly),* George Touliatos *(McBride),* Melanie Morse MacQuarrie *(Henri-Anne),* David Gardner *(Fairchild),* Joy Thompson *(Jude),* Sheldon Rybowski, Rob Garrison, David Bolt.

Fresh from being terrorized in HALLOWEEN, Jamie Lee Curtis stars in this slasher clone set to the wonderful thump of disco music. The film opens, a la HALLOWEEN, with an expository scene from the past: taunted by four other kids, a girl falls to her death from an abandoned building. Approximately eight years later, on the night of the high-school prom, a hooded killer stalks and slashes the four teens responsible for the little girl's death. Who could the killer be? Is it the victim's sister Kim (Curtis), who was crowned prom queen? Is it her brother Alex (Michael Tough), who works as the DJ at the prom? Is it her father (Leslie Nielsen), who just happens to be the school principal? Or is it, perhaps, one of the four culprits trying to kill off the others so that no one will ever know what happened that day? The answer is pretty obvious, so you'll just have to enjoy scenes of Curtis disco dancing and wonderful moments like the severed head of a victim rolling across the dance floor. Still, PROM NIGHT is better than most slasher movies, mainly because it's funnier.

p, Peter Simpson; d, Paul Lynch; w, William Gray (based on a story by Robert Guza, Jr.); ph, Robert New; ed, Brian Ravok; m, Carl Zittrer, Paul Zaza.

(PR:O MPAA:R)

## PROPHECY*

(1979) 102m PAR c

Talia Shire *(Maggie),* Robert Foxworth *(Rob),* Armand Assante *(Hawks),* Richard Dysart *(Isley),* Victoria Racimo *(Ramona),* George Clutesi *(M'Rai),* Tom McFadden *(Pilot),* Evans Evans *(Cellist),* Burke Byrnes *(Father),* Mia Bendixsen *(Girl),* Johnny Timko *(Boy),* Everett L. Creach *(Kelso),* Charles H. Gray *(Sheriff),* Lyvingston Holms *(Black Woman),* Graham Jarvis *(Shusette),* James H. Burk, Bob Terhune, Lon Katzman *(Rescuers),* Jaye Durkus *(Sheriff's Deputy),* Cheri Bergen *(Social Worker),* Cliff Hutchison *(Stage Manager),* Thomas P. May *(Lumberjack).*

PROPHECY harks back to the monster genre of the 1950s in which such creatures as Godzilla were a warning of the possible effects of radiation, only this time out the focus is on industrial pollution in the backwoods of Maine. Rob (Robert Foxworth) is hired by the EPA to investigate the wildlife of Maine in order to settle a dispute between local Indians and a paper mill. He is accompanied by his preg-

nant wife, Maggie (Talia Shire), as they set up camp in the woods. There they encounter giant fish and a man-eating raccoon, attributing their disproportionate size to the presence of mercury in the water. Next they take in a hideously malformed bear cub—and get themselves in trouble with mama bear, a gigantic gooey mess of a beast. Director John Frankenheimer has made some intelligent non-horror films in the past (THE MANCHURIAN CANDIDATE and THE TRAIN, as well as 1986's not-so-good 52 PICK-UP) and here he tries to apply an environmental issue and a government cover-up to the conventions of the horror genre. Instead of trying to thrill his audience, he concentrates on the effects of various horrors on his main characters: there is the unseen environmental horror (the mercury-poisoned water), a killer which few people seem to fear, and then there's the giant mutant bear, a killer that terrifies everyone. Frankenheimer also examines the different fears of his male and female characters—Rob is concerned with the poisoned waters' effect on society, while the pregnant Maggie is concerned with its effect on her unborn child. Credit must be given to Frankenheimer for trying something different, but overall the film is a disappointment and a failure. Worst of all is the downright embarrassing "monster," which is an insult to horror fans. No matter how bad this gets, however, don't shut off the VCR until the end—one of the funniest, most cliched final shots you'll ever see.

p, Robert L. Rosen; d, John Frankenheimer; w, David Seltzer; ph, Harry Stradling, Jr. (Panavision, Movielab Color); ed, Tom Rolf; m, Leonard Rosenman.

(PR:O MPAA:PG)

## PROWLER, THE**

(1981) 88m Graduation/Sandhurst c (AKA: ROSEMARY'S KILLER)

Vicki Dawson *(Pam McDonald),* Christopher Goutman *(Mark London),* Cindy Weintraub *(Lisa),* Farley Granger *(Sheriff George Fraser),* John Seitz *(Kingsley),* Lawrence Tierney, Lisa Dunsheath, David Sederholm, Bill Nunnery, Thom Bray, Diane Rode, Bryan Englund, Donna Davis, Carlton Carpenter, Joy Glaccum, Timothy Wahrer, Bill Hugh Collins, Dan Lownsberry, Douglas Stevenson, Susan Monts, John Christian, Richard Colligan, Steven Bock, Matthew Iddings.

A WW II veteran returns home to find his girl friend carrying on with someone else at a graduation dance in this routine slasher picture. He then kills the two-timing gal and her lover with a pitchfork and the annual dance is cancelled for the next 35 years. Thirty-six years later, the dance is revived and the crazed vet dons his brain-bucket and heads off to teach those damn teens a lesson they'll never forget. The real reason for the existence of this unexceptional film is to show off the artistry of special effects man Tom Savini. Unfortunately, several of his most gruesome moments were cut from the film at the last minute to appease a touchy MPAA. A better-than-average cast, including veterans Farley Granger and Lawrence Tierney, helps make this one a bit more palatable.

p, Joseph Zito, David Streit; d, Joseph Zito; w, Glenn Leopold, Neal Barbera; ph, Raoul Lumas; ed, Joel Goodman; m, Richard Einhorn.

(PR:O  MPAA:R)

## PSYCHIC, THE*

(1977, It.) 90m Group I c (SEITE NOTE IN NERO)

Jennifer O'Neill, Marc Porel, Evelyn Stewart [Ida Galli], Jenny Tamburi, Gabriele Ferzetti, Gianni Garko, Fabrizio Jovine, Luigi Diberti, Laura Vernier.

Made by Lucio Fulci before ZOMBIE, this film is not as gross as the one that would follow, but it's just as boring. Jennifer O'Neill plays a woman haunted by visions of the impending deaths of several people. In a flashback, we learn that when she was a girl, her mother apparently committed suicide by jumping off a cliff. As the adult O'Neill experiences more visions—the camera slowly zooming into a close-up of her eyes—she learns more about the true nature of her mother's death.

p, Fulvio Frizzi; d, Lucio Fulci; w, Lucio Fulci, Roberto Gianuiti, Dardano Sacchetti; ph, Sergio Salvati (DeLuxe Color); m, Fabio Frizzi.

(PR:O  MPAA:R)

## PSYCHIC KILLER**

(1975) 90m AE c

Jim Hutton (Arnold), Julie Adams (Laura, Psychiatrist), Paul Burke (Detective Morgan), Nehemiah Persoff (Dr. Gubner), Aldo Ray (Anderson, Morgan's Assistant), Neville Brand (Lemonowski, Butcher), Della Reese (Mrs. Gibson), Rod Cameron (Dr. Commanger), Joe Della Sorte (Sanders), Harry Holcombe (Judge), Robyn Raymond (Jury Foreman), Jerry James (Dead Doctor), Diane Deininger (Arnold's Mother), John Dennis (Frank), Judith Brown (Anne), Mary Wilcox (Martha), Bill Quinn (Coroner), Marland Proctor (Motorcycle Cop), Bill Bonner (Ambulance Driver), Walter Miles (Coroner), Whit Bissell (Dr. Taylor), Stack Pierce (Emilio), Ed Cross (Old Man), Mello Alexandria (Cop), Sheldon Lee (Inmate), Greydon Clark (Sowash).

Wrongly accused of murder, Arnold (Jim Hutton) is placed inside a mental institution, where another inmate teaches him the secrets of astral projection. Upon his release, Arnold goes about exacting revenge from those who had him committed, permitted by his psychic powers to gruesomely murder his victims without ever leaving his apartment. PSYCHIC KILLER is marred by its blatant references to Hitchcock films, especially Arnold's PSCYHO-derived mother complex. Actor-turned-director Ray Danton's presentation of this material is pretty mundane and leaves his competent cast of supporting players to inject whatever life they can into the movie.

p, Mardi Rustam; d, Ray Danton; w, Greydon Clark, Mike Angel, Raymond Danton; ph, Herb Pearl (Eastmancolor); ed, Michael Brown; m, William Kraft.

(PR:C  MPAA:PG)

## PSYCHO*****

(1960) 109m PAR bw

Anthony Perkins (Norman Bates), Janet Leigh (Marion Crane), Vera Miles (Lila Crane), John Gavin (Sam Loomis), Martin Balsam (Milton Arbogast), John McIntire (Sheriff Chambers), Lurene Tuttle (Mrs. Chambers), Simon Oakland (Dr. Richmond), Frank Albertson (Tom Cassidy), Patricia Hitchcock (Caroline), Vaughn Taylor (George Lowery), John Anderson (California Charlie, the Car Salesman), Mort Mills (Policeman), Francis De Sales (District Attorney), George Eldridge (Chief of Police), Sam Flint (Official), Helen Wallace (Woman Customer), Ted Knight (Police Guard), Alfred Hitchcock (Man Outside Office in Cowboy Hat), Frank Killmond (Bob Summerfield), Virginia Gregg (Mother's Voice), Ann Dore (Perkins' Double in Shower Scene), Marli Renfro (Leigh's Double in Shower Scene).

Perhaps no other film changed Hollywood's perception of the horror film so drastically as did PSYCHO. More surprising is the fact that this still unnerving horror classic was directed by Alfred Hitchcock, a filmmaker whose cruel sense of humor was at the forefront in this picture. Its violence and bloodletting may look tame to those who have grown up on Jason and Freddy Kreuger, but no one had ever seen anything quite like it in 1960. The familiar plot revolves around Norman Bates (Anthony Perkins), a nervous, birdlike motel proprietor who lives under the influence of his domineering old mother. Norman must care for Mother, and, in return, Mother helps keep Norman away from the filthy, sluttish women that come to stay at the motel. When Marion Crane (Janet Leigh) stops at the motel, Mother stabs her to death in the shower, after which the son sinks her bloody corpse in a nearby lagoon. The situation gets tense for Norman when Marion's sister, Lila (Vera Miles); Marion's lover, Sam Loomis (John Gavin); and private investigator Milton Arbogast (Martin Balsam) arrive to ask some questions. Inspired by the life of the demented, cannibalistic Wisconsin killer Ed Gein (whose heinous acts would also inspire THE TEXAS CHAINSAW MASSACRE and DERANGED), PSYCHO's importance to the genre cannot be overestimated. The influence comes not only from the Norman Bates character (who has since been reincarnated in a staggering variety of forms), but also from Hitchcock's psychological themes (the cause of Norman's madness is Freudian—familial and sexual—he is not a zombie or a possessed demon), Bernard Herrmann's score (his groundbreaking strains of violin "screams" have been oft-mimicked), the camera angles (Hitchcock's overhead shots, for example, are now standard), and the sets (the gothic house and, especially, the motel are now common settings). Curiously, the main difference between PSYCHO and the horror film of today is in the age of the characters. There isn't a teenager in sight in PSYCHO—a curious comment on the evolution of the genre and the shifting age of moviegoing audiences.

p, Alfred Hitchcock; d, Alfred Hitchcock; w, Joseph Stefano (based on the novel by Robert Bloch); ph, John L. Russell; ed, George Tomasini; m, Bernard Herrmann.

(PR:O  MPAA:NR)

## PSYCHO II**½

(1983) 113m UNIV-Oak/UNIV c

Anthony Perkins *(Norman Bates)*, Vera Miles *(Lila Loomis)*, Meg Tilly *(Mary)*, Robert Loggia *(Dr. Raymond)*, Dennis Franz *(Toomey)*, Hugh Gillin *(Sheriff Hunt)*, Claudia Bryar *(Mrs. Spool)*, Robert Alan Browne *(Statler)*, Ben Hartigan *(Judge)*, Lee Garlington *(Myrna)*, Tim Maier *(Josh)*, Jill Carroll *(Kim)*, Chris Hendrie *(Deputy Pool)*, Tom Holland *(Deputy Norris)*, Michael Lomazow *(District Attorney)*, Robert Destri *(Public Defender)*, Osgood Perkins *(Young Norman)*, Ben Frommer *(Sexton)*, Gene Whittington *(Diver)*, Robert Traynor *(Desk Clerk)*, George Dickerson *(County Sheriff)*, Thaddeus Smith *(Deputy Sheriff)*, Sheila K. Adams *(Deputy Woman)*, Victoria Brown *(Deputy Clerk)*.

It should come as no surprise that someone would decide to film a sequel to Alfred Hitchcock's classic. What *is* a surprise is that it's as good as it is. After 22 years in an asylum, Norman Bates (Anthony Perkins, reprising his familiar role) is released and allowed to return home, over the loud objections of Lila Loomis (Vera Miles), sister of the murdered Marion Crane (who apparently married her dead sister's lover, Sam Loomis, after Marion's demise in PSYCHO). Lila vows to avenge her sister's death and to get Norman returned to the asylum. Although Norman is somewhat apprehensive about returning to the old house and motel where he committed his murders, he seems to be completely recovered. He is even given work at a local diner, where he meets Mary (Meg Tilly), a cute but spacy waitress who seems completely ignorant of the horrors that occurred in the area 22 years before. As Norman gets close to Mary, strange things begin to occur. Norman finds notes signed by Mother, receives phone calls from Mother, even sees Mother standing in her bedroom window. Then the bodies begin to pile up. PSYCHO II could have resorted to the cheap slasher techniques of the day, but instead it concentrates on developing the character of Norman Bates—a sympathetic soul who is fighting with all his might to overcome his past and live as a normal person. In PSYCHO II, Norman is a victim of crazed people who insist on persecuting him and, as a result, looks incredibly sane by comparison. Unfortunately the end to PSYCHO II contradicts the entire feel of the film, turning Norman into a leering loon in preparation for another sequel.

p, Hilton A. Green; d, Richard Franklin; w, Tom Holland (based on characters created by Robert Bloch); ph, Dean Cundey (Technicolor); ed, Andrew London; m, Jerry Goldsmith.

**(PR:O  MPAA:R)**

## PSYCHO III***

(1986) 93m UNIV c

Anthony Perkins *(Norman Bates)*, Diana Scarwid *(Maureen Coyle)*, Jeff Fahey *(Duane Duke)*, Roberta Maxwell *(Tracy Venable)*, Hugh Gillin *(Sheriff Hunt)*, Lee Garlington *(Myrna)*, Robert Alan Browne *(Statler)*, Gary Bayer *(Father Brian)*, Patience Cleveland *(Sister Margaret)*, Juliette Cummins *(Red)*, Steve Guevara *(Deputy Leo)*, Kay

Heberle *(Ruthie)*, Donovan Scott *(Kyle)*, Karen Hensel *(Sister Catherine)*, Jack Murdock *(Lou)*, Katt Shea Ruben *(Patsy Boyle)*, Hugo L. Stanger *(Harvey Leach)*, Lisa Ives *(Belltower Nun)*, Angele Ritter *(Bartender)*, Diane Rodriguez *(Nun)*, Virginia Gregg *(Mother's Voice)*.

. . . And sure enough that sequel followed, this time with Anthony Perkins making his directorial debut as well as starring in the role for which he will forever be remembered. Understanding the Norman Bates character probably better than anyone (including Alfred Hitchcock and novelist Robert Bloch ), having lived in Norman's shadow for 26 years , Perkins is here given his chance to interpret the story. Beginning one month after the end of PSYCHO II, this film introduces Norman to the blonde Maureen Coyle (Diana Scarwid), a pretty young novice who is looking for some sign from above that God exists. Having left the convent, Maureen arrives at the Bates Motel. Not only does she have the same initials of one of Norman's victims (M.C.—Marion Crane), she also looks a bit like her. Norman tries to keep himself under control, fighting with his memory of the murdered Marion. He discusses the problem with Mother, who is still propped up at her bedroom window, and who wants very much to get rid of that "whore" Maureen. Meanwhile, Maureen is tormented by the thoughts of her own "mother"—the Virgin Mary—to whom she has devoted her life. Naturally these two opposites attract and Norman feels love for the first time. The Richard Franklin-Tom Holland PSYCHO II was commendable in that it revered Hitchcock and employed the master's techniques adroitly, and Perkins is an equally adroit director. PSYCHO III, however, differs significantly from PSYCHO II in Perkins' wicked, malicious sense of humor. Not just some actor who has been given a chance to direct, Perkins has a style and, like fellow director-actors Orson Welles and Clint Eastwood, knows his own persona, knows how to photograph and light himself for the proper effect. Adding to the excitement of PSYCHO III is Perkins' willingness to take chances with his style and material. Risking the wrath of religious groups, Perkins makes Maureen a nun who has fallen from grace. She thinks her life has been saved by the Virgin, but the credit is actually due to Norman—a schizophrenic murderer. Unfortunately, PSYCHO III is much gorier than the two previous PSYCHOs, the murder scenes relying on creative killings rather than any real terror. PSYCHO II did mediocre business, and PSYCHO III did even worse—factors that stop Hollywood from adding another entry to the series.

p, Hilton A. Green; d, Anthony Perkins; w, Charles Edward Pogue (based on the characters created by Robert Bloch); ph, Bruce Surtees; ed, David Blewitt; m, Carter Burwell.

**(PR:O  MPAA:R)**

## PSYCHOMANIA**

(1972, Brit.) 91m Scotia International c (AKA: DEATH WHEELERS, THE; FROG, THE; LIVING DEAD, THE)

George Sanders *(Shadwill)*, Beryl Reid *(Mrs. Latham)*, Nicky Henson *(Tom )*, Mary Larkin *(Abby )*, Roy Holder *(Bertram)*, Ann Michelle *(Jane Pettibone)*, Robert Hardy *(Chief Insp. Hesseltine)*, Patrick Holt *(Sergeant)*, Denis Gil-

**THE HORROR FILM**

more *(Hatchet)*, Miles Greenwood *(Chopped Meat)*, Rocky Taylor *(Hinley)*, Peter Whitting *(Exesh)*, Jacki Webb *(Mother)*, David Millett *(Father)*, Linda Gray *(Grandmother)*, Andrew Laurence *(Grandfather)*, Alan Bennion, John Levene *(Constables)*, Bill Pertwee *(Publican)*, Roy Evans *(Motorist)*, Stanley Stewart *(Petrol Pump Attendant)*, Serretta Wilson *(Stella)*, Lane Meddick *(Mr. Pettibone)*, June Brown *(Mrs. Pettibone)*, Denis Carey *(Coroner's Assistant)*, Martin Boddey *(Coroner)*.

This has to be the only British biker-gang horror movie ever made. Tom Latham (Nicky Henson) is the long-haired leader of "The Living Dead," an obnoxious motorcycle gang whose favorite hangout is a remote field containing a Stonehenge-like aggregation of rocks. Under the guidance of his spiritualist mother (Beryl Reid) and her Satanist butler (George Sanders), Tom discovers the secret of eternal life: all you have to do is willingly commit suicide in the belief that you'll come back from the dead. Once zombified, nothing can kill you. Tom decides to test the theory by driving his bike off an overpass into a river. Soon after his burial—with his corpse sitting upright on his motorcycle—Tom revs up his bike and bursts out of the grave at full throttle. Thrilled with his success, the rest of the gang begins committing suicide (driving into a truck, drowning, jumping off a building, etc.). Although all but one succeed in returning from the dead—his belief wavers at the last minute—Tom's girl friend, Abby (Mary Larkin), really doesn't want to kill herself, leading to tension between her and Tom. Meanwhile, the newly immortal Living Dead raise even more hell than usual; riding through grocery stores and brick walls, the zombie bikers wreak havoc in their little town, moving Tom's mother to put a stop to their nonsense. With the exception of a fairly creepy credit sequence, there's not much particularly frightening here. What is fun, however, is taking in all the "hip" 1960s and 70s lingo and watching the nihilistic bikers displaying their studied rebellious attitude. The whole affair plays like it was meant to be tongue-in-cheek, but it's difficult to tell at times. Don't miss the stunning biker anthem "Riding Free" (music by David Whittaker, lyrics by John Worth) sung by Harvey Andrews at Tom's funeral.

p, Andrew Donally; d, Don Sharp; w, Arnaud D'Usseau; ph, Ted Moore (Technicolor); ed, Richard Best; m, David Whitaker.

**(PR:A   MPAA:PG)**

## PSYCHOS IN LOVE*½

(1987) 87m Generic/Wizard Home Video-ICN Bleecker Infinity c

Carmine Capobianco *(Joe)*, Debi Thibeault *(Kate)*, Frank Stewart *(Herman)*, Cecilia Wilde *(Nikki)*, Donna Davidge *(Heather)*, Patti Chambers *(Girl in Bed)*, Carla Bragoli *(Girl in Woods)*, Carrie Gordon *(Girl in Toilet)*, Angela Nicholas *(Dianne)*, Peach Gribauskas *(Bar Waitress)*, Professor Morono *(Joey the Creep)*, Shawn Light *(Girl in Sauna)*, Scott Sears *(Frightened Man)*, Lee Ann Baker *(Heavy Metal Girl)*, Linda Strouth *(Cathy)*, Eric Lutes *(Mechanic)*, Mike Brady *(Redneck)*, Ruth Collins *(Susan)*, Jerry Rakow *(Henry)*, Irma St. Paule *(Sara)*, Tressa Zannino *(Hooker)*.

An ambitious low-budget horror parody, PSYCHOS IN LOVE actually contains a few redeeming moments of social satire and is fairly interesting stylistically. Joe (Carmine Capobianco) is a balding, overweight bar owner and self-confessed psycho who despises grapes (". . . all kinds of grapes! Purple grapes! Green grapes! Peeled grapes and nonpeeled grapes! Grapes with seeds! Grapes without seeds! Grapes in bunches or in small clumps of twos and threes!") and has problems sustaining a relationship. He picks up attractive women, and, when the dates go badly, kills them. Joe's life changes, however, when he meets female psycho killer Kate (Debi Thibeault), who shares his hatred of grapes. Sophomoric, gross, warped, and more than a bit depraved, PSYCHOS IN LOVE succeeds as a low-budget satire of American dating rituals, modern relationships, suburbia, and slasher movies. Although at times the pacing is sluggish and only about half the jokes are funny, it does have a zany originality. Narrated by both Joe and Kate, the film is often self-reflexive—the viewer reminded throughout that it's all "just a movie" as actors make asides to the camera, or put their hands over the lens, or slap away the mike-boom when it comes into frame. While certainly not for the squeamish, PSYCHOS IN LOVE does have a certain grotesque charm, and may achieve a minor sort of cult status among fans of the bizarre.

p, Gorman Bechard; d, Gorman Bechard; w, Carmine Capobianco, Gorman Bechard; ph, Gorman Bechard (Precision color); ed, Gorman Bechard; m, Carmine Capobianco, Gorman Bechard.

**(PR:O   MPAA:NR)**

## PULSE***

(1988) 91m Aspen Film Society/COL c

Cliff DeYoung *(Bill)*, Roxanne Hart *(Ellen)*, Joey Lawrence *(David)*, Matthew Lawrence *(Stevie)*, Charles Tyner *(Old Man)*, Dennis Redfield *(Pete)*, Robert Romanus *(Paul)*, Myron D. Healey *(Howard)*.

PULSE is an original, highly visual, intense thriller that becomes horrific as it weaves its tale of everyday household items run amok. One evening, Bill (Cliff DeYoung) and his wife (Roxanne Hart) are awakened by a neighbor who is destroying his house, having presumably gone mad. The next day, Bill's son, David (Joey Lawrence), arrives from Colorado to visit his father and step-mother. He's not happy to be there, especially when he learns that the crazy neighbor's wife was killed just before the man himself lost control. It seems that the woman died when a piece of metal was spewed from her garbage disposal, piercing her eye. Slowly, the electrical world around David begins to change—the TV burns out, the furnace shoots flames. David, eager to discover the truth of these ruptures, breaks into the house across the street, where he meets an elderly electrician who tells of voices in the wires and hints about "them." "I've seen dozens of houses just like this one," he says eerily. By the climax, the family is trapped in the house, battling fire, water, and electricity. Writer-director Paul Golding succeeds where many horror directors fail: in making the incredible believable. The idea of

**PULSE—**

electricity having a mind of its own is silly, of course, but with Golding's guidance the notion becomes frighteningly possible as he generates fear from the recognition that most of us don't know exactly how an electrical device works. Especially effective is the refusal to provide an exact reason as to why the chaos is happening. The filmmakers leave it to our imagination (providing a possible alien connection), and because we are put in the same position as the characters themselves, we can identify with their fear.

p, Patricia A. Stallone; d, Paul Golding; w, Paul Golding; ph, Peter Collister (DeLuxe Color); ed, Gib Jaffe; m, Jay Ferguson.

(PR:C  MPAA:PG-13)

**PUMPKINHEAD\*\***

(1988) 86m UA-Lion/MGM-UA c

Lance Henriksen *(Ed Harley)*, Matthew Hurley *(Billy Harley)*, Jeff East *(Chris)*, John DiAquino *(Joel)*, Kimberly Ross *(Kim)*, Joel Hoffman *(Steve)*, Cynthia Bain *(Tracy)*, Kerry Remsen *(Maggie)*, Madeleine Taylor Holmes *(Witch-woman)*, Tom Woodruff, Jr. *(Pumpkinhead)*, Florence Schauffler.

The fairly promising directorial debut of Oscar-winning special-effects man Stan Winston (THE TERMINATOR; ALIENS; and PREDATOR), PUMPKINHEAD is an old-fashioned, atmospheric, moralistic tale that presents horror steeped in rural folklore and legend. Ed (Lance Henriksen) is a kindly, widowed farmer who runs a general store and who loves his 10-year-old son more than anything in the world. Tragedy strikes, however, when the boy is accidentally run over by a motorcyclist who leaves the youngster to die. Blinded by hatred and the desire for vengeance, Ed goes to the remote cabin of an ancient witch and begs her to bring his boy back to life. That she cannot do, but Ed also knows the legend of "Pumpkinhead," a vicious demon that can be summoned to avenge wrongful death. Having worked closely with director James Cameron, Winston has a strong visual sense, and a surprisingly good feel for character development. The relationship between Ed and his son is especially effective, encouraging viewers to feel just as vindictive as the father. Winston then turns the tables on his audience, however, by showing Ed as he calms down, has second thoughts, and then tries to stop the terror he created. The message: Revenge is wrong. Not a common theme in modern horror. Unfortunately, Winston begins to lose control in the film's latter half, when the monster is on the rampage. By now the "Ten Little Indians" method of killing characters one at a time has gotten so stale that no matter how impressive the monster is, the resulting sequence is inevitably tedious.

p, Richard C. Weinman, Howard Smith; d, Stan Winston; w, Mark Patrick Carducci, Gary Gerani (based on a story by Mark Patrick Carducci, Stan Winston, Richard C. Weinman); ph, Bojan Bazelli (Technicolor); ed, Marcus Manton; m, Richard Stone.

(PR:O  MPAA:R)

**PYX, THE\*\*\***

(1973, Can.) 111m Cinerama c

Karen Black *(Elizabeth Lucy)*, Christopher Plummer *(Jim Henderson)*, Donald Pilon *(Pierre Paquette)*, Jean-Louis Roux *(Keerson)*, Yvette Brind'Amour *(Meg)*, Jacques Godin *(Superintendent)*, Lee Broker *(Herbie Lafram)*, Terry Haig *(Jimmy)*, Robin Gammell *(Worther)*, Louise Rinfret *(Sandra)*.

This quickly made but compelling Canadian horror-mystery presents Karen Black as a hooker who is murdered after participating in a Black Mass, her body found clutching a pyx—the container used to hold the host. Henderson (Christopher Plummer), the tough detective sent to investigate, soon unravels a conspiracy of Satanists, many in high places. Although the plot is sometimes convoluted, and somewhat confusing (lots of flashbacks), the film does have a palpable sense of unease and foreboding. The acting, especially by Plummer and supporting cast members Yvette Brind'Amour and Jean-Louis Roux, is terrific and the dialog is sharp, literate, and witty. Black wrote and sang three songs for this film, which she would do again in Robert Altman's NASHVILLE.

p, Maxine Samuels, Julian Roffman; d, Harvey Hart; w, Robert Schlitt (based on the novel by John Buell); ph, Rene Verzier; ed, Ron Wisman; m, Harry Freedman.

(PR:O  MPAA:R)

**Q\*\*\*\***

(1982) 100m United Film Distribution c (AKA: THE WINGED SERPENT)

Michael Moriarty *(Jimmy Quinn)*, Candy Clark *(Joan)*, David Carradine *(Detective Shepard)*, Richard Roundtree *(Sgt. Powell)*, James Dixon *(Lt. Murray)*, Malachy McCourt *(Police Commissioner)*, Fred J. Scollay *(Capt. Fletcher)*, Peter Hock *(Detective Clifford)*, Ron Cey *(Detective Hoberman)*, Mary Louise Weller *(Mrs. Pauley)*, Bruce Carradine *(Victim)*, John Capodice *(Doyle)*, Tony Page *(Webb)*, Larkin Ford *(Curator)*, Larry Pine *(Professor)*, Eddie Jones *(Watchman)*, Shelly Desai *(Kahea)*, Nancy Stafford *(Eyewitness)*, Bobbi Burns *(Sunbather)*.

Larry Cohen once again proves himself to be among the most creative, original, and intelligent American horror film directors in this bizarre masterwork, which successfully combines a *film noir* crime story with a good old-fashioned "giant monster" movie. Michael Moriarty turns in a brilliant performance as Jimmy Quinn, an ex-con, former junkie, and small-time hood looking to make one big score. After robbing a Manhattan diamond center, he hides out in the tower of the Chrysler building and discovers a large hole in the dome of the structure, containing a huge nest with an equally large egg and several partially devoured human corpses. Meanwhile, the New York City police have been plagued by a bizarre string of deaths, and Detective Shepard (David Carradine) and Sgt. Powell (Richard Roundtree) have been investigating reports of people being snatched off rooftops. What all soon find out is that the Aztec god Quetzalcoatl, the winged serpent, is flying over Manhattan. Though Q's premise seems fairly silly (so does KING KONG's), Cohen's handling of the material is superior; he really convinces us that the idea of a giant bird living in a nest at the top of the Chrysler building isn't as implausible as it sounds. Cohen packs the film with stunning visuals and makes the most of New York City's architecture, capitalizing on its dozens of facades with birds and birdlike carvings. Q bombed at the box office because it was nearly impossible to package into a nice, simple ad campaign, but the film is a skillful combination of genres, sporting some fine acting and a literate, fascinating script with dashes of biting humor, that is well worth seeing.

p, Larry Cohen; d, Larry Cohen; w, Larry Cohen; ph, Fred Murphy; ed, Armand Lebowitz; m, Robert O. Ragland.

(PR:O MPAA:R)

# R

## RABID***

(1976, Can.) 91m Cinepix-Dibar/New World c (AKA: RAGE)

Marilyn Chambers *(Rose)*, Frank Moore *(Hart Read)*, Joe Silver *(Murray Cypher)*, Howard Ryshpan *(Dr. Dan Keloid)*, Patricia Gage *(Dr. Roxanne Keloid)*, Susan Roman *(Mindy Kent)*, J. Roger Periard *(Lloyd Walsh)*, Lynne Deragon *(Nurse Louise)*, Terry Schonblum *(Judy Glasberg)*, Victor Desy *(Claude LaPointe)*, Julie Anna *(Rita)*, Gary McKeehan *(Smooth Eddy)*, Terrence G. Ross *(Farmer)*, Miguel Fernandes *(Man in Cinema)*, Robert O'Ree *(Police Sergeant)*, Greg Van Riel *(Young Man in Plaza)*, Jerome Tiberghien *(Dr. Carl)*, Jack Messinger *(Policeman on Highway)*, Grant Lowe *(Trucker)*, John Gilbert *(Dr. Royce Gentry)*, Tony Angelo *(Dispatcher)*, Peter McNeill *(Leader)*, Una Kay *(Jackie)*, Madeline Pageau *(Beatrice Owen)*, Mark Walker *(Steve)*.

A virtual remake of THEY CAME FROM WITHIN, RABID finds director David Cronenberg more in control of his narrative and his visual style than he was in his previous film, but the results are still somewhat uneven. Once again Cronenberg explores sexually transmitted horror, but this time through none other than hardcore porno starlet Marilyn Chambers, making her legitimate debut here as Rose, a woman seriously injured in a motorcycle accident. A local plastic surgeon uses the opportunity to experiment with some new skin grafts he's developing, but somehow the surgery goes awry and soon Rose sports a grotesque, phalluslike organ in her armpit that sucks blood out of her unsuspecting lovers (the original treatment of the film was entitled "Mosquito"). This soon leads to an epidemic that turns the citizens of Montreal into rabid, blood-seeking,

sex-crazed monsters that drool green slime. Once again, Cronenberg has made a rather frustrating film. Although RABID is full of interesting ideas, they are not particularly well developed or presented by Cronenberg's unfocused script. And while the film has an uneasy sense of humor, Cronenberg again overplays his most visceral sequences, including the well-shot but pointless car crash. He does, however, make more of an attempt to develop his characters here, but they are still little more than cardboard cutouts whose reactions to the story's bizarre situations are surprisingly nonchalant (Rose kind of shrugs off her affliction). As with THEY CAME FROM WITHIN, the performances are rather weak, and while Chambers does add some resonance to the film as a sexual icon, her acting ability is limited and mars the movie. Part of what makes Cronenberg's work so fascinating is his progression as an artist—with each of his films better than its predecessor—and his next horror film, THE BROOD, showed him to be an even more assured filmmaker.

p, John Dunning; d, David Cronenberg; w, David Cronenberg; ph, Rene Verzier (Panavision, Eastmancolor); ed, Jean LaFleur.

(PR:O MPAA:R)

## RACE WITH THE DEVIL**½

(1975) 88m FOX c

Peter Fonda *(Roger)*, Warren Oates *(Frank)*, Loretta Swit *(Alice)*, Lara Parker *(Kelly)*, R.G. Armstrong *(Sheriff)*, Clay Tanner *(Delbert)*, Carol Blodgett *(Ethel)*, Ricci Ware *(Ricci Ware)*, James N. Harrell *(Gun Shop Owner)*, Paul A. Partain *(Cal Mathers)*, Karen Miller *(Kay)*, Arkey Blue *(Arkey Blue)*, Jack Starrett *(Gas Station Attendant)*, Phil Hoover *(Mechanic)*, Wes Bishop *(Deputy Dave)*, Bob Jutson, Peggy Kokernot, Carol Cannon, Tommy Splittberger.

Peter Fonda, Lara Parker, Warren Oates, and Loretta Swit star in this fairly effective action-horror film as two married couples who travel to Texas in a large camper. The first night out they accidentally stumble upon a cult of Devil worshipers, and witness a human sacrifice. When the vacationers try to escape, the Satanists give chase, leading to an incredible, lengthy action sequence in which the cultists leap onto the moving camper from pick-up trucks and cars. This exceptionally well-done sequence bears a remarkable resemblance to the climactic chase scene in THE ROAD WARRIOR, wherein the crazed desert rats leap onto Mel Gibson's gasoline tanker in an effort to stop him. In fact, the scenes are similar enough in style and execution that THE ROAD WARRIOR's director, George Miller, must have seen RACE WITH THE DEVIL and been inspired by it.

p, Wes Bishop; d, Jack Starrett; w, Wes Bishop, Lee Frost; ph, Robert Jessup (DeLuxe Color); ed, Allan Jacobs; m, Leonard Rosenman.

(PR:C MPAA:PG)

## RATS ARE COMING! THE WEREWOLVES ARE HERE!, THE zero

(1972) 92m William Mishkin c

Hope Stansbury *(Monica Mooney)*, Jacquelis Skarvellis *(Diana)*, Noel Collins *(Mortimer Mooney)*, Joan Ogden *(Phoebe Mooney)*, Douglas Phair *(Pa Mooney)*, Berwick Kaler *(Malcolm Mooney)*, Ian Innes *(Gerald)*.

This stupid horror movie with a great title opens as the daughter of a strange family brings her new husband to the family estate. Gradually (and after many boring scenes), it is revealed that the entire clan (except the daughter) is the victim of a family curse that turns them into werewolves when the moon is full. To deal with this unfortunate condition, they take tranquilizers and lock themselves in their rooms. The daughter decides it's time to end the curse, so she has husband's silver crucifix melted down into silver bullets. Originally to be titled CURSE OF THE FULL MOON, the finished film ran a scant 67 minutes, so some rat scenes were added to pad it out and to capitalize on the success of WILLARD. The most interesting thing about the movie is trying to pick out the fake British accents from the real ones.

p, William Mishkin; d, Andy Milligan; w, Andy Milligan; ph, Andy Milligan.

**(PR:O    MPAA:PG)**

## RATTLERS*

(1976) 82m Boxoffice International c

Sam Chew *(Dr. Sam Parkinson)*, Elisabeth Chauvet *(Ann)*, Dan Priest *(The Colonel)*, Ron Gold *(Dr. Delaney)*, Tony Ballen *(Sheriff)*, Richard Lockmiller *(Deputy)*, Jo Jordan *(Mother)*, Al Dunlap *(The General)*, Ancel Cook *(Janitor)*, Gary Van Ormand, Darwin Joston *(Soldiers)*, Travis Gold, Alan Dekkar *(Boys)*, Celia Kaye *(Woman in Bathtub)*, Scott McCarter *(Son)*, Matt Knox *(Pilot)*.

Rattlesnakes are the stars of this unspectacular killer-reptile film set in the Mojave Desert. Zoology professor Sam Parkinson (Sam Chew) is determined to get to the bottom of a rash of mysterious murders; Ann (Elisabeth Chauvet), a photographer, aids him in his investigation, and together they discover that snakes, attacking in packs, are the culprits. Following the clues to a nearby Army base, they learn of a hidden crate of nerve gas to which the rattlers were exposed and which has chemically driven to them to murder. This dull revenge-of-nature film is far too static and slow-paced to be worthwhile.

p, John McCauley; d, John McCauley; w, Jerry Golding; ph, Richard Gibb, Irv Goodnoff; ed, Sandy Glieberman.

**(PR:C    MPAA:PG)**

## RAVEN, THE***½

(1935) 62m UNIV bw

Boris Karloff *(Edmond Bateman)*, Bela Lugosi *(Dr. Richard Vollin)*, Irene Ware *(Jean Thatcher)*, Lester Mathews *(Dr. Jerry Holden)*, Samuel S. Hinds *(Judge Thatcher)*, Inez Courtney *(Mary Burns)*, Ian Wolfe *("Pinky" Geoffrey)*, Spencer Charters *(Col. Bertram Grant)*, Maidel Turner *(Harriet Grant)*, Arthur Hoyt *(Chapman)*, Walter Miller.

The second teaming of Bela Lugosi and Boris Karloff finds the horror greats in fine form in this film "inspired by" by the work of Edgar Allan Poe. Dr. Richard Vollin (Lugosi) is a demented brain surgeon whose admiration for Poe has led him to construct a dungeon filled with devices right out of the author's stories. At the behest of Judge Thatcher (Samuel S. Hinds), Vollin agrees to save the life of his beautiful daughter, Jean (Irene Ware), a dancer. Having fallen in love with the girl—her interpretive dance to a recitation of Poe's "The Raven" mere icing on the cake—Vollin asks her for her hand in marriage, but is scoffed at by the judge. It seems Jean is already engaged to be married to another doctor, Jerry Holden (Lester Mathews). To get revenge, Vollin invites the judge, his daughter, and her fiance to a dinner party, at which he offers to show them his collection of Poe artifacts, intending to use them on his guests. But his plans are upset by Bateman (Boris Karloff), an escaped criminal who had begged Vollin to perform plastic surgery on him, only to be transformed into a monster by the evil surgeon. Held in check by Vollin, who promises to make him handsome again, Bateman reluctantly does the doctor's bidding, but has a change of heart and helps foil Vollin's revenge. Whereas Karloff dominated his previous film with Lugosi, THE BLACK CAT (1934), Lugosi is definitely the star of THE RAVEN, in one of his best roles. First seen reciting some lines from Poe's famous poem, Lugosi's Dr. Vollin is a bit arrogant and cruel, but it is the pain of unrequited love that drives him completely insane. Karloff, who does not make his appearance until well into the film, is also excellent, sporting two Jack Pierce makeup creations—first seen with a heavy beard and then clean-shaven with half his face horribly contorted. The scene wherein Vollin reveals what he has done to Karloff—in a operating room full of mirrors—is the highlight of the film. While not as poetic or haunting as Edgar Ulmer's THE BLACK CAT (with which it is available as a videocassette double-bill), THE RAVEN is a remarkably demented tale of revenge, and memorable in its own right.

p, David Diamond; d, Louis Friedlander; w, David Boehm (based on the poem by Edgar Allan Poe); ph, Charles Stumar; ed, Alfred Akst; m, Gilbert Harland.

**(PR:A    MPAA:NR)**

## RAVEN, THE***½

(1963) 86m Alta Vista/AIP c

Vincent Price *(Dr. Erasmus Craven)*, Peter Lorre *(Dr. Adolphus Bedlo)*, Boris Karloff *(Dr. Scarabus)*, Hazel Court *(Lenore Craven)*, Olive Sturgess *(Estelle Craven)*, Jack Nicholson *(Rexford Bedlo)*, Connie Wallace *(Maidservant)*, William Baskin *(Grimes)*, Aaron Saxon *(Gort)*, Jim Jr. *(The Raven)*.

Another of Roger Corman's Poe films, THE RAVEN is a wonderfully funny sendup of the genre, which begins as a recently retired wizard, Dr. Erasmus Craven (Vincent Price), has gone into seclusion after the apparent death of his wife, Lenore (Hazel Court). His gloomy meditations are interrupted by the arrival of an obnoxious talking raven, which claims to be a wizard put under a spell by the most powerful magician in the land, Dr. Scarabus (Boris Karloff). After some clever banter, Craven restores the raven-wizard to his human form ... almost, as the raven becomes Dr. Adolphus Bedlo (Peter Lorre), a pudgy character with winged arms—an ornithological mutation that is corrected by another dose of potion. Adolphus informs Craven that a woman who greatly resembles Lenore is Scarabus' mistress, and Craven decides to investigate and pays a visit to Scarabus' castle. When the rival wizards meet face to face, a stunning battle erupts, filled with fireballs and flashing lights. The charming comedic success of THE RAVEN sprang from a Corman cast and crew that had grown tired of the repetitive Poe series and wanted to have some fun. Most of the laughs on the set (and in the film) came from watching an impish Lorre improvising one-liners that would catch cool professionals Price and Karloff by surprise and test their straight-faced skills. Lorre is a joy to watch, and obviously relished the role, his infectious wit infusing the screen. Corman brought the film in under budget and ahead of schedule, and, since he had Karloff contracted for three more days of work, decided to make another quickie horror film, THE TERROR. This was the first time the three horror film stars—billed as "The Great Triumvirate of Terror"—appeared together.

p, Roger Corman; d, Roger Corman; w, Richard Matheson (based on the poem by Edgar Allan Poe); ph, Floyd Crosby (Panavision, Pathe Color); ed, Ronald Sinclair; m, Les Baxter.

(PR:C MPAA:NR)

## RAWHEAD REX*

(1987, Brit.) 89m Alpine-Paradise-Green Man/Empire c

David Dukes *(Howard Hallenbeck)*, Kelly Piper *(Elaine Hallenbeck)*, Hugh O'Conor *(Robbie Hallenbeck)*, Cora Lunny *(Minty Hallenbeck)*, Ronan Wilmot *(Declan O'Brien)*, Niall Toibin *(Rev. Coot)*, Niall O'Brien *(Det. Insp. Isaac Gissing)*, Heinrich Von Schellendorf *(Rawhead Rex)*, Donal McCann *(Tom Garron)*, Eleanor Feely *(Jenny Nicholson)*, Gladys Sheehan *(Ena Benedict)*, Madelyn Erskine *(Alice Gibson)*, Gerry Walsh *(Dennis McHugh)*, Noel O'Donovan *(Mitch Harney)*, John Olohan *(Dennis Nicholson)*, Peter Donovan *(Liam Blanchfield)*, Bob Carlile *(Garda Conroy)*, Patrick Dawson *(Det. Larkin)*, Barry Lynch *(Andy Johnson)*, Maeve Germaine *(Katrina)*, Simon Kelly *(Neil Johnson)*, Derry Power *(Sean Power)*, Sheila Flitton *(Nancy Power)*, Derek Halligan *(Caravaner)*, Bairbee Ni Chaoimh *(Laurie)*, Tom Lawlor *(1st Man Possessed)*, Dave Carey *(Caravaner Gunman)*, Vincent Smith, Mary Ryan *(Survivors)*, Michael Ford *(Gissing's Driver)*.

There are two good reasons why British horror author Clive Barker decided to direct his own stories (beginning with HELLRAISER): one is UNDERWORLD (1985) and the other is RAWHEAD REX, both produced and directed by the same inept team. Although Barker wrote both screenplays and director George Pavlou is his friend, neither film captures the essence of the Barker stories from which they are derived. Set in Ireland, RAWHEAD REX begins promisingly enough as a farmer decides to dig up an ancient stone that has been standing in his field for centuries and ends up unearthing a huge, snarling, legendary monster, an ancient god of the days before Christianity—Rawhead Rex (played by seven-foot-tall German actor Heinrich Von Schellendorf). The monster goes on a rampage, taking big, fatal bites out of several locals, including the young son of American university professor Howard Hallenbeck (David Dukes). An expert in history and anthropology, Hallenbeck uncovers the history of Rawhead Rex and figures out how to destroy him. For starters, the monster suit concocted by special-effects whiz Peter Litten is downright laughable. The beast is supposed to have been buried beneath the earth for hundreds of years (Barker's description of this in the story is *very* vivid), but this Rawhead Rex is a squeaky clean latex rubber-man fresh out of the mold—looking more like a drooling college football mascot than an evil ancient god. Director Pavlou moves his film at a snail's pace, demonstrating little flair for suspense or even simple shock. The last word on Pavlou's directorial cleverness is that he is not beyond intercutting shots of gory violence with a housewife cutting up some meat for a stew. Gosh, what an ingenious juxtaposition. Ugh.

p, Kevin Attew, Don Hawkins; d, George Pavlou; w, Clive Barker (based on a short story by Clive Barker); ph, John Metcalfe (Rank color); ed, Andy Horvitch; m, Colin Towns.

(PR:O MPAA:R)

## RAZORBACK**½

(1984, Aus.) 95m UAA/WB c

Gregory Harrison *(Carl Winters)*, Arkie Whiteley *(Sarah Cameron)*, Bill Kerr *(Jake Cullen)*, Chris Haywood *(Benny Baker)*, Judy Morris *(Beth Winters)*, John Howard *(Danny)*, John Ewart *(Turner)*, Don Smith *(Wallace)*, Mervyn Drake *(Andy)*, Redmond Phillips *(Magistrate)*, Alan Beecher *(Counsel)*, Peter Schwartz *(Lawyer)*, Beth Child *(Louise Cullen)*, Rick Kennedy *(Farmer)*, Chris Hession *(TV Cowboy)*, Brian Adams *(Male Newscaster)*, Jinx Lootens *(Female Newscaster)*, Angus Malone *(Scotty)*, Peter Boswell *(Wagstaff)*, Don Lane *(Himself)*, David Argue.

American journalist Beth Winters (Judy Morris) travels to Australia to do a story on the illegal hunting of kangaroos. After she meets with hostility from outback locals, her car is run off the road, and while she pulls herself to safety, Beth is attacked and killed by an enormous wild pig. Her husband, Carl (Gregory Harrison), goes to find out what happened and meets Jake (Bill Kerr), whose baby grandson had earlier been carried off by the mutant porker, and who has dedicated his life to hunting it down. Carl isn't convinced, however, until he barely escapes the monster himself; then he helps Jake track it to a dog-food factory run by a couple of sleazy types who actually feed the awful creature. Only fitfully interesting, RAZORBACK boasts a truly original monster (the giant pig runs through a house like a freight train), but the real horror lies with the totally repulsive brothers who run the dog-food factory and slaughter kangaroos. Although director Russell Mulcahy and cinematographer Dean Semler (THE ROAD WAR-

RIOR) present a slick-looking film, the action is sometimes too repetitive (and sometimes simply too silly) to be truly engaging. Mulcahy would go on to helm the equally superficial HIGHLANDER (1986).

p, Hal McElroy; d, Russell Mulcahy; w, Everett DeRoche (based on the novel by Peter Brennan); ph, Dean Semler (Panavision); ed, William Anderson; m, Iva Davies.

**(PR:O  MPAA:R)**

## RE-ANIMATOR***½

(1985) 86m Re-Animated Productions/Empire c

Jeffrey Combs *(Herbert West),* Bruce Abbott *(Dan Cain),* Barbara Crampton *(Megan Halsey),* David Gale *(Dr. Carl Hill),* Robert Sampson *(Dean Halsey),* Gerry Black *(Mace),* Carolyn Purdy-Gordon *(Dr. Harrod),* Peter Kent *(Melvin the Re-Animated),* Barbara Pieters *(Nurse),* Ian Patrick Williams *(Swiss Professor),* Bunny Summers *(Swiss Woman Doctor),* Al Berry *(Dr. Gruber),* Derek Pendleton, Gene Scherer *(Swiss Policemen),* James Ellis, James Earl Cathay *(Psycho Ward Guards),* Annyce Holzman *(E-R Patient Corpse),* Velvet Debois *(Slit Wrist Girl Corpse),* Lawrence Lowe *(Failed Operation Corpse),* Robert Holcomb *(Motorcycle Accident Corpse),* Mike Filloon *(Bullet Wound to the Face Corpse),* Greg Reid *(One Arm Guy Corpse),* Jack Draheim *(Tall Skinny Guy Corpse),* Robert Pitzele *(Bald O-R Corpse).*

H.P. Lovecraft, a Rhode Island native and recluse, wrote a large number of short stories, most of which were published only in lurid pulp magazines like "Weird Tales." He has since been acclaimed as the most important and influential writer of horror and fantasy to appear post-Poe and pre-King. Several attempts to film Lovecraft's eerie tales of monsters and madness have been made, ranging from DIE, MONSTER, DIE (1965) to THE DUNWICH HORROR (1970). RE-ANIMATOR is the latest effort to bring Lovecraft to the big screen, and while it also fails as a faithful adaptation of Lovecraft, it is an incredibly demented film in its own right that combines a plethora of downright disgusting grand guignol with disturbing black humor. Herbert West (Jeffrey Combs) is an intense young med student determined to make a scientific breakthrough and bring the dead back to life. He works at home on mysterious experiments and finally, using the glowing green fluid he has developed, revivifies a dead cat. The next stop is the med school morgue, where Herbert reanimates a human corpse. Of course, this and every other cadaver he reanimates become a bit difficult to subdue. A major-league splatter-fest, RE-ANIMATOR has a number of horrifying moments, made even more macabre by the grisly humor evident in almost every unforgettable scene (the most memorable and bizarre being the sex scene with a cadaver's detached head). Perhaps the film's only drawback is the somewhat arch self-consciousness of the performers, who are constantly winking at the audience as the horrible is defused into the safely ludicrous. Director-coscreenwriter Stuart Gordon again turned his attention to Lovecraft in 1986's FROM BEYOND.

p, Brian Yuzna; d, Stuart Gordon; w, Dennis Paoli, William

J. Norris, Stuart Gordon (based on the story "Herbert West, The Re-Animator" by H.P. Lovecraft); ph, Mac Ahlberg (DeLuxe Color); ed, Lee Percy; m, Richard Band.

**(PR:O  MPAA:NR)**

## REDEEMER, THE zero

(1976) 83m Dimension c (AKA: REDEEMER. . .SON OF SATAN!, THE)

Michael Hollingsworth, Jeannetta Arnette, T.G. Finkbinder, Damien Knight, Gyr Patterson, Eric Kjoenes, Larry Mooney, Nick Carter, Nikki Barthen, Christopher Flint.

Six former students return to their alma mater for a reunion organized, unknown to them, by a psychotic former classmate. Displeased with his classmates' immorality (including homosexuality), the psycho kills and mutilates them, using, among other murder weapons, a flame thrower and a wash basin. Possessed of disturbingly puritanical sensibility, this inept, unpleasant film is sticky going indeed.

p, Sheldon Tromberg; d, Constantine S. Goochis; w, William Vernick; ph, John Michael Seymer.

**(PR:O  MPAA:R)**

## REPULSION*****

(1965, Brit.) 104m Compton-Tekli/Royal bw

Catherine Deneuve *(Carol Ledoux),* Ian Hendry *(Michael),* John Fraser *(Colin),* Patrick Wymark *(Landlord),* Yvonne Furneaux *(Helen Ledoux),* Renee Houston *(Miss Balch),* Helen Fraser *(Bridget),* Valerie Taylor *(Mme. Denise),* James Villiers *(John),* Monica Merlin *(Mrs. Rendlesham),* Imogen Graham *(Manicurist),* Roman Polanski *(Spoons Player).*

Quite simply, REPULSION is one of the most frightening pictures ever made. It has in many instances been compared to Hitchcock's PSYCHO, but, instead of presenting a *portrait* of a psychotic killer, REPULSION pulls the audience *into the mind* of the crazed individual. Carol Ledoux (Catherine Deneuve) is a Belgian manicurist working in London and sharing an apartment with her sister who slowly becomes unhinged from reality as a result of her feelings about sex, a simultaneous repulsion and attraction. When her sister leaves for a few days with her lover, Carol is left to fend for herself, becoming more and more detached from the outside world. She takes little interest in her surroundings (a potato begins to mold, as does a skinned rabbit ready for cooking) or her appearance, wandering around in a zombie-like trance. She eventually locks herself in the apartment and begins to hallucinate. The most frightening shot in the picture lasts for just a fraction of a second—as Carol is opening a wardrobe, she glimpses the reflection of a man standing in her room. She turns and he is gone. These hallucinations become more intense as her grasp on sanity loosens: the walls crack with a blistering crispness; lights turn on and off; a man (who previously whistled at her on the street) appears in her room and rapes her. Meanwhile the potato continues to rot and flies buzz around the decapitated rabbit carcass. Then the killing starts. Essentially, REPULSION tells a simple story, but Roman Polanski's direction makes it undeniably brilliant. He took great pains in creating the proper composition for the shot of the razor blade, for getting the plaster to crack just right, and for constructing (with art director Seamus Flannery) a hallway that not only seemed to expand and elongate throughout the picture, but actually did, with the help of wall panels. A powerfully engrossing film, which owes much to the realistic, nearly silent performance of Catherine Donouve.

p, Gene Gutowski; d, Roman Polanski; w, Roman Polanski, Gerard Brach, David Stone; ph, Gilbert Taylor; ed, Alastair McIntyre; m, Chico Hamilton.

(PR:O MPAA:NR)

## RETRIBUTION*

(1988) 107m Renegade/United c

Dennis Lipscomb (George Miller), Leslie Wing (Dr. Jennifer Curtis), Suzanne Snyder (Angel), Jeffrey Pomerantz (Dr. Alan Falconer), George Murdock (Dr. John Talbot), Pamela Dunlap (Sally Benson), Susan Peretz (Mrs. Stoller), Clare Peck (Carla Minelli), Chris Caputo (Dylan), Hoyt Axton (Lt. Ashley), Ralph Manza (Amos), Mario Roccuzzo (Johnny Blake), Harry Caesar (Charlie), Jeffrey Josephson (Joe Martinez), Danny D. Daniels (Rasta Doctor), Mike Muscat (Vito Minelli, Sr.), Pearl Adell (Waitress), Ed Berke (Mickey), George Caldwell (Paramedic), Brian Christian (Bus Driver), Tony Cox (Hotel Resident), David Dunard (Lt. Lupo), Trish Fillmore (Desiree), Kenneth Gray (Rev. Dr. Baxley), Richard Jamison (4th Killer), Joan-Carol Kent (Paramedic), Steve Lerman (Bus Passenger).

This incredibly tedious, low-budget ($1.5 millon) horror film tries to make up for its lack of narrative inspiration with hyperactive camerawork. Set in Los Angeles, the film opens on Halloween night as destitute, wimpy artist George Miller (Dennis Lipscomb) makes a suicide leap from the roof of his flophouse. He survives, but his soul—somehow, in a green laser light show with clouds of smoke—becomes possessed. After a stay in a sanitarium he is allowed to go home to his flophouse, where he is welcomed back by an extended family of hookers, bums, thugs, junkies, and drunks. Everything is looking up for George—until he falls asleep, when he has nasty dreams in which he goes places he's never been, meets people he's never seen, and murders them in a variety of horrible ways. When he wakes up, news of the murders is all over the front page. RETRIBUTION is the feature debut of director Guy Magar, who racked up 25 hours of television helming ("Lady Blue," "Hunter," "The A-Team") before trying his hand at the big screen, but it sure seems like he didn't learn much in TV. The film is dull, repetitive, and much, much too long, with every scene pointlessly drawn out and padded with loads of unnecessary camera movement. It has no drama, no suspense, and no surprises—it's just plain slow and terribly pretentious. The whole premise of the film is woefully underdeveloped and doesn't make much sense, even for a supernatural horror film.

p, Guy Magar; d, Guy Magar; w, Guy Magar, Lee Wasserman; ph, Gary Thieltges (Fujicolor); ed, Guy Magar, Alan Shefland; m, Alan Howarth.

(PR:O MPAA:R)

## RETURN OF THE FLY**½

(1959) 80m FOX bw

Vincent Price (Francois Delambre), Brett Halsey (Philippe Delambre), David Frankham (Alan Hinds, Scientist), John Sutton (Inspector Charas), Dan Seymour (Max Berthold, Underworld Fixer), Danielle De Metz (Cecile Bonnard), Janine Graudel (Mme. Bonnard), Richard Flato (Sgt. Dubois), Florence Storm (Nun), Pat O'Hara (Detective Evans), Barry Bernard (Lt. Maclish), Jack Daly (Granville), Michael Mark (Gaston), Francisco Villalobos (Priest), Joan Cotton (Nurse).

Filmed in black and white, this disappointing sequel to THE FLY (1958) retained only Vincent Price from the original cast. Some 20 years after the action of the first film, Philippe (Brett Halsey), the son of the scientist who inadvertently became part-man, part-fly, decides to renew his father's experiments, though his uncle, Francois (Price), warns against it. Philippe re-creates the matter transformation mechanisms, then meets the same fate as his dad when his assistant, Alan (David Frankham), a foreign agent intent on getting the secret of the invention, forces him into the device. Now sporting a huge fly-head, a fly-arm, and a fly-leg, Philippe wanders the area exacting revenge from Alan and his cohorts, while Francois tries to capture the tiny fly with Philippe's head, arm, and leg, so that his nephew can be returned to normal. Edward Bernds, who directed many of The Three Stooges shorts, provided rather plodding direction for this movie, which is far less entertaining than the original. Perhaps believing that the audience needed a *bigger* jolt during the transformation, the filmmakers employed a huge fly-head mask (the script excuses it with some nonsense about the machine causing "giantism"). Unfortunately, the head is so large that the actor underneath it sometimes has trouble holding his head up (he can occasionally be seen holding the mask straight with his good hand while running) and getting through doorways. Still, the film was successful enough to prompt Fox to bring back the Fly again in THE CURSE OF THE FLY (1965).

p, Bernard Glasser; d, Edward Bernds; w, Edward Bernds (based on a story by George Langelaan); ph, Brydon Baker (CinemaScope); ed, Richard C. Meyer; m, Paul Sawtell, Bert Shefter.

(PR:A MPAA:NR)

## RETURN OF THE LIVING DEAD**

(1985) 91m Hemdale-Fox Films Ltd./Orion c

Clu Gulager (Burt), James Karen (Frank), Don Calfa (Ernie), Thom Mathews (Freddy), Beverly Randolph (Tina), John Philbin (Chuck), Jewel Shepard (Casey), Miguel A. Nunez, Jr. (Spider), Brian Peck (Scuz), Linnea Quigley (Trash), Mark Venturini (Suicide), Jonathan Terry (Col. Glover), Cathleen Cordell (His Wife), Drew Deighan,

James Dalesandro *(Paramedics)*, John Durbin, David Bond *(Radio Corpses)*, Bob Libman *(Tac Squad Captain)*, John Stuart West, Michael Crabtree, Ed Krieger *(Riot Cops)*, Robert Craighead, Paul Cloud *(Cops)*, Leigh Drake *(Dispatcher)*, Derrick Brice *(Gunnery Sergeant)*.

Screenwriter Dan O'Bannon has been a sporadic genre talent at best, his screenplays ranging from the interesting (ALIEN; BLUE THUNDER) to the awful (DEAD AND BURIED). RETURN OF THE LIVING DEAD, his directorial debut, is a horror parody of George Romero's "Living Dead" trilogy based on a story by John Russo, who coauthored the script to Romero's original film and shares story rights. Set mostly in a medical supply house owned by Burt (Clu Gulager) and run by Frank (James Karen), the film details the events of a night in which an experimental nerve gas pioneered by the military leaks and brings the dead back to life. Frank explains to a young employee, Freddy (Thom Mathews), that a similar incident occurred several years ago, and that a movie was made about it (NIGHT OF THE LIVING DEAD), only the movie didn't tell the whole truth— in the film, the dead could be stopped by a blow to the head; in real life, *nothing* stopped them. The whole thing is played for laughs, with a pseudohip sense of humor satirizing everything from suburban punks to the military, while delivering a few legitimate chills. Not only does RETURN OF THE LIVING DEAD contain shades of the "Living Dead" trilogy, but the premise of the toxic gas developed by the military and the crisis' nuclear solution is stolen directly from Romero's film THE CRAZIES. RETURN OF THE LIVING DEAD gets off to a promising start and contains some macabre comedy, but it's basically a one-joke film that hinges on dozens of high-tech special effects. While the effects are superior (the half-woman corpse that moves and talks while on the morgue table falls into the amazing-but-disgusting category), they cannot, and do not, carry the entire film. This strange comedy did quite well at the box office, and since it hit screens just before Romero's third "Living Dead" film, DAY OF THE DEAD, it stole much of his thunder.

p, Tom Fox, Graham Henderson; d, Dan O'Bannon; w, Dan O'Bannon (based on a story by Rudy Ricci, John Russo, Russell Streiner); ph, Jules Brenner (DeLuxe Color); ed, Robert Gordon; m, Matt Clifford, The Flesheaters, 45 Grave, The Damned, The Cramps.

**(PR:O   MPAA:R)**

## RETURN OF THE LIVING DEAD PART II**

(1988) 89m Greenfox/Lorimar c

Michael Kenworthy *(Jesse Wilson)*, Thor Van Lingen *(Billy)*, Jason Hogan *(Johnny)*, James Karen *(Ed)*, Thom Mathews *(Joey)*, Suzanne Snyder *(Brenda)*, Marsha Dietlein *(Lucy Wilson)*, Suzan Stadner *(Aerobics Instructor)*, Jonathan Terry *(Colonel)*, Dana Ashbrook *(Tom Essex)*, Sally Smythe *(Billy's Mom)*, Allan Trautman *(Tarman)*, Don Maxwell *(Billy's Dad)*, Reynold Cindrich *(Soldier)*, Philip Bruns *(Doc Mandel)*, Mitch Pileggi *(Sarge)*, Arturo Bonilla *(Les)*, Terrence Riggings *(Frank)*, James McIntire *(Officer)*.

Burdened with a most unwieldy sequel title (why not simply "Return of the Return of the Living Dead"?), this movie is not so much a continuation of the surprise horror hit of 1985 as it is a remake, considering that the original movie ended with the nuclear annihilation of the entire cast. Maintaining the goofy black humor that made the first film tolerable, the sequel again begins with the opening of the same deadly canisters that caused all the problems last time out. The mist from the canister seeps into the cemetery, contaminating the humans who breathe it and reanimating the buried corpses. In a comic dead-rising-from-their-graves sequence, dozens of corpses interred during a variety of historical periods come stumbling out of their coffins with a sudden craving for brains. Gore fans will appreciate the special effects (by Kenny Myers), which are superior to the ones employed in RETURN OF THE LIVING DEAD—the highlight being a pair of zombie legs that continue to walk around *after* being separated from the zombie's torso. The humor here, as in the first film, is strictly sophomoric and mostly slapstick. Director Ken Wiederhorn is a competent, if unremarkable, talent and he handles the action scenes in a professional manner. His writing talent, however, is not equal to that of the first film's writer-director, Dan O'Bannon, and the sequel lacks its predecessor's snappy, biting dialog and O'Bannon's satiric edge. Wiederhorn, instead, gives us lines like, "No, duh." Although not nearly as successful financially as the first film, RETURN OF THE LIVING DEAD PART II made enough to turn a profit.

p, Tom Fox; d, Ken Wiederhorn; w, Ken Wiederhorn; ph, Robert Elswit (Foto-Kem Color); ed, Charles Bornstein; m, J. Peter Robinson.

**(PR:O   MPAA:R)**

## RETURN OF THE VAMPIRE, THE***

(1944) 69m COL bw

Bela Lugosi *(Armand Tesla)*, Frieda Inescort *(Lady Jane Ainsley)*, Nina Foch *(Nicki Saunders)*, Roland Varno *(John Ainsley)*, Miles Mander *(Sir Frederick Fleet)*, Matt Willis *(Andreas Obry)*, Ottola Nesmith *(Elsa)*, Gilbert Emery *(Professor Saunders)*, Leslie Denison *(Lynch)*, William C.P. Austin *(Gannett)*, Billy Bevan, George McKay.

Bela Lugosi, who played a phony vampire in Tod Browning's MARK OF THE VAMPIRE, essays the real thing here for the first time since DRACULA (1931), though the famous count's name couldn't be used because Universal owned the rights to it. In WW II London, German bombing releases vampire Armand Tesla (Lugosi) from his grave. Aided by a werewolf named Andreas (Matt Willis) and opposed by Lady Jane (Frieda Inescort), who operates an asylum, Tesla goes in search of young ladies to supply him with blood. It is not Lady Jane but Andreas, however, who proves to be Tesla's undoing, as the werewolf decides to go straight and finishes off the vampire by dragging him from his coffin and into the sunlight while he sleeps. For the final scene depicting the vampire's deterioration, a wax mask was made of Lugosi, placed over a skull, and melted; however, the effect was deemed too graphic for British audiences and edited out of the UK release. Lugosi is properly menacing as the vampire, and Lew Landers' atmospheric direction makes this a fairly memorable, although minor, horror venture. Surprisingly, though he is most often identified with his vampire roles, Lugosi only played a bloodsucker three times—in this film, DRACULA, and ABBOTT AND COSTELLO MEET FRANKENSTEIN (1948).

p, Sam White; d, Lew Landers; w, Griffin Jay, Randall Faye (based on an idea by Kurt Neumann); ph, John Stumar, L.W. O'Connell; ed, Paul Borofsky.

(PR:A MPAA:NR)

## RETURN TO HORROR HIGH*½

(1987) 95m NW/Balcor c

Lori Lethin (Callie Cassidy/Sarah/Susan), Brendan Hughes (Steven Blake), Alex Rocco (Harry Sleerik), Scott Jacoby (Josh Forbes), Andy Romano (Principal Kastleman), Richard Brestoff (Arthur Lyman), Al Fann (Amos), Pepper Martin (Chief Deyner), Maureen McCormick (Officer Tyler), Vince Edwards (Richard Birnbaum), Philip McKeon (Richard Farley), Panchito Gomez (Choo Choo), Michael Eric Kramer (Donny Porter), Marvin McIntyre (Robbie Rice), George Clooney (Oliver), Remy O'Neill (Esther Molvania), Darcy DeMoss (Sheri Haines), Cliff Emmich (Dillon), Will Etra (Mangled Face/Hatchet Face), George Fisher (Masked Figure), Dexter Hamlett (Freddie), Joy Heston (Becky), Frank Kniest (Camera Assistant), John Mueller (Jimmy).

This is one of those horror films that tries way too hard to be something different and merely winds up as a confused mess. Combining gore with comedy and presenting it in a movie-within-a-movie-within-a-dream-within-a-movie format, RETURN TO HORROR HIGH opens as local police arrive at a high school brimming with the bloody bodies of a horror film crew, a massacre only the screenwriter survived. Through a flashback, we see the hapless low-budget crew shooting at the school, where a real-life unsolved mass murder took place several years before. The innumerable twists and turns of the plot, combined with several shifts in time and perspective, wind up more confusing than intriguing, and most of the humor is purely (pardon the pun) sophomoric, but some of the "in" jokes about the industry in general and horror films in particular are good for a few laughs. Fans of "The Brady Bunch" will be particularly shocked—or delighted, depending upon one's perspective—by the over-the-top performance by Maureen McCormick, aka Marsha Brady. Blood seems to turn her on, and at one point she excitedly clutches her breast and smears her uniform with the stuff.

p, Mark Lisson; d, Bill Froehlich; w, Bill Froehlich, Mark Lisson, Dana Escalante, Greg H. Sims; ph, Roy Wagner; ed, Nancy Forner; m, Stacy Widelitz.

(PR:O MPAA:R)

## RETURN TO SALEM'S LOT, A**½

(1988) 95m Larco/WB c

Michael Moriarty (Joe Weber), Ricky Addison Reed (Jeremy), Samuel Fuller (Van Meer), Andrew Duggan (Judge Axel), Evelyn Keyes (Mrs. Axel), Jill Gatsby (Sherry), June Havoc (Aunt Clara), Ronee Blakley (Sally), James Dixon (Rains), David Holbrook (Deputy), Katja Crosby (Cathy), Tara Reid (Amanda), Brad Rijn (Clarence), Georgia Janelle Webb (Sarah), Robert Burr (Dr. Fenton), Jacqueline Britton (Mrs. Fenton), Gordon Ramsey (Allen), David Ardao (Car Salesman), Kathleen Kichta (Vampire Woman), Edward Shils, Richard Duggan (Farmer Vampires), Stewart G. Day (Jeremiah), Nancy Duggan (Farm Girl).

A RETURN TO SALEM'S LOT is another one of those bizarre, personal, and very quirky genre films from the fevered brain of Larry Cohen—this one produced directly for home video. A sequel in name only to "Salem's Lot," the made-for-TV movie of Stephen King's novel, the film stars Michael Moriarty as Joe Weber, an ambitious anthropologist who travels to Maine with his estranged teenage son, Jeremy (Ricky Addison Reed), to renovate a house left to him by his aunt. To their surprise, the small New England town is populated by vampires. The 300-year-old vampire community, led by the grandfatherly Judge Axel (Andrew Duggan), has grown rich from real estate values alone, and its members have become wealthy old Republicans, the literal embodiment of "old money" in America. Although they drink human blood from time to time, they have primarily turned to cattle blood for sustenance since, as Judge Axel explains, human blood has become unsafe, what with alcohol, drugs, hepatitis, and "that AIDS virus." Because he is a famed anthropologist, the vampires want Weber to write their history—to dispel the myths about their race and set the facts down once and for all. Intrigued, Weber agrees, but he begins to have second thoughts when he realizes that his son is slowly being seduced into the vampire lifestyle. Not your typical vampire movie, A RETURN TO SALEM'S LOT is a somewhat satiric poke at the genre without many thrills. Character is everything in Cohen's films, and once again he gets an eccentric performance from Moriarty, but the movie is stolen by a pair of older performers: Duggan, in one of his last roles, and director Samuel Fuller, as a crotchety, cigar-chomping vampire hunter. Thematically, Cohen continues his use of the fantasy genres to explore modern-day political and social ills, so those expecting a reverent sequel to the King tale will no doubt be disappointed.

p, Paul Kurta; d, Larry Cohen; w, Larry Cohen, James Dixon; ph, Daniel Pearl; ed, Armond Leibowitz; m, Michael Minard.

(PR:O MPAA:R)

## REVENGE zero

(1986) 100m United Entertainment c

Patrick Wayne (Michael Hogan), John Carradine (Sen. Bradford), Bennie Lee McGowan (Gracie Moore), Josef Hanet (Dr. White), Stephanie Kropke (Liz), Fred Graves (Dean Bayley), Charles Ellis (Ron), David Stice (Deputy), John Bliss (Psychiatrist), Andrea Adams (Reporter).

Although shot on film, this sequel to the shot-on-video BLOOD CULT never received a theatrical release and went straight to videocassette. Its confused plot—serving only as filler between the gore sequences—involves a group of dog worshipers, the "Cult of Caninus." Predictably, the members are all upstanding citizens of their small community and their leader, Bradford (John Carradine, obviously reading his lines from cue cards), even happens to be a senator. The cult members are, however, set on acquiring a piece of land owned by a poor widow (Bennie Lee McGowan), anxious to use it as the site for their sacred rites. With the assistance of stranger Michael Hogan (Patrick Wayne), the distraught widow tries to fend off the crazed dog lovers. Simpleminded, mean-spirited, and downright laughable in spots, REVENGE is, in a word, pathetic. The violence is from the Herschell Gordon Lewis school of gratuitous gore and the filmmakers even stoop so low as intercutting a shot of a woman having her leg amputated with one of her ignorant boy friend cutting up some sausage for breakfast. Detestable.

p, Linda Lewis; d, Christopher Lewis; w, Christopher Lewis; ph, Steve McWilliams; ed, James Lenertz; m, Rod Slane.

(PR:O  MPAA:NR)

## REVOLT OF THE ZOMBIES*½

(1936) 65m Academy bw

Dorothy Stone (Claire Duval), Dean Jagger (Armand Louque), Roy D'Arcy (Col. Mazovia), Robert Noland (Clifford Grayson), George Cleveland (Gen. Duval), Fred Warren (Dr. Trevissant), Carl Stockdale (Ignacio McDonald), Teru Shimada (Buna), William Crowell (Hsiang), Selmer Jackson (Officer), Hans Schumm (German Soldier).

Set at the end of WW I, this terribly disappointing follow-up to the Halperin brothers' WHITE ZOMBIE (1932) relates the tale of a secret regiment of French-Cambodian zombie fighters who are impervious to German bullets. When the war ends, the French government orders that all remaining zombie soldiers be deactivated and that the secret for creating them—kept in Angkor, Cambodia—also be destroyed. General Duval (George Cleveland) is put in charge of the mission sent to destroy the secret. But Armand Louque (Dean Jagger), an expert in ancient languages, discovers the secret first and uses it for his own nefarious purposes when Duval's daughter (Dorothy Stone) spurns him, creating an army of zombies and setting himself up as their king. Although the premise is intriguing, the film itself is hopelessly static and dull, with much of the action taking place in front of obvious rear-screen projected slides of Cambodian temples. Director Victor Halperin utterly fails to evoke any atmosphere or suspense, and the incredibly stiff performances make it hard to determine which of the actors are supposed to be the zombies. The only remotely chilling moments occur when Halperin rather incongruously cuts to an extreme close-up of Bela Lugosi's eyes from WHITE ZOMBIE. REVOLT OF THE ZOMBIES is a curiosity, but nothing more.

p, Edward Halperin; d, Victor Halperin; w, Howard Higgin,

Rollo Lloyd, V. Halperin; ph, Arthur Martinelli, J.A. Feindel; ed, Douglas Biggs.

(PR:A  MPAA:NR)

## ROAD GAMES**½

(1981, Aus.) 101m Quest/AE c

Stacy Keach (Pat Quid), Jamie Lee Curtis (Hitch/Pamela), Marion Edward (Frita Frugal), Grant Page (Smith or Jones), Thaddeus Smith (Abbott), Bill Stacey (Capt. Careful), Stephen Millichamp (Costello), Alan Hopgood (Lester).

Stacy Keach stars in this Hitchcockian Australian thriller as Pat Quid, a road-addled trucker making a Melbourne-to-Perth run who begins following the news of a series of murders of pretty female hitchhikers. After a while, Pat begins to suspect that the driver of the black van he has seen periodically is responsible for the killings, and he takes it upon himself to investigate, especially after a hitchhiker he has befriended (Jamie Lee Curtis) accepts a ride in the van. Suspenseful throughout most of its running time and exceedingly well-shot, ROAD GAMES collapses at the end—the confrontation between Pat and the killer a letdown. Although director Richard Franklin has definitely studied his Hitchcock (he would go on to direct PSYCHO II), his film lacks the psychological depth of the master's work. Keach, however, is quite engaging as the eccentric hero.

p, Barbi Taylor, Richard Franklin; d, Richard Franklin, Jon Dowding; w, Everett DeRoche; ph, Vincent Monton (Panavision, Eastmancolor); ed, Edward McQuinn-Mason; m, Brian May.

(PR:C  MPAA:PG)

## ROBOT VS. THE AZTEC MUMMY, THE**

(1958, Mex.) 65m Cinematografica Calderon/K. Gordon Murray bw (EL ROBOT HUMANO; LA MOMIA AZTECA CONTRA EL ROBOT HUMANO; AKA: AZTEC MUMMY VS THE HUMAN ROBOT, THE)

Ramon Gay (Flor's Lover), Rosita Arenas (Flor), Luis Aceves Castaneda (Dr. Krupp), Crox Alvarado, Emma Roldan, Angel d'Esteffani, Arturo Martinez, Jaime Gonzalez Quinones, Julian de Meriche, Alberto Yanez, Enrique Yanez, Guillermo Hernandez.

"How far can the human mind penetrate the mysteries of the great beyond? Who knows? This picture is based upon an extraordinary experiment, carried out by doctors Hughes and Tooney of the University of Los Angeles. There is no doubt as to its authenticity. Testimony of people participating in the experiment, sworn to by a notary public, precludes the possibility of any fraud. This picture is a combination of factual data, mixed with fiction." So said the publicity for THE ROBOT VS. THE AZTEC MUMMY. But we know better, don't we? It's really just a silly sequel to THE AZTEC MUMMY (1957) and CURSE OF THE AZTEC MUMMY (1957) in which the evil Dr. Krupp (Luis Aceves Castaneda) is once again after the treasure buried in a crypt guarded by Popoca, the Aztec mummy. To combat the powerful mummy, Krupp creates a robot with a human brain (actually a man in a clunky suit with huge lightbulbs in his ears). The climactic battle between the robot and the Aztec mummy is a real hoot. Although given the seal of approval by the "Young American Horror Club" upon its American release (in 1965), this feeble effort is rescued only by its inherent strangeness. It is also padded with lots of footage from the first two films.

p, Guillermo Calderon; d, Rafael Portillo; w, Guillermo Calderon, Alfredo Salazar (based on a story by Salazar); ph, Enrique Wallace; ed, Jorge Bustos, Jose Li-Ho; m, Antonio Diaz Conde.

**(PR:A   MPAA:NR)**

## ROCK 'N' ROLL NIGHTMARE zero

(1987, Can.) 83m Thunder/Shapiro c (AKA: EDGE OF HELL, THE)

Jon-Mikl Thor *(John Triton),* Jillian Peri *(Lou Anne),* Frank Dietz *(Roger Eburt),* Dave Lane *(Max),* Teresa Simpson *(Randy),* Clara Pater *(Mother),* Jesse D'Angelo *(Little Boy),* Chris Finkel *(Father),* Liane Abel *(Mary Eburt),* Denise Dicandia *(Dee Dee),* Jim Cirile *(Stig),* Gene Kroth *(Karl),* Rusty Hamilton *(Seductress),* Carrie Schiffler *(Cindy Connelly),* Tralle O'Farrell, Layra Daans, Nancy Bush *(Groupies).*

Even the most hardened veteran of bad cinema will sit slack-jawed as this incredibly amateurish vanity production, boasting cheap thrills and even cheaper rock'n'roll, unfolds. In a remote Canadian farmhouse, an unseen evil force slaughters an entire family. Years later, a heavy-metal rock band has converted the barn into a recording studio. The leader of the band, muscle-bound, long-haired John Triton (Jon-Mikl Thor), is a committed musician with little tolerance for the tomfoolery of the other band members—most of whom spend the weekend cavorting with their girl friends. Unbeknownst to the band, however, several poorly crafted puppet creatures are crawling around the set possessing hapless cast members. It's all a silly ego trip for obscure heavy-metal rocker Thor, who wrote, produced, and starred in this overlong rock video featuring several of his insipid songs. Director John Fasano's only contributions are several Sam Raimi/EVIL DEAD-inspired camera moves in which the camera races through the farmhouse, taking the point-of-view of the evil force. The acting is uniformly awful. Most of the female cast members readily shed their clothes; however, no one shows as much flesh as Thor himself, who dresses in nothing but a studded loin cloth for his climactic battle scene with Satan.

p, Jon-Mikl Thor; d, John Fasano; w, Jon-Mikl Thor; ph, Mark MacKay (Medallion color); ed, Robert Williams.

**(PR:O   MPAA:R)**

## ROSEMARY'S BABY*****

(1968) 136m PAR c

Mia Farrow *(Rosemary Woodhouse),* John Cassavetes *(Guy Woodhouse),* Ruth Gordon *(Minnie Castevet),* Sidney Blackmer *(Roman Castevet),* Maurice Evans *(Hutch),* Ralph Bellamy *(Dr. Sapirstein),* Angela Dorian *(Terry Fionoffrio),* Patsy Kelly *(Laura-Louise),* Elisha Cook, Jr. *(Mr. Nicklas),* Charles Grodin *(Dr. Hill),* Emmaline Henry *(Elise Dunstan),* Marianne Gordon *(Joan Jellico),* Phil Leeds *(Dr. Shand),* Hope Summers *(Mrs. Gilmore),* Wendy Wagner *(Tiger),* Hanna Landy *(Grace Cardiff),* Gordon Connell *(Guy's Agent),* Joan T. Reilly *(Pregnant Woman),* Patricia Ann Conway *(Mrs. John F. Kennedy),* Walter Baldwin *(Mr. Wees),* Charlotte Boerner *(Mrs. Fountain),* Sebastian Brooks *(Argyron Stavropoulos),* Patricia O'Neal *(Mrs. Wees),* Robert Osterloh *(Mr. Fountain),* Almira Sessions *(Mrs. Sabatini),* Bruno Sidar *(Mr. Gilmore),* D'Urville Martin *(Diego),* George Savalas *(Workman),* Viki Vigen *(Lisa),* Paul A. Denton *(Skipper),* Frank White *(Hugh Dunstan),* Mary Louise Lawson *(Portia Haynes),* Gale Peters *(Rain Morgan),* George Ross Robertson *(Lou Comfort),* Carol Brewster *(Claudia Comfort),* Clay Tanner *(Devil),* Michael Shillo *(Pope).*

Roman Polanski's first American movie and his second masterpiece of horror (REPULSION was released in 1965) is set under the sunny skies of modern-day New York City. There are no creepy characters and no eerie locations, just a happy young couple expecting their first child. Newlyweds Rosemary Woodhouse (Mia Farrow) and unemployed actor Guy (John Cassavetes) have just moved into their new apartment in a gothic Central Park building (shot in the famous Dakota). Their neighbors, the elderly Minnie (Ruth Gordon) and Roman Castevet (Sidney Blackmer), are friendly but a bit intrusive. Rosemary learns that she is pregnant, but feels a certain sense of anxiety. She seems to remember a vague dream in which she was raped by a savage beast. She has mysterious scratches on her stomach. Her doctor prescribes a curious elixir. It's perhaps not surprising that Rosemary becomes fixated by the idea that she has been impregnated by Satan, is carrying the Antichrist in her womb, and is living among a coven of witches. Terribly frightening because it is so plausible and full of normalcy, ROSEMARY'S BABY is one of the premier examples of modern horror and was an important force in the evolution of the genre. Although the subject matter is rooted in the supernatural, the treatment is very real. The unspectacular Rosemary lives in a highly populated area—a change from the usual secluded locales—and surrounded by nice people (a husband, friendly old neighbors, doctors), but the horror continues. What is most brilliant about the film's premise is that the horror, in the form of the fetal Antichrist, exists inside Rosemary's womb, leaving the young woman with no way out and filling her with deeply conflicting feelings towards her son's birth. As in REPULSION, the story is told through the eyes of the heroine, yielding a disturbing atmosphere in which the audience feels the same anxiety as the character on the screen.

p, William Castle; d, Roman Polanski; w, Roman Polanski (based on the novel by Ira Levin); ph, William A. Fraker (Technicolor); ed, Sam O'Steen, Robert Wyman; m, Krzysztof Komeda.

**(PR:O   MPAA:R)**

## RUBY**½

(1977) 84m Steve Krantz/Dimension c

Piper Laurie *(Ruby Claire)*, Stuart Whitman *(Vince Kemper)*, Roger Davis *(Dr. Keller)*, Janit Baldwin *(Leslie Claire)*, Crystin Sinclaire *(Lila June)*, Paul Kent *(Louie)*, Len Lesser *(Barney)*, Jack Perkin *(Avery)*, Edward Donno *(Jess)*, Sal Vecchio *(Nicki)*, Fred Kohler *(Jake Miller)*, Rory Stevens *(Donny)*, Raymond Kark *(1st Man)*, Jan Burrell *(1st Woman)*, Kip Gillespie *(Herbie)*, Tamar Cooper *(Woman)*, Patricia Allison *(Pickup Man's Wife)*, Stu Olson *(Man)*, Mary Robinson *(Sheriff's Wife)*, Michael Alldredge *(Sheriff's Wife's Date)*, Allison Hayes *(The Fifty-Foot Woman)*.

Fresh from her role as the fanatical mother in CARRIE (1976), Piper Laurie returns to the horror genre as Ruby Claire, the owner of a Florida drive-in theater, who, when she was a torch singer in 1935, had an affair with a gangster who was gunned down. Sixteen years later, his spirit returns through their deaf-mute daughter and sets out to get revenge from the survivors of the gang that killed him, most of whom are now employed by the kind-hearted Ruby. In time, the projectionist is discovered hanging by celluloid in the projection room, and the concessionaire is found dead in the Coke machine. While keeping the action moving at a brisk pace, director Curtis Harrington evokes a nice gothic flavor in this low-budget but effectively atmospheric effort. Allison Hayes fans will note that the drive-in shows ATTACK OF THE 50-FOOT WOMAN, which is a bit strange considering that RUBY is set in 1951, while ATTACK OF THE 50-FOOT WOMAN wasn't made until 1958.

p, George Edwards; d, Curtis Harrington, Stephanie Rothman; w, George Edwards, Barry Schneider (based on a story by Steve Krantz); ph, William Mendenhall; ed, Bill McGee; m, Don Ellis.

(PR:O MPAA:R)

# S

## SATAN'S CHEERLEADERS zero

(1977) 92m World Amusements c

John Ireland *(Sheriff Bub/High Priest)*, Yvonne De Carlo *(Emm Bub)*, Jack Kruschen *(Billy the Janitor)*, John Carradine *(Bum)*, Sydney Chaplin *(Mond)*, Jacquelin Cole *(Ms. Johnson)*, Kerry Sherman *(Patti)*, Hillary Horan *(Chris)*, Alisa Powell *(Debbie)*, Sherry Marks *(Sharon)*, Lane Caudell *(Stevie)*, Joseph Carlo *(Coach)*, Michael Donavon O'Donnell *(Farmer)*, Robin Greer *(Baker Girl)*.

This is a wretched drive-in movie that doesn't even live up to the potential for unintentional laughs promised by the title. Jack Kruschen is Billy, the strange Benedict High School janitor angered by smarty-pants teenage cheerleaders (Kerry Sherman, Sherry Marks, Hillary Horan, and Alisa Powell) who make fun of him. Seeking vengeance, he decides to impress the members of the satanic cult he's just joined by sacrificing these nubile young big mouths to the Devil himself. Obnoxious and irritating in all respects, SATAN'S CHEERLEADERS is just another embarrassing entry in the filmographies of John Ireland, John Carradine, and Yvonne De Carlo.

p, Alvin L. Fast; d, Greydon Clark; w, Greydon Clark, Alvin L. Fast; ph, Dean Cundey (Movielab Color); m, Gerald Lee.

(PR:O MPAA:R)

## SATURDAY THE 14TH*

(1981) 75m NW c

Richard Benjamin *(John)*, Paula Prentiss *(Mary)*, Severn Darden *(Van Helsing)*, Jeffrey Tambor *(Waldemar)*, Kari Michaelsen *(Debbie)*, Kevin Brando *(Billy)*, Nancy Lee Andrews *(Yolanda)*, Craig Coulter *(Duane)*, Roberta Collins *(Cousin Rhonda)*, Thomas Newman *(Cousin Phil)*, Rosemary De Camp *(Aunt Lucille)*, Carol Androsky *(Marge)*, Annie O'Donnell *(Annette)*, Michael Miller *(Ernie)*, Stacy Keach *(Attorney)*, Paul "Mousie" Garner *(Major)*, Patrick Campbell *(Mailman)*, Irwin Russo *(Truck Driver)*.

More a standard haunted-house comedy than a parody of FRIDAY THE 13TH, this uninspired farce rarely succeeds. John and Mary (Richard Benjamin and Paula Prentiss) inherit an old mansion and move in with their son, Billy (Kevin Brando). While rummaging around, Billy finds the *Book of Evil* and inadvertently summons forth a bevy of monsters left over from other movies (such as GALAXINA). With everything from vampires to space aliens plaguing the household, it is up to Billy to exorcise the demons and send them back where they came from. Pitifully childish on all counts, SATURDAY THE 14TH really doesn't contain anything fresh or funny, save one gag in which the gill-man emerges from a bubble bath.

p, Julie Corman, Jeff Begun; d, Howard R. Cohen; w, Howard R. Cohen (based on a story by Begun); ph, Daniel Lacambre (DeLuxe Color); ed, Joanne D'Antonio, Kent Beyda.

(PR:A MPAA:PG)

## SAVAGE WEEKEND zero

(1981) 83m Upstate Murder Co./Cannon c (AKA: KILLER BEHIND THE MASK, THE; UPSTATE MURDERS, THE)

Christopher Allport *(Nicky)*, James Doerr *(Robert)*, Marilyn Hamlin *(Marie)*, Kathleen Heaney *(Shirley)*, David Gale *(Mac)*, Devin Goldenberg *(Jay)*, Jeffrey Pomerantz *(Greg)*, William Sanderson *(Otis)*.

A truly reprehensible exploitation item, SAVAGE WEEKEND was originally shot in 1976, but went unreleased until 1981, when Cannon picked it up for distribution following the success of the slasher-movie cycle. Several couples go off to a remote country house in upstate New York for the weekend. As the couples engage in various soft-core sex acts, a masked killer begins stalking and killing them one by one. While it can be looked upon as a precursor to the mad-slasher films that would dominate the genre in the

1980s, SAVAGE WEEKEND is a distinctly sleazy and truly offensive effort. Ultra-low-budget and shot on grainy color stock, the film is borderline pornography and the gore effects are extremely gruesome. Director David Paulsen would surface again with SCHIZOID (1980).

p, John Mason Kirby, David Paulsen; d, David Paulsen; w, David Paulsen; ph, Zoli Vidor (Technicolor, Berkey/Pathe Humphreys Color); ed, Zion Avrahamian, Jonathan Day; m, Dov Seltzer.

**(PR:O   MPAA:R)**

## SCALPEL**

(1976) 95m P.J./United Intl. c (AKA: FALSE FACE)

Robert Lansing (Dr. Phillip Reynolds), Judith Chapman (Heather/Jane). Arlen Dean Snyder (Uncle Bradley), David Scarroll (Dr. Robert Dean), Sandy Martin (Sandy), Bruce Atkins (Plumber).

Crazed plastic surgeon Dr. Reynolds (Robert Lansing) attempts to collect a $5 million inheritance by reconstructing a go-go dancer's face in the image of his missing daughter, Jane (Judith Chapman). Having previously murdered his wife and his daughter's boy friend—the incidents that drove Jane away—Reynolds plans to show off his "daughter" at family functions and to the trustees of his father's estate, the bulk of which was left to Jane. Before long the dancer-daughter begins bestowing sexual favors on the insane surgeon, adding an uncomfortable air of incest to the bizarre proceedings. Shot in Georgia on a $400,000 budget, the film is hampered somewhat by the lack of funds, but it does manage to deliver a few genuine surprises.

p, Joseph Weintraub, John Grissmer; d, John Grissmer; w, John Grissmer (based on a story by Weintraub); ph, Edward Lachman, Jr. (Movielab Color); ed, Joseph Weintraub; m, Robert Cobert.

**(PR:O   MPAA:R)**

## SCALPS*

(1983) 82m American Panther/21st Century c

Kirk Alyn (Dr. Howard Machen), Carroll Borland (Dr. Reynolds), Jo Ann Robinson (D.J.), Richard Hench (Randy), Roger Maycock (Kershaw), Barbara Magnusson (Ellen), Frank McDonald (Ben), Carol Sue Flockhart (Louise), George Randall (Billy Iron Wing), Forrest J. Ackerman (Prof. Treatwood).

King of the Amateurs Fred Olen Ray grinds out another cheapo here, this time a slasher movie separated from the pack only by virtue of its genuinely home-movie look and a supporting cast of B-movie veterans who show up with nothing to do. A group of teenagers poke their noses around a sacred Indian burial ground and stir up a warrior's spirit, leading to the bloody removal of the kids' scalps through some laughable special effects. The film does boast the casting of Kirk Alyn, of 1948's "Superman" serials, and Carroll Borland, of Tod Browning's 1935 MARK OF THE VAMPIRE. Famous Monsters of Filmland editor Forrest J. Ackerman makes another one of his cameos

with a copy of the magazine in his hand. Unfortunately, the film is mostly boring.

p, T.L. Lankford; d, Fred Olen Ray; w, Fred Olen Ray; ph, Brett Webster, Larry van Loon (Quality Color); ed, John Barr; m, Drew Neumann, Eric Rasmussen.

**(PR:O   MPAA:R)**

## SCANNERS***

(1981, Can.) 102m Filmplan International/AE c

Stephen Lack (Cameron Vale), Jennifer O'Neill (Kim), Patrick McGoohan (Dr. Paul Ruth), Lawrence Dane (Keller), Charles Shamata (Gaudi), Adam Ludwig (Crostic), Michael Ironside (Darryl Revok), Victor Desy (Dr. Gatineau), Mavor Moore (Trevellyan), Robert Silverman (Pierce).

SCANNERS is a bit of a disappointment from David Cronenberg, who presents a typically intriguing premise only to have it disintegrate because of its flawed screenplay, an overabundance of crowd-pleasing pyrotechnics, and some really poor acting from the lead, Stephen Lack. During the 1940s an experimental tranquilizer, Ephemerol, was tested on pregnant women and was found to have severe side affects. Although the drug was taken off the market, the babies born to the women tested were found to possess an ability to read minds telepathically. Dubbed "scanners," there are 236 of these powerful telepaths spread out through North America and in two mysterious companies: Consec, headed by Dr. Paul Ruth (Patrick McGoohan), and Biocarbon Amalgamate, headed by the obviously evil Darryl Revok (Michael Ironside). Caught in the middle of this is Cameron Vale (Lack), one of the 236 whose "gift" has driven him to join the ranks of the homeless. Rescued and rehabilitated by Ruth, Vale learns that Revok has plans to take over the world with an army of evil scanners. After many confusing episodes, including an elaborate car crash and several shootouts, Vale finally confronts Revok in his office at Biocarbon Amalgamate, where he learns that they are brothers. Their father is none other than Ruth, the man who invented Ephemerol and tested it on his pregnant wife. Because she took the highest dosage, Revok and Vale are the most powerful scanners, and the climax is a bizarre telepathic showdown between the siblings. Notorious for its set-piece, the scene in which Revok uses his awesome scanning power to literally explode the head of another man, SCANNERS is a relatively conventional and somewhat confusing effort that delivers action-film thrills without bothering to tidy up the many loose ends of its plot. While the film finds Cronenberg ever more confident as a visual stylist, his ideas here are muddled and unconvincing. Several scenes—such as that in which Vale scans a computer system over the phone lines, causing the lines to burn, the phone to melt, and a nearby gas station to explode—are merely silly. Worse yet is the extremely weak lead performance from Lack, who fails to make even the simplest line reading remotely convincing. While SCANNERS was certainly a crowd-pleaser, the film was an alarming step back for Cronenberg, whose previous film, THE BROOD (1979), had been the crowning achievement of his career. Luckily,

Cronenberg followed the rather conventional SCANNERS with his most ambitious and visionary film up to that point, VIDEODROME (1982).

p, Claude Heroux; d, David Cronenberg; w, David Cronenberg; ph, Mark Irwin (CFI Color); ed, Ronald Sanders; m, Howard Shore.

(PR:O   MPAA:R)

## SCARED TO DEATH**

(1947) 65m Screen Guild c

Bela Lugosi *(Leonide)*, Douglas Fowley *(Terry Lee)*, Joyce Compton *(Jane)*, George Zucco *(Dr. Van Ee)*, Nat Pendleton *(Raymond)*, Roland Varno *(Ward Van Ee)*, Molly Lamont *(Laura Van Ee)*, Angelo Rossitto *(Indigo)*, Gladys Blake *(Lilybeth)*, Lee Bennett *(Rene)*, Stanley Andrews, Stanley Price *(Autopsy Surgeons)*.

The only Bela Lugosi movie shot in color—billed as "Natural Color" but really Cinecolor—this is an obscure and truly bizarre little programmer told entirely in flashbacks from the point of view of a female corpse (Molly Lamont), killed without any identifiable marks. Set in a sanitarium run by the macabre Dr. Van Ee (George Zucco, sporting incredibly thick spectacles), the film parades secret panels, trap doors, red-herring villains (Lugosi and Angelo Rossitto), comedic relief (Nat Pendleton and Gladys Blake), and a fluorescent green death mask that seems to float on its own. A quick glance at the title will tell you how the woman died. Extremely claustrophobic, eccentric, and at times downright incoherent, SCARED TO DEATH is oddly compelling in a warped sort of way, with the crude orange/green two-strip "Natural Color" making the whole thing look like it's taking place in another dimension. Ironically, the narrative device of having a dead person as a narrator was later to be used in the classic SUNSET BOULEVARD (1950), in which William Holden played a murdered gigolo.

p, William B. David; d, Christy Cabanne; w, W.J. Abbott; ph, Marcel Le Picard (Cinecolor); ed, George McGuire; m, Carl Hoefle.

(PR:A   MPAA:NR)

## SCARED TO DEATH**

(1981) 95m Lone Star c (AKA: TERROR FACTOR, THE)

John Stinson *(Ted Lonergan)*, Diana Davidson *(Jennifer Stanton)*, Jonathon David Moses *(Lou Capell)*, Toni Jannotta *(Sherry Carpenter)*, Kermit Eller *(Syngenor)*, Walker Edmiston, Pamela Bowman.

This cheaply made monster movie features a synthetic creature made through DNA experiments, appropriately named "Syngenor." When the creature's creator dies, it goes on a rampage, killing humans by sucking fluid out of their spinal columns. The police try to pin the murders on a psychotic killer, leaving ex-cop-turned-novelist Ted Lonergan (John Stinson) and genetics student Jennifer Stanton (Diana Davidson) to scrounge around sewers to look for the beast. The rubber monster suit is fairly effective, although highly derivative of H.R. Giger's designs for ALIEN (1979).

p, Rand Marlis, Gil Shelton; d, William Malone; w, William Malone; ph, Patrick Prince (Getty Color); ed, Warren Chadwick; m, Tom Chase, Ardell Hake.

(PR:O   MPAA:R)

## SCARS OF DRACULA, THE**

(1970, Brit.) 96m Hammer-EMI/Anglo-EMI/American Continental c

Christopher Lee *(Count Dracula)*, Dennis Waterman *(Simon Carlson)*, Jenny Hanley *(Sarah Framsen)*, Christopher Matthews *(Paul Carlson)*, Patrick Troughton *(Klove)*, Michael Gwynne *(Priest)*, Wendy Hamilton *(Julie)*, Anoushka Hempel *(Tania)*, Delia Lindsay *(Alice)*, Bob Todd *(Burgomaster)*, Toke Townley *(Elderly Wagon Master)*, Michael Ripper *(Landlord)*, David Leland, Richard Durden *(Officers)*, Morris Bush *(Farmer)*, Margot Boht *(Landlord's Wife)*, Clive Barrie *(Fat Young Man)*.

Arguably the worst of the Hammer "Dracula" films featuring Christopher Lee, THE SCARS OF DRACULA is marred by a lousy script, bad acting, some shockingly gratuitous violence, and laughably inept special effects. Plundering some nuggets from the original Bram Stoker novel, this film opens with a rather silly resurrection scene—a huge bat drools blood on Dracula's ashes—and then follows a callow young man named Paul (Christopher Matthews) who wanders into Dracula's castle and is asked to stay the night by the Count himself. That night, Dracula's mistress, Tania (Anoushka Hempel), climbs into bed with Paul. When he awakens the following morning, he is shocked to find Dracula stabbing the girl to death. Meanwhile, Paul's girl friend, Sarah (Jenny Hanley), and his brother, Simon (Dennis Waterman), trace Paul to the castle. Although Dracula denies having seen the young man, he invites the two to spend the night. Foolishly, Dracula's crippled servant Klove (Patrick Troughton) advises Simon to take Sarah and flee. Simon stashes Sarah in a nearby church for safekeeping and returns to find Paul, who has been horribly mutilated by the Count. Back at the church, a horde of vicious bats (actually, silly-looking rubber bats on strings) attack the parish priest (Michael Gwynn), killing him. Sarah runs back to the castle just in time for the violent climax. Loaded with more sex and violence than the previous four films put together, THE SCARS OF DRACULA is a dreadful film, though somewhat redeemed by the fact that Lee is given more screen time and dialog than any other film in the series. For some reason, with both the Hammer "Frankenstein" and "Dracula" series, only the best (CURSE OF FRANKENSTEIN; HORROR OF DRACULA) and worst (THE EVIL OF FRANKENSTEIN; SCARS OF DRACULA) entries are available thus far on home video.

p, Aida Young; d, Roy Ward Baker; w, Anthony Hinds (based on the characters created by Bram Stoker); ph, Moray Grant (Technicolor); ed, James Needs; m, James Bernard.

(PR:O   MPAA:R)

## SCHIZO*

(1976, Brit.) 105m Niles International c (AKA: AMOK; BLOOD OF THE UNDEAD)

Lynne Frederick *(Samantha)*, John Leyton *(Alan)*, Stephanie Beacham *(Beth)*, John Fraser *(Leonard)*, Victoria Allum *(Samantha as a Child)*, Jack Watson *(Haskin)*, Paul Alexander *(Peter)*, Queenie Watts *(Mrs. Wallace)*, Tricia Mortimor *(Joy)*, John McEnery *(Stephens)*, Colin Jeavons *(Commissioner)*, Raymond Bowers *(Manager)*, Terry Duggan *(Editor)*, Robert Mill *(Maitre d')*, Diana King *(Mrs. Falconer)*, Lindsay Campbell *(Falconer)*, Victor Winding *(Sergeant)*, Pearl Hackney *(Lady at Seance)*, Primi Townsend *(Secretary)*, Wendy Gilmore *(Samantha's Mother)*.

A dull and simpleminded psycho-thriller, SCHIZO shows Samantha (Lynne Frederick) being pursued by an axe-wielding nut case who killed her mother. She was unlucky enough to witness the murder and now has to pay. Given the title, it isn't too difficult to guess the twist ending. A terribly predictable effort from Peter Walker and David McGillivray, which contains the standard gore effects (a darning needle in the eye, a sledgehammer to the head, etc.) and the obligatory shower scene.

p, Peter Walker; d, Peter Walker; w, David McGillivray; ph, Peter Jessop (Technicolor); ed, Alan Brett; m, Stanley Myers.

**(PR:O   MPAA:R)**

## SCHIZOID*½

(1980) 91m Cannon c (AKA: MURDER BY MAIL)

Klaus Kinski *(Dr. Peter Fales)*, Mariana Hill *(Julie)*, Craig Wasson *(Doug)*, Donna Wilkes *(Alison Fales)*, Richard Herd *(Donahue)*, Joe Regalbuto *(Jake)*, Christopher Lloyd *(Gilbert)*, Flo Gerrish *(Pat)*, Kiva Lawrence *(Rosemary)*, Claude Duvernoy *(Francoise)*, Cindy Dolan *(Sally)*, Danny Assael *(Barney)*, Jon Greene *(Archie)*, Richard Balin *(Freddy)*, Kathy Garrick *(Maxine)*, Tobar Mayo *(Francis)*, Fredric Cook *(Willy)*, Jonathan Millner *(Francis' Friend)*, Gracie Lee *(Bruce)*, Frances Nealy *(Housekeeper)*, Jay May *(Boy)*, Kimberly Jensen *(Girl)*, Cindy Riegel *(Secretary)*, Tony Swartz *(Bartender)*.

A succession of murderer's-point-of-view slashing scenes adds just another cliche to the heap already piled up in this slow-paced psychothriller involving psychiatrist Dr. Peter Fales (Klaus Kinski), whose group-therapy patients (all nubile women) are being sheared by a scissors-wielding maniac. Those self-same scissors may be the very ones used for the cut-out, paste-up letters forecasting the crimes posted to advice columnist Julie (Mariana Hill), who, as a member of the therapy group, herself appears to be at risk. Who is the crazy cut-up? Is it the kinky shrink who likes to look at his daughter (Donna Wilkes) as she showers (in a possible tribute to Hitchcock)? You won't really care by the time it's over.

p, Menahem Golan, Yoram Globus; d, David Paulsen; w,

David Paulsen; ph, Norman Leigh (TVC Color); ed, Robert Fitzgerald, Dick Brummer; m, Craig Hundley.

**(PR:O   MPAA:R)**

## SCHLOCK**

(1973) 77m Gazotskie/Jack Harris c (AKA: BANANA MONSTER, THE)

John Landis *(The Schlockthropus)*, Saul Kahan *(Detective Sgt. Wino)*, Joseph Piantadosi *(Prof. Shlibovitz)*, Eliza Garrett *(Mindy Binerman)*, Eric Allison *(Joe Puzman)*, Enrica Blankey *(Mrs. Binerman)*, Charles Villiers *(Cal)*, John Chambers *(National Guard Captain)*, Richard Gillis, Alvici, Forrest J. Ackerman, Jack Harris.

Completed in 1971, SCHLOCK was the feature debut of John Landis and, quite frankly, remains one of his more interesting pictures. A sometimes hilarious, but more often merely silly spoof of science-fiction and horror films of the 1950s, the film contains plenty of cameos only horror buffs will appreciate, including Forrest J. Ackerman, Jack Harris, and John Chambers. Twenty-two-year-old Landis himself stars, dressed in an ape suit, as a 20-*million*-year-old missing link known as Schlockthropus. He wanders around town, goes to see monster movies, and kills several people, leaving a trail of banana peels behind him. He also is befriended by a blind girl who thinks he's a dog—that is, until she regains her sight. The makeup was done by Rick Baker, who would go on to save Landis' AN AMERICAN WEREWOLF IN LONDON from being a total washout. Out on videotape as THE BANANA MONSTER.

p, James C. O'Rourke; d, John Landis; w, John Landis; ph, Bob Collins (DeLuxe Color); ed, George Folsey, Jr.; m, David Gibson.

**(PR:A   MPAA:PG)**

## SCREAM AND SCREAM AGAIN***

(1969, Brit.) 94m Amicus-AIP/AIP c

Vincent Price *(Dr. Browning)*, Christopher Lee *(Fremont)*, Peter Cushing *(Maj. Benedek Heinrich)*, Judy Huxtable *(Sylvia)*, Alfred Marks *(Superintendent Bellaver)*, Anthony Newlands *(Ludwig)*, Peter Sallis *(Schweitz)*, David Lodge *(Detective Inspector Strickland)*, Uta Levka *(Jane)*, Christopher Matthews *(David Sorel)*, Judi Bloom *(Helen Bradford)*, Clifford Earl *(Detective Sgt . Jimmy Joyce)*, Kenneth Benda *(Prof. Kingsmill)*, Michael Gothard *(Keith)*, Marshall Jones *(Konratz)*, Julian Holloway *(Griffin)*, Edgar D. Davies *(Rogers)*, Yutte Stensgaard *(Erika)*, Lincoln Webb *(Wrestler)*, Nigel Lambert *(Ken Sparten)*, Steve Preston *(Fryer)*, Lee Hudson *(Matron)*, Leslie Ewin *(Tramp)*, Kay Adrian *(Nurse)*, Rosalind Elliot *(Valerie)*, The Amen Corner.

A very bizarre movie, SCREAM AND SCREAM AGAIN attempts to juggle the many loose strands of Christopher Wicking's ambitious screenplay, but Gordon Hessler's disappointing direction simply isn't up to it. A man out jogging has a heart attack and wakes up in a hospital to find his leg amputated, then the other, then both arms. A girl is raped and murdered, and her body contains two mysterious puncture wounds on her wrist. In an unnamed European country sporting Nazi-like regalia, one of the military officials is murdered by another with a simple squeeze to the neck. After a second girl is murdered, police inspector Bellaver (Alfred Marks) enlists the aid of a policewoman to go undercover and entrap the killer, who frequents nightclubs. Picked up by a young man in a purple silk shirt (Michael Gothard), the policewoman is taken to a remote area where she is strangled before the cops can intervene. As the police close in they see the young man sucking the blood out of her wrist, and when they try to arrest him, he simply shrugs them off with incredible strength and gets away in his sports car. A lengthy chase ensues, and the man is eventually captured and handcuffed to a squad car. Incredibly, he escapes again, this time severing his own hand to be free of the handcuff. The cops chase him to the estate of Dr. Browning (Vincent Price), where the fugitive jumps into a vat of acid kept by the doctor. Under questioning, Browning pleads ignorance of any knowledge of the mysterious killer, but it is later revealed that he in fact *created* the man—who was an android made from a mixture of both synthetic materials and human flesh. Apparently, there is a worldwide conspiracy of androids, which includes the leader of the Nazi-like government (Peter Cushing) and the head of British Intelligence (Christopher Lee). With its ambitious structure, intriguing premise, and prevailing sense of paranoia, SCREAM AND SCREAM AGAIN is a fascinating, but frustratingly flawed film. While it is the only movie to boast Price, Lee, and Cushing all in the same cast, the actors actually never appear together, with the exception of Lee and Price during the last minute of the movie (shades of their "duet" in THE OBLONG BOX). Cushing is in only one scene, Lee in about three, and Price has most of the strange climax to himself. Although the complicated plot is mysterious enough to retain interest, by the time all the narrative strands dovetail, the climax seems rather perfunctory and is a bit disappointing. Director Fritz Lang, however, thought the film marvelous, because its political paranoia echoed his own "Dr. Mabuse" films.

p, Max J. Rosenberg, Milton Subotsky; d, Gordon Hessler; w, Christopher Wicking (based on the novel *The Disoriented Man* by Peter Saxon); ph, John Coquillon (Eastmancolor); ed, Peter Elliott; m, David Whitaker.

**(PR:O   MPAA:PG)**


**SCREAM, BLACULA, SCREAM**\*\*½

(1973) 95m AIP c

William Marshall *(Manuwalde)*, Don Mitchell *(Justin)*, Pam Grier *(Lisa)*, Michael Conrad *(Sheriff Dunlop)*, Richard Lawson *(Willis)*, Lynn Moody *(Denny)*, Jane Michelle *(Gloria)*, Barbara Rhoades *(Elaine)*, Bernie Hamilton *(Ragman)*, Arnold Williams *(Louis)*, Van Kirksey *(Prof. Walston)*, Bob Minor *(Pimp)*, Al Jones *(Pimp)*, Eric Mason *(Milt)*, Sybil Scotford *(Librarian)*, Beverly Gill *(Maggie)*, Don Blackman *(Doll Man)*, Judith Elliotte *(Prostitute)*, Dan Roth *(Cop)*, Nicholas Worth *(Dennis)*, Kenneth O'Brien *(Joe)*, Craig T. Nelson *(Sarge)*, James Payne *(Attendant)*,

Richard Washington *(Cop)*, Bob Hoy *(Cop)*, James Kingsley *(Sgt. Williams)*, Arnita Bell *(Woman)*.

The sequel to BLACULA begins at a meeting of an American voodoo sect. When the high priestess of the sect dies, her son, Willis (Richard Lawson), demands that he be made leader. His bid for power is rejected, however, and another woman, Lisa (Pam Grier), is installed. Angry and looking for revenge, Willis purchases a bag of bones from another voodoo priest (Bernie Hamilton) and performs a rite over them. The bones ignite and the resurrected black vampire Manuwalde, aka Blacula (William Marshall), materializes. Blacula promptly vampirizes Willis, turning him into his slave, then once again makes the rounds in Los Angeles, vampirizing many young people, who then gather at Willis' mansion. Eventually, Blacula meets Lisa and is quite taken with the woman, begging her to cure him of his vampirism through her voodoo powers. Directed by Bob Kelljan, who performed similar duty on COUNT YORGA, VAMPIRE (1970), SCREAM, BLACULA, SCREAM benefits from a slicker presentation than its predecessor had, but the script is fairly unimaginative and fails to capitalize on the more intriguing aspects of the clash between voodoo religion and the vampire legend.

p, Joseph T. Naar; d, Bob Kelljan; w, Joan Torres, Raymond Koenig, Maurice Jules (based on the story by Koenig, Torres); ph, Isidore Mankofsky (Movielab Color); ed, Fabian Tordjmann; m, Bill Marx.

**(PR:C   MPAA:PG)**


**SCREAM BLOODY MURDER zero**

(1972) 90m Indepix c

Paul Vincent, Marlena Lustik, Nick Kleinholz III, Paul Ecenta, Nancy Whetmore.

Released from an insane asylum where he was placed after killing his father with a tractor, a young man with a hook for one of his hands takes up where he left off before his incarceration. First he kills his mother and stepfather, then he terrorizes the small town he left behind, leaving a string of corpses in his path. This substandard horror film suffers from a lack of money and imagination.

p, Robert J. Emery; d, Robert J. Emery; w, Robert J. Emery.

**(PR:O   MPAA:R)**


**SCREAMERS**\*

(1978, It.) 91m Dania-Medusa/New World bw (L'ISOLA DEGLI UOMINI PESCE; AKA: ISLAND OF THE FISHMEN; SOMETHING WAITS IN THE DARK)

Barbara Bach *(Amanda)*, Claudio Cassinelli *(Claude)*, Richard Johnson *(Edmund)*, Joseph Cotten *(Prof. Marvin)*, Beryl Cunningham *(Shakira)*, Mel Ferrer *(Radcliffe)*, Cameron Mitchell *(Decker)*, Eunice Bolt *(Samantha)*, Tom J. Delaney *(Patterson)*, Charles Cass.

One of the more memorable rip-offs in recent horror film history, this pretty dreadful Italian monster movie was picked up by New World for distribution in the US. To spice the rather dull film up, the studio added a 12-minute prolog featuring Mel Ferrer and Cameron Mitchell, and then a few gore scenes of a crazed fishman killing some folks. They then packaged the film with a poster showing an eyeless, skinless, screaming man with nothing but sinew and veins for a body, and a tag line reading, "Warning: In this film you will actually see a man turned inside out!" Well, that's a bold-faced lie since no such thing occurs. The plot features Joseph Cotton as Prof. Marvin, the stereotypical mad scientist on a deserted island, who creates a race of fish-like mutants to serve the island's megalomaniacal owner, Edmund Rackham (Richard Johnson). He trains these "fishmen" to recover the lost fortune of Atlantis. Barbara Bach, as Prof. Marvin's daughter, is on hand mainly to appear in soaking wet clothes and communicate telepathically with the gilled creatures. The whole thing is really very silly and the fishmen costumes are laughable. The inserted gore effects are also poorly done and certainly aren't worth wasting one's time over.

p, Lawrence Martin; d, Sergio Martino, Dan T. Miller; w, Sergio Donati, Cesare Frugoni, Sergio Martino; ph, Giancarlo Ferrando (Eastmancolor); ed, Eugenio Alabiso; m, Luciano Michelini, Sandy Berman.

(PR:A   MPAA:R)

## SCREAMING DEAD, THE zero

(1972, Sp.) 84m Fenix c (SANTANA CONTRA DR. EXORTIO; DRACULA CONTRA FRANKENSTEIN; AKA: DRACULA AGAINST FRANKENSTEIN; DRACULA VS. FRANKENSTEIN; DRACULA, PRISONER OF FRANKENSTEIN)

Dennis Price *(Dr. Frankenstein)*, Howard Vernon *(Dracula)*, Alberto Dalbes *(Jonathan)*, Mary Frances *(Gypsy)*, Brandy *(Werewolf)*, Luis Barboo *(Morpho)*, Fernando Bilbao *(The Monster)*, Britt Nichols, Genevieve Deloir, Jossiane Gibert.

A bad, even for Jesus Franco, all-star monster romp with a plot that makes no sense, this film begins as Dr. Frankenstein (Dennis Price), finds a crucified vampire bat in a coffin and surmises that this is the remains of Count Dracula (Howard Vernon). Using the blood of a female singer captured by his mute servant, Morpho, Frankenstein brings Dracula back to life by drowning the little bat in a jar full of the stuff. Now revived, Dracula finds himself Frankenstein's slave—but wait!—the werewolf (Brandy) and Jonathan (Alberto Dalbes) are attacking the castle to defeat the mad scientist. There's lots of gore, gratuitous nudity, and sick, sick "erotic" scenes (one involving necrophilia)—some of which have been trimmed on the video release.

p, Robert de Nesle, Arturo Marcos; d, Jesus Franco; w, Jesus Franco; ph, Jose Climent (Techniscope, Eastmancolor).

(PR:O   MPAA:NR)

## SCREAMS OF A WINTER NIGHT zero

(1979) 91m Full Moon/Dimension c

Matt Borel *(John)*, Gil Glascow *(Sam)*, Patrick Byers *(Carl)*, Mary Agen Cox *(Elaine)*, Robin Bradley *(Sally)*, Ray Gaspard *(Harper)*, Beverly Allen *(Jookie)*, Brandy Barrett *(Liz)*, Charles Rucker *(Alan)*, Jan Norton *(Lauri)*.

Ten fun-loving teenagers head for Louisiana's backwoods (the film was shot on 16mm in Natchitoches) to an area supposed to be haunted by a devil wind. While waiting for something scary to happen, the kids sit around the campfire and tell ghost stories, ineptly visualized to form the bulk of the film. Among the tales told: a bigfoot creature terrorizes a local community, some boys try to spend the night in a haunted apartment, and a homicidal child-woman kills anyone she catches having sex. The legend of an ancient Indian wind-demon is also related. This is an ultracheap and ultradull effort, which barely saw a theatrical release before turning up on home video.

p, Richard H. Wadsack, James L. Wilson; d, James L. Wilson; w, Richard H. Wadsack; ph, Robert E. Rogers (PSI Color); ed, Gary Ganote, Craig Mayes; m, Don Zimmers.

(PR:A   MPAA:PG)

## SCREAMTIME**

(1985, Brit.) 89m Manson International/Rugged c

Vincent Russo *(Ed)*, Michael Gordon *(Bill)*, Marie Scinto *(Marie)*, Kevin Smith *(Shop Owner)*, Robin Bailey *(Jack Grimshaw)*, Ann Lynn *(Lena)*, Johnathon Morris *(Damien)*, Dione Inman *(Suzy)*, Boscoe Hogan *(Doctor)*, John Styles *(Punch Voice)*, Ian Saynor *(Tony)*, Yvonne Nicholson *(Susan)*, Lally Bowers *(Mrs. Kingsley)*, Veronica Doran *(Miss Burns)*, Brenda Kempner *(Woman)*, Dora Bryan *(Emma)*, Jean Anderson *(Mildred)*, David Van Day *(Gavin)*, Matthew Peters *(Tim)*, Phillip Bloomfield *(Colin)*, Gary Linley *(Frank)*, Kim Thompson *(Lady Anne)*.

The heyday of the horror anthology—a mostly British phenomenon, dating back to DEAD OF NIGHT (1945)—was around 1970, with films such as TALES FROM THE CRYPT; ASYLUM; and THE HOUSE THAT DRIPPED BLOOD offering three to five little shockers framed by one connecting story. Here the tradition is revived in an inferior effort, opening as two lowlifes (Vincent Russo and Michael Gordon) steal three videocassettes from a Times Square shop. They take a subway to Brooklyn and go to a girl friend's apartment to watch their new tapes, "Killer Punch," "Scream House," and "Garden of Blood." "Killer Punch" concerns a Punch and Judy puppeteer (Robin Bailey) who, with the help of Mr. Punch, takes his anger out on his wife and stepson. "Scream House" is the story of a young couple (Ian Saynor and Yvonne Nicholson) who move into a big house whose halls are haunted by the image of a knife-wielding homicidal maniac. The final and best episode, "Garden of Blood," tells of a young handyman and gardener (David Van Day) whose new place of employment, an old house owned by two spinsters, has a strange garden haunted by fairies, gnomes, and a 16th-century femme fatale. Not a shock or scare to be found anywhere.

p, Al Beresford; d, Al Beresford; w, Michael Armstrong; ph, Don Lord, Alan Pudney, Mike Spera (Rank Color); m, KPM.

**(PR:O  MPAA:R)**

## SEANCE ON A WET AFTERNOON****

(1964, Brit.) 115m Beaver-Allied/Artixo bw

Kim Stanley *(Myra Savage)*, Richard Attenborough *(Billy Savage)*, Mark Eden *(Charles Clayton)*, Nanette Newman *(Mrs. Clayton)*, Judith Donner *(Amanda Clayton)*, Patrick Magee *(Supt. Walsh)*, Gerald Sim *(Sgt. Beedle)*, Margaret Lacey *(Woman at 1st Seance)*, Maria Kazan *(Other Woman at Seance)*, Lionel Gamlin *(Man at Seances)*, Marian Spencer *(Mrs. Wintry)*, Ronald Hines *(Policeman at Clayton's)*, Hajni Biro *(Maid at Clayton's)*, Diana Lambert *(Clayton's Secretary)*, Godfrey James *(Clayton's Chauffeur)*, Arnold Bell *(Mr. Weaver)*, Stanley Morgan *(Man in Trilby)*, Michael Lees *(Plainclothes Policeman)*, Margaret McGrath *(Woman at 2nd Seance)*, Frank Singuineau *(Bus Conductor)*.

In this eerie tale, Myra Savage (Kim Stanley), a medium, claims contact with "the other side" through her late son Arthur, a stillborn child whose death Myra cannot come to accept. Myra's husband, Billy (Richard Attenborough, the British actor who would later direct MAGIC; CRY FREEDOM; and GANDHI), does his best to keep her happy, knowing well that she is walking a tightrope between insanity and rationality. He is a weak man and adores Myra, so he can deny her nothing. Myra would like some publicity for her flagging business, so she concocts a plan to have Billy kidnap a wealthy child and collect his ransom. Myra will then offer the services of her psychic powers to the bereaved family and, of course, "find" the child. An atmospheric film, SEANCE ON A WET AFTERNOON succeeds because of Bryan Forbes' excellent direction and the superb performances of both Kim Stanley (in a rare film appearance) and Attenborough (who also produced). While the film can be slow going in spots, Stanley's portrayal of the emotionally unfit Myra Savage is riveting as she gradually loses her grip on reality and slips into a dark psychological abyss.

p, Richard Attenborough, Bryan Forbes; d, Bryan Forbes; w, Bryan Forbes (based on the novel by Mark McShane); ph, Gerry Turpin; ed, Derek York; m, John Barry.

**(PR:C  MPAA:NR)**

## SENDER, THE***

(1982, Brit.) 91m PAR c

Kathryn Harrold *(Gail Farmer)*, Zeljko Ivanek *(The Sender)*, Shirley Knight *(Jerolyn)*, Paul Freeman *(Dr. Denman)*, Sean Hewitt *(The Messiah)*, Harry Ditson *(Dr. Hirsch)*, Olivier Pierre *(Dr. Erskine)*, Tracy Harper *(Young Girl)*, Al Matthews *(Vietnam Veteran)*, Marsha Hunt *(Nurse Jo)*, Angus MacInnes *(Sheriff Prouty)*, Jana Sheldon *(Nurse Reimbold)*, Monica Buferd *(Dr. Warren)*, Colin Bruce *(Computer Technician)*, Jerry Harte *(Security Guard)*, Darcy Flynn *(TV Anchorwoman)*.

An underrated psychological horror thriller, THE SENDER

bombed at the box office because its studio had no idea how to sell a crisply directed shocker that didn't wallow in pointless gore effects. An unidentified 20-year-old who has attempted suicide (Zeljko Ivanek) is brought to a psychiatric clinic for treatment and placed under the supervision of Gail Farmer (Kathryn Harrold), a pretty young psychiatrist who dubs the patient "John Doe." It soon becomes apparent that John Doe, the Sender of the title, possesses the ability to telepathically send his disturbed nightmares and feelings into the minds of others. Unfortunately, the young man can't control these powers, and his dreams—involving hideous bugs, rats, and fires—are invading the brains of most of the people in the hospital. When his mysterious mother, Jerolyn (Shirley Knight), a domineering woman who has always thought her son was the second coming of Christ, is found dead, John Doe is the only suspect. Director Roger Christian (the set decorator for STAR WARS and the art director for ALIEN) slowly builds the suspense, keeping the performances calm and underplayed, so that when the fairly simple effects sequences do arrive, they are all the more horrifying and powerful. An intelligent film that refuses to resort to the kind of bloody, overblown direction that marks the work of so many other horror film directors.

p, Edward S. Feldman; d, Roger Christian; w, Thomas Baum; ph, Roger Pratt (Rank Color); ed, Alan Strachan; m, Trevor Jones.

**(PR:O  MPAA:R)**

## SENTINEL, THE*

(1977) 91m UNIV c

Chris Sarandon *(Michael Lerman)*, Cristina Raines *(Alison Parker)*, Martin Balsam *(Professor)*, John Carradine *(Halliran)*, Jose Ferrer *(Robed Figure)*, Ava Gardner *(Miss Logan)*, Arthur Kennedy *(Franchino)*, Burgess Meredith *(Chazen)*, Sylvia Miles *(Gerde)*, Deborah Raffin *(Jennifer)*, Eli Wallach *(Gatz)*, Christopher Walken *(Rizzo)*, Jerry Orbach *(Director)*, Beverly D'Angelo *(Sandra)*, Hank Garrett *(Brenner)*, Robert Gerringer *(Hart)*, Nana Tucker *(Girl At End)*, Tom Berenger *(Man At End)*, William Hickey *(Perry)*, Gary Allen *(Malcolm Stinnett)*, Tresa Hughes *(Rebecca Stinnett)*, Kate Harrington *(Mrs. Clark)*, Jane Hoffman *(Lillian Clotkin)*, Elaine Shore *(Emma Clotkin)*, Sam Gray *(Dr. Aureton)*, Reid Shelton *(Priest)*, Fred Stuthman *(Alison's Father)*, Lucie Lancaster *(Alison's Mother)*, Anthony Holland *(Party Host)*, Jeff Goldblum *(Jack)*, Zane Lasky *(Raymond)*, Mady Heflin *(Professor's Student)*, Diane Stilwell *(Brenner's Secretary)*, Ron McLarty *(Real Estate Agent)*.

Although it boasts an incredible cast featuring actors ranging in age and experience from John Carradine and Burgess Meredith to Christopher Walken and Beverly D'Angelo, THE SENTINEL is a truly repulsive film. Alison Parker (Cristina Raines) is a top-flight New York City fashion model who takes a breather from her relationship with her fiance (Chris Sarandon) and moves into a gorgeous brownstone in Brooklyn Heights. She soon discovers that her neighbors are more than a little strange. There is a lesbian couple (Sylvia Miles and D'Angelo), an eccentric and

**THE HORROR FILM**

nosy old man (Meredith), and a blind priest (Carradine) up-stairs who always seems to be standing guard. Well it doesn't take long before the weirdness begins and Alison eventually learns that the apartment building is the door-way to hell and the blind priest is the "sentinel" assigned to guard it. Furthermore, Alison discovers that she is des-tined to replace the priest and become the new sentinel. Although the script has potential, Michael Winner per-forms his usual hack job on the material—making the whole thing rather cheap and repugnant. In the climax, the horribly deformed and grotesque denizens of hell come forth; it was later revealed that the creatures were a mix of Dick Smith special makeup and actual deformed people Winner had recruited from freak shows and hospitals. Whereas Tod Browning showed the warm humanity of such people in FREAKS (1932), Winner cruelly exploits their handicaps for the purpose of repulsing his audience. This alone makes the film detestable.

p, Michael Winner, Jeffrey Konvitz; d, Michael Winner; w, Michael Winner, Jeffrey Konvitz (based on novel *The Sentinel* by Konvitz); ph, Dick Kratina (Technicolor); ed, Bernard Gribble, Terence Rawlings; m, Gil Melle.

(PR:O MPAA:R)

## SERPENT AND THE RAINBOW, THE***½

(1988) 98m UNIV c

Bill Pullman *(Dennis Alan)*, Cathy Tyson *(Marielle)*, Zakes Mokae *(Dargent Peytraud)*, Paul Winfield *(Lucien Celine)*, Brent Jennings *(Mozart)*, Conrad Roberts *(Christophe)*, Badja Djola *(Gaston)*, Theresa Merritt *(Simone)*, Michael Gough *(Schoonbacher)*, Paul Guilfoyle *(Andrew Cassedy)*, Dey Young *(Mrs. Cassedy)*, Aleta Mitchell *(Celestine)*.

The moviegoing public has been fascinated with voodoo and zombies since the release of the Halperin brothers' WHITE ZOMBIE in 1932. The incredible success of that film spawned a rash of inferior imitations and comedies, until producer Val Lewton and director Jacques Tourneur resuscitated the genre with the lyrical and haunting mas-terpiece I WALKED WITH A ZOMBIE (1943). Ever since, cinematic zombies have been detached from their reli-gious roots (voodoo) and been made the marauding, can-nibalistic hordes popularized by the "Living Dead" films of George Romero. With THE SERPENT AND THE RAIN-BOW, director Wes Craven returns the zombie to the Ca-ribbean, exploring the culture from which it sprang in this ambitious tale of Haitian voodoo. Dennis Alan (Bill Pull-man) is a young scientist hired by an American pharma-ceutical company to go to Haiti and uncover the secrets of zombification. Recent studies have proven the exis-tence of actual zombies and scientists suspect a drug or potion—the discovery of which could mean a fortune to drug manufacturers looking for a new anesthetic—is in-volved in the process. Dennis' trip, however, happens to coincide with the collapse of the Duvalier government, and he finds himself tossed into the resulting violent social up-heaval. In Haiti, Dennis teams up with beautiful local psy-chiatrist Marielle (Cathy Tyson), who introduces him to the mysterious world of voodoo. The more he probes into voo-doo rituals, however, the greater the opposition from voo-

doo priests, who attempt to invade his mind and transform him into a zombie. An ambitious mix of pop anthropology, scientific exploration, political observation, and good old-fashioned Lewtonesque horror, THE SERPENT AND THE RAINBOW succeeds more often than it fails. Writer-director Craven sees Haiti as a vital, mysterious society where harsh economic reality and belief in the supernatu-ral walk hand-in-hand, and where the elite has corrupted deep traditional religious beliefs to oppress the masses through fear of violence, death, or, even worse, zombifica-tion. From this vivid sociopolitical morass emerges a chill-ing horror story in which the dead appear to walk and peo-ple are possessed by spirits regularly. In conveying this sense of unease and dread, Craven combines the terrify-ing dream sequences of A NIGHTMARE ON ELM STREET with the subtle and evocative atmospherics of Val Lewton.

p, David Ladd, Doug Claybourne; d, Wes Craven; w, Richard Maxwell, A.R. Simoun (based on a book by Wade Davis); ph, John Lindley (Duart color); ed, Glenn Farr; m, Brad Fiedel.

(PR:O MPAA:R)

## SEVENTH SIGN, THE*

(1988) 97m Tri-Star-ML Delphi Premiere-Interscope/Tri-Star c

Demi Moore *(Abby Quinn)*, Michael Biehn *(Russell Quinn)*, Jurgen Prochnow *(David, the Boarder)*, Peter Friedman *(Father Lucci)*, Manny Jacobs *(Avi)*, John Taylor *(Jimmy Zaragoza)*, Lee Garlington *(Dr. Inness)*, Akosua Busia *(Penny)*, Harry W. Basil *(Kid's Korner Salesman)*, Arnold Johnson *(Janitor)*, John Walcutt *(Noviciate)*, Michael Laskin *(Israeli Colonel)*, Hugo Stanger *(Old Priest)*, Patricia Allison *(Administrator)*, Ian Buchanan *(Meteorologist)*, Glenn Edwards, Robin Groth, Dick Spangler *(Newscasters)*, Rabbi William Kramer *(Rabbi Ornstein)*, Blanche Rubin *(Mrs. Ornstein)*, John Heard *(Reverend)*, Joe Mays *(Motel Clerk)*, Jane Frances *(Game Show Wom-an)*.

Willem Dafoe (THE LAST TEMPTATION OF CHRIST) wasn't the only actor to play Jesus in a major motion pic-ture in 1988. Jurgen Prochnow had the same honor in this truly odd—and truly terrible—biblical horror epic. Calling himself David for some unexplained reason, Christ wan-ders a troubled world, cracking, one by one, the seals on seven ancient parchments, each describing the catastro-phes leading up to—you guessed it—the Apocalypse. As each seal is broken, the described disaster occurs, usually in political hot spots like the Middle East, where a desert village is suddenly encased in ice. David shows up on pregnant Abby Quinn's (Demi Moore) doorstep (located in that other well-known global trouble spot, Venice, Califor-nia) to rent her garage apartment and, since he's in the neighborhood, to claim her unborn child in fulfillment of the seventh, and final, catastrophe—the stillbirth of a baby without a soul. As if that weren't enough to fill 97 minutes, Fr. Lucci (Peter Friedman) is also following the progress of the Apocalypse with an unhealthy relish, just a step be-hind Christ. THE SEVENTH SIGN almost qualifies as a guilty pleasure. With its fast-moving profusion of subplots, it's frequently silly, but never boring. Gaping plot holes are abundant and add to the amusement. Moreover, director Carl Schultz and cinematographer Juan Ruiz Anchia pull out the stops when it comes to visual flourishes. Breathtaking special effects, gorgeous matte shots, stylish chiaroscuro lighting, and fluidly ominous camera movements abound to no great effect, but they're great fun to watch.

p, Ted Field, Robert W. Cort; d, Carl Schultz; w, W.W. Wicket, George Kaplan; ph, Juan Ruiz Anchia (Panavision, Technicolor); ed, Caroline Biggerstaff; m, Jack Nitzsche.

(PR:C   MPAA:R)

## SEVENTH VICTIM, THE*****

(1943) 71m RKO bw

Tom Conway (Dr. Louis Judd), Kim Hunter (Mary Gibson), Jean Brooks (Jacqueline Gibson), Hugh Beaumont (Gregory Ward), Erford Gage (Jason Hoag), Isabel Jewell (Frances Fallon), Chef Milani (Mr. Romari), Marguerite Sylva (Mrs. Romari), Evelyn Brent (Natalie Cortez), Mary Newton (Mrs. Redi), Jamesson Shade (Swenson), Eve March (Mrs. Gilchrist), Ottola Nesmith (Mrs. Lowood), Edythe Elliott (Mrs. Swift), Milton Kibbee (Joseph), Marianne Mosner (Miss Rowan), Elizabeth Russell (Mimi), Joan Barclay (Gladys), Barbara Hale (Young Lover), Mary Halsey (Bit), William Halligan (Radeaux), Wheaton Chambers, Ed Thomas (Men), Edith Conrad (Woman), Lou Lubin (Irving August), Lloyd Ingraham (Watchman), Dewey Robinson (Conductor), Ann Summers (Miss Summers), Tiny Jones (News Vendor).

"I runne to death and death meets me as fast / And all my pleasures are like yesterday." This epigraph from the first "Holy Sonnet" by John Donne sets the tone for what is producer Val Lewton's most personal film, and one of his greatest. While very little in the way of horrific action takes place in THE SEVENTH VICTIM, the film has a haunting, lyrical, overwhelming sense of melancholy and despair to it—in which death is looked upon as a sweet release from the oppression of a cold, meaningless existence. Kim Hunter makes her film debut as Mary Gibson, an orphan attending a gloomy Catholic boarding school. Informed by the nuns that her older sister, Jacqueline (Jean Brooks), has disappeared and stopped sending tuition money, Mary is forced to go to New York City and find her. With the help of Jacqueline's husband, Gregory (Hugh Beaumont), Mary discovers that her sister has fallen in with a group of satanists who meet in secret and virtually control the lives of their members. No plot description can fully convey the uneasy sense of dread that pervades every frame of this film. Although Mark Robson, who made his directorial debut here, is no Jacques Tourneur, his direction is restrained and effective. Lewton ensured this by seeing to it that all the delicate nuance of mood and character was written into the screenplay. The film includes a number of unforgettable moments: the scene in which Mary persuades Jacqueline's landlord to open up her room—only to find a noose hanging from the ceiling and a chair placed beneath it, Mary watching in horror as the body of a murder victim is transported by its killers on the subway, a precursor to the shower scene in PSYCHO that must have been seen by Hitchcock, and the film's final moment—without a doubt the bleakest ending to any film ever made in Hollywood.

p, Val Lewton; d, Mark Robson; w, Dewitt Bodeen, Charles O'Neal; ph, Nicholas Musuraca; ed, John Lockert; m, Roy Webb.

(PR:A   MPAA:NR)

## SHADOWS RUN BLACK zero

(1986) 89m Mesa/Troma c

William J. Kulzer (Rydell King), Elizabeth Trosper (Judy Cole), Shea Porter (Morgan Cole), George J. Engelson (Priest), Dianne Hinkler (Helen Cole), Julius Metoyer (Billy), Terry Congie (Lee Faulkner), Kevin Costner (Jimmy Scott), Nealie Gerard (Prostitute), Gerard Thomas (Janitor), Richard Escobedo (Arresting Officer), Marc Christopher (Detective at Station), Olwen Armstrong (Lady Attorney), Hank Robinson (Capt. Dorsey), James M. Cooper (Policeman at Counter), John "Magic" Wright (Magician), Rhonda Selesnow (Girl Stabbed in Chest), Joe Marmo (Coroner), Kim Patterson (Franklin), David Gaines (Man Watching Television), Ann Hull (Girl Killed in Kitchen), Joseph Long (Detective at Interrogation), Vince McKay (Sgt. Bishop), Wendy Tolkin (Georgie), Barbara Peckinpaugh (Sandy), Eric Robert Louzil (Baby in Crib), Tim Mallacy (Biker in Jail), Rick Searles (Photographer at Pool).

A young woman (Elizabeth Trosper) stands by helplessly as all of her girl friends are being murdered. The case is being investigated by an overly enthusiastic cop (William J. Kulzer) who zeros in on Jimmy Scott (Kevin Costner) as his chief suspect. Not only is this film repugnant in its exploitation of women, it's hopelessly inept in nearly every other department. Although it pretends to be a police thriller about a serial killer, SHADOWS RUN BLACK is basically an excuse to parade several well-endowed young women naked before the camera while they wait to be murdered in a variety of bloody ways. When the filmmakers don't even bother giving the victims names and bill the actresses as "Girl Stabbed in Chest" and "Girl Killed in Kitchen," you can expect a totally gratuitous flesh-and-blood-fest. The film, which was shot in 1981 but not released until 1986, is notable only because a young Costner makes a brief appearance, and his talents are in evidence as he manages to create the only believable character in the film.

p, Eric Louzil; d, Howard Heard; w, Craig Kusaba, Duke Howard (based on a story by Craig Kusaba); ph, John Sprung (United Color); ed, Raul Davalos, Davide Ganzino.

(PR:O   MPAA:NR)

## SHINING, THE****

(1980) 146m WB c

Jack Nicholson (Jack Torrance), Shelley Duvall (Wendy Torrance), Danny Lloyd (Danny), Scatman Crothers (Halloran), Barry Nelson (Ullman), Philip Stone (Grady), Joe Turkel (Lloyd), Anne Jackson (Doctor), Tony Burton

*(Durkin)*, Lia Beldam *(Young Woman in Bathtub)*, Billie Gibson *(Old Woman in Bathtub)*, Barry Dennen *(Watson)*, David Baxt, Manning Redwood *(Forest Rangers)*, Lisa Burns, Louise Burns *(Grady Girls)*, Robin Pappas *(Nurse)*, Alison Coleridge *(Secretary)*, Burnell Tucker *(Policeman)*, Jana Sheldon *(Stewardess)*, Kate Phelps *(Receptionist)*, Norman Gay *(Injured Guest)*.

This eerie, disturbing picture from Stanley Kubrick practically throws away its Stephen King source material and becomes an exceedingly controlled, intelligent, and distancing tale of the reality of family horror and the inexplicability of psychic phenomena. Jack Torrance (Jack Nicholson) is a former schoolteacher who, hoping to find the solitude necessary to write a novel, accepts a position as the off-season caretaker of a Colorado resort, the Overlook Hotel. Because the winter storms are so violent, the hotel, situated in an isolated mountain region, often is cut off from the rest of civilization. When he accepts the job, Jack is warned that the isolation can be devastating (some years earlier, the caretaker axed to death his wife and two daughters). Jack, his wife, Wendy (Shelley Duvall), and their son, Danny (Danny Lloyd), eventually arrive at the Overlook. Danny, who is able to ''shine'' (to see things that have happened in the past) senses something evil about the hotel, and while riding his bike through its labyrinthine halls, ''sees'' the carnage of past murders. While Danny takes refuge in his imaginary friend, Tony, and repeatedly growls the word ''redrum'' (''murder'' backwards), the mentally vulnerable Jack succumbs to the hotel's supernatural forces and becomes possessed by thoughts of chopping Wendy and Danny into pieces. Sustaining a disturbing atmosphere from the opening shot to the close, without ever letting the viewer relax in the safety of a ''normal'' scene, Kubrick directs this unlike any other horror film. The film does, however, recall some of Kubrick's other pictures—his characters here, like those at headquarters in PATHS OF GLORY, in the War Room of DR. STRANGELOVE, or outer space in 2001, are corrupted by the vast, empty space that surrounds them. In its plot, themes, and performances, THE SHINING is full of the same kind of ambiguity and uncertainty that characterize paranormal experience and psychic phenomena. At the same time, the film presents an intriguing father-son relationship: Jack, a novelist, struggles to create, while Danny is blessed (or cursed?) with the gift of ''shining'' that allows him to see tales unfold uncontrollably in his head. Not surprisingly, THE SHINING met with much negative criticism (especially from King fans who felt betrayed), but there is much more here than meets the eye, and with the passage of time, the film's virtues may reappear like a ghost.

p, Stanley Kubrick; d, Stanley Kubrick; w, Stanley Kubrick, Diane Johnson (based on the novel by Stephen King); ph, John Alcott; ed, Ray Lovejoy; m, Bela Bartok, Wendy Carlos, Rachel Elkind, Gyorgy Ligeti, Krzysztof Penderecki.

(PR:C-O  MPAA:R)

## SHOCK WAVES**½

(1977) 86m Lawrence Friedricks Enterprises/Cinema Shares c (AKA: DEATH CORPS; ALMOST HUMAN)

Peter Cushing *(Scar)*, John Carradine *(Capt. Ben)*, Brooke Adams *(Rose)*, Fred Buch *(Chuck)*, Jack Davidson *(Norman)*, Luke Halpin *(Keith)*, D.J. Sidney *(Beverly)*, Don Stout *(Dobbs)*, Tony Moskal, Gary Levinson, Jay Maeder, Bob Miller, Talmadge Scott, Bob White *(Death Corps Members)*.

During WW II, the Nazis decided to use the ultimate secret weapon: a troop consisting of super zombies. Predictably, they didn't quite live up to the Fuehrer's needs and at the war's end, the battalion was sunk with their ship off the Caribbean coast. During a storm some 35 years later, however, a group of passengers from a luxury liner are stranded on a deserted island where an underground explosion resurrects the squadron. This NIGHT OF THE LIVING DEAD-style film is surprisingly well made considering its tiny budget. Brooke Adams, Fred Buch, and FLIPPER star Luke Halpin are among the nice people attacked by the zombies. The scene in which the creatures rise from the water is memorable, and the zombie makeup was done by Alan Ormsby. John Carradine has a nice cameo as a grizzled captain of a decrepit steamer, and Peter Cushing plays the squadron leader of the zombie Nazis. Good fun.

p, Reuben Trane; d, Ken Wiederhorn; w, Ken Wiederhorn, John Harrison; ph, Reuben Trane (TVC Color); ed, Norman Gay; m, Richard Einhorn.

(PR:C  MPAA:PG)

## SHOUT, THE***

(1978, Brit.) 87m Recorded Picture Company/Films, Inc. c

Alan Bates *(Crossley)*, Susannah York *(Rachel)*, John Hurt *(Anthony)*, Robert Stephens *(Medical Man)*, Tim Curry *(Robert)*, Julian Hough *(Vicar)*, Carol Drinkwater *(Wife)*, Nick Stringer *(Cobbler)*, John Rees *(Inspector)*, Susan Woolridge *(Harriet)*.

THE SHOUT is a strange, disturbing, and elusive tale of a mental patient, Charles Crossley (Alan Bates), who, having once lived with a tribe of Aborigines, has learned the secret of ''the shout,'' which has the power to kill. Told in flashback during a cricket match that takes place on the grounds of a mental asylum, the film follows Crossley's relationship with experimental composer Anthony (John Hurt) and his wife, Rachel (Susannah York). Crossley moves in with the couple and gradually his disturbing presence takes its toll. He tells the couple that he killed his own children, demonstrates his ability to kill with his shout, seduces Rachel, and tries to destroy Anthony. Directed by Polish director Jerzy Skolimowski (MOONLIGHTING), THE SHOUT has a certain compelling element that both mystifies and involves the viewer, its unusual story told with equal amounts of obscurity and skill. There are no tidy conclusions or explanations, leaving the audience as baffled at the end as they were at the start, but the film is definitely worth experiencing. Tony Banks and Mike Rutherford of the group Genesis contributed to the electronic score, and ROCKY HORROR star Tim Curry has a supporting role.

p, Jeremy Thomas; d, Jerzy Skolimowski; w, Michael Austin, Jerzy Skolimowski (based on a story by Robert Graves); ph, Mike Molloy; ed, Barrie Vince; m, Rupert Hine, Anthony Banks, Michael Rutherford.

(PR:O   MPAA:R)

## SHRIEK OF THE MUTILATED zero

(1974) 92m AM Films/Film Brokers c

Alan Brock *(Ernst Prell)*, Tawn Ellis *(Dr. Karl Werner)*, Jennifer Stock *(Karen Hunter)*, Michael Harris *(Keith Henshaw)*, Morton Jacobs *(Laughing Crow)*, Darcy Brown.

The ads claimed, "A Frenzied Hunt for a Hideous Beast Uncovers an Evil Cannibal Cult and Death is the Devil's Blessing," and that pretty much sums it up. This is one of the all-time worst, but the unintentional laughs may just make it worth a look for those who can stomach inept filmmaking. Ernst Prell (Alan Brock) is a college professor who takes four of his students on an expedition to Boot Island to search for the Abominable Snowman. There they meet with Prell's associate, Dr. Karl Werner (Tawn Ellis), and his native servant, Laughing Crow (Morton Jacobs), a dangerous-looking mute. Together, the small group begins exploring the island, and soon two of the students are ripped to pieces by a large, white beast who blow-dries its bushy mane. This leaves only two students remaining, and they begin to suspect things on this island aren't quite what they seem. One of them, Karen (Jennifer Stock), is cornered in the bathroom by two of the fuzzy brutes and scared to death. Her boy friend, Keith (Michael Harris), who was conveniently knocked out in the woods, comes to in time to witness the two professors and Laughing Crow cannibalizing one of the corpses, with their fuzzy white costumes hanging in a nearby closet. Keith takes off and finds a cop, but when they arrive on the scene it is revealed that the cop is a member of this cannibal cult as well. Wretched stuff and the credits read like a *Who's Who* of bad cinema. Lead actor Brock was a bit player in the 1930s who gave up the screen to become an agent, his cohort Ellis starred in CAT WOMEN OF THE MOON (1954), writer-producer Ed Adlum (a former rock critic for *Creem* magazine) was also responsible for the equally vile INVASION OF THE BLOOD FARMERS, and director Michael Findlay also made the bogus snuff film SNUFF (1976). Findlay, who, along with his wife, Roberta, helmed several porno and exploitation features, was killed in a gruesome accident atop the Pan Am building in New York when he was decapitated by a helicopter. Roberta carries on, having recently directed BLOOD SISTERS (1987).

p, Ed Adlum; d, Michael Findlay; w, Ed Adlum, Ed Kelleher.

(PR:O   MPAA:R)

## SILENT NIGHT, BLOODY NIGHT**

(1974) 88m Cannon c (AKA: NIGHT OF THE DARK FULL MOON; DEATH HOUSE)

Patrick O'Neal *(Carter)*, John Carradine *(Towman)*, Walter

Abel *(Mayor)*, Mary Woronov *(Diane)*, Astrid Heeren, James Patterson, Candy Darling, Ondine, Tally Brown, Jack Smith, Walter Klavun, Philip Burns, Fran Stevens.

This fitfully interesting film contains some nicely atmospheric moments and some fairly shocking gore. Patrick O'Neal plays a lawyer who spends the night in a house he's trying to sell for its mysterious owner (James Patterson). The place was once an insane asylum, and its history is told in unsettling flashbacks starring New York underground film actors Ondine, Jack Smith, Candy Darling, and Tally Brown. It seems that the doctors in the asylum were as sadistic and cruel as some of the patients, and the original owner of the place finally let the inmates go. A slaughter of the doctors ensued, and the freed patients wound up assimilating themselves into the town. Now, of course, someone wielding an axe is out for revenge and the former mental patients are killed off one by one. John Carradine and Mary Woronov are featured in the modern-day scenes.

p, Ami Artzi, Jeffrey Konvitz; d, Theodore Gershuny; w, Theodore Gershuny, Jeffrey Konvitz, Ami Artzi, Ira Teller; ph, Adam Giffard.

(PR:O   MPAA:R)

## SILENT NIGHT, DEADLY NIGHT*

(1984) 79m Tri-Star c

Lilyan Chauvin *(Mother Superior)*, Gilmer McCormick *(Sister Margaret)*, Toni Nero *(Pamela)*, Robert Brian Wilson *(Billy at 18)*, Brett Leach *(Mr. Sims)*, Nancy Borgenicht *(Mrs. Randall)*, H.E.D. Redford *(Capt. Richards)*, Danny Wagner *(Billy at 8)*, Linnea Quigley *(Denise)*, Leo Geter *(Tommy)*, Randy Stumpf *(Andy)*, Will Hare *(Grandpa)*, Tara Buckman *(Mother/Ellie)*, Charles Dierkop *(Father/Jim)*, Eric Hart *(Levitt)*, Jonathon Best *(Billy at 5)*, A. Madeline Smith *(Sister Ellen)*, Amy Stuyvesant *(Cindy)*, Max Robinson *(Barnes)*, Oscar Rowland *(Dr. Conway)*.

It's not a very Merry Christmas for anyone who gets a visit from Santa in this film. Billy (Robert Brian Wilson) is a toystore Santa Claus whose qualifications for the job are a mite shady. It seems that, when he was a lad, Billy witnessed his parents' Yuletide murder at the hands of a killer in a Santa suit. This, along with a cruel upbringing in an orphanage, has given him a decidedly negative view of the holiday season. Unhappy with his new job, Billy takes to frightening the children who sit upon his knee, then takes the scares a step further. He goes off on a murder spree dressed as St. Nick, committing a series of gruesome slayings and beheadings before his holiday visits come to an end. As slasher films go, this is about average. The sets are cheap, with most of the film's budget seemingly going to the gore effects. Ironically, SILENT NIGHT, DEADLY NIGHT was directed by the same man who produced such wholesome fare as THE LIFE AND TIMES OF GRIZZLY ADAMS. The film was the subject of much controversy, including protesters who demanded that the film be withdrawn.

p, Ira Richard Barmak; d, Charles E. Sellier; w, Michael Hickey (based on a story by Paul Caimi); ph, Henning

Schellerup (Metrocolor); ed, Michael Spence; m, Perry Botkin.

**(PR:O  MPAA:R)**

## SILENT NIGHT, DEADLY NIGHT PART II zero

(1987) 88m Ascot Entertainment Group-Silent Night Releasing c

Eric Freeman, James L. Newman, Elizabeth Clayton, Jean Miller.

All is not calm and all is not bright in this alleged sequel to the infamous 1984 release. Least bright of all are the filmmakers who thought they could capitalize on the controversy surrounding the original movie. This is not so much a sequel as it is a rerun of the first film, since a great deal of footage from SILENT NIGHT, DEADLY NIGHT appears here, but PART II is even poorer than its predecessor in every way. The acting is blah, the script is lame, the direction is dumb, and the editing is as pretentious as anything you may have ever seen. PART II picks up the action years after the first film, as a nutso young man (Eric Freeman) realizes it's Christmas Eve, dons his red-and-white suit, and departs on a murderous Yuletide rampage. The ways in which the psycho Santa kills are ingenious as well as disgusting: he blows off the top of one man's head by cramming live battery chargers down the guy's gullet, and impales another with an umbrella, then opens it. If the writers had taken as much care with the dialog and the plot as they did with the murders, the movie might have risen from dreadful to mediocre.

p, Lawrence Appelbaum; d, Lee Harry; w, Lee Harry, Joseph H. Earle (based on a story by Lee Harry, Joseph H. Earle, Dennis Paterson, Lawrence Appelbaum and a character created by Michael Hickey, Paul Caimi); ph, Harvey Genkins (United color); m, Michael Armstrong.

**(PR:O  MPAA:R)**

## SILENT SCREAM**½

(1980) 87m American Cinema Releasing c

Rebecca Balding *(Scotty Parker)*, Cameron Mitchell *(Lt. McGiver)*, Avery Schreiber *(Sgt. Rusin)*, Barbara Steele *(Victoria Engles)*, Steve Doubet *(Jack)*, Brad Reardon *(Mason)*, John Widelock *(Peter)*, Juli Andelman *(Doris)*, Yvonne De Carlo *(Mrs. Engels)*, Jack Stryker *(Police Chief)*, Tina Taylor *(Victoria at age 16)*, Jason Zahler *(Mason at Age 3)*, Thelma Pelish, Joan Lemmo, Ina Gould, Virginia Rose, Ernie Potvin, Rachel Bard.

Scotty (Rebecca Balding), Jack (Steve Doubet), Peter (John Widelock), and Doris (Juli Andelman) are some college kids who can't get on-campus housing. They need to live somewhere, so the coed quartet takes up residence in the creepy mansion of Mrs. Engles (Yvonne De Carlo) and her disturbed son, Mason (Brad Reardon). Shortly after moving in, Peter is brutally murdered and the cops (Cameron Mitchell and Avery Schreiber) investigate. They discover that Mrs. Engles also has a daughter, Victoria (Barbara Steele), who ran away years before. Is the murderer Mrs. Engles, her crazed son, or her vengeful daugh-

ter? Surprisingly bloodless and fairly atmospheric, SILENT SCREAM is a bit better than most films of this ilk. Director Denny Harris actually takes the time to develop the characters, so that the audience has a certain amount of empathy for them before they are murdered, and the offbeat casting of Mitchell and Schreiber actually works quite well.

p, Jim Wheat, Ken Wheat; d, Denny Harris; w, Jim Wheat, Ken Wheat, Wallace C. Bennett; ph, Michael D. Murphy, David Short (MGM Color); ed, Edward Salier; m, Roger Kellaway.

**(PR:O  MPAA:R)**

## SISTER SISTER**

(1988) 91m Odyssey/NW c

Eric Stoltz *(Matt Rutledge)*, Jennifer Jason Leigh *(Lucy Bonnard)*, Judith Ivey *(Charlotte Bonnard)*, Dennis Lipscomb *(Sheriff Cleve Doucet)*, Anne Pitoniak *(Mrs. Bettleheim)*, Benjamin Mouton *(Etienne LeViolette)*, Natalia Nogulich *(Fran Steuben)*, Richard Minchenberg *(Lenny Steuben)*, Bobby Pickett *(Roger)*, Jason Saucier *(Jud Nevins)*, Jerry Leggio *(Mr. Bonnard)*, Fay Cohn *(Mrs. Bonnard)*, Ashley McMurry *(Young Lucy)*, Ben Cook *(Young Matt)*, Casey Levron *(Young Etienne)*, Aggie the Dog *(Beau)*.

SISTER SISTER is pure southern gothic horror (in the tradition of HUSH . . . HUSH, SWEET CHARLOTTE) that begins promisingly enough, but then quickly disintegrates into a dull, predictable, and at times absurd chiller. Two sisters, Charlotte (Judith Ivey) and Lucy (Jennifer Jason Leigh), live together in the Louisiana bayou in a giant old plantation house left them by their parents. Charlotte devotes much of her time to caring for the younger and more "delicate" Lucy. It is hinted that Lucy has had some emotional problems in the past, and because Charlotte fears that separation from her sister will cause a relapse, she refuses the marriage proposals of the kindly local sheriff (Dennis Lipscomb). Lucy, a pale, lonely girl, spends much of her time fantasizing about ghosts and dreaming up "Harlequin Romance"-style sexual scenarios with handyman Etienne (Benjamin Mouton). All this sexual repression threatens to explode when handsome young congressional aide Matt Rutledge (Eric Stoltz) arrives on holiday. Beautifully shot in a wide-screen format, SISTER SISTER is easy to look at, but hard to take. Directed and coscripted by STRANGE INVADERS writer Bill Condon in his feature directorial debut, the picture is all misty mood and little else. Luckily, Condon has cast two excellent actresses in the leads, and Ivey and Leigh are impressive, striking all the right contrasts and similarities as two adult siblings. While Condon should be commended for trying to steer the horror film away from the routine slasher fare that has nearly ruined the genre, he has failed to notice that he drove it right back into the ranks of boring gothic thrillers that slasher prototype HALLOWEEN rebelled against in the first place.

p, Walter Coblenz; d, Bill Condon; w, Bill Condon, Joel Cohen, Ginny Cerrella; ph, Stephen M. Katz (DeLuxe Color); ed, Marion Rothman; m, Richard Einhorn.

**(PR:O  MPAA:R)**

## SISTERS****

(1973) 92m Pressman-Williams/AIP c (GB: BLOOD SISTERS)

Margot Kidder *(Danielle Breton)*, Jennifer Salt *(Grace Collier)*, Charles Durning *(Joseph Larch)*, Bill Finley *(Emil Breton)*, Lisle Wilson *(Phillip Woode)*, Barnard Hughes *(Mr. McLennen)*, Mary Davenport *(Mrs. Collier)*, Dolph Sweet *(Detective Kelley)*.

Although one of his earliest films, SISTERS still stands as director Brian De Palma's greatest contribution to the horror genre. Grace Collier (Jennifer Salt) is a nosy reporter who sees neighbor Danielle Breton (Margot Kidder) murder her black boy friend, Phillip (Lisle Wilson). She calls the police, but when the cops arrive there is no evidence of foul play, Danielle and a male accomplice (Bill Finley) having cleaned the apartment up and disposed of the body. Determined to crack the case, Grace continues to investigate on her own, with the help of private eye Joseph Larch (Charles Durning). The trail leads her to a mental hospital/retreat where Grace learns that Danielle was a Siamese twin who was separated from her sister, and that it may be her twin who committed the murder. Though clearly inspired by PSYCHO (1960) and REAR WINDOW (1954), De Palma actually comes up with some great cinematic embellishments of his own, especially his inventive use of the split-screen technique, which builds a great deal of suspense while toying with audience perception and loyalties. Also powerful are the remarkable flashback and hallucination scenes, which provide the intriguing backstory. For a De Palma film, SISTERS is surprisingly rich in character and thematics, has an uncharacteristic sense of humor that delights in tweaking the ineptitude of the local police force and government bureaucracy, and contains a magnificent performance from Kidder. The wonderful musical score is by Hitchcock's favorite composer, Bernard Herrmann.

p, Edward R. Pressman; d, Brian De Palma; w, Brian De Palma, Louisa Rose (based on a story by De Palma); ph, Gregory Sandor (Movielab Color); ed, Paul Hirsch; m, Bernard Herrmann.

**(PR:O MPAA:R)**

## SLAUGHTER HIGH**½

(1987) 88m Vestron c

Caroline Munro *(Carol)*, Simon Scuddamore *(Marty)*, Carmine Iannaccone *(Skip)*, Donna Yaeger *(Stella)*, Gary Hartman *(Joe)*, Billy Martin *(Frank)*, Michael Saffran *(Ted)*, John Segal *(Carl)*, Kelly Baker *(Nancy)*, Sally Cross *(Susan)*, Josephine Scandi *(Shirley)*, Marc Smith *(Coach)*, Dick Randall *(Manny)*, Jon Clark *(Digby)*.

A group of high-school kids, the elite clique of the popular and successful, make nerd Marty (Simon Scuddamore) the butt of their humiliating April Fool's gags. When one trick in the science lab turns bad, Marty is scalded with acid. Years later, the same group of students is invited to the shuttered high school for a reunion. There they find no party and, later, no exit. One by one they are done away with in gruesome fashion, until it slowly begins to dawn on them that they are being victimized by killer nerd Marty. They make efforts to escape, but eventually all are killed, whereupon Marty takes off his mask and begins laughing with delight at his accomplishment—until the ghosts of his victims begin to torment him and chase after him. Although superficially indistinguishable from the usual run of this type of film, SLAUGHTER HIGH is actually a superior example. The high-school revenge plot is always potent, for who wasn't humiliated during those years, and who didn't dream of wreaking a nasty revenge? The story line is as direct as can be and little time is wasted with extraneous subplots. Very effective use is made of the location, a decaying old school building that would give anyone the creeps, and good performances by Scuddamore, Carmine Iannaccone, and veteran B-movie starlet Caroline Munro further enhance the film. The effects are rather good but not too gross, tending to the near-comic.

p, Steve Minasian, Dick Randall; d, George Dugdale, Mark Ezra, Peter Litten; w, George Dugdale, Mark Ezra, Peter Litten; ph, Alan Pudney; ed, Jim Connock; m, Harry Manfredini.

**(PR:O MPAA:R)**

## SLAUGHTERHOUSE*½

(1988) 85m American Artists-Slaughterhouse/Manson c

Sherry Bendorf *(Liz Borden)*, Don Barrett *(Lester Bacon)*, William Houck *(Sheriff)*, Joe Barton *(Buddy)*, Jane Higginson *(Annie)*, Eric Schwartz *(Skip)*, Jeff Grossi *(Buzz)*.

With SLAUGHTERHOUSE, director Rick Roessler has tried to capture the same mix of horror and humor that Tobe Hooper's classic TEXAS CHAIN SAW MASSACRE achieved, but delivers a film that falls far short of those high standards, despite some obvious talent behind the camera. Lester Bacon (Don Barrett) is the owner of a long-closed pig slaughterhouse. The land it sits on is valuable and when a local competitor offers to buy him out, Lester refuses. The businessmen are upset, as is Lester, who, with the help of his obese son, Buddy (Joe Barton), begins to kill off his perceived enemies one by one. Although a typical slasher film, SLAUGHTERHOUSE offers a few moments of genuine fright. Roessler presents Buddy Bacon as an unstoppable killing monster who communicates only through pig grunts and groans, and the results are unsettling, especially when the 370-pound Barton starts swinging his oversized mallet. It's obvious that Roessler has talent (his visual technique is quite good) but it's a shame that talent is invested in a movie that has little else to set it apart from the horde of slasher films.

p, Ron Matonak; d, Rick Roessler; w, Rick Roessler; ph, Richard Benda (Cinema Color); ed, Sergio Uribe; m, Joseph Garrison.

**(PR:O MPAA:R)**

## SLAUGHTERHOUSE ROCK*

(1988) 90m First American-Arista/Arista c

Nicholas Celozzi *(Alex Gardner)*, Tom Reilly *(Richard Gardner)*, Donna Denton *(Carolyn Harding)*, Toni Basil

(Sammy Mitchell), Hope Marie Carlton (Krista Halpern), Steven Brian Smith (Jack), Ty Miller (Marty), Al Fleming (The Commandant).

Confused and at times incomprehensible, SLAUGHTER-HOUSE ROCK tries so hard to include a little bit of everything that it ends up delivering nothing. Alex Gardner (Nicholas Celozzi) is having horrible dreams of a prison plagued by the dead in which he is an inmate. These visions grow so disturbing that they begin to interfere with his daily life. With the help of his brother (Tom Reilly) and his girl friend (Donna Denton), Alex seeks the guidance of an expert in the occult, who discerns that the place in his dreams is the abandoned isle of Alcatraz and suggests that Alex go there to face his fear head on, whereupon his nightmares should cease. Backed up by a few wise-cracking friends, Alex duly heads out to the island and encounters the ghost of dead rock star Sammy Mitchell (Toni Basil), who explains that Alcatraz is haunted by the evil spirit of a US cavalry commandant (it seems he had a thing for eating people raw). It is up to Alex to kill the demon and save his friends, who, one by one, are being killed and/or possessed by the rampaging beast. This movie is all over the place. One moment it's about a young man trying to deal with his nightmares, the next it's about a dead rock star chasing down evil spirits. For its first 20 minutes or so, SLAUGHTERHOUSE ROCK is a serious-minded horror tale (and a pretty promising one at that), then, when the kids arrive on Alcatraz, the film switches gears and decides to be a comedy—a switch that annoys and finally damages a film that asks its audience to take an already implausible story seriously.

p, Louis George; d, Dimitri Logothetis; w, Ted Landon; ph, Nicholas von Sternberg; ed, Daniel Gross; m, Mark Mothersbaugh, Gerald V. Casale.

**(PR:O   MPAA:R)**

### SLAYER, THE**½

(1982) 80m International Picture Show/21st Century c
(AKA: NIGHTMARE ISLAND)

Sarah Kendall (Kay), Frederick Flynn (Eric), Carol Kottenbrook (Brooke), Alan McRae (David), Michael Holmes (Marsh), Carl Kraines (The Slayer).

An artist named Kay (Sarah Kendall) paints surreal pictures inspired by her phobia-filled dreams. As Kay, her husband, her brother, and her brother's wife vacation on a small island off the coast of Georgia, many of her worst dreams suddenly begin to come true when they are stalked by an unseen monster during a vicious thunderstorm. Director J.S. Cardone manages to present this overly familiar material with considerable flair, considering his low budget, and the film does have a genuinely surreal, nightmarish quality. Available on a double-bill videotape with Fred Olen Ray's inferior SCALPS.

p, William R. Ewing; d, J.S. Cardone; w, Cardone, William R. Ewing; ph, Karen Grossman (DeLuxe Color); ed, Edward Salier; m, Robert Folk.

**(PR:O   MPAA:R)**

### SLEEPAWAY CAMP zero

(1983) 85m American Eagle/United Film c

Mike Kellin (Mel), Felissa Rose (Angela), Jonathan Tierston (Ricky), Karen Fields (Judy), Christopher Collet (Paul), Paul De Angelo (Ron), Robert Earl Jones (Ben), Katherine Kamhi (Meg), John E. Dunn (Kenny).

A mad slasher stalks the boys and girls of Camp Arawak, slaughtering them in messy ways, including a drowning, a scalding, a killer bee attack, and the good old standby—a large knife. Writer-director Robert Hiltzik apparently tries to mask the poorly staged murder scenes and lousy effects (by the king of lousy effects, Ed French) with a perverse sense of humor, but it doesn't work. Some scenes, especially one involving a girl and a curling iron, are simply irredeemable. Believe it or not, a sequel followed.

p, Michele Tatosian, Jerry Silva; d, Robert Hiltzik; w, Robert Hiltzik; ph, Benjamin Davis (Technicolor); ed, Ron Kalish, Sharyn L. Ross; m, Edward Bilous.

**(PR:O   MPAA:R)**

### SLEEPAWAY CAMP 2: UNHAPPY CAMPERS zero

(1988) 80m Double Helix/Nelson c

Pamela Springsteen (Angela Baker), Brian Patrick Clarke (T.C.), Renee Estevez (Molly), Walter Gotell (Uncle John), Susan Marie Snyder (Mare), Heather Binion (Phoebe), Tony Higgins (Sean), Terry Hobbs (Rob), Kendall Bean (Demi), Valerie Hartman (Ally), Julie Murphy (Lea), Carol Chambers (Brooke), Amy Fields (Jodi).

Camp Rolling Hills has a problem. It seems that all of the organization's bad kids are being murdered in every grisly way imaginable: slashed, drilled, beaten, choked—even drowned in an outhouse. But who exactly are the "bad kids"? They are the ones who smoke, drink, swear, and fornicate at every opportunity, and Rolling Hills is full of these brats. One by one, they are taught their lesson by murderess Angela Baker (Pamela Springsteen, Bruce's younger sister), a harsh yet cheerful counselor who lives by the motto, "Keep your morals strong and you'll never go wrong." As the kids are murdered and the other counselors begin to wonder about their diminishing enrollment, Angela explains that she has sent the missing miscreants home for breaking the camp rules. Only then do they learn that Angela is a transsexual who committed the murders in the original SLEEPAWAY CAMP . . . as a man! SLEEPAWAY CAMP 2 is a tired, lame excuse for a film, a shameless rip-off of FRIDAY THE 13TH (which in itself doesn't win any awards for originality). This isn't a movie, it's a show reel for special-effects man Bill "Splat" Johnson.

p, Jerry Silva, Michael A. Simpson; d, Michael A. Simpson; w, Fritz Gordon (based on a story idea by Robert Hiltzik); ph, Bill Mills (Cinefilm color); ed, John David Allen; m, James Oliverio.

**(PR:O   MPAA:R)**

## SLUMBER PARTY MASSACRE, THE**½

(1982) 84m Sante Fe/PFC c

Michele Michaels (Trish), Robin Stille (Valerie), Michael Villela (Russ), Andre Honore (Jackie), Debra Deliso (Kim), Gina Mari (Diane), David Millbern (Jeff), Joe Johnson (Neil), Pamela Roylance (Coach Jana), Brinke Stevens (Linda), Rigg Kennedy (David), Howard Furgeson (Devereaux), Ryan Kennedy, Jean Vargas, Anna Patton, Pam Cazano, Aaron Lipstadt, Francis Menedez, Joe Dante, Jim Boyce, Jennifer Meyers.

THE SLUMBER PARTY MASSACRE garnered much attention because it was the first slasher film to be made by women—written by feminist author Rita Mae Brown (Rubyfruit Jungle), produced and directed by Amy Jones—but a slasher film is still a slasher film and the boasts that this one is somehow "feminist" are dubious at best. As plotless as any other splatter movie, the film shows a high-school girls' slumber party being invaded by a mad killer wielding a power drill. The big twist here is that the surviving teen bands with her sister and a neighbor girl to dispatch the creep successfully. While Jones' direction is nothing special, the script by Brown does have its share of male ego-deflating laughs—mainly some obvious Freudian jokes—and actually takes some time to develop the victims as characters instead of mere gore-fodder. A sequel followed.

p, Amy Jones, Aaron Lipstadt; d, Amy Jones; w, Rita Mae Brown; ph, Steve Posey (DeLuxe Color); ed, Wendy Green; m, Ralph Jones.

**(PR:O  MPAA:R)**

## SLUMBER PARTY MASSACRE II**

(1987) 90m Concorde/EM c

Crystal Bernard (Courtney), Jennifer Rhodes (Mrs. Bates), Kimberly McArthur (Amy), Patrick Lowe (Matt), Juliette Cummins (Sheila), Heidi Kozak (Sally), Cynthia Eilbacher (Valerie), Atanas Ilitch (The Driller Killer), Joel Hoffman (T.J.), Marshall La Plante (Car Driver), Don Daniel (Mr. Damnkids), Michael Delano (Officer Kroeger), Hamilton Mitchell (Officer Voorhies).

The original SLUMBER PARTY MASSACRE is one of the few films in the slasher genre directed and written by women (Amy Jones and Rita Mae Brown, respectively). The sequel carries on that vaguely feminist tradition, having been produced, directed, and written by Deborah Brock. The film gets under way as Courtney (Crystal Bernard), the sister of the girl who survived SPM I, goes off on a weekend trip with the other members of her all-girl rock band. They plan to stay at the new condominium owned by one member's father, and some guys are going to join them. Plagued by dreams in which a black-leather-clad rockabilly singer (Atanas Ilitch) with an auger at the end of his guitar attacks her and her friends, Courtney repeatedly wakes up in hysterics, and her friends begin to grow upset with her. Suddenly, though, he actually appears, gleefully drilling the boys and girls while doing little dance steps. The rockabilly killer is probably the most entertaining slasher ever to grace the screen—sort of like Elvis Presley playing Nor-

man Bates, complete with musical numbers. Usually it's no mystery why some films go straight to video without theatrical release, but this film is far above the caliber of most straight-to-video releases. Perhaps on tape it will gain the cult audience this original and funny horror film deserves.

p, Deborah Brock, Don Daniel; d, Deborah Brock; w, Deborah Brock; ph, Thomas Callaway.

**(PR:O  MPAA:NR)**

## SOMETHING WEIRD*½

(1967) 83m HUR-LEW/Mayflower c (AKA: EERIE WORLD OF DR. JORDAN, THE)

Tony McCabe (Cronin Mitchell), Elizabeth Lee (Ellen Parker, the Beautiful/Ugly Witch), William Brooker (Dr. Alex Jordan), Mudite Arums (Hag), Ted Heil (Maddox), Lawrence J. Aberwood (Chief Vinton), Stan Dale (Government Official), Larry Wellington (Rev. Ammond), Jeffery Allen (Dr. White), Roy Collodi (Dr. Roxin), Norm Lenet (Stein), Carolyn Smith (Nurse), Richard Nilsson (Kim), Janet Charlton (Secretary), Kathy Koenio (Ghost), George Cohon (Banker), William B. Petan (Lawyer), Semaj Velruth (Editor), Peo Stewart (Vinton's Wife), Lee Ahsmann (Photographer), Daniel Milano (Maitre D'Hotel), Joe Adamik (Policeman), Dan Carrington (Man in Bar), Roger L. Papsch, Louis Newman (Drunks), Ione.

"Something weird" is right—there's barely a drop of blood in the entire movie! This is a strange and fairly obscure Herschell Gordon Lewis effort, which combines witchcraft and ESP with a touch of espionage. Cronin Mitchell (Tony McCabe) is an electrical engineer whose face is disfigured in a high-tension wire accident. As a result of the accident, he discovers that he has acquired ESP and telekinetic powers, enabling him to see into the future and move objects. Depressed about his scarred face, he pays a visit to Ellen Parker (Elizabeth Lee), a witch who agrees to fix his face if he will be her lover. The witch appears beautiful to the rest of the world, but because of his powers, Mitchell is able to see her as she really is, horribly ugly. Together they travel around the country, and Mitchell becomes a famous psychic. Called to a small town to help solve a murder case, Mitchell is, unbeknownst to him, observed by Dr. Alex Jordan (William Brooker), an expert in psychic phenomena who has been employed by the government to determine if Mitchell's powers are real. Jordan falls in love with Ellen, which causes problems for Mitchell. Shot in Chicago, this is one of Lewis' most conventional films and consequently one of his dullest. Overly ambitious, SOMETHING WEIRD was produced and written by James F. Hurley, a college professor, karate buff, and a former associate of psychic Peter Hurkos. Hurley attempts to combine all of his obsessions into one script that alternates between a tale of the supernatural, an action film (it opens with a lengthy karate lesson), and a tribute to the Playboy lifestyle. Unfortunately, it fails on all counts, because Lewis really isn't much of a director and the acting is, as usual, atrocious. Oddly enough, the videotape release of this film is actually letterboxed.

p, James F. Hurley; d, Herschell Gordon Lewis; w, James

F. Hurley; ph, Herschell Gordon Lewis, Andy Romanoff; m, Edward J. Petan.

**(PR:C    MPAA:NR)**

## SOMETHING WICKED THIS WAY COMES**

(1983) 94m WB-Bryna/BV c

Jason Robards Jr, *(Charles Halloway)*, Jonathan Pryce *(Mr. Dark)*, Diane Ladd *(Mrs. Nightshade)*, Pam Grier *(Dust Witch)*, Royal Dano *(Tom Fury)*, Vidal Peterson *(Will Halloway)*, Shawn Carson *(Jim Nightshade)*, Angelo Rossitto *(Little Person No. 1)*, Peter Risch *(Little Person No. 2)*, Tim T. Clark, Jill Carroll *(Teenage Couple)*, Tony Christopher *(Young Ed)*, Sharan Lea *(Young Miss Foley)*, Scott DeRoy *(Cooger as a Young Man)*, Sharon Ashe *(Townswoman)*, Arthur Hill *(Narrator)*, Mary Grace Canfield *(Miss Foley)*, Richard Davalos *(Mr. Crosetti)*, Jake Dengel *(Mr. Tetley)*, Jack Dodson *(Dr. Douglas)*, Bruce M. Fischer *(Mr. Cooger)*, Ellen Geer *(Mrs. Halloway)*, Brendan Klinger *(Cooger as a Child)*, James Stacy *(Ed, the Bartender)*.

The talents of the wonderful Jonathan Pryce are wasted in this poor adaptation of Ray Bradbury's tale of fantasy and the supernatural. Pryce stars as Mr. Dark, the mysterious and sinister owner of a traveling carnival that comes to a small Illinois town in the early 20th century and immediately enthralls the townsfolk. Most of the people in this small town have unfulfilled dreams or wishes for a better life, which Mr. Dark can give to them, but only if they join his dark circus as freaks. Bradbury's surprisingly bland script, the perfunctory direction, and so-so special effects cripple what could have been a great movie had director Sam Peckinpah—who long dreamed of filming the book—been allowed to see it through. Instead, the property was snapped up by Disney, which promptly sucked the life out of it, turning it into a scrubbed and innocuous coming-of-age tale. Too bad.

p, Peter Vincent Douglas; d, Jack Clayton; w, Ray Bradbury (based on the novel by Bradbury); ph, Stephen H. Burum (Technicolor); ed, Argyle Nelson, Barry Mark Gordon; m, James Horner.

**(PR:C    MPAA:PG)**

## SON OF DRACULA***½

(1943) 78m UNIV bw

Lon Chaney, Jr. *(Count Alucard)*, Robert Paige *(Frank Stanley)*, Louise Allbritton *(Katherine Caldwell)*, Evelyn Ankers *(Claire Caldwell)*, Frank Craven *(Dr. Harry Brewster)*, J. Edward Bromberg *(Prof. Lazlo)*, Samuel S. Hinds *(Judge Simmons)*, Adeline DeWalt Reynolds *(Queen Zimba)*, Patrick Moriarity *(Sheriff Dawes)*, Etta McDaniel *(Sarah)*, George Irving *(Col. Caldwell)*, Walter Sande *(The Jailor)*, Cyril Delevanti *(The Coroner)*, Jack Rockwell *(Deputy Sheriff)*, Jess Lee Brooks *(Steven)*, Joan Blair *(Mrs. Land)*, Sam McDaniel *(Andy)*, Charles Moore *(Mathew)*, Robert Dudley *(Kirby)*, Charles Bates *(Tommy Land)*, Emmett Smith *(Servant)*.

Although Lon Chaney, Jr., is easily the heaviest actor ever to play Count Dracula, this unjustly forgotten entry in the classic Universal horror series is a surprisingly good film—despite the fact that there is no "son" of Dracula involved. This time the king of the vampires, calling himself Count Alucard ("Dracula" spelled backwards), heads to Louisiana to take occult worshipper Katherine Caldwell (Louise Allbritton) as his new bride. The family thinks he is a member of Hungary's high society, but Katherine knows the truth and perversely embraces the undead count, willingly accepting vampirism in exchange for eternal life. Her former boy friend (Robert Paige) suspects that the count is up to no good and decides to investigate. Sporting a mustache and slicked-back hair with a touch of grey at the temples, Chaney makes a rather effective—if somewhat husky—Dracula. The film boasts some impressive camerawork from George Robinson and excellent special effects by John Fulton, which have the vampire turning into either a bat or a wisp of white smoke at will. Perhaps the most memorable scene in the movie takes place as Dracula's coffin comes bubbling up from the swamp and white mist emerges from it to form Dracula, who glides across the water to meet his bride, who stands on the bank, hypnotized. Also on hand are the beautiful Evelyn Ankers and a Maria Ouspenskaya-like sorceress called Queen Zimba played by 80-year old Adeline DeWalt Reynolds. One of the reasons for this film's relative obscurity may be its regrettable racism: the black servants are referred to as "boys" and the whole lot of them flee the household after the first vampire killing.

p, Ford Beebe; d, Robert Siodmak; w, Eric Taylor (based on a story by Curtis Siodmak); ph, George Robinson; ed, Saul Goodkind.

**(PR:A    MPAA:NR)**

## SON OF FRANKENSTEIN****

(1939) 95m UNIV bw

Basil Rathbone *(Baron Wolf von Frankenstein)*, Boris Karloff *(The Monster)*, Bela Lugosi *(Ygor)*, Lionel Atwill *(Inspector Krogh)*, Josephine Hutchinson *(Elsa von Frankenstein)*, Donnie Dunagan *(Peter von Frankenstein)*, Emma Dunn *(Amelia)*, Edgar Norton *(Thomas Benson)*, Perry Ivins *(Fritz)*, Lawrence Grant *(Burgomaster)*, Lionel Belmore *(Emil Lang)*, Michael Mark *(Ewald Neumuller)*, Caroline Cook *(Frau Neumuller)*, Gustav von Seyffertitz *(Councilor)*, Edward Cassidy *(Dr. Berger)*, Tom Ricketts, Lorimer Johnson *(Burghers)*, Jack Harris, Betty Chay, Harry Cording, Ward Bond, Dwight Frye, Bud Wolfe, Eddie Parker.

The third film in the Universal "Frankenstein" series and the last feature film appearance by Boris Karloff as the monster, SON OF FRANKENSTEIN boasts some stunning set design by Russell Gausman, a good script, and a magnificent cast. Set 25 years after the end of THE BRIDE OF FRANKENSTEIN, the film begins as the late Baron von Frankenstein's son, Wolf (Basil Rathbone), returns to his homeland and receives a weak welcome from the burgomaster, who presents him with a box containing his father's papers. Once safe in his castle, Wolf is visited by Inspector Krogh (Lionel Atwill), who warns him that he is not welcomed by the villagers, who fear that he will continue his father's experiments. Wolf laughs off their suspicions, but the next day, while wandering the ruins of his father's laboratory, he meets Ygor (Bela Lugosi). The deceased Baron's assistant now hides among the ruins, guarding his "friend"—the comatose Frankenstein monster (Karloff), laid out on a slab, immobile, but very much alive. Wolf becomes obsessed with the idea of bringing the monster back to full power, then vindicating his father by teaching the creature to behave. SON OF FRANKENSTEIN is a rousing, memorable addition to the series, and features a collection of superb portrayals from Lugosi (who delivers the performance of his career and nearly steals the film), Rathbone (in a part originally planned for Peter Lorre), and Lionel Atwill (who milks his false arm for all it's worth), though Karloff is a bit of a disappointment—his beloved monster turned into little more than a mute robot. Dwight Frye, who had been Frankenstein's assistant in the first two films, unfortunately had his entire role as one of the villagers cut out. While the offbeat vision and humor of James Whale (the director of the first two "Frankenstein" films) are missing, Rowland Lee manages to create a memorable world all his own. The series would go downhill from here and end with a rousing parody of the whole genre in ABBOTT AND COSTELLO MEET FRANKENSTEIN (1948).

p, Rowland V. Lee; d, Rowland V. Lee; w, Willis Cooper (based on characters created by Mary Shelley); ph, George Robinson; ed, Ted Kent; m, Frank Skinner.

**(PR:C   MPAA:NR)**

## SON OF KONG***

(1933) 70m RKO bw

Robert Armstrong *(Carl Denham)*, Helen Mack *(Hilda Peterson)*, Frank Reicher *(Capt. Englehorn)*, John Marston *(Helstrom)*, Victor Wong *(Chinese Cook)*, Ed Brady *(Red)*, Lee Kohlmar *(Mickey)*, Clarence Wilson *(Peterson)*, Katherine Ward *(Mrs. Hudson)*, Gertrude Short *(Girl Reporter)*, Gertrude Sutton *(Servant Girl)*, James B. Leong *(Chinese Trader)*, Noble Johnson *(Native Chief)*, Steve Clemento *(Witch King)*, Frank O'Connor *(Process Server)*, Constantine Romanoff *(Bell)*, Harry Tenbrook *(Tommy)*, Leo ""Dutch" Hendrian *(Dutch)*.

Hot to capitalize on the massive success of KING KONG, RKO Studios, now headed by Merian C. Cooper, decided to rush a sequel before the cameras under the direction of Ernest B. Schoedsack. The result is a funny, entertaining little film that pales in comparison with the original, but has enough value in its own right. Picking up where KING KONG left off, the film opens as the irrepressible Carl Denham (Robert Armstrong) finds nearly every lawyer in New York City ready to sue him for the damage done by the late Eighth Wonder of the World. In an effort to avoid these lawsuits, Denham and Capt. Englehorn (Frank Reicher) set off for the China seas, hoping to find a hidden treasure stashed on Skull Island, the very place that spawned King Kong. Sure enough, they meet the son of Kong. Standing a mere 25 feet tall (his dad towered over 50 feet), this new gorilla's most striking feature is his white fur. Kong's son also has a much more pleasant disposition than his father,

and tags along with the humans, offering his large helping hands. Of course, there are several giant beasts roaming the island to threaten the humans (including a brontosaurus, a stegosaurus, a lizard-like creature, and a sea monster), and the friendly Kong, Jr., comes to the expedition's rescue. Where KING KONG was heavy and dramatic, filled with excitement and action, SON OF KONG relies on comedy and cuteness. Kong *fils* is a very friendly, comical creature with an extremely expressive face who mimics the behavior of those around him. This approach to the material was probably budgetary—Cooper was handed a tiny budget of $250,000, more than $400,000 *less* than he spent on KING KONG. Knowing there was little time or money to make an elaborate adventure filled with animated monsters, Cooper and his wife, screenwriter Ruth Rose, went to work on a story that emphasized and developed the human characters, with the special effects kept to a minimum. Willis O'Brien, who did the marvelous effects for KING KONG, reluctantly returned for SON OF KONG and, though unhappy with the limitations, still did some of his best work.

p, Archie S. Marshek; d, Ernest B. Schoedsack; w, Ruth Rose; ph, Edward Linden, Vernon Walker, J.O. Taylor; ed, Ted Cheesman; m, Max Steiner.

**(PR:A   MPAA:NR)**

## SORORITY HOUSE MASSACRE zero

(1986) 74m Concorde c

Angela O'Neill *(Beth)*, Wendy Martel *(Linda)*, Pamela Ross *(Sara)*, Nicole Rio *(Tracy)*, John C. Russell *(Bobby)*, Marcus Vaughter *(Andy)*, Vincent Bilancio *(John)*, Joe Nassi *(Craig)*, Mary Anne *(Mrs. Lawrence)*, Gillian Frank *(Dr. Lindsey)*, Joseph Mansier *(Technician)*, Axel Roberts *(Larry)*, Fitzhough Houston *(Detective Gilbert)*, Marsha Carter *(Nurse)*, Maureen Hawkes *(Professor)*, Alan Engster *(Night Orderly)*, Phyllis Frank *(Teacher)*, Thomas R. Mustin *(Steve)*, Susan Bollman *(Cindy)*, Ray Spinka *(Shop Owner)*, Hammer *(Gas Station Woman)*, Todd Darling *(U-Hauler)*, Jon Hofferman *(U-Helper)*, Patrick Fahey, Bob Moore *(Policemen)*, Hillary Hollingsworth *(Laura)*, Aimee Brooks *(Cathy)*, Kara Joy *(Janet)*, Ivory Berry *(Susan)*, Shirley Aldridge *(Mother)*, Scott Martin *(Father)*.

Since just about every holiday around has been used up by slasher films, SORORITY HOUSE MASSACRE forgoes a festive theme in its title. That doesn't stop writer-director Carol Frank from conjuring up memories of HALLOWEEN, however, by blatantly ripping off that film's plot, characters, and camera style with unashamed abandon. The skimpy story line follows the teenaged Beth (Angela O'Neill), who goes off to visit some friends at their college sorority house. Beth is disturbed by dreams of a mad killer who slaughters a family. Meanwhile, at a nearby insane asylum, trouble is brewing. Bobby (John C. Russell), one of the longtime residents, is also being plagued with bad dreams. After some scientific mumbo jumbo (it's hard to pad these things out to 74 minutes, isn't it?), Bobby escapes and starts heading you-know-where. Back at the sorority house, it's learned that this abode was the scene of a horrible mass murder years before. If director Frank had tried for even borderline originality, this might be tolerable. Instead, she simply goes through the motions, generating nothing more than a bad Xerox copy of John Carpenter's far superior work. There's no suspense, no excitement, just a lot of bloody knives to slice through the tedium.

p, Ron Diamond; d, Carol Frank; w, Carol Frank; ph, Marc Reshovsky; ed, Jeff Wishengra; m, Michael Wetherwax.

**(PR:O MPAA:R)**

## SPASMS*½

(1982, Can.) 89m Cinequity-NTC-CFDC-Famous Players/PDC c (AKA: DEATH BITE)

Peter Fonda *(Dr. Brasilian)*, Oliver Reed *(Jason)*, Kerrie Keane *(Susanne)*, Al Waxman *(Crowley)*, Miguel Fernandes *(Mendes)*, Marilyn Lightstone *(Dr. Rothman)*, Angus MacInnes *(Duncan)*, Laurie Brown *(Allison)*, Gerard Parkes *(Capt. Noveck)*, George Bloomfield *(Rev. Thomas)*.

This brainless picture concerns a killer devil-snake that surfaces every seven years to claim the souls of the dead. The snake is captured, but soon escapes, sending parapsychologist Dr. Brasilian (Peter Fonda) and an American millionaire (Oliver Reed) on a ridiculous search for the demonic reptile. The millionaire has an edge in the pursuit, because he was bitten by the snake seven years earlier and now possesses the ability to "see through the snake's eyes." Terribly hammy performances from both Fonda and Reed don't help the silly cause and the steadicam snake point-of-view shots get pretty tiresome after a while.

p, John G. Pozhke, Maurice Smith; d, William Fruet; w, Don Enright (based on the novel *Death Bite* by Michael Maryk, Brent Monahan); ph, Mark Irwin (Medallion Color); ed, Ralph Brunjes; m, Eric N. Robertson, Tangerine Dream.

**(PR:O MPAA:R)**

## SPECTRE OF EDGAR ALLAN POE, THE*½

(1974) 87m Cintel/Cinerama c

Robert Walker, Jr. *(Edgar Allan Poe)*, Cesar Romero *(Dr. Grimaldi)*, Tom Drake *(Dr. Forrest)*, Carol Ohmart *(Lisa Grimaldi)*, Mary Grover *(Lenore)*, Mario Milano *(Joseph)*, Karen Hartford *(Night Nurse)*, Dennis Fimple *(Farron)*, Marsha Mae Jones *(Sarah)*.

This disappointing low budgeter purportedly details Edgar Allan Poe's traumatic romance with his great love, Lenore. Mary Grover plays Lenore, who, after almost being buried alive, goes insane and must be put in a mental institution run by the mysterious Dr. Grimaldi (Cesar Romero). Poe (Robert Walker, Jr.) has misgivings about leaving his love in the institution after a series of bloody killings. Upon investigating, he discovers a basement torture chamber complete with a snake pit and other charming devices. It is revealed that Dr. Grimaldi's wife (Carol Ohmart) is homicidally insane, and it is she who is hacking up inmates and visitors alike. Although THE SPECTRE OF EDGAR ALLAN POE has virtually nothing to do with the facts of Poe's life, this could have been an intriguing little "what if?" entry had

it been handled with more aplomb. As it is, however, the film is woefully dull and most of the key players are miscast.

p, Mohy Quandour; d, Mohy Quandour; w, Mohy Quandour, Kenneth Hartford; ph, Robert Birchall (Eastmancolor); ed, Abbas Amin; m, Allen D. Allen.

**(PR:C MPAA:PG)**

## SPIDER BABY****

(1968) 80m Lasky-Monka/American General-Distributors Intl. bw (AKA: LIVER EATERS, THE; SPIDER BABY, OR THE MADDEST STORY EVER TOLD; CANNIBAL ORGY, OR THE MADDEST STORY EVER TOLD)

Lon Chaney, Jr. *(Bruno)*, Carol Ohmart *(Emily)*, Quinn Redeker *(Peter)*, Mantan Moreland *(Messenger)*, Beverly Washburn *(Elizabeth)*, Mary Mitchell *(Ann)*, Karl Schanzer *(Schlocker)*, Sid Haig *(Ralph)*, Jill Banner *(Virginia)*, Carolyn Cooper, Joan Keller.

Probably the strangest film detailed in this book, SPIDER BABY is a disturbing, funny, and wholly unique horror film that remained hidden in virtual obscurity until it made its way onto home video. The film opens with a man reading aloud from a psychology textbook. He informs the audience about Merrye's Syndrome, an extremely rare disease that causes its adult victims to regress mentally to a preinfantile state—"a rotting of the brain, so to speak," as Lon Chaney, Jr.'s character later explains—causing violent behavior and cannibalism. In a watery flashback, we meet the principal victims of Merrye's Syndrome, the three children of the late Titus W. Merrye. The three (two girls and one boy) live in a remote mansion and are cared for by their chauffeur, Bruno (Chaney). The first fright occurs when a messenger (Mantan Moreland) attempts to deliver a telegram and has his neck caught in a window frame. Virginia (Jill Banner) darts into the room carrying two sharp knives with a small net strung between them. Pretending she's a spider, Virginia runs up to the "big, fat bug" and catches him in her "web," then proceeds to give the "bug" a "sting" and viciously cuts the messenger to pieces. She is caught and reprimanded by both her sister, Elizabeth (Beverly Washburn), and Bruno, who arrives in the family car with their brother, a bald cretin named Ralph (Sid Haig), in the back seat. Shortly thereafter, the plot proper kicks in and we learn that the children have two distant cousins who plan to steal their inheritance, including the mansion. This, of course, leads to much trouble. Filmed in 1964 but unreleased until 1968, SPIDER BABY was written and directed by Jack Hill, the man behind the wretched series of Mexican films Boris Karloff made just before his death. A genuine oddity, the film is exceedingly well shot by cinematographer Alfred Taylor, and has a creepy PSYCHO-like feel about it as well as some nightmarish surrealism. Better yet are the performances. While some have chosen to view Chaney's appearance here as degrading (he even sings the bizarre theme song), his performance is easily one of the best he gave toward the end of his career (it is genuinely touching) and is nowhere near as embarrassing as his role in the execrable DRACULA VS. FRANKENSTEIN. Also remarkable is Banner as the "spider baby" Virginia, who combines a little-girlish innocence with a budding sexuality and puts a disturbingly homicidal spin on it. Mere words cannot properly convey the uniqueness of this film, which should be sought out and seen by all with an interest in the genre.

p, Gil Lasky, Paul Monka; d, Jack Hill; w, Jack Hill; ph, Alfred Taylor; ed, Elliot Fayad; m, Ronald Stein.

(PR:C  MPAA:NR)

## SPLATTER UNIVERSITY zero

(1984) 77m Aquifilm/Troma c

Francine Forbes *(Julie Parker),* Dick Biel *(Father Janson/ Daniel Grayham),* Cathy Lacommare *(Cathy),* Ric Randig *(Mark),* Joanna Mihalakis, George Seminara, Don Eaton, Sal Lumetta, Denise Texeira, John Michaels, Richard W. Haines, Laura Gold, Mary Ellen David.

One assumes that after SLAUGHTER HIGH the surviving students might further their education at SPLATTER UNIVERSITY. This charming Troma picture follows poor Julie Parker (Francine Forbes), a generic sociology instructor who arrives at a small Catholic college to take over the teaching duties of an instructor murdered the previous semester. More killings take place, further dwindling enrollment. This grainy 16mm slasher film stomps over the same familiar turf with a mind-numbing lack of imagination. Lots of college kids bite the dust between poorly written dialog scenes that fail to advance the story. On the plus side, the picture is quite short.

p, Richard W. Haines, John Michaels; d, Richard W. Haines; w, Richard W. Haines, John Michaels, Michael Cunningham; ph, Fred Cohen, Jim Grib; ed, Richard W. Haines; m, Chris Burke.

(PR:O  MPAA:R)

## SQUIRM***

(1976) 93m AIP c

Don Scardino *(Mick),* Patricia Pearcy *(Geri),* R.A. Dow *(Roger),* Jean Sullivan *(Naomi),* Peter MacLean *(Sheriff),* Fran Higgins *(Alma),* William Newman *(Quigley),* Barbara Quinn *(Sheriff's Girl),* Carl Dagenhart *(Willie Grimes),* Angel Sande *(Millie),* Carol Jean Owens *(Bonnie),* Kim Iocouvozzi *(Hank),* Walter Dimmick *(Danny),* Julia Klopp *(Mrs. Klopp).*

Man-eating worms are created from the regular variety when an electrical storm downs wires and fills the ground that harbors them with high voltage. A Georgia farm community falls victim to the slimy creatures, which have a way of responding to underlying tensions among the townspeople. The somewhat tongue-in-cheek tone for this movie is set from its beginning, when it is claimed in the opening titles that the story is based on an actual occurrence in Georgia in 1975. Jeff Lieberman, who would go on to direct the excellent BLUE SUNSHINE (1977), handles both the inherent humor of the situation and the actual scares with equal aplomb. The viewer is jerked back and forth between laughs and frights, as in the PSYCHO shower scene

*hommage,* which features worms wriggling out of the shower head, or the genuinely terrifying scene in which the vicious worms are seen burrowing into a character's face (courtesy of Rick Baker's effects). The climax doesn't skimp on the worms either, for literally thousands of them invade a house and take it over. As with most of Lieberman's work, this is an underrated effort.

p, George Manasse; d, Jeff Lieberman; w, Jeff Lieberman; ph, Joseph Mangine (Movielab Color); ed, Brian Smedley-Aston; m, Robert Prince.

(PR:C  MPAA:PG)

## STANLEY*

(1973) 108m Crown c

Chris Robinson *(Tim Ochopee),* Alex Rocco *(Richard Thomkins),* Steve Alaimo *(Crail Denning),* Susan Carroll *(Susie Thomkins),* Mark Harris *(Bob Wilson),* Marcie Knight *(Gloria Calvin),* Rey Baumel *(Sidney Calvin),* Paul Avery *(Psycho Simpson),* Gary Crutcher *(Dr. Everett),* Melvin Pape *(Medical Center Guard),* Butterball Smith *(Nightclub Stage Manager),* Pamela Talus *(Thomkins' Girl Friend),* Bill Marquez *(Wauchula).*

Hot on the heels of the phenomenally successful boy-and-his-killer-rat movie WILLARD (1972) and its sequel, BEN (1972) came this stomach-churning epic about a crazed Vietnam vet of Seminole Indian descent and his pet rattlesnake, Stanley. War experiences in Southeast Asia have left the mental load of Tim Ochopee (Chris Robinson) shy one brick. Tim finds solace in the company of snakes, and soon breeds a whole shack full of them, setting up a snake empire with Stanley and his mate, Hazel, as the reptilian king and queen. Trouble looms on the horizon when a rich snakeskin apparel manufacturer, Richard Thomkins (Alex Rocco), offers to buy Tim's shack o' snakes. The nature-loving vet refuses; he would never consider selling his friends to a man who would slaughter them for wallets, purses, and shoes. Outraged, Thomkins swears vengeance and hires a psychopathic hit man, appropriately named "Psycho" (Paul Avery), to do the dirty work. Luckily, Stanley the snake and his minions know a bad guy when they see one and they slither off to nutty Tim's rescue. Wretched in every respect, STANLEY would be an entirely laughable affair if it wasn't so disturbingly gross. Not only does the very concept of this film insult Vietnam vets, Seminole Indians, snake aficionados, strippers, and wallet manufacturers, but the human performers are so awful that after five minutes the viewer hopes the snakes will get embarrassed enough to kill the entire cast quickly and slither off.

p, William Grefe; d, William Grefe; w, Gary Crutcher (based on a story by Grefe); ph, Cliff Poland (DeLuxe Color); ed, Julio C. Chavez; m, Post Production Associates, Jack Vino.

(PR:O  MPAA:PG)

## STEPFATHER, THE****

(1987) 90m ITC/New Century-Vista c

Terry O'Quinn (Jerry Blake), Jill Schoelen (Stephanie Maine), Shelley Hack (Susan Blake), Charles Lanyer (Dr. Bondurant), Stephen Shellen (Jim Ogilvie), Stephen Miller (Al Brennan), Robyn Stevan (Karen), Jeff Schultz (Paul Baker), Lindsay Bourne (Art Teacher), Anna Hagan (Mrs. Leitner), Gillian Barber (Anne Barnes), Blu Mankuma (Lt. Jack Wall), Jackson Davies (Mr. Chootorton), Gabriollo Rose (Dorothy), Richard Sargent (Mr. Anderson), Rochelle Greenwood (Mr. Anderson), Don Williams (Mr. Stark), Don MacKay (Joe), Dale Wilson (Frank), Gary Hetherington (Herb), Andrew Snider (Mr. Grace), Marie Stillin (Mrs. Fairfax), Paul Batten (Mr. Fairfax).

Just when you thought slasher movies were wholly irredeemable, director Joseph Ruben comes along to prove there is some intelligent life in this otherwise bereft subgenre. Featuring a fascinating script by novelist Donald Westlake, some taut direction, and an absolutely absorbing performance by Terry O'Quinn, THE STEPFATHER is not just another slice-and-dice thriller. Loosely based on a real-life case, the film begins in a picturesque suburb in autumn as a rugged-looking, bearded man (O'Quinn) washes blood from his hands, cuts his hair, shaves, and changes his clothes to emerge a completely different person. As he walks downstairs, we see that the man's entire family has been massacred. One year later, the man resurfaces as Jerry Blake—in a new suburb, with a new job, a new wife (Shelley Hack), and a teenage stepdaughter (Jill Schoelen). Gradually the secret madness and alternate lives of Jerry Blake begin to emerge. THE STEPFATHER fits in nicely among such examinations of the seedy underbelly of "perfect" family life as Alfred Hitchcock's SHADOW OF A DOUBT and David Lynch's BLUE VELVET. Although the last part of the film disintegrates into some typical slasher movie conventions and a plethora of clumsy Hitchcock homages, the majority of the film is definitely not typical. Fueled by an intense and intricate performance by O'Quinn, the movie is a fascinating examination of America's predilection for superficial appearances over genuine substance. Jerry Blake is the consummate actor, masking his crazed state with an air of friendliness and easy charm. He strives for a false veneer of bliss—one that has been spoon-fed to his diseased mind via television. He wants the perfect television family, but when reality rears its ugly head and day-to-day problems cannot be dealt with in a matter of minutes, his repressed rage erupts.

p, Jay Benson; d, Joseph Ruben; w, Donald E. Westlake (based on a story by Carolyn Lefcourt, Brian Garfield, Donald E. Westlake); ph, John Lindley; ed, George Bowers; m, Patrick Moraz.

**(PR:O MPAA:R)**

## STEPHEN KING'S SILVER BULLET zero

(1985) 95m DD/PAR c

Gary Busey (Uncle Red), Everett McGill (Reverend Lowe/Werewolf), Corey Haim (Marty Coslaw), Megan Follows (Jane Coslaw), Robin Groves (Nan Coslaw), Leon Russom (Bob Coslaw), Terry O'Quinn (Sheriff Joe Haller), Bill Smitrovich (Andy Fairton), Joe Wright (Brady Kincaid), Kent Broadhurst (Herb Kincaid), Heather Simmons (Tammy Sturmfuller), James A. Baffico (Milt Sturmfuller), Rebecca Fleming (Mrs. Sturmfuller), Lawrence Tierney (Owen Knopfler), William Newman (Virgil Cuts), Sam Stoneburner (Mayor O'Banion), Lonnie Moore (Billy McLaren), Rick Pasotto (Aspinall), Wendy Walker (Stella Randolph), Myra Mailloux (Mother), William Brown (Bobby Robertson), Herb Harton (Elmer Zinneman), David Hart (Pete Sylvester), Graham Smith (Porter Zinneman), Paul Butler (Edgar Rounds).

Short of his grocery lists, horror writer Stephen King seems to publish everything he's ever written. His enormous output undoubtedly staggers the imagination of any would-be writer. However, quantity does not equal quality, and STEPHEN KING'S SILVER BULLET, which King adapted himself from his own novelette, is a dismal and woefully inept werewolf picture. Marty Coslaw (Corey Haim) is a disabled youngster who rides around in a rocket-powered wheelchair dubbed "The Silver Bullet," which, as we all know, is also the only kind of ammunition that can knock off a werewolf. When a crazed murderer starts a bloody reign of terror in little Marty's home town, his parents do the only sensible thing: take off on a vacation and leave their handicapped son with his drunken Uncle Red (Gary Busey). King's smug style permeates the film like a rank odor as the story lurches from one poorly created sequence to another. The werewolf effects, in keeping with the film's other standards, are just awful; any resemblance between a scary, hairy beast and the creature that lurches on-screen here is wholly in the imagination of the filmmakers. A real waste of time, to put it mildly. King would further massacre his own words on film in MAXIMUM OVERDRIVE. The monster was designed by Carlo Rambaldi.

p, Martha Schumacher; d, Daniel Attias; w, Stephen King (based on his novelette Cycle of the Werewolf); ph, Armando Nannuzzi (J-D-C Widescreen, Technicolor); ed, Daniel Loewenthal; m, Jay Chattaway.

**(PR:O MPAA:R)**

## STRAIT-JACKET**½

(1964) 89m COL bw

Joan Crawford (Lucy Harbin), Diane Baker (Carol), Leif Erickson (Bill Cutler), Howard St. John (Raymond Fields), John Anthony Hayes (Michael Fields), Rochelle Hudson (Emily Cutler), George Kennedy (Leo Krause), Edith Atwater (Mrs. Fields), Mitchell Cox (Dr. Anderson), Lee Yeary (Frank Hardin), Patricia Krest (Stella Fulton), Vickie Cos (Carol Aged 3), Patty Lee (1st Little Girl), Laura Hess (2nd Little Girl), Robert Ward (Shoe Clerk), Lyn Lundgren (Beauty Operator), Howard Hoffman.

Joan Crawford stars in this Robert Bloch-scripted (PSYCHO) tale of a crazed axe-murderer. Released after spending 20 years in an insane asylum for lopping the heads off her husband and his lover, Lucy Harbin (Crawford) returns home to her daughter, Carol (Diane Baker), who witnessed the slayings as a three-year-old. Shortly after her return, heads begin to roll again, with all the evidence pointing to Lucy, who begins to think she's gone insane. Although it's not particularly scary and relatively gimmick-free for a William Castle film, STRAIT-JACKET is lent plenty of camp value by Crawford's swaggering, suffering, self-parodic performance, as she pushes her established screen persona to new extremes. Sporting vintage 1940s clothes, a black wig, and jangling bracelets, Crawford chain-smokes her way through the movie, glaring at everyone through eyes outlined in heavy mascara. The highlight of the film occurs when she dreams that the severed heads of her husband and his lover are sitting in bed with her. Also keep an eye out for the prominently displayed carton of Pepsi in one scene—surely one of moviedom's first blatant product endorsements. Think that it may have had something to do with Crawford being a member of the board of the Pepsi Co.? Nah.

p, William Castle; d, William Castle; w, Robert Bloch; ph, Arthur Arling; ed, Edwin Bryant; m, Van Alexander.

**(PR:A-C  MPAA:NR)**

## STRANGE BEHAVIOR***

(1981, Aus./New Zealand) 105m Greater Union/South Street c (AKA: DEAD KIDS)

Michael Murphy *(Brady)*, Louise Fletcher *(Barbara Moorhead)*, Dan Shor *(Pete Brady)*, Fiona Lewis *(Gwen Parkinson)*, Arthur Dignam *(LeSange)*, Scott Brady *(Shea)*, Dey Young *(Caroline)*, Marc McClure *(Oliver)*, Charles Lane *(Donovan)*, Elizabeth Cheshire *(Lucy)*, Beryl Te Wiata *(Mrs. Haskell)*.

The directorial debut of Michael Laughlin, who had previously produced Monte Hellman's excellent TWO LANE BLACKTOP, is an intelligent little film starring Michael Murphy as the chief of police in a Midwestern town (though the film was shot in New Zealand) who is trying to solve a series of teenage stabbings. The bloody trail leads to the local college where the science department is doing government research on the effects of mental conditioning. Interesting, suspenseful, and quite witty, STRANGE BEHAVIOR contains several strong performances, with Murphy as the sheriff, Fiona Lewis as the head of the college science department, and Louise Fletcher as a concerned parent all standouts. Director Laughlin also made the underrated science-fiction film STRANGE INVADERS (1983).

p, Anthony I. Ginnane, John Barnett; d, Michael Laughlin; w, Michael Laughlin, Bill Condon (based on story "School Days," by Robert Hughes); ph, Louis Horvath (Panavision, Eastmancolor); ed, Petra Von Oellfen.

**(PR:O  MPAA:NR)**

## STRANGER IS WATCHING, A**

(1982) 92m MGM/UA c

Kate Mulgrew *(Sharon Martin)*, Rip Torn *(Artie Taggart)*, James Naughton *(Steve Peterson)*, Shawn von Schreiber *(Julie Peterson)*, Barbara Baxley *(Lally)*, Stephen Joyce *(Detective)*, James Russo *(Ronald Thompson)*, Frank Hamilton *(Bill Lufts)*, Maggie Task *(Mrs. Lufts)*, Roy Poole *(Kurner)*, Stephen Strimpell, Jason Robards III.

Artie (Rip Torn) is a psychopathic killer who kidnaps and scares the daylights out of 11-year-old Julie (Shawn von Schreiber) and television reporter Sharon Martin (Kate Mulgrew), who happens to be in love with the girl's father, Steve (James Naughton). What's more, the hostages are kept in the dark, dingy bowels of New York's Grand Central Station. The entire film has a sadistic bent to it, but curiously—given that it was directed by Mr. FRIDAY THE 13TH, Sean S. Cunningham—only a few murders occur, not nearly enough to sustain the interest of fans of this sort of thing. This was definitely Cunningham's bid for respectability and, of course, it failed at the box office. Luckily, it does contain yet another wonderful performance from Rip Torn, who plays the most sympathetic psychopath in recent memory.

p, Sidney Beckerman; d, Sean S. Cunningham; w, Earl MacRauch, Victor Miller (based on the novel by Mary Higgins Clark); ph, Barry Abrams (Metrocolor); ed, Susan E. Cunningham; m, Lalo Schifrin.

**(PR:O  MPAA:R)**

## STRANGLER, THE**

(1964) 89m AA bw

Victor Buono *(Leo Kroll)*, David McLean *(Lt. Benson)*, Diane Sayer *(Barbara)*, Davey Davison *(Tally)*, Ellen Corby *(Mrs. Kroll)*, Michael Ryan *(Posner)*, Baynes Barron *(Sgt. Clyde)*, Russ Bender *(Dr. Sanford)*, Jeanne Bates *(Clara)*, Wally Campo *(Eggerton)*, Mimi Dillard *(Thelma)*, Byron Morrow *(Dr. Morton)*, John Yates *(Intern)*, James Sikking *(Artist)*, Selette Cole *(Helen)*, Robert Cranford *(Jack Rosten)*, Victor Masi *(Attendant)*.

Leo (Victor Buono) is a fat lab technician at a Boston hospital whose severe mother complex compels him to strangle pretty nurses. Since her recent heart attack, Mom (Ellen Corby) has been cared for by a nurse (Jeanne Bates), who the jealous Leo believes has replaced him in his mother's affections. Leo also has a doll fetish and frequents an amusement park to win more. This, however, proves to be his undoing when the cops tie a doll found at a murder scene to Leo. Filmed while the "Boston Strangler" murders were still unsolved, THE STRANGLER is a sleazy attempt to capitalize on the then-current hysteria over the case. Although Buono is quite good as the killer, the script relies on too many PSYCHO cliches and the production is very low budget.

p, Samuel Bischoff, David Diamond; d, Burt Topper; w, Bill S. Ballinger; ph, Jacques Marquette; ed, Robert S. Eisen; m, Marlin Skiles.

**(PR:C  MPAA:NR)**

## STREET TRASH**½

(1987) 91m Chaos/Lightning c

Mike Lackey *(Fred)*, Vic Noto *(Bronson)*, Bill Chepil *(Bill the*

Cop), Mark Sferrazza *(Kevin, Fred's Brother)*, Jane Arakawa *(Wendy)*, Nicole Potter *(Winette)*, R.L. Ryan *(Frank Schnizer)*, Clarenze Jarmon *(Burt)*, Bernard Perlman *(Wizzy)*, Miriam Zucker *(Drunken Wench)*, M. D'Jango Krunch *(Ed)*, James Lorinz *(Doorman)*, Morty Storm *(Black Suit)*, Tony Darrow *(Nick Duran)*, Frank Farel, Roy Frumkes.

Judging a film like STREET TRASH is quite problematic. Normally, one would not hesitate to praise the debut of interesting new young talent Jim Muro, a director who can take a budget of less than $100,000 and produce a professional-looking film of cinematic excitement and verve. Unfortunately, STREET TRASH also happens to be one of the most repugnant exploitation movies ever filmed, one that offends the sensibilities and will shock even the most hardened veteran of so-called "cult" films. Pushing the envelope of bad taste, STREET TRASH is perhaps the most revoltingly funny film since John Waters' PINK FLAMINGOS. As "Midnight Movies" go, STREET TRASH is the most fiercely original and inventive in years, although only those with strong stomachs should dare to investigate. Inspired by Akira Kurosawa's DODES'KA-DEN, the film is set among the homeless of Brooklyn and concentrates on a group of winos living in a trash heap just outside a junkyard. The virtually plotless action loosely revolves around a case of contaminated wine a local liquor-store owner has discovered in his basement and sold to the derelicts for $1 a bottle. Unbeknownst to all, the so-called "Tenafly Viper" is so potent that one sip causes the unfortunate drinker literally to melt into a puddle of paint goo (the well-executed gore effects are colorfully cartoonish and relatively inoffensive). An unabashed celebration of bad taste, STREET TRASH has something to offend everyone, including lots of misogyny and shock humor. Besides directing, the industrious, 21-year-old Muro operated his own steadicam—an expensive and relatively complicated piece of camera equipment that allows supreme mobility while maintaining a smooth, gliding shot. As a director-cinematographer, Muro seems most influenced by EVIL DEAD director Sam Raimi, and has a good eye for composition, movement, and color. This is renegade cinema, made to offend the establishment. The fact that STREET TRASH is so very offensive says much about what young talent must do to get noticed.

p, Roy Frumkes; d, Jim Muro; w, Roy Frumkes; ph, David Sperling (Technicolor); ed, Dennis Werner; m, Rick Ulfik.

**(PR:O   MPAA:NR)**

## STUDENT BODIES*

(1981) 86m Universal Southwest Cinema/PAR c

Kristen Riter *(Toby)*, Matthew Goldsby *(Hardy)*, Richard Brando *(The Breather)*, Joe Flood *(Mr. Dumpkin)*, Joe Talarowski *(Principal Peters)*, Mimi Weddell *(Miss Mumsley)*, Carl Jacobs *(Dr. Sigmund)*, Peggy Cooper *(Ms. Van Dyke)*, Janice E. O'Malley *(Nurse Krud)*, The Stick *(Malvert the Janitor)*, Kevin Mannis *(Scott)*, Sara Eckhardt *(Patti)*, Brian Batytis *(Wheels)*, Cullen G. Chambers *(Charles)*, Joan Browning Jacobs *(Mrs. Hummers)*, Angela Bressler *(Julie)*, Kay Ogden *(Ms. LeClair)*, Douglas Cotner *(Mr.*

Hummers), Charles I. Trotter *(Announcer)*, Jonathan Walling *(Al)*, Keith Singleton *(Charlie)*, Dario O. Jones *(Mawamba)*, Thomas D. Cannon II *(Ralph)*, Oscar James *(Coach)*, Robyn Flanery *(Joan)*, Tammie M. Tignor *(Dagmar)*.

As if the plethora of mindless slasher films weren't enough, they were followed by a flood of mindless slasher film parodies, including STUDENT BODIES, which manages to drain the humor from potentially funny situations and repeats its gags endlessly. As with other films of this genre, horny teenagers are killed before their moment of glory. In a cut-away, an official-looking man appears and tells the audience that since the film contains no sex or violence, the only thing to do to get an all-important "R" rating is swear, which he does. The film attempts to mock both slasher movies and the mentality that produces them, but its humor is so sophomoric that it's a little like the pot calling the kettle stupid. STUDENT BODIES was written and directed by Mickey Rose, who cowrote such Woody Allen classics as BANANAS; WHAT'S UP TIGER LILY?; and TAKE THE MONEY AND RUN, and produced by none other than director Michael Ritchie (DOWNHILL RACER; FLETCH; THE GOLDEN CHILD), who decided to hide behind that time-honored Hollywood pseudonym, Allen Smithee.

p, Allen Smithee [Michael Ritchie]; d, Mickey Rose; w, Mickey Rose; ph, Robert Ebinger (Movie Lab Color); ed, Kathryn Ruth Hope; m, Gene Hobson.

**(PR:C   MPAA:NR)**

## STUFF, THE**½

(1985) 93m Larco/NW c

Michael Moriarty *(David Rutherford)*, Andrea Marcovicci *(Nicole Kendall)*, Garrett Morris *(Chocolate Chip Charlie)*, Paul Sorvino *(Col. Spears)*, Scott Bloom *(Jason)*, Danny Aiello *(Vickers)*, Patrick O'Neal *(Stuff Executive)*, Alexander Scourby *(Evans)*, Russell Nype *(Richards)*, Gene O'Neill *(Scientist)*, Cathy Schultz *(Waitress)*, Colette Blonigan *(Jason's Mother)*, Frank Telfer *(Jason's Father)*, Brian Bloom *(Jason's Brother)*, Marilyn Staley *(Stuff Girl)*, Rutanya Alda *(Psychologist)*, David Snell *(Doctor)*, Abe Vigoda, Clara Peller, Brooke Adams *(Actors in Stuff Commercial)*, Tammy Grimes *(Herself)*.

This sociopolitical black comedy from Larry Cohen presents us with an America that is addicted to a new yogurt-like dessert called "The Stuff." Low in calories and good tasting, the Stuff has become such a force in the dessert market that a group of ice-cream company executives hire industrial spy David Rutherford (Michael Moriarty) to uncover the secret ingredients of the popular food item. With the help of marketing whiz Nicole Kendall (Andrea Marcovicci) and cookie king Chocolate Chip Charlie (Garrett Morris), David learns that the Stuff is active bacteria, mined from the earth's core, that literally takes over the bodies of those who eat it and then, after destroying the person, exits in a huge steady stream from the victims' gaping mouths. THE STUFF attacks American business practices, advertising, mindless consumers, and even right-wing fanaticism (Paul Sorvino is a nutty colonel) by combining a horror/science-fiction tale with large doses of biting black humor. Cohen evokes the feel of a 1950s science fiction film, self-consciously echoing everything from INVASION OF THE BODY SNATCHERS to THE BLOB. Unfortunately, the film is wildly disjointed (witness Danny Aiello's scene, which seems to be pulled from another movie), as if Cohen had a difficult time integrating all his fascinating ideas into a single, coherent plot line. Clara Peller, the elderly "Where's the beef?" lady from the Wendy's commercials, makes a cameo in a Stuff commercial, as does actress Brooke Adams in a spot that appears after the closing credits.

p, Paul Kurta; d, Larry Cohen; w, Larry Cohen; ph, Paul Glickman (Technicolor); ed, Armand Lebowitz; m, Anthony Guefen.

(PR:C    MPAA:R)

## SUPERNATURALS, THE**

(1987) 80m Republic Ent. Intl. c

Maxwell Caulfield *(Lt. Ray Ellis)*, Nichelle Nichols *(Sgt. Leona Hawkins)*, Talia Balsam *(Pvt. Angela Lejune)*, Bradford Bancroft *(Pvt. Tom Weir)*, LeVar Burton *(Pvt. Michael Osgood)*, Bobby Di Cicco *(Pvt. Tim Cort)*, Margaret Shendal *(Melanie)*, Patrick Davis *(Old Man)*, James Kirkwood *(Captain)*, Scott Jacoby *(Pvt. Chris Mendez)*, Richard Pachorek *(Pvt. Ralph Sedgewick)*, John Zarchen *(Pvt. Julius Engel)*, Robert Barron *(Old Vet)*, Chad Sheets *(Jeremy)*, Mark Schneider, Jesse Lawrence Ferguson *(Recruits)*, David Ault *(Soldier on Horse)*, Frank Caggiano, Greg Landerer, Gary Bentley *(Union Soldiers)*, Laura Francis *(Townswoman)*, Nicky Blair *(Townsman)*.

Tough female sergeant Leona Hawkins (Nichelle Nichols) leads a group of Army trainees on a survival mission through the Alabama woodlands, where they have a number of strange experiences. Lt. Ray Ellis (Maxwell Caulfield) sees a ghostly woman appear and disappear; Pvt. Tim Cort (Bobby Di Cicco) finds a human skull; unexplained winds and scorched earth baffle the recruits; and an underground bunker is discovered. Then a series of unexplained murders occur, with the unseen attackers terrorizing the recruits' bivouac. When a deep fog descends on the camp, the recruits are at their most vulnerable. Only then do they see their attackers—skeletal Confederate soldiers who have risen from their graves to continue their Civil War battles. Lacking the excessive gore, gratuitous nudity, amateurish acting, and tepid direction upon which many recent horror entries have thrived, THE SUPERNATURALS (despite its nondescript title) proves to be an entertaining time if one can ignore the ridiculous premise. Displaying professional technical qualities, the film also boasts some superb performances from Max Caulfield (GREASE II and ELECTRIC DREAMS), Bobby Di Cicco (THE PHILADELPHIA EXPERIMENT and SPLASH), Nichelle Nichols (STAR TREK IV), Talia Balsam, and Bradford Bancroft. Director Armand Mastroianni's has great success in his decision to keep the Confederate attackers out of sight for most of the picture—the greatest fear comes from the un-

seen attacker. The film's strength lies in its solid characterizations and a fairly concise script that leaves no room for gore or nudity.

p, Michael S. Murphey, Joel Soisson; d, Armand Mastroianni; w, Michael S. Murphey, Joel Soisson; ph, Peter Collister; m, Robert O. Ragland.

(PR:O    MPAA:R)

## SUPERSTITION zero

(1985) 84m Penaria/Almi c (AKA: WITCH, THE)

James Carl Houghton *(Rev. David Thompson)*, Albert Salmi *(Inspector Sturgess)*, Larry Pennell *(George Leahy)*, Lynn Carlin *(Melinda Leahy)*, Maylo McCaslin *(Sheryl Leahy)*, Heidi Bohay *(Ann Leahy)*, Billy Jacoby *(Justin Leahy)*, Jacquelyn Hyde *(Elvira Sharack)*, Kim Marie *(Mary)*, Stacy Keach *(Rev. Maier)*, Joshua Cadman *(Arlen)*, Robert Symonds *(Pike)*, Carole Goldman *(Elondra)*, John Alderman *(Romberg)*, Johnny Doran *(Charlie)*, Bennett Liss *(Arty)*, Casey King *(Hollister)*.

Shot in 1981 as THE WITCH, this film was so wretched it sat on the shelf for four years before being dumped into the horror market. The insipid story involves the 200-year-old spirit of a witch who was the cause of some supernatural dilemmas in 1784. Her powers linger to the present day, when hapless minister George Leahy (Larry Pennell) and his family move onto the site where the witch burned a church, killing her accuser, two centuries before. Of course all kinds of spooky things start cropping up and it's learned that the family who lived there previously was killed under gruesome circumstances. Local minister David Thompson (James Carl Houghton) and detective Sturgess (Albert Salmi) investigate the case and try to contain the force behind the murders. SUPERSTITION is silly, predictable, and created without imagination, beyond its gore effects. Executive producers Mario Kassar and Andrew Vajna wisely kept this one out of circulation, though they scored big with their next project, FIRST BLOOD, in 1982.

p, Ed Carlin, John D. Schwartz, Robert L.J. Lewis; d, James W. Roberson; w, Michael Sajbel, Bret Plate, Brad White, Donald G. Thompson (based on the story "The Witch" by Sajbel); ph, Lee Madden (CFI Color); ed, Al Rabinowitz; m, David Gibney.

(PR:O    MPAA:NR)

## SURVIVOR***

(1980, Aus.) 93m Ginnane c

Robert Powell *(Keller)*, Jenny Agutter *(Hobbs)*, Joseph Cotten *(The Priest)*, Angela Punch McGregor *(Beth Rogan)*, Peter Sumner *(Tewson)*, Ralph Cotterill *(Slater)*, Adrian Wright *(Goodwin)*.

SURVIVOR is one of a series of interesting pictures that actor-director David Hemmings made in Australia, including THIRST and HARLEQUIN. Sort of a supernatural disaster film, it stars Robert Powell as Keller, the pilot of a 747 that crashes as the result of an on-board explosion, leaving him the only survivor. As it turns out, Keller is actually dead too, but, haunted by the spirits of the passengers, he has risen to punish the person who planted the bomb on his plane. With a good cast, solid direction, and a decent score from Brian May (ROAD WARRIOR), this is a surprisingly effective film that evokes a truly eerie mood. Regrettably, it never got a stateside release and was sold straight to cable TV.

p, Anthony I. Ginnane; d, David Hemmings; w, David Ambrose (based on the novel by James Herbert); ph, John Seale.

(PR:C-O   MPAA:NR)

## SWAMP THING**

(1982) 90m Swampfilms/EM c

Louis Jourdan *(Arcane)*, Adrienne Barbeau *(Alice Cable)*, Ray Wise *(Dr. Alec Holland)*, David Hess *(Ferret)*, Nicholas Worth *(Bruno)*, Don Knight *(Ritter)*, Al Ruban *(Charlie)*, Dick Durock *(Swamp Thing)*, Ben Bates *(Arcane Monster)*, Nannette Brown *(Dr. Linda Holland)*, Reggie Batts *(Jude)*, Mimi Meyer *(Secretary)*, Karen Price *(Messenger)*, Bill Erickson *(Young Agent)*, Dov Gottesfeld *(Commando)*, Tommy Madden *(Little Bruno)*.

Another disappointment from Wes Craven (THE HILLS HAVE EYES; A NIGHTMARE ON ELM STREET), SWAMP THING tries its best to play as a camp parody of 1950s creature features, complete with hokey dialog and men running around in rubber monster-suits, but it simply doesn't work. Based on the popular DC comic book created by Bernie Wrightson, the film is set in the Louisiana bayous, where scientist Alec Holland (Ray Wise) is working on a secret government experiment to combine plant and animal cells. When bad guy Arcane (Louis Jourdan) and his cohorts try to steal the formula that Alec has created, the solution is spilled on the scientist, transforming him into the burly green Swamp Thing (played by Dick Durock in an unexceptional rubber suit), who can magically heal the dead with his glowing touch. Adrienne Barbeau, who had the dubious distinction of doing her first topless scene in this film, gives some heart to her role as the government agent trying to beat Arcane to the title creature. In the silly climax, Arcane changes into a goofy-looking beast with a body like a lizard, a face like a wild-boar, and a mane like a lion (special makeup by William Munns). Although SWAMP THING was definitely aimed at a different audience than THE HILLS HAVE EYES, Craven fails to capture the gothic quality of its comic book inspiration—which had some genuinely frightening and grotesque moments. Instead, the whole thing is merely silly and not much fun.

p, Benjamin Melniker, Michael E. Uslan; d, Wes Craven; w, Wes Craven (based on DC Comics characters); ph, Robin Goodwin (Technicolor); ed, Richard Bracken; m, Harry Manfredini.

(PR:C   MPAA:PG)

## SWEET SIXTEEN*

(1983) 90m Productions Two/Century International c

Bo Hopkins *(Dan)*, Susan Strasberg *(Joanne)*, Don Stroud *(Billy)*, Dana Kimmell *(Marci)*, Aleisa Shirley *(Melissa)*, Don Shanks *(Jason)*, Steve Antin *(Hank)*, Logan Clarke *(Jimmy)*, Michael Pataki *(George)*, Patrick Macnee *(John)*, Larry Storch *(Earl)*, Henry Wilcoxon *(Greyfeather)*, Sharon Farrell *(Kathy)*.

Sweet 16-year-old Melissa (Aleisa Shirley) has a problem: all of her boy friends are being found hacked to death. In typical teenage slasher film fashion, it's all the fault of a crazed schizophrenic, and as usual, Melissa is being punished for her sexual awakening. Fair direction and a decent cast (most notably Bo Hopkins as the sheriff) make this one at least somewhat watchable, but the body count isn't high enough—or gory enough—to satisfy fans of this sort of thing.

p, Jim Sotos; d, Jim Sotos; w, Erwin Goldman; ph, James Carter; ed, Drake Silliman; m, Tommy Vig.

(PR:O   MPAA:R)

# T

## TALES FROM THE CRYPT***

(1972, Brit.) 92m Amicus-Metromedia/Cinerama c

"Prolog": Ralph Richardson *(Crypt Keeper)*, Geoffrey Bayldon *(Guide)*, "All Through the House": Joan Collins *(Joanne Clayton)*, Marty Goddey *(Richard Clayton)*, Oliver MacGreevy *(Maniac)*, Chloe Franks *(Carol Clayton)*, "Reflection of Death": Ian Hendry *(Carl Maitland)*, Paul Clere *(Maitland's Son)*, Sharon Clere *(Maitland's Daughter)*, Angie Grant *(Susan)*, Susan Denny *(Mrs. Maitland)*, Frank Forsyth *(Tramp)*, "Blind Alleys": Nigel Patrick *(William Rogers)*, Patrick Magee *(George Carter)*, Tony Wall *(Attendant)*, Harry Locke *(Cook)*, "Poetic Justice": Peter Cushing *(Grimsdyke)*, Robin Phillips *(James Elliot)*, David Markham *(Edward Elliot)*, Edward Evans *(Mr. Ramsay)*, Ann Sears *(Mrs. Carter)*, Irene Gawne *(Mrs. Phelps)*, Kay Adrian *(Mrs. Davies)*, "Wish You Were Here": Richard Greene *(Ralph Jason)*, Roy Dotrice *(Charles)*, Barbara Murray *(Enid)*.

A somewhat disappointing attempt to translate William Gaines' infamous E.C. horror comics of the 1950s to the screen, TALES FROM THE CRYPT suffers from the flat direction of Freddie Francis, who fails to capture the gleeful ghoulishness of the comics. Framed by the appearance of Ralph Richardson, as the Crypt Keeper, who introduces each tale from his underground lair (to which all the principal characters have been summoned), the first story, "All Through the House," finds Joan Collins being terrorized by a psycho killer dressed as Santa Claus. "Reflection of Death" features Ian Hendry as a philanderer who was killed in a car crash but doesn't realize he's dead. "Poetic Justice," adapted from one of the all-time great E.C. comics stories, finds Peter Cushing as a kindly old man named Grimsdyke who loves the neighborhood children. His neighbors, a greedy real estate man and his son, hate Grimsdyke and want to drive him from the area. On Valentine's Day, they send him dozens of nasty cards and the old man is driven to suicide. Next Valentine's Day, however, Grimsdyke rises from the grave to get revenge. "Wish You Were Here" is a variation in the classic story "The Monkey's Paw," and stars Richard Greene as a crooked businessman whose wife buys a Chinese curio that will grant her three wishes—though things don't quite turn out the way she'd like. The last story, "Blind Alleys," features Nigel Patrick as the cruel director of a home for the blind whose charges exact a horrible revenge. While all the stories are fairly effective, "Poetic Justice" and "Blind Alleys" are the standouts. The film did well at the box office and spawned a sequel, THE VAULT OF HORROR (1973). Ten years later George Romero would tackle E.C. comics-type horrors in his omnibus, CREEPSHOW (1982).

p, Milton Subotsky, Max J. Rosenberg; d, Freddie Francis; w, Milton Subotsky (based on the stories "Tales from the Crypt" and "The Vault of Horror" by Al Feldstein, Johnny Craig, William Gaines, appearing in "Cartoon" Magazines); ph, Norman Warwick, John Harris (Eastmancolor); ed, Teddy Darvas; m, Douglas Gamley.

(PR:C    MPAA:PG)

## TALES OF TERROR***½

(1962) 90m Alta Vista/AIP c (AKA: POE'S TALES OF TERROR)

Vincent Price *(Locke/Fortunato/Valdemar)*, "Morella": Maggie Pierce *(Lenora)*, Leona Gage *(Morella)*, Ed Cobb *(Driver)*, "The Black Cat": Peter Lorre *(Montresor)*, Joyce Jameson *(Annabel)*, Lenny Weinrib, John Hacketl *(Policemen)*, Wally Campo *(Bartender)*, Alan Dewit *(Chairman)*, "The Case of Mr. Valdemar": Basil Rathbone *(Carmichael)*, Debra Paget *(Helene)*, David Frankham *(Dr. James)*, Scotty Brown *(Servant)*.

The fourth entry in Roger Corman's Edgar Allan Poe series, this film is an anthology of three short pieces based on tales by Poe, and all three—"Morella," "The Black Cat," and "The Case of Mr. Valdemar"—feature Vincent Price in the starring role. In "Morella," Price is Locke, an embittered widower who has lived alone in his gloomy mansion since the death of his wife, Morella (Leona Gage), after giving birth some 26 years ago. His daughter, Lenora (Maggie Pierce), arrives and finds that her father loathes her, because he blames her for his wife's death. Prowling around the house, Lenora finds Morella's mummified body lying on a bed. Locke explains he couldn't bear to have her beauty buried beneath the ground, so he had her corpse moved into the house. Lenora reveals to her father that she is dying and only has a few months left. Father and daughter are reconciled, but that night Lenora dies and her body becomes possessed by Morella, who has been waiting all these years to return and wreak her vengeance on Locke—the father of the baby that killed her. In "The Black Cat," Peter Lorre is superb as the drunken loser Montresor, whose behavior forces his wife to seek comfort in the arms of wine-taster Fortunato (Price). To get even, Montresor captures his wife and her lover and walls them up in the cellar. Unbeknownst to him, however, the family cat is also entombed and its wails give

the scheme away. The final story, "The Case of Mr. Valdemar," features Price as the title character, a dying man who has fallen under the spell of an evil mesmerist named Carmichael (Basil Rathbone). Valdemar agrees to be the subject of an experiment wherein Carmichael will put him in a state of hypnosis at the moment of death, which will, perhaps, prevent him from dying. The trick works, but when the evil Carmichael attempts to steal Valdemar's wife and estate, Valdemar snaps out of the spell and attacks the mesmerist, his dead flesh melting. "Morella," the scariest of the tales, is an interesting precursor to THE TOMB OF LIGEIA (1965). "The Black Cat" combines the title Poe tale with Poe's "The Cask of Amontillado," and is a wonderfully funny prototype of THE RAVEN (1963), with both Lorre and Price having a grand time poking fun at the material and themselves. The final story has several memorable moments—especially when Valdemar's disembodied voice can be heard pleading for release from his undead state—but the ending is marred by some unnecessary optical effects that obscure Valdemar's melted visage (indeed, the production stills from this tale are more frightening than what appears in the movie).

p, Roger Corman; d, Roger Corman; w, Richard Matheson (based on stories by Edgar Allan Poe); ph, Floyd Crosby (Panavision, Pathe Color); ed, Anthony Carras; m, Les Baxter.

(PR:A    MPAA:NR)

## TARGETS****

(1968) 90m Saticoy/PAR c

Boris Karloff *(Byron Orlok)*, Tim O'Kelly *(Bobby Thompson)*, Nancy Hsueh *(Jenny)*, James Brown *(Robert Thompson)*, Sandy Baron *(Kip Larkin)*, Arthur Peterson *(Ed Loughlin)*, Mary Jackson *(Charlotte Thompson)*, Tanya Morgan *(Ilene Thompson)*, Monte Landis *(Marshall Smith)*, Peter Bogdanovich *(Sammy Michaels)*, Paul Condylis *(Drive-in Manager)*, Mark Dennis, Stafford Morgan *(Gunshop Salesmen)*, Daniel Ades *(Chauffeur)*, Timothy Burns *(Waiter)*, Warren White *(Grocery Boy)*, Geraldine Baron *(Larkin's Girl)*, Frank Marshall *(Ticket Boy)*, Byron Betz *(Projectionist)*.

An unconventional horror picture that draws a comparison between the real-life horror of the 1966 Charles Whitman murder spree and the fictional horrors of movie legend Boris Karloff, TARGETS opens with a film clip (the flood scene) from Roger Corman's 1963 film, THE TERROR. The clip then ends, revealing a screening room occupied by aging horror star Byron Orlok (Karloff), filmmaker Sammy Michaels (Peter Bogdanovich), and some film executives. Orlok informs them that he's had enough of horror films and plans to return to his home in England. He is aware that his films no longer frighten people and that the public is only affected by the horrors in the headlines, stating, "The world belongs to the young. Make way for them. Let them have it. I am an anachronism." Meanwhile, in a gun shop across the street, a clean-cut young man, Bobby Thompson (Tim O'Kelly), adds a high-powered rifle to the already huge arsenal of weapons stashed in his car trunk. Thompson begins a bloody rampage, first murdering his wife, then sniping at innocent drivers from a tower near a highway. TARGETS' brilliant finale, set at a drive-in premiere of the latest Orlok opus, puts both of these horrors—the movieland fiction of Orlok and the real-life danger of Thompson—up on the screen together. Down below, the audience screams in fright, not at Orlok but at Thompson, whose rifle shots are picking them off one by one. TARGETS is an insightful comment on the changing state of the horror film: Where Karloff's films concerned gruesome monsters with frightening physical attributes, TARGETS is about—to use Bogdanovich's phrase—"the ghouls next door," the all-American killers who are all the more frightening because the deformities exist *inside* their heads.

p, Peter Bogdanovich; d, Peter Bogdanovich; w, Peter Bogdanovich (based on a story by Polly Platt, Bogdanovich); ph, Laszlo Kovacs (Pathe Color); ed, Peter Bogdanovich; m, Charles Greene, Brian Stone.

**(PR:O MPAA:NR)**

## TEEN WOLF**½

(1985) 91m Wolfkill/Atlantic c

Michael J. Fox *(Scott Howard)*, James Hampton *(Harold Howard)*, Susan Ursitti *(Lisa Marconi)*, Jerry Levine *(Rupert Stilinsky)*, Jim McKrell *(Russell)*, Lorie Griffin *(Pamela)*, Mark Arnold *(Mick)*, Matt Adler *(Lewis)*, Mark Holton *(Chubby)*, Jay Tarses *(Coach Finstock)*, Scott Paulin *(Kirk Lolley)*, Elizabeth Gorcey *(Tina)*, Melanie Manos *(Gina)*, Doug Savant *(Brad)*, Charles Zucker *(Malcolm)*, Harvey Vernon *(Clerk)*, Clare Peck *(Miss Hoyt)*, Gregory Itzin *(English Teacher)*, Doris Hess *(Science Teacher)*, Troy Evans *(Dragon Basketball Coach)*, Lynda Wiesmeier *(Rhonda)*, Rod Kageyama *(Janitor)*, Carl Steven *(Whistle Boy)*.

In this schizophrenic teen comedy, Michael J. Fox plays Scott Howard, an amiable young man desperate to gain popularity with his peers. His high-school basketball team is pathetic, and the girl of his dreams, Pamela Wells (Lorie Griffin), repeatedly ignores his overtures of affection. To compound his misery, Scott discovers he's a werewolf. He learns from his father that this strange condition is genetic. Though he tries to hide his newfound secret from his schoolmates, his true nature comes out and the result is instant popularity. Everyone wants to be friends with the teen wolf. TEEN WOLF (which bears more than a passing resemblance to Larry Cohen's little-seen 1982 picture FULL MOON HIGH) was made before Fox's big success in BACK TO THE FUTURE, but released a few months afterwards to capitalize on the young star's sudden popularity. Fox is enormously likable here, but the gimmickry of the werewolf transformation and Fox's lupine existence is just that—a gimmick, a wholly artificial contrivance that intrudes on the character. What's more, the transformation is one of the worst in recent memory, a far cry from WOLFEN. An indication of the film's mentality is that it inspired a Saturday morning cartoon series the following year. This is the first of four horror-related films to come from cast members of TV's "Family Ties." It was fol-

lowed in 1986 by TRICK OR TREAT with Marc "Skippy" Price; in 1987 by MY DEMON LOVER with Scott "Nick" Valentine; and in 1988 with SATISFACTION, which, though not really a horror film, may scare some viewers just by virtue of starring Justine Bateman in its thoroughly ridiculous story.

p, Mark Levinson, Scott M. Rosenfelt, George Perkins; d, Rod Daniel; w, Joseph Loeb III, Matthew Weisman; ph, Timothy Suhrstedt (United Color); ed, Lois Freeman-Fox; m, Miles Goodman.

**(PR:A-C MPAA:PG)**

## TEEN WOLF TOO*

(1987) 95m Atlantic c

Jason Bateman *(Todd Howard)*, Kim Darby *(Prof. Brooks)*, John Astin *(Dean Dunn)*, Paul Sand *(Coach Finstock)*, James Hampton *(Uncle Howard)*, Estee Chandler *(Nicki)*, Robert Neary *(Gustavson)*, Stuart Fratkin *(Stiles)*, Beth Ann Miller *(Lisa)*, Rachel Sharp *(Emily)*.

A carbon-copy of the Michael J. Fox feature. TEEN WOLF TOO stars another TV heartthrob, 18-year-old Jason Bateman ("Valerie" and brother of "Family Ties" star Justine), who plays the cousin of Fox's original character. Todd Howard (Bateman), who, as far as he knows, isn't a victim of the family curse, is off to Hamilton University on a boxing scholarship. The catch is that Todd isn't a boxer—his coach (Paul Sand) helped Todd get a free ride because he knows of cousin Scott's lupine-fostered athletic prowess and hopes that Todd is similarly gifted. It's hard to imagine a more calculated sequel than TEEN WOLF TOO. The storyline is almost identical to its precursor, except that the high-school environment has been replaced by a college one (preposterously unlike any real institution of higher education) and boxing has replaced basketball as the featured sport. Although Bateman has an endearing presence, he doesn't infuse his role with the naive charm Fox brought to the original. TEEN WOLF had an innocence about it that kept its message from being simplistic, and Fox's struggles with his changing body and personality became a metaphor for the confusion of adolescence. Unfortunately, the sequel is predictable, unfunny, and contains some special makeup effects that are hardly spectacular.

p, Kent Bateman; d, Christopher Leitch; w, R. Timothy Kring (based on a story by Joseph Loeb III, Matthew Weisman); ph, Jules Brenner (Consolidated Film Labs Color); ed, Steven Polivka, Kim Secrist, Harvey Rosenstock, Raja Gosnell; m, Mark Goldenberg.

**(PR:A-C MPAA:PG)**

## TELL-TALE HEART, THE***

(1962, Brit.) 78m Danziger/Brigadier-Union bw (AKA: HIDDEN ROOM OF 1,000 HORRORS, THE)

Laurence Payne *(Edgar Marsh)*, Adrienne Corri *(Betty Clare)*, Dermot Walsh *(Carl Loomis)*, Selma Vaz Dias *(Mrs. Vine)*, John Scott *(Inspector)*, John Martin *(Police Sergeant)*, Annette Carell *(Carl's Landlady)*, David Lander *(Jeweler)*, Rosemary Rotheray *(Jackie)*, Suzanne Fuller

(Dorothy), Yvonne Buckingham (Mina), Richard Bennett (Mike), Elizabeth Paget (Elsie), Frank Thornton (Barman), Joan Peart (Street Girl), Nada Beall (Old Crone), Graham Ashley (Neston).

A rare adaptation of Edgar Allan Poe from the British, this tautly paced expansion of "The Tell-Tale Heart" finds Laurence Payne as Edgar Marsh, a crippled librarian who is shy and sensitive about his handicap. Encouraged by his friend Carl (Dermot Walsh), Edgar introduces himself to the beautiful Betty (Adrienne Corri), who lives across the road, and arranges a date with her. Although Betty is polite to Edgar, she really has eyes for lothario Carl. Eventually, the lovesick Edgar catches Betty and Carl together and is driven to murder his best friend. Edgar hides Carl's body beneath the floorboards of his house, but is driven mad by the sound of the dead man's beating heart. Well directed by Ernest Morris, who conveys a palpable sense of claustrophobia and paranoia, the film is marred somewhat by its hokey and totally unnecessary twist ending.

p, Edward J. Danziger, Harry Lee Danziger; d, Ernest Morris; w, Brian Clemens, Eldon Howard (based on the story by Edgar Allan Poe); ph, James Wilson; ed, Derek Parsons; m, Tony Crombie, Bill Le Sage.

(PR:O    MPAA:NR)

## TEMPTER, THE*

(1974, It.) 96m AE c (L'ANTICRISTO; Trans: The Anti-Christ)

Carla Gravina (Ippolita), Mel Ferrer (Massimo), Arthur Kennedy (Bishop), George Coulouris (Father Mittner), Alida Valli (Irene), Anita Strindberg (Gretel), Mario Scaccia (Faith Healer), Umberto Orsini (Psychiatrist).

An obvious EXORCIST-ripoff considerably more sensational than its prototype, THE TEMPTER concerns Ippolita (Carla Gravina), the paralyzed, 20-year-old daughter of Prince Massimo (Mel Ferrer) who becomes possessed by an ancestor burnt at the stake for practicing witchcraft. A la her American counterpart, Regan, Ippolita spews forth an excess of nasty vomit, generous portions of which splatter holy visitors in the face. A couple of priests (Arthur Kennedy and George Coulouris) try to exorcise the demon from Ippolita's soul, while a psychiatrist (Umberto Orsini) concentrates on the young woman's mind. Meanwhile, an unseen demon has focused its attention on Ippolita's nubile body, resulting in a graphic rape scene in which Gravina must prove her acting talents. It should come as no surprise that THE TEMPTER (which was originally titled L'ANTICRISTO, "The Antichrist") is poorly dubbed and a technical mess, though Ennio Morricone's score—while no "Tubular Bells"—is rather effective.

p, Edmundo Amati; d, Alberto DeMartino; w, Alberto DeMartino, Vincenzo Mannino, Gianfranco Clerici; ph, Aristide Massaccesi; ed, Vincenzo Tomassi; m, Ennio Morricone.

(PR:O    MPAA:R)

## TENANT, THE***

(1976, Fr.) 124m PAR c (LE LOCATAIRE)

Roman Polanski (Trelkovsky), Isabelle Adjani (Stella), Shelley Winters (Concierge), Melvyn Douglas (Mr. Zy), Jo Ann Fleet (Mme. Dioz), Bernard Fresson (Scope), Lila Kedrova (Mme. Gaderian), Claude Dauphin (Husband), Claude Pieplu (Neighbor), Rufus (Badar), Romain Bouteille (Simon), Jacques Monod (Cafe Proprietor), Patrice Alexandre (Robert), Josiane Balasko (Viviane), Jean Pierre Bagot (Policeman), Michel Blanc (Scope's Neighbor), Jacky Cohen (Stella's Friend), Florence Blot (Mme. Zy), Bernard Donnadieu (Bar Waiter), Alain Frerot (Beggar), Gerard Jugnot (Office Clerk), Raoul Guylad (Priest), Eva Ionesco (Mme. Gaderian's Daughter), Gerard Pereira (Drunk), Maite Nahyr (Lucille).

This creepy psychological horror tale stars its director, Roman Polanski, as Trelkovsky, a shy Polish office clerk living in Paris who rents an apartment in a serene building populated by bitter elderly folks. The previous tenant, a young woman named Simone, tried to commit suicide by flinging herself out the window. He pays a visit to the dying Simone, an unidentifiable person covered head to toe in wrappings, and there meets the mousy Stella (Isabelle Adjani), a friend of Simone's. Simone soon lets out a blood-curdling scream and dies, a dreadful experience that forms a bond between Trelkovsky and Stella, who nearly become lovers, then drift apart. Meanwhile, Trelkovsky has increasing difficulty when it comes to pleasing his fellow tenants, who complain that he makes noise (though we don't see or hear anything) and threaten to "take steps." He grows steadily more interested in Simone—who she was, what she was interested in, why she died, and why she hid a tooth in a crack in the wall. Trelkovsky's paranoia increases when a neighborhood cafe owner insists on serving him Simone's favorites. He becomes convinced he is being watched from across the courtyard. His condition worsens as he imagines himself as Simone and, in the most frightening fashion, begins to act like her and wear her clothes. In many ways THE TENANT is REPULSION, with Polanski in the Catherine Deneuve role. The concept of a person's inner world clashing with the "real" world until no sense can be made of either is strongly present in both, and in both cases the conflict between the two forces leads to violence. Not as wholly successful as REPULSION, but just as eerie in many spots.

p, Andrew Braunsberg; d, Roman Polanski; w, Roman Polanski, Gerard Brach (based on the novel Le Locataire Chimerique by Roland Topor); ph, Sven Nykvist (Panavision, Eastmancolor); ed, Francoise Bonnot; m, Philippe Sarde.

(PR:O    MPAA:R)

## TENTACLES*

(1977, It.) 102m AIP-FOX c

John Huston (Ned Turner), Shelley Winters (Tillie Turner), Bo Hopkins (Will Gleason), Henry Fonda (Mr. Whitehead), Delia Baccardo (Vicky Gleason), Cesare Danova (John Corey), Alan Boyd (Mike), Claude Akins (Capt. Robards),

Sherry Buchanan *(Judy),* Franco Diogene *(Chuck),* Marc Fiorini *(Don),* Helena Makela *(Jane's Mother),* Alessandro Poggi, Roberto Poggi, Giancarlo Nacinelli, Consolato Marciano, Philip Dallas, Leonard Lightfoot, John White, William Van Raaphorst, Joanne Van Raaphorst, Patrick Mulvihill, Janet Myers, Kristin M. Brekke, Janet Raycraft, Kenneth Lundeen, Rita Real, Alan Scharf, Ross Gordon, Ronald Shapiro, Joseph Johnson.

The makers of this JAWS-ripoff were lucky enough to get John Huston, Shelley Winters, and Henry Fonda to sign on for this picture; otherwise it would be completely forgotten today. As it is, it's just a footnote in the actors' respective filmographies—outside of Fonda's minor role as an executive and Huston's equally small part as a newspaper reporter married to Winters, there isn't much to the ultraboring TENTACLES. Bo Hopkins does the best he can as Will Gleason, a marine biologist who trains a pair of whales to attack the killer octopus that's been strangling a town dry. Director Ovidio Assonitis (working under his pseudonym, Oliver Hellman) also produced PIRANHA II: THE SPAWNING and was obviously trying to milk the JAWS craze for all it was worth. Killer flying piranhas, a killer octopus, what else—a killer carp or killer seahorses, maybe?

p, E.F. Doria; d, Ovidio Assonitis; w, Jerome Max, Tito Carpi, Steve Carabatsos, Sonia Molteni; ph, Robert D'Ettore (Technicolor); ed, A.J. Curi; m, S.W. Cipriani.

(PR:C MPAA:PG)

## TERMINAL CHOICE*½

(1985, Can.) 95m Magder/Almi c (AKA: TRAUMA; CRITICAL LIST; DEATH LIST; DEATHBED)

Joe Spano *(Dr. Frank Holt),* Diane Venora *(Anna Lang),* David McCallum *(Dr. Dodson),* Robert Joy *(Dr. Harvey Rimmer),* Don Francks *(Chauncey Rand),* Nicholas Campbell *(Henderson),* Ellen Barkin *(Mary O'Connor),* Chapelle Jaffe *(Mrs. Dodson),* Clare Coulter *(Nurse Barton),* James Kidnie *(Dr. Kline),* Les Rubie *(Miles Kingsley),* Martha Gibson *(Kingsley's Daughter),* Chas Lawther *(Kingsley's Son-in-law),* Terry Austin *(Lylah Crane),* Tom Harvey *(Dr. Warren),* Sandra Warren *(Nurse Tipton),* Lynda Mason Green *(Hooker),* Gaye McDonald *(Lady in Restaurant),* Marilyn Boyle *(E.R. Nurse),* Cheryl Wilson *(Nurse Fields),* Heidi Palleske *(Student Nurse),* Monica Parker *(Nurse Mercer),* Bob Sher *(Radio Announcer),* Ingrid Izzard *(Radio Disc Jockey).*

High-tech med center Dodson Clinic is the setting for this COMA-styled suspenser, in which patients are turning into corpses at an alarming rate. The incompetence of hard-drinking Dr. Frank Holt (Joe Spano) seems initially to be the root of the problem, but computer whiz Anna Lang (Diane Venora), a former flame of Holt's, combs the hospital's computer system for a virus. Dr. Dodson (David McCallum), the head of the clinic, has ordered an investigation, but patients are still winding up on morgue slabs, including Mary O'Connor (Ellen Barkin), who stumbles across some evidence during an autopsy. There's an emphasis on the danger of high-tech systems, but the script and pacing don't develop enough tension to make this one

worthwhile. The result is an unnecessarily gory outing with an emphasis placed on bodily fluids. Filmed in 1982 and known under a variety of titles—TRAUMA; CRITICAL LIST; DEATH LIST; and DEATHBED—the film does boast some decent performances.

p, Gary Magder; d, Sheldon Larry; w, Neal Bell (based on a story by Peter Lawrence); ph, Zale Magder (Medallion Color); ed, Murray Magder; m, Brian Bennett.

(PR:O MPAA:R)

## TERROR, THE**½

(1963) 81m Filmgroup/AIP c (AKA: LADY OF THE SHADOWS)

Jack Nicholson *(Lt. Andre Duvalier),* Boris Karloff *(Baron Von Leppe),* Sandra Knight *(Helene),* Richard Miller *(Stefan),* Dorothy Neumann *(Old Woman),* Jonathan Haze *(Gustaf).*

More famous for the story behind its making than for the story it actually tells, THE TERROR stars a young Jack Nicholson as Andre Duvalier, a Napoleonic officer who wakes up on the Baltic Coast (really Big Sur) and sees the figure of a woman, who then disappears. After seeing her several times more, he follows her trail to the castle of Baron Von Leppe (Boris Karloff), where he spots a portrait of the woman on the wall. It turns out that she is Helene (Sandra Knight), Leppe's long-dead wife. Refusing to believe this, Duvalier searches the house for the woman, and learns from Leppe's servant (Dick Miller) that the baron isn't really the baron, but a man who killed the real baron years ago and took his place. After much confusion, the bogus baron is drowned when the sea invades the castle and Duvalier rescues Helene, who ends up falling apart in his arms, for she is nothing more than a rotting corpse. Perhaps the most legendary film in Roger Corman's entire career, THE TERROR began as a brainstorm the director had while finishing THE RAVEN. Hating to see the massive RAVEN set go to waste, Corman decided to shoot another picture on the set during the five days remaining before it was to be dismantled. With only a vague idea of a story, Corman had writer Leo Gordon write some scenes for Karloff and Nicholson, both of whom agreed to hang around for a few days after completion of THE RAVEN. Corman shot their scenes, then became involved with another project, so he had his assistant, Francis Ford Coppola, finish the film. Coppola took Nicholson and Knight to Big Sur and shot some more scenes, then he got an offer from producer Ray Stark and also left the picture. Several other directors helped finish the film, including Monte Hellman, Jack Hill, Dennis Jacob, and Nicholson himself. Months later, Corman sifted through the footage and realized the story didn't make any sense, so he called Nicholson and Miller back to shoot one more scene, in which an angry Duvalier forces the baron's servant to tell him what's going on. Thus, Miller explains the confusing plot to Nicholson—and the audience. AIP got even more mileage out of the RAVEN set when clips from the Karloff-Nicholson scenes of THE TERROR ended up in Peter Bogdanovich's TARGETS, four years later, as the film being shown at a drive-in during the climax.

# TERROR, THE—

p, Roger Corman, Jack Nicholson; d, Roger Corman (uncredited directorial assistance, Francis Coppola, Monte Hellman, Jack Hill, Dennis Jacob, Jack Nicholson); w, Leo Gordon, Jack Hill; ph, John Nickolaus (VistaScope, Pathe Color); ed, Stuart O'Brien; m, Ronald Stein.

**(PR:A    MPAA:NR)**

## TERROR*

(1978, Brit.) 86m Crown International c

John Nolan *(James)*, Carolyn Courage *(Ann)*, James Aubrey *(Philip)*, Sarah Keller *(Suzy)*, Tricia Walsh *(Viv)*, Glynis Barber *(Carol)*, Michael Craze *(Gary)*, Rosie Collins *(Diane)*, L.E. Mack *(Mad Dolly)*, Chuck Julian, Elaine Ives-Cameron, Patti Love, Mary Maude, William Russell, Peter Craze, Peter Attard, Peter Sproule, Colin Howells, Peter Mayhew, Milton Reid, Mike O'Malley.

Nearly as unexciting as its title, TERROR begins with a lengthy film-within-a-film about the family responsible for the death of Mad Dolly (L.E. Mack), an accused witch who burnt at the stake. After watching the film, Ann (Carolyn Courage), the cousin of the film's director (John Nolan), goes off the deep end and sets her slice-and-dice plan into motion. What begins promisingly turns into nothing more than the usual lunatic-on-the-rampage picture, with people getting their heads lopped off, a woman getting pinned to a tree, a poor sap getting caught in a bear trap, etc.

p, Les Young, Richard Crafter; d, Norman J. Warren; w, David McGillivray (based on a story by Les Young, Moira Young); ph, Les Young; ed, Jim Elderton; m, Ivor Slaney.

**(PR:O    MPAA:R)**

## TERROR HOUSE**

(1972) 90m Red Wolf/Scope III-Far West c (AKA: TERROR AT RED WOLF INN; FOLKS AT RED WOLF INN, THE)

Linda Gillin *(Regina)*, Arthur Space *(Henry)*, John Neilson *(Baby John)*, Mary Jackson *(Evelyn)*, Michael Macready *(Policeman)*, Earl Parker *(Pilot)*, Janet Wood *(Pamela)*, Margaret Avery *(Edwina)*.

In this gruesome parody, a likable young woman, Regina (Linda Gillin) wins a vacation trip to the Red Wolf Inn, a cozy little resort run by elderly proprietors Henry (Arthur Space) and Evelyn (Mary Jackson) and their mentally retarded grandson, Baby John (John Neilson). When two other guests inexplicably disappear, Linda's suspicions lead her to a freezerful of body parts. As far as Regina can tell, she's going to be tomorrow's special on the Red Wolf menu; luckily, however, Baby John is in love with her. The classy ending shows Baby John and Regina working in the kitchen and carrying on the legacy, while Grandpa Henry's grinning, winking head watches approvingly from a nearby shelf. Creepy and witty in all the right spots, TERROR HOUSE is no masterwork, but it does have some merit as part of the subgenre of family horror.

p, Michael Macready; d, Bud Townsend; w, Allen J. Actors; ph, John McNichol; ed, Al Maguire; m, Bill Marx.

**(PR:O    MPAA:R/PG)**

## TERROR ON TOUR zero

(1980) 88m IFD-Four Feathers/Tour Features c

Rick Styles *(Fred)*, Chip Greenman *(Ralph)*, Rich Pemberton *(Henry)*, Dave Galluzzo *(Cherry)*, Larry Thomasof *(Tim)*, Jeff Morgan *(Herb)*, Dave Thompson *(Jeff)*, Lisa Rodriguez *(Jane)*, John Green *(Lt. Lambert)*, Sylvia Wright *(Carol)*, Lindy Leah *(Nancy)*.

A hard-rock band known as the Clowns wears makeup a la KISS and performs Grand Guignol routines on stage. One of their fans takes these antics a bit too seriously, donning makeup like his idols and killing off such immoral sorts as pretty young prostitutes. The premise is relatively interesting, especially in light of the mass hysteria that results when the trappings of rock'n'roll and Satan worship are combined. Unfortunately, TERROR ON TOUR is directed by Don Edmonds, who is responsible for the degenerate ILSA, SHE WOLF OF THE SS and ILSA, HAREM KEEPER OF THE OIL SHEIKS. Edmonds proved with his ILSA cult films that he was something less than depraved and certainly no filmmaking talent; with TERROR ON TOUR he simply proves he has no talent. For example, the film doesn't even attempt to show a tour, much less a crowd, only occasionally providing a few cheering extras.

p, Sandy Cobe; d, Don Edmonds; w, Dell Lekus; ph, James Roberson (United Color); ed, Bob Ernst; m, The Names.

**(PR:O    MPAA:NR)**

## TERROR TRAIN**

(1980, Can.) 97m Astral Bellevue Pathe/FOX c (AKA: TRAIN OF TERROR)

Ben Johnson *(Carne)*, Jamie Lee Curtis *(Alana)*, Hart Bochner *(Doc)*, David Copperfield *(The Magician)*, Derek MacKinnon *(Kenny Hampson)*, Sandee Currie *(Mitchy)*, Timothy Webber *(Mo)*, Anthony Sherwood *(Jackson)*, Howard Busgang *(Ed)*, Steve Michaels *(Brakeman)*, Greg Swanson *(Class President)*, D.D. Winters *(Merry)*, Joy Boushel *(Pet)*, Victor Knight *(Engineer)*.

Better than most in the slice-and-dice genre, TERROR TRAIN has a couple of decent performances from Ben Johnson and Jamie Lee Curtis, great photography from John Alcott (BARRY LYNDON; THE SHINING), and some atmospheric direction from Roger Spottiswoode (UNDER FIRE). The script follows the fright essentials to a T: a disturbed student terrorizes a train full of partying college kids and kills them off one by one, using an assortment of gory, gruesome techniques. The killer, who dons various outfits, is a hypersensitive med student who goes off his rocker after a nasty fraternity hazing. While the technical aspects of the production are superior and the setting is fairly unusual, the film still succumbs to the standard slasher movie cliches.

p, Harold Greenberg; d, Roger Spottiswoode; w, T.Y.

Drake; ph, John Alcott (DeLuxe Color); ed, Anne Henderson; m, John Mills-Cockell.

(PR:O  MPAA:R)

## TEXAS CHAIN SAW MASSACRE, THE*****

(1974) 83m Vortex-Henkel-Hooper/Bryanston c

Marilyn Burns *(Sally)*, Allen Danziger *(Jerry)*, Paul A. Partain *(Franklin)*, William Vail *(Kirk)*, Teri McMinn *(Pam)*, Edwin Neal *(Hitchhiker)*, Jim Siedow *(Old Man)*, Gunnar Hansen *(Leatherface)*, John Dugan *(Grandfather)*, Jerry Lorenz *(Pickup Driver)*.

Though its exploitation title would suggest that THE TEX-AS CHAIN SAW MASSACRE is just another mindless gore-fest, it is in fact an intelligent, absorbing, and deeply disturbing horror film that is nearly bloodless in its depiction of violence. Using the age-old technique of suggestion, combined with a gritty, well-executed (no pun intended) visual style, the film seems much bloodier than it actually is. Disturbed by news reports that vandals have been desecrating the remote Texas cemetery where her grandfather is buried, Sally (Marilyn Burns) and her wheelchair-bound brother, Franklin (Paul A. Partain), gather some of their friends and take the family van to see if their grandfather's grave is still intact. While in the area they decide to visit the old farmhouse where Grandpa lived. Nearby is another farmhouse—one decorated with grisly items made from human and animal skin and bones—in which resides a family of unemployed slaughterhouse workers, the most frightening of whom is "Leatherface" (Gunnar Hansen), who wears a mask of human flesh and has a way with a chainsaw. Obviously based on real-life Wisconsin farmer Ed Gein (whose grotesque exploits also inspired Hitchcock's PSYCHO) THE TEXAS CHAIN SAW MASSACRE is one of the best examples of the "horror of the family" subgenre, which takes as its subject the American family—traditionally a wholesome, positive force—and examines its dark side, the side that is claustrophobic, stifling, and incestuous. Tobe Hooper's film is deeply disturbing and is meant to be. The best films in the horror genre don't exist just to "scare" people, but to examine the darker impulses, fears, taboos, and repressed desires found in human beings, and to purge them from our collective subconscious.

p, Tobe Hooper; d, Tobe Hooper; w, Kim Henkel, Tobe Hooper; ph, Daniel Pearl (CFI Color); ed, Sallye Richardson, Larry Carroll; m, Tobe Hooper, Wayne Bell.

(PR:O  MPAA:R)

## TEXAS CHAINSAW MASSACRE PART 2, THE zero

(1986) 95m Cannon c

Dennis Hopper *(Lt. "Lefty" Enright)*, Caroline Williams *(Vanita "Stretch" Brock)*, Bill Johnson *(Leatherface)*, Jim Siedow *(Drayton Sawyer the Cook)*, Bill Moseley *(Chop-Top)*, Lou Perry *(L.G. McPeters)*, Barry Kinyon *(Mercedes Driver)*, Chris Douridas *(Gunner)*, Kinky Friedman *(Sports Anchor)*, Joe Bob Briggs [John Bloom] *(Gonzo Moviegoer)*, Ken Evert *(Grandpa)*, Tobe Hooper.

1986 was a banner year for director Tobe Hooper—not only did he totally botch the remake of the 1953 science-fiction cult classic INVADERS FROM MARS, but he went on to prove that he couldn't even make a sequel to *his own* cult classic. This time around, a family of Texas maniacs are aiming their chainsaws at obnoxious yuppies who cruise through town in their Mercedes Benzes. The murders come to the attention of ex-Texas Ranger Lefty Enright (Dennis Hopper, in an awful performance), who is obsessed with the chainsaw killings of the previous film, and who tries to bring the insane family out of hiding. From the concept to the casting, CHAINSAW II was an ill-conceived mess. Although every one of the original cast members was willing to participate in the sequel, all except Jim Siedow were snubbed. Perhaps the most significant addition to the sequel was the participation of gore-effects master Tom Savini, who does some terrifically nauseating work here, though none of it belongs. Hooper took the easy path and went for out-and-out gore, rather than making a carefully constructed horror film that would claw at the mind instead of the gut. The film feels as if Hooper himself has nothing but contempt for the original and went out of his way to tear it down. And therein may lie the clue to this disaster. The 1974 film was Hooper's first feature, and to this date, the best thing he has done. Perhaps, in his bid for respectability, Hooper began to resent his association with the first MASSACRE, and decided to bury it forever by finally living up to his undeserved reputation as a gore-freak, rubbing the mainstream's nose in this bloody, sadistic, disgusting, and totally mindless film that would offend everyone, including the fans of the original.

p, Menahem Golan, Yoram Globus; d, Tobe Hooper; w, L.M. Kit Carson; ph, Richard Kooris (TVC Color); ed, Alain Jakubowicz; m, Tobe Hooper, Jerry Lambert.

(PR:O  MPAA:NR)

## THEATRE OF BLOOD****

(1973, Brit.) 104m UA c

Vincent Price *(Edward Lionheart)*, Diana Rigg *(Edwina Lionheart)*, Ian Hendry *(Peregrine Devlin)*, Harry Andrews *(Trevor Dickman)*, Coral Browne *(Miss Chloe Moon)*, Robert Coote *(Oliver Larding)*, Jack Hawkins *(Solomon Psaltery)*, Michael Hordern *(George Maxwell)*, Arthur Lowe *(Horace Sprout)*, Robert Morley *(Meredith Merridew)*, Dennis Price *(Hector Snipe)*, Diana Dors *(Mrs. Psaltery)*, Joan Hickson *(Mrs. Sprout)*, Renee Asherson *(Mrs. Maxwell)*, Madeleine Smith *(Rosemary)*, Milo O'Shea *(Inspector Boot)*, Eric Sykes *(Sgt. Dogge)*, Brigid Eric Bates *(Agnes)*, Tony Calvin *(Police Photographer)*, Bunny Reed, Peter Thornton *(Policemen)*, Tutte Lemkow, Jack Maguire, Joyce Graeme, John Gilpin, Eric Francis, Sally Gilmore, Stanley Bates, Declan Mulholland *(Meths Drinkers)*.

After the horrible deaths of three of his colleagues with the prestigious London Theatre Critics Circle, critic Peregrine Devlin (Ian Hendry) approaches the baffled police with a bizarre theory: perhaps the murders are being committed by Edward Lionheart (Vincent Price), an aging Shakespearean actor who was outraged when the Critic's Circle award went to another actor. So incensed was Lionheart, in fact, that he pushed his way onto the stage, stole the award, and jumped into the Thames, killing himself. Since the three murders closely parallel deaths detailed in the plays of Shakespeare, the cops think that Devlin may be right. As it turns out, the now-insane Lionheart, aided by his lovely and equally mad daughter, Edwina (Diana Rigg), and a group of derelicts who rescued him from the Thames, is indeed getting revenge upon the critics who robbed him of his due and sets about killing them in different, diabolical ways derived from Shakespeare. These include stabbing by a small group of assassins ("Julius Caesar"); dragging by a horse ("Troilus and Cressida"); decapitation ("Cymbeline"); the taking of a pound of flesh ("The Merchant of Venice"); drowning in wine ("Richard III"); strangulation ("Othello"); electrocution ("Henry IV, Part I"); force-feeding of two ground-up pet poodles ("Titus Andronicus"); and attempted blinding ("King Lear"). Clearly inspired by the success of the "Dr. Phibes" films, THEATRE OF BLOOD does them one better by allowing Price to have a field day and glory in his particular Gothic acting style. Price is wonderful here—he obviously delights in every grotesque killing and deliciously recites the appropriate passages of Shakespeare outfitted in a variety of outlandish costumes and makeups (perhaps the most bizarre is the giant afro wig used in his pose as a hairdresser). While Price dominates the film with his superb performance, he is ably supported by a top-notch cast—all of whom agreed to do the film in homage to Price. Director Douglas Hickox wisely chooses a very fluid, cinematic visual style to counterpoint the distinctly theatrical bent of the narrative, and skillfully intertwines the hilarious black humor with some surprisingly intense Grand Guignol effects. Wholly entertaining and memorable, THEATRE OF BLOOD is an excellent film and is a lasting tribute to the career of one of the most important actors in the horror genre, Vincent Price.

p, John Kohn, Stanley Mann; d, Douglas Hickox; w, Anthony Greville-Bell; ph, Wolfgang Suchitzky (DeLuxe Color); ed, Malcolm Cooke; m, Michael J. Lewis.

(PR:C-O  MPAA:R)

## THEATRE OF DEATH**

(1966, Brit.) 91m Pennea/Hemisphere c (AKA: BLOOD FIEND; FEMALE FIEND)

Christopher Lee (Philippe Darvas), Lelia Goldoni (Dani Cirreaux), Julian Glover (Charles Marquis), Evelyn Laye (Mme. Angele), Jenny Till (Nicole Chapel), Ivor Dean (Inspector Michaeud).

Philippe Darvas (Christopher Lee), the mysterious, domineering, and seemingly violent director of a Grand Guignol playhouse in Paris, is the prime suspect when a number of people are murdered in a vampire-like fashion. Although Darvas seems the obvious culprit, his ward Nicole (Jenny Till), a young gypsy girl with her own sanguineous inclinations, also appears to be a likely suspect. This relatively entertaining thriller provides an interesting look at the little-seen workings of Grand Guignol theater, and was beautifully photographed by Gilbert Taylor, who was behind the

camera on A HARD DAY'S NIGHT; REPULSION; THE OMEN; STAR WARS; and the 1979 version of DRACULA.

p, Michael Smedley-Aston, William Gell; d, Samuel Gallu; w, Ellis Kadison, Roger Marshall (based on a story by Kadison); ph, Gilbert Taylor (Techniscope, Technicolor).

(PR:C-O  MPAA:NR)

## THEY CAME FROM WITHIN**½

(1976, Can.) 87m DAL/AIP c (AKA: PARASITE MURDERS, THE; FRISSONS; SHIVERS)

Paul Hampton (Roger St. Luc), Joe Silver (Rollo Linsky), Lynn Lowry (Forsythe), Alan Migicovsky (Nicholas Tudor), Susan Petrie (Janine Tudor), Barbara Steele (Betts), Ronald Mlodzik (Merrick), Barrie Baldero (Detective Heller), Camille Ducharme (Mr. Guilbault), Hanka Posnanka (Mrs. Guilbault), Wally Martin (Doorman), Vlasta Vrana (Kresimar Sviben), Charles Perley (Delivery Boy), Al Rochman (Parkins), Julie Wildman (Miss Lewis), Arthur Grosser (Mr. Wolfe), Edith Johnson (Olive), Dorothy Davis (Vi), Joy Coghill (Mona Wheatley), Joan Blackman (Mother in Elevator), Fred Doederlein (Emil Hobbes), Sony Forbes (Man in Garbage Room), Silvie Debois (Benda Sviben), Kirsten Bishopric (Daughter in Elevator).

Canadian director David Cronenberg's first mainstream work, THEY CAME FROM WITHIN is an intriguing and ultimately disturbing work, which, while intensely personal, is also immature, suffering from a lack of balance and genuine insight. An obsessive, grotesque, and paranoid look at modern sexuality, the film seems more of a knee-jerk reaction than a studied examination. A research scientist who specializes in parasites develops an aphrodisiac parasite with an active venereal disease component that enters a patient's body and turns him into a sex fiend. The mad doctor then implants one of the parasites in the body of his teenage mistress. However, the teenager happens to be fairly promiscuous, and soon the parasite has spread to most of the residents of a modern, self-sufficient high-rise, turning everyone into libidinous maniacs. Cronenberg was rather prophetic in forecasting the AIDS crisis, and he paints a grim, disturbing portrait of modern sexuality, in which every sexual taboo is depicted as a breeding ground for the parasites. Unfortunately, THEY CAME FROM WITHIN seems reactionary and hysterical, and the director's criticism of modern lifestyles is not balanced by any representation of a healthy sexual relationship. At this point in his development as a filmmaker, Cronenberg's world was entirely populated by amoral, sexually degenerate characters with absolutely no redeeming qualities that would move an audience to sympathize with their plight. This seemingly puritanical revulsion, this lack of compassion, mars much of his early work. With THE FLY, however, the director seems to have found some genuine warmth and empathy for his characters, and the result is a richer and much more powerful film that achieves true greatness. THEY CAME FROM WITHIN is flawed aesthetically as well, suffering as it does from an extremely low budget and a director who had not yet fully developed a cogent visual style. It's an extremely interesting film, but certainly not the masterpiece some of its defenders claim.

p, Ivan Reitman, John Dunning, Andre Link; d, David Cronenberg; w, David Cronenberg; ph, Robert Saad (Movielab Color); ed, Patrick Dodd; m, Ivan Reitman.

**(PR:O MPAA:R)**

## THIRST**½

(1979, Aus.) 98m F.G. Film/New Line c

Chantal Contouri *(Kate Davis)*, David Hemmings *(Dr. Fraser)*, Henry Silva *(Dr. Gauss)*, Max Phipps *(Hodge)*, Shirley Cameron *(Mrs. Barker)*, Rod Mullinar *(Derek)*, Robert Thompson *(Sean)*, Walter Pym *(Dichter)*, Rosie Sturgess *(Lori)*, Lulu Pinkus *(Nurse)*, Amanda Muggleton *(Martha)*.

An intelligent, modern vampire tale is given a serious treatment in this well-acted, technically superior production. Beautiful businesswoman Kate Davis (Chantal Contouri) is kidnaped by the Hyma Brotherhood, a secret organization that exists in near solitude in a desolate rural area. The group, led by Dr. Fraser (David Hemmings), believe themselves to be a superior race because of their consumption of human blood, extracted from "donors" through a high-tech, sanitary dairy farm-type operation. Convinced that Kate is the direct descendent of the Hyma Brotherhood's revered founder, Countess Bathory, Dr. Fraser asks the businesswoman to join the cult. THIRST is not without its problems, but its highly original concept and occasionally creepy atmosphere carry the picture.

p, Anthony I. Ginnane; d, Rod Hardy; w, John Pinkney (based the "Instant Terror" stories by John Pinkney); ph, Vincent Monton (Panavision, Eastmancolor); ed, Phil Reid; m, Brian May.

**(PR:O MPAA:R)**

## THIRSTY DEAD, THE*

(1975) 90m International Amusements c (AKA: BLOOD CULT OF SHANGRI-LA, THE)

John Considine, Jennifer Billingsley, Judith McConnell, Fredricka Meyers, Tani Guthrie.

This amusingly bad pseudo-vampire effort stars John Considine as a jungle dweller who has attained eternal life by performing a bizarre blood ritual, in which sexy young women are the main ingredient. A beautiful actress and her friends are kidnapped and taken to Considine's Shangri La-like lair for use in the rituals. Made on a zero budget in the Philippines, this is a distinctly dull effort that boasts many unintentionally comic highlights, but little in the way of chills. Considine would later be featured in many Alan Rudolph films, including WELCOME TO L.A. (1977) and TROUBLE IN MIND (1985).

p, Wesley E. Depue; d, Terry Becker; w, Charles Dennis; ph, (Movielab Color).

**(PR:A-C MPAA:PG)**

## THIRTEEN GHOSTS**½

(1960) 85m COL bw-c

Charles Herbert *(Buck Zorba)*, Jo Morrow *(Medea Zorba)*, Martin Milner *(Ben Rush)*, Rosemary De Camp *(Hilda Zorba)*, Donald Woods *(Cyrus Zorba)*, Margaret Hamilton *(Elaine Zacharides)*, John Van Dreelen *(E. Van Allen)*.

Cyrus Zorba (Donald Woods) and his wife, Hilda (Rosemary De Camp), are the parents of young Buck (Charles Herbert) and college-age Medea (Jo Morrow). Barely keeping their heads above water financially because Cyrus' job at the Los Angeles County Museum doesn't pay much, the family is delighted to learn that Cyrus's eccentric uncle has left them his huge, gloomy mansion. Lawyer Ben Rush (Martin Milner) regrets to inform the family, however, that the former owner collected ghosts—11 of them, to be exact. Cyrus dismisses such nonsense and moves the family into the mansion, which comes with its own dour housekeeper, Elaine (Margaret Hamilton). Soon after their arrival, the ghosts—including No. 12, the dead uncle—start to wreak havoc on the house and the family is warned that there will be one more death, bringing the number of spirits to 13. Who will it be? THIRTEEN GHOSTS was another gimmicky William Castle movie—this time the audience draw was "Illusion-O," facilitated by a pair of red- and blue-colored glasses. When the ghosts appeared, a blue tint was imposed on the black-and-white film, so viewers could choose either to see the ghosts by looking through the red "Ghost Viewer" portion or remove them by looking through the blue "Ghost Remover" portion. Unfortunately, the effect is lost on the home video release, which also clumsily edits out William Castle's introduction explaining how to use the Ghost Viewer device. Gimmick or no, the film is really rather silly and not particularly scary.

p, William Castle; d, William Castle; w, Robb White; ph, Joseph Biroc (Eastmancolor); ed, Edwin Bryant; m, Von Dexter.

**(PR:A MPAA:NR)**

## THRILL KILLERS, THE*

(1965) 69m Hollywood Star bw (AKA: MONSTERS ARE LOOSE, THE; MANIACS ARE LOOSE, THE)

Cash Flagg *(Mort "Mad Dog" Click)*, Liz Renay *(Liz Saxon)*, Brick Bardo *(Joe Saxon)*, Carolyn Brandt *(Carol)*, Ron Burr *(Ron)*, Gary Kent *(Gary)*, Herb Robins *(Herbie)*, Keith O'Brien *(Keith)*, Laura Benedict *(Linda)*, Erina Enyo *(Erina Devore)*, Atlas King *(Dennis Kesdekian)*, Titus Moede *(Officer Frank West)*, Lonnie Lord *(Officer Tracy)*, George J. Morgan *(Himself)*, Arch Hall *(Himself)*.

Writer-director Ray Dennis Steckler, billed under his usual pseudonym, Cash Flagg, stars as "Mad Dog" Click, a murderous lunatic whose brother, Herbie (Herb Robins), has just escaped from a California insane asylum along with two other depraved goons. While trying to hook up with his brother, "Mad Dog" thumbs a ride from traveling salesman Dennis Kesdekian (Atlas King), kills him, and steals his car. Meanwhile, aspiring actor Joe Saxon (Brick Bardo) and his wife, Liz (Liz Renay), try to persuade film producer George J. Morgan (THE THRILL KILLERS' producer, playing himself) to star Joe in his next project. The action then shifts to a roadside diner run by Liz's cousin, where the three escaped killers turn up and behead an amorous young couple (Carolyn Brandt and Ron Burr). Soon Joe, Liz, and Morgan arrive on the scene, followed shortly thereafter by Mad Dog himself. With all the characters now assembled in one place, the lunatics, having added Mad Dog to their ranks, take a stab at beheading the filmmakers. This low-low-budget fun from Steckler offered even more surprises during its initial theatrical run, including the on-site presence of men in latex Cash Flagg masks who ran up and down the aisles brandishing fake axes. What's more, the film featured a prolog with a "real" hypnotist who used a spinning wheel to suggest to the audience that the axe-wielding goons were actually jumping out of the screen.

p, George J. Morgan; d, Ray Dennis Steckler; w, Ray Dennis Steckler, Gene Pollock; ph, Joseph V. Mascelli; ed, Austin McKinney; m, Henry Price.

(PR:O MPAA:NR)

## TO ALL A GOODNIGHT zero

(1980) 84m IRC-IWC and Four Features c

Buck West *(Weird Ralph)*, Sam Shamshak *(Polansky)*, Katherine Herington *(Mrs. Jensen)*, Jennifer Runyon, Forrest Swanson, Linda Gentile, William Lauer, J. Bridges.

TO ALL A GOODNIGHT is yet another entry in the disturbingly fertile series of "psycho-killer Santa Claus" films that includes BLACK CHRISTMAS; YOU BETTER WATCH OUT; SILENT NIGHT, DEADLY NIGHT (Parts 1 and 2); and the "All Through the House" episode of TALES OF THE CRYPT (1972). Here the setting is the swanky Calvin Finishing School for Girls as the students prepare for Christmas break. The holiday is spoiled for five of the girls, however, when the crazed parents of a student who was killed on campus two Christmases before dress up as Santa and begin slashing. By the time it's over most of the girls and several bystanders have been dispatched in a variety of bloody ways (by a crossbow, an axe, and even an airplane propeller), leaving the audience to ponder the other activities that could have filled the hour and a half required to witness this inanity.

p, Sandy Cobe; d, David Hess; w, Alex Rebar; ph, B. Godsey; m, Richard Tufo.

(PR:O MPAA:R)

## TO THE DEVIL A DAUGHTER***

(1976, Brit./Ger.) 92m Hammer-Terra/Cine Artists c
(DIE BRAUT DES SATANS)

Richard Widmark *(John Verney)*, Christopher Lee *(Father Michael Raynor)*, Honor Blackman *(Anna Fountain)*, Denholm Elliott *(Henry Beddows)*, Michael Goodliffe *(George de Grass)*, Nastassja Kinski *(Catherine Beddows)*, Eva-Marie Meineke *(Eveline de Grass)*, Anthony Valentine *(David)*, Derek Francis *(Bishop)*, Isabella Telezynska *(Margaret)*, Constantin de Goguel *(Kollde)*, Anna Bentinck *(Isabel)*, Irene Prador *(German Matron)*, Petra Peters *(Sister Helle)*, William Ridoutt *(Airport Porter)*, Brian Wilde *(Room Attendant)*, Howard Goorney *(Critic)*, Frances De La Tour *(Salvation Army Major)*, Zoe Hendry, Lindy Benson, Jo Peters, Bobby Sparrow *(Girls)*.

This intelligent, though flawed, Hammer entry features an excellent cast that includes Richard Widmark, Christopher Lee, Denholm Elliott, Honor Blackman, and the nubile young Nastassia Kinski. John Verney (Widmark) is an occult novelist enlisted by the desperate Henry Beddows (Elliott) to save his 16-year-old daughter, Catherine (Kinski). It seems that Catherine has fallen under the spell of high priest Michael Raynor (Lee), who plans to sacrifice the virgin to a homunculus he has created. In the process, a number of bizarre deaths occur, and poor Henry, who offered his daughter to the Devil in exchange for his own safety, self-destructs into a frightened and pathetic old man. Beautifully photographed in locations from Bavaria to London to the English countryside, and including some excellent special effects from Les Bowie, TO THE DEVIL A DAUGHTER deteriorates a bit in its relatively ludicrous ending. The film does, however, boast some truly frightening images of black magic rituals, a gruesome birth scene, and a very immodest Kinski.

p, Roy Skeggs; d, Peter Sykes; w, Christopher Wicking (based on the novel by Dennis Wheatley); ph, David Watkin (Technicolor); ed, John Trumper; m, Paul Glass.

(PR:O MPAA:R)

## TOMB OF LIGEIA, THE****

(1964, Brit.) 80m Alta Vista/AIP c (AKA: TOMB OF THE CAT)

Vincent Price *(Verden Fell)*, Elizabeth Shepherd *(Lady Ligeia Fell/Lady Rowena Trevanion)*, John Westbrook *(Christopher Gough)*, Oliver Johnston *(Kenrick)*, Derek Francis *(Lord Trevanion)*, Richard Vernon *(Dr. Vivian)*, Ronald Adam *(Parson)*, Frank Thornton *(Peperel)*, Denis Gilmore *(Livery Boy)*, Penelope Lee.

The last of Roger Corman's Poe films and the last horror movie by the director to date, THE TOMB OF LIGEIA is also the most unusual entry in the series and one of the best. Set in 1821, the film opens as Verden Fell (Vincent Price) stands grief-stricken while his beloved wife, Ligeia, is buried in the cemetery outside the ruined, ancient abbey where he lives. Before she expired, Ligeia told her husband that she would never die, and, as the coffin is lowered, a black cat sitting on the tombstone screams and the corpse's eyes snap open. Fell rushes to the casket, convinced that his wife still lives, but the eye movement was merely a nervous reaction. Months later, while on a fox hunt, the Lady Rowena (Elizabeth Shepherd) falls from her horse near Ligeia's grave. Her ankle injured, Rowena is found by Fell—dressed entirely in black and sporting bizarre wrap-around dark glasses because of his aversion to sunlight—and carried into the abbey, where he tends to her sprain. As the weeks go by, Rowena and Fell fall in love and become engaged, although she is disturbed by Fell's morbid obsession with Ligeia. After their wedding and honeymoon, the couple learns that they cannot sell the abbey because much of the property is in Ligeia's name and she was never officially declared dead. This seems to send Fell even further into madness, and he becomes convinced that Ligeia is still alive. Rowena also begins to suffer from dreams and hallucinations in which she imagines herself as Ligeia. Eventually, Rowena discovers that Ligeia's body lies in a secret underground passageway in the abbey (Fell had the corpse exhumed and put a wax figure in its place), where Fell tends to it every night. Desperate, Rowena tries to convince Fell that *she* is Ligeia, but their tragic love is destroyed in a bizarre and fiery climax. For his last stab at Poe, Corman decided to do something different and shot the film on location at the old Norfolk abbey in East Anglia, much to the delight of Price, who had always wanted to do a picture in a ruin. In addition to the impressive look of its physical production, THE TOMB OF LIGEIA is the most subtle in the entire Poe series, with a finely nuanced performance from Price and an excellent screenplay from Robert Towne (CHINATOWN, 1974) that is part romance, part horror. Footage from the climax was used by Martin Scorsese in MEAN STREETS (1973).

p, Roger Corman; d, Roger Corman; w, Robert Towne (based on the story "Ligeia" by Edgar Allan Poe); ph, Arthur Grant (Colorscope, Pathe Color); ed, Alfred Cox; m, Kenneth V. Jones.

(PR:A MPAA:NR)

## TOO SCARED TO SCREAM**

(1985) 104m Doorman/Movie Store c

Mike Connors *(Lt. Dinardo)*, Anne Archer *(Kate)*, Leon Isaac Kennedy *(Frank)*, Ian McShane *(Hardwick)*, Ruth Ford *(Irma)*, John Heard *(Lab Technician)*, Carrie Nye *(Graziella)*, Maureen O'Sullivan *(Mother)*, Murray Hamilton *(Jack)*, Ken Norris *(Mike)*, Val Avery *(Medical Examiner)*, Chet Doherty *(Edward)*, Sully Boyar *(Sydney Blume)*, Karen Rushmore *(Nadine)*, Rony Clanton *(Barker)*, Beeson Carroll *(Barry Moyer)*, Victoria Bass *(Cynthia Oberman)*, Dick Boccelli *(Benny)*, Fred Ford *(Man at Bar)*, Ernesto Gasco *(Waiter)*, Adrienne Howard *(Louise)*, Yvonne Talton Kersey *(Mamie)*, Gaetano Lisi *(Guard)*, Harry Madsen *(Lyman)*, John Ring *(Irishman)*.

The first and only feature directed by actor Tony Lo Bianco, TOO SCARED TO SCREAM is the fairly atmospheric but less than chilling tale of a maniac who is menacing a posh Manhattan apartment building. The police detective in charge of the investigation, Lt. Dinardo (Mike Connors of TV's "Mannix"), uses a female undercover cop (Anne Archer) to entrap the obvious killer, Hardwick (Ian McShane), a doorman with a predilection for Shakespeare but an unnatural fixation on his invalid mother (Maureen O'Sullivan). Although the plot isn't particularly believable, Lo Bianco milks the situation for all it's worth and manages to create some well-developed, eccentric characters who fall victim to the knife-wielding psycho. Connors, who also produced, does a nice job with a role for which he is a little too old, while the rest of the cast—Archer, McShane, Leon Isaac Kennedy, John Heard and Murray Hamilton—should have been above this sort of fare.

p, Mike Connors; d, Tony Lo Bianco; w, Neal Barbera, Glenn Leopold; ph, Larry Pizer (CFI Color); ed, Ed Beyer, Michael Economou; m, George Garvarentz.

(PR:O MPAA:R)

## TOOLBOX MURDERS, THE zero

(1978) 93m Cal-Am c

Cameron Mitchell *(Kingsley)*, Pamelyn Ferdin *(Laurie)*, Wesley Eure *(Kent)*, Nicholas Beauvy *(Joey Ballard)*, Aneta Corsaut *(JoAnn Ballard)*, Tim Donnelly *(Detective Jamison)*, Faith McSwain, Marciee Drake, Mariane Walter, Kelly Nichols *(Victims)*, Evelyn Guerrero *(Butch)*.

This is an extremely ugly film. Cameron Mitchell, in one of his most reprehensible roles, plays a deranged building superintendent who kills off his female victims with an array of implements—a hammer, drill, screwdriver, and nail gun—from his toolbox. All of this is motivated by the death of his daughter, which was somehow caused by "sinful" behavior. He even kidnaps the one girl he considers pure, dresses her up like his daughter, ties her to a bed, and forces her to listen to his sobbing rendition of "Sometimes I Feel Like a Motherless Child." Not only is this truly sick stuff, but the production is so low-budget, and the photography so muddy, that a sense of ultrasleaze prevails. The bizarre cast includes Aneta Corsaut, who played Helen Crump on "The Andy Griffith Show," and porno star Kelly Nichols, who is murdered with the nail-gun.

p, Tony Didio; d, Dennis Donnelly; w, Robert Easter, Ann N. Kindberg; ph, Gary Graver (EFI Color); ed, Skip Lusk; m, George Deaton.

(PR:O MPAA:R)

## TORSO*

(1973, It.) 90m CHAM/Joseph Brenner c (I CORPI PRESENTANO TRACCE DI VIOLENZA CARNALE)

Suzy Kendall *(Jane)*, Tina Aumont *(Dani)*, Luc Meranda *(Roberto)*, John Richardson *(Franz)*, Robert Bisacco *(Stefano)*, Angela Covello *(Katia)*, Carla Brait *(Ursula)*, Cristina Airoldi *(Carol)*, Patricia Adiutori *(Flo)*.

Beautiful young college girls are terrorized by a hooded rapist-killer who gets his kicks by dismembering his victims with saws. Director Sergio Martino is no Dario Argento and therefore this virtually bloodless film, directed without much flair, is pretty boring—despite the presence of THE BIRD WITH THE CRYSTAL PLUMAGE star Suzy Kendall and the exploitative title. The Italian title translates as "The Bodies Presented Traces of Carnal Violence"—perhaps a bit of an understatement when we're talking about women with their limbs hacked off.

p, Carlo Ponti, Antonio Cervi; d, Sergio Martino; w, Ernesto Gastaldi, Sergio Martino; ph, Giancarlo Ferrando (Technicolor).

(PR:O MPAA:R)

## TORTURE DUNGEON zero

(1970) 80m Constitution/Mishkin c

Jeremy Brooks *(Norman)*, Susan Cassidy *(Heather McGregor)*, Patricia Dillon *(Lady Jane)*, Donna Whitfield *(Lady Agatha)*, Haal Borske *(Alfred)*, Maggie Rogen *(Margaret)*, Neil Flanagan *(Peter the Eye)*, Richard Mason *(Ivan)*,

George Box, Patricia Garvey, Dan Lyra, Helen Adams, Robert Fricelle.

Another pathetic costumer from Andy Milligan, this film takes place on unconvincing medieval sets and tells a lame tale about a crazed duke who attempts to kill off and mutilate all the heirs to his kingdom's throne. One of Milligan's goriest movies, TORTURE DUNGEON was filmed on Staten Island, a poor substitute indeed for the England of yore.

p, William Mishkin; d, Andy Milligan; w, Andy Milligan, John Borske; ph, Andy Milligan.

**(PR:O  MPAA:R)**

## TORTURE GARDEN**½

(1967, Brit.) 92m Amicus/COL c

Jack Palance (Ronald Wyatt), Burgess Meredith (Dr. Diabolo), Beverly Adams (Carla Hayes), Peter Cushing (Lancelot Canning), Barbara Ewing (Dorothy Endicott), Michael Bryant (Colin Williams), Maurice Denham (Colin's Uncle), John Standing (Leo Winston), Robert Hutton (Bruce Benton), John Phillips (Eddie Storm), Michael Ripper (Gordon Roberts), Bernard Kay (Dr. Heim), Catherine Finn (Nurse Parker), Ursula Howells (Miss Chambers), Niall MacGinnis (Doctor), Timothy Bateson (Fairground Barker), David Bauer (Mike Charles), Nicole Shelby (Millie), Clytie Jessop (Atropos), Michael Hawkins (Constable), Hedger Wallace (Edgar Allan Poe).

Four stories from the pen of Robert Bloch (PSYCHO) are bookended by Burgess Meredith as Dr. Diabolo, a carnival barker who provides four patrons with glimpses into their future. The first episode, "Enoch," concerns a young playboy who falls under the spell of a cat, prompting him to murder people and turn them into cat food. The second, "Terror Over Hollywood," follows an aspiring actress as she falls in love with a famous star, only to discover that he is a robot, and to be turned into a robot herself, attaining fame in the bargain. In "Mr. Steinway," the third and worst episode, a female reporter falls in love with a concert pianist. Their relationship is cut short, however, when a piano, controlled by the jealous spirit of the pianist's mother, kills the reporter. The final story, "The Man Who Collected Poe," features Jack Palance as a collector of Edgar Allan Poe paraphernalia who murders a fellow collector (Peter Cushing) in an attempt to acquire some rare manuscripts, and is then visited by Poe himself. The fifth member of Dr. Diabolo's audience refuses to have his future told and stabs the prognosticator, causing the other four to flee in fear. After they've gone, Meredith reveals that the stabbing is just part of his act. Although marred by the uneven quality of the episodes, TORTURE GARDEN does have a few creepy moments. Especially effective is the final episode in which Poe's spirit is conjured up from the great beyond.

p, Max J. Rosenberg, Milton Subotsky; d, Freddie Francis; w, Robert Bloch (based on his stories "Enoch," "Terror Over Hollywood," "Mr. Steinway," "The Man Who Collected Poe"); ph, Norman Warwick (Technicolor); ed, Peter Elliott; m, Don Banks, James Bernard.

**(PR:O  MPAA:NR)**

## TOURIST TRAP, THE*

(1979) 85m Band Compass-Manson c

Chuck Connors (Slausen), Jon Van Ness (Jerry), Jocelyn Jones (Molly), Robin Sherwood (Eileen), Tanya Roberts (Becky), Keith McDermott (Woody), Dawn Jeffory (Tina), Shailar Coby (Davey).

A bizarre, eerie, but entirely pointless shocker, THE TOURIST TRAP stars Chuck Connors as Slausen, a hobbled southerner who operates a roadside tourist attraction called "Slausen's Lost Oasis"—a strange museum that houses a collection of lifelike mannequins. Why anyone would want to visit such a place is anyone's guess, but sure enough some dumb college kids roll on in. The Pino Donaggio music kicks in, the dummies come to life, and the visitors are violently dispatched. Why? Who knows? If the filmmakers know, they're not telling. As senseless as it all is, there are some fairly creepy scenes, as there are in any film in which mannequins spring to life. Tanya Roberts, soon to be one of "Charlie's Angels," makes a brief appearance here—the back of her head serving as a target for a knife-throwing dummy. If the living dummies don't get you, how about Connors wearing a macabre mask while he wanders through a cellar filled with disembodied mannequin parts. Director David Schmoeller would later direct Klaus Kinski in CRAWLSPACE.

p, Larry Carroll; d, David Schmoeller; w, David Schmoeller, Larry Carroll; ph, Nicholas von Sternberg (Metrcolor); ed, Ted Nicolaou; m, Pino Donaggio.

**(PR:C  MPAA:PG)**

## TOWN THAT DREADED SUNDOWN, THE*

(1977) 90m AIP c

Ben Johnson (Capt. Morales), Andrew Prine (Deputy Norman Ramsey), Dawn Wells (Helen Reed), Jimmy Clem (Sgt. Griffin), Charles B. Pierce (Patrolman Benson), Cindy Butler (Peggy Loomis), Earl E. Smith (Dr. Kress), Christine Ellsworth (Linda Mae Jenkins), Mike Hackworth (Sammy Fuller), Jim City (Police Chief Sullivan), Misty West (Emma Lou Cook), Rick Hildreth (Buddy Turner), Steve Lyons (Roy Allen), Bud Davis (The Phantom Killer), Joe Catalanatto (Eddie LeDoux), Roy Lee Brown (Rainbow Johnson), Jason Darnell (Gus Wells), Michael Brown (Police Officer), James B. McAdams (Sheriff's Deputy), John Stroud (Dr. Preston Hickson), Mason Andres (Rev. Harden), Richard Green (High School Principal), Dorothy Darlene Orr (Dispatcher), Don Adkins (Suspect), Vern Stierman (Narrator).

Producer-director Charles B. Pierce did well with the thriller THE LEGEND OF BOGGY CREEK (1972), then hit it big in the southern markets with this supposedly true story about a berserk killer terrorizing the border town of Texarkana. The killer murdered five people back in 1946, but was never caught because he left no clues. The film recounts the story in a dull documentary style, with breaks for clunky narration and some surprisingly bloody murders. Texas Ranger J.D. Morales (veteran character actor Ben Johnson) leads an inept group in the chase as the townspeople start suspecting one another of being the killer. Despite the intriguing premise, Pierce is a stupifyingly unimaginative director and the film is incredibly dull.

p, Charles B. Pierce; d, Charles B. Pierce; w, Earl E. Smith; ph, James Roberson (Movielab Color), ed, Thomas Boutress; m, Jaime Mendoza-Nava.

(PR:O MPAA:R)

## TOXIC AVENGER, THE*

(1985) 81m Troma c

Andree Maranda (Sara), Mitchell Cohen (The Toxic Avenger), Jennifer Baptist (Wanda), Cindy Manion (Julie), Robert Prichard (Slug), Gary Schneider (Bozo), Pat Ryan, Jr. (Mayor Belgoody), Mark Torgl (Melvin), Dick Martinsen (Officer O'Clancy), Chris Liano (Walter Harris), David Weiss (Chief of Police), Dan Snow (Cigar Face), Doug Isbecque (Knuckles), Charles Lee, Jr. (Nipples), Pat Kilpatrick (Leroy), Larry Sutton (Frank), Mike Russo (Rico), Norma Pratt (Mrs. Haskell), Andrew Craig (Fred), Ryan Sexton (Johnny), Sarabel Levinson (Melvin's Mom), Al Pia (Tom Wrightson), Reuben Guss (Dr. Snodburger), Kenneth Kessler (Toxic Avenger's Voice), Dennis Souder (Drug Dealer), Joe Zarro (Mr. Wilson), Dan Hogan (Aerobics Instructor), Myrna Williams (The Kansas Runaway), Richard Duggan (Ice Cream Man), Bruce Morton (Tony).

New York City-based low-budget schlock kings Troma, Inc. made a bid for midnight cult movie status with this bizarre combination of science fiction, horror, and comedy, of which the ads exclaimed, "He was 98 lbs. of solid nerd until he became . . . The Toxic Avenger—the first Super-Hero from New Jersey!" Filmed on location in that beautiful state (home of many a toxic-waste site), THE TOXIC AVENGER follows the story of hapless, nerdy janitor Melvin (Mark Torgl), who just can't seem to fit in among the nubile young fitness nuts at the health club where he works. A victim of a practical joke, Melvin accidentally falls into a vat of toxic waste, transforming him into a powerful monstrosity with bubbly skin (now played by the muscular Mitchell Cohen). The Toxic Avenger discovers that he now possesses incredible strength and, fortunately for New Jersey, is compelled to destroy evildoers and aid the helpless. Though it is silly, sleazy, and graphically violent, THE TOXIC AVENGER does hold a bit of warped charm for fans of this sort of thing.

p, Lloyd Kaufman, Michael Herz; d, Michael Herz, Lloyd Kaufman; w, Joe Ritter, Lloyd Kaufman, Gay Terry, Stuart Strutin; ph, James London, Lloyd Kaufman (Guffanti Film Labs Color); ed, Richard W. Haines, Alan J. Polyniak.

(PR:O MPAA:R)

## TRACK OF THE MOONBEAST zero

(1976) 90m Cinema Shares/Lizard c

Chase Cordell (Paul Carson), Donna Leigh Drake (Kathy Nolan), Gregorio Sala (Johnny Longbow), Francine Kessler (Janet Price), Joe Blasco (The Monster), Patrick Wright, Crawford MacCallum, Fred McCaffrey, Timothy Wayne Brown, Alan Swain, Jeanne Swain, Tim Butler.

Just when you think you've seen it all, along comes TRACK OF THE MOONBEAST. Paul Carson (Chase Cordell), a friendly New Mexican mineralogist, gets hit in the head by a piece of a meteor and undergoes some severe changes, transforming into a giant lizard—the embodiment of some goofy Indian lore about the Lizard God. Although this premise is ripe with comedic opportunities, the production is hampered by classically inept filmmaking, and the story unfolds so slowly one begins to think the film is running in reverse. The acting is even worse. Still, horror fanatics might find some interest in Rick Baker's lizard makeup.

d, Dick Ashe; ph, E.S. Wood; m, Bob Orpin.

(PR:C-O MPAA:NR)

## TRANSYLVANIA 6-5000*

(1985) 93m NW c

Jeff Goldblum (Jack Harrison), Joseph Bologna (Dr. Malavaqua), Ed Begley, Jr. (Gil Turner), Carol Kane (Lupi), Jeffrey Jones (Lepescu), John Byner (Radu), Geena Davis (Odette), Michael Richards (Fejos), Donald Gibb (Wolfman), Norman Fell (MacTurner), Teresa Ganzel (Elizabeth Ellison), Rudy DeLuca (Lawrence Malbot), Inge Apelt (Mme. Moravia), Bozidar Smiljanic (Inspector Percek), Peter Buntic (Hunyadi/Frankenstein's Monster), Dusko Valentic (Twisted Man), Ksenija Prohaska (Mummy), Sara Grdjan (Laura Ellison), Nada Arbus (Uta), Visnja Konigskneght (Peasant Girl), Slobodan Milovanovic (Front Guard), Vida Jerman (Rear Guard), Venco Kapural (Jailer), Thomas H. Brodek (BandLeader), Robert F. Lyons (Victim).

With a good cast and a fairly good (if familiar) premise, TRANSYLVANIA 6-5000 might have been a real winner, had it been executed with at least a modicum of intelligence. A tabloid newspaper editor (Norman Fell) needs a strong story for his sleazy publication and thinks that a "Dracula Lives" piece might increase circulation, so he sends his reluctant son, Gil (Ed Begley, Jr.), and another reporter, Jack Harrison (Jeff Goldblum), off to Transylvania. What they find doesn't measure up to their expectations: the town's mayor, Lepescu (Jeffrey Jones), manages the local inn and has plans to turn the area into a theme park. To bring in the tourists, however, the authorities have to keep under wraps a horde of odd creatures and bloodsuckers who are abetted by mad scientist-plastic surgeon Dr. Malavaqua (Joseph Bologna); his assistant, Radu (John Byner); sex-crazed vampirette Odette (Geena Davis); and the evil Lupi (Carol Kane). It's little more than 93 minutes of vampire jokes from writer-director Rudy DeLuca, a former writer for Mel Brooks, and the best that can be said of this lame-o comedy is that it will make

you run to the video store to rent Brooks' YOUNG FRAN-
KENSTEIN.

p, Mace Neufeld, Thomas H. Brodek; d, Rudy DeLuca; w,
Rudy DeLuca; ph, Tom Pinter; ed, Harry Keller; m, Lee
Holdridge, Alfie Kabiljo.

(PR:C   MPAA:PG)

## TRICK OR TREAT**

(1986) 97m DEG c

Marc Price *(Eddie Weinbauer)*, Tony Fields *(Sammi Curr)*,
Lisa Orgolini *(Leslie Graham)*, Doug Savant *(Tim Hainey)*,
Elaine Joyce *(Angie Weinbauer)*, Glen Morgan *(Roger
Mockus)*, Gene Simmons *(Nuke)*, Ozzy Osbourne *(Rev.
Aaron Gilstrom)*, Elise Richards *(Genie Wooster)*, Richard
Pachorek *(Ron Avery)*, Claire Nono *(Maggie Wong Her-
nandez)*, Alice Nunn *(Mrs. Cavell)*, Larry Sprinkle *(Marv
McCain)*, Charles Martin Smith *(Mr. Wimbley)*, Claudia
Templeton *(Hysterical Survivor)*, Denny Pierce, Ray Shaf-
fer, Brad Thomas *(Goons)*, Terry Loughlin *(Senator)*,
Graham Smith *(Stan)*, Kevin Yahger *(Lead Guitarist)*, Amy
Bertolette *(Fairy)*, Leroy Sweet, Barry Bell, Steve Boles
*(Cops)*, James D. Nelson *(Dave the Partier)*, Richard Doyle
*(Voice)*.

TRICK OF TREAT is a fairly clever sendup of both heavy-
metal music and the paranoid parental-action groups that
want it banned. The first directorial effort by actor Charles
Martin Smith (AMERICAN GRAFFITI; NEVER CRY WOLF;
STARMAN), the film stars Marc Price (Skippy of TV's
"Family Ties") as Eddie, an alienated, nerdy high-schooler
whose only refuge is head-banging. When his idol, heavy-
metal rocker Sammi Curr (Tony Fields), is killed in a hotel
fire, Eddie becomes despondent. He visits his DJ friend
Nuke (Gene Simmons of the group KISS), who gives the
nerd the last, unreleased recording by Sammi, and when
Eddie plays it backwards he discovers those evil satanic
messages that the television evangelists claim warp young
peoples' minds. Sure enough, Eddie unleashes the fire-
scarred spirit of Sammi Curr, who becomes the dream
weapon of every nerdy high-schooler as he helps Eddie
get revenge on the preppie jock types who torment him.
While not exactly frightening, TRICK OR TREAT is a well-
meaning, humorous look at the kind of rock music that isn't
worth the attention paid to it by lonely teens, worried parents, and the exploitative media. Smith (who appears on
screen in a cameo as a schoolteacher) pokes fun at all
groups equally, including the television evangelists, by
casting heavy-metal head-banger supreme Ozzy Osbourne as the TV preacher leading the witch-hunt. Smith's
direction borrows heavily from other horror films, mainly
HALLOWEEN and CARRIE, but he does show a sensitivity
toward humanity sorely lacking in most modern horror films.

p, Michael S. Murphey, Joel Soisson; d, Charles Martin
Smith; w, Michael S. Murphey, Joel Soisson, Rhet Topham
(based on a story by Rhet Topham); ph, Robert Elswit
(Technicolor); ed, Jane Schwartz Jaffe; m, Christopher
Young.

(PR:O   MPAA:R)

## TRICK OR TREATS**

(1982) 91m Lone Star International c

Jackelyn Giroux *(Linda)*, Peter Jason *(Malcolm)*, Chris
Graver *(Christopher)*, David Carradine *(Richard)*, Carrie
Snodgress *(Joan)*, Steve Railsback *(The Boyfriend)*, Jillian
Kesner *(Andrea)*, Dan Pastorini, Tim Rossovich *(Men in
White Shorts)*, Jerry L. Clark *(Bert)*, John Blyth Barrymore
*(Mad Doctor)*, Catherine Coulson *(Nurse Reeves)*, Maria
Dillon *(Newscaster)*, Allen Wisch *(Bum)*, Nike Zach-
manoglou *(Connie)*.

The title alone makes it known that this is another HAL-
LOWEEN rip-off. Again it's a case of a person brought to
the loony bin at the beginning of the film who escapes a
few years later to seek revenge against those who had him
committed; this time, Malcolm (Peter Jason) seduces a
nurse to gain passage out of the institution, donning her
uniform as a disguise and looking outrageously silly. His
object is a confrontation with his former wife, Joan (Carrie
Snodgress), only she's not at home, and there's a baby-
sitter, Linda (Jackelyn Giroux), watching over her kid. Linda is initially terrorized by the precocious youngster (Chris
Graver) she's supervising, priming her for the real terror
when the boy's father, Malcolm, arrives. Former football
players Dan Pastorini and Tim Rossovich and cult filmmaker Paul Bartel have cameo appearances during a
prolog. Though the movie has the usual amount of gore,
a modest sense of humor is maintained, making it more
enjoyable than most run-of-the-mill slasher films. A one-
man show from exploitation cinematographer Gray Graver
(SATAN'S SADISTS; BLOOD OF FRANKENSTEIN; INVA-
SION OF THE BEE-GIRLS; THE TOOLBOX MURDERS;
et al.), who was also involved in some of Orson Welles' in-
complete film projects of the 1970s.

p, Gary Graver; d, Gary Graver, Michael Railsback; w, Gary
Graver; ph, Gary Graver; ed, Gary Graver (CFI Color).

(PR:O   MPAA:R)

## TROLL*½

(1986) 86m Empire c

Noah Hathaway *(Harry Potter, Jr.)*, Michael Moriarty *(Harry
Potter, Sr.)*, Shelley Hack *(Anne Potter)*, Jenny Beck
*(Wendy Potter)*, Sonny Bono *(Peter Dickinson)*, Phil Fon-
dacaro *(Malcolm Malory/Torok the Troll)*, Brad Hall
*(William Daniels)*, Anne Lockhart *(Young Eunice St. Clair)*,
Julia Louis-Dreyfus *(Jeannette Cooper)*, Gary Sandy
*(Barry Tabor)*, June Lockhart *(Eunice St. Clair)*, Robert
Hathaway, James Beck *(Policemen)*, Dale Wyatt
*(Dickinson's Girl Friend)*, Barbara Sciorilli, Viviana Giusti,
Jessie Carfora *(Fairies)*, Debra Dion, Charles Band *(Young
Couple on TV)*, Jacquelyn Band, Albert Band *(Older Cou-
ple on TV)*.

Those folks at Empire Pictures don't waste anything, so
they took the title "ghoulies" from 1985's horror epic and
made them trolls and goblins in 1986. Harry Potter (Michael Moriarty) and wife, Anne (Shelley Hack), move their
family to a new apartment in San Francisco, where youngster Wendy (Jenny Beck) becomes possessed by an ugly
little troll. When Wendy behaves strangely by gobbling her

food and basically acting like a wild animal, Mom and Dad attribute their daughter's bizarre behavior to the "big move," but Wendy's big brother, Harry, Jr. (Noah Hathaway), become concerned when little Sis throws him across the room. As the Wendy-troll transforms other apartment residents into goblins and their apartments into fairy kingdoms, Harry, Jr., turns to neighbor Eunice (June Lockhart), a strange old lady who happens to be a witch who's been doing battle with this troll for centuries. Incredibly dull, TROLL is bit easier to take than an Amtrak ride through Oklahoma, but not by much. Except for another quirky performance from Moriarty—whose solo dance number to Blue Cheer's heavy-metal rendition of Eddie Cochran's classic "Summertime Blues" is almost worth the price of admission—and two likable performances from the children, the acting borders on the pathetic. The special effects, supervised by director John Buechler, who was the effects man on GHOULIES, are pretty poor, essentially slimy rubber creatures with a limited amount of movement and the seams from their molds clearly visible.

p, Albert Band; d, John Carl Buechler; w, Ed Naha; ph, Romano Albani (Technicolor); ed, Lee Percy; m, Richard Band.

**(PR:C  MPAA:PG-13)**

## TWILIGHT ZONE—THE MOVIE**

(1983) 102m WB c

Prolog: Dan Aykroyd *(Passenger)*, Albert Brooks *(Driver)*, Segment 1: Vic Morrow *(Bill)*, Doug McGrath *(Larry)*, Charles Hallahan *(Ray)*, Kai Wulff, Remus Peets *(German Officers)*, Sue Dugan, Debby Porter *(Waitresses)*, Steven Williams *(Bar Patron)*, Annette Claudier *(French Mother)*, Joseph Hieu, Albert Leong *(Vietnamese)*, Stephen Bishop *(Charming GI)*, Segment 2: Scatman Crothers *(Mr. Bloom)*, Bill Quinn *(Mr. Conroy)*, Martin Garner *(Weinstein)*, Selma Diamond *(Mrs. Weinstein)*, Helen Shaw *(Mrs. Dempsey)*, Murray Matheson *(Mr. Agee)*, Peter Brocco *(Mr. Mute)*, Priscilla Pointer *(Miss Cox)*, Scott Nemes *(Young Mr. Weinstein)*, Tanya Fenmore *(Young Mrs. Weinstein)*, Evan Richards *(Young Mr. Agee)*, Laura Mooney *(Young Mrs. Dempsey)*, Christopher Eisenmann *(Young Mr. Mute)*, Segment 3: Kathleen Quinlan *(Helen Foley)*, Jeremy Licht *(Anthony)*, Kevin McCarthy *(Uncle Walt)*, Patricia Barry *(Mother)*, William Schallert *(Father)*, Cherie Currie *(Sara)*, Bill Mumy *(Tim)*, Segment 4: John Lithgow *(Valentine)*, Abbe Lane *(Senior Stewardess)*, Donna Dixon *(Junior Stewardess)*, John Dennis Johnston *(Co-Pilot)*, Larry Cedar *(Creature)*, Charles Knapp *(Sky Marshall)*, Christina Nigra *(Little Girl)*, Lonna Schwab *(Mother)*, Margaret Wheeler *(Old Woman)*, Eduard Franz *(Old Man)*, Rod Serling, Burgess Meredith *(Narrators)*.

Based on television's most popular anthology series, TWILIGHT ZONE—THE MOVIE is a frightfully lopsided omnibus that begins with two wretched episodes, by John Landis and Steven Spielberg, and finishes with an engrossing pair, by Joe Dante and George Miller, bookended by a comic bit with Dan Aykroyd and Albert Brooks as ambulance drivers. Unfortunately, the film is best remembered today for the controversy (and subsequent trial) that surrounded the death of actor Vic Morrow and two Vietnamese extras (six-year-old Renee Chen and seven-year-old Myca Dinh Lee) during the shooting of a helicopter scene for Landis' episode. In the first episode (directed by Landis, the only segment *not* adapted from an original television episode), a loud-mouthed bigot (Morrow) with an intense hatred for Jews, blacks, and Vietnamese gets the tables turned on him when he is sent back in time as a Jew during WW II, a black during a KKK rally, and a Vietcong during an aerial attack. Spiolborg's piece, "Kick the Can," crystallizes almost every thing intolerable about the director's work. It's the sugary tale of an old man (Scatman Crothers) who arrives at a retirement home and transforms the oldsters into youthful incarnations of their days gone by. The anthology takes a sharp turn for the better in the third segment, directed by Joe Dante and based on the TZ episode "It's a Good Life." Helen (Kathleen Quinlan), a young traveler who has lost her way, meets a young boy named Anthony (Jeremy Licht) who initially seems sweet, but is really a tyrant who has imprisoned his family in a cartoon existence. The result is a wildly imaginative and stunningly directed segment with much credit due to set designer William J. Teegarden, special makeup effects master Rob Bottin, and Sally Cruikshank, who created the cartoon segments. The momentum continues with the fourth episode, "Nightmare at 20,000 Feet," directed by George Miller (MAD MAX) and starring John Lithgow as an airline passenger who is deathly afraid of flying. He wrestles with his phobia and manages to keep in control until he sees something standing out on the wing—a crazed demon who is wreaking havoc on the engines. Judging from the order of the segments, it seems coproducers Spielberg and Landis were well aware that their episodes were of a lesser caliber. The moderate success of TWILIGHT ZONE—THE MOVIE paved the way for a resurgence of the anthology series on television. Spielberg came up with the idea for "Amazing Stories," most of which were less than amazing, while "The Twilight Zone" and "Alfred Hitchcock Presents" also were resurrected.

p, Steven Spielberg, John Landis; d, John Landis, Steven Spielberg, Joe Dante, George Miller; w, John Landis, George Clayton Johnson, Josh Rogan, Richard Matheson (based on the teleplay "Kick the Can" by Johnson for "The Twilight Zone" created by Rod Serling), Richard Matheson (based on the teleplay "It's a Good Life" by Rod Serling for "The Twilight Zone" from a short story by Jerome Bixby), Richard Matheson (based on his teleplay "Nightmare at 20,000 Feet" For "The Twilight Zone"); ph, Steven Larner (Technicolor), Allen Daviau, John Hora; ed, Malcolm Campbell, Michael Kahn, Tina Hirsch, Howard Smith; m, Jerry Goldsmith.

**(PR:C-O  MPAA:PG)**

## TWINS OF EVIL***½

(1971, Brit.) 87m Hammer-Rank/UNIV c

Madeleine Collinson *(Frieda Gellhorn)*, Mary Collinson *(Maria Gellhorn)*, Peter Cushing *(Gustav Weil)*, Kathleen Byron *(Katy Weil)*, Dennis Price *(Dietrich)*, Damien Thomas *(Count Karnstein)*, David Warbeck *(Anton Hoffer)*,

Isobel Black *(Ingrid Hoffer)*, Harvey Hall *(Franz)*, Alex Scott *(Hermann)*, Katya Keith *(Countess Mircalla)*, Roy Stewart *(Joachim)*, Maggie Wright *(Alexa)*, Luan Peters *(Gerta)*, Kirsten Lindholm *(Young Girl at Stake)*, Inigi Jackson *(Woodman)*, Judy Matheson *(Woodman's Daughter)*.

The last and best of the Hammer "Karnstein" trilogy, TWINS OF EVIL features Madeleine and Mary Collinson, the first twin centerfold girls for *Playboy*, as Frieda and Maria Gellhorn, a pair of orphans who come to visit their repressive Witchfinder General uncle, Gustav Weil (Peter Cushing). He lives near Karnstein Castle and, of course, that means evil lurks just around the corner. Frieda, the more outgoing and adventurous of the twins, becomes curious about the old castle and takes a look around the place. There she meets Count Karnstein (Damien Thomas), a handsome young man who also happens to be a satanist. During a demonic rite, the young count inadvertently resurrects his ancestor Mircalla and is promptly vampirized. Karnstein then vampirizes Frieda, who ventures out to suck the blood of the locals. The puritanical Weil finally catches up with his niece and imprisons her, but Karnstein installs the innocent Maria in her place, setting up the exciting climax, in which Maria may be burned at the stake for the crimes of her twin. Fueled by a great performance from Cushing as the zealous witchfinder, TWINS OF EVIL is an effective examination of the conflict between repression and hedonism. Director John Hough, who made his mark in several episodes of the popular television series "The Avengers," keeps things moving at a brisk pace and stages the scenes of horror with considerable panache. Released by Universal in the US, the studio butchered the British print, removing all of the sex and most of the violence. Luckily, the print available on videocassette is the uncut British version.

p, Harry Fine, Michael Style; d, John Hough; w, Tudor Gates (based on characters created by J. Sheridan Le Fanu); ph, Dick Bush (Eastmancolor); ed, Spencer Reeve; m, Harry Robinson.

**(PR:O   MPAA:R)**

## TWITCH OF THE DEATH NERVE ★★★

(1973, It.) 82m Hallmark c (ANTEFATTO; AKA: LAST HOUSE ON THE LEFT PART II)

Claudine Auger, Claudio Volonto, Ana Maria Rosati, Laura Betti, Luigi Pistilli, Brigitte Skay.

A dispute over a piece of a desirable real estate spawns 13 vicious murders in this film, which comes about as close as Mario Bava ever came to making a virtually plotless cinematic essay in stylistic bloodletting. TWITCH OF THE DEATH NERVE had an incredible influence on Sean S. Cunningham, who ripped off many of the murders and the plotless format for his own FRIDAY THE 13TH (1980). The difference between Cunningham and Bava, however, are significant; Cunningham is an artless exploitation director, while Bava is obsessed with the purely lyrical aspects of violence on film. While some extol this film as Bava's latter-day masterpiece, his realization is flawed by an over-reliance on the annoying zoom lens in place of the gor-

geous floating camerawork found in his earlier films. Ironically, it was re-released in the US as a bogus sequel to Wes Craven's LAST HOUSE ON THE LEFT, which was produced by Cunningham. Available on videotape as LAST HOUSE ON THE LEFT PART II.

p, Giuseppe Zacciarello; d, Mario Bava; w, Mario Bava, Carlo Reali; ph, Mario Bava; m, Stelvio Cipriani.

**(PR:O   MPAA:R)**

## TWO THOUSAND MANIACS★★½

(1964) 88m Box Office Spectaculars c

Connie Mason *(Terry Adams)*, Thomas Wood *(Tom White)*, Jeffrey Allen *(Mayor Buckman)*, Ben Moore *(Lester)*, Shelby Livingston *(Bea Miller)*, Gary Bakeman *(Rufe)*, Jerome Eden *(John Miller)*, Michael Korb *(David Wells)*, Yvonne Gilbert *(Beverly Wells)*, Mark Douglas *(Harper)*, Linda Cochran *(Betsy)*, Vincent Santo *(Billy)*, Andy Wilson *(Policeman)*, The Pleasant Valley Boys *(Themselves)*.

Three vacationing couples are led into a small southern town, thanks to some maliciously placed detour signs. They discover Pleasant Valley isn't too pleasant when they become special guests of honor in the town's centennial. Before long, one gets hacked apart with an axe, her husband has his arms and legs tied to four horses that are sent galloping in different directions, another man is rolled down a hill in a barrel lined with sharp nails, and his wife is tied to a platform and has a boulder dropped on her. Only one couple, BLOOD FEAST stars Connie Mason and Thomas Wood, manages to escape. After the four murders, the centennial is complete, and we learn that the townsfolk are actually ghosts from the Civil War getting revenge on Northerners for the destruction of their town 100 years before. From its genuinely catchy theme song, "The Rebel Yell" (penned and sung by the director himself) to its effectively creepy ending, this is easily Herschell Gordon Lewis' best film. Although BLOOD FEAST (1963) is just as gory as TWO THOUSAND MANIACS, the violence here is more disturbing, especially the first instance, when one of the rednecks sadistically cuts off a woman's thumb on the pretext of showing her his knife. Filming on a budget of less than $40,000 on location in St. Cloud, Florida, Lewis proves to be a much more assured filmmaker here, contributing some surprisingly good camerawork and an effective opening credits sequence vaguely reminiscent of Sam Peckinpah's THE WILD BUNCH (1969). While TWO THOUSAND MANIACS remains the film of which Lewis is most proud, it didn't make nearly as much money as the cruder BLOOD FEAST.

p, David F. Friedman; d, Herschell Gordon Lewis; w, Herschell Gordon Lewis; ph, Gordon Lewis (Eastmancolor); ed, Robert Sinise; m, Herschell Gordon Lewis.

**(PR:O   MPAA:NR)**

# U

## UNCANNY, THE**

(1977, Brit./Can.) 85m Cinevideo-Tor-Subotsky and Heroux/RANK c

Peter Cushing *(Wilbur)*, Ray Milland *(Frank)*, Susan Penhaligon *(Janet)*, Joan Greenwood *(Miss Malkin)*, Roland Culver *(Wallace)*, Simon Williams *(Michael)*, Alexandra Stewart *(Mrs. Blake)*, Donald Pilon *(Mr. Blake)*, Chloe Franks *(Angela)*, Renee Giraud *(Mrs. Maitland)*, Katrina Holden *(Lucy)*, Donald Pleasence *(Valentine De'Ath)*, Samantha Eggar *(Edina)*, John Vernon *(Pomeroy)*, John LeClerc *(Barrington)*, Sean McCann *(Inspector)*, Catharine Begin *(Madeline)*.

This mediocre horror anthology concerns an author, Wilbur (Peter Cushing), who is trying to sell a manuscript, which maintains that cats are plotting to take over the world, to a skeptical publisher (Ray Milland). In order to persuade the reluctant publisher, Wilbur tells three stories involving cantankerous felines. In the first, set in foggy London, the eccentric and quite wealthy Miss Malkin (Joan Greenwood) is eaten by her pet kitties. In the second, a girl shrinks to tiny size and is terrorized by her now giant cat. The final episode follows a pair of Hollywood actors (Donald Pleasence and Samantha Eggar) who are trying to murder one of their spouses, only to have a cat interfere. The good cast, unfortunately, isn't served by the spotty material. Director Denis Heroux would go on to produce ATLANTIC CITY and QUEST FOR FIRE.

p, Claude Heroux, Rene Dupont; d, Denis Heroux; w, Michael Parry; ph, Harry Waxman, James Bawden; m, Wilfred Josephs.

**(PR:C MPAA:NR)**

## UNEARTHLY, THE*

(1957) 73m American Broadcast-Paramount Theatres/REP bw

John Carradine *(Prof. Charles Conway)*, Allison Hayes *(Grace Thomas)*, Myron Healey *(Mark Houston)*, Sally Todd *(Natalie)*, Marilyn Buferd *(Dr. Gilchrist)*, Arthur Batanides *(Danny Green)*, Tor Johnson *(Lobo)*, Harry Fleer *(Jedrow)*, Roy Gordon *(Dr. Loren Wright)*, Guy Prescott *(Capt. Rogers)*, Paul MacWilliams *(Police Officer)*.

A dull and slow-moving, but satisfyingly, camp madscientist-operates-on-humans picture, THE UNEARTHLY stars John Carradine as Prof. Charles Conway, a scientist driven to find the secret of eternal youth, who is assisted in his operations by a mutant named Lobo (Tor Johnson of PLAN 9 FROM OUTER SPACE). Grace Thomas (Allison Hayes) is a disturbed young woman who is sent to the professor's hideaway by an unscrupulous doctor. Undercover investigator Mark Houston (Myron Healey) fears Grace will be turned into another of the professor's failed experiments and doomed to live the life of a mutant in the laboratory's secret cellar. The pair fall in love and lumbering Lobo finally comes to their aid. Keeping to tradition, all the evil folks are killed off by the finish, but when the police finally arrive to search the premises, they uncover a cellar full of subhuman creatures. The film closes on one policeman's query: "What if they *do* live forever?"

p, Brooke L. Peters; d, Brooke L. Peters; w, Geoffrey Dennis, Jane Mann (based on a story by Mann); ph, Merle Connell; ed, Richard Currier.

**(PR:O MPAA:NR)**

## UNHOLY, THE*

(1988) 100m Limelite-Team Effort/Vestron c

Ben Cross *(Father Michael)*, Ned Beatty *(Lt. Stern)*, Jill Carroll *(Millie)*, William Russ *(Luke)*, Hal Holbrook *(Archbishop Mosley)*, Trevor Howard *(Father Silva)*, Peter Frechette *(Claude)*, Claudia Robinson *(Teresa Montez)*, Nicole Fortier *(Demon)*, Ruben Rabasa *(Father Dennis)*, Phil Becker *(Doctor)*, Susan Bearden *(Hotel Manager)*, Xavier Barquet *(Bell Boy)*, Larl White *(Housekeeper)*, Jeff D'Onofrio *(Paramedic)*, Martha Hester *(Young Nun)*, John Boyland *(Dr. Valerio)*, Norma Donaldson *(Abby)*, Earleen Carey *(Lucille)*, Anthony Deans, Jr. *(Manolo)*, Frank Barnes, Selma Jones, Willemina Riley, Steven Hadley, Anthony Deans *(Parishoners)*, Laura Plyscco *(Lorna)*, Joshua Sussman, David Sanderson *(Bodyguards)*, Alan Warhaftig *(Intern)*, Sandy Queen *(Nurse)*, Ellen Cody *(Old Woman)*.

A poor excuse for a horror film, THE UNHOLY again pits a Catholic priest against the forces of darkness, this time in a poor New Orleans parish. It seems that several years ago two priests were murdered while praying before the altar on Easter weekend. Although the crime was kept quiet by the church, an archbishop (Hal Holbrook) and a old blind priest (Trevor Howard) are convinced that young Fr. Michael (Ben Cross) is the one to fight whatever demons lurk in the killer parish. He follows the clues to a local nightclub which specializes in titillating simulations of Satanic rituals. Based on an old treatment by veteran screenwriter Phillip Yordan (JOHNNY GUITAR; KING OF KINGS; DAY OF THE TRIFFIDS), THE UNHOLY is a dreadfully boring effort that wastes the considerable talents of its betterthan-average (for a horror movie) cast. Cuban-born director Camilo Vila makes his Hollywood debut here, and it is less than impressive. Lots of fog, blue and red gels, and shadowy lighting pass for "mood" here; when that doesn't work, some jolting, bloody gore effects—a priest with his throat ripped out, an actor vomiting about 30 gallons of blood, a disemboweled man hanging upside down from a crucifix—are thrown in to wake up viewers. And yes, this film contains far more blasphemous imagery than Martin Scorsese's THE LAST TEMPTATION OF CHRIST, but zealous Christians didn't even notice, which is why it didn't make any money.

p, Mathew Hayden; d, Camilio Vila; w, Philip Yordan, Fernando Fonseca; ph, Henry Vargas (CFI Color); ed, Mark Melnick; m, Roger Bellon.

**(PR:O MPAA:R)**

## UNHOLY THREE, THE***

(1930) 75m MGM bw

Lon Chaney *(Prof. Echo)*, Lila Lee *(Rosie O'Grady)*, Elliott Nugent *(Hector McDonald)*, Harry Earles *(Midget)*, John Miljan *(Prosecuting Attorney)*, Ivan Linow *(Hercules)*, Clarence Burton *(Regan)*, Crauford Kent *(Defense Attorney)*.

For his first and only talking picture, Lon Chaney decided to return to the safety of one of his biggest grossing films, the 1925 Tod Browning-directed silent film THE UNHOLY THREE. The 1930 version tells essentially the same story: Chaney plays Professor Echo, a carnival ventriloquist who shares the stage with strongman Hercules (Ivan Linow) and a midget named Midget (Harry Earles, later to star in FREAKS) while the vampish Rosie (Lila Lee) picks the pockets of audience members. Eventually they are exposed and have to close down the carnival. Echo, however, comes up with a new idea. Disguised as a little old lady named Mrs. O'Grady, he opens a pet shop, with Hercules as "her" son-in-law, Rosie as the daughter, and Midget as their baby boy. Echo scams his wealthy clientele by selling them parrots that supposedly talk, though he is actually mimicking bird sounds and throwing his voice. When the customers later complain that their parrots can't talk, Echo visits their houses, checks out the valuables, and then robs them. This system eventually gets fouled up when Rosie falls in love with a pet shop clerk and Hercules and Midget commit a murder. After three years of refusing to appear in a talkie (saying, "I have a thousand faces, but only one voice"), Chaney finally gave in to audience and studio pressure with this film, in which the master of disguises would not be satisfied with talking only in his own voice and, to quiet his critics (who had begun rumors that Chaney was mute), spoke in five different voices—his own, the old woman's, a parrot's, a child's, and that of a ventriloquist's dummy. Although not as critically admired as the original (mainly because director Browning's visual style far surpassed that of Jack Conway), the 1930 THE UNHOLY THREE guaranteed Chaney a future in sound films. MGM quickly lined up for him THE SEA BAT; THE BUGLE SOUNDS; and CHERI BIBI, while Universal began negotiating for him to star in DRACULA. Fate, however, interfered and, seven weeks after the opening of THE UNHOLY THREE, Chaney succumbed, in perverse irony, to throat cancer.

d, Jack Conway; w, J.C. Nugent, Elliott Nugent (based on the story "The Terrible Three" by Clarence Aaron Robbins); ph, Percy Hilburn; ed, Frank Sullivan.

**(PR:A   MPAA:NR)**

## UNINVITED, THE zero

(1988) 89m Heritage c

George Kennedy *(Mike Harvey)*, Alex Cord *(Walter Graham)*, Clu Gulager *(Albert)*, Toni Hudson *(Rachel)*, Eric Larson *(Martin)*, Clare Carey *(Bobbie)*, Rob Estes *(Corey)*, Shari Shattuck *(Suzanne)*, Austin Stoker *(Carribean Officer)*, Greydon Clark *(Lab Doctor)*, Michael Holden *(Daryl Perkins)*, Cecile Callan *(Girl in Pizza Parlor)*, Jack Heller *(Concierge)*, Gina Schinasi *(Bartender)*, Ron Presson *(Man at Gas Station)*, Paul Martin *(Lab Assistant)*, Trevor Clark *(Boy on Beach)*, Beau Dremann.

A mutant cat that occasionally spits up a monster hand puppet from it's craw is the less-than-terrifying beastie in this straight-to-video release. Coeds Bobbie (Clare Carey) and Suzanne (Shari Shattuck) are on spring break in Florida, where they meet Walter Graham (Alex Cord), a well-known financier whose fingers are in some less-than-legal pies. With the authorities closing in on him, Graham plans to sail off and retire to some beach without an extradition agreement. The girls are invited along as cover, and they bring along three guys. George Kennedy and Clu Gulager also appear, rounding out the passengers and crew under skipper Rachel (Toni Hudson). The girls also bring along a stray cat, which escaped from a secret government lab in the first scene. The feline is infected with some sort of parasitic disease that allows the monster inside it to crawl out and kill with one bite or to infect the food supply. THE UNINVITED is a lousy film by any standards, but is made worse by the silliest monster since the moving rug in THE CREEPING TERROR. The thing is blatantly a hand puppet obtruding from an obviously stuffed cat, and the sight of once-respectable actors like Kennedy shrieking over this menace is too ridiculous for words. Horror veteran Gulager's bespectacled, besotted henchman is the only memorable human here—too bad he's the first to die.

p, Greydon Clark; d, Greydon Clark; w, Greydon Clark; ph, Nicholas von Sternberg; ed, Travis Clark; m, Dan Slider.

**(PR:O   MPAA:PG-13)**

## UNSANE***

(1982, It.) 91m Sigma c (SOTTO GLI OCCHI DELL'ASSASSINO; AKA: TENEBRAE)

Anthony Franciosa *(Peter Neal)*, John Saxon, Guiliano Gemma, Daria Nicolodi, Christian Borromeo, John Steiner, Veronica Laric, Lara Wendel, Ania Pieroni, Carola Stagnaro, Isabella Amadeo, Mirella Banti, Enio Girolami, Monica Maisani, Marino Mase, Fulvio Mingozzi, Gianpaolo Saccarola, Ippolita Santarelli, Francesca Viscardi.

Peter Neal (Tony Franciosa) a popular American writer of mystery novels, arrives in Rome to go on a tour promoting his latest novel, *Tenebrae*. Shortly after his arrival, a series of horrible murders occurs, patterned after the killings in his book. One victim is found with several pages of *Tenebrae* stuffed in her mouth. Although the police are baffled, Neal decides to launch his own investigation, with the aid of his agent (John Saxon) and his staff. After several virtually plotless, surrealistic splatter movies (SUSPIRIA; INFERNO), director Dario Argento made a return with UNSANE to the sort of suspense thriller—such as his seminal BIRD WITH THE CRYSTAL PLUMAGE—that made him famous. Although the mystery itself is nothing special, Argento uses the narrative structure as a jumping-off point for his virtuoso murder sequences, which are incredibly well orchestrated and inventive. In one scene a girl is attacked as she is putting a t-shirt on. The killer slashes at her with a razor blade just as the shirt is going over her head, and makes a hole in the shirt large enough for her to look at him in terror before being murdered. In the same scene, the camera moves from outside one victim's window, up the side of the building, into the window upstairs, and then prowls through the room searching for a new victim. Another great shot shows a detective standing in a room and looking for the killer. As the detective bends down, the killer—who was blocked from the camera's view by the detective—is shown to be standing directly behind him. Argento also introduces a mocking tone of black humor into the proceedings by having a female book critic verbally assault novelist Neal for his misogyny—a charge often leveled against Argento, since the vast majority of his victims are female. Once again, sources conflict as to the running time of this film and lengths of 110 minutes, 101 minutes, 100 minutes, and 91 minutes have been reported. This review was based on the videocassette release clocking in at 91 minutes, and it seemed to have suffered from some trimming by the censors.

p, Claudio Argento; d, Dario Argento; w, Dario Argento, George Kemp; ph, Luciano Tovoli.

(PR:O   MPAA:R)

## UNSEEN, THE**

(1981) 89m Triune/World Northal c

Barbara Bach *(Jennifer)*, Sydney Lassick *(Ernest Keller)*, Stephen Furst *(Junior)*, Lelia Goldoni *(Virginia Keller)*, Karen Lamm *(Karen)*, Doug Barr *(Tony)*, Lois Young *(Vicki)*.

A vile and perverse horror film that manages to be interesting and compelling nonetheless, THE UNSEEN follows Jennifer (Barbara Bach), a news reporter who travels with two female coworkers to Solveg, California, for a Danish festival. The festival is obviously a popular one, since the trio can't find lodging and are forced to stay overnight in an eerie mansion owned by TEXAS CHAIN SAW-type patriarch Ernest Keller (Sydney Lassick). Ernest and his sister, Virginia (Lelia Goldoni), harbor some taboo secrets— Ernest not only killed his father but also had an incestuous relationship with Virginia, resulting in a demented offspring named Junior (Stephen Furst) who remains "unseen" in the basement. Bach's character, poor as it is (as usual, she must have been hired for her exotic looks), is also negligible, included just to have a screaming woman that the audience is supposed to identify with. The film is tasteless and disturbing, but oddly compelling, in its concentration on the maliciousness of Ernest, who beats the moronic Junior zealously in the basement. Everybody in the film, with the exception of Jennifer, is sick and depraved—it's just a matter of degrees. One wonders, however, if any of this was intentional. Furst (of NATIONAL LAMPOON'S ANIMAL HOUSE) sports a fine makeup job in his role as Junior, while Goldoni (once known for her role in John Cassavetes' SHADOWS, but now better known to horror fans for THEATER OF DEATH and the remake of THE INVASION OF THE BODY SNATCHERS) does the bast she can in her role as the victimized sister.

p, Anthony Unger, Don Behrns; d, Peter Foleg; w, Michael

L. Grace; ph, Roberto Quezada, Irv Goodnoff, James Carter (Metrocolor); ed, Jonathan Braun; m, Michael J. Lewis.

(PR:O   MPAA:R)

## VAMP**

(1986) 93m NW c

Chris Makepeace *(Keith)*, Sandy Baron *(Vic)*, Robert Rusler *(A.J.)*, Dedee Pfeiffer *(Amaretto)*, Gedde Watanabe *(Duncan)*, Grace Jones *(Katrina)*, Billy Drago *(Snow)*, Brad Logan *(Vlad)*, Lisa Lyon *(Cimmaron)*, Jim Boyle *(Fraternity Leader)*, Larry Spinak, Eric Welch, Stuart Rogers *(Students)*, Gary Swailes *(Sock Salesman)*, Ray Ballard *(Coffee Shop Proprietor)*, Paunita Nichols *(Maven)*, Trudel Williams *(Dragon Girl)*, Marlon McGann *(Hard Hat)*, Thomas Bellin *(Shorty)*, Bryan McGuire *(Pool Player)*, Leila Hee Olsen *(Seko)*, Hilary Carlip *(Jett)*, Francine Swift *(Dominique)*, Tricia Brown *(Candi)*, Naomi Shohan, Janeen Davis *(Bartendresses)*, Ytossie Patterson, Tanya Papanicolas *(Waitresses)*, Robin Kaufman *(Little Girl)*, Hy Pike *(Desk Clerk)*, Pops *(Dead Man in Car)*, Bob Schott *(Gang Leader)*, Adam Barth, Bill Morphew *(Dragons)*, Simmy Bow *(Bum)*, Roger Hampton, Andy Rivas *(Police)*, Julius LeFlore *(Garbage Truck Driver)*, Greg Lewis *(Bus Driver)*, Dar Robinson *(Security Guard)*, Mitch Carter, Cathy Cavadini, Deborah Fallender, Greg Finley, David McCharen, Jan Rabson, Marilyn Schreffler, Dennis Tufano *(Voices)*.

Combining out-and-out horror with comedy is always a risky proposition. In most cases the horror becomes so gruesome that the film is no longer funny, or the humor so moronic that it diffuses the horror. VAMP suffers somewhat from the above symptoms, but it's basic problem is its sluggishness. The movie begins at the University of Southern California where best buddies Keith (Chris Makepeace) and A.J. (Robert Rusler) decide to pledge a fraternity, but being no-nonsense guys, they grow impatient with the frat's archaic and silly initiation rites. Stopping in the middle of a ridiculous ceremony, Keith and A.J. make the dim-witted frat boys an offer: they will do anything to make the frat's upcoming party the hit of the campus. Although Keith and A.J. are thinking of booze and munchies, the brothers demand a stripper. After visiting a nightclub and watching Katrina (Grace Jones) perform an incredibly erotic dance number, A.J. wanders backstage to hire the stripper for the party. Without saying a word, Katrina seduces the young man. Unfortunately for A.J., Katrina happens to be a 2,000-year-old Egyptian vampire in need of blood. With the exception of its clever premise (vampires working in a nightclub where their victims *come to them*) and the magnetic presence of international pop star Jones, VAMP has little new to offer. The humor is mostly of the sophomoric teen-sex-comedy variety, the violence (handled fairly well by special makeup artist Greg Cannom) is graphic and gruesome, and there is a fair amount of bumping and grinding.

p, Donald P. Borchers; d, Richard Wenk; w, Richard Wenk (based on a story by Donald P. Borchers, Richard Wenk); ph, Elliot Davis (Metrocolor); ed, Marc Grossman; m, Jonathan Elias.

(PR:O  MPAA:R)

## VAMPIRE BAT, THE***

(1933) 63m Majestic bw

Lionel Atwill (Dr. Otto von Niemann), Fay Wray (Ruth Bertin), Melvyn Douglas (Karl Brettschneider), Maude Eburne (Gussie Schnappmann), George E. Stone (Kringen), Dwight Frye (Herman Gleib), Robert Frazer (Emil Borst), Rita Carlisle (Martha Mueller), Lionel Belmore (Burgermeister Gustave Schoen), William V. Mong (Sauer), Stella Adams (Georgiana), Paul Weigel (Holdstadt), Harrison Greene (Weingarten), William Humphrey (Dr. Haupt), Fern Emmett (Gertrude), Carl Stockdale (Schmidt the Morgue Keeper).

Small independent Majestic Studios tried to capitalize on the horror boom of the earlier 1930s by creating this unusual hybrid film comprised of sets, props, and performers borrowed from Universal and Warner Bros. Lionel Atwill and Fay Wray make their third and last horror appearance together (after DR. X and THE MYSTERY OF THE WAX MUSEUM), with the former playing yet another mad scientist and the latter another terrified victim. The film opens with the small European village of Kleinschloss plagued by an epidemic of murder. Several villagers have been found dead in their beds, drained of all blood. Despite police inspector Brettschneider's (Melvyn Douglas) conviction that the killer is a common criminal, the villagers believe the murders to be the work of a vampire—their suspicions raised by the huge swarm of bats that has infested the village, and by village idiot Herman Gleib's (Dwight Frye) unusual affection for the creatures. An angry mob brings about the death of the supposed vampire, then a stake is driven through his heart to assure the village's safety, but the terror doesn't stop. Majestic Studios shot THE VAMPIRE BAT on Universal Studio's back lot—using the village set from FRANKENSTEIN, the house from THE OLD DARK HOUSE, and furnishings from the silent version of THE CAT AND THE CANARY—and, not surprisingly, the film has a familiar look to it. Moreover, the casting of Frye in a role almost identical to his "Renfield" in DRACULA and Lionel Belmore's reprise of his burgermeister role from FRANKENSTEIN makes the film look and sound even more like a Universal production. With Warner Bros' popular terror duo Atwill and Wray added to the brew, VAMPIRE BAT takes on a very strange feel indeed. It is as if two studios had collided and their productions became intertwined.

p, Phil Goldstone; d, Frank R. Strayer; w, Edward T. Lowe; ph, Ira Morgan; ed, Otis Garrett.

(PR:A  MPAA:NR)

## VAMPIRE LOVERS, THE**½

(1970, Brit.) 91m Hammer/AIP c

Ingrid Pitt (Carmilla/Mircalla/Marcilla Karnstein), Pippa Steele (Laura Spielsdorf), Madeleine Smith (Emma Morton), Peter Cushing (Gen. Spielsdorf), George Cole (Roger Morton), Dawn Addams (The Countess), Kate O'Mara (Mme. Perrodot), Douglas Wilmer (Baron Hartog), Jon Finch (Carl Ebbhardt), Kirsten Betts (1st Vampire), Harvey Hall (Renton), Janet Key (Gretchen), Charles Farrell (Kurt, the Landlord), Ferdy Mayne (Doctor), John Forbes Robertson (Man in Black), Shelagh Wilcox (Housekeeper), Graham James, Tom Browne (Young Men), Joanna Shelley (Woodman's Daughter), Olga James (Village Girl).

THE VAMPIRE LOVERS is the first entry in Hammer's "Karnstein" series, which was based on characters and incidents from Sheridan Le Fanu's Carmilla. The lovely Ingrid Pitt stars as Mircalla Karnstein, a sexy vampire who arrives at a remote Eastern European town to exact revenge upon the townsfolk, who killed off her family of vampires several years before. Mircalla seduces her way into the household of the respectable Gen. Spielsdorf (Peter Cushing) and his beautiful daughter, Laura (Pippa Steele). Soon afterwards, Mircalla manages to bed Laura and slowly drains her blood after numerous lesbian encounters. Having killed off the daughter of one upstanding villager, Mircalla next moves on to seduce Emma Morton (Madeleine Smith), the young best friend of the now-deceased Laura. Once again Mircalla begins to slowly suck the life out of a young woman during sex, and, after Mircalla kills the girl's doctor, her father enlists the aid of famed vampire killer Baron Hartog (Douglas Wilmer) to investigate. Together with Gen. Spielsdorf, the Baron seeks out Mircalla and destroys her. At the time of this film's making, Hammer was looking for a way to revitalize their horror series, and hit upon a combination of soft-core sex with lesbian overtones and violence even more graphic than in their previous films. While THE VAMPIRE LOVERS is an interesting and entertaining entry, containing excellent performances from both Pitt and Cushing, writers Harry Fine and Michael Style and director Roy Ward Baker seem to shy away from actually addressing the questions of sexuality and repression inherent in the material. Hammer exploits instead of explores. Nevertheless, the film was a hit and was quickly followed by LUST FOR A VAMPIRE (1970) and TWINS OF EVIL (1971).

p, Harry Fine, Michael Style; d, Roy Ward Baker; w, Tudor Gates, Harry Fine, Michael Style (based on the story "Carmilla" by J. Sheridan Le Fanu); ph, Moray Grant (Technicolor); ed, James Needs; m, Harry Robinson.

(PR:O  MPAA:R)

## VAMPYR*****

(1932, Fr./Ger.) 83m Dreyer-Tobis-Klangfilm bw (VAMPYR, OU L'ETRANG E AVENTURE DE DAVID GRAY; VAMPYR, DER TRAUM DES DAVID GRAY; AKA: CASTLE OF DOOM; VAMPIRE, THE; STRANGE ADVENTURE OF DAVID GRAY, THE; NOT AGAINST THE FLESH)

Baron Nicolas de Gunzberg *(David Gray),* Henriette Gerard *(Marguerite Chopin),* Jan Hieronimko *(Doctor),* Maurice Schutz *(Lord of the Manor),* Rena Mandel *(His Daughter Gisele),* Sibylle Schmitz *(His Daughter Leone),* Albert Bras *(Servant),* N. Babanini *(The Girl).*

Much to the dismay of his admirers, Danish director Carl Theodor Dreyer followed his silent classic THE PASSION OF JOAN OF ARC (1927) with this horror film, his first foray into sound. The result was a masterpiece of subtle terror, the stuff of true nightmares. Loosely based on *In a Glass Darkly,* a collection of stories by Joseph Sheridan Le Fanu, the film begins as a young man (Julian West) arrives in a dark, mysterious European village and takes a room that has been booked for him at the inn. That night he is visited by a strange old man (Maurice Schutz), who gives him a package to be opened upon the old man's death, then disappears. The visitor wanders the village, following a disembodied shadow of a one-legged man to a house where more shadows dance insanely to odd music. After observing other various strange goings-on, the young man opens his package, which turns out to be a copy of *Strange Tales of Vampires.* As the story proceeds, it becomes apparent that the town is at the mercy of just such a creature. In VAMPYR, Dreyer conveys a deep sense of terror by suggesting evil, not showing it. There is no gore, but the film leaves a much more effective sense of unease and dread, moving slowly and with little cinematic trickery or fanfare through its bizarre world where shadows leave bodies and things are not as they seem. The director's use of sound is brilliant: phrases are purposely muffled and half-heard from off-screen, giving the impression that something is going on that we can't quite comprehend. As in all of Dreyer's works, viewers must decelerate their normal narrative expectations and allow the film to wash over them; VAMPYR is a sensual film of mood and emotion rather than plot and thrills. Accordingly, the film did poorly at the box office worldwide. US distributors tried to cut footage from the film to pick up the pace, retitling it CASTLE OF DOOM and presenting it to audiences accustomed to the more visceral thrills of Universal's DRACULA and FRANKENSTEIN, but it failed miserably. Nonetheless, VAMPYR is one of the true classics of the horror genre, unparalleled in its subtle evocation of bone-chilling terror. No description can do justice to this example of filmmaking at its most evocative; it simply must be seen and savored. (In Danish; English subtitles.)

p, Baron Nicolas de Gunzberg, Carl Theodor Dreyer; d, Carl Theodor Dreyer; w, Carl Theodor Dreyer, Christen Jul (based on stories from *In a Glass Darkly* by Joseph Sheridan Le Fanu); ph, Rudolph Mate, Louis Nee; m, Wolfgang Zeller.

**(PR:A   MPAA:NR)**

## VAMPYRES, DAUGHTERS OF DRACULA**½

(1975, Brit.) 87m Cambist c (AKA: VAMPYRES)

Marianne Morris *(Fran),* Anulka *(Miriam),* Murray Brown *(Ted),* Brian Deacon *(John),* Sally Faulkner *(Harriett),* Michael Byrne *(Playboy),* Karl Lanchbury *(Rupert),* Bessie Love, Elliott Sullivan *(Elderly Couple).*

Following Hammer's THE VAMPIRE LOVERS (1970), the horror market was virtually flooded with erotic vampire movies featuring sexy female bloodsuckers. One of the better efforts among these, VAMPYRES, DAUGHTERS OF DRACULA features a pair of bisexual female vampires, Fran (Marianne Morris) and Miriam (Anulka, *Playboy*'s May 1973 centerfold), based in a decrepit mansion. Sleeping in their double coffin by day, they roam the area by night, seducing men and women into their lair with promises of untold carnal delights. However, one of their victims, Ted (Murray Brown), falls in love with Fran and agrees to stay with her, despite the fact that he knows she is a vampire who will eventually drain him of all his blood. A surprisingly effective combination of the genuinely erotic and horribly violent, this film is one of the few vampire movies that actually manages to convey powerfully the seductions of vampirism. Unfortunately, the movie is marred somewhat by its low budget and a rather mundane conclusion. Available on home video under the title VAMPYRES.

p, Brian Smedley-Aston; d, Joseph Larraz; w, D. Daubeney; ph, Harry Waxman; ed, Geoff R. Brown; m, James Clark.

**(PR:O   MPAA:R)**

## VAULT OF HORROR, THE**½

(1973, Brit.) 93m Metromedia-Amicus/Cinerama c (AKA: TALES FROM THE CRYPT II)

Daniel Massey *(Rogers),* Anna Massey *(Donna),* Mike Pratt *(Clive),* Edward Judd *(Alex),* Robin Nedwell *(Tom),* Geoffrey Davies *(Jerry),* Arthur Mullard *(Gravedigger),* Curt Jergens *(Sebastian),* Dawn Addams *(Inez),* Jasmina Hilton *(Indian Girl),* Terry-Thomas *(Critchit),* Glynis Johns *(Eleanor),* Marianne Stone *(Jane),* John Forbes-Robertson *(Wilson),* Tom Baker *(Moore),* Denholm Elliott *(Diltant).*

THE VAULT OF HORROR is another so-so film adaptation of the marvelous E.C. horror comics from the 1950s in which five tales (none of them taken from the "Vault of Horror" comics, but from the sister publication, "Tales from the Crypt") of the macabre are presented. The first stars Daniel Massey (son of Raymond) as Rogers, who goes to visit his sister in a spooky small town. His sister, Donna (Anna Massey, Daniel's real-life sister), turns out to be a vampire and soon Rogers finds himself strung up by his heels with a tap on his neck while vampires fill wine glasses with his blood. Another story stars Terry-Thomas as a compulsively neat man who drives his wife (Glynis Johns) insane with his obsession. She eventually kills him with an axe and neatly stores his dismembered body parts in little jars. In a third tale, Sebastian (Curt Jurgens) steals a rope trick from India that eventually spells doom. A fourth story (which contains several E.C. comics in-jokes) follows

Maitland (Michael Craig), who embarks upon an insurance scam by faking his death from an overdose of drugs, only to be disinterred later by his partner (Edward Judd). The last segment stars the most popular TV "Dr. Who," Tom Baker, as an insane artist who uses voodoo to mutilate part of a portrait, the subject of which duly becomes mutilated in turn. The sequel to TALES FROM THE CRYPT (1972), THE VAULT OF HORROR suffers from the same problems as its predecessor and is still no substitute for the comics themselves, which were filled with a lively sense of the macabre, heavy doses of black humor, and impressive illustrations.

p, Max J. Rosenberg, Milton Subotsky; d, Roy Ward Baker; w, Milton Subotsky (based on episodes from William Gaines' *E.C. Comics* by Al Feldstein, Gaines); ph, Denys Coop (Eastmancolor); ed, Oswald Hafenrichter; m, Douglas Gamley.

**(PR:C-O   MPAA:PG)**

## VELVET VAMPIRE, THE**½

(1971) 82m NW c (AKA: THROUGH THE LOOKING GLASS; CEMETERY GIRLS)

Michael Blodgett *(Lee Ritter),* Sherry Miles *(Susan Ritter),* Celeste Yarnall *(Diane),* Jerry Daniels *(Juan),* Gene Shane *(Carl),* Paul Prokop *(Cliff),* Sandy Ward *(Amos),* Chris Woodley *(Mechanic's Girl),* Bob Thessier *(Motorcycle Rapist).*

This is a disappointing horror film from director Stephanie Rothman, whose TERMINAL ISLAND (1973) is one of the more interesting exploitation items from the 1970s. In THE VELVET VAMPIRE, newlyweds Lee (Michael Blodgett) and Susan (Sherry Miles) meet the mysterious and sexy Diane (Celeste Yarnall) at a Los Angeles art gallery and agree to spend the weekend at her expensive home in the Mojave Desert. As it happens, Diane is a vampire and she wastes no time in seducing the eager Lee. Later, when Lee discovers the corpse of Diane's loyal servant drained of its blood, he decides to take his wife and leave, but Susan, too, has developed an attraction to Diane and refuses to depart. She soon snaps back to reality, however, when she stumbles across the bloodless corpse of her husband. Attempting to flee, Susan is followed back to LA by a vengeful Diane, who is able to survive in sunlight because of her wide-brimmed hat and sunglasses. Although the script is fairly interesting and Rothman's direction is frequently inventive and effective—especially the bizarre dream sequences set in the desert—the film is crippled by the truly awful performance of Miles, who literally whines her way through the entire movie. This is not to say that Blodgett or Yarnall are much better, for they too contribute boring and listless performances that fail to convey the erotic pull needed to make the story convincing. With its bright, arid desert setting and a vampire who can survive in sunlight, THE VELVET VAMPIRE is an interesting, but flawed, precursor to the excellent NEAR DARK (1987), which was also directed by a woman.

p, Charles S. Swartz; d, Stephanie Rothman; w, Maurice Jules, Charles S. Swartz, Stephanie Rothman; ph, Daniel Lacambre (Metrocolor); ed, Stephen Judson; m, Clancy B. Grass III, Roger Dollarhide.

**(PR:O   MPAA:R)**

## VIDEODROME****

(1983, Can.) 88m Filmplan International/UNIV c

James Woods *(Max Renn),* Sonja Smits *(Bianca O'Blivion),* Deborah Harry *(Nicki Brand),* Peter Dvorsky *(Harlan),* Les Carlson *(Barry Convex),* Jack Creley *(Prof. Brian O'Blivion),* Lynne Gorman *(Masha),* Julie Khaner *(Briley),* Rainer Schwartz *(Moses),* David Bolt *(Rafe),* Lally Cadeau *(Rena King),* Sam Malkin *(Bum),* Bob Church *(Newscaster),* Jayne Eastwood *(Caller),* Franciszka Hedland *(Bellydancer),* Harvey Chao, David Tsubouchi *(Salesmen),* Henry Gomez *(Brolley),* Kay Hawtrey *(Matron).*

Director David Cronenberg's most visionary and audacious film up to the time of its making, VIDEODROME is a fascinating rumination on humanity, technology, entertainment, sex, and politics that is virtually incomprehensible on the first viewing and needs to be seen several times before one can even begin to unlock its mysteries. James Woods, in one of the greatest performances of his career, stars as Max Renn, an ambitious cable TV programmer who, in his off hours, is a closet voyeur of sex and violence. Looking for something new, something "sensational" for his cable station, Renn stumbles across a show called "Videodrome" while pirating signals from satellite dishes. The show seems to depict the actual torture and murder of a different victim every night. Fascinated (and excited) by the program, Renn tries to find out where the show originates. During the investigation, he becomes deeply embroiled in a bizarre, intriguing, and sometimes utterly confusing fusion of television, politics, and mind-control that seems to herald some sort of "New Order" for society. VIDEODROME very well may be the most incomprehensible mainstream film ever made. As Cronenberg veers his narrative between hallucination and reality and back again—the line between them more blurred each time—he unleashes his bizarre visual imagination and we are bombarded with such delights as an open stomach cavity that becomes a repository for videocassettes and guns, throbbing television sets, a literal hand-gun, and humans who crack open and spew forth all manner of flesh, blood, and multicolored goo. While these images are undeniably powerful (the throbbing, *living* TV set is amazing) and the film is compulsively watchable, it does tend to become wholly impenetrable toward the end and may leave the uninitiated frustrated or even angry. Nevertheless, this is a remarkable film that will continue to be debated and analyzed for decades to come.

p, Claude Heroux; d, David Cronenberg; w, David Cronenberg; ph, Mark Irwin; ed, Ronald Sanders; m, Howard Shore.

**(PR:O   MPAA:R)**

## VIRGIN WITCH, THE**

(1970, Brit.) 87m Univista/Joseph Brenner c (AKA: LESBIAN TWINS)

Anne Michelle *(Christine)*, Patricia Haines *(Sybil Waite)*, Vicki Michelle *(Betty)*, Keith Buckley *(John)*, James Chase *(Peter)*, Neal Hallett *(Gerald Amberley)*, Helen Downing *(Abby Drake)*, Paula Wright *(Mrs. Wendell)*.

Another mix of virgins, lesbians, and witchcraft, THE VIRGIN WITCH concerns Christine and Betty (sisters Anne and Vicki Michelle), two attractive siblings who travel from the countryside to London in the hope of becoming models. They visit an agency and are introduced to Sybil (Patricia Haines), who tricks them into becoming members of a religious sect run by her husband, Gerald (Neil Hallett), a doctor who deflowers the pretty virgins and plans to use them as good witches. Christine, however, has other ideas, and becomes seduced by the evils of black magic. THE VIRGIN WITCH is not very good, but it is relatively watchable thanks to some atmospheric touches and Anne Michelle's mildly erotic presence.

p, Ralph Solomons, Dennis Durack, Edward Brady; d, Ray Austin; w, Klaus Vogel (based on the novel by Vogel); ph, Gerald Moss (Eastmancolor); ed, Philip Barknel; m, Ted Dicks.

(PR:O MPAA:R)

## VISITING HOURS*

(1982, Can.) 105m Filmplan International/FOX c (AKA: FRIGHT, THE; GET WELL SOON)

Michael Ironside *(Colt Hawker)*, Lee Grant *(Deborah Ballin)*, Linda Purl *(Sheila Munroe)*, William Shatner *(Gary Baylor)*, Lenore Zann *(Lisa)*, Harvey Atkin *(Vinnie Bradshaw)*, Helen Hughes *(Louise Shepherd)*, Michael J. Reynolds *(Porter Halstrom)*, Kirsten Bishopric *(Denise)*, Debra Kirschenbaum *(Connie Wexler)*, Elizabeth Leigh Milne *(Patricia Ellis)*, Maureen McRae *(Elizabeth Hawker)*, Dustin Waln *(Hawker)*, Neil Affleck *(Officer)*, Damir Andrei *(Paramedic)*, Dorothy Barker *(Sally)*, Steve Bettcher *(Anesthetist)*.

This tasteless, mindless slasher movie is made more so by its stupid borrowings from better pictures like PEEPING TOM and PSYCHO. Crusading feminist journalist Deborah Ballin (Lee Grant) is attacked and raped by Colt Hawker (Michael Ironside), a misogynistic creep who blames his hatred of women on a lousy childhood. Deborah survives the attack and is hospitalized, but Colt—who likes to photograph his victims in their death throes—continues his reign of terror at the hospital, cleverly evading the security system and killing others while he tries to get to Deborah. While Ironside (SCANNERS) contributes a memorably depraved performance, VISITING HOURS is a fairly repugnant film that seems to share its killer's attitude toward women. Director Jean Claude Lord does manage to build some effective suspense sequences, but overall his direction is hyperactive—as is the annoyingly insistent musical score by Jonathan Goldsmith.

p, Claude Heroux; d, Jean Claude Lord; w, Brian Taggert;

ph, Rene Verzier; ed, Claude Lord, Lise Thouin; m, Jonathan Goldsmith.

(PR:O MPAA:R)

## VISITOR, THE*

(1980, It./US) 90m International Picture Show-Marvin c (IL VISITATORE)

Mel Ferrer *(Dr. Walkor)*, Glenn Ford *(Detective)*, Lance Henriksen *(Raymond)*, John Huston *(Jersey Colsowitz)*, Paige Conner *(Katie Collins)*, Joanne Nail *(Barbara Collins)*, Shelley Winters *(Jane Phillips)*, Sam Peckinpah *(Sam)*, J. Townsend, Jack Dorsey, Johnny Popwell, Steve Somers, Wallace Williamson, Lew Walker, Walter Gordon, Sr., Calvin Fenbry, Betty Turner, Steve Cunningham, Neal Bortz, Bill Ash, Charley Hardnett, Jack H. Gordon, Steve Belzer, Hsio Ho Chao.

More junk from Ovidio Assonitis (PIRANHA II: THE SPAWNING; TENTACLES), THE VISITOR boasts a bizarre all-star cast of actors just going through the motions. Basically an OMEN rip-off, the plot concerns a wealthy Atlanta sports magnate (Mel Ferrer) who is involved with an international satanic cult. As it happens, his eight-year-old daughter (Paige Conner) is the Antichrist. Glenn Ford plays the hapless detective who gets too nosy and has his eyes pecked out by birds. While most of the film is patently absurd, the ending really goes over the top. Although his name was displayed prominently in the cast list, have good luck spotting Sam Peckinpah (director of THE WILD BUNCH and STRAW DOGS) as an abortionist seen only from the back.

p, Ovidio Assonitis; d, Giulio Paradisi; w, Lou Comici, Robert Mundi (based on a story by Paradisi, Assonitis); ph, Ennio Guarnieri; ed, Robert Curi; m, Franco Micalizzi.

(PR:O MPAA:R)

# W

## WACKO*

(1983) 84m Jensen Farley c

Joe Don Baker *(Harbinger)*, Stella Stevens *(Marg Graves)*, George Kennedy *(Dr. Graves)*, Julia Duffy *(Mary Graves)*, Scott McGinnis *(Norman)*, Andrew Clay *(Tony)*, Elizabeth Daily *(Bambi)*, Michele Tobin *(Rosie)*, Anthony James *(Zeke)*, David Drucker *(Looney)*, Sonny Davis *(Weirdo)*, Victor Brandt *(Dr. Moreau)*, Jeff Altman *(Harry)*, Charles Napier *(Patrick)*, Wil Albert *(Dr. Denton)*, Michael Lee Gogin *(Damien)*.

Everything conceivable was thrown into this spoof of teenage slasher horror films, in which a small town is held in the grip of the notorious "Lawnmower Killer," who murdered a girl 13 years before. Although nobody will believe him, local cop Dick Harbinger (Joe Don Baker) is convinced that the killer will strike again. Marg Graves (Julia

Duffy), the sister of the murdered girl, is plagued by nightmares involving lawnmowers, which puts a damper on her preparations for Hitchcock High School's annual Halloween Pumpkin Dance. With such obvious gags as naming the high school football team the Hitchcock Birds and their rivals the De Palma Knives, or naming the science teacher Dr. Moreau, or visually quoting everything from PSYCHO to ALIENS, WACKO is merely dumb and not very funny. Director Greydon Clark (SATAN'S CHEERLEADERS) is better at making inadvertent parodies than attempting the real thing.

p, Greydon Clark; d, Greydon Clark; w, Dana Olsen, Michael Spound, M. James Kauf, Jr., David Greenwalt; ph, Nicholas von Sternberg; ed, Earl Watson, Curtis Burch; m, Arthur Kempel.

(PR:C   MPAA:PG)

## WARNING SIGN**

(1985) 100m FOX c

Sam Waterston *(Cal Morse)*, Kathleen Quinlan *(Joanie Morse)*, Yaphet Kotto *(Maj. Connolly)*, Jeffrey De Munn *(Dan Fairchild)*, Richard Dysart *(Dr. Nielsen)*, G.W. Bailey *(Tom Schmidt)*, Jerry Hardin *(Vic Flint)*, Rick Rossovich *(Bob)*, Cynthia Carle *(Dana)*, Scott Paulin *(Capt. Walston)*, Kavi Raz *(Dr. Ramesh Kapoor)*, Keith Szarabajka *(Tippett)*, Jack Thibeau *(Pisarczyk)*, J. Patrick McNamara *(Connolly's Aide)*, Tom McFadden *(Deputy Grazio)*, Lori Hallier *(TV Reporter)*, Jeannie Epper *(Woman on Video Screen)*, Gilbert Smith *(Man on Schmidt's Team)*, Nancie Kawata *(Woman in Cafeteria)*, James B. Dirker *(Helicopter Pilot)*.

An uneasy mix of social criticism, conspiracy paranoia, and horror, WARNING SIGN is interesting at times, but eventually collapses because it can't decide which aspect to concentrate on. Set in a small Utah town, the film's action surrounds the BioTek Agronomics company where many of the members of the community work. Joanie Morse (Kathleen Quinlan) is employed as a security guard; her husband, Cal (Sam Waterston), is the local sheriff. While most citizens and employees believe that the company is trying to develop a strain of corn that will grow in salt water, the powers that be are actually performing some dangerous gene splicing in an effort to create a bacterium to be used in germ warfare. Of course, there is an accident at the plant, and the bacterium turns much of the population into slobbering zombies. Quinlan takes top honors in the acting department as the scared-but-tough security guard, with Richard Dysart adroitly handling his second zombie-like role in a year's time (he was also in RETURN OF THE LIVING DEAD).

p, Jim Bloom; d, Hal Barwood; w, Hal Barwood, Matthew Robbins; ph, Dean Cundey (Panavision, DeLuxe Color); ed, Robert Lawrence; m, Craig Safan.

(PR:O   MPAA:R)

## WATCHER IN THE WOODS, THE*½

(1980, Brit.) 100m Disney/BV c

Bette Davis *(Mrs. Aylwood)*, Carroll Baker *(Helen Curtis)*, David McCallum *(Paul Curtis)*, Lynn-Holly Johnson *(Jan Curtis)*, Kyle Richards *(Ellie Curtis)*, Ian Bannen *(John Keller)*, Richard Pasco *(Tom Colley)*, Frances Cuka *(Mary Fleming)*, Benedict Taylor *(Mike Fleming)*, Eleanor Summerfield *(Mrs. Thayer)*, Georgina Hale *(Young Mrs. Aylwood)*, Katherine Levy *(Karen Aylwood)*.

A disappointing attempt by the Disney Studios to remain a filmmaking force, this tepid ghost story fails to focus on either its story or its target audience. The Curtis family—mom Helen (Carroll Baker), dad Paul (David McCallum), and kids Jan (Lynn-Holly Johnson) and Ellie (Kyle Richards)—arrives from America and rents an English country home from the aging Mrs. Aylwood (Bette Davis). The place is surrounded by dark, encroaching woods, and there are indications from the start that this is no ordinary glen teeming with cute little Disney squirrels. Jan, however, isn't intimidated by the woods, but strange incidents begin occurring when she becomes possessed by the spirit of Mrs. Aylwood's long-dead daughter. A bland attempt at a horror story, THE WATCHER IN THE WOODS never gets the directorial spark needed to enliven it. Although some effort is made to create a creepy atmosphere, the filmmakers fail at one of horror's most basic formats—the haunted house story. Director John Hough already had experience in this sub-genre with LEGEND OF HELL HOUSE, but he is found wanting here, and comedy director Vincent McEveety (THE MILLION DOLLAR DUCK; HERBIE GOES BANANAS) was brought in to redo the film's still unsatisfying ending.

p, Ron Miller; d, John Hough, Vincent McEveety (uncredited); w, Brian Clemens, Harry Spalding, Rosemary Anne Sisson (based on the novel by Florence Engel Randall); ph, Alan Hume (Technicolor); ed, Geoffrey Foot; m, Stanley Myers.

(PR:C   MPAA:PG)

## WEREWOLF OF WASHINGTON*

(1973) 90m Millco/Diplomat c (AKA: WEREWOLF AT MIDNIGHT)

Dean Stockwell *(Jack Whittier)*, Biff McGuire *(The President)*, Clifton James *(Attorney General)*, Beeson Carroll *(Comdr. Salmon)*, Jane House *(Marion)*, Michael Dunn *(Dr. Kiss)*, Barbara Siegel *(Girl Hippie)*, Stephen Cheng *(Chinese Foreign Minister)*, Nancy Andrews *(Mrs. Captree)*, Ben Yaffe *(Judge Captree)*, Jacqueline Brooks *(Publisher)*, Thurman Scott *(Boy Hippie)*, Tom Scott *(Reporter)*, Dennis McMullen *(Astronaut)*, Jack Waltzer *(Appointments Secretary)*, Randy Phillips *(Federal Agent)*, Glenn Kezer *(Admiral)*.

The laughs are few and far between in this horror spoof-political satire about White House press secretary Jack Whittier (Dean Stockwell), who is bitten by a werewolf and then turns into one himself. Eventually, after gobbling up various politicians on Capitol Hill and attacking a Chinese foreign minister, the hairy, fanged Jack goes after the president. It's such a bizarre idea that one really wants it to be funny, but the promise is never fulfilled and the picture ultimately disappoints. Perhaps the filmmakers chose the wrong monster—politicians seem more likely to become vampires or square-headed Frankenstein monsters.

p, Nina Schulman; d, Milton Moses Ginsberg; w, Milton Moses Ginsberg; ph, Bob Baldwin; m, Arnold Freed ; ed, Milton Moses Ginsberg.

(PR:C  MPAA:PG)

## WEREWOLF VS. THE VAMPIRE WOMEN, THE*½

(1970, Sp./Ger.) 86m Hifi Stereo 70-Plata c (LA NOCHE DE WALPURGIS; NACHT DER VAMPIRE; AKA: WEREWOLF'S SHADOW, THE; BLACK HARVEST OF COUNTESS DRACULA, THE; GB: SHADOW OF THE WEREWOLF)

Paul Naschy [Jacinto Molina] (Waldemar Daninsky/Werewolf), Gaby Fuchs (Elvire), Barbara Capell (Genevieve), Paty Shepard (Wandesa Darvula de Nadasdy), Yelena Samarina, Julio Pena, Andrew Reese [Andres Resino], Jose Marco, Barta Barri.

Former weight-lifting champion Paul Naschy [Jacinto Molina] became the horror movie king of Spain playing Count Waldemar Daninsky, a sympathetic werewolf who can only be killed by someone he loves. Naschy made his debut as the character in LA MARCA DEL HOMBRE LOBO (known in the US as FRANKENSTEIN'S BLOODY TERROR), and continued in LOS NOCHES DEL HOMBRE LOBO and EL HOMBRE QUE VINO DE UMMO. THE WEREWOLF VS. THE VAMPIRE WOMAN is the fourth entry in the series in which Daninsky, having been dispatched by a silver bullet in his previous outing, is inadvertently revived by a doctor who removes the bullet during an autopsy. The werewolf kills his captors and then travels back to his castle where he joins up with two female students searching for the tomb of the legendary vampire woman, Countess Waldessa (Paty Shepard), a Countess Bathory type rumored to have bathed in the blood of virgins. When one of the women accidentally cuts herself and the blood falls on Waldessa's face, the vampire is revived. She quickly vampirizes one and kidnaps the other, leaving Daninsky to rescue her. Although it was a huge hit in Spain—it was that country's eighth-highest grossing film in 1970—the film simply isn't very good, for the script (co-authored by Naschy) is predictable and the direction by Leon Klimovsky is grating, mainly due to his overuse of the zoom lens. By this time Naschy was quite a power in Spain's horror cinema and he would soon begin directing as well as writing and acting.

p, Salvadore Romero; d, Leon Klimovsky; w, Jacinto Molina, Hans Munkol; ph, Leopoldo Villasenor (Eastmancolor); ed, Antonio Jimeno; m, A. Garcia Abril.

(PR:O  MPAA:R)

## WEREWOLVES ON WHEELS*

(1971) 85m Fanfare c

Stephen Oliver (Adam), Severn Darden (One), D.J. Ander-

son (Helen), Duece Barry (Tarot), Billy Gray (Bill), Gray Johnson (Movie), Barry McGuire (Scarf), Owen Orr (Mouse), Anna Lynn Brown (Shirley), Leonard Rogel (Gas Station Operator), Dan Kopp, Ingrid Grunewald, Tex Hall, Keith Guthrie.

In this biker movie, the leather-clad motorcyclists turn into werewolves, thanks to a spell cast by a satanist high priest (Severn Darden). Adam (Stephen Oliver) is the leader of a gang called The Devil's Advocates. His girl (D.J. Anderson) receives an offer from a cult to offer herself to the Devil. She dances naked with a snake and before long is chomping on lover boy Adam, turning him into a werewolf, too, and the only one who can put an end to the mayhem is Tarot (Duece Barry), a biker with a background in the supernatural. Lots of sex, violence, and wide-open desert highways. The cast includes Barry McGuire, whose hit, "Eve of Destruction," topped the charts in the mid-1960s with its antiwar message.

p, Paul Lewis; d, Michel Levesque; w, Michel Levesque, David M. Kaufman; ph, Isidore Mankofsky (DeLuxe Color); ed, Peter Parasheles; m, Don Gere.

(PR:O  MPAA:R)

## WHATEVER HAPPENED TO BABY JANE?****

(1962) 132m Aldrich Associates/Seven Arts/WB bw

Bette Davis (Jane Hudson), Joan Crawford (Blanche Hudson), Victor Buono (Edwin Flagg), Anna Lee (Mrs. Bates), Maidie Norman (Elvira Stitt), Marjorie Bennett (Mrs. Della Flagg), Dave Willock (Ray Hudson), Anne Barton (Cora Hudson), Barbara D. Merrill (Liza Bates), Julie Allred (Young Jane), Gina Gillespie (Blanche as a Child), Bert Freed (Producer), Wesley Addy (Director), Debbie Burton (Singing Voice), William Aldrich, Ernest Anderson, Don Ross, Russ Conway, James Seay, Maxine Cooper.

Bringing Bette Davis and Joan Crawford together for the first time on-screen, this superb gothic horror film revitalized the careers of both. The Hudson sisters—Jane (Davis) and Blanche (Joan)—are aging actresses who live in a rotting Los Angeles mansion. Jane, the younger sister, had been a big child star known as "Baby Jane," but as she grew older her career faded; Blanche lived in Jane's shadow as a girl but had an enormously successful career as an adult. At the peak of her stardom, however, Blanche suffered a career-ending accident for which Jane was seemingly responsible. Ever since then the two have lived together in mutual enmity, tended to by their maid, Elvira (Maidie Norman). When Jane learns that her wheelchair-bound sister is planning to sell the mansion and put her in a sanitarium, she begins terrorizing Blanche, feeding her dead rats and birds, eventually confining her to her room. Meanwhile, Jane enlists the service of Edwin Flagg (Victor Buono), a young pianist who she hopes will help her make a comeback. The film then nicely builds suspense on its way to a conclusion that puts a new spin on the relationship between the two sisters. As in the best Alfred Hitchcock movies, suspense, rather than actual blood and gore, is the key to success here. Davis, as usual, plays her role broadly and proves a dynamic counterpoint to Crawford's understated portrayal. Two such mannered performers in one film might have made for a scenery-chewing contest but Robert Aldrich exercises a strong directorial hand.

p, Robert Aldrich; d, Robert Aldrich; w, Lukas Heller (based on the novel by Henry Farrell); ph, Ernest Haller; ed, Michael Luciano; m, Frank DeVol.

(PR:C  MPAA:NR)

## WHEN A STRANGER CALLS***

(1979) 97m COL c

Carol Kane *(Jill Johnson)*, Rutanya Alda *(Mrs. Mandrakis)*, Carmen Argenziano *(Dr. Mandrakis)*, Kirsten Larkin *(Nancy)*, Charles Durning *(John Clifford)*, Bill Boyett *(Sgt. Sacker)*, Ron O'Neal *(Lt. Charlie Garber)*, Heetu *(Houseboy)*, Rachel Roberts *(Dr. Monk)*, Tony Beckley *(Curt Duncan)*, Colleen Dewhurst *(Tracy)*, Michael Champion *(Bill)*, Joe Reale *(Bartender)*, Ed Wright *(Retired Man)*, Louise Wright *(Retired Woman)*, Carol O'Neal *(Mrs. Garber)*, Dennis McMullen *(Maintenance Man)*, Wally Taylor *(Cheater)*, John Tobyansen *(Bar Customer)*, Sarah Dammann *(Bianca Lockart)*, Richard Bail *(Stevie Lockart)*, Steven Anderson *(Stephen Lockart)*, Lenora May *(Sharon)*, Randy Holland *(Maitre d')*.

Unbearably scary in spots, WHEN A STRANGER CALLS begins with a sequence that will test anyone's fright threshold. A baby-sitter, Jill (Carol Kane), gets a creepy phone call from a man who asks a rather ominous question, "Have you checked the children?" Jill considers the call to be a prank and hangs up. When the caller persists, she telephones the police, who offer to put out a tracer. After another phone call, the police contact Jill and tell her the calls are coming from inside the house. To her horror, Jill learns that the kids have been slaughtered by a crazed merchant marine seaman (Tony Beckley), who is captured by detective John Clifford (Charles Durning) before he can kill the baby-sitter. Seven years later the killer escapes from the mental hospital and returns to terrorize Jill, now married, with kids of her own. The first part of the film is an exceedingly taut little chiller that stands on its own, mainly because it was originally a short film called "The Sitter." Director Fred Walton decided to expand the premise into a feature, and regrettably, this is where the film begins to fall apart. Dependent on an increasingly unlikely series of coincidences and lapses of logic, the movie lurches along to its climax. WHEN A STRANGER CALLS is the perfect film for mischievous parents to leave in the VCR for their baby-sitter.

p, Doug Chapin, Steve Feke; d, Fred Walton; w, Steve Feke, Fred Walton; ph, Don Peterman; ed, Sam Vitale; m, Dana Kaproff.

(PR:O  MPAA:R)

## WHITE ZOMBIE****

(1932) 73m UA bw

Bela Lugosi *(Murder Legendre)*, Madge Bellamy *(Madeline Short)*, John Harron *(Neil Parker)*, Joseph Cawthorn *(Dr. Bruner)*, Robert Frazer *(Charles Beaumont)*, Clarence Muse *(Coach Driver)*, Brandon Hurst *(Silver)*, Dan Crimmins *(Pierre)*, John Peters *(Chauvin)*, George Burr McAnnan *(Von Gelder)*, John Printz, Claude Morgan, John Fergusson *(Zombies)*, Annette Stone, Velma Gresham *(Maids)*.

Although it opened in the wake of such classics as DRACULA; FRANKENSTEIN; and DR. JEKYLL AND MR. HYDE and made a fortune at the box office on its initial release, WHITE ZOMBIE is all but forgotten today. The film opens as young couple Madeline (Madge Bellamy) and Neil (John Harron) pass by a funeral in Haiti in which the body is being buried in the road. Their driver explains that this will protect the corpse from ghouls. Soon the coach in which the couple is riding passes some strange creatures led by a mysterious figure, Murder Legendre (Bela Lugosi, fresh from his immortal success in DRACULA). The driver hurries past and later explains that these creatures are zombies, living dead who have been resurrected through voodoo. The couple finally arrives at the mansion of Charles Beaumont (Robert Frazer), where they are to be married. Madeline met Charles on the ship that took her to Haiti to join her fiance, and the wealthy man insisted the wedding be held in his home, though it's obvious his interest in her is less than honorable. Later, Charles gets Legendre, who provides zombies to work in the sugar mills, to turn Madeline into a zombie after she refuses his love. He realizes his mistake when she becomes one of the living dead, but the evil Legendre, who is also taken with the girl, will not change her back to her former self. WHITE ZOMBIE was the first film ever made about zombies and was inspired by William Seabrook's 1929 book on Haitian voodoo, *The Magic Island*. Produced and directed by brothers Edward and Victor Halperin, the film is a neglected classic that deserves to be placed alongside the early Universal horror pictures and the later Val Lewton chillers. With excellent lighting and camerawork by Arthur Martinelli, imaginative use of sound and music, makeup by Jack Pierce, and opulent sets (left over from a wide range of pictures, including THE KING OF KINGS, 1927; DRACULA, 1931; and FRANKENSTEIN, 1931), WHITE ZOMBIE creates a sense of nightmarish foreboding and dreamy disorientation (indeed, the last line in the film is "Neil, I . . . I dreamed") rivaled only by Carl Dreyer's masterpiece VAMPYR (1931). While the Halperins demonstrate a keen sense of the possibilities of the cinema, however, their handling of actors is woefully inadequate. With the exception of Bela Lugosi, who turns in one of his finest performances, most of the acting in WHITE ZOMBIE is weak. Luckily, the dialog is kept to an absolute minimum and many scenes are played out with only eerie sound effects as accompaniment. The success of WHITE ZOMBIE landed the Halperins a contract with Paramount, but their subsequent efforts—both in the horror genre and outside of it—never equalled the artistic or financial success of WHITE ZOMBIE. A sequel of sorts, THE REVOLT OF THE ZOMBIES, was made by the Halperins in 1936 and was a crushing disappointment.

p, Edward Halperin; d, Victor Halperin; w, Garnett Weston (based on the novel *The Magic Island* by William Seabrook); ph, Arthur Martinelli; ed, Harold MacLernon; m,

Guy Bevier Williams, Xavier Cugat, Nathaniel Dett, Gaston Borch, Hugo Riesenfeld, Leo Kempenski, H. Herkan, H. Maurice Jacquet.

(PR:A    MPAA:NR)

## WHO SLEW AUNTIE ROO?**½

(1971, US/Brit.) 89m Hemdale-AIP/AIP c (AKA: GINGERBREAD HOUSE; GB: WHOEVER SLEW AUNTIE ROO?)

Shelley Winters *(Rosie Forrest)*, Mark Lester *(Christopher)*, Ralph Richardson *(Mr. Benton)*, Lionel Jeffries *(Inspector Willoughby)*, Judy Cornwell *(Clarine)*, Michael Gothard *(Albie)*, Hugh Griffith *(The Pigman/Mr. Harrison)*, Chloe Franks *(Katy)*, Rosalie Crutchley *(Miss Henley)*, Pat Heywood *(Dr. Mason)*, Jacqueline Cowper *(Angela)*, Richard Beaumont *(Peter)*, Charlotte Sayce *(Katherine)*, Marianne Stone *(Miss Wilcox)*.

Set in 1920s England, this macabre combination of black comedy and suspense thriller features Shelley Winters (in a wonderfully hammy performance) as Auntie Roo, an ex-music hall singer who has become a recluse since the death of her only daughter years before. A la PSYCHO, she keeps the child's room exactly as it was when the girl was alive, rocking and singing to the cradle that holds her daughter's mummified remains. Every year she invites eight children from the local orphanage to spend Christmas with her, but one year, two extras appear—Christopher (Mark Lester) and his sister, Katy (Chloe Franks), a pair of problem kids who stowed away on the car bound for Auntie Roo's mansion. Katy bears an uncanny resemblance to Auntie Roo's daughter and is not only allowed to stay but also receives more affection from Auntie Roo than any of the others. Christopher, however, becomes jealous and goes prowling around the place after hours, discovering the mummy. Putting two and two together, he realizes that he's caught up in a real-life version of "Hansel and Gretel," with Auntie Roo as the witch who wants to eat both him and his sister. The film, obviously a bid to capture the same audience that thrilled to Robert Aldrich's WHATEVER HAPPENED TO BABY JANE? and HUSH . . . HUSH, SWEET CHARLOTTE, walks a fine line between good and bad taste, manipulating audience expectations and loyalties gleefully and shamelessly.

p, Samuel Z. Arkoff, James H. Nicholson; d, Curtis Harrington; w, Robert Blees, Jimmy Sangster, Gavin Lambert (based on a story by David Osborn); ph, Desmond Dickinson (Movielab Color); ed, Tristam Cones; m, Kenneth V. Jones.

(PR:O    MPAA:GP)

## WICKER MAN, THE***½

(1974, Brit.) 102m BL/WB c

Edward Woodward *(Sgt. Neil Howie)*, Christopher Lee *(Lord Summerisle)*, Diane Cilento *(Miss Rose)*, Britt Ekland *(Willow MacGregor)*, Ingrid Pitt *(Librarian-Clerk)*, Lindsay Kemp *(Alder MacGregor)*, Russell Waters *(Harbormaster)*, Aubrey Morris *(Old Gardener)*, Irene Sunters *(May Morri-*

*son)*, Walter Carr *(Schoolmaster)*, Roy Boyd *(Broome)*, Ian Campbell *(Oak)*, Leslie Mackie *(Daisy)*, Geraldine Cowper *(Rowan Morrison)*, Kevin Collins *(Old Fisherman)*, Donald Eccles *(T.H. Lennox)*, Jennifer Martin *(Myrtle Morrison)*, Leslie Blackwater *(Hairdresser)*, Barbara Ann Brown *(Woman with Baby)*, S. Newton Anderson *(Landers)*, Penny Cluer *(Gillie)*, Myra Forsyth *(Mrs. Grimmond)*, John Hallam *(Police Constable McTaggart)*, Alison Hughes *(Sgt. Howie's Fiancee)*, John MacGregor *(Baker)*, Charles Kearney *(Butcher)*, Fiona Kennedy *(Holly)*, Jimmie MacKenzie *(Brian)*, Tony Roper *(Postman)*.

Sgt. Neil Howie (Edward Woodward) is a devoutly Christian policeman and lay minister, still an unmarried virgin though middle-aged. After receiving a lead on the whereabouts of a missing girl, he heads out to Summerisle, a Scottish island community within his jurisdiction. What he finds on the island is a pagan cult led by Lord Summerisle (Christopher Lee) that offers a human sacrifice every year. Here we have an unusual instance of a film about a pagan cult that has developed a cult following of its very own. Drastically cut by its original distributors (from 102 minutes to 87 minutes), poorly marketed, and subsequently little seen, THE WICKER MAN developed a reputation as a lost masterpiece of mystery and the macabre. Fueled by Lee's contention that the film contained his best performance, a rabid group of fans zealously extolled the movie's virtues. When director Robin Hardy's reconstructed original cut of the much-anticipated film was finally released on videocassette (actually seven minutes are still missing), opinion was split—people either loved it or hated it. While no masterpiece, THE WICKER MAN is a fascinating examination of the conflict between fundamental Christianity and paganism. The performances are uniformly excellent and Hardy's direction is evocative, bizarre, witty, erotic, and downright chilling.

p, Peter Snell; d, Robin Hardy; w, Anthony Shaffer; ph, Harry Waxman; ed, Eric Boyd-Perkins; m, Paul Giovanni.

(PR:O    MPAA:R)

## WILLARD**½

(1971) 95m Bing Crosby/Cinerama c

Bruce Davison *(Willard Stiles)*, Elsa Lanchester *(Henrietta Stiles)*, Ernest Borgnine *(Al Martin)*, Sondra Locke *(Joan)*, Michael Dante *(Brandt)*, Jody Gilbert *(Charlotte Stassen)*, Joan Shawlee *(Alice Rickles)*, William Hansen *(Mr. Barskin)*, J. Pat O'Malley *(Jonathan Farley)*, John Myhers *(Mr. Carlson)*, Helen Spring *(Mrs. Becker)*, Pauline Drake *(Ida Stassen)*, Almira Sessions *(Carrie Smith)*, Alan Baxter *(Walter T. Spencer)*, Sherry Presnell *(Mrs. Spencer)*, Lola Kendrick *(Mrs. Martin)*, Robert Golden *(Motorcycle Rider)*, Minta Durfee Arbuckle, Arthur Tovey, Shirley Lawrence, Louise De Carlo *(Guest)*.

WILLARD could have been a great horror film; instead, it will just make your flesh crawl, sweat form on your brow, and lift your feet safely off the floor. With THE BIRDS, Alfred Hitchcock made famous this genre in which masses of creatures attack humans. Since that film movie audiences have witnessed enough frenzied bees and frogs and spiders and snakes to give even the bravest pet shop owner the shakes. Rats, however, are especially nasty, particularly when they are trained to kill by the psychotic young Willard Stiles (Bruce Davison), whose widowed mother, Henrietta (Elsa Lanchester), looks like (and indeed has been) the bride of Frankenstein. Fed up with his pushy, conniving boss, Al Martin (Ernest Borgnine), office boy Willard decides to make friends with a couple of rats, whom he calls Ben and Socrates, and trains them to savagely rip the flesh from his enemies' bodies. Martin is the prime target, and in one of Borgnine's most memorable performances, he cowers in the corner of his office as the fury monsters stage a mass attack. Willard, however, begins to neglect his rats when he falls in love with Joan (Sondra Locke, who would later direct RAT BOY—hmm, what does this mean?). Surprisingly (or perhaps not), hordes of filmgoers descended on WILLARD, standing in line to see their worst fears depicted on-screen—a good reason to see any horror film. Moe and Nora Di Sesso, WILLARD's animal trainers, deserve special mention for getting the vermin to "act." Dozens of rats were used, each taught specific skills (plank crawling, face chewing, etc.), and assisted by, of all things, the Di Sessos' pet cat.

p, Mort Briskin; d, Daniel Mann; w, Gilbert A. Ralston (based on the novel *Ratman's Notebooks* by Stephen Gilbert); ph, Robert B. Hauser (DeLuxe Color); ed, Warren Low; m, Alex North.

(PR:O    MPAA:GP)

## WITCHBOARD**½

(1987) 98m Paragon Arts/Cinema Group c

Todd Allen *(Jim Morar)*, Tawny Kitaen *(Linda Brewster)*, Steven Nichols *(Brandon Sinclair)*, Kathleen Wilhoite *(Zarabeth)*, Burke Byrnes *(Lt. Dewhurst)*, Rose Marie *(Mrs. Moses)*, James W. Quinn *(Lloyd)*, Judy Tatum *(Dr. Gelineau)*, Gloria Hayes *(Wanda)*, J.P. Luebsen *(Malfeitor)*, Susan Nickerson *(Chris)*, Ryan Carroll *(Roger)*, Kenny Rhodes *(Mike)*, Clare Bristol *(Anchorwoman)*.

This ambitious little horror film rejects graphic violence and instead spins a spooky tale of the supernatural. In it Linda Brewster (Tawny Kitaen) becomes obsessed with a Ouija board that has a direct line to the spirit of David, a friendly 10-year-old who died 30 years previously. Linda ignores the rule never to use the board alone, and gets tricked by the evil spirit of a savage axe-murderer, who pretends to be David. Instead of killing off a series of cardboard cut-outs, WITCHBOARD takes the high road and actually tries to develop relatively complex relationships between the main characters. While the film suffers at times from some clumsy scripting, weak (but not bad) acting, and a cliche presentation, it still *tries* to be something more than just a thrill ride (its gore and violence definitely de-emphasized). First-time feature director-writer Kevin S. Tenney imbues his film with a surprisingly slick sense of style and employs some clever camerawork when the narrative warrants it, refusing to bore the viewer with endless evil-point-of-view shots favored by so many other horror directors.

p, Gerold Geoffray; d, Kevin S. Tenney; w, Kevin S.

Tenney; ph, Roy Wagner; ed, Daniel Duncan, Stephen J. Waller; m, Dennis Michael Tenney.

(PR:O    MPAA:R)

## WITCHCRAFT THROUGH THE AGES*****

(1922, Swed.) 76m Svensk bw (HAXAN)

Benjamin Christensen *(Satan)*, Maria Pedersen *(The Witch)*, Clara Pontoppdian *(The Nun)*, Elith Pio *(The Monk)*, Oscar Stivolt *(The Fat Monk)*, Tora Teje *(The Kleptomaniac)*, Johs Anderson *(Chief Inquisitor)*, Poul Reumert, Karen Winther, Kate Fabian, Astrid Holm, Gerda Madsen, Aage Hertel, Ib Schonberg, Emmy Schonfeld, Frederick Christensen, Ella la Cour, Elizabeth Christensen, Alice O'Fredericks, William S. Burroughs *(Narrator)*.

A stunning combination of documentary and fiction, WITCHCRAFT THROUGH THE AGES is an unjustly forgotten classic of the cinema and contains some truly remarkable grotesque imagery. Swedish director Benjamin Christensen created a film that caused a considerable stir—the review in *Variety* praised the film's quality and then called it "absolutely unfit for public exhibition"—and that fellow director Carl Dreyer (THE PASSION OF JOAN OF ARC; VAMPYR) praised mightily. Although many versions of the film have circulated over the years, the most easily accessible is the 1969 re-release print, narrated by the author of *Naked Lunch*, William S. Burroughs, and boasting an excellent new modern jazz score composed by Daniel Humair and featuring violinist Jean-Luc Ponty. The film opens with a brief lecture on the history of witchcraft, illustrated with medieval woodcuts, paintings, engravings, and models by such artists as Bosch, Cranach, Breughel, and Durer. Christensen then presents several fictional vignettes designed to dramatize some of the events depicted in the artwork. These sequences are extraordinary, containing some of the most sophisticated filmmaking techniques then known to the cinema. Through the gorgeous photography of Johan Ankerstjerne, Christensen presents a nightmarish medieval world full of hideous witches, weird rites, monsters, ghouls, and demons. The special-effects makeup for the various demons is amazingly frightening and impressive, even to this day. The sets, costumes, and casting are magnificent, and Christensen uses a dynamic combination of both stage tricks and innovative camera techniques (such as double-exposure, reverse-motion, and stop-motion animation) to create his fantastical world. Christensen takes us through some astonishing episodes, including a woman's seduction by the Devil (played by Christensen himself) while her husband sleeps beside her, a woman's giving birth to demons, the sacrifice of a baby in a nightmarish black mass, and an outbreak of mass hysteria among nuns in a convent. The film then brings us into (then) modern times and explains that what was taken as witchcraft in the Middle Ages is now known to be the expression of various, and easily explainable, mental illnesses. Because it contains a surprising amount of nudity and violence, is highly critical of church oppression of "witches," and sees the entire witchcraft phenomenon as a conspiracy to control women and their sexuality, WITCHCRAFT THROUGH THE AGES was banned in several countries and sank into obscurity. Director Christensen later came to Hollywood, where he made several interesting fantasy films, including THE HAUNTED HOUSE (1928) and SEVEN FOOTPRINTS TO SATAN (1929), but none of his subsequent work was as truly memorable or remarkable as WITCHCRAFT THROUGH THE AGES. Running times vary, with 76 minutes, 83 minutes, 94 minutes, and 131 minutes all listed by various sources. The current video release is 76 minutes.

p, Ernest Mattison, Anthony Balch (English Sound Version); d, Benjamin Christensen; w, Benjamin Christensen; ph, Johan Ankerstjerne; m, Daniel Humair (English Sound Version), Jean-Luc Ponty.

(PR:C MPAA:NR)

## WITCHES OF EASTWICK, THE*

(1987) 118m WB c

Jack Nicholson *(Daryl Van Horne)*, Cher *(Alexandra Medford)*, Susan Sarandon *(Jane Spofford)*, Michelle Pfeiffer *(Sukie Ridgemont)*, Veronica Cartwright *(Felicia Alden)*, Richard Jenkins *(Clyde Alden)*, Keith Jochim *(Walter Neff)*, Carel Struycken *(Fidel)*, Helen Lloyd Breed *(Mrs. Biddle)*, Caroline Struzik *(Carol Medford)*, Becca Lish *(Mrs. Neff)*, Ruth Maynard *(Mrs. Biddle's Friend)*, Carole Ita White *(Cashier)*, Margot Dionne *(Nurse)*, John Blood *(Deli Counterman)*, Ron Campbell *(Ice-Cream Counterman)*, Eugene Boles *(Minister)*, Lansdale Chatfield, James T. Boyle *(Doctors)*, Carolyn Ditmars, Cynthia Ditmars, Christine Ditmars *(Ridgemont Children)*, Craig Burket, Abraham Mishkind, Christopher Verrette *(String Quartet)*, Babbie Green, Jane A. Johnston, Merrily Horowitz, Harriet Medin *(Women at Market)*.

A haphazard and bewitchingly dumb adaptation of John Updike's best-selling novel, THE WITCHES OF EASTWICK is a star-studded, special–effects extravaganza about the battle of the sexes. A trio of bored, sexually repressed New England women—Alex (Cher), Jane (Susan Sarandon), and Sukie (Michelle Pfeiffer), each of them left to live without their respective husbands—innocently conjures up a mysterious stranger who, they are convinced, will relieve their frustrations. This mystery man arrives in town in the form of Daryl Van Horne (Jack Nicholson), the filthy rich, wild-eyed Devil incarnate, who buys a local mansion. Within days, Alex, Jane, and Sukie have all been to bed with the Devil and discovered in themselves the almighty power of the female trinity. By the finale, the female trinity is pitted against the Devil, a mildly sympathetic misogynist who only wants to be loved *and* have someone to iron his shirts. While the underlying themes and message of THE WITCHES OF EASTWICK may be of interest, the execution by George (MAD MAX) Miller is downright pathetic, adding new meaning to the concept of sloppy and disjointed direction. Supposedly a film about sexual power and the battle of the sexes, told through a metaphorical Faustian battle in which a woman must sell her soul to the Devil in order to live a full life, the film instead is a pedestrian collection of supposedly lewd and direct sexual power struggles. Instead of addressing the central issues, the film plays like a TV sitcom, with an overdose

of raunch added to the proceedings; when the Devil spews forth his profanities, one almost expects to hear a diabolical laugh track. While the film promises to be, at the very least, thoughtful, it is quickly reduced to nothing but an over-reliance on special effects and bursts of vomit, uninspired acting, and embarrassingly unfunny situations. The familiar special visual effects were handled by Industrial Light & Magic, the special effects supervisor was Mike Lanteri, and special makeup effects were handled by Rob Dottin.

p, Neil Canton, Peter Guber, Jon Peters; d, George Miller; w, Michael Cristofer (based on the novel by John Updike); ph, Vilmos Zsigmond (Panavision, Technicolor); ed, Richard Francis-Bruce, Hubert C. De La Bouillerie; m, John Williams.

(PR:O MPAA:R)

## WITCHFIRE*

(1986) 100m Panda/Shapiro c

Shelley Winters *(Lydia)*, Gary Swanson *(The Hunter)*, Francesca De Sapio *(Hattie)*, Corinne Neuchateau *(Julietta)*, Al Shannon *(Harold)*, James Mendenhall *(Jarnigan)*, David Mendenhall *(Hunter's Son)*, Paula Shaw *(Nurse Hemmings)*.

When an asylum psychiatrist dies in a car wreck, three of his patients—Lydia (Shelley Winters, who doubles as associate producer), Hattie (Francesca De Sapio), and Julietta (Corinne Neuchateau), all completely bonkers—refuse to believe that he is dead. When they are taken to the funeral for verification, Lydia leads her friends in an escape to an abandoned mansion in the woods, where Lydia, who fancies herself a witch, conducts seances to contact their deceased doctor, and where the three crazies meet and proceed to terrorize a hunter (Gary Swanson) and his son (David Mendenhall). Shelley Winters' performance is the centerpiece of the film, the only thing of interest about it, and that dooms it. Her best line comes when she tells the hunter, "I may be insane, but I'm not stupid." Perhaps not, but people who rent this tape can't say the same.

p, James R. Orr; d, Vincent J. Privitera; w, Vincent J. Privitera, James R. Orr; ed, Gregg McGee; m, Dave Puchan.

(PR:O MPAA:NR)

## WITCHMAKER, THE*½

(1969) 97m Las Cruces-Arrow Films/Excelsior c (AKA: LEGEND OF WITCH HOLLOW)

John Lodge *(Luther the Beserk)*, Alvy Moore *(Dr. Ralph Hayes)*, Thordis Brandt *(Anastasia/"Tasha")*, Anthony Eisley *(Victor Gordon)*, Shelby Grant *(Maggie)*, Robyn Millan *(Sharon the Students)*, Tony Benson *(Owen)*, Helen Winston *(Jessie One)*, Warrene Ott *(Jessie Two)*, Burt Mustin *(Boatman)*, Kathy Lynn *(Patty Ann)*, Sue Bernard *(Felicity Johnson)*, Howard Viet *(San Blas)*, Nancy Crawford *(Goody Hale)*, Patricia Wymer *(Hag of Devon)*, Carolyn Rhodimer *(Marta)*, Diane Webber *(Nautch of Tangier)*, Larry Vincent *(Amos Coffin)*, Del Kaye *(Le Singe)*,

Gwen Lipscomb *(Fong Quai)*, Valya Garanda *(El A Haish Ma)*.

A group of witch hunters, led by parapsychology professor Dr. Ralph Hayes (Alvy Moore), journeys into the bayous of Louisiana to find out who or what is behind the murders of eight young woman, all apparently the victims of witchcraft. The women's corpses are found hung upside down, their throats slit and their blood drained. Dr. Hayes and his group encounter Luther the Beserk (John Lodge), a warlock who has made a pact with a 200-year-old witch to provide a supply of human blood. Luther sets his aims on Tasha (Thordis Brandt), a member of the group with an ancestor who was a witch, and who thus possesses a few secret powers of her own. After much mayhem and blood-draining, everyone is killed except Luther the Beserk, Ralph the Frightened, and Tasha the Malicious. Actor L.Q. Jones (a regular in the films of Sam Peckinpah) was executive producer.

p, William O. Brown; d, William O. Brown; w, William O. Brown; ph, John Arthur Morrill (Techniscope, Technicolor); m, Jaime Mendoza-Nava.

**(PR:C  MPAA:M)**

## WIZARD OF GORE, THE*

(1970) 96m Mayflower c

Ray Sager *(Montag the Magnificent)*, Judy Cler *(Sherry Carson)*, Wayne Ratay *(Jack)*, Phil Laurenson *(Greg)*, Jim Rau *(Steve)*, John Elliot *(Detective Harlan)*, Don Alexander *(Detective Kramer)*, Monika Blackwell, Corinne Kirkin, Karin Alexana, Sally Brody, Karen Burke *(Girls)*, Jack Gilbreth *(Maitre d'Hotel)*, Alex Ameripoor *(Man on Stage)*.

Herschell Gordon Lewis' next-to-last gore film, THE WIZARD OF GORE is one of his most disgusting efforts. Shot in and around Chicago and its suburbs, the film begins at a Grand Guignol stage show performed by Montag the Magnificent (Ray Sager). Witnessing the spectacular performance are local TV hostess Sherry Carson (Judy Cler), who is reviewing the act for her "Housewife's Coffee Break" show, and her sportswriter boy friend, Jack (Wayne Ratay). While Jack is repulsed, Sherry is impressed as Montag seems to saw a woman from the audience in half with a chainsaw. Although after the trick the woman—who had been disemboweled before the audience's eyes—seems fine, an hour later she collapses at a nearby restaurant, her guts spilling out on the floor. Unaware of this development, Sherry calls on the clever magician, inviting him to make a guest appearance on her talk show in a few days. The next night, Sherry and Jack attend another performance, in which Montag drives a spike through a woman's head. She too initially appears to be fine, but an hour later she dies of her wound. Jack gets suspicious and goes to the police with his theory, and soon the police department, Jack, and Sherry are all trying to figure out what the illusionist is up to. Although it's an amusingly ambitious attempt to blur the distinction between illusion and reality, this film is one of Lewis' most incompetent productions. Poorly shot and edited—flash frames and jump cuts are in abundance—THE WIZARD OF GORE ex-

ists merely for its gore effects, which are really not as good as those in BLOOD FEAST or TWO THOUSAND MANIACS. While quality acting has never been a requirement in a Lewis film, Sager is unbelievably bad as Montag, playing a character much older than he is and bellowing every one of his lines. Despite these fatal flaws, Lewis fans will no doubt love it.

p, Herschell Gordon Lewis; d, Herschell Gordon Lewis; w, Allen Kahn; ph, Alex Ameripoor, Dan Krogh (Eastmancolor); ed, Eskandar Ameripoor; m, Larry Wellington.

**(PR:O  MPAA:R)**

## WOLF MAN, THE****

(1941) 71m UNIV bw

Claude Rains *(Sir John Talbot)*, Lon Chaney, Jr. *(Larry Talbot)*, Evelyn Ankers *(Gwen Conliffe)*, Ralph Bellamy *(Capt. Paul Montford)*, Warren William *(Dr. Lloyd)*, Patric Knowles *(Frank Andrews)*, Maria Ouspenskaya *(Maleva)*, Bela Lugosi *(Bela)*, Fay Helm *(Jenny Williams)*, Leyland Hodgson *(Kendall)*, Forrester Harvey *(Victor Twiddle)*, J.M. Kerrigan *(Charles Conliffe)*, Kurt Katch *(Gypsy with Bear)*, Doris Lloyd *(Mrs. Williams)*, Olaf Hytten *(Villager)*, Harry Stubbs *(Rev. Norman)*, Tom Stevenson *(Graveyard Digger)*, Eric Wilton *(Chauffeur)*, Harry Cording *(Wykes)*, Ernie Stanton *(Phillips)*, Ottola Nesmith *(Mrs. Bally)*, Connie Leon *(Mrs. Wykes)*.

Bearing no resemblance to Universal's 1935 film THE WEREWOLF OF LONDON, THE WOLF MAN was given a whole new look and treatment by the studio. Lon Chaney, Jr., stars as Larry Talbot, a young British heir who returns to the mansion of his father (Claude Rains) after getting a college education in America. Learning about the legend of the werewolf from antique store employee Gwen (Evelyn Ankers), gypsy fortune teller Maleva (Maria Ouspenskaya), and Maleva's son, Bela (Bela Lugosi), Larry laughs it off as superstition. When the young man hears a bone-chilling wolf's howl and a blood-curdling scream emanating from the foggy moors, however, he rushes to the source of the hideous noises and is attacked and bitten by a vicious, hairy beast. Later, Maleva tells Larry that he will transform into a savage, murderous wolf when the moon is full and that he can only be killed by silver—be it a silver bullet, knife, or cane. Larry tries to deny her superstitious forecast, but when the next full moon arises, his nose becomes a wet snout, his hands and feet turn to paws, and his body is covered with thick fur. An animal trapped in a bedroom, the wolf man crashes through the window and runs off into the night in search of his prey. Fearing comparison with his famous father, Lon Jr. avoided appearing in horror films, but as he gained confidence in his abilities he agreed to try the genre and created the character with whom he would always be identified—the wolf man. Through the genius of Universal makeup artist Jack Pierce, Chaney underwent a complete transformation nearly as complete as his character's—gaining a rubber snout, fangs, claws, and lots of yak hair. Screenwriter Curt Siodmak patched together the legend of the werewolf by combining elements from lycanthropic folklore, witchcraft, and Bram Stoker's *Dracula*, creating a new monster for the screen. All elements combined to make a thrilling, scary, and ultimately tragic horror classic. Chaney essayed the role of the werewolf five more times, in FRANKENSTEIN MEETS THE WOLFMAN (1943); HOUSE OF FRANKENSTEIN (1944); HOUSE OF DRACULA (1945); and ABBOTT AND COSTELLO MEET FRANKENSTEIN (1948), as well as a guest appearance on the television show "Route 66."

p, George Waggner; d, George Waggner; w, Curt Siodmak; ph, Joseph Valentine; ed, Ted Kent; m, Charles Previn.

**(PR:A MPAA:NR)**

## WOLFEN***½

(1981) 115m Orion/WB c

Albert Finney *(Dewey Wilson)*, Diane Venora *(Rebecca Neff)*, Edward James Olmos *(Eddie Holt)*, Gregory Hines *(Whittington)*, Tom Noonan *(Ferguson)*, Dick O'Neill *(Warren)*, Dehl Berti *(Old Indian)*, Peter Michael Goetz *(Ross)*, Sam Gray *(Mayor)*, Ralph Bell *(Commissioner)*, Max. M. Brown *(Christopher Vanderveer)*, Anne Marie Photamo *(Pauline Vanderveer)*, Sarah Felder *(Cicely Rensselaer)*, Reggie Vel Johnson *(Morgue Attendant)*, James Tolkan *(Baldy)*, John McCurry *(Sayad Alve)*, Chris Manor *(Janitor)*, Donald Symington *(Lawyer)*, Jeffery Ware *(Interrogation Operator)*, E. Brian Dean *(Fouchek)*, Jeffery Thompson *(Harrison)*, Victor Arnold *(Roundenbush)*, Frank Adonis *(Scola)*, Richard Minchenberg *(Policeman)*, Ray Brocksmith *(Fat Jogger)*, Michael Wadleigh *(Terrorist Informer)*, George Stonefish, Julie Evening Lilly *(Native Americans)*.

This straightforward, intelligent film puts a new spin on the werewolf legend, turning the creatures into a superior species living in the slums of New York City. Police detective Dewey Wilson (Albert Finney) is called to investigate the savage murder of a rich industrialist who had just broken ground on a multimillion dollar development project in the South Bronx slums. When the city coroner (Gregory Hines, in his film debut) suggests that the dead man was mutilated by a wild animal, Wilson and criminal psychologist Rebecca Neff (Diane Venora) connect the killing with several murders that have occurred in the South Bronx in which the bodies of winos, drug addicts, and bums have been found with their throats ripped out. Wilson and Neff are led to a group of Native American construction workers, who explain that the "Wolfen" once roamed the land that is now New York City. Learning how to survive in an urban environment, the Wolfen inhabit only the slum areas and feed off those members of society who will not be missed. Since the Indians and wolves shared the same fate at the hands of white settlers, they understand each other, and the workers surmise that the industrialist was killed by the Wolfen to prevent the new development project from once again pushing them off their land. Directed by Michael Wadleigh, whose only other feature is the 1970 rock documentary WOODSTOCK, WOLFEN is an intelligent, insightful, and visually creative twist on the werewolf legend, which, while occasionally preachy (addressing urban decay, the homeless, the problems of Native Americans,

ecological issues, and big business), is a fascinating horror tale that is as engrossing as it is thrilling. The visual effects are sensational and bring to the screen a previously unseen "Wolfen Vision" that, through a variety of optical printing techniques, conveys the wolves' heightened sense of heat, smell, movement, and texture. The gore effects by Carl Fullerton are effective, if somewhat gratuitous.

p, Rupert Hitzig; d, Michael Wadleigh; w, David Eyre, Michael Wadleigh (based on the novel by Whitley Strieber); ph, Gerry Fisher (Panavision, Technicolor); ed, Chris Lebenzon, Dennis Dolan, Martin Bram, Marshall M. Borden; m, James Horner.

**(PR:O MPAA:R)**

## WOLFMAN*½

(1979) 101m E.D./Omni c (AKA: WOLFMAN, THE)

Earl Owensby *(Colin Glasgow)*, Ed L. Grady *(Rev. Leonard)*, Julian Morton *(Edwin Glasgow)*, Kristine Reynolds *(Lynn Randolph)*, Richard Dedmon *(Uncle Clement)*, Maggie Lauterer *(Aunt Elizabeth)*, Sid Rancer *(Dr. Tate)*, Victor Smith *(Luthor)*, Helen Tryon *(Grandmother)*, Brownlee Davis.

This bit of drive-in trash from one of the sub-Mason-Dixon line moguls of movies, Earl Owensby, stars none other than himself. Set in Georgia in 1910, WOLFMAN revolves around the life of Colin Glasgow (Owensby), whose father, a scion of southern wealth, is slain by the sinister Rev. Leonard (Ed L. Grady). Rev. Leonard is responsible for maintaining a curse on Colin's family, instituted when a long-dead relative reneged on a Faustian pact with Satan. Colin inherits his murdered father's estate and his lycanthropic mantle along with it, and goes loping through the night biting out throats. It's not that WOLFMAN is all that terrible, it's just a pointless and ultimately worthless rehashing of an age-old legend that offers nothing new. In other words, it has no reason to exist. Naturally, however, being an Owensby movie, it made big bucks in Southern drive-ins.

p, Earl Owensby; d, Worth Keeter; w, Worth Keeter; ph, Darrell Cathcart (DeLuxe Color); ed, Richard Aldridge; m, Arthur Smith, David Floyd.

**(PR:O MPAA:R)**

## WORM EATERS, THE zero

(1977) 94m Cinema Features-Genini/New American c

Herb Robins, Lindsay Armstrong Black, Joseph Sacket, Robert Garrison, Muriel Cooper, Mike Garrison, Barry Hostetler, Carla.

Hermann Umgar (Herb Robins) is a worm breeder (??) who surrounds himself with (what else?) worms—worms he has pet names for, talks to, even sings to. Like his father before him, Umgar is the victim of real estate developers who want to construct condominiums on his property, but Umgar and his squirmy wormies don't like the idea. Umgar therefore makes a pact with three mysterious wormlike men from the Champion Bass Fishing Club (who have been transformed into slithery creatures after eating bass caught with some of his worms), agreeing to provide the threesome with worm-women for procreating purposes in exchange for their promise to help destroy local crops. The worm breeder has (what else but) worms in his mouth much of the time and, in the glorious finale, gets mushed by a truck. This godawful piece of annelid waste was filmed in 1977 and subsequently managed to achieve some of the cult status for which it undoubtedly aims.

p, Ted V. Mikels; d, Herb Robins; w, Herb Robins (based on a story by Nancy Kapner); ph, Willis Hawkins (Eastmancolor); ed, Soly Bina; m, Theodore Stern.

(PR:O MPAA:NR)

## WRAITH, THE*

(1986) 104m Alliance-John Kemeny/New Century-Vista c

Charlie Sheen *(The Wraith/Jake Kesey)*, Nick Cassavetes *(Packard Walsh)*, Sherilyn Fenn *(Keri Johnson)*, Randy Quaid *(Sheriff Loomis)*, Matthew Barry *(Billy Hankins)*, David Sherrill *(Skank)*, Jamie Bozian *(Gutterboy)*, Clint Howard *(Rughead)*, Griffin O'Neal *(Oggie Fisher)*, Chris Nash *(Minty)*, Vickie Benson *(Waitress)*, Jeffrey Sudzin *(Redd)*, Peder Melhuse *(Murphy)*, Michael Hungerford *(Stokes)*, Steven Eckholdt *(Boy in Daytona)*, Elizabeth Cox *(Girl in Daytona)*, Dick Alexander *(Sandeval)*, Christopher Bradley *(Jamie)*, Joan H. Reynolds *(Policewoman)*.

A ridiculous mishmash of drag racing, ghosts, and science fiction, THE WRAITH swiftly disappeared, sparing Charlie Sheen a lot of embarrassment. In the Arizona desert, a gang of tough kids led by Packard Walsh (Nick Cassavetes) race against all comers, betting their cars on the outcome. One day Jake Kesey (Sheen) rides into town on a motor scooter and falls in love with Keri (Sherilyn Fenn), Packard's girl friend. Everyone seems to recall Jake's face, but no one can quite place it. At about the same time, a mysterious and very fast black car starts turning up on the highways outside of town. Eventually it is revealed that Jake is the reincarnation of a boy killed by the gang sometime before the action of the film, and now . . . as "The Wraith," he has been returned to life by some aliens and sent back to get revenge. The performances range from poor to lousy (to be fair, Sheen isn't *too* bad), mostly the fault of an incomprehensible script that, instead of working anything out, simply throws in another bone to distract from the story's stupidity. Director-writer Mike Marvin is obviously working out of his element, which consists of ski films and features with titles of things you eat or drink (SIX PACK; HOT DOG—THE MOVIE; and HAMBURGER). The best thing here are the cars, which have no dialog and just stand around looking fast. Sheen's is a specially built Dodge pace car that cost over $1.5 million.

p, John Kemeny; d, Mike Marvin; w, Mike Marvin; ph, Reed Smoot (Metrocolor); ed, Scott Conrad, Gary Rocklin; m, Michael Hoenig, J. Peter Robinson.

(PR:C MPAA:PG-13)

## WRESTLING WOMEN VS. THE AZTEC MUMMY, THE*

(1964, Mex.) 77m Cinematografica Calderon bw (LAS LUCHADORAS CONTRA LA MOMIA)

Lorena Velazquez, Elisabeth Campbell, Armando Silvestre, Maria Eugenia San Martin, Chucho Salinas, Ramon Bugarini, Victor Velaquez, Ton-La Tapatia, Irma Gonzalez, Chabela Romero.

A gang of criminals, led by a Fu Manchu-like character, is determined to find the ancient treasure buried in an Aztec tomb, and proceeds to dispose of several archaeologists and to steal information that will lead them to the goal. Enter two popular female wrestlers (Lorena Velazquez and Elisabeth Campbell), who vow to stop them. Before departing for the ruins, the wrestling women enter into a match with the head villain's sisters—two burly experts in karate. Eventually, everyone winds up at the tomb, where, when someone tries to snatch a sacred medallion off the corpse of a princess, her mummy guard comes to life to protect it. Able to turn into a bat or tarantula at will, the Aztec mummy gives both the villains and the heroes a run for their money. This extremely silly film presents both its wrestling and its horror at a fast and furious pace. The Aztec mummy must be the only mummy in cinema history who can transform himself into other animals at will, and these scenes are made even funnier by the English dubbing, which has the startled humans gasping, "Now he's a vampire!" and "Oh! He's a mummy again!" The most widely available videotape version of this film was released by Rhino Video, who saw fit to retitle the movie ROCK 'N' ROLL WRESTLING WOMEN VS. THE AZTEC MUMMY, truncate the footage, and add their own campy rock songs and music cues (including H.G. Lewis' score for BLOOD FEAST) to the soundtrack. The overall effect of this tampering is slightly amusing, but one has to question the wisdom of trying to impose self-conscious camp in a film that is plenty campy on its own unadulterated form. Songs include: "The Aztec Mummy," "Head Locks and Hard Knocks," "We Wanna Be Wrestling Women" (David Starns, Richard Foos, performed by Jo Anne Kurman), "Godzilla Stomp," "Night of the Living Wedge" (The Wedge), "5,000 Years Ago," "Ancient Weird Religious Rites," "A Fitting Death for the Garbage He Was" (Herschell Gordon Lewis), "Wrestling Women" (Starns, Foos).

p, Guillermo Calderon, K. Gordon Murray (English Version); d, Rene Cardona, Manuel San Fernando (English Version); w, Guillermo Calderon, Alfredo Salazar; ph, Ezequiel Carrasco; ed, Jorge Bustos; m, Antonio Diaz Conde.

(PR:A MPAA:NR)

# XYZ

## YOU BETTER WATCH OUT**

(1980) 100m Pressman c (AKA: CHRISTMAS EVIL)

Brandon Maggart *(Harry Stadling)*, Dianne Hull *(Jackie*

*Stadling)*, Scott McKay *(Fletcher)*, Joe Jamrog *(Frank Stol-ler)*, Peter Friedman *(Grosch)*, Ray Barry *(Gleason)*, Bobby Lesser *(Gottleib)*, Sam Gray *(Grilla)*, Ellen McElduff *(Harry's Mother)*, Patty Richardson *(Moss' Mother)*.

It should go without saying that this unpleasant holiday picture revolves around a Santa who's definitely naughty, not nice—who is, in fact, a murdering lunatic. Surprisingly intelligent and gripping, the tale stars the unknown and convincing Brandon Maggart as the fat, bearded Kris Kringle, who, as a young boy, underwent a trauma that has forever haunted him. Because of the attention it pays to the development of the murderous Santa's character, the film is somewhat better than the rest of its subgenre; it's also expertly photographed by Ricardo Aronovich, a cameraman better known for his work with European directors Alain Resnais, Costa-Gavras, and Ettore Scola. Originally released as YOU BETTER WATCH OUT, the film has resurfaced on videocassette as CHRISTMAS EVIL.

p, Burt Kleiner, Pete Kameron; d, Lewis Jackson; w, Lewis Jackson; ph, Ricardo Aronovich; ed, Corky O'Hara, Linda Leeds.

**(PR:O MPAA:R)**

## YOUNG FRANKENSTEIN****

(1974) 108m FOX bw

Gene Wilder *(Dr. Frederick Frankenstein)*, Peter Boyle *(Monster)*, Marty Feldman *(Igor)*, Madeline Kahn *(Elizabeth)*, Cloris Leachman *(Frau Blucher)*, Teri Garr *(Inga)*, Kenneth Mars *(Inspector Kemp)*, Gene Hackman *(Blind Hermit)*, Richard Haydn *(Herr Falkstein)*, Liam Dunn *(Mr. Hilltop)*, Danny Goldman *(Medical Student)*, Leon Askin *(Herr Waldman)*, Oscar Beregi *(Sadistic Jailer)*, Lou Cutell *(Frightened Villager)*, Arthur Malet *(Village Elder)*, Richard Roth *(Kemp's Aide)*.

Mel Brooks' follow-up to his enormously successful western spoof BLAZING SADDLES tackles the horror genre, specifically, the "Frankenstein" film. This time, Brooks tones down much of his broad humor to create a work that is both an affectionate parody and an homage to its cinematic forebears. Gene Wilder plays Dr. Frederick Frankenstein (now defiantly pronounced "FRONK-en-steen"), a med school lecturer who thinks his infamous grandfather's work is "doo-doo." The younger Frankenstein must face his fate, however, when he is left his grandfather's Transylvanian estate. Once there, he meets Igor (pronounced "eye-gore" and played by the eye-popping Marty Feldman), whose hunchback inexplicably changes from the left side to the right throughout the movie; Inga (Teri Garr), a young woman who will assist the doctor; and Frau Blucher (Cloris Leachman), a hideous old woman who causes horses to whinny in fright at the mere mention of her name. Eventually, Frederick finds his grandfather's private library and a copy of his book, *How I Did It*. Of course, Frederick cannot keep himself from righting his grandfather's wrongs and creating a new monster (Peter Boyle), a big, dumb corpse with a zipper round his neck and an abnormal brain in his head. The laughs are fast and furious, with the film's highlight being the "Puttin' On The Ritz" duet

performed by Frederick and the Monster. YOUNG FRANKENSTEIN is Brooks' most accomplished work, combining his well-known brand of comedy with stylish direction and a uniformly excellent cast. The direction achieves a seemingly impossible task, balancing Brooks' off-the-wall humor within the framework of a classic Universal-styled "Frankenstein" film. The Frankenstein castle, with its cobwebs, dust, skulls, original lab equipment, and strange goings-on, could easily have been inhabited by Boris Karloff or Bela Lugosi. Wilder later attempted his own genre spoof, HAUNTED HONEYMOON (1986), which, while it had its moments, came nowhere near YOUNG FRANKENSTEIN.

p, Michael Gruskoff; d, Mel Brooks; w, Gene Wilder, Mel Brooks (based on the characters from the novel *Frankenstein* by Mary Wollstonecraft Shelley); ph, Gerald Hirschfield; ed, John C. Howard; m, John .

**(PR:C MPAA:PG)**

## ZOMBIE*½

(1979, It.) 91m Variety/Jerry Gross Organization c (ZOMBI 2; AKA: ISLAND OF THE LIVING DEAD; ZOMBIE FLESH EATERS)

Tisa Farrow *(Anne)*, Ian McCullough *(Peter)*, Richard Johnson *(Dr. Menard)*, Al Cliver [Pier Luigi Conti] *(Brian)*, Auretta Gay *(Susan)*, Olga Karlatos *(Mrs. Menard)*, Stefania d'Amario *(Nurse)*, Ugo Bologna, Monica Zanchi.

Although sold in Italy as a sequel to George Romero's DAWN OF THE DEAD, which was known as ZOMBIE in that country, this Lucio Fulci-directed gross-out has nothing whatsoever to do with Romero's film. After the opening sequence undoubtedly inspired by NOSFERATU (1922), a lone sailboat drifts into a New York City harbor. On it is a zombie who proceeds to devour a hapless cop before falling into the water. As it turns out, the boat is owned by the father of Anne (Tisa Farrow), who decides to go to the small island of Matoul, near St. Thomas, to find out what happened to her dad. Joined by a reporter (Ian McCulloch) and another couple (Al Cliver and Annetta Gay), Anne charters a small boat and sets sail. On the island, they discover a scientist (Richard Johnson) who, while conducting experiments on the dead, has inadvertently revived scores of corpses through ancient voodoo rites. Soon dozens of zombies are shuffling around the island, dismembering the living in some of the most grotesque gore effects ever filmed, the much talked-about highlights of which are a woman's eye being impaled with a long sliver in extreme close-up and a parody of JAWS in which a swimming woman is attacked by both a shark and an underwater zombie. The woman escapes, leaving the zombie to fight the shark. Although the effects work of Giannetto De Rossi is generally excellent and certainly stomach-churning, most of ZOMBIE is slow-moving and unintentionally funny. Fulci's work has its champions, but like most purveyors of no-holds-barred gore, his films are basically dim-witted and hold little interest for anyone other than hardcore gorehounds. Running times on ZOMBIE have been reported as 98 minutes, 95 minutes, 93 minutes, and 91 minutes.

## ZOMBIE—

Sources for the US release say 91 minutes; the current home video version is 93 minutes and may contain some gore excised from the American release.

p, Ugo Tucci, Fabrizio De Angelis; d, Lucio Fulci; w, Elisa Briganti; ph, Sergio Salvati (Technicolor); ed, Vincenzo Tomassi; m, Fabio Frizzi, Giorgio Tucci.

**(PR:O   MPAA:X)**


## ZOMBIES OF MORA TAU**

(1957) 70m COL bw

Gregg Palmer *(Jeff Clark)*, Allison Hayes *(Mona Harrison)*, Autumn Russell *(Jan Peters)*, Joel Ashley *(George Harrison)*, Morris Ankrum *(Jonathan Eggert)*, Marjorie Eaton *(Mrs. Peters)*, Gene Roth *(Sam)*, Leonard Geer *(Johnny)*, Lewis Webb *(Art)*, Ray "Crash" Corrigan *(Sailor)*, Mel Curtis *(Johnson)*, Frank Hagney *(Capt. Jeremy Peters)*, Karl Davis, William Baskin *(Zombies)*.

This good cheap zombie picture follows two explorers— Jeff Clark (Gregg Palmer) and pre-Beatle George Harrison (Joel Ashley)—off to search for diamonds under the sea off the coast of Africa. Little do they know that zombies guard the treasure and won't let anyone who tries to take it get out alive. Jeff escapes in the end, scattering the diamonds so no one can get at them and thus giving the creatures the first moments of peace they've had in eons. It's all of a standard horror quality for grade B films, with some cheesy underwater wave effects that are far more charming than they are offensive.

p, Sam Katzman; d, Edward L. Cahn; w, Raymond T. Marcus (based on a story by George Plympton); ph, Benjamin Kline; ed, Jack Ogilvie.

**(PR:O   MPAA:NR)**

# ALTERNATE TITLE

Listed below are alternate, foreign, and Great Britain titles of films, followed by the title under which the film appears in this volume.

## A

ABBOTT AND COSTELLO MEET THE GHOSTS (SEE: ABBOTT AND COSTELLO MEET FRANKENSTEIN)

AMANTI D'OLTRETOMBA (SEE: NIGHTMARE CASTLE)

AMOK (SEE: SCHIZO)

ANDY WARHOL'S YOUNG DRACULA (SEE: ANDY WARHOL'S DRACULA)

ANGEL OF VENGEANCE (SEE: MS. 45)

ANGUSTIA (SEE: ANGUISH)

ANTEFATTO (SEE: TWITCH OF THE DEATH NERVE)

ANTHROPOPHAGOUS (SEE: GRIM REAPER, THE)

APOCALIPSIS CANIBAL (SEE: NIGHT OF THE ZOMBIES)

ARE YOU DYING YOUNG MAN? (SEE: BEAST IN THE CELLAR, THE)

ASYLUM OF THE INSANE (SEE: FLESH AND BLOOD SHOW, THE)

ATTACK OF THE MAYAN MUMMY (SEE: AZTEC MUMMY, THE)

AZTEC MUMMY VS THE HUMAN ROBOT, THE (SEE: ROBOT VS. THE AZTEC MUMMY, THE)

## B

BANANA MONSTER, THE (SEE: SCHLOCK)

BARBARIC BEAST OF BOGGY CREEK PART II, THE (SEE: BOGGY CREEK II)

BE MY VALENTINE, OR ELSE. . . (SEE: HOSPITAL MASSACRE)

BEAST, THE (SEE: EQUINOX)

BEYOND THE GATE (SEE: HUMAN EXPERIMENTS)

BIRTHMARK (SEE: OMEN, THE)

BLACK CHRISTMAS (SEE: BLACK SABBATH)

BLACK FRANKENSTEIN (SEE: BLACKENSTEIN)

BLADE IN THE BODY, THE (SEE: MURDER CLINIC, THE)

BLIND MAN'S BLUFF (SEE: CAULDRON OF BLOOD)

BLOOD BRIDES (SEE: HATCHET FOR A HONEYMOON)

BLOOD COUPLE (SEE: GANJA AND HESS)

BLOOD CULT OF SHANGRI-LA, THE (SEE: THIRSTY DEAD, THE)

BLOOD DOCTOR (SEE: MAD DOCTOR OF BLOOD ISLAND, THE)

BLOOD FIEND (SEE: THEATRE OF DEATH)

BLOOD FOR DRACULA (SEE: ANDY WARHOL'S DRACULA)

BLOOD OF FRANKENSTEIN (SEE: DRACULA VS. FRANKENSTEIN)

BLOOD OF THE UNDEAD (SEE: SCHIZO)

BLOOD SISTERS (SEE: SISTERS)

BLOODSUCKERS, THE (SEE: INCENSE FOR THE DAMNED)

BLUE EYES OF THE BROKEN DOLL, THE (SEE: HOUSE OF PSYCHOTIC WOMEN, THE)

BRAIN, THE (SEE: BRAIN OF BLOOD)

BRENN, HEXE, BRENN (SEE: MARK OF THE DEVIL)

BRIDE OF FENGRIFFIN (SEE: AND NOW THE SCREAMING STARTS)

BUMP IN THE NIGHT (SEE: FINAL TERROR, THE)

BURN, WITCH, BURN (SEE: MARK OF THE DEVIL)

## C

CAMPSITE MASSACRE (SEE: FINAL TERROR, THE)

CANNIBAL ORGY, OR THE MADDEST STORY EVER TOLD (SEE: SPIDER BABY)

CARNE PER FRANKENSTEIN (SEE: ANDY WARHOL'S FRANKENSTEIN)

CARNE PER FRANKENSTEIN (SEE: ANDY WARHOL'S FRANKENSTEIN)

CASTLE OF DOOM (SEE: VAMPYR)

CAUCHEMARES (SEE: CATHY'S CURSE)

CHI SEI? (SEE: BEYOND THE DOOR)

CHRISTMAS EVIL (SEE: YOU BETTER WATCH OUT)

CITY OF THE DEAD, THE (SEE: HORROR HOTEL)

CITY OF THE LIVING DEAD (SEE: GATES OF HELL, THE)

CODE NAME: TRIXIE (SEE: CRAZIES, THE)

COMMUNION (SEE: ALICE, SWEET ALICE)

COMPUTER KILLERS (SEE: HORROR HOSPITAL)

CORPSE, THE (SEE: CRUCIBLE OF HORROR)

CREATURES (SEE: FROM BEYOND THE GRAVE)

CREATURES FROM BEYOND THE GRAVE, THE (SEE: FROM BEYOND THE GRAVE)

CREATURE'S REVENGE, THE (SEE: BRAIN OF BLOOD)

CREEPS (SEE: BLOODY BIRTHDAY)

CRIES IN THE NIGHT (SEE: FUNERAL HOME)

CRIMES IN THE WAX MUSEUM (SEE: NIGHTMARE IN WAX)

CRYPT OF DARK SECRETS (SEE: MARDI GRAS MASSACRE)

## D

DADDY'S GIRL (SEE: DADDY'S DEADLY DARLING)

DARK EYES OF LONDON (SEE: HUMAN MONSTER, THE)

DAS BILDNESS DES DORIAN GRAY (SEE: DORIAN GRAY)

DAS CABINETT DES DR. CALIGARI (SEE: CABINET OF DR. CALIGARI, THE)

DAUGHTER OF FRANKENSTEIN, THE (SEE: LADY FRANKENSTEIN)

DAUGHTER OF HORROR (SEE. DEMENTIA)

DEAD KIDS (SEE: STRANGE BEHAVIOR)

DEATH BITE (SEE: SPASMS)

DEATH HOUSE (SEE: SILENT NIGHT, BLOODY NIGHT)

DEATH OF NIGHT (SEE: DEATHDREAM)

DEATH TRAP (SEE: EATEN ALIVE)

DEATH WHEELERS, THE
(SEE: PSYCHOMANIA)

DEEP RED (SEE: DEEP RED:
HATCHET MURDERS)

DEMONI (SEE: DEMONS)

DEMONI 2—L'INCUBO RITORNA
(SEE: DEMONS 2: THE
NIGHTMARE RETURNS)

DER GOLEM: WIE ER IN DE WELT
(SEE: GOLEM, THE)

DEVIL AND DR. FRANKENSTEIN,
THE (SEE: ANDY WARHOL'S
FRANKENSTEIN)

DEVIL WITHIN HER, THE
(SEE: BEYOND THE DOOR)

DEVIL'S MEN, THE (SEE: LAND OF
THE MINOTAUR)

DEVIL'S PEOPLE, THE (SEE: LAND
OF THE MINOTAUR)

DIE BRAUT DES SATANS (SEE: TO
THE DEVIL A DAUGHTER)

DIE SCHLANGENGRUBE UND DAS
PENDEL (SEE: BLOOD DEMON)

DIE ZWOELFTE STUNDE
(SEE: NOSFERATU, THE
VAMPIRE)

DOCTOR FROM SEVEN DIALS,
THE (SEE: CORRIDORS OF
BLOOD)

DOCTOR MANIAC (SEE: HOUSE
OF THE LIVING DEAD)

DOCTORS WEAR SCARLET
(SEE: INCENSE FOR THE
DAMNED)

DOOR WITH SEVEN LOCKS, THE
(SEE: CHAMBER OF HORRORS)

DOUBLE POSSESSION
(SEE: GANJA AND HESS)

DRACULA (SEE: NOSFERATU,
THE VAMPIRE)

DRACULA AGAINST
FRANKENSTEIN
(SEE: SCREAMING DEAD, THE)

DRACULA AND THE SEVEN
GOLDEN VAMPIRES
(SEE: LEGEND OF THE SEVEN
GOLDEN VAMPIRES, THE)

DRACULA CERCA SANGUE DI
VERGINE E. . .MORI DI SETE
(SEE: ANDY WARHOL'S
DRACULA)

DRACULA CONTRA
FRANKENSTEIN
(SEE: SCREAMING DEAD, THE)

DRACULA, PRISONER OF
FRANKENSTEIN
(SEE: SCREAMING DEAD, THE)

DRACULA VS. FRANKENSTEIN
(SEE: SCREAMING DEAD, THE)

DRACULA VUOLE VIVERE: CERCA
SANGUE DI VERGINA
(SEE: ANDY WARHOL'S
DRACULA)

DRACULA'S CASTLE (SEE: BLOOD
OF DRACULA'S CASTLE)

DRACULA'S LAST RITES
(SEE: LAST RITES)

DRIPPING DEEP RED (SEE: DEEP
RED: HATCHET MURDERS)

E

EAST SIDE KIDS MEET BELA
LUGOSI, THE (SEE: GHOSTS ON
THE LOOSE)

EDGAR ALLAN POE'S
CONQUEROR WORM
(SEE: CONQUEROR WORM,
THE)

EDGAR ALLEN POE'S "THE
OBLONG BOX" (SEE: OBLONG
BOX, THE)

EDGE OF HELL, THE (SEE: ROCK
'N' ROLL NIGHTMARE)

EERIE WORLD OF DR. JORDAN,
THE (SEE: SOMETHING WEIRD)

EINE NACHT DES GRAUENS
(SEE: NOSFERATU, THE
VAMPIRE)

EL BUQUE MALDITO
(SEE: HORROR OF THE
ZOMBIES)

EL CASTELLO DELL' ORRORE
(SEE: HOUSE OF FREAKS)

EL COLECCIONISTA DE
CADAVERES (SEE: CAULDRON
OF BLOOD)

EL ROBOT HUMANO
(SEE: ROBOT VS. THE AZTEC
MUMMY, THE)

ELLA (SEE: MONKEY SHINES: AN
EXPERIMENT IN FEAR)

EYES WITHOUT A FACE
(SEE: HORROR CHAMBER OF
DR. FAUSTUS, THE)

F

FACE OF FEAR (SEE: PEEPING
TOM)

FACELESS MONSTERS, THE
(SEE: NIGHTMARE CASTLE)

FALL OF THE HOUSE OF USHER,
THE (SEE: HOUSE OF USHER)

FALSE FACE (SEE: SCALPEL)

FANATIC (SEE: DIE! DIE! MY
DARLING)

FANATIC, THE (SEE: LAST
HORROR FILM, THE)

FARM, THE (SEE: CURSE, THE)

FEAR, THE (SEE: GATES OF HELL,
THE)

FEAR IN THE CITY OF THE LIVING
DEAD (SEE: GATES OF HELL,
THE)

FEMALE FIEND (SEE: THEATRE
OF DEATH)

FENGRIFFIN (SEE: AND NOW THE
SCREAMING STARTS)

FLESH FOR FRANKENSTEIN
(SEE: ANDY WARHOL'S
FRANKENSTEIN)

FORBIDDEN LOVE (SEE: FREAKS)

FOREST OF FEAR
(SEE: BLOODEATERS)

FOREST PRIMEVAL, THE
(SEE: FINAL TERROR, THE)

FRANKENSTEIN (SEE: ANDY
WARHOL'S FRANKENSTEIN)

FRANKENSTEIN EXPERIMENT,
THE (SEE: ANDY WARHOL'S
FRANKENSTEIN)

FRANKENSTEIN'S CASTLE OF
FREAKS (SEE: HOUSE OF
FREAKS)

FRIGHT, THE (SEE: VISITING
HOURS)

FRIGHTMARE II
(SEE: FRIGHTMARE (1974))

FRISSONS (SEE: THEY CAME
FROM WITHIN)

FROG, THE (SEE: PSYCHOMANIA)

FROM A WHISPER TO A SCREAM
(SEE: OFFSPRING, THE)

FULL CIRCLE (SEE: HAUNTING OF
JULIA, THE)

FUN HOUSE, THE (SEE: LAST
HOUSE ON DEAD END STREET)

G

GAMMA 693 (SEE: NIGHT OF THE
ZOMBIES)

GHOSTS IN THE NIGHT
(SEE: GHOSTS ON THE LOOSE)

GINGERBREAD HOUSE
(SEE: WHO SLEW AUNTIE
ROO?)

GLI ORRORI DEL CASTELLO DI
NOREMBERGA (SEE: BARON
BLOOD)

GOLEM: HOW HE CAME INTO THE
WORLD, THE (SEE: GOLEM,
THE)

GOMAR-THE HUMAN GORILLA
(SEE: NIGHT OF THE BLOODY
APES)

GREEN MONKEY (SEE: BLUE
MONKEY)

GRIP OF THE STRANGLER
(SEE: HAUNTED STRANGLER,
THE)

# H

HATCHET MURDERS, THE
(SEE: DEEP RED: HATCHET
MURDERS)
HAUNTED AND THE HUNTED,
THE (SEE: DEMENTIA 13)
HAUNTING OF HAMILTON HIGH,
THE (SEE: HELLO MARY LOU,
PROM NIGHT II)
HAXAN (SEE: WITCHCRAFT
THROUGH THE AGES)
HEAD THAT WOULDN'T DIE, THE
(SEE: BRAIN THAT WOULDN'T
DIE, THE)
HELL OF THE LIVING DEAD
(SEE: NIGHT OF THE ZOMBIES)
HEXEN BIS AUFS BLUT GEQUALT
(SEE: MARK OF THE DEVIL)
HIDDEN ROOM OF 1,000
HORRORS, THE
(SEE: TELL-TALE HEART, THE)
HOLLYWOOD MEAT CLEAVER
MASSACRE, THE (SEE: MEAT
CLEAVER MASSACRE)
HOLLYWOOD STRANGLER, THE
(SEE: DON'T ANSWER THE
PHONE)
HOLOCAUST 2,000
(SEE: CHOSEN, THE)
HOLY TERROR (SEE: ALICE,
SWEET ALICE)
HORROR HOTEL MASSACRE
(SEE: EATEN ALIVE)
HORROR OF DEATH, THE
(SEE: ASPHYX, THE)
HORROR ON SNAPE ISLAND
(SEE: BEYOND THE FOG)
HORROR STAR, THE
(SEE: FRIGHTMARE (1983))
HORRORS OF BURKE AND HARE,
THE (SEE: BURKE AND HARE)
HOUSE OF CRAZIES
(SEE: ASYLUM)
HOUSE OF DOOM (SEE: BLACK
CAT, THE)
HOUSE OF DOOM (SEE: HOUSE
OF PSYCHOTIC WOMEN, THE)
HOUSE OF EVIL (SEE: HOUSE ON
SORORITY ROW, THE)
HOUSE OF MORTAL SIN
(SEE: CONFESSIONAL, THE)
HOUSE OF THE DARK STAIRWAY
(SEE: BLADE IN THE DARK, A)

# I

I CORPI PRESENTANO TRACCE DI
VIOLENZA CARNALE
(SEE: TORSO)
I HAVE NO MOUTH BUT I MUST
SCREAM (SEE: AND NOW THE
SCREAMING STARTS)

I TRE VOLTI DELLA PAURA
(SEE: BLACK SABBATH)
IL DIO CHIAMATO A DORIAN
(SEE: DORIAN GRAY)
IL FIUME DEL GRANDE CAIMANO
(SEE: GREAT ALLIGATOR, THE)
IL ROSO SEGMO DELLA POLLIAS
(SEE: HATCHET FOR A
HONEYMOON)
IL VISITATORE (SEE: VISITOR,
THE)
INCREDIBLE TORTURE SHOW,
THE (SEE: BLOODSUCKING
FREAKS)
INFERNAL IDOL, THE
(SEE: CRAZE)
INFERNO DEI MORTI-VIVENTI
(SEE: NIGHT OF THE ZOMBIES)
ISLAND OF THE FISHMEN
(SEE: SCREAMERS)
ISLAND OF THE LIVING DEAD
(SEE: ZOMBIE)
IT'S ALIVE II (SEE: IT LIVES
AGAIN)

# J

JACK'S WIFE (SEE: HUNGRY
WIVES)
JASON LIVES: FRIDAY THE 13TH
PART VI (SEE: FRIDAY THE
13TH PART VII—THE NEW
BLOOD)
JENNIFER (THE SNAKE
GODDESS) (SEE: JENNIFER)

# K

KAIDAN (SEE: KWAIDAN)
KILL AND GO HIDE! (SEE: CHILD,
THE)
KILLBOTS (SEE: CHOPPING MALL)
KILLER BATS (SEE: DEVIL BAT,
THE)
KILLER BEHIND THE MASK, THE
(SEE: SAVAGE WEEKEND)
KILLER GRIZZLY (SEE: GRIZZLY)
KILLER ORPHAN (SEE: FRIDAY
THE 13TH . . . THE ORPHAN)
KNIFE IN THE BODY, THE
(SEE: MURDER CLINIC, THE)

# L

LEGEND OF THE BAYOU
(SEE: EATEN ALIVE)
LA CABEZA VIVIENTE
(SEE: LIVING HEAD, THE)
LA CAMARA DEL TERROR
(SEE: FEAR CHAMBER, THE)
LA CASA CON LA SCALA NEL
BUIO (SEE: BLADE IN THE
DARK, A)
LA CASA DELL' EXORCISMO
(SEE: HOUSE OF EXORCISM,
THE)

LA FIGLIA DI FRANKENSTEIN
(SEE: LADY FRANKENSTEIN)
LA HORRIPLANTE BESTIA
HUMANA, HORROR Y SEXO
(SEE: NIGHT OF THE BLOODY
APES)
LA LAMA NEL CORPO
(SEE: MURDER CLINIC, THE)
LA MALDICION DE LA MOMIA
AZTECA (SEE: CURSE OF THE
AZTEC MUMMY, THE)
LA MANSION DE LA LOCURA
(SEE: DR. TARR'S TORTURE
DUNGEON)
LA MOMIA (SEE: AZTEC MUMMY,
THE)
LA MOMIA AZTECA CONTRA EL
ROBOT HUMANO (SEE: ROBOT
VS. THE AZTEC MUMMY, THE)
LA NOCHE DE LOS MIL GATOS
(SEE: NIGHT OF A THOUSAND
CATS, THE)
LA NOCHE DE WALPURGIS
(SEE: WEREWOLF VS. THE
VAMPIRE WOMAN, THE)
LA NOVIA ESANGENTADA
(SEE: BLOOD SPATTERED
BRIDE, THE)
LADY OF THE SHADOWS
(SEE: TERROR, THE)
LAMP, THE (SEE: OUTING, THE)
L'ANTICRISTO (SEE: TEMPTER,
THE)
LAS LUCHADORAS CONTRA LA
MOMIA (SEE: WRESTLING
WOMEN VS. THE AZTEC
MUMMY, THE)
LAST HOUSE ON THE LEFT PART
II (SEE: TWITCH OF THE DEATH
NERVE)
LAST VICTIM, THE (SEE: FORCED
ENTRY)
LE LOCATAIRE (SEE: TENANT,
THE)
LE ROUGE AUX LEVRES
(SEE: DAUGHTERS OF
DARKNESS)
LEGACY OF MAGGIE WALSH, THE
(SEE: LEGACY, THE)
LEGEND OF WITCH HOLLOW
(SEE: WITCHMAKER, THE)
LES NUITS DE L'EPOUVANTE
(SEE: MURDER CLINIC, THE)
LES YEUX SANS VISAGE
(SEE: HORROR CHAMBER OF
DR. FAUSTUS, THE)
LESBIAN TWINS (SEE: VIRGIN
WITCH, THE)
LISA AND THE DEVIL
(SEE: HOUSE OF EXORCISM,
THE)

SEASON OF THE WITCH
(SEE: HUNGRY WIVES)
SECRET OF DORIAN GRAY, THE
(SEE: DORIAN GRAY)
SEDDOK, L'EREDE DI SATANA
(SEE: ATOM AGE VAMPIRE)
SEED OF TERROR (SEE: GRAVE
OF THE VAMPIRE)
SEITE NOTE IN NERO
(SEE: PSYCHIC, THE)
SEL DONNE PER L'ASSASSINO
(SEE: BLOOD AND BLACK
LACE)
SEVEN BROTHERS MEET
DRACULA, THE (SEE: LEGEND
OF THE SEVEN GOLDEN
VAMPIRES, THE)
SEVEN SISTERS (SEE: HOUSE ON
SORORITY ROW, THE)
SHADOW OF THE WEREWOLF
(SEE: WEREWOLF VS. THE
VAMPIRE WOMAN, THE)
SHE MONSTER OF THE NIGHT
(SEE: FRANKENSTEIN'S
DAUGHTER)
SHIVERS (SEE: THEY CAME
FROM WITHIN)
SHOCK (SEE: BEYOND THE DOOR
II)
SILENT NIGHT, EVIL NIGHT
(SEE: BLACK CHRISTMAS)
SNAKE PIT AND THE PENDULUM,
THE (SEE: BLOOD DEMON)
SNAKE PIT, THE (SEE: BLOOD
DEMON)
SOMETHING IS OUT THERE
(SEE: DAY OF THE ANIMALS)
SOTTO GLI OCCHI
DELL'ASSASSINO
(SEE: UNSANE)
SPIDER BABY, OR THE MADDEST
STORY EVER TOLD
(SEE: SPIDER BABY)
SPIRIT OF THE DEAD
(SEE: ASPHYX, THE)
STARTLIGHT SLAUGHTER
(SEE: EATEN ALIVE)
STRANGE ADVENTURE OF DAVID
GRAY, THE (SEE: VAMPYR)
STRANGER IN THE HOUSE
(SEE: BLACK CHRISTMAS)
SWEENEY TODD, THE DEMON
BARBER OF FLEET STREET
(SEE: DEMON BARBER OF
FLEET STREET, THE)

T

TALES FROM THE CRYPT II
(SEE: VAULT OF HORROR, THE)
TENEBRAE (SEE: UNSANE)
TERROR AT RED WOLF INN
(SEE: TERROR HOUSE)

TERROR FACTOR, THE
(SEE: SCARED TO DEATH)
TERROR IN THE FOREST
(SEE: FOREST, THE)
TERROR OF DR. CHANEY, THE
(SEE: MANSION OF THE
DOOMED)
TERROR OF DRACULA
(SEE: NOSFERATU, THE
VAMPIRE)
THEY'RE COMING TO GET YOU
(SEE: DRACULA VS.
FRANKENSTEIN)
THREE FACES OF FEAR, THE
(SEE: BLACK SABBATH)
THREE FACES OF TERROR, THE
(SEE: BLACK SABBATH)
THROUGH THE LOOKING GLASS
(SEE: VELVET VAMPIRE, THE)
THURSDAY THE 12TH
(SEE: PANDEMONIUM)
TO LOVE A VAMPIRE (SEE: LUST
FOR A VAMPIRE)
TOMB OF THE CAT (SEE: TOMB
OF LIGEIA, THE)
TOMB OF THE LIVING DEAD
(SEE: MAD DOCTOR OF BLOOD
ISLAND, THE)
TORTURE CHAMBER OF BARON
BLOOD, THE (SEE: BARON
BLOOD)
TORTURE CHAMBER OF DR.
SADISM, THE (SEE: BLOOD
DEMON)
TORTURE ROOM, THE
(SEE: BLOOD DEMON)
TOWER OF EVIL (SEE: BEYOND
THE FOG)
TRAIN OF TERROR
(SEE: TERROR TRAIN)
TRAUMA (SEE: TERMINAL
CHOICE)
TWELFTH HOUR, THE
(SEE: NOSFERATU, THE
VAMPIRE)
TWILIGHT OF THE DEAD
(SEE: GATES OF HELL, THE)
TWINKLE, TWINKLE, KILLER KANE
(SEE: NINTH CONFIGURATION,
THE)

U

UNA HACKA PARA LA LUNA DE
MIEL (SEE: HATCHET FOR A
HONEYMOON)
UP FRANKENSTEIN (SEE: ANDY
WARHOL'S FRANKENSTEIN)
UPSTATE MURDERS, THE
(SEE: SAVAGE WEEKEND)

V

VAMPIRE-BEAST CRAVES BLOOD,
THE (SEE: BLOOD BEAST
TERROR, THE)
VAMPIRE PLAYGIRLS
(SEE: DEVIL'S NIGHTMARE,
THE)
VAMPYR, DER TRAUM DES DAVID
GRAY) AKA: NOT AGAINST THE
FLESH (SEE: VAMPYR)
VAMPYR, OU L'ETRANG E
AVENTURE DE DAVID GRAY
(SEE: VAMPYR)
VAMPYRES (SEE: VAMPYRES,
DAUGHTERS OF DRACULA)
VANISHING BODY, THE
(SEE: BLACK CAT, THE)
VEIL, THE (SEE: HAUNTS)
VELVET HOUSE (SEE: CRUCIBLE
OF HORROR)
VETERAN, THE
(SEE: DEATHDREAM)
VIRUS, INFERNO DEI
MORTI-VIVENTI (SEE: NIGHT OF
THE ZOMBIES)

W

WARD 13 (SEE: HOSPITAL
MASSACRE)
WARHOL'S FRANKENSTEIN
(SEE: ANDY WARHOL'S
FRANKENSTEIN)
WEREWOLF AT MIDNIGHT
(SEE: WEREWOLF OF
WASHINGTON)
WHO? (SEE: BEYOND THE DOOR)
WHOEVER SLEW AUNTIE ROO?
(SEE: WHO SLEW AUNTIE
ROO?)
WINGED SERPENT, THE (SEE: Q)
WITCHFINDER GENERAL
(SEE: CONQUEROR WORM,
THE)

X

X-RAY (SEE: HOSPITAL
MASSACRE)

Y

YOUNG DRACULA (SEE: ANDY
WARHOL'S DRACULA)
YOUNG MAN, I THINK YOU'RE
DYING (SEE: BEAST IN THE
CELLAR, THE)

Z

ZOLTAN, HOUND OF DRACULA
(SEE: DRACULA'S DOG)
ZOMBI 2 (SEE: ZOMBIE)
ZOMBIE CREEPING FLESH
(SEE: NIGHT OF THE ZOMBIES)
ZOMBIE FLESH EATERS
(SEE: ZOMBIE)

# INDEX

Individuals listed in the Index are grouped by function as follows:

**Actors** (major players only)
**Cinematographers**
**Directors**
**Editors**
**Music Composers**
**Producers**
**Screenwriters**
**Source Authors** (authors of the original material or creators of the characters upon which the film is based)

Individual names are followed by a listing of the films in which they were involved.

## ACTORS (Major players)

**Abbott, Bruce**
RE-ANIMATOR
BAD DREAMS

**Abbott, Bud**
ABBOTT AND COSTELLO MEET
FRANKENSTEIN
ABBOTT AND COSTELLO MEET DR.
JEKYLL AND MR. HYDE

**Abel, Walter**
SILENT NIGHT, BLOODY NIGHT

**Ackland, Joss**
GHOST SHIP

**Adams, Brooke**
DEAD ZONE, THE

**Adams, Julie**
CREATURE FROM THE BLACK
LAGOON
PSYCHIC KILLER

**Adams, Nick**
DIE, MONSTER, DIE

**Adjani, Isabelle**
POSSESSION
NOSFERATU, THE VAMPIRE
TENANT, THE

**Agar, John**
DAUGHTER OF DR. JEKYLL
CURSE OF THE SWAMP CREATURE

**Agutter, Jenny**
AMERICAN WEREWOLF IN LONDON,
AN
SURVIVOR

**Akins, Claude**
CURSE, THE
MONSTER IN THE CLOSET

**Albert, Eddie**
DEVIL'S RAIN, THE

**Albert, Edward**
HOUSE WHERE EVIL DWELLS, THE

**Albertson, Jack**
DEAD AND BURIED

**Alda, Robert**
HOUSE OF EXORCISM, THE

**Alda, Rutanya**
AMITYVILLE II: THE POSSESSION

**Allen, Nancy**
DRESSED TO KILL
CARRIE
BLOW OUT
POLTERGEIST III

**Allen, Todd**
WITCHBOARD

**Allnutt, Wendy**
FROM BEYOND THE GRAVE

**Ameche, Don**
PICTURE MOMMY DEAD

**Amplas, John**
MARTIN

**Anders, Luana**
DEMENTIA 13
PIT AND THE PENDULUM, THE

**Anderson, Judith**
INN OF THE DAMNED

**Anderson, Melissa Sue**
HAPPY BIRTHDAY TO ME

**Andrews, Dana**
CURSE OF THE DEMON

**Angeli, Pier**
OCTAMAN

**Ann-Margret**
MAGIC

**Ansara, Michael**
DEAR, DEAD DELILAH
DAY OF THE ANIMALS
MANITOU, THE

**Anspach, Susan**
BLUE MONKEY

**Ant, Adam**
NOMADS

**Archer, Anne**
TOO SCARED TO SCREAM

**Armstrong, Bess**
JAWS 3-D

**Armstrong, R.G.**
CHILDREN OF THE CORN
CAR, THE

**Armstrong, Robert**
KING KONG

**Arnaz, Jr., Desi**
HOUSE OF THE LONG SHADOWS

**Arquette, Patricia**
NIGHTMARE ON ELM STREET 3:
DREAM WARRIORS, A

**Assante, Armand**
PROPHECY

**Astaire, Fred**
GHOST STORY

**Astin, John**
TEEN WOLF TOO

**Astor, Mary**
HUSH . . . HUSH, SWEET CHARLOTTE

**Atkins, Tom**
MANIAC COP

**Attenborough, Richard**
SEANCE ON A WET AFTERNOON

**Atwill, Lionel**
DOCTOR X
FRANKENSTEIN MEETS THE WOLF
MAN
MARK OF THE VAMPIRE
MYSTERY OF THE WAX MUSEUM, THE
VAMPIRE BAT, THE
SON OF FRANKENSTEIN

**Auger, Claudine**
TWITCH OF THE DEATH NERVE

**Aumont, Jean-Pierre**
CAULDRON OF BLOOD

**Axton, Hoyt**
GREMLINS

**Aykroyd, Dan**
GHOSTBUSTERS
TWILIGHT ZONE—THE MOVIE

**Ayres, Leah**
BURNING, THE

**Bach, Barbara**
GREAT ALLIGATOR, THE
UNSEEN, THE
SCREAMERS

**Baker, Carroll**
WATCHER IN THE WOODS, THE

Baker, Diane
STRAIT-JACKET

Baker, Joe Don
PACK, THE
WACKO

Balding, Rebecca
BOOGENS, THE
SILENT SCREAM

Baldwin, Alec
BEETLEJUICE

Balsam, Martin
PSYCHO
SENTINEL, THE

Balsam, Talia
CRAWLSPACE

Bankhead, Tallulah
DIE! DIE! MY DARLING

Banks, Leslie
CHAMBER OF HORRORS

Bannen, Ian
FROM BEYOND THE GRAVE
WATCHER IN THE WOODS, THE

Barbeau, Adrienne
CREEPSHOW
FOG, THE
OPEN HOUSE
SWAMP THING

Barker, Lex
BLOOD DEMON

Baron, Sandy
VAMP

Barrymore, Drew
CAT'S EYE

Barrymore, John
DR. JEKYLL AND MR. HYDE

Barrymore, Lionel
DEVIL DOLL, THE
MARK OF THE VAMPIRE

Bartel, Paul
EATING RAOUL

Bartok, Eva
BLOOD AND BLACK LACE

Basehart, Richard
MANSION OF THE DOOMED
ISLAND OF DR. MOREAU, THE

Bate, Anthony
GHOST STORY

Bateman, Jason
TEEN WOLF TOO

Bates, Alan
SHOUT, THE

Bates, Ralph
DR. JEKYLL AND SISTER HYDE

Batsford, Sara
DEADLY EYES

Bay, Sarah
LADY FRANKENSTEIN

Bayldon, Geoffrey
TALES FROM THE CRYPT

Beals, Jennifer
BRIDE, THE

Beatty, Ned
UNHOLY, THE

Beck, Jenny
TROLL

Beery, Wallace
LOST WORLD, THE

Beghe, Jason
MONKEY SHINES: AN EXPERIMENT IN
FEAR

Begley, Ed
DUNWICH HORROR, THE

Begley, Jr., Ed
TRANSYLVANIA 6-5000

Bellamy, Ralph
ROSEMARY'S BABY
WOLF MAN, THE

Beltran, Robert
EATING RAOUL

Bendorf, Sherry
SLAUGHTERHOUSE

Benjamin, Richard
SATURDAY THE 14TH
LOVE AT FIRST BITE

Bennett, Alma
LOST WORLD, THE

Benton, Barbi
HOSPITAL MASSACRE

Berger, Helmut
DORIAN GRAY

Berger, William
MURDER CLINIC, THE

Bergman, Ingrid
DR. JEKYLL AND MR. HYDE

Berridge, Elizabeth
FUNHOUSE, THE

Beswick, Martine
DR. JEKYLL AND SISTER HYDE

Black, Karen
BURNT OFFERINGS
PYX, THE
IT'S ALIVE III: ISLAND OF THE ALIVE

Blackman, Honor
TO THE DEVIL A DAUGHTER

Blackmer, Sidney
ROSEMARY'S BABY

Blair, Linda
EXORCIST II: THE HERETIC
EXORCIST, THE
HELL NIGHT

Blakley, Ronee
NIGHTMARE ON ELM STREET, A
RETURN TO SALEM'S LOT, A

Blankfield, Mark
FRANKENSTEIN GENERAL HOSPITAL

Blodgett, Michael
VELVET VAMPIRE, THE

Bloom, Claire
HAUNTING, THE

Bochner, Hart
TERROR TRAIN

Boehm, Karl
PEEPING TOM

Bolling, Tiffany
KINGDOM OF THE SPIDERS

Bologna, Joseph
TRANSYLVANIA 6-5000

Bonet, Lisa
ANGEL HEART

Bonet, Nai
NOCTURNA

Bono, Sonny
TROLL

Boo the Monkey
MONKEY SHINES: AN EXPERIMENT IN
FEAR

Borgnine, Ernest
DEVIL'S RAIN, THE
WILLARD

Bottoms, Joseph
OPEN HOUSE

Bottoms, Timothy
IN THE SHADOW OF KILIMANJARO

Bowie, David
HUNGER, THE

Boyle, Peter
YOUNG FRANKENSTEIN

Brady, Scott
CASTLE OF EVIL
NIGHTMARE IN WAX

Brand, Neville
EATEN ALIVE
NINTH CONFIGURATION, THE

Brasseur, Pierre
HORROR CHAMBER OF DR.
FAUSTUS, THE

Brazzi, Rossano
FINAL CONFLICT, THE
HOUSE OF FREAKS

Bridges, Jeff
KING KONG

Britt, May
HAUNTS

Brocco, Peter
HOMEBODIES

Brolin, James
AMITYVILLE HORROR, THE
CAR, THE

Brooks, Albert
TWILIGHT ZONE—THE MOVIE

Brosnan, Pierce
NOMADS

Browne, Coral
THEATRE OF BLOOD

Bujold, Genevieve
DEAD RINGERS

**Bunny, George**
LOST WORLD, THE

**Buono, Victor**
ARNOLD
EVIL, THE
STRANGLER, THE
WHATEVER HAPPENED TO BABY JANE?

**Burden, Hugh**
GHOST SHIP

**Burke, Paul**
PSYCHIC KILLER

**Burns, Mark**
HOUSE OF THE LIVING DEAD

**Burr, Raymond**
BRIDE OF THE GORILLA

**Burstyn, Ellen**
EXORCIST, THE

**Burton, Richard**
EXORCIST II: THE HERETIC

**Busey, Gary**
STEPHEN KING'S SILVER BULLET

**Byrne, Eddie**
MUMMY, THE

**Byrne, Gabriel**
KEEP, THE
GOTHIC

**Cabot, Bruce**
KING KONG

**Caine, Michael**
DRESSED TO KILL
HAND, THE
JAWS: THE REVENGE

**Calhoun, Rory**
MOTEL HELL

**Campbell, Bruce**
MANIAC COP

**Campbell, William**
DEMENTIA 13

**Cardille, Lori**
DAY OF THE DEAD

**Cariou, Len**
LADY IN WHITE

**Carlson, Richard**
CREATURE FROM THE BLACK LAGOON

**Carradine, David**
Q
TRICK OR TREATS

**Carradine, John**
HOUSE OF THE LONG SHADOWS
BLUEBEARD
BLOOD OF DRACULA'S CASTLE
BILLY THE KID VS. DRACULA
BIG FOOT
HOUSE OF SEVEN CORPSES, THE
HILLBILLYS IN A HAUNTED HOUSE
MONSTER CLUB, THE
NOCTURNA
NESTING, THE
SILENT NIGHT, BLOODY NIGHT

SHOCK WAVES
SENTINEL, THE
SATAN'S CHEERLEADERS
REVENGE
UNEARTHLY, THE

**Carradine, Robert**
MASSACRE AT CENTRAL HIGH

**Carrera, Barbara**
ISLAND OF DR. MOREAU, THE

**Carrillo, Leo**
PHANTOM OF THE OPERA

**Casey, Bernie**
DR. BLACK AND MR. HYDE

**Cassavetes, John**
FURY, THE
INCUBUS, THE
ROSEMARY'S BABY

**Cassavetes, Nick**
WRAITH, THE

**Cates, Phoebe**
GREMLINS

**Celozzi, Nicholas**
SLAUGHTERHOUSE ROCK

**Chambers, Marilyn**
RABID

**Chandler, Helen**
DRACULA

**Chaney, Jr., Lon**
DRACULA VS. FRANKENSTEIN
ABBOTT AND COSTELLO MEET FRANKENSTEIN
BRIDE OF THE GORILLA
HILLBILLYS IN A HAUNTED HOUSE
FRANKENSTEIN MEETS THE WOLF MAN
SPIDER BABY
WOLF MAN, THE
SON OF DRACULA

**Chaney, Lon**
PHANTOM OF THE OPERA, THE
UNHOLY THREE, THE
HUNCHBACK OF NOTRE DAME, THE

**Cher**
WITCHES OF EASTWICK, THE

**Chiles, Lois**
CREEPSHOW 2

**Chiodo, Michael**
CARNAGE

**Christensen, Benjamin**
WITCHCRAFT THROUGH THE AGES

**Christie, Julie**
DON'T LOOK NOW

**Cilento, Diane**
WICKER MAN, THE

**Clark, Candy**
Q

**Clarke, Mae**
FRANKENSTEIN

**Clive, Colin**
BRIDE OF FRANKENSTEIN, THE
FRANKENSTEIN

**Cobb, Lee J.**
EXORCIST, THE

**Coe, Barry**
DOCTOR DEATH: SEEKER OF SOULS

**Collins, Joan**
TALES FROM THE CRYPT

**Combs, Jeffrey**
FROM BEYOND
RE-ANIMATOR

**Comer, Anjanette**
BABY, THE
NIGHT OF A THOUSAND CATS, THE

**Connelly, Christopher**
MANHATTAN BABY

**Connelly, Jennifer**
CREEPERS

**Connors, Chuck**
TOURIST TRAP, THE

**Connors, Mike**
TOO SCARED TO SCREAM

**Considine, John**
DOCTOR DEATH: SEEKER OF SOULS

**Conti, Tom**
HAUNTING OF JULIA, THE

**Contouri, Chantal**
THIRST

**Convy, Bert**
JENNIFER

**Conway, Tom**
CAT PEOPLE
BRIDE OF THE GORILLA
I WALKED WITH A ZOMBIE
SEVENTH VICTIM, THE

**Coogan, Jackie**
HUMAN EXPERIMENTS

**Cooke, Jennifer**
FRIDAY THE 13TH PART VI: JASON LIVES

**Cooper, Alice**
MONSTER DOG

**Copperfield, David**
TERROR TRAIN

**Cord, Alex**
UNINVITED, THE
INN OF THE DAMNED

**Corey, Jeff**
PREMONITION, THE

**Costello, Lou**
ABBOTT AND COSTELLO MEET FRANKENSTEIN
ABBOTT AND COSTELLO MEET DR. JEKYLL AND MR. HYDE

**Cotten, Joseph**
BARON BLOOD
ABOMINABLE DR. PHIBES, THE
HEARSE, THE
LADY FRANKENSTEIN
SURVIVOR
SCREAMERS
HUSH ... HUSH, SWEET CHARLOTTE

**Court, Hazel**
CURSE OF FRANKENSTEIN, THE
GHOST SHIP

**Cowles, Jules**
LOST WORLD, THE

**Cox, Ronny**
BEAST WITHIN, THE

**Crampton, Barbara**
FROM BEYOND

**Crawford, Joan**
BERSERK
STRAIT-JACKET
WHATEVER HAPPENED TO BABY
JANE?

**Crenna, Richard**
EVIL, THE
DEATH SHIP

**Crisp, Donald**
DR. JEKYLL AND MR. HYDE

**Crosby, Harry**
FRIDAY THE 13TH

**Crosby, Lindsay**
BIG FOOT

**Cross, Ben**
UNHOLY, THE

**Crothers, Scatman**
DEADLY EYES
SHINING, THE
TWILIGHT ZONE—THE MOVIE

**Culver, Roland**
DEAD OF NIGHT

**Cummins, Peggy**
CURSE OF THE DEMON

**Currie, Finley**
CORRIDORS OF BLOOD

**Curtis, Jamie Lee**
FOG, THE
HALLOWEEN II
HALLOWEEN
PROM NIGHT
TERROR TRAIN
ROAD GAMES

**Curtis, Tony**
MANITOU, THE

**Cushing, Peter**
HOUSE OF THE LONG SHADOWS
BLOOD BEAST TERROR, THE
BEAST MUST DIE, THE
ASYLUM
AND NOW THE SCREAMING STARTS
CURSE OF FRANKENSTEIN, THE
EVIL OF FRANKENSTEIN, THE
DR. TERROR'S HOUSE OF HORRORS
HORROR EXPRESS
GORGON, THE
GHOUL, THE
FROM BEYOND THE GRAVE
LAND OF THE MINOTAUR
MUMMY, THE
SHOCK WAVES
UNCANNY, THE

**Cyr, Myriam**
GOTHIC

**D'Arcy, Alex**
BLOOD OF DRACULA'S CASTLE

**Dale, Jennifer**
OF UNKNOWN ORIGIN

**Dallesandro, Joe**
ANDY WARHOL'S FRANKENSTEIN
ANDY WARHOL'S DRACULA

**Damon, Mark**
DEVIL'S WEDDING NIGHT, THE
HOUSE OF USHER

**Dane, Lawrence**
OF UNKNOWN ORIGIN

**Dano, Royal**
HOUSE II: THE SECOND STORY
GHOULIES II

**Darby, Kim**
TEEN WOLF TOO

**Darden, Severn**
SATURDAY THE 14TH
WEREWOLVES ON WHEELS

**Davenport, Nigel**
ISLAND OF DR. MOREAU, THE

**Davis, Bette**
WATCHER IN THE WOODS, THE
WHATEVER HAPPENED TO BABY
JANE?
HUSH ... HUSH, SWEET CHARLOTTE

**Davis, Geena**
FLY, THE
BEETLEJUICE

**Davison, Bruce**
WILLARD

**Dawson, Greg**
BERSERKER

**De Carlo, Yvonne**
AMERICAN GOTHIC
NOCTURNA
SATAN'S CHEERLEADERS
PLAY DEAD

**de Gunzberg, Baron Nicolas**
VAMPYR

**de Havilland, Olivia**
HUSH ... HUSH, SWEET CHARLOTTE

**De Niro, Robert**
ANGEL HEART

**Dee, Frances**
I WALKED WITH A ZOMBIE

**Dee, Sandra**
DUNWICH HORROR, THE

**DeLuise, Dom**
HAUNTED HONEYMOON

**Den Dooven, Leslie**
CARNAGE

**Deneuve, Catherine**
HUNGER, THE
REPULSION

**Denning, Richard**
CREATURE FROM THE BLACK
LAGOON

**Dennis, John**
GARDEN OF THE DEAD

**Derek, Bo**
ORCA

**Dern, Bruce**
BLACK SUNDAY

**Dewhurst, Colleen**
DEAD ZONE, THE

**DeYoung, Cliff**
PULSE
HUNGER, THE

**Dickinson, Angie**
DRESSED TO KILL

**Diffring, Anton**
BEAST MUST DIE, THE
CIRCUS OF HORRORS

**Diller, Phyllis**
MAD MONSTER PARTY

**Dillman, Bradford**
PIRANHA

**Domergue, Faith**
HOUSE OF SEVEN CORPSES, THE

**Dors, Diana**
BERSERK
CRAZE

**Douglas, Kirk**
FURY, THE
CHOSEN, THE

**Douglas, Melvyn**
CHANGELING, THE
GHOST STORY
TENANT, THE
VAMPIRE BAT, THE

**Dourif, Brad**
CHILD'S PLAY

**Down, Lesley-Anne**
NOMADS

**Drake, Tom**
SPECTRE OF EDGAR ALLAN POE, THE

**Dreyfuss, Richard**
JAWS

**Duff, Howard**
MONSTER IN THE CLOSET

**Dukes, David**
RAWHEAD REX

**Dullea, Keir**
BLACK CHRISTMAS
HAUNTING OF JULIA, THE

**Dunn, Michael**
HOUSE OF FREAKS

**Dunne, Dominique**
POLTERGEIST

**Dunne, Griffin**
AMERICAN WEREWOLF IN LONDON,
AN

**Durning, Charles**
SISTERS

WHEN A STRANGER CALLS

**Duvall, Shelley**
SHINING, THE

**Eddy, Nelson**
PHANTOM OF THE OPERA

**Edgerton, Earle**
CARNIVAL OF BLOOD

**Eggar, Samantha**
CURTAINS
BROOD, THE
DEMONOID

**Ekland, Britt**
ASYLUM
WICKER MAN, THE

**Elam, Jack**
CREATURE FROM BLACK LAKE, THE

**Elliot, Peter**
KING KONG LIVES

**Elliott, Denholm**
HOUSE THAT DRIPPED BLOOD, THE
TO THE DEVIL A DAUGHTER

**Elliott, Sam**
FROGS
LEGACY, THE

**Ellison, James**
I WALKED WITH A ZOMBIE

**Englund, Robert**
NIGHTMARE ON ELM STREET 4: THE
DREAM MASTER, A

**Erickson, Leif**
STRAIT-JACKET

**Estevez, Emilio**
MAXIMUM OVERDRIVE

**Evans, Clifford**
CURSE OF THE WEREWOLF, THE

**Evans, Edith**
CRAZE

**Evans, Maurice**
ROSEMARY'S BABY

**Evers, Jason**
BRAIN THAT WOULDN'T DIE, THE

**Fairbanks, Jr., Douglas**
GHOST STORY

**Faire, Virginia Browne**
LOST WORLD, THE

**Faithfull, Marianne**
GHOST STORY

**Farentino, James**
DEAD AND BURIED

**Farrell, Sharon**
IT'S ALIVE
PREMONITION, THE

**Farrow, Mia**
ROSEMARY'S BABY
HAUNTING OF JULIA, THE

**Farrow, Tisa**
GRIM REAPER, THE
ZOMBIE

**Feldman, Marty**
YOUNG FRANKENSTEIN

**Fenn, Sherilyn**
WRAITH, THE

**Ferrare, Cristina**
MARY, MARY, BLOODY MARY

**Ferrer, Jose**
BLOODY BIRTHDAY
BLOOD TIDE
DRACULA'S DOG
SENTINEL, THE

**Ferrer, Mel**
CITY OF THE WALKING DEAD
EATEN ALIVE
GREAT ALLIGATOR, THE
TEMPTER, THE
VISITOR, THE

**Field, Shirley Ann**
HOUSE OF THE LIVING DEAD

**Finney, Albert**
WOLFEN

**Firth, Peter**
BORN OF FIRE

**Fishburne, Larry**
NIGHTMARE ON ELM STREET 3:
DREAM WARRIORS, A

**Flemyng, Robert**
BLOOD BEAST TERROR, THE

**Fletcher, Louise**
EXORCIST II: THE HERETIC
STRANGE BEHAVIOR

**Foch, Nina**
JENNIFER
RETURN OF THE VAMPIRE, THE

**Fonda, Henry**
TENTACLES

**Fonda, Peter**
RACE WITH THE DEVIL
SPASMS

**Ford, Glenn**
HAPPY BIRTHDAY TO ME
VISITOR, THE

**Forrest, Frederic**
IT LIVES AGAIN

**Foster, Jodie**
LITTLE GIRL WHO LIVES DOWN THE
LANE, THE

**Foster, Preston**
DOCTOR X

**Foster, Susanna**
PHANTOM OF THE OPERA

**Fox, Michael J.**
TEEN WOLF

**Foxworth, Robert**
PROPHECY
INVISIBLE STRANGLER, THE

**Franciosa, Anthony**
UNSANE

**Franklin, Pamela**
LEGEND OF HELL HOUSE, THE

**Franz, Dennis**
DRESSED TO KILL
PSYCHO II
BODY DOUBLE
BLOW OUT

**Frederick, Lynne**
SCHIZO

**French, Victor**
HOUSE ON SKULL MOUNTAIN, THE

**Friedrich, John**
FINAL TERROR, THE

**Frye, Dwight**
CRIME OF DR. CRESPI, THE

**Fuller, Samuel**
RETURN TO SALEM'S LOT, A

**Furneaux, Yvonne**
MUMMY, THE

**Gabor, Zsa Zsa**
PICTURE MOMMY DEAD

**Galligan, Zach**
GREMLINS

**Ganz, Bruno**
NOSFERATU, THE VAMPIRE

**Gardenia, Vincent**
LITTLE SHOP OF HORRORS

**Gary, Lorraine**
JAWS: THE REVENGE
JAWS II

**Gavin, John**
JENNIFER
PSYCHO

**Geer, Will**
DEAR, DEAD DELILAH

**George, Christopher**
DAY OF THE ANIMALS
GRIZZLY
PIECES

**George, Lynda Day**
BEYOND EVIL
DAY OF THE ANIMALS
PIECES

**George, Susan**
HOUSE WHERE EVIL DWELLS, THE

**Gertz, Jami**
LOST BOYS, THE

**Getz, John**
FLY, THE

**Gibson, Henry**
MONSTER IN THE CLOSET

**Glenn, Scott**
KEEP, THE

**Goldblum, Jeff**
FLY, THE
TRANSYLVANIA 6-5000

**Gorcey, Leo**
GHOSTS ON THE LOOSE

**Gordon, Keith**
CHRISTINE

**Gordon, Ruth**
ROSEMARY'S BABY

**Gortner, Marjoe**
MAUSOLEUM

**Gossett, Jr., Louis**
JAWS 3-D

**Gower, Andre**
MONSTER SQUAD, THE

**Grahame, Gloria**
MANSION OF THE DOOMED
NESTING, THE

**Granger, Farley**
ARNOLD

**Grant, Donald**
MONSTER IN THE CLOSET

**Grant, Lee**
DAMIEN—OMEN II
VISITING HOURS

**Grantham, Lucy**
LAST HOUSE ON THE LEFT

**Gray, Charles**
BEAST MUST DIE, THE

**Gray, Lorna**
MAN THEY COULD NOT HANG, THE

**Greene, Ellen**
LITTLE SHOP OF HORRORS

**Greenwood, Joan**
UNCANNY, THE

**Grier, Pam**
SOMETHING WICKED THIS WAY
COMES
SCREAM, BLACULA, SCREAM

**Griffith, Hugh**
ABOMINABLE DR. PHIBES, THE
CRAZE
DOCTOR PHIBES RISES AGAIN

**Griffith, Melanie**
BODY DOUBLE

**Grodin, Charles**
KING KONG

**Groom, Sam**
DEADLY EYES

**Gross, Arye**
HOUSE II: THE SECOND STORY

**Groves, Robin**
NESTING, THE

**Guest, Lance**
JAWS: THE REVENGE

**Guilfoyle, Paul**
CRIME OF DR. CRESPI, THE

**Gulager, Clu**
INITIATION, THE
OFFSPRING, THE
NIGHTMARE ON ELM STREET PART 2:
FREDDY'S REVENGE, A
RETURN OF THE LIVING DEAD

**Haas, Lukas**
LADY IN WHITE

**Hack, Shelley**
TROLL
STEPFATHER, THE

**Hackman, Gene**
YOUNG FRANKENSTEIN

**Hagen, Uta**
OTHER, THE

**Hale, Creighton**
CAT AND THE CANARY, THE

**Hall, Huntz**
GHOSTS ON THE LOOSE

**Halsey, Brett**
RETURN OF THE FLY

**Hamilton, George**
LOVE AT FIRST BITE

**Hamilton, Linda**
CHILDREN OF THE CORN
KING KONG LIVES

**Hannah, Darryl**
FINAL TERROR, THE

**Hardin, Ty**
BERSERK

**Hardwicke, Sir Cedric**
HUNCHBACK OF NOTRE DAME, THE
GHOUL, THE

**Hargitay, Mickey**
LADY FRANKENSTEIN

**Harper, Tess**
AMITYVILLE 3-D

**Harris, John**
CARNIVAL OF BLOOD

**Harris, Julie**
HAUNTING, THE

**Harris, Richard**
ORCA

**Harrison, Gregory**
RAZORBACK

**Harrold, Kathryn**
NIGHTWING
SENDER, THE

**Harry, Deborah**
VIDEODROME

**Hartman, Lisa**
DEADLY BLESSING

**Hatfield, Hurd**
PICTURE OF DORIAN GRAY, THE

**Hathaway, Noah**
TROLL

**Hauer, Rutger**
HITCHER, THE

**Havoc, June**
RETURN TO SALEM'S LOT, A

**Hawkins, Jack**
THEATRE OF BLOOD

**Hayman, Cyd**
GODSEND, THE

**Haynes, Linda**
HUMAN EXPERIMENTS

**Heard, John**
CAT PEOPLE

**Heckart, Eileen**
BURNT OFFERINGS

**Hedison, David**
FLY, THE

**Hedren, Tippi**
BIRDS, THE

**Helm, Anne**
NIGHTMARE IN WAX

**Helmond, Katherine**
LADY IN WHITE

**Hemmings, David**
DEEP RED
THIRST

**Hendry, Ian**
THEATRE OF BLOOD
REPULSION

**Henreid, Paul**
EXORCIST II: THE HERETIC

**Henriksen, Lance**
PUMPKINHEAD

**Henry, Buck**
EATING RAOUL

**Henry, Gregg**
BODY DOUBLE

**Herbert, Charles**
THIRTEEN GHOSTS

**Herbst, Rick**
BRAIN DAMAGE

**Herrmann, Edward**
LOST BOYS, THE

**Hershey, Barbara**
ENTITY, THE

**Hess, David**
LAST HOUSE ON THE LEFT

**Heston, Charlton**
AWAKENING, THE

**Hicks, Catherine**
CHILD'S PLAY

**Hill, Mariana**
SCHIZOID

**Hines, Gregory**
WOLFEN

**Hingle, Pat**
MAXIMUM OVERDRIVE

**Hobson, Valerie**
BRIDE OF FRANKENSTEIN, THE

**Holbrook, Hal**
CREEPSHOW
FOG, THE
UNHOLY, THE

**Holden, William**
DAMIEN—OMEN II

**Holmes, Jennifer**
DEMON, THE

**Hopkins, Anthony**
AUDREY ROSE

**Hopkins, Bo**
TENTACLES
SWEET SIXTEEN

# ACTORS

**Hopper, Dennis**
TEXAS CHAINSAW MASSACRE PART 2, THE

**Horton, Peter**
CHILDREN OF THE CORN

**Houseman, John**
FOG, THE
GHOST STORY

**Howard, Trevor**
CRAZE
UNHOLY, THE

**Hoyt, Arthur**
LOST WORLD, THE

**Huffman, David**
BLOOD BEACH

**Hunnicutt, Gayle**
LEGEND OF HELL HOUSE, THE

**Hunter, Ian**
DR. JEKYLL AND MR. HYDE

**Hunter, Kim**
SEVENTH VICTIM, THE

**Hurley, Matthew**
PUMPKINHEAD

**Hurt, John**
GHOUL, THE
SHOUT, THE

**Husky, Ferlin**
HILLBILLYS IN A HAUNTED HOUSE

**Hussey, Olivia**
BLACK CHRISTMAS

**Huston, John**
TENTACLES
VISITOR, THE

**Hutton, Jim**
PSYCHIC KILLER

**Hutton, Lauren**
ONCE BITTEN

**Hyer, Martha**
PICTURE MOMMY DEAD

**Inescort, Frieda**
RETURN OF THE VAMPIRE, THE

**Ireland, John**
HOUSE OF SEVEN CORPSES, THE
SATAN'S CHEERLEADERS

**Irons, Jeremy**
DEAD RINGERS

**Ironside, Michael**
HELLO MARY LOU, PROM NIGHT II
VISITING HOURS

**Irving, Amy**
FURY, THE
CARRIE

**Ivanek, Zeljko**
SENDER, THE

**Ivey, Judith**
SISTER SISTER

**Jaeckel, Richard**
DAY OF THE ANIMALS
GRIZZLY

**Jagger, Dean**
REVOLT OF THE ZOMBIES

**Jessel, Patricia**
HORROR HOTEL

**Johns, Mervyn**
DEAD OF NIGHT

**Johnson, Ben**
TERROR TRAIN
TOWN THAT DREADED SUNDOWN, THE

**Johnson, Joseph**
BERSERKER

**Johnson, Richard**
HAUNTING, THE

**Jones, Carolyn**
EATEN ALIVE
HOUSE OF WAX

**Jones, Duane**
GANJA AND HESS

**Jones, James Earl**
BLOOD TIDE

**Jourdan, Louis**
SWAMP THING

**Kahn, Madeline**
YOUNG FRANKENSTEIN

**Kane, Carol**
WHEN A STRANGER CALLS
TRANSYLVANIA 6-5000

**Karloff, Boris**
CORRIDORS OF BLOOD
HOUSE OF EVIL
DIE, MONSTER, DIE
BLACK ROOM, THE
BLACK CAT, THE
BEFORE I HANG
BEDLAM
APE, THE
ABBOTT AND COSTELLO MEET DR. JEKYLL AND MR. HYDE
CAULDRON OF BLOOD
BRIDE OF FRANKENSTEIN, THE
BODY SNATCHER, THE
FEAR CHAMBER, THE
HAUNTED STRANGLER, THE
GHOUL, THE
FRANKENSTEIN 1970
MUMMY, THE
ISLE OF THE DEAD
RAVEN, THE
RAVEN, THE
TERROR, THE
TARGETS
MAN THEY COULD NOT HANG, THE
SON OF FRANKENSTEIN
MAD MONSTER PARTY
FRANKENSTEIN

**Katt, William**
HOUSE

**Kaufmann, Christine**
MURDERS IN THE RUE MORGUE

**Keach, Stacy**
ROAD GAMES
NINTH CONFIGURATION, THE

**Keaton, Camille**
I SPIT ON YOUR GRAVE

**Keaton, Michael**
BEETLEJUICE

**Kedrova, Lila**
BLOOD TIDE

**Keller, Marthe**
BLACK SUNDAY

**Kemp, Valli**
DOCTOR PHIBES RISES AGAIN

**Kendall, Suzy**
BIRD WITH THE CRYSTAL PLUMAGE, THE

**Kennedy, Arthur**
TEMPTER, THE

**Kennedy, George**
UNINVITED, THE
CREEPSHOW 2
DEATH SHIP
WACKO

**Kenworthy, Michael**
RETURN OF THE LIVING DEAD PART II

**Kerr, John**
PIT AND THE PENDULUM, THE

**Kidder, Margot**
BLACK CHRISTMAS
AMITYVILLE HORROR, THE
SISTERS

**Kiel, Richard**
HYSTERICAL

**Kiger, Robby**
MONSTER SQUAD, THE

**King, Adrienne**
FRIDAY THE 13TH

**King, Alan**
CAT'S EYE

**Kinski, Klaus**
CRAWLSPACE
COUNT DRACULA
NOSFERATU, THE VAMPIRE
SCHIZOID

**Kinski, Nastassja**
CAT PEOPLE
TO THE DEVIL A DAUGHTER

**Kirk, Phyllis**
HOUSE OF WAX

**Kitaen, Tawny**
WITCHBOARD

**Knowles, Patric**
FRANKENSTEIN MEETS THE WOLF MAN

**Korman, Harvey**
MUNCHIES

**Koscina, Sylva**
HOUSE OF EXORCISM, THE

**Kotto, Yaphet**
WARNING SIGN

**Krauss, Werner**
CABINET OF DR. CALIGARI, THE

**Kristel, Sylvia**
DRACULA'S WIDOW

**Kruschen, Jack**
SATAN'S CHEERLEADERS

**La Plante, Laura**
CAT AND THE CANARY, THE

**Ladd, Diane**
SOMETHING WICKED THIS WAY
COMES

**Lake, Veronica**
FLESH FEAST

**Lally, Michael David**
NESTING, THE

**Lamour, Dorothy**
CREEPSHOW 2

**Lampert, Zohra**
LET'S SCARE JESSICA TO DEATH

**Lancaster, Burt**
ISLAND OF DR. MOREAU, THE

**Lanchester, Elsa**
ARNOLD
BRIDE OF FRANKENSTEIN, THE
WILLARD

**Landau, Martin**
ALONE IN THE DARK

**Landis, John**
SCHLOCK

**Landon, Laurene**
MANIAC COP

**Lange, Hope**
NIGHTMARE ON ELM STREET PART 2:
FREDDY'S REVENGE, A

**Lange, Jessica**
KING KONG

**Langella, Frank**
DRACULA

**Langenkamp, Heather**
NIGHTMARE ON ELM STREET, A
NIGHTMARE ON ELM STREET 3:
DREAM WARRIORS, A

**Lansbury, Angela**
PICTURE OF DORIAN GRAY, THE

**Lansing, Joi**
BIG FOOT
HILLBILLYS IN A HAUNTED HOUSE

**Lapotaire, Jane**
ASPHYX, THE

**Larroquette, John**
TWILIGHT ZONE—THE MOVIE

**Laughton, Charles**
HUNCHBACK OF NOTRE DAME, THE

**Laurie, Piper**
CARRIE
RUBY

**Le Gros, James**
PHANTASM II

**Lee, Anna**
BEDLAM

**Lee, Christopher**
CORRIDORS OF BLOOD
HOUSE OF THE LONG SHADOWS
BLOOD DEMON
CURSE OF FRANKENSTEIN, THE
CREEPING FLESH, THE
COUNT DRACULA
DR. TERROR'S HOUSE OF HORRORS
HOWLING II . . . YOUR SISTER IS A
WEREWOLF
HORROR EXPRESS
GORGON, THE
KEEPER, THE
OBLONG BOX, THE
MUMMY, THE
TO THE DEVIL A DAUGHTER
THEATRE OF DEATH
SCREAM AND SCREAM AGAIN
SCARS OF DRACULA, THE
WICKER MAN, THE
HORROR HOTEL

**Leigh, Janet**
FOG, THE
PSYCHO

**Leigh, Jennifer Jason**
EYES OF A STRANGER
SISTER SISTER

**Lemmon, Chris**
JUST BEFORE DAWN

**Lenz, Kay**
HOUSE

**Lester, Mark**
WHO SLEW AUNTIE ROO?

**Lewis, Geoffrey**
HUMAN EXPERIMENTS

**Lewis, Jerry**
NUTTY PROFESSOR, THE

**Leyton, John**
SCHIZO

**Lindfors, Viveca**
CAULDRON OF BLOOD

**Lithgow, John**
TWILIGHT ZONE—THE MOVIE
BLOW OUT

**Little, Michelle**
MY DEMON LOVER

**Lloyd, Danny**
SHINING, THE

**Lloyd, Kathleen**
CAR, THE

**Locke, Sondra**
WILLARD

**Lockhart, Calvin**
BEAST MUST DIE, THE

**Loggia, Robert**
BELIEVERS, THE
PSYCHO II
NINTH CONFIGURATION, THE

**Lom, Herbert**
ASYLUM
AND NOW THE SCREAMING STARTS
COUNT DRACULA

DORIAN GRAY
MARK OF THE DEVIL
MURDERS IN THE RUE MORGUE

**Loomis, Christopher**
NESTING, THE

**Lorre, Peter**
RAVEN, THE
TALES OF TERROR

**Love, Suzanna**
BOOGEYMAN II
BOOGEY MAN, THE
DEVONSVILLE TERROR, THE

**Lovejoy, Frank**
HOUSE OF WAX

**Lugosi, Bela**
BLACK DRAGONS
BLACK CAT, THE
APE MAN, THE
ABBOTT AND COSTELLO MEET
FRANKENSTEIN
CORPSE VANISHES, THE
BOWERY AT MIDNIGHT
BODY SNATCHER, THE
DRACULA
DEVIL BAT, THE
HUMAN MONSTER, THE
FRANKENSTEIN MEETS THE WOLF
MAN
MARK OF THE VAMPIRE
INVISIBLE GHOST, THE
RAVEN, THE
SCARED TO DEATH
RETURN OF THE VAMPIRE, THE
WHITE ZOMBIE
SON OF FRANKENSTEIN

**Lugosi, Boris**
HOUSE OF FREAKS

**Lupino, Ida**
DEVIL'S RAIN, THE

**Lupton, John**
JESSE JAMES MEETS
FRANKENSTEIN'S DAUGHTER

**Luz, Franc**
GHOST TOWN

**Lynch, Richard**
PREMONITION, THE

**Lyon, Sue**
INVISIBLE STRANGLER, THE

**McCallum, David**
WATCHER IN THE WOODS, THE
TERMINAL CHOICE

**McCarthy, Kevin**
PIRANHA

**McClure, Doug**
HUMANOIDS FROM THE DEEP
HOUSE WHERE EVIL DWELLS, THE

**MacCorkindale, Simon**
JAWS 3-D

**McCulloch, Ian**
ZOMBIE

**McDowall, Roddy**
ARNOLD

FRIGHT NIGHT
LEGEND OF HELL HOUSE, THE

**McDowell, Malcolm**
CAT PEOPLE

**MacDowell, Nelson**
LOST WORLD, THE

**McGavin, Darren**
DEAD HEAT

**McGee, Vonette**
BLACULA

**MacGinnis, Niall**
CURSE OF THE DEMON

**McGuire, Biff**
WEREWOLF OF WASHINGTON

**Macht, Stephen**
NIGHTWING

**McKellen, Ian**
KEEP, THE

**McKern, Leo**
OMEN, THE

**Macnee, Patrick**
HOWLING, THE
INCENSE FOR THE DAMNED

**McNeil, Kate**
MONKEY SHINES: AN EXPERIMENT IN FEAR

**McRaney, Gerald**
NIGHT OF BLOODY HORROR

**McWade, Margaret**
LOST WORLD, THE

**Magee, Patrick**
ASYLUM
AND NOW THE SCREAMING STARTS

**Maher, Bill**
HOUSE II: THE SECOND STORY

**Makepeace, Chris**
VAMP

**Mancuso, Nick**
NIGHTWING

**Mansfield, Martha**
DR. JEKYLL AND MR. HYDE

**Marcovicci, Andrea**
HAND, THE
STUFF, THE

**Marley, John**
CAR, THE
DEATHDREAM

**Marsh, Jean**
CHANGELING, THE

**Marshall, Herbert**
FLY, THE

**Marshall, William**
BLACULA
SCREAM, BLACULA, SCREAM

**Martin, Damon**
GHOULIES II

**Martin, Steve**
MAN WITH TWO BRAINS, THE
LITTLE SHOP OF HORRORS

**Martin, Strother**
BROTHERHOOD OF SATAN, THE
NIGHTWING

**Mason, Marsha**
AUDREY ROSE

**Massey, Anna**
VAULT OF HORROR, THE
PEEPING TOM

**Massey, Daniel**
VAULT OF HORROR, THE

**Massey, Ilona**
FRANKENSTEIN MEETS THE WOLF MAN

**Mathews, Kerwin**
MANIAC

**Mathews, Thom**
FRIDAY THE 13TH PART VI: JASON LIVES

**Matthews, Brian**
BURNING, THE

**Matthews, Kerwin**
OCTAMAN
NIGHTMARE IN BLOOD

**Maury, Derrel**
MASSACRE AT CENTRAL HIGH

**Maynard, Ken**
BIG FOOT

**Mayne, Ferdinand**
FRIGHTMARE

**Mayo, Virginia**
CASTLE OF EVIL

**Melvin, Murray**
GHOST STORY

**Menzies, Heather**
PIRANHA

**Meredith, Burgess**
BURNT OFFERINGS
TORTURE GARDEN
MAGIC

**Mesmer, Michael**
DEADTIME STORIES

**Miles, Vera**
INITIATION, THE
PSYCHO II
PSYCHO

**Milland, Ray**
FROGS
PREMATURE BURIAL, THE
UNCANNY, THE

**Miller, Jason**
EXORCIST, THE
NINTH CONFIGURATION, THE

**Miller, Patsy Ruth**
HUNCHBACK OF NOTRE DAME, THE

**Mills, Juliet**
BEYOND THE DOOR

**Milner, Martin**
THIRTEEN GHOSTS

**Mitchell, Cameron**
BLOOD AND BLACK LACE

DEMON, THE
HAUNTS
NIGHTMARE IN WAX
SILENT SCREAM
TOOLBOX MURDERS, THE

**Mitchell, Don**
SCREAM, BLACULA, SCREAM

**Mitchell, Thomas**
HUNCHBACK OF NOTRE DAME, THE

**Mitchum, Chris**
BIG FOOT

**Moffat, Donald**
MONSTER IN THE CLOSET

**Mokae, Zakes**
SERPENT AND THE RAINBOW, THE

**Moll, Richard**
HOUSE

**Montana, Bull**
LOST WORLD, THE

**Montecelli, Anna Maria**
NOMADS

**Montgomery, Julie**
GIRLS NIGHT OUT

**Moore, Clayton**
BLACK DRAGONS

**Moore, Demi**
SEVENTH SIGN, THE

**Moore, Roger**
MAN WHO HAUNTED HIMSELF, THE

**Moorehead, Agnes**
DEAR, DEAD DELILAH
HUSH . . . HUSH, SWEET CHARLOTTE

**Moranis, Rick**
LITTLE SHOP OF HORRORS

**Moriarty, Michael**
Q
STUFF, THE
TROLL
RETURN TO SALEM'S LOT, A
IT'S ALIVE III: ISLAND OF THE ALIVE

**Morris, Garrett**
STUFF, THE

**Morrow, Jo**
THIRTEEN GHOSTS

**Morrow, Vic**
HUMANOIDS FROM THE DEEP
TWILIGHT ZONE—THE MOVIE

**Mulgrew, Kate**
STRANGER IS WATCHING, A

**Munro, Caroline**
LAST HORROR FILM, THE

**Murphy, Michael**
STRANGE BEHAVIOR

**Murray, Bill**
GHOSTBUSTERS

**Musante, Tony**
BIRD WITH THE CRYSTAL PLUMAGE, THE

**Myers, Kim**
NIGHTMARE ON ELM STREET PART 2:
FREDDY'S REVENGE, A

**Naish, J. Carrol**
DRACULA VS. FRANKENSTEIN

**Nalder, Reggie**
DRACULA'S DOG

**Naschy, Paul**
PEOPLE WHO OWN THE DARK
WEREWOLF VS. THE VAMPIRE
WOMAN, THE

**Naughton, David**
AMERICAN WEREWOLF IN LONDON,
AN

**Neil, Hildegard**
MAN WHO HAUNTED HIMSELF, THE

**Neill, Sam**
FINAL CONFLICT, THE
POSSESSION

**Nelligan, Kate**
DRACULA

**Nelson, Craig T.**
POLTERGEIST II
POLTERGEIST

**Nettleton, Lois**
DEADLY BLESSING

**Newman, Melissa**
ONE DARK NIGHT

**Newmar, Julie**
HYSTERICAL

**Nicholson, Jack**
RAVEN, THE
TERROR, THE
SHINING, THE
WITCHES OF EASTWICK, THE

**Nielsen, Leslie**
CREEPSHOW
DAY OF THE ANIMALS
PROM NIGHT

**North, Sheree**
MANIAC COP

**Nye, Carrie**
CREEPSHOW

**O'Brien, Edmond**
HUNCHBACK OF NOTRE DAME, THE

**O'Hara, Maureen**
HUNCHBACK OF NOTRE DAME, THE

**O'Keefe, Dennis**
LEOPARD MAN, THE

**O'Neal, Patrick**
SILENT NIGHT, BLOODY NIGHT

**O'Neill, Jennifer**
PSYCHIC, THE

**O'Quinn, Terry**
STEPFATHER, THE

**O'Rourke, Heather**
POLTERGEIST II
POLTERGEIST
POLTERGEIST III

**O'Sullivan, Maureen**
DEVIL DOLL, THE

**Oates, Warren**
RACE WITH THE DEVIL

**Ogilvy, Ian**
AND NOW THE SCREAMING STARTS
CONQUEROR WORM, THE

**Oliver, Stephen**
WEREWOLVES ON WHEELS

**Olivier, Laurence**
DRACULA

**Olmos, Edward James**
WOLFEN

**Olson, James**
AMITYVILLE II: THE POSSESSION

**Owens, Patricia**
FLY, THE

**Oxenberg, Catherine**
LAIR OF THE WHITE WORM, THE

**Page, Geraldine**
BRIDE, THE

**Palance, Jack**
ALONE IN THE DARK
CRAZE
TORTURE GARDEN

**Palmer, Betsy**
FRIDAY THE 13TH

**Palmer, Lilli**
CHAMBER OF HORRORS
MURDERS IN THE RUE MORGUE

**Pankow, John**
MONKEY SHINES: AN EXPERIMENT IN
FEAR

**Parker, Jameson**
PRINCE OF DARKNESS

**Parker, Jean**
BLUEBEARD

**Pataki, Michael**
DRACULA'S DOG

**Patric, Jason**
LOST BOYS, THE

**Patton, Mark**
NIGHTMARE ON ELM STREET PART 2:
FREDDY'S REVENGE, A

**Paul, Alexandra**
CHRISTINE

**Payton, Barbara**
BRIDE OF THE GORILLA

**Peck, Gregory**
OMEN, THE

**Pelikan, Lisa**
JENNIFER

**Penhaligan, Susan**
CONFESSIONAL, THE

**Penhaligon, Susan**
PATRICK
UNCANNY, THE

**Perkins, Anthony**
PSYCHO II

**PSYCHO III
PSYCHO**

**Persoff, Nehemiah**
PSYCHIC KILLER

**Peterson, Cassandra**
ELVIRA: MISTRESS OF THE DARK

**Pettet, Joanna**
EVIL, THE

**Pfeiffer, Michelle**
WITCHES OF EASTWICK, THE

**Philbin, Mary**
PHANTOM OF THE OPERA, THE

**Philbin, Phil**
FLESH FEAST

**Pierce, Charles B.**
BOGGY CREEK II

**Pierce, Maggie**
TALES OF TERROR

**Pilon, Donald**
PYX, THE

**Piscopo, Joe**
DEAD HEAT

**Pleasence, Angela**
GODSEND, THE

**Pleasence, Donald**
HALLOWEEN IV: THE RETURN OF
MICHAEL MYERS
ALONE IN THE DARK
CREEPERS
CIRCUS OF HORRORS
DRACULA
DEVONSVILLE TERROR, THE
HALLOWEEN II
HALLOWEEN
FROM BEYOND THE GRAVE
LAND OF THE MINOTAUR
PRINCE OF DARKNESS

**Pleshette, Suzanne**
BIRDS, THE

**Plummer, Christopher**
PYX, THE

**Polanski, Roman**
TENANT, THE

**Pollard, Michael J.**
AMERICAN GOTHIC

**Porter, Eric**
HANDS OF THE RIPPER

**Powell, Robert**
ASPHYX, THE
SURVIVOR

**Powers, Stefanie**
DIE! DIE! MY DARLING
INVISIBLE STRANGLER, THE

**Prentiss, Paula**
SATURDAY THE 14TH

**Prevost, Francoise**
MURDER CLINIC, THE

**Price, Vincent**
HOUSE OF THE LONG SHADOWS
ABOMINABLE DR. PHIBES, THE
CONQUEROR WORM, THE

# ACTORS

ESCAPES
DOCTOR PHIBES RISES AGAIN
HOUSE ON HAUNTED HILL
HOUSE OF WAX
HOUSE OF USHER
MONSTER CLUB, THE
MASQUE OF THE RED DEATH, THE
RAVEN, THE
PIT AND THE PENDULUM, THE
OFFSPRING, THE
OBLONG BOX, THE
THEATRE OF BLOOD
TALES OF TERROR
SCREAM AND SCREAM AGAIN
FLY, THE
TOMB OF LIGEIA, THE
RETURN OF THE FLY
MADHOUSE
DEAD HEAT

**Prine, Andrew**
EVIL, THE
GRIZZLY
TOWN THAT DREADED SUNDOWN, THE

**Prochnow, Jurgen**
SEVENTH SIGN, THE
KEEP, THE

**Prosky, Robert**
CHRISTINE
KEEP, THE

**Pryce, Jonathan**
SOMETHING WICKED THIS WAY COMES

**Pullman, Bill**
SERPENT AND THE RAINBOW, THE

**Purdom, Edmund**
DON'T OPEN TILL CHRISTMAS
PIECES

**Purl, Linda**
VISITING HOURS

**Quaid, Dennis**
JAWS 3-D

**Quaid, Randy**
WRAITH, THE

**Quarry, Robert**
DOCTOR PHIBES RISES AGAIN

**Quinlan, Kathleen**
WARNING SIGN

**Radner, Gilda**
HAUNTED HONEYMOON

**Railsback, Steve**
BLUE MONKEY

**Raines, Cristina**
NIGHTMARES
SENTINEL, THE

**Rains, Claude**
PHANTOM OF THE OPERA
WOLF MAN, THE
INVISIBLE MAN, THE

**Ramis, Harold**
GHOSTBUSTERS

**Rampling, Charlotte**
ANGEL HEART
ORCA

**Randolph, Jane**
CURSE OF THE CAT PEOPLE, THE

**Rathbone, Basil**
SON OF FRANKENSTEIN

**Ratzenberger, John**
HOUSE II: THE SECOND STORY

**Ray, Aldo**
HUMAN EXPERIMENTS
HAUNTS
PSYCHIC KILLER
HAUNTED

**Reed, Donna**
PICTURE OF DORIAN GRAY, THE

**Reed, Oliver**
CURSE OF THE WEREWOLF, THE
BURNT OFFERINGS
BROOD, THE
DR. HECKYL AND MR. HYPE
SPASMS

**Reed, Ricky Addison**
RETURN TO SALEM'S LOT, A

**Rees, Angharad**
HANDS OF THE RIPPER

**Reicher, Frank**
KING KONG

**Reid, Beryl**
BEAST IN THE CELLAR, THE

**Remberg, Erika**
CIRCUS OF HORRORS

**Remick, Lee**
OMEN, THE

**Resnick, Judith**
CARNIVAL OF BLOOD

**Revill, Clive**
LEGEND OF HELL HOUSE, THE

**Rhys-Davies, John**
IN THE SHADOW OF KILIMANJARO

**Richardson, Natasha**
GOTHIC

**Richardson, Ralph**
TALES FROM THE CRYPT
WHO SLEW AUNTIE ROO?

**Rigg, Diana**
THEATRE OF BLOOD

**Robards, Jr., Jason**
MURDERS IN THE RUE MORGUE
SOMETHING WICKED THIS WAY COMES

**Roberts, Tony**
AMITYVILLE 3-D

**Robinson, Andrew**
HELLRAISER

**Robson, Flora**
BEAST IN THE CELLAR, THE

**Rocco, Alex**
LADY IN WHITE

**Roman, Ruth**
BABY, THE

**Romero, Cesar**
SPECTRE OF EDGAR ALLAN POE, THE

**Ross, Katharine**
LEGACY, THE

**Roundtree, Richard**
Q
MANIAC COP

**Rourke, Mickey**
ANGEL HEART

**Rubenstein, Zelda**
ANGUISH

**Rubin, Jennifer**
BAD DREAMS

**Ryan, John**
IT'S ALIVE

**Saint James, Susan**
LOVE AT FIRST BITE

**St. John, Betta**
CORRIDORS OF BLOOD
HORROR HOTEL

**Salt, Jennifer**
SISTERS

**Sampson, Will**
ORCA

**Sanders, George**
PSYCHOMANIA
PICTURE OF DORIAN GRAY, THE

**Sands, Julian**
GOTHIC

**Sarandon, Chris**
FRIGHT NIGHT
SENTINEL, THE

**Sarandon, Susan**
HUNGER, THE
WITCHES OF EASTWICK, THE

**Savalas, Telly**
HOUSE OF EXORCISM, THE
HORROR EXPRESS

**Saxon, John**
UNSANE
BLOOD BEACH
BEYOND EVIL
NIGHTMARE ON ELM STREET, A

**Scarfe, Alan**
CATHY'S CURSE

**Scarwid, Diana**
PSYCHO III

**Scheider, Roy**
CURSE OF THE LIVING CORPSE, THE
JAWS II
JAWS

**Schrage, Lisa**
HELLO MARY LOU, PROM NIGHT II

**Schreck, Max**
NOSFERATU, THE VAMPIRE

**Schreiber, Avery**
SILENT SCREAM

THE HORROR FILM

Scott, Debralee
PANDEMONIUM

Scott, George C.
CHANGELING, THE

Seyrig, Delphine
DAUGHTERS OF DARKNESS

Sharp, Anthony
CONFESSIONAL, THE

Shatner, William
DEVIL'S RAIN, THE
KINGDOM OF THE SPIDERS
VISITING HOURS

Shaver, Helen
BELIEVERS, THE

Shaw, Robert
BLACK SUNDAY
JAWS

Shawn, Dick
LOVE AT FIRST BITE

Shearer, Moira
PEEPING TOM

Sheen, Charlie
WRAITH, THE

Sheen, Martin
BELIEVERS, THE
DEAD ZONE, THE
LITTLE GIRL WHO LIVES DOWN THE
LANE, THE

Sheldon, Valerie
BERSERKER

Shelton, Deborah
BODY DOUBLE

Sheppard, Paula
ALICE, SWEET ALICE

Shields, Brooke
ALICE, SWEET ALICE

Shire, Talia
PROPHECY

Shor, Dan
STRANGE BEHAVIOR

Silva, Henry
THIRST

Silver, Ron
ENTITY, THE

Sim, Gerald
DR. JEKYLL AND SISTER HYDE

Simon, Simone
CURSE OF THE CAT PEOPLE, THE
CAT PEOPLE

Skerritt, Tom
POLTERGEIST III

Slaughter, Tod
DEMON BARBER OF FLEET STREET,
THE

Smiles, Finch
LOST WORLD, THE

Smith, Alexis
LITTLE GIRL WHO LIVES DOWN THE
LANE, THE

Smith, Kent
CURSE OF THE CAT PEOPLE, THE
CAT PEOPLE

Smits, Sonja
VIDEODROME

Smothers, Tom
PANDEMONIUM

Snodgress, Carrie
TRICK OR TREATS

Soles, P.J.
HALLOWEEN

Sommer, Elke
BARON BLOOD
HOUSE OF EXORCISM, THE
INVISIBLE STRANGLER, THE

Sorvino, Paul
STUFF, THE

Spacek, Sissy
CARRIE

Spano, Joe
TERMINAL CHOICE

Spinell, Joe
MANIAC
LAST HORROR FILM, THE

Standing, John
LEGACY, THE

Stanley, Kim
SEANCE ON A WET AFTERNOON

Stanton, Harry Dean
CHRISTINE

Stark, Jonathan
HOUSE II: THE SECOND STORY

Steele, Barbara
PIT AND THE PENDULUM, THE

Steiger, Rod
AMERICAN GOTHIC
AMITYVILLE HORROR, THE

Stephens, Robert
ASPHYX, THE

Stevens, Andrew
MASSACRE AT CENTRAL HIGH

Stevens, Craig
ABBOTT AND COSTELLO MEET DR.
JEKYLL AND MR. HYDE

Stevens, Stella
ARNOLD
MANITOU, THE
WACKO
NUTTY PROFESSOR, THE

Stevenson, Venetia
HORROR HOTEL

Sting
BRIDE, THE

Stockwell, Dean
DUNWICH HORROR, THE
WEREWOLF OF WASHINGTON

Stockwell, Guy
IT'S ALIVE

Stockwell, John
CHRISTINE

Stoddard, Malcolm
GODSEND, THE

Stoltz, Eric
SISTER SISTER

Stone, Dorothy
REVOLT OF THE ZOMBIES

Stossel, Ludwig
BLUEBEARD

Straight, Beatrice
POLTERGEIST

Strasberg, Susan
BLOODY BIRTHDAY
MANITOU, THE
SWEET SIXTEEN

Stratton, Charles
MUNCHIES

Strode, Woody
KINGDOM OF THE SPIDERS

Stroud, Don
SWEET SIXTEEN

Stuart, Gloria
INVISIBLE MAN, THE

Sutherland, Donald
DON'T LOOK NOW
DR. TERROR'S HOUSE OF HORRORS

Sutherland, Kiefer
LOST BOYS, THE

Swanson, Gary
WITCHFIRE

Swanson, Kristy
DEADLY FRIEND

Swit, Loretta
RACE WITH THE DEVIL

Tabor, Eron
I SPIT ON YOUR GRAVE

Talbot, Gloria
DAUGHTER OF DR. JEKYLL

Tamblyn, Russ
HAUNTING, THE

Tandy, Jessica
BIRDS, THE

Taylor, Dub
CREATURE FROM BLACK LAKE, THE

Taylor, Kent
BRAIN OF BLOOD

Taylor, Rod
BIRDS, THE

Terry-Thomas
ABOMINABLE DR. PHIBES, THE

Tewes, Lauren
EYES OF A STRANGER

Thor, Jon-Mikl
ROCK 'N' ROLL NIGHTMARE

Tilly, Meg
PSYCHO II
ONE DARK NIGHT

Todd, Richard
DORIAN GRAY

# ACTORS

**Torn, Rip**
STRANGER IS WATCHING, A

**Tracy, Lee**
DOCTOR X

**Tracy, Spencer**
DR. JEKYLL AND MR. HYDE

**Travolta, Ellen**
HUMAN EXPERIMENTS

**Travolta, John**
CARRIE
BLOW OUT

**Turkel, Ann**
HUMANOIDS FROM THE DEEP

**Turner, Kathleen**
MAN WITH TWO BRAINS, THE

**Turner, Lana**
DR. JEKYLL AND MR. HYDE

**Tyson, Cathy**
SERPENT AND THE RAINBOW, THE

**Valentine, Scott**
MY DEMON LOVER

**Valli, Alida**
HOUSE OF EXORCISM, THE
HORROR CHAMBER OF DR.
FAUSTUS, THE

**Van Devere, Trish**
CHANGELING, THE
HEARSE, THE

**Van Fleet, Jo**
TENANT, THE

**Van Patten, Joyce**
MONKEY SHINES: AN EXPERIMENT IN
FEAR

**Van Patten, Vincent**
HELL NIGHT

**Van Peebles, Mario**
JAWS: THE REVENGE

**Van Vooren, Monique**
ANDY WARHOL'S FRANKENSTEIN

**Vaughan, Peter**
DIE! DIE! MY DARLING

**Veidt, Conrad**
CABINET OF DR. CALIGARI, THE

**Velazquez, Lorena**
WRESTLING WOMEN VS. THE AZTEC
MUMMY, THE

**Venora, Diane**
WOLFEN
TERMINAL CHOICE

**Vernon, John**
CURTAINS

**Veruschka**
BRIDE, THE

**von Stroheim, Erich**
CRIME OF DR. CRESPI, THE
GREAT GABBO, THE

**von Sydow, Max**
EXORCIST II: THE HERETIC
EXORCIST, THE

**Walken, Christopher**
DEAD ZONE, THE

**Walker, Jr., Robert**
SPECTRE OF EDGAR ALLAN POE, THE

**Wallace, Dee**
CUJO
HOWLING, THE

**Walsh, Dermot**
GHOST SHIP

**Ward, Rachel**
FINAL TERROR, THE

**Ware, Irene**
RAVEN, THE

**Warner, David**
FROM BEYOND THE GRAVE
OMEN, THE
NIGHTWING
MAN WITH TWO BRAINS, THE

**Wasson, Craig**
GHOST STORY
NIGHTMARE ON ELM STREET 3:
DREAM WARRIORS, A
SCHIZOID
BODY DOUBLE

**Waterston, Sam**
WARNING SIGN

**Wayne, Patrick**
REVENGE

**Weaver, Fritz**
CREEPSHOW

**Weaver, Sigourney**
GHOSTBUSTERS

**Wegener, Paul**
GOLEM, THE

**Weller, Peter**
OF UNKNOWN ORIGIN

**Wellesley, Charles**
LOST WORLD, THE

**Welsh, Kenneth**
OF UNKNOWN ORIGIN

**Wendt, George**
HOUSE

**Wheaton, Wil**
CURSE, THE

**Whitelaw, Billie**
OMEN, THE

**Whitman, Stuart**
EATEN ALIVE
DEMONOID
RUBY

**Widmark, Richard**
TO THE DEVIL A DAUGHTER

**Wiest, Dianne**
LOST BOYS, THE

**Wilder, Gene**
HAUNTED HONEYMOON
YOUNG FRANKENSTEIN

**Williams, Caroline**
TEXAS CHAINSAW MASSACRE PART
2, THE

**Williams, JoBeth**
POLTERGEIST II
POLTERGEIST

**Williams, Treat**
DEAD HEAT

**Wilson, Scott**
NINTH CONFIGURATION, THE

**Winfield, Paul**
SERPENT AND THE RAINBOW, THE

**Winters, Shelley**
TENTACLES
TENANT, THE
WHO SLEW AUNTIE ROO?
VISITOR, THE
WITCHFIRE

**Woods, James**
CAT'S EYE
VIDEODROME

**Woodward, Edward**
WICKER MAN, THE

**Woronov, Mary**
MOVIE HOUSE MASSACRE
SILENT NIGHT, BLOODY NIGHT
EATING RAOUL

**Wray, Fay**
DOCTOR X
MYSTERY OF THE WAX MUSEUM, THE
VAMPIRE BAT, THE
KING KONG

**Wymark, Patrick**
BLOOD ON SATAN'S CLAW, THE

**Wynn, Keenan**
DEVIL'S RAIN, THE
PIRANHA
ORCA

**York, Michael**
ISLAND OF DR. MOREAU, THE

**York, Susannah**
AWAKENING, THE
SHOUT, THE

**Young, Burt**
AMITYVILLE II: THE POSSESSION

**Yulin, Harris**
BAD DREAMS

**Zerbe, Anthony**
DEAD ZONE, THE

**Zmed, Adrian**
FINAL TERROR, THE

**Zucco, George**
DEAD MEN WALK

# CINEMATOGRAPHERS

**Abrams, Barry**
CHILDREN, THE
FRIDAY THE 13TH
STRANGER IS WATCHING, A

**Ackerman, Thomas**
BEETLEJUICE

**Ahlberg, Mac**
GHOST TOWN
DOLLS
HOUSE II: THE SECOND STORY
HOUSE
HELL NIGHT
GHOULIES
FROM BEYOND
RE ANIMATOR
NOCTURNA
PRISON

**Alavi, Mori**
CHILD, THE

**Albani, Romano**
CREEPERS
INFERNO
TROLL

**Alcott, John**
TERROR TRAIN
SHINING, THE

**Alonzo, John A.**
BLACK SUNDAY

**Ameripoor, Alex**
WIZARD OF GORE, THE

**Anchia, Juan Ruiz**
SEVENTH SIGN, THE

**Anderson, Jamie**
PIRANHA

**Anderson, William**
GRIZZLY

**Ankerstjerne, Johan**
WITCHCRAFT THROUGH THE AGES

**Anneman, Bill**
CORPSE GRINDERS, THE

**Archambault, Arch**
COUNT YORGA, VAMPIRE

**Arling, Arthur**
STRAIT-JACKET

**Aronovich, Ricardo**
YOU BETTER WATCH OUT

**Artigot, Raul**
HORROR OF THE ZOMBIES

**Asbjorsen, Stuart**
FOREST, THE

**Asher, Jack**
CURSE OF FRANKENSTEIN, THE
HORROR OF DRACULA, THE
MUMMY, THE

**Askins, Monroe**
HOUSE ON SKULL MOUNTAIN, THE

**August, Joseph**
HUNCHBACK OF NOTRE DAME, THE

**Baer, Hanania**
ELVIRA: MISTRESS OF THE DARK

**Baggott, King**
HAND, THE

**Bailey, John**
CAT PEOPLE

**Baker, Brydon**
RETURN OF THE FLY

**Baldwin, Bob**
LET'S SCARE JESSICA TO DEATH
NIGHTMARE WEEKEND
WEREWOLF OF WASHINGTON

**Banes, Lionel**
HAUNTED STRANGLER, THE

**Barboni, Enzo**
NIGHTMARE CASTLE

**Barich, Robert**
MAUSOLEUM

**Bassuk, Craig**
DEATHROW GAMESHOW

**Battaglia, Gianlorenzo**
BLADE IN THE DARK, A
DEMONS 2: THE NIGHTMARE
RETURNS
DEMONS

**Bava, Mario**
HATCHET FOR A HONEYMOON
TWITCH OF THE DEATH NERVE

**Bawden, James**
UNCANNY, THE

**Bazelli, Bojan**
PUMPKINHEAD

**Bechard, Gorman**
PSYCHOS IN LOVE

**Becker, Joshua M.**
EVIL DEAD, THE

**Beeson, Paul**
DIE, MONSTER, DIE

**Benda, Richard**
SLAUGHTERHOUSE

**Berenguer, Manuel**
MURDERS IN THE RUE MORGUE

**Bergman, Robert**
GRAVEYARD SHIFT

**Bethard, Bob**
PLAY DEAD

**Birbichi, Enrico**
GRIM REAPER, THE

**Birchall, Robert**
SPECTRE OF EDGAR ALLAN POE, THE

**Biroc, Joseph**
THIRTEEN GHOSTS
HUSH ... HUSH, SWEET CHARLOTTE

**Bode, Ralf**
DRESSED TO KILL

**Boulton, Davis**
HAUNTING, THE

**Brenner, Jules**
RETURN OF THE LIVING DEAD
TEEN WOLF TOO

**Bridenbecker, Milton**
PHANTOM OF THE OPERA, THE

**Burks, Robert**
BIRDS, THE

**Burman, Hans**
CITY OF THE WALKING DEAD

**Burum, Stephen H.**
BRIDE, THE
ENTITY, THE
SOMETHING WICKED THIS WAY
COMES
BODY DOUBLE

**Bush, Dick**
LAIR OF THE WHITE WORM, THE
BLOOD ON SATAN'S CLAW, THE
LEGACY, THE
TWINS OF EVIL

**Butler, Bill**
DAMIEN—OMEN II
JAWS
CHILD'S PLAY

**Butler, Michael**
JAWS II

**Cabrera, John**
NIGHT OF THE ZOMBIES

**Callaway, Thomas**
SLUMBER PARTY MASSACRE II

**Canton, Daniel B.**
DEADTIME STORIES

**Caramico, Robert**
EATEN ALIVE
ORGY OF THE DEAD
OCTAMAN

**Cardiff, Jack**
AWAKENING, THE
CAT'S EYE
GHOST STORY

**Cardwell, Herbert**
ERASERHEAD

**Carpenter, John**
HALLOWEEN II

**Carpenter, Russell**
LADY IN WHITE

**Carpenter, Stephen**
DORM THAT DRIPPED BLOOD, THE
POWER, THE

**Carras, Robert**
DR. HECKYL AND MR. HYPE

**Carrasco, Ezequiel**
WRESTLING WOMEN VS. THE AZTEC
MUMMY, THE

**Carter, James**
DON'T ANSWER THE PHONE
SWEET SIXTEEN
UNSEEN, THE

**Casey, Thomas**
FLESH FEAST

**Cathcart, Darrell**
FINAL EXAM
WOLFMAN

**Chapman, Michael**
LOST BOYS, THE
MAN WITH TWO BRAINS, THE

**Chavez, Julio C.**
DEATH CURSE OF TARTU

# CINEMATOGRAPHERS

**Civit, Josep Maria**
ANGUISH

**Climent, Jose**
SCREAMING DEAD, THE

**Cohen, Fred**
SPLATTER UNIVERSITY

**Collins, Bob**
SCHLOCK

**Collister, Peter**
PULSE
HALLOWEEN IV: THE RETURN OF
MICHAEL MYERS
SUPERNATURALS, THE

**Connell, Merle**
UNEARTHLY, THE

**Contner, James A.**
JAWS 3-D
MONKEY SHINES: AN EXPERIMENT IN
FEAR

**Coop, Denys**
ASYLUM
AND NOW THE SCREAMING STARTS
VAULT OF HORROR, THE

**Cooper, Wilkie**
MANIAC

**Coquillon, John**
CONQUEROR WORM, THE
CHANGELING, THE
OBLONG BOX, THE
SCREAM AND SCREAM AGAIN

**Corkidi, Rafael**
DR. TARR'S TORTURE DUNGEON

**Coscarelli, Don**
PHANTASM

**Cox, Vincent**
DEMON, THE

**Cronjager, Jules**
MONSTER WALKS, THE

**Crosby, Floyd**
HOUSE OF USHER
RAVEN, THE
PREMATURE BURIAL, THE
PIT AND THE PENDULUM, THE
TALES OF TERROR

**Cundey, Dean**
CREATURE FROM BLACK LAKE, THE
FOG, THE
HALLOWEEN II
HALLOWEEN III: SEASON OF THE
WITCH
HALLOWEEN
PSYCHO II
SATAN'S CHEERLEADERS
WARNING SIGN

**Cunha, Richard**
GIANT FROM THE UNKNOWN

**D'Ettore, Robert**
TENTACLES

**Dalzell, Archie**
LITTLE SHOP OF HORRORS

**Daviau, Allen**
TWILIGHT ZONE—THE MOVIE

**Davidescu, A.**
FINAL TERROR, THE

**Davidson, Carson**
FLESH EATERS, THE

**Davis, Andrew**
MANSION OF THE DOOMED

**Davis, Benjamin**
SLEEPAWAY CAMP

**Davis, Elliot**
VAMP

**de Grasse, Robert**
LEOPARD MAN, THE

**DeBont, Jan**
CUJO

**DeGrasse, Robert**
BODY SNATCHER, THE

**Del Ruth, Thomas**
MOTEL HELL

**Demarecaux, Jacques**
I DRINK YOUR BLOOD

**Deming, Peter**
EVIL DEAD 2: DEAD BY DAWN

**DeNove, Tom**
LAST HORROR FILM, THE

**Di Leo, Mario**
EVIL, THE

**Dickinson, Desmond**
BEYOND THE FOG
BERSERK
CHAMBER OF HORRORS
BURKE AND HARE
WHO SLEW AUNTIE ROO?
INCENSE FOR THE DAMNED

**DiGiacomo, Franco**
AMITYVILLE II: THE POSSESSION

**DiLeo, Mario**
NIGHTMARES

**Dohler, Don**
FIEND

**Dominguez, Raul**
HOUSE OF EVIL
FEAR CHAMBER, THE

**Dorfman, Ron**
NIGHT OF THE ZOMBIES

**Dragonetti, Vittorio**
ORCA

**Dunk, Albert J.**
INCUBUS, THE

**Ebinger, Robert**
STUDENT BODIES

**Edeson, Arthur**
LOST WORLD, THE
INVISIBLE MAN, THE
FRANKENSTEIN

**Elizondo, Jesus**
IN THE SHADOW OF KILIMANJARO

**Elliott, Paul**
FRIDAY THE 13TH PART VII—THE NEW
BLOOD

**Elms, Frederick**
ERASERHEAD

**Elswit, Robert**
TRICK OR TREAT
RETURN OF THE LIVING DEAD PART II

**Faithfull, Geoffrey**
CORRIDORS OF BLOOD

**Feil, Gerald**
HE KNOWS YOU'RE ALONE
FRIDAY THE 13TH PART III

**Feindel, J.A.**
BLUEBEARD
REVOLT OF THE ZOMBIES

**Fernandes, Joao**
HUMAN EXPERIMENTS
FRIDAY THE 13TH—THE FINAL
CHAPTER
NESTING, THE

**Ferrando, Giancarlo**
GREAT ALLIGATOR, THE
TORSO
SCREAMERS

**Fierberg, Steven**
NIGHTMARE ON ELM STREET 4: THE
DREAM MASTER, A

**Findlay, Roberta**
BLOOD SISTERS

**Finnerman, Gerald Perry**
NIGHTMARES

**Fiore, Gianni**
NIGHTMARE

**Fisher, Gerry**
ISLAND OF DR. MOREAU, THE
WOLFEN
NINTH CONFIGURATION, THE

**Fishman, Bill**
MOVIE HOUSE MASSACRE

**Ford, Roy**
LEGEND OF THE SEVEN GOLDEN
VAMPIRES, THE

**Forges, Robert D.**
CURSE, THE

**Foster, Phillipe Carr**
BOOGEYMAN II

**Fraker, William A.**
EXORCIST II: THE HERETIC
ROSEMARY'S BABY

**Fraser, Tom**
FRANKENSTEIN GENERAL HOSPITAL

**Fredricks, Ellsworth**
PICTURE MOMMY DEAD

**Freund, Karl**
DRACULA
GOLEM, THE

**Friberg, John**
ALICE, SWEET ALICE

**Friedberg, Lionel**
HOUSE OF THE LIVING DEAD

**Fujimoto, Tak**
DR. BLACK AND MR. HYDE

**Galisteo, Jose Garcia**
MONSTER DOG

**Garzon, Miguel**
MARY, MARY, BLOODY MARY

**Geiwitz, Richard**
FIEND

**Gelpi, Juan**
CRYPT OF THE LIVING DEAD

**Genkins, Harvey**
SILENT NIGHT, DEADLY NIGHT PART II

**Gerstad, Merritt B.**
FREAKS

**Gertsman, Maury**
BRUTE MAN, THE

**Gheerbrant, Denis**
NIGHTMARE WEEKEND

**Gibb, Kenneth Lloyd**
DRIVE-IN MASSACRE

**Gibb, Richard**
RATTLERS

**Gibbons, Rodney**
MY BLOODY VALENTINE

**Gibbs, Gerald**
DEVIL DOLL

**Giffard, Adam**
SILENT NIGHT, BLOODY NIGHT

**Giordano, Aldo**
ATOM AGE VAMPIRE

**Glennon, Bert**
HOUSE OF WAX

**Glickman, Paul**
DRACULA VS. FRANKENSTEIN
STUFF, THE

**Glouner, Richard C.**
DUNWICH HORROR, THE

**Godar, Godfrey**
HOWLING IV: THE ORIGINAL
NIGHTMARE

**Godsey, B.**
TO ALL A GOODNIGHT

**Goldblatt, Stephen**
HUNGER, THE

**Goodich, Fred**
FEAR NO EVIL

**Goodnoff, Irv**
EVILSPEAK
JENNIFER
RATTLERS
UNSEEN, THE

**Goodwin, Robin**
SWAMP THING

**Gornick, Michael**
DAWN OF THE DEAD
CREEPSHOW
DAY OF THE DEAD
MARTIN

**Grant, Arthur**
CURSE OF THE WEREWOLF, THE
TOMB OF LIGEIA, THE

**Grant, Moray**
HORROR OF FRANKENSTEIN, THE
SCARS OF DRACULA, THE
VAMPIRE LOVERS, THE

**Grant, Stanley**
GHOST SHIP

**Graver, Gary**
DRACULA VS. FRANKENSTEIN
MORTUARY
TRICK OR TREATS
TOOLBOX MURDERS, THE

**Greenberg, Adam**
ONCE BITTEN
NEAR DARK

**Greene, Craig**
OFFSPRING, THE

**Greene, W. Howard**
PHANTOM OF THE OPERA

**Greenhalgh, Jack**
DEAD MEN WALK
MAD MONSTER, THE

**Grib, Jim**
SPLATTER UNIVERSITY

**Grossman, Karen**
MICROWAVE MASSACRE
SLAYER, THE

**Gruszynski, Alexander**
BAD DREAMS

**Guarnieri, Ennio**
VISITOR, THE

**Guthe, Fred**
CURTAINS

**Guthrie, Carl E.**
HOUSE ON HAUNTED HILL
FRANKENSTEIN 1970

**Haitkin, Jacques**
HOUSE WHERE EVIL DWELLS, THE
NIGHTMARE ON ELM STREET, A
NIGHTMARE ON ELM STREET PART 2:
FREDDY'S REVENGE, A
MY DEMON LOVER

**Hajnal, Stephen**
BRAIN THAT WOULDN'T DIE, THE

**Hall, Chuck**
ALICE, SWEET ALICE

**Haller, Ernest**
WHATEVER HAPPENED TO BABY
JANE?

**Hameister, Willy**
CABINET OF DR. CALIGARI, THE

**Hamilton, Fenton**
IT'S ALIVE
IT LIVES AGAIN

**Hannawalt, Charles**
DEMENTIA 13

**Hannon, Peter**
HAUNTING OF JULIA, THE

**Hansen, Gary**
NEXT OF KIN

**Harmon, Robert**
BLACK ROOM, THE

**Harris, John**
TALES FROM THE CRYPT

**Harrison, Harvey**
AMERICAN GOTHIC
BURNING, THE

**Hart, Dick**
CREEPSHOW 2

**Hauser, Robert B.**
WILLARD

**Havens, James O.**
CREATURE FROM THE BLACK
LAGOON

**Haviv, Yuri**
I SPIT ON YOUR GRAVE

**Hawkins, Willis**
WORM EATERS, THE

**Hayashi, Teru**
PREY, THE

**Hayes, Robert**
OPEN HOUSE

**Hebb, Brian**
HUMONGOUS

**Heller, Otto**
PEEPING TOM

**Herzog, John**
HELLO MARY LOU, PROM NIGHT II

**Hieronymous, Richard**
LOVE BUTCHER, THE

**Hilburn, Percy**
UNHOLY THREE, THE

**Hildyard, Jack**
BEAST MUST DIE, THE

**Hilliard, Richard L.**
CURSE OF THE LIVING CORPSE, THE
HORROR OF PARTY BEACH, THE

**Hines, W.E.**
HAUNTED

**Hinton, James E.**
GANJA AND HESS

**Hinzman, Bill**
HUNGRY WIVES

**Hinzman, S. William**
CRAZIES, THE

**Hipp, Paul**
BOOGENS, THE
GRAVE OF THE VAMPIRE

**Hirschfield, Gerald**
CAR, THE
YOUNG FRANKENSTEIN

**Hochstatter, Zoran**
DEADLY DREAMS

**Hong, Wilson S.**
BIG FOOT

**Hoover, Mike**
EQUINOX

**Hora, John**
HOWLING, THE
GREMLINS
TWILIGHT ZONE—THE MOVIE

# CINEMATOGRAPHERS

**Horvath, Louis**
STRANGE BEHAVIOR

**Howarth, Alan**
HALLOWEEN II

**Howe, James Wong**
MARK OF THE VAMPIRE

**Hugo, Michel**
MANITOU, THE
PANDEMONIUM

**Hume, Alan**
DR. TERROR'S HOUSE OF HORRORS
FROM BEYOND THE GRAVE
LEGEND OF HELL HOUSE, THE
LEGACY, THE
WATCHER IN THE WOODS, THE

**Hunt, J. Roy**
I WALKED WITH A ZOMBIE

**Hurst, Peter**
GHOST STORY

**Hurwitz, Tom**
CREEPSHOW 2

**Hurwitz, Victor**
LAST HOUSE ON THE LEFT

**Ibbetson, Arthur**
DIE! DIE! MY DARLING

**Irving, Louis**
HOWLING III, THE

**Irwin, Mark**
BROOD, THE
DEAD ZONE, THE
FUNERAL HOME
FLY, THE
SPASMS
SCANNERS
VIDEODROME

**Jessop, Peter**
CONFESSIONAL, THE
FLESH AND BLOOD SHOW, THE
HOUSE OF WHIPCORD
SCHIZO
FRIGHTMARE

**Jessup, Robert**
DEADLY BLESSING
RACE WITH THE DEVIL

**Johnson, William R.**
DEAR, DEAD DELILAH

**Jones, Don**
HOUSE OF SEVEN CORPSES, THE
LOVE BUTCHER, THE

**Jordan, Albert R.**
GIRLS SCHOOL SCREAMERS

**Julius, H.**
DEAD OF NIGHT

**Jurgenson, William**
ARNOLD

**Kalinke, Ernst W.**
BLOOD DEMON
MARK OF THE DEVIL

**Katz, Stephen M.**
SISTER SISTER

**Kaufman, Lloyd**
TOXIC AVENGER, THE

**Kawa, Mori**
HEARSE, THE

**Keisser, Jan**
FRIGHT NIGHT

**Kelley, W. Wallace**
NUTTY PROFESSOR, THE

**Kelsch, Ken**
DRILLER KILLER

**Kemper, Victor J.**
AUDREY ROSE
MAGIC

**Kibbe, Gary B.**
PRINCE OF DARKNESS

**King, D.**
JUST BEFORE DAWN

**King, J.**
JUST BEFORE DAWN
FRIGHTMARE

**Kleinman, A.**
FORCED ENTRY

**Kline, Benjamin**
BEFORE I HANG
MAN THEY COULD NOT HANG, THE
ZOMBIES OF MORA TAU

**Kline, Richard H.**
FURY, THE
KING KONG

**Knapp, Douglas**
ASSAULT ON PRECINCT 13

**Koenekamp, Fred J.**
AMITYVILLE HORROR, THE

**Kojayan, Shirah**
BOGGY CREEK II

**Kooris, Richard**
TEXAS CHAINSAW MASSACRE PART
2, THE

**Kornman, Tony**
HUNCHBACK OF NOTRE DAME, THE

**Kovacs, Laszlo**
GHOSTBUSTERS
BLOOD OF DRACULA'S CASTLE
TARGETS

**Krampf, Gunther**
GHOUL, THE

**Kranhouse, Jon R.**
FRIDAY THE 13TH PART VI: JASON
LIVES

**Kratina, Dick**
SENTINEL, THE

**Krogh, Dan**
WIZARD OF GORE, THE

**Kuveiller, Luigi**
DEEP RED
ANDY WARHOL'S FRANKENSTEIN
ANDY WARHOL'S DRACULA

**Lacambre, Daniel**
HUMANOIDS FROM THE DEEP
SATURDAY THE 14TH

VELVET VAMPIRE, THE

**Lachman, Jr., Edward**
SCALPEL

**Langley, Bryan**
HUMAN MONSTER, THE

**Langley, Norman**
HOUSE OF THE LONG SHADOWS

**Larner, Steven**
TWILIGHT ZONE—THE MOVIE

**Laszlo, Andrew**
FUNHOUSE, THE
POLTERGEIST II

**Lathrop, Philip**
DEADLY FRIEND
MONSTER OF PIEDRAS BLANCAS,
THE
JEKYLL AND HYDE . . . TOGETHER
AGAIN

**Le Picard, Marcel**
INVISIBLE GHOST, THE
SCARED TO DEATH

**Leigh, Norman**
SCHIZOID

**Lente, Miklos**
HAPPY BIRTHDAY TO ME

**Leonetti, Matthew F.**
POLTERGEIST

**Leslie, Bill**
NAIL GUN MASSACRE

**Lewis, David**
HILLS HAVE EYES II, THE

**Lewis, Gordon**
TWO THOUSAND MANIACS

**Lewis, Herschell Gordon**
BLOOD FEAST
COLOR ME BLOOD RED
SOMETHING WEIRD

**Lewnes, Peter**
I WAS A TEENAGE ZOMBIE

**Linden, Edward**
SON OF KONG
KING KONG

**Lindley, John**
KILLER PARTY
STEPFATHER, THE
SERPENT AND THE RAINBOW, THE

**Lindsay, Robert**
MANIAC

**Logan, Bruce**
DRACULA'S DOG

**Lomas, Raoul**
CHILDREN OF THE CORN

**Lommel, Ulli**
DEVONSVILLE TERROR, THE

**London, James**
TOXIC AVENGER, THE

**Long, Stanley A.**
BLOOD BEAST TERROR, THE

**Lord, Don**
SCREAMTIME

**Louzon, Gary**
OPEN HOUSE

**Lumas, Raoul**
PROWLER, THE

**McAlpine, Don**
PATRICK

**Macari, Giuseppe**
DRACULA'S WIDOW

**McCollough, Paul**
MIDNIGHT

**McDonald, David**
HORROR HOSPITAL

**McGowan, Bruce**
BORN OF FIRE

**McGowan, Jack**
DEATHDREAM
MARDI GRAS MASSACRE

**McKay, Doug**
KEEPER, THE

**MacKay, Mark**
ROCK 'N' ROLL NIGHTMARE

**Mackenzie, Jack**
ISLE OF THE DEAD

**McKinney, Austin**
HOUSE OF EVIL
FEAR CHAMBER, THE
LOVE BUTCHER, THE

**McLeish, Ronald W.**
MONSTER IN THE CLOSET

**McNichol, John**
TERROR HOUSE

**McPherson, John**
JAWS: THE REVENGE

**McWilliams, Steve**
REVENGE

**Madden, Lee**
SUPERSTITION

**Magder, Zale**
TERMINAL CHOICE

**Mancori, Guglielmo**
MANHATTAN BABY

**Mangine, Joseph**
ALONE IN THE DARK
ALLIGATOR
MOTHER'S DAY
SQUIRM

**Mankofsky, Isidore**
HOMEBODIES
SCREAM, BLACULA, SCREAM
WEREWOLVES ON WHEELS

**Marino, Juan**
PIECES

**Marion, Manuel**
COUNT DRACULA

**Marley, Peverell**
HOUSE OF WAX

**Marquard, Brick**
CASTLE OF EVIL

**Marquette, Jacques**
CREATURE FROM THE HAUNTED SEA
STRANGLER, THE

**Martinelli, Arthur**
DEVIL BAT, THE
WHITE ZOMBIE
REVOLT OF THE ZOMBIES

**Mascelli, Joseph V.**
THRILL KILLERS, THE

**Masciocchi, Marcello**
MURDER CLINIC, THE

**Massaccesi, Aristide**
DEVIL'S WEDDING NIGHT, THE
TEMPTER, THE

**Mate, Rudolph**
VAMPYR

**Maxwell, Robert**
POINT OF TERROR

**May, Bradford**
MONSTER SQUAD, THE

**Mayers, Michael**
CLASS OF NUKE 'EM HIGH

**Meaj, Urgent**
DEMON WITCH CHILD

**Meheux, Phil**
FINAL CONFLICT, THE

**Menczer, Enrico**
CHOSEN, THE

**Mendenhall, William**
RUBY

**Mescall, John**
BLACK CAT, THE
BRIDE OF FRANKENSTEIN, THE

**Metcalfe, John**
RAWHEAD REX

**Metty, Russell**
BEN

**Miller, Virgil**
PHANTOM OF THE OPERA, THE

**Milligan, Andy**
BLOODTHIRSTY BUTCHERS
CARNAGE
MAN WITH TWO HEADS, THE
RATS ARE COMING! THE
WEREWOLVES ARE HERE!, THE
TORTURE DUNGEON
GHASTLY ONES, THE

**Mills, Alec**
KING KONG LIVES

**Mills, Bill**
SLEEPAWAY CAMP 2: UNHAPPY
CAMPERS

**Mills, D.**
GHASTLY ONES, THE

**Milt, Victor C.**
PREMONITION, THE

**Minsky, Charles**
APRIL FOOL'S DAY

**Miyajima, Yoshio**
KWAIDAN

**Mohr, Hal**
PHANTOM OF THE OPERA

**Molloy, Mike**
SHOUT, THE

**Momel, James**
MS. 45
MADMAN

**Monton, Vincent**
THIRST
ROAD GAMES

**Moore, Ted**
PSYCHOMANIA
ORCA

**Morgan, Donald**
CHRISTINE
HYSTERICAL

**Morgan, Ira**
GREAT GABBO, THE
VAMPIRE BAT, THE

**Morrill, John Arthur**
BROTHERHOOD OF SATAN, THE
KINGDOM OF THE SPIDERS
WITCHMAKER, THE

**Morris, Reginald H.**
BLACK CHRISTMAS
PHOBIA

**Moss, Gerald**
VIRGIN WITCH, THE

**Muir, David**
LUST FOR A VAMPIRE

**Muller, Robby**
BELIEVERS, THE

**Murphy, Fred**
Q

**Murphy, Michael D.**
MIRRORS
SILENT SCREAM

**Musuraca, Nicholas**
BEDLAM
CURSE OF THE CAT PEOPLE, THE
CAT PEOPLE
SEVENTH VICTIM, THE

**Nannuzzi, Armando**
MAXIMUM OVERDRIVE
STEPHEN KING'S SILVER BULLET

**Neame, Ronald**
DEMON BARBER OF FLEET STREET,
THE

**Nee, Louis**
VAMPYR

**Nepomniaschy, Alex**
POLTERGEIST III

**Neumann, Harry**
APE, THE

**New, Robert**
PROM NIGHT

**Newbrook, Peter**
CRUCIBLE OF TERROR

**Newhard, Robert**
HUNCHBACK OF NOTRE DAME, THE

# CINEMATOGRAPHERS

**Nicholson, Meredith**
FRANKENSTEIN'S DAUGHTER

**Nickolaus, John**
TERROR, THE

**Nuyteen, Bruno**
POSSESSION

**Nykvist, Sven**
TENANT, THE

**O'Connell, L.W.**
RETURN OF THE VAMPIRE, THE

**Okada, Daryn**
PHANTASM II

**Oster, Emil**
DOCTOR DEATH: SEEKER OF SOULS

**Overbaugh, Roy**
DR. JEKYLL AND MR. HYDE

**Pallotini, Riccardo**
LADY FRANKENSTEIN

**Paniagua, Cecilio**
HOUSE OF EXORCISM, THE

**Paris, Dominic**
LAST RITES

**Parker, Jack**
DEAD OF NIGHT

**Parslow, Ray**
HOUSE THAT DRIPPED BLOOD, THE
MADHOUSE

**Patka, Beda F.**
FRIDAY THE 13TH . . . THE ORPHAN

**Paulino, Justo**
MAD DOCTOR OF BLOOD ISLAND,
THE

**Paynter, Robert**
AMERICAN WEREWOLF IN LONDON,
AN
CURTAINS
FINAL CONFLICT, THE
LITTLE SHOP OF HORRORS

**Pearl, Daniel**
TEXAS CHAIN SAW MASSACRE, THE
RETURN TO SALEM'S LOT, A
IT'S ALIVE III: ISLAND OF THE ALIVE

**Pearl, Herb**
PSYCHIC KILLER

**Peterman, Don**
WHEN A STRANGER CALLS

**Phillips, Jr., Alex**
FADE TO BLACK
DEVIL'S RAIN, THE
DEMONOID
NIGHT OF A THOUSAND CATS, THE

**Philo, Tim**
EVIL DEAD, THE

**Piazzoli, Roberto d'Ettore**
BEYOND THE DOOR
PIRANHA II: THE SPAWNING

**Piel, Don**
MARDI GRAS MASSACRE

**Pierce, Charles B.**
LEGEND OF BOGGY CREEK, THE

**Pinter, Tom**
TRANSYLVANIA 6-5000

**Pizer, Larry**
PHANTOM OF THE PARADISE
TOO SCARED TO SCREAM

**Plotin, Ken**
BEYOND EVIL

**Poland, Cliff**
STANLEY

**Posey, Stephen**
BLOODY BIRTHDAY
FRIDAY THE 13TH, PART V—A NEW
BEGINNING

**Posey, Steve**
SLUMBER PARTY MASSACRE, THE

**Poster, Steve**
BLOOD BEACH
DEAD AND BURIED

**Prather, Maurice**
CARNIVAL OF SOULS

**Pratt, Roger**
SENDER, THE

**Prince, Patrick**
SCARED TO DEATH

**Probyn, Brian**
INN OF THE DAMNED

**Pudney, Alan**
DON'T OPEN TILL CHRISTMAS
SLAUGHTER HIGH
SCREAMTIME

**Quezada, Roberto**
UNSEEN, THE

**Rabe, Vincent J.**
MANIAC COP

**Raditschnig, Herbert**
OUTING, THE

**Ramos, Jose Ortiz**
LIVING HEAD, THE

**Ramsey, Stephen**
NOMADS

**Rasca, Nonong**
NIGHT OF THE COBRA WOMAN

**Reed, Art**
BLACK DRAGONS
CORPSE VANISHES, THE

**Reed, Michael**
GORGON, THE

**Rennahan, Ray**
DOCTOR X
MYSTERY OF THE WAX MUSEUM, THE

**Reshovsky, Marc**
SORORITY HOUSE MASSACRE

**Richards, Jack L.**
BEAST WITHIN, THE

**Richmond, Anthony**
DON'T LOOK NOW

**Richmond, Tom**
CHOPPING MALL

**Rinaldi, Antonio**
HATCHET FOR A HONEYMOON

**Rivers, Joe**
GIRLS NIGHT OUT

**Roberson, James**
TERROR ON TOUR
TOWN THAT DREADED SUNDOWN,
THE

**Robinson, George**
ABBOTT AND COSTELLO MEET DR.
JEKYLL AND MR. HYDE
FRANKENSTEIN MEETS THE WOLF
MAN
SON OF FRANKENSTEIN
SON OF DRACULA

**Roeg, Nicolas**
MASQUE OF THE RED DEATH, THE

**Rogers, Robert E.**
SCREAMS OF A WINTER NIGHT

**Roizman, Owen**
EXORCIST, THE

**Rojas, Mini**
EYES OF A STRANGER

**Roland, Jr., Glenn**
DADDY'S DEADLY DARLING

**Romanoff, Andy**
FLESH FEAST
SOMETHING WEIRD

**Romero, George A.**
NIGHT OF THE LIVING DEAD
HUNGRY WIVES

**Rosher, Charles**
NIGHTWING

**Rosson, Edward**
LOVE AT FIRST BITE

**Rudnick, Charles**
NIGHTMARE IN BLOOD

**Russell, John L.**
PSYCHO

**Ruttenberg, Joseph**
DR. JEKYLL AND MR. HYDE

**Saad, Robert**
THEY CAME FROM WITHIN

**Saarinen, Eric**
HILLS HAVE EYES, THE

**Salvati, Sergio**
CELLAR DWELLER
CRAWLSPACE
HOUSE BY THE CEMETERY, THE
PSYCHIC, THE
ZOMBIE
GATES OF HELL, THE
GHOULIES II

**Sanchez, Francisco**
HOUSE OF PSYCHOTIC WOMEN, THE

**Sanderson, David**
PLUMBER, THE

**Sandor, Gregory**
SISTERS

**Schellerup, Henning**
SILENT NIGHT, DEADLY NIGHT

THE HORROR FILM

**Schmidt-Reitwein, Jorg**
NOSFERATU, THE VAMPIRE

**Schnall, Peter**
MUTILATOR, THE

**Schuler, Fred**
AMITYVILLE 3-D
HAUNTED HONEYMOON

**Sciafe, Ted**
CURSE OF THE DEMON

**Seale, John**
HITCHER, THE
SURVIVOR

**Secrist, Larry**
HAUNTS

**Seigler, Al**
BLACK ROOM, THE

**Semler, Dean**
RAZORBACK

**Sempere, Francisco**
CAULDRON OF BLOOD

**Seresin, Michael**
ANGEL HEART

**Seymer, John Michael**
REDEEMER, THE

**Shellerup, Henning**
BERSERKER

**Shlugleit, Eugene**
EVIL DEAD 2: DEAD BY DAWN

**Short, David**
SILENT SCREAM

**Shuftan, Eugene**
HORROR CHAMBER OF DR.
FAUSTUS, THE

**Slocombe, Douglas**
CIRCUS OF HORRORS

**Smith, Glen**
NIGHTMARE IN WAX

**Smith, Leonard**
DEVIL DOLL, THE

**Smoot, Reed**
WRAITH, THE

**Snyder, William E.**
CREATURE FROM THE BLACK
LAGOON

**Solares, Raul Martinez**
NIGHT OF THE BLOODY APES

**Sorrentino, Bob**
DAY OF THE ANIMALS

**Southon, Mike**
GOTHIC

**Spagnoli, Alberto**
BEYOND THE DOOR II

**Spencer, Brenton**
BLUE MONKEY

**Spera, Mike**
SCREAMTIME

**Sperling, David**
BLOODEATERS
BOOGEYMAN II

**BOOGEY MAN, THE**
STREET TRASH

**Spila, Otello**
DORIAN GRAY

**Spratling, Tony**
MAN WHO HAUNTED HIMSELF, THE

**Sprung, John**
SHADOWS RUN BLACK

**Stahl, Jr., Jorge**
LIVING HEAD, THE

**Stavrou, Ari**
BLOOD TIDE
LAND OF THE MINOTAUR

**Stein, Peter**
FRIDAY THE 13TH PART II

**Stengler, Mack**
APE MAN, THE
BOWERY AT MIDNIGHT
GHOSTS ON THE LOOSE
KING OF THE ZOMBIES

**Stensvold, Alan**
INVISIBLE STRANGLER, THE

**Stephenson, G.**
HOWLING II . . . YOUR SISTER IS A
WEREWOLF

**Stevens, John**
BLACULA

**Storaro, Vittorio**
BIRD WITH THE CRYSTAL PLUMAGE,
THE

**Stradling, Harry**
PICTURE OF DORIAN GRAY, THE

**Stradling, Jr., Harry**
PROPHECY

**Struss, Karl**
FLY, THE

**Stumar, Charles**
MUMMY, THE
RAVEN, THE

**Stumar, John**
RETURN OF THE VAMPIRE, THE

**Suchitzky, Wolfgang**
THEATRE OF BLOOD

**Suhrstedt, Timothy**
HOUSE ON SORORITY ROW, THE
TEEN WOLF

**Surtees, Bruce**
PSYCHO III

**Surtees, Robert L.**
OTHER, THE

**Suschitzky, Peter**
DEAD RINGERS

**Swenning, William**
I DISMEMBER MAMA

**Talbot, Kenneth**
HANDS OF THE RIPPER

**Tarzana, Herman**
BLOOD AND BLACK LACE

**Taylor, Alfred**
SPIDER BABY

**Taylor, Gilbert**
DRACULA
OMEN, THE
THEATRE OF DEATH
REPULSION

**Taylor, J.O.**
SON OF KONG
KING KONG

**Terzano, Ubaldo**
BLACK SABBATH

**Thieltges, Gary**
EATING RAOUL
RETRIBUTION

**Thompson, William**
DEMENTIA
MANIAC

**Thomson, Alex**
DOCTOR PHIBES RISES AGAIN
KEEP, THE

**Tirl, George**
INITIATION, THE

**Toll, Gerry**
BLOODSUCKING FREAKS

**Tomsic, Gary**
ESCAPES

**Torbet, Bruce**
BASKET CASE
BRAIN DAMAGE

**Tosi, Mario**
CARRIE
FROGS

**Tovoli, Luciano**
UNSANE

**Tower, Richard**
DOCTOR X

**Trane, Reuben**
SHOCK WAVES

**Trussel, Hal**
ONE DARK NIGHT

**Turpin, Gerry**
SEANCE ON A WET AFTERNOON

**Tynes, Jim**
DEMENTED

**Ulloa, Alejandro**
HORROR EXPRESS

**Valentine, Joseph**
WOLF MAN, THE

**Valtenburgs, John**
KEEP MY GRAVE OPEN

**Vamos, Thomas**
GATE, THE

**Van Der Enden, Edward**
DAUGHTERS OF DARKNESS

**Van Enger, Charles**
ABBOTT AND COSTELLO MEET
FRANKENSTEIN
BRIDE OF THE GORILLA
PHANTOM OF THE OPERA, THE

# CINEMATOGRAPHERS

**van Loon, Larry**
SCALPS

**Van Munster, Burt**
MASSACRE AT CENTRAL HIGH

**Vargas, Henry**
UNHOLY, THE

**Varriano, Emilio**
BARON BLOOD

**Verzier, Rene**
DEATH SHIP
DEADLY EYES
RABID
PYX, THE
OF UNKNOWN ORIGIN
VISITING HOURS
LITTLE GIRL WHO LIVES DOWN THE
LANE, THE

**Vidgeon, Robin**
HELLBOUND: HELLRAISER II
HELLRAISER

**Vidor, Zoli**
SAVAGE WEEKEND

**Villasenor, Leopoldo**
WEREWOLF VS. THE VAMPIRE
WOMAN, THE

**von Sternberg, Nicholas**
UNINVITED, THE
SLAUGHTERHOUSE ROCK
HOSPITAL MASSACRE
WACKO
TOURIST TRAP, THE

**Wagner, Fritz Arno**
NOSFERATU, THE VAMPIRE

**Wagner, Roy**
NIGHTMARE ON ELM STREET 3:
DREAM WARRIORS, A
RETURN TO HORROR HIGH
WITCHBOARD

**Wagreitch, Herb**
GHOSTBUSTERS

**Wakeford, Kent**
DOCTOR DEATH: SEEKER OF SOULS

**Walker, Vernon**
SON OF KONG
KING KONG

**Wallace, Enrique**
AZTEC MUMMY, THE
CURSE OF THE AZTEC MUMMY, THE
ROBOT VS. THE AZTEC MUMMY, THE

**Walther, Jurg**
BLOOD DINER

**Wanvick, Norman**
CREEPING FLESH, THE

**Warren, John F.**
DAUGHTER OF DR. JEKYLL

**Warrenton, Gilbert**
CAT AND THE CANARY, THE

**Warwick, Norman**
ABOMINABLE DR. PHIBES, THE
DR. JEKYLL AND SISTER HYDE
TALES FROM THE CRYPT
TORTURE GARDEN

GODSEND, THE

**Watkin, David**
TO THE DEVIL A DAUGHTER

**Waxman, Harry**
BEAST IN THE CELLAR, THE
WICKER MAN, THE
UNCANNY, THE
VAMPYRES, DAUGHTERS OF
DRACULA

**Weaver, Robert A.**
NIGHT OF BLOODY HORROR

**Webster, Brett**
SCALPS

**Weis, Jack**
MARDI GRAS MASSACRE

**West, Jonathan**
MUNCHIES

**Wexler, Howard**
DREAMANIAC

**Wilcots, Joe**
MOUNTAINTOP MOTEL MASSACRE

**Wilcox, John**
CRAZE
EVIL OF FRANKENSTEIN, THE
LEGEND OF THE SEVEN GOLDEN
VAMPIRES, THE
GHOUL, THE

**Wilkins, Vaughn**
HILLBILLYS IN A HAUNTED HOUSE

**Williams, Billy**
EXORCIST, THE

**Williams, Larry**
CRIME OF DR. CRESPI, THE

**Wilson, Ian**
CAPTAIN KRONOS: VAMPIRE HUNTER

**Wilson, James**
TELL-TALE HEART, THE

**Wood, E.S.**
TRACK OF THE MOONBEAST

**Wood, James**
DR. JEKYLL'S DUNGEON OF DEATH

**Wood, Oliver**
DON'T GO IN THE HOUSE

**Woolsey, Ralph**
PACK, THE

**Worth, Lothrop**
BILLY THE KID VS. DRACULA
JESSE JAMES MEETS
FRANKENSTEIN'S DAUGHTER

**Yarussi, Daniel**
GRADUATION DAY

**Yeoman, Robert D.**
DEAD HEAT

**Young, Freddie**
ASPHYX, THE

**Young, Les**
TERROR

**Zsigmond, Vilmos**
WITCHES OF EASTWICK, THE
BLOW OUT

**Zuccoli, F.**
DR. BUTCHER, M.D.

# DIRECTORS

**Adamson, Al**
DRACULA VS. FRANKENSTEIN
BLOOD OF DRACULA'S CASTLE
BRAIN OF BLOOD

**Adlum, Ed**
INVASION OF THE BLOOD FARMERS

**Alcocer, Santos**
CAULDRON OF BLOOD

**Aldrich, Robert**
WHATEVER HAPPENED TO BABY
JANE?
HUSH . . . HUSH, SWEET CHARLOTTE

**Alston, Emmett**
NEW YEAR'S EVIL

**Alves, Joe**
JAWS 3-D

**Anderson, Clyde**
MONSTER DOG

**Anderson, Michael**
ORCA

**Angel, Mikel**
LOVE BUTCHER, THE

**Annett, Paul**
BEAST MUST DIE, THE

**Aranda, Vincent**
BLOOD SPATTERED BRIDE, THE

**Argento, Dario**
UNSANE
DEEP RED
BIRD WITH THE CRYSTAL PLUMAGE,
THE
CREEPERS
INFERNO

**Armstrong, Michael**
MARK OF THE DEVIL

**Arnold, Jack**
CREATURE FROM THE BLACK
LAGOON

**Ashe, Dick**
TRACK OF THE MOONBEAST

**Asher, William**
BUTCHER, BAKER (NIGHTMARE
MAKER)

**Assonitis, Ovidio**
BEYOND THE DOOR
TENTACLES

**Attenborough, Richard**
MAGIC

**Attias, Daniel**
STEPHEN KING'S SILVER BULLET

**Auer, John H.**
CRIME OF DR. CRESPI, THE

**Aured, Carlos**
HOUSE OF PSYCHOTIC WOMEN, THE

**Austin, Ray**
HOUSE OF THE LIVING DEAD
VIRGIN WITCH, THE

**Avedis, Howard**
MORTUARY

**Badham, John**
DRACULA

**Baker, Graham**
FINAL CONFLICT, THE

**Baker, Roy Ward**
ASYLUM
AND NOW THE SCREAMING STARTS
LEGEND OF THE SEVEN GOLDEN
VAMPIRES, THE
DR. JEKYLL AND SISTER HYDE
MONSTER CLUB, THE
SCARS OF DRACULA, THE
VAULT OF HORROR, THE
VAMPIRE LOVERS, THE

**Balch, Anthony**
HORROR HOSPITAL

**Ballard, John**
FRIDAY THE 13TH . . . THE ORPHAN

**Band, Albert**
DRACULA'S DOG
GHOULIES II

**Barker, Clive**
HELLRAISER

**Bartel, Paul**
EATING RAOUL

**Barton, Charles T.**
ABBOTT AND COSTELLO MEET
FRANKENSTEIN

**Barwood, Hal**
WARNING SIGN

**Bass, Jules**
MAD MONSTER PARTY

**Batzella, Luigi**
DEVIL'S WEDDING NIGHT, THE

**Bava, Lamberto**
BLADE IN THE DARK, A
BEYOND THE DOOR II
DEMONS 2: THE NIGHTMARE
RETURNS
DEMONS

**Bava, Mario**
BLOOD AND BLACK LACE
BLACK SABBATH
BEYOND THE DOOR II
BARON BLOOD
HOUSE OF EXORCISM, THE
HATCHET FOR A HONEYMOON
TWITCH OF THE DEATH NERVE

**Bearde, Chris**
HYSTERICAL

**Beaudine, William**
BILLY THE KID VS. DRACULA
APE MAN, THE
GHOSTS ON THE LOOSE
JESSE JAMES MEETS
FRANKENSTEIN'S DAUGHTER

**Beaumont, Gabrielle**
GODSEND, THE

**Bechard, Gorman**
PSYCHOS IN LOVE

**Becker, Terry**
THIRSTY DEAD, THE

**Belson, Jerry**
JEKYLL AND HYDE . . . TOGETHER
AGAIN

**Bercovici, Luca**
GHOULIES

**Beresford, Al**
SCREAMTIME

**Bernds, Edward**
RETURN OF THE FLY

**Berwick, Irvin**
MONSTER OF PIEDRAS BLANCAS,
THE

**Berwick, Wayne**
MICROWAVE MASSACRE

**Bigelow, Kathryn**
NEAR DARK

**Black, Noel**
MIRRORS

**Blatty, William Peter**
NINTH CONFIGURATION, THE

**Bloom, Jeffrey**
BLOOD BEACH

**Boese, Carl**
GOLEM, THE

**Bogdanovich, Peter**
TARGETS

**Boorman, John**
EXORCIST II: THE HERETIC

**Bourke, Terry**
INN OF THE DAMNED

**Bowers, George**
HEARSE, THE

**Brismee, Jean**
DEVIL'S NIGHTMARE, THE

**Brock, Deborah**
SLUMBER PARTY MASSACRE II

**Brooks, Mel**
YOUNG FRANKENSTEIN

**Brown, Edwin Scott**
PREY, THE

**Brown, William O.**
WITCHMAKER, THE

**Browning, Tod**
DRACULA
DEVIL DOLL, THE
FREAKS
MARK OF THE VAMPIRE

**Brownrigg, S.F.**
DON'T LOOK IN THE BASEMENT
KEEP MY GRAVE OPEN

**Buchanan, Larry**
CURSE OF THE SWAMP CREATURE

**Buechler, John Carl**
CELLAR DWELLER
TROLL
FRIDAY THE 13TH PART VII—THE NEW
BLOOD

**Burr, Jeff**
OFFSPRING, THE

**Burton, Tim**
BEETLEJUICE

**Cabanne, Christy**
SCARED TO DEATH

**Cahn, Edward L.**
ZOMBIES OF MORA TAU

**Caiano, Mario**
NIGHTMARE CASTLE

**Cameron, James**
PIRANHA II: THE SPAWNING

**Carayiannis, Costa**
LAND OF THE MINOTAUR

**Cardona, Jr., Rene**
NIGHT OF A THOUSAND CATS, THE

**Cardona, Rene**
WRESTLING WOMEN VS. THE AZTEC
MUMMY, THE
NIGHT OF THE BLOODY APES

**Cardone, J.S.**
SLAYER, THE

**Cardos, John ""Bud"**
KINGDOM OF THE SPIDERS

**Carpenter, John**
ASSAULT ON PRECINCT 13
CHRISTINE
FOG, THE
HALLOWEEN
PRINCE OF DARKNESS

**Carpenter, Stephen**
DORM THAT DRIPPED BLOOD, THE
POWER, THE

**Carreras, Michael**
MANIAC

**Castle, William**
HOUSE ON HAUNTED HILL
THIRTEEN GHOSTS
STRAIT-JACKET

**Cavalcanti, Alberto**
DEAD OF NIGHT

**Christensen, Benjamin**
WITCHCRAFT THROUGH THE AGES

**Christian, Roger**
SENDER, THE

**Ciccoritti, Gerard**
GRAVEYARD SHIFT

**Clark, Bob**
BLACK CHRISTMAS
CHILDREN SHOULDN'T PLAY WITH
DEAD THINGS
DEATHDREAM

**Clark, Greydon**
UNINVITED, THE
SATAN'S CHEERLEADERS
WACKO

# DIRECTORS

**Clark, Jim**
MADHOUSE

**Clayton, Jack**
SOMETHING WICKED THIS WAY
COMES

**Clemens, Brian**
CAPTAIN KRONOS: VAMPIRE HUNTER

**Clouse, Robert**
DEADLY EYES
PACK, THE

**Cohen, Howard R.**
SATURDAY THE 14TH

**Cohen, Larry**
IT'S ALIVE
IT LIVES AGAIN
Q
STUFF, THE
RETURN TO SALEM'S LOT, A
IT'S ALIVE III: ISLAND OF THE ALIVE

**Condon, Bill**
SISTER SISTER

**Connor, Kevin**
HOUSE WHERE EVIL DWELLS, THE
FROM BEYOND THE GRAVE
MOTEL HELL

**Conway, Jack**
UNHOLY THREE, THE

**Conway, James L.**
BOOGENS, THE

**Cooper, Buddy**
MUTILATOR, THE

**Cooper, Merian C.**
KING KONG

**Coppola, Christopher**
DRACULA'S WIDOW

**Coppola, Francis Ford**
DEMENTIA 13

**Corman, Roger**
CREATURE FROM THE HAUNTED SEA
HOUSE OF USHER
MASQUE OF THE RED DEATH, THE
LITTLE SHOP OF HORRORS
RAVEN, THE
PREMATURE BURIAL, THE
PIT AND THE PENDULUM, THE
TERROR, THE
TALES OF TERROR
TOMB OF LIGEIA, THE

**Coscarelli, Don**
PHANTASM
PHANTASM II

**Cosmatos, George Pan**
OF UNKNOWN ORIGIN

**Crain, William**
BLACULA
DR. BLACK AND MR. HYDE

**Craven, Wes**
DEADLY FRIEND
DEADLY BLESSING
HILLS HAVE EYES II, THE
HILLS HAVE EYES, THE
NIGHTMARE ON ELM STREET, A

SWAMP THING
LAST HOUSE ON THE LEFT
SERPENT AND THE RAINBOW, THE

**Crichton, Charles**
DEAD OF NIGHT

**Cronenberg, David**
BROOD, THE
DEAD RINGERS
DEAD ZONE, THE
FLY, THE
RABID
THEY CAME FROM WITHIN
SCANNERS
VIDEODROME

**Cruze, James**
GREAT GABBO, THE

**Cunha, Richard**
FRANKENSTEIN'S DAUGHTER
GIANT FROM THE UNKNOWN

**Cunningham, Sean S.**
FRIDAY THE 13TH
STRANGER IS WATCHING, A

**Curtis, Dan**
BURNT OFFERINGS

**Curtis, J.**
FLESH EATERS, THE

**Curtiz, Michael**
DOCTOR X
MYSTERY OF THE WAX MUSEUM, THE

**Daalder, Renee**
MASSACRE AT CENTRAL HIGH

**Dahlin, Bob**
MONSTER IN THE CLOSET

**Daley, Tom**
OUTING, THE

**Dallamano, Massimo**
DORIAN GRAY

**Damiani, Damiano**
AMITYVILLE II: THE POSSESSION

**Daniel, Rod**
TEEN WOLF

**Dante, Joe**
HOWLING, THE
GREMLINS
PIRANHA
TWILIGHT ZONE—THE MOVIE

**Danton, Ray**
CRYPT OF THE LIVING DEAD
PSYCHIC KILLER

**Davidson, Boaz**
HOSPITAL MASSACRE

**Davis, Andrew**
FINAL TERROR, THE

**Dawson, Anthony**
ANDY WARHOL'S FRANKENSTEIN
ANDY WARHOL'S DRACULA

**Day, Robert**
CORRIDORS OF BLOOD
HAUNTED STRANGLER, THE

**De Gaetano, Michael**
HAUNTED

**de Leon, Geraldo**
MAD DOCTOR OF BLOOD ISLAND,
THE

**de Martino, Alberto**
CHOSEN, THE

**De Ossorio, Armando**
DEMON WITCH CHILD
PEOPLE WHO OWN THE DARK
HORROR OF THE ZOMBIES

**De Palma, Brian**
FURY, THE
DRESSED TO KILL
CARRIE
PHANTOM OF THE PARADISE
SISTERS
BODY DOUBLE
BLOW OUT

**de Toth, Andre**
HOUSE OF WAX

**Dearden, Basil**
DEAD OF NIGHT
MAN WHO HAUNTED HIMSELF, THE

**DeCoteau, David**
DREAMANIAC

**Dehlavi, Jamil**
BORN OF FIRE

**Dekker, Fred**
MONSTER SQUAD, THE

**Delman, Jeffrey**
DEADTIME STORIES

**DeLuca, Rudy**
TRANSYLVANIA 6-5000

**DeMartino, Alberto**
TEMPTER, THE

**DeSimone, Tom**
HELL NIGHT

**Deubel, Robert**
GIRLS NIGHT OUT

**Dieterle, William**
HUNCHBACK OF NOTRE DAME, THE

**Dohler, Don**
FIEND

**Donnelly, Dennis**
TOOLBOX MURDERS, THE

**Donner, Richard**
OMEN, THE

**Douglass, John S.**
MUTILATOR, THE

**Dowding, Jon**
ROAD GAMES

**Dowling, William**
LOST WORLD, THE

**Dragoti, Stan**
LOVE AT FIRST BITE

**Drake, Tom**
KEEPER, THE

**Dreyer, Carl Theodor**
VAMPYR

**Duffell, Peter**
HOUSE THAT DRIPPED BLOOD, THE

**Dugan, Michael**
MAUSOLEUM

**Dugdale, George**
SLAUGHTER HIGH

**Durston, David**
I DRINK YOUR BLOOD

**Edmonds, Don**
TERROR ON TOUR

**Ellison, Joseph**
DON'T GO IN THE HOUSE

**Emery, Robert J.**
SCREAM BLOODY MURDER

**Esper, Dwain**
MANIAC

**Essex, Harry**
OCTAMAN

**Ezra, Mark**
SLAUGHTER HIGH

**Farris, John**
DEAR, DEAD DELILAH

**Fasano, John**
ROCK 'N' ROLL NIGHTMARE

**Fenady, Georg**
ARNOLD

**Ferrara, Abel**
DRILLER KILLER
MS. 45

**Findlay, Michael**
SHRIEK OF THE MUTILATED

**Findlay, Roberta**
BLOOD SISTERS

**Finegan, John P.**
GIRLS SCHOOL SCREAMERS

**Fisher, Terence**
CURSE OF THE WEREWOLF, THE
CURSE OF FRANKENSTEIN, THE
HORROR OF DRACULA, THE
GORGON, THE
MUMMY, THE

**Fleischer, Richard**
AMITYVILLE 3-D

**Fleming, Andrew**
BAD DREAMS

**Fleming, Victor**
DR. JEKYLL AND MR. HYDE

**Florea, John**
INVISIBLE STRANGLER, THE

**Foleg, Peter**
UNSEEN, THE

**Forbes, Bryan**
SEANCE ON A WET AFTERNOON

**Fox, Wallace**
CORPSE VANISHES, THE
BOWERY AT MIDNIGHT

**Francis, Freddie**
CRAZE
EVIL OF FRANKENSTEIN, THE
DR. TERROR'S HOUSE OF HORRORS
GHOUL, THE
TALES FROM THE CRYPT

TORTURE GARDEN

**Franco, Jesus**
COUNT DRACULA
SCREAMING DEAD, THE

**Franics, Freddie**
CREEPING FLESH, THE

**Franju, Georges**
HORROR CHAMBER OF DR.
FAUSTUS, THE

**Frank, Carol**
SORORITY HOUSE MASSACRE

**Frankenheimer, John**
BLACK SUNDAY
PROPHECY

**Franklin, Richard**
PSYCHO II
PATRICK
ROAD GAMES

**Freed, Herb**
BEYOND EVIL
HAUNTS
GRADUATION DAY

**Freund, Karl**
MUMMY, THE

**Friedkin, William**
EXORCIST, THE

**Friedlander, Louis**
RAVEN, THE

**Fritsch, Gunther V.**
CURSE OF THE CAT PEOPLE, THE

**Froehlich, Bill**
RETURN TO HORROR HIGH

**Fruet, William**
BLUE MONKEY
FUNERAL HOME
KILLER PARTY
SPASMS

**Fuest, Robert**
ABOMINABLE DR. PHIBES, THE
DOCTOR PHIBES RISES AGAIN
DEVIL'S RAIN, THE

**Fulci, Lucio**
HOUSE BY THE CEMETERY, THE
MANHATTAN BABY
PSYCHIC, THE
ZOMBIE
GATES OF HELL, THE

**Furie, Sidney J.**
ENTITY, THE

**Gallu, Samuel**
THEATRE OF DEATH

**Gershuny, Theodore**
SILENT NIGHT, BLOODY NIGHT

**Gessner, Nicolas**
LITTLE GIRL WHO LIVES DOWN THE
LANE, THE

**Giannone, Joe**
MADMAN

**Gibson, Brian**
POLTERGEIST II

**Ginsberg, Milton Moses**
WEREWOLF OF WASHINGTON

**Ginter, Brad F.**
FLESH FEAST

**Girdler, William**
DAY OF THE ANIMALS
GRIZZLY
MANITOU, THE

**Goldblatt, Mark**
DEAD HEAT

**Golding, Paul**
PULSE

**Goochis, Constantine S.**
REDEEMER, THE

**Goodell, Gregory**
HUMAN EXPERIMENTS

**Gordon, Bert I.**
PICTURE MOMMY DEAD

**Gordon, Stuart**
DOLLS
FROM BEYOND
RE-ANIMATOR

**Gornick, Michael**
CREEPSHOW 2

**Governor, Richard**
GHOST TOWN

**Graver, Gary**
TRICK OR TREATS

**Green, Joseph**
BRAIN THAT WOULDN'T DIE, THE

**Grefe, William**
DEATH CURSE OF TARTU
STANLEY

**Griffith, Charles**
DR. HECKYL AND MR. HYPE

**Grinde, Nick**
BEFORE I HANG
MAN THEY COULD NOT HANG, THE

**Grissmer, John**
SCALPEL

**Guillermin, John**
KING KONG LIVES
KING KONG

**Gunn, Bill**
GANJA AND HESS

**Haines, Richard W.**
CLASS OF NUKE 'EM HIGH
SPLATTER UNIVERSITY

**Haller, Daniel**
DIE, MONSTER, DIE
DUNWICH HORROR, THE

**Halperin, Victor**
WHITE ZOMBIE
REVOLT OF THE ZOMBIES

**Hamer, Robert**
DEAD OF NIGHT

**Hammer, Robert**
DON'T ANSWER THE PHONE

**Hancock, John**
LET'S SCARE JESSICA TO DEATH

## DIRECTORS

Hardy, Robin
WICKER MAN, THE

Hardy, Rod
THIRST

Harlin, Renny
PRISON
NIGHTMARE ON ELM STREET 4: THE
DREAM MASTER, A

Harmon, Robert
HITCHER, THE

Harrington, Curtis
RUBY
WHO SLEW AUNTIE ROO?

Harris, Denny
SILENT SCREAM

Harrison, Paul
HOUSE OF SEVEN CORPSES, THE

Harry, Lee
SILENT NIGHT, DEADLY NIGHT PART II

Hart, Harvey
PYX, THE

Hartford-Davis, Robert
INCENSE FOR THE DAMNED

Harvey, Herk
CARNIVAL OF SOULS

Hayers, Sidney
CIRCUS OF HORRORS

Hayes, John
GRAVE OF THE VAMPIRE
GARDEN OF THE DEAD

Heard, Howard
SHADOWS RUN BLACK

Hemmings, David
SURVIVOR

Henenlotter, Frank
BASKET CASE
BRAIN DAMAGE

Heroux, Denis
UNCANNY, THE

Herz, Michael
TOXIC AVENGER, THE

Herzog, Werner
NOSFERATU, THE VAMPIRE

Hess, David
TO ALL A GOODNIGHT

Hessler, Gordon
OBLONG BOX, THE
MURDERS IN THE RUE MORGUE
SCREAM AND SCREAM AGAIN

Hewitt, Jean
BLOOD OF DRACULA'S CASTLE

Hickox, Douglas
THEATRE OF BLOOD

Hildebrand, Frank E.
ONCE BITTEN

Hill, Jack
HOUSE OF EVIL
FEAR CHAMBER, THE
SPIDER BABY

Hiller, Arthur
NIGHTWING

Hiltzik, Robert
SLEEPAWAY CAMP

Hirsch, Bettina
MUNCHIES

Hitchcock, Alfred
BIRDS, THE
PSYCHO

Holland, Tom
FRIGHT NIGHT
CHILD'S PLAY

Honthaner, Ron
HOUSE ON SKULL MOUNTAIN, THE

Hooker, Ted
CRUCIBLE OF TERROR

Hooper, Tobe
EATEN ALIVE
FUNHOUSE, THE
POLTERGEIST
TEXAS CHAINSAW MASSACRE PART
2, THE
TEXAS CHAIN SAW MASSACRE, THE

Houck, Jr., Joy
CREATURE FROM BLACK LAKE, THE
NIGHT OF BLOODY HORROR

Hough, John
AMERICAN GOTHIC
HOWLING IV: THE ORIGINAL
NIGHTMARE
LEGEND OF HELL HOUSE, THE
INCUBUS, THE
WATCHER IN THE WOODS, THE
TWINS OF EVIL

Hoyt, Harry O.
LOST WORLD, THE

Hunt, Ed
BLOODY BIRTHDAY

Hunter, T. Hayes
GHOUL, THE

Huston, Jimmy
FINAL EXAM

Huston, John
PHOBIA

Ibanez, Juan
HOUSE OF EVIL
FEAR CHAMBER, THE

Irvin, John
GHOST STORY

Jackson, Donald
DEMON LOVER, THE

Jackson, Lewis
YOU BETTER WATCH OUT

Janos, Victor
LAST HOUSE ON DEAD END STREET

Jeffreys, Arthur
DEMENTED

Jeffries, Richard
BLOOD TIDE

Jones, Amy
SLUMBER PARTY MASSACRE, THE

Jones, Don
FOREST, THE
LOVE BUTCHER, THE

Julian, Rupert
PHANTOM OF THE OPERA, THE

Kalmanowicz, Max
CHILDREN, THE

Karlson, Phil
BEN

Karr, Tom
DEATHDREAM

Kaufman, Charles
MOTHER'S DAY

Kaufman, Lloyd
CLASS OF NUKE 'EM HIGH
TOXIC AVENGER, THE

Keeter, Worth
WOLFMAN

Keith, David
CURSE, THE

Kelljan, Bob
COUNT YORGA, VAMPIRE
SCREAM, BLACULA, SCREAM

Kelly, James
BEAST IN THE CELLAR, THE

Kenner, Elly
BLACK ROOM, THE

Kiersch, Fritz
CHILDREN OF THE CORN

King, George
DEMON BARBER OF FLEET STREET,
THE

King, Stephen
MAXIMUM OVERDRIVE

Kirman, Leonard
CARNIVAL OF BLOOD

Klimovsky, Leon
WEREWOLF VS. THE VAMPIRE
WOMAN, THE

Kobayashi, Masaki
KWAIDAN

Koch, Howard W.
FRANKENSTEIN 1970

Kong, Jackie
BLOOD DINER

Kubrick, Stanley
SHINING, THE

Kumel, Harry
DAUGHTERS OF DARKNESS

La Loggia, Frank
FEAR NO EVIL
LADY IN WHITE

Lamont, Charles
ABBOTT AND COSTELLO MEET DR.
JEKYLL AND MR. HYDE

Landers, Lew
RETURN OF THE VAMPIRE, THE

**Landis, John**
AMERICAN WEREWOLF IN LONDON, AN
SCHLOCK
TWILIGHT ZONE—THE MOVIE

**Larraz, Joseph**
HOUSE THAT VANISHED, THE
VAMPYRES, DAUGHTERS OF DRACULA

**Larry, Sheldon**
TERMINAL CHOICE

**Laughlin, Michael**
STRANGE BEHAVIOR

**Lawrence, Marc**
DADDY'S DEADLY DARLING

**Leder, Paul**
I DISMEMBER MAMA

**Lee, Evan**
MEAT CLEAVER MASSACRE

**Lee, Norman**
CHAMBER OF HORRORS

**Lee, Rowland V.**
SON OF FRANKENSTEIN

**Leitch, Christopher**
TEEN WOLF TOO

**Leni, Paul**
CAT AND THE CANARY, THE

**Lenzi, Umberto**
CITY OF THE WALKING DEAD

**Leslie, Bill**
NAIL GUN MASSACRE

**Levesque, Michel**
WEREWOLVES ON WHEELS

**Levy, William A.**
BLACKENSTEIN

**Lewin, Albert**
PICTURE OF DORIAN GRAY, THE

**Lewis, Christopher**
REVENGE

**Lewis, Herschell Gordon**
BLOOD FEAST
COLOR ME BLOOD RED
SOMETHING WEIRD
WIZARD OF GORE, THE
TWO THOUSAND MANIACS
GRUESOME TWOSOME

**Lewis, Jerry**
NUTTY PROFESSOR, THE

**Lewis, Joseph H.**
INVISIBLE GHOST, THE

**Lieberman, Jeff**
BLUE SUNSHINE
JUST BEFORE DAWN
SQUIRM

**Litten, Peter**
SLAUGHTER HIGH

**Little, Dwight H.**
HALLOWEEN IV: THE RETURN OF MICHAEL MYERS

**Lo Bianco, Tony**
TOO SCARED TO SCREAM

**Lofton, Terry**
NAIL GUN MASSACRE

**Logothetis, Dimitri**
SLAUGHTERHOUSE ROCK

**Lommel, Ulli**
BOOGEYMAN II
BOOGEY MAN, THE
DEVONSVILLE TERROR, THE

**Loncraine, Richard**
HAUNTING OF JULIA, THE

**Lord, Jean Claude**
VISITING HOURS

**Loventhal, Charles**
MY DEMON LOVER

**Lubin, Arthur**
PHANTOM OF THE OPERA

**Luna, Bigas**
ANGUISH

**Lustig, William**
MANIAC
MANIAC COP

**Lynch, David**
ERASERHEAD

**Lynch, Paul**
HUMONGOUS
PROM NIGHT

**Lyon, Francis D.**
CASTLE OF EVIL

**McCauley, John**
RATTLERS

**McCowan, George**
FROGS

**McCrann, Chuck**
BLOODEATERS

**McCullough, Sr., Jim**
MOUNTAINTOP MOTEL MASSACRE

**McEveety, Bernard**
BROTHERHOOD OF SATAN, THE

**McEveety, Vincent**
WATCHER IN THE WOODS, THE

**Mack, Brice**
JENNIFER

**McLoughlin, Tom**
FRIDAY THE 13TH PART VI: JASON LIVES
ONE DARK NIGHT

**McNamara, Richard**
ATOM AGE VAMPIRE

**McTiernan, John**
NOMADS

**Magar, Guy**
RETRIBUTION

**Majano, Anton Guilio**
ATOM AGE VAMPIRE

**Malone, William**
SCARED TO DEATH

**Mann, Daniel**
WILLARD

**Mann, Michael**
KEEP, THE

**Marquand, Richard**
LEGACY, THE

**Martin, Eugenio**
HORROR EXPRESS

**Martinelli, Franco**
DR. BUTCHER, M.D.

**Martino, Sergio**
GREAT ALLIGATOR, THE
TORSO
SCREAMERS

**Marvin, Mike**
WRAITH, THE

**Mascelli, Joseph V.**
ATOMIC BRAIN, THE

**Massaccesi, Aristide**
GRIM REAPER, THE

**Mastroianni, Armand**
HE KNOWS YOU'RE ALONE
KILLING HOUR, THE
SUPERNATURALS, THE

**Matalon, Eddy**
CATHY'S CURSE

**Mattei, Bruno**
NIGHT OF THE ZOMBIES

**Maylam, Tony**
BURNING, THE

**Medak, Peter**
CHANGELING, THE

**Meyer, Andrew**
NIGHT OF THE COBRA WOMAN

**Michalakias, John Elias**
I WAS A TEENAGE ZOMBIE

**Mihalka, George**
MY BLOODY VALENTINE

**Mikels, Ted V.**
BLOOD ORGY OF THE SHE-DEVILS
CORPSE GRINDERS, THE

**Miller, Dan T.**
SCREAMERS

**Miller, George**
WITCHES OF EASTWICK, THE
TWILIGHT ZONE—THE MOVIE

**Milligan, Andy**
BLOODTHIRSTY BUTCHERS
CARNAGE
MAN WITH TWO HEADS, THE
RATS ARE COMING! THE WEREWOLVES ARE HERE!, THE
TORTURE DUNGEON
GHASTLY ONES, THE

**Miner, Steve**
HOUSE
FRIDAY THE 13TH PART III
FRIDAY THE 13TH PART II

**Moctezuma, Juan Lopez**
DR. TARR'S TORTURE DUNGEON
MARY, MARY, BLOODY MARY

## DIRECTORS

**Mora, Philippe**
BEAST WITHIN, THE
HOWLING III, THE
HOWLING II . . . YOUR SISTER IS A
WEREWOLF

**Morris, Ernest**
TELL-TALE HEART, THE

**Morrissey, Paul**
ANDY WARHOL'S FRANKENSTEIN
ANDY WARHOL'S DRACULA

**Moxey, John**
HORROR HOTEL

**Mulcahy, Russell**
RAZORBACK

**Mulligan, Robert**
OTHER, THE

**Mundhra, Jag**
OPEN HOUSE

**Murnau, F.W.**
NOSFERATU, THE VAMPIRE

**Muro, Jim**
STREET TRASH

**Narizzano, Silvio**
DIE! DIE! MY DARLING

**Neill, Roy William**
BLACK ROOM, THE
FRANKENSTEIN MEETS THE WOLF
MAN

**Neumann, Kurt**
FLY, THE

**Newbrook, Peter**
ASPHYX, THE

**Newell, Mike**
AWAKENING, THE

**Newfield, Sam**
DEAD MEN WALK
MAD MONSTER, THE

**Nicholson, Jack**
TERROR, THE

**Nicol, Alex**
POINT OF TERROR

**Nigh, William**
BLACK DRAGONS
APE, THE

**O'Bannon, Dan**
RETURN OF THE LIVING DEAD

**O'Connolly, Jim**
BEYOND THE FOG

**O'Connor, Jim**
BERSERK

**Obrow, Jeffrey**
DORM THAT DRIPPED BLOOD, THE
POWER, THE

**Oliver, Robert**
HOUSE OF FREAKS

**Oz, Frank**
LITTLE SHOP OF HORRORS

**Paradisi, Giulio**
VISITOR, THE

**Paris, Dominic**
LAST RITES

**Parker, Alan**
ANGEL HEART

**Parker, John**
DEMENTIA

**Parkinson, Tom**
DISCIPLE OF DEATH

**Pataki, Michael**
MANSION OF THE DOOMED

**Patel, Raju**
IN THE SHADOW OF KILIMANJARO

**Paulsen, David**
SCHIZOID
SAVAGE WEEKEND

**Pavlou, George**
RAWHEAD REX

**Peeters, Barbara**
HUMANOIDS FROM THE DEEP

**Perkins, Anthony**
PSYCHO III

**Peters, Brooke L.**
UNEARTHLY, THE

**Peterson, Kristine**
DEADLY DREAMS

**Pierce, Charles B.**
BOGGY CREEK II
LEGEND OF BOGGY CREEK, THE
TOWN THAT DREADED SUNDOWN,
THE

**Piers Haggard**
BLOOD ON SATAN'S CLAW, THE

**Pirro, Mark**
DEATHROW GAMESHOW

**Pittman, Bruce**
HELLO MARY LOU, PROM NIGHT II

**Polanski, Roman**
TENANT, THE
ROSEMARY'S BABY
REPULSION

**Portillo, Rafael**
AZTEC MUMMY, THE
CURSE OF THE AZTEC MUMMY, THE
ROBOT VS. THE AZTEC MUMMY, THE

**Post, Ted**
BABY, THE

**Powell, Michael**
PEEPING TOM

**Privitera, Vincent J.**
WITCHFIRE

**Purdom, Edmund**
DON'T OPEN TILL CHRISTMAS

**Quandour, Mohy**
SPECTRE OF EDGAR ALLAN POE, THE

**Railsback, Michael**
TRICK OR TREATS

**Raimi, Sam**
EVIL DEAD 2: DEAD BY DAWN
EVIL DEAD, THE

**Rakoff, Alvin**
DEATH SHIP

**Raley, Alice**
MOVIE HOUSE MASSACRE

**Randel, Tony**
HELLBOUND: HELLRAISER II

**Ray, Fred Olen**
SCALPS

**Reed, Joel M.**
BLOODSUCKING FREAKS
NIGHT OF THE ZOMBIES

**Reeves, Michael**
CONQUEROR WORM, THE

**Reiner, Carl**
MAN WITH TWO BRAINS, THE

**Reinl, Harold**
BLOOD DEMON

**Reitman, Ivan**
GHOSTBUSTERS

**Richard, Jef**
BERSERKER

**Ritelis, Viktor**
CRUCIBLE OF HORROR

**Roberson, James W.**
SUPERSTITION

**Roberts, Deborah**
FRANKENSTEIN GENERAL HOSPITAL

**Robertson, John S.**
DR. JEKYLL AND MR. HYDE

**Robins, Herb**
WORM EATERS, THE

**Robson, Mark**
BEDLAM
ISLE OF THE DEAD
SEVENTH VICTIM, THE

**Roddam, Franc**
BRIDE, THE

**Roeg, Nicolas**
DON'T LOOK NOW

**Roessler, Rick**
SLAUGHTERHOUSE

**Romero, Eddie**
MAD DOCTOR OF BLOOD ISLAND,
THE

**Romero, George A.**
DAWN OF THE DEAD
CREEPSHOW
CRAZIES, THE
DAY OF THE DEAD
MARTIN
NIGHT OF THE LIVING DEAD
HUNGRY WIVES
MONKEY SHINES: AN EXPERIMENT IN
FEAR

**Rose, Mickey**
STUDENT BODIES

**Rosenberg, Stuart**
AMITYVILLE HORROR, THE

**Rosenthal, Rick**
HALLOWEEN II

**Rosman, Mark**
HOUSE ON SORORITY ROW, THE

**Rothman, Stephanie**
RUBY
VELVET VAMPIRE, THE

**Ruben, Joseph**
STEPFATHER, THE

**Rubens, Percival**
DEMON, THE

**Russell, Chuck**
NIGHTMARE ON ELM STREET 3:
DREAM WARRIORS, A

**Russell, Ken**
LAIR OF THE WHITE WORM, THE
GOTHIC

**Russo, John A.**
MIDNIGHT

**Saeta, Eddie**
DOCTOR DEATH: SEEKER OF SOULS

**Sala, Henry**
NIGHTMARE WEEKEND

**San Fernando, Manuel**
WRESTLING WOMEN VS. THE AZTEC
MUMMY, THE

**Sangster, Jimmy**
HORROR OF FRANKENSTEIN, THE
LUST FOR A VAMPIRE

**Sargent, Joseph**
JAWS: THE REVENGE
NIGHTMARES

**Sasdy, Peter**
HANDS OF THE RIPPER

**Scardamaglia, Elio**
MURDER CLINIC, THE

**Scavolini, Romano**
NIGHTMARE

**Schlesinger, John**
BELIEVERS, THE

**Schmoeller, David**
CRAWLSPACE
TOURIST TRAP, THE

**Schnitzer, Robert Allen**
PREMONITION, THE

**Schoedsack, Ernest B.**
SON OF KONG
KING KONG

**Schrader, Paul**
CAT PEOPLE

**Schultz, Carl**
SEVENTH SIGN, THE

**Schumacher, Joel**
LOST BOYS, THE

**Scott, Tony**
HUNGER, THE

**Segall, Stuart**
DRIVE-IN MASSACRE

**Sellier, Charles E.**
SILENT NIGHT, DEADLY NIGHT

**Sewell, Vernon**
BLOOD BEAST TERROR, THE
BURKE AND HARE
GHOST SHIP

**Sharp, Don**
PSYCHOMANIA

**Sherman, Gary**
DEAD AND BURIED
POLTERGEIST III

**Sholder, Jack**
ALONE IN THE DARK
NIGHTMARE ON ELM STREET PART 2:
FREDDY'S REVENGE, A

**Shonteff, Lindsay**
DEVIL DOLL

**Signorelli, James**
ELVIRA: MISTRESS OF THE DARK

**Silverstein, Elliot**
CAR, THE

**Simon, Juan Piquer**
PIECES

**Simpson, Michael A.**
SLEEPAWAY CAMP 2: UNHAPPY
CAMPERS

**Siodmak, Curt**
BRIDE OF THE GORILLA

**Siodmak, Robert**
SON OF DRACULA

**Skolimowski, Jerzy**
SHOUT, THE

**Slatzer, Robert F.**
BIG FOOT

**Smith, Charles Martin**
TRICK OR TREAT

**Sole, Alfred**
ALICE, SWEET ALICE
PANDEMONIUM

**Sotos, Jim**
FORCED ENTRY
SWEET SIXTEEN

**Spielberg, Steven**
JAWS
TWILIGHT ZONE—THE MOVIE

**Spottiswoode, Roger**
TERROR TRAIN

**Stanley, John**
NIGHTMARE IN BLOOD

**Starr, Bruce**
BOOGEYMAN II

**Starrett, Jack**
RACE WITH THE DEVIL

**Stayer, Frank B.**
MONSTER WALKS, THE

**Steckler, Ray Dennis**
THRILL KILLERS, THE

**Steensland, David**
ESCAPES

**Steinmann, Danny**
FRIDAY THE 13TH, PART V—A NEW
BEGINNING

**Stephen, A.C.**
ORGY OF THE DEAD

**Stewart, Larry**
INITIATION, THE

**Stone, Oliver**
HAND, THE

**Storm, Howard**
ONCE BITTEN

**Strayer, Frank R.**
VAMPIRE BAT, THE

**Stryker, Johnathan**
CURTAINS

**Summers, Walter**
HUMAN MONSTER, THE

**Sykes, Peter**
TO THE DEVIL A DAUGHTER

**Szwarc, Jeannot**
JAWS II

**Takacs, Tibor**
GATE, THE

**Tampa, Harry**
NOCTURNA

**Taylor, Don**
DAMIEN—OMEN II
ISLAND OF DR. MOREAU, THE

**Teague, Lewis**
ALLIGATOR
CUJO
CAT'S EYE

**Tenney, Del**
CURSE OF THE LIVING CORPSE, THE
HORROR OF PARTY BEACH, THE

**Tenney, Kevin S.**
WITCHBOARD

**Thomason, Harry**
ENCOUNTER WITH THE UNKNOWN

**Thompson, J. Lee**
HAPPY BIRTHDAY TO ME

**Topper, Burt**
STRANGLER, THE

**Tourneur, Jacques**
CURSE OF THE DEMON
CAT PEOPLE
I WALKED WITH A ZOMBIE
LEOPARD MAN, THE

**Townsend, Bud**
NIGHTMARE IN WAX
TERROR HOUSE

**Trikonis, Gus**
EVIL, THE

**Ulmer, Edgar G.**
BLUEBEARD
BLACK CAT, THE
DAUGHTER OF DR. JEKYLL

**Urueta, Chano**
LIVING HEAD, THE

**Vane, Norman Thaddeus**
BLACK ROOM, THE
FRIGHTMARE

# DIRECTORS

**Vanorio, Frank**
CURSE, THE

**Vila, Camilio**
UNHOLY, THE

**Villard, Dimitri**
ONCE BITTEN

**Voskanian, Robert**
CHILD, THE

**Wadleigh, Michael**
WOLFEN

**Waggner, George**
WOLF MAN, THE

**Wald, Robby**
ONCE BITTEN

**Walker, David**
HOUSE OF WHIPCORD

**Walker, Peter**
HOUSE OF THE LONG SHADOWS
CONFESSIONAL, THE
FLESH AND BLOOD SHOW, THE
SCHIZO
FRIGHTMARE

**Wallace, Tommy Lee**
HALLOWEEN III: SEASON OF THE
WITCH

**Walton, Fred**
APRIL FOOL'S DAY
WHEN A STRANGER CALLS

**Warren, Norman J.**
TERROR

**Weeks, Stephen**
GHOST STORY

**Wegener, Paul**
GOLEM, THE

**Weir, Peter**
PLUMBER, THE

**Weis, Jack**
MARDI GRAS MASSACRE

**Welles, Mel**
LADY FRANKENSTEIN

**Wenk, Richard**
VAMP

**Weston, Armand**
NESTING, THE

**Weston, Eric**
EVILSPEAK

**Whale, James**
BRIDE OF FRANKENSTEIN, THE
INVISIBLE MAN, THE
FRANKENSTEIN

**Wiederhorn, Ken**
EYES OF A STRANGER
SHOCK WAVES
RETURN OF THE LIVING DEAD PART II

**Wiene, Robert**
CABINET OF DR. CALIGARI, THE

**Wilder, Gene**
HAUNTED HONEYMOON

**Wiley, Ethan**
HOUSE II: THE SECOND STORY

**Williams, Tony**
NEXT OF KIN

**Wilson, James L.**
SCREAMS OF A WINTER NIGHT

**Winner, Michael**
SENTINEL, THE

**Winston, Stan**
PUMPKINHEAD

**Winters, David**
LAST HORROR FILM, THE

**Wise, Robert**
AUDREY ROSE
CURSE OF THE CAT PEOPLE, THE
BODY SNATCHER, THE
HAUNTING, THE

**Wittman, Peter**
PLAY DEAD

**Wood, Edward**
NIGHT OF THE GHOULS

**Wood, James**
DR. JEKYLL'S DUNGEON OF DEATH

**Woods, Jack**
EQUINOX

**Worsley, Wallace**
HUNCHBACK OF NOTRE DAME, THE

**Wynorski, Jim**
CHOPPING MALL

**Yarbrough, Jean**
BRUTE MAN, THE
DEVIL BAT, THE
HILLBILLYS IN A HAUNTED HOUSE
KING OF THE ZOMBIES

**Younkins, Jerry**
DEMON LOVER, THE

**Yust, Larry**
HOMEBODIES

**Zacharias, Alfred**
DEMONOID

**Zarchi, Meir**
I SPIT ON YOUR GRAVE

**Zimmerman, Vernon**
FADE TO BLACK

**Zito, Joseph**
FRIDAY THE 13TH—THE FINAL
CHAPTER
PROWLER, THE

**Zulawski, Andrzej**
POSSESSION

# EDITORS

**Ackland, Noreen**
PEEPING TOM

**Akst, Alfred**
RAVEN, THE

**Alabiso, Eugenio**
SCREAMERS

**Albert, Ross**
POLTERGEIST III

**Albertson, Eric**
KILLER PARTY

**Aldridge, Richard**
WOLFMAN

**Allen, John David**
SLEEPAWAY CAMP 2: UNHAPPY
CAMPERS

**Allen, Stanford C.**
MORTUARY

**Ameripoor, Eskandar**
WIZARD OF GORE, THE

**Amin, Abbas**
SPECTRE OF EDGAR ALLAN POE, THE

**Amy, George**
DOCTOR X
MYSTERY OF THE WAX MUSEUM, THE

**Anderson, Leonard**
BRAIN THAT WOULDN'T DIE, THE

**Anderson, Marc**
BRAIN THAT WOULDN'T DIE, THE

**Anderson, William**
RAZORBACK

**Andrews, Christopher**
MS. 45

**Appleby, George**
INCUBUS, THE

**Asman, Bub**
DAY OF THE ANIMALS
MANITOU, THE

**Astori, Gabrio**
MONSTER DOG

**Austin, William**
MANIAC

**Avrahamian, Zion**
SAVAGE WEEKEND

**Baird, Stuart**
OMEN, THE

**Balsam, Alan**
DEAD AND BURIED

**Barknel, Philip**
VIRGIN WITCH, THE

**Barnard, Michael**
PREY, THE

**Barnes, Chris**
LEGEND OF THE SEVEN GOLDEN
VAMPIRES, THE
HORROR OF FRANKENSTEIN, THE
LAST HORROR FILM, THE

**Barr, John**
SCALPS

**Bateman, Michael John**
NOMADS

**Bava, Lamberto**
BLADE IN THE DARK, A

**Bechard, Gorman**
PSYCHOS IN LOVE

**Benedict, Max**
OBLONG BOX, THE
MURDERS IN THE RUE MORGUE

**Berger, Peter E.**
PACK, THE

**Bergman, Robert**
GRAVEYARD SHIFT

**Berndt, George**
HEARSE, THE

**Best, Richard**
PSYCHOMANIA

**Beyda, Kent**
FRIGHT NIGHT
SATURDAY THE 14TH

**Beyer, Ed**
TOO SCARED TO SCREAM

**Bieber, Francis**
GHOST SHIP

**Biggerstaff, Caroline**
SEVENTH SIGN, THE

**Biggs, Douglas**
REVOLT OF THE ZOMBIES

**Bina, Soly**
WORM EATERS, THE

**Blangsted, Folmar**
OTHER, THE

**Blewitt, David**
GHOSTBUSTERS
PSYCHO III

**Block, Larry**
ALLIGATOR

**Bloom, John**
DRACULA
ORCA
MAGIC

**Bock, Richard C.**
MAUSOLEUM

**Bogdanovich, Peter**
TARGETS

**Bonan, Denis**
DAUGHTERS OF DARKNESS

**Bonnot, Francoise**
TENANT, THE

**Borden, Marshall M.**
WOLFEN

**Bornstein, Charles**
FOG, THE
RETURN OF THE LIVING DEAD PART II

**Borofsky, Paul**
RETURN OF THE VAMPIRE, THE

**Borroni, Claudio**
NIGHT OF THE ZOMBIES

**Boutress, Thomas**
LEGEND OF BOGGY CREEK, THE
TOWN THAT DREADED SUNDOWN, THE

**Bowers, George**
STEPFATHER, THE

**Boyd-Perkins, Eric**
WICKER MAN, THE

**Boyer, Lyle**
BEDLAM
ISLE OF THE DEAD

**Bozza, Pietro**
DEMONS 2: THE NIGHTMARE RETURNS
DEMONS

**Bracken, Richard**
DEADLY BLESSING
HILLS HAVE EYES II, THE
SWAMP THING

**Bradsell, Michael**
GOTHIC

**Brady, Bob**
NIGHTMARE ON ELM STREET PART 2: FREDDY'S REVENGE, A

**Bram, Martin**
WOLFEN

**Braun, Jonathan**
UNSEEN, THE

**Brett, Alan**
SCHIZO

**Bronson, Gerald**
CARNAGE

**Brown, Geoff R.**
VAMPYRES, DAUGHTERS OF DRACULA

**Brown, Michael**
PSYCHIC KILLER
NIGHTMARES

**Brown, O. Nicholas**
OTHER, THE

**Brown, Robert**
BEAST WITHIN, THE
AMITYVILLE HORROR, THE
DAMIEN—OMEN II
LOST BOYS, THE

**Brummer, Dick**
SCHIZOID

**Brunjes, Ralph**
FUNERAL HOME
SPASMS

**Bryant, Edwin**
THIRTEEN GHOSTS
STRAIT-JACKET

**Buba, Pasquale**
CREEPSHOW
DAY OF THE DEAD
MONKEY SHINES: AN EXPERIMENT IN FEAR

**Bullingham, Ernest**
DEVIL DOLL

**Burch, Curtis**
IT LIVES AGAIN
WACKO

**Burns-Errington, Malcolm**
HOWLING IV: THE ORIGINAL NIGHTMARE

**Burnstein, Charles**
HALLOWEEN

**Bushelman, John**
FRANKENSTEIN 1970
PICTURE MOMMY DEAD

**Bustos, Jorge**
WRESTLING WOMEN VS. THE AZTEC MUMMY, THE
CURSE OF THE AZTEC MUMMY, THE
ROBOT VS. THE AZTEC MUMMY, THE
NIGHT OF THE BLOODY APES

**Cahn, Philip**
BRUTE MAN, THE

**Cahoon, Richard**
BLACK ROOM, THE

**Calmes, Lynn Leneau**
NAIL GUN MASSACRE

**Cambas, Jacqueline**
CAT PEOPLE

**Campbell, Malcolm**
AMERICAN WEREWOLF IN LONDON, AN
TWILIGHT ZONE—THE MOVIE

**Campbell, Mike**
DEATH SHIP

**Caputo, Bernard**
DEADLY DREAMS

**Carpenter, Stephen**
POWER, THE

**Carras, Anthony**
HOUSE OF USHER
PIT AND THE PENDULUM, THE
TALES OF TERROR

**Carroll, Larry**
TEXAS CHAIN SAW MASSACRE, THE

**Carruth, Milton**
DRACULA
MUMMY, THE

**Chadwick, Warren**
SCARED TO DEATH

**Chance, John T.**
ASSAULT ON PRECINCT 13

**Chavez, Julio C.**
DEATH CURSE OF TARTU
STANLEY

**Cheesman, Ted**
SON OF KONG
KING KONG

**Chegwidden, Ann**
MASQUE OF THE RED DEATH, THE

**Cinquini, Renato**
NIGHTMARE CASTLE

**Clark, Travis**
UNINVITED, THE

**Clayton, Curtiss**
HALLOWEEN IV: THE RETURN OF MICHAEL MYERS

**Clifford, Graeme**
DON'T LOOK NOW

# EDITORS

**Coates, Anne V.**
LEGACY, THE

**Cole, Stan**
BLACK CHRISTMAS
PHOBIA

**Collins, Allan**
BROOD, THE

**Cones, Tristam**
ABOMINABLE DR. PHIBES, THE
DOCTOR PHIBES RISES AGAIN
WHO SLEW AUNTIE ROO?

**Connell, Thelma**
DR. TERROR'S HOUSE OF HORRORS

**Connock, Jim**
SLAUGHTER HIGH

**Conrad, Scott**
CAT'S EYE
WRAITH, THE

**Converse, Cleo**
LADY FRANKENSTEIN

**Cooke, Malcolm**
THEATRE OF BLOOD
KING KONG LIVES

**Coscarelli, Don**
PHANTASM

**Cotter, Ed**
FRANKENSTEIN GENERAL HOSPITAL

**Cox, Alfred**
DIE, MONSTER, DIE
CURSE OF THE WEREWOLF, THE
MUMMY, THE
TOMB OF LIGEIA, THE

**Craven, Wes**
HILLS HAVE EYES, THE
LAST HOUSE ON THE LEFT

**Cunningham, Susan E.**
FRIDAY THE 13TH PART II
STRANGER IS WATCHING, A

**Curi, A.J.**
TENTACLES

**Curi, Robert**
VISITOR, THE

**Currier, Richard**
KING OF THE ZOMBIES
UNEARTHLY, THE

**Curtis, Ray**
BLACK CAT, THE

**Curtiss, Edward**
FRANKENSTEIN MEETS THE WOLF
MAN

**Cutry, Claudio**
CURSE, THE
OUTING, THE

**D'Antonio, Joanne**
SATURDAY THE 14TH

**Dalrymple, Ian**
GHOUL, THE

**Dante, Joe**
HOWLING, THE
PIRANHA

**Darvas, Teddy**
TALES FROM THE CRYPT
MAN WHO HAUNTED HIMSELF, THE

**Daucus, Mindy**
MOUNTAINTOP MOTEL MASSACRE

**Davalos, Raul**
SHADOWS RUN BLACK

**David, Battle**
ELVIRA: MISTRESS OF THE DARK

**Davidow, Kenneth**
DAWN OF THE DEAD

**Davies, Jr., Freeman**
JAWS II

**Davies, Peter**
LAIR OF THE WHITE WORM, THE

**Davis, Kaye**
EVIL DEAD 2: DEAD BY DAWN

**Davis, T. Battle**
NINTH CONFIGURATION, THE

**Day, Jonathan**
SAVAGE WEEKEND

**De La Bouillerie, Hubert C.**
WITCHES OF EASTWICK, THE

**De Nieva, Petra**
HORROR OF THE ZOMBIES

**De Zarraga, Tony**
COUNT YORGA, VAMPIRE

**Dearberg, Robert**
HOUSE OF THE LONG SHADOWS
FRIGHTMARE

**DeJarnette, Bill**
CARNIVAL OF SOULS

**DiMarco, Tony**
DOCTOR DEATH: SEEKER OF SOULS
HELL NIGHT

**Dodd, Everett**
FRANKENSTEIN'S DAUGHTER

**Dodd, Patrick**
THEY CAME FROM WITHIN

**Dohler, Don**
FIEND

**Dolan, Dennis**
WOLFEN

**Dorfman, Ron**
DEAR, DEAD DELILAH

**Dubus, Marie-Sophie**
POSSESSION

**Duncan, Daniel**
WITCHBOARD

**Economou, Michael**
TOO SCARED TO SCREAM

**Eisen, Robert S.**
CASTLE OF EVIL
STRANGLER, THE

**Elderton, Jim**
TERROR

**Elias, Michael T.**
JAWS II

**Eliot, Michael**
DEADLY FRIEND

**Elliott, Peter**
SCREAM AND SCREAM AGAIN
TORTURE GARDEN

**Ellis, Michael**
BRIDE, THE
GODSEND, THE

**Ernst, Bob**
TERROR ON TOUR

**Estrin, Robert**
MIRRORS

**Fallick, Mort**
LOVE AT FIRST BITE

**Farr, Glenn**
SERPENT AND THE RAINBOW, THE

**Fayad, Elliot**
SPIDER BABY

**Fehr, Rudi**
HOUSE OF WAX

**Feitshans, Jr., Fred**
DUNWICH HORROR, THE
FROGS

**Fields, Verna**
JAWS

**Findlay, Roberta**
BLOOD SISTERS

**Fineman, Joseph**
DON'T ANSWER THE PHONE

**Finkle, Claudia**
HOWLING IV: THE ORIGINAL
NIGHTMARE

**Fitzgerald, Robert**
SCHIZOID

**Flaum, Erica**
FINAL TERROR, THE

**Folsey, Jr., George**
SCHLOCK

**Foot, Geoffrey**
LEGEND OF HELL HOUSE, THE
WATCHER IN THE WOODS, THE

**Forest, Frank**
FLESH EATERS, THE

**Forner, Nancy**
RETURN TO HORROR HIGH

**Foster, Jack**
NESTING, THE

**Francis-Bruce, Richard**
WITCHES OF EASTWICK, THE

**Fraticelli, Franco**
DEEP RED
BIRD WITH THE CRYSTAL PLUMAGE,
THE
CREEPERS
INFERNO

**Frazen, Stanley**
HYSTERICAL

**Freda, Bill**
FRIDAY THE 13TH

**Freeman, Jeff**
BAD DREAMS

**Freeman, Robert**
LOVE BUTCHER, THE

**Freeman-Fox, Lois**
TEEN WOLF

**Friedman, Louis**
IT LIVES AGAIN

**Fruet, Michael**
BLUE MONKEY

**Gallitti, Alberto**
MURDER CLINIC, THE

**Ganote, Gary**
SCREAMS OF A WINTER NIGHT

**Ganzino, Davide**
SHADOWS RUN BLACK

**Garrett, Otis**
VAMPIRE BAT, THE

**Garrett, W.O.**
OFFSPRING, THE

**Garson, Arline**
ALONE IN THE DARK
NIGHTMARE ON ELM STREET PART 2:
FREDDY'S REVENGE, A

**Gay, Norman**
EXORCIST, THE
SHOCK WAVES

**Gerstad, Henry**
BEN

**Gilbert, David**
NIGHTMARE WEEKEND

**Ginsberg, Arthur**
GIRLS NIGHT OUT

**Ginsberg, Moses**
WEREWOLF OF WASHINGTON

**Gittens, George**
MONSTER OF PIEDRAS BLANCAS,
THE

**Glastein, Bert**
CRAWLSPACE

**Glieberman, Sandy**
RATTLERS

**Gluck, Joseph**
DEMENTIA

**Goldblatt, Mark**
HUMANOIDS FROM THE DEEP
HOWLING, THE
HALLOWEEN II
PIRANHA

**Golden, Robert**
CORPSE VANISHES, THE
INVISIBLE GHOST, THE

**Goodkind, Saul**
SON OF DRACULA

**Goodman, Joel**
FRIDAY THE 13TH—THE FINAL
CHAPTER
PROWLER, THE

**Goodnoff, Irvin**
DADDY'S DEADLY DARLING

**Gordon, Barry Mark**
SOMETHING WICKED THIS WAY
COMES

**Gordon, Michael**
CURSE OF THE DEMON

**Gordon, Robert**
RETURN OF THE LIVING DEAD

**Gosnell, Raja**
TEEN WOLF TOO
MONSTER IN THE CLOSET

**Graver, Gary**
TRICK OR TREATS

**Green, Bruce**
APRIL FOOL'S DAY
FRIDAY THE 13TH PART VI: JASON
LIVES
FRIDAY THE 13TH, PART V—A NEW
BEGINNING

**Green, Wendy**
SLUMBER PARTY MASSACRE, THE

**Greenberg, Jerry**
DRESSED TO KILL
BODY DOUBLE

**Greenbury, Christopher**
HAUNTED HONEYMOON

**Gribble, Bernard**
MOTEL HELL
SENTINEL, THE

**Griffen, Gary**
BLOOD BEACH

**Grimaldi, Hugo**
BIG FOOT

**Gross, Daniel**
SLAUGHTERHOUSE ROCK

**Gross, Frank**
ABBOTT AND COSTELLO MEET
FRANKENSTEIN

**Grossman, Marc**
ONCE BITTEN
VAMP

**Hafenrichter, Oswald**
CREEPING FLESH, THE
VAULT OF HORROR, THE

**Haines, Richard W.**
CLASS OF NUKE 'EM HIGH
SPLATTER UNIVERSITY
TOXIC AVENGER, THE

**Hall, Kiplan**
ESCAPES

**Haller, Hermann**
BLOOD DEMON

**Hambling, Gerry**
ANGEL HEART

**Hamilton, William**
HUNCHBACK OF NOTRE DAME, THE

**Hartzell, Duane**
JENNIFER

**Hasse, Charles**
DEAD OF NIGHT

**Hay, Rod**
INN OF THE DAMNED

**Henderson, Anne**
TERROR TRAIN

**Henenlotter, Frank**
BASKET CASE
BRAIN DAMAGE

**Hernandez, Robert**
JAWS II

**Hirsch, Paul**
FURY, THE
CREEPSHOW
CARRIE
PHANTOM OF THE PARADISE
SISTERS
BLOW OUT

**Hirsch, Tina**
GREMLINS
TWILIGHT ZONE—THE MOVIE

**Hising-lung, Chiang**
LEGEND OF THE SEVEN GOLDEN
VAMPIRES, THE

**Hively, George**
FRIDAY THE 13TH PART III

**Hobson, Colin**
ASPHYX, THE

**Hoenig, Dov**
KEEP, THE

**Hoffman, Bud**
BIG FOOT

**Hofstra, Jack**
FUNHOUSE, THE

**Holmes, Christopher**
DUNWICH HORROR, THE

**Honess, Peter**
BELIEVERS, THE
IT'S ALIVE

**Hope, Kathryn Ruth**
STUDENT BODIES

**Horger, Jack**
DR. BLACK AND MR. HYDE

**Horvitch, Andy**
RAWHEAD REX
PRISON

**Howard, John C.**
NIGHTWING
YOUNG FRANKENSTEIN

**Ireland, John**
FROM BEYOND THE GRAVE

**Isaacs, Bud S.**
INVISIBLE STRANGLER, THE

**Jackson, Gerald**
GHASTLY ONES, THE

**Jackson, Robert**
FRIGHTMARE

**Jacobs, Allan**
BLACULA
RACE WITH THE DEVIL
LOVE AT FIRST BITE

# EDITORS

**Jacobson, Sherrie Sanet**
JAWS II

**Jaffe, Gib**
PULSE

**Jaffe, Jane Schwartz**
TRICK OR TREAT

**Jakubowicz, Alain**
TEXAS CHAINSAW MASSACRE PART 2, THE

**Jenkins, Eric**
PANDEMONIUM

**Jimeno, Antonio**
WEREWOLF VS. THE VAMPIRE WOMAN, THE

**Johnson, George**
KEEPER, THE

**Johnson, Jed**
ANDY WARHOL'S FRANKENSTEIN
ANDY WARHOL'S DRACULA

**Johnson, Ron**
GRAVE OF THE VAMPIRE

**Joyce, John**
EQUINOX

**Judson, Stephen**
VELVET VAMPIRE, THE

**Jympson, John**
LITTLE SHOP OF HORRORS

**Kahn, Michael**
DEVIL'S RAIN, THE
POLTERGEIST
TWILIGHT ZONE—THE MOVIE

**Kahn, Sheldon**
GHOSTBUSTERS

**Kalish, Ron**
SLEEPAWAY CAMP

**Kanefsky, Victor**
BLOODSUCKING FREAKS
NIGHT OF THE ZOMBIES
GANJA AND HESS

**Kantor**
KINGDOM OF THE SPIDERS

**Karen, Debra**
HAPPY BIRTHDAY TO ME

**Katz, Sidney**
PREMONITION, THE

**Katzman, Alfred**
NIGHTMARE IN BLOOD

**Keller, Harry**
TRANSYLVANIA 6-5000

**Kent, Ted**
CREATURE FROM THE BLACK LAGOON
BRIDE OF FRANKENSTEIN, THE
WOLF MAN, THE
SON OF FRANKENSTEIN

**Keramidas, Harry**
CHILDREN OF THE CORN
DRACULA'S DOG
MASSACRE AT CENTRAL HIGH

**Kern, David**
BLACK ROOM, THE
MANIAC COP
IT'S ALIVE III: ISLAND OF THE ALIVE

**Kirshner, Jack**
EVIL, THE

**Knue, Michael N.**
HOUSE
NIGHTMARE ON ELM STREET 4: THE DREAM MASTER, A

**Kojayan, Shirah**
BOGGY CREEK II

**Kolster, Clarence**
FRANKENSTEIN

**Kress, Carl**
AUDREY ROSE

**Kress, Harold F.**
DR. JEKYLL AND MR. HYDE

**Kunin, Howard**
FADE TO BLACK

**Kurson, Jane**
DON'T GO IN THE HOUSE
BEETLEJUICE

**Kwei, James Y.**
BRAIN DAMAGE

**Kwit, Leonard**
NIGHTMARE IN WAX

**LaFleur, Jean**
RABID
MY BLOODY VALENTINE

**Landeras, Federico**
MARY, MARY, BLOODY MARY

**Lang-Willar, Suzanne**
POSSESSION

**Langlois, Yves**
LITTLE GIRL WHO LIVES DOWN THE LANE, THE

**Lanning, Howard**
BLOOD BEAST TERROR, THE
CONQUEROR WORM, THE

**LaVine, Ronald**
INITIATION, THE

**Lawrence, Robert**
WARNING SIGN

**Lebenzon, Chris**
WOLFEN

**Lebowitz, Armand**
Q
STUFF, THE

**Ledersen, Lilla**
CHANGELING, THE

**Lee-Thompson, Peter**
NINTH CONFIGURATION, THE

**Leeds, Linda**
YOU BETTER WATCH OUT

**Leibowitz, Armond**
RETURN TO SALEM'S LOT, A

**Leighton, Robert**
BLOOD TIDE

**Lemon, Max**
NEXT OF KIN

**Lenertz, James**
REVENGE

**Lenny, Bill**
HORROR OF DRACULA, THE

**Leondopoulos, Jordan**
EXORCIST, THE

**Lewis, Ben**
MARK OF THE VAMPIRE

**Li-Ho, Jose**
ROBOT VS. THE AZTEC MUMMY, THE

**Livingston, Roy**
BILLY THE KID VS. DRACULA
HOUSE ON HAUNTED HILL
HILLBILLYS IN A HAUNTED HOUSE
JESSE JAMES MEETS FRANKENSTEIN'S DAUGHTER

**Livitt, Bert**
BEAST WITHIN, THE

**Lockert, John**
SEVENTH VICTIM, THE

**Loewenthal, Daniel**
FRIDAY THE 13TH—THE FINAL CHAPTER
STEPHEN KING'S SILVER BULLET

**Lombardo, Elizabeth**
LAST RITES

**London, Andrew**
PSYCHO II

**Lopez, Soledad**
HATCHET FOR A HONEYMOON

**Lord, Claude**
VISITING HOURS

**Lottman, Evan**
EXORCIST, THE
MAXIMUM OVERDRIVE

**Lovejoy, Ray**
SHINING, THE

**Low, Warren**
WILLARD

**Lowenthal, Dan**
MADMAN

**Luciano, Michael**
WHATEVER HAPPENED TO BABY JANE?
HUSH . . . HUSH, SWEET CHARLOTTE

**Lusk, Skip**
TOOLBOX MURDERS, THE

**Lynch, David**
ERASERHEAD

**Lyon, Francis D.**
BRIDE OF THE GORILLA

**Lyon, William**
MAN THEY COULD NOT HANG, THE

**McCarthy, Matt**
HOUSE OF WHIPCORD

**McCollough, Paul**
MIDNIGHT

**McCrann, Chuck**
BLOODEATERS

**McCroskey, Michael**
CAR, THE

**McGee, Bill**
RUBY

**McGee, Gregg**
WITCHFIRE

**McGuire, George**
LOST WORLD, THE
SCARED TO DEATH

**McIntyre, Alastair**
REPULSION

**Mack, Stephen**
MUTILATOR, THE

**McKinney, Austin**
THRILL KILLERS, THE

**MacLaverty, Michael**
CURTAINS

**MacLernon, Harold**
WHITE ZOMBIE

**McQuinn-Mason, Edward**
ROAD GAMES

**Magar, Guy**
RETRIBUTION

**Magder, Murray**
TERMINAL CHOICE

**Maguire, Al**
TERROR HOUSE

**Mainka-Jellinghaus, Beate**
NOSFERATU, THE VAMPIRE

**Maitland, Ian**
NOCTURNA

**Mann, Steve**
LADY IN WHITE

**Manton, Marcus**
PUMPKINHEAD
BERSERKER

**Marden, Richard**
HELLRAISER

**Marinelli, Lorenzo**
MANIAC

**Marks, Richard**
HAND, THE

**Mayes, Craig**
SCREAMS OF A WINTER NIGHT

**Mayhew, Peter**
CORRIDORS OF BLOOD
HAUNTED STRANGLER, THE

**Medico, Ronald**
ALLIGATOR

**Megginson, Robert T.**
NIGHTMARE

**Melnick, Mark**
UNHOLY, THE

**Meshelski, Thomas**
BLOOD DINER

**Metzger, Radley**
FLESH EATERS, THE

**Meyer, Richard C.**
RETURN OF THE FLY

**Michalakias, John Elias**
I WAS A TEENAGE ZOMBIE

**Michell, Ornella**
GRIM REAPER, THE

**Mikels, Ted V.**
CORPSE GRINDERS, THE

**Mills, Ann E.**
BLOODY BIRTHDAY

**Mills, Reginald**
CIRCUS OF HORRORS

**Mirkovich, Steve**
PRINCE OF DARKNESS

**Mitchell, James**
DAY OF THE ANIMALS
MONSTER SQUAD, THE

**Molin, Bud**
MAN WITH TWO BRAINS, THE

**Moore, Millie**
HALLOWEEN III: SEASON OF THE WITCH

**Napier-Bell, Nicholas**
BEAST IN THE CELLAR, THE

**Natot, Gilbert**
HORROR CHAMBER OF DR. FAUSTUS, THE

**Needs, James**
CURSE OF FRANKENSTEIN, THE
CAPTAIN KRONOS: VAMPIRE HUNTER
EVIL OF FRANKENSTEIN, THE
DR. JEKYLL AND SISTER HYDE
DIE! DIE! MY DARLING
HORROR OF DRACULA, THE
GORGON, THE
MUMMY, THE
SCARS OF DRACULA, THE
VAMPIRE LOVERS, THE

**Neilan, Jr., Marshall**
LITTLE SHOP OF HORRORS

**Nelson, Argyle**
SOMETHING WICKED THIS WAY COMES

**Nelson, Charles**
BEFORE I HANG

**Nervig, Sandy**
DEMONOID

**Nicholson, Marty**
HOUSE II: THE SECOND STORY

**Nicolaou, Ted**
GHOULIES
TOURIST TRAP, THE

**Nielson, Steven**
MICROWAVE MASSACRE

**Noble, Thom**
POLTERGEIST II

**Norris, George T.**
HE KNOWS YOU'RE ALONE

**O'Blath, Carol**
IT LIVES AGAIN

**O'Brien, Stuart**
DEMENTIA 13
TERROR, THE

**O'Connell, Maureen**
FRIDAY THE 13TH PART VII—THE NEW BLOOD

**O'Connor, John**
FINAL EXAM

**O'Hara, Corky**
YOU BETTER WATCH OUT

**O'Steen, Sam**
AMITYVILLE II: THE POSSESSION
ROSEMARY'S BABY

**Obrow, Jeffrey**
DORM THAT DRIPPED BLOOD, THE
POWER, THE

**Ochoa, Antonio Jose**
MONSTER DOG

**Ogilvie, Jack**
ZOMBIES OF MORA TAU

**Palewski, Stephanie**
MONSTER IN THE CLOSET

**Palmquist, Dan**
CARNIVAL OF SOULS

**Pankow, Bill**
BODY DOUBLE

**Parasheles, Peter**
HOMEBODIES
WEREWOLVES ON WHEELS

**Parsons, Derek**
TELL-TALE HEART, THE

**Patterson, Sally**
KEEPER, THE

**Paul, Edna Ruth**
FEAR NO EVIL
EVIL DEAD, THE

**Percy, Lee**
DOLLS
FROM BEYOND
RE-ANIMATOR
TROLL

**Peters, Barry**
HOUSE WHERE EVIL DWELLS, THE

**Peterson, Roy E.**
CHILD'S PLAY

**Pierson, Carl**
BLUEBEARD
BLACK DRAGONS
APE MAN, THE
BOWERY AT MIDNIGHT
GHOSTS ON THE LOOSE

**Pivar, Maurice**
DRACULA
PHANTOM OF THE OPERA, THE
FRANKENSTEIN

**Polivka, Steven**
TEEN WOLF TOO

**Pollard, Samuel**
NIGHT OF THE ZOMBIES

**Polyniak, Alan J.**
TOXIC AVENGER, THE

# EDITORS

Pomeroy, John
HORROR HOTEL

Potter, Steve
JAWS II

Poulton, Raymond
BERSERK

Power, Pamela
HUNGER, THE

Priego, Alfredo Rosas
LIVING HEAD, THE

Priestley, Tom
EXORCIST II: THE HERETIC

Queen-Mason, Edward
PATRICK

Rabinowitz, Al
SUPERSTITION

Radecki, R.A.
POINT OF TERROR

Ravok, Brian
PROM NIGHT

Rawlings, Terence
AWAKENING, THE
SENTINEL, THE

Reali, Carlo
BARON BLOOD

Reeve, Spencer
LUST FOR A VAMPIRE
TWINS OF EVIL

Reid, Phil
THIRST

Richards, E.G.
HUMAN MONSTER, THE

Richardson, Henry
BEYOND THE FOG
CRAZE
GHOUL, THE

Richardson, Sallye
TEXAS CHAIN SAW MASSACRE, THE

Roberts, Randy
JAWS 3-D

Robinson, Byron
MONSTER WALKS, THE

Robson, Mark
CAT PEOPLE
I WALKED WITH A ZOMBIE
LEOPARD MAN, THE

Rocklin, Gary
WRAITH, THE

Rojo, J. Antonio
CAULDRON OF BLOOD

Rolf, Tom
BLACK SUNDAY
GHOST STORY
PROPHECY

Romero, George A.
DAWN OF THE DEAD
CREEPSHOW
CRAZIES, THE
MARTIN
NIGHT OF THE LIVING DEAD

HUNGRY WIVES

Romolo, Frank
BLOOD FEAST

Rondinella, Thomas R.
GIRLS SCHOOL SCREAMERS

Roose, Ronald
MY DEMON LOVER

Rosenstock, Harvey
TEEN WOLF TOO
DEAD HEAT

Rosenthal, Leslie
CHOPPING MALL

Ross, Sharyn L.
SLEEPAWAY CAMP

Rothman, Marion
CHRISTINE
ISLAND OF DR. MOREAU, THE
ORCA
SISTER SISTER

Rotundo, Nick
HUMONGOUS
HELLO MARY LOU, PROM NIGHT II

Rubell, Paul
FINAL TERROR, THE

Ryan, Joe
LET'S SCARE JESSICA TO DEATH

Sabin, Tom
ANGUISH

Sadoff, Martin Jay
GRADUATION DAY
FRIDAY THE 13TH PART VII—THE NEW
BLOOD

Salier, Edward
ALICE, SWEET ALICE
LAST HORROR FILM, THE
SILENT SCREAM
SLAYER, THE

Sanders, Ronald
DEAD RINGERS
DEAD ZONE, THE
FLY, THE
SCANNERS
VIDEODROME

Scellars, Angela
CREATURE FROM THE HAUNTED SEA

Schmidt, Arthur
JAWS II

Schoengarth, Russell
APE, THE
ABBOTT AND COSTELLO MEET DR.
JEKYLL AND MR. HYDE
PHANTOM OF THE OPERA

Schoolnik, Skip
DR. HECKYL AND MR. HYPE
HALLOWEEN II

Sear, Walter
BLOOD SISTERS

Secrist, Kim
TEEN WOLF TOO

Selakovich, Dan
OPEN HOUSE

Selfe, Ray
DON'T OPEN TILL CHRISTMAS

Serandrei, Mario
BLACK SABBATH

Shah, Pradip Roy
IN THE SHADOW OF KILIMANJARO

Shaine, Rick
EYES OF A STRANGER
NIGHTMARE ON ELM STREET, A

Shapiro, Melvin
ARNOLD

Shefland, Alan
RETRIBUTION

Shoemaker, Tim
DEATHROW GAMESHOW

Sholder, John
BURNING, THE

Siiter, Tom
DRACULA'S WIDOW

Silliman, Drake
SWEET SIXTEEN

Silvi, Franca
ANDY WARHOL'S FRANKENSTEIN
ANDY WARHOL'S DRACULA

Silvi, Robert
OF UNKNOWN ORIGIN
PIRANHA II: THE SPAWNING
NINTH CONFIGURATION, THE

Simpson, Tom
MANIAC

Sinclair, Ronald
RAVEN, THE
PREMATURE BURIAL, THE

Sinise, Robert
BLOOD FEAST
COLOR ME BLOOD RED
TWO THOUSAND MANIACS

Smedley-Aston, Brian
SQUIRM

Smith, Bud
EXORCIST, THE

Smith, Clive
MADHOUSE

Smith, Frederick Y.
DEVIL DOLL, THE

Smith, Howard
NEAR DARK
TWILIGHT ZONE—THE MOVIE

Smith, John Victor
AMERICAN GOTHIC

Smith, Lee
HOWLING III, THE

Smith, Norman
GRAVEYARD SHIFT

Soloman, Murray
LET'S SCARE JESSICA TO DEATH

Spence, Michael
BOOGENS, THE
ONE DARK NIGHT
SILENT NIGHT, DEADLY NIGHT

**Sperling, David**
BLOODEATERS

**Spolan, Michael**
CREEPSHOW

**Stephens, Rod**
NIGHTMARES

**Stokes, Terry**
NIGHTMARE ON ELM STREET 3:
DREAM WARRIORS, A

**Strachan, Alan**
FINAL CONFLICT, THE
SENDER, THE

**Sullivan, Frank**
UNHOLY THREE, THE

**Suran, Mark**
BLOOD AND BLACK LACE

**Szarka, William**
DEADTIME STORIES

**Tannen, Terrell**
BOOGEYMAN II
BOOGEY MAN, THE

**Tanner, Peter**
BEAST MUST DIE, THE
ASYLUM
AND NOW THE SCREAMING STARTS
HOUSE THAT DRIPPED BLOOD, THE
MONSTER CLUB, THE

**Teschner, Peter**
GHOST TOWN
DREAMANIAC
MONSTER DOG
PHANTASM II

**Tetoni, Charles**
ONE DARK NIGHT

**Thouin, Lise**
VISITING HOURS

**Todd, Holbrook N.**
DAUGHTER OF DR. JEKYLL
DEVIL BAT, THE
DEAD MEN WALK
MAD MONSTER, THE

**Tomasini, George**
BIRDS, THE
PSYCHO

**Tomassi, Vincenzo**
CHOSEN, THE
HOUSE BY THE CEMETERY, THE
MANHATTAN BABY
TEMPTER, THE
ZOMBIE

**Toomayan, Alan**
EATING RAOUL

**Tordjmann, Fabian**
SCREAM, BLACULA, SCREAM

**Travis, Nell**
CUJO
JAWS II

**Trejo, Paul**
HOUSE ON SORORITY ROW, THE

**Trumper, John**
TO THE DEVIL A DAUGHTER

**Tunney-Smith, G.**
PLUMBER, THE

**Uribe, Sergio**
SLAUGHTERHOUSE

**Urioste, Frank J.**
AMITYVILLE 3-D
ENTITY, THE
HITCHER, THE

**Vansier, Gerald**
MY BLOODY VALENTINE

**Vasseur, Jean-Marc**
HOUSE ON SORORITY ROW, THE

**Verkler, Dennis**
BURNT OFFERINGS

**Verschueren, Gust**
DAUGHTERS OF DARKNESS

**Vince, Barrie**
SHOUT, THE

**Vitale, Sam**
WHEN A STRANGER CALLS

**Von Oellfen, Petra**
STRANGE BEHAVIOR

**Wallace, Tommy Lee**
FOG, THE
HALLOWEEN

**Waller, Stephen J.**
WITCHBOARD

**Wallis, Kit**
GATE, THE
MY BLOODY VALENTINE

**Walowitz, Marvin**
BROTHERHOOD OF SATAN, THE

**Walter, Ernest**
HAUNTING, THE

**Warschilka, Edward**
CHILD'S PLAY

**Washonig, Hannah**
FINAL TERROR, THE

**Watson, Earl**
WACKO

**Weatherly, Peter**
CREEPSHOW 2

**Weaver, Robert A.**
NIGHT OF BLOODY HORROR

**Weber, Billy**
JEKYLL AND HYDE . . . TOGETHER
AGAIN

**Webster, Ferris**
PICTURE OF DORIAN GRAY, THE

**Weintraub, Joseph**
SCALPEL

**Weiss, Chuck**
NIGHTMARE ON ELM STREET 3:
DREAM WARRIORS, A
NIGHTMARE ON ELM STREET 4: THE
DREAM MASTER, A

**Wentworth, Nicholas**
DORIAN GRAY

**Werner, Dennis**
STREET TRASH

**Wessling, Nikki**
CHILDREN, THE

**Westover, Rick**
BEYOND EVIL

**Westvic, Dane**
ESCAPES

**Wheeler, Leonard**
CRIME OF DR. CRESPI, THE

**White, Merrill G.**
FLY, THE

**Whittredge, J.R.**
CURSE OF THE CAT PEOPLE, THE
BODY SNATCHER, THE

**Wilder, King**
GHOST TOWN

**Williams, Robert**
ROCK 'N' ROLL NIGHTMARE

**Wilson, Gerard**
HOUSE ON SKULL MOUNTAIN, THE

**Winters, Ralph E.**
ORCA
KING KONG

**Wise, Robert**
HUNCHBACK OF NOTRE DAME, THE

**Wishengra, Jeff**
SORORITY HOUSE MASSACRE

**Wisman, Ron**
DEADLY EYES
PYX, THE
HAUNTING OF JULIA, THE

**Wood, James**
DR. JEKYLL'S DUNGEON OF DEATH

**Woodcock, John**
NUTTY PROFESSOR, THE

**Wrangell, Basil**
FREAKS

**Wyman, Robert**
ROSEMARY'S BABY

**York, Derek**
SEANCE ON A WET AFTERNOON

**Youngman, Gary**
CURSE OF THE LIVING CORPSE, THE
HORROR OF PARTY BEACH, THE

**Zaillian, Steve**
KINGDOM OF THE SPIDERS

**Zarchi, Meir**
I SPIT ON YOUR GRAVE

**Zetlin, Barry**
CELLAR DWELLER
GHOULIES II
FRIDAY THE 13TH PART VII—THE NEW
BLOOD

## MUSIC COMPOSERS

**45 Grave**
RETURN OF THE LIVING DEAD

**Abril, A. Garcia**
WEREWOLF VS. THE VAMPIRE WOMAN, THE
HORROR OF THE ZOMBIES

**AC/DC**
MAXIMUM OVERDRIVE

**Achley, James**
BLACK ROOM, THE

**Alcivar, Robert**
HYSTERICAL

**Alessandroni, Alessandro**
LADY FRANKENSTEIN

**Alexander, Van**
STRAIT-JACKET

**Allen, Allen D.**
SPECTRE OF EDGAR ALLAN POE, THE

**Allen, Marty**
DR. JEKYLL'S DUNGEON OF DEATH

**Allerd, Byron**
DON'T ANSWER THE PHONE

**Antheil, George**
DEMENTIA

**Arevalo, Tito**
MAD DOCTOR OF BLOOD ISLAND, THE

**Argento, Dario**
DAWN OF THE DEAD

**Armstrong, Michael**
HOUSE OF THE LONG SHADOWS
SILENT NIGHT, DEADLY NIGHT PART II

**Auric, Georges**
DEAD OF NIGHT

**Badalamenti, Angelo**
NIGHTMARE ON ELM STREET 3: DREAM WARRIORS, A

**Bahler, Tom**
MARY, MARY, BLOODY MARY

**Baker, Abe**
BRAIN THAT WOULDN'T DIE, THE

**Band, Richard**
DR. HECKYL AND MR. HYPE
HOUSE ON SORORITY ROW, THE
GHOULIES
FROM BEYOND
RE-ANIMATOR
TROLL
PRISON

**Banks, Anthony**
SHOUT, THE

**Banks, Don**
DIE, MONSTER, DIE
EVIL OF FRANKENSTEIN, THE
TORTURE GARDEN

**Barry, John**
SEANCE ON A WET AFTERNOON
KING KONG

**Bartok, Bela**
SHINING, THE

**Baxter, Les**
BLACK SABBATH
BEAST WITHIN, THE
BARON BLOOD
DUNWICH HORROR, THE
HOUSE OF USHER
FROGS
RAVEN, THE
PIT AND THE PENDULUM, THE
TALES OF TERROR

**Beal, John**
FUNHOUSE, THE
KILLER PARTY

**Bechard, Gorman**
PSYCHOS IN LOVE

**Bell, Wayne**
TEXAS CHAIN SAW MASSACRE, THE

**Belling, Andrew**
DRACULA'S DOG

**Bellon, Roger**
UNHOLY, THE

**Bennett, Brian**
TERMINAL CHOICE

**Berman, Sandy**
SCREAMERS

**Bernard, James**
HORROR OF FRANKENSTEIN, THE
HORROR OF DRACULA, THE
GORGON, THE
SCARS OF DRACULA, THE
TORTURE GARDEN

**Bernstein, Charles**
APRIL FOOL'S DAY
DADDY'S DEADLY DARLING
CUJO
ENTITY, THE
DEADLY FRIEND
NIGHTMARE ON ELM STREET, A
LOVE AT FIRST BITE

**Bernstein, Elmer**
GHOSTBUSTERS
AMERICAN WEREWOLF IN LONDON, AN

**Bilous, Edward**
SLEEPAWAY CAMP

**Biohazard**
CLASS OF NUKE 'EM HIGH

**Black, Gabriel**
INITIATION, THE

**Black, Stanley**
MANIAC

**Blake, Howard**
AMITYVILLE 3-D

**Boekelheide, Todd**
DEADLY DREAMS

**Bolling, Claude**
AWAKENING, THE

**Borch, Gaston**
WHITE ZOMBIE

**Borne, Hal**
HILLBILLYS IN A HAUNTED HOUSE

**Boswell, Simon**
DEMONS 2: THE NIGHTMARE RETURNS

**Botkin, Perry**
SILENT NIGHT, DEADLY NIGHT

**Bowie, David**
CAT PEOPLE

**Brockman, David**
FRANKENSTEIN

**Brooks Group, The**
CARNIVAL OF BLOOD

**Broughton, Bruce**
MONSTER SQUAD, THE

**Bucci, Marc**
HUMAN EXPERIMENTS

**Burke, Chris**
SPLATTER UNIVERSITY

**Burnette, Dorsey**
KINGDOM OF THE SPIDERS

**Burwell, Carter**
PSYCHO III

**Buttolph, David**
HOUSE OF WAX

**Cabiati, Henry**
HOUSE OF EVIL

**Cacavas, John**
HORROR EXPRESS
MORTUARY

**Cam**
PIECES

**Campbell, James**
ELVIRA: MISTRESS OF THE DARK
DRACULA'S WIDOW

**Caper, John**
EQUINOX
POINT OF TERROR

**Capobianco, Carmine**
PSYCHOS IN LOVE

**Carlos, Wendy**
SHINING, THE

**Carpenter, John**
ASSAULT ON PRECINCT 13
CHRISTINE
FOG, THE
HALLOWEEN III: SEASON OF THE WITCH
HALLOWEEN
PRINCE OF DARKNESS

**Carras, Nicholas**
FRANKENSTEIN'S DAUGHTER

**Carrion, Gustavo Cesar**
LIVING HEAD, THE

**Casale, Gerald V.**
SLAUGHTERHOUSE ROCK

**Chapin, Steve**
LAST HOUSE ON THE LEFT

**Chase, Tom**
SCARED TO DEATH

**Chattaway, Jay**
MANIAC
STEPHEN KING'S SILVER BULLET
MANIAC COP

**Chudnow, David**
MAD MONSTER, THE

**Cipriani, S.W.**
TENTACLES

**Cirino, Chuck**
CHOPPING MALL

**Clark, James**
VAMPYRES, DAUGHTERS OF
DRACULA

**Clifford, Matt**
RETURN OF THE LIVING DEAD

**Cobert, Robert**
BURNT OFFERINGS
SCALPEL

**Cockwell, John Mills**
HUMONGOUS

**Coffey, Dennis**
MARDI GRAS MASSACRE

**Cohen, Harvey R.**
GHOST TOWN

**Colcord, Ray**
DEVONSVILLE TERROR, THE

**Coleman, Patrick**
BLUE MONKEY

**Conde, Antonio Diaz**
WRESTLING WOMEN VS. THE AZTEC
MUMMY, THE
CURSE OF THE AZTEC MUMMY, THE
ROBOT VS. THE AZTEC MUMMY, THE
NIGHT OF THE BLOODY APES

**Conti, Bill**
NOMADS

**Cooper, Alice**
MONSTER DOG

**Copriani, Stelvio**
TWITCH OF THE DEATH NERVE

**Cramps, The**
RETURN OF THE LIVING DEAD

**Crane, Lor**
HAUNTED

**Crisman, H.**
CARNIVAL OF BLOOD

**Crombie, Tony**
TELL-TALE HEART, THE

**Cugat, Xavier**
WHITE ZOMBIE

**Damned, The**
RETURN OF THE LIVING DEAD

**Dante, Carlo**
CELLAR DWELLER

**Davies, Iva**
RAZORBACK

**De Angelis, Guido**
BLADE IN THE DARK, A

**De Angelis, Maurizio**
BLADE IN THE DARK, A

**De Lory, Al**
DEVIL'S RAIN, THE

**de los Rios, Waldo**
MURDERS IN THE RUE MORGUE

**De Masi, Francesco**
MURDER CLINIC, THE

**De Roubaix, Francois**
DAUGHTERS OF DARKNESS

**De Vol, Frank**
HUSH . . . HUSH, SWEET CHARLOTTE

**De Vorzon, Barry**
NINTH CONFIGURATION, THE

**Deaton, George**
TOOLBOX MURDERS, THE

**Delia, Joseph**
DRILLER KILLER
MS. 45

**DeLuca, Peppino**
DORIAN GRAY

**Derbyshire, Delia**
LEGEND OF HELL HOUSE, THE

**Dett, Nathaniel**
WHITE ZOMBIE

**DeVol, Frank**
WHATEVER HAPPENED TO BABY
JANE?

**DeVorzon, Barry**
JEKYLL AND HYDE . . . TOGETHER
AGAIN

**Dicks, Ted**
VIRGIN WITCH, THE

**Dilulio, Ron**
MOUNTAINTOP MOTEL MASSACRE

**Dolan, Des**
DON'T OPEN TILL CHRISTMAS

**Dolby, Thomas**
GOTHIC

**Dollarhide, Roger**
VELVET VAMPIRE, THE

**Donaggio, Pino**
DRESSED TO KILL
CRAWLSPACE
CARRIE
DON'T LOOK NOW
HOWLING, THE
PIRANHA
TOURIST TRAP, THE
BODY DOUBLE
BLOW OUT

**Drasnin, Robert**
PICTURE MOMMY DEAD

**Dress, Michael**
HOUSE THAT DRIPPED BLOOD, THE

**Du Prez, John**
ONCE BITTEN

**Duning, George**
ARNOLD

**Dunlap, Paul**
CASTLE OF EVIL

**Easdale, Brian**
PEEPING TOM

**Einhorn, Richard**
EYES OF A STRANGER
DON'T GO IN THE HOUSE
PROWLER, THE
SHOCK WAVES
SISTER SISTER

**Elfman, Danny**
BEETLEJUICE

**Elias, Jonathan**
CHILDREN OF THE CORN
VAMP

**Elkind, Rachel**
SHINING, THE

**Ellis, Don**
RUBY

**Ellis, Ray**
CAULDRON OF BLOOD

**Emerson, Keith**
INFERNO

**Eno, Brian**
LAND OF THE MINOTAUR

**Farrar, Robert**
KEEP MY GRAVE OPEN

**Ferguson, Jay**
PULSE
BAD DREAMS

**Ferris, Paul**
BLOOD BEAST TERROR, THE
CREEPING FLESH, THE
CONQUEROR WORM, THE

**Fidenco, Nico**
DR. BUTCHER, M.D.

**Fiedel, Brad**
FRIGHT NIGHT
JUST BEFORE DAWN
SERPENT AND THE RAINBOW, THE

**Fielding, Jerry**
FUNERAL HOME

**Flesheaters, The**
RETURN OF THE LIVING DEAD

**Floyd, David**
WOLFMAN

**Folk, Robert**
SLAYER, THE

**Francour, Chuck**
BERSERKER

**Frankel, Benjamin**
CURSE OF THE WEREWOLF, THE

**Frederick, Jesse**
LAST HORROR FILM, THE

**Freed, Arnold**
WEREWOLF OF WASHINGTON

**Freedman, Harry**
PYX, THE

**Fricke, Florian**
NOSFERATU, THE VAMPIRE

# MUSIC COMPOSERS

**Fried, Gerald**
BABY, THE

**Frizzi, Fabio**
MANHATTAN BABY
PSYCHIC, THE
ZOMBIE
GATES OF HELL, THE

**Fu-ling, Wang**
LEGEND OF THE SEVEN GOLDEN
VAMPIRES, THE

**Gagnon, Andre**
PHOBIA

**Gale, John**
DOCTOR PHIBES RISES AGAIN

**Gallo, Phil**
MOTHER'S DAY

**Gamley, Douglas**
BEAST MUST DIE, THE
FROM BEYOND THE GRAVE
TALES FROM THE CRYPT
VAULT OF HORROR, THE
MADHOUSE
HORROR HOTEL

**Garrison, Joseph**
SLAUGHTERHOUSE

**Garvarentz, George**
TOO SCARED TO SCREAM

**Gaslini, Giorgio**
DEEP RED

**Gaubert, Christian**
LITTLE GIRL WHO LIVES DOWN THE
LANE, THE

**Geesin, Ron**
GHOST STORY

**George, David**
HOWLING IV: THE ORIGINAL
NIGHTMARE

**Gere, Don**
WEREWOLVES ON WHEELS

**Gershenson, Joseph**
ABBOTT AND COSTELLO MEET DR.
JEKYLL AND MR. HYDE

**Gibney, David**
SUPERSTITION

**Gibson, David**
SCHLOCK

**Gilbert, Herschel Burke**
I DISMEMBER MAMA

**Gillis, Richard**
DEMONOID

**Giovanni, Paul**
WICKER MAN, THE

**Gizzi, Carlo**
ANDY WARHOL'S FRANKENSTEIN

**Gizzi, Claudio**
ANDY WARHOL'S DRACULA

**Glass, Paul**
TO THE DEVIL A DAUGHTER

**Glasser, Albert**
GIANT FROM THE UNKNOWN

**Goblin, The**
CREEPERS
NIGHT OF THE ZOMBIES

**Goblins, The**
DEEP RED

**Goldenberg, Mark**
TEEN WOLF TOO

**Goldsmith, Jerry**
DAMIEN—OMEN II
FINAL CONFLICT, THE
GREMLINS
PSYCHO II
POLTERGEIST II
POLTERGEIST
OMEN, THE
TWILIGHT ZONE—THE MOVIE
OTHER, THE
MAGIC

**Goldsmith, Joel**
MAN WITH TWO BRAINS, THE

**Goldsmith, Jonathan**
VISITING HOURS

**Goodman, Miles**
TEEN WOLF
LITTLE SHOP OF HORRORS

**Gorn, Steve**
HUNGRY WIVES

**Gounod, Charles**
NOSFERATU, THE VAMPIRE

**Grass III, Clancy B.**
VELVET VAMPIRE, THE

**Greene, Charles**
TARGETS

**Griffin, Gary**
BERSERKER

**Gross, Charles**
BLUE SUNSHINE

**Gross, Gregg**
DEATHROW GAMESHOW

**Grupo Dichotomy**
MONSTER DOG

**Guard, Barrie**
HOWLING IV: THE ORIGINAL
NIGHTMARE
MONSTER IN THE CLOSET

**Guefen, Anthony**
STUFF, THE

**Gunning, Christopher**
HANDS OF THE RIPPER

**Hake, Ardell**
SCARED TO DEATH

**Hamilton, Chico**
REPULSION

**Hardman, Karl**
NIGHT OF THE LIVING DEAD

**Harland, Gilbert**
RAVEN, THE

**Harline, Leigh**
ISLE OF THE DEAD

**Harling, W. Frank**
INVISIBLE MAN, THE

**Harris, Johnny**
EVIL, THE

**Harrison, John**
CREEPSHOW
DAY OF THE DEAD

**Harvey, Richard**
HOUSE OF THE LONG SHADOWS

**Harwood, Bo**
HAPPY BIRTHDAY TO ME

**Herkan, H.**
WHITE ZOMBIE

**Herrmann, Bernard**
BIRDS, THE
IT'S ALIVE
IT LIVES AGAIN
PSYCHO
SISTERS
IT'S ALIVE III: ISLAND OF THE ALIVE

**Hess, David**
LAST HOUSE ON THE LEFT

**Hieronymous, Richard**
FOREST, THE
INVISIBLE STRANGLER, THE

**Hill, Ed**
DEVONSVILLE TERROR, THE

**Hine, Rupert**
SHOUT, THE

**Hobson, Gene**
STUDENT BODIES

**Hodgson, Brian**
LEGEND OF HELL HOUSE, THE

**Hodian, John**
GIRLS SCHOOL SCREAMERS

**Hoefle, Carl**
SCARED TO DEATH

**Hoenig, Michael**
GATE, THE
WRAITH, THE

**Holdridge, Lee**
PACK, THE
TRANSYLVANIA 6-5000

**Holm, Michael**
MARK OF THE DEVIL

**Holmes, Bill**
CURSE OF THE LIVING CORPSE, THE

**Hooper, Tobe**
TEXAS CHAINSAW MASSACRE PART
2, THE
TEXAS CHAIN SAW MASSACRE, THE

**Horelick, Stephen**
MADMAN

**Horner, James**
DEADLY BLESSING
HUMANOIDS FROM THE DEEP
HAND, THE
SOMETHING WICKED THIS WAY
COMES
WOLFEN

**Horvath, Leif**
MICROWAVE MASSACRE

**Hotchkis, John**
CRUCIBLE OF HORROR

**Howarth, Alan**
HALLOWEEN IV: THE RETURN OF
MICHAEL MYERS
CHRISTINE
HALLOWEEN III: SEASON OF THE
WITCH
PRINCE OF DARKNESS
RETRIBUTION

**Hoyt, Eric**
KEEPER, THE

**Humair, Daniel**
WITCHCRAFT THROUGH THE AGES

**Hundley, Craig**
ALLIGATOR
BOOGEYMAN II
SCHIZOID

**Immel, Jerrold**
HOUSE ON SKULL MOUNTAIN, THE

**Isham, Mark**
HITCHER, THE

**Jacquet, H. Maurice**
WHITE ZOMBIE

**Jaeger, Denny**
HUNGER, THE

**Jarre, Maurice**
BRIDE, THE
HORROR CHAMBER OF DR.
FAUSTUS, THE

**Johnson, Laurie**
CAPTAIN KRONOS: VAMPIRE HUNTER
IT LIVES AGAIN
IT'S ALIVE III: ISLAND OF THE ALIVE

**Jones, Guy**
HUMAN MONSTER, THE

**Jones, Ken**
BEYOND THE FOG
HORROR HOTEL

**Jones, Kenneth V.**
WHO SLEW AUNTIE ROO?
TOMB OF LIGEIA, THE

**Jones, Ralph**
SLUMBER PARTY MASSACRE, THE

**Jones, Trevor**
ANGEL HEART
SENDER, THE

**Josephs, Wilfred**
DIE! DIE! MY DARLING
UNCANNY, THE

**Jost, Paul**
LAST RITES

**Justin, Susan**
FINAL TERROR, THE

**Justis, Bill**
DEAR, DEAD DELILAH

**Kabiljo, Alfie**
TRANSYLVANIA 6-5000

**Kamen, Michael**
DEAD ZONE, THE

**Kaplowitz, Matt**
NIGHT OF THE ZOMBIES

**Kaproff, Dana**
PANDEMONIUM
WHEN A STRANGER CALLS

**Katz, Fred**
CREATURE FROM THE HAUNTED SEA
LITTLE SHOP OF HORRORS

**Kay, Edward**
APE MAN, THE
APE, THE

**Kellaway, Roger**
EVILSPEAK
SILENT SCREAM

**Kempel, Arthur**
WACKO

**Kempenski, Leo**
WHITE ZOMBIE

**Kershaw, Martin**
NIGHTMARE WEEKEND

**Kirchin, Basil**
ABOMINABLE DR. PHIBES, THE

**Komeda, Krzysztof**
ROSEMARY'S BABY

**Korzynski, Andrzej**
POSSESSION

**Koz, Jeff**
LAST HORROR FILM, THE

**KPM**
SCREAMTIME

**Kraft, William**
PSYCHIC KILLER

**Kraushaar, Raoul**
BILLY THE KID VS. DRACULA
BRIDE OF THE GORILLA
JESSE JAMES MEETS
FRANKENSTEIN'S DAUGHTER

**Krog, Tim**
BOOGEYMAN II
BOOGEY MAN, THE

**La Loggia, Frank**
FEAR NO EVIL
LADY IN WHITE

**Labuschagne, Nick**
DEMON, THE

**Lambert, Jerry**
TEXAS CHAINSAW MASSACRE PART
2, THE

**LaSalle, Richard**
DOCTOR DEATH: SEEKER OF SOULS

**Lattanzi, Michael**
CLASS OF NUKE 'EM HIGH

**Lawrence, Stephen**
ALICE, SWEET ALICE
MIRRORS

**Le Sage, Bill**
TELL-TALE HEART, THE

**Lee, David**
MASQUE OF THE RED DEATH, THE

**Lee, Gerald**
SATAN'S CHEERLEADERS

**Leonetti, Tommy**
MASSACRE AT CENTRAL HIGH

**Lewis, Herschell Gordon**
BLOOD FEAST
TWO THOUSAND MANIACS

**Lewis, Michael J.**
LEGACY, THE
THEATRE OF BLOOD
UNSEEN, THE
MAN WHO HAUNTED HIMSELF, THE

**Lewis, W. Michael**
NEW YEAR'S EVIL

**Lewis, Webster**
HEARSE, THE

**Ligeti, Gyorgy**
SHINING, THE

**Litovsky, Michael**
BLOOD SISTERS

**Lo Duca, Joseph**
EVIL DEAD 2: DEAD BY DAWN
EVIL DEAD, THE

**Love, Wayne**
BOOGEYMAN II

**Lutyens, Elisabeth**
DR. TERROR'S HOUSE OF HORRORS

**Macauley, Tony**
BEAST IN THE CELLAR, THE

**Macero, Ted**
FRIDAY THE 13TH . . . THE ORPHAN

**McGuffie, Bill**
ASPHYX, THE

**McKelvey, Frank**
BOGGY CREEK II

**Malken, Jack**
NESTING, THE

**Mancini, Henry**
NIGHTWING

**Manfredini, Harry**
CHILDREN, THE
HOUSE II: THE SECOND STORY
HOUSE
HILLS HAVE EYES II, THE
FRIDAY THE 13TH PART VI: JASON
LIVES
FRIDAY THE 13TH, PART V—A NEW
BEGINNING
FRIDAY THE 13TH—THE FINAL
CHAPTER
FRIDAY THE 13TH PART III
FRIDAY THE 13TH PART II
FRIDAY THE 13TH
SWAMP THING
SLAUGHTER HIGH
FRIDAY THE 13TH PART VII—THE NEW
BLOOD

**Manzie, Jim**
OFFSPRING, THE

# MUSIC COMPOSERS

**Marx, Bill**
COUNT YORGA, VAMPIRE
SCREAM, BLACULA, SCREAM
TERROR HOUSE

**Mathieson, Muir**
CIRCUS OF HORRORS

**May, Brian**
PATRICK
THIRST
ROAD GAMES

**Melle, Gil**
BLOOD BEACH
SENTINEL, THE

**Mendoza-Nava, Jaime**
CREATURE FROM BLACK LAKE, THE
BROTHERHOOD OF SATAN, THE
MAUSOLEUM
LEGEND OF BOGGY CREEK, THE
WITCHMAKER, THE
TOWN THAT DREADED SUNDOWN,
THE

**Menken, Alan**
LITTLE SHOP OF HORRORS

**Meyers, Stanley**
INCUBUS, THE

**Micalizzi, Franco**
CURSE, THE
VISITOR, THE

**Michelini, Luciano**
SCREAMERS

**Mills-Cockell, John**
TERROR TRAIN

**Minard, Michael**
MUTILATOR, THE
RETURN TO SALEM'S LOT, A

**Mollicone, Henry**
PREMONITION, THE

**Mollin, Fred**
FRIDAY THE 13TH PART VII—THE NEW
BLOOD

**Moore, Gene**
CARNIVAL OF SOULS

**Moraz, Patrick**
STEPFATHER, THE

**Moroder, Giorgio**
CAT PEOPLE

**Morricone, Ennio**
BIRD WITH THE CRYSTAL PLUMAGE,
THE
CHOSEN, THE
EXORCIST II: THE HERETIC
TEMPTER, THE
ORCA
NIGHTMARE CASTLE

**Morris, John**
HAUNTED HONEYMOON
YOUNG FRANKENSTEIN

**Morse, Fuzzbee**
DOLLS
GHOULIES II

**Moseley, Jerry**
BLOOD TIDE

FRIGHTMARE

**Mothersbaugh, Mark**
SLAUGHTERHOUSE ROCK

**Myers, Stanley**
CONFESSIONAL, THE
HOUSE OF WHIPCORD
SCHIZO
WATCHER IN THE WOODS, THE
FRIGHTMARE

**Myrow, Fred**
PHANTASM
PHANTASM II

**Names, The**
TERROR ON TOUR

**Navarro, Jose Luis**
CAULDRON OF BLOOD

**Neumann, Drew**
SCALPS

**Newman, Alfred**
HUNCHBACK OF NOTRE DAME, THE

**Newman, David**
MY DEMON LOVER

**Newman, Thomas**
LOST BOYS, THE

**Nicolai, Bruno**
COUNT DRACULA

**Nicolosi, Roberto**
BLACK SABBATH

**Nitzsche, Jack**
SEVENTH SIGN, THE
EXORCIST, THE

**Nolin, Maggie**
NIGHT OF THE ZOMBIES

**North, Alex**
WILLARD

**Novotny, Paul**
BLUE MONKEY

**Nugent, Ted**
NOMADS

**Ober, Arlon**
BLOODY BIRTHDAY
HOSPITAL MASSACRE
IN THE SHADOW OF KILIMANJARO
EATING RAOUL

**Oldfield, Alan**
FOREST, THE
INVISIBLE STRANGLER, THE

**Oliverio, James**
SLEEPAWAY CAMP 2: UNHAPPY
CAMPERS

**Onomatopoeia, Inc.**
NIGHT OF THE ZOMBIES

**Orpin, Bob**
TRACK OF THE MOONBEAST

**Orr, Buxton**
CORRIDORS OF BLOOD
HAUNTED STRANGLER, THE

**Ortolani, Riz**
BEYOND THE DOOR

**Pagan, J.M.**
ANGUISH

**Page, Gene**
BLACULA

**Parker, Alan**
AMERICAN GOTHIC
JAWS 3-D

**Parker, Clifton**
CURSE OF THE DEMON

**Parsons, Steve**
HOWLING II . . . YOUR SISTER IS A
WEREWOLF

**Pate, Johnny**
DR. BLACK AND MR. HYDE

**Peake, Don**
HILLS HAVE EYES, THE
PREY, THE

**Penderecki, Krzysztof**
SHINING, THE

**Pes, Carlo**
DORIAN GRAY

**Peskanov, Alexander**
HE KNOWS YOU'RE ALONE

**Peskanov, Mark**
HE KNOWS YOU'RE ALONE

**Petan, Edward J.**
SOMETHING WEIRD

**Phillips, Art**
POSSESSION

**Pike, Nicholas**
GRAVEYARD SHIFT

**Pitts, Clay**
I DRINK YOUR BLOOD

**Podell, Art**
BLACK ROOM, THE

**Podolor, Richard A.**
BIG FOOT

**Ponty, Jean-Luc**
WITCHCRAFT THROUGH THE AGES

**Popple, Todd**
ESCAPES

**Post Production Associates**
OCTAMAN
STANLEY

**Powder, Steve**
PIRANHA II: THE SPAWNING

**Preston, Don**
BLOOD DINER

**Previn, Charles**
WOLF MAN, THE

**Price, Henry**
THRILL KILLERS, THE

**Prince, Robert**
SQUIRM

**Productions, Lonjohn**
DRIVE-IN MASSACRE

**Puchan, Dave**
WITCHFIRE

THE HORROR FILM

**Ragland, Robert O.**
GRIZZLY
MANSION OF THE DOOMED
Q
SUPERNATURALS, THE
HYSTERICAL

**Rasmussen, Eric**
SCALPS

**Reed, Les**
CREEPSHOW 2

**Regan, Pat**
OFFSPRING, THE

**Reiser, Clutch**
BRAIN DAMAGE

**Reitman, Ivan**
THEY CAME FROM WITHIN

**Reizenstein, Franz**
CIRCUS OF HORRORS
MUMMY, THE

**Renzetti, Joe**
DEAD AND BURIED
POLTERGEIST III
CHILD'S PLAY

**Restaino, Tony**
BRAIN THAT WOULDN'T DIE, THE

**Riesenfeld, Hugo**
WHITE ZOMBIE

**Rinder, Laurin**
NEW YEAR'S EVIL

**Rizzati, Walter**
HOUSE BY THE CEMETERY, THE

**Roberts, Bruce**
CRAZIES, THE

**Roberts, Jonathan**
I WAS A TEENAGE ZOMBIE

**Robertson, Eric N.**
SPASMS

**Robinson, Harry**
GHOUL, THE
LUST FOR A VAMPIRE
OBLONG BOX, THE
VAMPIRE LOVERS, THE
TWINS OF EVIL

**Robinson, J. Peter**
BELIEVERS, THE
GATE, THE
WRAITH, THE
RETURN OF THE LIVING DEAD PART II

**Romitelli, Sante**
HATCHET FOR A HONEYMOON

**Rosenbaum, Joel**
OUTING, THE

**Rosenman, Leonard**
CAR, THE
RACE WITH THE DEVIL
PROPHECY

**Rosenthal, Laurence**
ISLAND OF DR. MOREAU, THE

**Ross, John**
FRANKENSTEIN GENERAL HOSPITAL

**Rubin, Lance**
HAPPY BIRTHDAY TO ME
MOTEL HELL

**Rubini, Michel**
HUNGER, THE

**Rubinstein, Donald**
MARTIN

**Russo, Gus**
BASKET CASE
BRAIN DAMAGE

**Rustichelli, Carlo**
BLOOD AND BLACK LACE

**Rutherford, Michael**
SHOUT, THE

**Safan, Craig**
NIGHTMARES
WARNING SIGN
NIGHTMARE ON ELM STREET 4: THE
DREAM MASTER, A

**Sahl, Michael**
BLOODSUCKING FREAKS

**Sales, Gary**
MADMAN

**Salzedo, Leonard**
CURSE OF FRANKENSTEIN, THE

**Sand Castle, The**
MIDNIGHT

**Sarde, Philippe**
GHOST STORY
TENANT, THE

**Savina, Carlo**
HOUSE OF EXORCISM, THE

**Sawtell, Paul**
FLY, THE
RETURN OF THE FLY

**Scharf, Walter**
BEN
NUTTY PROFESSOR, THE

**Schifrin, Lalo**
AMITYVILLE II: THE POSSESSION
AMITYVILLE HORROR, THE
DAY OF THE ANIMALS
MANITOU, THE
STRANGER IS WATCHING, A

**Scholes, Kim**
NESTING, THE

**Schulze, Klaus**
NEXT OF KIN

**Scott, Gary**
FINAL EXAM

**Scott, John**
CRAZE
KING KONG LIVES

**Scott, Patrick John**
BERSERK

**Seagrave, Malcolm**
PHANTASM

**Sear, Walter**
BLOOD SISTERS

**Searle, Humphrey**
HAUNTING, THE

**Seeman, Craig**
I WAS A TEENAGE ZOMBIE

**Segall, Bernardo**
HOMEBODIES

**Seltzer, Dov**
SAVAGE WEEKEND

**Serio, Renato**
ALONE IN THE DARK

**Shefter, Bert**
RETURN OF THE FLY

**Shire, David**
MONKEY SHINES: AN EXPERIMENT IN
FEAR

**Shore, Howard**
BROOD, THE
DEAD RINGERS
FLY, THE
SCANNERS
VIDEODROME

**Silvestri, Alan**
CAT'S EYE

**Simonetti, Claudio**
DEMONS

**Skiles, Marlin**
STRANGLER, THE

**Skinner, Frank**
ABBOTT AND COSTELLO MEET
FRANKENSTEIN
SON OF FRANKENSTEIN

**Slane, Rod**
REVENGE

**Slaney, Ivor**
TERROR

**Slider, Dan**
UNINVITED, THE

**Small, George**
LAST RITES

**Small, Michael**
AUDREY ROSE
JAWS: THE REVENGE

**Smiley, Pril**
PREMONITION, THE

**Smith, Arthur**
WOLFMAN

**Spear, David**
FEAR NO EVIL

**Spear, Eric**
GHOST SHIP

**Stein, Julian**
FLESH EATERS, THE

**Stein, Ronald**
DEMENTIA 13
PREMATURE BURIAL, THE
TERROR, THE
SPIDER BABY

**Steiner, Max**
SON OF KONG
KING KONG

**Stern, Theodore**
WORM EATERS, THE

**Stoeber, Orville**
LET'S SCARE JESSICA TO DEATH

**Stoloff, Morris W.**
BEFORE I HANG

**Stone, Brian**
TARGETS

**Stone, Christopher L.**
PRISON
PHANTASM II

**Stone, Richard**
PUMPKINHEAD

**Stothart, Herbert**
PICTURE OF DORIAN GRAY, THE

**Studer, Jim**
OPEN HOUSE

**Summers, Bob**
BOOGENS, THE
ONE DARK NIGHT

**Syrewicz, Stanislas**
LAIR OF THE WHITE WORM, THE

**Taj**
DEADTIME STORIES

**Takemitsu, Toru**
KWAIDAN

**Tangerine Dream**
KEEP, THE
NEAR DARK
SPASMS

**Tchaikovsky, Peter Illich**
DRACULA

**Tenney, Dennis Michael**
WITCHBOARD

**Theodore, Mike**
MARDI GRAS MASSACRE

**Thomas, Peter**
BLOOD DEMON

**Thomas, Whitey**
NAIL GUN MASSACRE

**Thorne, Ken**
HOUSE WHERE EVIL DWELLS, THE

**Tipton, George Aliceson**
PHANTOM OF THE PARADISE

**Tolland, Gerry**
PLUMBER, THE

**Towns, Colin**
RAWHEAD REX
HAUNTING OF JULIA, THE

**Troost, Ernest**
DEAD HEAT

**Trovajoli, Armando**
ATOM AGE VAMPIRE

**Tucci, Giorgio**
ZOMBIE

**Tufo, Richard**
DEMENTED
TO ALL A GOODNIGHT

**Ulfik, Rick**
STREET TRASH

**Uretta, Alice**
FEAR CHAMBER, THE

**Vicari, Clem**
MOTHER'S DAY

**Victor and Diego**
DEMON WITCH CHILD

**Vig, Tommy**
FORCED ENTRY
SWEET SIXTEEN

**Vino, Jack**
STANLEY

**Von Dexter**
HOUSE ON HAUNTED HILL
THIRTEEN GHOSTS

**Vuh, Popol**
NOSFERATU, THE VAMPIRE

**Waggner, George**
PHANTOM OF THE OPERA

**Wagner, Richard**
DRACULA
MAXIMUM OVERDRIVE
NOSFERATU, THE VAMPIRE

**Wakeman, Rick**
CREEPSHOW 2
BURNING, THE

**Walker, Shirley**
GHOULIES

**Wallace, Rob**
CHILD, THE

**Waller, Fats**
ERASERHEAD

**Wannberg, Ken**
OF UNKNOWN ORIGIN

**Ward, Edward**
PHANTOM OF THE OPERA

**Waxman, Franz**
BRIDE OF FRANKENSTEIN, THE
DR. JEKYLL AND MR. HYDE
DEVIL DOLL, THE

**Waymon, Sam**
GANJA AND HESS

**Webb, Roger**
BURKE AND HARE
GODSEND, THE

**Webb, Roy**
BEDLAM
CURSE OF THE CAT PEOPLE, THE
CAT PEOPLE
BODY SNATCHER, THE
I WALKED WITH A ZOMBIE
SEVENTH VICTIM, THE
LEOPARD MAN, THE

**Wellington, Larry**
WIZARD OF GORE, THE
GRUESOME TWOSOME

**Wetherwax, Michael**
SORORITY HOUSE MASSACRE

**Whitaker, David**
DR. JEKYLL AND SISTER HYDE

PSYCHOMANIA
SCREAM AND SCREAM AGAIN

**Widelitz, Stacy**
RETURN TO HORROR HIGH

**Wilkins, Rick**
CHANGELING, THE

**Wilkinson, Marc**
BLOOD ON SATAN'S CLAW, THE

**Williams, Guy Bevier**
WHITE ZOMBIE

**Williams, Jack Eric**
NIGHTMARE

**Williams, John**
FURY, THE
BLACK SUNDAY
DRACULA
JAWS: THE REVENGE
JAWS II
JAWS
WITCHES OF EASTWICK, THE

**Williams, Paul**
PHANTOM OF THE PARADISE

**Woznicki, Paul**
FIEND

**Wyman, Dan**
HELL NIGHT

**Young, Bob**
INN OF THE DAMNED

**Young, Christopher**
HELLBOUND: HELLRAISER II
DORM THAT DRIPPED BLOOD, THE
HELLRAISER
POWER, THE
NIGHTMARE ON ELM STREET PART 2:
FREDDY'S REVENGE, A
TRICK OR TREAT

**Zavod, Allan**
HOWLING III, THE

**Zaza, Paul**
CURTAINS
HELLO MARY LOU, PROM NIGHT II
PROM NIGHT
MY BLOODY VALENTINE

**Zeller, Wolfgang**
VAMPYR

**Zimmers, Don**
SCREAMS OF A WINTER NIGHT

**Zittrer, Carl**
BLACK CHRISTMAS
PROM NIGHT

## PRODUCERS

**Adamson, Al**
DRACULA VS. FRANKENSTEIN
BLOOD OF DRACULA'S CASTLE
BRAIN OF BLOOD

**Adlum, Ed**
SHRIEK OF THE MUTILATED
INVASION OF THE BLOOD FARMERS

**Albright, Carlton J.**
CHILDREN, THE

**Alchimede, Diego**
CITY OF THE WALKING DEAD

**Aldrich, Robert**
WHATEVER HAPPENED TO BABY
JANE?
HUSH . . . HUSH, SWEET CHARLOTTE

**Alland, William**
CREATURE FROM THE BLACK
LAGOON

**Amati, Edmundo**
CHOSEN, THE
TEMPTER, THE

**Andrews, Peter**
BLOOD ON SATAN'S CLAW, THE

**Appelbaum, Lawrence**
SILENT NIGHT, DEADLY NIGHT PART II

**Argento, Claudio**
UNSANE
INFERNO

**Argento, Dario**
CREEPERS
DEMONS 2: THE NIGHTMARE
RETURNS
DEMONS

**Argento, Salvatore**
DEEP RED
BIRD WITH THE CRYSTAL PLUMAGE,
THE

**Argyle, John**
CHAMBER OF HORRORS
HUMAN MONSTER, THE

**Arkoff, Samuel Z.**
DUNWICH HORROR, THE
WHO SLEW AUNTIE ROO?

**Arthur, Robert**
ABBOTT AND COSTELLO MEET
FRANKENSTEIN

**Artzi, Ami**
SILENT NIGHT, BLOODY NIGHT

**Assonitis, Ovidio**
BEYOND THE DOOR
CURSE, THE
VISITOR, THE

**Attenborough, Richard**
SEANCE ON A WET AFTERNOON

**Attew, Kevin**
RAWHEAD REX

**Auer, John H.**
CRIME OF DR. CRESPI, THE

**Aured, Carlos**
MONSTER DOG

**Avedis, Howard**
MORTUARY

**Backlar, Marshal**
HOMEBODIES

**Balch, Anthony**
WITCHCRAFT THROUGH THE AGES

**Balcon, Michael**
DEAD OF NIGHT

GHOUL, THE

**Ball, David**
CREEPSHOW 2

**Band, Albert**
DRACULA'S DOG
TROLL
GHOULIES II

**Band, Charles**
MANSION OF THE DOOMED

**Barich, Robert**
MAUSOLEUM

**Barmak, Ira Richard**
SILENT NIGHT, DEADLY NIGHT

**Barnett, John**
STRANGE BEHAVIOR

**Bateman, Kent**
TEEN WOLF TOO

**Baughn, David**
BEYOND EVIL
GRADUATION DAY

**Bava, Mario**
ATOM AGE VAMPIRE

**Beaumont, Gabrielle**
CRUCIBLE OF HORROR
GODSEND, THE

**Bechard, Gorman**
PSYCHOS IN LOVE

**Becker, Vernon**
NOCTURNA

**Beckerman, Sidney**
STRANGER IS WATCHING, A

**Beebe, Ford**
SON OF DRACULA

**Begun, Jeff**
SATURDAY THE 14TH

**Behrns, Don**
FRIDAY THE 13TH PART VI: JASON
LIVES
UNSEEN, THE

**Belski, Micky**
LOVE BUTCHER, THE

**Bender, Michael**
BEETLEJUICE

**Benson, Jay**
STEPFATHER, THE

**Beresford, Al**
SCREAMTIME

**Bergquist, Peter L.**
MONSTER IN THE CLOSET

**Berman, Pandro S.**
HUNCHBACK OF NOTRE DAME, THE
PICTURE OF DORIAN GRAY, THE

**Bernardi, Barry**
POLTERGEIST III

**Bernhard, Harvey**
BEAST WITHIN, THE
DAMIEN—OMEN II
FINAL CONFLICT, THE
LOST BOYS, THE
OMEN, THE

**Bernhardt, Steven**
FUNHOUSE, THE

**Bessi, Roberto**
CRAWLSPACE

**Billitteri, Salvatore**
BLACK SABBATH

**Birdt, Marvin**
CAR, THE

**Bischoff, Samuel**
STRANGLER, THE

**Bishop, Tony**
FRIDAY THE 13TH—THE FINAL
CHAPTER
FRIDAY THE 13TH PART III

**Bishop, Wes**
RACE WITH THE DEVIL

**Blanke, Henry**
MYSTERY OF THE WAX MUSEUM, THE

**Blatt, Daniel H.**
CUJO

**Blatty, William Peter**
EXORCIST, THE
NINTH CONFIGURATION, THE

**Bloom, Jim**
WARNING SIGN

**Bockner, Michael**
GRAVEYARD SHIFT

**Bogdanovich, Peter**
TARGETS

**Boisvert, Nicole**
CATHY'S CURSE

**Bollinger, Henri**
MARY, MARY, BLOODY MARY

**Bombyk, David**
HITCHER, THE

**Boorman, John**
EXORCIST II: THE HERETIC

**Borchers, Donald P.**
CHILDREN OF THE CORN
VAMP

**Borkon, Jules**
HORROR CHAMBER OF DR.
FAUSTUS, THE

**Bourke, Terry**
INN OF THE DAMNED

**Boyman, Marc**
DEAD RINGERS
INCUBUS, THE

**Brady, Edward**
VIRGIN WITCH, THE

**Braun, Zev**
LITTLE GIRL WHO LIVES DOWN THE
LANE, THE

**Braunsberg, Andrew**
ANDY WARHOL'S FRANKENSTEIN
ANDY WARHOL'S DRACULA
TENANT, THE

**Braunstein, George**
FADE TO BLACK

# PRODUCERS

**Breimer, Stephen**
BUTCHER, BAKER (NIGHTMARE MAKER)

**Briskin, Mort**
BEN
WILLARD

**Brittany, John**
ASPHYX, THE

**Brock, Deborah**
SLUMBER PARTY MASSACRE II

**Brodek, Thomas H.**
TRANSYLVANIA 6-5000

**Broder, Jack**
BRIDE OF THE GORILLA

**Broughton, Cliff**
MONSTER WALKS, THE

**Brown, David**
JAWS II
JAWS

**Brown, Summer**
HUMAN EXPERIMENTS
PREY, THE

**Brown, William O.**
WITCHMAKER, THE

**Browning, Tod**
FREAKS

**Brownrigg, S.F.**
DON'T LOOK IN THE BASEMENT
KEEP MY GRAVE OPEN

**Buchanan, Larry**
CURSE OF THE SWAMP CREATURE

**Burr, William**
OFFSPRING, THE

**Butler, Aaron C.**
BLACK ROOM, THE

**Cady, Daniel**
GRAVE OF THE VAMPIRE
GARDEN OF THE DEAD

**Cahn, Barry**
HILLS HAVE EYES II, THE

**Caiano, Carlo**
NIGHTMARE CASTLE

**Calderon, Guillermo**
WRESTLING WOMEN VS. THE AZTEC MUMMY, THE
AZTEC MUMMY, THE
CURSE OF THE AZTEC MUMMY, THE
ROBOT VS. THE AZTEC MUMMY, THE
NIGHT OF THE BLOODY APES

**Camhe, Beverly**
BELIEVERS, THE

**Campbell, R. Wright**
DEMENTIA 13

**Canton, Neil**
WITCHES OF EASTWICK, THE

**Cardoza, Anthony**
BIG FOOT

**Carlin, Ed**
EVIL, THE
SUPERSTITION

**Carlton, Rex**
BLOOD OF DRACULA'S CASTLE
BRAIN THAT WOULDN'T DIE, THE

**Carpenter, John**
HALLOWEEN II
HALLOWEEN III: SEASON OF THE WITCH

**Carpenter, Peter**
POINT OF TERROR

**Carreras, Michael**
MUMMY, THE

**Carroll, Larry**
TOURIST TRAP, THE

**Carroll, Matt**
PLUMBER, THE

**Case, Carroll**
BILLY THE KID VS. DRACULA
JESSE JAMES MEETS FRANKENSTEIN'S DAUGHTER

**Castle, William**
HOUSE ON HAUNTED HILL
THIRTEEN GHOSTS
STRAIT-JACKET
ROSEMARY'S BABY

**Cervi, Antonio**
TORSO

**Chambliss, John L.**
FINAL EXAM

**Chaney, Warren**
OUTING, THE

**Chapin, Doug**
PANDEMONIUM
WHEN A STRANGER CALLS

**Chase, Brandon**
ALLIGATOR

**Chester, Hal E.**
CURSE OF THE DEMON

**Childers, Michael**
BELIEVERS, THE

**Christie, Howard**
ABBOTT AND COSTELLO MEET DR. JEKYLL AND MR. HYDE

**Clark, Bob**
BLACK CHRISTMAS
CHILDREN SHOULDN'T PLAY WITH DEAD THINGS
DEATHDREAM

**Clark, Greydon**
UNINVITED, THE
WACKO

**Clark, John G.**
HOUSE ON SORORITY ROW, THE

**Claybourne, Doug**
SERPENT AND THE RAINBOW, THE

**Clemens, Brian**
CAPTAIN KRONOS: VAMPIRE HUNTER
DR. JEKYLL AND SISTER HYDE

**Clement, Jack**
DEAR, DEAD DELILAH

**Cobe, Sandy**
OPEN HOUSE

TO ALL A GOODNIGHT
TERROR ON TOUR

**Coblenz, Walter**
SISTER SISTER

**Cohen, Herman**
BERSERK
CRAZE

**Cohen, Larry**
IT'S ALIVE
IT LIVES AGAIN
Q
MANIAC COP

**Cohen, Martin B.**
HUMANOIDS FROM THE DEEP
HOUSE WHERE EVIL DWELLS, THE
NIGHTMARE IN WAX

**Coilet, Paul**
DAUGHTERS OF DARKNESS

**Connors, Mike**
TOO SCARED TO SCREAM

**Conrad, Jack**
HOWLING, THE

**Constantine, Frixos**
LAND OF THE MINOTAUR

**Cooper, Buddy**
MUTILATOR, THE

**Cooper, Merian C.**
KING KONG

**Corke, Penny**
GOTHIC

**Corman, Julie**
CHOPPING MALL
SATURDAY THE 14TH

**Corman, Roger**
CREATURE FROM THE HAUNTED SEA
DEMENTIA 13
HOUSE OF USHER
MASQUE OF THE RED DEATH, THE
LITTLE SHOP OF HORRORS
RAVEN, THE
PREMATURE BURIAL, THE
PIT AND THE PENDULUM, THE
MUNCHIES
TERROR, THE
TALES OF TERROR
TOMB OF LIGEIA, THE

**Cornfeld, Stuart**
FLY, THE

**Coromina, Pepon**
ANGUISH

**Corotona, Sergio**
NIGHT OF THE ZOMBIES

**Cort, Robert W.**
SEVENTH SIGN, THE

**Coscarelli, Don**
PHANTASM

**Crafter, Richard**
TERROR

**Croft, Alvin C.**
CRAZIES, THE

**Cronenberg, David**
DEAD RINGERS

**Crowe, Christopher**
NIGHTMARES

**Croydon, John**
CORRIDORS OF BLOOD
HAUNTED STRANGLER, THE

**Cruze, James**
GREAT GABBO, THE

**Cullen, James V.**
DEVIL'S RAIN, THE

**Cunningham, Sean S.**
HOUSE II: THE SECOND STORY
HOUSE
FRIDAY THE 13TH
LAST HOUSE ON THE LEFT

**Curtis, Bruce Cohn**
HELL NIGHT

**Curtis, Dan**
BURNT OFFERINGS

**Curtis, Jack**
FLESH EATERS, THE

**Curtis, Terry**
FLESH EATERS, THE

**Cushing, Harry**
LADY FRANKENSTEIN

**Dadashian, Robert**
CHILD, THE

**Daniel, Don**
SLUMBER PARTY MASSACRE II

**Danziger, Edward J.**
TELL-TALE HEART, THE

**Danziger, Harry Lee**
TELL-TALE HEART, THE

**Das, Gautam**
IN THE SHADOW OF KILIMANJARO

**Daubeney, Diana**
HOUSE THAT VANISHED, THE

**David, William B.**
SCARED TO DEATH

**Davis, Kenn**
NIGHTMARE IN BLOOD

**Davison, Jon**
PIRANHA

**De Angelis, Fabrizio**
HOUSE BY THE CEMETERY, THE
MANHATTAN BABY
ZOMBIE

**De Castro, J.L. Bermudez**
HORROR OF THE ZOMBIES

**De Felitta, Frank**
AUDREY ROSE

**De Gaetano, Michael**
HAUNTED

**de Gunzberg, Baron Nicolas**
VAMPYR

**De Laurentiis, Dino**
KING KONG

**de Nesle, Robert**
SCREAMING DEAD, THE

**De Palma, Brian**
BODY DOUBLE

**DeCoteau, David**
DREAMANIAC

**Dehlavi, Jamil**
BORN OF FIRE

**Depue, Wesley E.**
THIRSTY DEAD, THE

**Di Milia, Robert**
HE KNOWS YOU'RE ALONE

**Diamond, David**
RAVEN, THE
STRANGLER, THE

**Diamond, Ron**
SORORITY HOUSE MASSACRE

**Didio, Tony**
TOOLBOX MURDERS, THE

**Dietz, Jack**
BLACK DRAGONS
APE MAN, THE
CORPSE VANISHES, THE
BOWERY AT MIDNIGHT
GHOSTS ON THE LOOSE

**Dillman, Jr., Dean**
ATOMIC BRAIN, THE

**Donally, Andrew**
PSYCHOMANIA

**Doria, E.F.**
TENTACLES

**Douglas, Peter Vincent**
SOMETHING WICKED THIS WAY
COMES

**Drabinsky, Garth H.**
CHANGELING, THE

**Drai, Victor**
BRIDE, THE

**Drake, Arnold**
FLESH EATERS, THE

**Dreyer, Carl Theodor**
VAMPYR

**Druker, Matt**
HOUSE OF THE LIVING DEAD

**Dunas, Ronald S.**
ABOMINABLE DR. PHIBES, THE

**Dunlap, Scott R.**
APE, THE

**Dunning, John**
HAPPY BIRTHDAY TO ME
RABID
MY BLOODY VALENTINE
THEY CAME FROM WITHIN

**Dupont, Rene**
UNCANNY, THE

**Durack, Dennis**
VIRGIN WITCH, THE

**Eckert, John M.**
INCUBUS, THE

**Edwards, George**
FROGS
RUBY

**Eglee, Charles**
DEADLY EYES

**Elster, J.G.**
DR. TARR'S TORTURE DUNGEON

**Emery, Robert J.**
SCREAM BLOODY MURDER

**Esper, Dwain**
MANIAC

**Evans, Charles**
MONKEY SHINES: AN EXPERIMENT IN
FEAR

**Evans, Robert**
BLACK SUNDAY

**Ewing, William R.**
SLAYER, THE

**Fairman, Charles**
DISCIPLE OF DEATH

**Fast, Alvin L.**
SATAN'S CHEERLEADERS

**Feke, Steve**
WHEN A STRANGER CALLS

**Feldman, Edward S.**
SENDER, THE

**Fenady, Andrew J.**
ARNOLD

**Fennell, Albert**
CAPTAIN KRONOS: VAMPIRE HUNTER
DR. JEKYLL AND SISTER HYDE
LEGEND OF HELL HOUSE, THE

**Fentress, Robert**
DEAD AND BURIED

**Fetterman, Peter**
HAUNTING OF JULIA, THE

**Field, Ted**
SEVENTH SIGN, THE

**Figg, Christopher**
HELLBOUND: HELLRAISER II
HELLRAISER

**Fine, Harry**
LUST FOR A VAMPIRE
VAMPIRE LOVERS, THE
TWINS OF EVIL

**Finegan, James W.**
GIRLS SCHOOL SCREAMERS

**Finegan, John P.**
GIRLS SCHOOL SCREAMERS

**Fink, Joseph**
DEATH CURSE OF TARTU

**Finnell, Michael**
HOWLING, THE
GREMLINS

**Flaxman, Harvey**
GRIZZLY

**Fleming, Victor**
DR. JEKYLL AND MR. HYDE

## PRODUCERS

**Folsey, Jr., George**
AMERICAN WEREWOLF IN LONDON,
AN

**Forbes, Bryan**
SEANCE ON A WET AFTERNOON

**Foster, David**
LEGACY, THE

**Fox, Tom**
RETURN OF THE LIVING DEAD
RETURN OF THE LIVING DEAD PART II

**Foy, Bryan**
HOUSE OF WAX

**Francis, Kevin**
GHOUL, THE

**Franco, Larry**
PRINCE OF DARKNESS

**Franklin, Richard**
PATRICK
ROAD GAMES

**Frederic, Marc**
FRANKENSTEIN'S DAUGHTER

**Frederick, Jerome**
GHASTLY ONES, THE

**Freed, Herb**
BEYOND EVIL
HAUNTS
GRADUATION DAY

**Freeman, Joel**
LOVE AT FIRST BITE

**Freeman, Paul**
HALLOWEEN IV: THE RETURN OF
MICHAEL MYERS

**Friedman, David F.**
BLOOD FEAST
COLOR ME BLOOD RED
TWO THOUSAND MANIACS

**Fries, Charles**
CAT PEOPLE

**Frizzi, Fulvio**
PSYCHIC, THE

**Fromkess, Leon**
BLUEBEARD

**Fruet, William**
FUNERAL HOME

**Frumkes, Roy**
STREET TRASH

**Gallagher, Jack**
DEVIL BAT, THE

**Gardner, Eric**
ELVIRA: MISTRESS OF THE DARK

**Garroni, Andrew**
MANIAC

**Geffen, David**
LITTLE SHOP OF HORRORS

**Geisinger, Elliot**
AMITYVILLE HORROR, THE

**Gell, William**
THEATRE OF DEATH

**Geoffray, Gerold**
WITCHBOARD

**George, Louis**
SLAUGHTERHOUSE ROCK

**Gibson, Derek**
DEATH SHIP

**Ginnane, Anthony I.**
STRANGE BEHAVIOR
PATRICK
THIRST
SURVIVOR

**Ginter, Brad F.**
FLESH FEAST

**Girdler, William**
MANITOU, THE

**Glass, Joe**
ENCOUNTER WITH THE UNKNOWN

**Glasser, Bernard**
RETURN OF THE FLY

**Glick, Michael S.**
DEVIL'S RAIN, THE

**Globus, Yoram**
DR. HECKYL AND MR. HYPE
HOSPITAL MASSACRE
NEW YEAR'S EVIL
TEXAS CHAINSAW MASSACRE PART
2, THE
SCHIZOID

**Glucksman, Ernest D.**
NUTTY PROFESSOR, THE

**Goch, Gary**
CHILDREN SHOULDN'T PLAY WITH
DEAD THINGS

**Golan, Menahem**
HOUSE OF THE LONG SHADOWS
DR. HECKYL AND MR. HYPE
NEW YEAR'S EVIL
TEXAS CHAINSAW MASSACRE PART
2, THE
SCHIZOID

**Goldstone, Phil**
VAMPIRE BAT, THE

**Goodell, Gregory**
HUMAN EXPERIMENTS

**Gordon, Bernard**
HORROR EXPRESS

**Gordon, Bert I.**
PICTURE MOMMY DEAD

**Gordon, Lawrence**
JEKYLL AND HYDE ... TOGETHER
AGAIN

**Gordon, Richard**
BEYOND THE FOG
DEVIL DOLL
HORROR HOSPITAL

**Grais, Michael**
POLTERGEIST II

**Graver, Gary**
TRICK OR TREATS

**Green, Hilton A.**
PSYCHO II

PSYCHO III

**Green, Pat**
DIE, MONSTER, DIE

**Greenberg, Harold**
DEATH SHIP
TERROR TRAIN

**Greenwald, Stephen R.**
AMITYVILLE II: THE POSSESSION

**Grefe, William**
STANLEY

**Grissmer, John**
SCALPEL

**Gross, Jerry**
I DRINK YOUR BLOOD

**Gruskoff, Michael**
YOUNG FRANKENSTEIN

**Guber, Peter**
WITCHES OF EASTWICK, THE

**Guilleaume, Alain C.**
DAUGHTERS OF DARKNESS

**Gurvis, Anthony N.**
GIRLS NIGHT OUT

**Gutowski, Gene**
REPULSION

**Haines, Richard W.**
SPLATTER UNIVERSITY

**Halperin, Edward**
WHITE ZOMBIE
REVOLT OF THE ZOMBIES

**Hamady, Ron**
FADE TO BLACK

**Hamilton, Judd**
LAST HORROR FILM, THE

**Hammer, Robert**
DON'T ANSWER THE PHONE

**Hammill, Ellen**
DON'T GO IN THE HOUSE

**Hamori, Andras**
GATE, THE

**Hannawalt, Charles**
DEMENTIA 13

**Hardman, Karl**
NIGHT OF THE LIVING DEAD

**Harris, Graham**
BEAST IN THE CELLAR, THE

**Harris, Jack H.**
EQUINOX

**Harrison, Paul**
HOUSE OF SEVEN CORPSES, THE

**Harrop, Christopher**
AMERICAN GOTHIC

**Harvey, Herk**
CARNIVAL OF SOULS

**Hashimoto, Richard**
BEETLEJUICE

**Hawkins, Don**
RAWHEAD REX

**Hay, Rod**
INN OF THE DAMNED

**Hayden, Mathew**
UNHOLY, THE

**Heller, Paul**
PACK, THE

**Helpern, David**
DEAD HEAT

**Henderson, Graham**
RETURN OF THE LIVING DEAD

**Herman, Norman T.**
LEGEND OF HELL HOUSE, THE

**Heroux, Claude**
BROOD, THE
OF UNKNOWN ORIGIN
SCANNERS
VISITING HOURS
VIDEODROME
UNCANNY, THE

**Herskovic, Pat**
DEADLY BLESSING

**Herz, Michael**
CLASS OF NUKE 'EM HIGH
TOXIC AVENGER, THE

**Herzog, Werner**
NOSFERATU, THE VAMPIRE

**Hessler, Gordon**
OBLONG BOX, THE

**Heyward, Louis M.**
ABOMINABLE DR. PHIBES, THE
DOCTOR PHIBES RISES AGAIN
MURDERS IN THE RUE MORGUE

**Heyworth, Malcolm**
BLOOD ON SATAN'S CLAW, THE

**Hildalgo-Gato, Juan**
DEATH CURSE OF TARTU

**Hill, Debra**
FOG, THE
DEAD ZONE, THE
HALLOWEEN II
HALLOWEEN III: SEASON OF THE
WITCH
HALLOWEEN

**Hinds, Anthony**
CURSE OF THE WEREWOLF, THE
CURSE OF FRANKENSTEIN, THE
EVIL OF FRANKENSTEIN, THE
DIE! DIE! MY DARLING
HORROR OF DRACULA, THE

**Hirsh, Richard**
I WAS A TEENAGE ZOMBIE

**Hitchcock, Alfred**
BIRDS, THE
PSYCHO

**Hitzig, Rupert**
JAWS 3-D
WOLFEN

**Hooper, Tobe**
TEXAS CHAIN SAW MASSACRE, THE

**Houck, Jr., Joy**
NIGHT OF BLOODY HORROR

**Houghton, Don**
LEGEND OF THE SEVEN GOLDEN
VAMPIRES, THE

**Hoven, Adrian**
MARK OF THE DEVIL

**Hreljanovic, Doro Vlado**
JUST BEFORE DAWN

**Hurd, Gale Anne**
BAD DREAMS

**Hurley, James F.**
SOMETHING WEIRD

**Ibanez, Juan**
HOUSE OF EVIL

**Ievins, Edgar**
BASKET CASE
BRAIN DAMAGE

**Jackson, Donald**
DEMON LOVER, THE

**Jacobs, Arthur P.**
GIANT FROM THE UNKNOWN

**Jaffe, Herb**
FRIGHT NIGHT

**Jaffe, Robert**
MOTEL HELL

**Jaffe, Steven-Charles**
MOTEL HELL
NEAR DARK

**Jeffreys, Arthur**
DEMENTED

**Jones, Amy**
SLUMBER PARTY MASSACRE, THE

**Jones, Don**
FOREST, THE

**Jones, L.Q.**
BROTHERHOOD OF SATAN, THE

**Kahnert, Paul**
DEADLY EYES

**Kaiser, Norman F.**
LAST HOUSE ON DEAD END STREET

**Kalmanowicz, Max**
CHILDREN, THE

**Kameron, Pete**
YOU BETTER WATCH OUT

**Kaplan, J.S.**
ASSAULT ON PRECINCT 13

**Karr, Tom**
DEATHDREAM

**Kastner, Elliott**
ANGEL HEART
NOMADS

**Katz, Peter**
DON'T LOOK NOW

**Katzka, Gabriel**
BEAST WITHIN, THE

**Katzman, Sam**
BLACK DRAGONS
APE MAN, THE
CORPSE VANISHES, THE
BOWERY AT MIDNIGHT

GHOSTS ON THE LOOSE
INVISIBLE GHOST, THE
ZOMBIES OF MORA TAU

**Kaufman, Charles**
MOTHER'S DAY

**Kaufman, Lloyd**
CLASS OF NUKE 'EM HIGH
TOXIC AVENGER, THE

**Keating, Pierce J.**
GIRLS SCHOOL SCREAMERS

**Keller, Max**
DEADLY BLESSING

**Keller, Micheline**
DEADLY BLESSING

**Kemeny, John**
GATE, THE
WRAITH, THE

**Kesten, Stephen F.**
AMITYVILLE 3-D

**Kevan, Jack**
MONSTER OF PIEDRAS BLANCAS,
THE

**Keys, Anthony Nelson**
GORGON, THE

**Kimmel, Anne**
EATING RAOUL

**King, George**
DEMON BARBER OF FLEET STREET,
THE

**Kirby, John Mason**
SAVAGE WEEKEND

**Kirby, Terence**
CHILDREN OF THE CORN

**Kirkwood, Gene**
KEEP, THE

**Kirman, Leonard**
CARNIVAL OF BLOOD

**Kirschner, David**
CHILD'S PLAY

**Kleiner, Burt**
YOU BETTER WATCH OUT

**Kobritz, Richard**
CHRISTINE

**Koch, Jr., Howard W.**
KEEP, THE

**Kohlberg, Stanford S.**
BLOOD FEAST

**Kohn, John**
THEATRE OF BLOOD

**Kong, Jackie**
BLOOD DINER

**Konvitz, Jeffrey**
SILENT NIGHT, BLOODY NIGHT
SENTINEL, THE

**Kraike, Michael**
OCTAMAN

**Kramreither, Anthony**
HUMONGOUS

# PRODUCERS

**Krantz, Steve**
JENNIFER

**Kravitz, Michael**
MOTHER'S DAY

**Kubrick, Stanley**
SHINING, THE

**Kuhnlenz, Wolfgang**
BLOOD DEMON

**Kurta, Paul**
STUFF, THE
RETURN TO SALEM'S LOT, A

**La Loggia, Charles M.**
FEAR NO EVIL

**La Loggia, Frank**
FEAR NO EVIL
LADY IN WHITE

**La Marca, Andrew G.**
LADY IN WHITE

**Ladd, David**
SERPENT AND THE RAINBOW, THE

**Laemmle, Carl**
BLACK CAT, THE
BRIDE OF FRANKENSTEIN, THE
DRACULA
MUMMY, THE
PHANTOM OF THE OPERA, THE
INVISIBLE MAN, THE
HUNCHBACK OF NOTRE DAME, THE
FRANKENSTEIN

**Lake, Vernoica**
FLESH FEAST

**Landis, John**
TWILIGHT ZONE—THE MOVIE

**Lane, Steven**
HOWLING II . . . YOUR SISTER IS A
WEREWOLF

**Langdon, Donald**
BLOOD TIDE

**Lankford, T.L.**
SCALPS

**Lasky, Gil**
SPIDER BABY

**Lawrence, Marc**
DADDY'S DEADLY DARLING

**Le Tet, Robert**
NEXT OF KIN

**Lecocq, Charles**
DEVIL'S NIGHTMARE, THE

**Lederer, Richard**
EXORCIST II: THE HERETIC

**Lee, Rowland V.**
SON OF FRANKENSTEIN

**Leipzig, Matt**
DEADLY DREAMS

**Leone, Alfred**
BARON BLOOD
HOUSE OF EXORCISM, THE

**Lepiner, Michael**
KILLER PARTY

**Levine, Joseph E.**
MAGIC

**Levine, Richard P.**
MAGIC

**Levine, Terry**
DR. BUTCHER, M.D.

**Levinson, Mark**
TEEN WOLF

**Levy, David**
MONSTER IN THE CLOSET

**Levy, Gene**
HYSTERICAL

**Levy, Jefery**
GHOULIES

**Lewis, Herschell Gordon**
BLOOD FEAST
WIZARD OF GORE, THE
GRUESOME TWOSOME

**Lewis, Jerry**
NUTTY PROFESSOR, THE

**Lewis, Linda**
REVENGE

**Lewis, Paul**
HOUSE OF SEVEN CORPSES, THE
WEREWOLVES ON WHEELS

**Lewis, Robert L.J.**
SUPERSTITION

**Lewton, Val**
BEDLAM
CURSE OF THE CAT PEOPLE, THE
CAT PEOPLE
BODY SNATCHER, THE
ISLE OF THE DEAD
I WALKED WITH A ZOMBIE
SEVENTH VICTIM, THE
LEOPARD MAN, THE

**Link, Andre**
HAPPY BIRTHDAY TO ME
MY BLOODY VALENTINE
THEY CAME FROM WITHIN

**Lipstadt, Aaron**
SLUMBER PARTY MASSACRE, THE

**Lisson, Mark**
RETURN TO HORROR HIGH

**Litto, George**
DRESSED TO KILL
BLOW OUT

**Locke, Peter**
HILLS HAVE EYES II, THE
HILLS HAVE EYES, THE

**Lofton, Terry**
NAIL GUN MASSACRE

**Lommel, Ulli**
BOOGEYMAN II
BOOGEY MAN, THE
DEVONSVILLE TERROR, THE

**Louzil, Eric**
SHADOWS RUN BLACK

**Lowry, A. Hunt**
HUMANOIDS FROM THE DEEP

**Lustig, William**
MANIAC

**Lynch, David**
ERASERHEAD

**Lyon, Earle**
CASTLE OF EVIL
INVISIBLE STRANGLER, THE

**McCauley, John**
RATTLERS

**McCrann, Chuck**
BLOODEATERS

**McCullough, Jr., Jim**
MOUNTAINTOP MOTEL MASSACRE

**McCullough, Sr., Jim**
CREATURE FROM BLACK LAKE, THE
MOUNTAINTOP MOTEL MASSACRE

**MacDonald, Wallace**
BEFORE I HANG
MAN THEY COULD NOT HANG, THE

**McElroy, Hal**
RAZORBACK

**McEuen, William E.**
MAN WITH TWO BRAINS, THE

**Machlis, Neil A.**
MONSTER SQUAD, THE

**Macready, Michael**
COUNT YORGA, VAMPIRE
TERROR HOUSE

**Madero, Robert**
MAUSOLEUM

**Magar, Guy**
RETRIBUTION

**Magder, Gary**
TERMINAL CHOICE

**Magder, Zale**
PHOBIA

**Magness, Kerry**
NIGHT OF THE COBRA WOMAN

**Manasian, Steve**
PIECES

**Manasse, George**
BLUE SUNSHINE
HE KNOWS YOU'RE ALONE
SQUIRM

**Mancuso, Jr., Frank**
APRIL FOOL'S DAY
FRIDAY THE 13TH—THE FINAL
CHAPTER
FRIDAY THE 13TH PART III

**Mann, Stanley**
THEATRE OF BLOOD

**Mannix, Edward J.**
DEVIL DOLL, THE
MARK OF THE VAMPIRE

**Marconi, Chris**
POINT OF TERROR

**Marcos, Arturo**
SCREAMING DEAD, THE

**Margolin, Alan**
BLOODSUCKING FREAKS

Marks, Harvey
NIGHT OF THE COBRA WOMAN

Marlis, Rand
SCARED TO DEATH

Marshall, Alan
ANGEL HEART

Marshall, Frank
POLTERGEIST

Marshek, Archie S.
SON OF KONG

Martin, Lawrence
GREAT ALLIGATOR, THE
SCREAMERS

Masini, Giovanni
GATES OF HELL, THE

Maslon, Jimmy
BLOOD DINER

Mastorakis, Nico
BLOOD TIDE

Matalon, Eddy
CATHY'S CURSE

Mathieu, N.
CATHY'S CURSE

Matonak, Ron
SLAUGHTERHOUSE

Mattison, Ernest
WITCHCRAFT THROUGH THE AGES

Mazzola, Eugene
BUTCHER, BAKER (NIGHTMARE
MAKER)

Meisel, Myron
FINAL EXAM

Melniker, Benjamin
SWAMP THING

Meltzer, Michael
DEAD HEAT

Mendez, Luis
CITY OF THE WALKING DEAD

Michaels, Joel B.
CHANGELING, THE

Michaels, John
SPLATTER UNIVERSITY

Michalakias, John Elias
I WAS A TEENAGE ZOMBIE

Mikels, Ted V.
BLOOD ORGY OF THE SHE-DEVILS
CORPSE GRINDERS, THE
WORM EATERS, THE

Miller, Arnold Louis
BLOOD BEAST TERROR, THE
CONQUEROR WORM, THE

Miller, Ron
WATCHER IN THE WOODS, THE

Miller, Stephen
MY BLOODY VALENTINE

Minasian, Steve
DON'T OPEN TILL CHRISTMAS
SLAUGHTER HIGH

Miner, Steve
FRIDAY THE 13TH PART II

Mirisch, Walter
DRACULA

Mishkin, Lew
CARNAGE

Mishkin, William
BLOODTHIRSTY BUTCHERS
MAN WITH TWO HEADS, THE
RATS ARE COMING! THE
WEREWOLVES ARE HERE!, THE
TORTURE DUNGEON

Monash, Paul
CARRIE

Monka, Paul
SPIDER BABY

Montoro, Edward E.
DAY OF THE ANIMALS

Moore, Alvy
BROTHERHOOD OF SATAN, THE

Mora, Philippe
HOWLING III, THE

Morgan, George J.
THRILL KILLERS, THE

Moss, Jr., Charles B.
LET'S SCARE JESSICA TO DEATH

Moss, Lou
BLOOD AND BLACK LACE

Muckler, Craig
MICROWAVE MASSACRE

Mulligan, Robert
OTHER, THE

Muren, Dennis
EQUINOX

Murphey, Michael S.
TRICK OR TREAT
SUPERNATURALS, THE

Murphy, Dennis
FRIDAY THE 13TH PART II

Murray, K. Gordon
WRESTLING WOMEN VS. THE AZTEC
MUMMY, THE

Naar, Joseph T.
BLACULA
SCREAM, BLACULA, SCREAM

Nalevansky, Steven
BLOOD BEACH

Neufeld, Mace
TRANSYLVANIA 6-5000

Neufeld, Sigmund
DEAD MEN WALK
MAD MONSTER, THE

Neumann, Kurt
FLY, THE

Newbrook, Peter
INCENSE FOR THE DAMNED

Nicholson, Jack
TERROR, THE

Nicholson, James H.
DUNWICH HORROR, THE
WHO SLEW AUNTIE ROO?

North, Robert
BLACK ROOM, THE

Nugent, Ginny
MUNCHIES

O'Rourke, James C.
SCHLOCK

Obrow, Jeffrey
DORM THAT DRIPPED BLOOD, THE
POWER, THE

Ohman, Kip
HITCHER, THE

Olea, Antonio Perez
BLOOD SPATTERED BRIDE, THE

Olson, Gerald T.
BLOODY BIRTHDAY

Orr, James R.
WITCHFIRE

Owensby, Earl
WOLFMAN

Pariser, Alfred
HAUNTING OF JULIA, THE

Parker, John
DEMENTIA
MIRRORS

Parkinson, Tom
CRUCIBLE OF TERROR
DISCIPLE OF DEATH

Parkyn, Leslie
CIRCUS OF HORRORS

Parsons, Lindsley
KING OF THE ZOMBIES

Paterson, Iain
FRIDAY THE 13TH PART VII—THE NEW
BLOOD

Paul, Bill
DEADTIME STORIES

Paulsen, David
SAVAGE WEEKEND

Pearlman, Nan
HE KNOWS YOU'RE ALONE

Pepperman, Paul
PHANTASM

Perilli, Frank Ray
DRACULA'S DOG

Perkins, George
TEEN WOLF

Peters, Brooke L.
UNEARTHLY, THE

Peters, Jon
WITCHES OF EASTWICK, THE

Pickard, Therese
BORN OF FIRE

Picker, David V.
MAN WITH TWO BRAINS, THE

Pierce, Charles B.
BOGGY CREEK II

LEGEND OF BOGGY CREEK, THE
TOWN THAT DREADED SUNDOWN,
THE

**Pierson, Mark**
ELVIRA: MISTRESS OF THE DARK

**Pivar, Ben**
BRUTE MAN, THE

**Pollexfen, Jack**
ATOMIC BRAIN, THE
DAUGHTER OF DR. JEKYLL

**Polsky, Abe**
BABY, THE

**Polsky, Milton**
BABY, THE

**Pommer, Erich**
CABINET OF DR. CALIGARI, THE

**Ponti, Carlo**
ANDY WARHOL'S FRANKENSTEIN
ANDY WARHOL'S DRACULA
TORSO

**Powell, Michael**
PEEPING TOM

**Powers, Derek**
FUNHOUSE, THE

**Pozhke, John G.**
SPASMS

**Pressman, Edward R.**
HAND, THE
PHANTOM OF THE PARADISE
SISTERS

**Price, Lorin E.**
NIGHT OF THE ZOMBIES

**Pupillo, Massimo**
DEVIL'S WEDDING NIGHT, THE

**Quandour, Mohy**
SPECTRE OF EDGAR ALLAN POE, THE

**Quested, John**
AMERICAN GOTHIC

**Quezada, Roberto A.**
PHANTASM II

**Raley, Alice**
MOVIE HOUSE MASSACRE

**Randall, Dick**
DON'T OPEN TILL CHRISTMAS
PIECES
SLAUGHTER HIGH

**Randall, Robert**
HOUSE OF FREAKS

**Rankin, Jr., Arthur**
MAD MONSTER PARTY

**Ransohoff, Martin**
NIGHTWING

**Rassam, Jean-Pierre**
ANDY WARHOL'S FRANKENSTEIN
ANDY WARHOL'S DRACULA

**Rebar, Alex**
DEMENTED

**Red, Eric**
NEAR DARK

**Redinger, Donald**
MIDNIGHT

**Redondo, Modesto Perez**
HOUSE OF PSYCHOTIC WOMEN, THE

**Reitman, Ivan**
GHOSTBUSTERS
THEY CAME FROM WITHIN

**Relph, Michael**
MAN WHO HAUNTED HIMSELF, THE

**Reyre, Marie-Laure**
POSSESSION

**Risher, Sara**
NIGHTMARE ON ELM STREET, A
NIGHTMARE ON ELM STREET 3:
DREAM WARRIORS, A
NIGHTMARE ON ELM STREET PART 2:
FREDDY'S REVENGE, A

**Rive, Kenneth**
DEVIL DOLL

**Rivera, Jules**
BERSERKER

**Roffman, Julian**
PYX, THE

**Romero, Eddie**
MAD DOCTOR OF BLOOD ISLAND,
THE

**Romero, Nancy M.**
HUNGRY WIVES

**Romero, Salvadore**
PEOPLE WHO OWN THE DARK

**Rosen, Robert L.**
PROPHECY

**Rosenberg, Max J.**
BEAST MUST DIE, THE
ASYLUM
AND NOW THE SCREAMING STARTS
DR. TERROR'S HOUSE OF HORRORS
HOUSE THAT DRIPPED BLOOD, THE
FROM BEYOND THE GRAVE
TALES FROM THE CRYPT
SCREAM AND SCREAM AGAIN
VAULT OF HORROR, THE
TORTURE GARDEN
MADHOUSE

**Rosenberg, Richard K.**
ALICE, SWEET ALICE

**Rosenfelt, Scott M.**
TEEN WOLF

**Rosman, Mark**
HOUSE ON SORORITY ROW, THE

**Rossi, Giorgio**
BEYOND THE DOOR

**Roth, Joe**
FINAL TERROR, THE

**Roth, Leon**
I DISMEMBER MAMA

**Rovins, Randy**
PREY, THE

**Rubens, Percival**
DEMON, THE

**Rubinstein, Richard P.**
DAWN OF THE DEAD
CREEPSHOW
DAY OF THE DEAD
MARTIN

**Ruskin, Susan**
HAUNTED HONEYMOON

**Russell, Charles**
HEARSE, THE

**Russell, Ken**
LAIR OF THE WHITE WORM, THE

**Rustam, Mardi**
EATEN ALIVE
PSYCHIC KILLER

**Saeta, Eddie**
DOCTOR DEATH: SEEKER OF SOULS

**Saland, Ronald**
AMITYVILLE HORROR, THE

**Salazar, Abel**
LIVING HEAD, THE

**Salazar, Alfredo**
NIGHT OF THE BLOODY APES

**Sales, Gary**
MADMAN

**Saletri, Frank R.**
BLACKENSTEIN

**Samuels, Maxine**
PYX, THE

**Sanciriaco, Manuel Cano**
HATCHET FOR A HONEYMOON

**Sanders, Angela**
ESCAPES

**Sangster, Jimmy**
HORROR OF FRANKENSTEIN, THE
MANIAC

**Santaniello, Oscar**
GRIM REAPER, THE

**Sargent, Joseph**
JAWS: THE REVENGE

**Scardamaglia, Elio**
MURDER CLINIC, THE

**Scarpelli, Henry**
FORCED ENTRY

**Schectman, Jeff**
PIRANHA II: THE SPAWNING

**Scheinman, Andrew**
AWAKENING, THE

**Schlesinger, John**
BELIEVERS, THE

**Schmidt, Marlene**
MORTUARY

**Schneider, Harold**
ENTITY, THE

**Schnitzer, Robert Allen**
PREMONITION, THE

**Schoedsack, Ernest B.**
KING KONG

**Schroeder, Michael**
ONE DARK NIGHT

**Schulman, Nina**
WEREWOLF OF WASHINGTON

**Schultz, Chris**
GANJA AND HESS

**Schumacher, Martha**
CAT'S EYE
MAXIMUM OVERDRIVE
STEPHEN KING'S SILVER BULLET
KING KONG LIVES

**Schwartz, John D.**
SUPERSTITION

**Scott, Darin**
OFFSPRING, THE

**Sear, Walter**
BLOOD SISTERS

**Segall, Stuart**
DRIVE-IN MASSACRE

**Sellier, Jr., Charles E.**
BOOGENS, THE

**Sen, Bachoo**
NIGHTMARE WEEKEND

**Sewell, Vernon**
GHOST SHIP

**Shafer, Martin**
AWAKENING, THE

**Shaw, Lou**
CRYPT OF THE LIVING DEAD

**Shaw, Vee King**
LEGEND OF THE SEVEN GOLDEN
VAMPIRES, THE

**Shaye, Robert**
ALONE IN THE DARK
NIGHTMARE ON ELM STREET, A
NIGHTMARE ON ELM STREET 3:
DREAM WARRIORS, A
NIGHTMARE ON ELM STREET PART 2:
FREDDY'S REVENGE, A
MY DEMON LOVER
NIGHTMARE ON ELM STREET 4: THE
DREAM MASTER, A

**Sheldon, David**
GRIZZLY
JUST BEFORE DAWN

**Shelton, Gil**
SCARED TO DEATH

**Shenck, Aubrey**
FRANKENSTEIN 1970

**Shepard, Richard A.**
HUNGER, THE

**Sherman, Robert M.**
DEADLY FRIEND

**Sherman, Sam**
BRAIN OF BLOOD

**Shipman, Kenneth**
BURKE AND HARE

**Shonteff, Lindsay**
DEVIL DOLL

**Shusett, Ronald**
DEAD AND BURIED

**Silva, Jerry**
SLEEPAWAY CAMP
SLEEPAWAY CAMP 2: UNHAPPY
CAMPERS

**Silver, Timothy**
FRIDAY THE 13TH, PART V—A NEW
BEGINNING

**Silverstein, Elliot**
CAR, THE

**Simpson, Michael A.**
SLEEPAWAY CAMP 2: UNHAPPY
CAMPERS

**Simpson, Peter**
CURTAINS
HELLO MARY LOU, PROM NIGHT II
PROM NIGHT

**Singer, Robert**
CUJO

**Singer, Steven L.**
MEAT CLEAVER MASSACRE

**Singer, Thomas**
MICROWAVE MASSACRE

**Skeggs, Roy**
TO THE DEVIL A DAUGHTER

**Smedley-Aston, Brian**
VAMPYRES, DAUGHTERS OF
DRACULA

**Smedley-Aston, Michael**
THEATRE OF DEATH

**Smith, Brian J.**
DEATHROW GAMESHOW

**Smith, Howard**
PUMPKINHEAD

**Smith, Ira N.**
AMITYVILLE II: THE POSSESSION

**Smith, Maurice**
SPASMS

**Smith, Stirling W.**
MIRRORS

**Smithee, Allen**
STUDENT BODIES

**Snell, Peter**
WICKER MAN, THE

**Sneller, Jeffrey**
KINGDOM OF THE SPIDERS
IN THE SHADOW OF KILIMANJARO

**Sobel, Harold**
MASSACRE AT CENTRAL HIGH

**Soisson, Joel**
TRICK OR TREAT
SUPERNATURALS, THE

**Solo, Robert**
AWAKENING, THE

**Solomons, Ralph**
VIRGIN WITCH, THE

**Sotos, Jim**
FORCED ENTRY
SWEET SIXTEEN

**Spielberg, Steven**
POLTERGEIST

TWILIGHT ZONE—THE MOVIE

**Stader, Paul**
IT'S ALIVE III: ISLAND OF THE ALIVE

**Stallone, Patricia A.**
PULSE

**Stanley, John**
NIGHTMARE IN BLOOD

**Steensland, David**
ESCAPES

**Steloff, Skip**
ISLAND OF DR. MOREAU, THE

**Stephen, A.C.**
ORGY OF THE DEAD

**Storey, Ray**
HOUSE ON SKULL MOUNTAIN, THE

**Streiner, Russell**
NIGHT OF THE LIVING DEAD

**Streit, David**
PROWLER, THE

**Style, Michael**
LUST FOR A VAMPIRE
VAMPIRE LOVERS, THE
TWINS OF EVIL

**Subotsky, Milton**
BEAST MUST DIE, THE
ASYLUM
AND NOW THE SCREAMING STARTS
DR. TERROR'S HOUSE OF HORRORS
HOUSE THAT DRIPPED BLOOD, THE
FROM BEYOND THE GRAVE
MONSTER CLUB, THE
TALES FROM THE CRYPT
SCREAM AND SCREAM AGAIN
VAULT OF HORROR, THE
TORTURE GARDEN
MADHOUSE
HORROR HOTEL

**Sussan, Herbert**
NIGHTMARE IN WAX

**Swartz, Charles S.**
VELVET VAMPIRE, THE

**Tabet, Sylvio**
EVILSPEAK

**Talalay, Rachel**
NIGHTMARE ON ELM STREET 4: THE
DREAM MASTER, A

**Tapert, Robert G.**
EVIL DEAD 2: DEAD BY DAWN
EVIL DEAD, THE

**Tatosian, Michele**
SLEEPAWAY CAMP

**Taylor, Barbi**
ROAD GAMES

**Taylor, Donald**
HORROR HOTEL

**Temple-Smith, John**
ISLAND OF DR. MOREAU, THE

**Tennant, Timothy D.**
GHOST TOWN

**Tenney, Del**
CURSE OF THE LIVING CORPSE, THE

HORROR OF PARTY BEACH, THE

**Tenser, Mark**
HEARSE, THE

**Tenser, Tony**
BLOOD BEAST TERROR, THE

**Thomas, Jeremy**
SHOUT, THE

**Thomas, Peter**
FROGS

**Thor, Jon-Mikl**
ROCK 'N' ROLL NIGHTMARE

**Towers, Harry Alan**
COUNT DRACULA
DORIAN GRAY
HOWLING IV: THE ORIGINAL
NIGHTMARE

**Trane, Reuben**
SHOCK WAVES

**Traxler, Stephen**
DRACULA'S WIDOW

**Tromberg, Sheldon**
REDEEMER, THE

**Tucci, Ugo**
ZOMBIE

**Unger, Anthony**
UNSEEN, THE

**Uslan, Michael E.**
SWAMP THING

**Van Horn, Kelly**
LAST RITES

**van Leuwen, Chako**
PIRANHA II: THE SPAWNING

**Vandom, John**
DRACULA VS. FRANKENSTEIN

**Vasile, Juri**
BEYOND THE DOOR II

**Vergara, Luis Enrique**
HOUSE OF EVIL
FEAR CHAMBER, THE

**Vetter, Charles**
CORRIDORS OF BLOOD

**Victor, Mark**
POLTERGEIST II

**Villard, Dimitri**
FRANKENSTEIN GENERAL HOSPITAL

**Vincenzoni, Luciano**
ORCA

**Viskin, Roberto**
DR. TARR'S TORTURE DUNGEON

**Wadsack, Richard H.**
SCREAMS OF A WINTER NIGHT

**Waggner, George**
FRANKENSTEIN MEETS THE WOLF
MAN
PHANTOM OF THE OPERA
WOLF MAN, THE

**Wakatsuki, Shigeru**
KWAIDAN

**Walker, Charles**
DR. BLACK AND MR. HYDE

**Walker, David**
HOUSE OF WHIPCORD

**Walker, Peter**
CONFESSIONAL, THE
FLESH AND BLOOD SHOW, THE
SCHIZO
FRIGHTMARE

**Walters, Martin**
BLUE MONKEY

**Waterstreet, Charles**
HOWLING III, THE

**Watkins, John L.**
NIGHTMARE

**Weeks, Stephen**
GHOST STORY

**Weinbach, Robert D.**
CAULDRON OF BLOOD

**Weinman, Richard C.**
PUMPKINHEAD

**Weinstein, Harvey**
BURNING, THE

**Weintraub, Fred**
PACK, THE

**Weintraub, Joseph**
SCALPEL

**Weis, Jack**
MARDI GRAS MASSACRE

**Weisberg, Rochelle**
DRILLER KILLER

**Weissbourd, Burt**
HAUNTS
GHOST STORY

**Welles, Mel**
LADY FRANKENSTEIN

**Weston, Armand**
NESTING, THE

**Weston, Eric**
EVILSPEAK

**Wheat, Jim**
SILENT SCREAM

**Wheat, Ken**
SILENT SCREAM

**White, Sam**
RETURN OF THE VAMPIRE, THE

**Williams, Gary**
LOVE BUTCHER, THE

**Wilson, Donald**
KEEPER, THE

**Wilson, James L.**
SCREAMS OF A WINTER NIGHT

**Wilson, Larry**
BEETLEJUICE

**Winant, Scott**
INITIATION, THE

**Winner, Michael**
SENTINEL, THE

**Winters, David**
LAST HORROR FILM, THE

**Wintle, Julian**
CIRCUS OF HORRORS

**Wise, Robert**
HAUNTING, THE

**Wizan, Joe**
AUDREY ROSE

**Wood, Edward**
NIGHT OF THE GHOULS

**Wood, James**
DR. JEKYLL'S DUNGEON OF DEATH

**Woolner, Bernard A.**
HILLBILLYS IN A HAUNTED HOUSE

**Wright, Patrick**
FRIGHTMARE

**Wright, Tallie**
FRIGHTMARE

**Wynn, Bob**
CELLAR DWELLER

**Yablans, Frank**
FURY, THE

**Yablans, Irwin**
HELL NIGHT
PRISON

**Yamin, Robert**
MARY, MARY, BLOODY MARY

**Yanne, Jean**
ANDY WARHOL'S FRANKENSTEIN
ANDY WARHOL'S DRACULA

**Young, Aida**
HANDS OF THE RIPPER
SCARS OF DRACULA, THE

**Young, Les**
TERROR

**Younkins, Jerry**
DEMON LOVER, THE

**Yuzna, Brian**
DOLLS
FROM BEYOND
RE-ANIMATOR

**Zacaria, Mario Z.**
NIGHT OF A THOUSAND CATS, THE

**Zacciarello, Giuseppe**
TWITCH OF THE DEATH NERVE

**Zacharias, Alfred**
DEMONOID

**Zanuck, Richard D.**
JAWS II
JAWS

**Zbeda, Joseph**
I SPIT ON YOUR GRAVE

**Zerra, Ronald**
EYES OF A STRANGER

**Zimbert, Jonathan A.**
MONSTER SQUAD, THE

**Zito, Joseph**
PROWLER, THE

## SCREENWRITERS

**Abbott, W.J.**
SCARED TO DEATH

**Abdulla, Raficq**
BORN OF FIRE

**Abraham, Edward**
MONSTER CLUB, THE

**Abraham, Valerie**
MONSTER CLUB, THE

**Ackerman, Forrest J.**
MAD MONSTER PARTY

**Actors, Allen J.**
TERROR HOUSE

**Adlum, Ed**
SHRIEK OF THE MUTILATED
INVASION OF THE BLOOD FARMERS

**Albright, Carlton J.**
CHILDREN, THE

**Alcocer, Santos**
CAULDRON OF BLOOD

**Ambrose, David**
SURVIVOR

**Amiel, J.J.**
DAUGHTERS OF DARKNESS

**Anderson, Clyde**
MONSTER DOG

**Andrews, Robert D.**
BEFORE I HANG

**Angel, Mike**
PSYCHIC KILLER

**Aranda, Vincent**
BLOOD SPATTERED BRIDE, THE

**Argento, Dario**
UNSANE
BIRD WITH THE CRYSTAL PLUMAGE,
THE
CREEPERS
DEMONS 2: THE NIGHTMARE
RETURNS
DEMONS
INFERNO

**Argyle, John**
CHAMBER OF HORRORS
HUMAN MONSTER, THE

**Armstrong, Michael**
SCREAMTIME

**Artzi, Ami**
SILENT NIGHT, BLOODY NIGHT

**Arywitz, Mark L.**
JUST BEFORE DAWN

**Ashman, Howard**
LITTLE SHOP OF HORRORS

**Ashton, James**
DEVIL'S RAIN, THE

**Assonitis, Ovidio**
BEYOND THE DOOR

**Atkins, Peter**
HELLBOUND: HELLRAISER II

**Austin, Michael**
SHOUT, THE

**Avedis, Howard**
MORTUARY

**Avrech, Robert J.**
BODY DOUBLE

**Aykroyd, Dan**
GHOSTBUSTERS

**Babbes, Thom**
DEADLY DREAMS

**Bach, Danilo**
APRIL FOOL'S DAY

**Baines, John**
DEAD OF NIGHT

**Bairn, William A.**
BARON BLOOD

**Baker, Tom**
CONQUEROR WORM, THE

**Balch, Anthony**
HORROR HOSPITAL

**Balderston, John L.**
BRIDE OF FRANKENSTEIN, THE
MUMMY, THE
FRANKENSTEIN

**Baldwin, Earl**
DOCTOR X

**Ballard, John**
FRIDAY THE 13TH . . . THE ORPHAN

**Ballinger, Bill S.**
STRANGLER, THE

**Barbera, Neal**
PROWLER, THE
TOO SCARED TO SCREAM

**Barbieri, Francesco**
BEYOND THE DOOR II

**Barclay, George**
DEVIL DOLL

**Barich, Robert**
MAUSOLEUM

**Barilla, Joe**
BLOOD AND BLACK LACE

**Barker, Clive**
HELLRAISER
RAWHEAD REX

**Barr, Matthew**
DEADLY BLESSING

**Barrie, M.E.**
FRANKENSTEIN'S DAUGHTER

**Bartel, Paul**
EATING RAOUL

**Barwood, Hal**
WARNING SIGN

**Bassan, Giuseppe**
DEEP RED

**Baum, Thomas**
SENDER, THE

**Bava, Lamberto**
BEYOND THE DOOR II

DEMONS 2: THE NIGHTMARE
RETURNS
DEMONS

**Bava, Mario**
BLOOD AND BLACK LACE
BLACK SABBATH
HOUSE OF EXORCISM, THE
HATCHET FOR A HONEYMOON
TWITCH OF THE DEATH NERVE

**Baxt, George**
CIRCUS OF HORRORS
HORROR HOTEL

**Bayonas, Jose Luis**
CAULDRON OF BLOOD

**Beaird, John**
MY BLOODY VALENTINE

**Beaumont, Charles**
MASQUE OF THE RED DEATH, THE
PREMATURE BURIAL, THE

**Bechard, Gorman**
PSYCHOS IN LOVE

**Befilacqua, Alberto**
ATOM AGE VAMPIRE

**Behm, Marc**
HOSPITAL MASSACRE

**Behnke, Dietmar**
COUNT DRACULA

**Bell, Neal**
TERMINAL CHOICE

**Bellwood, Peter**
PHOBIA

**Belson, Jerry**
JEKYLL AND HYDE . . . TOGETHER
AGAIN

**Benchley, Peter**
JAWS

**Benest, Glenn M.**
DEADLY BLESSING

**Bennett, Charles**
CURSE OF THE DEMON

**Bennett, Wallace C.**
SILENT SCREAM

**Beranger, Clara S.**
DR. JEKYLL AND MR. HYDE

**Bercovici, Luca**
GHOULIES

**Bernds, Edward**
RETURN OF THE FLY

**Bevilacqua, Alberto**
BLACK SABBATH

**Bigari, Walter**
DEVIL'S WEDDING NIGHT, THE

**Bigelow, Kathryn**
NEAR DARK

**Binder, Lou**
HORROR OF PARTY BEACH, THE

**Birkin, Andrew**
FINAL CONFLICT, THE

**Bishop, Wes**
RACE WITH THE DEVIL

**Black, Shane**
MONSTER SQUAD, THE

**Black, Terry**
DEAD HEAT

**Blackburn, Richard**
EATING RAOUL

**Blatty, William Peter**
EXORCIST, THE
NINTH CONFIGURATION, THE

**Blees, Robert**
DOCTOR PHIBES RISES AGAIN
FROGS
WHO SLEW AUNTIE ROO?

**Bleich, Bill**
HEARSE, THE

**Bloch, Robert**
ASYLUM
HOUSE THAT DRIPPED BLOOD, THE
STRAIT-JACKET
TORTURE GARDEN

**Block, Larry**
FUNHOUSE, THE

**Bloom, Eric L.**
EYES OF A STRANGER

**Bloom, Jeffrey**
BLOOD BEACH
NIGHTMARES

**Boam, Jeffrey**
DEAD ZONE, THE
LOST BOYS, THE

**Boasberg, Al**
FREAKS

**Bodeen, Dewitt**
CURSE OF THE CAT PEOPLE, THE
CAT PEOPLE
SEVENTH VICTIM, THE

**Boehm, David**
RAVEN, THE

**Bogdanovich, Peter**
TARGETS

**Boileau, Pierre**
HORROR CHAMBER OF DR.
FAUSTUS, THE

**Bolster, Joe**
GIRLS NIGHT OUT

**Bond, Timothy**
HAPPY BIRTHDAY TO ME

**Borske, John**
BLOODTHIRSTY BUTCHERS
TORTURE DUNGEON

**Bourke, Terry**
INN OF THE DAMNED

**Brach, Gerard**
TENANT, THE
REPULSION

**Bradbury, Ray**
SOMETHING WICKED THIS WAY
COMES

**Bradford, Ernie**
BURKE AND HARE

**Brandner, Gary**
HOWLING II . . . YOUR SISTER IS A
WEREWOLF

**Breimer, Stephen**
BUTCHER, BAKER (NIGHTMARE
MAKER)

**Brewer, Jameson**
ARNOLD

**Bricker, George**
BRUTE MAN, THE

**Briganti, Elisa**
BLADE IN THE DARK, A
MANHATTAN BABY
ZOMBIE

**Briganti, Paolo**
BEYOND THE DOOR II

**Brock, Deborah**
SLUMBER PARTY MASSACRE II

**Brooke, Ralph**
GIANT FROM THE UNKNOWN

**Brooks, Mel**
YOUNG FRANKENSTEIN

**Brown, Edwin Scott**
PREY, THE

**Brown, Karl**
MAN THEY COULD NOT HANG, THE

**Brown, Rita Mae**
SLUMBER PARTY MASSACRE, THE

**Brown, Summer**
PREY, THE

**Brown, William O.**
WITCHMAKER, THE

**Browning, Tod**
DEVIL DOLL, THE

**Bryan, Peter**
BLOOD BEAST TERROR, THE

**Bryant, Chris**
AWAKENING, THE
DON'T LOOK NOW

**Burnham, Jeremy**
HORROR OF FRANKENSTEIN, THE

**Burr, Jeff**
OFFSPRING, THE

**Butler, Michael**
CAR, THE

**Caiano, Carlo**
NIGHTMARE CASTLE

**Caillou, Alan**
KINGDOM OF THE SPIDERS

**Calderon, Guillermo**
WRESTLING WOMEN VS. THE AZTEC
MUMMY, THE
AZTEC MUMMY, THE
ROBOT VS. THE AZTEC MUMMY, THE

**Campbell, R. Wright**
MASQUE OF THE RED DEATH, THE

**Candy, Reuben**
MAD DOCTOR OF BLOOD ISLAND,
THE

**Capobianco, Carmine**
PSYCHOS IN LOVE

**Carabatsos, Steve**
TENTACLES

**Cardona, Jr., Rene**
NIGHT OF A THOUSAND CATS, THE
NIGHT OF THE BLOODY APES

**Cardona, Rene**
NIGHT OF THE BLOODY APES

**Cardone, J.S.**
SLAYER, THE

**Carducci, Mark Patrick**
PUMPKINHEAD

**Carlton, Rex**
BLOOD OF DRACULA'S CASTLE
NIGHTMARE IN WAX

**Carpenter, John**
ASSAULT ON PRECINCT 13
FOG, THE
HALLOWEEN II
HALLOWEEN
PRINCE OF DARKNESS

**Carpenter, Stephen**
DORM THAT DRIPPED BLOOD, THE
POWER, THE

**Carpi, Tito**
TENTACLES

**Carroll, Larry**
TOURIST TRAP, THE

**Carroll, Richard**
APE, THE

**Carson, L.M. Kit**
TEXAS CHAINSAW MASSACRE PART
2, THE

**Casey, Thomas**
FLESH FEAST

**Cassner, Sergio**
MARK OF THE DEVIL

**Castle, Michael**
DON'T ANSWER THE PHONE

**Cedar, Jon**
MANITOU, THE

**Cerrella, Ginny**
SISTER SISTER

**Chace, Haile**
MONSTER OF PIEDRAS BLANCAS,
THE

**Chaney, Warren**
OUTING, THE

**Charles, Ernest A.**
POINT OF TERROR

**Chase, David**
GRAVE OF THE VAMPIRE

**Chaskin, David**
CURSE, THE
NIGHTMARE ON ELM STREET PART 2:
FREDDY'S REVENGE, A

**Chester, Hal E.**
CURSE OF THE DEMON

**Christensen, Benjamin**
WITCHCRAFT THROUGH THE AGES

**Christodoulou, Raymond**
FROM BEYOND THE GRAVE

**Ciccoritti, Gerard**
GRAVEYARD SHIFT

**Clark, Bob**
CHILDREN SHOULDN'T PLAY WITH DEAD THINGS

**Clark, Greydon**
UNINVITED, THE
PSYCHIC KILLER
SATAN'S CHEERLEADERS

**Clarke, Robin**
FROM BEYOND THE GRAVE

**Clarke, T.E.B.**
DEAD OF NIGHT

**Clasen, Tom**
LAST HORROR FILM, THE

**Clavell, James**
FLY, THE

**Clawson, Elliott J.**
PHANTOM OF THE OPERA, THE

**Clemens, Brian**
CAPTAIN KRONOS: VAMPIRE HUNTER
DR. JEKYLL AND SISTER HYDE
TELL-TALE HEART, THE
WATCHER IN THE WOODS, THE

**Clement, Myra**
CATHY'S CURSE

**Clerici, Gianfranco**
TEMPTER, THE

**Clifford, John**
CARNIVAL OF SOULS

**Clouse, Robert**
PACK, THE

**Cohen, Barney**
FRIDAY THE 13TH—THE FINAL CHAPTER
KILLER PARTY

**Cohen, David**
FRIDAY THE 13TH, PART V—A NEW BEGINNING

**Cohen, Herman**
BERSERK
CRAZE

**Cohen, Howard R.**
SATURDAY THE 14TH

**Cohen, Joel**
SISTER SISTER

**Cohen, Larry**
CARRIE
GHOST STORY
IT'S ALIVE
IT LIVES AGAIN
Q
STUFF, THE
RETURN TO SALEM'S LOT, A
MANIAC COP

IT'S ALIVE III: ISLAND OF THE ALIVE

**Cohn, Alfred A.**
CAT AND THE CANARY, THE

**Collins, Boon**
BUTCHER, BAKER (NIGHTMARE MAKER)

**Columbus, Chris**
GREMLINS

**Comfort, Brian**
ASPHYX, THE

**Comici, Lou**
VISITOR, THE

**Condon, Bill**
STRANGE BEHAVIOR
SISTER SISTER

**Cooper, Buddy**
MUTILATOR, THE

**Cooper, John C.**
HAUNTED STRANGLER, THE

**Cooper, Willis**
SON OF FRANKENSTEIN

**Coppola, Christopher**
DRACULA'S WIDOW

**Coppola, Francis Ford**
DEMENTIA 13

**Corti, Antonio**
CITY OF THE WALKING DEAD

**Coscarelli, Don**
PHANTASM
PHANTASM II

**Coscia, Marcello**
DORIAN GRAY

**Cranston, Joseph L.**
CORPSE GRINDERS, THE

**Craven, Wes**
DEADLY BLESSING
HILLS HAVE EYES II, THE
HILLS HAVE EYES, THE
NIGHTMARE ON ELM STREET, A
NIGHTMARE ON ELM STREET 3: DREAM WARRIORS, A
SWAMP THING
LAST HOUSE ON THE LEFT

**Crechales, Tony**
POINT OF TERROR

**Creelman, James**
KING KONG

**Cristofer, Michael**
WITCHES OF EASTWICK, THE

**Cronenberg, David**
BROOD, THE
DEAD RINGERS
FLY, THE
RABID
THEY CAME FROM WITHIN
SCANNERS
VIDEODROME

**Crowe, Christopher**
NIGHTMARES

**Crudo, Aldo**
BEYOND THE DOOR

**Crutcher, Gary**
STANLEY

**Cuccia, Milo G.**
COUNT DRACULA

**Cunilles, J.M.**
NIGHT OF THE ZOMBIES

**Cunningham, Michael**
SPLATTER UNIVERSITY

**Curiel, Frederick**
LIVING HEAD, THE

**Currier, Lauren**
CUJO

**D'Usseau, Arnaud**
HORROR EXPRESS
PSYCHOMANIA

**Daalder, Renee**
MASSACRE AT CENTRAL HIGH

**Dahlin, Bob**
MONSTER IN THE CLOSET

**Dallamano, Massimo**
DORIAN GRAY

**Danton, Raymond**
PSYCHIC KILLER

**Darabont, Frank**
NIGHTMARE ON ELM STREET 3: DREAM WARRIORS, A

**Daubeney, D.**
VAMPYRES, DAUGHTERS OF DRACULA

**Davenport, Harry Bromley**
HAUNTING OF JULIA, THE

**Davidson, L.W.**
HANDS OF THE RIPPER

**Davis, Ivan**
HUNGER, THE

**Davis, Kenn**
NIGHTMARE IN BLOOD

**de Agostini, Fabio**
NIGHTMARE CASTLE

**de Angelis, Fabrizio**
DR. BUTCHER, M.D.

**De Felitta, Frank**
AUDREY ROSE
ENTITY, THE

**De Gaetano, Michael**
HAUNTED

**de Guzman, Michael**
JAWS: THE REVENGE

**De Ossorio, Armando**
DEMON WITCH CHILD
HORROR OF THE ZOMBIES

**De Palma, Brian**
DRESSED TO KILL
PHANTOM OF THE PARADISE
SISTERS
BODY DOUBLE
BLOW OUT

**De Roche, Everett**
PATRICK

de Sanctis, Gino
ATOM AGE VAMPIRE

de Souza, Steven E.
BAD DREAMS

Dearden, Basil
MAN WHO HAUNTED HIMSELF, THE

Deel, Robert
FRANKENSTEIN GENERAL HOSPITAL

Dein, Edward
LEOPARD MAN, THE

Dekker, Fred
MONSTER SQUAD, THE

Delgado, Luis Maria
CITY OF THE WALKING DEAD

Delman, Jeffrey
DEADTIME STORIES

DeLuca, Rudy
TRANSYLVANIA 6-5000

DeMartino, Alberto
TEMPTER, THE

Dennis, Charles
THIRSTY DEAD, THE

Dennis, Geoffrey
UNEARTHLY, THE

DeRoche, Everett
RAZORBACK
ROAD GAMES

Di Lorenzo, Edward
LADY FRANKENSTEIN

Di Martino, Aldo
CHOSEN, THE

Dickinson, Desmond
HORROR HOTEL

Dillman, Jr., Dean
ATOMIC BRAIN, THE

Dixon, James
RETURN TO SALEM'S LOT, A

Dohler, Don
FIEND

Donati, Sergio
CHOSEN, THE
SCREAMERS
ORCA

Donnelly, Ben
LAST RITES

Down, Allison Louise
BLOOD FEAST

Downe, Allison Louise
GRUESOME TWOSOME

Downing, Rupert
GHOUL, THE

Drake, Arnold
FLESH EATERS, THE

Drake, T.Y.
TERROR TRAIN

Drake, Tom
KEEPER, THE

Dreyer, Carl Theodor
VAMPYR

Drouot, Pierre
DAUGHTERS OF DARKNESS

DuBois, Kit
CELLAR DWELLER

Dugdale, George
SLAUGHTER HIGH

Dunaway, Don Carlos
CUJO

Durston, David
I DRINK YOUR BLOOD

Dwiggens, Sue
ATOMIC BRAIN, THE

Earle, Joseph H.
SILENT NIGHT, DEADLY NIGHT PART II

Easter, Robert
TOOLBOX MURDERS, THE

Ebert, Gunter
DORIAN GRAY

Edwards, George
RUBY

Egan, Sam
ELVIRA: MISTRESS OF THE DARK

Eglee, Charles
DEADLY EYES

Elder, John
EVIL OF FRANKENSTEIN, THE
GHOUL, THE

Ellis, Robert
MONSTER WALKS, THE

Ellison, Joseph
DON'T GO IN THE HOUSE

Emery, Robert J.
SCREAM BLOODY MURDER

Endore, Guy
DEVIL DOLL, THE
MARK OF THE VAMPIRE

Enright, Don
SPASMS

Erickson, Carl
MYSTERY OF THE WAX MUSEUM, THE

Escalante, Dana
RETURN TO HORROR HIGH

Essoe, Gabe
DEVIL'S RAIN, THE

Evans, David Mickey
OPEN HOUSE

Evergreen, James
LOVE BUTCHER, THE

Ewing, William R.
SLAYER, THE

Exton, Clive
AWAKENING, THE

Eyre, David
WOLFEN

Ezra, Mark
SLAUGHTER HIGH

Fadda, Carlo
COUNT DRACULA

Faget-Benard, George
NIGHTMARE WEEKEND

Fairfax, Marion
LOST WORLD, THE

Fairman, Churton
DISCIPLE OF DEATH

Faragoh, Francis Edwards
FRANKENSTEIN

Farrell, Henry
HUSH . . . HUSH, SWEET CHARLOTTE

Farris, John
FURY, THE
DEAR, DEAD DELILAH

Fast, Alvin L.
EATEN ALIVE
SATAN'S CHEERLEADERS

Faye, Randall
RETURN OF THE VAMPIRE, THE

Fein, David Lee
DEMONOID

Feke, Steve
WHEN A STRANGER CALLS

Feldman, Randolph
HELL NIGHT

Ferrini, Franco
CREEPERS
DEMONS 2: THE NIGHTMARE
RETURNS
DEMONS

Fidello, Manuel
FRIDAY THE 13TH PART VII—THE NEW
BLOOD

Findlay, Roberta
BLOOD SISTERS

Fine, Bobby
HOUSE ON SORORITY ROW, THE

Fine, Harry
VAMPIRE LOVERS, THE

Finegan, John P.
GIRLS SCHOOL SCREAMERS

Finochi, August
COUNT DRACULA

Fischer, Janice
LOST BOYS, THE

Flaxman, Harvey
GRIZZLY

Fleming, Andrew
BAD DREAMS

Florey, Robert
FRANKENSTEIN

Flower, Buck
DRIVE-IN MASSACRE

Fondato, Marcello
BLOOD AND BLACK LACE
BLACK SABBATH

Fonseca, Fernando
UNHOLY, THE

Fonvielle, Lloyd
BRIDE, THE

**Forbes, Bryan**
SEANCE ON A WET AFTERNOON

**Ford, Derek**
DON'T OPEN TILL CHRISTMAS
HOUSE THAT VANISHED, THE

**Fort, Garrett**
DRACULA
DEVIL DOLL, THE
FRANKENSTEIN

**Forte, Vincent**
BARON BLOOD

**Fragasso, Olaudio**
NIGHT OF THE ZOMBIES

**Francini, Mario**
HOUSE OF FREAKS

**Franco, Jesus**
COUNT DRACULA
SCREAMING DEAD, THE

**Franju, Georges**
HORROR CHAMBER OF DR.
FAUSTUS, THE

**Frank, Bruno**
HUNCHBACK OF NOTRE DAME, THE

**Frank, Carol**
SORORITY HOUSE MASSACRE

**Franklin, George**
INCUBUS, THE

**Freed, Herb**
BEYOND EVIL
HAUNTS
GRADUATION DAY

**Froehlich, Bill**
RETURN TO HORROR HIGH

**Frost, Lee**
RACE WITH THE DEVIL

**Frost, Mark**
BELIEVERS, THE

**Frugoni, Cesare**
GREAT ALLIGATOR, THE
SCREAMERS

**Frumkes, Roy**
STREET TRASH

**Fuest, Robert**
DOCTOR PHIBES RISES AGAIN

**Fulci, Lucio**
HOUSE BY THE CEMETERY, THE
PSYCHIC, THE
GATES OF HELL, THE

**Galeen, Henrik**
NOSFERATU, THE VAMPIRE
GOLEM, THE

**Garofalo, Joseph**
EVILSPEAK

**Gastaldi, Ernesto**
GREAT ALLIGATOR, THE
MURDER CLINIC, THE
TORSO

**Gates, Harvey**
BLACK DRAGONS
CORPSE VANISHES, THE

**Gates, Tudor**
LUST FOR A VAMPIRE
VAMPIRE LOVERS, THE
TWINS OF EVIL

**Gendron, Pierre**
BLUEBEARD

**George, Jon**
FINAL TERROR, THE

**Gerani, Gary**
PUMPKINHEAD

**Gershuny, Theodore**
SILENT NIGHT, BLOODY NIGHT

**Giachino, Stacey**
DORM THAT DRIPPED BLOOD, THE

**Gianettino, Ronald**
HORROR OF PARTY BEACH, THE

**Giannone, Joe**
MADMAN

**Gianuiti, Roberto**
PSYCHIC, THE

**Gidding, Nelson**
HAUNTING, THE

**Gilling, John**
GORGON, THE

**Ginsberg, Milton Moses**
WEREWOLF OF WASHINGTON

**Ginter, Brad F.**
FLESH FEAST

**Gipe, George**
MAN WITH TWO BRAINS, THE

**Girdler, William**
MANITOU, THE

**Glueckman, Alan Jay**
BUTCHER, BAKER (NIGHTMARE
MAKER)

**Goff, John**
DRIVE-IN MASSACRE

**Goldbeck, Willis**
FREAKS

**Golding, Jerry**
RATTLERS

**Golding, Paul**
PULSE

**Goldman, Erwin**
SWEET SIXTEEN

**Goldman, William**
MAGIC

**Goldsmith, George**
BLUE MONKEY
CHILDREN OF THE CORN

**Goldstein, William**
ABOMINABLE DR. PHIBES, THE

**Goodhart, William**
EXORCIST II: THE HERETIC

**Gordon, Fritz**
SLEEPAWAY CAMP 2: UNHAPPY
CAMPERS

**Gordon, Leo**
TERROR, THE

**Gordon, Leon**
FREAKS

**Gordon, Stuart**
FROM BEYOND
RE-ANIMATOR

**Gottlieb, Carl**
JAWS 3-D
JAWS II
JAWS

**Grace, Michael L.**
UNSEEN, THE

**Graham, Lewis**
CRIME OF DR. CRESPI, THE

**Grais, Michael**
POLTERGEIST II
POLTERGEIST

**Grant, John**
ABBOTT AND COSTELLO MEET
FRANKENSTEIN
ABBOTT AND COSTELLO MEET DR.
JEKYLL AND MR. HYDE

**Graver, Gary**
TRICK OR TREATS

**Gray, William**
HUMONGOUS
PROM NIGHT

**Green, Joseph**
BRAIN THAT WOULDN'T DIE, THE

**Greenwalt, David**
WACKO

**Grefe, William**
DEATH CURSE OF TARTU

**Greville-Bell, Anthony**
THEATRE OF BLOOD

**Grey, William**
CHANGELING, THE

**Gries, Alan**
DEATHROW GAMESHOW

**Griffith, Charles**
CREATURE FROM THE HAUNTED SEA
DR. HECKYL AND MR. HYPE
LITTLE SHOP OF HORRORS

**Grissmer, John**
SCALPEL

**Guerra, Tonino**
ANDY WARHOL'S FRANKENSTEIN

**Gunn, Bill**
GANJA AND HESS

**Gunn, Gilbert**
CHAMBER OF HORRORS

**Gurvis, Anthony N.**
GIRLS NIGHT OUT

**Guza, Jr., Robert**
CURTAINS

**Haines, Richard W.**
CLASS OF NUKE 'EM HIGH
SPLATTER UNIVERSITY

**Hall, Arch**
CORPSE GRINDERS, THE

# SCREENWRITERS

Halperin, V.
REVOLT OF THE ZOMBIES

Halvey, Julian
HORROR EXPRESS

Hamilton, Judd
LAST HORROR FILM, THE

Hammer, Robert
DON'T ANSWER THE PHONE

Hammill, Ellen
DON'T GO IN THE HOUSE

Haney, Daryl
FRIDAY THE 13TH PART VII—THE NEW
BLOOD

Hanson, Curtis Lee
DUNWICH HORROR, THE

Hargreaves, Lance Z.
DEVIL DOLL

Harrison, John
SHOCK WAVES

Harrison, Paul
HOUSE OF SEVEN CORPSES, THE

Harry, Lee
SILENT NIGHT, DEADLY NIGHT PART II

Harry, T. Michael
IN THE SHADOW OF KILIMANJARO

Hart, John
ATOM AGE VAMPIRE

Hartford, Kenneth
SPECTRE OF EDGAR ALLAN POE, THE

Hause, Jeffrey
ONCE BITTEN

Hawes, Michael
ONE DARK NIGHT

Hayes, Patrick
GRAVE OF THE VAMPIRE

Hayward, Frederick
DEMON BARBER OF FLEET STREET,
THE

Heath, Michael
NEXT OF KIN

Helgeland, Brian
NIGHTMARE ON ELM STREET 4: THE
DREAM MASTER, A

Heller, Lukas
WHATEVER HAPPENED TO BABY
JANE?
HUSH . . . HUSH, SWEET CHARLOTTE

Henenlotter, Frank
BASKET CASE
BRAIN DAMAGE

Henkel, Kim
TEXAS CHAIN SAW MASSACRE, THE

Herbert, Hugh
GREAT GABBO, THE

Herzog, Werner
NOSFERATU, THE VAMPIRE

Heyward, Louis M.
CONQUEROR WORM, THE

Hickey, Michael
SILENT NIGHT, DEADLY NIGHT

Hicks, Neill
FINAL TERROR, THE

Higgin, Howard
REVOLT OF THE ZOMBIES

Higgins, Kenneth
GHOSTS ON THE LOOSE

Hill, Debra
FOG, THE
HALLOWEEN II
HALLOWEEN

Hill, Jack
HOUSE OF EVIL
FEAR CHAMBER, THE
TERROR, THE
SPIDER BABY

Hill, Robert F.
CAT AND THE CANARY, THE

Hilliard, Richard L.
HORROR OF PARTY BEACH, THE

Hiltzik, Robert
SLEEPAWAY CAMP

Hinds, Anthony
CURSE OF THE WEREWOLF, THE
SCARS OF DRACULA, THE

Hines, David
ONCE BITTEN

Hittleman, Carl
BILLY THE KID VS. DRACULA
JESSE JAMES MEETS
FRANKENSTEIN'S DAUGHTER

Hodges, Michael
DAMIEN—OMEN II

Hoffenstein, Samuel
PHANTOM OF THE OPERA

Holland, Tom
BEAST WITHIN, THE
FRIGHT NIGHT
PSYCHO II
CHILD'S PLAY

Hooker, Ted
CRUCIBLE OF TERROR

Hooper, Tobe
TEXAS CHAIN SAW MASSACRE, THE

Hopman, Gerald
DEVIL'S RAIN, THE

Houck, Jr., Joy
NIGHT OF BLOODY HORROR

Houghton, Don
LEGEND OF THE SEVEN GOLDEN
VAMPIRES, THE

Houston, Tony
CURSE OF THE SWAMP CREATURE

Howard, Duke
SHADOWS RUN BLACK

Howard, Eldon
TELL-TALE HEART, THE

Hudson, Brett
HYSTERICAL

Hudson, Mark
HYSTERICAL

Hudson, William
HYSTERICAL

Humphries, Dave
HAUNTING OF JULIA, THE

Hunebelle, Andre
DEVIL'S NIGHTMARE, THE

Hunt, Bob
BOOGENS, THE

Hunt, Ed
BLOODY BIRTHDAY

Hunter, Evan
BIRDS, THE

Huntingdon, Lawrence
OBLONG BOX, THE

Hurlbut, William
BRIDE OF FRANKENSTEIN, THE

Hurley, James F.
SOMETHING WEIRD

Huston, Jimmy
FINAL EXAM

Hutchison, Robert
FROGS

Illescas, Charles
DR. TARR'S TORTURE DUNGEON

Irving, Gregg
JUST BEFORE DAWN

Jackson, Donald
DEMON LOVER, THE

Jackson, Lewis
YOU BETTER WATCH OUT

Jackson, Mark
EYES OF A STRANGER

Jaffe, Robert
MOTEL HELL

Jaffe, Steven-Charles
MOTEL HELL

James, Frederick
HUMANOIDS FROM THE DEEP

Janowitz, Hans
CABINET OF DR. CALIGARI, THE

Jay, Griffin
RETURN OF THE VAMPIRE, THE

Jeffies, Richard
BLOOD TIDE

Jeremias, James
LOST BOYS, THE

Jobin, Peter
HAPPY BIRTHDAY TO ME

Johnson, Diane
SHINING, THE

Johnson, George Clayton
TWILIGHT ZONE—THE MOVIE

Johnson, Kay Cousins
JENNIFER

Johnson, Monica
JEKYLL AND HYDE . . . TOGETHER
AGAIN

Johnston, Trace
HYSTERICAL

Jonas, Norman
LET'S SCARE JESSICA TO DEATH

Jones, Don
LOVE BUTCHER, THE

Jones, Evan
FOREST, THE

Jones, John
GARDEN OF THE DEAD

Jordan, Lothrop W.
PLAY DEAD

Joyner, Courtney
OFFSPRING, THE
PRISON

Jul, Christen
VAMPYR

Jules, Maurice
SCREAM, BLACULA, SCREAM
VELVET VAMPIRE, THE

Kadison, Ellis
THEATRE OF DEATH

Kahn, Allen
WIZARD OF GORE, THE

Kaminsky, Howard
HOMEBODIES

Kandel, Aben
BERSERK
CRAZE

Kaplan, George
SEVENTH SIGN, THE

Kauf, Jr., M. James
WACKO

Kaufman, Charles
MOTHER'S DAY

Kaufman, David M.
WEREWOLVES ON WHEELS

Kaufman, Lloyd
CLASS OF NUKE 'EM HIGH
TOXIC AVENGER, THE

Kaufman, Robert
LOVE AT FIRST BITE

Keeter, Worth
WOLFMAN

Keith, Carlos
BEDLAM

Kelleher, Ed
SHRIEK OF THE MUTILATED
INVASION OF THE BLOOD FARMERS

Kelljan, Bob
COUNT YORGA, VAMPIRE

Kelly, James
BEAST IN THE CELLAR, THE

Kelly, Michael
FRANKENSTEIN GENERAL HOSPITAL

Kelly, Thomas J.
HOUSE OF SEVEN CORPSES, THE

Kelso, Edmund
KING OF THE ZOMBIES

Kemp, George
UNSANE

Kindberg, Ann N.
TOOLBOX MURDERS, THE

King, Stephen
CREEPSHOW
CAT'S EYE
MAXIMUM OVERDRIVE
STEPHEN KING'S SILVER BULLET

Kirman, Leonard
CARNIVAL OF BLOOD

Kirtzman, Harvey
MAD MONSTER PARTY

Kirwan, Patrick
HUMAN MONSTER, THE

Kitrosser, Martin
FRIDAY THE 13TH, PART V—A NEW
BEGINNING
FRIDAY THE 13TH PART III

Klein, Jaime
PANDEMONIUM

Koenig, Laird
LITTLE GIRL WHO LIVES DOWN THE
LANE, THE

Koenig, Raymond
BLACULA
SCREAM, BLACULA, SCREAM

Kohler, Manfred R.
BLOOD DEMON

Konvitz, Jeffrey
SILENT NIGHT, BLOODY NIGHT
SENTINEL, THE

Korobkin, Len
MAD MONSTER PARTY

Kring, R. Timothy
TEEN WOLF TOO

Kubrick, Stanley
SHINING, THE

Kumel, Harry
DAUGHTERS OF DARKNESS

Kurgis, Kevin
GIRLS NIGHT OUT

Kurz, Ron
FRIDAY THE 13TH PART II

Kusaba, Craig
SHADOWS RUN BLACK

La Loggia, Frank
FEAR NO EVIL
LADY IN WHITE

Lafia, John
CHILD'S PLAY

Lambert, Gavin
WHO SLEW AUNTIE ROO?

Landau, Richard
FRANKENSTEIN 1970

Landis, John
AMERICAN WEREWOLF IN LONDON,
AN
SCHLOCK
TWILIGHT ZONE—THE MOVIE

Landon, Ted
SLAUGHTERHOUSE ROCK

Langdon, Donald
BLOOD TIDE

Laughlin, Michael
STRANGE BEHAVIOR

Lawrence, Brian
LAST HOUSE ON DEAD END STREET

Lawrence, Marc
DADDY'S DEADLY DARLING

Lawrence, Peter
BURNING, THE

LeBron, Larry
DR. BLACK AND MR. HYDE

Lecocq, Charles
DEVIL'S NIGHTMARE, THE

Lee, Norman
CHAMBER OF HORRORS

Lees, Robert
ABBOTT AND COSTELLO MEET
FRANKENSTEIN

Lehman, Ernest
BLACK SUNDAY

Lehman, Lew
PHOBIA

Leight, Warren D.
MOTHER'S DAY

Lekus, Dell
TERROR ON TOUR

Leone, Alfred
HOUSE OF EXORCISM, THE

Leopold, Glenn
PROWLER, THE
TOO SCARED TO SCREAM

Lesson, Michael
JEKYLL AND HYDE . . . TOGETHER
AGAIN

Levesque, Michel
WEREWOLVES ON WHEELS

Levien, Sonya
HUNCHBACK OF NOTRE DAME, THE

Levison, Ken
MADHOUSE

Levy, Jefery
GHOULIES

Lewin, Albert
PICTURE OF DORIAN GRAY, THE

Lewis, Christopher
REVENGE

Lewis, Herschell Gordon
COLOR ME BLOOD RED
TWO THOUSAND MANIACS

Lewis, Jerry
NUTTY PROFESSOR, THE

# SCREENWRITERS

**Lewton, Val**
BODY SNATCHER, THE
ISLE OF THE DEAD

**Lieberman, Jeff**
BLUE SUNSHINE
SQUIRM

**Lindsey, George T.**
DEVONSVILLE TERROR, THE

**Lisson, Mark**
RETURN TO HORROR HIGH

**Litten, Peter**
SLAUGHTER HIGH

**Lloyd, Rollo**
REVOLT OF THE ZOMBIES

**Loeb III, Joseph**
TEEN WOLF

**Loeb, Lee**
ABBOTT AND COSTELLO MEET DR.
JEKYLL AND MR. HYDE

**Lofton, Terry**
NAIL GUN MASSACRE

**Lommel, Ulli**
BOOGEY MAN, THE
DEVONSVILLE TERROR, THE

**Love, Suzanna**
DEVONSVILLE TERROR, THE

**Lowe, Edward T.**
VAMPIRE BAT, THE
HUNCHBACK OF NOTRE DAME, THE

**Lucas, Ralph**
CHILD, THE

**Luna, Bigas**
ANGUISH

**Lynch, David**
ERASERHEAD

**Lynn, Kane W.**
BRAIN OF BLOOD

**McCormack, Frank M.**
PHANTOM OF THE OPERA, THE

**McCoy, Steve**
I WAS A TEENAGE ZOMBIE

**McCrann, Chuck**
BLOODEATERS

**McCullough, Jr., Jim**
CREATURE FROM BLACK LAKE, THE
MOUNTAINTOP MOTEL MASSACRE

**MacDonald, Philip**
BODY SNATCHER, THE

**McDowell, Michael**
BEETLEJUICE

**McElroy, Alan B.**
HALLOWEEN IV: THE RETURN OF
MICHAEL MYERS

**McGillivray, David**
CONFESSIONAL, THE
HOUSE OF WHIPCORD
TERROR
SCHIZO
FRIGHTMARE

**McGoohan, Al**
DON'T OPEN TILL CHRISTMAS

**McLoughlin, Tom**
FRIDAY THE 13TH PART VI: JASON
LIVES
ONE DARK NIGHT

**MacPhail, Angus**
DEAD OF NIGHT

**MacRauch, Earl**
STRANGER IS WATCHING, A

**McTiernan, John**
NOMADS

**Maddox, Diana**
CHANGELING, THE

**Madero, Robert**
MAUSOLEUM

**Magar, Guy**
RETRIBUTION

**Magness, Kerry**
NIGHT OF THE COBRA WOMAN

**Mahin, John Lee**
DR. JEKYLL AND MR. HYDE

**Mahon, Anthony**
PREMONITION, THE

**Majano, Anton Guilio**
ATOM AGE VAMPIRE

**Malone, William**
SCARED TO DEATH

**Maltby, H.F.**
DEMON BARBER OF FLEET STREET,
THE

**Mancini, Don**
CHILD'S PLAY

**Mann, Jane**
UNEARTHLY, THE

**Mann, Michael**
KEEP, THE

**Mann, Stanley**
DAMIEN—OMEN II

**Mannino, Vincenzo**
TEMPTER, THE

**Marais, Marc**
HOUSE OF THE LIVING DEAD

**Marcus, Raymond T.**
ZOMBIES OF MORA TAU

**Marini, Giorgio**
BEYOND THE DOOR

**Marisse, Anne**
HAUNTS
GRADUATION DAY

**Mariuzzo, Giorgio**
HOUSE BY THE CEMETERY, THE

**Marks, Leo**
PEEPING TOM

**Marmorstein, Malcolm**
MARY, MARY, BLOODY MARY

**Marsh, Terence**
HAUNTED HONEYMOON

**Marshall, Roger**
AND NOW THE SCREAMING STARTS
THEATRE OF DEATH

**Martin, Al**
INVISIBLE GHOST, THE

**Martin, Helen**
INVISIBLE GHOST, THE

**Martin, James**
I WAS A TEENAGE ZOMBIE

**Martin, Steve**
MAN WITH TWO BRAINS, THE

**Martinelli, Franco**
DR. BUTCHER, M.D.

**Martino, Sergio**
GREAT ALLIGATOR, THE
MURDER CLINIC, THE
TORSO
SCREAMERS

**Marvin, Mike**
WRAITH, THE

**Marzac, Mario**
NIGHT OF A THOUSAND CATS, THE

**Masefield, Joseph**
DON'T GO IN THE HOUSE

**Massaccesi, Aristide**
GRIM REAPER, THE

**Mastorakis, Nico**
BLOOD TIDE

**Matalon, Eddy**
CATHY'S CURSE

**Mathers, James**
DR. JEKYLL'S DUNGEON OF DEATH

**Matheson, Richard**
DIE! DIE! MY DARLING
HOUSE OF USHER
LEGEND OF HELL HOUSE, THE
JAWS 3-D
RAVEN, THE
PIT AND THE PENDULUM, THE
TALES OF TERROR
TWILIGHT ZONE—THE MOVIE
TWILIGHT ZONE—THE MOVIE
TWILIGHT ZONE—THE MOVIE

**Max, Jerome**
TENTACLES

**Maxwell, Richard**
SERPENT AND THE RAINBOW, THE

**Mayer, Carl**
CABINET OF DR. CALIGARI, THE

**Melson, John**
CAULDRON OF BLOOD

**Meyer, Andrew**
NIGHT OF THE COBRA WOMAN

**Michaels, John**
SPLATTER UNIVERSITY

**Mikels, Ted V.**
BLOOD ORGY OF THE SHE-DEVILS

**Miller, Harvey**
JEKYLL AND HYDE ... TOGETHER
AGAIN

**Miller, Victor**
FRIDAY THE 13TH
STRANGER IS WATCHING, A

**Milligan, Andy**
BLOODTHIRSTY BUTCHERS
CARNAGE
MAN WITH TWO HEADS, THE
RATS ARE COMING! THE
WEREWOLVES ARE HERE!, THE
TORTURE DUNGEON
GHASTLY ONES, THE

**Milton, H.A.**
PIRANHA II: THE SPAWNING

**Mischel, Josef**
ISLE OF THE DEAD

**Mitchell, Steve**
CHOPPING MALL

**Mizuki, Yoko**
KWAIDAN

**Moctezuma, Juan Lopez**
DR. TARR'S TORTURE DUNGEON

**Moffat, Ivan**
BLACK SUNDAY

**Molina, Jacinto**
WEREWOLF VS. THE VAMPIRE
WOMAN, THE
HOUSE OF PSYCHOTIC WOMEN, THE

**Molteni, Sonia**
BEYOND THE DOOR
TENTACLES

**Moncada, Santiago**
HATCHET FOR A HONEYMOON

**Montefiori, Luigi**
GRIM REAPER, THE

**Monviso, Piero**
ATOM AGE VAMPIRE

**Moore, Roy**
BLACK CHRISTMAS

**Mora, Philippe**
HOWLING III, THE

**More, Julian**
INCENSE FOR THE DAMNED

**Morrison, Greg**
MADHOUSE

**Morrissey, Paul**
ANDY WARHOL'S FRANKENSTEIN
ANDY WARHOL'S DRACULA

**Morse, Lawrence**
OCTAMAN

**Mullally, Don**
MYSTERY OF THE WAX MUSEUM, THE

**Mundi, Robert**
VISITOR, THE

**Munkell, Hans**
WEREWOLF VS. THE VAMPIRE
WOMAN, THE

**Murphey, Michael S.**
TRICK OR TREAT
SUPERNATURALS, THE

**Murray, John Fenton**
ARNOLD

**Musy, Mario**
HATCHET FOR A HONEYMOON

**Myers, Henry**
BLACK ROOM, THE

**Myton, Fred**
DEAD MEN WALK
MAD MONSTER, THE

**Naha, Ed**
DOLLS
TROLL

**Nankin, Michael**
GATE, THE

**Naranda, Vencenzio**
PEOPLE WHO OWN THE DARK

**Narcejac, Thomas**
HORROR CHAMBER OF DR.
FAUSTUS, THE

**Nelson, Ida**
FUNERAL HOME

**Neubauer, Leonard**
NEW YEAR'S EVIL

**Neville, John Thomas**
DEVIL BAT, THE

**Nolan, William**
BURNT OFFERINGS

**Norris, William J.**
RE-ANIMATOR

**Norton, Eleanor E.**
DAY OF THE ANIMALS

**Norton, William**
DAY OF THE ANIMALS
I DISMEMBER MAMA

**Nugent, Elliott**
UNHOLY THREE, THE

**Nugent, J.C.**
UNHOLY THREE, THE

**O'Bannon, Dan**
DEAD AND BURIED
RETURN OF THE LIVING DEAD

**O'Connolly, Jim**
BEYOND THE FOG

**O'Malley, David**
BOOGENS, THE

**O'Neal, Charles**
SEVENTH VICTIM, THE

**Obrow, Jeffrey**
DORM THAT DRIPPED BLOOD, THE
POWER, THE

**Oliver, Ron**
HELLO MARY LOU, PROM NIGHT II

**Olmstead, Edward**
CRIME OF DR. CRESPI, THE

**Olsen, Dana**
WACKO

**Ormsby, Alan**
CHILDREN SHOULDN'T PLAY WITH
DEAD THINGS

CAT PEOPLE
DEATHDREAM

**Orr, James R.**
WITCHFIRE

**Paoli, Dennis**
FROM BEYOND
RE-ANIMATOR
GHOULIES II

**Paragon, John**
ELVIRA: MISTRESS OF THE DARK

**Pares, Mildred**
HOUSE ON SKULL MOUNTAIN, THE

**Paris, Dominic**
LAST RITES

**Parker, Alan**
ANGEL HEART

**Parker, John**
DEMENTIA

**Parker, Percy**
MARK OF THE DEVIL

**Parker, Scott**
HE KNOWS YOU'RE ALONE

**Parkinson, Tom**
CRUCIBLE OF TERROR
DISCIPLE OF DEATH

**Parry, Michael**
UNCANNY, THE

**Pastore, Louis**
PREMONITION, THE

**Patriarca, Walter**
DR. BUTCHER, M.D.

**Paulsen, David**
SCHIZOID
SAVAGE WEEKEND

**Peach, L. DuGarde**
GHOUL, THE

**Pearson, Barry**
BLOODY BIRTHDAY

**Perilli, Ray**
DRACULA'S DOG
MANSION OF THE DOOMED

**Pertwee, Roland**
GHOUL, THE

**Peterson, Cassandra**
ELVIRA: MISTRESS OF THE DARK

**Phillips, Bill**
CHRISTINE

**Piazzoli, Roberto d'Ettore**
BEYOND THE DOOR

**Pierce, Arthur C.**
INVISIBLE STRANGLER, THE

**Pierce, Charles B.**
BOGGY CREEK II

**Pierce, Scott**
NIGHTMARE ON ELM STREET 4: THE
DREAM MASTER, A

**Pinkney, John**
THIRST

# SCREENWRITERS

**Pirro, Mark**
DEATHROW GAMESHOW

**Plate, Bret**
SUPERSTITION

**Pogue, Charles Edward**
FLY, THE
PSYCHO III

**Polanski, Roman**
TENANT, THE
ROSEMARY'S BABY
REPULSION

**Pollexfen, Jack**
DAUGHTER OF DR. JEKYLL

**Pollock, Gene**
THRILL KILLERS, THE

**Polsky, Abe**
BABY, THE

**Ponti, Sal**
DOCTOR DEATH: SEEKER OF SOULS

**Pooley, Olaf**
CRUCIBLE OF HORROR
GODSEND, THE

**Pope, Tim**
DON'T LOOK IN THE BASEMENT

**Pope, Tom**
MANITOU, THE

**Portillo, Adolfo Lopez**
LIVING HEAD, THE

**Powell, Amos**
DEMONOID
KEEP MY GRAVE OPEN

**Pratt, Jr., Charles**
INITIATION, THE

**Pressfield, Steven**
KING KONG LIVES

**Price, Daria**
NESTING, THE

**Privitera, Vincent J.**
WITCHFIRE

**Pugsley, William**
DRACULA VS. FRANKENSTEIN

**Pupillo, Massimo**
DEVIL'S WEDDING NIGHT, THE

**Quandour, Mohy**
SPECTRE OF EDGAR ALLAN POE, THE

**Raimi, Sam**
EVIL DEAD 2: DEAD BY DAWN
EVIL DEAD, THE

**Raley, Alice**
MOVIE HOUSE MASSACRE

**Ralston, Gilbert A.**
BEN
WILLARD

**Ramis, Harold**
GHOSTBUSTERS

**Ramrus, Al**
ISLAND OF DR. MOREAU, THE

**Randall, Dick**
PIECES

**Ray, Fred Olen**
SCALPS

**Ray, Leslie**
MY DEMON LOVER

**Read, Jan**
HAUNTED STRANGLER, THE

**Reali, Carlo**
TWITCH OF THE DEATH NERVE

**Rebar, Alex**
DEMENTED
TO ALL A GOODNIGHT

**Red, Eric**
HITCHER, THE
NEAR DARK

**Redon, Jean**
HORROR CHAMBER OF DR.
FAUSTUS, THE

**Reed, Joel M.**
BLOODSUCKING FREAKS
NIGHT OF THE ZOMBIES

**Reed, Tom**
PHANTOM OF THE OPERA, THE

**Reeves, Michael**
CONQUEROR WORM, THE

**Regnoli, Piero**
CITY OF THE WALKING DEAD

**Reiner, Carl**
MAN WITH TWO BRAINS, THE

**Relph, Michael**
MAN WHO HAUNTED HIMSELF, THE

**Rhomm, Patrice**
DEVIL'S NIGHTMARE, THE

**Richard, Jef**
BERSERKER

**Richmond, Bill**
NUTTY PROFESSOR, THE

**Richter, W.D.**
DRACULA

**Rinaldo, Frederic I.**
ABBOTT AND COSTELLO MEET
FRANKENSTEIN

**Ritter, Joe**
TOXIC AVENGER, THE

**Rityo, Rosemary**
ALICE, SWEET ALICE

**Robbins, Matthew**
WARNING SIGN

**Roberts, Jonathan**
ONCE BITTEN

**Robins, Herb**
WORM EATERS, THE

**Robins, John**
DEATH SHIP

**Robins, Sam**
CORPSE VANISHES, THE

**Robinson, Helen**
DREAMANIAC

**Robinson, Richard**
KINGDOM OF THE SPIDERS

**Robson, Mark**
BEDLAM

**Robson, Michael**
CHOSEN, THE

**Roessler, Rick**
SLAUGHTERHOUSE

**Rogan, Josh**
TWILIGHT ZONE—THE MOVIE

**Rogers, Jean Scott**
CORRIDORS OF BLOOD

**Romero, George A.**
DAWN OF THE DEAD
CREEPSHOW 2
CRAZIES, THE
DAY OF THE DEAD
MARTIN
NIGHT OF THE LIVING DEAD
HUNGRY WIVES
MONKEY SHINES: AN EXPERIMENT IN
FEAR

**Rose, Louisa**
SISTERS

**Rose, Mickey**
STUDENT BODIES

**Rose, Ralph**
LET'S SCARE JESSICA TO DEATH

**Rose, Ruth**
SON OF KONG
KING KONG

**Rosenbaum, Henry**
DUNWICH HORROR, THE

**Rosenberg, C.A.**
MANIAC

**Rosman, Mark**
HOUSE ON SORORITY ROW, THE

**Ross, Harry Essex Arthur**
CREATURE FROM THE BLACK
LAGOON

**Ross, Kenneth**
BLACK SUNDAY

**Ross, Paul**
BEYOND EVIL

**Rothman, Stephanie**
VELVET VAMPIRE, THE

**Rothstein, Richard**
HUMAN EXPERIMENTS

**Rowe, Arthur**
LAND OF THE MINOTAUR

**Rowe, Freddie**
HOWLING IV: THE ORIGINAL
NIGHTMARE

**Rubens, Percival**
DEMON, THE

**Rubin, Bruce Joel**
DEADLY FRIEND

**Rudnitsky, Mark**
CLASS OF NUKE 'EM HIGH

**Rumbold, Jonathon**
CREEPING FLESH, THE

**Ruric, Peter**
BLACK CAT, THE

**Russell, Chuck**
NIGHTMARE ON ELM STREET 3:
DREAM WARRIORS, A

**Russell, Ken**
LAIR OF THE WHITE WORM, THE

**Russell, Ray**
PREMATURE BURIAL, THE

**Russell, Vi**
ATOMIC BRAIN, THE

**Russo, John A.**
MIDNIGHT
NIGHT OF THE LIVING DEAD

**Rustam, Mardi**
EATEN ALIVE

**Sacchetti, Dardano**
BLADE IN THE DARK, A
BEYOND THE DOOR II
DEMONS 2: THE NIGHTMARE
RETURNS
DEMONS
HOUSE BY THE CEMETERY, THE
MANHATTAN BABY
PSYCHIC, THE
GATES OF HELL, THE

**Sackler, Howard**
JAWS II
JAWS

**St. John, Nicholas**
DRILLER KILLER
MS. 45

**Sajbel, Michael**
SUPERSTITION

**Salazar, Alfredo**
WRESTLING WOMEN VS. THE AZTEC
MUMMY, THE
AZTEC MUMMY, THE
CURSE OF THE AZTEC MUMMY, THE
ROBOT VS. THE AZTEC MUMMY, THE

**Saletri, Frank R.**
BLACKENSTEIN

**Sandefur, Duke**
GHOST TOWN

**Sangster, Jimmy**
CURSE OF FRANKENSTEIN, THE
HORROR OF FRANKENSTEIN, THE
HORROR OF DRACULA, THE
LEGACY, THE
MUMMY, THE
WHO SLEW AUNTIE ROO?
PHOBIA
MANIAC

**Sarecky, Barney**
APE MAN, THE

**Sarno, Robert**
HOWLING II . . . YOUR SISTER IS A
WEREWOLF

**Sautet, Claude**
HORROR CHAMBER OF DR.
FAUSTUS, THE

**Saxton, John**
HAPPY BIRTHDAY TO ME

**Sayles, John**
ALLIGATOR
HOWLING, THE
PIRANHA

**Scandariato, Romano**
DR. BUTCHER, M.D.

**Scarpelli, Henry**
FORCED ENTRY

**Scavolini, Romano**
NIGHTMARE

**Schlitt, Robert**
PYX, THE

**Schmidt, Marlene**
MORTUARY

**Schmoeller, David**
CRAWLSPACE
TOURIST TRAP, THE

**Schneider, Barry**
RUBY

**Schnitzer, Allen**
PREMONITION, THE

**Schnitzer, Gerald**
CORPSE VANISHES, THE
BOWERY AT MIDNIGHT

**Schrock, Raymond**
PHANTOM OF THE OPERA, THE

**Schubert, Bernard**
MARK OF THE VAMPIRE

**Scott, Allan**
AWAKENING, THE
DON'T LOOK NOW

**Scott, Darin**
OFFSPRING, THE

**Seltzer, David**
OMEN, THE
PROPHECY

**Seminara, George**
I WAS A TEENAGE ZOMBIE

**Semple, Jr., Lorenzo**
KING KONG

**Sens-Cazenave, A.**
CATHY'S CURSE

**Sewell, Vernon**
GHOST SHIP

**Shadow, John**
PIECES

**Shaffer, Anthony**
WICKER MAN, THE

**Shagan, Steve**
NIGHTWING

**Shaner, John Herman**
ISLAND OF DR. MOREAU, THE

**Shaughnessy, Alfred**
FLESH AND BLOOD SHOW, THE

**Shaw, Lou**
CRYPT OF THE LIVING DEAD

**Sheehan, Perley Poore**
HUNCHBACK OF NOTRE DAME, THE

**Sheldon, David**
GRIZZLY

**Shelton, Charles F.**
DEADTIME STORIES

**Sherman, Gary**
POLTERGEIST III

**Sherman, Robert**
PICTURE MOMMY DEAD

**Sherman, Samuel M.**
DRACULA VS. FRANKENSTEIN

**Sherriff, R.C.**
INVISIBLE MAN, THE

**Sherwood, Hal**
GHASTLY ONES, THE

**Sholder, Jack**
ALONE IN THE DARK

**Shrake, Bud**
NIGHTWING

**Shryack, Dennis**
CAR, THE

**Shusett, Ronald**
FINAL TERROR, THE
DEAD AND BURIED
KING KONG LIVES

**Silkosky, Ronald**
DUNWICH HORROR, THE

**Simmons, Robert Wynne**
BLOOD ON SATAN'S CLAW, THE

**Simoun, A.R.**
SERPENT AND THE RAINBOW, THE

**Sims, Bennett**
HOMEBODIES

**Sims, Greg H.**
RETURN TO HORROR HIGH

**Singer, Thomas**
MICROWAVE MASSACRE

**Siodmak, Curt**
APE, THE
BRIDE OF THE GORILLA
FRANKENSTEIN MEETS THE WOLF
MAN
I WALKED WITH A ZOMBIE
WOLF MAN, THE

**Sisson, Rosemary Anne**
WATCHER IN THE WOODS, THE

**Skaaren, Warren**
BEETLEJUICE

**Skolimowski, Jerzy**
SHOUT, THE

**Slate, Lane**
CAR, THE

**Slatzer, Robert F.**
BIG FOOT

**Slesar, Henry**
MURDERS IN THE RUE MORGUE

**Smith, Earl E.**
LEGEND OF BOGGY CREEK, THE

TOWN THAT DREADED SUNDOWN, THE

**Smith, Lance**
MUNCHIES

**Smith, Martin Cruz**
NIGHTWING

**Sneller, Jeffrey**
IN THE SHADOW OF KILIMANJARO

**Snider, Norman**
DEAD RINGERS

**Sohl, Jerry**
DIE, MONSTER, DIE

**Soisson, Joel**
TRICK OR TREAT
SUPERNATURALS, THE

**Sole, Alfred**
ALICE, SWEET ALICE

**Sonye, Michael**
BLOOD DINER

**Spalding, Harry**
WATCHER IN THE WOODS, THE

**Spenceley, Peter**
CREEPING FLESH, THE

**Spencer, Jr., Gil**
GIRLS NIGHT OUT

**Spiegel, Scott**
EVIL DEAD 2: DEAD BY DAWN

**Spielberg, Steven**
POLTERGEIST

**Spinell, Joe**
MANIAC

**Spound, Michael**
WACKO

**Stadie, Hildegarde**
MANIAC

**Stanley, John**
NIGHTMARE IN BLOOD

**Stebel, Sidney L.**
MIRRORS

**Steckler, Ray Dennis**
THRILL KILLERS, THE

**Steensland, David**
ESCAPES

**Stefano, Joseph**
PSYCHO

**Steinmann, Danny**
FRIDAY THE 13TH, PART V—A NEW BEGINNING

**Stern, Sandor**
AMITYVILLE HORROR, THE

**Stone, David**
REPULSION

**Stone, Oliver**
HAND, THE

**Strawn, Arthur**
BLACK ROOM, THE

**Strutin, Stuart**
CLASS OF NUKE 'EM HIGH
TOXIC AVENGER, THE

**Style, Michael**
VAMPIRE LOVERS, THE

**Subotsky, Milton**
DR. TERROR'S HOUSE OF HORRORS
TALES FROM THE CRYPT
VAULT OF HORROR, THE

**Suhosky, Robert**
HOUSE WHERE EVIL DWELLS, THE

**Summers, Walter**
HUMAN MONSTER, THE

**Sutcliff, Rosemary**
GHOST STORY

**Swartz, Charles S.**
VELVET VAMPIRE, THE

**Taggert, Brian**
OF UNKNOWN ORIGIN
VISITING HOURS
POLTERGEIST III

**Tampa, Harry**
NOCTURNA

**Tasker, Robert**
DOCTOR X

**Taussig, Frank Hart**
GIANT FROM THE UNKNOWN

**Taylor, Eric**
PHANTOM OF THE OPERA
SON OF DRACULA

**Teller, Ira**
SILENT NIGHT, BLOODY NIGHT

**Tenney, Del**
CURSE OF THE LIVING CORPSE, THE

**Tenney, Kevin S.**
WITCHBOARD

**Terry, Edward**
CHILDREN, THE

**Terry, Gay**
TOXIC AVENGER, THE

**Thomas, Kathryn Ann**
DRACULA'S WIDOW

**Thomas, Michael**
HUNGER, THE

**Thompson, Donald G.**
EVIL, THE
SUPERSTITION

**Thor, Jon-Mikl**
ROCK 'N' ROLL NIGHTMARE

**Thornton, Philip**
GHOST SHIP

**Tilley, Patric**
LEGACY, THE

**Tintini, Alberto**
HOUSE OF EXORCISM, THE

**Topham, Rhet**
TRICK OR TREAT

**Torres, Joan**
BLACULA
SCREAM, BLACULA, SCREAM

**Towers, Alan**
COUNT DRACULA

**Towne, Robert**
TOMB OF LIGEIA, THE

**Tristan, Dorothy**
JAWS II

**Troisio, Antonio**
BEYOND THE DOOR

**Tryon, Thomas**
OTHER, THE

**Turner, Clive**
HOWLING IV: THE ORIGINAL
NIGHTMARE

**Turner, John Hastings**
GHOUL, THE

**Tuten, Frederic**
POSSESSION

**Ulmer, Edgar G.**
BLACK CAT, THE

**Van Rogers, Joe**
BRAIN OF BLOOD

**Vane, Norman Thaddeus**
BLACK ROOM, THE
FRIGHTMARE

**Vergara, Luis Enrique**
HOUSE OF EVIL
FEAR CHAMBER, THE

**Vernick, William**
REDEEMER, THE

**Victor, Mark**
POLTERGEIST II
POLTERGEIST

**Vincenzoni, Luciano**
ORCA

**Vines, Michael**
AMERICAN GOTHIC

**Vogel, Klaus**
VIRGIN WITCH, THE

**Volk, Stephen**
GOTHIC

**von Stroheim, Erich**
DEVIL DOLL, THE

**Wadleigh, Michael**
WOLFEN

**Wadsack, Richard H.**
SCREAMS OF A WINTER NIGHT

**Wagner, Bruce**
NIGHTMARE ON ELM STREET 3:
DREAM WARRIORS, A

**Wales, William**
AMITYVILLE 3-D

**Wallace, Charles A.**
CASTLE OF EVIL

**Wallace, Tommy Lee**
AMITYVILLE II: THE POSSESSION
HALLOWEEN III: SEASON OF THE WITCH

**Walton, Fred**
WHEN A STRANGER CALLS

**Wasserman, Lee**
RETRIBUTION

Watson, Alan
HORROR HOSPITAL

Watson, Carol
FRIDAY THE 13TH PART III

Weaver, Robert A.
NIGHT OF BLOODY HORROR

Webster, M. Coates
BRUTE MAN, THE

Weeks, Stephen
GHOST STORY

Wegener, Paul
GOLEM, THE

Weinstein, Bob
BURNING, THE

Weir, Peter
PLUMBER, THE

Weis, Jack
MARDI GRAS MASSACRE

Weisman, Matthew
TEEN WOLF

Welch, William
BROTHERHOOD OF SATAN, THE

Wenk, Richard
VAMP

Westlake, Donald E.
STEPFATHER, THE

Weston, Armand
NESTING, THE

Weston, Eric
EVILSPEAK

Weston, Garnett
WHITE ZOMBIE

Wetanson, Bert
AMERICAN GOTHIC

Wheat, Jim
SILENT SCREAM

Wheat, Ken
SILENT SCREAM

Wheeler, Paul
LEGACY, THE

White, Brad
SUPERSTITION

White, James Gordon
BIG FOOT

White, Robb
HOUSE ON HAUNTED HILL
THIRTEEN GHOSTS

Whitley, Richard
PANDEMONIUM

Whiton, James
ABOMINABLE DR. PHIBES, THE

Wicket, W.W.
SEVENTH SIGN, THE

Wicking, Christopher
OBLONG BOX, THE
MURDERS IN THE RUE MORGUE
TO THE DEVIL A DAUGHTER
SCREAM AND SCREAM AGAIN

Wiederhorn, Ken
SHOCK WAVES
RETURN OF THE LIVING DEAD PART II

Wilbur, Crane
HOUSE OF WAX

Wilder, Gene
HAUNTED HONEYMOON
YOUNG FRANKENSTEIN

Wiley, Ethan
HOUSE II: THE SECOND STORY
HOUSE

Williams, Tony
NEXT OF KIN

Winder, Michael
BEAST MUST DIE, THE

Winkless, Terence H.
HOWLING, THE

Winner, Michael
SENTINEL, THE

Winters, David
LAST HORROR FILM, THE

Wood, Edward
NIGHT OF THE GHOULS

Wood, Jr., Edward Davis
ORGY OF THE DEAD

Woods, Jack
EQUINOX

Woolf, Edgar Allan
FREAKS

Wray, Ardel
ISLE OF THE DEAD
I WALKED WITH A ZOMBIE
LEOPARD MAN, THE

Wylie, Philip
INVISIBLE MAN, THE

Wynorski, Jim
CHOPPING MALL

Yates, George Worthing
FRANKENSTEIN 1970

Yelton, Duke
HILLBILLYS IN A HAUNTED HOUSE

Yordan, Philip
UNHOLY, THE

Younkins, Jerry
DEMON LOVER, THE

Yust, Larry
HOMEBODIES

Yuzna, Brian
FROM BEYOND

Zacharias, Alfred
DEMONOID

Zarchi, Meir
I SPIT ON YOUR GRAVE

Zimmerman, Vernon
FADE TO BLACK

Zulawski, Andrzej
POSSESSION

## SOURCE AUTHORS

Alcocer, Santos
CAULDRON OF BLOOD

Alston, Emmett
NEW YEAR'S EVIL

Anson, Jay
AMITYVILLE HORROR, THE

Appelbaum, Lawrence
SILENT NIGHT, DEADLY NIGHT PART II

Argento, Dario
DEEP RED

Armstrong, Anthony
MAN WHO HAUNTED HIMSELF, THE

Arnold, Frank
HUMANOIDS FROM THE DEEP

Ashman, Howard
LITTLE SHOP OF HORRORS

Assonitis, Ovidio
VISITOR, THE

Auer, John H.
CRIME OF DR. CRESPI, THE

Babcock, Dwight V.
BRUTE MAN, THE

Baines, John
DEAD OF NIGHT

Balderston, John
DRACULA
DRACULA

Barker, Clive
HELLBOUND: HELLRAISER II
HELLRAISER
RAWHEAD REX

Bassett, Ronald
CONQUEROR WORM, THE

Baughn, David
BEYOND EVIL

Baxt, George
BEYOND THE FOG

Begun, Jeff
SATURDAY THE 14TH

Belden, Charles S.
MYSTERY OF THE WAX MUSEUM, THE

Benchley, Peter
JAWS: THE REVENGE
JAWS 3-D
JAWS II
JAWS

Benson, E.F.
DEAD OF NIGHT

Bergquist, Peter L.
MONSTER IN THE CLOSET

Biggers, Earl Derr
HOUSE OF THE LONG SHADOWS

Bixby, Jerome
TWILIGHT ZONE—THE MOVIE

Blaisdell, Anne
DIE! DIE! MY DARLING

# SOURCE AUTHORS

**Blatty, William Peter**
EXORCIST II: THE HERETIC
EXORCIST, THE

**Bloch, Robert**
PSYCHO II
PSYCHO III
PSYCHO
TORTURE GARDEN

**Bloom, Jeffrey**
BLOOD BEACH

**Bodeen, DeWitt**
CAT PEOPLE

**Bogdanovich, Peter**
TARGETS

**Borchers, Donald P.**
VAMP

**Bradbury, Ray**
SOMETHING WICKED THIS WAY
COMES

**Brandel, Marc**
HAND, THE

**Brandner, Gary**
HOWLING III, THE
HOWLING II . . . YOUR SISTER IS A
WEREWOLF
HOWLING, THE
HOWLING IV: THE ORIGINAL
NIGHTMARE

**Brennan, Peter**
RAZORBACK

**Bricker, George**
DEVIL BAT, THE

**Briganti, Elisa Livia**
HOUSE BY THE CEMETERY, THE

**Brown, Karl**
APE MAN, THE

**Buell, John**
PYX, THE

**Caimi, Paul**
SILENT NIGHT, DEADLY NIGHT PART II
SILENT NIGHT, DEADLY NIGHT

**Calderon, Guillermo**
CURSE OF THE AZTEC MUMMY, THE

**Carducci, Mark Patrick**
PUMPKINHEAD

**Carlton, Rex**
BRAIN THAT WOULDN'T DIE, THE

**Carpenter, Peter**
POINT OF TERROR

**Carpenter, Stephen**
POWER, THE

**Chase, David**
GRAVE OF THE VAMPIRE

**Chekov, Anton**
BLACK SABBATH

**Chetwynd-Hayes, Ronald**
FROM BEYOND THE GRAVE
MONSTER CLUB, THE

**Clark, Mary Higgins**
STRANGER IS WATCHING, A

**Cohen, David**
FRIDAY THE 13TH, PART V—A NEW
BEGINNING

**Cohen, Martin B.**
HUMANOIDS FROM THE DEEP

**Comstock, Howard W.**
DOCTOR X

**Conde, Nicholas**
BELIEVERS, THE

**Craig, Johnny**
TALES FROM THE CRYPT

**Craven, Wes**
NIGHTMARE ON ELM STREET 3:
DREAM WARRIORS, A

**Curnick, David**
KEEPER, THE

**Dahlin, Bob**
MONSTER IN THE CLOSET

**Davis, Wade**
SERPENT AND THE RAINBOW, THE

**De Felitta, Frank**
AUDREY ROSE
ENTITY, THE

**De Palma, Brian**
SISTERS
BODY DOUBLE

**Deane, Hamilton**
DRACULA
DRACULA

**Dekker, Fred**
HOUSE

**Delman, Jeffrey**
DEADTIME STORIES

**Devine, J. Liewellyn**
GORGON, THE

**Dibdin-Pitt, George**
DEMON BARBER OF FLEET STREET,
THE

**Dick, Michael**
BAD DREAMS

**Dolan, Charlie**
GHOULIES II

**Doyle, Sir Arthur Conan**
LOST WORLD, THE

**du Maurier, Daphne**
BIRDS, THE
DON'T LOOK NOW

**Earle, Joseph H.**
SILENT NIGHT, DEADLY NIGHT PART II

**Endore, Guy**
CURSE OF THE WEREWOLF, THE

**Farris, John**
FURY, THE

**Feldstein, Al**
TALES FROM THE CRYPT
VAULT OF HORROR, THE

**Finegan, John P.**
GIRLS SCHOOL SCREAMERS

**Fischer, Janice**
LOST BOYS, THE

**Fisher, Dave**
PACK, THE

**Fleming, Andrew**
BAD DREAMS

**Furst, Werner H.**
BLUEBEARD

**Gaines, William**
TALES FROM THE CRYPT
VAULT OF HORROR, THE

**Galeen, Henrik**
NOSFERATU, THE VAMPIRE

**Garfield, Brian**
STEPFATHER, THE

**Geasland, Jack**
DEAD RINGERS

**Gibson, Lois**
CRYPT OF THE LIVING DEAD

**Gilbert, Stephen**
BEN
WILLARD

**Gindes, Mark**
LOVE AT FIRST BITE

**Goldman, William**
MAGIC

**Goldstein, William**
DOCTOR PHIBES RISES AGAIN

**Graves, Robert**
SHOUT, THE

**Green, Joseph**
BRAIN THAT WOULDN'T DIE, THE

**Grefe, William**
STANLEY

**Grey, Brad**
BURNING, THE

**Guza, Jr., Robert**
PROM NIGHT

**Haines, Richard W.**
CLASS OF NUKE 'EM HIGH

**Hall, Angus**
MADHOUSE

**Hardiman, James**
HOUSE WHERE EVIL DWELLS, THE

**Harry, Lee**
SILENT NIGHT, DEADLY NIGHT PART II

**Hearn, Lafcadio**
KWAIDAN

**Hecht, Ben**
GREAT GABBO, THE

**Helgeland, Brian**
NIGHTMARE ON ELM STREET 4: THE
DREAM MASTER, A

**Henderson, Don**
MARY, MARY, BLOODY MARY

**Henstell, Diana**
DEADLY FRIEND

**Herbert, James**
DEADLY EYES

SURVIVOR

**Hickey, Michael**
SILENT NIGHT, DEADLY NIGHT PART II

**Hiltzik, Robert**
SLEEPAWAY CAMP 2: UNHAPPY CAMPERS

**Hines, Leonard J.**
GHOUL, THE

**Hittleman, Carl**
BILLY THE KID VS. DRACULA

**Hjortsberg, William**
ANGEL HEART

**Holzer, Hans**
AMITYVILLE II: THE POSSESSION

**Hopkins, John**
POWER, THE

**Hughes, Robert**
STRANGE BEHAVIOR

**Hugo, Victor**
HUNCHBACK OF NOTRE DAME, THE
HUNCHBACK OF NOTRE DAME, THE

**Hunter, Russell**
CHANGELING, THE

**Hutchison, Robert**
FROGS

**Jackson, Shirley**
HAUNTING, THE

**Jacoby, John**
PHANTOM OF THE OPERA

**James, Montague R.**
CURSE OF THE DEMON

**Jay, Griffin**
MUMMY, THE

**Jeremias, James**
LOST BOYS, THE

**Johnson, George Clayton**
TWILIGHT ZONE—THE MOVIE

**Kadison, Ellis**
THEATRE OF DEATH

**Kapner, Nancy**
WORM EATERS, THE

**Kaufman, Robert**
LOVE AT FIRST BITE

**Keating, Katie**
GIRLS SCHOOL SCREAMERS

**Keating, Pierce**
GIRLS SCHOOL SCREAMERS

**King, Dr. Frank**
GHOUL, THE

**King, Stephen**
CUJO
CREEPSHOW 2
CHRISTINE
CHILDREN OF THE CORN
CAT'S EYE
CARRIE
DEAD ZONE, THE
STEPHEN KING'S SILVER BULLET
SHINING, THE

**Kitrosser, Martin**
FRIDAY THE 13TH, PART V—A NEW BEGINNING
FRIDAY THE 13TH—THE FINAL CHAPTER

**Koenig, Laird**
LITTLE GIRL WHO LIVES DOWN THE LANE, THE

**Koenig, Raymond**
SCREAM, BLACULA, SCREAM

**Konvitz, Jeffrey**
SENTINEL, THE

**Kotzwinkle, William**
NIGHTMARE ON ELM STREET 4: THE DREAM MASTER, A

**Krantz, Steve**
JENNIFER
RUBY

**Kurz, Ron**
FRIDAY THE 13TH—THE FINAL CHAPTER
FRIDAY THE 13TH PART III

**Langelaan, George**
FLY, THE
FLY, THE

**Lawrence, Peter**
TERMINAL CHOICE

**Le Fanu, J. Sheridan**
LUST FOR A VAMPIRE
VAMPYR
VAMPIRE LOVERS, THE
TWINS OF EVIL

**Lefcourt, Carolyn**
STEPFATHER, THE

**Leroux, Gaston**
PHANTOM OF THE OPERA
PHANTOM OF THE OPERA, THE

**Levin, Ira**
ROSEMARY'S BABY

**Levy, Edward**
BEAST WITHIN, THE

**Lipsius, Dhani**
HALLOWEEN IV: THE RETURN OF MICHAEL MYERS

**Loeb III, Joseph**
TEEN WOLF TOO

**Lovecraft, H.P.**
DIE, MONSTER, DIE
DUNWICH HORROR, THE
FROM BEYOND
RE-ANIMATOR

**Lyon, Earle**
INVISIBLE STRANGLER, THE

**McCollough, Paul**
CRAZIES, THE

**McDowell, Michael**
BEETLEJUICE

**McElroy, Alan B.**
HALLOWEEN IV: THE RETURN OF MICHAEL MYERS

**McGee, Mark Thomas**
EQUINOX

**McGregor, Sean**
BROTHERHOOD OF SATAN, THE

**MacPhail, Angus**
DEAD OF NIGHT

**Mancini, Don**
CHILD'S PLAY

**Mann, Jane**
UNEARTHLY, THE

**Marasco, Robert**
BURNT OFFERINGS

**Marconi, Chris**
POINT OF TERROR

**Maryk, Michael**
SPASMS

**Marzac, Mario**
NIGHT OF A THOUSAND CATS, THE

**Masterson, Graham**
MANITOU, THE

**Matheson, Richard**
LEGEND OF HELL HOUSE, THE
TWILIGHT ZONE—THE MOVIE

**Maylam, Tony**
BURNING, THE

**Merritt, Abraham**
DEVIL DOLL, THE

**Meyrink, Gustav**
GOLEM, THE

**Middleton, Joseph**
JUST BEFORE DAWN

**Millar, Jeff**
DEAD AND BURIED

**Miller, Allen C.**
DOCTOR X

**Miller, Stephen**
MY BLOODY VALENTINE

**Miller, Victor**
FRIDAY THE 13TH—THE FINAL CHAPTER
FRIDAY THE 13TH PART III
FRIDAY THE 13TH PART II

**Monahan, Brent**
SPASMS

**Montoro, Edward E.**
DAY OF THE ANIMALS

**Moses, Charles A.**
FRANKENSTEIN 1970

**Muckler, Craig**
MICROWAVE MASSACRE

**Mundhra, Jag**
OPEN HOUSE

**Nalevansky, Steven**
BLOOD BEACH

**Neubauer, Leonard**
NEW YEAR'S EVIL

**Neumann, Kurt**
RETURN OF THE VAMPIRE, THE

# SOURCE AUTHORS

**Obrow, Jeffrey**
POWER, THE

**Osborn, David**
WHO SLEW AUNTIE ROO?

**Paradisi, Giulio**
VISITOR, THE

**Parker III, Chauncey G.**
OF UNKNOWN ORIGIN

**Paterson, Dennis**
SILENT NIGHT, DEADLY NIGHT PART II

**Penny, John**
POWER, THE

**Pettiette, P.J.**
BAD DREAMS

**Phillips, Arnold**
BLUEBEARD

**Pierce, Arthur C.**
INVISIBLE STRANGLER, THE

**Pinkney, John**
THIRST

**Platt, Polly**
TARGETS

**Plympton, George**
ZOMBIES OF MORA TAU

**Poe, Edgar Allan**
BLOOD DEMON
BLACK CAT, THE
CRIME OF DR. CRESPI, THE
DR. TARR'S TORTURE DUNGEON
HOUSE OF USHER
MASQUE OF THE RED DEATH, THE
RAVEN, THE
RAVEN, THE
PREMATURE BURIAL, THE
PIT AND THE PENDULUM, THE
OBLONG BOX, THE
MURDERS IN THE RUE MORGUE
TELL-TALE HEART, THE
TALES OF TERROR
TOMB OF LIGEIA, THE

**Putnam, Nina Wilcox**
MUMMY, THE
MUMMY, THE

**Randall, Florence Engel**
WATCHER IN THE WOODS, THE

**Rankin, Jr., Arthur**
MAD MONSTER PARTY

**Rattner, Larry**
HALLOWEEN IV: THE RETURN OF
MICHAEL MYERS

**Raven, Simon**
INCENSE FOR THE DAMNED

**Read, Jan**
HAUNTED STRANGLER, THE

**Redon, Jean**
HORROR CHAMBER OF DR.
FAUSTUS, THE

**Ricci, Rudy**
RETURN OF THE LIVING DEAD

**Rico, Don**
MARY, MARY, BLOODY MARY

**Robbins, Clarence Aaron**
UNHOLY THREE, THE

**Robbins, Ted**
FREAKS

**Romero, George A.**
NIGHT OF THE LIVING DEAD

**Rosenwink, Katherine**
MAUSOLEUM

**Ruffner, Benjamin**
HALLOWEEN IV: THE RETURN OF
MICHAEL MYERS

**Russell, Ray**
INCUBUS, THE

**Russo, John**
MIDNIGHT
RETURN OF THE LIVING DEAD

**Sacchetti, Dardano**
DEMONS

**Sajbel, Michael**
SUPERSTITION

**Sakow, Bruce Hidemi**
FRIDAY THE 13TH—THE FINAL
CHAPTER

**Salazar, Alfredo**
CURSE OF THE AZTEC MUMMY, THE
ROBOT VS. THE AZTEC MUMMY, THE

**Sangster, Jimmy**
LEGACY, THE

**Saxon, Peter**
SCREAM AND SCREAM AGAIN

**Saxton, John**
HAPPY BIRTHDAY TO ME

**Sayre, George W.**
MAN THEY COULD NOT HANG, THE

**Schayer, Richard**
MUMMY, THE

**Schmoeller, David**
GHOST TOWN

**Seabrook, William**
WHITE ZOMBIE

**Seltzer, Dave**
FINAL CONFLICT, THE

**Serling, Rod**
TWILIGHT ZONE—THE MOVIE

**Seymour, Henry**
CRAZE

**Shelley, Mary**
FRANKENSTEIN GENERAL HOSPITAL
ABBOTT AND COSTELLO MEET
FRANKENSTEIN
CURSE OF FRANKENSTEIN, THE
BRIDE OF FRANKENSTEIN, THE
BRIDE, THE
HORROR OF FRANKENSTEIN, THE
YOUNG FRANKENSTEIN
SON OF FRANKENSTEIN
FRANKENSTEIN

**Shenck, Aubrey**
FRANKENSTEIN 1970

**Sherman, Gary**
PHOBIA

**Shewl, Edward Spencer**
HANDS OF THE RIPPER

**Shirk, Adam Hull**
APE, THE

**Shryack, Dennis**
CAR, THE

**Shusett, Ronald**
PHOBIA

**Siodmak, Curtis**
SON OF DRACULA

**Smith, Frederick E.**
DEVIL DOLL

**Smith, Martin Cruz**
NIGHTWING

**Snyder, F.G.**
BLACK SABBATH

**Spinell, Joe**
MANIAC

**Stern, Alex**
DEAD AND BURIED

**Stevenson, Robert Louis**
ABBOTT AND COSTELLO MEET DR.
JEKYLL AND MR. HYDE
BODY SNATCHER, THE
DR. JEKYLL AND SISTER HYDE
DR. JEKYLL AND MR. HYDE
MAN WITH TWO HEADS, THE
JEKYLL AND HYDE . . . TOGETHER
AGAIN
DR. JEKYLL AND MR. HYDE

**Stewart, Michael**
MONKEY SHINES: AN EXPERIMENT IN
FEAR

**Stoker, Bram**
LAIR OF THE WHITE WORM, THE
AWAKENING, THE
COUNT DRACULA
DRACULA'S DOG
LEGEND OF THE SEVEN GOLDEN
VAMPIRES, THE
DRACULA
DRACULA
HORROR OF DRACULA, THE
NOSFERATU, THE VAMPIRE
SCARS OF DRACULA, THE
NOSFERATU, THE VAMPIRE

**Straub, Peter**
GHOST STORY
HAUNTING OF JULIA, THE

**Strawn, Arthur**
BLACK ROOM, THE

**Streiner, Russell**
RETURN OF THE LIVING DEAD

**Strieber, Whitley**
HUNGER, THE
WOLFEN

**Subotsky, Milton**
HORROR HOTEL

**Taylor, Bernard**
GODSEND, THE

**Tenser, Mark**
HEARSE, THE

**Topham, Rhet**
TRICK OR TREAT

**Topor, Roland**
TENANT, THE

**Torres, Joan**
SCREAM, BLACULA, SCREAM

**Trueblood, Guerdon**
JAWS 3-D

**Tryon, Thomas**
OTHER, THE

**Updike, John**
WITCHES OF EASTWICK, THE

**Villard, Dimitri**
ONCE BITTEN

**Vogel, Klaus**
VIRGIN WITCH, THE

**Wagner, Bruce**
NIGHTMARE ON ELM STREET 3:
DREAM WARRIORS, A

**Walker, Peter**
FRIGHTMARE

**Wallace, Edgar**
CHAMBER OF HORRORS
HUMAN MONSTER, THE
KING KONG LIVES
KING KONG
KING KONG

**Wallace, Inez**
I WALKED WITH A ZOMBIE

**Warren, Bill**
LADY FRANKENSTEIN

**Watson, Carol**
FRIDAY THE 13TH—THE FINAL
CHAPTER

**Webling, Peggy**
FRANKENSTEIN

**Weinman, Richard C.**
PUMPKINHEAD

**Weinstein, Harvey**
BURNING, THE

**Weisman, Matthew**
TEEN WOLF TOO

**Weldon, Charles**
HOUSE OF WAX

**Wells, H.G.**
DEAD OF NIGHT
ISLAND OF DR. MOREAU, THE
INVISIBLE MAN, THE

**Wenk, Richard**
VAMP

**Westlake, Donald E.**
STEPFATHER, THE

**Wheatley, Dennis**
TO THE DEVIL A DAUGHTER

**White, Leslie T.**
MAN THEY COULD NOT HANG, THE

**Whiton, James**
DOCTOR PHIBES RISES AGAIN

**Wilde, Oscar**
DORIAN GRAY
PICTURE OF DORIAN GRAY, THE

**Willard, John**
CAT AND THE CANARY, THE

**Williams, Robert**
MURDER CLINIC, THE

**Wilson, Donald**
KEEPER, THE

**Wilson, F. Paul**
KEEP, THE

**Wilson, Larry**
BEETLEJUICE

**Winston, Stan**
PUMPKINHEAD

**Wood, Bari**
DEAD RINGERS

**Wood, Jr., Edward Davis**
ORGY OF THE DEAD

**Woolrich, Cornell**
LEOPARD MAN, THE

**Yablans, Irwin**
PRISON

**Young, Les**
TERROR

**Young, Moira**
TERROR

**Zacharias, Alfred**
DEMONOID

**Zapponi, Bernardo**
DEEP RED

**Zeltser, Yuri**
BAD DREAMS

**Zimm, Maurice**
CREATURE FROM THE BLACK
LAGOON

**THE HORROR FILM**